INDIA
Including
Nepal

REVISED AND
COMPLETELY UPDATED

Editor: Andrew E. Beresky
Area Editors: Kathy Cox, Trevor Fishlock, Greta Goldsmith, Bachi J. Karkaria, Ravi Khanna, Karl Samson, Lisa Samson, John Seekings, Amit Shah
Drawings: Lorraine Calaora
Maps: C. W. Bacon

FODOR'S TRAVEL PUBLICATIONS, INC.
New York & London

MANUFACTURED IN THE UNITED STATES OF AMERICA
10 9 8 7 6 5 4 3 2 1

CONTENTS

FACTS AT YOUR FINGERTIPS

The Land, 8; Basic Statistics for India, 9; The Climate, 9; What It Will Cost, 10; Currency, 12; Planning Your Trip, 12; Travel Documents, 13; Touring Itineraries, 15; Tour Operators, 18; Restricted Areas, 19; Travel Agents, 20; When to Go, 21; What to Pack, 22; Health Regulations, 22; Insurance, 23; Travel to India, 23; Customs on Arrival, 26; Special-Interest Travel, 27; Staying in India, 27; Hill and Beach Resorts, 30; Student Lodging, 31; Meeting the People at Home, 31; Roughing It, 31; Dining Out, 32; Tour Guide Services, 32; Special Events, 32; Calendar of Festivals, 33; Business Hours and Holidays, 34; Tipping, 35; Measurements, 35; Electricity, 35; Time Zones, 35; Postage, 35; Metric Conversion Chart, 36; Overseas Telephone and Telex, 37; Laundry and Dry Cleaning, 37; Drinking Laws, 37; Museums and Galleries, 38; Behavior, 38; Begging, 38; Sports, 38; Hints to Photographers, 39; Wildlife Sanctuaries, 39; Medical Treatment, 40; Hints to the Disabled, 40; Pollution Report, 41; Shopping, 41; Nightlife, 42; Traveling in India, 42; *Map of Rail Routes*, 46–47; *Map of Major Highways*, 51; On Departure from India, 52

NORTHERN REGION

WESTERN AND CENTRAL REGION

CONTENTS

FOREWORD

The subcontinent of India offers the tourist a million miles of scenic natural wonders: some of the world's highest mountains; awesome rivers and valleys; deserts, jungles, and wildlife. Everything seems to be on an epic scale. Five thousand years of continuous civilization have left a legacy of aesthetic grandeur in architecture, literature, music, and art. India's strongest attraction for the visitor is in its interplay of contrasts. Nowhere do the past and present coexist in more colorful abandonment.

This edition includes Nepal, fabled for its mountain adventures, and Bhutan, a true "Shangri-la" nation.

We wish to express our gratitude to the various offices of the Government of India Tourist Office in New York, London, and throughout India for their assistance in the preparation of this guidebook, especially to Mrs. Sudha Kothary, Mrs. Lila Nadan, C.R.V. Rao, and Mrs. Susan Mehta of the New York Office. Our thanks also to Mahendrasinhji (Chota) Chudasama and Lauraine Schallop of Air-India, New York, Pallan Katgara and Captain Vijay Prasada of Travel Corporation of India, Om P. Munjal and Dileep Rao of the Welcomgroup Hotels, Marie Brown of Bhutan Travel Service, and Pradip and Tapashi Chaudhuri of Calcutta.

Government of India tourist officials on the subcontinent especially helpful were S.K. Misra, Secretary of Tourism, and Man Mohan Verma, Director in the Department of Tourism. Our thanks go also to the following officials for their assistance on the state and city level: Vivek Srivastava, and S.K. Verma, Himachal Pradesh; Mohiuddin Shah, Jammu and Kashmir; Chiranjiv Singh, Karnataka; Naranda Luther, Andhra Pradesh; M.T. Rayudu and Mrs. T.R. Devichand, Bombay; V.A.P. Mahajan, Goa; B.K. Bagchi, Madhya Pradesh; M. Ramamcortz, Pondicherry; G.A. Rajkumar, Tamil Nadu; and Surendra Mohan and Satyendra Kuma, Uttar Pradesh.

While every care has been taken to ensure the accuracy of the information contained in this guide, the publishers cannot accept responsibility for any errors which may appear.

All prices quoted in this guide are based on those available to us at the time of writing. In a world of rapid change, however, the possibility of inaccurate or out-of-date information can never be totally eliminated. We trust, therefore, that you will take prices quoted as indicators only, and will double-check to be sure of the latest figures.

Similarly, be sure to check all opening times of museums and galleries. We have found that such times are liable to change without notice, and you could easily make a trip only to find a locked door.

When a hotel closes or a restaurant produces a disappointing meal, let us know, and we will investigate the establishment and the complaint. We are always ready to revise our entries for the following year's edition should the facts warrant it.

Send your letters to the editors of Fodor's Travel Publications, 201 E 50th Street, New York, NY 10022. European readers may prefer to write to Fodor's Travel Guides, 9–10 Market Place, London W1N 7AG, England.

IMMENSE LAND, IMMENSE DRAMA

An Introduction to India

by
TREVOR FISHLOCK

Journalist, author, and broadcaster, Trevor Fishlock in 1987 won the International Reporter of the Year prize in the British Press Awards. Five years earlier, while a staff correspondent in Delhi for The Times of London, *he won the David Holden Award for outstanding foreign reporting from India. He is now chief roving correspondent for* The Daily Telegram, London. *He visits India frequently and has had stints in Australia and the Soviet Union. His most recent books are* India File *and* The State of America.

India will change you. It is not possible to be unmoved by it. For old hands already in its thrall and for new explorers about to set off, there is nothing quite so stimulating or sharpening as the prospect of India's immense drama. All journeys to this vast and varied land are adventures. The very name of it stirs the imagination and holds out the promise of astonishments, great spectacles, and sudden challenges to preconceptions. It is neither bland nor always comfortable. It is not for everybody. Many of its sights, flavors, and evident contradictions are strong and sometimes provocative. There are subtleties and baffling complexities and opaquenesses not easily penetrated. But India pays large and enduring dividends to travelers who come with open minds,

1

particularly those who take things in their stride and keep in their minds Rudyard Kipling's admonition, "A fool lies here who tried to hustle the East."

Nearly 2,000 years ago, the Greek geographer Strabo struck a cautious note when he wrote, "We must hear accounts of India with indulgence for not only is it very far away, but even those who have seen it saw only some parts of it."

Modern transport has shrunk the distances, but Strabo's observation still has some validity. India's great size and variety mean that even today, most travelers may see only a small area of it. And it really is large. Walled off in the north by the massive bulwarks of the Himalayas, the source of the great rivers Indus and Ganges, India unrolls for more than 2,000 miles—over deserts and jungles, rain forests and well-tilled fields, and plains so vast they make your eyes ache—to the hot southern tip of Cape Comorin. It also spreads for 2,000 miles from the edges of Burma and China to a remote area of mudflats near the mouth of the Indus, the river, now mostly in Pakistan, from which India derives its name.

The peoples who came in waves through the mountain passes to conquer and to settle have created an amazingly complex society in a single country the size of Europe. India embraces great religions. Hinduism, which has its roots in the country's earliest history and remains one of the unifying elements, is the dominant faith. But Islam and Sikhism have helped to shape the country and are significant forces, part of India's fabric. The modern republic acknowledges 15 official languages, but there are hundreds of minor tongues. Among the 23 states and eight territories there are fierce regional loyalties. But in spite of the disparities, strains, and rivalries, the great bulk of Indians are loyal to the idea of India.

One of the keys to understanding today's India is to recognize that it is a country that exists in several centuries at once. India is, in part, a sophisticated and modern society, an industrial leader. It is also the home of primitive tribes, of millions of wretchedly poor people who live seemingly without hope. Between ancient and modern, rich and poor, lives a remarkable spectrum of humanity. The paradoxes of modern India can be seen in the existence of two important research centers: one for space, the other devoted to building a better bullock cart.

Cultures Meshed by Caste

The wonderful tapestry of cultures, languages, religions, diets, and costumes form a heterogeneity linked by the mesh of the caste system. This system has evolved over thousands of years, under racial, social, and religious pressures, as a way of ordering a huge mass of people in a large land area.

Caste provides people with an identity—the knowledge of where they stand in society and how they should live. It can provide security, govern a person's eating customs and other rituals, and determine the choice of a husband or wife (there is a widespread insistence on marriage within one's caste). India has more than 3,000 of these social divisions, from Brahmans to the untouchables.

Caste is so powerful a part of Indian life that it long ago penetrated the Moslem, Sikh, and Christian communities that are meant to be outside it. It is undoubtedly a force for stability in Indian life, strong and conservative, and possibly a defense against revolution. But it is one of the paradoxes of India in that it is also a cause of dissension and deadly rivalry. Caste prejudice, the labyrinth of petty apartheids, is one of the unpleasant facts of Indian life. The struggle of the lower castes and the untouchables to find justice and a decent life is enduring. Caste plays a significant part in the politics of the modern democracy because it is part of the very fiber of India, woven into Hindu ideas of life, rebirth, and predestination.

India is an ancient land, its roots going back 5,000 years. It is fabulous, intricate, and teeming. When, in 1947, the British bid farewell to the jewel in the crown of their empire, India had 350 million people. Now it has 850 million and is growing by more than a million a month. The government is trying to put the brakes on this phenomenal growth with a birth-control program. But nothing will stop India, the second most populous country on earth, from growing to a billion and beyond. It is expected to outstrip China as the world's giant early in the next century. Today, one person in every six in the world is an Indian.

Recent Impressive Advances

The pressures of population create enormous problems for the country's leaders. It is not just a matter of food. In a society whose expectations are constantly raised, there is an ever-increasing demand for better education, health care, jobs, housing, and transport, and these demands are translated into political pressures.

India can point with pride to advances made in recent years. Improvements in public health and disease control have obviously been a big factor in the growth of the population. The years of appalling food shortages and the burden of having to import grain belong to the past. India has learned how to feed its swelling millions through its agricultural revolution, the investment in healthier and stronger crops and improved irrigation. People are manifestly better clothed, fed, educated, and housed. Huge sections of Indian society are moving up and the nation can feel justifiably proud of what has been achieved. But there is also a darker side. It is impossible to ignore the evidence of poverty and the fact that there are millions in want.

Indians take pride in their country's place as the largest democratic society on earth. In the postcolonial, post-World War II era, many newly independent countries pledged their devotion to the democratic ideal, only to retreat to old ways as traditions and enmities in their societies reemerged and took over. In India, the democratic ideal may be battered in practice, but it endures. It is a fact of modern history that sets India apart, and Indians are deeply conscious of it. In such a large and complex society, it is not an easy road. But it can also be argued that in such a society, it is the only practical road.

India is by far the giant of south Asia, its population, economy, and military strength dwarfing the surrounding countries of Pakistan, Nepal, Bangladesh, and Sri Lanka. Its population is three and a half times greater than the total of the populations of all its neighbors, and its land mass is three times larger than all the others combined.

The political shape of the subcontinent in modern times was changed first by partition in 1947, when the two wings of Pakistan were carved out to create a Moslem homeland, and then by the war of 1971 in which East Pakistan broke away to become Bangladesh. The most important political matter in subcontinental relations is the enduring tension between India and Pakistan. This tension, whose roots are deep in historical rivalries and suspicions, is compounded by mutual mistrust and by the quarrel over the possession of Kashmir, the cause of two of the three wars the countries have fought since partition.

Diversity of People

It is hard to generalize about India and its people. One always runs into the exceptions and contradictions, for the diversity is astonishing.

The people of Kashmir, Assam, and Nagaland are different from those of Kerala, Punjab, and Maharashtra. Languages, customs, traditions, histories, diets, and clothing are different, just as, in Europe, Norwegians are different from Spaniards. One has to keep in mind the sheer vastness of India.

Which brings us back to what the wise old geographer Strabo said about seeing only part of India. You can see some of the country by making the great triangular trip of Delhi-Agra-Jaipur. It is a familiar route for travelers and is not to be despised simply because it is well worn. Delhi is more than the capital. It is a repository of history and has been rebuilt several times. The Taj Mahal really is a marvel, well worth the trip, and Jaipur is a particular splendor. If you travel by road around these places, and pause often, you can see and learn much. But travelers do themselves and India an injustice if they do not get out of their comfortable hotels and walk in the streets and lanes and meet the people around them. They sell themselves short if they travel only on the jets of Indian Airlines and shut themselves away in luxurious lobbies and expensive restaurants.

Glamour and wealth are as much a part of the real India as anything else, even if the very rich are only a small minority. And in the smart hotels of great cities like Delhi, Bombay, Calcutta, and Madras, you can see the gatherings of tycoons, film producers, and other entrepreneurs and get a feeling of India's strong business tradition.

You can also see beautiful women, expensively dressed in saris or the long shirt and trousers favored by Punjabis, their bangles gently tinkling. In Bombay, particularly, you might think that these women are stars or starlets, part of the largest movie industry in the world. And you will probably be right.

Bustling City Life

Study the rush hour in any city for a while and you will get a good idea of India at work. One of the striking developments of recent times is the way cities and towns have swelled to create a large and important commercial and industrial population, a burgeoning middle class. The buses are crammed with office workers. Squadrons of bicycles weave to and fro. Young managers perch on motor scooters, often with a wife and children on board. Cars are expensive, but there are plenty of them, ranging from the veteran Ambassador—the great car of India based on a British 1950s design—to the newer Japanese models. And all the vehicles compete for road space with pony carts, rickshaws, camels, and elephants. The noise is tremendous.

The great majority of Indians, however, live in rural areas. Nearly 75 percent of the people depend on farming. They live in 576,000 villages, some large and prosperous, some little more than poor hamlets. In many respects, the routines of their lives have changed little over the centuries. When you go to a village, you might imagine that here is the simplest of existences, but village life is a complex pattern of hard work, family problems, disputes, caste consciousness and rivalries, and religious rituals.

The rhythms of crop growing and the weather are central concerns. But the overriding concern is the monsoon—the wind that brings the annual rains—which plays a part in the politics of the country. Politicians and economists, as well as the millions who live off the land, wait anxiously and hopefully as the monsoon moves northward. Radio and newspaper reports are followed with keen interest. Everyone prays for a good monsoon. The air grows hot and the sky turns dark. Then the monsoon breaks with lightning and thunder. People dance in the heavy rain and give thanks. But, from time to time, the rains are scanty and the harvests are poor.

Farming Prospers in the North

The most prosperous farming region is Punjab, home of the "green revolution," which enabled India to feed itself. Punjabis are big, outgoing people, energetic and business minded. They have made Punjab the most prosperous state in the country. They are great farmers and took readily to mechanization, modern fertilizers, and new varieties of crops, the bases of the green revolution. Punjabis have spread throughout the north. Delhi has a strong Punjabi presence, and Punjabis are a major force in the film business in Bombay, India's Hollywood.

Punjab is also the home state of the Sikhs, perhaps the most distinctive Indians, who form over half the state's population. Sikhs are only about 2 percent of the Indian population, but their contribution to national life is in much larger proportion. They have a strong military tradition and retain an important presence in the army, navy, and air force. They are also big in medicine, engineering, and trucking. Sikhs are adherents of a religion founded in the sixteenth century, as an offshoot of Hinduism, and codified by 10 *gurus,* or teachers. To keep their unshorn hair tidy, Sikhs tuck it into a turban, their distinctive headgear (although other Indians also wear turbans).

The complex politics of the Sikhs and the fundamentalists' belief that their religion is in danger of being swallowed up by Hinduism are reasons for the troubles in Punjab. Hindus and Sikh Punjabis have traditionally lived in harmony, often worshiping in each other's temples. It was once common for one son in a Hindu family in Punjab to be raised as a Sikh. Sikh extremists, however, have been trying to drive a wedge between the two communities.

You will see a different style of turban in Rajasthan, the home of the Rajput people. The turbans here are big, bright edifices made out of 40 feet of muslin.

Bengalis are also distinctive. Their chief city is Calcutta, vigorous and teeming, with a strong cultural tradition. Bengalis are great debaters, poets, artists, and writers, and their politics are lively and contentious. Many Bengalis have names ending in *ji,* or *jee,* as in Chatterji.

Clothing, of course, is governed by the climate. Warm woolen jackets and shawls are worn in the north and cool sarongs are worn in the south. Although many men wear Western-style clothing (trousers and shirts or suits), most women wear the traditional sari or shirt and trousers, the trousers being baggy or narrow. The sari endures because it is graceful, cool, modest, and available in a vast array of patterns and colors.

Many men in the north favor the cool *kurta*—a long shirt and loose trousers, usually white. Also popular is the *dhoti,* the comfortable garment that is often worn loose and baggy or as a loincloth. Many Bengalis like wearing the dhoti, and you'll often see it worn in the countryside.

Land of Many Languages

The languages of India form part of its complexity. By and large, the country's political and regional boundaries are drawn on linguistic lines. With 15 major languages and hundreds of minor ones, as well as dialects, every state in the union is multilingual.

Each main language has an ancient literature and is spoken by millions of people. There is no majority language. Even Hindi, the main official language and the fifth major language of the world after Chinese, English, Russian, and Spanish, is not spoken by a majority. Only English is known throughout India, and only about three people in every hundred speak it. But this Anglophone minority has the greatest influence on running the country. They are the administrators, judges, industrialists, businessmen, leading politicians, and educators.

The languages of India are great unifiers within their home regions; but there are places where language is a sensitive—and political—issue.

Legacy of the Raj

The English language is one of the chief legacies of the British raj, and spoken English in India often has a distinctive and musical lilt. Many Indian words have entered English as part of the cross-fertilization: *bungalow, chintz, pajama,* and *calico* are familiar ones.

English was only one important legacy. A system of justice and the democratic ideal were others. And Indians from north to south love another legacy, the game of cricket. They are as devoted to it as any Englishman—more so, some would say. Listen to Indians discussing cricket, in any language, and you will hear something of the international cricket language: "sticky wicket," "keep a straight bat," and "well played, sir!" Test matches attract huge crowds, and employers complain about people taking the day off to attend. As you travel about, you can see even the poorest boys playing cricket in the dust or on a patch of grass, with makeshift bats and other gear, and dreaming of being cricket stars. The top players are national heroes. Cricket is one of the things that Pakistan and India have in common. When the two countries play each other, the crowds forget other rivalries and concentrate on sporting ones. When there was tension on the shared frontier in 1987, a cricket match defused it.

The British left little or no residue of bitterness when they quit India in 1947. The relations between the two countries have usually been cordial and remain special. Many Indians suffered during the years of the struggle for independence; Nehru and Gandhi were only two of the many thousands who were imprisoned for their activities against the British. But once independence was achieved, there was no attempt to erase the evidence of British management. Nehru, for example, always had a good relationship with the British, and many Indians look back with affection on their years in British schools and universities. India has done what it has usually done throughout history. It absorbed what the British had to offer and took it in its stride.

Traditional Values vs. Modern Cities

India respects its past and reveres old values and rituals, no more so than in the countryside. If you bear in mind that most of the people derive their living from the land, the social and family structures in the villages form a massive bedrock of stability. People live together in a joint family, an efficient way of sharing resources, work, and problems. Major decisions, such as a woman's wish to be sterilized in the birth-control program, may involve the whole family. For decisions affecting the whole community, villagers turn to the *panchayat,* the elected village council. This practice supervises development projects and lobbies the authorities for improvements like wells, irrigation pumps, and health facilities.

Although the countryside in many parts of India has a timeless appearance, with plodding oxen drawing carts and women balancing water jars on their heads, time does not stand still. Agricultural production has been modernized in many areas, new power stations drive irrigation pumps, most villages have electricity, and many villages now own a community television set. In some areas, you will be impressed by the sheer number of shiny new tractors. But bear in mind that these improvements and changes are based on centuries of tradition, of caste divisions and the close loyalties of the joint family—a strict social pecking order.

In the country in particular, you can plainly see that customs, religion, and economic demands put a heavy emphasis on the male. Men rule the roost. Couples fervently desire sons, and girls are often regarded as a burden. The birth of a son is always a matter of celebration; the birth of a girl is usually not. In general, boys in rural India get better treatment, food, education, and medical care. The life expectancy of women in the countryside is shorter than that of men.

It is a different story in the towns and cities whose populations are growing rapidly. It is difficult to keep caste barriers in crowded buses, trains, offices, factories, and restaurants. The rise of urban India has eroded caste differences. The extended family, with parents and sons and daughters-in-law all living together, is still important in the cities, as is the tradition of arranged marriages, with parents finding brides for their sons through personal contacts and newspaper advertisements. However, many young middle-class are opting for Western-style courtship and marriage.

It is in urban India that women are at their most emancipated and can compete as equals with men. Women are steadily advancing in medicine, education, law, science, civil service, commerce, and politics. And instead of being kept apart, many men and women in the cities get to know each other socially and professionally in universities and other places of work. The growth of the middle class in the cities is bringing about great changes in Indian life.

The cities are the dynamos, and people stream in from the countryside in search of the better life and more money. The result is that the cities have become overcrowded and, in some places like Bombay and Calcutta, overcrowding creates a permanent and desperate crisis. In Bombay, for example, about half the city's 10 million people live in slums. Indeed, some of these shanty settlements are almost towns in their own right: the largest has a population of more than half a million. But people continue to pour in because they believe they will earn more than they can in the fields at home. And they are right. Even a lowly job in Bombay pays more than a laboring job in the country, enough to enable a man to send money back home. So many people, rich and poor, want to be in Bombay that property prices have soared to astonishing levels. Bombay's best areas have become as expensive as New York and Tokyo.

Since the early 1970s, the cities of India have grown by 40 percent and 12 cities now have populations of more than a million. Nearly a quarter of the Indians are town or city dwellers, and the migration into cities—with all the problems it creates—is one of the significant forces that is changing Indian life. It is shaping new attitudes and breaking ancient molds.

FACTS AT YOUR FINGERTIPS

THE LAND. Though you may think of India as a place that's hot and tropical, all of it is in the northern hemisphere. India's territory makes it the seventh largest country in the world, with a land frontier of 9,425 miles, a total land area of 1,261,000 square miles, and a coastline of 3,535 miles—approximately the cross-country distance of the United States. In the north, the Himalayas separate India from China. Situated between the two countries is Nepal; to its east is Bhutan, which is still closely connected to India by special treaty. All three countries lie along the chain of the Himalayas, and still more mountains separate India from Burma on India's eastern border. Also in the east lies Bangladesh, wedged between the Indian states of Assam and West Bengal. In the northwest, Pakistan and a small hook of Afghanistan border India and separate it from the USSR.

Stretching southward, the country crosses the Tropic of Cancer, then tapers off into a peninsula with the Arabian Sea to the west and the Bay of Bengal to the east. Just off the eastern tip of the subcontinent lies Sri Lanka (formerly Ceylon), separated from the mainland by a sliver of water, the Palk Straits. Sri Lanka, just 31 miles away, is an independent nation, whereas islands much farther away from India, like the Laccadive, Minicoy, and Amindivi Islands—now known as the Lakshadweep Islands—in the Arabian Sea and the distant Andaman and Nicobar Islands in the Bay of Bengal are part of the Indian Union.

The mainland itself is a geographer's and geologist's paradise. The Himalayan range (*hima* = snow; *laya* = abode) is dramatically high, the altitude of the Indo-Gangetic plain varies little from sea to sea, and the southern peninsula is a high plateau with coastal strips. The Himalayan mountains are three parallel ranges with wide plateaus and valleys that are fertile and spectacular. The mountain wall, which is 1,500 miles long with a depth of 150 to 200 miles, boasts one of the world's highest altitudes. Until recently, Mount Everest, at 29,108 feet, was undisputedly the highest peak in the world, but astronomers making calculations via satellite measurements in early 1987 claimed that K-2 in Pakistan is taller. The dispute was resolved later in 1987 when an Italian expedition confirmed that Everest is still tops—840 feet higher than K-2.

The Garo, Khasi, and Naga hills in the northeast are dwarfs in comparison to their Himalayan neighbors. They run east–west to join the north–south Lushai and Arakan Hills that separate India from Burma.

The unvarying Indo-Gangetic Plain is 150 to 200 miles broad and formed by the basins of three river systems; it is the home of probably more people per square mile than any other spot on earth. The basins of the Indus, the Ganges, and the Brahmaputra make the land rich and fertile. Between India's capital of Delhi and the Bay of Bengal, nearly 1,000 miles, the elevation of the Gangetic plain drops only 700 feet. The peninsular plateau is marked off from this plain by mountain and hill ranges, among them the Aravali and the Vindhya ranges. The Eastern Ghats move down the peninsula and follow its shape, marking off a broad coastal strip between it and the Bay of Bengal, while on the opposite side of the peninsula, the Western Ghats define a narrower coast off the Arabian Sea. The two ranges meet near the southern tip of India in the Nilgiri Hills.

Geologically, the country has this three-part division: The Himalayas are formed by layers of marine deposits and were once covered by the sea, the soil of the Indo-Gangetic plain comes from river deposits, and the rocks of the southern peninsula are among the oldest in the world. The Himalayan rivers are snow fed and flow continuously, often causing great floods during the monsoons; the Deccan rivers are rain fed and fluctuate greatly in volume; and the coastal rivers are short and drain little territory.

The Ganges is the mother of India's rivers, the bedrock of mythology and veneration. Its basin drains about a quarter of the country's entire area. The second-largest basin is that of the Godavari, which claims about 10 percent of the total land mass. The most important rivers are the Brahmaputra in the east, the Indus in the west, and the Krishna in the south.

Basic Statistics for India

Land area: 1,261,000 square miles (3,287,000 square km)
Population: 1988 (est.) 850 million
Population, average annual growth: 2.1 percent
Population, literate adults: 36 percent
Average life expectancy: 56 years
Average per capita income (1988 estimate): $270 (in U.S. dollars)
Population of 18–25 year olds: 80 million
Agriculture as a percentage of the gross national product (GNP): 41.9 percent (73 percent of the work force)
Industry as a percentage of the GNP: 22 percent
Religions (percentage of population):
  Hindu   83.3
  Muslim   11.0
  Christian 2.6
  Sikh   1.9
  Buddhist 0.9
  Other   0.3
Languages: 15 major regional languages plus 250 minor regional languages

 THE CLIMATE. India's climate can be described as monsoon-tropical, in spite of some local variations like the winter rains in the northwest. Keep in mind that India is a subcontinent and make allowances for that fact in the following broad classification of the seasons: the cool weather lasts from October to the end of February, and the really hot weather from the beginning of April to the beginning of June, at which point the monsoon (rainy)

Temperature and Rainfall Chart (Averages)

		Bombay	Calcutta	Darjeeling	Delhi	Madras
Jan.	*	82	81	46	70	84
	†	0.14	0.37	0.53	0.99	1.41
Feb.	*	82	84	48	75	88
	†	0.08	1.17	1.19	0.83	0.41
Mar.	*	86	93	57	88	91
	†	0.05	1.36	1.88	0.51	0.29
Apr.	*	90	97	63	97	95
	†	0.03	1.75	4.14	0.33	0.61
May	*	91	97	64	106	100
	†	0.65	5.49	9.63	0.52	1.03
June	*	90	91	64	102	100
	†	19.06	11.69	24.18	3.03	1.86
July	*	84	90	66	97	97
	†	24.27	12.81	32.92	7.03	3.60
Aug.	*	84	90	64	93	95
	†	13.39	12.92	26.56	7.23	4.58
Sept.	*	84	90	64	93	90
	†	10.39	9.95	18.90	4.84	4.68
Oct.	*	90	90	61	93	90
	†	2.54	4.48	5.41	0.40	12.04
Nov.	*	90	84	54	84	84
	†	0.53	0.81	0.81	0.10	13.96
Dec.	*	88	79	48	73	84
	†	0.08	0.18	0.27	0.43	5.45

*Average maximum temp. Fahrenheit   †Average rainfall in inches

season sets in until the end of September. The clear cool weather arrives again and moves gradually eastward and southward. The monsoon deserves special emphasis. This seasonal trade wind blows across the Arabian Sea and reaches India with almost mathematical regularity in May and traverses the country in June and July. It brings with it rain-laden clouds that water practically every part of India to some degree and return to the Arabian Sea in September and October. In the far north, the Himalayas, Nepal, Sikkim, Bhutan, and Kashmir can be extremely cold during winter, when many mountain passes and valleys are closed because of deep snow. The temperatures in these mountainous areas also vary a great deal, depending on elevation; evenings are generally cool.

WHAT IT WILL COST. This is about the hardest travel question to answer in advance. Budgeting is much simplified if you take a prepackaged trip. Air and rail travel and taxis are cheaper than in other countries. Good accommodations in Western-style hotels with air-conditioned rooms and deluxe hotel services and dining in restaurants that serve Western food will be expensive, but, throughout the country, adequate Indian-style hotels provide accommodations at reasonable rates. Some hotels quote prices for rooms only, while others offer some or all meals, and service charges may or may not be added. Check carefully what is included in the quote you receive from hotels. The prices quoted here are based on an exchange rate (at press time, mid-1987) of Rs. 12.70 to U.S. $1; or Rs. 21 to the U.K. pound sterling.

You can estimate expenses for two persons as being roughly Rs. 2,000–2,200 per day for luxury hotel accommodations, three a la carte meals, and city sightseeing. For moderately priced accommodations, three meals, and sightseeing, a couple would spend around Rs. 1,300–1,400 per day in any of the big cities. Costs are comparatively lower in smaller towns and resorts. On the whole, the southern region of India is approximately 15 percent cheaper than is North India.

HOTEL PRICES

	Major City	Major Resort	Provincial Capital	Small Resort
DELUXE				
Single	Rs.900–1400	500–750	600–700	300–400
Double	Rs.1200–1400	600–750	700–800	300–500
EXPENSIVE				
Single	Rs.450–650	250–300	250–350	100–200
Double	Rs.550–750	250–350	225–450	160–260
MODERATE				
Single	Rs.250–335	105–220	150–265	180–200
Double	Rs.350–450	175–350	200–300	225–270
INEXPENSIVE				
Single	Rs.95–200	60–100	40–120	50–110
Double	Rs.130–250	80–125	75–170	120–150

Expensive and Moderate hotels are worth the money and are usually centrally located, thus allowing you to save on transportation.

Many of India's hotels, in resorts and in major cities, give off-season rates that are 10–15 percent lower than the regular rates.

In addition to the rates just quoted, most hotels now levy a 10 percent service charge. Some states also levy a sales tax, which varies from 2 to 10 percent, and a luxury tax of from 3 to 20 percent for certain items.

Taxi service. Government-controlled taxis are yellow topped and have meters. The rates vary among major cities but usually start at around Rs. 3.50 for the first 1.2 km (approximately ¾ mile) and thereafter increase by Rs. 2 for every subsequent km. Rates are based on gasoline costs, which are regulated by the central government. Since costs rise frequently, rates are constantly being changed. In some cities, meters don't keep up with these changes, so taxis have rate charts to refer to in determining the correct fare (as much as 40 percent above the meter costs in some locations). These rate charts are sometimes available at tourist counters in hotels. Taxi rates vary slightly in different states. Scooter or auto rickshaws in main cities are metered and cheaper than are taxis. Whether traveling by taxi or scooter rickshaw, be sure that the meter is started after you enter the cab, or that you have agreed on a price in advance, especially for airport taxis.

Private cars from tour operators approved by the Department of Tourism are also available for package trips. The rates are fixed, usually Rs. 150–200 for a half day (4 hours), depending on mileage and inclusive of gasoline. If you hire such a car for the entire day, you will most probably be expected to pay for gasoline at the end.

Cinema. First-run shows and imported movies will cost approximately Rs. 8 for the most expensive seats; seats should be reserved most of the time. The price drops considerably in provincial theaters, but so does the comfort.

RESTAURANT PRICES
(for dinner, per person; drinks not included)

	Major city	Major Resort	Small Resort or Provincial Capital
Deluxe	Rs. 110–140	100–145	80–100
Expensive	Rs. 80–100	80–115	55–80
Moderate	Rs. 40–60	55–80	45–70
Inexpensive	Rs. 35–50	35–60	35–55

Drinks. Because of localized prohibition, alcoholic drinks are not always available (except for beer), even in hotel restaurants. Indian beer, which is good and plentiful, is about Rs. 20–45 per bottle at hotel bars, Rs. 15 in shops. Canned beer is available, but imported beer is usually not available. Imported whiskey and gin are expensive, around Rs. 750 per bottle. Indian whiskey, gin, and rum are good and cost about Rs. 75–140 per bottle, outside hotels. Prices vary from state to state. Sikkim makes good rum, and Goa is producing sweet wines that should be tried. Western (American-style) coffee costs roughly Rs. 9. Italian espresso—when obtainable—is better and costs about the same. Indian coffee has a caramel tang and is inexpensive. Tea is excellent and inexpensive, although those who take it black or without sugar should indicate so, since it is frequently served with milk and sugar already in it. A delicious tea, for those adventurous types, is to be found in *dhabas* (roadside truck stops), where the tea is brewed by boiling tea leaves in milk with sugar in it. India has a tremendous variety of good soft drinks that cost Rs. 1.50, and recently some delicious bottled fruit juices have come on the market, including a refreshing mango fruit drink, costing Rs. 2. In metropolitan markets, bottles are being replaced with "bricks" —paper boxes packaged by a Swedish company and offering a range from chocolate milk to juices, for Rs. 2.50 a brick.

Cigarettes. Imported cigarettes are usually not available outside major metropolitan cities. Indian cigarettes are excellent and cost Rs. 12–20 for a packet of 20. Indian cigars are cheap and good.

Magazines. *Time* and *Newsweek* (Asian editions) cost about Rs. 15; other foreign magazines are rare, expensive, and late. Indian magazines in English, covering a broad range of subjects from computers to film stars, run Rs. 4–6. Indian English-language newsmagazines such as *India Today, Frontline,* and *Sunday* are excellent in their national coverage.

Newspapers. The only foreign newspaper available in India is the *International Herald Tribune* (Rs. 15), available in major hotel shopping arcades. Indian English-language daily newspapers, with a history of over 200 years behind them and the second-highest circulation of newspapers in any language, are easily available. Many of them carry news analyses from the *New York Times Service,* the *Washington Post* and news service bureaus. They cost Rs. 1.50–2. National dailies are *Times of India, Indian Express, Statesman, Hindusthan*

Standard, and *Hindu.* The feistiest and most analytical is a regional daily, *The Telegraph,* which is less than a decade old and is published in Calcutta.

Haircut and shampoo. Haircuts do not cost much. Even the fanciest establishments will charge about Rs. 15–20 for a man's haircut. A woman's shampoo costs Rs. 15–20, and a woman's haircut, Rs. 15–30.

NOTE: Traveler's checks are the best way to safeguard travel funds. Widely accepted American traveler's checks are those of *Bank of America* and *American Express.* However, in some places, where there is no American Express office, a surcharge is added to the cost of a purchase. *Thos. Cook & Son* are the best known and most easily exchanged British traveler's checks.

Foreign credit cards are increasingly accepted in Indian hotels, restaurants, and major shops and in many of the larger state emporiums. Payment for travel "concession" tickets, such as the *Indrail* train pass and the *Discover India* airline ticket, must usually be paid in foreign currency. Credit cards are acceptable. Shops that accept credit cards will often give an extra discount if you pay in cash. Some hotels insist on being paid in foreign currency. *American Express, Diner's Club, MasterCard,* and *VISA* are the most common credit cards.

$P£ **CURRENCY.** On arriving in India you must fill out a Currency Declaration Form if you are bringing in over U.S. $1,000 or its equivalent in foreign currency. Travelers are strongly urged to retain all receipts of foreign currency exchanges to convert excess rupees on departure because these receipts are necessary when one converts rupees into foreign currency. Visitors are not allowed to bring in, or take out, any Indian currency. As we go to press, the value of the Indian rupee is about Rs. 12.70 to U.S. $1 and Rs. 21 to the British pound sterling. Exchange rates fluctuate regularly, so we suggest that you keep an eye on current values when you plan your trip. Your bank or travel agent can advise you, or check in the business section of your local paper. All banks and most of the large Western-style hotels are authorized to exchange travelers checks, U.S. dollars, and pounds sterling. If you want quick service, change your money directly at your hotel. The rate is usually the same as in banks, and the service is considerably faster.

Note: For foreign travelers and Indian residents abroad, internal air travel expenses and accommodations in many hotels must be paid in foreign currency. Some hotels do not accept credit cards, so carry plenty of small-denomination travelers checks. Change will probably be given in rupees.

Indian Money: 1 rupee = 100 paise. Coins come in denominations of 5, 10, 20, 25, and 50 paise and 1 rupee. Notes come in denominations of 1, 2, 5, 10, 20, 50, 100, and 500 rupees.

A major problem throughout India is the asserted lack of small change by taxi and rickshaw drivers and soft drink or souvenir vendors. It is therefore wise to carry a generous supply of coins and small notes. Another problem in India is that bank notes that are torn or damaged are frequently refused but often tendered as change. Since torn notes are plentiful, make sure you refuse them or you will be stuck with them and will have to go to a bank to exchange them for new ones.

Planning Your Trip

India is one country where you *must* plan your trip in advance. It is too vast and complex a land to start organizing your itinerary after you arrive. Unless you are traveling on a package tour, with a fixed itinerary and schedule, read every possible brochure first and then settle on priorities.

Most first-time visitors to India try to pack in too many objectives. Distances are huge, traveling tiring, and sightseeing exhausting. Wise travelers plan a couple of days' complete relaxation, in a beach resort or hill station, for every 7–10 days of touring, to digest all the wonders they have seen and to catch up on rest and laundry before the next phase of the trip.

The *Government of India Tourist Office* is one of the best of the national tourism-promotion organizations. Here, you will get informative leaflets covering the diverse attractions and regions of India. We hope you will find most of the planning information you need in this book, but public libraries will provide more in-depth information about social or political aspects. State-run tourist offices vary in reliability and information; some are informative about local events and some offer reasonably priced tour packages.

Major Goverment of India Tourist Offices are located at the following addresses:

USA	30 Rockefeller Plaza, 15 North Mezzanine, New York, NY 10112; tel. 212–586–4901
	3550 Wilshire Blvd., Los Angeles, CA 90010; tel. 213–380–8855
	230 North Michigan Ave., Chicago, IL 60601; tel. 312–236–6899
UK	7 Cork St., London W1X 2AB; tel. 01–437–3677 or 78
CANADA	60 Bloor St. West, Suite 1003, Toronto, Ontario M4W3B8; tel. 416–962–3787 or 88
AUSTRALIA	Carlton Center, 55 Elizabeth St., Sydney, NSW 2000; tel. 02–232–1600

There are also overseas offices in Bangkok, Dubai, Frankfurt, Geneva, Kuwait, Milan, Paris, Singapore, Stockholm, Tokyo, and Vienna. Visitors will find Government of India Tourist Offices in all the major towns of India; these offices will be even more helpful than the overseas branches because they have more detailed information for their own areas.

Except for the northeast area where special travel restrictions apply, it is possible to make your own arrangements for a tour of India, rather than use a travel agent. However, you would be well advised to make hotel bookings well in advance for major tourist centers, especially if you travel in the high season, October–March.

The services of Indian Airlines, the major domestic carrier, have improved greatly in recent years. Bookings can be made through Air-India offices abroad, since Indian Airlines does not have overseas facilities. It is critical that you reconfirm all airline flights, domestic or international, throughout your stay in India. Train reservations and ticket purchases usually have to be made on the spot in each major city. Special lines for tourists are set up at major airports and railroad terminals. Indian railways are in the process of computerizing reservations, cancellations, and the like. Delhi is already on-line, and Calcutta and Bombay will be on-line by mid-1988.

The growth of major hotel chains in recent years has made advance booking much simpler, and accommodations for a complete tour itinerary can now be reserved through just one or two central reservations systems. Details of the major chains are given in the *Hotels* section of this chapter.

City sightseeing, car hire, and guide services can be easily arranged on arrival at each destination, either through hotel travel desks, the local Government of India Tourist Office, or the state tourist organization. The excursions and tours detailed in this section can also be arranged easily, but one should make airline reservations well in advance, especially during peak travel times.

The wise traveler to India builds in several reserve days in case of unexpected delays or the impulse to see more of a particular place. We would most strongly advise that you do not try to work within a tight itinerary. Take it easy and, if you cannot see all of India in one trip (an impossibility!), come back again, just as many do, to this fascinating land.

This book will help you to decide what you want to see in India. Study our maps of the tourist highlights, consult the list of itineraries appearing later in this chapter while building up your own itinerary, and then try to reconcile the itinerary you plan with the time at your disposal. Remember that airline schedules change slightly according to season, so be sure to check them.

 TRAVEL DOCUMENTS. Apply for your passport and visa several months in advance of your departure date. Passports are valid for 10 years for adults (over age 18) and for five years for children. U.S. citizens who are applying for their first passport must appear in person either at a U.S. Passport Agency in Boston, Chicago, Honolulu, Houston, Los Angeles, Miami, New

Orleans, New York, Philadelphia, San Francisco, Seattle, Stamford (CT), or Washington DC or at designated post offices or local county courthouses. You will need 1) proof of citizenship, such as a certified copy of your birth certificate (an original birth certificate, if not certified, is not acceptable); for those born abroad, a certificate of naturalization can be used; 2) two identical 2″ × 2″ black-and-white or color full-face photos (you must appear in regular street attire) taken within the last six months, with the background of the photo either plain white or off white; 3) current identification with a photo, such as a driver's license or a government or school ID card, with a physical description and signature; 4) a fee of $42 for those 18 years or older and $27 for children payable in cash (the exact amount only if applying at the U.S. Passport Agency) or by check. Allow at least three to four weeks for processing. For children up to 13 years, a parent, with an ID, must apply in person. Those who were issued a passport within the past 12 years when they were 16 years or older may apply for a new passport through the mail by filling out Form DSP 82, which is available at designated post offices and offices of the U.S. Passport Agency, or by writing to Passport Services, U.S. Department of State, 1425 K St., NW, Washington, DC 20524. You will need two new photos, your old passport, and $35, payable by check or money order. Allow at least two to three weeks for processing.

If you are a resident of the United States, but are not a citizen, you will need your alien registration card and a valid passport from your country in order to reenter the United States. If you intend to remain abroad longer than one year, contact the nearest office of the Immigration and Naturalization Service at least six weeks in advance of your departure to determine if additional forms are necessary.

VISAS

Citizens of the United States entering India *must* have a visa.

Applications for tourist or entry/business visas should be made on prescribed visa application forms that can be obtained from your nearest Consulate General of India (3 East 64th St., New York, NY 10021; 150 North Michigan Ave., Chicago IL; 540 Arguello Blvd., San Francisco CA) or to the Embassy of India, 2107 Massachusetts Ave., Washington, DC. You must have a valid passport and one passport-size photograph and pay a $15 fee ($2 additional to have a passport with a visa returned by mail). Visas are issued within 24–48 hours if you apply in person. If you apply by mail, allow three weeks.

All tourist visas are triple entry, are valid for a three-month stay in India, and can be extended to six months (multiple-entry, five-year visas are being considered). The current triple-entry visa simplifies the procedure of visiting neighboring countries like Nepal. Entry/business visas, meant for those traveling on business or to visit family or friends, are single entry, but additional entries may be requested. These visas are valid for a three-month stay. Those traveling on business will need a letter from their sponsoring firm indicating the nature of the business, a guarantee of maintenance expenses, and return travel ticket.

Persons who intend to stay in India for a prolonged period will have to apply for an entry visa at least two months in advance of their proposed departure.

Special Note: No visas are issued in India, so be sure that you have one before you leave. Should you arrive in India without one, you will be allowed to stay in the airport for up to 72 hours (or until a flight can take you home), but you will not be granted a visitor's permit.

If you have visited India before and are now traveling with a new passport, bring along your previous passport or a photocopy of its Indian visa and entry and departure information for India. Indian Immigration will sometimes delay your processing on arrival if you have been to India but cannot produce such visa, arrival, and departure information.

British Citizens. Passports and visas are necessary for all British citizens visiting India. British subjects should apply for passports on special forms obtainable from main post offices or a travel agent. The application should be sent or taken to the Passport Office according to residential area (as indicated on the guidance form) or lodged with them through a travel agent. It is best to apply for the passport four–five weeks before it is required, although in some cases it will be issued sooner. The regional Passport Offices are located in London, Liverpool, Peterborough, Glasgow and Newport. The application must be countersigned by your bank manager or by a solicitor, barrister, doctor, clergyman, or justice of the peace who knows you personally. You will need two full-face photos. The fee is £15; the passport is valid for 10 years.

Individual tourists should preferably apply for a tourist visa to avoid delaying their departure. Tourist visas can be arranged within 48 hours if you are able to appear at the High Commission for India, India House, Aldwych, London WC2. Applications by mail take three–four weeks. Tourist visas are valid for six months. A visa for India, if valid for one entry, must be used within six months of issue. If valid for more than one entry, it must be used for the first time within six months of issue and will expire 90 days after the date of the first entry. A "restricted area permit" is required if you wish to visit the northwestern region, Punjab. Apply for this visa well in advance because it can take two–three months to issue.

Canadian Citizens. Canadian citizens apply in person to regional passport offices or post offices or by mail to Passport Office, 200 DuPortage, 6th Floor, Place du Center, Hull, Quebec K1A 0G3 (819–994–3500). A $21 fee, two photographs and evidence of citizenship are required. Canadian passports are valid for five years and are nonrenewable. For visas, Canadians may apply at the Indian consulates at 10 Springfield Rd., Ottawa, Quebec KLM 109; 2 Bloor St., Suite 500, West Cumberland, Toronto, Ontario M4W 3E2; or 325 Howe St., Vancouver, British Columbia VG 127. The fee is $7, and the same restrictions for British citizens apply.

 TOURING ITINERARIES. In planning tours of India one should either select one city as a base, radiating out to other places of interest, or make up an itinerary that includes major attractions between key cities. This plan is particularly valid for brief visits of up to a week, such as might be undertaken by a business or transit traveler. The following tours will need Indian Airlines and Vayudoot timetables for detailed planning, but flight frequencies are convenient, mostly daily, between adjacent points.

One-Week Tours (based on major cities):

Out of Bombay (West India): Bombay city sightseeing plus boat ride to Elephanta Caves (Sept.–May only) or Khaneri Caves. Fly to Aurangabad, visiting Ajanta and Ellora caves by car or bus. Fly to Jaipur, returning to Bombay, or return directly to Bombay and fly to Goa to relax at the seaside. Alternative destinations to the south are Cochin or Trivandrum, for the Kovalam Beach resort and the Periyar Game Sanctuary.

Out of Delhi (Northwest India): Old and New Delhi sightseeing, including evening Sound and Light Show at the Red Fort. Trips out of Delhi include Agra, with the magnificent Taj Mahal and the haunting beauty of Fatehpur Sikri; Khajuraho, its temples covered lavishly with erotic sculpture; Varanasi, the holiest Hindu pilgrimage site and perhaps the world's oldest living city; Srinagar in Kashmir with side trips to Gulmarg (skiing in the winter) and Pahalgum; Leh, capital of Ladakh, with its Buddhist monasteries (*gompas*) and stark mountainous setting; Chandigarh, the modern city planned by Le Corbousier; and Jaipur or Udaipur in Rajasthan, with their Rajput palaces.

Out of Calcutta (East India): City sightseeing. After the stimulus of this great city, trips to the mountains or beaches are reviving; Darjeeling, a cool Himalayan hill station; mountainous Sikkim and Bhutan, with their spectacular scenery and intriguing cultures; and the Andaman Islands, a developing beach resort with excellent coral reefs. Bhubaneswar, south of Calcutta, offers a rich opportunity to study the architecture of Hindu temples, and driving to the nearby cities of Puri and Konarak, one passes through rich farmlands (the beaches between Puri and Konarak are beautiful). Pilgrimage spots in Bihar, such as Bodhgaya, can be reached most easily from Calcutta. Assam's wildlife sanctuaries, Kaziranga and Manas, and Orissa's, Simlipal, are special-interest spots. *For Darjeeling, Sikkim, Bhutan, and Assam, one needs special permits.*

Out of Madras (Southeast Madras): Local sightseeing in Madras and in the temple towns of Kanchipuram and Mahabalipuram, both easily reached by road. Mahabalipuram has a delightful beach resort. Farther south by road are the ex-French city of Pondicherry and Chidambaram, with its fine temples. There are many easy excursions by air from Madras: flying to Coimbatore, one connects by bus or car to the "Queen of Hill Stations," Ootacamund; via Trivandrum one can reach Kovaluam, a beach resort, and the Periyar game reserve; Tiruchirapalli and Madurai, can be seen for their temples and other interesting sights; from Bangalore one can drive to Mysore; the Andaman Islands are a few hours away; and Hyderabad is also reached easily from Madras. Colombo, Sri Lanka, can be reached by air from Madras, Madurai, or Trivandrum, with international connections to Singapore and Bangkok.

"Connecting" One-Week Tours

Delhi–Calcutta (or reverse): A convenient air service provides "bus stop" service between major attractions across North India, from Delhi to Calcutta. Included could be Agra, to see the Taj Mahal, with a car ride to Fatehpur Sikri, or by air to Jaipur, Khajuraho, and Varanasi. From Varanasi, one could fly to Calcutta directly or via Kathmandu in Nepal or take a train to Patna with an onward domestic flight to Calcutta.

Bombay–Madras (southern circle tour): Out of Bombay, one has a number of choices: Goa with its beach resorts, Cochin, or Trivandrum. By road, one can reach Kavalam Beach Resort, Periyar Game Sanctuary, or Cape Comorin in the extreme south. Other trips include Bombay–Bangalore–Bombay–Hyderabad–Madras. From Trivandrum, one can fly to Madras or Colombo, Sri Lanka.

15-Day Tour of India. Two days in Delhi and New Delhi seeing sights. Sound and Light Show at Red Fort one evening. Proceeding from Delhi, spend two more days visiting Agra and Fatehpur Sikri. One day each in Jaipur, Khajuraho, Varanasi. Spend the next seven days visiting Kashmir and Ladakh; Calcutta and Darjeeling or the Andaman Islands; Calcutta and Bhubaneswar, Puri, Konarak, and Chilka Lake; Madras, Mahabalipuram, Bangalore, and Mysore; Bombay, Ajanta and Ellora Caves, Sanchi.

21-Day Air Tour (with side trips) could include Bombay, the Ajanta and Ellora Caves outside Hurangabad, Jaipur, Udaipur, Delhi, Agra, Khajuraho, Varanasi and Sarnath, Kathmandu, Calcutta, Darjeeling or the Andaman Islands, Madras, Madurai, Cochin, and Bangalore.

30-Day All-India Air Tour could bring you to the following places, but at least one day of complete rest a week is strongly recommended:

Day:	Place:	Program:
1	Bombay	City sightseeing and, between mid-September and mid-May, excursion to Elephanta Caves.
2	Bombay	Fly in the morning to Aurangabad (30 min.). During the day, visit Ellora by bus or car and take a city tour.
3	Aurangabad	Visit Ajanta by bus or car; return to Aurangabad for overnight stay.
4	Udaipur	Fly in the morning to Bombay. Change flights. Leave by air for Udaipur (45 min.).
5	Udaipur	City sightseeing and excursions by car to Sas Bahu Temples, Nathdwara, or Eklingji.
6	Jaipur	Fly to Jaipur (35 min.).
7	Jaipur-Delhi	City sightseeing and visit Amber. Fly in the evening to Delhi (35 min.).
8 and 9	Delhi	Sightseeing of Old and New Delhi. Evening, attend "Son et Lumière" show at the Red Fort (except in monsoon).

Day:	Place:	Program:
10	Srinagar	Fly to Srinagar in the morning (1 hr.). City sightseeing; boat ride on Dal and Nagin Lakes.
11	Srinagar	Excursion by car or bus to Pahalgam or Gulmarg.
12	Srinagar-Delhi	Rest or shopping. Return to Delhi.
13	Agra	Fly in the morning to Agra (35 min.). City sightseeing, and visit Fatehpur Sikri. See Taj, by moonlight if possible.
14	Khajuraho	Fly in the morning to Khajuraho (45 min.). Visit temples.
15	Varanasi (Benares)	Fly in the morning to Varanasi (50 min.). City sightseeing and visit Sarnath.
16	Varanasi-Kathmandu	Early morning boat ride on the Ganges. Fly to Kathmandu (Nepal) in the forenoon (55 min.). City sightseeing.
17	Kathmandu	Visit places of interest around Kathmandu.
18	Calcutta	Fly to Calcutta in the afternoon (1 hr.).
19	Calcutta-Bhubaneswar	Forenoon: City sightseeing. Fly in the afternoon to Bhubaneswar (1 hr.). Visit temples in Bhubaneswar.
20	Bhubaneswar	Excursion by car to Konarak and Puri. Have lunch or snacks at Toshali Sands.
21	Bhubaneswar	Fly in the afternoon to Hyderabad (1 hr.).
22	Hyderabad-Madras	City sightseeing. Fly late evening to Madras (1 hr.).
23 and 24	Madras	City sightseeing and excursion by car to Mahabalipuram, Pondicherry, and Kanchipuram.
25	Madurai	To Madurai. City sightseeing.
26	Trivandrum	Continue to Trivandrum. City sightseeing and relax at Kovalam Beach. (We suggest staying overnight at Kovalam.)
27	Cochin	Fly in the morning to Cochin (30 min.). City sightseeing and boat ride on backwaters.
28	Bangalore-Mysore	Fly in the morning to Bangalore (40 min.). Go by car to Mysore; en route visit Srirangapatnam and Somnathpur. City tour.

Day:	Place:	Program:
29	Mysore	Excursion by car to Halebid and Belur, via Sravanabelgola.
30	Bangalore-Bombay	Leave in the morning by car for Bangalore. Fly in the afternoon to Bombay (1 hr. 25 min.).

TOUR OPERATORS. A number of agencies specialize in the India-Nepal-Sri Lanka region. Those marked "B" in this list also offer tours to Bhutan.

Abercrombie & Kent (B), 1420 Kensington Rd., Oak Brook, IL 60521 (312–954–2944), has six tours ranging from 15 to 22 days. "Magnificent India and Nepal" journeys to Delhi, Kathmandu, Varanasi, Agra, and Jaipur cost around $2,200 for the two-week tour. The "Essence of India and Nepal" and "Splendors of India and Nepal" tours, which offer comprehensive visits to cultural cities of Northern India and Kathmandu and Tiger Tops in Nepal, cost $3,440–$3,990. "Temples and Tigers," which includes the Tiger Tops Jungle Reserve in Nepal as well as the Rhanthambhore Tiger Reserve in India in an 18-day trip, costs approximately $3,200. "Mountains, Rivers, and Jungles—Exploration of Nepal" is an 18-day adventure tour that includes trekking and river rafting; it costs about $2,800. The "Himalayan Kingdoms" tour covers Kashmir, Nepal, and Bhutan and costs approximately $4,000. "Off the Beaten Track" excursions to Kashmir and Ladakh may be booked independently or in conjunction with the other tours.

Distant Horizons, 5455 Wilshire Blvd., Los Angeles, CA 90036 (213–935–8845), offers cultural tours to India, Nepal, and Tibet. Its tours, running from 17 to 23 days, cost $1,429–$2,699. A wildlife tour stays in Tiger Tops in Nepal and game parks in the deserts of Rajasthan and the jungles of South India. Cultural tours include visits to cities of India and Nepal. The "Summer of the Raj" tour visits hill stations and tea plantation districts in the Indian Himalayas.

Esplanade Tours, 581 Boylston St., Boston, MA 02116 (617–266–7465), has a variety of tours throughout India for groups or individuals. Costs vary with the length of time and needs. Call for rates.

Hemphill Harris Travel Corp. (B), 16000 Ventura Blvd., Encino, CA 91436 (800–421–0454 or, inside California, 800–252–2103), has 11 tours ranging from 16 to 43 days, with the longer tours tied in with other countries in Asia. Its newly introduced 21-day "Best of India and Nepal" tour costs $1,990 for land arrangements, and its 29-day "India and Nepal Explored" tour costs $3,060.

Maupintour, 1515 St. Andrews Dr., Lawrence, KS 66044 (800–255–4266), offers 19-day tours in 1988: "Indian Dynasties," which takes you to Bombay, Aurangabad, Udaipur, Jaipur, Agra, Delhi, and Srinagar, and "Footsteps of the Moghuls," which takes you to Bombay, Aurangabad, Calcutta, Kathmandu, Varanasi, Khajuraho, Delhi, Agra, and Jaipur. The tour costs $2,298 per person (double occupancy) and includes most meals.

Mountain Travel (B), 1398 Solano Ave., Albany, CA 94706 (800–227–2384), offers carefully supervised treks that are graded for both difficulty and the experience required.

Odyssey Tours (B), 1821 Wilshire Blvd., Santa Monica, CA 90403 (800–654–7975), specializes in medical, cultural, and business exchange excursions of about 20 days. Costs, including land and air, range from $3,565 to $3,975. A popular tour is "Women-to-Women" excursion.

Olson-Travelworld (B), 5855 Green Valley Circle, Culver City, CA 90230 (213–670–7100), has deluxe-style tours from 17 to 35 days, at a cost of $2,295–$4,395. It also offers an intriguing tour, "The Great Himalayan Adventure," which visits the fascinating Himalayan areas of Bhutan, Sikkim, and Ladakh. Its affiliate, Jet Tours, offers an 18-day trek in Nepal.

For the nature lover, *Questers Tours* (B), 257 Park Ave. South, New York, NY 10010 (212–673–3120), offers tours to the Himalayas which explore the diversity of the area's natural history and cultures. The tours, offered in the spring and the fall, to coordinate with the best times for seeing wildflowers in bloom, the migration of birds, and clear weather, visit Nepal, Bhutan, Sikkim, and the Jaldapara Wildlife Refuge in Bengal.

Tours of Distinction (B), 141 E. 44th St., New York, NY 10017 (212–661–4680), features "Connoisseur" visits to Delhi, Kathmandu, Varanasi, Kajuraho, Agra, Udaipur, Jaipur, and Srinagar in 17 days, for $1,195.

Zutshi's Travel Service (B), 71 Keystone Ave., Reno, NV 89503 (702–323–0110), offers trips to Tibet as well as India, Nepal, Sri Lanka, Bhutan, and Pakistan. It also arranges "home accommodations" with Indian families, a unique way to explore the richness of Indian culture.

Other agencies specializing in tours to the subcontinent and other nearby countries include *Himalayan Travel* (B), P.O. Box 481, Greenwich, CT 06836 (800–551–1769); *Journeyworld International, Ltd.* (B), 410 East 51st St., New York, NY 10022 (212–752–8308); and *Percival,* 1 Tandy Center Plaza, Fort Worth, TX 76102 (800–433–5656).

RESTRICTED AREAS. Certain parts of India, which are politically sensitive or strategic for defense, are designated by the government as "restricted or protected areas," and foreign travelers need special permits to enter them. These areas include Darjeeling and other areas of northern West Bengal; the northeast states of Arunachal Pradesh, Assam, Manipur, Meghalaya, Mizoram, Nagaland, and Tripura; the northwest state of Punjab; Sikkim; Tribal Reserve Areas; the Lakshadweep Islands, and, depending on your length of stay and the islands to be visited, the Andaman Islands. The northernmost border areas are off limits to foreign travelers.

Each area has a slightly different procedure to follow for gaining permission to travel, and since local conditions change, these procedures and access regulations can change with them. The Government of India Tourist Office is developing a brochure, to be available by 1988, that will outline them in detail. Contact them at any of the addresses listed under "Planning Your Trip." The following are the current guidelines:

Visitors to the Andaman Islands must get a permit upon arrival in Port Blair, South Andaman, which allows visits to the capital, Port Blair, and the islands of Jolly Boy and Cinque for a maximum of 15 days. Those wishing to visit longer or to visit the islands need a Restricted Area Permit. (The Nicobar Islands are not open to foreign travelers.) Permission for groups of six to 20 may be obtained through the Immigration Department in Port Blair for day trips to the islands of Grub, Snob, Redskin, and Boat. To stay in the Andamans for over 15 days or to travel to other areas in Great and Little Andamans, you must get permission from the Ministry of Home Affairs, North Block, New Delhi, 110 001.

Assam and Meghalaya are the only northeast states for which permission to travel is being given. A Restricted Area Permit is required, and additional travel restrictions may apply. Visitors to Assam's Kaziranga and Manas Wildlife Sanctuaries and to Meghalaya must travel in groups of six or more on tours arranged for by recognized tour agents and are accompanied by a government liaison officer during their visit.

Visitors to Darjeeling need not apply beforehand for permits if they fly into Bagdogra Airport and stay for no longer than 15 days. Those traveling overland through northern West Bengal will need to apply for a Restricted Area Permit. You may also apply for a permit at the Foreigners' Registration Office, 237 Acharya J. C. Bose Road, Calcutta.

If you are traveling by train through Punjab, no permission is needed, but to visit, you need a Restricted Area Permit.

Sikkim permits, for sightseeing only, are for seven days. They can be extended to 10 days with relative ease in Sikkim by applying to the Inspector General of Police in Gangtok. Those wishing to go trekking are given a 15-day permit. It is advisable to send an additional copy of your permit application to the Liaison Officer, Sikkim Tourism Office, Hotel Janpath, Room No. 10, New Delhi, 110 001, to facilitate your application.

Restricted Area Permit applications, available at Indian consulates or embassies, should be filed when applying for your Indian visa. The consulate or embassy will then serve as a conduit, routing applications to the Ministry of Home Affairs, North Block, New Delhi, 110 001, and receiving notification from them. There is no charge for this permit, but three photographs must be submitted with it. Allow three months at a minimum for these permits.

Visitors to Bhutan need a visa and must travel in groups of six or more on tours arranged by approved agents. A government liaison officer will accompany the tour. Visas, which cost $20, are processed in the United States by the Bhutan Travel Service, 120 East 56th St., No. 810, New York, NY 10022.

Trekking permits are needed for parts of Nepal but can be obtained after your arrival.

Permits are required to photograph railway stations and trains. Contact the Railway Board through the Government Tourist Office where you are staying.

 TRAVEL AGENTS. Travel agents are experts in the increasingly complicated business of tourism. They have contacts with carriers and tourist offices all over the world, they know about sudden changes in schedules and fares, they keep a check on cancellations at times of the year when planes and ships are booked to capacity, and their racks and files are bulging with information on the latest tours and excursions. A good travel agent can save you time and money through his or her knowledge of details about which you could not be expected to know. In the all-important phase of planning your trip, even if you wish to travel independently, it is wise to take advantage of the services of these specialists. Whether you select one of the larger American, European, or Indian specialist agencies or a smaller organization is a matter of preference. But there are good reasons why you should engage a reliable agent.

If you wish an agent merely to arrange an oceanliner or airline ticket or to book you on a package tour, this service should cost you nothing. Most carriers and tour operators grant agents a fixed commission for saving them the expense of having to open individual offices in every town and city.

If you wish an agent to plan an individual itinerary for you and make all the arrangements down to hotel reservations and transfers to and from rail and air terminals, you are drawing on the agent's skills and knowledge of travel, as well as asking your agent to shoulder a great mass of details. Commissions from carriers (5–7½ percent) won't come close to covering an agent's expenses. Accordingly, a service charge will be levied on top of the actual cost of your trip, the amount varying with the agent and the complexity of your tour.

If you cannot locate a travel agent near your home, if in America, contact the *American Society of Travel Agents,* P.O. Box 23992, Washington, DC 20026 –3992; tel. 703–793–2782. If in Britain, contact the *Association of British Travel Agents,* 55 Newman St., London W1. Any agency affiliated with these organizations should be thoroughly reliable.

Nevertheless, if you do decide to make your own arrangements, you will find that the booking services of centralized hotel chains and improved domestic air services will reduce the problems you might formerly have had. Try to book major elements—air travel and hotels—in advance to cut down on the time you have to spend on practical arrangements after you arrive. Even on the best travel-agency-organized tour of India you can expect minor problems and hitches, so anticipate having to involve yourself with at least some practical arrangements. Through the aid of hotel travel desks and Government of India Tourist offices, located in all major cities and in many smaller locales, you will find the local, on-the-spot tour planning rather easy. Check the "Useful Addresses" section in each chapter for local contacts.

For general information on the subcontinent or names of member travel agents specializing in arranging tours, American readers can also contact the *Pacific Asia Travel Association,* 228 Grant Ave., San Francisco CA 94108; 415–986–4646.

U.S. AGENTS WHO PROMOTE TRAVEL TO INDIA

(B) = tours to Bhutan as well

American Express Travel Related Services, Inc., 100 Church St., New York, NY 10007.

Odyssey Tours (B), 1821 Wilshire Blvd., Santa Monica, CA 90403.

Lindblad Travel Inc. (B), 1 Sylvan Road No., P.O. Box 912, Westport, CT 06881.

Sita World Travel Bureau (B), 3932 Wilshire Blvd., Suite 100, Los Angeles, CA 90010.

General Tours, 770 Broadway, 10th Floor, New York, NY 10003.

Bennett Tours, 270 Madison Ave., New York, NY 10016.

Esplanade Tours, 581 Boylston St., Boston, MA 02116.

Four Winds Travel, 175 Fifth Ave., New York, NY 10010.

Shiba Travel, 1776 Broadway, New York, NY 10019.

Hemphill Harris Travel Corp. (B), 1600 Ventura Blvd., Encino, CA 91436.

Journeyworld International (B), 410 East 51st St., New York, NY 10022.

Tours of Distinction (B), 141 East 44th St., New York, NY 10017.

Tiger Mountain, Tiger Tops International, Inc., 2627 Lombard St., San Francisco, CA 94123.
Innerasia Travel (B), 2627 Lombard St., San Francisco, CA 94123.
Mercury Travels (B), 300 East 42nd St., New York, NY 10017.
Zutshi's Travel Service (B), 71 Keystone Ave., Reno, NV 89503.

BRITISH TRAVEL AGENTS
SPECIALIZING IN TOURS TO INDIA

American Express Co., Inc.
6 Haymarket
London SW1Y 4BS

Kuoni Travel Ltd.
33 Maddox St.
London W1

Bales Tours Ltd.
Bales House
Burrington Rd.
Dorking
Surrey RH4 3EJ

Swan Hellenic Tours Ltd.
Beaufort House
St. Botolph St.
London EC3A 7DX

Cox & Kings Ltd.
Vulcan House
46 Marshall St.
London W1V 2PA

Thos. Cook Ltd.
45 Berkeley St.
London W1A 1EB

ExplorAsia Ltd.
Blenheim House
Burnsall St.
London SW3 5XS

Most of these firms have branch offices in the provinces.

AUSTRALIAN AND NEW ZEALAND TRAVEL AGENTS
SPECIALIZING IN TOURS TO INDIA

Australian Express
239 Elizabeth St.
Brisbane, Queensland QLD 4000

Russell & Sommers Ltd.
Box 1284
83 Customs St.
Auckland, NZ

Elders Travel Service
117 St. George's Terrace
Perth, WA 6000

Thos. Cook & Sons Ltd.
Branches in Melbourne, Sydney,
    Adelaide, Perth, etc.

Orbit Travel Service
MLC Centre, Castlereagh St.
Sydney, NSW 2000

CANADA

Crossways Travel (specializes in trekking), 2340 Dundas St. West, Toronto, Ontario M6P4A9.

 WHEN TO GO. The regular tourist season in India runs from mid-September through March. The summer season can be excruciatingly hot, but lasts only from April through May. At that time, the central plains are especially hot, and many people leave for the hill stations, where cooler altitudes provide a welcome respite from the heat. Some beach spots can also be comfortable at this time. The monsoon season in the southwest, with its torrential rains, sets in at the end of May/early June and lasts on and off until early September. The southeast areas receive most of their rainfall between November and January, during the northeast monsoons. Western-type hotels are fully or partially air-conditioned. During the winter months, one can enjoy good skiing at the hill stations in the Himalayas (such as Gulmarg in Kashmir). Springtime anywhere in the Himalayas is spectacular, as orchards and hillsides come into bloom. In these regions, travel is best from April through October. Kashmir, Ladakh, and other mountainous locations can be cold during the winter months, especially December and January.

Since India is such a vast land, additional information on the best times to visit are included in each chapter.

 WHAT TO PACK. Travel light. Airlines generally limit your luggage to two pieces (plus one carry-on bag), with a combined weight of about 70 pounds. One should leave home with less than this to allow room for souvenirs. It's a good idea to pack the bulk of your things in one large bag and put everything you need for two or three nights in another bag. In your carry-on baggage, bring your cosmetics, any medicines you need, and, if it's summer, a light wrap (the air-conditioning systems of airplanes are sometimes too efficient). If you wear eyeglasses, take along a spare pair. There is no difficulty in getting over-the-counter medicines in India, but if you take prescription drugs, bring along enough for your stay, and then some.

Clothing. In Northern India, and elsewhere in India's hill stations and wild-life sanctuaries at higher altitudes, evening and night temperatures drop steeply in the winter, so woolens are necessary—either light or heavy, depending on the latitude and altitude of your destination. During the summer months in India, only light tropical clothing is comfortable. During the monsoon season, you will need light flannels and a raincoat, umbrella, and overshoes in the mountains and summer clothing and a raincoat in the rest of India.

Delicate fabrics do not stand up well to laundering facilities in India except at deluxe hotels. Leave them at home. Plain cottons or cotton/synthetic blends are the most practical and the coolest. Synthetic materials that don't "breathe" should be avoided.

India also offers travelers a wide selection of inexpensive comfortable casual clothing for both men and women, made of cotton and cotton blends. You might want to consider traveling light and outfitting yourself there.

Cosmetics. Imported toilet articles, if obtainable at all, are nearly twice the price of their cost back home, so come with enough of your favorite brands. Basic toiletries, such as soap, shampoo, toothpaste, hand lotions, sanitary napkins and tampons, and razor blades, are found in abundance in major metropolitan cities. Less available are suntan or sunscreen lotions, mosquito repellents, other specialty items for those who are not used to the Indian environment, and some types of double-edged razor blades. Bring along a roll or two of toilet paper, since many rest rooms do not have it, and a package of disposable moist towelettes for the quick refresher to clean your hands and face on hot and dusty days on the road.

 HEALTH REGULATIONS. Only persons arriving from yellow fever-infected areas in Africa or Latin America are required to produce a valid vaccination certificate. Otherwise, there are no restrictions, but you are advised in your own interest to get inoculated against cholera. You may be leaving for countries that require incoming passengers from India to produce a certificate. For budget travelers in India, plague, tetanus, typhoid, and typhus immunization and Gamma Globulin shots are advisable; for others, they are not necessary. Check your doctor on which shots should be taken and get them well ahead of departure to allow for possible reactions.

Special Tourist Assistance. Foreign visitors to India receive more special assistance and concessions than is probably available to them anywhere else in the world. There are special booking and information sections for foreigners in railway stations and in major offices of the domestic carrier, *Indian Airlines,* which enable the visitor to jump the often considerable waiting lines. Concession air and rail fares are available (for purchase in foreign exchange only), which can greatly reduce the costs of transportation throughout India. In Gujarat, the only "dry" state where alcohol is banned, foreign visitors can obtain a liquor permit, which effectively counters the prohibition laws.

Medical Precautions. It is advisable to carry a few basic remedies with you in India. Stomach upsets may be due as much to the richness of Indian food as to the lack of hygiene. Ask your doctor to prescribe suitable pills for stomach upsets. Parts of India still have malaria, particularly prior to the monsoon season. Reliable antimalaria pills are now available; it is recommended that you take them, particularly during an extended tour. A good insect repellent is also recommended.

The sun can be very dangerous in India if you are not careful. Beware of overexposure while sightseeing or on the beach even on overcast days. Take a sunscreen and use it. A hat is also a worthwhile precaution.

Always carry a tube of antiseptic cream, with adhesive or lint bandages, and treat any minor scratches, cuts, or blisters at once. India is a dusty place and dust carries infection.

Some doctors recommend taking daily multivitamin tablets, especially those with B-complex, during a tropical tour, when you are using more-than-usual energy and your diet may be changed from its usual pattern.

Water is said to be safe in most big Indian cities, but we still recommend drinking bottled or boiled water. If in doubt, drink hot tea, refreshing as well as safe. Be cautious over Indian food at first, if you are not used to such spiciness. Eat only fruit that can be peeled (do it yourself) and beware of green salad. Be especially careful about eating from roadside stalls or vendors. Soft drinks in India are plentiful and good; drink them rather than water from street vendors.

Warning: Japanese encephalitis, a mosquito-borne disease, occurs in epidemics during the summer months in some rural sections of India, Nepal, and Sri Lanka. The risks to travelers to urban centers is low. However, precautions should be taken to guard against mosquito bites: sleep in screened quarters, wear protective clothing, and use insect repellents liberally. If you wish to inquire about a new investigational vaccine for Japanese encephalitis, contact the Division of Vector-Borne Viral Diseases in Fort Collins, CO (303–221–6429) or the American Embassies in India, Nepal, or Sri Lanka.

INSURANCE. We suggest that you be fully covered with theft, loss, and especially, medical policies before your arrival in India. Americans can insure baggage and personal possessions for up to $2,000 against loss or damage anywhere in the world. Usually covered are clothing, luggage, jewelry, cameras, and recreational equipment. Trip-cancellation insurance, up to about $5,000, pays for nonrefundable travel and hotel expenses that you may lose because of illness or injury. Liability coverage carried by forms of local transportation, including taxis, either does not exist or is so low that you should take out your own coverage at home before leaving. Insurance for all types of policies can be bought in every large city in India from local branches of British and American insurance firms or a duly authorized local agent.

Travel to India

BY AIR. The Indian subcontinent is halfway round the world from the American Midwest, yet the country's four major cities are geographically situated at the crossroads of the Eastern Hemisphere, with direct air links to all continents except South America. Nonstop service to Bombay and Delhi is available from Great Britain and Europe; from Asia and Australia, one can fly nonstop to these two cities and to Calcutta and Madras. Hardly any point on the globe is more than a day away.

India's international flag carrier is *Air-India,* which maintains the greatest frequency of flights. Started in 1932 as a private pioneering venture to improve communications internally, the airline began to take its current form at about the time India was granted independence in 1947. Air-India serves Africa, Asia, Australia, Europe, the Middle East, Russia, the United Kingdom, and the United States. The airline has built its reputation for superior service and Indian and European cuisine around its famous symbol of a welcoming maharajah. Its fleet consists mainly of Boeing 742s and 747s and Airbus A310s, with striking interior decor, and its attendants are elegantly attired and service minded.

Based at Bombay's International Airport, Air-India serves the major international airports at Delhi, Calcutta, and Madras. Flights from the Middle East fly through to Goa and Trivandrum in the South. Air-India also operates a limited number of domestic flights between Bombay and Delhi, Madras, Calcutta, and Hyderabad, as well as between Goa and Trivandrum.

A number of smaller international airports have opened to serve flights from the Middle East, Southeast Asia, and neighboring countries. At present, these airports include those in Trivandrum, Goa, Hyderabad, Varanasi, Patna, and Srinagar. An airport at Bangalore also is now being developed.

FROM NORTH AMERICA. New York is the direct gateway to Delhi and Bombay from the East Coast. Air-India has daily Boeing 747 service via London. Flights to India from London are nonstop, but most return flights from India make a stop in Dubai. *Pan American*'s direct flights stop in Frankfurt, Germany, and in Riyadh, Saudia Arabia, or Karachi, Pakistan. One can also fly Pan Am to London and make connections there for India. From the West Coast, *Thai International* (out of Seattle), *Singapore,* and *Japan* airlines have direct flights with some stops in Asia. Of these three airlines, Thai International, with its excellent service, flies into Calcutta, while the other two fly into Delhi or Madras. From other points in North America, connections can be made with many airlines in Europe or Asia.

Stopovers from North America. Most carriers now allow one stopover en route to and from one's destination, with additional stopovers costing as little as $50 each. With this allowance, a stopover is a temptation one shouldn't resist. Whether from the East or West coast, this is a terrific opportunity to see that European or Asian city you wouldn't otherwise have a chance to see. Standard stopovers from New York include London, Frankfurt, Rome, and Paris. Out of Seattle, Los Angeles, or San Francisco, stopovers include Tokyo, Seoul, Hong Kong, Taipei, Bangkok, or Singapore.

Fares. Deregulation of air carriers has left air fares in a constant state of flux, and the best advice we can give is to consult a travel agent and have him or her make your reservations for you. Agents have up-to-date information about fares, special discounts, and rules governing various discount plans. Generally, on regularly scheduled flights, you have the option, in descending order of cost, of First Class, Business or Club class, and Economy tickets.

The cheapest economy fares to Delhi on Air-India or Pan Am from New York require that you stay in India from 14 to 120 days. The round-trip fare on Air-India is about $1,400 and Pan Am's fare is $1,200 (slightly lower during the summer months). For an unrestricted ticket, the regular one-way fare from the United States to India, on Air-India runs $1,000–$1,200, and if you purchase your return ticket in India, a cheaper fare applies—between $700 and $900, depending on when you purchase your tickets (discounts apply if you buy tickets seven days in advance) and what time you travel (summer rates are cheaper). Pan Am's regular round-trip economy fare, based on two one-way tickets, is around $2,400, though one can travel Business Class for a few dollars more.

A burgeoning number of companies, which are listed in the Sunday travel sections of most major metropolitan newspapers, offer inexpensive round-the-world fares over a set route. A typical ticket, valid for one year, costs $1,400 flying on *TWA* and *Singapore Airlines* over the following route: New York–London–Delhi–Bangkok–Hong Kong–Tokyo–Los Angeles or San Francisco–New York. It's a great buy for those with a lot of time and stamina. These companies also offer good prices on tickets to Asia on lesser known carriers, such as *Korean Airlines* and *China Air.* From Asia, one can pick up an Air-India, Thai International, Japan, or Singapore airlines flight to India. A drawback to these companies is that many accept cash only and there are no refunds, should your plans change.

As stated before, fares and routes change frequently. Thus, those listed here are only guides. Fares fluctuate from month to month. Moreover, the specifics of the itineraries of excursion fares change all the time. The particular cities that you can visit on stopover flights can change, depending on an airline's schedule or the availability of space on a given flight.

FROM BRITAIN. *Air-India* maintains about eight flights a week from London to Delhi and Bombay, where connections can be made for all other important centers in the country. In addition to flights that operate via the Continent, the Middle East, the Gulf, or Moscow, *Air-India, British Airways* and *Thai International* offer nonstop flights to Delhi (flying time about 10 hours). *Air-India* and *British Airways* have frequent flights to Bombay, including some nonstop—an important point on routes to Australia and the Far East. *Singapore Airlines* links Bombay with London twice a week, and *Pan Am* serves Delhi and Bombay on its round-the-world flights (though not both on the same flight).

Fares. There are no Advance Purchase Excursion Fares between London and India, nor are there any charter flights. However, there are promotional excursion fares and beyond this, some undercutting by a few travel agents in conjunction with lesser-known airlines, which entail a change of plane in the Middle East. We do not vouch for the legality of this practice, but we cannot ignore the fact that it goes on and have been quoted return fares from London to Delhi for as low as £350. A good place to look for budget fares is in the London weekly entertainment magazine, *Time Out,* and the national Sunday press. *British Airways* return fares: between London and Bombay: (first class) £2,214; (Superclub class) £1,286; (full economy class) £1,118; excursion fare (valid for six months) £634; and the PEX fare (valid for four months) £507.

Stopovers. Traveling on the full first or economy class fare, you could make stops in Northern Europe and the Soviet Union in one direction, and the Middle East, Central and Southern Europe on the return journey at no extra charge.

FROM EUROPE. The classical passenger route is the Suez Canal—Aden—Bombay, with additional calls at Karachi or Colombo. But the amount of shipping with available passenger space on this route is now very limited. *P&O* and other cruise operators feature parts of the route on their way round the world. More ships pass via the Cape, but there are not many of them either. If you really want to make the journey to India by sea, then we suggest you ask your travel agent to root round for the odd, occasional sailing that might fill your requirements. There are still a very few passenger-carrying cargo ships serving Asia, for those who do not like the cruise atmosphere, but these are becoming increasingly rare.

 OVERLAND. It is unfortunately not at present feasible to travel overland from Europe to India by successive local train and bus connections. We hope politics will allow one to undertake the journey again in the future. You will need time, patience, flexibility, and a certain amount of stamina, but this trip would be a memorable one.

For many years, until political problems disrupted the route, it was possible to travel overland to India from Europe, via Turkey, Iran, Afghanistan, and Pakistan. This was popular with budget travelers or those seeking an adventure. You could use your own vehicle, or take trains or buses. The truly adventurous hitchhiked or took a motorcycle. There were also overland adventure tours packaged by various organizations based in England.

Hann Overland, 268–270 Vauxhall Bridge Road, London SW1V 1EJ, arranges overland trips to India. It runs 87-day (about £890) and 64-day (about £620) tours from London to Kathmandu. These prices do not include food and accommodations (usually in campsites or modest hotels), the prices of which are kept to a minimum. A food kitty system is used, and everyone is expected to take his or her turn cooking and washing. Prices are for one-way travel, and all tours are escorted. Alternative travel arrangements may have to be made if the political situation in some countries will not allow travel through certain areas. All travelers must be flexible, and be prepared for last-minute changes in their itineries.

The major roads along the route from Istanbul to Delhi are mostly in good condition, forming part of the Asian Highway network. Substantial parts of the journey could also be undertaken by train. If political and security conditions improve and borders are more open, the best sources of information on how to follow the ancient silk and spice routes overland to India are the major motoring organizations and student travel groups.

 BY SEA. Ships to India, though nowhere near as plentiful or popular as they once were, can still be found with European and Mediterranean departures.

From the U.S. Another strategy would be to cross the Atlantic by ship and then proceed by air. From the heyday of ocean travel between the United States and "the Continent" when sailings were frequent, the possibilities have shrunk to one: the *Cunard Line*'s *Queen Elizabeth II*. Cunard has had ships on the North Atlantic route since 1839. Now, setting out two or three times a month from April to December, the QE II makes the journey to

Southampton, England, from New York, in five days. Between October 1986 and April 1987, the QE II underwent a costly refurbishment in which its steam power was converted to diesel-electric, its cabins were redecorated, and its lounges and restaurants were redesigned. A one-way crossing, which includes the cost of a return air ticket, runs $1,250 to $7,555 per person in double-room accommodations. For arrangements, contact your travel agent.

For those with the time and money, nothing compares with the relaxing indulgence of sea travel. If you have any apprehension about motion sickness, provide yourself with Dramamine or another of the well-known stabilizers.

Travel on freighters, increasingly difficult to arrange in the past few years, is no longer possible for U.S. travelers to Europe.

 CUSTOMS ON ARRIVAL. Airport procedures on arrival in India are increasingly simple for visitors and are generally no more time consuming than in other international airports. The exception is Calcutta's Dum Dum Airport. The government has recently released plans for improving that airport, but at present, we recommend that you enter through Delhi, Madras, or Bombay. From the Middle East and various areas in Asia, you can also arrive at Varanasi, Patna, Srinagar, Bangalore, and Trivandrum. Hyderabad will soon accept international flights, and Goa is open for international charter flights. Computerization is significantly reducing the amount of time spent in line waiting to clear immigration at some of the larger airports.

In general, travelers from the United States, Great Britain, Europe, and Australia will arrive at Delhi, Madras, Bombay, or Calcutta, where a "red" (for those with items to declare) and "green" (for those with nothing to declare) channel system is used for customs. Tourists are seldom delayed. Customs officials may ask you to open at least one piece of luggage, but this should usually not take more than a minute or two. Currency or travelers checks in excess of U.S. $1,000 or its equivalent must be declared, on a Currency Declaration Form. Remember that it is illegal to enter or leave the country with Indian rupees.

A traveler may bring in personal jewelry, cameras, binoculars, and tape recorders but should fill out a Tourist Baggage Re-Export form on arrival. If these items are lost, stolen, or otherwise disposed of during your stay in India, you will have to pay duty on their value at the time of departure. Customs officials will appraise these items for you unless you have receipts indicating what you paid for them. For electronic or photographic equipment, these appraisals are based on Indian import costs and, therefore, are much higher than what one pays for such equipment elsewhere. That's why it's best to bring receipts for these items.

Keep your baggage claim tag because you may have to surrender it on leaving the airport. Licensed porters are always at hand. The charge is Rs. 1 per suitcase, and tipping is not encouraged unless the baggage is carried a great distance. It is strongly advised that you use only licensed porters. Self-service baggage carts are available at the baggage claim areas of all four international airports if you do not want to use a porter.

You may cash traveler's checks and most currencies at airport banks. Be sure to keep all receipts for currency exchange throughout your stay in India. These receipts are needed to show that you obtained the currency through legal channels, and you will be asked to show them when you pay hotel bills in local currency (although foreign travelers usually are required to settle their bills in foreign currency) or if you want to convert local currency back to foreign currency when you leave India.

All major Indian airports have a tourist office or desk, usually open until late at night, where useful general information may be obtained. Some also have a hotel accommodation booking service (no commission) for those without confirmed reservations.

Airport-to-town transportation is plentiful, but if you take a taxi or auto rickshaw to your hotel or to the center of the city, be sure that the meter is working or agree on a price beforehand. Fares will vary from Rs. 25 to 80, depending on where you are and how far you have to go. Buses, run by exservicemen's organizations, are run from some airports into city centers or major hotels. Departures are usually well timed with arriving flights, though not always with departing ones, and tickets cost Rs. 15–20. At Bombay, Delhi, and Madras, there are taxi counters where you pay in advance a fixed price based on your destination and are assigned a taxi; the fixed price takes care of the problem of bargaining. In Calcutta, bargain hard or wait for a metered taxi.

SPECIAL-INTEREST TRAVEL. If you want to learn more about India, its culture and peoples, or would like to explore a particular aspect of India—a list would be endless—you should consider alternatives to a normal sightseeing program. Begin by discussing your desires with your travel agent, who can correspond with contacts in India, so that a special program can be set up for you in addition to or instead of a regular program of sightseeing. Arrangements for a special-interest visit—to an industrial plant, a hospital, a social institution, or an ordinary home—should be made well in advance.

The largest travel agency in India is *TCI (Travel Corporation of India), Pvt. Ltd.;* main office: Chander Mukhi, Nariman Point, Bombay 400 021; tel. 201–1881; cable TURING; telex. 011–2366, 011–3983 TOUR IN; overseas offices in Barcelona, Frankfurt, London, Los Angeles, Milan, New York, Paris, and Tokyo. TCI offers over 20 special-interest tours covering everything from anthropology and architecture to study tours for learning yoga or wildlife photography. TCI prefers to run these tours in groups of 20 and over, and the tours usually last 10–21 days, depending on the subject. Costs are reasonable for groups but are considerably higher for an individual traveler. The cost of these tours ranges from $45 to $70 per person per day for a group of 20. TCI has recently opened Adventure Tourism in Delhi, which offers trekking, wildlife tours, white-water rafting, camel safaris in the desert, and scuba diving in the Andaman Islands (TCI also operates one hotel, the lovely, relaxing Andaman Beach Resort, on Corbyn's Cove, just outside Port Blair). Typical special-interest tours include a 20-day countrywide golf tour for about $3,000, a fishing tour in Kashmir, and tours for studying Ayurveda medicine or Buddhism. Other travel agents organize specialized tours covering history, archaeology, crafts, and festivals.

Another unique way to experience India is through small India-based travel agents. Zutshi's Travel Service, located in New Delhi and Reno, Nevada (71 Keystone Ave., Reno, NV), is one such agent that can set up home visits, specialized tours, and treks to Ladakh, Leh, and the interior of Tibet. It also has "correspondents" (agents) who are affiliated with major travel agencies throughout India and can make India-wide arrangements from their international offices.

Specializing in cultural and study tours is another India-based travel agent, *Indoculture Tours,* C–1/69 Safdarjung Dev. Area, New Delhi 110 016; tel. 66–7901; telex. 31–65007 icld in; Cable: INDCULTURE.

Fraternal organizations, such as the *Red Cross, Rotary Club, YMCA,* and *Lions Club* can also provide a wealth of personalized information through their Indian counterparts.

Staying in India

HOTELS AND OTHER ACCOMMODATIONS. The greatest single advance made by the tourism industry of India in the past decade has been in providing new and renovated hotels. In the cities and the major tourist centers, including beach and hill resorts, these hotels are well up to international standards, yet the prices are lower than similar hotels elsewhere. The need for hotel rooms is great, since India's tourist traffic was close to two million this year. Delhi is a major international convention center, and vacant rooms are virtually nonexistent in the peak season of December–February (see *Calcutta* section for growth of hotels there). Bombay and Madras are now commercially important, and business travelers (through block reservations of their companies) are in great demand. Western-style hotels are much like their American and European counterparts. The deluxe hotels often surpass the West in luxuries and round-the-clock service. "Indian-style" often means that the bathroom has a shower instead of a shower/bathtub and that the rooms have the basic necessities, including air-conditioning, but not the opulent appointments and the 24-hour service. Often the Indian-style hotels have a "floor waiter," who is in charge of extra blankets, soaps, and early morning tea, instead of a "room waiter" and personalized room service.

As was pointed out in the "Planning Your Trip" section, India is a country for which advance planning is a *must*. This holds true for accommodations as well as itineraries. Hotel reservations should be made—as much as possible—before you leave on your trip. Furthermore, when you arrive at your first destination, ask the hotel desk to reconfirm the rest of the reservations on your itinerary. Sometimes, telex reservations made by travel agencies tend to get "lost" in India.

All five-star hotels, especially those of the Oberoi, Taj, and Welcomgroup chains, have a full array of services for the business traveler. Secretarial services, access to copiers and computers, conference rooms, and executive suites are among the amenities that are available. These services certainly are a nod to the largest clientele of these chains—business travelers and their companies.

The ratings in this guide and the equivalents to the Government of India star classification are as follows: *Luxury* or *Deluxe*—all five-star hotels, *Expensive*—all four-star and most of the three-star hotels, *Moderate*—most of the two-star hotels, *Inexpensive*—most of the one-star hotels.

In some cities, the Government of India Tourist Office maintains lists of "paying guest" accommodations, which can be a delightful way of meeting local people. It is best to check these locally after arrival. Prices tend to be reasonable. In most small places, you will find government-owned establishments ("circuit houses") designed primarily for traveling officials, who will have precedence over tourists. But tourists may find accommodations in these establishments as well. These facilities can be divided into the following categories:

Circuit Houses and Government Guest Houses: generally hard to get into, since priority is given to high-echelon government officials. Usually comfortable, sometimes luxurious. Meals available.

Tourist Bungalows: constructed and managed for tourists, the Class I category bungalows are well furnished with attached bath, linens, and Indian and Western-style catering. Class 2 category bungalows are usually plainly furnished. Meals are provided, but bedding is not included. Standards of hygiene vary. These bungalows are often run by the various state tourism development corporations and usually give good value.

PWD (Public Works Department) or Forest Department Inspection Bungalows: lower standards are maintained in these bungalows than in circuit houses or first-class tourist bungalows, with few exceptions. Sometimes no meals are available. Usually you must bring your own bedding. Few are suitable for foreign travelers.

DAK or Travelers' Bungalows and Rest Houses: these are generally the bottom of the ladder. Bedding usually is not provided, but catering is available.

GROUP HOTELS

Booking hotels in India has become greatly simplified because of the number of hotel chains that cover all the main tourist centers and many of the smaller ones. Some of the major hotel groups are outlined next, with addresses of their centralized reservations systems.

ASHOK GROUP (INDIA TOURISM DEVELOPMENT CORPORATION).

The ITDC is India's largest accommodation chain, covering most key tourist destinations with properties ranging from five-star luxury hotels, such as the Ashok or Akbar in Delhi and the Airport in Calcutta; ex-Maharajah's palaces in Mysore and Udaipur, and delightful beach resorts in Kovalam and Mahabalipuram, to simple and inexpensive lodges for travelers in places of pilgrimage, hill stations, and major archaeological sites. The ITDC also operates a nationwide travel agency, restaurants, duty-free shops at airports, city sightseeing and transportation in many major tourism centers, and sound and light shows. The group's accommodation facilities include the following:

Cities. *Centaur.* Bombay (airport); *Airport Ashok,* Calcutta; *Hotel Ashok,* Bangalore; *Akbar, Ashok, Janpath, Lodhi, Qutab, Ranjit, Samrat, Kanishka,* and *Ashok Yatri Niwas* in Delhi; *Lalitha Mahal Palace,* Mysore; *Patiliputra Ashok,* Patna; *Pinewood Ashok,* Shillong.

Resorts and Tourist Centers. *Agra Ashok,* Agra; *Aurangabad Ashok,* Aurangabad; *Kalinga Ashok,* Bhubaneswar; *Ashok,* Hassan; *Jaipur Ashok,* Jaipur; *Jammu Ashok,* Jammu; *Khajuraho Ashok,* Khajuraho; *Kovalam Ashok Resort,*

Kovalam; *Ashok*, Madurai; *Temple Bay Ashok Beach Resort*, Mahabalipuram; *Laxmi Vilas Palace Hotel*, Udaipur; *Varanasi Ashok*, Varanasi.

ITDC also operates forest and travelers' lodges in the following locations: Bharatpur, Bijapur, Bodhgaya, Kanchipuram, Kaziranga, Konarak, Kulu, Kushinagar, Manali, Mandu, Mukki, Sanchi, Sasan Gir, Thanjavur, and Tiruchirapalli.

Reservations. ITDC *Central Reservations Service,* Hotel Janpath, New Delhi 110 001; tel. 35–0070, Cable: CENTRES, telex. 031–2468.

CENTAUR GROUP. A subsidiary of Air-India with four hotels.

Cities. *Centaur Hotel,* Bombay (airport); *Centaur Hotel,* Delhi (airport).

Resorts and Tourist Centers. *Centaur Hotel,* Juhu Beach, Bombay; *Centaur Lake View Hotel,* Srinagar.

Reservations. Information about reservations may be obtained from Air-India offices in India. In the United States, reservations may be made through Air-India for any of these hotels, provided one is traveling on Air-India.

CLARKS GROUP. One of the older chains of good-quality deluxe hotels, with more modest rates and located in major provincial tourism centers.

Resorts and Tourist Centers. *Clarks Chiraz,* Agra; *Clarks Amer,* Jaipur; *Clarks Avadh,* Lucknow; *Clarks Varanasi,* Varanasi.

Reservations. *U.P. Hotels Ltd.* 1101 Surya Kiran, 19, Kasturba Gandhi Marg, New Delhi 110 001; tel. 331–2367, telex. 031–2447 or, in Bombay, 103 Embassy Center, Nariman Point, Bombay 400 021; tel. 23–0030, telex. 011–2733.

OBEROI GROUP. This chain should take the credit for raising the standards of luxury-grade hotel accommodations in India. The rates are at the top of the scale, but their services and a comprehensive range of facilities puts these hotels well above others.

Cities. *Oberoi Towers,* Bombay; *Oberoi Grand,* Calcutta; *Oberoi Intercontinental,* New Delhi; *Oberoi Maidens,* Delhi. In Nepal, *Soaltee Oberoi,* Kathmandu. In Sri Lanka, *Lanka Oberoi,* Colombo; *Queens Hotel,* Kandy.

Resorts and Tourist Centers. *Oberoi Bhubaneswar,* Bhubaneswar; *Oberoi Mount View,* Chandigarh; *Oberoi Mount Everest,* Darjeeling; *Oberoi Bogmalo Beach,* Goa; *Oberoi Palm Beach,* Gopalpur-on-Sea; *Jass Oberoi,* Khajuraho; *Oberoio Shambha-La,* Ladakh; *Oberoi Cecil* and *Oberoi Clarkes,* Simla; *Oberoi Palace,* Srinagar.

Reservations. In the United States, contact *Loews Representation International,* 666 Fifth Ave., New York, NY 10103. For individuals, call 800–223–0888 (outside New York state), 800–522–5455 (in New York state), or 841–1111 (in New York City); for group bookings of 10 rooms or more, contact 800–223–7188 (outside New York) or 212–841–1586. In India, at "instant" reservations offices at all major hotels, such as Oberoi Inter-Continental, contact Dr. Zakir Hussain Marg, Delhi, telex. 2372, 3829; Oberoi-Towers, Nariman Point, Bombay, telex. 4153, 4154. In the United Kingdom, contact *LRI/Lawson,* 103/105 Clarence St., Kingston-upon-Thames, Surrey KT1 1QY, tel. 01–541–1199; or 30 Old Bond Rd., London W1X 3AD; tel. 01–491–7431.

TAJ GROUP. Superb luxury hotels and resorts in key tourist areas, offering the finest-quality facilities and services. Top price range.

Cities. *Taj Residency* and *West End Hotel,* Bangalore; *Taj Mahal, Hotel President,* and *Taj Mahal Inter-Continental,* Bombay; *Taj Coromandel,* Connemara; *The Fisherman's Cove,* Madras; *Taj Palace Hotel* and *Taj Mahal Hotel,* New Delhi.

Resorts and Tourist Centers. *Taj View Hotel,* Agra; *Malabar Hotel,* Cochin; *The Aguada Hermitage, Taj Holiday Village,* and the *Fort Aguada Beach Resort,* Goa; *Rambagh Palace* and *Jai Mahal Palace Hotel,* Jaipur; *Savoy Hotel,* Doty; *Lake Palace,* Udaipur; *Hotel Taj Ganges,* Varanasi.

Reservations. Worldwide offices of *Utell International.* In the United States, tel. 800–44U–TELL; also, Taj Group of Hotels Sales, 230 Park Ave. South, Suite 466, New York, NY 10169; tel. 212–972–6830. In India, use *Central Reservation Service,* Taj Mahal Inter-Continental, Apollo Bundar, Bombay, telex. 11–2442 TAJB IN, or 11–3791 TAJB IN.

WELCOMGROUP. One of the newest hotel groups, less than 20 years old, and the most aggressive in marketing and expansion of facilities. It has spawned international-grade hotels throughout India, all with excellent facilities. Rates are at the top end of the scale, and the services are excellent.

Cities. *Windsor Manor,* Bangalore; *SeaRock,* Bombay; *Chola Sheraton* and *Adayar Park,* Madras; *Manjarun,* Mangalore; *Maurya Sheraton,* New Delhi; *Maurya Patna,* Patna. In Bhutan, *Druk,* Phuntsholing; in Nepal, *Everest Sheraton,* Kathmandu; in Sri Lanka, *The Dolphin.* In the planning stages is a hotel in Calcutta, where Welcomgroup has its headquarters.

Resorts and Tourist Centers. *Mughal Sheraton* and *Mumtaz,* Agra; *Bay Island,* Andaman Islands; *Rama International,* Aurangabad; *Vadodara,* Barodas; *Nilambag Palace,* Bhavnagar; *Cidade de Goa,* Goa; *Usha Kiran Palace,* Gwalior; *Mansingh,* Jaipur; *Umaid Bhawan Palace,* Jodhpur; *Highlands,* Kargil (Ladakh); *Royal Castle,* Khimsar; *Gurkha Houseboats,* Srinagar. In the planning stages are hotels in Gulmarg, Kashmir, Bhubaneswar, Vishakhapatnam, and Ahmadabad.

Reservations. Through any Sheraton hotel overseas. In the United States, call toll free, 800–325–3535, or, in New York, call ITC, 212–986–3724. In India, through *Welcomgroup Central Reservations Service,* c/o Maurya Sheraton, Diplomatic Enclave, New Delhi 110 021; telex. 031–3147. Domestic reservations through *Welcomnet* in New Delhi, tel. 47–3691. Cable: WELCOTEL.

In addition to the major groups listed above, privately operated hotels may be booked direct, or reservations may be made through hotel counters in many of the major airports in India on arrival. During peak seasons, especially in Delhi, it is best to arrive with hotel reservations.

HILL AND BEACH RESORTS. India owes its hill stations to the British who found the enervating summer heat of the plains unbearable and retreated to mountainous hideouts where they could work more efficiently. The lower spurs of the Middle Himalayas, Kashmir, the Vindhyas in Central India, the Nilgiri hills in the south, with their pleasant climate, sparkling streams and alpine forests, offered ample scope for the development of such resorts which they called "hill stations." It then became customary for central and provincial governments to shift their headquarters to these summer seats, islands of modern civilization. While these places have ceased to be administrative centers in summer, the practice of retreating to hill stations during the hot period—with some of India's best hotels, plenty of sports, and exquisite scenery —survived and has become increasingly fashionable.

From Calcutta, the most easily accessible hill stations are at 7,000 ft.-high Darjeeling, which has a good range of hotels, and Shillong, 2,000 ft. lower, with pine forests and a delightful countryside. From Delhi, the nearest hill station is at Mussoorie, a lively and cosmopolitan little town; not much farther is Simla, the most famous hill station and once the summer capital of the British Raj, so there is still a good range of hotels. Smaller and more relaxed is Dalhousie, on the lower slopes of the Dhauladhar range and with a pleasant climate. The nearest hill station to Bombay is Mahabaleshwar, which offers jungle scenery, a refreshing climate, boating, and fishing. In the South, there is Ootacamund, the "Queen of Hill Stations," located 7,400 feet up in the rolling Nilgiri hills and surrounded by acres of forests and tea plantations.

It is only very recently that India has begun to establish an international reputation for its beach resorts. India has always had beaches, in boundless variety, but modern and comfortable accommodations and other facilities were lacking. As part of its overall planning for the development of international tourism, India launched an intensive program to create fully integrated beach resorts, especially in the south. The results can now be seen in the shape of some of Asia's most delightfully escapist resorts.

The availability of good beach resorts has added an entirely new dimension to traveling through India. The visitor on an extensive tour itinerary can now spend a few days of total relaxation in comfortable hotels or beach cottages, with superb beaches and guaranteed tropical sunshine. The government's Ministry of Tourism has plans for the extensive development of water sports in Goa, Kovalam, Puri, the Andaman Islands, Srinagar, and Jaipur. Currently, you can go trout fishing and waterskiing in Kashmir; para-sailing and windsurfing in Sri Lanka at Welcomgroup's Hotel Dolphin, north of Colombo on Waikkal Beach;

and in India at Goa's Cidade de Goa, near Panaji, where canoeing, water tobaganning, and waterskiing are featured.

At present, the most developed resorts can be found at the following places. On the former Portuguese colony of Goa, the most comfortable resorts are the Taj Group's Fort Aguada Beach, set amid the ruins of a 17th-century Portuguese fortress, Oberoi's Bogmalo Beach, and the Welcomgroup *Cidade de Goa* resort. These offer a choice of hotel or cottage-style accommodations with a range of facilities for sport and leisure. In southwest India, there is a delightful resort at Kovalam in the heart of Kerala. Beaches are backed by coconut plantations and there is a modern ITDC hotel with spacious accommodations and beach cottages. South of Madras, there is Covelong Beach with several small hotels, the most pleasant being the Taj Group's Fisherman's Cove set in the ruins of an 18th-century fort, and farther south, at Mahabalipurum, ITDC's Temple Bay Ashok, overlooking the famous ruins. The Andaman Islands, though not enjoying the easy access that mainland beach resorts have, offer spectacular opportunities for seeing coral reefs. This quiet location is a short airplane ride from Madras or Calcutta. Hotels include the lovely Bay Island, run by Welcomgroup, and the Andaman Beach Resort, TCI's hotel situated overlooking Corbyn's Cove.

For further details of hill and beach resorts and how to reach them, see the regional chapters for the areas concerned. There are also delightful hill and beach resorts in Sri Lanka, details of which are listed in that chapter.

STUDENT LODGING. STILE (Students International Lodgings Exchange), a nonprofit organization, operates through some 2,000 universities and other institutions of higher learning to help students exchange their lodging during their travel to India and more than 50 other countries. The membership fee of $29 includes two directories from which students may choose their partners. For further details, write STILE, 210 Fifth Ave., New York, NY (no phone), or contact its headquarters at 9 Rue Charcot 92200 Neilly/Seine, Paris, France (tel. 33–1.47472888).

MEETING THE PEOPLE AT HOME. Although there are enough museums, scenery, historic sites, and artistic monuments in India to keep the average tourist on the run, many travelers want to penetrate the surface to learn what Indian people are like in their own homes. A number of organized meet-the-people projects exist, and those who are interested in them should contact the *Government of India Tourist Office* in major cities. Some offices maintain lists of "paying guest" accommodations, which allow a traveler to stay with a family.

ROUGHING IT. This means traveling overland or hitchhiking, moving about the country in the cheapest-class trains or on buses, or bicycling, carrying your luggage on your back and sleeping in youth hostels or pilgrim accommodations. A number of specialized student-travel guidebooks and a few general guidebooks are now available for this particular kind of travel. Those who tour this way need to gather and collate material from various sources—guidebooks, local tourist centers, and meetings with people who have gone on similar trips. A visit to a specialized travel bookstore is recommended before leaving the home country. For further information on youth hostels, write *American Youth Hostels,* 1332 I (Eye) St., NW, 8th floor, Washington DC 20005. In England, contact *Youth Hostels Association,* Trevelyan House, 8 St. Stephen's Hill, St. Alban's, Herts. In Canada, write *Canadian Youth Hostels Association,* Tower A, 333 River Rd., 3d Floor, Ottawa, Ontario U1L 8H9. In India, contact *Youth Hostels Association of India,* 5 Nyaya Marg, Chanakyapuri, New Delhi 110 021; *World University Service,* University of Delhi, Delhi 110 008. A free Youth Hostel directory listing 16 places in the four regions of India is available from the YHA. In addition to maintaining hostels throughout India, the YHA sponsors cultural programs and organizes treks.

DINING OUT. Metropolitan cities in India are full of restaurants serving a wide variety of tastes. Independent restaurants and restaurants affiliated with major hotels do not usually require a prescribed set of clothes. The fussy British dress code instituted during the Raj has disappeared, replaced with casual but neat dress, which is much more appropriate in a climate such as India's. Reservations are usually not required unless you go with a large party. It is advisable to reserve, though, to avoid disappointments. If you are traveling with a young child, find out if the restaurant has a high chair or small booster seat. Indians are very attentive to children in restaurants, so children shouldn't pose a problem. Tips are based on charges for the meal, not on the total with the tax included. Tips are usually 10 percent.

Restaurants in this guidebook are classified by price categories: *Deluxe, Expensive, Moderate,* and *Inexpensive.* The types of cuisine are usually listed in the general description of the specialties of each restaurant. Although the various restaurant categories are standard throughout the guidebook, the prices may vary, depending on the area (see restaurant price listings).

Deluxe: This category applies to major metropolitan cities and beach and hill resorts. Usually lavishly decorated and with specialty themes—rooftop specialty cuisines, designer-decorated appointments. Entrees at these gourmet restaurants are anywhere from Rs. 50 to Rs. 70. Cocktails will cost about Rs. 20, and desserts, Rs. 20–Rs. 25. A bill for two can easily be around Rs. 250. These restaurants will often serve wine and imported liquor as well. The high prices usually assure you of extremely courteous service and a kitchen that often has world-class chefs.

Expensive: In addition to the expected dishes and service, these restaurants are known for a specialty cuisine.

Moderate: Beer and perhaps liquor; basic amenities, such as air-conditioning; and a reputation for wholesome, good food. Entrees will not cost more than Rs. 15.

Inexpensive: The bargain-basement restaurants, usually a traveler's delight. Sometimes air-conditioned but often only with ceiling fans, and tables in rows or in curtained cubicles. Adequate service and usually memorable food for little money. Entrees will cost Rs. 6–Rs. 8.

Food is one of the adventures of visiting India. The cuisines of India encompass all Asia, the Middle East, and the Mediterranean. Meats, fish, vegetables, lentils, and grains proliferate in splendid combinations—subtle and enticing. Dining out is not a humdrum chore in India; it is part of your daily adventure. (See chapter, *Discovering the Spice Route—Indian Cuisine.*)

TOUR-GUIDE SERVICES. English-speaking guides may be arranged in advance by your travel agent or by the agent's correspondent in India, but it is easier to get suitable services locally through *Government of India Tourist Offices* or through regional state-level tourist offices. Guides who are fluent in French, Italian, German, Russian, and Japanese will cost more. The following is a sample of approximate rates for guides:

Local sightseeing	Half day	Full day
Group of four or fewer	Rs. 50	Rs. 75
Group of five to 15	Rs. 75	Rs. 100

Inquire at *Government of India Tourist Offices* about overnight, long-distance travel guides. Tipping and paying for meals is customary. The *Archaeological Survey of India* has authorized guides, wearing green identification badges, at many national monuments. This service is free and saves you the problem of having to determine the level of competence of the many "guides" who throng tourist sites.

SPECIAL EVENTS. Among the special attractions that might influence you in selecting the date for a vacation in India is the January 26 *Republic Day Parade* in New Delhi, the most impressive and colorful pageant you are ever likely to see. Reserve a seat through your travel agent or by contacting the Government of India Tourist Office, 88 Janpath, New Delhi (tel. 32–0005).

Make reservations early. Groups of folk dancers from all parts of India participate in events in Delhi following Republic Day.

Arts festivals for classical or folk music and dance are held in various parts of India, usually in the cooler months of October and November or February and March. Among the most important of these is the *Festival of Dances,* held in Khajuraho, Madhya Pradesh, usually in February or March. During this week-long event, some of India's most celebrated proponents of classical dance perform before the backdrop of Khajuraho's sensuously decorated temples. The colorful *Desert Festival* in Jaisalmer, Rajasthan, held in January/February, is a recent celebration of Rajasthan's culture that unfolds in the starkness of the Thar desert. Folk dancers, balladeers, and folk musicians are among the performers; the climax of this three-day event is a sound and light show dramatically set against a moonlit night.

Special local sporting events, such as the *Onam boat races,* held in Kerala in October, are also worth considering when you plan your visit. Among the most unusual sights are the *major tribal fairs,* such as that held in Pushkar, Rajasthan, in November. Most of the subcontinent's festivals and special events are timed for full-moon dates and so vary from year to year. Exact dates and details are usually available from the overseas offices of the Government of India Tourist Office. (See calendar of festivals that follows or regional sections for more information.)

 CALENDAR OF FESTIVALS. India, one of the world's great spiritual sanctuaries, holds religious festivals all year round, and some of them probably coincide with the date of your visit. Since most Indian festivals are based on lunar or religious calendars, dates vary from year to year, but the following list indicates approximate times and some of the best places to see the festivities.

Winter. *Muharram.* Commemorating the martydom of a grandson of the Prophet Mohammed, seen at its best in Delhi, Hyderabad, or Lucknow, with "mourning" processions. In southern India, men in tiger masks lead the procession. Most colorful.

Mid-January. *Pongal Sankranti.* A three-day harvest festival, celebrated at its best in Tamil Nadu, Karnataka, and Andhra Pradesh. Cows are often decorated and garlanded and led in procession to the accompaniment of drums and music.

Late January. *Vasanta Panchami.* Hindu festival devoted to the goddess of scholars. In Bengal, her images are taken in a procession to bathe in the rivers. Kite flying is popularly associated with this festival.

February. *Tirumala Nayak.* In the great southern temple city of Madurai, a spectacular procession of floats, music, and dancing. Extremely colorful.

February/March. *Shivratri.* Celebrated throughout India by Hindus. The festival celebrates Shiva at temples in Khajuraho, Konarak, Chidambaram, and Varanasi.

Spring. **March.** *Carnival.* In Goa, a Mardi Gras to rival all others, with masked dancers and floats.

March/April. *Holi.* Also colorful, with dye, water, and perfume thrown around by everyone; celebrated all over India. Watch your cameras and wear old clothes because the locals love to single out foreigners for special treatment. A warm and friendly festival.

March/April. *Gangaur.* Festival for Parvati, consort of the god Shiva. Celebrated in Jaipur with processions of gorgeously dressed girls visiting the main temple. Also celebrated in other Rajasthani cities and in Bengal and Orissa.

March and April. *Spring Festival.* In Kashmir, locals flock to see the first blossoms of the almond orchards. A lovely time to visit this spectacular state.

April. *Baisakhi.* Celebrated all over India as the Hindu solar New Year. Ritual bathing and visits to the temple are undertaken by everyone. Of special significance to the Sikhs, who have spectacular festivals in Amritsar.

April/May. *Meenakshi Kalyanam.* Annual marriage celebrations of the god Shiva. A huge procession in Madurai, with vast chariots carrying the temple images through the streets to the accompaniment of music.

May. *Puram.* The most spectacular temple festival in Kerala, in the south. In Truchi, fireworks follow an elephant procession that carries the image of Shiva.

May. *Buddha Purnima.* Marking the birth, enlightenment, and death of the Lord Buddha. Observed in all Buddhist temples. Special celebrations are held at major centers of Buddhist pilgrimages, such as Sarnath and Bodhgaya, in Bihar.

Summer. June. *Hemis.* Hemis is the biggest monastery in Ladakh, site of an annual festival of great intensity to celebrate the birth of Guru Padamasambhava. Masked dancers as spirits of good and evil are highlights.

June/July. *Rath Yatra.* The most spectacular temple festival in Puri, Orissa, in honor of Lord Krishna. A procession of huge chariots.

July/August. *Teej.* Celebrated, especially by women, to welcome the monsoon in Rajasthan. A time of local fairs, bright clothes, and special swings set up in every village.

July/August. *Naag Panchami.* A colorful fair and festival in Jodhpur in honor of the cobra deity.

August. *Raksha Bandhan.* A festival for brothers and sisters, when the girls tie threads round the boys' wrists and receive gifts in return.

August 15. *Independence Day.* Special commemorative celebrations to mark the country's independence from British rule in 1947.

August. *Janmashtami.* The birthday of Lord Krishna, when the people flock to temples to see dance dramas enacting scenes from his life.

August/September. *Ganesha Chaturthi.* Festival in honor of the popular elephant-headed god of good fortune. Around Bombay are processions, with images finally being immersed in the sea or lake. Also a time for fairs and cultural events all over India.

Autumn. September. *Onam.* Harvest festival in Kerala, four days of feasting, dance, and boat races by "snake" boats with up to 100 paddlers.

September/October. *Id-Ud-Fitr.* Moslem festival celebrated in mosques all over India to mark the end of the month-long fast of Ramadan. A time of feasting.

September/October. *Dussehra.* The annual battle between the traditionally represented forces of good and evil. The classic *Ramayana* is enacted all over India during a 10-day period, ending in a great celebration in which evil is vanquished. At its best in Delhi, with dance, drama, and the burning in effigy of the "baddies" on the final day. Also celebrated with local variations in the northern mountain valley of Kulu, Mysore, in the south, and in eastern India, especially Bengal, where it's known as *Durga Puga.*

October 2. *Gandhi Jayanti.* The birthday of the great Mahatma Gandhi. Pilgrimages are made from all over the country to pay respects at the Raj Ghat, in Delhi, where he was cremated.

October or November. *Diwali.* The festival of lights, when every house is decorated with oil lamps. Celebrations are also held in many temples dedicated to Lakshmi and Kali.

November. *Guru Purab.* A major Sikh festival marking the birthday of the founder of the religion, Guru Nanak. Celebrated especially in Amritsar and Patna.

November. *Pushkar Fair.* One of the world's most spectacular remaining tribal fairs. In a small village near Ajmer, in Rajasthan, tribal folk assemble from all over the state for a camel fair and pilgrimage to a nearby lake.

For more information on fairs and festivals, see regional sections.

 BUSINESS HOURS AND HOLIDAYS. The Indian calendar is full of festivals and local, regional holidays, but has no hallowed day—Sabbath—in the Christian, Hebrew, or Muslim sense. Sunday has been adopted as the day of rest when most shops, banks, and offices are closed. On workdays, shops open by 10 A.M. and stay open till after 7 P.M. Small traders stay open longer. Office and banking hours are 10 A.M.–1 P.M. and 2–5 P.M. Monday–Friday; Saturdays, 10 A.M.–noon.

Try to get your business done in offices and banks as early in the day as possible. The afternoon lunch hours can extend into the late afternoon, especially in government offices. Carry business cards. Indians are conscious of this protocol.

TIPPING. India does not have a rigid system of imposing a service charge on restaurant bills, although most major hotels include a service charge on your bill. The service charge is usually 10 percent. Waiters, room service, housekeepers, porters, and doormen all expect to be tipped, as they do in the rest of the world. You won't go wrong if you tip Rs. 5 per night to your room waiter. Bellboys and bell captains should be paid Rs. 1 per bag. If you are staying in a private home, it is customary to tip the domestic workers. Taxi drivers do not expect tips unless they go through a great deal of trouble to get you to your destination. However, tip a hired driver Rs. 10 for a half day's trip and Rs. 20–Rs. 25 for a full day's trip. It is also customary to give a hired driver money for his meals if you are on a day trip.

There are no service charges at government-run houses, DAK bungalows, or hostelries. Tip individuals according to the rates just cited. Railroad porters should be given Rs. 1 per bag. Bargain for the rate before you let your bags be picked up. Unusually heavy luggage should be tipped at a higher rate. In all major airports, baggage porterage tickets must be purchased near the entrance to the terminal. Their rate is regulated by the airport authorities and is usually Rs. 1 per item. Porters need not be tipped on top of this charge, although many will insist. When you arrive at the airport in Delhi, Bombay, or Madras, you can get your own baggage cart and wheel your luggage. At the Calcutta airport, however, regardless of such a system, porters jostle for business within the baggage claims area. If you opt for a porter, bargain the price to Rs. 1 per bag.

MEASUREMENTS. India has fully adopted the metric system. In this book, we have given most distances in miles and heights in feet, but you will often be faced with the kilometer, meter, and centimeter. The kilometer is 0.62 mile, and an easy rule of thumb is that 8 kilometers equal 5 miles. There are, of course, 1,000 meters in a kilometer, and 100 centimeters in a meter. A meter is just over 3 feet in length and a centimeter is about four-tenths of an inch.

Temperature in India is now measured by the Centigrade system. Water boils at 100 degrees Centigrade, which is 212 degrees Fahrenheit. Water freezes at 0 degrees Centigrade and at 32 degrees Fahrenheit. To convert to Fahrenheit, multiply Centigrade by nine-fifths (9/5) and add 32. To convert to Centigrade, subtract 32 and multiply Fahrenheit by five-ninths (5/9). There are 2.2 pounds in every kilogram, but we doubt that you will be buying anything in terms of weight here.

When you hire a car and buy gasoline (petrol), you should remember that four liters are slightly over a U.S. gallon and just under a British imperial gallon.

Indians refer to large numbers with two words peculiar to the country. You will often read in English-language newspapers and magazines about a *crore* of rupees and a *lakh* of people. Crore is 10 million; lakh is 100,000.

ELECTRICITY. Electric voltage in most places is 220 AC, 50 cycles. American appliances (110 volts, 60 cycles) will function only with transformers, which some of the major hotels have. You can get hairdryers that can be switched from one voltage to another, but they still need plug adapters to fit Indian outlets.

TIME ZONES. Indian Standard Time is five and one-half hours ahead of Greenwich Mean Time and nine and one-half hours ahead of the U.S. Eastern Standard Time. Thus, noon in India is 2:30 A.M. in New York. Nepal has recently stopped adhering to the ancient sundial and is now 15 minutes ahead of Indian Standard Time.

POSTAGE. Domestic and international mail delivery is good if you use post offices in major cities and through hotel services. The rate for inland letters is 0.35 paise. Domestic postcards are 0.15 paise. Domestic letters up to 10 grams are 0.70 paise. Airmail rates per 10 grams for letters to foreign countries are Rs. 6.50 for North America and the United Kingdom. An air letter

METRIC CONVERSION

CONVERTING METRIC TO U.S. MEASUREMENTS

Multiply:	by:	to find:
Length		
millimeters (mm)	.039	inches (in.)
meters (m)	3.28	feet (ft.)
meters	1.09	yards (yd.)
kilometers (km)	.62	miles (mi.)
Area		
hectare (ha)	2.47	acres
Capacity		
liters (L)	1.06	quarts (qt.)
liters	.26	gallons (gal.)
liters	2.11	pints (pt.)
Weight		
gram (g)	.04	ounce (oz.)
kilogram (kg)	2.20	pounds (lb.)
metric ton (MT)	.98	tons (t.)
Power		
kilowatt (kw)	1.34	horsepower (hp)
Temperature		
degrees Celsius	9/5 (then add 32)	degrees Fahrenheit

CONVERTING U.S. TO METRIC MEASUREMENTS

Multiply:	by:	to find:
Length		
inches (in.)	25.40	millimeters (mm)
feet (ft.)	.30	meters (m)
	Length	
yards (yd.)	.91	meters
miles (mi.)	1.61	kilometers (km)
Area		
acres	.40	hectares (ha)
Capacity		
pints (pt.)	.47	liters (L)
quarts (qt.)	.95	liters
gallons (gal.)	3.79	liters
Weight		
ounces (oz.)	28.35	grams (g)
pounds (lb.)	.45	kilograms (kg)
tons (t.)	1.11	metric tons (MT)
Power		
horsepower (hp)	.75	kilowatts
Temperature		
degrees Fahrenheit	5/9 (after subtracting 32)	degrees Celsius

(ask for an aerogram) costs Rs. 5. Postcards by air to the United States and United Kingdom are Rs. 4. For important letters, request a certificate of posting. Parcels should be posted from major post offices; do not rely on shops to ship purchases. In spite of regulations for excess baggage, pay the surcharge and carry your souvenirs with you.

If you need to send a package that has to get to Europe or North America in a few days, there are now some courier services. Desk-to-desk service is provided by *CATS Courier Service*, with offices in London and New York. Domestic offices are in New Delhi (tel. 33–1501), Calcutta (tel. 44–4225), Bombay (tel. 26–2727), and Madras (tel. 41–2476). Branches are also in Bangalore, Buwahati, Cochin, Hyderabad, and Patna. *Bor-Air Freight Co., Inc.,* also provides courier service, with agents in three cities: Bombay (tel. 25–1037), Calcutta (tel. 23–7171), and New Delhi (tel. 252–7372 or 571–8669). Also in New Delhi, contact *DHL International* (331–8945).

OVERSEAS TELEPHONES AND TELEX. Telex facilities and international calls may be subject to uncomfortably long delays. Go through your hotel switchboard. All major hotels have excellent telex and telegraph services. Insist on a copy after the dispatch. Main post offices have cable services. India is linked to the United Kingdom, Australia, France, Japan, Hong Kong, Singapore, and other parts of Southeast Asia and Europe with direct dial codes.

Domestic long-distance telephones are not reliable, and the service is bad. An Italian subsidiary of the U.S. ITT has a contract to produce sets and reenginccr the countrywide exchanges. It is advisable to use hotel services or the public telephones at major post offices. Ask for *Lightning Call* (the fastest, top priority) or *Demand Call* (the second fastest). The rates are appropriately higher.

LAUNDRY AND DRY CLEANING. In deluxe and expensive hotels in India, you can get your laundry or dry cleaning done usually within a day or even faster if you pay a nominal surcharge. Outside these places, or at some resort areas, you must wait two to three days to have it done. Laundry methods in Asia differ from those of local laundromats in the United States and the United Kingdom. Mark Twain meant it when he said that the Indian *dhobi* (washerman) breaks stones with people's shirts. Ordinary cottons and linens are safely turned over to the dhobi, and will cost a fraction of what you are accustomed to paying. Dry cleaning chemicals are generally harsh, so you should not entrust delicate fabrics to the ordinary establishment. At higher-priced hotels, you can expect the standards of both services to be up to those of North America or Europe.

No matter how you are traveling, deluxe or budget, it's a good idea to carry a small container of laundry detergent to wash out clothes. Except for the monsoon seasons, light cottons or cotton blends will dry in one's bathroom overnight.

DRINKING LAWS. The only state that now has prohibition is Gujarat. Foreign travelers may apply to the Gujarat Tourism Development Corporation for a permit that allows them to buy liquor in the state. The Government of India Tourist Offices in the United States can issue a three-month liquor permit allowing you to carry liquor into the state. Elsewhere, most localities have six "dry" days per month: one day per week (often coinciding with the one meatless day of the week, when no slaughtering is done and no meat is sold or served in most restaurants), and the first and last days of the month (coinciding with pay days).

Tourist hotels are usually exempt, but this varies from state to state. Imported liquor is expensive and is not generally available in restaurants and bars outside metropolitan areas or top hotels in resort areas. Liquor is available in major cities in "wine shops," at high prices. Outside metropolitan centers, one finds signs reading, "Foreign Liquor Shops." This does not mean that imported liquor is sold, but, rather, that the liquor being sold is not "home brew" but is Indian gin, rum, or whiskey, much of which is quite good, as is Indian beer. The wines that are produced in Goa are sweet. An interesting liqueur to try in Goa is *feni,* which is made from cashew nuts.

MUSEUMS AND GALLERIES. India has superb museums, especially for history, archaeology, and art. In addition to the large-scale museums in most cities, you will find smaller ones close to most major archaeological sites that can give much greater meaning to the study of the ruins themselves.

Most museums, galleries, and historical sites have a modest entrance fee, usually 0.50 paise to Rs. 1, and charge extra for photography, when it is allowed (some require that you check your camera before entering and retrieve it at the end of your visit). Museums are usually closed once a week, on Mondays; check the regional sections for each museum's closing day. Tourist information counters have local listings of museums and their hours. Temples that are open to non-Hindus usually do not charge admission, but donations are customary. They will charge for photography, whenever it's allowed (most will not allow you to photograph in the inner sanctum). Entrance fees are charged at forts and other monuments, ranging from 0.50 to Rs. 2. Many locations charge neither for entrance nor photography.

BEHAVIOR. We advise that you have a general awareness of Indian sensibilities. Comparisons with the more developed West will not ease your difficulties; they will only accentuate them. Each country has its own rhythm and pace, and in India there are many "countries," almost separate cultures, mores, and ways of behaving. Some general rules are these: remove your shoes before entering shrines, temples, and holy places, even if they seem in ruins (in some places, such as the Taj Mahal, cloth overshoes are provided for a small charge); casual clothes should not include brief shorts or revealing tops; do not drink alcoholic beverages, such as beer, on temple grounds; be restrained while photographing holy places (much as you would be in a cathedral or a synagogue). Many inner sanctums of Hindu temples are off limits to non-Hindus, and some temples are entirely off limits. Most temples have signs in English telling you so or guards at the entrance. Many Hindu temples and *gurudwaras* (Sikh temples) do not allow any leather to be worn inside—shoes, belts, handbags, or camera cases.

BEGGING. India has a large number of beggars, partly because many Indians give money to them for religious reasons and partly because begging can be profitable for the beggar. On the whole, begging is a racket, and the central government and local authorities are trying to wipe it out. You should not give money to beggars; there are many worthy charities in India that can use the money. Remember that beggars near hotels and tourist sights are professionals who have been reared to the trade; those near the temples are satisfying a certain demand of simple and pious pilgrims to acquire merit by giving alms.

Occasionally, astrologers or palmists might turn up to tell you a few things. They can be entertaining to talk with, if you don't mind parting with a rupee or two, but don't expect them to be gifted with extraordinary powers of divination. Foreign visitors to Indian cities are often approached by "students" or supporters of political parties who offer little paper flags in exchange for a "contribution." These requests should be politely resisted. At temples, Brahmin priests might approach you to give a blessing that involves touching your forehead with sandalwood paste and vermillion; a few rupees donation to the temple is expected in exchange. Do not be afraid to refuse such an offer or to return a "gift" for which you are subsequently expected to pay.

SPORTS. Because of the variety in its seasons and geophysical conditions, India provides ample facilities for sports. Popular spectator sports are cricket, soccer, field hockey, polo, and horse racing. If you want to be more energetic, golf is available in large towns and in the hill stations. The Royal Calcutta Golf Club is the oldest club outside the British Isles, and New Delhi's course is listed in the *World Atlas of Golf* as one of the most outstanding 100 courses in the world. Other good courses are in Ooty, Ranikhet, Dalhousie, Shillong, Bangalore, Gulmarg, and Ladakh.

You can swim everywhere—in seas, lakes, and hotel pools. Hotels and private clubs that offer temporary memberships have tennis, squash, and badminton courts. At seaside and lake-front resorts like the Andamans, Srinagar, Goa, Kovalam, and Mahabalipuram, sailing, rowing, canoeing, scuba diving, snorkeling, para-sailing, some windsurfing (especially in Sri Lanka), fishing, and water-skiing are available. See regional sections for specific information on how to obtain gear for these activities.

Other sports that can be pursued where local conditions are appropriate are skiing in Gulmarg, Kashmir, horseback riding and trekking the hill towns such as Darjeeling, and fishing in mountain rivers. The Solang Valley of Himachal Pradesh and Kufri, near Simla, is good for skiing, tobogganing, and ice skating. These sports also can be done in the Kulu and Manali areas and in the Garhwal Himalayas. Trekking and fishing are available in the Nilgiri (Blue Mountains) of the south.

New features in adventure sports are rock climbing near Delhi and on the Western Ghats near Pune, hang gliding, ballooning, motor rallies, camel rides across the Rajasthan desert, rafting on rivers, and hunting for snipe, geese, and ducks in Kashmir. There are clubs in Pune, New Delhi, Bombay, Sirula, and Bangalore for all of these sports.

Organizations that provide information on these sports are the *Youth Hostels Association,* 5 Nyaya Marg, Chanakyapuri, New Delhi 110 021, with branches throughout India, which offers treks even for children as young as 12 years (a 15–day YHA trek costs about Rs. 470); *Bangalore's Spark Club,* which includes people in their 60s; *Indian Mountaineering Foundation,* Benito Juarez Rd., New Delhi 110 021; the *Himalayan Club,* Box 1905, Bombay; *Jammu and Kashmir Tourist Office,* Kanishka Shopping Plaza, 19 Ashok Rd., New Delhi 110 001 (tel. 34–5373, telex. 031–61854 JKI–IN); *Himachal Pradesh Tourist Information Office,* Kanishka Shopping Plaza, 19 Ashok Rd., New Delhi 110 001 (tel. 34–5320); *Uttar Pradesh Tourist Bureau,* Chanderlok Building, 36 Janpath, New Delhi 110 001 (tel. 32–2251); *West Bengal Tourist Office,* 3/2 BBD Bagh (East), Calcutta (tel. 23–8271). *See* "Useful Addresses" in the regional sections for other tourist centers.

 HINTS TO PHOTOGRAPHERS. Some people whom you want to photograph may demand money, so carry a pocketful of small coins if you feel you must pay. Most Indians are good natured about having their photographs taken and will say "thank you," but Moslem people may object, especially where women are veiled. Be cautious about photography in tribal areas. Military installations, airports, bridges, railway stations, and trains are not supposed to be photographed for security reasons.

Color and black-and-white film is available in larger towns and cities, made locally or imported from eastern Europe or Japan. A roll of 35 mm, 36-exposure film will cost Rs. 50–Rs. 90. We recommend that you take all you need with you and that you have the developing done when you get home, although facilities are available in all major Indian cities.

Warning. Don't leave already exposed film in your pockets or in any hand luggage while passing through airport X-ray machines. The process sometimes fogs or darkens your film, and you may find a whole trip's photographs ruined. U.S. Federal Aviation Administration regulations permit you to insist on a hand inspection of film while in the United States. Carry film in a plastic bag for easy access. Sima Products sells a luggage tag that bears this FAA ruling; it is available for $1 from Sima Products, 4001 West Devon Ave., Chicago, IL 60646. The article "Traveling With Color," in the August 1987 issue of *Popular Photography,* details additional precautions to take with film while traveling.

In some airports in India, you will be asked to open the back of your camera as part of a security check, or, if there is film in the camera, you will have to shoot one or two frames.

 WILDLIFE SANCTUARIES. India has 59 national parks and 254 sanctuaries, a striking number for its land mass and population. Before 1947, wildlife were not protected. Travelers on safaris indiscriminately hunted on trips sponsored by maharajahs and their English guests, decimating the rich splendor of wild animals from the Himalayas to the central grasslands, the sparsely forested south and the marshes to the east.

The government has done much to develop sanctuaries and reserves in the face of the constant demands of the population for land and the needs of the rural people who live on the perimeters of these habitats. Poaching and illegal logging are severe problems. Currently, all the reserves are jammed into 4 percent of the country's geographic area.

In 1952, 13 species were on the endangered list; today, the list contains 70 species of mammals, 16 species of reptiles, and 36 species of birds. Among the endangered species are the snow leopard (fewer than 300 are left), male musk deer (widely hunted for a gland whose secretions are used in the manufacture of cosmetics in the West and elsewhere); desert fox, golden langur, bison, Himalayan ibex, sloth bear, lesser florican, and black-necked crane. The Asian lion has risen to only 200 in number after it dwindled to 50 in the 1920s. Tigers, the symbolic mascot of India, were killed so frequently that by 1970, there were only 1,500. Under the ambitious "Project Tiger," the government banned killing and set up nine reserves; the total number has risen dramatically to 1,800.

India's sanctuary program is caught between the economic problems of a developing country—the rural poor and their needs versus the need for habitats for wildlife. Much of India's wildlife is peculiar to the subcontinent, and you should avail yourself of every opportunity to visit some of the sanctuaries. Among India's unique animals are the swamp deer, the Asian lion, the four-horned antelope, and nilpai. The spotted chital deer has its home in India, Pakistan, and Nepal, and the prehistoric-looking one-horned Indian rhinoceros is found only in India and Nepal. The Indian bison is not a bison at all but a gaur, a species of wild ox.

There are also excellent reserves in Nepal and Sri Lanka (see appropriate chapters). All states have booklets on their specific sanctuaries, and the Government of India Tourist Office publishes a number of brochures outlining all the reserves. We highly recommend a visit to this unique aspect of India's mosaic. See regional sections for complete listings of each sanctuary and provisions for accommodations and travel. Though roads and bungalows in these sanctuaries are improving greatly, travel here is not for those who expect deluxe facilities.

MEDICAL TREATMENT. All hotels have doctors on call. The *IAMAT* (International Association for Medical Assistance to Travelers), publishes a list of approved English-speaking doctors who received postgraduate training in the United States, Canada, or Great Britain. Membership is free; the plan is worldwide; in India, it has correspondent hospitals in 15 cities. An office call costs $20, hotel calls are $30, and weekend and holiday calls are $40. For information, apply in the United States to 417 Center St., Lewiston, NY 14092; in Canada, 1287 St. Claire Ave. West, Toronto, Ontario M6E1B9, and 188 Nicklin Rd., Guelph, Ontario N1H 7L5; in Europe, at Gotthardstrasse 17, 6300 Zug, Switzerland; and in New Zealand, to Box 5049, Christchurch 5.

A similar service to travelers, but one that charges an initial membership fee of $6 per person or $10 per family, is offered by *Intermedic,* 777 Third Ave., New York, NY 10017. Office calls cost $30–$40; house or hotel calls cost $40–$50 between 7 A.M. and 7 P.M. and $50–$60 between 7 P.M. and 7 A.M. In India, Intermedia has 18 correspondent physicians in six cities.

HINTS TO THE DISABLED. Most countries in Asia, including India, are not prepared for travelers who are disabled. There are no special boarding ramps in buses, trains, airplanes, or hotel elevators, on public sidewalks, or at museums or monuments. Disabled travelers to India must rely on careful preplanning and have a companion to assist them. Unfortunately, there are no specialized guidebooks in this area for travelers to Asia. Simon and Schuster's 1984 *A Guide for the Disabled Traveler,* by Frances Barish, is significant in that it is written for travelers who use special equipment—wheelchairs, crutches, canes, ileostomy bags, pacemakers, and so on—but it is geared to travel in the United States and Europe. Wheelchair travelers in India must have a collapsible, easily folding, compact wheelchair with lightweight, sturdy wheels for city sidewalks. Easily removable accessories should also be brought because replacements will not be available.

For more information, we advise that you contact the *Society for the Advancement of Travel for the Handicapped,* 26 Court St., Brooklyn, NY 11242. This organization provides, free of charge, a list of travel agents who are experienced in handling itineraries for disabled travelers. *Travel Information Center,* Moss

Rehabilitation Hospital, 12th St. and Tabor Rd., Philadelphia, PA 19141, provides information on the accessibility of international cities, hotels, and airlines.

Airports, published by Airport Operators Council International, Inc., lists design features and services at 472 airport terminals in 46 countries; it is available from the Consumer Information Center, Pueblo, CO 81009. *Rehabilitation International, USA* (RIUSA), 20 West 40th St., New York, NY 10018, publishes *Travel Tips for the Handicapped,* which also may be obtained from the Consumer Information Center, Pueblo, CO 81009.

POLLUTION REPORT. Except for such cities as New Delhi and Bangalore, Indian cities will appear polluted to the Western tourist. Garbage-littered streets are usual, cows and other livestock roam freely in some areas, and personal hygiene is frequently taken care of in public places. Millions of crows begin their day of scavenging at dawn, their raucous cawing being as effective as an alarm clock in metropolitan cities like Calcutta. Beaches close to cities are usually severely polluted, but the newer beach resorts, such as Kovalam, Goa, Mahabalipuram, the Andaman Islands, are pollution free because they are far from the major population centers. The evening air throughout India becomes thick with the haze of tens of millions of cooking fires, which helps to produce spectacular sunsets but does nothing beneficial for those with respiratory problems such as asthma. In all the older cities, one's eyes and nose are frequently assaulted by a wide variety of unusual sights and smells that might shock at first, but to which you probably will quickly adapt.

 SHOPPING. India is a rewarding terrain for the enterprising bargain hunter and has an array of exotica well designed to embellish the collection of even the most discriminating souvenir hunter. Many of the items combine good design, marvelous color, and elegant usefulness—others may look perfect in a romantic "moonlight on the Ganges" type setting, but not quite so well on your hall table. We have no warnings to proffer: we just suggest that before you take a tumble for some irresistible object, you picture it in its eventual setting—you will come away with the best India has to offer!

State-run emporiums have the advantage of bringing the country's regional crafts to you. Here the souvenirs are of good quality and the prices are fixed. You will find these Handloom-Handcraft Emporia in many large cities, including Bombay, Calcutta, Madras, and New Delhi. For "local color" and some bargaining, visit the bazaars where silversmiths, goldsmiths, gem-cutters, enamelers, and copper beaters work and sell in tiny shops, practicing their trade.

Street peddlers usually ask about three times the price they hope to get. It is best to decide beforehand how much the coveted object is worth to you and to remember that the vendor has been at the game much longer than you have.

Indians seem to be able to make almost anything from ivory—miniature animals, cigarette holders, boxes, paper cutters, book marks, lamp stands, and so forth. First cousins to the ivory carvings are the delicate birds made of translucent horn in shades of gray. From Agra comes exquisite marble inlay work. Jewels are sliced petal thin and embedded in the marble with such precision that you cannot see the joints even with a magnifying glass. This craft goes back to the days of the Moguls. A set of dessert plates would be a memorable possession. Talking of plates, enamel Nirmalware looks like Rajput paintings and is handsome; the three-metal plates from Thanjavur depict scenes with an Oriental love of detail.

Genuine pieces of the Pallava, Chola, or even Vijayanagar period bronzes are usually not obtainable on the market. You will be lucky if you obtain a good imitation at a reasonable price. Genuine antiques need export permits, which are not likely to be granted for any but the most ordinary pieces.

You should take a look at India's hand-loomed rugs. It is India, not Iran, that has the world's largest rug industry—whose products are close in design to their Persian counterparts because they were introduced by the Moguls. Rather more than a simple souvenir, an Indian rug is an attractive investment. And in Delhi and many of the Himalayan towns, where there are groups of Tibetan refugees, you will find superb rugs and other craft objects in an entirely different and remarkably attractive artistic tradition.

To get back to the pocket-sized items, there are enchanting terracotta or brightly painted wooden toys for children and for grown-ups with taste. For something less breakable, there is metalwork like the jet and silver "Bidriware" and the wares of Moradabad which combine bright enamel and brass. You can also pick up attractive and simple souvenirs made of more unpretentious materials like pottery, hand-painted tiles, ceramics, and cane or bamboo ware.

If you want to brighten your wardrobe and express your personality, you might choose a pair of embroidered slippers or gilt sandals that would look spectacular in a Western boudoir or beach house. You will be dazzled when confronted with bags, belts, scarves, shawls (like the Kashmiri "Paisley" ones, recently put back into the high-fashion category), and all sorts of costume jewelry in precious metals, filigree, gems, jade, or ivory.

If you can resist buying a sari—or at least an embroidered silk stole—you will be one of the very few women of cast-iron willpower in the Western world. Indian textiles have a variety and beauty unmatched anywhere else—you can have the fiber, the color, and the texture you choose. The south specializes in heavy silks and brilliant contrasting colors. Utter Pradesh is famed for its "chikan" embroidery on white voile (which could make a beautiful bridal veil), and Benares for its brocades. Bengal offers off-white shot with gold, while the Deccan provides a choice of summer saris. The Chanderi cottons have tiny floral motifs in gold while their first cousins of Maheshwari prefer interesting variations in texture to a pattern. Either could make an unforgettable summer evening dress. True Oriental splendor is attained in the Jamdani muslins—as costly as they are beautiful, since eight men may spend all day weaving a single inch—and in the Baluchar saris of eastern India whose intricate designs are woven by a secret process handed down from generation to generation. Rajasthan introduces a bright and gay note in its saris made by the "tie and dye" method, which results in startling and successful patterns.

Indian women manage to wear their saris with spectacular grace—but, of course, they have been doing so for several millennia. If you feel bound to imitate them, then you will need a choli (blouse) and a long skirt petticoat, threaded through the top like men's pajamas, a draping lesson, and a good memory (or a notebook) to avoid tying yourself up in knots. So try draping your sari once, and if you truly feel utterly unself-conscious, wear it that way.

Particular handicraft emporiums, shopping streets, and bazaar areas are listed under each town heading in the regional sections of this guide, together with particular local specialties.

A word of warning: Be alert when shopping. Bargain hard and generally do not trust shopkeepers' descriptions of age, quality, and so forth. Check goods after paying, and check change. Do *not* let taxi drivers take you to their favorite shops—you will pay much more.

See regional sections for more of India's eye-catching crafts, from Rajasthani miniature paintings, hand-blended perfumes to Bengal's simple but elegant blue pottery.

NIGHTLIFE. India's nightlife is tame in comparison to that of the Western capitals, Bangkok, and Hong Kong. Delhi, Bombay, Madras, and Calcutta all have a handful of discos and sedate dinner dances, and floor shows are usually featured in the major resort areas. Bars are dimly lit, unappealing places. Most Indians entertain at home. What the cities offer most at night are cultural shows of outstanding Indian music, dance dramas and recitals, folk theater, and regional-language theater. Philharmonic orchestras can be heard in Bombay. Zubin Mehta, a native son, recently brought down the house. See regional sections for detailed information such as *jatras* in Calcutta, *Kathakali* in Kerala, and *Ram-lila* in Delhi.

Traveling in India

BY AIR. Since India is more of a continent than a country, good internal air transportation has proved to be as vital to India's development as a nation as it is to you, the tourist. The state-owned *Indian Airlines* has been building up its services for more than a quarter of a century. With over 50,000 kilometers of unduplicated routes, it is now one of the largest domestic carriers in the world. Over 240 flights daily from 73 cities are served, including neighboring countries, from the four major bases of Delhi, Bombay, Calcutta, and Madras.

Indian Airlines carries some six million passengers annually. A feeder airline, *Vayudoot*, operates over 45 routes out of major and regional airports throughout India and is planning 45 more by the end of 1988. Fleet is mostly 19-seat Dornier 228s that complement the wide-bodied A300 228-seater Airbuses of Indian Airlines.

Indian Airlines' one major drawback is that though it has recently computerized its reservation system, mechanical malfunctioning can cause numerous delays in bookings. After this, they are controlled by the city of departure. It is vitally important to reconfirm your flights individually, at least 48 hours before departure—an often tiresome chore, considering the high volume of traffic and lack of technology in this sphere. And if you wish to change your itinerary as you go along, you run the risk of failing to get a seat on the desired flight, since each journey can only be changed once you get to your next destination. Waiting lists are common, but the airline has a high number of "no show" passengers, so one often does get on at the last minute, especially the larger jet aircraft. Fortunately, *Air-India* operates a computer reservation system covering its domestic destinations, but it is not always functioning because of the power cuts, which occur throughout India. Domestic flights usually operate on a daily basis, but in small, remote destinations, the flights are less frequent, the aircraft smaller, and there are more delays or cancellations. Reconfirm your confirmation from the city of departure at least 72 hours in advance and be at the airport well ahead of your departure time.

Check-in procedures are slower everywhere now because of security measures. Do not pack a pocket knife in your hand luggage. Security is extremely tight at all Indian airports. Even golf clubs are not allowed as hand luggage! Checked-in baggage has to be identified on the tarmac, next to the aircraft, before boarding. Indian Airlines and Vayudoot have, thus far, a high safety rate. Check in no later than 90 minutes for domestic flights and two hours for international flights. If you take a coach from the city air terminal, it will usually be timed to arrive two hours before departure. In the larger centers, ex-servicemen's organizations run the town-to-airport transport service. Indian Airlines and local tourist offices do the job in smaller places, but there are seldom any buses for flights departing early in the morning, of which there are many. Coach fares usually range from Rs. 10 to Rs. 20, depending on the distance. Taxi fares should be based on the meter or agreed to in advance. Taxi fares are usually two to three times the coach fare, and are a good value for two or more persons traveling together. Provincial airports are now mostly modern and convenient, but in view of frequent overbooking, it pays to arrive in plenty of time for check-in. Even on domestic flights, there is advance seat selection and rigid, often time consuming security checks of both passengers and hand baggage. On arrival, you can expect to wait 15 to 20 minutes for your baggage, so rather than stand impatiently in the heat, under slowly turning fans, use the time to visit the local tourist desk or hotel accommodations desks or attend to banking. Hang on to your baggage tags since your porter may need to show them before you will be permitted to leave the airport with your belongings. Although early morning mist can cause delays at certain times of the year, most flights depart more or less on schedule, even during the stormy monsoon. High season "extra" flights are more frequently delayed, sometimes for many hours.

The airport tax is Rs. 100 for international flights and Rs. 50 for flights to neighboring countries. There is no airport tax on domestic services.

You can now book your Indian Airlines and Vayudoot flights through Air-India if you travel to India on this airline.

Fares. Indian Airlines is run on the basis that air travel should be as inexpensive as possible. Despite soaring fuel costs and the purchase of expensive aircraft, they have kept true to their word and offer some of the lowest air fares on a mileage basis in the world. Air fares are increased each year because of the price increase in gasoline. In-flight service is perfectly adequate with light meals and refreshments served by English-speaking hostesses, but few concessions are made to Western tastes. The cuisine is Indian. The choice of vegetarian food is always available, and usually tastier. Alcohol is not available.

A sample of one-way fares based on mid-1987 currency exchange rates: Delhi–Bombay, $80; Delhi–Calcutta, $90; Delhi–Madras, $113; Delhi–Agra, $15; Delhi–Srinagar, $53; Calcutta–Madras, $95; Delhi–Jaipur, $19; Bombay–

Dabolim, Goa, $45; Bombay–Madras, $75; Calcutta–Pt. Blair, Andaman Islands, $92; Calcutta–Bagdogra, Darjeeling, $36.

Special concessional fares are available, such as a "21 day South India, 30 percent discount."

By far the best deal for foreigners in India is Indian Airlines $375 "Discover India" fare. This ticket lets you fly anywhere you like in the country for 21 days. The ruling is that you must travel more or less in a circular pattern, not returning to the same city, except to make a connection, which may or may not mean staying overnight. The ticket can be purchased (and reservations made) when booking your trip to India, or on arrival, but in *the latter instance,* it must be bought in foreign currency to the equivalent value of U.S. dollars. Credit cards are accepted. As stated before, some areas of the country are served only from one major city. Therefore, the following itinerary would be acceptable: Delhi—Agra—Jaipur—Bombay—if you did all this in 21 days, you would have had a glimpse of all corners of the country, for $375. On a point-to-point basis, *the same itinerary* would cost you more than $750! And if you wish, you can change your flights and even your routing at any time along the way, with no extra charge. Indians resident abroad are eligible for this fare. The "Discover India" fare covers only domestic destinations, not those to neighboring countries. A new plan, Tour India, for 14 days, $390, is offered now.

Other concession fares are available for students and people under 30, who get 25 percent off on normal economy class fares. Groups of 10 or more can get discounts of up to 50 percent under certain conditions. The *Complete Travel Handbook* is a handy quarterly updated guide to all schedules, fares, and concessions for Indian Airlines and Vayudoot. It costs Rs. 25 at bookstores or inquire through Charnock's Cocktails, 7A Ganga Jamina Building, 28/1 Shakespeare Sarani, Box 16051, Calcutta 700 017. Indian Airlines and Vayudoot offices in all sectors also have free information.

BY TRAIN. India's first passenger train ran in 1853, from Bombay to Thana—a distance of 21 miles. In the following year, the line from Calcutta (Howrah) to Raniganj was opened and, by 1880, all the major cities of India had been connected. The present railway system is the fourth largest in the world, having a route total of 37,700 miles. It is the second largest system in the world under one management, the USSR claiming first place. Every day, 10 million people in India travel by train. There are over 7,000 stations in the country.

The original trunk lines were built to the gauge of 5 ft. 6 in., the widest in the world at the present time; a substantial network of meter gauge lines was added and still account for about 40 percent of the total capacity. There are also a few narrow gauge lines of 2 ft. 6 in. and 2 ft., but except for the scenic mountain railways, these would not ever come within the range of the usual tourist.

All the major cities are linked by the broad gauge, so changing trains because of a break of gauge is rare. On the other hand, there are some areas which are served entirely or mainly by the meter gauge, so train changes are more likely on "secondary" routes.

Speeds are slow compared with Western countries, and the climate and distance are not generally conducive to rail travel for tourists or business travelers. It is also impossible to keep non-air-conditioned cars free of the all-pervading dust. Distances in India are such that air travel is much more sensible between the main cities. The distance between Bombay and Delhi is covered in 18–24 hours by train, but in two hours by air. For those with time and an interest in seeing India's countryside and the variety it embraces, however, train travel is the only way to go. Most of the fast trains stop about once an hour for about 10 minutes, giving travelers an opportunity to stretch their legs and observe the continually changing landscape and markings of Indian culture, such as the variations in dress.

India is a paradise for the railway enthusiast. There are still many steam locomotives to be seen, and while most of the fast trains are now electric or diesel hauled on the broad gauge, steam is still king on the meter. The mountain railways, the Simla and Darjeeling lines in the Himalayas, the Matheran Hill Railway near Bombay—all narrow gauge—and the Nilgiri Railway meter gauge track in the south are all well worth a visit.

Classes of Accommodation. There are five classes of passenger service on Indian trains—air-conditioned (AC) sleepers, first, AC two-tier sleeper, AC chair, and second. Air-conditioned is found mainly on the top express services between major cities and is excellent in facilities, cleanliness, and service. In this class, reasonable food and all bedding are supplied at no extra cost. First and AC two-tier sleeper classes are charged on the same fare basis. A number of special "superfast" trains between major cities entail a surcharge. Air-conditioned cars consist of two- and four-berth compartments, with transverse upper and lower berths opening off a corridor which has toilets, Western style and Indian at each end. These coaches are usually vestibuled. They are well equipped and bedding, including towels and toilet paper, is provided without extra charge. An attendant is on duty in each car. The compartments are larger than those in Western countries and the standard of comfort compares favorably. First-class cars are similar in layout and have an attendant, but the standard of accommodation is comparable to the European "couchette"; some first-class cars, but by no means all, are vestibuled. Two-tier AC sleepers provide couchette-type berths in open saloons and second-class AC chair cars have reclining seats. In both first-class and second AC sleepers, the lower berth must be utilized to full seating capacity between 6 A.M. and 9 P.M.; thus a four-berth compartment will seat six by day. Bedding may be hired either on the train, in the case of certain important trains, or at the starting station, on payment of a small fee. Western travelers should provide their own toilet paper except in AC class. Ordinary second-class has hard seats and is usually very crowded. It is not recommended for Western travelers.

Train Services. All the major cities are linked by "Mail" trains which, except for the special expresses, are normally the fastest trains. Most have AC (airconditioned) class accommodation and many, but not all, have dining cars. The most famous is *The Frontier Mail*—Bombay (Central) to Amritsar. *The Deccan Queen* is a luxury day train but is not air-conditioned—Bombay (Victoria Terminus) to Poona (Pune); this is a scenic route as the line rises about 1,000 ft. in 16 miles, winding up the hillside, through 25 tunnels and over eight high viaducts. This line is electrified. In recent years a tourist train, *The Taj Express,* with first-class accommodation has been put on between New Delhi and Agra. It takes three hours to cover the 124 miles. A similar "tourist" express, The Pink City, also daily links Delhi and Jaipur.

There are also the special expresses, of which pride of place must be given to *The Rajdhani,* which carry only AC class and second AC class and two-tier passengers. These trains have cut the overall time from Bombay to Delhi by five hours and from Calcutta to Delhi by seven hours to 18 hours each. They only run two days in each week.

One of the most fascinating rail travel experiences available in India, if not in the world, is the *Palace on Wheels,* which uses several historic, and extremely luxurious, private rail coaches of ex-maharajas for two to seven-day inclusive package tours from Delhi to major tourist destinations in Rajasthan. One travels and lives in this unique environment, with sightseeing side trips arranged in such places as Jaipur, Agra, Jaisalmer, Udaipur, and Jodhpur. For information and bookings, contact Central Reservations, Rajasthan Tourism, Chandralok Building, 36 Janpath, New Delhi 110 001.

COMPARATIVE DISTANCES AND TIMES

Broad Gauge
Bombay-Delhi 860 m (1,384 km)
Rajdhani Express...................................... 18 hrs.
Frontier Mail.. 24 hrs.
Bombay-Calcutta, 1,223 m (1,968 km) .... 36 hrs.
Delhi-Calcutta 892 m (1,437 km)
Rajdhani Express...................................... 17 hrs.
Mail .... 23 hrs.
Delhi-Madras 1,294 m (2,185 km)....................... 40 hrs.
AC Express .... 30 hrs.
Calcutta-Madras 1,039 m (1,662 km) .... 25 hrs.

Meter Gauge
Delhi-Bikanir 289 m (463 km)......................... 12 hrs.
Delhi-Jodhpur 388 m (625 km)....................... 15½ hrs.
Delhi-Udaipur 466 m (750 km)....................... 20 hrs.

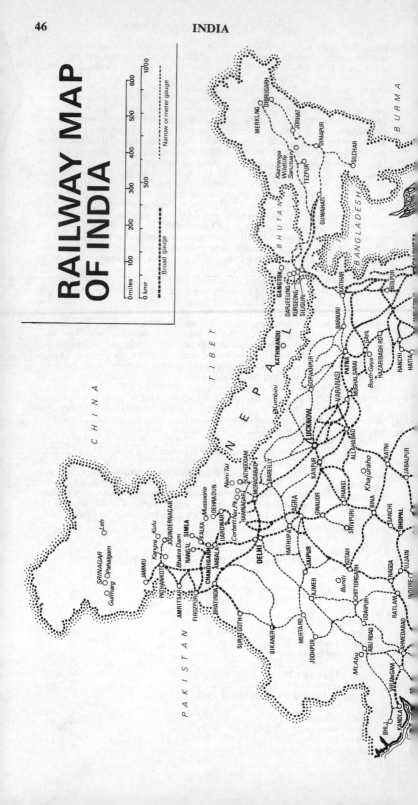

RAILWAY MAP OF INDIA

0 miles	100	200	300	400	500	600	1000
0 kms	100	200	300	500			

▬▬▬ Broad gauge

········· Narrow or meter gauge

Itineraries. Indian Tourist Offices abroad or the tourist guides at the offices of the Western and Central Railways at Bombay, the Eastern Railway at Calcutta, and the Northern at Delhi will assist in planning itineraries.

There are few day trips that can be taken owing to the distances involved, but a visit to Agra from Delhi can be made in a day by using *The Taj Express;* this allows nine hours for sightseeing. The scenic route to Poona (Pune) can also be enjoyed in a day by leaving Bombay at 7 A.M., arriving at Pune at 11:35 A.M. and returning at 3:25 P.M., reaching Bombay at 7:40 P.M. The Matheran Hill Railway is on this route and can be visited in the day. There is also a daily return train service from Delhi to Jaipur, which allows time for sightseeing by taxi or tour coach in the Pink City.

Timetables, Fares, and Reservations. A *Tourist Railway Timetable* can be obtained at the Government of India Tourist Offices abroad. It gives much useful information. For the railway enthusiast, the *All India Railway Timetable* is published by the Railway Board, but it is difficult to obtain outside India. Thomas Cook's superb *International Railway Timetable* also gives details of many Indian rail services. In India, railway station bookstores sell Eastern, Western, Northern, and Southern Zone timetables. Also available is the *Complete Travel Handbook* (Rs. 25) from bookstores in metropolitan cities. This book lists quarterly updated timetables.

Fares are low by Western standards, only AC class approximating those charged in the West. They are calculated on a kilometer basis, but become cheaper the greater the distance. Approximate rates are given below:

Kilometers	AC class	and sleepers	Chair class	Second class
200	Rs. 170	86	48	23
1,000	Rs. 619	312	170	76
1,500	Rs. 837	420	230	102
2,000	Rs. 1,042	522	285	126

The above fares admit to all trains, except the Rajdhani Expresses. The second-class fare shown is for Mail or Express trains, fares for passenger trains only are about two-thirds of the Mail or Express fare.

Special fares apply for the Rajdhani Expresses, which include bedding, meals, and the reservation fee. They are:

	AC sleeper	two-tier	AC chair
Bombay–Delhi	Rs. 1,065	605	320
Calcutta–Delhi	Rs. 1,190	455	330

For a few fast trains, such as the Frontier Mail, Taj Express, Tamil Nadu Express, a "Rapide" supplement is charged, irrespective of the distance traveled.

AC class	Rs. 25
First class	Rs. 12
Second AC class	Rs. 12
Second class	Rs. 6

Prior reservation is essential for all Mail and Express trains. Fees are

AC class	Rs. 10
First class 1A two-tier sleeper	Rs. 4
Second AC chair class	Rs. 2
Second class	Rs. 2

Sample fares between major cities are

	Distances kms	AC class	First class and sleepers	Second class
Delhi–Agra	199	Rs. 170	86	23
Delhi–Madras	2,188	Rs. 1,083	543	126

Delhi–Bombay	1,388	Rs. 797	400	97
Calcutta–Delhi	1,441	Rs. 837	420	102
Calcutta–Bombay	1,968	Rs. 1,042	522	126
Bombay–Madras	1,279	Rs. 755	380	91
Calcutta–Madras	1,662	Rs. 920	462	111

All fares and charges are approximate and are given as a guide only. Allow for projected increases by early 1988.

Concessional Tickets. The "Indrail Pass" is a wonderful value for the visitor wishing to make an extended rail tour of India. It is sold only to foreign nationals who reside outside India. It entitles the holder, within the period of the validity, to travel by all trains, including the Rajdhani Expresses, throughout India. Holders are not charged the fast train supplement or reservation fees and are entitled to free meals on the Rajdhani Expresses. Rates are calculated in U.S. dollars but may be purchased in other approved foreign currencies, such as pound sterling.

Period	AC superior class	First class/ AC sleeper/AC chair	Second class
7 days.........	US $180	$ 95	$ 45
15 days........	230	115	55
21 days........	280	140	65
30 days........	350	175	75
60 days........	520	260	115
90 days........	690	345	150

Fares for children under 12, approximately half the above rates.

Indrail passes cannot be purchased outside India; they can be bought only through leading travel agents or the Railway Central Reservation Offices at Delhi, Bombay, Calcutta, Madras, Secunderabad, Hyderabad, Rameswaram, Bangalore, Vasco-Da-Gama, Jaipur, Trivandrum Central, Chandigarh, and Agra Cantonment.

Rail Travel Tips. Travel by rail in India is safe and comfortable, but can be confusing until one knows the ropes, owing to the booking procedures and crowded, confused conditions of stations. Local travel agents can obtain bookings and tickets on your behalf, but may have to borrow your passport. It is quite feasible to undertake these arrangements for oneself because special facilities are set up by railway authorities for foreign tourists in major rail centers. The local tourist office or your hotel will tell you which ticket office to go to for your particular journey. When booking, look for the "Tourist Information" section of the reservations office, where staff are usually helpful, if slow. They will issue a voucher, which one usually takes to the adjacent ticket purchase counter, where the actual booking will be made and the ticket paid for. Check which station you will need and allow plenty of time for finding your seat on the train—the sleeper and seat numbers are displayed on the platform and on each carriage, along with the passengers' names.

It is advisable to take overnight sleepers, AC or two-tier first class, since travel by night is cooler. In AC class, bedding is usually provided, but not in two-tier first class, unless one arranges this in advance and pays a little extra.

At the departure station, get any help from the station superintendent. Passengers' names are posted on notice boards on the platform from which your train will leave, and on each carriage. Local people will generally be tolerant of foreigners jumping the queue for information, but not at ticket purchase windows.

Travel by rail is not recommended during the summer months when the heat is the most oppressive and it is overcrowded.

CATERING. No one need starve on a journey in India. All large stations have refreshment rooms at which Indian food can be bought, and many have a restaurant serving Western-style food. Dining cars are provided on the principal trains but the number of these is relatively small. There are buffet cars on some others. On trains without a dining car, the train conductor or car attendant will telegraph ahead to the nearest restaurant or refreshment room, free of charge, and the meal will be served to passengers in their compartment. The cost of meals is very reasonable although the choice may be limited and hygiene dubious. Refreshment rooms and tea stalls at stations where Western food cannot be obtained, can usually provide omelettes, toast or bread and butter; tea or coffee and iced mineral drinks are obtainable on all major trains. Drinking water provided from official sources, such as dining cars and refreshment rooms, is safe to drink. Alcohol is not sold on any trains or at any station.

ACCOMMODATIONS AT STATIONS. Some major stations have "Retiring Rooms" which approximate to economy hotel accommodations but not to five-star. They cannot be reserved in advance and are for short-term occupation only. Charges are well below hotel prices. All first-class waiting rooms have couches for passengers, using their own bedding. These facilities are in great demand, so do not count on them being available.

THE HILL RAILWAYS are of special interest. The Kalka-Simla Railway starts from Kalka and climbs to Simla in just under 60 miles. Kalka is at 2,400 ft. above sea level and 5,200 ft. is reached in 23 miles; the line then drops down to 4,600 ft. only to climb again to reach Simla at an altitude of 6,700 ft. The scenery is superb and the ruling gradient is 1 in 33. The gauge is 2 ft. 6 in. and trains are now diesel hauled.

The Darjeeling Himalayan Railway is a steam operated 2 ft. gauge line, with features of great interest, notably the reversing stations and the double loop by which the railway gains height. It climbs to 7,400 ft. at Ghoom, the highest altitude attained by any railway in the Indian subcontinent, before dropping down to 6,800 ft. at Darjeeling. The ruling gradient is 1 in 25 with some lengths of 1 in 22 and a short length of 1 in 20.

The Matheran Hill Railway near Bombay is a 2 ft. gauge line of only 12 miles, with gradients of 1 in 20. It is now diesel operated. Regrettably the Matheran Hill Railway can be visited only as a day excursion.

BY CAR. Renting a self-drive car in India is neither possible nor recommended, especially in congested cities such as Calcutta or on highways, where long-distance bus and truck drivers make driving a nerve-wracking experience. Hiring a car with a driver is not expensive, especially for three to five people, and can be arranged by your travel agent before your departure or upon arrival. Smaller cars are available from about Rs. 350 per day, which includes fuel and the driver's fee; vehicles are mostly Indian-produced Hindustan-Ambassadors or Fiats, though each year an increasing number of Indian collaborations can be found, such as the Japanese Maruti-Suzuki, Italian Fiats, and English Contessas.

Rules of the Road. Traffic keeps to the left and passes on the right, as in the British system. Subject to local regulations, tram cars can be passed on either side. There is no general speed limit for cars apart from the 30 MPH limit in the cities. In rural areas, slow-moving cyclists, bullock carts, and occasional camels or elephants share the road with daredevil long-distance trucks and buses. Speeds vary according to what you find yourself behind. The horn is used as a warning whenever one is passing. The constant horn-honking, particularly in the cities, greatly adds to the nerve-wracking experience of road travel. Remember that for Hindus, cows are considered sacred; for them or any other animals on the road, slow down and use your horn; bypassers will help to shoo them off the road. In a rural society, the loss or damage of any livestock can bring economic hardship.

Roads. Main trunk roads are generally good, but secondary roads may be bad, especially during monsoons and in the hot, dusty season. In addition to other drivers (of whatever transportation) and animals, one may encounter rural roads being used as an extension of farms, with food grains laid out to dry or sisal rope being strung out over the pavement.

The present national highway system includes roads whose total length is 31,000 km (approximately 20,000 miles).

Monsoons usually play havoc with roads and bridges, and it is advisable, before you set out for a long car trip, to consult one of the following automobile associations (AAs) that periodically issue regional motoring maps, excellent road information, and detailed charts:

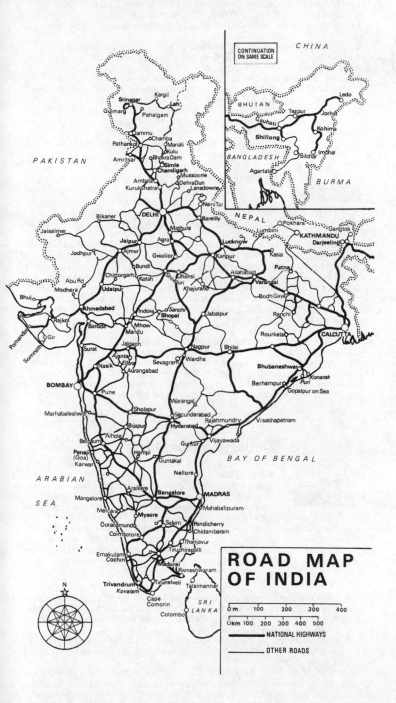

ROAD MAP OF INDIA

0 m 100 200 300 400

0 km 100 200 300 400 500

━━━ NATIONAL HIGHWAYS

─── OTHER ROADS

A.A. of Eastern India, 13 Promothesh Barua Sarani, Calcutta 700 019

A.A. of South India, 38-A Mount Rd., Madras 600 006

A.A. of Upper India, Lilaram Building, 14–F, Connaught Pl., New Delhi 110 001

A.A. of Uttar Pradesh, 32–A, Mahatma Gandhi Marg, Allahabad

A.A. of Western India, L.N. Memorial Building, 76 Veer Nariman Rd., Bombay 400 020

Gasoline (Petrol) costs, at the time of writing, are about Rs. 7.60 per liter. The government controls the price, which changes every year during March when the central government releases the annual budget figures.

Driving License and Insurance. An International Driving License is recognized in India. In case of loss, one of the automobile associations will issue a replacement license on presentation of your national driving permit. Third-party insurance is compulsory and must be obtained locally; international motor insurance is not acceptable in India.

 BY SHIP. There are a number of ways to travel by ship around the coasts of India. It is possible to sail from Madras or Calcutta to Port Blair in the Andaman Islands. Contact the *Shipping Corporation of India,* 13 Strand Rd., Calcutta 700 001; tel. 23–2354, telex: VMO495, cable: SHIPINDIA.

Regular, frequent sailings are available for the one-day journey from Bombay to Goa between October and May. Rates vary from Rs. 300 for the "owner's cabin" to Rs. 48 for the lower deck class. For reservations to Goa (no round-trip fares), in Bombay, contact *Mogul Lines Ltd.,* 16 Bank St., Fort Bombay; tel. 25–6835, telex: 011–4049, cable: MOGHI. Boarding is at New Ferry Wharf, Mallet Bunder, Bombay. In Goa, contact *M/s V.S. Dempo and Co. Prt. Ltd.,* Campal, Panaji, Goa; tel. 3842, telex: 0194–217, cable: AIRTRADE. Boards at Passenger Jetty, Campel, Panaji.

At the time of writing, ferry service between Rameshwaram and Sri Lanka's southern port of Talaimannar is suspended. When operating, it sails three times a week except from the third week in September to the first week in January. The trip takes three hours. Inquire at the *Government of India Tourist Office* in Madras for current information on this service.

Cabins are available for the above journeys, but conditions are not that of a luxury cruise ship, and on some ships, you must provide your own food.

Departing from India

 CUSTOMS. If you propose to take on your holiday any *foreign-made* articles, such as cameras, binoculars, expensive timepieces and the like, it is wise to put with your travel documents the receipt from the retailer or some other evidence that the item was bought in your home country. If you bought the article on a previous holiday abroad and have already paid duty on it, carry the receipt for this. Without such a receipt, customs officials may appraise the items at a higher value than their worth, and, should you lose them during your stay in India, you will have to pay duty on this higher rate when you leave.

American residents may now bring in up to $400 worth of purchases duty free; and for the next $1,000 worth of goods beyond the initial $400, customs inspectors will assess a flat 10 percent duty across the board, rather than hitting you with different percentages for different types of goods.

You can import free of duty the following—antiques (over 100 years old), original paintings, sculpture, prints over 20 years old, professional books, and tools and typewriters.

Since 1976, under the GSP (Generalized System of Preferences) plan, some 2,700 items from *developing* countries may be brought into the United States duty free. The purpose of this is, of course, to help the economic development of such countries by encouraging their exports. Because the lists, both of countries and of products, are reviewed annually, write to the Treasury Department, U.S. Customs Service, Washington DC 20229 and ask for the latest edition of the leaflet, *GSP and the Traveler.* GSP articles must be acquired in their country of origin.

Gifts that cost less than $50 may be mailed to friends or relatives at home, but not more than one per day or receipt to any one addressee. Mark the package "unsolicited gift—value less than $50." Those gifts must not include perfumes costing more than $5, tobacco, or liquor.

Note that the United States now has strict limitations on the import of any items made from protected animal species, including ivory and most furs of wild animals.

The following articles, up to a value of Rs. 15,000 (about $1,200), can be exported without any formality: souvenirs, silks, woolens, artwork, precious stones, and jewelry up to a value of Rs. 10,000 (about $800), articles made of silver up to a value of Rs. 1,000 (about $80), gold jewelry up to a value of Rs. 2,000 (about $160). All animal products, souvenirs, and trophies are subject to the protected list under the Wildlife (Protection) Act, 1972. The export of skins made from protected wildlife species is not allowed, and India is becoming increasingly rigorous in its monitoring of such exports. Such items cannot be imported into many countries, including the United States. As a general rule, avoid any souvenir made of wild animal skins (except crocodile leather goods). Ivory, unless it can be proved to be old, is also not allowed into the United States, although it is widely available for purchase. Ivory poaching, especially in southern India, is reducing the size of elephant herds. The illegal ivory market is in souvenirs.

Export of Antiquities. Generally, items more than 100 years old cannot be exported without a permit from the director-general of the Archeological Survey, Janpath, New Delhi; the director, Prince of Wales Museum, Port Bombay; or the superintendent, Archeological Survey of India, Museums Branch, Indian Museum, Calcutta. Articles will be detained by Indian Customs if they are believed to be over 100 years.

Airport Tax. All travelers must pay on departure from the airport a tax of Rs. 100 for international flights, Rs. 50 to the neighboring countries of Afghanistan, Bangladesh, Bhutan, Burma, Maldives, Nepal, Pakistan, and Sri Lanka. No tax is levied for domestic flights.

Banking Facilities. Rupees are not allowed to leave India. You cannot exchange them in other countries and, therefore, you must exchange them before you leave India. Banking facilities for changing rupees back into foreign currency before your departure are usually only available before you enter the departure hall, so be sure to check before going through the immigration procedures.

British subjects, except those under age 17, may bring home *duty free* from *any* country, 200 cigarettes or 100 cigarillos or 50 cigars or 250 grams of tobacco; one liter of spirits or two liters of wine not in excess of 38.8° proof, and two liters of still table wine. Also 50 grams of perfume, ¼ liter of toilet water and £32 worth of other dutiable goods.

Returning to Britain from any EEC country, you may, *instead* of the above exemptions, bring in the following, provided you can prove they were not bought in a duty-free shop: 300 cigarettes or 150 cigarillos or 75 cigars or 400 grams of tobacco; 1½ liters of strong spirits or three liters of other spirits or fortified wines plus four liters of still table wine; 75 grams of perfume and 0.375 liter of toilet water and £250 worth of other normally dutiable goods.

You can import free of duty the following: antiques (made before 1870), original paintings and other original works of art, including prints not mass produced, and unset gems.

Canadian residents may after seven days out of the country, and upon written declaration, claim an exemption of $150 a year plus an allowance of 40 ounces of liquor, 50 cigars, 200 cigarettes and two lbs. of tobacco. Personal gifts should be mailed as "unsolicited gift—value under $25." For details, ask for the Canadian Customs brochure, *I Declare.*

THE SHAPING OF
MODERN INDIA

A Look Backward and Forward

by
TREVOR FISHLOCK

Modern India is the new political and social ordering of one of the world's most ancient societies. Measured against the 5,000-year antiquity of Indian civilization, the four decades since independence in 1947 are but a brief time. And the British raj, which had considerable influence on the shaping of modern India, was a relatively short episode. India's history is a marvelous progression. It has been fashioned by the interaction of invaders, by the dynamics of Hinduism and Islam, by the monsoon, and by the impact of Europeans. It has also been conditioned by India's peninsular shape, which made it a net rather than a place of transit, and which has contributed to its unique development and character.

India's historical roots lie in the Indus civilization, known to archaeologists as the Harappa culture. This civilization grew out of earlier and more primitive developments and sprang up on the plain of the Indus River and in other parts of northern and western India. It flourished for about 1,000 years, until around 1550 B.C., but disappeared from historical view until archaeologists began to unearth its treasures in the 1920s. At that time, they found the remnants of the subcontinent's first major urban growth. In the years of its greatest vigor, this civilization spread over an area of 500,000 square miles.

The chief seats of its power were Mohenjo Daro and Harappa, both in modern Pakistan. These were great cities, run by merchants and priests, and well planned. Their principal features were large raised citadels that were the focus of government and religion, streets laid out in grids, and an elaborate drainage system: the Harappans liked to keep clean, and many of the houses had bathrooms. There were planned residential sections and districts of nondescript brick houses for workers, foreshadowing the monotonous urban districts of so many modern cities. At harvest time, carts brought in grain for the cities' huge granaries. The Indus people were traders and, as far as we know, the world's first cultivators of cotton.

The Harappan script survives on some 2,000 seals that have yet to be deciphered. These seals have pictures of people and animals and may have been merchants' tokens, a form of currency. The archaeological excavations have revealed that Harappans liked making carvings of monkeys, squirrels, and cattle. They made little carts and bird-shaped whistles for their children. The bull played an important part in their religion. And in many houses, there was a statuette of a nude woman, wearing an ornate headdress, perhaps worshipped as the Mother Goddess—one of the elements of the Indus civilization that persists to this day in the Hindu religion.

Arrival of the Aryans

The decline and fall of the Harappan culture was caused by the arrival of the Aryans. This powerful race of hunters and herders lived originally in the vast sweep of steppeland that stretches from Poland into central Asia. In one of humankind's great migrations, they spread south, west, and east in the early part of the second millenium B.C. It was a movement spread over several centuries. As they traveled, the Aryans conquered local peoples, intermarried, and adapted their language to local ones. In Europe, they were the ancestors of Greeks, Celts, Teutons, and Latins.

As the Aryans advanced and settled in India, they gradually took to agriculture and became traders. Their society developed on distinct lines, with groupings of warriors, priests, craftsmen, and serfs—the seeds of a caste system that, vastly more complex and subtle, is the social framework of India. Sacrifice was the fundamental part of their religion, and the strongly patriarchal family was the basic unit of their society. Their language was Sanskrit, which is related to Latin and Greek, and their developing philosophical thought was expressed in the *Upanishads,* the mystical verses set down in their early writings, known as *Vedas.* One of the great documents of India is the *Rig Veda,* a collection of 1,028 hymns dedicated to the Aryan gods. It is the earliest of the Hindu scriptures and is in an ancient form of Sanskrit.

According to many authorities, some of the *Rig Veda* was written before 1000 B.C.; but in dealing with the early history of the Indo-Aryans, we need to remember that much of the evidence is sketchy and that dating can, for the most part, only be speculative. Through their language, the evolution of religious thought and rituals, their cultural institutions and caste, the Indo-Aryans started to create a way of life that was self-contained and that sustained them as they progressed across India and through the centuries. They developed a social matrix that has shaped India for 30 centuries, and, in many respects, persists today.

The Indo-Aryans pushed eastward across the Punjab, clearing the forests as they went. They spread eastward along the Ganges, which developed as a major route for expansion. Around the ninth and eighth centuries B.C., the Aryans began to migrate south into the Deccan. The great Hindu epic poem, the *Ramayana,* says Aryans conquered Sri Lanka during this period, but there is no evidence of it.

Network of Kingdoms

In any event, the Aryans were certainly on the move, penetrating all of northern India and bringing their ideas to the Dravidian people in the south. During the period from the seventh to the fifth century B.C., there emerged in the fertile Ganges plain a network of about 16 kingdoms and tribal republics with a coherent political and religious basis. Indeed, there was a common cultural pattern across all northern India. But there was always volatility.

Religion was in a state of flux, and many people wanted more than the ritualism of early Hinduism, with its sacrifices to Indra, the thunderbolt god; to Mitra, the sun; and to Agni, the god of fire. Out of a cauldron of religious speculation and assertion emerged a number of influential spiritual leaders. One of these was Mahavira, born about 540 B.C., who founded the Jain religion, which is today a significant minor faith with many adherents among India's traders. Another was Gautama Buddha, born in what is now Nepal, about 566 B.C. Buddha's teachings laid the foundations for one of the world's major faiths.

During the fifth century B.C., the disparate territories ruled by chiefs and kings were steadily reduced by conquest to four and, finally, to one great superpower kingdom: Magadha. The capital of Magadha was at Pataliputra, on the Ganges, where Patna now stands. It was a magnificent city, mostly made of timber, and was protected by wooden walls.

Meanwhile, the Indus valley had been brought under the control of the Persian empire. Given the name of India, it was ruled as a province. In the fourth century B.C., Alexander the Great conquered the Persians and marched to the Indus. Thus Europe met Asia. And, what was important for India, a young Indian prince, Chandragupta Maurya, who is said to have met Alexander near the Indus in 325 B.C., took advantage of the confusion caused by Alexander's conquest and the further confusion caused by the conqueror's departure. Chandragupta seized the throne in Magadha, proclaiming himself emperor. He seized territory east of the Indus and then progressed triumphantly southward to bring all central India under his rule. In 303 B.C., he beat Seleucus Nicator, Alexander's successor in the northwest, and annexed the immense Greek province that included much of what is now Afghanistan.

Mauryan Empire Founded

Chandragupta was the founder of the Mauryan empire. He lived in luxury in his grand wooden palace in Pataliputra and reigned for 24 years. But he was always in fear of assassination and, according to legend, he abdicated to become a Jain monk. His son, Bindusara, extended the empire, and Chandragupta's grandson, Asoka, completed the process with a series of bloody conquests along the coast of the Bay of Bengal. Thus, for the first time, most of the subcontinent, from Kabul almost to the southern tip, came under a single political authority. India was then, much as it is today, a land of farming villages.

The empire lived for a century and a half. Its third leader, the emperor Asoka, is reckoned by Indians to have been their greatest ruler. Certainly, he ranks as one of the great kings of world history. After his early years of war and conquest, he became a Buddhist and adopted a humanitarian code for living and for government. In other words, he advocated the abandonment of warfare in favor of setting an example of moral leadership through a creed of peace and tolerance. He practiced the code of *ahimsa* (nonviolence to humans and animals), stopped animal sacrifice, and encouraged pilgrimages in place of hunting for sport. He was a far-sighted man, a ruler well ahead of his time, a reformer, a builder of roads, and a planter of trees. He was also a shrewd administrator. He set out his philosophy in edicts inscribed on stone pillars in many parts of the country. These edicts are the oldest inscriptions of any importance in India and remain Asoka's monuments. The emperor's symbol of four lions sitting together, a mark of his authority, is the symbol of modern India, the government's official crest. Another of his symbols, a chariot wheel, is incorporated in the country's green, white, and saffron tricolor.

The emperor died about 232 B.C., and the Mauryan empire steadily declined, its age of glory perishing with Asoka. New invaders entered northern India from Greece, Persia, and central Asia. New kingdoms sprang up in many parts of the country, and the Greek and Indian cultures and religions fertilized each other. Hinduism established itself in greater strength in the Ganges plain, and Sanskrit literature enjoyed a renaissance. Buddhism developed two distinct codes that still exist. The fundamentalist Inayana Buddhism is strongest in Southeast Asia, Sri Lanka, and Burma. Mahayana Buddhism is dominant in Japan, China, and Tibet.

Trade Flourishes

During this period, there was a surge in trade between India and the Middle East, which increased as Greek power gave way to Roman expansion. India sent vast quantities of silk, spices, jewelry, indigo, and animals. The goods were sent through the port of Barbaricum, at the mouth of the Indus, and by camel caravan from Taxila, now in Pakistan.

Kingdoms and dynasties rose and fell. The Satavahanas who emerged in the Deccan plateau of central India became a formidable force and spread and conquered in the north. The lands of the south became divided between Cholas, Padyas, and Cheras. In the fourth century A.D., northern India gradually came under the authority of the imperial dynasty of the Guptas. The seat of power became, as it had been years before, Magadha and the city of Pataliputra, and the Gupta empire extended from the Punjab to Assam. It lasted into the sixth century.

The most outstanding of the Gupta monarchs was Samudra Gupta, who ruled from A.D. 335 to 375. Under his rule and that of his successors, particularly Chandragupta II, A.D. 375–415, India enjoyed another golden age. Trading with the Middle East and the Mediterranean flourished, and the empire was efficiently managed.

The next event of significance was the rise of Harsha, son of a Punjab king, who succeeded to the throne at age 16 in the early seventh century and ruled for 41 years. Harsha extended his rule over much of northern India and restored some of the lost splendor of the Guptas. He was the first Indian ruler to open diplomatic links with China, and we know much about the life at his court from the journals of the Chinese traveler Hsuan Tsang, which have survived intact.

King Harsha was a cultured man, a playwright among other things, and he loved the showy ceremony of his court. He was an indefatigable traveler through his vast domain. He was the last Hindu king to govern all of northern India. But he had no heirs, and the glitter faded. After his death, his empire collapsed and India became once more a confusion of warring states. During this period and the following centuries, Hinduism expanded vigorously. Buddhism and Hinduism were integrated in the eighth century under the influence of the teacher and philosopher Sankaracharya, from Kerala, but as Hinduism steadily gained ascendancy, Buddhism began to wane in India, the country of its birth.

Advance of Islam

The most significant, most far-reaching, event in the centuries after the fall of the Roman empire was the advance of Islam. The Prophet Mohammed was born in Mecca in A.D. 570 and, by the time of his death in 632, the faith he founded was strong and expanding. In the seventh century, Moslems conquered Afghanistan, Iran, and central Asia and under Mahmud of Ghazni thrust into India. In the eighth century, they took the province of Sind, which has remained Moslem ever since. In the tenth century, Punjab was conquered, and in the years that followed, the twilight of Hindu independence, Islamic invaders increasingly took control. Hindu India was weakened by disunity, by its patchwork of rival rulers, that made it vulnerable to invaders. Late in the twelfth century, Mohammed of Ghor and his general Qutbuddin Aibak, a freed slave, marched into the Hindu states. In a decisive battle at Tarain in 1191, the Hindus, under Prithvaraja—a Rajput hero sung about to this day—beat back the invaders. But in the following year, the Moslems returned with a larger force, beat the Hindu army, and killed Prithvaraja. The road to Delhi and all the riches of India were now open.

Within a decade, the Ganges plain was dominated by Islamic rulers, and in 1206, Qutbuddin became the first Sultan of Delhi. The Sultanate of Delhi imposed stability on much of northern India for several hundred years and, indeed, the Moslem hegemony was only ended by the conquests of the British in the 18th century. There is a historical thread extending from the founding of the Delhi Sultanate in 1206 to the Indian Mutiny in 1857.

Between the fourteenth and sixteenth centuries, Hinduism made the adjustments that enabled it to survive and to grow. There were important reforms in the religion, and many holy men denied any contradiction between Moslem and Hindu ideas of deity. But politically, India was a loose collection of kingdoms, both Hindu and Moslem, often at war with each other, so that the country lacked unity and was ripe for invasion. In 1523, Babur the Mogul, a descendant of the Mongol warlord Genghis Khan and of the conqueror Timur (Tamerlane), marched into the Punjab from Afghanistan. He defeated the Sultan of Delhi at Panipat, north of the city, in 1526, and proclaimed himself emperor of India. The age of the great Moguls had begun.

Rule of the Moguls

It was difficult at first for the conquerors to gain a secure footing because the warriors of northern India fought back fiercely. Indeed, the invaders were thrown out in 1539 by the brilliant leader Sher Shah. But they returned in massive force. Babur's young grandson, Akbar, headed the invasion and restored and consolidated the rule of the Moguls. He took full power at the early age of 18 and became one of the great figures of Indian, and world, history. He extended his power throughout northern India, including Bengal, Kashmir, Baluchistan, Afghanistan, and Gujarat. His fortress-palace at Agra and his now-deserted capital at Fatehpur Sikri are physical memorials to the power of this, the greatest of the Mogul emperors. But there was much else. Akbar was a masterful administrator. He was also a unifier. He sought peaceful coexistence with the Hindu majority. He abolished a discriminatory tax, encouraged Hinduism to flourish alongside Islam, and recruited Hindu Rajputs to important posts in his administration. He was a foreigner, but he had a deep understanding of India. He was an enthusiastic patron of the arts, adored painting and architecture, and filled his court with artists and poets. The Mogul school of miniature painting blossomed. The wonderful city of Fatehpur Sikri was a blend of Islamic and Hindu architecture. Akbar's reign, from 1556 to 1605, was a classical age, a brilliant time.

Akbar sought to bring the Deccan kingdoms of central India under his rule, and this policy of expansion was continued by his successors, Jahangir and Shah Jahan (who built the Taj Mahal). And under Aurangzeb, Akbar's great-grandson, the Mogul empire reached its broadest extent. But Aurangzeb reversed the policy of tolerance toward his Hindu subjects. He reimposed the discriminatory taxes lifted by his great-grandfather and squeezed out the Hindus who held positions in his court and administration. Inevitably, the earlier mood of cooperation was replaced by bitterness. The court and government became weaker. Angry Rajputs, the proud warrior people of the northwest who had been important supporters of the Mogul emperors, revolted against Aurangzeb's discrimination. The Sikhs, whose religion had been founded in the early sixteenth century, one of the by-products of the meeting between Hinduism and Islam, also rose in rebellion. So did the Jat people of the north. The powerful Marathas, renowned as skilled and disciplined cavalrymen, also pitted themselves against the emperor. Their leader, Shivaji (1627–80), is revered today as a hero of Hindu resistance and revival. His son was captured, blinded, and killed by Aurangzeb.

War, intolerance, and the decaying of a once-magnificent administration began to put an end to the Mogul empire. Aurangzeb died in 1707, but his empire was already well past its best, and it was effectively finished within a few years. The Maratha troops pushed northward, occupied Gujarat and invaded Hindustan, reaching Lahore, Orissa, the Ganges plain, and much of central India. They took over a large part of the Mogul empire, having marched into Delhi in 1719. The emperor himself had to concede allegiance to a Maratha chief. With the close of the empire, there ended a marvelous time in the story of India. For the most part, the epoch of the great Moguls, 1560–1707, was one of creativity and economic expansion. The courts were dazzling in their luxury, and we only have to look at some of the buildings that remain— the Taj Mahal, the Red Fort in Delhi, Fatehpur Sikri, the mosques, the palaces, and the forts—to gain an idea of the power and the glory of it all.

In the years of the empire's decline, in the eighteenth century, a new force began to emerge in India: the Europeans. Merchant venturers from Portugal, France, Britain, Holland, and Denmark set up stations around the coasts, opened up trade to a Europe hungry for the spices and fabrics and raw materials of India, and, from time to time, challenged each other for superiority.

European Influence

The story of Europe in India really began in 1498 with the arrival in Calicut, on the west coast, of the Portuguese navigator Vasco da Gama. The Portuguese established bases in other places, most importantly in Goa, their headquarters, and for 100 years had the India trade mostly to themselves. The Dutch, British, and French secured a hold in the seventeenth century. The English East India Company, which was to play such a large part in the development of commerce and political power in India, was granted its first charter by Queen Elizabeth I in 1600. Trade was carried on from coastal bases under concessions granted by local rulers or by the Mogul emperors.

The British acquired Bombay from the Portuguese as part of the dowry of Catherine of Braganza on her marriage to King Charles II in 1661. The British also built major bases in Madras and Bengal for the export of textiles, sugar, indigo, and the spices that were so valuable in the preservation and flavoring of food. In those early years, the authority of Indian rulers was strong enough to prevent Europeans from interfering politically in local affairs. But later, the rulers began to appreciate the military skills and equipment of Europeans and gradually began to court them for assistance in their own struggles.

Around the middle of the eighteenth century, when the power of the Moguls had waned, French and British trading companies began fighting along the Carnatic coast of the southeast. Their warfare was an offshoot of two European struggles, the War of the Austrian Succession (1740–48) and the Seven Years War (1756–63). The outstanding British figure of this time was Robert Clive, a former clerk in the East India Company, whose military brilliance effectively ended France's ventures in India. After 1763, the French were never a serious threat to British ambitions in the subcontinent. With the help of Indian leaders, Clive went on to defeat the Mogul emperor's army at Plassey, in Bengal, in 1757, and thus secured Orissa, Bihar, and Bengal, where the East India Company had a trading center in Calcutta since 1690.

British Power Asserted

As conqueror of Bengal, Clive was the original force behind British power in India. More battles against local rulers won more territory for the East India Company. And as the British newcomers pushed their way into the interior, local rulers threatened by the might of the Marathas put themselves under British protection. Thus, the flabby outposts of the Mogul empire came under British control. The East India Company (John Company, as it was known), became a power in the land.

In the early nineteenth century, consolidation of the gains was achieved by Richard Wellesley, the Duke of Wellington's brother. His forces broke the power of the Marathas in 1803 and the Mogul emperor in Delhi agreed to put himself under Wellesley's protection. Wellesley left India in 1805, satisfied that much of India lay under British rule. Sind was conquered in 1843, and the kingdom of Punjab, the homeland of the Sikhs, was annexed five years later; the Sikhs were the last, and probably the toughest, opponents. They later became firm allies of the British. But not all of India lay under direct British rule. Princes continued to govern in many parts, and the British could not have managed India without their cooperation. India, as a colony of Britain, became part of the global economy. It was the imperial pivot, the jewel in the crown of the empire.

In 1857 the Indian Mutiny shook Britain's composure and arrogance. Its causes were complex. In the background, there was the resentment of rulers who had lost power to the British and a natural dislike of a foreign ruler. Some deplored British interference with Hindu customs, like *suttee,* in which a widow immolated herself on her husband's funeral pyre. Some Indian historians see the mutiny as a war of independence or as an explosive reaction against change.

The trigger was the scandal of cartridges, greased with the fat of tabooed animals, the cow in the case of Hindus, the pig in the case of Moslems. These cartridges were issued to *sepoys,* the native soldiers. Enraged sepoys rose up at Meerut, east of Delhi, and there was bitter fighting. At one time, a large part of northern India was caught up in the revolt, which took the British 14 months to put down. They did so with rigor. The rebellion had the nominal leadership of the last of the Mogul emperors, Bahadur Shah, who hardly knew what was going on.

The British exiled him to Rangoon. As a result of the mutiny, the power of the discredited East India Company came to an end, and India came under the direct rule of the British crown. In due course, Queen Victoria was proclaimed Empress of India.

Results of British Rule

This was the beginning of modern India. The British built an extensive network of railways and a postal and telegraph service. They undertook irrigation projects and other public works. They established an administration with a huge bureaucracy, trained Indians in British techniques, spread the English language and education, and set up a system of justice. The railways, of course, enabled the British to expand their commerce. The British Indian empire grew even larger with the annexation of Burma in the 1850s and 1880s.

But, at the time of its greatest strength, the seeds of its demise were firmly planted. British education for Indians had been encouraged since 1835, and some of the sons of rich men went to Britain for their education in the best schools and universities. These young people imbibed British ideas of the liberal tradition and of democracy. Naturally they were struck by the incongruity of India being a colony, contributing to British wealth. There was a surge of intellectual curiosity in India's past, sparked by European and Indian scholars, so that more Indians developed the pride that springs from a grasp of history. Meanwhile, the Indian middle class and a new breed of capitalists grew and expanded. Indian entrepreneurs developed mills and mines. This significant class of young intellectuals was trained, aware of their country's position, and increasingly frustrated.

New Nationalism Rises

The springboard for the new nationalism was the Indian National Congress, founded in 1885 by an Englishman, to be a focus for the ideas and aspirations of the educated class. At first, the Indian National Congress was a debating society, a safety valve for the steam of intellectuals. But it quickly became a significant movement that questioned the British presence in India. In 1905, there was the first large-scale demonstration calling for self-rule, sparked by the partition of Bengal along Hindu-Moslem lines. There were also terrorist incidents.

The pace quickened during World War I, in which many Indians fought and died for Britain. The disruption caused by the war and the growing revolutionary spirit among the people led to a more insistent demand for home rule. The government responded with a proclamation that responsible government was a long-term aim and with reforms setting up provincial councils. These reforms were not enough. Meanwhile, Indian Moslems were angered by the British treatment of the Turkish sultan (*khalifa*), their spiritual head, after World War I.

Gandhi and the People's Struggle

In answer to the disturbances, the government became more repressive. In 1919, hundreds of civilians were massacred in the walled garden of Jallianwallabagh, in Amritsar, on the orders of General Reginald Dyer. This massacre was the turning point, and nothing was ever the same after that. Far from showing strength, the British showed they had lost their authority. The outrage united Indians. In the aftermath, Mahatma Gandhi became a national figure, the leader of the independence movement. It was Gandhi who transformed a mostly middle-class and intellectual movement into a people's struggle. He took it from the city into the villages, into the heart of India. His simplicity and charisma, his saintly quality, made him an adored leader.

Gandhi was one of those men who, in his youth, had gone to England to study. His devoted follower, Jawaharlal Nehru, who later became the first prime minister of independent India, was another. Gandhi's technique of opposition to the British was one he had used in South Africa in his struggle against race laws: *satyagraha,* or nonviolent mass demonstration and non-cooperation. There was also a boycott of British goods. Given the mood of the times, the British concessions to Indian demands looked stingy. The Indian National Congress was the unstoppable vehicle of the push for self-rule, a moral as well as a political force, and Gandhi was its president from 1924 to 1934. Radicals like Jawaharlal Nehru and Subhas Chandra Bose persuaded the congress to harden its attitude and demand complete independence.

There were countless demonstrations in the great civil disobedience campaign of 1930–34. Gandhi and tens of thousands of his supporters were arrested, and many freedom fighters were jailed. Gandhi went to London in 1931 for talks with the British, but these failed and Gandhi returned to the struggle. Confrontation was the order of the day.

For a time, there had been unity in the independence movement, with Hindus and Moslems working together. But the split that Gandhi feared began to show itself more clearly. Elections to provincial councils embittered relationships. Although a minority, Moslems formed the majority in some areas, and the Moslem League became increasingly strident in its assertion that Moslems would not accept domination by the Hindus. In Mohammed Ali Jinnah, they found a brilliant, steely, and single-minded leader.

India's entry into World War II was automatic. The lack of consultation infuriated many Indians. The Indian National Congress decided not to take part in the war effort. Meanwhile, the differences between Hindus and Moslems grew more raw. In 1940, the Moslem League called for the founding of a separate homeland: Pakistan. This idea was Gandhi's nightmare because he stood for a united India, as did a large number of his Moslem supporters. But Jinnah was immovable. At the end of the war, it was clear to the British that the game was up, that they would have to quit a country whose people would no longer consent to be governed by them. It was clear, too, that the Moslem leaders would stand for nothing less than partition.

The confusion and quarreling in the interim government in 1946 demonstrated the impossibility of India remaining a single state. In 1947, Lord Mountbatten was sent by the British Labour government to be the last viceroy, with orders to bring about a final settlement. It was he who cut the Gordian knot. He reconciled himself to the inevitability of partition, as the lesser of two evils. In the meantime, he persuaded some 500 princes who ruled about two-fifths of India to give allegiance to the new, democratic India, thus buttressing the country's political integrity.

Independence Arrives

On August 15, 1947, India and Pakistan became independent. In Delhi, the ancient capital built and rebuilt down the centuries on a great crossroads of the northern plains, Prime Minister Nehru addressed his countrymen: "Long years ago, we made a tryst with destiny, and now the time comes when we shall redeem our pledge, not wholly or in full measure, but very substantially. At the stroke of midnight, while the world sleeps, India will wake to life and freedom."

It was a time of celebration and the birth of hope. It was also a time of turbulence and terror. When the borders between India and Pakistan were drawn by a British civil servant, millions of Hindus and Moslems packed their bags and exchanged countries. It was one of the most astonishing migrations of history. Five million Sikhs and Hindus left Pakistan for India, and five million Moslems left India for Pakistan. It was a bitter exchange, with fighting and massacres. About 500,000 people were killed. At the same time, there was a quarrel over Kashmir. The Hindu maharajah of this key Moslem state vacillated over whether to join India or Pakistan. In the end, he opted for India, and there was fighting between the two new countries. Pakistan still claims Kashmir, and the dispute endures.

Mahatma Gandhi was still working for peace. On January 30, 1948, while he was in Delhi to use his influence to prevent attacks on Moslems, he was murdered by a Hindu fanatic, one of a group incensed by his conciliatory approach to Moslems. Nehru, to an extent, took on Gandhi's mantle. Nehru was a natural aristocrat, an energetic and magnetic man, with firm ideas about the way India should develop. India was fortunate to have such a strong leader in the tumultuous years after independence. Nehru had a dream and was able to communicate it to the people. He was devoted to the democratic ideal and to parliament as a way of governing this complex heterogeneous country.

India as a Republic

In 1950, India became a republic, a federal union of states with a strong center. Today, 23 states and eight union territories are administered from Delhi. The national parliament is set up along the lines of the British Parliament and is bicameral. The Lok Sabha (lower house or house of the people) has 544 members. The Rajya Sabha (upper house) has 250 members, most of whom are elected by the state legislatures, and 12 who are nominated by the president of India. As in Britain, the life of a parliament is five years, unless a general election is called beforehand. All Indian adults have the vote, and an election in the world's largest democracy is a truly amazing feat of organization.

In the new republic's first general election, in 1951, Nehru and the Congress party were given their mandate to raise India from its economic stagnation and to make changes in a country that was vulnerable to famine and drought and in a society where the social and political problems were daunting. There were problems of low industrialization and low productivity. The swelling population wanted food, better education, and better health care. Nehru believed in a strong public sector, with power, steel, manufacturing, and transport having priority. He saw great industrial plants as the new temples. In 1951, he launched India on the first of a series of five-year plans.

Nehru's plans were grand and ambitious. The first plan aimed to free India from its burden of importing food and to establish a strong industrial base. Nehru was seen everywhere as he traveled the country opening factories, laying foundation stones, and always encouraging. Three excellent harvests followed, and optimism was in the air. At the same time, Nehru steered social legislation through Parliament. His reforms of Hindu law were not popular with some conservatives, but they provided important rights for women in regard to marriage and property. Nehru was a strong supporter of giving greater political and public power to women. He was also a leader of the drive to spread education, to build universities and technical colleges.

The five-year plans had mixed success. Poor harvests, the result of poor monsoons, damaged the second and third plans. The trouble was that they were too ambitious. Nehru bit off more than he could chew. He was a visionary and inspirer—a most necessary figure—but he did not have a disciplined grasp of detail. India certainly made great progress, but Nehru's economic aims were undermined by a lack of capital, overconfidence, and insufficient realistic planning. Meanwhile, the public sector and a great bureaucracy simply grew more sprawling.

Foreign policy was Nehru's abiding interest. He was certain that India had an important role to play in the world and he set out, successfully, to increase India's international prestige. India was active in the United Nations and a founder in the 1950s of the Non-Aligned Movement. But it was in foreign policy that Nehru ran into damaging trouble. India and China quarreled over disputed borders in the northeast and in the area where Kashmir meets China. In 1962, the quarrel caused fighting, and Chinese troops marched into the Indian northeast. They eventually pulled back, but India was humiliated. Nehru never recovered from the episode. Some say it hastened his death in 1964. He was 74 and had been prime minister for 17 years. He certainly had disappointments, and not all of his ambitious goals were reached. But his achievements were remarkable and he played a giant role in India's history.

Rule Under Indira Gandhi

In 1965, India and Pakistan fought a second war, in Punjab and Kashmir, which was settled at a peace conference. The following year, Indira Gandhi, Nehru's daughter, became prime minister. The Congress party bosses thought she would be easy to manipulate, but they were wrong. She had learned politics at her father's side; indeed, she had been involved in politics and political argument since she was a small girl receiving the letters her father wrote her from jail. She herself had been imprisoned, like Nehru, for her part in the independence struggle. Far from being soft, she was tough. Henry Kissinger noted her "cold-blooded calculation of the elements of power."

Mrs. Gandhi gained her magical surname through her marriage to the journalist and member of parliament, Feroze Gandhi, by whom she had two sons, Rajiv and Sanjay. She became popular with ordinary people, traveling constantly through India and meeting villagers. Her popularity reached its apogee in 1971 through her policies with respect to the Bangladesh war of independence. India supported the guerrillas of East Pakistan, who were fighting to break away from West Pakistan and found a new country. The Indian army defeated Pakistani forces in 12 days, and Bangladesh was born. India earned praise for the way it coped with caring for 10 million refugees from the war zone. For Mrs. Gandhi, it was a triumphant time. Her election victory in 1971 was overwhelming.

But in the way of such things, the euphoria ended. The economy soured, harvests failed, food prices rose, India was squeezed by the oil crisis. People grew angry and reacted with demonstrations and strikes. In June 1975, Mrs. Gandhi declared a state of emergency, suspending basic rights and rounding up her opponents. The press was censored and strikes banned. Her blow was swift and stunning. The 19 months of the emergency were notable for the rise of Mrs. Gandhi's younger son and confidant, Sanjay. Always ambitious, ruthless and pushy, he was the enthusiastic mover behind a population-control campaign that left a legacy of fear with its stories of compulsory sterilizations.

In 1977, Mrs. Gandhi felt she could win an election and she restored the democratic process. The people decisively threw her out and installed the Janata coalition, headed by Morarji Desai. But the Janata squandered its opportunities. It was riven by factionalism and unable to pursue workable policies. Meanwhile, Mrs. Gandhi was fighting back and rebuilding her support. In 1980 she and the Congress party stormed back to power.

In the summer of that year the daredevil Sanjay was killed performing an aerobatic stunt in Delhi. Having lost her right-hand man, Mrs. Gandhi replaced him with Rajiv, then a self-effacing airline pilot with little interest in politics. At his mother's side he became an apprentice to power.

Sikh Terrorism

During the early 1980s, trouble festered in Punjab. Sikh grievances were compounded by rivalries among Sikh politicians and by the flaring of religious extremism under the turbulent Jarnail Singh Bhindranwale, whose headquarters were in the Golden Temple, the very heart of the Sikh faith, in Amritsar. Sikh terrorists tried to drive a wedge between Hindus and Sikhs with a campaign of massacre and murder.

In June 1984, with Punjab a powder keg, Mrs. Gandhi sent the army to root out the extremists in the Golden Temple. There was a fierce battle. Bhindranwale was one of many men killed. Punjab was put under martial law, and some Sikhs vowed vengeance for the attack on their most sacred place. On October 31, 1984, Mrs. Gandhi was murdered by her Sikh bodyguards in her garden in Delhi. She was 66 and had ruled for 17 years. Within hours of her death, Rajiv Gandhi was sworn in as prime minister.

He was 40 years old, a Nehru, a man of modern outlook, technology minded, who had grown up in independent India. In the general election in December 1984, he won a huge mandate. Indians looked on him as the symbol of their fresh start, and he plunged into a task he knew would be formidably difficult.

Rajiv Gandhi made a positive attempt to handle India's most serious problem—the growth of Sikh terrorism in Punjab. Extremists, who aimed to make their Punjab homeland a separate Sikh state (to be known as Khalistan), stepped up a ruthless campaign of terrorism. In a state where Hindu and Sikh had traditionally enjoyed an amicable relationship, the extremists tried to whip up hatred by indiscriminate shootings of Hindus and of Sikh moderates. Hindus demanded action. Gandhi's policy was tough police action coupled with a backing of the moderate leaders of the Sikh-led Punjab government. But the terrorism grew worse and Mr. Gandhi had to impose direct rule from Delhi.

Meanwhile, other problems grew. The new prime minister and his ruling Congress party were demoralized by corruption scandals—allegations that the party had profited from kickbacks in arms deals—and the press and the opposition were relentless in their criticism. There were also attacks on the prime minister's management style; Gandhi frequently changed his government team. On top of this, his party crashed to defeat after defeat in state elections. To some old Congress hands Mr. Gandhi looked a loser. The euphoria that had accompanied the new leader's arrival to power vanished. Concern about runaway population growth and the great drought of 1987 added to his difficulties.

On the positive side, Rajiv Gandhi forged a settlement in the bloody civil strife in neighboring Sri Lanka. This had a fair chance of securing the peace, though the situation was fragile. But the settlement was a much-needed foreign policy success for Gandhi, a bright spot in a political career that had reached a nadir of troubles.

SUMMARY OF HISTORICAL AND ARTISTIC PERIODS

Note:	In the following table, 1 describes the *Historical Period,* 2 the developments in *Art, Religion and Literature.*

Approximate Period:

3500–2500 B.C.	1.	Indus Valley (Sumerian) Civilization
	2.	(Harappa, Mohenjo-Daro)
2000–1500	2.	*Rig Veda* compiled
1500–1000	2.	Early *Upanishads;* development of caste system
1000–500	2.	Later *Upanishads, Ramayana, Mahabharata* and *Bhagavad Gita*
514–512	1.	Persian king Darius invades the Punjab
	2.	Gautama Buddha (563–483); Mahavira Jina (550–475); first Buddhist *jatakas;* emergence of Shaivism and Vishnuism
327–325	1.	Alexander the Great in India
320–184	1.	Mauryan Dynasty
	2.	Asoka's column edicts; Sanchi Stupa; Buddhist Mission arrives in Ceylon
250 B.C.–A.D. 60	1.	Bactrian and Parthian (Indo-Greek) dynasties in the Punjab
250 B.C.–A.D. 250	1.	Andhra Dynasty in S.E. Deccan
	2.	Amaravati Stupa; first Buddhist caves (Bhaja)
184 B.C.–A.D. 70	1.	Sunga Period
	2.	Early Ajanta wall paintings; Buddh-Gaya shrine; Buddhist caves at Karla, Bedsa, Kanheri, etc.
A.D. 64–225	1.	Kushan Dynasty in N.W. India; South India Kingdoms of the Cholas (Madras region), Cheras (Malabar coast) and Pandyas (southern tip)
	2.	Gandhara (Helleno-Buddhist) art; Mathura school of art; Buddhism arrives in China; commerce with Rome (Malabar); Manu's religious laws; *Kama Sutra* written
320–475	1.	Gupta Dynasty
	2.	Early Gupta art (Sarnath, Gaya); Nalanda University; writers, musicians, scientists; Ajanta Cave frescos; Ellora Cave carvings
4th century	1.	Hun invasion
5th–10th century	1.	Pallava Dynasty in the South
	2.	Appearance of Dravidian architecture (Mahabalipuram)
6th–12th century	1.	Chalukya Dynasty in the Deccan
	2.	Temples at Aihole, Badami, Pattadkal; decline of Buddhism in India; disappearance of Jainism in the South
8th century	1.	Emergence of Rajputs; Sind invaded by Arabs
	2.	Hindu cave temples at Ellora and Elephanta
8th–12th century	1.	Pala Dynasty in Bengal
	2.	Bengal school of sculpture; Shankara, teacher of Advaita; Shaivism in Kashmir and the South
9th–end of 17th century	1.	Hindu medieval period
	2.	Chandella art at Khajuraho; Chalukya art in Gujarat; Kalinga art at Konarak; Nepal school of art; Sena art in Bengal; Chola art at Tanjore; Hoysala art at Belur, Halebid and Somnathpur; Pandya art at Madurai; Vijayanager art at Hampi
11th–15th century	2.	Hindu art penetrates Cambodia and Java
11th–14th century	1.	Moslems conquer Delhi, Khilji and other dynasties; Timur destroys Delhi
	2.	The Italian Marco Polo visits South India; Guru Nanak, first Sikh teacher; Ramanuja and Madhava, mystic philosophers
15th–16th century	1.	Three Moslem Dynasties; Lodis in Delhi, Brahmanis in the Deccan, Adil Shahis at Bijapur. The Portuguese arrive in South India

Approximate Period:

	2.	Flowering of Hindu and Bengali literature
16th–17th century	1.	Mogul Dynasty (Babur, Humayun, Akbar, Jahangir, Shahjahan, Aurangzeb)
	2.	Reigns over North and Central India; Akbar brings Hindus and Moslems together, epoch finds expression in architecture and Mogul and Rajput miniature painting
17th century	1.	Establishment in the South of British East India Company, followed by Dutch and French; emergence of two Indian military powers: Marathas under Shivaji and Sikhs in Punjab
18th century	1.	See-saw wars all over India; British tighten their hold (Clive); Nadir Shah sacks Delhi
1857	1.	First stirrings of Indian nationalism: Sepoy Rising
1858	1.	British Crown takes over from East India Company
Second half of 19th century	2.	Hindu religious reform movements: Arya Samaj, Brahmo Samaj, Ramakrishna Mission
1885	1.	Establishment of Indian National Congress
1913	1.	Rabindranath Tagore Nobel Prize winner for literature
1915	1.	Mahatma Gandhi returns from South Africa to lead struggle for emancipation and independence
	2.	Excavations culminate in Archeological Survey of India; Bengal school of modern painting
1930	2.	Chandrasekara Vekata Raman wins Nobel Prize for physics
1947	1.	Independence and partition of subcontinent into India and Pakistan (predominantly Moslem)

Post-Independence Period:

1948	January, Assassination of Mahatma Gandhi
1950	January 26, India declared a Republic, with its own constitution
1951	First General Election. Nehru confirmed as Premier
1954	Repossession of Pondicherry, from the French
1961	Annexation of Goa, taken back from Portuguese
1962	November–December. War with China over northern border disputes
1964	Death of J. Nehru
1965	War between India and Pakistan over Kashmir
1966	January. Mrs. Gandhi becomes Prime Minister
1971	Second major war with Pakistan. Bangladesh becomes separate state
1974	India explodes first nuclear device in Rajasthan desert
1975	June. Declaration of "State of Emergency" by Mrs. Gandhi
1977	March. General Election, Mrs. Gandhi out, Mararji Desai becomes Prime Minister
1980	January. Mrs. Gandhi returned to power
1981	June. India launches communications satellite
1984	Mrs. Gandhi assassinated. Rajiv Gandhi elected Prime Minister by largest post-independent majority
1984	Dec. 3. Methyl isocyanate gas escapes from tank owned by Union Carbide in Bhopal. Worst industrial accident in history of technology
1987	Peace accord signed by governments of India and Sri Lanka aimed at ending the communal conflict between the central government and the Tamil separatist fighters in the northern and eastern provinces of Sri Lanka.

RELIGIONS BLEND
WITH CULTURE

by
TREVOR FISHLOCK

Religion is a dominant force in India and plays an integral part in everyday life. Its influence and symbolism are pervasive, and visitors will soon see that they have come to a deeply religious society.

On city pavements, devotees create small religious paintings out of chalk, colored powder, and petals. There are shrines in the streets, where people offer *puja,* or homage. The dashboards of taxis are decorated with pictures of gods. Many homes contain a niche to hold a sacred picture or idol. There is a large number of wandering religious men, or *sadhus,* dressed in saffron robes, their bodies smeared with ash, who carry their worldly possessions—a bowl, a staff, and a blanket—with them. Some are silent; some preach and sing religious songs.

The greatest inspiration for India's architecture has come from the various religions of the country. India has marvelous temples built by Hindus, Buddhists, and Jains. These temples are encrusted with carvings of gods, animals, plants, and religious motifs. There are wonderful temple complexes as well. The important Jain temple city of Shatrunjaya Hill, in Gujarat, contains 863 lavishly decorated temples.

There are innumerable religious festivals and rites, in addition to small celebrations, associated not only with gods and goddesses, but also with water, animals, the planets, the sun, and the moon. The visitor should try to be present at one of these occasions because they are a lavish spectacle.

Of the 850 million people who live in India today, roughly 82.7 percent are Hindu, 11.2 percent are Moslems, 2.6 percent are Christians, 1.9 percent Sikhs, .7 percent are Buddhist, .5 percent are Jains, and .3 percent are Zoroastrians.

Hinduism Allows Liberties

Hinduism is one of the world's most powerful religious and social forces. A Hindu's religion rules his or her whole life, from the ceremonies performed at birth to food, clothing, employment, marriage, and death. Hinduism provides a means of supporting and improving one's existence in the world, and the religious part of the system is no more important than the social. The whole provides a framework for dealing with all manner of superstitions and beliefs.

Hinduism is not dogmatic, and although there is a belief in the power of the the Supreme Being, it is not the central focus. Millions of gods are admitted to the Hindu pantheon, allowing great freedom of worship. Indeed, Hindus often have a businesslike arrangement with their gods. They offer sacrifices and gifts when prayers are answered, but shout abuse at them when things do not go according to plan.

For simplicity, Hindus have assigned the major attributes of the Deity to a trinity of principal gods: Brahma, the creator; Vishnu, the preserver; and Shiva, the destroyer. Brahma is often shown with four heads, each holding sway over a quarter of the universe. The four *Vedas* are believed to have emanated from his heads, and he is therefore the god of wisdom. His bride, Saraswati, is the goddess of learning. Vishnu is the highest of the gods, who periodically visits the world to destroy evil and preserve truth. His incarnations as Rama and Krishna have inspired great fervor among Hindus. Rama is the hero of the great epic, the *Ramayana,* which is staged annually all over India. Krishna is represented as a handsome youth, holding or playing a flute. The Krishna cult is Hinduism's expression of human love. Krishna has inspired much of India's art.

Shiva is the terrible god of destruction, and he controls war, pestilence, famine, and death as well as related calamities like floods and drought. His consort, Parvati, is benevolent and affectionate, but she can take on the form of Durga, goddess of battle. She can also become Kali, the black goddess who has conquered time.

Ganesh, the son of Shiva and Parvati, wears an elephant's head; he is the god of luck and success. Hanuman, the monkey who, according to the *Ramayana,* helped Rama construct a bridge between Ceylon and India, is worshiped as a god in some parts of India.

The Hindu code for living is based on *dharma,* doing one's duty, as dictated by conscience, custom, and social background. Dharma is linked to *karma,* the belief that present actions affect future existence. The soul is eternal and goes through a cycle of births, deaths, and rebirths. Hindus believe that present difficulties are caused by the sins committed in a former life. The future may be improved by a series of selfless actions. If one's motives are truly altruistic, they can lead to a state of *moksha,* or serene peace and liberation from the pain and problems of the world. Many techniques are prescribed for the attainment of moksha: pilgrimages, yoga, ascetic practices, and the following of a *guru,* or spiritual teacher.

The Western notion is that the most profound part of Hinduism is an esoteric religious experience. But Hindus say that this mysterious aspect, the harnessing of forces through meditation and yoga, is not the most important. Hinduism is realistic; it provides a way of living in the

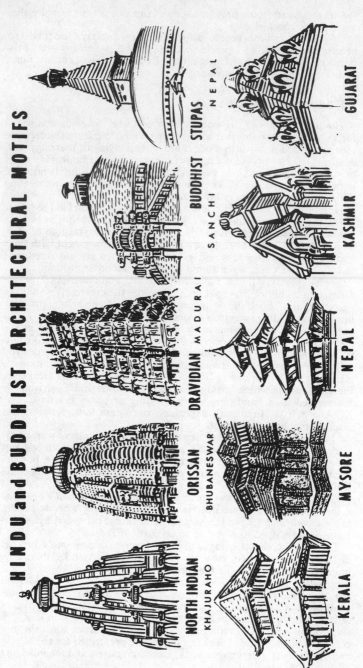

HINDU and BUDDHIST ARCHITECTURAL MOTIFS

STUPAS
NEPAL
GUJARAT
BUDDHIST
SANCHI
KASHMIR
DRAVIDIAN MADURAI
NEPAL
ORISSAN BHUBANESWAR
MYSORE
NORTH INDIAN KHAJURAHO
KERALA

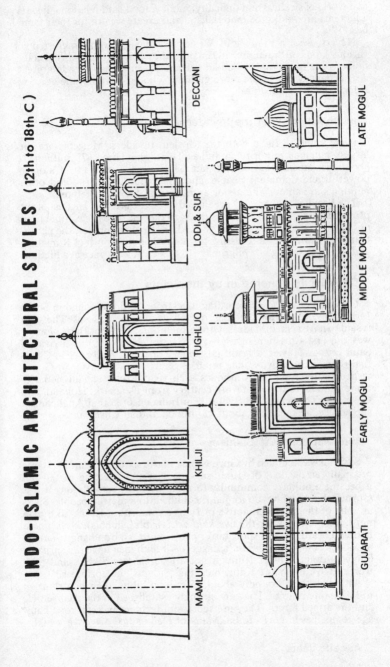

INDO-ISLAMIC ARCHITECTURAL STYLES (12th to 18th C)

DECCANI

LATE MOGUL

LODI & SUR

MIDDLE MOGUL

TUGHLUQ

KHILJI

EARLY MOGUL

MAMLUK

GUJARATI

real world of sickness and difficulty, money, food, and relationships. Its adherents are told to be materialistic and create wealth for their families.

Nevertheless, a number of Westerners have become interested in various kinds of Indian mysticism, and they travel India seeking solutions to the mysteries of human existence. Gurus have made a great deal of money out of the more gullible, who go to India, they say, to escape the materialism and decaying values of the West.

Islam Enters with the Invaders

Islam came to India with the Moslem invaders. Moslems are the largest religious minority in India. Their population, 77 million, is about the same as that of Pakistan. They are the remnant of a once-powerful and dominant people, and their mosques, forts, and other buildings are among the major architectural features of India.

The Prophet Mohammed is believed to be the last and greatest of the prophets, and the Holy Koran is the sacred book. The basic injunctions of Islam are a belief in one true god, Allah, frequent prayer, the performance of charitable acts, fasting through the holy month of Ramadan, and the undertaking of a pilgrimage to Mecca at least once in a lifetime.

Christianity Ushered in by the Saints

Christianity in India, according to a strong tradition found in South India, is as old as Saint Thomas, one of the apostles of Jesus. The saint is said to have visited Madras. Others maintain that Saint Bartholomew was the first Christian missionary in India. However, the arrival of Saint Francis Xavier, a Jesuit missionary, in 1542, really began Christian missionary activity. The tomb of Saint Francis Xavier in Goa is visited by thousands of Catholics each year. Protestant missionaries came to India in the eighteenth century from Denmark, Holland, and Germany. The years of British rule in India ensured that Anglicanism spread. Today there are about 18 million Indian Christians.

Hinduism Sprouts Sikhism

Sikhism was founded by Guru Nanak in the sixteenth century. It was originally an offshoot of Hinduism—pacifist and rejecting caste—but it became a military community to resist Moslem persecution. It was Guru Gobind Singh who forged the Sikhs into a martial people. Sikhs are one of the most distinctive of India's minorities. Every Sikh man must observe and wear the five *kakkari* (visible symbols): *kesh,* uncut hair and beard; *kachh,* short boxer pants; *kara,* an iron bangle; *kanga,* a wooden comb; and *kirpan,* a dagger. All Sikh men have the surname Singh, meaning "lion" (though not all Singhs are Sikhs), and Sikh women have the name Kaur, meaning "lioness" or "princess."

Although there are only about 15 million Sikhs, their contribution to Indian life is large. They are strongly established in the civil service and the armed forces. They are successful farmers and run road haulage companies in north India. Many of Delhi's taxi drivers are Sikhs.

Ascetic Jains

Jainism is a severely ascetic religion, practiced by about 3.5 million people in India. Its followers maintain that right faith, right knowledge, and right conduct lead to salvation. Right conduct means the rejection of falsehood, theft, lust, greed, and violence. The highest virtue is the rejection of any action that could harm a living being. Some Jains, therefore, wear masks over their mouths to prevent them breathing in, and therefore killing, insects. Some devotees do not eat after dark in case insects get into their food and die. But Jains are also successful in commerce and are an important minority.

Zoroastrianism on Decline

Zoroastrianism is an ancient Persian religion founded by Zoroaster in the fifth century B.C. Its followers, about 90,000 people, are known as Parsis and live primarily in the Bombay region. Their holy book, the *Avesta*, describes the conflict between the Wise Lord, Ahura Mazda, and Ahriman, the Evil Force. Parsis are renowned for their ability to prosper, and India's most successful business family, the Tatas, are Parsis. But the Parsi community is dwindling, and there has been a decline in their interest in their own religion and traditions.

Four Truths of Buddhism

Buddhism was founded in India in the sixth century B.C. Siddhartha, who became known as Buddha, the Enlightened One, was born in the foothills of the Himalayas. It was prophesied that he would reject worldly pleasures and search for the way to true knowledge and happiness. He saw suffering around him and eventually began his search for enlightenment. After meditating under the Bodhi tree for several days, he became the Buddha and started preaching a new faith.

Buddhism is based on four truths: suffering is universal; it is caused and sustained by "birth sin," an accumulation of sins committed during previous existences; pain is ended only by nirvana, enlightenment; and the way to nirvana is the eightfold path—right faith, judgment, language, purpose, practice, memory, obedience, and meditation.

Buddha wandered from place to place preaching his gospel until his death in 487 B.C. He is usually shown sitting cross-legged on a lotus plinth. When his hands are raised in a graceful position, he is teaching; his hands are folded when he is meditating; and witnessing, his right arm is forward and his left hand is in his lap. There are about 5 million Buddhists in India.

Judaism was brought to India about 2,000 years ago by a group of Jewish refugees who landed on the west coast. Today small Jewish communities live in Bombay, Poona, Calcutta, Delhi, and Cochin, where they have built synagogues and prayer halls. They have assimilated into the mainstream of Indian life.

Merger of Cultures

The visitor to India cannot fail to be impressed by the individuality of its people, their character and culture. In the upheavals of its long history, India's traditions and mores have been continuously evolving. India has absorbed, adopted, and adapted outside cultures and influences, which have merged into Indian society, contributing to its Indianness. Religion and social life are closely interwoven, and religious symbolism can be seen in every aspect of the people's lifestyle, from great architecture, sculpture, and dance to the humblest Indian home where arts and crafts are used to great effect.

The people show a great flair for cultural expression, which illustrates the richness and variety of their cultural heritage. Tradition is evident, in spite of India's rapid modernization.

Since Independence, Indians have become increasingly keen to promote their sense of national identity, and there has been a revival of interest in Indian art, music, and dance. The successful Festival of India in 1985 was the most extensive series of cultural events ever to be staged in several cities in Britain, France, and the United States.

A brief survey of the main elements of Indian culture follows. Many specialist publications are available for those who want to gain greater knowledge of a particular aspect.

Architecture

Indians take great pride in their ancient civilization. Archaeological research has revealed that the roots of Indian life can be traced back almost 5,000 years to the settlements in the Indus valley. The Indus and Harappa civilization, with its great cities of Mohenjo Daro and Harappa, lasted from the third to the middle of the second millenium B.C. Mohenjo *Daro and Harappa* had two main intersecting streets, and houses constructed from sun-dried bricks and wood. The streets had drainage systems, and the houses had wells.

The Vedic Aryan and Buddhist period, from about 1400 B.C. to A.D. 300, saw the beginning of the fashioning of *stupas* (shrines) and pillars. The earliest Aryans were content with a simple wooden railing enclosing their idols, but later the style became far more elaborate. Caskets containing precious metals or bones, ashes, golden leaves engraved with prayers, beads, and coins were placed just below the summit of the stupa. On top, a square enclosed by a railing represented the heaven from where the gods governed the world.

The Hindu civilization, from about A.D. 400, saw stone coming into its own for whole buildings. The constructions are large, with thick walls, sturdy pillars, heavy lintels and ceiling slabs, corbeled arches and domes. Some of the carvings were erotic, symbolizing, in Hindu eyes, the sanctity of the creative force.

The Islamic Civilization, from the twelfth century, endowed India and Pakistan with some of their most beautiful buildings. The Moslems built mosques, forts, gardens, and tombs. The early Mogul emperors were cultivated men, patrons of art, architecture, and literature. Akbar encouraged artists and poets, and the deserted city of Fatehpur Sikri, an important tourist attraction, was his capital for 12 years. The mausoleum of Empress Mumtaz Mahal—the Taj Mahal—was built by Emperor Shahjahan in memory of his wife who died in childbirth in 1630.

The Mogul style of architecture was regal and imperial, worthy of the wealthy, refined rulers. The most important buildings were constructed in white marble, sometimes encrusted with semiprecious stones, while others were built of red sandstone.

The European colonizers brought their architectural styles with them. The Portuguese built their towns on the west coast in late Renaissance and baroque styles, and the French introduced Louis XVI architecture in the eighteenth century.

The architecture of British India shows that there was constant experimentation with different building styles. One of the grandest edifices is the Victoria railway terminus in Bombay. It is an architectural sensation, the finest Victorian Gothic building in India. Bombay glories in other Gothic Revival buildings, while in Calcutta there are many decaying buildings in the English Classical style. On a smaller scale, vice-regal lodges, hotels, and churches abound, and an Englishman can usually find something architecturally familiar in an Indian city.

The grandly imperialistic city of New Delhi was designed by Sir Edwin Lutyens in the 1920s to make an emphatic statement about the grandeur of empire. It was the new capital of British India. Some of its landmarks are Rashtrapati Bhavan, the official residence of India's president, which was the former Vice-Regal Lodge; India Gate; Parliament House; and Connaught Circus.

Sculpture and Painting

The fact that India has an ancient tradition of sculpture has been known in the West since the thirteenth century, but no real understanding or appreciation of it existed until the nineteenth century. Before that, it was dismissed as the product of bizarre religions and of having no aesthetic value.

But the study of excavated Indian antiquities by the British and other Europeans slowly changed intellectual attitudes. As people began to understand Indian religions, they came to appreciate Indian sculpture.

The earliest examples of Indian sculpture date from the Harappan period. The objects are assured and mature. Artists depicted animals—the mythical unicorn, revered throughout ancient Asia, being one of the most popular. The elegant figure of a dancing girl from Mohenjo Daro is world famous.

After the founding of Buddhism in the sixth century B.C., much sculpture was Buddhist in feeling, and artists sought to express the eternal and infinite. The Buddha represented one of the highest aspirations of human thought and art.

During the reign of the emperor Asoka (268–232 B.C.), about 84,000 stupas (the emperor converted to Buddhism) were erected. Asoka ordered his philosophy and edicts to be carved on stone pillars throughout India. Sculpture of the time showed the glory of ancient India, covering every aspect of life.

The fourth century A.D. marked the rise of the classical phase of Indian sculpture. The centuries of the Gupta dynasty (320–600) produced sculptors who excelled not only in stone but also in metal casting by the technically advanced cire perdue process. Unfortunately, much of this sculpture was destroyed by Moslem invaders.

During the medieval period, different styles of sculpture evolved in different parts of India. The work is unrivaled for sheer exuberance, and its vibrancy leaves no aspect of life unexplored. Gods with attendant dancers festooned with jewelery were given the full baroque treatment. At Bhubaneswar, in Orissa, sculptors carved lithe figures representing traditional ideals and at Konarak, also in Orissa, a temple to Surya, the sun god, takes the form of a giant chariot, covered with erotic sculptures depicting a variety of sexual postures. Other temples were covered with figures of loving couples, heavenly beings, deities, and animals. They are all a lasting testament to the vigor of Indian sculptors.

Indian painting can be traced back to the beautiful work found in the Ajanta caves. About 200 B.C., artists were producing work of lyrical beauty, naturalism, and grace. This rhythmic line formed the basis of Indian painting through the ages. The Ajanta paintings had a wide influence on Indian art.

India is renowned for the scope of its large murals—and for its long tradition of painting in miniature. Walls of palaces and temples were decorated with scenes from Buddhist, Hindu, and Jain religious teachings. The majority of these murals have disappeared, but miniature paintings are more accessible. The earliest are the Buddhist religious texts painted on palm leaves.

Under the Moguls, miniature painting flourished. Akbar encouraged painting and installed more than 100 artists, mostly Hindus, at Fatehpur Sikri, to work under two Persian masters, Abdus Samad and Mir Sayyid Ali. The paintings reflected the exuberance of their patron.

Other schools of painting were developing in India at the same time. In Rajasthan, the miniatures showed happy people in bright clothing and had a wider appeal than the courtly scenes of the Moguls.

As the power of the British grew, Western ideas and values became popular among fashionable and wealthy Indians. So traditional painting became less appealing. Many Indian artists switched to painting the sort of subjects and scenes that the British liked—costume, occupations, festivals, flowers, birds, and animals.

Later, Indian artists, reacting against foreign domination, began a revival of interest in the traditional folk art of their ancestors. Nevertheless, the great figures in Indian art in this century belong to the international tradition, although their Indian roots can be seen. Some of the most original current work creates a dynamic synthesis between the Indian past and Western materials and techniques.

Music

The music of India is the result of a sophisticated and ancient tradition. Music and dance are all pervading, bringing vitality to festivals and ceremonies. The beginnings of Indian music can be traced to the Vedas, and music has developed definite laws of theory and practice. There are many legends—the notes of the scale and basic rhythms are said to have come from the Lord Himself.

Music developed as an adjunct to worship, and temples became the most important repositories of music and dance. It is the logical development of a long historical process that is a distinctive and integral part of Indian history and culture. Music should not be judged in Western terms; time and perseverance are needed to appreciate it.

Indian music is broadly divided into two forms—Carnatic in south India and Hindustani in the north—both having a common heritage and philosophy. North Indian music uses a wide range of beautiful instruments like the sitar and the flute. In the south, the forms of music are stricter, with little improvisation. In general, the composition of Indian music is lyrical and exciting and offers the Western ear a new dimension in musical appreciation.

There has been a growing interest lately in all kinds of Eastern music among the young in North America and Europe. Some of this interest is faddish, but there are musicians who are genuinely experimenting. Renowned masters like Yehudi Menuhin are working out ways of collaborating with Indian musicians, while Indian artists like Ravi Shankar tour the West with great success.

Dance

Indian dance has a rich and varied background. Folk dances derive from various sources, but the origin of all the classical systems is the temple, where they were conceived and attained their full stature. Dance formed an intrinsic part of worship. Indian dance demands a spirit of devotion and surrender because it is believed that a high spiritual experience can be gained from a sincere practice of the art.

Dancing is mentioned in the Vedas, and there are references to it in the great epics, the *Ramayana* and the *Mahabharata*. There are several well-defined dance forms, each from a different part of the country. The four main ones are Bharata Natyam in the south, particularly in Tamil

Nadu; Kathakali in Kerala; Manipur in the northeast; and Kathak in the north.

Bharata Natyam is a dynamic, precise dance style. The dancer wears anklets of bells that emphasize the rhythm. In many south Indian temples, one can see Bharata Natyam dance poses in sculpture.

Kathakali is one of the most popular dance forms. It developed during the sixteenth and seventeenth centuries and was inspired by the heroic myths and legends of Hindu religious writings, with gods, warriors, demons, wise men and villains. Boys aged 12–20 are trained for six years in this dance form. Kathakali makeup is an elaborate process, the characters being classified into distinct types according to the color of their makeup and costumes. Performances are held all over Kerala in temple courtyards, clubs, and open spaces.

Manipur dances are vigorous when performed by men and lyrical when performed by young women. They revolve around episodes in the life of Vishnu. The women's costumes are picturesque and richly embroidered.

Kathak is exciting and entertaining—the most secular of all the dance forms. The footwork is complicated, and long strings of bells adorn the dancers' ankles.

There has recently been a revival of interest in Indian classical dance, and artists have traveled to the West. In spite of some experiments, dance remains close to its traditional form and does not portray contemporary themes.

Literature

The great tradition of Indian writing centers on the epic, romantic dramas and poems. The *Ramayana* and *Mahabharata,* like the great Homeric epics, take their place among the great literature of the world. They are available in English translation and help the reader to understand the rich traditional background that has inspired India's creative arts.

Poetry has grown and flourished, and the Bengali poet, Rabindranath Tagore, who won the Nobel Prize for Literature in 1913, is ranked among the great poets of the world. Sri Aurobindo, who was born in Calcutta in 1872, spent much of his youth in England, and English was his mother tongue. His poem, *Savitri,* is an epic. He founded the famous *ashram* (retreat) in Pondicherry.

British rule meant that English became the common language, and a number of Indian authors have written in English. However, over the past 50 years, several have developed a style and approach that is quintessentially Indian. R. K. Narayan, who began writing in 1930, delights his readers with scenes from Indian middle-class life. Raja Rao and Kamala Markandaya use social and political themes.

An excellent way to get the authentic feel of the country is to read the autobiographies of India's famous creative citizens. Mahatma Gandhi and Jawaharlal Nehru both wrote fascinating books. Ved Mehta, a regular contributor to *New Yorker* magazine, gives vivid accounts of his experiences during partition and as a student in the United States. V. S. Naipaul, who was born in Trinidad in 1932, analyzed the Indian scene brilliantly in such books as *India, A Wounded Civilization.* More recently, Salman Rushdie's *Midnight's Children,* which won the Booker prize, was hailed as a masterpiece. The work of Anita Desai also has received critical acclaim.

A number of English authors have written fascinating accounts of India as they experienced it. Rudyard Kipling was the first. E. M. Forster produced the classic, *A Passage to India,* and Paul Scott wrote the superb *Raj Quartet.*

The Mass Media

For most Indians, movies are an accessible form of entertainment. India's film industry, centered in Bombay, is the largest in the world, making about 700 features a year, most of them very long. The majority of the movies fulfill a need for escapism, romance, drama, and color. They follow a set formula: a love story, a battle between good and evil, a lot of action, a little comedy, and breaks in the action when the stars sing a song. Happy endings are almost compulsory. Social issues are explored, but the audience prefers the filmmaker not to dwell too long on them.

In addition, a number of high-quality films are being made by idealistic filmmakers like Satyajit Ray and Mrinal Sen. Their work is strong and original.

Radio and television are government controlled and the programs are, for the most part, dull and unimaginative. One listener threatened to put a bomb in his local radio station because the programs were so boring. Many other listeners sympathized with him!

The government says that radio and television should educate and enlighten and not be a forum for political controversy. Many of India's radio sets are communally owned and listened to by whole villages. All-India Radio broadcasts in many of India's languages and dialects. Television is slowly growing more important, and Indian-made soap operas are becoming popular. But those who can afford to do so buy video equipment and watch Western programs, pirated or otherwise.

Newspaper and book publishing are growing industries. The circulation of newspapers is about 40 million, the highest ever, and in some regions sales of the vernacular press are larger than that of the English-language newspapers. Indians feel proud that their country has a free press, although some, especially politicians, argue that India is "not ready" for it.

DISCOVERING THE
SPICE ROUTE

Indian Cuisine

by
BACHI J. KARKARIA

Bachi Karkaria is an assistant eiditor of The Statesman, *one of India's leading national daily newspapers, where she also writes editorial comment. She also contributes to magazines in India and abroad and has co-authored a book on Mother Teresa. She loves food—cooking it, eating it, and writing about it.*

You don't have to be an Indian prince to eat like one. There is nothing pedestrian about the food you will find in roadside stalls. Indeed, it just might be more delicious than any that emerges from the kitchens of the palaces or their inheritors of opulence, the deluxe hotels.

Mercifully, to think of Indian food today is no longer to think of curry. The food has instead become synonymous with *tandoori,* which is almost as inaccurate. Still, tandoori is more deeply entrenched in tradition, not merely because it emerges from the red-hot depths of the cavernous clay oven, or *tandoor.*

Currying Flavor

There is no such thing as Indian curry; if the word is taken generically to mean something in gravy, you will find little in common among the hundreds of kinds you will encounter on your journey through this varied subcontinent. However, although all gravies are what Westerners call "curries," not all curries are in gravy. The "curried" potato that the Anglicized menu writers refer to is really a dry dish, but by no means dull on that account.

The word was really no more than a convenient label placed on the concoctions stirred up in the kitchens of the raj. *Curry and Rice* is not only the name of a rare and delightful book on Anglo India. It is a standard dish, found only in the cuisines of two of the country's most colonially influenced and, incidentally, smallest minorities—the Goans and the Parsis; in both cuisines, it is a thick sauce heavily dependent on coconut. And nowhere will you find what passes for "curry" in the less fastidious hostelries of the West, meat cooked in its juices, with a teaspoonful of curry powder added. Indeed, if an item on your shopping list is "authentic Indian curry powder," strike it off right away, for it is unlikely that you will be able to buy a can of it in any part of India. Like chop suey, curry powder is an invention of the West. Indians use their spices freshly ground, either individually as with turmeric or dried chili, or in combination such as *garam masala,* a form of allspice.

You might find "Chicken/Mutton/Fish Curry" on the menus of a certain type of establishment. The dish will be some phony version, catering to the taste of the foreigner who is adventurous enough to "go Indian" and yet worried enough about "Bombay belly." Spurn it. Indeed, except for the fancier restaurants, avoid any establishment that features hamburgers and curry on the same menu. The former will be not what you expect, and the latter will be not what you deserve. Such places are geared for those who don't know any better and don't care either.

If the gastronomical tour is as important to you as is the guided one, ask at your hotel for the names of small authentic eating places. These could be individual restaurants or entire lanes in which the aroma of grilling, frying, and simmering triggers off an instant drool. And if you are worrying about your stomach's reaction the following day, don't, provided that you don't get carried away and you stay away from the obviously murderous-looking gravies.

The high turnover of patrons in these restaurants ensures that you won't get the previous day's leftovers, and the food is usually cooked before your eyes. Your safest bet are the grilled kebabs. These are skewerloads of beef or lamb strips marinated in nothing more sinister than a paste of cooling ginger, therapeutic garlic, and well, all right, the spices of the Orient: cinnamon, cardamom, cloves, and black pepper. The mighty chili that reduced the brave and the beautiful to running eyes and tummies is not a major ingredient.

Variety, the Spice of Life

Your trip to India will have been wasted if you do not try, in all its infinite variety, the food that India has to offer. The history and the culture that you gawk at in awe extends to the culinary fare on which waves of traders, adventurers, and conquerors also have left their mark.

The nostalgia for the raj, which has popularized Indian food, has created another kind of wave, this time of informed appreciation of the subtlety and succulence, to say nothing of the sheer variety, of the Indian table. To get the most from your trip, order the right food in the right places. There is no cause for self-congratulation if you've strayed from the straight and narrow roast chicken and ordered a tandoori chicken everywhere you've been. The north, the south, the east, and the west all have their broadly individual specialities.

Fleshed-Out North

North Indian cooking is robust, getting its muscle from the conquerors who surged through the frontier passes. Predominantly Moslem, the conquerors brought with them their massive cooking utensils and their cooks of equally formidable proportions and reputations. Today you may be not find powdered pearls in your *Murg Shahjehani,* but silver leaf is a common enough garnish for dessert sweets or the celebrated *biryani,* or meat and rice.

North India is the place to gorge on all the tandooris that you fancy; whether it is the whole chicken, the drumsticks known as *tangri* (leg) *kebab,* or succulent morsels in the form of *reshmi* (silken) *kebabs* all cooked in the tandoor, a huge mud oven that needs to be lit a good two hours before it is used so its searing heat pierces swiftly through the marinated meats, reducing them to mouth-melting tenderness in a matter of minutes.

Mutton, too, is cooked this way, and the most velvet form is the *bara kebab,* which traditionally was the unborn lamb, though nothing quite so barbaric is done today. Now merely very young animals are sacrificed at the altar of good taste—or bad, depending on your priorities. Tandoori fish and prawn are less popular but still delicious, the texture of the seafood improving tremendously in this form of quick grill.

The tandoor is a Persian import, and most of the gravied meat dishes are too; *dopiaza* or *korma,* for instance, are legacies of the Moslem rulers, whether they were the Turks, the slave dynasties, or the Mongols and later Moguls, in whose courts the cuisine was raised to the pinnacle of perfection. The last of the Mogul emperors bartered not a flawless ruby, but his secret recipes for his passage to safety. Both emperors and their great cooks had their private recipes, guarded with the same possessiveness as the Coca-Cola formula is today, and as much intrigue was plotted in extracting the secret of a particular court's spiced leg of lamb as in toppling a rival chieftain.

The ultimate meat dish was, and remains, the *biryani* or its variant, the *pulao.* Both are Persian words, and their meanings point to the different methods of cooking them. Whereas *biryani* is a dish of roasted meat and rice, the *pulao* is rice boiled with meat. Whereas both sound bland, it is the spices that add to their richness—ginger and garlic; liberal lashings of cinnamon, cloves, and cardamom; fistfuls of nuts, and the ultimate flavor *zafran,* or saffron. A thousand stigmas of the autumnal crocus go into making a gram of this spice, but just a thread or two is enough to elevate a humble plate of rice into a platter fit for a king.

In the north, concentrate on the meats; northern communities have a disregard for vegetables. An interesting northern vegetarian dish, however, is *paneer,* or cottage cheese, which is usually cubed, lightly fried, and served in a butter-based gravy, by itself or together with peas or spinach. A winter specialty in the Punjab is fresh mustard leaves, cooked for hours into a mash (*sarso da saag*) and eaten with corn bread (*makki di roti*).

Winning West

Western India's cuisine is polarized between that of the fish-eating Maharashtrians and the purely vegetarian Gujaratis. But if Bombay is your port of call, you can eat all India's food here. Don't concentrate on the Maharashtrian food, since not much of it is available outside homes and it isn't, comparatively speaking, much to write home about. Seek out, instead, the food of the minor communities that originated here or have migrated from their settlements in the surrounding region and struck root in this "city of gold."

In the Moslem areas, you can run your skewer through the entire gamut of kebabs, tuck into a hearty soup simmered in milk, and, if you are lucky, get to savor the unique speciality of *patthar gosht*—stone meat, a name that does not reflect its texture but describes the way it is cooked. Marinated slivers are slapped on a preheated special stone that is found only in North Africa and parts of West Asia; it is brought back when devout Moslems make their pilgrimage to Mecca.

Bombay is also the home of a unique and disappearing minority, the Parsis. Try their *dhansak* (if you can digest it), which is a rich lentil gravy cooked with mutton pieces, vegetables, herbs, and spices. Goa is a unique culinary oasis, with its delightful blend of Portuguese and native cuisine: fiery *vindaloos,* in which the spices are ground in vinegar instead of water; *sorpotel,* which needs a good lacing of pig's blood; charcoal-roasted mackerel straight from the bountiful nets; plenty of coconut and seafood; more pork than you will find anywhere else in India; a fermented brew called *feni;* and a hearty *joie de vivre* that is reflected in the eating, drinking, and dancing on the sands.

Gujarat, the home of Gandhi, is ascetic. It is predominantly vegetarian, and no one can make vegetables with the same uncluttered crispness as do the different Gujarati communities. The Gujarati treat the delicate flavor with respect, lightly tempering them with whole-seed spices. Order a *thali*—a gleaming stainless-steel platter encircling little bowls with their individual portions of a dry vegetable, a gravied one, some lentils, and a setting of yoghurt—all to be eaten with small soft *chapatis,* which are a delicate form of griddle rotis, or *poories,* dough that is rolled into rounds and fried, the expanding air inside puffing it up into balls. A small helping of aromatic rice comes later. The meal is rounded off with *doodhpak,* a thin and creamy rice pudding, or a cloying dessert called *shrikhand,* highly sweetened yoghurt, whipped to velvet texture and lightly flavored with cardamom or saffron.

Down South

The southern states are not all vegetarian, as many people seem to believe. The capital of Andhra Pradesh is Hyderabad, home of a distinctive Moslem style of cooking, brought in by the fabled nabobs (provincial governors). Kerala makes the most of its coastal location, reveling in the cornucopia of seafood. Karnataka and Tamil Nadu, however, are largely vegetarian. In Hyderabad, go a little easy on the meat dishes, for this is the home of the most murderous of chilis. But don't miss the *biryani.*

Clean, wholesome vegetarian food, known as the "rice plate," is available in the smallest southern eating places. It is unfussy but tasty. Wash it down with buttermilk or the famous coffee, which you don't really buy "by the yard," though it appears that way, since it is poured from one tumbler to another at dextrous arm's length.

But the south is really most famous for its two breakfast foods, the *idli* and the *dosa,* which have become so popular all over India that you will find them even in a distant Himalayan hill station. Both are made from the same slightly fermented batter of ground rice and a lentil called *urad dal,* but although the *idli* is steamed so it emerges as a light, fluffy, snow white, savory cupcake, the *dosa* is spread to paper thinness and crispness on a flat griddle and served rolled over, sometimes with a stuffing, traditionally of potatoes and onions.

Feast of the East

West Bengal, Bihar, and Orissa constitute the eastern states, and close by lie the exotic northeastern states of Assam Tripura, Manipur, Nagaland, and Arunachal Pradesh, for which you need an inner-line permit to visit. Bengali food has not been "discovered" even by other Indians, who seem to think it consists of fish heads and mustard sauce. However, this cuisine is highly prized, and its flavors and textures are varied and wonderful. Unfortunately, you cannot get a Bengali meal outside a home, not even in Calcutta.

The Bengalis love fish, which they simmer in a mustard sauce or yoghurt, steam in banana leaves, or bake in coconut shells. There is great rivalry between the cooking of the native Bengalis of the western half of the state and those who came over after Partition from what used to be East Bengal, became East Pakistan, and is now Bangladesh. Since the two groups have intermarried a great deal, the competition flourishes even in individual homes, with the husband maintaining a discreet balance between appreciation of his mother's cooking and his wife's.

If you go to Darjeeling, don't miss the Tibetan food—the pork and chicken dumplings, steamed or fried, called *momos* (like the Chinese won ton but more generously stuffed) and the *thumpa,* which is a hearty noodle soup.

NORTHERN REGION

DELHI

India's Capital—Ancient and New

by
KATHLEEN COX

Kathleen Cox is a contributing editor and writer for Indian Express,
The World of India, Indrama, Travel and Leisure, *and* Vogue. *A
former columnist for* The Village Voice *and* Playboy, *she is also the
writer and co-producer of the documentary television comedy,* Gizmo!

In the mid-1600s, when Bombay and Madras were trading posts and
Calcutta a village of mud flats, Delhi flourished in a state of magnificent
pomp and glory—the 450-year-old capital of a string of empires. First,
it served the various Hindu and Moslem dynasties, then the powerful
Moguls who ruled India until the 1800s when the British wheedled
their way in. One after another, each new power created its own new
Delhi, with each successive capital (there are eight) pushing the boundary farther north until the British came along. While building their
predominantly residential district called Civil Lines on this northerly
route, the British hit marshy flood-prone land that forced them to stop.
Years later, they changed the course of development, building the bulk
of their capital, the Imperial City, to the south.

Although the demands of the post-Independence population—over
6 million people now live in Delhi—have squeezed new neighborhoods
into every available pocket of Delhi, fusing all the cities into one,
celebrated monuments remain—especially the 18 tombs or mausoleums of various emperors—that attest to the significance of Delhi's

political heritage. Even Mahatma Gandhi's *samadhi* (place of cremation) lies here.

Delhi's massive collection of monuments—there are more than a
thousand—began in earnest when Qutub-ud-din Aibak, an Afghan and
follower of Islam, defeated the Hindu Chauhan Dynasty in the late
twelfth century. He declared himself sultan and founded the Sultanate
of Delhi. After a parade of Turkish and Afghan rulers, Babur, the first
great Mogul, seized power in 1526. But he loathed Delhi and moved
his capital to Agra, where the Moguls continued to rule until Shah
Jahan controlled the empire in 1650. He switched the capital back to
Delhi.

This Mogul emperor who possessed an exquisite artistic eye, especially in architecture, created the seventh city (much of it still stands
in Old Delhi) and, in the process, brought about Delhi's glorious
renaissance. But Shah Jahan was not destined to rule long. In 1658, his
son, Aurangzeb, who was anxious for the throne, deposed his father,
imprisoning him in the Agra Fort, where he died. After 20 years,
Aurangzeb grew sick of Delhi, too, and moved his capital to the Deccan plateau, where he kept busy waging a series of military campaigns.

With Aurangzeb's departure, the fortunes of Delhi began to decline.
First, the Emperor of Persia, Nadir Shah, sacked the city in 1739. Then
Ahmad Shah Abdali, an Afghan, swept in and wreaked havoc in 1757.
By 1803, Delhi's position of eminence was shattered; chaos ruled better
than any leader. The British-owned East India Company, actively
expanding its power over the subcontinent, grabbed hold of Delhi in
1803. Although the British agreed to protect and support the remnants
of the Mogul dynasty, they were propping up a hollow regime—a frail
vestige of former glory.

Then Delhi suffered through the Indian Mutiny of 1857 (a four-
month-long savage battle pitting the British against their subjects,
considered India's first struggle for Independence). The outcome essentially put an end to the age of the Moguls. The victorious British may
have proclaimed the withering Bahadur Shah "the Emperor of Hindustan," but the conquering forces were clearly in charge and the so-called
emperor died in exile in Burma.

For the next 54 years, Delhi ranked second to Calcutta, the British
chosen seat of power. But in 1911, King George V announced the
transfer of the capital back to the once-powerful city. With this decision, Sir Edwin Lutyens, the king's architect, and Lutyens's colleague,
Sir Herbert Baker, set in motion the construction of the eighth city—
New Delhi. A firm believer in the empire and all it represented, Lutyens
designed an Imperial City that verged on grandiosity; palatial-sized
buildings set amid broad tree-lined avenues punctuated by Mogul-style
gardens, complete with fountains and shallow pools. He intended to use
marble on many of the facades, but the cost forced him to use less-
ostentatious sandstone.

In about 20 years, Lutyens's capital was completed. But the British
hardly finished decorating the vast interiors when they had to pack up
and ship out. In 1947, England relinquished the subcontinent, the
largest chunk of its empire. India won its independence and Lutyens's
Imperial City now served the proud leaders of a young democracy.

EXPLORING DELHI

To write about all Delhi's monuments would create a guide of staggering dimensions, so what follows is a selective list that gives a glimpse

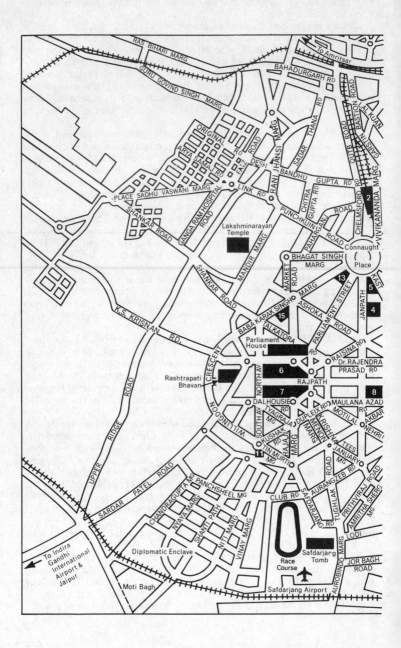

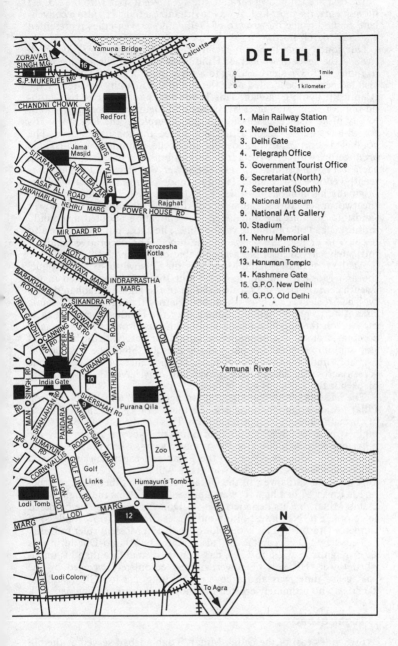

DELHI

0 _____ 1 mile
0 _____ 1 kilometer

1. Main Railway Station
2. New Delhi Station
3. Delhi Gate
4. Telegraph Office
5. Government Tourist Office
6. Secretariat (North)
7. Secretariat (South)
8. National Museum
9. National Art Gallery
10. Stadium
11. Nehru Memorial
12. Nizamudin Shrine
13. Hanuman Temple
14. Kashmere Gate
15. G.P.O. New Delhi
16. G.P.O. Old Delhi

of the best of Delhi down through the ages. We'll start with the earliest monuments, the most logical way to organize a tour. It's also a convenient method, since the growth of Delhi's first seven cities represented a steady march north.

Our tour begins in South Delhi at Qutab Minar, a 234-foot-high tower—the seventh wonder of Hindustan and the tallest stone tower in India, with 376 steps leading to a great view of Delhi. Qutab Minar also happens to be located near the site of the first city, created by the Rajput Prithviraj Chauhan. This Tower of Victory, started by Qutub-ud-din Aibak in 1199 after his capture of Delhi, can be called a joint family project since Qutub-ud-din only completed the first story. His son-in-law and successor, Iltutmish, added the top four stories. The combined effort led to a handsome sandstone example of Indo-Islamic architecture with terra-cotta frills and outbursts of balconies that mark each story. Unfortunately, after the tower was damaged in the fourteenth century, Firuz Shah Tughluq made repairs that destroyed the originally harmonious lines. He added not only height and marble to the two upper stories, but a heavy dose of incongruity. The lower sandstone sections are fluted, but his renovation adopted a "round" motif. Instead of continuing vertical lines, he chose horizontal. He also decided to change the degree of the taper. The decorative bands of intricately carved inscription are Arabic quotations from the Koran.

At the foot of the Qutab Minar lies the Quwwat-ul-Islam Mosque, the first Moslem building in Delhi and India. It was erected in the twelfth century after the Moslem defeat of the Hindu Chauhan dynasty. The Moslems clearly relished their victory that introduced Islamic rule. As if to prove their supremacy over the Hindus, they built their mosque on the site of a Hindu temple and used materials, especially columns, from 27 other demolished Hindu shrines. Note the Hindu and Jain sculptures in various parts of the mosque. Since the mosque was probably built by Hindu craftsmen, the presence of the large stone screen across the front of the prayer hall may have been intended to block out the strong Hindu influence.

The mosque is also famous for a strange object, a fifth-century Iron Pillar, which originally stood before a temple of Vishnu and was possibly brought here in the tenth century. This solid shaft of iron, 24 feet high, is inscribed with six lines of Sanskrit. No one knows why the pillar has remained rust free for so many years. According to legend, if you stand with your back to the pillar and can reach around and touch your fingers, any wish you make will come true.

A hundred yards west of the Qutab Minar is another strange structure, a tower 87 feet high. It was supposed to be twice the height of the Qutab Minar, but its designer, Ala-ud-Din, died and no one bothered to complete it. Northwest of the mosque is the tomb (now roofless) of Emperor Iltutmish. This is the oldest tomb of a Moslem ruler in Delhi.

The second Delhi capital, Siri, also created by Ala-ud-Din during his short reign from 1296 to 1316, had a more dismal fate than his unfinished tower. His seat of power, almost completely ravaged by the passage of time, was also a coveted building site for Ghiyas-ud-din Tughlak who ultimately created the third Delhi capital, Tughlaqabad.

Tughlaqabad

Five miles east of the Qutab Minar, Tughlaqabad served as the hill fortress-palace-town of this first Tughlaq king, a soldier of fortune and the founder of the Tughlak dynasty (1320–1400). The extensive city, with its vast number of mosques, palaces, and residences set behind seven miles of heavy battlements and inwardly sloping walls, was built in a speedy two years that was nearly mirrored in its similarly quick demise. In five short years, Tughlaqabad turned into an Indian ghost town. One legend claims that a Sufi saint put a curse on the village. Another attributes the hasty decline to a guilty conscience. When the king returned victorious from battle, a newly erected pavilion, which just happened to be built by his own son, proved to be more perilous than any military campaign. It collapsed on top of Ghiyas-ud-din, putting an unexpected end to the celebration, not to mention his life. His son, Muhammad Shah, the successor, fled the royal headquarters.

Despite the disposable nature of Tughlaqabad, the actual ruins have managed to survive on an impressive scale. Stark walls stand out on the landscape, and the fortress remains still provide a sense of the city within the enclosure. You can imagine the lay of the streets and the series of structures and even see the large stone-lined reservoir that supplied the water to this capital and the remnants of an ingenious network of underground passages. Facing the ruins of the fort, its founder's tomb, a small, solid pentagonal mausoleum, has remained miraculously intact. The structure is made of red sandstone with a marble dome, the first of its kind in India. By a quirk of fate, this tomb also contains the remains of Muhammad-bin-Tughlaq, the patricidal son.

Two miles south of Tughlaqabad on the road to Badarpur, you'll find Suraj Kund, a sacred tank that is the largest Hindu monument around Delhi, built in the eleventh century by a Rajput king. It is believed that a Sun temple, one of the few in India, once stood here, its steps leading down to the rock-cut pool that is shaped like an amphitheater.

Little remains of the fourth city, Jahanpanah, created by Muhammad-bin Tughlak and his successor, Firozshah Tuglak, who decided in 1351 to shift the capital closer to the Yamuna River. With the move, the capital acquired a new name, Firozabad, in tribute to himself ("bad" means city).

Lodi Gardens

In the intervening years leading up to the creation of the sixth capital in the 1500s, Delhi went through a terrible phase. After Timur (Tamerlane) ransacked the city at the end of the fourteenth century, he ordered the massacre of the entire population—just retribution, he thought, for the murder of some of his soldiers. As if in subconscious response to this mournful period, the subsequent Lodi dynasty built no city, only mausoleums and tombs.

A visit to Lodi Gardens, which contains the fifteenth- and sixteenth-century tombs of the Lodi rulers, offers a peaceful stroll along winding walks that cut through landscaped lawns with flowers and trees. See, especially, the dignified tomb of Mohammad Shah, the third ruler of the Lodi Dynasty—a tomb that also houses the graves of various other members of the ruling family. The octagon rises up near the southern entrance. Also see the imposing octagonal tomb of Sikandar Lodi, set in the northwest corner. Delhi is a city of gardens, and Lodi Gardens is one of the finest.

The Mogul Monuments

Delhi's sixth capital rests on the site of the Purana Qila, an old fort near the Delhi Zoo. This area of Delhi was the scene of a fierce sixteenth-century power struggle between the Afghan Sher Shah and the Mogul Emperor Humayan. In the 1530s Humayun began to build his own capital, Dinpanah, on these grounds, but Sher Shah defeated him in 1540. After destroying the Moguls' fledgling city, Sher Shah constructed his own city, Shergarh, over the remains, only to have Humayun strike back 15 years later and seize control.

Unfortunately, once you enter the massive Bara Darwaza (western gate), only two buildings remain intact: the Qila-i-Kuhna Masjid, Sher Shah's private mosque, an excellent example of Indo-Afghan architecture with lovely proportions; and a two-story octagonal red sandstone tower, the Sher Manzil, which ultimately became Humayun's library. This small building also served as Humayun's deathtrap a few years later. Hearing the call to prayer, Humayun started down the steep steps, slipped, and fell—so much for Humayun. This untimely accident leads us to a magnificent structure just south of the zoo: Humayun's tomb, built by his grieving widow, Haji Begum, who is also buried inside.

Humayun's Tomb

This tomb, erected in the middle of the sixteenth century, marks the beginning of a new architectural era that culminated in the glorious Mogul masterpieces at Agra and Fatehpur Sikri. The Moguls, who brought to India their love of gardens, fountains, and water, produced sublime structures, such as this mausoleum, which combines severe symmetry with Oriental splendor.

Built in a style reminiscent of Persian architecture, the tomb stands on a raised platform set amid spacious gardens enclosed by walls, the first "tomb-in-a-garden" complex in India. The color effect of Humayun's Tomb—a soothing blend of red sandstone and white, black, and yellow marble—is stunning. The marble dome, a lovely departure from former heavy domes, is India's first example of the dome within a dome (the interior dome is set inside the soaring larger dome seen from the exterior), a style that is also used in the Taj Mahal.

Many other notable Moguls are buried here, including the builder and possibly Humayun's barber, who is supposedly emtombed inside the blue domed, square structure. Finally, as you enter or leave, stand a moment in the gateway. Notice how the entire monument is framed in the arch; this, too, happens again at the Taj Mahal. And, as you contemplate the serene setting, consider how many of the dead buried inside were murdered princes, victims of foul play.

Shahjahanabad—Lal Qila (Red Fort)

After you pass through Delhi Gate, you soon see the silhouette of the massive outer walls of the Lal Qila (Red Fort) just ahead on the right. Lal Qila is the greatest wonder of all the cities of Delhi, even outdoing Ludyens's Imperial City. Here is Shah Jahan's symbol of Mogul power and elegance, built behind red sandstone walls that gave the fort its name. It's easy to imagine imperial elephants swaying by with their *mahouts* (elephant drivers) or any conceivable vestige of Shah Jahan's pomp.

The formerly unobstructed view of the main entrance, called the Lahore Gate, flanked by semioctagonal towers and facing Chandni Chowk, is blocked by a barbican (a kind of gatehouse), which the paranoid Aurangzeb added for greater security—much to the grief of Shah Jahan, his father. From his prison, where he was held captive by his power-hungry offspring, Shah Jahan wrote, "You have made a bride of the palace and thrown a veil over her face."

Once you enter the main gate, continue along a vaulted arcade, Chhatta Chowk, originally the shopping district for the royal ladies and now a bazaar selling goods of significantly lower quality. The arcade leads to the Naubat Khana, the main gateway of the palace—a red sandstone structure, where music was played five times daily. Beyond this point, everyone but the emperor and princes had to proceed on foot, a rule that was observed until 1857. A spacious lawn, once a courtyard serving as the boundary where all but the nobility had to stop, leads to the great Diwan-i-Am, the Hall of Public Audiences.

Now, you've entered the seventh city of Delhi, the Delhi of Shah Jahan. Marble dominates. Seen against a background of green grass and blue sky, the hall, raised on a platform and open on three sides, evokes a time of irretrievable glory—like the moment described by Bernier, a seventeenth-century French traveler, who was overwhelmed by the hall's magnificence. Here the emperor sat on a royal throne, set in a marble alcove in the center of the back wall—a throne studded with decorative panels that sparkled with countless inlaid precious stones. These panels, stolen by British soldiers after the Indian Mutiny of 1857, were restored 50 years later by Lord Curzon. It was here that the emperor listened to and judged the plight of subjects brought before him in full view of the throngs of people who watched from the courtyard below. The rest of the hall, Bernier explained, was reserved for rajahs and foreign envoys, all standing with "their eyes bent downwards and their hands crossed." High above them, under a pearl-fringed canopy resting on golden shafts in the royal recess, "glittered the dazzling figure of the Grand Mogul, a figure to strike terror, for a frown meant death." Facing the emperor's throne is the marble seat of the prime minister.

Behind the Diwan-i-Am stands a row of palaces that overlook the not-too-distant Yamuna River. To the extreme south is the Mumtaz Mahal—now the Red Fort Museum of Archaeology, with relics from the Mogul period and numerous paintings and drawings. The next palace is the Rang Mahal (the Painted Palace), which used to be richly decorated. The hall, which had a silver ceiling until the treasury ran too low, may have been a sitting room for the royal ladies. It contains a marble basin constructed into the center of the floor (the bottom is carved in the shape of a lotus), with a water channel—called the Canal of Paradise—running through this palace and many of the others.

The third palace is the Khas Mahal, the exclusive palace of the emperor, divided into three sections: the sitting room, the dream chamber (obviously for sleeping), and the prayer chamber, with lavishly decorated walls and painted ceilings still intact. The lovely marble screen contains the carved Scale of Justice—two swords and a scale that symbolize punishment and justice. From the attached octagonal tower, Muthamman Burj, the emperor, would appear before his subjects every morning. He also came here to watch elephant fights held in the fields.

The next palace is the famous Diwan-i-Khas (Hall of Private Audience), the most exclusive pavilion. Here Shah Jahan consulted with his ministers and held private meetings. He would sit on his famous solid-gold Peacock Throne, which was inlaid with hundreds of stones. Back then, its value was 12 million pounds sterling, or $19.8 million at today's rate of exchange. It was too precious, too beautiful! When Nadir Shah sacked Delhi in 1739, he hauled the throne to Persia. A Persian couplet written in gold above an arch sums up Shah Jahan's sentiments about his city:

If there be a paradise on earth
It is this! It is this! It is this!

Finally, you reach the Royal Hammams, exquisite Mogul baths with inlaid marble floors. Imagine the self-indulgence as you wander through the three rooms. There's a fountain that supposedly had rose-scented water, and a state-of-the-art hot steam bath. No wonder Shah Jahan called his city paradise.

From here, a short path leads to the Moti Masjid (the Pearl Mosque), designed by Aurangzeb for his personal use and the use of the royal ladies. Once the ceiling was copper plated. The prayer hall is inlaid with *musalla* (prayer rugs) outlined in black marble. Though the mosque has the purity of white marble, some claim the excessively ornate style reflects the decadence that set in before the end of Shah Jahan's reign.

Jama Masjid

Looming majestically on a high platform across the street stands an exquisite statement in red sandstone and white marble: the Jama Masjid, India's largest mosque, completed in 1658 by Shah Jahan. Broad steps lead up to the double-story gateways and a magnificent courtyard (where thousands still gather to pray), which is enclosed by pillared corridors with domed pavilions in each corner. The best time to visit is Friday, the holy day; the exact hour is tricky. Check beforehand to be certain you'll be able to go inside. For a small fee, you can also climb to the top of a minaret (however, a woman must be escorted by a "responsible" male). From here, you have an extended view of Old Delhi.

The mosque, with its onion-shaped dome and tapering minarets, is characteristically Mogul. But Shah Jahan added an innovation. Note the novel stripes running up and down the well-proportioned marble domes. Just standing in the courtyard, you are engulfed in the quiet power of Islam; tranquility prevails, enhanced by the architecture. Each dome, portico, and minaret of this mosque is subordinated to the whole, producing an overal impression of harmony.

Inside the prayer hall (entered by the devout after a ritual washing in the big water basin—a symbolic purification), the pulpit is carved from a single slab of marble. In one corner of the hall is a room where Shah Jahan installed the footprints of Hazrat Muhammad.

The northern gate of the mosque leads into Chandi Chowk, the former imperial avenue, down which Shah Jahan would ride at the head of a lavish cavalcade. Today, everything rushes indiscriminately into the congested avenue—bullock carts, wandering cows, limousines, taxis, private cars, dogs, auto rickshaws, bicycles, bicycle rickshaws, horse-drawn tongas, and crowds of pedestrians. It's a great place to explore (see the section on Delhi markets and bazaars).

As we move toward the twentieth century, two other monuments should be seen, built during the decline of the Mogul period.

Jantar Mantar and Safdarjang's Tomb

The first monument is on Parliament Street near Connaught Place (the center hub of New Delhi): the Jantar Mantar (observatory) built by Maharajah Jai Singh II of Jaipur in 1725. This astronomer-king, who left five similar structures in India, created precise masonry instruments that look like they stepped out of science fiction. The largest structure is a huge right-angle sundial, the Samrat Yantra (supreme instrument). Next, head south to the tomb of Safdarjang, one of the last prime ministers of the Moguls in Delhi. Erected in 1754 by Nabob Shuja-ud-Daula, the son of Mirza Shuja-ud-Daula, it is also the last Mogul mausoleum built in this city.

Now, leap to the twentieth century. . . .

The Imperial City and Modern Delhi

Start at the War Memorial Arch, better known as India Gate: a memorial to the Indian Army dead of the First World War, modeled along the lines of the Menin Gate in Belgium. The names of the dead, all 90,000, are inscribed on the arch. Majestic Raj Path—the broadest avenue of Delhi and the scene of the yearly parade on Republic Day (January 26)—heads west to the sight of the eighth and last capital of Delhi: Luydens's Imperial City. As you move up the avenue, you come first to the enormous Secretariat buildings that face one another on Raj Path. Identical in design, the two buildings have 1,000 rooms and miles of corridors. Directly behind the North Secretariat is the Sansad Bhavan (Parliament House), a huge circular building in red and gray sandstone with an open colonnade that extends around the circumference. Proceedings in the two houses of Parliament—Lok Sabha (House of the People) and the Rajya Sabha (Council of States)—are in Hindi, the national language, or English.

Continue up Raj Path to Rashtrapati Bhavan, the Presidential Palace. Though built in the twentieth century, its daunting proportions seem to come from an earlier and more lavish time. The Bhavan contains 340 rooms and its grounds cover 330 acres. The shape of the central brass dome, the main feature of the palace, copies a Buddhist *stupa* (shrine). A majestic courtyard bearing the Jaipur Column leads to the yawning Greek portico of the building. The overall effect is nearly overwhelming, with the building practically spilling over the small Raisini Hill.

A newer part of Delhi is the Diplomatic Enclave to the south, where a few excellent examples of modern architecture can be seen in the residences and office buildings of the diplomatic corps assigned to the Indian capital.

Our tour of Delhi concludes with a stop at a hospital across from the Red Fort. This is no ordinary hospital for humans; it is a bird hospital—the Charity Bird Hospital run by Jains for over 35 years. Vegetarian birds (and rabbits) are treated inside, and nonvegetarian birds are treated in the courtyard. Bathed, fed, and given vitamins, the healthy birds refuse to leave. That's how you can spot the building—flocks of birds fly happily over its roof. Visiting hours, unlike most hospitals, are liberal, and donations are welcome.

Delhi's Markets and Bazaars

If you were born to shop or if you just like to wander through markets and bazaars, Delhi will keep you happy for days. After a brief introduction to the Old Delhi markets, especially Chandni Chowk, you'll find a list of other shopping districts, some where you can barter or just gaze. For those who don't like to shop or for those who are stuck with a long list and too little time, the best bet is a single trip to the Central Cottage Industries Emporium on Jan Path near Connaught Place. Here, you'll find all India's handicrafts under one gigantic roof. But no bartering; prices are fixed.

Old Delhi and Chandni Chowk

Chandni Chowk, that perpetually congested avenue heading west from the Red Fort, is the best way to get into Old Delhi, with its twisting lanes, small streets, and crowded bazaars. As in the days of the Moguls, astrologers set up their booths on the narrow pavement.

Shoemakers squat outside and repair sandals, blithely ignoring the human swirl around them. If you peer through a portico, you may see men getting shaved, silver being weighed, plus every other conceivable form of intense commerce, while outside, a cow sits complacently in the street.

If you visit the old town on an auspicious day, you will meet wedding processions with bridegrooms dressed like princes—their turbans flashing with cut-glass jewels—astride jade-festooned horses. The groom is accompanied by relatives and friends and colorful brass bands who demonstrate the exuberance and the importance of this cavalcade. Often such processions take place at night, with portable chandeliers held high like torches.

Strange aromas fill the air, the pungent odor of Oriental spices and the unfortunate and overwhelming smell of garbage. Cattle stroll in the middle of the road, chewing some grocer's vegetables or abandoned refuse. Jewelry, delicate ivory carvings, and rich silks and brocades are exhibited in closely packed profusion. Medicine booths conceal doctors attending to a row of patients, who sit resignedly in open-air waiting rooms. Old Delhi is nothing if not superoriental—the glory and the guile, grandeur and grime, of the fascinating and slowly changing East. Chandni Chowk is a place to wander, to lose yourself, for you're never really lost.

Around Connaught Place

The sorrowfully neglected Connaught Circus, which encircles a park in the central hub of New Delhi, is another shopper's mecca, with fixed prices, for the most part. A little sprucing up of the dilapidated facades would improve the atmosphere, but once you step inside the fancier shops (like the Ivory Palace or Banaras Silk House), the former elegance takes over.

Built underneath a portion of the green park is the Palika Bazaar, India's bad idea of a modern market. Entering this underground shopping arcade is like descending into Times Square subway station—dreary, dirty, and crowded. But Palika Bazaar has a lot to offer. Check out the silver jewelry at the Jewel Mine in the central hall. For great *kurtas,* visit Lal Behari Tandon, halfway around the same circle. Every item is down there, if you can tolerate hunting through dingy surroundings.

Also visit Shankar Market, northwest of the Block of the Outer Circle of Connaught Place. If you don't see signs for this market, ask. Here you can buy great fabrics, especially cottons—handblocked and superfine. Often the merchant doubles as a tailor.

Finally, browse along Jan Path. At the southern end, you'll find the Tibetan Market. Sometimes a careful search can turn up a Tibetan treasure. But basically, buy what you like; most of the "antiques" are brand-new. Besides, you can't take any article out of India if it's 100 years old.

PRACTICAL INFORMATION FOR DELHI

WHEN TO GO. Delhi is at its best between October and April, and the choice months are November–March. At this time, there's a minimum of rainfall, the countryside is green, the gardens in bloom, and the climate is agreeable. A heavy coat is recommended for evening wear from mid-December to February. The big event of the year is the Republic Day Parade on January 26.

Visitors are advised to make their hotel bookings for this date well in advance. October and November are good months for the festivals—*Dussehra* and *Diwali.*

 HOW TO GET THERE. By air. Delhi is on the crossroad of most of the major airlines serving Asia and can be reached with equal ease from the Pacific Coast, Japan, Australia, the United States, Western Europe, the Middle East, and East Africa. *Air India* and *Indian Airlines* have domestic flights and operate flights into India from Kathmandu (Nepal), Kabul (Afghanistan), Lahore and Karachi (Pakistan), Dacca (Bangladesh), Colombo (Sri Lanka), Mali (Maldives), and Bangkok (Thailand). *Vayudoot* feeder airline connects small cities in India, including hill stations like Kullu, Shimla, and Shillong.

By Bus. Every day, deluxe buses from Haryana, Himachal Pradesh, Jammu and Kashmir, Uttar Pradesh, and Rajasthan—all with their videos blaring—come rolling into the *Inter State Bus Terminus* at Kashmeri Sate. For information and details, call the following numbers: Haryana, 221292, open: 6 A.M.–noon and 1–9 P.M.; Himachal Pradesh, 226241, open 7 A.M.–7 P.M.; Jammu and Kashmir, 224559 or 343400, ext. 2243, open 10 A.M.–5 P.M.; Rajasthan, 222276, open 6 A.M.–10 P.M.; Uttar Pradesh, 226175, open 6 A.M.–8 P.M.

By Train. Some of India's best trains converge on Delhi. To mention a few: From Bombay: (Central Station), daily air-conditioned Pashim/Express (nearly 24 hours). From Calcutta: (Howrah), the air-conditioned Rajdhani Express, five times a week (18 hours). From Madras: the air-conditioned Grand Trunk Express (37 hours). There are numerous trains from Agra, Bangalore, Bhopal, Jaipur, Lucknow, and Varanasi. For inquiries in Delhi, call 343727 or 351035.

By Hired Car with Driver. Delhi is 200 km from Agra, 249 km from Chandigarh, 261 km from Jaipur, 586 km from Jammu, 569 km from Lucknow, 368 km from Shimla, 765 km from Varanasi. Although renting a car with a driver in Delhi costs slightly more than in most other areas in India (Rs. 2.50 per km), it's still an economical way of getting around if you've the money to spare and want to really see the area. You can get a car and driver through *Delhi Tourism Development Corporation* (DTDC), N–36 Bombay Life Building, Connaught Place (Middle Circle), New Delhi, (tel. 3313637); *India Tourism Development Corporation* (ITDC), L Block, Connaught Place, New Delhi (tel. 350331); or through the following reliable tour agencies, which can also help you plan your travels: *Jetair Tours,* Hotel Janpath, Room No. 4, Jan Path, New Delhi; tel. 343971. *Mercury Travels,* Jeevan Tara Building, Parliament Building, New Delhi; tel. 312008. *Sita World Travels,* F–12 Connaught Pl., New Delhi; tel. 43103. *Trade Wings,* 60 Jan Path, New Delhi; tel. 321322. *Travel House,* M–3 Connaught Circus, New Delhi; tel. 311130.

If you've got real adventure on your mind (treks, safaris, water rafting) three tour operators specializing in the unusual in Delhi can get you all set up: *Himalayan River Runners,* 188–A Jor Bagh, New Delhi 110003; tel. 615736. *Shikhar Travels Private Limited,* 209 Competent House, F–14, Middle Circle, Connaught Pl., New Delhi 110001; tel. 3312666. *Tiger Tops Mountain Travel India,* 1/1 Rani Jhansi Rd., New Delhi 110055; tel. 523057.

 TOURIST INFORMATION. Lots of information is available in Delhi on everywhere in India and nearby countries for that matter. The Government of India Tourist office is usually crowded, but the staff are helpful and have good current information. Some of the separate state offices are better than others, with Jammu and Kashmir and Kerala outshining the rest.

Government of India Tourist Office, main office: 88 Jan Path; tel. 320005. Summer hours: 8 A.M.–7 P.M.; winter hours: 9 A.M.–7 P.M. Excellent map of Delhi plus information covering just about everywhere in India. The International Airport has an office that is open around the clock.

State Tourist Offices. Go to the Chandralok Building at 36 Jan Path, New Delhi and you'll find the following offices: Rajasthan (tel. 322332), Uttar Pradesh (tel. 322251), Haryana (tel. 344911), and Himachal Pradesh (tel. 345320). At Kanishka Plaza, 19 Ashok Rd., you'll find Gujarat (tel. 322107), Jammu and Kashmir (tel. 345373), Kerala (tel. 310151), and Madhya Pradesh (tel. 351187). The Andhra Pradesh office is at Ashok Road (tel. 343894). Offices for the other states are located at the State Emporia Complex on Baba Kharak Singh Marg: Assam (B–1; tel. 321967), Bihar (A–5; tel. 3010147), Karnataka (C–4; tel.

343862), Maharashtra (tel. 343774), Orissa (tel. 344580), Tamil Nadu (tel. 343913), and West Bengal (tel. 343775). Sikkim's office is located at Hotel Janpath (tel. 324589). In general, the state offices are open Monday–Friday, 10 A.M.–5 P.M., and most Saturday mornings.

FOREIGN CURRENCY EXCHANGE. Most of the Western-style hotels have money exchange counters that will cash your traveler's checks with twice the speed and half the hassle. *American Express* (at Wenger House, Connaught Place, tel. 344119) and Thomas Cook Pvt. Ltd. (Hotel Imperial, Jan Path, tel. 312468) will cash their own traveler's checks. At American Express, bring a book or lunch; the lines can get long. Open generally Monday–Friday 10 A.M.–5 P.M., Saturday mornings. *Banks:* If you must, they're all over Delhi. Hours are Monday–Friday, 10 A.M.–2 P.M.; Saturdays, 10 A.M.–noon. The Central Bank in the Ashok Hotel is open around the clock, as is the State Bank of India at the airport.

ACCOMMODATIONS. Delhi has luxurious Western-style hotels, moderately priced hotels, and even some lovely guest houses that are cozy and a real bargain. Book reservations early if you want to stay at a fancy Western-style hotel. Room rates are based on double occupancy: *Super Deluxe,* over Rs. 1000; *Deluxe,* Rs. 800–Rs. 1,000; *Expensive,* Rs. 500–Rs. 800; *Moderate,* Rs. 200–Rs. 500; *Inexpensive,* under Rs. 200. Most hotels in Delhi accept major credit cards.

Super Deluxe

Ashok Hotel. 50–B Chanakyapur, New Delhi, 10 km from the airport; tel. 600121. 576 rooms; air-conditioned. Fancy, attractive hotel with all the amenities, including restaurants, a bar, baby-sitters, a swimming pool, and a secretary to do your typing.

Hyatt Regency Delhi. Bhikaiji Cama Pl., Ring Road, New Delhi, eight km from the airport; eight km from downtown; tel. 609911. A 550-room air-conditioned luxury hotel. Again, whatever you need, it's probably here: a swimming pool, restaurants, and a bakery. There is a special superexpensive floor called the Regency Club for those who want special pampering.

The Oberoi. Dr. Zakir Hussain Marg, New Delhi, 16 km from the airport; four km from downtown; tel. 699571. A 289-room air-conditioned hotel, with all the trimmings: a swimming pool, numerous restaurants, and an attractive bar. This is an elegant hotel with lovely understated decor. Possibly Delhi's best.

Taj Mahal. No. 1. Mansingh Rd., New Delhi, 15 km from the airport; five km from downtown; tel. 3016162. A 307-room air-conditioned swank hotel, with all the Western amenities—even a disco. Glitzy and modern.

Taj Palace Hotel. 2 Sardar Patel Marg (Diplomatic Enclave), New Delhi, eight km from the airport; eight km from downtown; tel. 3010404. A 442-room air-conditioned fashionable hotel, again with all the amenities—even word-processor facilities.

Welcomgroup Maurya Sheraton. Diplomatic Enclave, New Delhi, seven km from the airport; seven km from downtown; tel. 3010101. A 500-room air-conditioned posh hotel. It's all here, including some of the best restaurants, a disco, and a bar with a library.

Deluxe

Meridien. Windsor Pl., Delhi, 15 km from the airport; five km from downtown; tel. 383960. 371-rooms. A new hotel scheduled to open in late 1987. Restaurants already functioning. Most amenities, including a swimming pool.

Hotel Sofitel Surya. New Friends Colony, New Delhi, 18 km from the airport; eight km from downtown; tel. 635070. A 237-room pretty hotel that's a bit off the beaten path. But in Delhi, that's not so important because of transportation services. Most amenities, including a swimming pool.

Expensive

Hotel Ambassador. Sujan Singh Park, New Delhi, 14 km from the airport; five km from downtown; tel. 690391. A 73-room air-conditioned older hotel, with numerous amenities but no swimming pool.

Centaur Hotel. Delhi Airport, Gurgaon Rd., New Delhi, two km from the International Airport; 19 km from downtown; tel. 391411. 376 rooms. Most amenities, including a swimming pool, plus bus into central Delhi.

Claridges. 12 Aurangzeb Rd. New Delhi, 12 km from the airport; four km from downtown; tel. 3010609. A 140-room pleasant hotel with most amenities, including a swimming pool.

Hotel Hans Plaza. 15 Barakhamba Rd., New Delhi, 15 km from the airport; ½ km from downtown; tel. 3316861. 57 rooms, central air-conditioning, TV, and a restaurant. Relatively new and pleasant.

Imperial. Jan Path, New Delhi, 18 km from the airport; in town; tel. 311511. 165 rooms. A swimming pool and most amenities. A bit tarnished, but old-world charm gives it a special ambience.

Hotel Kanishka. 19 Ashok Rd., New Delhi, 17 km from the airport; near downtown; tel. 343400. 318 rooms with most modern amenities; no swimming pool, but attractive and centrally located.

Oberoi Maidens. 7 Shamnath Marg, New Delhi, 24 km from the airport; 10 km from downtown; tel. 2525464. 60 rooms. Some amenities, including a swimming pool. An old hotel with a tired elegance. Near Old Delhi.

Qutab. Off Sri Aurobindo Marg, New Delhi, 10 km from the airport, 14 km from downtown; tel. 660060. 64 rooms. Adequate with some amenities, including a swimming pool and bowling alleys.

Siddharth Hotel. 3 Rajendra Pl., New Delhi; 13 km from the airport; four km from downtown; tel. 5712501. Some amenities, including a swimming pool.

Moderate

Diplomat Hotel. 9 Sardar Patel Rd., New Delhi; eight km from the airport; five km from downtown; tel. 3011070. A 25-room air-conditioned hotel with a restaurant. In diplomatic area. Quiet and adequate.

Jukaso Inn. 50 Sunder Nagar, New Delhi, 16 km from the airport; four km from downtown; tel. 690308. 55 rooms. Air-conditioned. 24-hour room service serving Indian, Continental, and Chinese food. A quiet, peaceful neighborhood. Nice lawns. A pleasant cozy feeling with friendly management. A great value.

Kailish Inn. 10 Sunder Nagar, New Delhi; 16 km from the airport; four km from downtown; tel. 617401. 10 rooms. Air-conditioned, 24-hour room service serving Indian, Chinese, and Continental food. The same quiet neighborhood. A great escape from the bustle of the city. Pleasant rooms and pleasant management. A great value.

Lodhi Hotel. Lala Lajput Raj Marg, New Delhi, 15 km from the airport; five km from downtown; tel. 619422. 207 rooms. Air-conditioned. Some amenities, including restaurants, a bar, a swimming pool, and TVs in rooms.

Maharani Guest House. 3 Sunder Nagar, New Delhi; 16 km from the airport; four km from downtown; tel. 693128. 25 rooms. Air-conditioned, 24-hour room service serving good Indian food. Lovely guest house with a roof terrace. A quiet neighborhood. A great value.

Nirulas Hotel. L-Block, Connaught Circus, New Delhi, 16 km from the airport; downtown; tel. 352419. 29 rooms. Air-conditioned. Restaurants galore. Right in the center of town. A well-managed hotel.

Hotel Ranjit. Maharaja Ranjit Singh Road, New Delhi, 21 km from airport; near center of town; tel. 3311256. 188 rooms. Some air-conditioned rooms; some amenities, including a swimming pool.

La Sagrita Tourist Home. 14 Sunder Nagar, New Delhi, 16 km from the airport; four km from downtown; approximately 25 rooms. tel. 694541. Another good guest house. Has 24-hour room service serving Chinese, Mughlai, and Continental food. Nice lawns. A quiet peaceful neighborhood. A great value.

Hotel Vikram. Ring Road, Lajpat Nagar, New Delhi, 12 km from the airport; seven km from downtown; tel. 6436451. 72 rooms. Air-conditioned. Many amenities, including TVs, a swimming pool, and a restaurant.

Woodstock Motel. 11 Golf Links, New Delhi, 14 km from the airport; 4.5 km from downtown; tel. 619571. 16 rooms. Air-conditioned. Another lovely guest house with 24-hour room service serving Indian and Continental food. Personal attention, a nice ambience, and a lovely quiet garden outside. A great value.

Inexpensive

Ashok Yatri Niwas. 19 Ashok Rd., New Delhi, 15 km from the airport; near downtown; tel. 344511. 558 rooms. No air-conditioning. Has restaurants, a bar, and some amenities but minimal aesthetics and service.

YMCA International Guest House. Parliament Street, New Delhi; tel. 311561. Numerous rooms. Air-conditioned. A good budget value.

 DINING OUT. Delhi has all kinds of cuisine: North Indian, South Indian vegetarian, Chinese, Continental, fast foods, and Indian-style "pizza." If you want a drink with dinner, you're stuck with dining in a hotel. Outside restaurants don't have liquor licenses. If you can do without a drink or be content with one before or after dinner, then Delhi is wide open—great neighborhoods, great haunts, and memorable eating to satisfy any budget. Prices are based on a three-course meal for one person excluding beverage, tax, or tip: *Expensive,* over Rs. 60; *Moderate,* Rs. 30–60; *Inexpensive,* under Rs. 30. Most hotels and many expensive outside restaurants accept most of the major credit cards, particularly Diner's Club and American Express.

MIXED MENU (CHINESE, CONTINENTAL, INDIAN)

Expensive

Captain's Table. Taj Mahal Hotel, No. 1 Mansingh Rd.; tel. 3016162 for reservations. Seafood specialties, Goan style. Indian and Continental cuisine. Nautical decor. Open noon–midnight.

Moderate

Cafe Promenade. Hyatt Regency, Bhikaiki Cama Pl., Ring Rd.; tel. 609911. Open 24 hours. Airy restaurant spilling into a downstairs lobby. Every month, there's a food fest celebrating the food of another country. Live band. Fun. Reservations recommended.

The Embassy. 11–D Connaught Pl., New Delhi; tel. 350480. 10 A.M.–11:30 P.M. Pleasant decor. A Delhi favorite.

Gaylord Restaurant. 16 Regal Building, Connaught Pl.; tel. 310717. 10 A.M.–midnight. Another Delhi staple as much an institution as is Connaught Place.

The Host. F–8 Connaught Circus; tel. 46576. 9:30 A.M.–midnight. Excellent, especially the Indian curries. A nice ambience.

Standard Restaurant. 44 Regal Building, Connaught Circus; tel. 352688. 9:30 A.M.–11 P.M. Another good Connaught Place standby.

United Coffee House. E–15 Connaught Pl.; tel. 352075. 9:30 A.M.–midnight. Turn-of-the-century regency decor. Good food, good ambience.

Williamsburg Room. Qutab Hotel, off Aurobindo Marg; tel. 660060. 1–2:30 P.M.; 8–11 P.M. Not colonial Virginia exactly, but the food is good.

Inexpensive to Moderate

Berco's. E–8, Connaught Pl.; tel. 353757. Chinese, Japanese, and Indian fast food. Very good. A fast-food atmosphere but tolerable; a popular hangout. Open noon–11 P.M. daily, except holidays.

Nirula's. L-Block, Connaught Pl.; tel. 352419. 11 A.M.–10:30 P.M. A collection of popular "fast-food" type restaurants that serve all sorts of food, most of it very good.

Garden Restaurant. Run by Essex Farms on Aurobindo Marg. Outdoor restaurant; eat under an umbrella or a thatched hut and have chicken from one of Delhi's famous chicken farms. Good ambience. Open noon–10:30 P.M.

CHINESE

Expensive

Bali Hi. Maurya Sheraton, Diplomatic Enclave; tel. 3010101 for reservations. Polynesian emphasis. Roof-top restaurant with live band and dancing. Fine food, loud music. Open 8:30 P.M. – 2 A.M.

House of Ming. Taj Mahal Hotel, 1 Mansingh Rd.; tel. 3016162 for reservations. Lovely restaurant with reliably good food. Cantonese and Szechwan. 12:30–3 P.M.; 7:30 P.M.–midnight.

Pearls. Hyatt Regency Hotel, Bhikaiji Cama Place, Ring Rd.; tel. 609911 for reservations. Cozy, yet elegant restaurant. Szechwan, Cantonese, and Hakka cuisine. Lunch: noon–2:45 P.M.; dinner: 7:45 to 11:45 P.M.

Tea House of the August Moon. Taj Palace Hotel, Sadar Patel Marg, Diplomatic Enclave, tel. 3010404 for reservations. Pagoda decor with ponds and dragons on the walls. Cantonese, Pekinese, and Szechwan. Excellent dim sum. 12:30–2:45 P.M., 7:30–11:45 P.M.

Moderate

Chinese Room. Nirula's, L-Block, Connaught Circus; tel. 352491. Good Chinese dishes. noon–3:30 P.M.; 7–11 P.M.

Chungwa. D–13, Defence Colony, tel. 625976. Excellent spicy Chinese food, possibly the best in Delhi. Lunch and dinner.

CONTINENTAL

Expensive

Casa Medici. Taj Mahal, 1 Mansingh Rd.; tel. 3816162 for reservations. Italian specialties. Elegant decor, live band, dancing. Lunch: 1–3 P.M.; dinner: 7 P.M.–midnight.

Orient Express. Taj Palace Hotel, Sadar Patel Marg, Diplomatic Enclave; tel. 3010404 for reservations. Romantic train-car motif. Noon–3 P.M.; 7:30–11:30 P.M.

Takshila. Maurya Sheraton, Diplomatic Enclave; tel. 3010101 for reservations. Mediterranean cuisine. Rooftop restaurant with a terrace garden. 12:30–3 P.M.; 8 P.M.–midnight.

Taverna Cypress. Ashok Hotel, 50–B Chanakyapuri; tel. 600121 for reservations. Cypriot food; solo guitarist in a cozy setting. Lunch: 1–2:45 P.M.; dinner: 8–11:30 P.M.

INDIAN

Expensive

Aangan. Hyatt Regency, Bhikaiji Cama Pl., Ring Rd.; tel. 609911 for reservations. Lunch: 12:30–2:45 P.M.; dinner: 8–11:45 P.M.

Bukhara. Maurya Sheraton, Diplomatic Enclave; tel. 3010101 for reservations. Excellent northwest frontier specialities include tandooris and kebabs, leg of lamb. Lunch: 12:30–2:30 P.M.; dinner 8 P.M.–midnight.

Dhaba. Claridges Hotel, 12 Akbar Rd., tel. 3010609 for reservations. Excellent Indian food. Lunch: noon to 3 P.M.; dinner: 7:30–11:30 P.M.

Frontier. Ashok Hotel, 50 B Chanakyapuri; tel. 600121 for reservations. Northwest frontier specialities, excellent leg of lamb, kebabs, and tandoori. Lunch: 1–2:45 P.M.; dinner: 8–11:30 P.M.

Haveli. Taj Mahal Hotel, 1 Man Singh Rd.; tel. 3016162 for reservations. Peshawari, Mughlai, and tandoori specialities. Indian music and dance performances at night. Lunch: 12:30–3 P.M.; dinner: 7:30 P.M.–midnight.

Mayur. Maurya Sheraton, Diplomatic Enclave; tel. 3010101 for reservations. Mughlai and tandoori specialities, plus Dum Pukht cuisine (meals sealed and cooked in a pot). Indian music and dance performances. Lunch and dinner. Excellent.

Peacock. Hotel Ashok, 50–B Chanakyapur; tel. 600121 for reservations. Mughlai and tandoori plus Persian specialties. Indian music. Noon–2:30 P.M.; 7:30–11:30 P.M.

Moderate

Ankur. The Village, Asian Games Village Complex, Siri Fort Rd.; tel. 651945. Excellent butter chicken and tandoori. 12:30–3 P.M.; 7:30–11:45 P.M.

Dasaprakash. Ambassador Hotel, Sujan Singh Park; tel. 690391. Great vegetarian food. Breakfast, lunch, and dinner.

Gulati Restaurant. 6 Pandara Rd. Market; tel. 388839. Great Indian Mughlai food. Excellent food. Political ambience, the government bigwigs hang out here. Open noon–midnight. (All the restaurants in this market are good.)

Karim's Newat Kada. Hazrat Nizamuddin West, near the police station; tel. 698300. Mughlai and tandoori. A fun restaurant with good food. Open noon–midnight.

Moti Mahal. Netaji Subhash Marg, Daryaganj (Old Delhi); tel. 273661. Garden restaurant in a courtyard. The atmosphere is better than the food, but this is a Delhi hallmark. Open noon–midnight.

The Panorama. Roof-top restaurant, Kanishka Hotel, 19 Ashok Rd.; tel. 343400 for reservations. Splendid view, fair food. Open 12:30–2:45 P.M.; 8 – P.M.

Woodlands. Lodhi Hotel, Lala Lajput Rai Marg, New Delhi; tel. 619422. Pure vegetarian. Often overcrowded. Open 8 A.M.–10:30 P.M.

Inexpensive

Kake da Hotel. 74 Outer Circle, Connaught Pl., between L & M Blocks; no phone. Don't be put off by the looks. Best butter chicken in town.

Karim Hotel. Gali Kababian, Jama Masjid, Old Delhi; no phone. Good mughlai food; lunch and dinner.

Moet's Bar-be-que. Shop 27, Defence Colony Market (no phone). Great spicy food. A popular hangout for lunch and dinner.

Peshawari Restaurant. Upstairs, 3711 Netaji Subhash Marg, Daryaganj, Old Delhi; tel. 273661. Very good butter chicken; open noon–midnight.

Sona Restaurant. Jusuf Sarai Market, Sri Aurobindo Marg. A no-frills restaurant serving excellent Punjabi food. Lunch: noon – 3 P.M.; dinner: 7–11 P.M.

HOW TO GET AROUND. From the Airports. It's approximately 18 km to the center of New Delhi from either airport. Two options: a **bus,** which is cheaper, under Rs. 10, and runs frequently to the main hotels and Connaught Place, or a prepaid **taxi.** To take the bus, go to the tourist-information counter for details. For the prepaid taxi, go to the "Prepaid" taxi counter. Tell them your destination, pay in advance according to the official destination chart, give the slip to the taxi driver, and don't pay one rupee more.

Once you're in Delhi, you've arrived in an enormous sprawl of a city, with numerous neighborhoods that have restaurants, monuments, and parks that appeal to tourists. There are a few good ways to get around the city.

By Taxi. Of course, a taxi will take you from place to place in relative comfort (make sure the driver uses the meter; minimum fare is Rs. 3).

By Auto Rickshaw. This is the best way to scoot around town. The driver can be surly, can claim that the meter is broken, and can rig the meter to go faster than the scooter. But still, they're the most fun and cheap. Just insist that the driver use the meter; don't take any rickshaw driver who won't use it. Rs. 2.30 is the minimum charge.

By Bus. Unless you're quick on your feet and love the idea of jumping into a moving overcrowded bus, don't take a bus. Busses take forever to get wherever they're going and have a decidedly strange tilt that suggests they might just topple over.

By Bike Rickshaw. In Old Delhi if you're not up to walking, this is the best alternative. A real bargain. It should be cheaper than the auto rickshaw.

By Deisel Rickshaw (twice as big as an auto rickshaw). From behind Palika Bazar, you'll find these oversized rickshaws that will take you to fixed points at set fees. Slow moving, although faster than a bus.

TOURS. The following three companies offer similar tours of Delhi. Delhi Tourism Development Corporations (DTDC), N–36 Connaught Pl. (Middle Circle), tel. 3313637; also at the Government of India Tourist Office, 88 Janpath, the New Delhi Railway Station, Indira Gandhi International Airport, and the Domestic Airport. Open 7 A.M.–3 P.M. every day. Offers morning or afternoon tour of Delhi in non-air-conditioned coaches. Morning tour: Jantar Mantar, Laxmi Narain Temple, Baha'i Temple or Safdarjang's Tomb, Qutab Minar, J.B. Nehru Stadium, Nehru Pavilion. Afternoon tour: Red Fort, Raj Ghat, Shantivan, and Jama Masjid. Each tour is Rs. 15. Combined tours, Rs. 30.

Museum and Appu Ghar Tour of Delhi on Sundays: Rail Transport Museum, Indira Gandhi Memorial, National Museum, Nehru Planetarium, National Museum of Natural History, Dolls Museum, and Appu Ghar. All day, Rs. 30.

Delhi by Evening Tour (Mondays, Wednesdays, Fridays, and Sundays): Aarti at Birla Mandir, Drive past the presidential Palace, Parliament, India Gate, Old Fort, and exhibition grounds. See the sound and light show at Red Fort and have dinner at a DTDC restaurant. Rs. 75.

India Tourism Development Corporation (ITDC), L Block Connaught Place, (tel. 350331); also at Jan Hotel (tel. 350070), Ashok Hotel (tel. 600121), Lodhi Hotel (tel. 619422). Offers similar tours at slightly higher rates for air-conditioned coach.

Karachi Taxi Co., 36 Jan Path (tel. 352389), also offers tours of Old Delhi and New Delhi, plus an evening tour of Delhi. The tours are in air-conditioned buses that will make hotel pick ups but they cost twice as much. All these conducted tours (DTDC, ITDC, and Karachi) include a guide.

To hire your own guide, contact the Government of India Tourist Office. For four persons, the cost is Rs. 40 for four hours.

 SEASONAL EVENTS. Lots of events happen regularly in Delhi. Just let a foreign dignitary arrive and advance preparations have truckloads of workers planting flowers, hanging posters, spiffying up the city. The following events are the most interesting (a more thorough list is available at the Government of India Tourist Office):

January 26. *Republic Day Parade* on Raj Path. You need a ticket to see this event, and tickets go from the ordinary to the VIP. Maybe there's a VVIP, too, but don't bother. The security check to be that close to the head of state would mean hours of waiting. Lots of military hoopla, floats from each state with great cultural highlights: dancers, musicians, planes flying overhead. **Cameras not allowed,** nor conspicuous handbags of any kind. The entire week is a celebration including festivals held in various auditoriums and hotels.

March. *Holi,* the festival that marks the start of spring and marks you as the target for water bombs filled with red color (permanent or washable)—stay indoors or wear old clothes.

May (full moon). *Buddha Jayanti,* the birth and enlightenment of the Buddha with celebratory prayer meetings at Ladakh Buddha Vihara (Bela Road).

August. *Raksha Bandhan.* Once, according to Hindu mythology, Indra, the king of the heavens, warred with demons and his consort tied a silk amulet around his wrist to help him win back his kingdom. Now, sisters and brothers pledge their love to one another and the sister ties a silk string around the brother's wrist. That explains all the stalls you'll see selling glittery paper wrist bands.

Aug. 15. *Independence Day.* Lots of speeches, and that's about it.

October 2. *Gandhi Jayanti,* birthday of Mahatma Gandhi, with special singing and ceremonies at the Raj Ghat.

October (dates vary). *Dussehra,* a 10-day celebration with plays and music recitals of *Ramalila,* recalling the mythological life of Rama. The most spectacular rendering is held at the Delhi Gate (performances for one month). On the 10th day, an elaborate procession heads to the Ram Lila grounds, where enormous effigies of the demon Ravana, his brother, and son (all stuffed with firecrackers) are exploded before a crowd of people.

October/November. The start of the *Hindu New Year.* Thousands of candles are lit at night on balconies of houses. The city crackles with the explosion of fireworks. Lots of fun.

 HISTORIC SITES. This list follows the suggested places to see in Exploring section.

Baha'i Temple of Worship. On Bahapur hill near Nehru Pl. This all-white building of cement, sand, dolomite, and marble is lotus-shaped and gigantic. Open 9:30 A.M. – 12:30 P.M.; 2 – 5 P.M. every day, except Mondays. On Saturdays, Sundays and public holidays, hours are extended until 7 P.M.

Firozabad. 3 km from Connaught Pl., near Delhi Gate. See the Kotla Firoz Shah (the remains of Firozshah Tuglak's palace), with its third-century Ashoka pillar mounted on the top. Also see the partially ruined Jami Masjid—the largest mosque from the Tughlak era and still a Moslem religious shrine. Free; open sunrise to sunset.

Hazrat Nizamudin Aulia. 4.8 km from Connaught Pl., near Humayun's Tomb. Shrine of Sheikh Nizamuddin Chisti, fourth in the line of Chisti saints, and an important place of Moslem pilgrimage. Chisti died in 1325. Many other notables are buried nearby, including Jahanara, Shahjahan's daughter. Free; open sunrise to sunset.

Humayun's Tomb. 4.8 km from Connaught Pl. in Nizamuddin. Built in the mid-sixteenth century by Haji Begum for her husband (she's also buried here), the tomb represents a new architectural era that culminated in Agra and Fatehpur Sikri. Definite Persian influences include the first "tomb-in-a-garden" complex in India. Entry fee: Rs.0.50, free Fridays; open sunrise to sunset.

Jama Masjid. In Old Delhi. Built of red sandstone and marble in 1658 by Shah Jahan. The largest mosque in India and the last building constructed by Shah Jahan. Some areas within the mosque are restricted to non-Moslems. Rs. 0.50 to climb the minarets. Free on Fridays. Check with tourist department for the appropriate visiting hours, which vary.

Jantar Mantar (Observatory). 0.4 km from Connaught Pl. Scientific instruments built by the astronomer-king, Maharajah Jai Singh II of Jaipur in 1725. Accurate instruments that measure celestial movements act as a sundial. Free; open sunrise to 10 P.M.

Lakshmi Narayan Temple. 2 km from Connaught Pl. Built in 1938 by the industrialist Birla Mandir in the Orissan style. Contains the deities of Narayan, Lakshmi, Durga, and Shiva. Remove your shoes once you enter the courtyard.

Lal Qila (Red Fort). Across from Jama Masjid. The site of the seventh capital of Delhi begun by the Mogul Emperor Shah Jahan around 1638. Built of red sandstone (Lal Qila); inside are a series of beautiful buildings in red sandstone and marble. Entry fee: Rs. 0.50, free on Fridays. Open sunrise to sunset. Sun and lumiere show nightly 7:30 – 8:30. Tickets, Rs. 4 and Rs. 8. Call 600121, ext. 667 for details.

Lodi Tombs. 4.8 km from Connaught Pl. on Rodi Road. Fifteenth- and sixteenth- century tombs of the rulers of the Sayyid and Lodi Dynasties: Mohammad Shah and Sikander Lodi. Also some believe that within the Bara Gumbad Mosque lie the remains of the unknown architect. Free; open sunrise to sunset.

Luydens's Imperial City. Near Lodi Tombs. See particularly the Sandad Bhavan and the Rashtrapati Bhavan (Presidential Palace). To gain entry into the Rashtrapati, you need an entry pass from the Government of India Tourist Office. These buildings were designed and built in the 1920s in red and gray sandstone.

Purana Qila. 3.2 km from Connaught Pl., off Mathura Rd. The ruins of this fifteenth- century fort constructed by the Afghan Sher Shah still have three imposing gateways. Inside is the octagonal red sandstone tower (Sher Manzil) that the Mogul Emperor Humayun used as his library, with the steep steps that became the instrument of his death—he slipped, fell, and died. Also see the Qila-i-Kuhna Masjid (Sher Shah's private mosque) built in Indo-Afghan style. Free; open sunrise to sunset.

Qutab Minar. 14.4 km from Connaught Place in South Delhi. Construction of this 234-foot tower was begun in 1199 by Qutub-ud-din Aibak, was finished by his son-in-law, then redesigned in the fourteenth century by Firuz Shah Tughlaq. Also see the Quwwat-ul-Islam Mosque nearby, the first Moslem building in Delhi and India, erected in the twelfth century, with its Iron Pillar. (See description under *Qutab Minar* for further details.) Rs. 0.50 (free on Fridays); open sunrise to sunset.

Raj Ghat. 4 km from Connaught Pl. on the banks of the Yamuna River. A square platform of polished black marble that marks the site where Mahatma Gandhi was cremated on Jan. 31, 1948.

Safdarjang's Tomb. 4.8 km from Connaught Pl. on Aurobindo Marg. The last Mogul mausoleum built in Delhi, constructed in 1754 by Nabob Shuja-ud-Daula for his father Mirsa Shuja-ud-Daula (Safdarjang). Entry fee: Rs. 0.50, free on Fridays; open sunrise to sunset.

Tughlaqabad. 5 km east of Qutab Minar. The ruins of Delhi's third capital begun in 1320 by Giyas-ud-din Tughlak. Thirteen gates of the fortress still guard the remains and the landscape; you can see the tomb of the capital's founder. Free; open sunrise to sunset.

MUSEUMS. Crafts Museum. Pragati Maidan, Mathura Rd.; tel. 804586. Terrific examples of traditional Indian crafts—folk and tribal arts from all over India. The museum spreads over an eight-acre complex and includes a craft demonstration complex plus 15 structures that represent the village dwellings of various states in India. Inside these huts are the day-to-day cultural objects from the specific areas. A fascinating museum. Open 11 A.M.–6 P.M.

Gandhi Smarak Sangrahalya. Opposite Raj Ghat; tel. 274746. A display of some of Gandhi's personal possessions, plus a library. Open 9:30 A.M.–5:30 P.M.; closed Mondays and holidays.

National Gallery of Modern Art. Jaipur House, former residential palace of the Jaipur Maharajah; tel. 382835. Exhibits the work of modern Indian artists: paintings, graphics, and sculpture. Open 10 A.M.–5 P.M., closed Mondays.

National Museum. Jan Path; tel. 385441. (Free on Sunday.) Wide-ranging collection of India's and Central Asia's artistic treasures, art and archeology, anthropology, decorative art, calligraphy, and textiles. Among the Indian collections are 5,000-year-old relics of the Indus Valley civilization (Mohenjo-daro, Harappa, and so forth). Brahmanical, Jain, and Buddhist sculptures in stone, bronze, and terra cotta of the early and medieval periods of Indian history. Good miniatures of the Mogul, Rajput, Deccani, and Pahari schools, as well as earlier work. Among the old manuscripts, you can see the famous Gita Govinda and the profusely illustrated *Mahabharata;* the *Bhagavad Gita,* written and illuminated in golden ink; the miniature octagonal *Koran* and Mogul Emperor Babur's *Babarnama* in his handwriting. Temple hangings and brocaded saris, costumes from different parts of India, beautifully worked weapons, set with precious stones from the Mogul and earlier periods, ancient jewelry, and painted pottery are part of the collection. In addition, the Aurel Stein collection of antiquities he recovered during his explorations in Central Asia and the western borders of China includes mural paintings from Buddhist shrines (some of the few examples removed from that area), silk paintings, and sculpture. Open 10 A.M.–5 P.M.; closed Mondays.

Nehru Memorial Museum. Teen Murti House on Teen Murti Marg; tel: 375333. 10 A.M. – 5 P.M.; closed Mondays. Official residence of Nehru, preserved as it was when he lived there—books, mementos, and pictures.

Rail Transport Museum. Chanakyapuri; tel. 601816. A must for railway buffs. 26 vintage locomotives and numerous old carriages and saloon cars on 10 acres of track. A lot of fancy forms of transport that no longer race along the rails. Open 9:30 A.M.–5:30 P.M.; closed Mondays.

Red Fort Museum of Archeology. Red Fort, tel. 27769. Small historical collection devoted to the Mogul period. Exhibits consist of old arms, dresses, paintings, documents, and seals. Open 9 A.M.–5 P.M.; closed Fridays.

Tibet House Museum. Institutional Area, Lodi Rd.; tel. 611515. Open 10 A.M.–1 P.M.; 2–5 P.M.; closed Sundays.

PARKS, GARDENS, ZOOS. Delhi has numerous lovely parks and gardens in which you can sit and watch the passing sights after too much big-city running around. They're open every day between sunrise and sunset, except when noted. Here are some of the best:

Children's Park, near India Gate, has nice walkways and good play equipment for the kids.

Deer Park, in the Chinkara complex near Hauz Khas, features deer and peacocks. It is a pleasant place to stop after seeing Qutab Minar.

Mughal Gardens, located in the Rashtrapati Bhavan estate, is laid out along the lines of the former sixteenth-century Mughal Gardens. There are red stone paths, fountains, and a lovely rose garden. This garden is open to the public only during February when the flowers are in bloom. For permission to visit at that time, contact the Government of India Tourist Office.

Nehru Park, comprises 85 acres of walks and landscaping with rocks inscribed with remembered words of Jawaharlal Nehru. There are lots of birds and many lovely places just to sit.

Yamuna Waterfront, has Mogul-style gardens near the Raj Ghat, where Gandhi was cremated; the Shanti Vana, where Nehru was cremated; and the Vijay Ghat, where Prime Minister Shastri was cremated. No wonder it's peaceful, despite lots of birds.

Delhi Zoo Not a great modern zoo with lots of freedom for the animals, but, set against the Purana Qila (old fort), you get some pleasure just in walking around. Open 8 A.M.–6:30 P.M. in summer, 9 A.M.–5 P.M. in winter.

PARTICIPANT SPORTS. Golf. Play golf against a backdrop of ancient monuments at *Delhi Golf Club,* Zakir Hussain Marg. Open 6 A.M.–3 P.M.; call 699236 for reservations and details.

Horseback Riding. *Delhi Riding Club,* Safdarjang Road. For details, call 371891.

Swimming. All deluxe and expensive hotels have swimming pools, which usually allow nonresidents for a fee. Check hotel listings.

SPECTATOR SPORTS. Delhi is a **polo** town, and just by virtue of its existence as capital of India, you'll find a **cricket** match somewhere almost any time. For details about polo, call *Delhi Polo Club,* President's Estate, Rashtrapati Bhavan; tel. 3015604. For cricket matches, check the newspapers. Tickets may be hard to come by, however, for some games when the rivalry is intense.

THEATER, DANCE, MUSIC. For serious cultural events, Delhi is rich. Just open up the newspaper and find out what's happening where. Numerous auditoriums put on cultural events and many hotels have performers. Or just contact the Government of India Tourist Office to see what's doing. This is a great city to see good dance and theater and to hear some of India's finest musical performers.

RECOMMENDED READING. *Delhi Diary* (Rs. 2), a weekly small magazine available free in many hotels and at most newsstands, is excellent. It tells you what is happening; lists restaurants, hotels, shopping information; and has a handy, albeit limited, map in the back. It's small enough to fit in your pocket. The tiny green *Sangam City Guide of Delhi* (Rs. 25) is also terrific and available at many newsstands. Good details on monuments, good maps (although you long for one big map), thorough information on just about everything in Delhi, most of it accurate and current; it's also small enough to fit in your pocket. Finally, if you're into shopping (and Delhi is a great shopping city), try to find a copy of *Explore and Shop in the Delhi Markets* by Colette Galas (Rs. 45). A little dated, but the best shops never die (at least rarely) and she knows her stuff. The book is also available in paperback. The best bookstores (in the Connaught place area): *Book Worm,* B–29 Connaught Pl.; *New Book Depot,* B–18 Connaught Pl.; *Oxford Book and Stationery Co.,* N Block, Connaught Pl., excellent for books on India—a serious place; *Piccadilly Book Stall,* Shop No. 64, Shankar Market, deceptive tiny-sized stall crammed with treasures, many out of print, on India and this part of the world, plus heavy into the occult.

SHOPPING. Delhi is the marketplace for all of India; shopping here can be fun. Bargain is the cardinal rule, unless you're obviously in a fixed-price shop. Go for a 30–50 percent reduction from the first price they give you. Walk away. Let them chase after you. It's part of the game. Besides the *Central Cottage Industries Emporium,* on Janpath (closed on Sundays), which has every handicraft of India somewhere under its roof, also visit the *State Emporia,* a string of shops on Baba Kharak Singh Marg. The state shops are also closed on Sundays and take a lunch break usually 1:30–2:30 P.M. The better shops on Connaught Place take a lunch break during that time and observe Sundays as a day of rest. *Explore and Shop in the Delhi Markets* is a handy guide to have before you begin your shopping. It may be available at the Government of India Tourist Office. The following is a list of a few interesting shops that sell some of the best of what Delhi has to offer:

For cottons and handlooms: *Pindi Cloth House,* 84 Shankar Market. The owner is a great shirt tailor; lots of fabric upstairs, keep asking to see more. *Joyce International Handloom* Shop, 49 Shankar Market, great handwoven goods; closed on Sundays.

For silk: *Banaras House Limited,* N–13 Connaught Pl., and *Handloom House* (government run), 9–A Connaught Pl., both shops close for lunch and close on Sundays.

For *good* curios: *Sunder Nagar,* lots of interesting shops throughout Delhi, all closed on Sundays. Also, *Mehra's Art Palace,* M–1 Market, Greater Kailash -2, closed Tuesday.

For art: *Kumar Gallery,* 11 Sunder Nagar Market, closed Sundays.

For tailoring: Women, *Charisma,* 9–N Connaught Pl., inside a jewelry shop; expensive but terrific. Men, *Style,* 13–E Connaught Pl., suits and jackets.

For handmade shoes: Don't be lured by the shops on Connaught Pl.; Mr. Lee's your man to see—*K.K. See,* 30–B, Khan Market. He's reliable and honest; closed Sundays.

For the best *kurtas* and *chikan* work (hand embroidery): *Lal Behari Tandon,* 20 Palika Bazar (central hall); closed Sundays.

For interesting ready-made clothes, from antique saris to exquisite sequin work: *Once Upon a Time,* H5/6 Mehrauli Rd., opposite the Qutab Minar; call first, 655077.

For ivory and jewelry: *Ivory Mart,* 22–F Connaught Pl.; *Ivory Palace,* 19–F Connaught Pl.; *Girdhari Lal & Sons,* 9–N Connaught Pl.; *Kanjimull & Sons Jewelers,* and *Scindia House,* Jan Path. All closed on Sundays and all take a lunch break.

TEATIME AND SNACKS. There are lots of fast-food shops in Delhi. Some are fun and are local hangouts worth a visit:

American Pie. Asian Games Village, Siri Fort Rd., New Delhi; tel. 6447230. Whatever you miss from home, it's here "Indian style." Open 11 A.M.–midnight.

Nirula's. L Block, Connaught Pl., tel. 352419. Snacks, pastry, ice cream (India's version of Baskin Robbin's). Numerous shops all huddled together. 11 A.M.–10:30 P.M.

Pizza King, Jan Path. Indian pizza. 8:30 A.M.–11 P.M.

Laziz Restaurant. 1 Jor Bagh Market; tel. 623715. Excellent inexpensive South Indian snacks and coffee.

Sona Rupa. Jan Path. Vegetarian snacks and light meals. 9 A.M.–10 P.M.

Top floor of Mohan Singh Place Building. On Baba Khara Singh Marg (across the street from the state emporia complex). Excellent Indian coffee and snacks. Popular local spot. Morning–early evening.

NIGHTLIFE AND BARS. All the major hotels have bars; check listings under *Hotels.* The classiest of these are at the *Oberoi;* sedate and elegant. Most hotel bars are open from lunch through late at night. You won't find liquor in any other restaurants; Delhi's dry that way. The two hot disco spots are *Number One,* Taj Mahal Hotel, 1 Man Singh Rd., from 10 P.M. until late; and at the *Sheraton,* Ghungroo, from 10 P.M. until 3 A.M. Dancing to the latest Western hit discs at either one.

THE PUNJAB AND HARYANA

Sikhs, Hindus, and Mountain Shrines

by
KATHLEEN COX

For centuries, the Punjab, the northwest border state of India, has been the scene of communal strife pitting Moslem against Hindu. In the mid-1500s, around the time of Babur, a new movement began that initially gave rise to the hope of a peaceful future. A Punjabi Hindu, Baba Nanak, began to preach a new gospel—a fusion of the best of Hinduism and Islam—a gospel that spurned the notion of castes and the worship of idols. Nanak developed a following, a title—Guru (*gu:* one who dispells darkness, by teaching enlightment: *ru*)—and numerous disciples called Sikhs. By 1708, the Sikhs had their own city, Amritsar, with its beautiful Golden Temple, their headquarters.

Unfortunately, communalism flared up anew. As the relationship between Islam and Sikhism soured, the Sikhs turned militant. Communalism continued into the twentieth century, erupting finally into a wholesale slaughter of Hindus, Sikhs, and Moslems during the post-World War II partitioning. As Hindus and Sikhs tried to flee Moslem Pakistan for India and Moslems tried to flee India for Pakistan, an estimated 500,000 were killed.

The Punjab still suffers from religious intolerance. Only now, instead of Hindu and Sikh against Moslem, the hostility rages between Hindu and Sikh—with disastrous consequences. The Golden Temple was stormed and seriously damaged, Indira Gandhi was assassinated, and relations between Pakistan and India were strained (India considers Pakistan a training ground and refuge for Sikh terrorists). Fear grips the people who are caught in the struggle of the Sikh extremists who want their people, a minority, to have their own Sikh state called Khalistan.

For all these reasons, travel to the Punjab is ill advised and, as of this writing, *prohibited to foreigners without a special permit.* For a vicarious trip under these circumstances—or if differences between the groups are settled—this can serve as your guide.

The Golden Temple of Amritsar

Amritsar was founded in 1579 by Ram Das, the fourth teacher (guru) of the Sikh religion (the Sikhs have had 10 gurus), as a central place of worship for the followers of his faith. He constructed a pool, the "Pool of Nectar" (which is what Amritsar means) and planned the temple that his son and successor expanded.

Known as the Golden Temple (Darbar Sahib), it is the glory of Amritsar and nucleus of Sikh worship. The pool is surrounded by a pavement of white marble, and the temple itself is reached by a marble causeway. Its bronze plates, heavily covered with pure gold leaf, burn in the tropical sun and flash their light in piercing gleams while their reflection in the still waters leaps up at you. Over the whole there reigns a stillness, a power of peace that seems to stem from that uplift that inhales the cosmic *prana* of the universe. For the Sikhs still practice that consciously physical correspondence with environment that is the inner meaning of this word and that feeds the adept with the celestial food they believe can conquer doubt, disease, and even death. In the Sanctuary, under a canopy, lies the *Granth Sahib,* the sacred book of the Sikhs, which is read out from time to time by a priest, to the accompaniment of devotional music.

The buildings around the Sacred Tank shelter pilgrims who come to worship from distant places. The Akal Takht (the Immortal Throne) is the supreme seat of Sikh religious authority and contains several relics. Incidentally, the only restriction imposed on those who visit these sacred places is that they must remove their shoes. As is the way with mosques and shrines, slippers are provided, but here no charge is made and no donation is accepted. The gardens that surround the Baba Atal Tower—richly painted with frescoes depicting scenes from the life of Guru Nanak—are of a strange and wistful beauty. The whole is impregnated with an energy that typifies the soul of the Sikh.

Haryana

Haryana has a minimal share of attractions, but it has roadside tourist conveniences (à la Howard Johnson motels) that put the state light years ahead of the rest of the country.

Take the Grand Trunk Road from Delhi, the start of a journey north to Chandigarh, the joint capital of the Punjab and Haryana. The first point of interest is Panipat, a sprawling industrial city, with numerous architectural reminders of decisive battles that changed the fate of India. Just outside the city, you can see the Kabuli Bagh Mosque, built by Babur to commemorate his victory in 1526 over Ibrahim Lodi, king of Delhi—a victory that gave birth to the Mogul Empire. You can also visit the tomb of the vanquished Lodi, who lost his life as well as his kingdom during the decisive battle.

The next attraction on the road is Kurukshetra, where the epic battle described in the *Mahabharata* was supposedly fought. Another legend claims that under an ancient spreading banyan tree, Krishna delivered his sermon of Bhagavad Gita. And, finally, a dip in Kurukshetra's sacred tank, especially during a solar eclipse, has an unbelievable redeeming effect, or so it is claimed.

Chandigarh, a few miles north, is either an urban planner's dream or a futuristic blight, depending on your point of view. An old city, it's not! In fact, if you've traveled through India for a few weeks before arriving here, Chandigarh is bound to astonish you. Where are the bullock carts, roadside stalls, and bustling produce markets? You might even think, Where is India? But it's right before your eyes. Chandigarh is always described as Le Corbusier's city (Le Corbusier contributed to the design of the United Nations), but Chandigarh is more accurately the creation of Nehru. At the time of partition, when the greater part of the Punjab, including its graceful capital Lahore, fell to Pakistan, a new capital had to be found—or created. A site was chosen under the Siwalki Hills, with two small rivers flowing on cither side. This site was Chandigarh and, according to an enthusiastic Nehru, who was Prime Minister at the time, the new capital would be "a new town, symbolic of the freedom of India, unfettered by the traditions of the past."

The city is divided into 47 sectors. Each one is 800 by 2,200 meters—a self-contained unit for living with housing, marketing, schools, and banks. It's all there. Building height, population density, traffic flow—all have been considered. To some visitors, this may sound like a vision out of *Brave New World,* but Chandigarh must be viewed within the context of India. It is, and should be, a source of pride—living evidence that India doesn't see itself confined to confusion, poverty, crushing crowds, heart-wrenching contrasts, and improvised solutions that often characterize urban life in many of its great cities. In this sense, Chandigarh is as much a symbol as a specific place. And though it may not be everyone's dream to live life in a symbol, Chandigarh is well worth visiting and knowing.

A few of the specifics about Chandigarh: Get yourself a map from the tourist office. Sector One is the Capital Complex—Secretariat, Assembly, High Court, and Open Hand Monument (which resembles Picasso's dove of peace). Because of political tensions, entry into the buildings is restricted. Sector 10 is the Museum and Art Gallery, with a good collection of contemporary Indian art. Sector 14 is the Punjab University campus. The Gandhi Bhawan here is perhaps the most elegant building in the city. Designed by Pierre Janerat, Le Corbusier's cousin, it is a gem of a building, small and shaped like an open lotus blossom. Sector 16 is the Zakir Rose Garden, supposedly the largest such garden in all Asia, extending over 30 acres with 1,500 varieties of roses.

Nek Chand's Rock Garden

It's ironic and wonderful that Chandigarh, the totally planned city, should have spawned this spectacular homage to imagination and intuitive construction—the Rock Garden located on the edge of Sector One. Some 30 years ago, Nek Chand (the name means benign moon) was a Public Works Department official whose job was to inspect roads and write maintenance reports. As he went about his work, he began collecting rocks, stones, and refuse that people dumped along the roadside. Soon, he began assembling his bits of junk—tiles, torn clothes, broken bangles, shards of glass, electric and plumbing fixtures—into a vision, his "kingdom of the gods and goddesses." Without the knowledge of any of Chandigarh's city planners, Nek Chand's Rock Garden took shape on the edge of the city. Chand had absolutely no artistic training when he embarked on his project, and, even today, he shrugs when the discussion turns to art. Yet, Nek Chand's talent was recognized early by the Indian government. Land was set aside for his project, and he was given several assistants to help bring his dream to life.

Visiting the Rock Garden today, you'll enter a low Alice-in-Wonderland entranceway ("it is good to bow down when you enter the kingdom of the gods and goddesses") and walk along a winding path through a series of environments. You'll see waterfalls, pools, imaginary forests, and miniature villages. You'll go up steps, around corners, and stoop under several more arches. Wherever you go, you'll be in the midst of hundreds of delightful figures—humans and animals—fashioned from recycled junk. Americans who are acquainted with the work of Red Grooms will have an idea of what to expect. But whereas Red Grooms is a sophisticated self-conscious artist using the idiom of naif art, Nek Chand is the real McCoy.

That the Rock Garden is in a state of perpetual expansion seems altogether appropriate. It's so filled with the energy of life that one feels good to know that the garden is alive and growing. Nek Chand has been honored throughout the world (including a Fantasy Garden in Washington D.C., which he supervised), but, in all likelihood, he'll be in the Rock Garden when you visit. His office is a cozy rock grotto that any Hobbit would gladly call home. You might think Nek Chand is a "simple" man, but once you've seen his elaborate fantasy kingdom, you realize that he's a man with a vision—and the skill and perseverance to execute it. He is a rare individual who gave Chandigarh a gift that neither Nehru nor Le Corbusier could provide—a spirit of gaiety, surprise, and love—a testament of faith in uniqueness and eccentricity of human beings. Nek Chand gave India's determinedly modern city a bit of personality.

PRACTICAL INFORMATION FOR
THE PUNJAB AND HARYANA

WHEN TO GO. October–March is the time to visit the Punjab and Haryana. They're both *very hot* in the summer.

HOW TO GET THERE. As of this writing, foreigners are not allowed into the Punjab without prior permission, which is difficult to obtain. To travel through Haryana to Chandigarh, you can go by air, train, car, or bus.

By Air. *Indian Airlines* and *Vayudoot* have numerous flights to Chandigarh from Delhi, Srinagar, Leh, and Kullu.

By Bus. Numerous deluxe buses make the daily run from Shimla, Delhi, and other northern cities into Chandigarh. From Delhi, call *Haryana Roadways,* (221292); hours, 6 A.M.–9 P.M. Or *Himachal Pradesh Road Transport Corporation.* (HPRTC) (2516725), 4 A.M.–10 P.M. From Shimla, call HPRTC, 3566 or 2887. In Chandigarh, Haryana Roadways, tel. 26370; HPRTC, tel. 20946. Buses operate from the Main Bus Stand, Sector 17.

By Train. Daily trains run from Delhi and Calcutta (Howrah) to Chandigarh. Railway inquiry in Chandigarh, tel. 22105.

By Car. Chandigarh is 248 km from Delhi by very good roads; 380 km from Jammu; and 119 km fronm Shimla.

TOURIST INFORMATION. Tourists are well advised to go to one of the following tourist departments on their arrival in Chandigarh to get a good map and up-to-date information.

Chandigarh Tourism has good information on Chandigarh. Sector 17, General Bus Stand, Chandigarh; tel. 22548.

Haryana Tourism, Sector 17, Chandigarh; tel. 21955. Also has good information on the entire state.

FOREIGN CURRENCY EXCHANGE. Most banks are open Monday – Friday, 10–2 P.M.; Saturdays 10 A.M. – noon. *Bank of India,* Sector 17, Chandigarh; tel. 32215. *Bank of India,* Sector 20, Chandigarh; tel. 29626. *Hotel Chandigarh Mountview,* Sector 10, tel. 21257, has money changing counter, as does Hotel Pankaj, Sector 22–C, tel. 41906. Numerous banks in Chandigarh will change foreign currency and travelers checks.

ACCOMMODATIONS. Chandigarh has adequate hotels; however, most have a dreary shopping mall setting, that is, they are large buildings that front an unattractive parking lot. Two exceptions are noted below. The rest of Haryana is dotted with numerous roadside stops (named after birds) that offer the travelers rest and relaxation. Facilities run the gamut from those à la Howard Johnson to an inexpensive–moderately priced resort by a lake. See *Delhi* chapter for rate classification.

CHANDIGARH

Expensive

Hotel President. Madhya Marg, Sector 26, nine km from the airport, three km from the main shopping area; tel. 40840. 20 air-conditioned rooms, TVs. Room service, many Western amenities, a coffee shop, two restaurants, a bar, and a health club. Poor maintenance for the money.

Moderate

Hotel Chandigarh Mountview. Sector 10, one km from the main shopping area; tel. 21257. 33 air-conditioned rooms with TVs, room service, a bar, a restaurant, and a broad lawn. The best place in town.

Hotel Piccadilly. Himalaya Marg, Sector 22, next to the main shopping area; tel. 32223. 48 air-conditioned rooms with TVs. Room service, a restaurant, a bar, and a coffee shop. Poorly kept up.

Hotel Sunbeam. Udyog Path, Sector 22, close to the main shopping area; tel. 32057. 57 air-conditioned rooms, TVs, room service, a restaurant, and a coffee shop.

Inexpensive

Hotel Pankaj. Sector 22, near the main shopping area; tel. 41906. 14 air-conditioned rooms, room service, a restaurant, and a bar.

Puffin Guest House. Kothi No. 2, Sector 2; tel. 27653. Eight air-conditioned rooms. Channel music, a restaurant, and lawns. Run by Haryana Tourism—one of their roadside environments.

All hotels that follow are in the *Moderate* to *Inexpensive* range.

DHARUHERA

(70 km from Delhi on the Delhi–Jaipur Highway)

Tangle Babbler. Dharuhera; tel. 25. Nine rooms, some air-conditioned. Designed to resemble rural Haryana, set in a landscaped garden. A restaurant, bar, and children's park.

HODAL

(92 km from Delhi on the Delhi–Agra Highway)

Dabchick. tel. 91. 12 air-conditioned rooms. Also two camper huts. And **Dream Castle Motel,** plus cottages on stilts. Mini lake with boating, camel and elephant rides, snake charmer, restaurant, bar—everything to break a long trip's monotony.

PANIPAT

(92 km from Delhi on Hwy. 1 on the way to Chandigarh)

Skylark. tel. 3579. 14 air-conditioned rooms. Set on four acres, in the style of Howard Johnsons. Motel rooms, a restaurant, bar, filling station, and juice counter.

PINJORE

(270 km from Delhi on Hwy. 22)

Yadavindra Gardens. tel. 455. 18 air-conditioned rooms. Motel facilities—new and old—set around the Pinjore Gardens. A restaurant, cafe, bar, mini zoo, children's park, shopping arcade, camel rides, boating, ice-cream parlor, and croquet. Full service tourism Haryana-style.

SAMALKHA

(70 km from Delhi on Hwy. 1)

Blue Jay. tel. 10. 6 rooms, some air-conditioned. Motel style setup, with a bar, restaurant, and gift shop.

SULTANPUR

(48 km from Delhi near Hwy. 8)

Sultanpur Bird Sanctuary. tel. 42. 4 rooms. Also two camper huts, a bird sanctuary, restaurant, bar, and even binoculars for hire for bird watchers.

 DINING OUT. The following price categories (*Expensive*, Rs. 50 or more; *Moderate*, Rs. 25–Rs. 50; and *Inexpensive*, Rs. 25 and under) are based on a three-course meal for one person not including beverage, taxes, or tips. Only Western-style hotels accept credit cards or traveler's checks. Most restaurants are informal.

CHANDIGARH

Moderate

Gazal. Sector 17, Chandigarh; tel. 29396. Lunch and dinner. Indian, Continental, and Chinese dishes. Clean and cozy.

Mehfil, Sector 17, Chandigarh; tel. 29439. Indian, Continental, and Chinese lunches and dinners. Comfortable and well managed with pleasant decor. The best place in town.

Kwality Restaurant. Sector 22, Chandigarh; tel. 23434. Good ice cream to top off an Indian, Continental, or Chinese meal.

Noor Restaurant. Hotel Pankaj, Sector 22, Chandigarh; tel. 41906. Cozy and well-managed place serving Indian, Continental, and Chinese meals.

Inexpensive

Indian Coffee House. Sector 22, Chandigarh; tel. 25804. Good south Indian snacks and light meals.

Hot Millions. Sector 17; no phone. Fast food served here morning until night.

 HOW TO GET AROUND. By Taxi. Unmetered taxis charge Rs. 50 from airport to the city or back; Rs. 10 as flat fee from one point in the city to another.

    By Auto Rickshaw. Auto rickshaws are metered. Fare: Rs. 2 for the first 1.5 km and 0.15 paise for every part thereof, with a waiting charge of 10 paise for every eight minutes. Plus a 7 percent surcharge on the overall meter reading.

    By Cycle Rickshaw. Cycle rickshaws will also pedal you around Chandigarh. Fares: negotiable, with a minimum sector-to-sector fare of Rs. 1.50.

By Bus. *Chandigarh Transport Undertaking* (tel. 26117) has an efficient local bus service with 41 routes. Fare about Rs. 1.

TOURS. *Chandigarh Tourism* conducts tours in deluxe buses and eight-seater Matador vans in and around Chandigarh and Haryana. For details contact them at Hotel Chandigarh Mountview, Sector 10 (tel. 21257), or *Chandigarh Tourist Information Office,* General Bus Stand, Sector 17 (tel. 22548). The following tours are available: Local sightseeing, Rs. 8; Chatbir Zoo, Rs. 8; Pinjore Gardens, Rs. 8; Pinjore Gardens via Mansa Devi, Rs. 10; Pinjore Gardens via Nada Sahib, Rs. 11; Mansa Devi, Rs. 6; Bhakra Dam, Nagal, Gobind Sagar Lake, Ropar Boat Club, and Anandpur Sahib shrine, Rs. 35.

SEASONAL EVENT. **February–March.** Two-day *Rose Festival* at the Zakir Rose Garden, Chandigarh. Contact the tourist department for the exact date.

PARKS AND GARDENS. *Leisure Valley* in Chandigarh is a 300-acre sprawl that runs through the length of the city and is filled with untouched greenery and gardens. The most famous is the Zakir Rose Garden, named after the late President Zakir Hussain. Located in Sector 16, the garden is the biggest in Asia, with 1,500 varieties planted over 30 acres. Rock Garden is the creation of Nek Chand, carved out of rocks and whatever refuse he found. The garden covers six acres and is still a work in progress. Entry fee: 50 paise. Summer: 9 A.M.–1 P.M.; 3–7 P.M. Winter: 9 A.M.–1 P.M.; 2–6 P.M.

The Pinjore (Yadavindra) Gardens are the former great Mogul gardens designed by Nawab Fidai Khan, the architect for Emperor Aurangzeb in the seventeenth century. Open every day. Motel accommodations also are available.

ZOO. *Chattbir Zoo,* on the Chandigarh-Patiala road, has Bengal tigers, Himalayan black bears, and birds galore. Open every day. Entry fee: Rs. 1.

SPORTS. Fishing on Sukhna Lake, Chandigarh. Rs. 3 per day. Contact Lake Club, Sector 1 (tel. 26661), for details.

TEMPLES. *Bhima Devi Temple,* 22 km from Chandigarh on the Pinjore-Kalka Rd., was built between the eleventh and the fourteenth centuries.

MUSEUMS. *Government Museum and Art Gallery,* Sector 10 (tel. 25568), has an excellent collection of contemporary paintings and sculpture; plus a good collection of old miniature paintings from the Kangra, Rajasthani, and Mogul schools. Fine sculptures, too. Open 10 A.M.–4:30 P.M. Closed Mondays. Entry fee. Rs 0.50.

CAFES AND COFFEEHOUSES. *Indian Coffee House,* Sector 22, Chandigarh (tel. 25804), has good south Indian snacks and coffee. *Sindhi Sweets* (two shops, both in sector 17) are great places to sample a vast array of desserts and milk drinks. Try *karachi halwa,* made of *ghee* (a semifluid liquified butter), nuts, and arrowroot. It has the color and consistency of apricot taffy—delicious!) Or *keser milk badam* (ice-cold milk laced with crushed cashews and pistachios and various seasonings).

BARS. Most of the hotels have bars, but the *Suroor Bar* at the Hotel Pankaj, Sector 22, is probably the closest you'll come to visiting a downtown New York City bar. Everything is modern, minimal, and carefully lighted. Where else, but in Le Corbusier's city of tomorrow?

AGRA AND FATEHPUR SIKRI

The Road into the Past

by
KATHLEEN COX

As distances go, the trip from Delhi to Agra is not more than a stone's throw—124 miles by car from the capital of modern India to the former seat of the Mogul Empire. But few trips in India—or anywhere else in the world—offer such an extensive journey into history and ethereal historic beauty. This is the royal road of the Mogul emperors established in the sixteenth and seventeenth centuries, when their capital fluctuated between Delhi and Agra. Today, Delhi reigns over India, but Agra still reigns over that unforgettable past created by warriors as skilled in art and architecture as they were on the battlefield.

A trip to Agra should include Fatehpur Sikri, the abandoned capital of Akbar the Great, and extend farther south to Gwalior, Shivpuri, and Jhansi, home of Lakshmi Bai, India's Joan of Arc.

Vrindaban

Eighty-two miles south of Delhi, you enter Vrindaban and holy ground. This is a city of 1,000 shrines, the biggest being Gobind Deo. Erected to Hindu glory, with the encouragement of the tolerant Mogul Akbar, the temple suffered a dismal reversal during the reign of one of Akbar's descendants. The continual glare of a giant oil lamp burning from an upper story so annoyed Aurangzeb that he overreacted and lopped off the entire top half of the shrine. The site of a walled-in garden, Nikunja Ban, Vrindaban is also significant to the Hindu pil-

113

grim. Here, Krishna, the most popular of the incarnations of Vishnu, the preserver, supposedly appeared before his worshipers. In fact, most every step you take in this city follows the path of this adored god, as does the road that takes you to Mathura, six miles south.

Mathura

Mathura, situated on the west bank of the Yamuna River, which flows from Delhi to Agra, is supposedly the birthplace of Krishna. Hindu pilgrims from the world over visit a shrine in a part of the city called Katra. Originally the site of a Hindu temple, it, too, was destroyed by the intolerant Aurangzeb, who built a mosque in its place. But the basement of the original Kesava Deo remains, as does a sign proclaiming that Krishna was born here.

The holiness of Mathura is all pervasive—drawing worshipers of Vishnu the way that Varanasi draws the adorers of Shiva, the destroyer. Even the Hare Krishnas are headquartered here. Just as the followers of Shiva flock to the Ganges, pilgrims to Mathura are drawn to the Yamuna—in particular to the Vishram Ghat. Here Krishna supposedly rested after killing the tyrant Kansa (in whose prison he is believed to have been born). Religious ceremonial acts on the Yamuna are less intense than those on the Ganges: at sunset, hundreds of flickering oil lamps are launched on the river. But rites are performed and they are worth seeing.

Mathura is one of the oldest cities of India, far older than Agra, with a history that goes back to before the Maurya Dynasty, which ruled India from 325 to 184 B.C. This explains why the government museum has such an accumulation of artistic wealth left behind by foreign conquerors, including the Parthians and the Greeks. This also explains the flowering of Mathura sculpture, which started in the first century A.D. and lasted for a startling 1,200 years, going into decline when sculptors gave up sacred Buddhist and Hindu subjects to turn their chisels to the frivolous figures of full-bosomed dancing girls. Unfortunately, much of the grandeur of Mathura suffered the wrath of its conquerors, and few Hindu monuments remain.

Sikandra: Akbar's Tomb

Six miles down the royal road, you come to the glorious introduction to Agra: Sikandra, named after Sultan Sikander Lodi of the dynasty conquered by the Moguls. Sikandra is the site of the tomb of Akbar, the great Mogul emperor (1542–1605) who planned its design and began its construction in 1602. The tomb was finally completed by his son Jahangir in 1613.

A model of symmetry, built out of red sandstone and marble, the mausoleum stands in the center of a huge garden. The entrance is through an imposing, two-story gateway, 75 feet high, with exquisite mosaic and inlay work, and is topped by four slim marble minarets that rise up from each corner.

The main tomb is a fusion of Hindu and Moslem styles, as if reflecting the religious tolerance of Akbar, who dreamed of peaceful coexistence between the two religions. Each floor of the five-story structure has a series of arcades, tapering to a marble cloister that seems to float on the top of the cloister beneath it.

A narrow passageway leads to the cryptlike grave, now dimly lit by a hanging lamp (the gift of Lord Curzon). A replica of the white marble centaph rests precisely above it on the upper floor so no one can ever walk on Akbar's resting place. This identical crypt is inscribed with the 99 names attributed to Allah, plus the phrase, "Allah-o-Akbar" (God is Great), at the head; and the phrase, "Jalla Jalalahu" (Great Is His Glory), at the foot.

AGRA

Akbar the Great made Agra great. The city's origins before the Mogul conquest are dim: The conquering Babur, Akbar's grandfather, practically founded the ultimately important Moslem center. And, by some strange process of mutation, the warlike Moguls—Babur was a descendant of the wicked Tamerlane of Central Asia—were transformed into the most civilized and refined rulers of their day, revering the arts and thirsting for learning with a tolerance seldom found in history. The pitifully short golden age of Agra came to an end with the seventeenth-century reign of Shah Jahan, but it had an unforgettable climax in the Taj Mahal.

Not much happened in Agra before the Moguls and not much has happened since. Sacked by the Jats and occupied by the Marathas, the city entered a peaceful slumber in 1803, when it fell into the hands of the British. Today, its population has reached 1.2 million, but it is still a small city by Indian standards. The surrounding countryside of sandy stretches somehow produces a rice crop, cultivated by patient and hard-working farmers.

To the lover of art and to the traveler seeking the wonders of the world, Agra is the goal of a pilgrimage to the creative best: the Agra Fort and the Taj Mahal.

The Fort and Its Palaces

At the Agra Fort, the story of that portion of the Mogul Empire extending from Akbar to his son Jahangir to Shah Jahan is recorded in stone: the rusty-red sandstone of forbidding walls raised by Akbar, the shimmering white marble of palaces built by Shah Jahan. The fort, which is open from sunrise to sunset, is an excellent introduction to Agra. It took centuries for the castles of Europe to evolve from stern medieval citadels to graceful Renaissance palaces. At Agra, this process of evolution took place within the span of these three generations.

No one would question the fort's indomitable appearance. It stands on the banks of the Yamuna, surrounded by a wall 70 feet high, which guards a 40-foot moat with another 70-foot wall behind it. These double walls, pierced with slits and loopholes, seem capable of barring anyone from an inner paradise whose towers can only be glimpsed from the outside. Luckily, this daunting mass can be penetrated for the price of admission at the Amar Singh Gate, where visitors usually enter the fort.

In all, the walls around the Agra Fort measure 1½ miles in circumference. The original military structure was begun by Akbar, who is believed to have demolished an ancient castle on the site. He completed the fort eight years later, then built the palace called the Jahangiri Mahal, the first of the many interior constructions—built with the simpler architecture and intricate decoration so typical of the Mogul era.

Jahangiri Mahal

Once you enter the Amar Singh Gate, to the north is the biggest private residence inside the Agra Fort, the Jahangiri Mahal (palace), supposedly built by Akbar for his son (Akbar's Palace, closer to the entrance, is in ruins). Here, you see a striking example of Akbar's

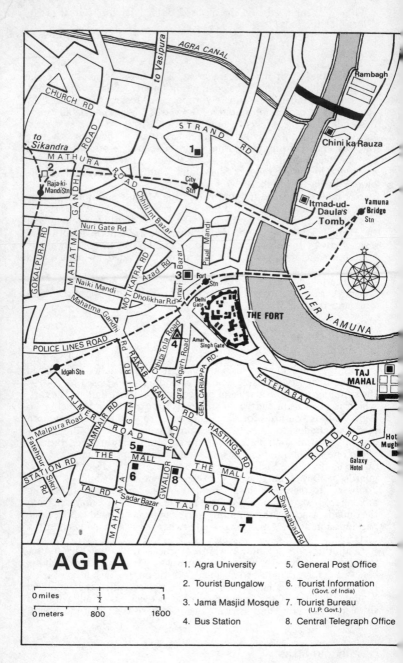

AGRA

0 miles   ½   1
0 meters   800   1600

1. Agra University
2. Tourist Bungalow
3. Jama Masjid Mosque
4. Bus Station

5. General Post Office
6. Tourist Information (Govt. of India)
7. Tourist Bureau (U.P. Govt.)
8. Central Telegraph Office

ability to blend Hindu architecture with the style imported by the Moguls from Central Asia. The palace is huge, measuring about 250 by 300 feet. You enter through a hall leading to a courtyard surrounded by columns. The central court of the palace is lined by two-story facades bearing remnants of the rich gilded decorations that once covered a great deal of the structure. On one side of the court is a hall known as Jodh Bai's dressing room (Jodh Bai was the Hindu mother of Jahangir), with a ceiling supported by serpents carved in stone. Also leading into the court is a hall known as Jodh Bai's reception room and a series of rooms, one of which is known as the library and is remarkable for its Mogul decoration. Most likely, these rooms were used both by Jahangir's mother and his empress, Nur Jahan (meaning light of the world).

Jahangir loved wine and the arts almost as much as he loved his wife. Nur Jahan attempted to convince him to settle down to the serious occupation of ruling an empire, but, finally, she had to do the job for him—sitting by his side in their palace in the Agra Fort, dispensing imperial justice. She was a strong-willed woman and made short shrift of anyone who stood in her way. One favorite method she employed was dropping rivals into a pit that conveniently led to the Yamuna River (the grim underground chambers near this pit are still intact).

Nur Jahan is also given credit for the discovery of distilling the attar of roses. After a quarrel with Jahangir, she went off to brood in the palace courtyard, where she noticed that, in the heat of the sun, rose petals floating in a pond oozed an oily substance. The fragrance was overwhelming. With a clever daub of this new perfume, she returned to Jahangir, who found her irresistible.

After Jahangir's death in 1628, Shah Jahan (whose mother was one of the other wives of Jahangir) assumed the throne and started his own collection of buildings inside the fort, some of them architectural pearls.

Shahjahani Mahal

The building known as Shahjahani Mahal is actually the remodeled northern part of Jahangiri Mahal; three rooms and a corridor enhanced by a tapering tower gallery topped with a pavilion bearing a spike. From this imperial vantage point, Shah Jahan watched elephant fights. In more tranquil moments, he received instruction from a Hindu holy man who was carried up in a litter.

Khas Mahal

Shah Jahan outdid himself in the Khas Mahal (the Private Palace), built in 1637: three pavilions overlooking the Yamuna with a fountain tank opposite the central pavilion. This white marble building follows the Mogul pattern in style: three arches on each side, five in front, and two turrets rising out of the roof. Once flowers created with precious stones were encrusted in its walls, but the jewels were looted in the eighteenth century. Of the other two pavilions, one is of white marble and is supposed to have been decorated with gold leaf, while the other is made of redstone. In one part of the Khas Mahal, a staircase leads down to the "air-conditioned" quarters of the palace, cool underground rooms that were probably inhabited during the scorching heat of summer.

Sheesh Mahal

On the northeastern end of the courtyard of the Khas Mahal stands
the Sheesh Mahal (Palace of Mirrors), built in 1637. This building was
the bath of the private palace and the dressing room of the harem, with
each of the two chambers containing a bathing tank that was once fed
by marble channels. In its glory, small mirrors that covered the ceilings
and walls caught the sunlight and turned the interior of the Sheesh
Mahal into a dazzling vision of brilliance. Cleanliness was evidently a
greater concern to the Moguls than to their contemporary counterparts
who lived in seventeenth-century castles and palaces in Europe (where
fountains were only for show).

Anguri Bagh

A rectangle in front of the Khas Mahal bears the mysterious name
of Anguri Bagh (Vineyard Garden), but no one has ever found any
trace of the grapevines. This was apparently a Mogul garden, with
fountains and flowerbeds on a marble-paved platform divided by stone
partitions. Apartments that might have been used by members of the
emperor's harem surround three sides of the garden. Below the terrace,
a marble cistern leads to the platform.

Diwan-i-Am

To the people of the empire and to the European emissaries who
came to see this powerful monarch, the most impressive part of the fort
was the Diwan-i-Am (Hall of Public Audience), set within the large
quadrangle. A huge low structure, it rests on a stage four feet high, with
nine cusped Mogul arches held aloft by rows of slender supporting
pillars. There is considerable disagreement about which of the three
Mogul emperors—Akbar, Jahangir, or Shah Jahan—built this hall, but
none at all about the creator of its throne room. Only Shah Jahan could
have conceived this alcove with its inlaid mosaics, one of the marvels
of Mogul art. Here, the emperor sat and dispensed justice to his subjects, rich and poor alike. Below the throne, his *wazir* (prime minister)
sat on a small platform with a silver railing, where he received the
petitioners as they came in.

The petitioner bowed three times before he reached the wazir, never
daring to raise his eyes to the Grand Mogul, while a herald proclaimed
that the poor mortal stood in the presence of the "Sun of the World."
Bernier, a French traveler of the day, dared to lift his gaze on the ruler,
however, and recorded what he saw: "The monarch, every day about
noon, sits upon his throne with some of his sons at his right and left,
while eunuchs, standing about the royal persons, flap away flies with
peacock tails, agitate the air with large fans or wait with profound
humility to perform the different services allotted to them."

Unlike the contemporaries of the Moguls, you get to wander freely
through the palace that was once reserved for the private life of the
emperor and his courts. For example, not far from the public audience
hall lies what is believed to have been the Inner Mina Bazaar, where
ladies of the court shopped for jewelry or silks. Sometimes, too, the
Grand Mogul and his intimates played store—a game in which the
wives of noblemen acted as vendors while the emperor amused himself
by haggling. The exact location of this regal shopping center is unknown; it may have been in the Maachi Bhavan.

In the Macchi Bhavan (Palace of Fish), gaily colored fish danced through water channels for the amusement of the court. Evidently, this was one part of the fort in which the emperor and his harem could escape all the inhibitions of pomp and ceremony.

Diwan-i-Khas

Contrasted with the Hall of Public Audience is the Diwan-i-Khas, or Hall of Private Audience, built by Shah Jahan in 1636–37. Here, the emperor received foreign ambassadors or dignitaries of his kingdom. The Diwan-i-Khas, which is due east of the Diwan-i-Am, contains two halls connected by three arches. White marble covers their red sandstone walls and lavish carvings can still be seen at the base of the columns that support the arches. Outside this light structure is the famous throne terrace with its pair of black-and-white thrones. The black throne was carved from a single block of marble and stands on a marble platform overlooking the Yamuna. A low railing of white marble contrasts with the black throne. According to the inscriptions found on it, this seat of power was apparently made for Jahangir. The white throne, consisting of several blocks of marble, was installed for Shah Jahan, who is said to have relaxed here by fishing below the terrace or by watching the magnificent elephant fights staged in the fort.

Musamman Burj

Near the Diwan-i-Khas is the tall Musamman Burj, originally built by Shah Jahan for Mumtaz Mahal, his wife, who is buried in the Taj Mahal. It is an octagonal tower with a courtyard on the lower floor paved with octagonal marble slabs. Here, too, are those delicate lattices of marble, no doubt used as screens to enable the ladies of the court to look out on the fort without being seen. In the center of the tower is a beautifully carved fountain. But all this beauty turned into the setting for a tragedy: Shah Jahan died here in 1666, after seven years as a prisoner of his own son, Aurangzeb. Here, he breathed his last, looking out at the Taj Mahal. Only his devoted daughter, Jahanara, remained with him during his final days.

The Mussamman Burj is another of the exceptional monuments left by Shah Jahan. One writer compared it to "a fairy tower hanging over grim ramparts." Unfortunately, only the barest trace still exists of the decorative designs that once adorned this tower: plunderers removed all the precious stones in 1761.

Nagina Masjid

To the northeast of the Diwan-i-Khas, you'll find the white marble Nagina Masjid, a private mosque raised by Shah Jahan with typical cusped arches. Walled in on three sides, it has a marble courtyard for worshipers and three graceful domes. This mosque was probably used by the royal ladies or by those seeking audience with the emperor.

Moti Masjid

A short distance away stands the Moti Masjid, a pearl mosque built in white marble by Shah Jahan and considered ideal in its proportions. The beauty of the Moti Masjid hits you suddenly—it's not at all evident from the outside. But a marble courtyard with arcaded cloisters on three sides unfolds before your eyes (the fourth side on the west has a place for the leader of the worshipers). Marble screens conceal what may have been the section reserved for women. Seven archways support the roof of this mosque, which bears three handsome domes. Over the arches of the prayer chamber, a Persian inscription compares the mosque to a pearl and states that as ordered by Shah Jahan, it took seven years to build. Unfortunately, as of this writing, the Moti Masjid is temporarily closed for renovations.

Also of interest are the two main gates, the Amar Singh and Delhi Gates, a pavilion known as Salim's Fort near the entrance, and the intriguing Hauz-i-Jahangiri. The Hauz-i-Jahangiri is a bath carved out of a huge block of stone five feet high and 25 feet in circumference that, according to the inscription, connects it to Jahangir. There are many theories regarding its purpose: some insist that Akbar ordered it carved to celebrate Jahangir's birth; others say it was Jahangir's wedding present to Nur Jahan in 1611.

Finally, just who is Lt. Governor Colvin, whose tomb is in the fort? The unfortunate soldier died here during the Indian Mutiny of 1857, when the fort was under seige.

THE TAJ MAHAL—MONUMENT TO LOVE

To some, the Taj Mahal is overrated. To others, it's a sublime experience to be ranked with the Pyramids of Egypt, the Palace of Versailles, or the Parthenon of Athens as the esthetic epitome of a civilization. To still others, it simply represents the greatest love story ever told. This should make it clear that the Taj Mahal, despite the imposing dimensions of its architecture and all the good and bad literature it has inspired, is very much a matter of taste.

One other preliminary word: give the Taj Mahal a chance. It speaks a different language when seen by moonlight, through the shimmer of dawn, in the bright light of midday, and at sunset. Although a full moon brings out its distinct and heavenly beauty, it also brings out the crowds who destroy the serenity and stately aura. So, taking everything into consideration, probably the best time to see the Taj Mahal is in the early morning when it emerges from the night ahead of the sun whose first pale rays give a soft luster to the marble, which glistens in a coat of pink, blue, or even mauve. And the surroundings at this time of day are calm and peaceful—nothing upstages its grandeur.

You can't experience the Taj Mahal if you don't know its story. Nearly all the world's great monuments were the product of the religious fervor of a people or the vanity of a king. But the Taj Mahal is an exception; it was built as a monument to love.

Arjuman Banu, the niece of Jangir's queen, Nur Jahan, was the second wife of Emperor Shah Jahan, the artist among the Mogul builders. In 1612, at the age of 21, she married him and took on the names that have passed down through time: Mumtaz Mahal, the Exalted of the Palace, and Mumtazul-Zamani, the Distinguished of the Age. Numerous tales speak of her generosity and her wisdom, both as a household manager and as an adviser to her imperial husband, but even these qualities were overshadowed by the love that bound her to Shah Jahan. She bore him 14 children, and it was in childbirth that she died in 1630 at Burhanpur, where her husband was waging a military campaign.

When she died, Shah Jahan was grief stricken. His hair supposedly turned gray within a few months and it is said that he put aside his royal robes for simple white muslin clothes. A huge procession brought her body from Burhanpur, where it had been temporarily buried, to Agra six months after her death. Shah Jahan vowed to build her a memorial surpassing anything the world had ever seen in beauty and in wild extravagance. He brought in skilled craftsmen from Persia, Turkey, France, and Italy. He put a huge army of 20,000 laborers to work, building a whole new village (Taj Ganj, which still stands) to house them. The cost of reproducing the Taj Mahal today has been estimated at nearly $70 million, but who would try?

A Masterpiece in Marble

The Taj Mahal lies on the banks of the Yamuna River, where it can be seen, like a fantastic mirage, from the nearby Agra Fort. Construction began in 1632; although no one knows who drew up the actual plans, Shah Jahan's chief architect, Ustad Ahmad Lahori, was clearly involved. Some people accuse the Taj Mahal of architectural exaggeration and coldness (not so inappropriate for a mausoleum), but no one has ever denied its perfect proportions. This huge mass of white marble resting on red sandstone is a jewel, fashioned over 17 years. The work ended on the exact anniversary of the Mumtaz Mahal's death.

Glimpsed from the enormous main gateway inscribed with verses of the Koran (the entire Koran is said to be reproduced on its walls), the Taj Mahal reveals itself with the suddenness of a jewel box opening before your eyes. This gate leads you inside a walled garden—and there, the magic spell is cast. A rectangular pool (unfortunately with too-shallow water), bordered by cypresses, catches the shimmering image of the tomb.

In the Agra Fort, virile red sandstone and elegant white marble symbolize different periods of Mogul architecture in a juxtaposition wrought by time. But here, the two materials have been brought together with deliberate effect. The Taj Mahal is built on two bases, one of sandstone and, above it, a marble platform measuring 313 feet square and worked into a black-and-white chessboard design. A slender marble minaret stands on each corner of the platform; these towers blend so well into the general composition that it's hard to believe their 130-foot height. Each one is also purposely constructed at a slight tilt away from the tomb (in case of an earth tremor, they'd fall away from the beautiful building).

In the mausoleum itself, the easy curves of pointed Mogul arches on the facade set off the square corners of the building. The entrance to the tomb is an archway soaring more than 90 feet high and inscribed with more verses from the Koran. Mogul inlay work, used so lavishly throughout the Taj Mahal, is carefully worked into the entrance. Notice the tiny, intricate flowers—the detailed stonework on each petal and leaf. Shine a flashlight and see the delicate translucence of some of the stones. Feel the perfectly smooth surfaces. Step inside and succumb to the pull of another dimension that draws your gaze to the graceful curve of the dome, a marble sky that is actually a dome within a dome. The dome seen from the exterior is above the dome you now see inside.

The Royal Tombs

Directly under the dome lie the tombs of Mumtaz Mahal and Shah Jahan, but they aren't immediately visible. The Taj Mahal plays a tantalizing game of illusion, revealing its treasures one by one. Originally, the tombs were surrounded by a barrier of gold encrusted with precious stones, but this barrier was apparently removed by Shah Jahan's rupee-pinching son Aurangzeb, who replaced it with a marble screen that is the height of a man. Carved from a single block of stone, the screen is a latticework as intricate as lace.

The tomb of Mumtaz Mahal is in the center of the enclosure behind the screen: diminishing rectangles leading up to what looks like a coffin. In fact, both Mumtaz Mahal and Shah Jahan are buried in a crypt below these tombs in obedience to a tradition that no one should ever walk over their graves. Supposedly, Shah Jahan originally planned to build a black marble mausoleum for himself on the other side of the Yamuna, linking it by bridge to the Taj. But Aurangzeb had other ideas, which explains why the emperor is buried next to his wife. It was most likely done as another money-saving measure—an ironic post-script to the munificence of Shah Jahan.

The cenotaph of Mumtaz Mahal bears this Persian inscription: "The illustrious sepulcher of Arjuman Banu Begum, called Mumtaz Mahal. God is everlasting, God is sufficient. He knoweth what is concealed and what is manifest. He is merciful and compassionate. Nearer unto him are those who say: Our Lord is God."

The epitaph of the builder of the Taj Mahal reads: "The illustrious sepulcher of His Exalted Majesty Shah Jahan, the Valiant King, whose dwelling is in the starry Heaven. He traveled from this transient world to the World of Eternity on the twenty-eighth night of the month of Rajab in the year of 1076 of the Hegira [February 1, 1666]."

Inlay Work and Marble Screens

The inlay work of the Taj achieved unrivaled grace with the tomb of Mumtaz Mahal. Designs, executed in jasper, agate, lapis lazuli, carnelian, and bloodstone, are rendered with such skill that neither your sense of touch nor a magnifying glass can detect breaks between two stones. For example, one flower that measures only a square inch contains 60 different inlays. There is less unanimity over the tomb of Shah Jahan, which dwarfs that of Mumtaz Mahal and has been called pompous and out of proportion. But maybe it's fitting that he should lie for eternity next to his favorite wife, and the romantically inclined give Aurangzeb credit for bringing the two together.

More than just the tombs of these royal lovers is under the dome of the Taj Mahal. In each corner of the mausoleum, small domes rise over round chambers about 30 feet in diameter. Light from these rooms filters into the chamber through marble screens. The play of light within the entire Taj is fascinating. Precious stones inlaid in the tombs, in the screens surrounding them, and in the walls glow against the background of white marble.

So fantastic is the decoration of the Taj that it inspired the imagination of marauders who raided the mausoleum in 1764 and managed to stagger off with two silver doors that once served as an entrance. Thieves also made away with the gold sheets that formerly lined the burial vault below the tombs. But they never got around to plucking out the pietra dura inlay work—probably because they didn't believe it was real.

Outside the mausoleum stand a pair of red sandstone mosques, one on each end. Much simpler than the central building, they frame the Taj from the river.

It is easy to leave the Taj Mahal with a sense of disbelief. Somehow, the wealth of marble and precious stones (35 different varieties of carnelian can be counted in a single carnation leaf on the tomb of Mumtaz Mahal) seems disassociated from the airy dream you first envision from a distance. But then, outside the gateway to the garden, where fountains used to play, look again. The Taj is real—a vivid, real dream.

OTHER AGRA LANDMARKS

Agra offers several other landmarks that would probably be far better known if it weren't for the illustrious Taj Mahal and the Agra Fort.

Another beautiful mausoleum, in a more subdued key than the Taj, is the tomb of Itmad-ud-Daula, father of Queen Nur Jahan and grandfather of Mumtaz Mahal. Though small, this monument (three miles north of the Taj on the left bank of the Yamuna) is wonderfully proportioned; some call it more pleasing than the Taj. Through a gate near the river, you enter a garden with a two-storied tomb of white marble standing on a plinth of red sandstone. Almost the entire surface is covered in mosaics inlaid with semiprecious stones: geometrics, flowers, and typically Persian designs. Four small minarets rise up from the corners of the lower story. Within the sepulchral chamber, light penetrates through more screens of marble latticework. Actually, the tomb, a forerunner of the Taj, is the first Mogul building of all white marble, with designs even more delicate than those of the Taj Mahal.

The Chini-ka-Rauza, or China Tomb, lies half a mile north of the tomb of Itmad-ud-Daula. Its name apparently comes from the brilliant glazed tiles used in its mosaics. Afzal Khan, the prime minister of Shah Jahan and a Persian poet, and his wife are buried here. Not far from this tomb is the Rambagh (originally Arambagh, Garden of Leisure), designed by the Mogul Babur, according to one version of its origin. Babur's body was taken here before it was removed to Kabul. The Rambagh is supposed to be India's first Mogul garden.

Finally, mention should be made of the Jami Masjid, the huge congregational mosque of Agra built in 1648 by Shah Jahan's daughter, Jahanara.

Fatehpur Sikri, the Ghost City

Twenty-four miles west of Agra lies an imperial capital frozen in time. When Elizabethan Englishmen came to Fatehpur Sikri in 1583 to meet the great emperor Akbar, they were amazed. Here was a city exceeding London both in population and in grandeur. They lost count of the rubies, the diamonds, and the plush silks. Today, Fatehpur Sikri is deserted, left in solitude to reminisce over its past.

The history of the city began when Akbar, desperate because he had no heir, decided to visit a Moslem holy man, Salim Chisti, who lived in a small village. Chisti blessed Akbar and, in turn, the emperor was blessed with a son, whom he named Salim in honor of the holy man. Salim later took the throne as Jahangir. The grateful Akbar decided to move his capital to the village, where he died in 1569.

Fatehpur Sikri lies on a rocky ridge about two miles long and one mile wide. But this ridge was no problem to the Mogul emperor, who simply sliced off the top to find room for his city. At the foot of the ridge, he waved his hand once more and created an artificial lake measuring 20 miles around. The lake formed one side of the city; the three others were protected by massive walls pierced by nine gates. In all, the circumference of the capital was seven miles. Here, as at the Agra Fort, you find the same specialization of buildings with impressive public halls and a delightful private residence under separate roofs. But there is more unity in the architecture of Fatehpur Sikri.

FATEHPUR SIKRI

(NOT TO SCALE)

1. KWABGAH
2. CHESSBOARD
3. DIWAN-I-KHAS
4. ANKH MICHAULI and ASTROLOGER'S SEAT
5. PANCH MAHAL
6. MARIAM'S HOUSE
7. JODH BAI'S PALACE
8. BIRBAL'S PALACE
9. LADIES MOSQUE
10. BULAND DARWAZA (GATE OF VICTORY)
11. SALIM CHISTI'S TOMB
12. COURT POETS' PAVILIONS

○ WELL   ◇ BATH

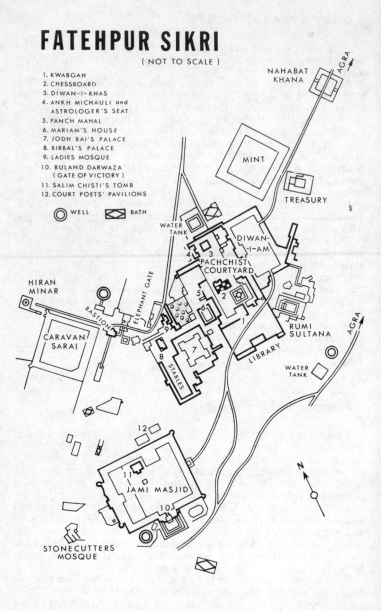

Momentos of Mogul Power

Probably the greatest structure in the city is the Jami Masjid, the imperial mosque built around 1575. For miles around, you can see the victory gateway, Buland Darwaza, rising above the capital. This massive triumphant portal, which sums up Mogul power, was built by Akbar after he conquered Gujarat. Its dimensions are in keeping with its purpose: 134 feet high over a base of steps that climb another 34 feet. Beware of the bees that have their own fortifications here and the phoney guides who badger and bluff.

Jama Masjid

This mosque was designed to hold 10,000 worshipers. Although not as sophisticated as the Jama Masjid of Delhi, it excels in its symmetry and in the geometric inlay designs that cover its interior. Note the deliberate use of Hindu elements in the design (especially the decorations on the pillars)—more examples of Akbar's wish for religious harmony so frequently mirrored in his architecture. The courtyard of the mosque contains a mausoleum that paradoxically, is the most living part of the city. Here, behind walls of marble lace, lies the tomb of Salim Chisti under an elaborate canopy inlaid with mother-of-pearl. Every year, thousands of childless women (Moslem and Hindu) come to pray at the tomb of this Mohammedan saint for the same blessing he conferred on the emperor four centuries ago.

Diwan-i-Am

The other main public building of Fatehpur Sikri is the Diwan-i-Am (Hall of Public Audiences), more than 350 long, which consists of cloisters surrounding a courtyard that contains the Hall of Judgment. Here, Akbar sat on a throne flanked by marble screens and handed down his decisions as the chief justice of his subjects. Those who were condemned to die were supposedly impaled, hanged, or trampled under the feet of an elephant. In a lighter vein, Akbar played pachisi (early form of Parcheesi) with slave girls as living pieces in the courtyard behind the Diwan-i-Am.

Diwan-i-Khas

The Hall of Private Audience (Diwan-i-Khas) has an unimpressive exterior; but inside the hall, divided by galleries, stands a strange stone column blossoming into a flat-topped flower. Elaborate designs on the column sweep up to the top, which served as Akbar's throne, used when he was receiving ambassadors or nobles. Four stone bridges connect the top of the pillar to the surrounding galleries. The intent behind such a lofty seat is not clear, but apparently it enabled the emperor to receive visitors without having to mingle with them.

Though small in size and not much more than a summer house in appearance (it is open and covered with an umbrella), the Astrologer's seat near the Diwan-i-Khas was an important cog in the Mogul empire. Open-minded Akbar was so intrigued by the trust his Hindu subjects placed in astrologers that he, too, consulted an astrologer daily. The astrologer determined what color the emperor wore each day (Akbar's favorite colors were yellow, purple, and violet).

Ankh Michauli

Nearby is the Ankh Michauli (its name means blindman's bluff). Supposedly, Akbar loved playing this "grope-and-feel" game inside this building with the ladies of his harem. Fantasy and whimsy prevail in the decorative stone monsters who were supposed to frighten thieves away from the crown jewels believed to have been kept in secret niches carved into the walls.

Jodh Bai's Palace

A feminine touch exists in the Jodh Bai Palace, built for Akbar's Hindu wife. Moslem and Hindu architecture blend together once again: the sculpture found inside the rooms is Hindu while Mogul domes extend above the top of the palace. Living quarters and bathrooms were located around a large interior court. An upper-story room, walled in by a red sandstone screen, is called the "Palace of Winds," and it may have been the coolest vantage point from which the ladies of the court could watch what was happening without being seen.

Joan of Arc—India-style

Fatehpur Sikri can be the end of your trip or the starting point for an excursion south to Jhansi. Here, the Rani of Jhansi, Lakshmi Bai, began her career as the Joan of Arc of India. The widow of the Rajah of Jhansi, she decided to succeed her husband as the head of his tiny state after he died in 1853, leaving no male heir. Unfortunately, the British had just proclaimed a new policy of taking over princely states whose rulers had left no son. They pensioned off the young widow rani, still in her twenties.

The rani joined the Sepoy Revolt (also known as the Indian Mutiny) in 1857. In April 1858, a British general captured Jhansi, but the rani slipped through his lines. After a wild ride on horseback, she reached Kalpi and joined another rebel leader, but their troops were defeated on May 22. The rani and her followers moved into Gwalior Fort, which was immediately attacked by the British. On June 17, 1858, the rani rode out of the fort, holding the reins of her horse in her teeth, and took the offensive: wielding her sword with both hands. Dressed as a man like the Maid of Orleans, she was shot and sliced by a saber. She slumped to her death clutching her horse. Her room in the old fort of Jhansi is now a shrine of Indian independence.

The medieval city, Orchha, is seven miles south of Jhansi. Built by the Bundela rajputs, it has a fortress with some exquisite palaces; most noteworthy is the seventeenth-century Jahangir Mahal, built by Bir Singh Ju Deo, friend of Prince Salim, the future Mogul Emperor Jahangir. Murals in the Lakshmi Temple are fine examples of Bundela art.

Deogarh and Shivpuri

Another different style of architecture is at Deogarh, 66 miles south of Jhansi and eight miles east of the famed Dasavatara Temple. Built 1,500 years ago, this temple is a classic of Gupta art, with its tapering tower and its four portals standing majestically over stone steps. Otherwise, you might prefer to stick to the main road and head west from Jhansi to Shivpuri, 32 miles away, the one-time summer capital of the Majarajah of Gwalior. Here, the beauty is natural.

Shivpuri, on a cool, wooded plateau at an altitude of 1,400 feet, is on the edge of a national park where you may encounter tigers or other wild animals. Thirteen miles before Shivpuri on the Jhansi road stands a ruined village, Surwaya, with an old Hindu monastery. But Shivpuri is far better known for relaxation than history. In the park, outside town, a silvery lake (Sakhya Sagar or Chandpatha), with seven miles of shoreline, is inlaid in Mogul fashion against a green setting of wooded hills. From Shivpuri, a delightful road or a toylike railway leads to Gwalior; then it's almost a straight line back to Delhi.

PRACTICAL INFORMATION FOR AGRA

WHEN TO GO. The best time to visit is from mid-October to March. The mornings and evenings are cool, the days warm and sunny. From early March to the end of May, it's hot. Temperatures in the day can soar to over 100 degrees F. Visitors are advised to sightsee in the early morning or late afternoon. Between mid-June and early July, the monsoon arrives, lasting until the end of September. If you want to see the Taj in the light of the full moon, check first that the monument is open. The authorities have been closing it at night because of political unrest.

HOW TO GET THERE. By Air. The best way to reach Agra is by early-morning *Indian Airlines* flights from Delhi (about 30 minutes). Daily Indian Airlines flights also connect Agra with Khajuraho and Varanasi, and daily (except Mondays) flights from Bombay and Jaipur. *Vayudoot* flies four times a week into Agra from Delhi and Varanasi, almost daily into Gwalior from Delhi, and three times weekly from Bhopal.

By Bus. Both *India Tourism Development Corporation* (ITDC) and *Delhi Tourism Development Corporation* (DTDC) provide inexpensive (about Rs. 200 for one day tour) deluxe air-conditioned bus tours from Delhi to Agra–Fatehpur Sikri–Sikandra. For details and booking, contact ITDC, L Block, Connaught Place, New Delhi (open 10 A.M. – 5 P.M., closed Sundays, tel. 350331); DTDC, N–36 Connaught Place (middle circle), New Delhi (open same hours, tel. 3313637). *U.P. Road Transport Corp.* runs intercity buses. In Agra, call UPRTC, West Station (Fort Bus Station), 74141; or East Station (Idgah Bus Station), 64198.

By Train. From Delhi, take the *Taj Express,* which runs daily, leaving early A.M. and returning that evening (about a three-hour journey). Taj Express and numerous other trains continue from Agra to Gwalior (inquire at Agra Railway station, tel. 72515). Once you arrive at the train station in Agra, you can take a day tour to the Agra monuments, Fatehpur Sikri, and Sikandra, conducted by Uttar Pradesh Road Transport Corp. (a deluxe bus with guide, fare: Rs. 40). Tour begins at 10:40 A.M. from the Agra Cant. Railway Station and returns in time for the Taj Express departure to Delhi.

From Jaipur, take the *Jaipur Agra Fort Express.* Inquire at the Jaipur Railway Station, tel. 72121.

By Car. Agra is 200 km from Delhi; 230 km from Jaipur; and 119 km from Gwalior. The roads are good from any direction. The round trip from Delhi to Agra (including Fatehpur Sikri) via hired car and driver is about Rs. 900.

TOURIST INFORMATION. In Agra, two good sources of information that offer different brochures are *Uttar Pradesh State Tourist Office,* 64 Taj Rd. (tel. 75852); and the *Government of India Tourist Office,* 191 The Mall, tel. 72377. The Government of India has the best map of Agra. It's wise to come armed with your own detailed information on the monuments if you want to get into the nitty-gritty of the architecture. Guides can be good, but their spiel has a worn-out and overused superficial edge. Hours of tourist offices are generally Monday–Saturday, 10 A.M.–5 P.M.

In **Jhansi,** *Tourist Bureau,* Prakash Hotel, Civil Lines, tel. 1267.

ACCOMMODATIONS. The full range of accommodations is available in Agra. For the other areas (Fatehpur Sikri, Gwalior, Mathura, Shivpuri) facilities are limited. Room rates are based on double occupancy: *Expensive,* Rs. 500 and above; *Moderate,* Rs. 250 – Rs. 500; *Inexpensive,* Rs. 250 and less. Most Western-style hotels accept traveler's checks and major credit cards (*Diner's Club* or *American Express*). During peak season (mid-October to March), book early at better hotels.

AGRA

Expensive

Agra Ashok. 6–B, Mall Rd., four km from the airport; tel. 67801. 58 rooms, most with Western amenities, air-conditioning, fans, TVs, a swimming pool, shopping arcade, restaurant, coffee shop, bar, and room service.

Clarks Shiraz. 54 Taj Rd. eight km from the airport; tel. 72421. 147 rooms. No TV, but amenities include air-conditioning, a swimming pool, shopping arcade, restaurant, coffee shop, bar, and room service.

Taj View. Fatehabad Rd., nine km from the airport; tel. 64171. 100 rooms, with air-conditioning, TVs, restaurants, a bar, swimming pool, health club, and room service.

Welcomgroup Mughal Sheraton. Taj Ganj, 12 km from the airport; tel. 64701; 200 rooms. Deluxe rooms have view of Taj. Award-winning super-duper design. Air-conditioning, TVs, a swimming pool, health club, restaurants, a bar, an observation deck, and cultural events. Even an elephant ride to take you to and from the Taj.

Moderate

Hotel Amar. Tourist Complex Area, Fatehabad Rd., six km from the airport; tel. 65696–8. Cable: MAYUR. 39 rooms with many amenities, air-conditioning, TVs, a restaurant, bar. New hotel.

Welcomgroup Mumtaz. Fatehbad Rd., 11 km from the airport; tel. 64771–6, 40 rooms. Many Western amenities, plus the use of many of the facilities at the more expensive Mughal Sheraton. A restaurant, bar, shopping arcade, TVs, and air-conditioning. Some rooms offer a view of the Taj.

Inexpensive

Grand Hotel. 137 Station Rd., five km from the airport; one km from the railroad station; tel. 74014. 31 rooms, some air-conditioned; a restaurant, bar, tennis court, and badminton. A popular place.

Laurie's Hotel. Mahatma Gandhi Rd., five km from the airport; 2½ km from the railroad station; tel. 72536. 28 rooms, some air-cooled, and a restaurant. Decent, but not great.

Mayur Tourist Complex. Fatehabad Rd., six km from the airport; tel. 67302. 25 rooms. A restaurant, bar, children's park, and garden. Charming bungalows, each with a little porch. Decor of cottages is regional style. The best inexpensive place in town—a good deal for the money.

JHANSI

Inexpensive

Jhansi Hotel. Shastri Marg, three km from the railroad station; tel. 1360. Cable: ABBOTT. 19 rooms, some air-conditioned. Has a restaurant and bar; TVs in some rooms. Okay for the price.

DINING OUT. Maybe it's because this city has one of the wonders of the world and is a heavy tourist draw, but food can be pricy by Indian standards. Tasty—but with a hefty bite out of your budget if you choose to eat at the first-class hotels. Prices are based on a three-course dinner for one person, excluding beverage, tip, and taxes: *Expensive,* over Rs. 60; *Moderate,* Rs. 30 – Rs. 60; *Inexpensive,* under Rs. 30. Most of the restaurants accept major credit cards.

JAGRAT

Expensive

Bagh-E-Bahar. Mughal Sheraton, Taj Ganj; tel. 64701. Specialty: Continental. Dance band at night. Breakfast, lunch, dinner. Luxurious, on the verge of a movie set. Reservations required.

Mahjong. Mughal Sheraton, Taj Ganj; tel. 64701. Chinese food. Oriental decor will definitely get you into the spirit of chopsticks. Lunch and dinner. Reservations required.

Mughal Room. Clarks Shiraz, 54 Taj Rd.; tel. 72421. Mughlai, Indian, Continental, and Chinese. Good food, quieter ambience, except sometimes there's live Western music. Better place when the music is Indian ghazels. Rooftop restaurant. Lunch, dinner. Reservations required.

Nauratna. Mughlai Sheraton, Taj Gang; tel. 64701. Specialty: Indian. Excellent Mughlai, Kashmiri, and Punjabi food. Indian music. Lunch and dinner. Reservations required. Again there's a heavy emphasis on decor—call it "high-tech" Indian.

Rang Mahal. Hotel Galaxy Ashok, Fetahabad Rd.; tel. 64171. Mughlai, Indian, Chinese, Continental. Lunch and dinner. Entertainment.

Moderate

Capri Restaurant. Hari Parbat; tel. 77077. Continental and Indian. Basic decor; emphasis is on good food. Lunch, dinner.

Kwality Caterers and Confectioners. 2 Taj Rd., Sadar Bazar; tel. 72525. Continental, Indian, Chinese, Tandoori. Very good. 9 A.M. – midnight. Recorded music and simple decor.

Mumtaz Restaurant. Hotel Galaxy Ashok, Fatehabad Rd., Taj Ganj; tel. 64171. Indian and Continental foods. Open 10 A.M. – midnight.

Inexpensive

Sonam. 51 Taj Rd. Breakfast, lunch, and dinner. Snacks and Chinese and Indian food. No frills-dining in a high-ceiling room.

HOW TO GET AROUND. From the Airport. There's good passenger coach service to hotels from the airport (Rs. 10). Taxis run about Rs. 30 – Rs. 35 to most main hotels and Agra.

By Bus. *City Bus Service* (tel. 64198) runs buses throughout Agra. Contact for details.

By Taxi. Rate: Rs. 1.50 per km. Make sure the meter is working or establish a prior before entering.

By Auto Rickshaw. Cheaper than cabs, and handy in the traffic-jammed streets.

By Bike Rickshaw. Quite pleasant. At most Rs. 10 per hour. They're the most fun and can take you all around Agra.

By Rented Car and Driver. Good only if you want to travel beyond Agra and maintain your own schedule. Cars are available through *ITDC,* 6–B, The Mall, tel. 73271; *Travel House,* Mughal Sheraton, Fatehabad Road, Taj Ganj, tel. 64701; *Sita World Travel,* A–2, Shopping Arcade, Sadar Bazar, tel. 64978; *Travel House,* Mughal Sheraton, Fatehabad Road, Taj Ganj, tel. 64701; and *Travel Corporation I, Pvt. Ltd,* Hotel Clarks Shiraz, 54 Taj Road, tel. 72421. Figure about Rs. 2 per km. plus night halt charges. Book ahead.

JHANSI

By Tongas (horse drawn carriages). Cheap and about the only way to get around here other than walking.

TOURS. *UPRTC* (tel. 74141 or 64198) and *ITDC* (tel. 72377) offer daily sightseeing tours of Agra–Fatepur Sikri–Sikandra with a guide in a deluxe coach. Rs. 40. Call for booking and further details.

$P£ **FOREIGN CURRENCY EXCHANGE. Agra.** The deluxe Western-style hotels (Taj, Welcomgroup, Clarks, Ashok) have money-exchange services. The following banks will also cash traveler's checks: *Central Bank of India,* on Mahatma Gandhi Road; *State Bank of India,* also on Mahatma Gandhi Road. Hours generally: Monday – Friday, 10 A.M. – 2 P.M.; sometimes open Saturdays until noon.

Jhansi. *State Bank of India,* Civil Lines, tel. 534. Banks have long lines. Clerks often take tea breaks, but that's India.

 SEASONAL EVENTS. February/March. At Mathura and environs, *Holi* celebrates the advent of spring. Wear old clothes: Messy red water thrown liberally, with everyone fair game. At Barsana (near Mathura), the legendary home of Radha (consort of the lovable avatar of Vishnu, Lord Krishna), the women challenge the men of nearby Nandgaon (home of Krishna) in numerous weird battles that get fairly frisky. Contact U.P. Tourist Bureau, Agra (tel. 75852) for exact dates for this and other seasonal events.

August/September. In Agra and Mathura, Janmashtami celebrates Krishna's birthday. Nightlong prayers, temple hymns. Festive.

October/November. In Mathura, *Diwali* marks the start of the Hindu New Year, most festive of Indian festivals. Thousands of candles, and flickering lights illuminate the city, homes, and public buildings. A noisy, firecracker good time.

In Mathura, see a *puja* (prayer service) held every evening at the Vishram Ghat on the Ganges. A beautiful ceremony that ends with the release of flickering oil lamps into the holy river.

 **HISTORIC SITES.** *Agra Fort.* Construction started with Akbar in 1565 and continued through the next two generations (Jahangir and Shah Jahan. Red sandstone fort and white marble palaces. Enter via the Amar Singh Gate, then follow the extensive description in this chapter under The Essay Section. Open daily, sunrise to sunset. Rs. 2. If you agree to a guide, make sure he's legitimate. Only pay a guide who has been approved by the government.

Chini-ka-Rauza (China Tomb) is a half mile north of Itmad-ud-Daulah. Constructed by Afzal Khan, the prime minister of Shah Jahan and a Persian poet. The building is sadly neglected. Open sunrise to sunset. Free.

Itmad-ud-Daulah. The tomb of Nur Jahan's father is three miles north of the Taj on the left bank of the Yamuna. Built 1622–1628 by the Empress Nur Jahan; her mother is also buried here. First Mogul structure constructed entirely of marble. Open sunrise to sunset. Rs. 2.

Jami Masjid, huge congregational mosque of Agra built in 1648 by Shah Jahan's daughter, Jahanara.

Ram Bagh, near China Tomb. Earliest example of a Mogul garden designed by the Emperor Babur in 1526. Not well maintained. Open sunrise to sunset. Free.

Akbar's Mausoleum was in Sikandra. 10 km from Agra, designed and begun by the emperor in 1602 before his death and completed by his son Hahangir in 1613. Graceful red sandstone and marble construction that represents a fusion of Hindu and Moslem architecture. Rs. 2.

 MUSEUMS. *Taj Mahal Museum,* within the Taj Mahal, Agra, contains a collection of findings from the Mogul period and a history of the Taj. In Jhansi, the *Archaeological Museum,* Rani Mahal, is the former home of the heroine Rani Lakshmi Bai. A good collection of sculptures from the ninth to the twelfth centuries. Open 8 A.M. – 5 P.M. Free. *Mathura Archeological Museum,* Dampier Park, Mathura. One of India's best museums. A great collection of sculpture going back to the fifth century B.C., beautiful sculptures of the Mathura school that flourished in the region, and the art of the Kushan period (the most comprehensive collection in existence). Plus good bronzes and terra cottas. Closed Monday and official holidays. Open July 1–April 15 (10:30 A.M.–4:30 P.M.); April 16 – June 30 (7:30 A.M. – 12:30 P.M.). Guides can be arranged at the museum for a nominal fee.

Taj Mahal. A memorial tomb created by Shah Jahan for his Queen Mumtaz Mahal. Started in 1632, completed around 1653. An architectural masterpiece of red sandstone and marble. Once you enter, follow the description under *Taj Mahal: Monument to Love.* Open sunrise to sunset. Rs 2. Might be open late on the nights of the full moon; but the government has been keeping it closed because of political unrest. Check with the tourist department.

Fatehpur Sikri, 24 miles west of Agra. After a sixteenth-century mystic, Salim Chisti, blessed the Mogul Emperor Akbar with a much-wanted male heir, Akbar decided to build his capital in the mystic's tiny community. He constructed his impressive city on a rocky eminence, enclosing three sides with walls, the fourth protected by a lake. The well-preserved royal edifices occupied a central position; lesser buildings were scattered around them; with the rest of the space taken up by the people's dwellings, now vanished. Open sunrise to sunset. Rs. 2.

Gobinda Palace in Datia was built in the seventeenth century by the Raj Bir Singh Deo. It's a lovely palace, seven stories high, sitting on the top of a hill.

SHOPPING. An excursion to Agra is not a great opportunity for shopping; too many hawkers sell junk. But if shopping is in your blood, Agra is famous for its special kind of marble inlay work on trinket and cigarette boxes and other souvenirs, reminiscent of what you have seen at the Taj or Itmad-ud-Daula's mausoleum. In the bazaar area, one can see craftsmen chiseling away at small pieces of marble or semiprecious stones before setting them. One of the outstanding local crafts is colored embroidery, generally done with gold and silver thread and often including semiprecious stones. Such pieces are ideal for summer handbags and evening bags. The area is also famous for its carpets.

Your best shopping bet in Agra is the *Uttar Pradesh Government Handicrafts Emporium* within the Taj complex, or the *Indian Handicraft Centre,* opposite Circuit House, near the Taj Mahal. If you are good at bargaining, you can try the shops at Sadar Bazar. Mathura's shopping centers are Tilak Dwar, Chatta and Naya Bazar.

NIGHTLIFE AND BARS. In Agra, bars in all the better hotels usually serve until 11 P.M., as does the bar in the Usha Kiran Palace, Gwalior. Otherwise, nightlife is rather sedate in this area.

RAJASTHAN

Shrine to Chivalry

by
KATHLEEN COX

Desert with dunes, scrub, cactus, and rock, fertile green tracks, hills, ravines, enchanting lakes, and jungles—all exist in Rajasthan, the second largest state in India. Geography, specifically the Aravalli Mountain Range, cuts the state into two distinct regions: northwestern and southwestern, with the western part (the Thar Desert) only sparcely populated.

Rajasthan is also rich in history, legend, and lore. Formerly called Rajputana ("Abode of Kings") the area was originally made up of at least 22 princely states, each ruled by a proud *Rajput* (prince). From the earliest centuries, the conflict for control over Northern India between the Hindu Rajput rulers, who were (and still are) great horsemen, and the powerful Moslems was passionately contested in a series of military campaigns and intrigues—some of them downright sneaky. One story has an eleventh-century Hindu guide, supposedly in league with an invading Moslem army, generously helping the soldiers get lost in the desert where they nearly died of thirst. Or consider the exploits of the seventeenth-century Mogul Emperor Akbar, whose "strategy" was the reverse of divide and conquer. To expand his empire, he took a Rajput princess of Jaipur as one of his wives (his son and successor Jahangir was the product of this union). And several of Akbar's most trusted generals were Rajputs who had previously fought against him. One of them, Man Singh, was even appointed governor of a great imperial province.

Whatever the outcome of a battle, the Rajputs were masterful warriors, who held onto an unwavering sense of honor and pride in a tradition that decreed, when the battle went against them, that they had to make the supreme sacrifice. Clothed in saffron robes of immolation, they went to battle and died to a man. If the sign of defeat was displayed on the battlefield, the women in the fortress performed the rite of *seti,* the Hindu act of throwing oneself into a flaming pyre—far superior to the indignity of capture. The Rajputs, who claim direct lineage with Hindu divinities and the heroes of India's great epic poems (the *Ramayana* and the *Mahabharata*), are in a class by themselves in world history.

Even when these independent rulers were forced to merge after Independence, each one kept title to an impressive accumulation of palaces, private lands, jewels, and miscellaneous mind-boggling possessions and, of course, none gave any thought to compromising his princely lifestyle. To compensate each ruler for the loss of control over his state and subjects, the maharajah also received a "privy purse," which was paid out annually until 1973, when Prime Minister Indira Gandhi decided that the princes had been paid enough. Mrs. Gandhi also cut off many of the royal privileges.

Without the stipend, some of the maharajahs proved they were poor businessmen and nearly went broke (many had to sell their palaces and live off their horded wealth). The elimination of pomp and privileges reduced them all to a humbler status; some turned their exclusive estates into fancy hotels catering to the upper crust.

In spirit, however, Rajasthan is still the legendary land of the Raj. Forts and palaces, lakes and gardens—all steeped in romance and chivalry—bear witness to a history of conquest and power. Here, the best martial qualities of a race are linked to the refinements of courtesy and an elegant culture. Nowhere else can you see people more intrinsically Indian and more true to their heritage than in Rajasthan.

EXPLORING RAJASTHAN

JAIPUR

Encircled on all but the southern side by the rugged Aravalli hills with numerous peaks crowned by imposing forts, Jaipur, the capital of Rajasthan, still looks cradled and well protected. Jaipur takes its name from Maharajah Jai Singh II, who, in the early 1700s, became king of Amber at the age of 13. Precocious and inquisitive, the young king soon proved to be so distinguished a scholar and diplomat, that Aurangzeb, the reigning Mogul emperor, called him Sawai (One and a Quarter), his way of claiming the young boy's superiority over all his Rajput predecessors. History proved him right.

At that moment, the Mogul Empire was approaching dissolution. With the milder rule from Delhi, it no longer was necessary for the Rajputs to bury themselves in mountain fortresses. They could now come down to the fertile plains with impunity. So, not long after Jai Singh came to the throne, he realized the need to shift the capital from Amber, the ancient rock-bound stronghold of his ancestors, down to the new site in the adjoining valley.

In no time, Sawai Jai Singh could add architect and astronomer to his list of credentials. In 1727, he conceived and designed the bulk of his new capital, with its exquisite buildings of rose-colored terra cotta described in historical writings as the "tone of the autumn sunset."

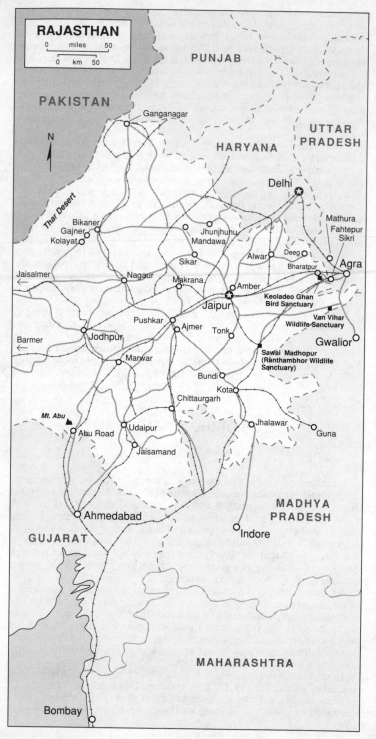

RAJASTHAN

0   miles   50

0   km   50

PAKISTAN

PUNJAB

Thar Desert

N

Ganganagar

HARYANA

UTTAR PRADESH

Delhi

Bikaner
Gajner
Kolayat

Jhunjhuhu
Mandawa

Mathura
Fahtepur
Sikri

Jaisalmer

Nagaur

Sikar

Alwar

Deeg

Agra

Bharatpur

Makrana

Amber

Keoladeo Ghan
Bird Sanctuary

Jaipur

Barmer

Pushkar

Ajmer

Tonk

Van Vihar
Wildlife Sanctuary

Jodhpur

Gwalior

Marwar

Sawai Madhopur
(Ranthambhor Wildlife
Sanctuary)

Bundi

Kota

Chittaurgarh

Mt. Abu

Jhalawar

Guna

Abu Road

Udaipur

Jaisamand

MADHYA
PRADESH

Ahmedabad

Indore

GUJARAT

MAHARASHTRA

Bombay

Although the Sawai's city is dusty and is crammed with camels, horses, dogs, and people, and is reminiscent of a gold-rush frontier town in its heyday, it remains an astonishing model of city planning. Enclosed inside fortified walls 20 feet high and guarded by eight gates, every aspect—the streets, sidewalks, height of the buildings, number and division of blocks—was based on geometric harmony, sound environmental and climatic considerations, and the intended use of each zone within the city. No detail escaped the sawai's attention. With pink and orange the dominant colors, the effect is magic at dusk even if the city is not kept up as it was in his time.

City Palace

Enter the City Palace complex through the Sireh Deorhi Gate, the principal entrance on the east. This complex, with its numerous pavilions, courtyards, chambers, and palace, was begun by the sawai, with further additions made by later maharajahs. Once you're inside the outer courtyard, the building directly in front is the Mubarak Mahal (guest pavilion), built by Maharajah Madho Singh II fewer than 100 years ago. This marble and sandstone building, with its delicate marble lacework, surrounds the original guest pavilion built earlier by the sawai. It now houses the textile and costume museum, which displays a collection of brocades, silks, and handblocked traditional royal garments and robes, plus musical instruments (all donated by the royal family). Some of the exhibits go back to the seventeenth century. Also visit the armory in the northwest corner of the courtyard. You'll see one of India's best collections of arms and weapons, including an 11-pound sword belonging to the Rajput General of Akbar.

Proceed to the inner courtyard (through the gateway guarded by two stone elephants) and enter the art gallery housed in the Diwan-i-Am (Hall of Public Audience). The building, constructed by another descendent, Pratap Singh, in the late 1700s, is gorgeous—huge—with rows of massive gray marble columns, the second largest chandelier in India, and a magnificent painted ceiling (painted in the 1930s for the maharajah's second marriage). The art gallery contains an extensive collection of miniatures from the Mogul and various Rajput schools, rare manuscripts, and gigantic carpets form the 1600s that were originally on the floors of the Amber Palace.

In the center of the inner courtyard, you'll notice a pair of mammoth silver urns inside the Hall of Private Audience, a raised platform with beautiful marble pillars. This building was used for formal banquets and ceremonial occasions. When Maharajah Madho Singh II sailed to England to attend the coronation of King Edward VII, these solid silver urns carried water from the Ganges (the only water the devout Hindu would dare drink)—a seemingly inefficient yet ostentatious method of hauling water.

From the inner courtyard, enter the Zanana courtyard on the left. Here you'll see the famous Chandra Mahal, or Moon Palace, with its seven stories that tower above the other structures. Built by Sawai Singh II, the lovely cream-hued building is still the official residence of the present Maharajah "Bubbles," or, more formerly, Lieutenant Colonel Sawai Bhawani Singh, who lives in the upper stories. The ground floor is also exquisite, with sumptuous chandeliers, murals, and a quasi-three-dimensional painting of an old maharajah.

Adjoining the palaces are the Jai Niwas gardens (off limits to the paying public), which offer the romantic prospect of splashing fountains and ornamental water. A legend claims that the Rajah Jagat Singh, oppressed by the heat of the palace, frequently escaped into some shady corner of this greenery. From here, he supposedly amused himself by exchanging love letters with his *zenana* (harem)—the letters dutifully carried back and forth in the mouth of his favorite dog. A monument to this trusty hound stands in the garden—his reward for his services as "post dog."

Jantar Mantar

Not content with designing this famous palace, Jai Singh also supervised the design and construction of five remarkable observatories in northern India. The largest and best preserved—the Jantar Mantar—is in Jaipur near the entrance to the City Palace. Built of masonry, marble, and brass, it is equipped with gigantic, futuristic scientific instruments, called *yantras,* each one designed by the Sawai "Newton of the East," who was well aware of European developments in this field and wanted to create observatories that would outdo anything already in existence—an attitude befitting this maharajah.

Abstract and weirdly beautiful, each yantra is uncannily accurate in measuring various celestial data. Samrat Yantra, a 90-foot-high right-angle triangle, is a sundial that tells local time that is accurate to within a few seconds. The *dhruva,* a peculiar brass slab, determines the position of the North Star at night. Numerous other *yantras* determine celestial latitude and longitude, and serve as alternative sundials (some relating to the zodiac). Of course, Jai Singh provided himself with an observer's seat from which he supervised his scientific calculations.

Hava Mahal—"Palace of Winds"

Another must visit in the old city is the Hawal Mahal (Palace of Winds), a landmark built by Maharajah Sawai Pratap Singh in Jaipur in 1799. The Hawa Mahal is located on the bustling commercial thoroughfare called Siredeori Bazar (directly after Johari Bazar heading north). The curious five-story structure, which gets its name from the westerly winds that send cool breezes through the windows, is elaborate and fanciful. Constructed of pink sandstone, its delicate honeycomb design glows in the evening light. Every story has semioctagonal overhanging windows, each with a perforated screen, from which the ever-discreet women of the court could view the activities on the street below. The roof is curvilinear, with domes and finials, which adds to the general effect of lightness and delicacy.

Ram Niwas Garden and the Albert Hall Museum

Outside the walled city, relax in quiet at the Ram Niwas Garden, then see the strange Albert Hall Museum located in the beautiful grounds. The sandstone and marble building, constructed in the Indo-Saracenic style in the late 1800s, contains eclectic displays, not your ordinary run of paintings and sculpture. Many of the unexpected exhibits offer convenient cultural explanations for the curious foreigner. Look at the one devoted to *Mehendi,* the Indian art of decorating hands and feet with henna, and the one that identifies the folk instruments you may have heard and dances you may have seen in Rajasthan. Upstairs you'll find a table display of numerous clay models that demonstrate the vast range of yoga positions mastered by the physically agile yogi.

Amber Palace

For six centuries, the capital of Rajasthan and the nucleus of Rajput history, Amber is now little more than a deserted palace, surrounded by majestic ramparts. The construction, started by Maharajah Man Singh in the early 1700s and completed 100 years later, is a blend of Rajput and Mogul influence. The palace, which rises on the slopes of a steep hill behind the Maota Lake, retains an aura of great beauty. As soon as you enter the Valley of Flowers and pass through the pink gate, Amber Palace glows with variegated colors and nobility.

To get to the palace, you can either walk or arrive, pompously enough, on the back of a gaily caparisoned elephant. This archaic means of transportation explains the unusual height of the palace gateways. Inside the palace, the principal hall, known as the Hall of Victory, presents a galaxy of decorative art—panels of alabaster with fine inlay work of the tenderest hues, together with every kind of workmanship for which Jaipur is famous. And, typical of the Mogul period, the rooms are essentially small and intimate, while the successive courtyards and narrow passages are particularly Rajput.

Each room shows some vestige of its former glory, especially the Sheesh Mahal (Chamber of Mirrors). When you step inside, close the doors, strike a match, and watch the ceiling twinkle and glow. Numerous narrow flights of stairs lead up to the royal apartments that provide the best views of the valley, the lovely palace courtyards, the formal gardens abutting an octagon pool that edges the lake, and the ancient fortress (the Jaigash Fort) that stands guard from the crest of the hill above you. Vast and somber, its vaults still hide the treasures of Jaipur —or at least that's the rumor.

Alwar, Deeg, and Bharatpur

Continuing northeast, the next place of interest is Alwar, built into the jagged Aravalli Hills. Alwar, founded in 1771, is dominated by its medieval fort that crowns a conical rock. Once the capital of the princely state of the same name, Alwar contains a city palace (Vinai Vilas Mahal) that was constructed in the late 1800s. The palace is separated from the hill by the Sagar Tank (an artificial water tank). The upstairs is a museum devoted to manuscripts (over 7,000, the most notable being an illuminated copy of the Koran in Arabic with Persian translation in red lettering) and paintings, including a rare collection of Mogul and Rajasthani miniatures. An armory contains the personal weapons of Akbar, Jahangir, Shah Jahan, and Aurangzeb, with hilts of gold studded with jewels.

Also visit Gunijankhana, the feudal academy of arts, and see excellent examples of the Alwar School of painting. Unlike conventional Rajput paintings, the pictures here of dancing girls do not conceal the limbs and sensuousness of Rajput women. Also see the marble mausoleum of Bakhtawar Singh (1781–1815)—an excellent example of Indo-Islamic architecture—south of the Sagar Tank. Another spot to visit is the Purjan Vihar, a public park on the outskirts of town, with its renowned Summer House.

Siliserh Lake, about eight miles from Alwar, is fringed by a dense forest and adorned with *chhatris* (domed cenotaphs). A magnificent former hunting lodge, built by a nineteenth-century maharajah for his queen, and now converted into a hotel, is nestled in the hills and overlooks the lovely lake. Travel another 18 miles to Sariska, a tiger reserve surrounded by the Aravallis. Here, too, you'll find a royal hunting lodge, the Sariska Palace (now a hotel), set on the edge of the sanctuary.

Continuing east from Alwar you reach Deeg, renowned for its massive fort and pleasure palaces (built by Badan Singh in the 1700s), surrounded by sumptuously laid-out gardens, tanks, and fountains, added by his son, Suraj Mal. Richly carved columns, cornices, and eaves are arranged with an exquisite sense of balance; kiosks are scattered about like sentinels, giving the palace an air of mystery and romance. The largest of the palaces, Gopal Bhavan, contains a curious marble swing. Originally the property of the Nabobs of Oudh, this eccentric plaything was carried off to Deeg by Maharajah Jawahar Singh. (Indeed, a good portion of the gorgeous inlaid marble you see here was stolen from Mogul Palace in Agra and Delhi.) Among the other buildings are the Suraj Bhavan, built of marble and ornamented with semiprecious inlaid stones; the Nand Bhavan, the big hall of audience; and the Machhi Bhavan, a decorative pavilion surrounded by fountains and ornamental ponds.

Bharatpur, capital of the former state of the same name and one of the chief cities of Rajasthan, is some 22 miles farther south. Founded by Suraj Mal, considered an outstanding military figure of the eighteenth century, Bharatpur is famous for its Lohagarh (Iron Fort), which successfully repulsed numerous Mogul and British attacks. No wonder—Suraj Mal's fortifications were an ingenious design: two massive mud ramparts, each encircled by a moat of formidable dimensions (over 150 feet wide and about 50 feet deep), which surrounded the central fortress built of solid masonry that had yet another ditch around it filled with water. Cannon balls stuck in the mud walls and caused no damage to the stone bastions of the inner fort. To get a better idea of the scale of the fortification, keep in mind this fact: The outer mud rampart, which is now demolished, had a seven-mile circumference. The inner fortress, which was octagonal in shape, had two gates, both trophies of war captured from Delhi. The central and most important tower of the fort, set up in 1765, commemorated the successful assault on the Mogul capital. The museum contains sculptures and other testimonies to the art and culture of the region.

Shekhavati

From Bharatpur, head back to Jaipur, then continue on a northwesterly route until you arrive at Sikar (about 60 miles from Jaipur). From here, give yourself a day or two to take an interesting and picturesque excursion through an area called Shekhavati (Garden of Shekha). First, head northeast from Sikar to Nawalgarh (about 18 miles away)—a beautiful village with hundreds of *havelis* (traditional Rajput homes with interior courtyards). Many of the older havelis have colorful frescoes covering the exterior and interior walls. You have now entered the land of the wealthy Marwaris, successful merchants on this formerly important and historic caravan route and great patrons. From the nineteenth-century houses that remain, the Marwaris were obviously devoted to the visual arts—recording contemporary world events and their passions on the walls of their homes. Go farther north to Mandawa, with its giant medieval fort, and spend a night as the guest of the maharajah in his well-appointed seventeenth-century castle/hotel, with its stunning views. See more havelis and then continue in your leisurely pace to Fatehpur, a small city. All along the route you will pass through villages with color and fanciful art.

Bikaner

About 100 miles due west of Fatehpur is Bikaner. Founded at the close of the fifteenth century by Rao Bika, a descendent of Jodhai, the founder of Jodhpur, Bikaner stands aloof on high ground surrounded by walls and the Thar Desert. Visit the sixteenth-century Junagarh Fort built by Raja Raj Singh, an outstanding general of the Mogul Emperor Akbar. Within this massive edifice (located in the heart of the city), protected by a moat, are housed some of the rarest gems of Rajput architecture. Especially beautiful are the ancient palaces of sandstone and marble, including the Chandra Mahal (Moon Palace) and the Phool Mahal (Flower Palace), with lavish mirror work, carvings, and paintings. There are also temples, a mosque, and Har Mandir, a handsome chapel in which royal weddings and important births were celebrated. Also visit Durbar Hall, built in the Mogul style and lavishly decorated with paintings. Floral bouquets, set in red and gold borders, gilded leaf work, and vases are the leading motifs. Two or three stories high, with slender columns, cusped arches, and intricate screens, palaces rise on all sides. The zenana is separated by a broad court with paneled niches. Gilt reliefs, glass mosaics, and lacelike mirrors adorn graceful and intimate apartments.

Bikaner is also the home of the famous Camel Corps, still useful in desert warfare. Outside the city are other palaces and temples—imposing edifices of carved red sandstone. Jain temples and monasteries abound in this city and neighborhood. Most of them early sixteenth century, they are rich in carvings. Five miles away are the *chhatris,* cenotaphs of the rulers of Bikaner.

For a squeamish experience, visit the Karni Mata Temple in Deshnok, about 20 miles from Bikaner, on the road to Jodhpur. This temple devoted to Karni Mata, an incarnation of Durga, is also the home of hundreds of rats, which are considered sacred and roam freely inside the temple. It is said that if a rat touches you or, better still, jumps on you, you'll be blessed with a lifetime of good luck (not rabies).

Jaisalmer: Island in the Sand

Some 300 miles in a southwesterly direction is the ancient city of Jaisalmer, founded by Rawal Jaisal in 1156. Lying at the extreme edge of Rajastan, Jaisalmer is a tiny jewel in the heart of the Thar, the great Indian desert. Once the capital of the Bhati Rajputs, the medieval city rises in a sea of sand on a low range of hills surrounded by a stone wall three miles around—a towering vision in delicate yellow hue—only infrequently broken by green oases.

Your first sighting of Jaisalmer sets off an ethereal vision, but one that is slightly seamy when you examine its past. Jaisalmer started out as an important caravan center—remnants of caravansaries still exist (some of them converted into hotels). Right through the eighteenth century, rulers amassed their wealth from taxes levied on those passing through. Jaisalmer was also a smuggler's paradise, with opium the long-time best-seller.

Two great gateways, from east to west, pierce the towered battlements of the twelfth-century citadel. Inside are numerous Jain and Hindu temples, palaces, and more charming havelis. It's a walker's utopia, with tiny lanes and visually rich rewards. Most of the buildings are exquisitely carved, especially the facades with elaborate workmanship, frequently filigreed like lace. Don't miss these gems: The seven-story palace built by Maharawal (1763–1820)—a conglomeration of buildings crowned by a vast umbrella of metal, mounted on a stone shaft. Notice the historic spot, Satiyar-ka-Pagthiya, just before the palace entrance. Here, the royal ladies performed seti, the act of self-immolation when husbands were slain, at the fall of the fortress in 1294. Also, see the eight Jain temples and four Hindu temples built in the fifteenth and sixteenth centuries. The Jain temples, dedicated to Rikhabdevji and Sambhavnathji, are filled with thousands of deities and dancing figures in mythological settings. The Gyan Bhandar (Jain library), inside the Jain temple complex contains over 1,000 old manuscripts—some of them dating back to the twelfth century and written on palm leaf in black ink with painted wooden covers. The library also has a good collection of Jain, pre-Mogul, and Rajput paintings.

Outside the fortress, walk through the narrow lanes with more of the delicate, lacy architecture that shimmers in soft yellow. See the Patva Havelis—a string of five connected havelis built by the Patva brothers in the 1800s. Two of the five are now owned by the government and are open to the public. It's also possible to visit the interiors of the others (offer a small fee to the current residents). Next, visit the Nathamal Ki Haveli, flanked by stone elephants, built by two brothers. Instead of working in tandem, each brother concentrated exclusively on the left or right side. Although the result is harmonious, look carefully. You'll see subtle differences in the windows and carvings. Here, too, a courteous request may get you inside. The interior of Salim Singh's Havelis is in sad disrepair. Perhaps that's a fitting denouement. Salim Singh, financier for Jaisalmer, nearly bankrupted the state with his excessive extortion. He also went overboard when he committed a series of murders to avenge the murder of his father. The exterior six-story eighteenth-century haveli, however, is still lovely, with 38 balconies and elaborate carvings.

Jodhpur

Once the capital of the state of Marwar, Jodhpur (about 130 miles southeast of Jaisalmer) tumbles down a low sandstone hill on the edge of the Thar Desert. Today, remnants of an immense fortification wall, almost six miles in circumference, with eight gates facing various directions, guard the old city from the sand that stretches over some 35,000 square miles and the new city growing around the base of the rocky eminence. At the summit soars the majestic Meherangarh Fort, built in 1459 by Rao Jodha when he shifted his capital from Mandore. Standing above a perpendicular cliff, the fort looks impregnable—an imposing landmark, especially at night when it is bathed in yellow light.

The walls of the fort enclose a variety of handsome, red sandstone buildings, palaces, barracks, temples, and havelis. The Victory Gate, leading up from the city to the fort, was erected by Maharajah Ajit Singh to commemorate his military successes over the Moguls at the beginning of the eighteenth century. Seven other gateways stand in honor of other victories—internecine—involving warfare between the various Rajput princes. On the walls of the final gate of entry are the palm marks of Rajput widows who immolated themselves on flaming pyres after their husbands were defeated in battle.

Delicately latticed windows and pierced screens worked in sandstone are the surprising motifs inside the rugged fort. The palaces—Moti Mahal, Phool Mahal, Sheesh Mahal, and the other apartments—are exquisitely decorated, with paintings still gracing some of the ceilings and walls. Outside the fort are more interesting old buildings and temples, such as the Jaswant Thada, a royal crematorium in marble, built in 1899 for Maharajah Jaswant Singh II. Also visit the Umaid Bhawan Palace, built in 1929–42 by the Maharajah Umaid Singh. This sandstone palace has been partially converted into a deluxe hotel. The Umaid Bhawan also houses the Government Museum, with its fancy collection of royal finery, local arts and crafts, and miniature paintings. You might also catch a glimpse of the family of the current maharajah who live in their accustomed splendor in one extensive wing of the palace.

While in Jodhpur, also wander through the Girdikot and Sardar markets, crowded with fruit and vegetable stalls and tiny shops, and noisy with the day-to-day bustle of a typical Indian market. Don't be surprised if you see some of the local folk wearing those favored equestrian pants, jodhpurs; they originated here.

About five miles to the north are the Mandore Gardens, the site of the ancient capital of the State of Marwar. Here, surrounded by lovely gardens and mischievous monkeys, you'll find the *devals,* or cenotaphs, of the former royalty.

Mount Abu—Hill Station

Situated on lush, verdant hills about 4,000 feet above sea level, Mount Abu, with its famous Dilwara Jain temples, is a hill resort endowed with antiquity. To reach Mount Abu, a place of pilgrimage for Jains, take the road that heads almost due south from Jodhpur. Originally a center of the cult of Shiva, Mount Abu became the Jainist religious stronghold by the eleventh century. Abu (a shortened form of Arbuda) was known in Hindu legend as the son of the Himalayas. This son, supposedly a serpent, rescued Shiva's sacred bull Nandi when it fell into a chasm. Here, too, Vasishta, the great sage of the epic period, established his *ashram* —something between a hermitage and a seat of learning. The four fire-born Rajput clans claim they were created from his sacrificial fire.

High in the steep valleys between the rocky peaks are five Jain shrines. For ornamental skill in intricate stonework and as pieces of architectural virtuosity, the Vimal Vasashi and the Tejpal temples stand out in the history of stone carving. The Vimal Vasashi was built in 1031 and is dedicated to Adinath, the first Jain Tirthanka. Composed of pure white marble, its exterior is deceptively simple, giving no hint of the wealth of ornamentation and sculpture hidden inside.

A procession of marble elephants leads up from the pavilion to the domed porch. On the backs of the carved animals sit the founder, Vimala, and his family. The central courtyard is surrounded by a high wall enclosing some 50 cells, each one enshrining its saintly image. In the central shrine, laden with jewels, sits the figure of Adinath. The octagonal dome, decorated with finely carved human and animal shapes and processions, is supported by eight sculptured pillars. The ceiling is a mass of intricate fretted marble lacework.

The second temple of major importance was built 200 years later. Here, exuberance knows no bounds, reaching the zenith of Indian inventive genius in decorative art. The most striking feature is the pendant of the temple's dome. To stimulate their talent, the carvers were supposedly offered rewards in silver equal in weight to that of the marble filings. Not content with this, Tejpal, the lavish founder offered the weight in gold of any further filings that could be pared off after work was completed. Whatever the truth, there's no doubt that the proportion of perspiration to inspiration was clearly well balanced.

Ranakpur

About 100 miles northeast of Mount Abu is Ranakpur, a famous Jain temple, nestled in a lovely glen. As at Mount Abu, the shrine is dedicated to Adinath and dates from the beginning of the fifteenth century. Despite its current state of tranquility, *dacoits* (Indian bandits) formerly used the sacred shrine for their headquarters. They were finally ejected about 25 years ago, when the temple was cleaned up and restored to its impeccable condition.

Inside the temple are 29 halls supported by 200 different pillars, plus subsidiary shrines, in the shape of side-altars, that face all four directions. A wall, about 200 feet high, encircles the entire structure. Its inner face contains a quantity of elaborately sculptured cells, each adorned with a graceful spire. Embedded in this galaxy of spires rise the central shrines; 20 domes constitute the complex roofing of the pillared hall. Intricate carvings, friezes, and sculptured figures in close formation adorn the ceilings of all these structures. And, beneath the floor are hidden meditation chambers. In front of this temple are two more Jain shrines and a temple dedicated to the sun god (displaying erotic sculpture).

Udaipur

Udaipur, southeast of Ranakpur, is called the "City of Dreams"; its ruler, the maharana, the "Sun of the Hindus," a descendent of the highest ranking "Solar" Rajputs. The maharana's island palaces sparkle in post and pinnacles of colored glass, amber, and pale jade. The gray waters of the Pichola Lake—the artificial creation of a fourteenth-century fantasy—reflect the famous eighteenth-century Jag Niwas Lake Palace (now a hotel), which seems to float on the water's surface. Not far from the Lake Palace is the smaller, equally lovely seventeenth-century Jag Mandir.

Udaipur, originally the capital of the state of Mewar, takes its name from Maharana Udai Singh, who founded the city in the middle of the sixteenth century after fleeing the third Moslem attack on the city of Chittaur. Although his act didn't live up to the Rajput code of bravery to the deadly finish, it brought about Udaipur and its gorgeous palaces that everyone now enjoys.

Another legend claims that Udai Singh chose this location for Udaipur after a wandering holy man (sadhu) told him that if he built his capital on the edge of the lake, it would never be captured. Given the maharana's predilection for staying alive, he readily took the sadhu's advice. Unfortunately, his son, Maharana Pratap Singh attempted a surprise victory over the Delhi Moslem Empire and succeeded. His success was short-lived. In 1615, his successor, Amar Singh, was forced to sign a conditional submission to the Emperor Jahangir in Delhi. So much for the sadhu's promise.

The maharana's City Palace stands on the crest of a ridge overlooking the lake, an imposing structure, the largest palace in Rajasthan. Built at various periods, it still preserves a harmony of design, enhanced by massive octagonal towers surmounted by cupolas.

In its sumptuous apartments, decorated by multicolor mosaics, mirror work and inlaid tiles abound on all sides, together with some fine paintings and historical relics. Roof gardens afford a wide panorama below. The later island palaces rival the ancient palace on the mainland. Almost in the middle of the lake, Jag Nivas (Lake Palace) consists of apartments, courts, fountains, and gardens. On another island at the southern end, Jag Mandir Palace, started in the seventeenth century, was added to and embellished during the next 50 years. Three stories high, of yellow sandstone with an inside lining of marble, it is crowned by an imposing dome. Its interior is decorated with arabesques of colored stones. It was to Jag Mandir that Sharja, son of Emperor Jahangir, came to hide after leading an unsuccessful revolt against his father.

Other lakes in the immediate neighborhood, all artificial like Pichola, are joined to it by canals. Sahelion-Ki-Bari Park, at a mile and a half's distance, is a good example of this Hindu art of landscape gardening on a princely scale. It was laid out by Maharana Sangram Singh. A good road snakes its way along the shores of Fatehsagar Lake. Close below the embankment is the Sahelion-ki-Bari, the "Garden of the Maids," designed for the special use of the maharana's ladies, who arrived in a bunch from Delhi as a peace offering from the emperor.

Ornamental pools, with finely sculptured cenotaphs of soft black stone surrounded by a profusion of fountains, are the main décor.

Udaipur's Environs

Around 40 miles north is Rajsamand, an artificial lake of considerable size possessing a masonry embankment, entirely paved with white marble, constructed by Maharana Raj Singh in 1660. Broad marble steps lead down to the water, while three delicately carved marble pavilions jut into the lake. Cut into the stones of the embankment is the longest Sanskrit inscription known in India, a poem, etched into 25 slabs, that recounts the history of Mewar.

Thirty-two miles southeast of Udaipur lies Dhebar, or Jai Samand Lake, one of the largest artificial sheets of water in Asia, created by a dam almost a quarter of a mile across and over 100 feet high—no small engineering feat considering it was built in the seventeenth century. A temple of Shiva, flanked by six cenotaphs with a carved elephant in front of each, stands on the embankment. Bhils tribesmen still inhabit the islands in the lake.

All around Udaipur, you come across lake and shrine, temple and cenotaph—a wealth of white marble overlooking calm waters and interspersed with trees. Not all are monuments of victory or relics of peace and splendor. Seti stones commemorate the self-sacrifice of women who hurled themselves into raging fires while their husbands, pledged to death, fought against the overwhelming odds of invading hordes.

Fourteen miles north of Udaipur is Eklingji, a temple dedicated to the diety of the rulers of the Mewar. The present building, standing on the site of the original fifteenth-century edifice, is of late eighteenth-century construction. Like most sacred buildings in this region, it's entirely of white marble. The roof is decorated by hundreds of circular knobs and crowned by a lofty tower. In the inner shrine is a four-faced black marble image of Shiva. Outside is the statue of Nandi, his sacred bull. At a short distance, Nagda, now in ruins, bore the brunt of too many Moslem invasions. One of the most ancient places in Mewar, it has two temples dating from the eleventh century, both ornamented with interesting carvings.

Continuing north, you arrive at Nathdwara and a famous temple of Krishna that draws pilgrims in the thousands from all parts of India. The image, supposedly dating back to the twelfth century, was rescued from the destructive hands of the Moslems and brought here in 1699. A legend claims that when it was carted away, the chariot sank suddenly at the site of the present temple. It couldn't be budged or removed, so here it stayed.

Forty-one miles from Udaipur is the historic pass of Haldighati. Here the valiant Maharan Pratap defied the might of Akbar, described then as "immeasurably the richest and most powerful monarch on the face of the earth." Outnumbered 100 to one, the Rajputs stood their ground until they all died except Pratap, who managed to escape on his horse, Chetak. From his outpost in the hills, he slowly won back all his strongholds except Chittaur.

Chittaurgarh—Cradle of Rajput Courage

Due east of Udaipur is Chittaugarh, a city steeped in heroism. The ancient capital of Mewar State, this city and its ruins represent the origin of Rajput courage. The foundations of the fort of Chittaur are traditionally linked to the seventh century, and it remained the capital until 1567.

The glory of Chittaurgarh is the Tower of Victory, set up by Rana Kumbha in the middle of the fifteenth century to commemorate his triumph over the Moslem kings of Gujarat and Malwa. Kumbha, like all the Rajput rulers, was a direct descendant of Bappa Rawal, that great chieftain who reigned in Chittaur in the eighth century. Supposedly, Boppa was "a giant who stood 20 cubits (the best part of 30 feet!), whose spear no mortal man could lift. Since the start of the dynasty, 59 princes, descendants of this man of mythical dimensions, have assumed the throne of Chittaur.

The front of Chittaurgarh presents a battered appearance. Built on the precipitous edge of a hill, the gigantic fort is over seven miles in circumference. Inside are ruins of temples, palaces, and tanks, ranging from the ninth to the seventeenth centuries and the almost-intact Tower of Fame, a Jain structure of the twelfth century.

Chittaur was sacked three times: the first was in 1303, when Allauddin Khilji, a Moslem ruler, attempted to abduct the Rani Padmini, considered the most beautiful woman in the world. The women of Chittaur matched the courage of their men. When the battle on the field went against them, a funeral pyre was lit in a vault. The Rajput women, decked in their bridal robes, plunged into the flames, singing their way to death. When the last warrior had died "for the ashes of his fathers and the temples of his gods," all the conqueror found inside the city was a wisp of smoke rising from the vault.

The second sack was in 1535 by Sultan Bahadur Shah of Gujarat. Once more, the Rajputs, realizing an impending defeat, accepted death. After the queen mother arranged for the safe escape of her infant son, the future Maharana Udai Singh, she led the women into the furnace. Thousands of women died in the flames, while many more men were killed on the field. The third sack took place in 1567, this time at the hands of Akbar, the great Mogul. The two commanders, Jaimal and Patta, who led the defense of the fort, so impressed Akbar that he erected statues of them on elephants and had them set up at the entrance to his palace in Agra.

Kota—Bundi

Kota, Rajasthan's industrial center, is about 184 km northeast of Chittaurgarh. Former capital of Kota state, the city is on the right bank of the Chambal River, with an imposing fort standing sentinel over the valley. Inside you can visit the old palace, which now contains the Maharana Madho Singh Museum, with an exquisite collection of Rajput miniatures of the Kota school, sculptures, frescoes, and superb antiques.

North of Kota is Bundi, embedded in a narrow and picturesque gorge, where time moves at a slower pace and history itself seems to have lingered. The old city is enclosed in huge walls, fortified by four gateways. The Chittar Mahal (Palace of Towers), set atop a hill, consists of acres of stone-built structures, one opening out from another. Gardens galore rise up in terraces on the hillside. The palace is covered with spy holes and mysterious foliage-shrouded windows. Even the garden terraces have trapdoors under your feet that presumably served as dungeons in less peaceful times. Shields, swords, and daggers hang on the walls, as well as the martial family portraits of men with inordinately long mustaches brushed up to fall back like cat's whiskers. Those glory days have passed. But within the charming walkable city, you still find hints of those former times, when Rudyard Kipling stayed at Bundi, while tigers lurked in the nearby forests, and crocodiles teemed in the Mej River.

Since those days, a new palace, the Phool Sagar, has been constructed on the lakeside, still in Rajput style with banquet rooms and halls
decorated with hunting trophies. And, in the streets of old lovely
Bundi, Rajput men with bright turbans and Rajput women, their
multicolored skirts flashing in the sun, crowd the dusty roads. With
shiny pots on their heads and a child in their arms, they sail by with
a smile, accompanied by the jingle of their jewelry.

Before you leave Rajasthar, head back toward Jaipur, by way of
Ajmer and Pushkar, northwest of Bundi.

Ajmer and Pushkar

Situated at the foot of a hill, Ajmer is an ancient city (founded in the
seventh century) and an important place of pilgrimage for Moslems—a
curious anomaly in the land of Hindu Rajputs, an anomaly that also
explains its stormy past. The Hindu Chauhans who created Ajmer
remained in power until the late twelfth century, when Mohammed
Ghori grabbed the city for himself. Then Ajmer changed hands repeatedly. In 1556, it was annexed by Akbar, who made it his royal residence, building the fort that still dominates the city. From here, he
could command the main routes from the north. Ajmer also served as
his key to the conquest of Rajputana and Gujarat. After the death of
the great Moslem saint, Khwaja Muin-ud-Din Chisti, who preached
here in the thirteenth century, a tomb, Dargah, was created in his
honor. During his reign, Akbar visited once a year and supposedly
walked from Agra to the saint's mausoleum, a distance of about 200
miles. Frequented later by Shah Jahan, it owes its beautiful marble
pavilions to his tender care. To this day, Moslems gather in Ajmer to
commemorate the death of their saint (the Urs Mela—a six-day fair).

It was in Ajmer that Sir Thomas Roe, the ambassador of King James
I of England, presented his credentials to the Emperor Jahangir in
1616. It was here, too, that the War of Succession, fought between the
sons of Shahjahan, came to an end with the decisive victory of Aurangzeb. Ajmer is one of the holy places of India; to this day, pilgrims arrive
yearly from all four corners of the land. Akbar himself made many
pilgrimages.

Closer to Ajmer, at the foot of Taragarh Hill, stands a rare specimen
of architecture, Adhai-din-Ka-Jhonpra, a mosque supposedly built in
two and one half days by Mohammed Ghori on the former site of 30
Hindu temples. James Tod, in his standard work of 100 years back,
waxed eloquent about its "gorgeous prodigality of ornament, richness
of tracery, delicate sharpness of finish, laborious accuracy of workmanship." Two short minarets with inscriptions were added later.

Few sights in Ajmer provide a greater delight to the dusty, hot
traveler than do the cool waters of Anasagar. This artificial lake was
formed in the first half of the twelfth century by the Rajput King Anaji,
who raised a vast embankment between two hills. The Mogul emperors
were so entranced by this landscape that one after another, they embellished it with gardens, a long parapet, and five elegant pavilions of
polished white marble created by Shah Jahan.

Vast crowds of devout Hindus and tourists assemble every autumn
during Kartik Poornima, when the devout bathe in Pushkar Lake's
holy water. This religious festival is also the occasion for a lively camel
market, which turns Pushkar into a festive city. According to sacred
scripts, Brahma—first of the Hindu trinity—on passing this place let
a lotus flower slip from his hand. Water sprang from the spot where
the petals fell. The lake was formed and called Pushkar, which means
lotus. Many temples surround the holy lake—one of them dedicated to
Brahma.

PRACTICAL INFORMATION FOR RAJASTHAN

 WHEN TO GO. The tourist season runs from September to March when temperatures are in the 80s in daytime and in the 60s at night—ideal weather, thanks to the absence of dampness. But Rajasthan is probably at its best during the monsoon (July–September) when the mountains and hills are covered with greenery and there's plenty of water in the lakes. Rainfall is light—from 12 to 24 inches per year, depending on the region. In the hot season, from the end of March to July, temperatures can rise above 100° F.

 HOW TO GET THERE. By air. Daily *Indian Airlines* flights operate from Delhi to Jaipur, on to Jodhpur, on to Udaipur, and on to Aurangagabad and Bombay. *Vayudoot* connects Delhi with Jaipur, Bikener, Jodhpur, Kota, and Jaisalmer.

By bus. Daily buses, equipped with video, to Jaipur from Delhi are clean, cheap, fast, but *noisy.* In Delhi, call for details; *Rajasthan Roadways* (tel. 222276), open 6 A.M.–10 P.M.; *Haryana State Roadways* (tel. 221292), open 6 A.M.–noon and 1 to 9 P.M.; *India Tourism Development Corporation* (tel. 352336). From Jaipur, there are good bus connections throughout the state. Call Central Bus Station, 75834 or 66579.

By car. Good roads connect Jaipur with every major city in Rajasthan. Car rental with driver costs about Rs. 2 per km, plus night halt charges (Rs. 30 per night).

By train. From Delhi. The daily *Pink City Express* (five hours, Delhi–Jaipur) enables you to visit the city within a day, which is not enough time and only recommended to those who have no alternative. Other trains are the *Ahmedabad Express* in the morning, the *Chetak Express* later in the morning (each takes 22 hours to Udaipur), and the *Ahmedabad Mail* at night, which gets to Jaipur after dawn and to Abu Road (for Mount Abu) at teatime. The *Jodhpur Mail* covers the distance from Delhi in 17 hours and the *Bikaner Mail* in 12 hours. From Bombay, there are excellent trains that stop at Kota, Sawai Madhopur, and Ahmedabad. In Rajasthan, there are good rail connections throughout the state. In Delhi, for information and reservation procedures *which may be complicated,* call 343727 or 351035. In Jaipur, call 72121.

 TOURIST INFORMATION. Excellent brochures on cities and special interests (wildlife, crafts), with comprehensive information and maps, when necessary, are available from the following tourist offices (hours usually Monday–Saturday, 10 A.M.–5 P.M.):

Ajmer. Khadim Tourist Bungalow, Savitri Girls College Rd.; tel. 21626.

Alwar. *Information Center,* Near Purjan Vihar; tel. 3863.

Amber. Near elephant stand; tel. 40764.

Bharatpur. Circuit House; tel. 2340.

Bikaner. Dhola Maru Tourist Bungalow, Poonam Singh Circle; tel. 5445.

Bundi. Circuit House; tel. 301.

Chittorgarh. Janta Aavas Grih; tel. 9

Jaipur. Railway Station, tel. 69714; Central Bus Stand, Sindhi Camp; Rajasthan Tourism, 100 Jawaharlal Nehru Marg, tel. 73873. Also, *Jaipur Vision,* a monthly tourist guide, is available for Rs. 3 at book stores on Mirza Ismail Rd.

Jodhpur. Ghoomar Tourist Bungalow, High Court Road; tel. 25183.

Jaisalmer. Moomal Tourist Bungalow, tel. 92.

Kota. Chambal Tourist Bungalow, tel. 7695.

Mount Ahu. Bus Stand, tel. 51.

New Delhi. Rajasthan Tourism, Chandralok Building, 36 Janpath, New Delhi; tel. 322332.

Udaipur. Kajri Tourist Bungalow, Shastri Circle, tel. 3605; Dabok Airport; Counter at Railway Station.

FOREIGN CURRENCY EXCHANGE. Most banks in Rajasthan are open 10 A.M.–2:30 P.M. Monday–Friday; some are also open Saturdays until noon. Most Western-style hotels will cash major traveler's checks.

Ajmer. *Bank of India,* Kaisarganj, tel. 20245, and *Bank of Rajasthan,* Mayo College, tel. 22424.

Alwar. *State Bank of India,* tel. 2448.

Bharatpur. *State Bank of Bikaner and Jaipur,* tel. 2441.

Bikaner. *Bank of Rajasthan,* tel. 3444, and *Central Bank of India,* tel. 4584.

Bundi. *State Bank of India,* tel. 200, and *Rajasthan Bank,* tel. 25.

Chittaurgarh. *State Bank of India,* tel. 402, and *Rajasthan Bank,* tel. 7.

Jaipur. *Bank of India,* Mirza Ismail Rd., tel. 75781, *Bank of Rajasthan,* Mirza Ismail Rd., tel. 76472, and *State Bank of India,* Mirza Ismail Rd., tel. 72912 (10 A.M.–2 P.M., 2:30–4:30 P.M.).

Jaisalmer. *State Bank of India,* Nachana House, tel. 98, and *State Bank of Bikaner and Jaipur,* tel. 29.

Jodhpur. *Bank of Rajasthan,* tel. 22296, *Central Bank of India,* tel. 20795, and *State Bank of India,* tel. 23790.

Udaipur. *Bank of Rajasthan,* Bapu Bazar, and *State Bank of India,* Hospital Road, tel. 6371.

ACCOMMODATIONS. Spending a night in Rajasthan frequently conjures up an interlude in a former raja palace. Sometimes the old castles/hunting lodges are great; sometimes they're a great disappointment, with character exchanged for sterile deluxe amenities; and at an awful cost—both in terms of what is lost and what it costs to stay there. Nonetheless, the state provides a good range of facilities to meet every budget. Rates are based on double occupancy: *Deluxe,* Rs. 1,000 plus; *Expensive,* Rs. 600–Rs. 1,000; *Moderate,* Rs. 250–Rs. 600; *Inexpensive,* under Rs. 250. At the conclusion of the hotel listings is a list of circuit houses—usually nice older buildings—for government VIPs. Foreigners can use them if space is available; charges for a nice double are usually under Rs. 100.

AJMER-PUCHKAR

Inexpensive

Khadim Tourist Bungalow. Savatri Girls College Rd., Ajmer; ¼ km from the bus stand; tel. 20490. 49 rooms, some air-conditioned; a restaurant and a bar. Run by Rajastan Tourism Development Corporation (RTDC).

Sarovar Tourist Bungalow. Pushkar, District Ajmer, Rajasthan; ½ km from the bus stand; tel. 40. 36 rooms in a former palace built around a courtyard and situated on a lake. Restaurant. Now run by RTDC.

During the Pushkar Festival, RTDC constructs a memorable tented tourist village in the *mela* (fairground). Accommodations are ordinary and deluxe tents, Rs. 580–Rs. 635, including vegetarian meals. Fair is held around November (see *Seasonal Events*). Book your tent well in advance through Central Reservation Office, Rajasthan Tourism Development Corporation, Ltd.; Chanderlok Building, 36 Jan Path, New Delhi, 110001 (tel. 32180), or through your travel agent.

ALWAR

(All places near Siliserh Lake or in Sariska Tiger Preserve)

Moderate

Hotel Sariska Palace. Sariska, District Alwar, Rajasthan; tel. 22. 25 rooms, some air-conditioned. Restaurant, game viewing. Former royal hunting lodge with modern amenities, period decor, a restaurant, game viewing. Very comfortable.

Inexpensive

Lake Palace Hotel. Siliserh, District, three km from the bus stand; tel. 22991. 10 rooms. A bar, dining room, and boating facilities. Off-season rates April

1–June 30. A former royal hunting lodge perched on a hill overlooking Siliserh Lake. Very nice getaway now run by RTDC.

Tiger Den Tourist Bungalow. Sariska, District, tel. 42. 17 rooms, plus cottages and tents. Some air-conditioned rooms, a restaurant, and a bar. Pleasant, modest RTDC facility set in Sariska Tiger Preserve.

BHARATPUR

(In or near the sanctuary)

Moderate

Bharatpur Forest Lodge. Bharatpur Bird Sanctuary, eight km from the railway station; tel. 2322. 18 rooms. Off-season rates June 1–September 30. Some air-conditioned rooms, a restaurant and bar, room service, and row boats for bird watching. Situated in the sanctuary. Operated by ITDC.

Inexpensive

Saras Tourist Bungalow. Fatehpur Sikri Rd.; tel. 3700. 20 rooms, some air-conditioned, a restaurant and bar, nice lawns, simple setup. Run by RTDC, which also sponsors sightseeing trips into the sanctuary.

BHARATPUR PROPER

Moderate

Golbagh Palace Hotel. Tel. 3349. 18 rooms, some air-conditioned. Lovely, well-managed hotel, formerly a palace, with old furnishings and modern amenities such as TVs, 24-hour room service, and a fine restaurant.

BIKANER–GAJNER

Moderate

Lalgrah Palace Hotel. Bikaner, 14 km from the airport, one km from downtown; tel. 3263. 14 air-cooled rooms, restaurant. Off-season discount May–July. Former red sandstone palace, part of it now renovated hotel. "Iffy" maintenance, but the place to stay if you want to be *in* Bikaner.

Gajner Palace Hotel. In Gajner Wildlife Sanctuary, 32 km from Bikaner; tel. 3263. For reservations book through Lalgarh Palace. Quiet, former maharajah hunting lodge built in 1890. 18 rooms. Great furnishings. But again "iffy" service. The trade-off: you're on a lake with wildlife and views.

Inexpensive

Dholamaru Tourist Bungalow. Near Major Puran Singh Circle, Bikaner; tel. 5002. 16 simple, clean rooms, restaurant. Run by RTDC.

CHITTAURGARH

Inexpensive

Janta Avas Grah. Station Rd., two km from the bus stand. 4 very basic rooms. Restaurant. Run by RTDC.

Panna Tourist Bungalow. Udaipur Rd., tel. 21900. 18 rooms, some air-conditioned; restaurant, bar. Functional and clean. Run by RTDC.

JAIPUR

Expensive

Clarks Ajmer. Jawahartal Lal Nehru Marg, Post Box No. 222, five km. from the airport, seven km from downtown; tel. 822617. 118 air-conditioned rooms, 24-hour room service, restaurants, coffee shop, a bar, swimming pool, and shopping arcade. Full amenities, but way out of town.

Jai Mahal Palace. 11 km from the airport, two km from downtown; tel. 73215. 40 air-conditioned rooms, 24-hour room service, a restaurant (fixed-price menu), and bar. Newly refurbished former palace. Much of the palace "look" is gone in the interior, but the exterior and grounds are beautiful.

Rajmahal Palace Hotel. Two km from downtown; tel. 61257. 11 large air-conditioned rooms (Rs. 625). A restaurant (fixed-price menu), a bar, and room service. Another former palace. Interior seems more '40s than Raj, but a grand setting.

Rambagh Palace Hotel. Bhawani Singh Rd., 11 km from the airport; three km from downtown; tel. 75141. 105 air-conditioned rooms, TVs, a restaurant, bar, room service, swimming pool, tennis courts, gardens, gorgeous grounds—the works. Former palace with exquisite public rooms, and magnificent suites with original furnishings. But request on an *old* room; new rooms are devoid of palatial character.

Welcomgroup Mansingh. Sansar Chandra Rd.; tel. 78771. 100 air-conditioned rooms, TVs, 24-hour room service, restaurants, a bar, shopping arcade, swimming pool, many amenities. A modern structure with limited character.

Moderate

Jaipur Ashok. Jai Singh Circle, Bani Park, 14 km from the airport; one km from the bus stand; tel. 75121. 63 air-conditioned rooms, room service, a restaurant, bar, coffee shop, and swimming pool. A modern newish building; run by ITDC.

Meru Palace. Sawai Ram Singh Rd., eight km from the airport; near downtown; tel. 61212. 48 air-conditioned rooms, 24-hour room service, restaurants, a coffee shop, and bar. A spiffy new hotel.

Moderate to Inexpensive

Hotel Khasa Kothi. Mirza Ismail Rd.; tel. 75151. 38 air-conditioned rooms, a restaurant, bar, room service, and swimming pool. Outside grounds are lovely, but rooms, although clean, are a bit tacky around the edges.

Hotel Khetri House. Outside Chandpole Gate, 15 km from the airport, one km from downtown; tel. 69183. 13 air-cooled rooms, and a restaurant. Lovely palace exterior, but clean rooms seem dingy and neglected.

Narain Niwas Palace Hotel. Kanota Bagh, Narain Singh Road; tel. 65448. 22 air-cooled rooms, and a restaurant with fixed-price menu in a former palace that has its original decor. It wins you over with its admittedly slightly musty, nineteenth-century decor. Clean rooms with great objets d'art, photos, paintings, and portraits. One of a kind in Jaipur.

Hotel Neelam. Motilal Atal Rd.; tel. 77774. 50 rooms, some with TVs; air-conditioning, and a vegetarian restaurant. Decor is a bit garish; keep the lights low.

Inexpensive

Arya Niwas. Sansar Chandra Rd.; ½ km from the bus stand, near the center of town; tel. 73456. 35 rooms. If you don't mind modern, this hotel is the best low-budget hotel in Jaipur. Helpful management, excellent vegetarian restaurant, and room service.

Hotel Bissau Palace. Outside Chand Pole, 15 km from the airport; one km from the bus stand; tel. 74191. 27 air-conditioned rooms, room service, a restaurant, and swimming pool in a lovely setting. Interesting common rooms with good old furnishings, but the bedrooms, though clean, cry out for better care.

Ghandragupt Hotel. Station Rd.; near Sindhi Camp Bus Stop; tel. 75001. 40 air-conditioned rooms, 24-hour room service, a restaurant, bar, coffee shop, terrace garden, and shopping arcade. Okay, newish hotel. The rooms are clean.

Gangaur Tourist Bungalow. Marza Ismail Rd., one km from the bus stand; tel. 60231. 63 rooms, some air-conditioned; a restaurant, bar, 24-hour coffee shop, and room service. Clean and modest. Run by RTDC.

LMB Hotel. Johari Basar; tel. 48844; cable: ALAMBE. In old city. 33 air-conditioned rooms. A great vegetarian restaurant, a bar, and a coffee shop. But beware of pesky monkeys—they'll sneak in if you open your window.

JAISALMER

Moderate

Jawahar Palace Hotel. Tel. 208. 15 rooms and a restaurant in a hotel owned by the Jaisalmer maharajah. A beautiful building with potential and nice grounds. Billiard room. Interior is clean, but right now it's a tired old palace, waiting to be revived.

Narawan Niwas Palace. Near Malka Prol, Jaisalmer; tel. 108; cable: JAIS-AL. 24 air-conditioned rooms, a restaurant, bar, lovely lawns. Former caravansary.

Inexpensive

Jaisal Castle. Tel. 62. Book through Narawan Niwas Palace above. 11 rooms. Very spartan old fort. Simple decor, but great views of Jaisalmer.

Moomal Tourist Bungalow. Tel. 92. 31 rooms, some rooms air-conditioned; a restaurant and bar. Clean, simple lodging, run by RTDC, which can arrange camel safaris and local sightseeing.

Note: A new hotel is under construction and was scheduled to open in 1988. Done up in golden sandstone like the rest of Jaisalmer, reminiscent of the fort architecture. Will have modern amenities. Check availability with tourist office or travel agent.

JHUNJHUNU

Inexpensive

Hotel Shiv Shekhawati. Muni Ashram; tel. 51. About 20 rooms. Room service, excellent vegetarian restaurant, camel rides. Very comfortable and clean for the money. In the thick of the Shekhawati region.

JODHPUR

Expensive

Welcomgroup Umaid Bhawan Palace. Five km from airport; five km from downtown; tel. 22526. 55 rooms. Off-season rates May – Sept. Air-conditioned, restaurant, bar, room service, health club, indoor pool, shopping arcade, billiards, incredible grounds. This palace is still the residence of the maharajah and is part museum. It tries hard to maintain its stately elegance. Exterior and public rooms are gorgeous! But many bedrooms are a bit unpalatial despite their generous size. Still, don't hope for modernization. Also, hotel guests can arrange overnight train trip to Jaisalmer in the maharajah's antique-furnished saloon car, with a day of sightseeing.

Moderate

Ajit Bhawan. Tel. 20409. 41 rooms and bungalows. Air-cooled, restaurant, lovely gardens, nightly cultural entertainment, village tours via jeep. For those who want an abundance of charm and more modest regal display, stay in this enchanting "village" complex, designed and owned by the maharajah's younger brother. Wonderful Rajasthani motif and Rajput objets d'art.

Hotel Ratanada International Ltd. Residency Rd.; tel. 25910; cable: POLO JODHPUR. 50 rooms. Air-conditioned, restaurant, bar, swimming pool, room service, shopping arcade. Comfortable new hotel.

Inexpensive

Ghoomar Tourist Bungalow. High Court Rd.; tel. 21900. 64 rooms, some air-conditioned; a restaurant, bar, room service, sightseeing. Tourist office located here. Clean, functional rooms. Run by RTDC.

KHIMSAR

Moderate

Welcomgroup Royal Castle. Khimsar, District Nagaur; tel. 28. 14 rooms. Room service, restaurant, jeep trips, camel rides and safaris, entertainment. Try to stay in a room designed in the '20s. A great escape hotel, which just happens to be a former fortress-castle.

KOTA

Moderate

Brijraj Bhawan Palace Hotel. Civil Lines; one km from downtown; tel. 3071. Seven large air-cooled rooms; restaurant (fixed-price meals). Not a posh palace;

more like a sprawling Victorian home filled with wonderful momentoes of the former raj. Gracious service. Nice ambience, especially when you sit in the drawing room or around the lovely dining room table. A place to relax and soak up the past. Cozy grounds overlooking river.

Inexpensive

Chambal Tourist Bungalow. Naya Pura, near downtown; tel. 26527. 49 rooms, some air-conditioned, clean, simple. Restaurant. Tourist office located here.

Hotel Navrang. Civil Lines, Kota; eight km from the airport; 1½ km from downtown; tel. 3294. 21 rooms, some air-conditioned. Restaurant, nice lawn. Okay place.

MANDAWA

Moderate

Castle Mandawa. Mandawa, District Jhunjhunu, Shekimvati; tel. 24; cable: CASTLE MANDAWA. 35 rooms and a restaurant. Great old castle, built in the late eighteenth century. Magnificent views. Another place to settle in and feel good, to go on a camel ride or safari, or to watch cultural events.

MOUNT ABU

Moderate

Hotel Hilltone. Box 18; tel. 137. Centrally located. 44 rooms, and a restaurant, bar, and lovely garden; some amenities.

Inexpensive

Mount Hotel. Dilwara Rd.; tel. 55. Seven rooms, a restaurant, a garden, some amenities.

Palace Hotel. Delwara Rd.; tel. 21. 28 rooms; some air-conditioned; a restaurant, tennis courts, and lovely gardens.

Shikhar Tourist Bungalow. Tel. 29. 79 rooms, some cottages. A restaurant and bar, boating. Set on a hill with good views. Clean and pleasant; run by RTDC.

SAWAI MADHOPUR

Inexpensive

Castle Jhoomar Baori. Forest Lodge, Ranthambhor Rd.; tel. 620. Eight rooms, some air-conditioned. In the Ranthambhor Tiger Preserve. A restaurant and bar. Former maharajah's lodge; now run by RTDC.

UDAIPUR

Expensive

Lake Palace Hotel. Pichola Lake; tel. 23241. 81 rooms. A restaurant and bar. 24-hour room service, a coffee shop, swimming pool, cultural entertainment, and shops. All Western amenities. The famous palace sits like a dream in the lake. Beautiful, but on the verge of glitzy.

Shivniwas Palace. Tel. 3203. 14 air-conditioned suites with private balconies and TVs. Room service, a bar, restaurant, swimming pool, and other amenities. Understated elegance. A former palace, now a hotel and the home of the Udaipur maharajah. Great views of the lake and a sense of privacy. Good decor in rooms, although there is no sense of the royal or historic until you enter the fancier suites, which are fabulous!

Moderate

Laxmi Vilas Palace Hotel. Tel. 24411. 34 rooms, some air-conditioned. TVs, room service, a bar, restaurant, and swimming pool. Palatial grounds with good views, but minimal interior character. Run by ITDC.

Shikarbadi Hotel. Goverdhanvilas; tel. 25321. 25 air-conditioned rooms, a restaurant, swimming, rowing, and horseback riding. The former hunting lodge of the royal family. Deer and monkeys are right at the door. Gracious service, rustic ambience. Terrific place.

Inexpensive

Hotel Anand Bhawan. Fatehsagar Rd.; tel. 23256. 20 air-conditioned rooms. Ask for a room facing the lake. A bar, restaurant, and room service.

Hotel Lakend. Alkapuri, Fatehsagar Lake; tel. 23841. 44 rooms, some air-conditioned, facing the lake, a restaurant, bar, and a terraced garden; fishing in private pond.

Kajri Tourist Bungalow. Shastri Circle; tel. 25122. 18 rooms, some air-conditioned. A restaurant, bar, boating, and local sightseeing. Clean rooms; okay for the price; run by RTDC.

Circuit Houses. Circuit houses are often attractive lodges—pleasantly furnished with a turn-of-the-century feel if not decor. They're also usually inexpensive (under Rs. 100 per double). Unfortunately, but perhaps appropriately, Indian government VIPs get first preference. Check on arrival to see if there's a vacancy or write in advance to: *Deputy Secretary, Circuit House Reservations,* General Administration Department, Secretariate, Jaipur, Rajasthan. Some good circuit houses are in Ajmer, Alwar, Bikaner, Bundi, Chittaurgarh, Jodhpur, Kota, and Mount Abu.

 DINING OUT. In Rajasthan, you can explore Indian vegetarian dining—*thalis, domas, paneer* (cheese), butter *masalas,* and lots of other exotic dishes. You can also find a decent nonvegetarian, Continental, or Chinese meal—at least in the bigger cities or at hotels. A selection of hotel dining rooms, as well as some independent restaurants, is included in this list. Categories are based on the price of a three-course dinner for one person, excluding beverage, tip, and taxes: *Expensive,* Rs. 60 and up; *Moderate,* Rs. 30–Rs. 60; *Inexpensive,* less than Rs. 30.

AJMER—PUSHKAR

Inexpensive to Moderate

Honey Dew. Ajmer; no phone. Good vegetarian selections served throughout the day and evening.

Khadim Tourist Bungalow. Savitri Girls College Rd., Ajmer; tel. 20490. Limited menu, but fine ambience and bar service.

Kwality. Ajmer; no phone. Indian and Continental dishes offered daily.

Sarovar Tourist Bungalow. Pushkar; tel. 40. Vegetarian food. Breakfast, lunch, and dinner.

ALWAR

Moderate

Hotel Sariska Palace. Sariska; tel. 22. Nice place for lunch or dinner. Indian, Continental, and Chinese cuisines.

Lake Palace Hotel. Siliserh; tel. 22991. Limited menu, but pleasant environment.

Tiger Den Tourist Bungalow. Sariska; tel. 42. Limited menu, modest surroundings, but restful.

BHARATPUR

Moderate

Bharatpur Forest Lodge. Bharatpur Bird Sanctuary; tel. 2322. Indian and Continental cuisines served amid all those birds.

Inexpensive

Saras Tourist Bungalow. Fatehpur Sikri Rd., Bharatpur; tel. 3700. Good inexpensive Indian food.

BIKANER
Moderate

Lalgarh Palace Hotel. Bikaner; tel. 3263. Indian and Continental foods served in a partly renovated old redstone palace.

Chhotu Motoo Restaurant. Station Rd.; tel. 4466. Wide selection of vegetarian dishes.

JAIPUR
Expensive

Shivar. Welcomgroup Mansingh, Sansar Chandra Rd.; tel. 78771. Mughlai and tandoori food, served in a rooftop restaurant with live Indian music. Reservations required.

Suvarna Mahal. Rambagh Hotel; tel. 75141. Continental, Chinese, and Indian food. Live sitar music at dinner. Originally a royal banquet hall; feast is also for the eyes. Reservations required.

Moderate

Aravalli. Hotel Jaipur Ashok, Jai Singh Circle; tel. 75121. Pleasant unassuming decor. Continental and Indian Regional cuisines. Reservations advised.

Cafe Nity. Mirza Ismail Rd., opposite government hostel; no phone. Good Mughlai food served. Outdoor setting under open-air rattan hut, with separate family "cabin." Fun.

Chanakya. Mirza Ismail Rd.; tel. 78461. Open noon–11 P.M. Simple, pleasant decor. Delicious Indian, Continental, and Chinese vegetarian food. Try the Chanakya special.

Jal Mahal. Mirza Ismail Rd.; no phone. Vegetarian and nonvegetarian specialties; tandoori and Mughlai food. Small and cozy—not fancy, but good.

Natraj Restaurant. Mirza Ismail Rd.; no phone. Fine vegetarian food served under subdued lighting; pleasant.

Niro's. Mirza Ismail Rd.; tel. 74493. Continental, Chinese, Indian, and Mughlai dishes. Subdued setting. Excellent food. May be Jaipur's best of the nonvegetarian restaurants. Reservations required.

Woodlands. Meru Palace, Sawai Ram Singh Rd.; tel. 61212. Open noon–10:30 P.M. Excellent South Indian food. Attractive contemporary setting. Reservations advised.

Inexpensive

Chandralok. Mirza Ismail Rd., opposite Laxmi Motor Company; no phone. Walk up an unmarked staircase to second floor to a simple modest restaurant with great typical Rajasthani fare. Menu in Hindu, but be daring. A local favorite.

Surya Mahal. Mirza Ismail Rd.; no phone. Borderline "fast-food" decor. Excellent North and South Indian vegetarian food. Great, and low, low prices.

JODHPUR
Expensive

Ajit Bhawan. Jodphur; tel. 20409. Lovely outdoor restaurant with great ambience and an excellent fixed menu food; nightly entertainment. Reservations required.

Marwar Hall. Umaid Bhawan Palace; tel. 22316. Gigantic formal-style dining room within the palace. Mughlai, Marwari, and Continental foods. Reservations required for dinner.

Moderate

Kalinga. Near Station Rd.; tel. 24066. Emphasis here is on North Indian Mughlai foods. Popular local spot.

Kashmiri Hotel. Near Annand Cinema; no phone. Good spicy Indian food, if you prefer it that way.

Ratanada International Hotel. Residency Rd.; tel. 25910. Decent variety of Chinese, Continental, Indian, vegetarian and tandoori foods served. Reservations advised.

KOTA

Moderate to Expensive

Brij Raj Bhawan Palace Hotel. Civil Lines; tel. 3071. A lovely place to eat; fixed-price meals; gracious service. If not staying there, call to see if they can squeeze you in for lunch or dinner.

Inexpensive

Chambal Tourist Bungalow. Naya Pura; tel. 26527. Limited Indian menu, but not bad lunch or dinner for the price.

MOUNT ABU

Moderate

Hotel Hilltone. Mount Abu; tel. 137. Indian and Continental foods served at lunch and dinner.
Mount Hotel. Dilward Road, Mount Abu; tel. 55. Indian foods, including Parsee and Gujarati cuisine; lunch and dinner.

UDAIPUR

Expensive

Neel Kamal. Lake Palace, Pichola Lake, Udaipur; tel. 23241. Lunch and dinner. Indian, Continental, and Chinese cuisines. Pleasant place with good food. Reservation suggested.
Shikarbadi Hotel. Udaipur; tel. 25321. Fixed-price meals of Indian, Continental, Mewari, and Rajasthani foods. Lovely setting, peaceful retreat. Reservations suggested for dinner.

Moderate

Berry's Restaurant. Chetak Circle, Udaipur; tel. 25132. Indian, Chinese, and Continental foods served. Popular restaurant among locals.

 HOW TO GET AROUND. From the airports. At Jaipur, a taxi costs about Rs. 60. Infrequent bus service is also available at Rs. 20. At Jodhpur, the taxi fare is about Rs. 80; also infrequent bus service, at Rs. 25. At Udaipur, the taxi fare is Rs. 100; bus fare, Rs. 20.

How you decide to get from city to city within Rajasthan depends on your budget and your time. It's a big state with a lot of territory between major attractions.

By Bus. Good, inexpensive deluxe (video!) coach services connect most major cities. In Jaipur, call *Rajasthan Tourism Development Corporation* at Gangaur Tourist Bungalow (60231), or *India Tourism Development Corporation* at Rajasthan State Hotel (65451).

By Train. Train reservations can be complicated to negotiate; trains are also slower than the buses, but they will get you to most cities. In Jaipur, call 72121.

By Rented Car with Driver. Figure about Rs. 2 per km for an Ambassador with driver, plus Rs. 50 per night halt charges. In Jaipur, call *ITDC*, 65154; *RTDC*, 60231; *Rajasthan Tours*, 69885; or the tourist department for a list of approved car agencies, 69714.

BIKANER

By Taxi. Unmetered taxis are available, with rates supposedly fixed by the Rajasthan Transport Department. Set the fare before you start.
By Auto Rickshaw and Tonga (horse cart). Establish fares in advance. Much fun and should be cheap.

JAIPUR

By Bus. Rajasthan State Roadways Transport Corporation provides regular bus service to Amber and around the city. For details, call 75834.

By Taxi. Taxis are unmetered, with rates set by the government. Establish the fare in advance.

By Auto Rickshaw. Rs. 1 per first km; Rs. 0.75 per each additional km. It's amazing how many meters don't work and how many drivers don't know the rates. Set the fares in advance. Can be hired for the day at about Rs. 100.

By Bike Rickshaw. Just haggle. Should be cheaper than auto rickshaw. Bike rickshaws can also be hired for the day at about Rs. 50.

JAISALMER

This is another walk-around town as far as the old city is concerned.

By Taxi. For sights only beyond Jaisalmer, rates are fixed by the Rajasthan Transport Department. For service, call the tourist officer (106) or arrange it through your hotel.

By Camel and Camel Cart. Lots of fun, but some discomfort. Call the tourist officer for details (106) or arrange for service through your hotel.

JODHPUR

By Bus. A city bus can take you to Mandore Gardens, Balsamund, and Mahamandir. Call the tourist department for details, 21583.

By Taxi. Unmetered taxis are available, with rates fixed by the government. Establish the price in advance.

By Auto Rickshaw. Rs. 1 for the first km; Rs. 0.75 for each additional km. Establish the fare in advance.

By Bike Rickshaw and Horse Tonga. Fix the rate in advance. Bargain.

KOTA

By Taxi. Rs. 2 per km.

By Auto Rickshaw and Bike Rickshaw. Cheap, but fix the fare in advance.

MOUNT ABU

By Taxi. Unmetered; set the fare in advance.

By Tonga or Pony. Haggle, and set the fare in advance.

UDAIPUR

By Taxi. Unmetered, with rates set by the government. Set the fare in advance.

By Auto Rickshaw and Tonga. Set the fare in advance. Bargain.

 TOURS. Two types of tours are available—local and more comprehensive "theme" or multiple-city packages: For those who can afford it, there's also the Palace on Wheels (a week-long train excursion in the former saloon cars of maharajahs and viceroys).

Tour packages are offered by RTDC. From Delhi, contact Manager, Package Tours, Rajasthan Tourism Development Corporation, 36 JanPath, Chandralok Building; tel. 321820. From Jaipur, Transport Unit, Ganaur Tourist Bungalow, Mirza Ismail Rd.; tel. 60239. From Udaipur, Manager, Kajri Tourist Bungalow, Udaipur; tel. 25122. When buses are used, they're air-conditioned, clean, and comfortable luxury buses.

Chittaurgarh Tour. Tour departs from Kajri Tourist Bungalow, Udaipur, on every alternate day. Itinerary: Udaipur–Chittaurgarh–Udaipur. Day-long tour. Tariff by minibus: Rs. 145 per adult; Rs. 100 per child (under 12). Tariff by taxi: Rs. 250 per person. Tour conducted September–March.

Golden Triangle. Three-day bus tour departing every Friday from Delhi. Itinerary: Delhi–Sariska–Jaipur–Bharatpur–Fatehpur Sikri–Agra–Delhi. Tariff: Rs. 525 per adult; Rs. 425 per child. (September–March)

Hadoti Package. Four-day tour departing from Delhi every first and third Friday. Itinerary: Delhi–Jaipur–Tonk–Bundi–Kota–Jaipur–Delhi. Tariff by minibus: Rs. 830 per adult; Rs. 730 per child. Tariff by taxi: Rs. 1285. (September–March)

Hawa Mahal Package. Three-day tour departing every Tuesday from Delhi. Itinerary: Delhi–Agra–Fatehpur Sikri–Bharatpur–Deeg–Sariska–Jaipur–Delhi. Tariff by bus: Rs. 525 per adult; Rs. 425 per child (September–March)

Mewar Package. Six-day tour departing every Saturday from Delhi. Itinerary: Delhi–Jaipur–Chittaurgarh–Udaipur–Haldighati–Nathdwara–Ajmer–Pushkar–Delhi. Tariff by minibus: Rs. 880 per adult; Rs. 700 per child. Those who join in Jaipur: Rs. 690 per adult; Rs. 590 per child. (September–June; in May and June, departures include a day's stop in Mount Abu.)

Mount Abu Express Package. Five departures of six-day trips from Delhi in April–June. Itinerary: Delhi–Jaipur–Mount Abu–Ajmer–Delhi, with three nights in Mount Abu. Cost: Rs. 885 per adult; Rs. 750 per child. Tariff from Jaipur: Rs. 785 per adult; Rs. 790 per child.

Palace on Wheels. Travel from Delhi to Jaipur–Udaipur–Chittaurgarh–Jaisalmer–Jodhpur Bharatpur–Fatehpur Sikri–Agra–and back to Delhi aboard one of 13 royal coaches that were once used by maharajahs and maharanis on bridal journeys, hunting trips, and general state visits. Some coaches also used by former British viceroy, with posh furnishings. Each "saloon" has a captain and an attendant. There are two restaurant cars, serving Continental and Indian foods, a bar, observation lounge, and library. Cabins are primarily twin bedded. Package price: Rs. 10,850 per person, including everything but laundry service and liquor. Seven-day trips with sightseeing at each stop, prepaid meals at deluxe hotels, cultural programs. For further details and reservations: SBS Central Reservation Office, Rajasthan Tourism Development Corporation, 36 Jan Path, Chandralok Building, New Delhi, 110001; tel. 321820. Telex: 031–63142. Train runs October–March.

Ranakpur Tour. One-day tour departs from Kajri Tourist Bungalow in Udaipur every alternate day. Itinerary: Udaipur–Ranakpur–Kumbhalgarh–Haldighati–Udaipur. By minibus: Rs. 141 per adult; Rs. 100 per child. By taxi: Rs. 237. (September–March)

Shekhawati Package. Three-day tour departing from Delhi every second and fourth Friday. Itinerary: Delhi–Jaipur–Samod–Nawalgarth–Mandawa–Fatehpur–Ramgarh–Jhunjhunu–Pilani–Delhi. Tariff by minibus: Rs. 660 per adult; Rs. 570 per child. Tariff by taxi: Rs. 900 per adult. (September–April)

Weekend Package. Two-day tour departing Saturdays from Delhi. Itinerary: Delhi–Siliserh–Sariska–Delhi. Tariff by minibus: Rs. 290 per adult; Rs. 275 per child. Taxi with tour escort: Rs. 540 per person; without tour escort: Rs. 405 per person.

Wildlife Package. Four-day tour departing Fridays from Delhi. Itinerary: Delhi–Bharatpur–Sawai Madhopur–Jaipur–Delhi. Tariff by minibus: Rs. 715 per adult; Rs. 650 per child. Tariff by taxi: Rs. 1310 per adult; Rs. 1000 per child. (October–June; from April to June, Bharatpur is replaced by Sariska.)

LOCAL SIGHTSEEING

In most of the large cities of Rajasthan, you can hire an approved guide for a half- or full-day through the local tourist office. Rates for one to four persons are about Rs. 25 for a half day and Rs. 45 for a full day.

Bharatpur: Keoladeo Ghana Bird National Park. Book through Sarus Tourist Bungalow, tel. 3700. Rs. 10 per person. Tour operates on demand.

Chittaurgarh. Fort, Meera Temple, Victory Tower, Padmini Palace, Rana Kumbha Palace. Book through Panna Tourist Bungalow; tel. 273. Rs. 15 per adult; Rs 10 per child. Time: 8 A.M.–noon; 2–6 P.M.

Jaipur. Half-day tour of Hawa Mahal, City Palace, Observatory, Amber Fort, and Palace, Central Museum, Nawab Sahab Ki Haveli. Rs. 15 per person. Time: 8 A.M.–1 P.M.; 1:30–6:30 P.M.

Full-day tour of Hawa Mahal, City Palace, Museum, Observatory, Amber Fort and Palace, Central Museum, Nahargarh Fort, Sisodia Rani Garden, Doll Museum, Galta. Rs. 35 per person. Time: 9 A.M.–6 P.M. Car taxi tours are also available (Rs. 1.85 per km), as is a minibus (Rs. 350 per km). Book through the Tourist Information Bureau, Railway Station Platform No. 1; tel. 69714.

Jaisalmer. Fort, Palace, Jain Temple, and Havelis. Book through Moomal Tourist Bungalow, tel. 92, 192. Rs. 12 per person. Tours on demand.

Jodhpur. Umaid Bhawan Palace, Mandore Gardens, Mehrangarh Fort, Jaswant Thanda, Government Museum. Time: 9:30 A.M.–1 P.M.; 2–6:30 P.M. Rs. 15. Book through Tourist Bungalow, tel. 21900.

Mount Abu. Nakki Lake, Delwara Temple, Achalgarh, Guru Shikhar. Time: 8 A.M.–1 P.M.. Nakki Lake, Delwara Temple, Achalgarh, Guru Shikhar, Sunset Point (Arbuda Devi). Time: 2–7 P.M. Rs. 15 per person. Book through Shikhar Tourist Bungalow, tel. 69, 29.

SEASONAL EVENTS. January 25 – 28. Nagaur (135 km from Jodhpur). *Nagaur Fair* is an enormous cattle fair, with camels and horses for sale. A popular event with rural folk; much entertainment, including cultural programs and camel races.

Jan. 31–Feb. 2. Jaisalmer. *Desert Festival* is one of Rajasthan's gala events—traditional Rajasthani music; a display of desert handicrafts, camel caravans, camel races, and turban-tying competitions. Don't miss it if your Rajasthan trip is planned around this time. Book rooms well in advance.

Jan. 31–Feb. 2. Baneshwar (about 70 km south of Udaipur). *Fair.* A chance to celebrate with the Bhil tribe.

Feb. 11–13. Kota. *Hadoti Festival.* Musicians and dancers celebrate the Hadoti culture.

Feb. 28–March 1. Bharatpur. *Brij Festival.* On the eve of Holi (this can be a messy festival with colored water thrown liberally at everyone). Processions, music, dancing.

Mar. 2–3. Jaipur. *Elephant Festival.* More Holi hoopla. Wear old clothes. Great fancy-dressed elephants in a procession.

Mar. 20–21. Udaipur and **Jaipur.** *Gangaur Festival.* Held a few days after Holi. In honor of the goddess Parvati, with festive processions involving young girls and this deity, who is the symbol of marital bliss.

June 1–3. Mount Abu. *Summer Festival,* with lots of folk music and lots of Rajasthani dance performances.

July/August. Jodhpur. *Naag Panchami,* is dedicated to the 1,000-headed mythical serpent, Sesha. Huge cloth *naags* (cobras) are displayed in a festive fair. Contact the tourist department for the exact date.

Aug. 15–16. Jaipur. *Teej Festival,* dedicated to Parvati, celebrates the beginning of the monsoon. Rajasthani women take to swings hanging from trees and have swinging contests. Procession of the goddess Parvati involving elephants, camels, and dancers. A big event in Jaipur.

November 20–23. Pushkar. *Pushkar Festival* is an amazing festive and religious event with a carnival atmosphere. Gaily festooned cattle and thousands of people gather for a sacred dip at dawn in the holy waters of the lake. Book a tent or room well in advance.

Nov. 23 – 24. Bikaner. *Bikaner Festival.* Folk music and dance, culminating in a fire dance, with men jumping in and out of flames.

PARKS, ZOOS, GARDENS. Alwar. *Purjan Vihar* (Company Garden), designed in 1868 by Maharajah Shiv, Dan Singh, has a lovely collection of ferns in an area called *Simla,* built by the Maharajah Mangal Singh in 1885. Great place to get away from the heat.

Bundi. *Kohaksar Bagh,* near Shikar Burj (Royal Hunting Lodge), is a well-maintained old garden surrounding the cenotaphs of former Bundi kings and queens.

Jaipur. *Ram Niwas Garden and Zoo.* Garden was designed in 1868 by Sawai Ram Singh II. The zoo has a number of birds and animals, plus a crocodile-and python-breeding farm. Zoo fee, Rs. 0.25. *Sisodia Garden and Palace* was built by Maharaja Sawai Singh in 1770 for his queen, Sisodia. A central room of the palace has galleries on three sides surrounded by terraced gardens with fountains and pools. Fee: Rs. 0.50. *Vidyadharji Ka Bagh* was built by Vidyadhar, chief architect of Sawai Jai Singh II. Terraced gardens, fountains, and pools. Entry fee, Rs. 0.50.

Jaisalmer. *Bada Bagh* (6 km from Jaisalmer). A garden surrounds the royal cenotaphs, some of which are elaborately carved, including sculptures of former rulers on horseback.

Jodhpur. Mandore Gardens (9 km from Jodhpur). The ancient capital of Marwar, with the "Hall of Heroes"—16 Hindu and folk deities carved out of one rock plus royal cenotaphs of the Maharajah Jaswant Singh and Maharajah Ajit Singh. The cenotaphs are ornate and built atop plinths with exquisite sculpture. Good examples of the best of the Marwar epoch.

Udaipur. *Gulab Bagh,* a rose garden designed by Maharana Sajjan Singh, contains a lovely building with a library. Children can ride the Aravalli Express, a minitrain. *Saheliyon Ki Bari* is a garden of the maid of honor, constructed especially for the use of the royal ladies who lived in the palaces. Four ornate pools with delicately carved kiosks and elephants in marble. Fountains surround a lotus pool, marble throne, and sitting room. Fee, Rs. 0.50; fountain fee, Rs. 2. Open 9 A.M.–6 P.M.

 HISTORIC SITES. There are lots of things to see throughout Rajasthan, whether you are on a guided tour or you take the more adventurous route of fending for yourself. Centuries-old forts, temples, palaces, gardens, and other sites are open for viewing by the public—some for a nominal fee and others, free. The following is a list of the major ones.

AJMER-PUSHKAR

Adhai-Din-Ka-Jhonpra. In 1193 after Muhammed Ghori destroyed an ancient Sanskrit college and 30 Hindu temples, he construed this mosque of Indo-Islamic style on the temple ruins supposedly in two and one half days. The mosque stands on the pillars, each different, of these temples.

Anasagar. An artificial lake built in the twelfth century by Anaji Chauhan and added to by Jahangir. Shah Jahan built the *Baradari* (pavilions).

Dargah. Tomb of the Sufi saint Khwaja Muin-ud-Din Chisti (1142–1246). Here, Akbar sought the blessings of a son.

Kishangarh. Princely state founded by Maharajah Kishan Singh in the seventeenth century. See Gundelao Lake, Phool Mahal Palace, fort, temple of Shri Kalyan Raiji (Krishna). Kishangarh School of painting flourished here under the patronage of Maharaja Sanwant Singh.

Nasiyan (Red Temple). Jain temple built in the nineteenth century with a two-story hall containing gilt representations of Jain mythology. Open 8 A.M.–4 P.M. Fee, Rs. 0.40.

ALWAR

Alwar Fort. A medieval fort, in which Babur hid treasures for his son Humayun. Jahangir stayed here three years. The fort was eventually conquered by Maharajah Pratap Singh in 1775. Gigantic citadel towering on a hill; 15 large and 51 small towers with 446 holes for muskets. Several gates—Jai Pol, Suraj Pol, Laxman Pol, Chand Pol, Hrishan Pol, Andheri Gate. See the remains of Jai Mahal, Nikumbh Mahal, Salim Sagar Pond, Suraj Kund, and numerous temples. Great view of city.

Vinay Vilas Mahal (City Palace). Built in the late eighteenth century in a Rajput and Moghal blend of architecture. Behind the Vinay Vilas, you can see temples and a cenotaph of Maharajah Bakhtawar Singh built by Maharajah Vinay Singh in 1815. Unusual Bengali roof and arches.

BHARATPUR

Jawahar Burj. Old fort built in 1726 by Suraj Mal to commemorate his victories over the Moghuls and later the British. Coronation ceremonies of Jat rulers of Bharatpur took place here.

Lohagarh Fort (Iron Fort). Designed in the early eighteenth century by Maharajah Suraj Mal, the founder of Bharatpur, the fort held off numerous British attacks. See Kishori Mahal, Mahal Khas, Kothi Khas. Open 9 A.M.–5 P.M.

Palace. A blend of Rajput and Moghal architecture. Magnificent apartments with beautifully designed floor tiles.

BIKANER AREA

Bhanda Sagar Jain Temple (five km from Bikaner). A sixteenth-century Jain temple, dedicated to the twenty-third Teerthankar Parsvanathji.

Devi Kund (eight km from Bikaner). Royal crematorium with a number of cenotaphs belonging to former rulers of the Bika dynasty. The *chhatri* of Maharajah Surat Singh is white marble with Rajput paintings adorning the ceiling.

Junagarh Fort. Built in the sixteenth century by Raja Raj Singh, an outstanding general of Mogul Emperor Akbar. Encircled by a moat with numerous red sandstone and marble palaces. Suraj Pol (Sun Gate) is the main entrance. Weddings and births were celebrated in Har Mandir (chapel). Numerous palaces adorned with columns, arches, graceful screens. Open 10 A.M.–5 P.M. Fee, Rs. 2.50; students, Rs. 1.

Karni Mata Temple (in Deshnok, 33 km from Bikaner). Dedicated to Karni Mata, an incarnation of Durga. The rats that crawl around here are sacred. Maharajah Ganga Singh donated the massive silver gates.

Lalgarh Palace (Red Fort). Built by Maharaja Ganga Singh in the nineteenth century. Red sandstone with terrific carvings. In the banquet hall, see the collection of old photographs and trophies. Open 10 A.M.–5 P.M. (closed Wednesdays). Entry fee: Rs. 1.

BUNDI

Chatter Mahal (Palace of Towers). Massive gates surround an enormous collection of stone buildings built by successive rulers starting in the 1600s. The palace is covered with spy holes and mysterious windows. Visit the Naubat Khana, the Hathi Pol (curious water clock which formerly struck each half hour), the Diwan-i-Am. Also see the Chitra Shala, built by Rao Rajah Shatroo Salji in the 1600s. Terrific Bundi mural paintings which adorn the walls and ceilings were added much later.

Naval Sagar, an artificial lake with a temple of Varuna (Aryan god of water) in the center.

Phool Sagar. A twentieth-century palace and present home of the Durbar (former ruler of Bundi). Also known as the Flower Palace, the magnificent home has banquet rooms, numerous halls, plus an intriguing collection of murals created by Italian prisoners of war. To visit, permission is required; call the secretary, tel. 1, 34.

Taragarh (Star Fort). Built in 1372, the fort with an enormous tank (originally the palace reservoir) provides a commanding view of Bundi.

CHITTAURGARH

Chittaurgarh Fort. Foundations attributed to the seventh century. Rests atop a hill. Enormous. Numerous gates providing a network of defense. Beyond the first gate, Padal Pol, a tablet marks the spot where Prince Bagh Singh died during the second attack on Chittaurgarh. Between the second gate (Bhairon Pol) and the third gate (Hanuman Pol) are two chattris (tombs) where Jaimal of Badnore and Kalla were killed by Akbar in 1567. Near the main gate (Ram Pol), there is another chhatri for Patta of Kelwa, a 15-year-old fighter who died here. The fort is seven miles in circumference and contains some great Rajput architecture. See the *Vijay Stambh* (Victory Tower), nine stories high, and covered with secular sculpture. Built by Maharana Jumbha to celebrate his victory over the Moslem rulers of Malwa and Gujarat in 1440. Kirti Stambh ("Tower of Fame"), built by a Jain merchant in the twelfth century and dedicated to Adinathji (the first of the Jain Teerthankaras). The tower is covered with figures from a Jain pantheon. Rana Kumbha's Palace unfortunately is in ruins. The palace also contained elephant and horse stables, plus a Shiva temple. Padmini's Palace, supposedly for Queen Padmini, overlooks a pool. Within the walls, a battle occurred between Allauddin Khilji and Rana Ratan Singh, which ended with the death of Padmini. Meera and Kumbha Shyam Temple, built in the Indo-Aryan style and associated with the mystic poet-wife of Bhojraj, the eldest son of Rana Sanga. Kalika Mata Temple built initially in the eighth century as Surya (Sun Temple) and later converted into Kalika Mata, or a mother goddess temple, in the fourteenth century.

Nagari (14 km north of Chittaurgarh). Ancient town that flourished from the Maurya to the Gupta era. Interesting archaeological sites with a distinct connection to Buddhism and Hinduism.

DEEG

Former summer resort of the rulers of Bharatpur (32 km from there). Numerous forts, palaces, and gardens. See *Ghopal Bhavan* and *Suraj Bhavan,* built of marble. Open 8 A.M.–noon; 1–6 P.M. Much of the beauty of these buildings was stolen from Mogul palaces in Agra and Delhi.

JAIPUR

Amber Palace and Fort (11 km from Jaipur). Construction begun by Maharajah Man Singh in early 1700s, completed 100 years later: an excellent blend of Rajput and Mogul influence. See the Hall of Victory, with panels of alabaster and inlay work; *Sheesh Mahal* (Hall of Mirrors)—step inside, close doors, strike a match—the ceiling glows. Rooms are small; typical of Mogul period. Courtyards and narrow passages: typical Rajput. Above the palace is the Jaigash Fort (supposedly still contains hidden treasures of Jaipur). Open: 9 A.M.–4:30 P.M.. Entry fee, Rs. 1.

City Palace and Museum. Begun by Sawai Jai Singh in the 1700s, with further additions by later maharajahs. Open: 9:30 A.M.–4:45 P.M.. Entry fee Rs. 5; students, Rs. 2.

Gaitor (eight km from Jaipur). Royal cenotaphs of kings at the foot of the Nahargarh hills. The cenotaph of Sawa Jai Singh II is of white marble, with intricate carvings over the dome, supported by 20 pillars. Other cenotaphs are for Madho Singh, Ram Singh, and Partap Singh.

Govind Devji Temple. Temple of Lord Krishna facing the City Temple complex. From here, you can get a good view of the City Palace, Chandra Mahal.

Hawa Mahal. (Palace of Winds). Built in 1799 by Maharajah Sawai Pratap Singh. Located on the Johari Bazar heading north. A five-story building with a pyramidal facade. Overhanging windows with latticed screens, domes, spires. Entrance fee: Rs. 0.30. Open: 10 A.M.–5 P.M.. Closed Fridays.

Jantar Mantar (Observatory). Built before the city of Jaipur in 1726. Located southeast of Chandra Mahal within the city palace complex. Largest and best preserved of the five astronomical observatories built by Sawai Jai Singh. Open: 9 A.M.–5 P.M. Entry fee, Rs. 1; free Mondays.

Nahargarh Fort (15 km from Jaipur). Originally called Sudarshangarh Fort, it was built in 1734 by Sawai Jai Singh. The upper floor was constructed by Sawai Ram Singh II in 1868–69; more apartments were added in 1902–03 by Sawai Madho Singh II. Great view of Jaipur from here. Open: 10 A.M.–5 P.M. Entry fee: Rs. 0.50.

Sisodia Palace and Garden (eight km from Jaipur). Built by Maharajah Sawai Jai Singh in 1770 for his queen, Sisodia. Central room with galleries on three sides surrounded by terraced gardens with fountains, pools, and sculpture. Entry fee, Rs. 0.50.

JAISALMER

Citadel. Constructed by Rawal Jaisal in 1156 on Trikuta hill surrounded by high golden walls. Inside are Jain temples dedicated to Rikhabdevji and Sambhavnathji, constructed from the twelfth to the fifteenth century. Filled with deities and mythological carvings. *Gyan Bhandar* (library), part of the Jain temple complex, contains some of the oldest manuscripts in India.

Havelis: Salim Singh Ki Haveli built by Salim Singh in the seventeenth century. Narrow dimension from ground floor widens at the top, with balconies jutting out. In sad disrepair within; a courteous request (or a few rupees) should get you inside. *Nathmal Ki Haveli* built in the nineteenth century by two architect brothers. The structure is flanked by stone elephants. Look carefully, they are not identical—just harmoniously in tune. Again, a courteous request or a small donation may get you inside. *Patva Havelis* —a string of five havelis built by the Patva brothers. Two of the five are owned by the government and are open to the public (inquire at the tourist department for the times). Handsome carved pillars. Painted murals on some of the interior walls. The other three are accessible, with a small donation, if the owner is in the mood.

JODHPUR

Jaswant Thada. Royal crematorium built in 1899 for Maharajah Jaswant Sinbgh II near the Meherangarh Fort. A white marble structure housing the portraits of past rulers. Plus other cenotaphs, also in marble, to commemorate acts of bravery and generosity of successive rulers. Open: 8 A.M.–6 P.M.; 9 A.M.–5 P.M. (Novemer 1–March 31).

Mahamandir Temple (two km from Jodhpur). Temple with 100 pillars. Richly ornamented with figures in various Yoga postures.

Meherangarh Fort. Overlooking Jodhpur and constructed by Rao Jodha in 1459. Seven gates lead into the fort. Numerous interior palaces and temples and an excellent museum. Open 6 A.M.–6 P.M.; 9 A.M.–5 P.M. (November 1 to March 31). Entry fee: Rs. 10 for the museum and guide; Rs. 4 for part of the fort and no guide. Get a guide. See the museum.

Umaid Bhawan Palace. Built by Maharajah Umaid Singh 1929–42. Also known as *Chhitar Palace* because of the sandstone that was used. Houses a museum.

KOTA AREA

Baroli (40 km from Kota). One of the oldest temple complexes in Rajasthan, constructed in the ninth century. Built in the Panchaytan (group of five) style, some still with rich carvings.

Jhalra Patan (60 km from Kota). "City of Bells," with the Jhalra patan, one of the best sun temples in India located within this ancient city. Also see old Jain temples, plus the ruins of Buddhist cave temples recently excavated.

MOUNT ABU

Adhar Devi Temple. Chiseled out of a rock, and dedicated to the goddess Durga. Good view of Mount Abu.

Dilwara Jain Temples. Constructed from the eleventh to the thirteenth centuries. Open: noon to 6 P.M. for non-Jains. Photography: Rs. 5 per camera.

RANAKPUR

Chanmukha. Jain temple constructed in the fifteenth century and dedicated to Adinathji. Great sculpture throughout interior and on the 1,444 pillars. Open from noon to 5 P.M. for non-Jains.

SHEKHAVATI DISTRICT

The following towns and villages are worth visiting to see the art of frescoes created in the mid-nineteenth century. The frescoes cover the facades and interiors of havelis (mansions of former Marwari merchants). Originally, the themes were religious, then moved to ornamental motifs. In the 1900s, painters called *chitera* began imitating British lithographs and etchings. First, only natural pigments were used; then, around 1890, a gradual switch was made to chemical dyes. The towns are located in this district, which lies between Delhi and Jaipur. Visit Sikar (the old quarter), Mandawa, Fatehpur Sikri, Khetri, and Nawalgarh.

UDAIPUR

City Palace Museum. Begun in the 1600s by Udai Singh and constructed of granite and marble. The main entrance is via the triple gate, Tripolia, with eight carved marble arches. Inside are numerous palaces: Suraj Gokhada (Sun Balcony), Badi Mahal (Garden Palace), Sheesh Mahal, Bhim Vilas, Chini Chitrasala, Mor Chowk (Peacock Courtyard). This is one place where it's worth having a guide. Entry fee: Rs. 2.50. Open: 9:30 A.M.–4:30 P.M.

Eklingji (22 km from Udaipur). Temple of sandstone and marble built in 1734. Ornate pillared hall under a huge pyramidical roof. Numerous interesting temples in this little village.

Jagdish Temple. Built in 1651 by Maharana Jagat Singh I. Largest temple in Udaipur, with good sculptures and carvings. Offers a great view of Udaipur.

 MUSEUMS. Practically every city and town in Rajasthan—besides being a museum in itself—contains a museum with centuries-old art objects and artifacts. Included are paintings, armor, sculpture, and manuscripts from many dynasties. Some of the buildings housing the museums are sights to behold, from palaces to forts. The following is a selection.

AJMER

Government Museum. Akbar's palace and royal quarters filled with Rajput and Mogul armor and regional sculptures. Open 10 A.M.–5 P.M.; Rs. .40.

ALWAR

Government Museum (second floor of City Palace). Great collection of Mogul and Rajput paintings from the eighteenth and nineteenth centuries and ancient manuscripts in Urdu, Sanskrit, and Persian. Good collection of armor. Open 10 A.M.–5 P.M.; closed Fridays and official holidays. Rs. .30.

BIKANER

Ganga Golden Jubilee Museum. One of Rajasthan's best museums, with a good collection of the pre-Harappan civilization, the Gupta and Kushan era: terra cotta, pottery, paintings, sculpture, armor, and coins. A separate collection of local arts and crafts. Open 10 A.M.–5 P.M.; closed Fridays and holidays.

CHITTAURGARH

Government Museum (former Fateh Prakesh Palace). Collection of sculptures from temples and other buildings in the fort. Open 10 A.M.–5 P.M.; closed Fridays and official holidays.

JAIPUR

Albert Hall Museum, in Ram Niwas Garden. Eclectic displays from clay models showing Yogi postures to carpets and displays of folk instruments and Rajasthani culture. Beautiful building. Open 10 A.M.–5 P.M.; closed Fridays and holidays. Rs. 1 per person. Free on Monday.
City Palace Museum. Collection of royal garments, textiles, carpets, armor, miniature paintings, and so forth. Open 9:30 A.M.– 4:45 P.M. Rs. 5; Rs. 2 for students.
Hawa Mahal Museum. Open 10 A.M.–5 P.M.; closed Friday, free on Monday. Rs. 60.

JODHPUR

Government Museum, in Umaid Public Garden. Collection of armor, textiles, local arts and crafts, miniatures, portraits, and manuscripts. Open 10 A.M.–4:30 P.M.; closed holidays. Rs. .50.
Meherangarh Fort Museum. Within various apartments and palaces of the regal fort are palanquins, howdahs, royal cradles, miniatures, folk instruments, costumes, and furniture. Open 8 A.M.–6 P.M. (April 1–October 30); 9 A.M.–5 P.M. (November 1–March 31). Rs. 10 with a guide (a guide is advisable).
Umaid Bhawan Palace Museum. Former possessions of the maharajah. Many clocks. Open 10 A.M.–5 P.M.

KOTA

Government Museum. Old coins, Hadoti sculpture. Open 10 A.M.–4:30 P.M. Rs. .60; Rs. .30 for students.

Maharana Madho Singh Museum. Set in old palace. Rich collection of Rajput miniatures in Kota school, sculptures, frescoes, weapons, and other antiques. Open 11 A.M.–5 P.M. Rs. 2; Rs. 1 for students.

UDAIPUR

Ahar Museum. Standing in the remains of the old city; royal cenotaphs of the maharanas of Mewar.

Bharatiya Lok Kala Museum. Indian folk art museum. Folk dresses, ornaments, puppets, masks, dolls, instruments, and paintings. Puppet show can be arranged on request. Open 9 A.M.–6 P.M. Rs. 2.

City Palace Museum. The only way to see this palace and its museum is with a guide; Rs. 20 for the tour. Open 9:30 A.M.–4:30 P.M.

 WILDLIFE SANCTUARIES. Sariska Tiger Reserve, Alwar. Best times to visit are before sunset and early morning. Closest game sanctuary to Delhi, with tigers, sambar, antelope, and wild boar. Closed July–August. Rs. 10 entry fee; Rs. 2 per person for night halt at watch towers; Rs. 20 for a guide; Rs. 5 for spotlight.

Keolodeo National Park, Bharatpur. Best time to visit is October–February. Bird sanctuary with over 350 species, plus some wild animals. Former hunting preserve of the royal family of Bharatpur. Entry fee: Rs. 5 per car; Rs. 10 per person; Rs. 20 per boat trip; Rs. 15 for a guide (up to four persons in the party).

Desert National Park, Jaisalmer (40 km south of Jaipur). Vast expanse of sand with desert animals—desert fox, cat, hare, lizards, sand grouse, great Indian bustard breeding ground, cranes, eagles, falcons. Sand dunes are in this park; camel rides are available.

Ranthambhor National Park, Sawai Madhopur (162 km from Jaipur). Famous tiger reserve—deer, wild boar, langur, tigers, leopards, jackals, sloth-bears, hyenas, python. Three lakes, old fort built in 944, and an eighth-century Ganesh temple.

Wildlife Sanctuary, Sariska. Rs. 35 per person. Book through Tiger Den Tourist Bungalow, tel. 42. Tour on demand.

Ranthambhor National Park, Sawai Madhopur. Rs. 50 per adult; Rs. 30 per child. Book through Castle Jhoomar Baori, tel. 620. Tour on demand.

Udaipur. Bhartiya Lik Kala Mandal, Sahelion Ki Bari, Fatch Sagar, Moti Magri, City Palace, Jagdish Temple, Gulab Garden, Haldi Ghati, Eklingji Nathdwara. Rs. 20 per person. Open 8 A.M.–1:30 P.M.. Book through Kajri Tourist Bungalow, Shastri Circle, tel. 23509.

 SPORTS. The polo season is in March, when five tournaments are held at the Rajasthan Polo Club, Jaipur. This Rajput sport can involve more than a horse. Polo is played here with elephants, camel, and bikes. The polo ground is near the Rambagh.

 SHOPPING. Rajasthan's craftsmen have been famous for centuries for stonecutting, enameling, setting precious stones, tie-dying textiles, block printing silks and muslins, ivory carving, and lacquer and filigree work. The Rajasthan Government has emporiums in the following cities (called *Rajasthan Government Handicrafts Emporiums):* Ajmer, Bikaner, Chittaurgarh, Jaipur, Jodhpur, Kota, and Udaipur. Also just take walks and browse, even buy, in the local bazaars. They're always fun; always interesting. And if you want something, remember to bargain, always! Jaipur and Jodhpur are the two big shopping cities. The following are a few reliable shops with good-quality merchandise, when you're after something truly special and valuable.

For fine art, including paintings, old photographs, Jain temple art, wooden sculptures, and good Rajasthani momentos, *Art Age, Ltd.,* 2 Bhawani Singh Rd., Jaipur 302005; tel. 75726.

For beautiful creations in Rajasthani fabrics (clothes and home furnishing), *Anokhi,* 2 Tilak Marg opposite Udyog Bhawan C Scheme; tel. 76619.

For fine gems and guaranteed satisfaction, *Gem Palace,* Mirza Ismail Rd., Jaipur 302001; tel. 74175. Its royal clientele makes Cartier seem third rate.

For handicrafts and "antiques": *Abani Handicrafts,* Anand Bhawan, High Court Rd., Jodhpur 342001; tel. 21150.

SNACKS AND TEATIME. In Rajasthan, if you're near a fancy hotel, you're also near some form of snack. But in Jaipur and Jodhpur, try the following places for local goodies:

Jaipur. *Chankakya,* Mirza Ismail Rd.; tel. 78461. Great snacks, Rajasthani ice-creams, shakes; Open noon to 11 P.M. *Gauri,* Gangaur Tourist Bungalow, near All India Rd., good snacks and espresso; open 24 hours. *LMB Hotel,* Johari Bazar, tel. 48844. Open 8:30 A.M.–10:30 P.M. Famous for its deserts and beverages. *Natraj Restaurant,* Mirza Ismail Rd., 9 A.M.–11 P.M. Great sweets and beverages. *Surya Mahal,* Mirza Ismail Rd., 9 A.M.–11 P.M., good snacks and coffee.

Jodhpur. *Rawat Mishtan Bhandar,* Station Rd., near Annand Cinema (9 A.M.–10 P.M.). Name means "treasure trove of sweets." That's what it is, plus a great selection of tasty beverages.

BARS AND NIGHTLIFE. Throughout Rajasthan the Western-style hotels usually have bars, which are open during lunch hour and in the evening until 10:30 or 11. Three worth trying are the posh *Polo Bar* at the Rambagh, where you can sit surrounded by trophies won by the maharajah's polo team and an indoor fountain; *Trophy Bar* at Umaid Bhawan Palace, Jodhpur, has a regal atmosphere. *Amrit Sagar* in Lake Palace Hotel, Udaipur, reached by a great boat ride on Pichola Lake; have your drink outside and just gaze into the lake.

UTTAR PRADESH

Abode of the Gods

by
KATHLEEN COX

Although smaller in size than overcrowded Britain, the state of Uttar Pradesh has 20 million more inhabitants, who somehow manage to make a living from the fertile soil and the recent benefits of land reform. Before Independence, *Zamindars,* absentee landowners, lorded over the peasantry, usually exploiting them mercilessly. Former tenant-farmers are now small holders, but they still have to cope with the lack of equipment, enormous families, and sometimes unsympathetic officials. They find solace in religion; two of the holiest rivers meet at Allahabad—the Yamuna (or Jumna) and the Ganges (or Ganga). At the *sangam* —their confluence—India's biggest religious bathing festival, the Magh Mela, is held each spring. Every twelfth year, on an auspicious date that is chosen by astrologers, millions converge on the riverbanks in Haridwar to join in the Kumbh Mela, an even more important ritual to the devout.

It was along the Ganges and Yamuna that the first Aryans made advances into India, calling their newly won territory Aryavarta. It was the kings of this valley who fought in the Great Battle of Kurukshetra recorded in the Mahabharata. It was in the foothill area (in present-day Nepal) that Siddhartha, a prince of the Skaya clan, was born, the man who became Gautama Buddha.

The Gangetic plain served as a pivot to the Mauryan Empire whose most outstanding figures were Chandragupta and Asoka. Harsha of Kanauj made himself master of northern India in the seventh century, and the region remained Hindu until Mahmud of Ghazni invaded and captured the imperial city in 1019. The Mohammedan conquest of Hindustan was consolidated over the centuries by various Moslem dynasties, but once the Mogul Empire gave visible signs of decline, the East India Company—with Calcutta as its base—began its irregular acquisitions, which culminated in the battle of Buxar (1764). The work of British conquest was now under way and a few months later when Robert Clive, founder of British India, was sent out again to India, he reported: "It is scarcely a hyperbole to say that tomorrow the whole Mogul empire is in our power."

EXPLORING UTTAR PRADESH

Leaving Delhi, bypass Meerut, a small city known as the cradle of that memorable insurrection, the Indian or Sepoy Mutiny, commonly referred to as India's First War of Independence. The British governor-general's order of 1856 that all units were liable for overseas service created consternation among the Indian troops, since, by Hindu religious law, those who leave their native land become outcasts. The Indians, especially the sepoy regiments, predominantly high-caste Rajputs, were offended by the British blunder and interpreted it as a deliberate act of religious intolerance.

Just a spark would trigger the move for sedition. This the British government provided the next year; it re-armed the troops with a new rifle that required a greased cartridge. The grease was rumored to be cow's fat, defiling the Hindu who touched it. The grease was also rumored to be pig's fat, which outraged the Moslem sepoys. Insubordination burst into open rebellion at the Meerut garrison. The Indians shot their officers and then marched on Delhi to transfer their allegiance to the Mogul emperor's descendant, who still kept his court and imperial title. This revolt, which can be regarded as the initial stirring of a nationalist movement, lasted several months. Although it didn't spread beyond the confines of Northern India, it resulted in grim battles and the liquidation of the East India Company. The British Crown took over, but the mood was never again the same.

ALIGARH, KANAUJ, AND KANPUR

For centuries a Rajput fortress, Aligarh lost its independence to the Moguls at the beginning of the sixteenth century. Then, in the middle of the eighteenth century, the Afghans, Jats, and Marathas fought over Aligarh. During the Maratha occupation, a French general, de Boigne, presided over the troops, and the fort was reputed to be impregnable. Finally, in the second Maratha War, Scindia was taken by Wellesley—the future Duke of Wellington—and Aligarh was captured by Lord Lake. Four miles to the west lies the massive Fort Scindia, heavily involved in these events. In the old city is the Bala Kala, a stronghold with a superimposed mosque (1728).

Today a small town on the Ganges, Kanauj (ancient Kanyakubja) was for many centuries the Hindu capital of northern India—a city of wealth and beauty, of fine temples and shining palaces. For five centuries, following its foundation by Harsha, Kanauj remained the symbol of imperial power, the capital of the greatest empire that came into being after the Mauryas. Its prestige remained until the Moslem invasion of the eleventh century. Ransacked and ruined, Kanauj passed into

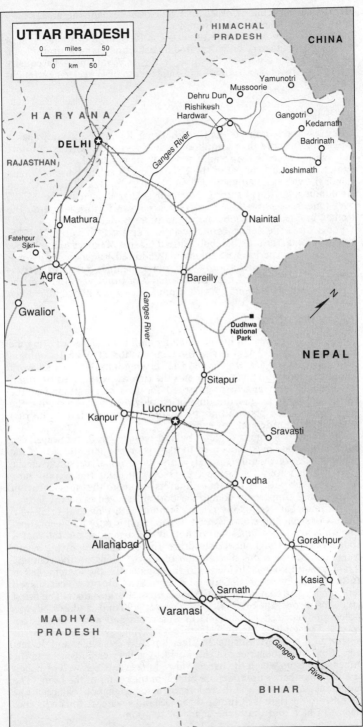

oblivion. Little remains of its ancient glories, except the melancholy ruins of a few ramparts and temples.

Some 50 miles farther, is Kanpur—the Pittsburgh of India—one of India's great industrial cities, created by trade and manufacture. Tragic events took place here at the time of the 1857 mutiny—the equally heroic exploits of Tantia Topi and the defense of Wheeler's entrenchment.

LUCKNOW

Far less industrialized than neighboring Kanpur, Lucknow has a population of more than a million, including a good portion of Shiite and Sunni Moslems living among Hindu neighbors. Lucknow is the eighteenth-century capital of the Persian sheiks called Nawab Wazirs (nabobs), who originally arrived in the Avadh area (Lucknow and surrounding territory) during Emperor Akbar's reign in the 1500s. Over time, successive Mogul rulers, whose own fortunes were on the decline, granted the nabobs more and more power.

For a time, the nabob capital was in Faizabad, but around 1775, Asaf-ud Daula, the fourth nabob, shifted his seat of power to Lucknow. His charity and perhaps megalomania endowed Lucknow with some of the best of its architecturally rich and sometimes outlandish structures, which are located near the left bank of the River Gomti in the northern part of the capital. Asaf's munificence was real and ingenious.

Asafi Imambara

In 1784, after a year of life-threatening famine that affected everyone regardless of status, Asaf began the construction of Asafi Imambara, his great relief project. He divided the starving into two distinct work forces: the poor who built by day and the rich who destroyed by night. Obviously, this arrangement retarded forward momentum. But the nabob wanted to extend the time of employment to keep paying the poor. Besides, the poor outnumbered the formerly rich and the rich weren't such hot demolition experts.

The Imambara stands directly behind two elaborate gateways. The outer gate, where musicians used to play, is on the opposite side of the public road, which unfortunately cuts the original perspective; the inner gate is purely for symmetry. Once you enter the second gate, Asaf's mosque with its 152-foot minarets stands to the right, a row of cloisters that supposedly conceals a bottomless well is on the left.

The Imambara (religious house) is built with clay and brick—no cement or iron, and wood is used in the interior only for decoration. The walls are 16 feet thick but of hollow construction, and the roof is 10 feet thick. Throughout the structure, there are no supporting beams or pillars. An ingenious distribution of weight holds up the ceiling.

The ground floor is divided into three halls. To the extreme left is an octagonal chamber of Chinese design. Its Chinese saucer-shaped ceiling has a 216-foot dome that extends up to the third floor. The priest sat on his throne (the original, which was of gold and sandalwood, was stolen and replaced with silver) in this room and addressed his devotees. The middle chamber features a ceiling whose shape is the reverse of a boat. Measuring 162 feet long, 53 feet wide, and 50 feet high, this hall is the largest in the world. A gallery extends around the upper story from which the harem viewed the events below. The nabob and the Imambara's architect are buried in the center of the room. The numerous mirrors are collected from assorted nabob palaces. The chamber to the right is of Indian design. Stand a watermelon on its end, slice it in half, and that's the shape of the dome.

As you leave the Imambara, notice on the left a small paper replica of a shrine (*tazia*), made and replaced annually for the woman who, reportedly on receiving the word from God, gave the land to the nabob who had been badgering her for years to sell it. She relented, but only on condition that he construct this tazia (memorial) to her. No one knows her name or what happened to her. Originally, tazias were constructed of wax that mysteriously refused to melt after hours in the sun. Now only one man understands this delicate craft, but he, too, is awaiting the word of God before he reveals his secret.

From outside the Imambara, a set of stairs leads up to an extraordinary labyrinth called Bhul-Bhulaiyan, which came about as a result of the building design required to support the ceilings. Try to find your way around. Every 20 steps or so leads to an intersection with four choices, three of which lead nowhere (here's a secret: think right). Guides do a brisk "escort" business. From the rooftop there's a great view of Lucknow.

Chhota Imambara

The Chhota Imambara, or Hussainabad Imambara, was built in 1836 by the Muhammad Ali Shan, the eighth nabob, as his burial place. A fish as a weathervane, just inside the gate, may seem odd, but the fish is auspicious in Hindu and Moslem mythology; its presence is a good omen. The chain that leads to the statue of the woman, at the left of the entrance, is no act of whimsy either. It served then and now as a lightning rod to protect the statue and the building from storms.

The tiny mosque on the right was for women. The next building on the right as you walk along the channel that leads to the Chhota is a burial tomb for the nabob's daughter, Zinat Asuja, and is a miniature replica of the Taj Mahal. The building directly across from it, which holds her husband's remains, was originally planned for symmetry.

The Chhota, with its gilded dome and vast number of turrets and minarets, is almost baroque. Its handsome black and white facade is, in fact, a vast collection of verses from the Koran. Inside, you are confronted by a dazzling collection of mirrors, chandeliers, and lamps. The tall red and white lamp near the middle of the floor, with its 500 moving pieces, was purchased by the nabob in 1836. The center chandelier in the entry room has 1,000 moving pieces. Here, too, you'll see a vast collection of tazias. Also on the left-hand wall, as you face the entrance, you'll see an extremely old print in blue lettering on white; it contains the entire Koran.

Jama Masjid, Picture Gallery

To the west of the Chhota is the elegant Jama Masjid, started by Muhammad Ali Shah and completed after his death. This royal mosque of the nabobs, closed to non-Moslems, is a lovely long building crowded by three onion-shaped domes and flanked by two lofty minarets.

For a glimpse of the fancy men who ruled over Lucknow, visit the Picture Gallery (originally a building built by Muhammad Ali Shah), reflecting into a pool of water and surrounded by a grove. It's a portrait gallery that could be called the Nabob Hall of Fame.

The Residency

Toward the heart of Lucknow stands the Residency, the battle-scarred remains of Asaf-ud Daula's other elaborate architectural contribution. Originally conceived as a pleasure house with a network of underground chambers that provided relief from the summer heat, it was acquired by the British when they annexed the province and deposed and deported the last nabob, Wajid Ali Shah. That act sealed the fate of this building. During the 1857 Indian Mutiny, British inhabitants crowded into the elegant building, which then became the scene of some of the fiercest fighting. For 87 days, the British held out until Sir Colin Campbell broke through the Indian lines and relieved the half-starved defenders. Of the 3,000 troops and noncombatants who had refused to surrender, less than 1,000 staggered out. Although the marks of cannon shots gouge every remaining wall, the surrounding gardens and lawns are kept in order. Peace and goodwill prevail; unpleasant memories lie buried with the past.

Tombs

In the center of Lucknow are the perfectly proportioned tombs of Nabob Ali Khan and his beautiful wife, Khurshed Begum, built in the beginning of the nineteenth century. The Kaisar Bagh adjoining the tombs contains rows of apartments that housed the ladies of the royal harem. Near the river is Shahnajaf Imambara, which derives its name from Najaf, a city in Iraq. It is the early-nineteenth-century tomb of Nabob Ghazi-ud-din Haider and his wives, including Mubarak Mahal (a European). This building, constructed in 1814, was a stronghold of independence fighters in 1857. Like the Residency, what you see today —its low frontage and large flattened-out dome—diffuses an atmosphere of great turmoil.

La Martiniere

On the outskirts of the city, in a park close to a small lake, rises a strange architectural jumble of styles built in 1795, not by a nabob but a Frenchman, Claude Martin, during the reign of Asaf-ud Daula. Nothing is missing in this compendium of styles; gargoyles rub shoulders with Corinthian columns and Roman arches are next to Oriental turrets. This fantastic hodgepodge was designed as a boys' school, with Kipling's *Kim* a student.

Chowk

Chowk is the bazaar in the old city of Lucknow, where the Moslem servants of the nabobs originally lived. Note the architectural detail of many of the buildings: stone lacework along the upper stories, later 1920s and '30s style facades that add up to a curious blend. Once you enter the main gate, you will hit the bustle of the bazaar—rows and rows of silver and jewelry merchants, shops and stalls selling hand-embroidered *chikan* work. The former haunt of the nabob feudal aristocracy, ancestral dwellings abound, some still inhabited by old-time families. Here, gracious nabob manners still persist, and you sense that eighteenth-century charm of an epoch when Lucknow was the center of culture and refinement.

ALLAHABAD

In ancient times Allahabad, which is at the confluence of the Ganges and Yamuna rivers, was known as Prayag. It was and still is an important place of Hindu pilgrimage. By the end of the twelfth century, Prayag fell under Moslem rule and in 1584 was given its new name.

The Patal Puri Temple is underneath an enormous fort that Akbar built all around it. Descending a long sloping passage, you see a tree in the dim square-shaped hall. This tree, watered continuously by the priests, was mentioned by the Chinese traveler, Hiuen T'sang, in A.D. 640 and is known as Akshaya Batt, the Undying Banyan Tree. Another shrine of tremendous importance to the Hindus is Bharadwaja. Named after the great sage who occupied a hermitage on the high bank overlooking the place where the waters meet, it is mentioned in the *Ramayana*. Bharadwaja had 10,000 pupils and, as the head of a clan, he provided his students with free board and lodging. His *ashram* became a cross between a hermitage, a seat of learning, and a welfare institution. Now, Allahabad University occupies this site.

Akbar's Fort and Mogul Monuments

Akbar's Fort is an impressive work of masonry. It houses the Ashoka Pillar, a single shaft of polished sandstone 35 feet high. Its capital disappeared during its 2,200 years of existence, but it still shows some of the edicts the emperor inscribed around its base—even though Jahangir's inscriptions of his family tree partially obliterated them. The mausoleum of Prince Khusro, Emperor Jahangir's eldest son, is covered with paintings and a Persian verse that ends with a chronogram giving the Moslem year of 1031 (A.D. 1622) as the date of his death.

If you're in Allahabad during the Magh Mela, held each spring at the confluence of the two rivers, don't miss the ceremonies. Bundle-laden pilgrims in the thousands arrive each day, setting up tents and makeshift huts. Holy men lie on beds of nails or read out scriptures to worshipers before they take the ritual plunge. Rows of barbers shave the heads of pilgrims to comply with orthodox precepts that bald is the beatific best. Hindu women throw rose petals and marigolds into the holy river as offerings. Improvised stalls sell food, souvenirs, and images of deities. There are no bathing *ghats* (riverbank steps), and most pilgrims are rowed by innumerable boats into mid-river to perform their immersion.

Allahabad is famous for its literary traditions. The Sahitya Sammalan is a pioneer institution for the study of the Hindi language. Outside the city, the ancestral home of the late Jawaharlal Nehru, called Anand Bhavan (Place of Joy), is now a museum set up in his memory. Next to it stands Swaraj Bhavan (House of Freedom), which he donated to the nation in 1930 as a children's home.

FAIZABAD AND AJODHYA

On leaving Lucknow, go due east and you will arrive at Faizabad, capital of the nabobs of Avadh before they switched to Lucknow. Of its numerous monuments, the mausoleum of Behbu Begum is the finest in the region. Adjoining Faizabad is Ajodhya, principal city of the ancient Kingdom of Kosala. Revered by Hindus as the birthplace of Lord Rama, hero of the Ramayana, it is one of India's seven sacred places. The most important buildings are the Hanuman temple and Kanak Vhavan Temple, said to have been the palace of the God-King Rama. Buddha supposedly traveled extensively in these parts, and Hiuen T'sang, that tireless seventh-century tourist, reported glowingly of the place.

SARNATH: CRADLE OF BUDDHIST FAITH

Sarnath, six miles from Varanasi, is the center of the Buddhist world, just as Varanasi is the spiritual center for Hindus. At Sarnath, Buddha ("the one who is enlightened" in Sanskrit) preached his first sermon more than 2,500 years ago. Here, he revealed the Eightfold Path that leads to the end of sorrow, the attainment of inner peace, enlightenment, and ultimate nirvana. Here, he established his doctrine of the Middle Way, the golden path between extremes of asceticism and self-indulgence.

Two hundred years later, Ashoka arrived—the Mauryan emperor who was the greatest convert to Buddhism. He erected a pillar at Lumbini on the Nepalese border where Buddha was born. In Sarnath, he built several *stupas* (shrines) and another pillar with the famous lion capital that symbolizes the ideals of peace and righteousness—adopted by India as the State emblem. You can see it in the excellent Sarnath Archaeological Museum. Six hundred years after that, under the Gupta Dynasty, Sarnath reached its zenith. Back then, the Chinese observer Fa-Hi-An claimed, 1,500 priests sat every day around the banyan tree close to the Vihara Temple. This tree is supposedly the actual Bo-Tree under which Gautama Siddhartha spent so many years of meditation and purification before he became the Buddha.

The twelfth century marked Sarnath's decline, with the devout Queen Kumaradevi building a large monastery: the final tribute, before Varanasi rulers dismantled the stupas—depredation for building materials. In the sixteenth century, the Moslem Emperor Akbar built a brick tower on top of some of the most sacred remaining stupas to commemorate his father's visit some years earlier. This downfall continued until 1836, when Sir Alexander Cunningham started extensive excavations. First, a stone slab was discovered with an inscription of the Buddhist creed; then numerous other relics were found.

Five great monuments remain: The Dhamekh Stupa (A.D. 500) is the largest survivor, with geometric ornaments on its walls. This stupa supposedly marks the location where Buddha set the Wheel of Law in motion, although excavations have unearthed the remains of an even earlier stupa of Mauryan bricks of the Gupta period (200 B.C.). The second monument is the Dharamrajika Stupa, set up by Ashoka to contain the bodily relics of Buddha. It's basically in ruins, thanks to the eighteenth-century king, Jagan Singh, who decided he had a better use for the construction materials. Also see the main shrine where Ashoka used to sit in meditation with the Ashoka pillar in front, and the Chankama, which marks the sacred promenade along which the gautama paced while preaching.

In recent years, Sarnath has undergone a revival. Near the Dhamekh Stupa and joining the old foundations of seven monasteries is a new temple, Mulagandha Kuti Vihara, built in 1931 by the Mahabodhi Society. The walls of the temple are decorated with frescoes depicting scenes of Buddha's life, painted by a Japanese artist, Kosetsu Nosu. The temple also contains a fine collection of Buddhist relics and a rare collection of Buddhist literature. On the anniversary of the temple's foundation—the first full moon in November—an assembly of monks and lay devotees from all parts of Asia come together. Also visit the Chinese temple, which contains an attractive marble image of the great teacher. Before you leave, buy a bunch of carrots (one rupee) and feed the deer in the nearby park.

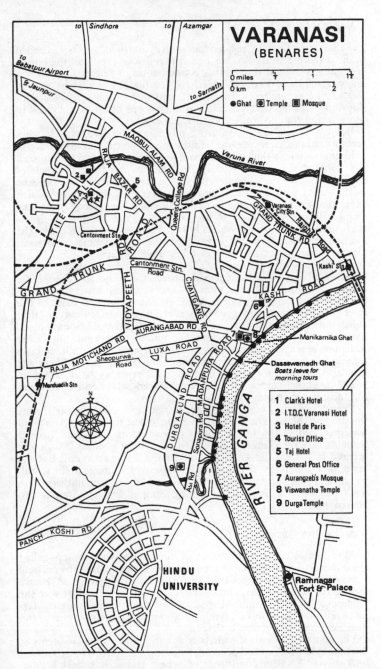

VARANASI
(BENARES)

0 miles   ¼   1   1¼
0 km   1   2

● Ghat   ◫ Temple   ▣ Mosque

1 Clark's Hotel
2 I.T.D.C. Varanasi Hotel
3 Hotel de Paris
4 Tourist Office
5 Taj Hotel
6 General Post Office
7 Aurangzeb's Mosque
8 Viswanatha Temple
9 Durga Temple

VARANASI

Varanasi, or Kasha ("resplendent with divine light"), as it was called in the seventh century B.C., has been the religious capital of the Hindu faith since recorded time and is a microcosm of Indian life. No one knows the date of Varanasi's birth. When Buddha came here around 500 B.C., he encountered an ancient settlement. Contemporary with Babylon, Nineveh, and Thebes, Varanasi is one of the oldest cities in the world, a hub of firmly rooted traditions.

But it's as a place of enduring pilgrimage that Varanasi's claim remains unique. Every devout Hindu wants to visit Varanasi once in a lifetime to purify the body and soul in the Ganges, shed all sin, and, if possible, to die here in old age and find release from the cycle of rebirth, which is the ultimate goal of the Hindus. This release means eternal unity with Brahma: "sinless, stirless rest, that change which never changes." Descending from the Himalayas on its long trek to the Bay of Bengal, each drop of the Ganga—as the Hindus call it—is august and propitious; the waters hold the powers of salvation, and the main sanctuary is Varanasi. Every year, the city welcomes millions of pilgrims, a lengthy trail many of them never retrace.

The old city of Varanasi (800,000 inhabitants) is a maze of small streets and alleyways, hiding in disorderly array no less than 2,000 temples and shrines. Domes, minarets, pinnacles and towers, and derelict eighteenth-century palaces dominate the sacred left bank of the river. The streets are noisy; color is rife. The air hangs heavy, as if in collaboration with the clang of temple gongs and bells. Some houses have naively decorated entrances; other buildings are ornate (notice the Indian-style gingerbread on balconies and verandahs). You'll see marriage processions and funeral processions and cows grabbing big flower necklaces destined for the gods, and you'll probably be hounded by would-be phony guides and assertive hawkers who don't understand that no can really mean no.

For all its variety of sacred spots, Varanasi is really one big shrine, the shrine of Shiva. This cult is one of the oldest form of worship, and was practiced in the Indus Valley thousands of years ago. Legend recounts how the Ganges was created. The water goddess Ganga was ordered to redeem the souls of some humans of great merit. But the fall of such a quantity of water would cause great damage to the world, so Shiva caught the goddess in his hair and let her seep out slowly to wash the ashes of the worthy mortals, and their souls ascended to heaven.

Along the Ganges

Along almost a four-mile stretch of the Ganges, you see steps called *ghats* that lead down from the steep city bank to the sacred river. These stone steps (there are about 70 sets of them) wed the great Hindu metropolis to the Ganges, and its religious connection is clear with the numerous *lingams* (phallic-shaped stones) that you see on most terraces. The lingam is Shiva's symbol and represents creative energy (no surprise, given the symbol's shape).

The best time to visit the ghats is at early dawn, when residents of the city shake off sleep and proceed, from some 80 narrow streets, down to the river. A solemn multitude of people and even animals—thousands of spots of color, lit by the sun's first rays—all move in one direction, bent on immersion in the holy stream.

If you decide to hire a boat, which is not expensive, go to the Dasashwamedh Ghat, the main ghat. As you slowly move along the river, you'll be drawn in by what you witness. Young men perform vigorous Hatha Yoga exercises; older men sit cross-legged in the lotus position, eyes closed in deep meditation. Brahmin priests sit under huge umbrellas offering prayers. Devotees drink from the obviously polluted water. A carcass may even float by. Women glide in and out of saris with such perfect finesse that they reveal nothing and you don't think to avert your eyes. Others beat and swoosh linen against the stone, purifying the clothes they wear.

Thin blue smoke twists up to the sky from the burning ghat, the Manikarnika, the chief cremation center of Varanasi (the other smaller cremation ghat is called Harish Chandra Ghat). Corpses wrapped in silk or linen—traditionally white for men and red for women—are carried on bamboo stretchers to the smoking pyres, where they are deposited and wait their turn: first an immersion into the Ganges, then, after a short wait, placement on the pyre for the ritual that precedes the cremation. These funeral ghats are not to be photographed; but you are allowed to watch.

Monuments Along the River

In the seventeenth century, Hindu-hater Aurangzeb pulled down the Vishwewara Temple and erected the Gyanvapi Mosque on its site. The foundation and rear of the mosque still reveal parts of the original temple. The tallest of its minarets, dominating the skyline of the holy city, collapsed during the great flood of 1948.

North of the Gyanvapi Mosque and also on the river is another of Aurangzeb's creations—the Alamgir Mosque—an odd blend of Hindu and Moslem design. Aurangzeb destroyed the seventeenth-century Beni Madhav ka Darera, which was dedicated to Vishnu, and replaced it with the mosque. The lower portions and wall are Hindu, the mosque is Islamic.

Ramnager Fort

Due south, on the opposite side of the Ganges, is the residential palace of the former maharajah of Varanasi. Called the Ramnager Fort, the Durbar Hall (Public Audience) and the Royal Museum have interesting collections that are open to the public. The palace was built to resist the floods of the monsoon, which play havoc with the city side of the river. The serrated skyline shows the damage wrought by inundation. Conical temples toboggan toward the river, houses are lopsided, water marks remind you of its power. There is an air of Venice in Varanasi, but without that sense of the carnival. Varanasi is solemn, and the sound of religious chanting places you clearly in the East.

The Inner City

Start your tour of the old city with a visit to the Kashi Vishwanath Temple, dedicated to Shiva. The temple is located back from the Ganges in between the Dasashwanedh and Manikarnika ghats. Follow along narrow streets crowded with animals, people, and little shops just as crammed with customers bargaining back and forth—often for the world-famous silver and gold brocades, for the appropriate wedding ornament, or even for a cremation cloth.

The most sacred shrine in all Varanasi, which is off limits to non-Hindus, is the Kashi Vishwanath. It is best seen from the top floor of the opposite house (pay a small fee to the usher). You'll see men and women make flower offerings to the lingam in the inner shrine. The present temple was built by Rani Ahalyabai of Indore in 1776 near the site of the original shrine destroyed by Aurangzeb. The spire is covered with gold plate, a gift from the Maharaja Ranjit Singh in 1835.

NORTHERN UTTAR PRADESH

Uttar Pradesh is a state of extremes that offers a lot of everything: Mogul architecture at its best in Agra, Hindu reverence at Varanasi, and a hefty dose of spectacular scenery and outdoor adventure. To discover these extremes, you should start at Bareilly, 100 km northwest of Lucknow, now an important rail and industrial center. Bareilly was formerly the chief city of the Rohillas, a marauding Afghan tribe that provoked a short but bloody war (1773–74) with the nabobs of Avdah and the British. The Khandan Mosque here has some Persian inscriptions that date back to the thirteenth century.

Twenty miles west, you'll find the ruins of the fortress city, Ahich Chatra, excavations of which have yielded sculptures, pottery, and Buddhist stupas ranging from the third century B.C. to A.D. 900. Not far from Ahich Chatra, you get your first glimpse of the distant Himalayas that divide India from Tibet and Nepal. Almost immediately, the road assumes those mountain characteristics, turning narrow in a constant circuitous up-and-down bend as you head into the foothill regions, the favorite area of Mahatma Gandhi. Finally, you enter the Lake District of the Kumaon Hills and arrive at Nainital, 6,500 feet above sea level.

Nainital

Divided into two parts, Malli Tal and Talli Tal (upper and lower lake), Nainital is an ideal base for forays into the Kumaon Hills, including a long climb to the top of Naina Peak, with its great view of the Himalayas and Nainital. The name of this peaceful town—the summer capital of the state until 1947—comes from an old temple of Goddess Naina Devi that stands on the shore of the lake. Naina Devi is the presiding deity of the hill people who consider the lake sacred. Other pretty nearby lakes are the Bhim Tal and Naukutchia Tal (the nine-cornered lake), only a few miles away.

Almora and Pindari Glacier

From Nainital, head north to Almora, surrounded by the Himalayas. Set on a hill where Vishnu supposedly stayed, Almora was founded in the sixteenth century as the chief city of the Chand rajahs who ruled in this area. The Gurkhas of Nepal also had a fling of power here, until the British seized control during the Gurkha War in 1815. Almora, compact and picturesque, is perched on a ridge with each surrounding hill topped by a temple. A small hill station with a distinct air of antiquity, it offers numerous walks leading to more of those exquisite views.

To the west is another tiny hill station, Ranikhet (queen's field, for the queen who supposedly came and never left). A visit to the Pindari Glacier, due north, is a journey controlled by weather conditions and made by jeep or on foot; it's a journey that takes you through dramatic scenery and leads to the very shadow of the snow-covered Himalayan giants. You proceed stage by stage, with well-equipped bungalows at frequent intervals. At each level, the tree line thins—pines cease, and you enter an enchanting garden of fern, wildflower, and rhododendron. The glacier itself, over two miles long, some 500 yards wide, and backed by mighty mountains, faces the unwary traveler with its indomitable gaze and leaves you touched by its grandeur.

Corbett National Park

India's oldest wildlife sanctuary (started in 1935), Corbett National Park is named after the fearless hunter and generous wildlife pioneer, Jim Corbett, author of *Man-Eaters of Kumaon*. Corbett grew up in these westernmost hills, and the local people, a number of whom he saved at the risk of his own life, held him in high esteem. But it wasn't until his death in Kenya in 1955 that India honored him by renaming the Hailey National Park for this well-liked man.

The park, with elephant grass, sal forests, and the Ramganga River covering its entire length, extends over an area of 125 square miles. From the back of an elephant, from inside a car, or from the height of a stationary watch tower, you may see elephants, tigers, leopards, black bear, wild boar, deer, snakes (including the python and king cobra), crocodiles, and birds and more birds. This is a *great* park, well worth a visit. The best time is from December to May; the park is closed during the monsoon (May to October).

HARIDWAR

Back in Ramnagar, travel northwest, hugging the edge of the mountains until you reach Haridwar, a sacred city of pilgrimage on the bank of the Ganges. Haridwar has the religious fervor of Varanasi, but its mood is joyous, not solemn. Here, King Bhagrath brought the Ganges down from heaven to provide a path of salvation for his ancestors. Here, the three supreme deities—Brahma, Vishnu, and Shiva—left their mark. In fact, a set of Vishnu's footprints is supposedly embedded in an upper portion of the wall of Haridwar's most important ghat, Har-ki-Pairi. *Swamis* (monks or teachers), *sadhus* (wandering holy men), devotees, over 150 *ashrams* (spiritual retreats) and *dharamsalas* (religious guest houses), temples, statues of deities, and numerous ghats—the entire city is set against the Ganges canal and river. The bustling scene serves as a constant reminder of Haridwar's importance in Hindu mythology. Religious strictures have also made Haridwar "dry" and strictly vegetarian, where even eggs are taboo.

One of the earliest names of this ancient city was Gangadwara, which means the Gate of the Ganges. A gate it is—sitting at the mouth of a gorge in the Shivalik mountains where the fast-moving Ganges rushes out, then slows dramatically as it enters the plains on its seaward course toward the Bay of Bengal. The devout believe that to bathe here once means salvation, and all along the banks, you see the faithful bathers congregating. At sunrise or at sunset, you must witness the celebration of *puja* (the offering of prayers to the Ganges) held at the Har-ki-pairi Ghat.

Moti Bazaar and Arti of the Ganges

The most festive puja is at evening and is called Arti of the Ganges. The event is heavily attended, so leave early and allow for at *least* an hour just to walk through the part of the city that hugs the Ganges canal and takes you to the Har-ki-Pairi Ghat. Here, every ashram and dharamsala is bathed in a tropical hue often outlined in contrasting trim. There's a vague aura of old Miami Beach. Many of the buildings were built in the 1920s and '30s and are distinctly art deco.

Start your walk at the Lalto Rao Bridge by the Bhola Giri Temple and Ashram, done up in the shade of natural terra cotta with its dharamsala set off by light blue trim. Next, as you head northeast along Jodhamal Road, is the Chiniot Bhawan, a yellow temple with lacy stone trim. Step inside and see ornate marble gods and goddesses dressed in their festive clothes.

Move along Jodhamal to the Moti Bazaar—pleasantly congested and busy, yet not overwhelming. Ayurvedic medicine shops sell *jalzeera* (Indian spice powder for stomachaches); religious shops sell small polished stones (omens and lingams) and beads of coral or sandalwood for devotees to hold while saying the mantras. Stalls sell fresh pickle chutneys, shawls, and saris. It's all fun to see.

At the end of the bazaar, the narrow street spills into a large square, where open-air stalls sell *dias*—leaves woven together like little boats and filled with fresh flowers and thimble-sized clay bowls and wicks. These beautiful vessels are set afloat on the Ganges during Arti. Men sell enormous balloons and boys sell wooden whistles and pipes. It's clearly festive. There's a carnival air. You've arrived at Har-ki-Pairi Ghat surrounded by a complex of temples—mostly new except for the sixteenth-century Shri Ganga Mandir.

A short bridge leads to the Pant Dweep (tiny terraced island), the best vantage point. If you can, sit on the top ghat step. The preliminary show is as fascinating as Arti, with all India walking by: Rajasthanis in colorful turbans and wild mustaches, Sikhs, Nagas, sadhus, and swamis. People bathe, and many set off their dias in hasty anticipation.

A few minutes before Arti begins, temple bells ring and priests from surrounding temples descend the steps of the ghat—each carrying bells and a large brass lamp filled with oil. The priests ignite the lamps—the start of Arti. Flames rise up as they hold the vessels over the Ganges. Bells ring continuously. The priests swing the vessels up and down across the surface of the water. The fragrance of *dwoop* (perfume) circulates. Chants, barely audible, silence the throngs. Burning dias flicker away on their downward journey along the swift moving Ganges. Within 15 minutes, Arti is over. A beautiful show!

In Haridwar, the temples aren't old, but they're always festive, and some are erected on mythologically important sites. See the Daksh Mahadev Temple and Sati Jund in Kankhal, a part of Haridwar, with yellow stone lions at the entrance. Here, the father of Sati (Shiva's first wife) performed a sacrifice and neglected to invite Shiva. Sati was so insulted that she arrived uninvited and performed her own sacrifice—throwing herself into the fire at Yagva Kund now inside the Deksh Mahadev. A large statue of the devoted Nandi (Shiva's bull) stands outside. There are other temples in this complex. One contains a Shiva lingam surrounded by a copper cobra, with the water dripping down on the stone; another shows this goddess in all her manifestations. There is also a ghat for devotees to step down to the Ganges to bathe.

For a good view of Haridwar, visit the Mansa Devi Temple dedicated to the goddess Mansi, which stands on the top of one of the nearby Shivalik Hills. You can go by cable car or on foot.

Pawan Dham

Pawan may mean holy and *Dham* may mean house, but once you step inside the Pawan Dham Ashram, constructed in 1970 by Swami Vedanta Maharaj, you almost need sunglasses, and you can't help but smile. No wonder this swami had such a large following. The entire gigantic building is pure religious fun. Most walls are covered with elaborate mythological frescoes made of inlaid and painted glass. Ceilings dazzle you with more colored glass. The few walls without a fresco have mirrors—perhaps so devotees see themselves as part of the Hindu pantheon. Step close to one of the numerous cubicles that contain gaily decorated marble gods and goddesses. Now look into the mirrored side walls inside the chamber. The statue appears in infinite reflection. The crowning *piéce de kitsch* is a large freestanding inlaid glass chariot drawn by horses, with Krishna and Arjun inside and Hanuman, the monkey god, riding on top of a stanchion. His weight kept the heavenly chariot earthbound.

RISHIKESH

Rishikesh, 24 km north of Haridwar, is a busy, newish city—in the worst sense. It may be another city of religious significance tied to the Ganges and it may have important ashrams, but Rishikesh also seems to pay homage to concrete and dust.

For hundreds of years, Rishikesh has been an important retreat for those on the spiritual path. There are over 100 ashrams here, including Maharishi Mahesh Yogi's Transcendental Meditation Center, which once hooked the Beatles; Swami Sivananda's Divine Life Society; and the Yoga Sadhan Ashram.

Triveni Ghat, with its sprawling terrace, is Rishikesh's main bathing ghat. Each evening, from 5 to 6 P.M., a local swami comes down to preach, his service followed by a small-scale Arti. The fish, considered sacred in this part of the river, seem to understand their peculiar status. Over the years, they've become so tame that they swarm to the surface to catch daily offerings.

Two mythological stories are connected to Rishikesh and commemorated by temples. Supposedly, Lakshman (a brother of Lord Rama) stood on one foot in the middle of the Ganges and meditated for 100 years as an act of penance for killing his guru—an unfortunate event that occured while he was attempting to help his brother, Rama. A suspension bridge, the Laxmanjhoola, crosses the Ganges where Lakshman evidently did his prolonged act of physical balance. The Bharat Temple is connected to Bharat, another brother of Rama, who also did penance in Rishikesh during the same period as did Lakshman and for the same approximate duration. Only he had committed no sin; his motivation was self-purification.

DEHRA DUN

Dehra Dun, 42 km from Rishikesh, is the largest Uttar Pradesh city in the lower Himalayan foothills. It's an important government administration center, home of the super-exclusive Doon School (Rajiv Gandhi is one of its alumni), and the location of Asia's largest forest research institute, with museums open to the public. Dehra Dun's no great beauty of a city, thanks to unregulated limestone quarrying. But it's a good stopover for those heading north and it offers two nearby diversions to break up a long ride.

Visit the Tapkeshwar Cave Temple, set in the woods along a stream. To the sound of piped religious music, you descend a stone staircase with pesky monkeys lying in wait, pass under a natural rock ledge with mossy grass hanging down, and reach a series of caves. Inside are shrines with small statues of Nandi, Ganesh, Hanuman and, in the main cave, a Shiva lingam set on a copper base—all tended by a gregarious *pujari* (priest). If you have a translator, this is one time to believe the stories. The pujari will explain how the temple is at least 5,000 years old and he'll recount how the water that used to drip steadily from the roof of the cave onto the lingum has decreased over the years with each disaster: the two world wars; the Chinese invasion of Tibet; the deaths of Mahatma Gandhi, Nehru, and Indira Gandhi; and a famine. Now you're lucky if you see much more than a droplet or two.

You can also cool yourself at Sahastradhara, where sulphur springs tumbling down from the mountains form a natural pool in which people can bathe. It's open from sunrise to sunset. There's a limited-menu Indian cafe and a temple on the side of the hill that leads up to yet another cave with another Shiva lingam. This time, plenty of water drenches the sacred stone.

Mussoorie

Mussoorie, 2,005 km above sea level, rises on a horseshoe-shaped foothill that overlooks the Ganges River, sluggishly moving through the plains on one side and the vibrant silhouette of the lower Himalayas on the other.

At first glance, Mussoorie looks like another former British hill station turned "honeymoon retreat," where the emphasis is on short walks and relaxation. You're bombarded with billboards that advertise hotels and see cars loaded with young couples. But then something happens. Tucked away here and there, some of that grand old elegance peeks out. Some of it is a bit musty around the edges and some of it even totters on old Victorian legs, but it's there and it's holding its own in a way that makes this particular hill station still special.

Stop at Hakmans Hotel and have a drink for old time's sake. As you sit and look around, it's as if time stood still—when the stiff upright British got up and left. Check the artwork on the walls and the old telephones. Walk through the former cabaret theater and linger a moment in the grand yet bizarre entrance to the hotel. For another trip into nostalgia—this one quite elegant—visit the chateaulike Hotel Savoy, a sprawl of Victorian charm sitting on a hill all its own.

While in old Mussoorie, walk west along Charleville Road to Happy Valley, a Tibetan township where Buddhist flags wave in the breeze and small restaurants entice you with good Tibetan cooking. At the other end of Mussoorie, you'll find bazaars. Stroll through the Mall to Kulri, set up for tourists, and the more interesting Landaur Bazaar. It's an ethnic market with a lengthy string of tiny shops built along a narrow winding ridge. Wherever you walk—along the Mall, up to Camel's Back Road, or Gun Hill—the views explain why British Captain Young decided that this particular ridge was an ideal retreat for his countrymen back in 1827.

Mussoorie is also a great base for day excursions. Visit Kempty Falls (15 km), a short drive to the north that ends at appealing falls that spill into a refreshing pool of water with an unassuming cafe set up alongside. Go east to Dhanolti (24 km) along a narrow road that climbs and winds, passing men leading pack horses that are laden with pails of collected milk. Occasionally, you will see tiny shrines mounted with flags erected along the road, terraced fields of wheat, small villages with simple stone or sod houses linked together, foot paths, and potato fields. This clearly rugged terrain brings you to a tiny village set in a pine forest: Dhanolti. There's an Uttar Pradesh Tourist Bungalow, which serves food and supplies an outdoor map that points the way to good walks away from it all.

Mussoorie is also the "gateway" to Yamnotri and Gangotri—two essential goals of pilgrimage that mark the source of the Yamuna and Ganges rivers. The shrines here draw thousands of devotees to this part of India, which also is scenically beautiful—reason enough to make the trip.

Yamnotri

Yamnotri is 128 km almost due north of Mussoorie. The road, which takes you to Hanuman Chatti within 13 km of the temple, is Himalayan beautiful with the Yamuna River escorting you on the left. You pass through tiny villages like Barkot, encircled by pine forests, with stunning snow-clad peaks forming a picturesque backdrop. Walking sadhus share the road. Once the road ends and you start out for the temple, you come to Kankibai Chatti, a good overnight halt, with rest houses and hot-water springs.

Yamnotri itself is huddled against the western bank of the snow-covered Banderpunch (20,720 feet above sea level). Here, an ancient Hindu sage is said to have built his hermitage and bathed daily in the Yamuna and Ganges. When old age prevented more treks to the Gangotri, a stream of the Ganges emerged from the Yamnotri rocks. Yamunaji Temple, dedicated to the goddess Yamuna, nearby hot springs gushing out of the mountain (the Surya Kund is considered the most sacred), and a rock (Divya Shila) are revered by Hindus, who flock here from May to November to offer prayers.

Gangotri

The Gangotri Temple, built in the eighteenth century and dedicated to the goddess Ganga, commemorates the source of the Ganges. Here, too, pilgrims flock during the season to pay respect to this shrine and their holiest river. The scenery on the way to Gangotri is magnificent, with canyons, cascades, and rushing rivulets at each turn of the way. At an elevation of 10,000 feet, Gangotri shows off its famous temple on the right bank of the river. On the opposite bank are a few huts, inhabited by sadhus who have settled here: some mere escapists from the turmoil of the world; others inflamed by zeal. You can also continue on from Gangotri, traveling by foot or pony, to Gaumukh (about 20 km) where you can offer tribute to that exact starting point of the river.

Kedarnath and Badrinath

Hindu pilgrims also hope to visit two other important shrines in this northern area of Uttar Pradesh—Kedarnath and Badrinath, the assumed abodes of Shiva and Vishnu. Set over 10,000 feet up in the mountains, they're magnets that draw adventurers who want to get off the beaten path.

Instead of taking the direct route to Kedarnath, try to go via Deoprayag, a charming Indian village built into the slope of a hill at the confluence of the Bhagipathi and Alaknanda rivers. You can even spend a night in the minimal but clean tourist bungalow. Deoprayag (God's place) is the site of the ancient and recently renovated Raghunath Temple, which commemorates the spot where Rama supposedly came to meditate. It is also in Deoprayag that the merging rivers assume the known name River Ganges. The whitewashed old village, connected to the new part of town by a pedestrian-sized suspension bridge, is filled with local *pandas* (priests), who lead visiting Hindus in their prayers on the bathing ghat that provides access to the river. As you walk through the narrow lanes, there's an abundance of charm in the architecture and hillside setting and a prevailing sense of tranquility, with the dominant sound that of the river thrashing along on its course. Deoprayag is really an appealing city, small, and worth a visit.

On leaving Deoprayag, you find that the road narrows and winds. Occasionally, you see distant pastoral hamlets in which life moves to a quiet rhythm. At Gauri Kund, with hot water springs and a temple, the road ends. From here, you go by foot or pony (there are rest huts along the way) on a 15-km journey near glaciers and waterfalls. You clomp through rocky forests until just after you cross a narrow bridge above a village, where you see a simple gray stone temple standing on a raised platform guarding the dwellings in Kedarnath. The temple, snowbound and closed from November to May, stands on the banks of the Mandakini. A statue of Nandi, Shiva's mount, is in the courtyard. Several holy bathing spots are around the temple, and inside the simple shrine are beautiful carvings of Shiva, Parvati, and the five *pandavas* (legendary rulers), who built this temple as atonement for the sins they committed during battle.

To get to Badrinath, return to Rudraprayag and take the road passing through the Alaknanda valley and the village of Karnaprayag, a busy meeting place for the surrounding hill people. Then, you enter the Pipalkoti Valley, with its important township, Joshimath, which is also the winter seat of the Badrinath shrine. Here, you come across the semipastoral nomadic Bhotias, an Indo-Mongoloid people whose life underwent severe change when trading with Tibet became impossible. Their greatest possession is the yak, their beast of burden that also provides milk, butter, and meat. To the east, the steep Nanda Devi Summit (25,650 feet) appears like a pyramid. Snow, blown by the winds, gives the impression of smoke blowing over gray rock; the locals call it the Nandi Devi, "kitchen of their deity."

In the winter, skiers can check out Joshimath's nearby Auli, India's newest ski resort—with some runs still under construction, including one 32 km long that will make the run one of the longest in the world.

PRACTICAL INFORMATION FOR

UTTAR PRADESH

WHEN TO GO. For the non-Himalayan areas (the plains region): This part of Uttar Pradesh has a variable climate. It can be very hot and dry in summer and fairly cool in winter. From November to February, the maximum temperature rarely exceeds 65°F in daytime; at night, it falls to 45°F. The main tourist season for the plains lasts from October to March. For the Central Himalayas: The best visiting seasons are from May to July and mid-September to early November. Temperatures are pleasant during the day and cool by night. The Valley of Flowers bursts into bloom in July and August.

HOW TO GET THERE. By Air. Occasional *Indian Airlines* flights into Allahabad from Delhi and Lucknow. Daily flights into Lucknow from Calcutta, Delhi, Ranchi, and Patna (in Bihar). Occasional flights into Lucknow from Allahabad and Bombay. Daily flights into Varanasi from Agra, Calcutta, Delhi, and Khajuraho. Occasional flights into Varanasi from Bombay, Hyderabad, and Lucknow. *Vayudoot* also flies into Allahabad from Delhi everyday but Sundays; into Pantnagar (71 km from Nainital), the twice-a-week flight originates in Delhi.

By Bus. The *Uttar Pradesh State Road Transport Corporation* (UPSRTC) runs deluxe interstate buses from Delhi and other large northern cities, including Shimla and Chandigarh; it also provides excellent and frequent service between most areas in the state that are of interest to the tourist. For fares and details: In Delhi, call 226175, 6 A.M.–8 P.M. at *Interstate Bus Terminus,* Kashmere Gate. In Lucknow, call *Kaiserbagh Bus Station,* 42503. In Varanasi, call UPSTRC, 63233.

By Train. Uttar Pradesh is well covered with railroad tracks. You can get to most important cities (Lucknow, Allahabad, Dehra Dun, and Varanasi) from either Delhi or Calcutta. Keep in mind, however, that some of these journeys are overnight. When you reserve a sleeper (first- or second-class and air-conditioned), you must also reserve a berth, or you might just find yourself ejected from the train. For train information in Delhi, call 343727 or 351035. In Calcutta, call 239530 or 224025. In Lucknow, call *Northern Railway Enquiry,* 51234 or *North Eastern Railway Enquiry,* 51433. In Varanasi, call *Varanasi Cantonment Railway Station,* 64920.

By Rented Car with Driver. Delhi is 541 km from Lucknow, 756 km from Varanasi (Calcutta is 677 km from Varanasi). Heading toward the Himalayas, Delhi is 222 km from Haridwar, 322 km from Nainital, 255 km from Dehra Dun, and 270 km from Mussoorie. The cost of renting a car is approximately Rs. 2 per km, plus night-halt charges (never more than Rs. 50 per night).

 TOURIST INFORMATION. Uttar Pradesh Tourist departments are extremely helpful, offering specific brochures and maps. (The only exception is in Varanasi, where the Government of India Tourist Department outshines.) Most offices are open 9–5, Monday–Saturday.

Allahabad. Uttar Pradesh Tourist Office, 35 Mahatma Gandhi Rd.; tel. 53883.

Dehra Dun. Regional Tourist Office, Hotel Drona, 45 Mahatma Gandhi Rd.; tel. 23217.

Haridwar. Regional Tourist Bureau, Lalta Rao Bridge, Station Rd.; tel. 19. Also, Information Counter, Railway Station; tel. 817.

Joshimath. (on the way to Badrinath and Kedarnath). Tourist Office; tel. 81.

Kotdwara (gateway to Garhwal). Tourist Office; tel. 162.

Lucknow. Directorate of Tourism, Uttar Pradesh Tourism, No. 3 Naval Kishore Rd., Chitrahar Building; tel. 47749. Also, Regional Tourist Office, Gompti Hotel, 6 Sapru Marg; tel. 46205; and Tourist Reception Center, Railway Station, Charbagh (no phone).

Mussoorie. Tourist Office, The Mall; tel. 2863.

Nainital. Tourist Bureau, The Mall; tel. 2337.

Pauri (Garhwal). Tourist Bureau, tel. 41.

Pithoragarh (near Tibet and Nepal). Tourist Bureau; tel. 227.

Rishikesh. Tourist Bureau, Yatayat Bus Station; tel. 209.

Srinagar (Garhwal). Tourist Bureau; tel. 10.

Varanasi. Government of India Tourist Office, 15–B, The Mall, Cantonment; tel. 43189. Government of India Tourist Information Counter, Babatpur Airport (open flight times only). Tourist Bureau, Parade Khothi; tel. 63186. Tourist Information Counter, Cantonment Railway Station (no phone).

 **ACCOMMODATIONS.** Uttar Pradesh has some Western-style hotels in the major tourist areas (including Lucknow, Varanasi, and Mussoorie) and a few charming old-fashioned guest houses. For some areas of the state—Badrinath, Kedarnath, Gangotri, and Yamunotri—the choice is limited because facilities are minimal. But to stay away from this part of Uttar Pradesh is foolish; it's beautiful and remote. Just prepare for a different type of adventure and get close to a part of the world that will be hard to forget. Rates are based on double occupancy: *Expensive,* Rs. 400 plus; *Moderate,* Rs. 200–Rs. 400; *Inexpensive,* under Rs. 200. Accommodations for Corbett National Park are listed under Wildlife Sanctuary.

ALLAHABAD

Moderate to Inexpensive

Hotel Yatrik. 33 Sadar Patel Marg, Civil Lines, one km from downtown; tel. 56020; 37 rooms, some air-conditioned; TVs in some rooms. Restaurant, swimming pool, and nice garden. Best bet.

Barnett Hotel. 14 Mahatma Gandhi Marg, two km from downtown; tel. 2231. 14 rooms, some air-conditioned; restaurant. Pleasant.

DEHRU DUN

Expensive

Hotel Madhuban. 97 Rajpur Rd., one km from downtown; tel. 24094. 37 air-conditioned rooms. Well-run older hotel, with many Western amenities, including TVs, 24-hour room service, car rental, restaurants, and a bar. Nice lawn out back.

Hotel Nidhi. 74–C Rajpur Rd., one km from downtown; tel. 24611. Approximately 25 air-conditioned rooms. New, modern, and attractive. TVs, room service, a restaurant, bar, coffee shop. Very nice.

Moderate to Expensive

Hotel Meedo's Grand. 28 Rajpur Rd.; tel. 27171. 35 rooms. Some Western amenities, room service, a restaurant, and a bar. Not great, but good enough.

Moderate

Motel Kwality. 19 Rajpur Rd., situated in a shopping area; tel. 27001. 18 rooms, some air-conditioned. TVs in simple clean rooms. Not much in the way of stylish decor.

Mandakini Hotel. 1 Haridwar Rd., tel. 27860. 24 rooms, some air-conditioned. Room service, TVs, and a bar. New hotel; nice, but not fancy.

Hotel President. 6 Astley Hall, Rajpur Rd., near downtown; tel. 27082. 10 rooms, some air-conditioned. TVs, room service. Small hotel with friendly management. Nice ambience.

Inexpensive

Hotel Drona. 45 Gandhi Rd.; tel. 24371. 78 rooms, some air-conditioned. Amenities include shops, an Uttar Pradesh tourist office, and a coffee shop. New, reasonably attractive hotel run by Uttar Pradesh. Excellent value.

Hotel Relax. Amrit Kaur Rd.; tel. 26608. 32 clean rooms, some air-conditioned. 24-hour room service, a restaurant, and a bar. Nice management.

DEOPRAYAG

Inexpensive

Tourist Rest House. Deoprayag. Reservations: Manager, Tourist Rest House, Deoprayag; tel. 33. Four rooms. Very minimal, but well-run, simple, clean rooms. Hot water brought by the bucket. Indian-style toilet (trench). No dining facilities, but local canteen will bring you an adequate Indian meal. Quiet surroundings, spectacular views. Set on a hill with a garden out front. The village of Deoprayag is charming, and this place fits in.

DHANOLTI

Inexpensive

Dhanolti Tourist Bungalow. Reservations: Manager of Tourist Complex, Dhanolti. Five rooms. "Super deluxe" room has a fireplace. Spacious, clean rooms; carpeting; hot and cold shower; Indian-style toilet. Peaceful, set on edge of pine and cedar forest. Dining room, room service, garden. Nice walks.

HARIDWAR

Moderate

Hotel Surprise. Haridwar-Delhi Rd., Jwala Pur; tel. 1146. 55 rooms. Haridwar's modern new showcase. Most Western amenities: TVs, air-conditioning, swimming pool, restaurants, coffee shop, room service, shopping arcade, and a spacious lawn. One drawback: hotel is on the outskirts of this lovely, fun-to-walk-through city. An advantage: it serves nonvegetarian food in this strictly vegetarian town.

Inexpensive

Hotel Aarti. Railway Rd., in the heart of the city; tel. 456. 34 rooms, some with air cooler. Unpretentious, nice hotel. Well-maintained, simple, clean rooms. 24-hour room service (only vegetarian).

Hotel Gurdev. Railway Rd.; in the heart of the city; tel. 101. 30 rooms, some facing an interior courtyard and some with balconies fronting the street. Some air-conditioned, some air-cooled, all have fans. Hot water by the bucket. Room service (vegetarian food only).

Hotel Kailish Haridwar. Railway Rd.; in the heart of the city; tel. 789. 64 air-cooled rooms. Hot and cold shower. Simple clean rooms.

Tourist Bungalow. tel. 379. Reservations: Office of the Manager, Uttar Pradesh State Tourism Development Corporation. 22 simple clean rooms; some air-cooled. Hot and cold water. Back lawn leads down to the Ganges Canal, a bathing ghat and promenade. Ideal quiet setting, within walking distance of the heart of the city. Limited vegetarian restaurant. Room service. Best bet.

KEDARNATH, BADRINATH, AND JOSHIMATH

These three places are beautiful. The accommodations are minimal—a room with a bed and sometimes an attached bath. If you're the fastidious sort, you'd be wise to bring a sleeping bag or your own clean sheets. Bedding is usually clean; but sometimes the trek to a *dhobi* (laundryman) is days away. For lodging reservations, contact Garhwal Mandal Vikas Nigam, Muni-ki-Reti, Rishikesh (tel. 372). This is a government-run operation. The cost of lodging is cheap—under Rs. 80 for a double. Don't stay away—think of forest camping huts and simple rest houses. These facilities are ideal given the surroundings.

At Badrinath, the best Garhwal Mandal Vikas Nigam facility is **Hotel Devlok,** which has about 25 rooms, each with an attached bathroom.

At Kedarnath, **Hotel Himlok** is the only accommodation, offering basic services.

LUCKNOW

Expensive

Clarks Avadh. 8 Mahatama Gandhi Marg; tel. 40130. 94 air-conditioned rooms, some with TVs. Many amenities, including a restaurant, bar, coffee shop, and golf. If you want modern, this is the best in the area.

Moderate to Expensive

Carleton Hotel Private, Ltd. Shahnajah Rd.; tel. 44021. 40 air-conditioned rooms. Breakfast included with rates. Has a restaurant and a bar. "Palace" look to the exterior, with nice lawns. Rooms are spacious with lavish bathrooms; but genteel air has been replaced by an air of neglect. Within walking distance of the main market.

Hotel Kohinoor. 6 Station Rd.; tel. 35421. 37 air-conditioned rooms. 24-hour room service, a restaurant, bar, and coffee shop. Modern decor, well run, and clean.

Inexpensive

Avadh Lodge Tourist Hotel. 1 Ram Mohan Rai Marg; tel. 43821. 12 rooms, some air-conditioned. Breakfast included. Great nabob exterior and charm to common rooms; delightful old tiling on the walls. Clean, but there is a seamy edge of neglect in the bedrooms. Nice garden and front lawn. Restaurant. Quiet location.

Capoor's Hotel and Restaurant. 52 Hazratganj; tel. 43958. 24 rooms. Distinct 1930s decor in the halls and lobby. Again, rooms are clean, but there is the same look of neglect. Restaurant.

Hotel Charan's International. 16 Vidhan Sabha Marg; tel. 32516. 46 rooms, some with air-conditioning and TVs; 24-hour room service, restaurant.

Hotel Gompti. 6 Sapra Marg; tel. 34282. 65 rooms, some air-conditioned. Clean, efficient, good value. Bar, restaurant, and room service.

MUSSOORIE

Expensive

Hakman's Grand Hotel. Mall Rd.; tel. 2559. 24 rooms. A 100-year-old Victorian statement. It's as if the British walked away and time stood still. The musty look has set in. A bit run down, but wildly of its era. Rooms are clean.

Check for good running water before you check in. Restaurant, bar, views (inside and out). Off-season discount.

Roselynn Estate Hotel. The Mall, Library; tel. 2201. 20 rooms. Old-time feel, with a fireplace, old furnishings, room service, a restaurant, and a bar.

Savoy Hotel. Tel. 2510. 121 rooms. Meals included. Almost 100 years old. Graceful, classy hotel. Each room has a fireplace and period furniture. Sweeping verandah around the upper floor. Lovely setting and views from its own mountain. Spacious lawns, a restaurant, bar, beer garden, tennis courts, and a Victorian ballroom with dancing and a cabaret in season. An equally gracious owner. Holds fast to the true meaning of a genteel hill-station resort.

Shilton Hotel. Library Club Chowk; tel. 2297. 48 rooms. Off-season discount. New hotel, for those who want modern. Cedar lobby. Simple clean rooms, but ask for a room with a view. A restaurant, bar, TVs, and room service.

Moderate

Carlton's Hotel Plaisance. Happy Valley Rd.; tel. 2800. 10 rooms. Off-season discount. Charming. Spacious bedrooms; drawing room. Victorian decor is impeccable; antiques galore. One trade-off: views are sacrificed for peaceful elegant living. Restaurant.

Hotel Clark's. The Mall; tel. 2393. 12 rooms. Off-season discount. 100-year-old building. Clean, simple rooms; ask for one with a view off the back. A billiard room, restaurant, and bar. Nice old-time ambience. In the center of the Mall.

Hotel Padmini Nivas. Library, The Mall; tel. 2793. 24 rooms. Off-season discounts. Cottages also available. Former maharajah's estate, but not very grand. Has old-time charm and nice ambience. Ask for an old room with a view. Vegetarian restaurant, room service.

Inexpensive

Sylverton Hotel. The Mall; tel. 2312. 14 rooms. Off-season discount. Old-time hotel with old-time prices. Simple, clean rooms with good views. Peaceful. Restaurant, room service.

Tourist Complex. Garhwal Mandal Vikas Nigam Ltd., Mall Rd.; tel. 2984. 24 rooms. Room service, restaurant. Simple, clean rooms with a view.

NAINITAL

Moderate

Grand Hotel. The Mall; tel. 2406. 31 rooms. Good decent hotel on the shores of the lake with good food. Closed during February.

Shervani Hilltop Inn. Shervani Lodge, Mallithal; tel. 2504. 20 rooms. Off-season discount. Good views. Many amenities, including a bar, free jeep service, and a children's park. No great character to the building, but management supplies good service and good food.

Swiss Hotel. Tel. 2603. 18 rooms. Off-season discount. Lovely chalet-style exterior, and great views. Rose garden. Restaurant, some rooms have TVs. Service can be indifferent.

Royal Hotel. The Mall, Mallital; tel. 2007. 46 rooms. Lots of amenities, tennis, a restaurant, library, and bar. Tries hard to please.

Inexpensive

Nagarpalika Tourist Home. Reservations: Assistant Director Tourism, Tourist Bureau, Nainital; tel. 2337. Six rooms. Very cheap. Simple, but nice.

RISHIKESH

Expensive

Hotel Natraj. Dehra Dun Rd.; tel. 728. 75 rooms. New modern hotel, still under construction at press time but scheduled to be ready by late 1988, with most Western amenities.

Moderate to Inexpensive

Hotel Baseraa. 1 Ghat Rd.; tel. 767. 35 rooms, some air-conditioned, others air-cooled. TVs in neat, clean rooms. Restaurant, room service.

Inderlok Hotel. Railway Rd.; tel. 555. 52 rooms, some air-conditioned, some with balconies. All rooms have fans and are clean. Interior courtyard. Older hotel. Not fancy, but good ambience. Nice management. Room service. Vegetarian restaurant.

Inexpensive

Luxmanjhula Hotel. Luxman Jhula; tel. 442. 28 rooms, some with air-conditioning and tubs. Restaurant, room service. Large rooms, spartan but clean. Don't be put off by the lobby. Located near interesting ashrams. Interesting Dharamsala feel.

Rishikesh Tourist Bungalow. Tourist Complex, Rishilok, Munikireti; tel. 373. 48 big, clean rooms with fans, and Indian toilets. Nice garden, room service, and a restaurant. Not far from the ashrams.

VARANASI

Expensive

Hotel Taj Ganges. Nadesar Palace; tel. 54385. 104 rooms. All Western amenities: air-conditioned, room service, TVs, a restaurant, bar, swimming pool, and shopping arcade. For those who need comfort. Not much atmosphere.

Clarks Varanasi. The Mall; tel. 62021. 130 rooms. Amenities include 24-hour room service, a swimming pool, restaurants, a shopping arcade, and a bar. Pleasant management. Fine older hotel.

Moderate

Diamond Hotel. Behlupur; tel. 56561. 41 rooms. Some amenities include air-conditioning, room service, two restaurants, and a terrace. Not bad for the price.

Hotel India. 59 Patel Nagar; tel. 42634. 20 air-conditioned rooms with overhead fans. A restaurant and room service. Very nice hotel, good management.

Pallavi International Hotel. Hathwa Market, Chetganj; tel. 54894. 85 air-conditioned rooms. Although the approach is through a shopping arcade, this is a former palace. Newly renovated in an attractive setting. The rooms are sparse, however. Some amenities: room service, a shopping arcade, and a restaurant.

Hotel de Paris. The Mall; tel. 56461. 47 air-conditioned rooms. Beautiful old-world exterior nicely done up in cream and pink. Interior needs equivalent attention. Rooms okay; nice old marble tubs. Each room opens out to the pretty lawns. Room service, a restaurant, and a bar.

Hotel Parvaaz. 56 Patel Nagar; tel. 43045. 33 bright, cheery air-conditioned rooms. Room service and a restaurant.

Hotel Varanasi Ashok. The Mall; tel. 42550. 84 air-conditioned rooms with TVs, 24-hour room service, private balconies, a restaurant, coffee shop, bar, and swimming pool. Good value.

Inexpensive

Hotel Pradeep. Jagatganj; tel. 66363. 20 air-conditioned, clean, cheery rooms with overhead fans. Restaurant. A bargain.

Gautam Hotel. Ramkatura; tel. 52816. 37 rooms. Room service. Common TV room. Adequate place.

YAMUNOTRI AND GANGOTRI

A reminder: The reason to visit these places is not to stay in some elegant hotel. These are beautiful, remote areas with minimal accommodations provided by the Uttar Pradesh Tourist Department. For reservations, contact *Garhwal Mandal Vikas Nigam Ltd.*, Muni-ki-Reti, Rishikesh (tel. 372). If you're fastidious, bring a sleeping bag or a clean sheet. Because these places are remote, it's hard to keep fresh linens when the nearest laundry is days away. But minimal doesn't mean bad. These places are maintained and even popular, so book early. In Gangotri, best is the **Travellers Lodge.** In Yamnotri, best is the **Tourist Bungalow,** with four "deluxe" rooms.

DINING OUT. Except for the big cities and Mussoorie, eating well can't be considered a major draw in Uttar Pradesh. Prices are based on a three-course meal for one person, not including taxes, beverage, or tip: *Expensive,* Rs. 50 plus; *Moderate,* Rs. 30–Rs. 50; *Inexpensive,* under Rs. 30. Fancy Western-style hotels generally accept credit cards and traveler's checks.

ALLAHABAD

Moderate

El Chico Restaurant. 24 Mahatma Gandhi Marg; tel. 3910. Indian, Continental, Chinese cuisines. Very good; informal setting.

Kwality Restaurant. 20 Mahatma Gandhi Marg, Civil Lines; tel. 2139. Indian, Tandoori, Continental, Chinese—all reliably good food.

DEHRA DUN

Moderate

Chanakya Restaurant. Hotel Relax, Amrit Kaur Rd.; tel. 26608. Indian and Chinese food.

Golden Hut. Hotel Madhuban, 97 Rajpur Rd.; tel. 24094. Chinese, with typical Chinese decor.

Kabab Wala. Hotel Madhuban, 97 Rajpur Rd.; tel. 24094. Open-air restaurant in nice garden. Tandoori and barbecue specialties.

Kwality Restaurant. 19–B Rajpur Rd.; tel. 27001. Chinese, Indian. Informal decor.

Pavilion. Hotel President, 6 Astley Hall, Rajpur Rd.; tel. 27082. Breakfast, lunch, and dinner. Indian, Mughlai, and Continental food. Nice ambience.

Rajputana Restaurant. Nidhi Hotel, 74–C Rajpur Rd.; tel. 24611. Breakfast, lunch, and dinner. Indian, Mughlai, Continental, and Chinese cuisine. Modern decor.

Temptation. Hotel Meedo's Grand, 28 Rajpur Rd.; tel. 27171. Nonvegetarian Indian, and Chinese food. Simple, informal decor. Open 24 hours.

Vatika Restaurant. Hotel Madhuban, 97 Rajpur Rd.; tel. 24094. Indian, Continental, and Mughlai food; light cheery decor. Indian *ghazels* (love songs) nightly.

Inexpensive

The Coffee Shop. Hotel Drona, 45 Gandhi Rd.; tel. 24371. Mainly good Indian food at low prices.

HARIDWAR

Haridwar is of such religious sanctity, it's a "dry" city and strictly vegetarian within the city limits. Nonvegetarians have one new nearby refuge, which is also the only expensive eatery in town.

Expensive

Gazal. Hotel Surprise, Haridwar-Delhi Rd., Jwala Pur; tel. 1146. Breakfast, lunch, and dinner. Continental, Indian, Chinese food. Decor is Indian modern. Also in the hotel is **Rooftop Restaurant,** serving grilled specialties; and in the *moderate* category, the **Barbeque,** serving outdoor barbeque and vegetarian food. Reservations advised at all times.

Inexpensive

Chotiwala Restaurant. Railway Station Rd.; tel. 242. Good reliable vegetarian food. Informal and popular.

Hotel Kailish. Railway Rd.; tel. 789. Breakfast, lunch, and dinner. Most expensive item: tea for six, Rs. 10. Interior offers no views, but food is reliable.

LUCKNOW

Expensive

Falaknuma Restaurant. Hotel Clarks Avadh, 8 Mahatma Gandhi Marg; tel. 40130. Buffet lunch and dinner. Continental, Chinese, and Indian food, specializing in Tandoori and regional casserole dishes (*Kadai Se*). Rooftop windows; be sure to ask for a view. Indian classical music.

Carlton Hotel. Shahnajah Rd.; tel. 44021. Buffet-style (Indian, Tandoori, Mughlai, Continental) lunch and dinner. Marble floor, stuffed animals on the wall. Informal, slightly worn-out decor, but nice ambience.

Moderate

Capoor's Restaurant. 52 Hazratganj; tel. 43958. Indian, Mughlai, South Indian vegetarian, and Chinese food. Cozy informal "neon" 1930-ish decor.

Dastarkhuun. Hotel Gomti, 6 Sapru Marg; tel. 34284. Indian and some Continental dishes.

Kabab Korner. Hotel Clarks Avadh, 8 Mahatma Gandhi Marg; tel. 40130. Outdoor dining, informal. Kebabs, tandoori, and pomfret (a fine, mild white fish).

Kwality Restaurant. Mayfair Building, Hazratganj; tel. 43331. Indian, Chinese, and Continental food.

Ranjana Restaurant. Hazratganj; tel. 45946. Vegetarian, nonvegetarian, South Indian, and Chinese food.

Inexpensive

Royal Cafe. 51 Hazaratganj; tel. 47070. Mixed menu, but good.

Seema Restaurant. Hotel Elora, 3 Lalbagh; tel. 31307. Mughlai, Continental, and Chinese foods.

MUSSOORIE

With most restaurants connected to inns or small hotels, you should call first to see if they'll serve nonhotel guests. Most will, but it's best to call, especially during the high season, May–October.

Expensive

Carlton's Hotel Plaisance. Happy Valley Rd.; tel. 2800. Breakfast, lunch, dinner; vegetarian and nonvegetarian dishes.

Savoy Hotel. Mussoorie; tel. 2510. Indian, Chinese, and Continental food. Excellent food in a handsome restaurant. Reservations advised.

Moderate

Hakman's Restaurant. Mall Road; tel. 2559. Breakfast, lunch, and dinner. Old-time restaurant with a view. Not fancy, just hill-station simple.

The Jungli Murgi Restaurant. Roselynn Estate Hotel; tel. 2201. Breakfast, lunch, and dinner. Indian and Continental cuisine. Nice "woodsy" feel, with striking views.

NAINITAL

Moderate

Royal Hotel. The Mall, Mallital; tel. 2007. A varied menu of Indian, Mughlai, Chinese, and Continental foods. Reliable service. Reservations advised.

Shervani Hilltop Inn. Shervani Lodge, Mallithal; tel. 2504. Tasty Indian, Chinese, Continental dishes.

RISHIKESH

Like the neighboring city of Haridwar, Rishikesh is devoutly "dry" and only strictly vegetarian foods—not even eggs—are served.

Moderate

Daana Paani. Baseraa Hotel, 1 Ghat Rd.; tel. 767. Informal downstairs restaurant. Indian, Continental, and Chinese foods.

Darpan Restaurant. Railway Rd.; (no phone). Popular in-town restaurant. Informal.

Indrandi Restaurant. Inderlok Hotel, Railway Rd.; tel. 555. Excellent Indian and Continental dishes. Cheery, informal restaurant.

Inexpensive

Luxmanjhula Restaurant. Luxman Jhula; tel. 442. Indian, Continental, and Chinese dishes.

VARANASI

Expensive

Amrapali. Clarks Varanasi, The Mall; tel. 62021. Fixed-price meals; also an à la carte menu. Best Indian, Continental, and Chinese food in town. Reservations advised.

Mandap Hotel. Taj Ganges, Nadeswar Palace Grounds; tel. 42480. Indian and some Continental dishes. Okay but not great. Reservations advised.

Moderate

Amber Restaurant. 59 Patel Nagar; tel. 42634. Indian, Chinese, and Continental food. Pleasant.

Anjuman Restaurant. Hotel Parvaaz, 56 Patel Nagar; tel. 43045. Chinese, Indian, and Continental dishes. Full-course meals or à la carte. Informal.

Darpan Restaurant. Pallavi International Hotel, Hathwa Market, Chetganj; tel. 54894. Tandoori specialties served in a nice old-fashioned ambience.

Poonam Restaurant. Hotel Pradeep, Jagatganj; tel. 66363. Pleasant, simple restaurant, serving good food.

Inexpensive

Tulsi Restaurant. At Lahurabir; no phone. Excellent vegetarian restaurant. Popular.

Winfa. At Lahurabir; no phone. Good Chinese food, without frills. Another popular restaurant with locals.

HOW TO GET AROUND. For some inexplicable reason, while Uttar Pradesh does very well at getting people from town to town by bus, train, and airplane, local transportation is sloppily controlled (or not controlled at all). *Tempos* (large **rickshaws** on fixed routes) in Lucknow and local **bus** service throughout the state are the exception. With everything else, tourist beware. Bargain.

By Taxi. Never pay more than Rs. 2 per km.

By Auto Rickshaw. Cheaper than taxis, but drivers in Varanasi can be downright cheats. Be firm in setting the price.

By Bike Rickshaw. Best bet for in town. By the hour, don't pay more than Rs. 10.

By Rented Car with Driver. For those who have the time and want to explore the state, especially the Himalayan area, a car with driver is best. Figure Rs. 2 per km, plus night-halt charges. Dehra Dun and Varanasi are two good departure points for excursions around Uttar Pradesh. Obviously, it's wise to book in advance. The following is a list of reliable car rental agencies. Also check with the local Uttar Pradesh tourist offices for a list of other approved agencies.

Dehra Dun: *Trans World Travels,* 9–B Astley Hall, Dehra Dun; tel. 23400.

Varanasi. *ITDC Transport Unit,* Varanasi Ashok, The Mall; Cantonment; tel. 52251. *Banaras Tours,* Clarks Varanasi, The Mall, Cantonment; tel. 62021.

TRAVEL AGENCIES. In Uttar Pradesh, the variety of experience is vast, especially the adventure in the Himalayas. Here are a few excellent travel agencies that offer terrific trips:

Adventure Holidays. Box 7, Dehra Dun 248001; tel. 23511. This outfit arranges treks galore and mountaineering led by a well-experienced staff. Expeditions can be arranged throughout Uttar Pradesh and surrounding states.

Himalayan River Rafters. 188–A Jor Bagh, New Delhi 11003; tel. 615736. This is the expert outfit on traveling down the great white waters of Uttar Pradesh and all the Himalayan areas. They take care of everything but day packs. Various price ranges from $45–$70 a day.

Shikhar Travels (India) Private Ltd. 209 Competent House, F–14 Middle Circle, Connaught Pl., New Delhi 110001; tel. 331–2444. Treks, bicycle tours, sailing in the Ganges River, water rafting, and more. Very good; very organized.

Garhwal Mandal Vikas Nigam Ltd. 74–1 Rajpur Rd., Dehra Dun 248001; tel. 26817. Cheaper, because more people involved. Not as detailed, but still the views and memorable experiences can be the equivalent. Also does trekking and skiing packages.

TOUR GUIDES. In general, play safe. Arrange all guides through the tourist department. They're cheaper and more reliable than guides arranged privately. Figure about Rs. 50 for four hours.

 TOURS. Throughout the state, deluxe coach tours are conducted by *Garhwar Mandal Vikas Nigam, Ltd.* Main office: 74–1, Rajpur Rd., Dehra Dun; tel. 24408 or 26817.

Dehra Dun. Daily city tour, including Malsi Deer Park, Tapkeshwar Temple Cave, and Sahastradhara (sulphur spring). Rs. 25. For further details, call 23217.

Haridwar. Local tours in Haridwar and Riskikesh, plus tours to Badrinath and Kedarnath, contact *Haridwar Tourist Bureau* for details (tel. 19), or *Garhwal Mandal Vikas Nigas Ltd.,* Muni-ki-reti in Rishikesh (tel. 372). The latter also conducts many tours to Kedarnath, Badrinath, Ganotri, Yamunotri, and Valley of Flowers.

Lucknow. Local sightseeing tours by *Uttar Pradesh State Tourism Development Corporation* (tel. 48849), plus longer tours to Dudhwa National Park.

Mussoorie. Kempty Falls tour (peaceful bathing spot) daily. Dhanolti, scenic pine forest with good views of the Himalayas, and Surkhanda Devi Temple, on a hill with more good views. Tel. 2863.

Nainital. Numerous tours run by *Kumaon Division Development Corporation;* tel. 2656. Local sightseeing, two-day tour to Corbett National Park, three-day tour to Badrinath.

Rishikesh. Four-day tour from Rishikesh to Badrinath; seven-day tour to Badrinath and Kedrinath; four-day tour to Yamunotri, Gangotri, Kedarnath, and Badrinath; seven-day tour to Yamunotri and Gangotri; seven-day tour to Valley of Flowers, Hemkund, and Badrinath.

Varanasi. *U.P.S. Road Transport Corporation* offers two deluxe coach tours: one of the Ganges, temples, and the university; the other to Sarnath and Ramnagar Fort. Call 63233 for fares and details.

 FOREIGN CURRENCY EXCHANGE. Throughout the state, better hotels will cash traveler's checks with less fuss and wait than at the banks. Otherwise join the line at the *Bank of Baroda, State Bank of India,* and any other bank your hotel recommends. Hours are usually 10 A.M.–2 P.M. Monday–Friday; sometimes banks are open Saturday mornings until noon.

 SEASONAL EVENTS. Exact dates of these events vary, since they are set by a lunar calendar. For further details for any of these or other unscheduled events, contact the appropriate tourist department.

February. *Lucknow Festival.* Classic Indian culture displayed on a grand scale for over a week: theater, music, and dance, including the *kathak,* one of India's four classical dance forms, which has its home in this region. From a temple dance, it developed under the patronage of Moslem rulers into a court dance with a different gesture code and foot technique. The knotted Hindu draperies are replaced by tight-fitting pajamas and loose tunics made of heavy brocades.

Mid-February. *Shiva Rati* at Dehra Dun. Shiva's birthday is celebrated with a fair at Tapkeswar Cave Temple.

Spring. *Magh Mela* held at the confluence of the Ganges and Yamuna, in Allahabad. An amazing spectacle of thousands of Hindu devotees undergoing a sacred immersion.

May. *Buddha Purnima,* Sarnath. Birthday of Gautama Buddha, founder of Buddhism. A large fair with a procession of his relics. Very big occasion.

May. Opening of Badrinath and Kedarnath Temples. A festive religious occasion.

June–July. *Id-ul-Fitr,* Lucknow. Moslem celebration marking the end of Ramadan (month of fasting). Religious; big splash of festivity.

July. *Rath Yatra.* Held at Ramnagar Fort, Varanasi. Festive celebration in honor of Lord Jagannath, the Lord of the Universe, attracts big crowds. Temple "chariot" procession with sacred deities in seats of honor.

September–October. *Dussehra,* Varanasi. Big Hindu festival commemorating the victory of Lord Rama over Ravana. Enactments of *Ramila* held all over the city. At Ramnagar, elephants are available for hire and on the tenth day, a large procession culminates with the burning of effigies and a big fireworks display. In Varanasi proper, deities are taken in procession to be immersed in the Ganges.

October. *Muharram,* Lucknow. Moslem commemoration of the martyrdom of the grandson of the Prophet Mohammed Imam Hussain. Procession of beautiful tazias and illumination of the two Imambaras.

Once every 12 years (next time, 1998) *Kumbh Mela* is observed in Haridwar. *Sadhus* (devotees) fill up the city to have a sacred dip in the Ganges. Fakirs and yogis practice their amazing acts. Very religious, very festive. India's biggest festival—possibly the biggest in Asia. Lasts for days. *Ardh Kumbh* is held every six years. (Next time, 1992.) Half as big as Kumbh Mela, but still amazing.

GARDENS AND MUNICIPAL ZOOS. Dehra Dun. *Forest Research Institute Botanical Garden* and *Malso Deer Park* are both open sunrise to sunset. Free.

Lucknow. *Zoological Garden of Lucknow* in the Banarasi Bagh, founded in 1921 as a memorial to visit by the Prince of Wales. Open 5 A.M.–7 P.M.

Kukrail Forest (14 km from Lucknow), artificial forest and lake to preserve crocodiles includes a Crocodile Rehabilitation Center, run by an intelligent young man who is informative and eager to talk with visitors and a deer park, peacocks, and outdoor snack bar (open early morning to sunset). Lucknow is a city of lovely gardens, see in particular *Sikandar Bagh* (open 6 A.M.–5 P.M.), former site of fierce fighting in 1857; gardens under the management of the National Botanical Research Institute. The *Gautma Buddha Park* is a delightful park for children.

Mussoorie. *Municipal Garden* has an artificial lake and boating and a cafeteria with snacks and beverages.

WILDLIFE NATIONAL PARK. *Corbett National Park,* 320 km from Delhi, has an elephant stationed at Dhikala (the main entrance) to take visitors around; Rs. 12.50 per person per trip. Park entrance fee, Rs. 30 for three days; vehicles, Rs. 10 per car. Park is open November 15–June 15. Best time: March–June. Numerous watch towers (*machan*) are scattered over the park, which has an area of 125 sq. miles. Only daylight photography is permitted. The fauna at Corbett National Park consists of a variety of species. There are wild elephants, a large number of tigers, a few leopards, hyenas and jackals with an occasional Himalayan black bear, a few sambar, some magnificent hog deer, wild cats, and squirrels. The Ramganga offers splendid mahseer fishing during spring and summer months. There are also huge goonch that lurk in the rapids and deep pools and a good many other fish that are not usually caught on rod and line (Rs. 25 for fishing per week). In the spring, the entire area—with the new leaves of the Sheesham, the scarlet flowers of Dhak, the famous Semal tree, the mauve blossoms of the Buahinias, and the sparkling waters of the Ramganga —is unforgetable.

The nearest airport is in Pantnagar (130 km from park), which has two weekly Vayudoot flights from Delhi. The nearest railhead is in Ramnagar. To get from Ramnagar to Dhikala, you can take a minibus or charter a vehicle, in advance, from the field director, Project Tiger (Uttar Pradesh), P.O. Ramnagar, District Nainital; tel. 76. During the park season, Garhwal Mandal Vikas Nigam Ltd., operates a three-day tour (Friday–Sunday) from New Delhi. For details, contact Uttar Pradesh Government, Chandralok Building, 36 Janpath, New Delhi; tel. 322251.

Accommodations for cabins or rest houses at Corbett National Park can be arranged through the Project Tiger field director or through the Uttar Pradesh Tourist Office in New Delhi.

At Khinanauli, the *Valley of Flowers National Park* is approached by a 16-km trek from Govind Khat. It's worth the hike during July and August, when the entire valley bursts into gorgeous bloom. Entrance fee, Rs.15. For further details, contact the Uttar Pradesh Tourist Office in New Delhi.

 HISTORIC SITES. Unless stated, temples are open to all and are free. Wherever donations are asked, a rupee or two will help in the upkeep of these shrines.

AJODHYA

This is the principal city of the ancient kingdom of Kosala and the birthplace of Lord Rama, hero of the *Ramayana.* It is one of India's seven most sacred places. See *Hamuman Temple* and *Kanak Vhavan Temple,* mentioned in writings that go back to the seventh century.

ALLAHABAD

Akbar's fort sits atop the *Patal Puri Temple* with a tree that is continuously watered by Hindu priests. The tree is called the Undying Banyan Tree (Akshaya Batt) and is mentioned in writings that go back to A.D. 640. Unfortunately, the rest of the fort is off limits.

BADRINATH

A colorfully decorated temple with stone carvings is believed to be Vishnu's former abode. In the inner sanctum is a black stone deity of Vishnu. A visit also involves an incredible trek. Nearby are purifying tapta kunds (hot water springs).

DEHRA DUN

Tapkeshwar Caves (5½ km from Dehra Dun) are shrines, dedicated to Shiva, that are claimed to be 5,000 years old. In a delightful pastoral setting.

DEOPRAYAG

Ancient *Raghunath Temple,* dedicated to Vishnu, commemorates the spot where Rama (avatar of Vishnu) supposedly came to meditate. Very simple structure of granite, the temple was recently renovated. A walk through the old village by the river is truly special. This is a charming place set on the confluence of the Alaknanda and the Bhagirathi, the point where the Ganges takes its name.

FAIZABAD

In this ancient capital of the nabobs, there's a lovely *mausoleum* of Behbu Begum, one of the best in Uttar Pradesh.

HARIDWAR

Har-ki-Pairi Ghat is where Vishnu left a set of his footprints—hard to see— but it *is* the most sacred ghat and backed by temples. See Arti at sunset, a beautiful prayer offering to the Ganges, which concludes with hundreds of little flower boats lit with candles set loose on the river. Visit the *Daksh Mahadev Temple,* dedicated to Shiva, and *Sati Kund* in Kankhal (part of Haridwar). Go up to the *Mansa Devi Temple,* dedicated to the goddess Mansi, an avatar of Durga, from which you get a good view of Haridwar. Also see three ashram on the northern edge of Haridwar: *Pawan Dhamin Kharkhali,* built in 1970, a sort of a Hindi psychadelic show—wonderful fun; *Parmarth Ashram,* more subdued; and *Sapt Rishi Ashram,* downright solemn in comparison.

KEDARNATH

In this supposed abode of Shiva is a simple gray temple on a raised platform set against the banks of the Mandakini, with a Nandi statue standing in the courtyard. A visit here represents an extremely important pilgrimage to be approached on foot or pony (15 km from the road). It's a beautiful walk and worth any effort! Temple closed November–May because of snow.

LUCKNOW

Asafi Imambara was built by Asaf-ud-Daula as his burial place in 1784 after a year-long famine. The project created "relief work" for the rich and poor—it contains neither cement, nor iron. Three interior chambers in different styles (from left to right after you enter): Chinese, Persian, and Indian. Find your way through the Bhul-Bhulaiyan maze upstairs. Open 6 A.M.–5 P.M.; Rs. 1.50.

Rumi Darwaza, beyond the outer gate of Imambara, was built in 1784 by Asaf-ud-Daula as another relief project. It is a facsimile of a gate in Constantinople.

Chhota Imambara was built in 1836 by Muhammad Ali Shah as his burial place. A miniature replica of the Taj Mahal is on the right after you enter the gate that contains the tomb of his daughter, Zinat Asuja. In the Imambara is a dazzling display of chandeliers, lamps, and *tazias.* Open 6 A.M.–5 P.M..

Residency is the remains of Asaf-ud-Daula's pleasure house, which was taken over by the British and subsequently became the scene of fierce fighting during the 1857 Indian Mutiny. If you want to go into the hall, called the Model Room (Rs. 2), entrance time is 8 A.M.–5 P.M. No restrictions to visit the rest of the Residency.

Also in the center of town, see the tombs of *Nawab Ali Khan* and his wife, Khurshed Begum, constructed in the nineteenth century. Nearby are the *Kaisar Bagh,* rows of apartments that housed the ladies of the royal harem.

Shahnajaf Imambara is the tomb of Nawab Ghazi-ud-din Haiden and his wives. Built in 1814, it became a stronghold for Indians during the 1857 mutiny. Open 6 A.M.–5 P.M.

La Martiniere was built in a jumble of styles by Claude Martin in 1795. An architectural compendium dedicated to whimsy, it is now a school.

RISHIKESH

Important Hindu ashrams that can be visited here: *Swami Sivananda's Divine Life Society; Maharshi Mahesh Yogi's Transcendental Meditation Center;* and *Triveni Ghat,* the main sacred ghat and scene of a mini-Arti performed each evening. Lit flower boats are set afloat during a lovely prayer ceremony.

SARNATH

At this center of the Buddhist world, six km from Varanasi, Buddha preached his first sermon 2,500 years ago in which he revealed the Eightfold Path leading to enlightenment. Ashoka is responsible for the construction of many of the third-century stupas. Sarnath reached its zenith under the Gupta dynasty in the sixth century. It's a lovely, peaceful place with new Buddhist temples.

VARANASI

Dasashwamedh Ghat is the main ghat to visit here. *Manikarnika Ghat* and *Harish Chandra Ghat* are the cremation ghats. You can watch cremations at no cost, but photographs are forbidden.

Gyanapi Mosque is Aurangzeb's seventeenth-century creation erected on the site of the Vishwewara Temple, which he destroyed.

Alamgir Mosque. After Aurangzeb destroyed a temple—the Beni Madhav Ka Darera, which was dedicated to Vishnu—he put up this mosque with an odd fusion of the abhorred Hindu (lower portion) and Moslem (upper portion) designs.

Ramnagar Fort is the former residential palace of the ex-maharajah of Varanasi; approached by boat, most of it is now a museum.

INNER CITY OF VARANASI

Kashi Vishwanath Temple, dedicated to Shiva, is in between the Dasash-wamedh and Manikarnika ghats. It is off limits to non-Hindus, but pay a small fee (about Rs. 2) and see the interior from the house opposite. Watch morning or evening prayers—flower offerings given to the lingam. The temple was constructed in 1776, with its spire covered in gold plate—a gift from Maharajah Ranjit Singh in 1835.

Durga Temple, dedicated to Durga, consort of Shiva; this eighteenth-century construction is located due west of Asi Ghat. Shikara is formed on top of five lower spires—a convergence that is a visual symbol of the belief that all five elements of the world merge with the Supreme. Durga is also called the Monkey Temple; the pests are everywhere and they'll steal anything.

Bharat Mata Mandir, on Vidya Peeth Road, is a temple inaugurated by Mahatma Gandhi and dedicated to India. Inside is a large relief map of India carved of marble.

MUSEUMS. In Allahabad, *Allahabad Museum,* Alfred Park, has terra cottas, good Rajasthani miniatures, and modern paintings. Open generally 10 A.M.–6 P.M. Closed Wednesdays. *Anand Bhavan* (Place of Joy), is the former home of Jawaharlal Nehru and contains personal momentoes of this freedom fighter/politician. Open mornings and afternoons. Closed Mondays.

In Lucknow, *Archaeological Museum,* Kaiserbagh, contains archeological finds, with a heavy concentration from Uttar Pradesh. Open 10 A.M.–5 P.M.; Rs. 0.50. *Picture Gallery,* between the two Imambaras, was built by Nawab Mohammad Ali Shah. Kind of a *Who's Who* portrait gallery of the megalomanical nabobs. Open 8 A.M.–5 P.M.; Rs. 0.75.

State Museum, Banarsi Bagh, is a general all-around museum with paintings and artifacts. Open 10 A.M. –5 P.M., closed Mondays.

In Sarnath, *Archaeological Museum* contains great Buddhist treasures. Open 10 A.M.–5 P.M., closed Fridays. Rs. 0.50.

In Varanasi, *Bharat Kala Bhavan* (Art Gallery) at Banaras Hindu University has a good collection of paintings and art objects. Closed Sundays and university holidays. Open 9:30 A.M.–4:30 P.M.; in summer, 8 A.M.–noon.

In Ramnagar, *Fort Museum* houses a fine collection of palanquins, furniture, arms, weapons, and costumes. Open 9 A.M.–noon; 2–5 P.M. Rs. 1.

SPORTS. Uttar Pradesh is an adventure state. Boating, fishing, skiing, trekking or wonderful walks, and white-water rafting are all here to experience in beautiful surroundings. New possibilities are opening up constantly. What follows is a partial list. Contact the Uttar Pradesh tourist departments for the most current range of possibilities.

Boating. Mussoorie and Nainital. Sailing down the Ganges.

Fishing. *Corbett National Park* (see under *Wildlife* section). *Dehra Dun.* For details and permit, contact Divisional Forest Officer (East), Dehra Dun, Uttar Pradesh. *Mussoorie.* For details and permit, contact Divisional Forest Officer, Yamuna Division, Mussoorie, Uttar Pradesh.

Skiing. Auli, near Joshimath, has a tow rope 3.8 km in length. This is a brand-new and developing resort. Garhwal Mandal Vikas Nigam, Ltd., runs ski courses from January to March for five, 10, and 15 days. They will supply the skiing equipment. For further details, reservations, and cost, contact Garhwal Mandal Vikas Nigam, Ltd. Yatra Office, Muni-ki-reti, Rishikesh; tel. 372. This resort will be spectacular once it's in full operation. For now, just to ski it's an inexpensive treat.

Trekking. Here are some of the most popular possibilities in Uttar Pradesh: *Rudraprayag to Badrinath* via Chamoh–Pipalkou–Gulabkoti–Joshimath (by bus). On foot: Joshimath–Pandukeshwar (eight miles)–Badrinath (11 miles). Elevation 6,000–10,250 feet. At all these stages there is a Public Works Department (P.W.D.) Inspection Bungalow. Reservation authority: Executive Engineer, P.W.D. Pauri. A three–four day hike.

Rudraprayag to Kedarnath via Kakaragad (last bus stop)–Gupta Kashi (four miles)–Phata (nine miles)–Gauri Kund (eight miles)–Kedarnath (seven miles).

Elevation 3,000–11,700 feet. Reservation authority for accommodations along this route: Secretary, District Board, and Executive Engineer, both at Pauri. A two-day hike. Hire porters at Rudraprayag.

Kedarnath to Chamoli via Gauri Kund–Phata–Nalapatan–Ukimath–Tung-nath–Gopeshwar–Chamoli (total 50 miles). Elevation 11,700–3,000 feet. P.W.D. Inspection Bungalow at all stages. Reservations authority: Executive Engineer, P.W.D., Pauri. Four days or less.

Almora to Pindari Glacier, by bus to Kapkot (where you must wait for ponies and porters)–Lharkhet (10 miles)–Dhakuri (six miles)–Khati (six miles)–Dwali (seven miles)–Phurkia (three miles)–Pindari Glacier (three miles). P.W.D. Bungalows at all stages. Reservations authority: P.W.D., Bageshwar. Bring a tent for camping at Martoli, near the glacier. Elevation 3,500–11,000 feet. Sundard-hhunga and Kaphini Glaciers can be visited en route.

A trip to Pindari Glacier is well within the capacity of any hiker, and the effort involved is amply rewarded by the views en route as well as the magnificence of the glacier itself. Six or seven days are required for this trek. The best time to visit is May 14–June 15, when the flowers are in bloom and the snow bridges have not melted away, or Sept. 15–early October, when the air is free from haze and the Trail Pass is still negotiable. The glacier is three miles from Phurkia, and the trek involves a climb of 2,500 feet. An early start enables you to spend some time on the glacier and to take in its grandeur and beauty. The return journey can be shortened by halting only at Dwali, Dhakuri, and Kapkot.

Mussoorie to Chakrata via Saingi (nine miles)–Lakhwar (seven miles)–Nayh-tat (six miles)–Chorani (nine miles)–Chakrata (seven miles). Ups and downs starting at 6,600 feet and ending at 7,000 feet. Dak Bungalows at all stages. Reservations not necessary but accommodations are usually primitive.

Chakrata to Himachal Pradesh boundary (toward Simla) via Desban (seven miles)–Mandali (12 miles)–Kalhyan–Tinuni (12 miles)–Arakot (9 miles). Elevation: 7,000 feet–2,900 feet. Forest Rest Houses at all stations. Reservations authority: District Forest Officer, Chakrata.

Garhwal Mandal Vikas Nigam, Ltd. (74/1 Rajpur Rd., Dehra Dun, UP.; tel. 26817, 26830) runs inexpensive treks of 5–14 days. They are good treks with a no-frills quality.

Shikhar Travels Private Limited (209 Competent House, F–14 Middle Circle, Connaught Place, New Delhi; tel. 3312444) runs interesting treks that are more upscale. You walk and carry your daypack, that's it. Prices, of course, are higher. But the trek groups are smaller and the attention is more personal.

SHOPPING. The main shopping areas are in the cities of Lucknow and Varanasi, two places where it's hard to say no. The main shopping bargains are, of course, the exquisite Varanasi silks, brocades, and saris. Lucknow's gold and silver and white embroidery (called chikan), table covers, and silverware, and Mirzapur's carpets. Brassware and lacquered toys complete the list. In the Himalayan area, look at handwoven products made of Garhwal wool: shawls, hats, and gloves. The main centers of shopping at Allahabad are the Civil Lines, Johnstonganj, and the Chowk. In Lucknow, fixed-price shopping is concentrated at Hazratganj. Aminabad (a market area) is the place to go for perfume essences (attars). The following three cities have great bazaars or *chowks:*

In Lucknow, *The Chowk* is great for browsing and getting a sense of lively Lucknow. Lots of special hand-embroidered chikan work. The best shops are *Lal Bihari Tandon,* Gota Bazar, Chowk, and *Delux Kurta Industry,* 11 Gota Bazar, Chowk, which has great *dhotis* (skirtlike garments) for babies and small children.

In Haridwar, *Moti Bazaar* is a delightful, manageable size, with medicine shops and religious stalls. Fun; mostly for browsing.

Varanasi has two good areas: *Chowk* and *Vishwanath Lane.* If you want to buy silk, play safe so you won't get stuck with shoddy goods. Get a list of approved shops from the Government of India Tourist Department. Good-quality silk costs money. If you get a steal, you're the one who's probably been robbed. The following are reputable good shops: *Brijraman Das & Sons,* K37/32, Golghar, tel. 63285, and *Vishwanath Lane,* tel. 63837; *Mohanlal Gopal Das,* Chowk, tel. 63484; *Oriental Emporium,* 10/252 Maqbool Alam Rd., tel. 64414.

TEA TIME. There are many places in Uttar Prudesh to take time out for tea, a cool drink, or snacks. A few are listed here.

DEHRA DUN

Chanakya Restaurant. Hotel Relax, Amrit Kaur Rd.; tel. 26608. Open 24 hours for tea and snacks.

Kwality Ice Cream Parlour. 19-B Rajpur Rd.; tel. 27001. 4–10 P.M.; holidays, open all day.

Rajputana Restaurant. Nidhi Hotel, 74/C Rajpur Rd.; tel. 24611. Good snacks 3–7:30 P.M.

LUCKNOW

Gulfam. Clark's Avadh, 8 Mahatma Gandhi Marg; tel. 40130. Snacks around the clock.

Hotel Gulmarg. Aminabad; tel. 31227. Amiable interior garden setting. Limited snack bar. 7–10 A.M.; 6–10 P.M.

Kwality Ice Cream Parlour. Hazratganj; 9 A.M.–9 P.M.

Old Coffee House on Hazaratganj. Coffee and snacks; 8 A.M.–9 P.M.

Thandai ke Dookam. Opposite Gol Darwaza (the gate that leads into Chowk), not far from the police station. A one-of-a-kind institution (really, just a simple stall). Offers *Thandai,* a delicious concoction of milk, dry fruits, pistachios, and spices—an Indian milkshake for Rs. 3. Try it! Open 8 A.M.–late at night.

BARS AND NIGHTLIFE. Don't expect too much nightlife in Uttar Pradesh, but most of the hotels have bars where you can enjoy an afternoon cocktail or a pleasant evening. Bars generally are open 11 A.M.–3 P.M. and 6–11 P.M. or midnight. A selection includes the *Polo Bar* in the Hotel President, Dehra Dun, which is in a cozy downstairs room. Also in Dehra Dun, the subdued lighting in the *Madhushala,* Hotel Madhuban, gives the feeling of intimacy. In Lucknow, the *Tashna Bar* in Hotel Gompti is also dark but not overbearing. To reminisce about the Raj era, have a drink in the Victorian barroom of *Hakman's Hotel* or try the comfortable cocktail lounge in the *Savoy,* which has a pleasant ambience. In Varanasi, the *Kambari* in Clarks Varanasi is an attractive and quiet place.

HIMACHAL PRADESH

Mountains, Vales—Unspoiled Serenity

by
KATHLEEN COX

Flanked by the lofty mountains of Jammu and Kashmir in the west, the Garhwal Himalayas of Uttar Pradesh in the east, and the rugged Tibetan mountains in the north, Himachal Pradesh, with its own towering peaks and romantic vales, is an enchanting state too often overlooked by Western tourists traveling in India. Every road in this state seems to bend, climb, and descend with few breaks of a straight stretch. The air, no matter the time of the year, is invigorating—a healthy relief from the plains. And, except for the occasional city, like Shimla or Mandi, the preferred pace of life remains slow and pastoral.

Villages mean a small huddle of shops and stalls supplying necessities and few luxuries, at least for the people who live here. But for foreigners who have the time to linger, Himachal Pradesh offers a hefty dose of outdoor sports at their best—treks, fishing, walks, even rafting and skiing. Its heady vistas change with the terrain, from snow-capped green mountains, to fertile valleys, to barren somber peaks where the monsoon never penetrates. And its people—Sikhs, Hindus, and Buddhists—are culturally diverse and wear distinct styles of dress. Himachal Pradesh is also an important haven for Tibetan refugees; it's the present home of the Dalai Lama.

Shimla, the capital of Himachal Pradesh, set atop a six-mile-long winding ridge at an altitude of 7,238 feet, was originally part of the kingdom of Nepal. In the 1800s, after the Gurkas of Nepal established one-too-many forts in their attempt to usurp new territory, the British

East India Company finally intervened and defeated them in the Gurka War of 1819. During the fierce fighting, a British lieutenant just happened to stumble across the thick wooded perch with its stunning vistas and ideal climate, a place already known for its temple dedicated to the goddess Shyamla (another Kali, the goddess of wrath, incarnation). The lieutenant decided this oasis was the ideal place to pitch the tents of the battle-fatigued British.

Three years later, a second British officer, Major Kennedy, constructed the first year-round residence (the house still stands; it serves as the seat of various Himachal Pradesh government offices). But decades still had to pass before Lord Lawrence, the British viceroy, finally adopted the hilltop ridge as his undeclared summer capital in 1864. Only then did Shimla make the grand leap in status, becoming the premiere British hill station, with Lord Curzon adding the piece de resistance when he ordered the construction of the Kalka-Shimla narrow gauge train in 1902 and inaugurated it two years later. This diesel train, still running today, is a great way to begin your exploration of Shimla and Himachal Pradesh.

EXPLORING HIMACHAL PRADESH

Shimla

The old-fashioned train—and don't think posh—chugs its way along a five-hour, 60-mile journey, passing through 103 tunnels, forests of flowering rhododendron, slowly winding into the mountains and only occasionally coming to a halt at a Swiss-chalet-style railway station (a deliberate Lord Curzon touch), one of many that dot the line. This is a nonhurried journey that slows you down, almost too much. For the new Shimla of independent India has changed, stepped up its tempo, making it more city than hill station.

Shimla's old Victorian face is tarnished. Paint is peeling and mortar is crumbling. New buildings have squeezed out lawns, gardens, and the genteel air that came with exclusivity. But democratic Shimla still has the mall—now crowded with shops, walks, horses, and monkeys—the ridge, all those zig-zag up-and-down streets open only to pedestrians, and those views into the surrounding valleys and distant mountains that are still serene.

Although Shimla is no longer the Shimla of Kipling, who set so many of his stories here, or the former viceroy's idea of a peaceful getaway, give it a chance. Let the new mood grow on you. Besides, a few buildings still try hard to remind you of their time of pomp and glory. See the former Viceroy's Lodge, now the Indian Institute of Advanced Studies. You can't go inside, but the grounds are lovely, the views are terrific, and the exterior of the main lodge is an English Renaissance (Elizabethan) treat. The building was constructed by Lord Dufferin between 1884 and 1888 out of Himalayan gray stone transported to Shimla by mules. At that time, the English thought it was built in too much of a hurry, which was reflected in the constant need for repair. Also, see the Kennedy house, the first house built in Shimla (across the street from the Shimla Railroad Station).

Then, after resting over espresso at an Indian coffee house, walk up to the Ridge and the Christ Church, supposedly the second oldest church in Northern India, consecrated in 1857. The women who attended this church, which isn't too large, were supposedly lectured in a sermon to cut back on the size of their crinolines, which took up too much room. The women responded by coming to church the next Sunday in their riding habits. From here, head up to the top of Jakhu Hill (two km), the highest peak offering the best nearby view of Shimla. On the top is a Hanuman Temple, dedicated to the monkey god, and appropriately guarded by a vigilant band of monkeys. Beware! They're always on the watch for an edible sacrificial offering.

For the true Indian experience, head back down those crooked alleys to the Middle and Lower Bazaar (especially if you're ready to shop, for prices are cheaper here). The mix of people brings you back to the heart of Asia—tall, stately Punjabs; hill tribes in homespun cloth; Tibetans; and an occasional lama with his prayer wheel, tender, and flint.

Shimla is an ideal base for sports and outdoor enthusiasts who are looking for a mountain to climb or a slope to ski down. No matter what direction you go, within minutes all sense of city life is gone. Hills, mountains, peace, and rural simplicity become the pervasive themes.

Take the winding road northeast to Narkanda (65 km). You pass through villages, then scattered dwellings built into the hillsides, and then occasional terraces of wheat and potato fields, usually bordered by pine forests. Snow-capped mountains gleam in the distance. Narkanda is a small village. Not much happens, but it offers great views, walks, and treks into the inner Himalayas.

Naldehra, only 22 km northeast of Shimla, has a nine-hole golf course—India's oldest, which Lord Curzon helped design. The fee for playing is nominal, and the spectacular scenery is enough of a diversion to wreak havoc with your score. This is also another great place for walks and picnics. If you're in the area in June, don't miss Naldehra's Sipi Fair, a gay, colorful festival at which costumed villagers from all over the state sell their handicrafts.

Nirath, Rampur, and Sarahan

Although the district of Kinnaur is off limits to foreigners, other culturally and visually appealing villages exist to the north of Narkanda. Proceed northeast until you reach the small village of Nirath (approximately 121 km from Shimla). Here you can visit an eighth-century *shikara* style Hindu temple, dedicated to the sun god, Surya. The temple is decorated with wooden walls and contains a *mandapa* (entrance hall), recently restored with a typical Himachal Pradesh blue slate roof.

Farther north is the town of Rampur, with tiers of houses that rise against the banks of the Sutlej River. At the lovely monastery, you begin to see the influence of Buddhism in the region. Rampur, the commercial center of the area, is the site of a November Lavi—one of the state's largest trade fairs, which draws thousands of local villagers in colorful traditional dress.

Northeast of Rampur is Sarahan (184 km from Shimla), located high above a valley, with exquisite views of snow-capped mountains and rolling fields. Atop a peak called Srikand (elevation 18,626 feet) is a stone image of Shiva, known as Srikand Mahadev. Worshippers offer their blessings by placing a cup of *charas* (a form of hashish) in front of the image. The charas is ignited and reduced to ashes. Other offerings are placed under stones.

In the village of Sarahan, visit the Bhimakali Temple set in a courtyard—an exquisite temple complex that combines Hindu and Buddhist architecture. Much of the detail of this serenely situated structure is magnificent. Note the elaborate silver doors made by Kinnauri silversmiths at the turn of the century during the reign of Maharajah Sir Padum Singh. The rectangular towers at one end of the courtyard represent the Hindu temple, which is served by Brahmin priests. The inner sanctum contains Hindu and Buddhist bronzes, numerous masks, and an image of the Bhimakali goddess 80 cm in height.

Chail

Chail (45 km to the southeast of Shimla) is a lovely mountain village and resort developed largely by the Maharajah Bhupinder Singh (the Maharajah of Patiala), who proved to be too dashing and handsome. He charmed the British ladies and enraged their jealous husbands, who made him feel less than welcome. The maharajah vowed to stay away from the fusty British and put all his energy and a ton of money into creating his own classy retreat that would put Shimla in its place.

At an altitude of 7,054 feet, Chail rests on three hills, with the former palace of the maharajah (now the Chail Palace Hotel) a beautiful sprawl atop Rahgarh Hill. The surrounding forests—the palace is situated on over 600 acres—are the home of barking deer, monkeys, occasional leopards, and numerous species of wild birds. You can relax in the quiet of an elegant stretch of lawn, walk for hours along well-marked paths that pass by orchards, gardens, and deep-green woods. Chail also boasts a well-kept cricket field, India's highest, possibly the highest in the world.

Bilasput

Northwest from Shimla, the road circles through forests, valleys, and mountains at times so rocky that the road seems scooped out of stone. You enter the Arkai Range and Arki, a tiny village with an old yellow stone palace perched on the edge of a hill overlooking a splendid green and yellow valley—the dominant spring colors. Moving on, you reach Bilaspur and a small cafe that overlooks the Gobindsagar Lake, a strange sight that reveals an odd partnership between art and nature. There, in the small lake (not much larger than a pond) are a slew of 200-year-old Hindu temples. This is actually the site of the old city of Palampur, submerged by the construction of the Bhakra Dam. During high season (the monsoon months of July–October), only the spires peek above the water. The rest of the year, as the water recedes, some of the simple stone temples are completely clear of the lake as though built on the water's edge.

Mandi—Gateway to Kullu Valley

On the left bank of the Beas River, Mandi at first glance looks like a New England mill town, with rickety houses packed tight along the river's edge. Mandi is a pleasing city with temple spires poking up everywhere. (There are over 100.) Many of the temples are of recent construction and brightly painted. Others are simple dark granite and date back to the sixteenth and seventeenth centuries, built in an odd blend of Mogul and Hindu styles. The latter have a faintly mausoleum exterior shape, but inside they go Hindu, with carved square pillars and an inner sanctum.

Visit in particular the sixteenth-century Panchvaktra on the right side of the riverbank, not far from the bridge leading into the city. Inside the temple, a monolithic and benign granite Nandi faces, not the expected *lingam* (phallic symbol), but an unusual five-faced Shiva sitting in his meditation pose. To the left of the inner sanctum is a stone replica of the deity that sits inside. Also, visit the Bhutnath, set on the river's edge in the heart of the city near a series of colorful new Shiva temples. This time Nandi stands outside the temple facing a small lingam in the inner sanctum. The temple is stark and has few exterior carvings. All the sculptural emphasis is on the double archway entrance, as if drawing our attention to Shiva's symbol. Finally, see the Trilknath Temple, another old temple set back from the river. In February or March, Mandi's Shivratri Fair, which pays homage to Shiva, turns the Bhutnath temple and the city itself into one big party. Devotees carry deities on temple chariots (small gaily dressed palanquins); folk dances and folk music brighten the mood.

All year round, the inner city markets and bazaars are a walker's treat. Take an evening stroll (shops close at 8 P.M.). Every lane is narrow and cobbled and lined with tiny shops or stalls, often with dark rough wood interiors; an occasional temple; a moss covered slope; and even a hearty tree that sneaks its roots into the crowded area. The architecture is stone and bare (or paint faded) wood. Sloping roofs overhang second stories frequently fronted by verandas, balconies, and push-open French-style windows. The overall effect is of an Italian hill town gone Asian. Also, while walking up and down these skinny streets that so often lead ultimately to the river, try to find Ravi Nagar, a pleasant spot, with its spacious rectangular garden and quiet communal courtyard.

Rewalsar Lake

If time permits, take a detour southeast to Rewalsar Lake. The drive is beautiful, winding into mountains that overlook terraced fields of wheat and modest square houses of wood or sod with carefully checkered slate roofs that flicker in the sun. Rewalsar Lake is tiny and famous for its floating reed islands. The power of prayer or a minuscule breeze can set them in motion (more often in the eyes of the believer). Three shrines for the three different faiths—Buddhists, Sikhs, and Hindus—dot the edge of the water, all of which are considered sacred. The Buddhist complex dominates. Prayer flags rise from courtyards. Prayer wheels encircle the exterior walls of the monastery. Inside sits a golden Buddha surrounded by numerous prayer stalls in which monks read scrolls. It's a peaceful village.

Kullu Valley

From Mandi, the Kullu road proceeds for 25 miles through the Mandi-Larji Gorge along the Beas River. The narrow road, blasted through solid rock, has left eerie precipices that tower overhead, while down below, the raging torrent rushes by. At Aut, you turn north along the river and head up the Kullu Valley that hugs the Beas—50 miles long and, when the vista opens up, just barely more than a mile at its broadest. Idyllic, yet wild and dominant. No wonder this valley is known as the Abode of the Gods.

In March, apricot and apple trees burst into pink and white blossoms. On the higher slopes, giant rhododendrons with crimson flowers give the appearance of trees decked out in small lanterns. Early in June, horse chestnuts are in flower, swarms of wild bees humming around them. By July masses of blue and purple irises are splashed over the hillside. Buttercups range in color from the familiar golden yellow to pink-red. The fall brings on an explosion of bright colors. With winter, the vista turns white except for the stately green forests of pine and cedar.

Manikaran

At Bhunjtar, about 10 km north of Bajaura, take the turn east across the bridge for an hour-long memorable trip to Manikaran (Jewel of the Ear). The road, winding along the Parvati River, is hardly wide enough for the public bus that makes the daily journey between Manikaran and Mandi. At intervals along the way, you see homes of mud and stone with straw roofs and fog hugging snow-capped mountains.

Manikaran is a spiritual center. Here Parvati and Shiva, on a journey through the Himalayas, stopped and meditated by the hot and cold streams for 1,000 years. Here, Parvati dropped a jewel from her earring into the river, where it was devoured by the Serpent King, Shesh Nag. Shiva prayed for its return with such power that the world shook and Shesh Nag hissed up Parvati's jewel, creating the bubbling springs. Along with her jewel thousands of others shot out, supposedly until 1905, when an earthquake put an end to the bounty.

In the Sri Ramchandra Temple, built in the sixteenth century, Vishnu sits in the inner sanctum below an electric clock. The famous Dussehra festival, now held at Kulla, was once held here. Also see the old Sri Raghunath Temple, dedicated to Vishnu, across from the Tourist Complex. Then head to the river and the little white new Himachal Pradesh temple, dedicated to Shiva and the nearby not-so-old Gurudwara Sri Guru Nanak Dev Ji Hari Har Ghat, built in the 1940s. You walk through waves of blinding white steam, passing rectangular hot water pits where pots of food are cooking. You enter a hall with chambers here and there, the steam rising up. Inside one, the devout sit in the heat and pray. Inside, other pilgrims purify themselves in bathing tanks. Another room is set up for free tea and meals (although a donation is welcome); there are rooms to spend the night at no charge. Upstairs is the sacred room, gaily decorated, where services are held periodically (evening and early morning). All are welcome.

Every temple has sacred bathing tanks, and all the streets and lanes have gurgling hot pits where clothing is washed and food is cooked. The pace of life nearly stops here: a few tourists, the chatter of crows, the lowing of a cow. It's a place to walk, relax, and enjoy natural beauty in an almost primeval state. Footpaths or friendly villagers gladly show you the way up and up into serene heavenly peaks. And by all means, refresh yourself in a hot spring bath set up in the new tourist complex; it's clean and revitalizing—a rare treat.

Kullu

Just before you enter the bustling little city of Kullu, you pass a large grass square on your right, called the Dhalpur Maidan, and a stadium on your left. This is the site of Himachal Pradesh's famous annual fair, the Kullu Dussehra, which celebrates the victory of good over evil. The October Dussehra is the most important gathering in the district. To the accompaniment of drums and bells, deities from neighboring villages temples are carried down to Kullu in an evening procession of decorated palanquins that marks the start—the Vijay Dashmi—of the festival. Once the deity arrives at the maidan, it is placed before the supreme deity Raghunathji, the presiding god of Kullu Valley, who sits in his honored position under a festive tent. The maidan is covered with booths, ringed with crowds, and alive with folk dances, music—the full spectrum of Himachal Pradesh village culture. Dussehra ends on an electric, yet squeamish note—the sacrifice of a bull and small creatures as gifts to the gods.

Every year on April 28–30, Kullu also holds a cattle fair on the same popular maidan. People from surrounding villages arrive to buy and sell their livestock. The spirit here is also festive, with folk dances and local cultural events the prime attraction.

While in Kullu, see the Raghunathji Temple, the shrine of the supreme deity, and the Vaishno Devi Temple, involving a delightful walk to a small cave that enshrines an image of the goddess Vaishno. Drive to the foot of Bijli Mahadev Shrine and spend a day climbing 11 km to an altitude of 8,000 ft. Besides panoramic views of the entire valley, you'll see a remarkable temple, the Bijli Mahadev. The temple is also called the Temple of Lightning because of a curious phenomenon: its 60-foot staff that glistens in the sun supposedly attracts divine blessings in the form of lightning. When lightning strikes, it shoots down the staff and shatters the Shiva lingam. Every year, this supposedly happens and every year the priests restore the image, putting it back together with butter and then awaiting the annual recurrence of the "miracle." And, in the small city of Kullu, spend time wandering through the Akhara Bazaar, a great place to buy Kullu handicrafts—shawls, *pattus* (bolts of cloth), *toppis* (Himachal Pradesh caps), and *pullans* (like bedroom slippers).

Naggar

Two roads lead to Manali. Take the less traveled one, which means turn right at Katrain, 20 km north of Kullu, and cross over to the right side of the Beas River. Before heading north, see Naggar, the former capital of the rajas of Kullu, and a sleepy village, with its door just slightly open to tourism. Perched on a mountainside, the 400-year-old castle, built of weathered wood and stone, is now a tourist hotel with minimal amenities but breathtaking views from its veranda. At its feet rests a tiny village with a slew of cozy wooden homes knit together by narrow lanes and paths. Orchards and fields of seasonal crops tumble down the slope to the river.

Naggar is peaceful and friendly. Walk through the narrow lanes to the old stone temple, dedicated to Shiva with Nandi nearby. Here boys play cricket in the temple courtyard and girls play jacks with red clay stones, while a priest, oblivious to all the activity, prays quietly near the idol in the inner sanctum. Stop at a tea stall, where a kettle simmers over a fire. Meander along footpaths that take you into backyards and by wooden huts filled with white rabbits whose angora fur is a precious commodity. Climb to the nearby Tripura Sundari Temple, with its pagodalike appearance and intriguing wood carvings. Walk, relax, and, above all, give in to Naggar's timelessness and that rare chance to discover beauty at every turn.

Manali

From Naggar, stay on the right side of the Beas and continue north 12 km until you reach Jagatsukh, another small village that was a former capital of Kullu and the site of ancient temples: The Shiva temple in Shikhara style and the nearby old Devi Sharvali Temple, dedicated to the Goddess Gayatri (a sister of Durga). Another six miles brings you to a bridge. On the other side is Manali, set against the magic of towering snow-capped peaks, many of them unscaled and unnamed. This mountain town, situated at an altitude of 6,000 feet, is an ideal stopping point—the perfect headquarters for hikes, treks, mountain climbing, inexpensive winter skiing at nearby Solang, and fishing in the summer.

Although the emphasis in Manali is on getting into nature, ancient artisans have added some of their own beautiful handiwork to the landscape. Walk one km from the heart of the town and visit the 600-year-old Hadimba Devi Temple with a four-tiered pagoda-shaped roof, a somber, wooden shrine set in a cedar grove. According to the *Mahabharata,* Bhima, who wanted to marry Hadimba, first had to kill her cruel demon brother Hadimb, which he did in this grove. Another legend claims that the artist who created the pretty shrine with its exterior and door covered with handsome carvings received a dubious token of gratitude from the king. He was so enamored with the results, he cut off the artist's hand to prevent him from duplicating another temple that might rival the Hadimba. Undaunted, the artist used his left hand and created a finer temple at Chamba (the Triloknath Temple). Again his work was so admired, no rival was wanted. This time they cut off his head.

Also visit the small village of Vashisht, on the right bank of the Beas. Just off the road in an interior courtyard is another lovely pyramidal stone temple, recently restored. Inside is a granite idol of Vashista with haunting silver eyes. A Shiva lingam sits in the corner and wooden carvings adorn the interior pillars. Vashisht is another source of sulphur springs; near the shrine are two sacred tanks (one for men, the other for women) where devotees purify themselves in hot sulphur water. Just down the road heading back toward Manali, the Himachal Pradesh Tourist Department has set up a delightful complex of hot sulphur baths—clean and refreshing—the perfect way to end any walk. The cost is nominal, and outside the bathing complex is a small outdoor cafe.

The influx of Tibetan refugees in Manali has left its stamp on the town. The new Tibetan Monastery just behind the bus stop in an area called Model Town and adjoining it, the Tibetan Bazaar, are examples. You'll have to look hard to find anything ethnic. The emphasis is decidedly on "West is best," no matter how shoddy.

Farther north from Manali is Kothi, a quiet village at the foot of the Rohtang Pass, offering dramatic views of massive snow-covered peaks. From Kothi, it's three kilometers to the Rahla Falls that shoot water from the Beas into a deep gorge. Solang Valley is Himachal Pradesh's developing ski resort, with reasonable runs at an unbelievably low price that includes all necessary equipment. And here, all year round, the Himalayas will catch hold of you. Finally, continue north another 38 kilometers to the Rohtang Pass, at an altitude of 13,400 feet, where you see the twin peaks of Geypan and the Sone Pani glaciers. This is the gateway to the next set of valleys—the remote Lahaul and Spiti. Nearly indomitable, the pass is open only from June to September, a little earlier for the intrepid who trek.

Lahaul and Spiti

To the uninitiated, Lahaul and Spiti mean little more than barren rocks, raging torrents, perilous mountain paths, and glaciers unrelieved by ordinary creature comforts. But to anyone who wants a profound confrontation with nature, these valleys on the Indo-Tibetan border represent an unforgettable experience. Here, the Himalayas assume their wildest and most inhabitable stance. And here, all but the cynical adventurer will feel that dimension of glory that approaches the mystical.

For a trek into the Lahaul valley (unfortunately, Spiti is closed to foreigners), cross the Rohtang Pass. Once you enter the bleak and windswept Khoksar, the first village in the valley, you've also entered that serene realm of Tantric Buddhism, the religion of Tibet. Lahaul reminds us vividly and often of its culture. Prayer wheels, *chortens* (stupas), prayer flags, gompas (monasteries)—they're all here in the valley, as are perpetual repetitions of mantras, which seem to beckon us to continue on.

Summers in Lahaul are cool and pleasant. Like Ladakh, no monsoon unleashes its fury here. The height of the mountains keeps out the rain clouds. Keylong, the capital of Lahaul, is 117 km from Manali—set in a green valley with fields of barley and buckwheat, an oasis surrounded by brown somber hills and massive snowy peaks. The Kharding Gompa, overlooking Keylong from the top of a hill across the river, has exquisite frescoes and murals and an enormous prayer drum with numerous strips of paper, each inscribed with the sacred *mantra:*

Only those rare, lucky foreigners who are able to procure an Inner-Line Permit from the Ministry of Home Affairs in New Delhi are able to proceed to Spiti, where the valley, in some places, is quite wide. In these flatlands, you find most of the settlements and cultivation bordered by steep rocky mountains that rise several thousand feet. The Spiti River is a fast-moving torrent that, through the years, has cut its way through the bottom of a deep ravine. The valley is less than a mile across, with narrow strips of arable land 1,000 feet above the riverbed. Steep rocky mountains, rise above this land, reaching several thousand feet. The sweeping vista of rugged crags and slopes changes color from pale pink to bright scarlet, tempered by the soft blues and greens of glaciers.

The men of Spiti wear a long double-breasted woolen gown, reinforced by a long woolen rope wrapped around the waist in multiple coils. This belt provides warmth and turns the upper part of the gown into an ample blouse in which all kinds of articles are stored, including a Buddhist prayer wheel; a silver bowl for water, tea, or liquor; a spare garment; or a newly born lamb. The women grease their hair with butter and wear it in numerous thin plaits that are then woven with yak's tailhair to increase the length. Their hairdo resembles a net of black strands that spreads down the back, often hanging to the knees.

Since food is scarce and arable land is limited, the people of Spiti have evolved a scheme to ward off the dangers of overpopulation; the eldest son inherits the land, while the younger sons are sent off to a local lamasery, where they take a vow of celibacy. Women who fail to find husbands often enter convents. Monogamy is the general rule, but both polygamy and polyandry occur occasionally. If the eldest son dies, a younger brother quits the lamasery and takes over the deceased brother's land, his widow, and the children.

Baijnath

Passing through the Kangra Valley, first stop is Baijnath, with its important Hindu temple, constructed in the Shikara style with a low pyramid-shaped roof. This is supposedly the oldest Shiva shrine in India, built in A.D. 804, possibly by the Pandavas. Like most stone temples in Himachal Pradesh, the Baijnath is not massive, sitting on the crest of a low mountain above the Binwakund River. Set against the backdrop of the Himalayas and nestled within the relatively tall stone wall of its courtyard, the overall effect accentuates its contained and diminutive size. The Baijnath is quite a contrast to the Dravidian temples of South India, with their soaring gopura that humble you before you set foot in the shrine. The four thick pillars supporting the Baijnath have handsome carvings, including an unusual composite image of Vishnu and Laxmi. Inside, the inner sanctum is a Shiva lingam (called the Vaidyanath).

Dharamsala

Dharamsala is a former British hill station (40 km from Kangra), spilling off a spur of the Dhauladhar range and surrounded on three sides by snow-capped peaks. When the white shrouded mountains first come into view, the rugged slopes appear black and foreboding, but as you draw nearer, the bleak mass softens to green and the white tops shimmer. Even Dharamsala, devastated by an earthquake in 1905, has a gentle aura, befitting the recent influx of Buddhist refugees who, along with their spiritual leader the Dalai Lama, fled Tibet after the Chinese invasion.

Dharamsala is broken into two distinct parts. In Lower Dharamsala, you find the Kotwali Bazaar, schools, businesses, government offices, and a feel that's distinctly Indian and Hindu in character. Upper Dharamsala at Mcleod Ganj (10 km away), on the far side of an Indian army base and just beyond St. John's Church in the Wilderness, is decidedly Tibetan and Buddhist. Throughout tiny Mcleod, you see European and American students of Buddhism, many with heads shaven, wandering about, discussing their texts.

Visit the Namgyal Monastery, where hundreds of purple-robed monks (men and women) gather inside their new temple and pray, sometimes for hours, reading from scrolls and sitting beneath an enormous golden image of the Buddha that towers over them from the front of the shrine. Non-Buddhists can enter the interior of the shrine from a side entrance, where they can see more large statues. Remove your shoes! Also inquire about Tibetan cultural performances at the Tibetan Institute of Performing Arts, perched on the top of a hill. You may be lucky and see great dancing, hear music, or witness a Tibetan opera. And every Sunday, you can wander through the Tibetan flea market, a short walk from Mcleod Ganj. Ask any person to point the way. This outdoor event is also heavily attended by inquisitive lemurs.

Finally, while in Upper Dharamsala, visit one special monument that survived the earthquake and remains a stalwart reminder of the days of British rule: St. John's Church in the Wilderness (set not in the wilderness, but in a cozy pine grove), built in 1860. The stained glass windows of this church are treasures; inside is a monument to Lord Elgin, a British viceroy originally from Scotland, who asked to be buried in this church, dedicated to the patron saint of Scotland.

Dalhousie

Dalhousie, the gateway to Chamba Valley (the vale of milk and honey), is set on five different hills rising from the main ridges of the Dhauladhar. Dalhousie is another former British hill station, although the small village and all the hotels have seen far better days. There's a seedy neglect to many of the old Victorian structures. The effect is dismal and depressing; not even the panorama of spectacular snow-capped peaks justifies much more than the briefest visit. Many of the hoteliers are also gougers, so watch out!

A bit of history. Dalhousie is named after a former viceroy, Lord Dalhousie, who, weary from one too many battle, sought peace and quiet here. After a number of years, the influx of British people who wanted to escape the scorching heat of the plains and the snobbish air of Shimla, turned Dalhousie into a hill station (which, at that time, was also lighter on the pocketbook).

After the invasion of Tibet, Dalhousie then became an official refugee camp and acquired an appealing new look. Buddhist artisans painted rocks, doors, and walls, creating a flourish of visual tribute to their god.

Unfortunately, the earlier residents weren't so impressed, and many of the best craftsmen left for Dharamsala. The paintings have pretty much disappeared except for those on the rocks along the walkway around the figure-eight ridge.

Chamba

After you reach the crest of the mountain, the road begins its slow descent to Chamba, winding continuously while hugging the edge of the mountain that slopes down to the near-dry Ravi River. The closer you get to the valley basin, the more terraced the land becomes. Still, the road seems untraveled; the chosen course appears to be dusty foot paths that race up and down the hills.

Just when you're lost in the peace and quiet, you round a bend, and there's Chamba, sprawling on the mountainside. Even the Ravi comes alive, with the water rushing now. This mountain village/city (with 5,000 people) is the center of the valley and rich in ancient stone temples.

Walk into the center of town and see the Lakshminarain temple complex, with three shrines dedicated to Vishnu and three dedicated to Shiva (the earliest of the six stone temples built in the tenth century and the last constructed in 1828). The temples follow two distinct architectural trends. The Vishnu temples are of the Shikara type, with two overhead "parasol" roofs that are intended to drain off snow; the others are indigenous hill style. Also visit the Bhuri Sing Museum, with its excellent collection of miniature paintings from the Kangra and Basoli schools. As you walk down Museum Street, note the shoe stalls. Chamba is a big sandal town and here is where you buy them.

Take a lazy walk on the Chaugan, grassy public promenade (maidan), above the river and near the center of town. This park often turns into an impromptu trading center for villagers who come in from the surrounding hills. The Chaugan is also the site of the colorful week-long Minjar Fair held annually in August or September at the time of the corn harvest to invoke the rain gods.

Chamba is no great beauty of a city, nor does it require much time to discover. It's very much the local business district. But go in any direction and you're surrounded by serenity and Himalayan magic. And this makes Chamba a good walking and trekking base. See Sahoo, a charming hill village where the Gujars (seminomadic Moslems) live six months a year. In the winter, they migrate with their families and buffalo to the plains of the Punjab. The people are tall and tend to dress in dark muted clothes; the men wrap thick turbans around their heads, and the women adorn themselves with heavy jewelry. While in Sahoo, also walk to the old Shiva temple with a lingam sitting on a copper base inside the inner sanctum. This walk means an idyllic stroll through green fields into the village proper—into pure village life Himachal Pradesh-style—even if some of the residents live here only half the year.

Bharmaur

From Chamba, one beautiful drive should not be missed. Go east from Chamba 65 km to Bharmaur. This is Shiva territory, and occasionally you'll pass three-pronged staffs called Trisuls (the three vertical prongs are the symbol of Shiva) stuck into the earth or small lingams set in tiny shrines—tributes to the favored god. This is Gaddi territory, although you'll still see many Gujars traveling through. Like the Gujars, the Gaddi shepherds are seminomads who move their flocks of goats and sheep down from Bharmaur in the cold months to warmer Dharamsala and the Kangra valley. Or they used to. Today, many Gaddi families stay put around Bharmaur, where they're developing cash crops: wheat, walnuts, almonds, maize, and apples. Gaddi men wear hand-woven beige coats that flair out and end at mid-thigh with rope belts coiled around the waist. The women wear patterned long skirts, heavily gathered at the waist.

For most of your journey, the road stays narrow but essentially level as it hugs the Ravi River flowing along the base of the valley. High rugged peaks crowd in from the other side of the road: thick jagged rock that remains about an arm's-length away. The water of the Ravi is cold and a vivid green. Mountain streams splash down the precipice and across the road. Gorges with small rivulets racing to meet the Ravi slice open the rocky border revealing a quick glimpse of the sky. Footpaths crisscross the difficult slopes and lead to isolated simple houses of wood or stone. Suspension bridges carry animals and villagers back and forth across the river.

You take a sharp turn and leave the Ravi, following the narrower Buddhal. Up ahead are snow-covered mountains, dominated by the not-too-distant Kailash Peak, that extends across the panorama. Minutes later, you arrive in Bharmaur, an ancient quiet haven with 84 temples (many of them small structures with simple lingams), nestled in a beautiful courtyard called Churasi (84 in Hindi).

Look at the wooden Laxshna Devi, erected in the seventh century; the stone Narsingh Temple constructed in the tenth or eleventh century, one of the few dedicated to Vishnu with a lionesque idol in the inner sanctum; and the stone Manimahesh, built in the seventh century. Sit in the peaceful courtyard and watch the people—so many of them Gaddis. Take in the views that unfold all around. This is nature and life at its best.

Pangi Valley

From Chamba, you can head north for the rugged Pangi Valley, a dry cold region about 8,000 feet above sea level. In the midst of wild hills, the Chenab River (Chandra Bhaga) flows in a deep narrow gorge where it lashes against rugged cliffs. This area is a trekker's paradise; the valley stays dry during the monsoon, and numerous peaks that tower to a level of 22,000 feet are still the challenge of mountaineers. Every village and hamlet has its own temple (the most important are Mindhal Vasni about 15 km from Killar and the Purthi about 30 km from Killar).

Killar, 137 km northeast of Chamba (a trekking route), lies in a valley set in a deep narrow gorge of the Chenab River in the high Himalayas. Grand, majestic! From Killar, you can trek northwest to Kistwar in Jammu and Kashmir, turn east halfway to Kistwar, and cross the Umasi La Pass into the Zanskar Valley. You can trek southeast to Keylong and Mandi, or trek from Killar to Lahaul, which will land you in Purthi and a convenient rest house on the bank of the Chandra Bhaga.

As is so often true in Himachal Pradesh, the Pangi Valley shows off northern India at its best: unspoiled, less traveled, and with nature clearly in charge. Days spent here are indelible, touching the soul. Time stops. Greater forces have more power.

PRACTICAL INFORMATION FOR

HIMACHAL PRADESH

WHEN TO GO. Most of Himachal Pradesh, except for Lahaul and remote areas, is open the entire year. Keep in mind that the nights can be cold most of the year—even in summer in Lahaul. Bring warm woolens. Hotels do their best to supply heat, but you may find that their best is not sufficient. For Chamba and the surrounding hill districts, the best seasons are April–mid-July and mid-September–December. The monsoon (July–September) brings rain and mist, but not continuous torrents.

Kangra Valley (Dharamsala area): the best season is March–June, September–November. If the monsoon, with its periodic rain doesn't bother you, the summer months are fine.

Kullu Valley and Manali: April–mid-November—the lush months—show off Kullu at its colorful best. Winter, however, means skiing and snowtime fun near Manali.

Lahaul: To get to Lahaul, you're at the mercy of the weather. The road is generally clear of snow mid-June–November. The days can be warm, but the nights are cold.

Mandi: Approachable all year round, but the best time is April–November.

Shimla, Chail, and nearby points: Year-round resort. An escape from the heat of India in the summer. July–August is the monsoon, but not constant rain. In spring and fall, the colorful flora are delightful, the nights are crisp and cool, and days are warm. Winter turns Shimla into a white getaway, with minimal winter sports but white Himalayan views.

HOW TO GET THERE. For **Himachal** in general: **By Air.** Daily *Indian Airlines* flights into Chandigarh (117 km from Shimla). From there, regular bus service into Shimla and fixed-rate private taxis (about Rs. 350). *Vayudoot* offers daily flights from Delhi to the new Shimla Airport at Jubbarhati (23 km from Shimla). Vayudoot also has scheduled flights into Bhuntar Airport (10 km from Kullu, 60 km from Mandi) from Chandigarh and Delhi.

By Bus. Numerous deluxe buses, unfortunately frequently video, make daily runs from Delhi, Pathankot, Dehra Dun, and Chandigarh to Shimla and other major Himachal Pradesh cities. Most inclusive is *Himachal Pradesh Road Transport Corporation* (HPRTC). Call the following numbers for schedules and fares: Delhi, 2516725; Pathankot, 20088; Chandigarh, 20946.

By Train. Frequent train service is available from Delhi and Chandigarh to Kalka. From there to Shimla, it's a slow-going but scenic trip by narrow gauge train. There is also frequent train service from Bombay, Delhi, and Calcutta to Pathankot. From Kalka, you can take a fixed-rate taxi to Shimla (about Rs. 250) or a bus. From Pathankot, you can take a bus to numerous northern cities.

By Car. From Delhi (370 km), plan for a seven-hour trip via national highway in Haryana (with its numerous motorist-restaurant-pitstops). The trip turns scenic and more slow going once you reach the Himachal Pradesh border.

CHAMBA

By Air. The nearest airport is at Jammu in Kashmir (245 km).

By Bus. Chamba is connected by HPRTC bus from Dalhousie (56 km), Pathankot (120 km), Shimla (422 km), and Delhi (640 km). HPRTC telephone in Chamba, 10.

By Train. Chamba is 118 km from Pathankot station, with daily trains from Delhi, Bombay, and Calcutta.

By Car. The same distances apply. The roads are good, but mountainous, so plan accordingly.

DALHOUSIE

By Bus. HPRTC runs buses from Pathankot, Chamba, and Dharamsala. Call nearby Banikhet, 80.
By Train. Pathankot is 80 km away, with trains from Delhi, Bombay, and Calcutta.
By Car. Again, good roads, but plan to take your time.

DHARAMSALA (KANGRA VALLEY)

By Air. The nearest airport is Bhunta airport (about 214 km) with Vayudoot flights from Delhi and Chandigarh. From there, take a bus or car to Dharamsala.
By Bus. HPRTC runs buses from Chandigarh (239 km), Delhi (514 km), Manali (253 km), Chamba (192 km), and Shimla (322 km). Call in Dharamsala, 2243.
By Train. Dharamsala is 90 km from Pathankot, with daily trains from Delhi, Bombay, and Calcutta.
By Car. Roads are winding and well maintained, with gorgeous scenery but slow going.

KULLU VALLEY (MANALI)

By Air. Kullu is connected by Vayudoot flights from Chandigarh and Delhi to Bhuntar Airport (10 km from Kullu).
By Bus. HPRTC buses from Mdnai, Chandigarh, Delhi, Dharamsala, Jogindernagar, Pathankot, Manali, and Shimla. Tel. in Kullu, 9; in Manali, 23.
By Train. Trains run to Shimla from Delhi and Chandigarh and to Pathankot from Calcutta, Bombay, and Delhi, with bus service into the Kullu Valley.
By Car. Kullu is 240 km via a scenic road (narrow, but good) from Shimla, 156 km from Mandi, 40 km from Manali, 798 km from Delhi, and 366 km from Pathankot.

LAHAUL VALLEY (KEYLONG)

By Air. Vayudoot flights from Delhi and Chandigarh via Bhuntar Airport, 50 km from Manali.
By Bus. In the summer, direct buses go from Manali to Udaipur and Keylong in Lahaul. Tel. in Manali, 23.
By Train. See Manali above.
By Car. Roads closed by snow usually from November to June.

MANDI

By Air. The nearest airport is Bhuntar (60 km from Mandi), with flights from Delhi and Chandigarh via Vayudoot.
By Bus. Regular HPRTC buses run from Shimla, Chandigarh, Pathankot, and Kullu; tel. in Mandi, 2403.
By Train. Via Shimla, with trains from Chandigarh and Delhi; then a bus or car to Mandi (160 km). Or via Pathankot, with trains from Delhi, Calcutta, or Bombay; then a bus to Mandi (213 km).
By Car. Mandi is connected by good but winding roads to Shimla, Pathankot, Kullu (70 km), and Dharamsala (147 km).

SHIMLA

By Air. Daily Indian Airlines flights from Delhi, Jammu, and Srinigar to Chandigarh; then a bus or fixed-price (Rs. 350) taxi to Shimla (120 km). Vayudoot also offers daily flights to the new Shimla Airport at Jubbarhati (23 km).
By Bus. Numerous deluxe buses from Delhi to Shimla. The best is HPRTC, which leaves from Kashmiri Gate (Inter-State Bus Terminus) in Delhi (tel. 2516725); HPRTC tel. in Shimla, 3566 or 2887. The cost is about Rs. 100; the trip takes about nine hours.

By Train. Via Kalka. Direct train connections from Delhi and Calcutta. From Kalka to Shimla is 90 km on a narrow-gauge line that takes about six hours.

By Car. From Delhi (370 km), about a seven-hour trip on the excellent Haryana highway; in Himachal Pradesh, the road turns winding and scenic, and the pace slows. Shimla is 495 km from Jammu, 380 km from Pathankot, 240 km from Kullu, and 280 km from Dharamsala—all well-maintained roads but slow going. Private cars for hire (at about Rs. 2.50 per km) can take you throughout the state. Contact *Kalka Taxi Union,* Shimla (tel. 3985), or *Vishal Taxi Union,* Shimla (tel. 5123).

 **ACCOMMODATIONS.** Himachal Pradesh has some Western-style hotels in the more established tourist areas and some charming old-fashioned guest houses, many of them former private homes. Throughout the state, you'll find dependable adequate facilities—much of them run by the state government—with clean rooms, decent bathroom facilities, and simple restaurants. The government-run stopovers are moderate to inexpensive, so don't expect more than the minimal extras. But given the mood of Himachal Pradesh —an adventure-oriented, undervisited state for travelers who want to get off the beaten path and be close to the best of nature—the accommodations are appropriate. What follows is a list of hotels, guest houses, and some government bungalows in major scenic areas. This list is supplemented with a second list of rest houses that are suitable for trekkers or travelers going the remote route. Rates are based on double occupancy, and in most cases don't include food; however, some places only offer the American plan: *Expensive,* Rs. 500 plus; *Moderate,* Rs. 200–Rs. 500; *Inexpensive,* under Rs. 200. Most-Western-style hotels accept traveler's checks and credit cards.

Bharmaur

Inexpensive

Government Rest House. Reservations: Executive Engineer, Chamba. Three rooms, minimal but clean; a fireplace, and some Western amenities. Perfectly nestled in an old village with great views. Cook on hand to prepare simple food.

CHAIL

Moderate to Expensive

Palace Hotel. Chail (45 km from Shimla); tel. 37; Cable, Himtour Chail. 19 large rooms with tubs; 10 rustic and private cottages with one to four bedrooms. Former palace of the maharajah of Patiala, now a hotel run by HPTDC. Though rooms and hotel are not lavishly furnished, the old-world charm sneaks in. The Honeymoon Den (cottage) comes with a copy of the *Kama Sutra.*

Rajgarh Cottage, former maharajah's guest house is a four-bedroom Victorian house caught in a time warp. Has a restaurant, billiard room, badminton, bar, sitting room with grand piano and unfortunate TV, outdoor cafe, spacious lawns, lovely private walks through the 62-acre property, giftshop, library, and room service.

CHAMBA

Inexpensive

Hotel Iravati. Chamba; tel. 94. Overhead fans in 12 clean, spacious rooms, some with balconies. Hot and cold water. Restaurant and room service (takes a long time).

Dalhousie

As of this printing, it's difficult to recommend any hotel in this hill station. If you must spend a night, stay in any of the three we list. While the rooms are essentially clean, the hotels are neglected and the decor is depressing. Your best bet is to stay in Khajjiar (see below).

Moderate

Aroma 'n Clair's. Court Rd., The Mall, Dalhousie; tel. 99. 20 rooms. This hotel is decidedly 1930s kitsch (that's the best part). Individual rooms, though large, have minimal comfort. Service is erratic; some amenities. TVs, restaurant, library, bank, shops. Nice views, good location. Off-season rates October 15–April.

Grand View Hotel. Near bus stop, Dalhousie; tel. 23. 20 rooms. Dalhousie Victorian-seedy, cavernous rooms, clean linen. Attached front porch. Garden with the "grand" view. Restaurant (bad food, disinclined service). But less objectionable decor than the Hotel Mount View.

Hotel Mount View. Near the bus stop, Dalhousie; tel. 27. 24 cavernous rooms and a restaurant. Redeemed by nice management and the views. Off-season rates October 15–April 1.

DHARAMSALA

Inexpensive

Hotel Bhagsu. Mcleod Ganj, Dharamsala; tel. 2190. 15 clean, attractive rooms. Hot and cold showers. Room service, restaurant, spacious lawns, nice views. Run by HPTCD.

Hotel Dhauladhar. In lower Dharamsala; tel. 363. A slightly fancier HPTDC hotel with 21 clean, attractive rooms with telephones. Room service; hot and cold showers. Has a restaurant, bar, outdoor terrace (where you can eat), gardens, TV lounge, and views.

Hotel Tibet. Mcleod Ganj, Dharamsala; tel. 2587. 21 simple, but clean rooms. In the center of the Tibetan area.

JOGINDERNAGAR

Inexpensive

Hotel Ross Common. Kasauli. Reservations: Manager, Hotel Ross Common, Kasauli; tel. 7. Seven rooms. A pleasant hotel with restaurant operated by HPTDC.

Tourist Bungalow. Jogindernagar; tel. 575. Reservations: Manager, Tourist Bungalow, Mandi, 175001. 16 pleasant, clean minimal rooms with overhead fans and hot and cold showers. Restaurant, nice gardens, views.

KATRAIN

Expensive

Span Resort. On Kullu Manali Hwy., 15 km from Manali, P.P. Katrain, Kullu; tel. 38. 25 rooms, three rooms to a cottage. Full-service secluded resort on the Beas River; American plan. New non-Indian style setup. Restaurant, dining room, bar, minigolf, badminton, fishing, croquet, video lounge, room service. Except for employees, you get little sense of India.

Moderate

Hotel Apple Blossom. Katrain. Reservations: Area Manager, Tourist Information Office, Kullu. Nine rooms and 4 cottages. Fishing spot overlooking the Beas River. Porches on backside of hotel are great places to relax and just gaze at the views. Rooms are simple, basic, and adequate. Cottages are more private, with the facilities in keeping with the locale. Restaurant.

KEYLONG

Inexpensive

Tourist Bungalow. Keylong, Lahaul Valley. Reservations: Tourist Information Office, Manali 175131; tel. 25. Seasonal, so inquire ahead. Three rooms. Simple Indian food prepared on request. Tents also available.

KHAJJIAR

Inexpensive

Hotel Deodar. Khajjiar. Reservations: Area Manager, HPTDC Tourist Information Office, Dalhousie; tel. 36. 11 clean, simple rooms with views. Idyllic surroundings 22 km from Dalhousie on the way to Chamba. Bungalow overlooks green fields and a pond bordered by a pine forest. Serene. Horseback riding available. Room service, hot and cold water, and heaters available. Restaurant has minimal menu.

KUFRI

Moderate to Expensive

Kufri Holiday Resort. 16 km from Shimla, Kufri, District: Shimla; tel. 8341, 8342, 8344. Eight cottages, 21 rooms; every room has view. Modern new facility with most Western amenities, including TVs, telephones, music, 24-hour room service, pickup service from Shimla, meditation grove, scenic walks, restaurant, barbecue, health club.

KULLU

Moderate

Ashok Travellers Lodge. Kullu 175101; tel. 79. Large spacious rooms, with sitting room and overhead fans. Heater Rs. 30 extra. Basic minimal decor. Restaurant, TV lounge. Off-season rates July 15–September 30 and December 15–March 31. Run by ITDC.

Inexpensive

Hotel Salvari. Reservations: Area Manager, Tourist Information Office, Kullu 175101; tel. 7. Eight simple, clean rooms with overhead fans. Restaurant, bar, TV lounge. Beautiful garden and views. Great value.

MANALI

Moderate to Expensive

Log Huts and Cottages. Reservations: The Manager, Tourist Information Office, Manali 17531; tel. 25. 12 huts with two bedrooms, living and dining room, two bathrooms, and a kitchen. Rustic, privacy, near the river. Nearby cafeteria and room service. 16 cottages with two units per cottage with same exterior setup.

Moderate

Ashok Travellers Lodge. Manali; tel. 31. 10 simple, clean rooms, each with a porch and a tub. Hot and cold water. Room service, TV, lounge. Restaurant. Quiet, away from town.
Hotel Highland. Manali 175131; tel. 99. 15 clean, simple rooms. *Bukara* (heater) put into room in winter. TV, minimal charm, room service, restaurant. Away from the center of town.
Hotel Holiday Home. Manali; tel. 101. 14 rooms. New construction, with fireplace in each room; clean, nice furnishings. Good bathrooms, good views, but not rustic. Restaurant. Quiet, away from the center of town.
John Banon's Guest House. Manali Orchards, P.O. Manali; tel. 35. 10 simple rooms with fireplaces and an interior stone wall. Minimal rustic. Room service, dining room. Very pleasant management. Quiet, away from the center of town.
Mayflower Guest House. Manali 175131; tel. 104. Each of the six cozy rooms has a fireplace. Charming and rustic, Manali's best old inn. Room service, dining room. Sweeping front porch overlooking orchards and views. Home-away-from-home atmosphere. Quiet, away from center of town. Open March–November 15.
New Hope Guest House. Manali; tel. 78. 14 rooms. Wood trim interiors; fireplace in each room; clean, simple decor. Phones in room. Minimal rustic feel. Restaurant. Quiet, away from the center of town.

Hotel Pinewood. Manali; tel. 118. Nine rooms; most are spacious and have fireplaces. Friendly service. Minimal rustic feel; restaurant. Open April 15–November. Quiet, away from the center of town.

Inexpensive

Aroma Hotel. Manali 175131; tel. 12. In town, near the Tibetan monastery. 12 rooms. Garish pink walls, but clean and newly refurbished, with attached bathrooms and hot and cold water. Off season rates November–March.

Hotel Manalsu. Reservations: The Manager, Tourist Information Office, Manali 175331; tel. 25. 27 neat, clean rooms. Room service, laundry, restaurant, nice view and garden. Quiet, away from town.

Hotel Mount View. Manali; tel. 44. In town but set back on a hill. 21 simple, clean rooms with hot and cold water and showers. Roof terrace and restaurant. Don't be put off by the dingy staircases.

Hotel Sagar. Model Town, Manali; (no phone). In town near the Tibetan monastery. 10 clean, and simple rooms. Hot water 7 A.M.–12 noon, brought by bucket at night.

Sunshine Guest House. Manali 175131; tel. 20. 10 rooms. Old folksy charm; rustic, comfortable living room. Nice family-style dining room, with fireplace. Rooms have rustic charm with basic furnishings. Another home-away-from-home atmosphere at a great price. Sweeping porch across the front. Quiet, away from the center of town.

MANDI

Inexpensive

Tourist Bungalow. Reservations: The Manager, Tourist Bungalow, Mandi, 175001; tel. 575. Seven clean rooms with simple furnishings; some rooms have balconies. Restaurant and bar. Nice old building, good staff. Peaceful. Run by HPTDC.

MANIKARAN

Inexpensive

Hotel Parvati Manikaran. Reservations: Tourism Development Officer, Hotel Parvati, Manikarin, Kullu; tel. 35. 12 modern, simple clean rooms with decor. Hot-and-cold water showers; room service; great views; terraces; restaurant. 14 hot spring sulphur baths, open 24 hours, have individual clean cubicles.

NAGGAR

Inexpensive

Castle Hotel. Reservations: Tourist Information Office, Kullu 175101; tel. 7. Seven rooms, some with a fireplace. 400-year-old castle. However, rooms are spartan and *very* basic; hot and cold water. Veranda with excellent views; restaurant with limited menu.

Poonam Fruit Garden Hotel. Six–eight room hotel scheduled to open 1988. Direct inquiries to hotel c/o Tej Ram Sharma, V & P.O., Naggar, Kullu.

NALDEHRA

Inexpensive

Hotel Golf Glade. Reservations: Tourist Information Office, The Mall, Shimla 171001; tel. 3311. Five rooms in a tourist bungalow, five log huts, and one golf hut with a kitchen. Rustic, simple, yet clean; well run; restaurant (HPTDC).

NARKANDA

Inexpensive

Hotel Himview. Reservations: same as Hotel Golf Glade. Four marginal, basic rooms, but in a great location. A quiet retreat for those who want to rough it. Run by HPTDC.

PALAMPUR

Inexpensive

Palace Motel. Taragarh, Kangra Valley, near Palampur; tel. Baijnath 34. 12 rooms. Restaurant, room service, TV in lounge. Lovely ex-palace with antique furnishings and a nice ambience.

Hotel T-Bud. Reservations: Manager, Hotel T-Bud, Palampur 176061; tel. 81. 12 quiet, clean rooms with hot and cold water; front and back terraces. Nice garden and lawn. Restaurant. Room service.

PARWANOO

Moderate to Expensive

Timber Trail Resort and Timber Trail Heights. Parwanoo, just across border from Haryana; tel. 497. 25 rooms; 10 tents. Interesting resort setup on the way to Shimla. The resort below has views, a restaurant, cafe, bar, and attractive rooms. The resort on top of the mountain via a rope-way that runs from sunrise to sunset. Spectacular views, a miniamusement park. Nice gardens in both areas.

RAISON

Inexpensive

Raison Tourist Huts. Raison (16 km north of Kullu). Reservations: Area Manager, Tourist Information Office, Kullu 175101; tel. 7. 14 huts. Simple clean shelter. Double bed with linen, Western toilet. Hot water by bucket. On a spacious lawn near the Beas River. Peaceful; great for campers, trekkers, and the hearty.

SARAHAN

Inexpensive

Tourist Lodge. Sarahan. Reservations: Manager of the tourist lodge or Manager of the Hotel Wildflower Hall, Chharabra; tel. 8–212. Four simple rooms; a pleasant getaway operated by HPTDC.

SHIMLA

Expensive

Chapslee Guest House. Lakkar, Bazar, Shimla; tel. 3242. Seven rooms. Rates include meals. Stepping back into the time of the raj. Elegant home with Victorian and art decor. You are the guest of a gracious raja who is rightfully selective about his clientele; put your best manners forward. Every room is filled with family memories. Great views and great meals also in the offering. Forget the Western amenities; this is Indian class. You must have reservations. You must respect the intended ambience. Closed January 1–March 15.

Oberoi Clarkes. The Mall, Shimla 171001; tel. 609195. 31 rooms. Rates include three meals and two teas. TV. Simple tasteful decor, good views, room service, restaurant, bar, good management.

Woodville Palace Hotel. Himachal Bhawañ Rd., The Mall, Shimla 170002; tel. 2722. 11 rooms. American plan. Another stately villa owned by a raja and converted into a hotel. Step back into the time of elegance and grand living, beautifully appointed with original Victorian and art deco decor. Excellent food. Billiard room, tennis court, gardens, views.

Moderate

Asia the Dawn. Shimla; tel. 5858. Four km from the Mall, but excellent bus service. 37 rooms in new hotel with excellent facilities. Courteous aim-to-please management. Restaurant, bar, terrace restaurant with barbecue on request, health club, and many other Western amenities. A peaceful location with great views.

Hotel Holiday Home. Below High Court, Shimla; tel. 6031, 6036. 65 clean, spacious rooms; decent decor. Room service, restaurant and bar. Run by HPTDC.

Hotel Surya. Circular Rd., Shimla; tel. 4762. 42 rooms in new hotel with simple yet modern accommodations. Restaurant, room service, and terrace.

Hotel Wildflower Hall. 13 km from Shimla center; tel. 8212. 32 rooms and 11 cottages. Former residence of Lord Kitchener, who also landscaped the gardens. Rustic hotel interior. Cottages have kitchen facilities and sitting rooms. Excellent tranquil views with woods and walks. Restaurant and outdoor cafe. Run by HPTDC.

Inexpensive

Hotel Harsha. Chaura Maidan, The Mall, 1½ km from downtown, Shimla; tel. 3016. 20 clean, simple rooms. Restaurant, some Western amenities. Off-season rates.

Marina Hotel. The Mall, Shimla; tel. 3557. Simple older hotel, with 35 modest rooms, dining hall, billiards, terrace, and room service.

Hotel Mayur. The Ridge, Shimla 171001; tel. 6047. 25 clean, modern rooms; TV.

Hotel Shingar. The Mall, Shimla 171001; tel. 2881. 32 rooms with clean, simple decor. Room service, music, TV.

 REST HOUSES AND CIRCUIT HOUSES. Throughout Himachal Pradesh, there are basic yet adequate forest rest houses (sometimes called tourist huts), which are often located in sublime rustic settings, and circuit houses, which are often lovely holdovers from the grand Victorian era. Fees for rest houses—very spartan but clean linen, private rooms and bathroom—(about Rs. 40 per double) and for circuit houses—quality varies but can be the best in town—(Rs. 75 per double). Unfortunately, government officials get first preference at the circuit house. Inquiries should be made via the H.P. Tourist Office (see *Tourist Information*). The rest houses are usually managed by the Public Works Department and the circuit houses by the General Administration Department. Take your chances and book well in advance, or have an alternative booking and check the circuit house on your arrival. Circuit houses are in Chamba, Mandi, Solan, Kasauli, Bilaspur, Dharamsala, Narkanda (near Shimla), Kullu, Manali, and Keylong. Rest houses are numerous, tucked here and there; just write and inquire.

 DINING OUT. Himachal Pradesh isn't the state to visit for great culinary experiences. This doesn't mean forced starvation or bad food, but, except for Shimla and a few select resort places, menus are limited. Expect to see some Continental items, some Chinese (Tibetan food exists in Dharamsala and Manali); and primarily Indian (vegetarian and nonvegetarian). By the same token, food is generally moderately priced or downright cheap, with the tourist areas the exception. The following price categories (*Expensive,* Rs. 50 or more; *Moderate,* Rs. 30–Rs. 50; and *Inexpensive,* Rs. 30 and under) are based on a three-course meal for one person and do not include beverage, taxes, or tips. Only fancy-style Western hotels accept credit cards or traveler's checks. Most restaurants are informal. We've included a few of the hotel dining rooms that may be of interest for their cuisine or ambience. Unless specified, restaurants are open for all three meals.

BILASPUR

Inexpensive

Cafe Lake View. Bilaspur; no phone. Basic simple Indian food—good, but not great. However, excellent midway stopping point between Shimla and Mandi. Cafe overlooks the lake with temples sticking up in the water.

CHAIL

Moderate

Chail Palace Hotel. Chail; tel. 37. Indoor restaurant. Large unpalatial-like room, but decent food. Indian, Chinese, and Continental.

CHAMBA

Inexpensive

Cafe Ravi View. On Chaugan Maidan near the Ravi River, Chamba. Limited menu, basically Indian, but nice ambience and view.

DHARAMSALA

Inexpensive

Hotel Dhauladhar. Lower Dharamsala; tel. 363. Chinese, Indian, and Continental cuisines. Nice ambience. You can also eat on the terrace—good views.
Toepa Restaurant. Center of Mcleod Gunj. Good ambience, very informal. Tibetan food. Try fried *momo,* the soups, fried *shabakleb,* noodle dishes, good Western cake.

KATRAIN

Expensive

Span Resort Dining Room and Riverside Restaurant. 15 km from Manali on Kullu-Manali Highway; tel. 38. Fixed-price Indian and Continental meals. Attractive setup, good views.

KHAJJIAR

Inexpensive

Hotel Deodar Restaurant. Khajjiar, 22 km from Dalhousie on the way to Chamba; tel. 36. Extremely limited offerings, but great view amidst tranquility.

KUFRI

Moderate

Kufri Holiday Resort. Kufri; tel. 8341. 24-hour coffee shop. Pleasant indoor cafeteria and restaurant with views. Also outdoor barbecue where they'll cook or, on Saturdays and Sundays, you can cook—they'll provide the food, Indian and Continental.

MANALI

With most of the restaurants connected to hotel guest houses, call (see hotel listings above) early in the day to see if they can accommodate you for lunch or dinner if you are not a guest. The hotel and guest houses generally serve Indian, Continental, and Chinese foods.

Moderate

Highland Restaurant. Manali; tel. 99. Choice of Continental, Chinese, Indian, Italian, or Gujarat foods.

Inexpensive

Adarsh Restaurant. Center of town. Chinese and Indian foods in an informal and folksy atmosphere.
Chandratal Restaurant. Center of town. Indian, Chinese, and Continental foods. Informal; run by HPTDC.
Mount View Restaurant. Center of town. Indian, Chinese, Japanese, and Tibetan fare. Owned by the Dalai Lama. Great local ambience.

MANDI

Inexpensive

Cafe Shiraz. In the heart of old Mandi. Simple, basic Indian food; run by HPTDC.

PARWANOO

Moderate

Timber Trail Resort & Timber Trail Heights. Parwanoo, on road to Shimla; tel. 497. Great lunch or dinner stop. Open 24 hours. Eat down by the road in nice gardens with views, or take time to go via ropeway to the upper restaurant. Great panoramas; a pleasant break from a long drive.

NARKANDA

Inexpensive

Cafe Vasant Bar and Restaurant. Narkanda. Limited selection of Indian, Continental, and Chinese foods. Informal; views of the Himalayas.

PALAMBUR

Moderate

Palace Motel. Taragarh, Kangra Valley, near Palampur; tel. Baijnath 34. Lovely restaurant, serving Indian and Continental foods. Call in advance.

SHIMLA

Moderate to *Expensive*

Honey Dew. Asia the Dawn, Mahavir Ghati, Shimla; tel. 5858. Terrace and outdoor barbecue restaurant also open during the warmer months, with good views of Shimla. Great ambience.

The following two guest houses with lovely intimate dining rooms might serve lunch or dinner to nonguests, but you must call early in the day. The food is great, the ambience is always refined, but dress can be "tastefully" informal: **Chapslee,** Kakkar Bazar Shimla (tel. 3242); and **Woodville Palace,** Himachal Bhawan Road (tel. 2722).

Moderate

Asiana. The Mall. Circular restaurant on the mall with panoramic views, serving Indian and Chinese foods as well as snacks.

Balgee's Restaurant. The Mall; tel. 2202. Indian, Chinese, and Continental foods.

Fascination Restaurant. The Mall; tel. 2202. Indian, Chinese, and Continental foods served; local color.

HOW TO GET AROUND. Chamba. Taxis and Himachal Pradesh Road Transport Corporation (HPRTC) buses are available. Contact Tourist Information at the Hotel Iravati (tel. 36), or the HPRTC bus stand (tel. 10).

Dharamsala. Buses and taxis are available at the bus stand (tel. 2243); or the local tourist office (tel. 2007).

Kullu Valley (Manali). Buses and private taxis are available for hire. Manali HPRTC bus stand, tel. 23; or Manali tourist office, tel: 25.

Mandi. Buses and taxis are available in Mandi at the HPRTC bus stand (tel. 2403), or the local tourist office (tel. 2575).

Shimla. HPRTC provides local bus service in and around Shimla (tel. 3566). Private taxis are available through the *Kalaka Taxi Union* (tel. 3985), or through the *Vishal Taxi Union* (tel. 5123). Approximate rate, Rs. 2.50 per km. The Mall and the Ridge are strictly prohibited to vehicles. Pony rides are available (fees negotiable).

Private Tour Operators. Himachal Pradesh is an adventure state with lots of fun-oriented opportunities. There are four excellent private tour operators who offer dependable services and superior trekking, water rafting, skiing, even jeep "safaris": *Arohi Travels,* The Mall, Manali 175131, Kullu; tel. 139; *Himalayan Adventuress, Pvt., Ltd.,* Mayflower Guest House, Manali 175131; tel. 104; *Himalayan River Runners,* 188–A Jor Bagh, New Delhi 110003; tel. 615736; and *Shikhar Travels Private Ltd.,* 209 Competent House, F–14 Middle Circle, Connaught Place, New Delhi 110001; tel. 3312444.

TOURIST INFORMATION. The tourist information offices of Himachal Pradesh are extremely helpful. This is an outdoor state, and the tourist department is a good source of what to do, where, when, and how. The offices also have excellent general information on hotels, sightseeing, and travel. Outside Himachal Pradesh, write or visit the following offices (generally open 9 A.M.–5 P.M., Monday–Saturday).

Tourist Information Officer
Government of Himachal Pradesh
26 World Trade Center
  Cuffe Parade
Bombay 400005, tel. 211123

Tourist Information Officer
Himachal Tourism
28 C-in-C Rd.
Madras 600105; tel. 472966

Tourist Information Officer
Himachal Tourism
25 Cama St.
Flat IC/3 Cama Court
Calcutta 16; tel. 472966

Area Manager
Himachal Pradesh Tourism
  Development Corporation
Tourist Office, Chanderlok Building
New Delhi; tel. 34520, 344764

Area Manager
Himachal Pradesh Tourism Development
  Corporation
Tourist Office, S.C., 1048–49
Sector–22–B, Chandigarh; tel. 26494

Once you're within the borders of Himachal Pradesh, contact the following local tourist offices, generally open six days a week, 10 A.M.–5 P.M.:

Chamba. Himachal Tourism, Hotel Iravati, Chamba; tel. 36.

Dalhousie. Himachal Tourism, Tourist Information Office, Dalhousie; tel. 36.

Dharamsala. Himachal Pradesh Tourism Development Corporation, Tourist Information Office, Kotwali Bazar, Dharamsala; tel. 2363; or Tourist Information Assistant, Himachal Pradesh Government Tourism, Dharamsala; tel. 2007

Kullu. Himachal Pradesh Tourism, Kullu; tel. 7.

Manali. Tourist Information Assistant, Himachal Pradesh Tourism Department, Manali; tel. 25.

Mandi. Himachal Pradesh Tourism, HPTDC Tourist Bungalow, Mandi; tel. 2575

Shimla. Tourist Information Assistant, Himachal Pradesh Government Tourist Office, Panchayat Bhawan, Shimla; tel. 4589 or Railway Station, Shimla; tel. 4559 or The Mall, Shimla; tel. 3311.

FOREIGN CURRENCY EXCHANGE. Throughout Himachal Pradesh, you can exchange major traveler's checks at banks and Western-style hotels. Bank hours are generally Monday–Friday, 10 A.M.–2:30 P.M., and sometimes Saturday mornings. Call for exact times. State Bank of India, Chamba, tel. 62; State Bank of India, Dalhousie, tel. 24; Dharamsala, Bank of India, tel. 2577; State Bank of India, Manali, tel. 36; State Bank of India, Mandi, tel. 2681; and Bank of India, Shimla, tel. 3600; or State Bank of India, Shimla, tel. 2480.

TOURS. For touring Himachal Pradesh, the *Himachal Pradesh Tourism Development Corporation (HPTDC)* is highly recommended and reasonably priced. To make reservations, contact the following offices:

Chandigarh. Area Manager, HPTDC, Tourist Office, SCO–1048–1049, Sector 22–B, Chandigarh; tel. 26494.

Manali. Tourist Information Office, Manali; tel. 25.

New Delhi. Area Manager, HPTDC, Tourist Office, Chanderlok Building, 36, Janpath, New Delhi 110001; tel. 345320.

Shimla. Area Manager, HPTDC, Tourist Information Officer, The Mall, Shimla 171001; tel. 3311.

Following is a list of HPTDC Tours conducted out of Dahousie, Manali, and Shimla, all in cars or in luxury coaches, depending on the fares you sign up for.

DALHOUSIE

Dalhousie–Knajjiar (pastorale setting; meadow with a lovely lake)–Dalhousie. Daily, 9 A.M.–3 P.M.

MANALI

Tour No. 1. Manali—Nehru Kund (a spring named after Nehru)–Rahla Falls–Marhi (views of the valley and mountains)–Rohtang Pass (pass to Lahaul with great views of glaciers and mountains)–Manali. Daily during the season, 9 A.M.–4 P.M.

Tour No. 2. Manali–Jagatsukh (ancient capital of Kullu)–Naggar (beautiful ancient capital of the Raja with great views of the valley)–Manali. Daily during season, 9 A.M.–4 P.M.

Tour No. 3. Manali–Manikaran (beautiful old village, excellent hot springs)–Manali. Daily during season, 9 A.M.–6 P.M.

SHIMLA

Tour No. 1. Shimla–Wildflower Hall (former home of Lord Kitchener)–Kufri (great views)–Indira Holiday Home (cedar forest)–Fagu (another great view)–Mashobra (forest of oak and pine)–Craignano (picnic spot)–Fruit Research Station (North India's largest)–Naldehra (golf course and nearby temple in beautiful setting)–Shimla. Daily, 10 A.M.–5 P.M.

Tour No. 2. Shimla–Fagu–Theog (potato-marketing center)–Matiana (beautiful orchards)–Narkanda (great Himalayan views)–Shimla. Wednesdays, Fridays, and Sundays, 10 A.M.–5 P.M.

Tour No. 3. Shimla–Chail (former palace of the maharajah of Patiala atop a beautiful mountain)–Kufri–Indira Holiday Home–Kiari Bungalow (picnic spot)–Shimla. Mondays, Thursdays, and Saturdays, 10 A.M.–5 P.M.

FESTIVALS AND EVENTS. Numerous festivals and Buddhist events are conducted in Himachal Pradesh throughout the year. Because most of the events are scheduled by the lunar calendar, only the months are given here. Specific dates may be obtained by contacting the local tourist offices. Major events are listed here alphabetically by the name of the town or city.

Chamba. *Minjar (Harvest) Festival* is a week-long celebration held in July–August. The festival appeases the god of rain with cultural programs, attended by local hill people. The colorful festival, filled with ritual, culminates in a procession with the immersion of *Minjars* (corn tassels) in the holy Ravi River.

Kangra Valley. *Shakti Festival,* is held March–April at various temples in the valley. The events are religious but festive and well attended, with the largest held at Jwalamukhi Temple in Kangra.

Kullu. During the *Dussehra Festival,* in October, all Himachal Pradesh is wrapped up in a week-long celebration of the victory of good over evil. There are processions, dance, music, and costumes.

Manali. A week-long winter *sports carnival* is held in February. In May, the *Doongri Forest Fair* is held at the Hadimba Devi Temple and celebrated by hill women to honor the goddess Hadimba.

Mandi. *Shivratri Mela* is a week-long religious festival in February–March, beginning with a colorful procession of hundreds of deities on Shivratri Day, accompanied by local folk music.

Lake Manimahesh (35 km from Bharmour). During July–August, thousands of Hindus make a 35-km trek to the sacred lake to have a dip in the waters.

Naldehra. Villagers from all around arrive for the *Sipi Fair* in June to sell handicrafts amid festive and colorful surroundings.

Hampur. Along the banks of the Sutlej River in November, you can witness one of North India's largest trade fairs, called the *Lavi Mela.* The town comes alive with cultural events, sports, and the influx of many people.

Lake Renuka. *Renuka Fair,* in November, is a big religious event with deities carried for ritual dipping in the lake, accompanied by festive dances and folk songs.

Lake Rewalsar. The *Sisu Fair,* in March–April, is the most important Buddhist fair in Himachal Pradesh, celebrated and observed by thousands.

 SPORTS. Himachal Pradesh does its best to keep the sports enthusiast happy. The scenery is gorgeous. It's just a matter of time before the facilities and offerings match the vistas and environment.

Fishing. Mahaseer (a good white fish) are plentiful in the Ravi River and its tributaries, Chamba, and at the Pong Dam Reservoir and nearby rivers, Dharamsala.

Trout can be netted on Beas River and Parvati, plus numerous other tributaries and rivers in the Kullu Valley Mandi. Trout in the Uhal River, 75 km from Mandi, and the Kamand River, 17 km from Mandi; and on the Pabar River, Seema, and on Baapa River in the nearby Sangla Valley. For a license and details, contact the District Fisheries Officer for each area.

Golf. Khajjiar, 27 km from Dalhousie, has a nine-hole golf course, as does Naldehra, 23 km from Shimla. For details and reservations, contact the local tourist offices.

Hang Gliding is a new sport in development stage at Billing, about 50 km from Palampur. Contact the Tourist Information Office in Dharamsala for further details.

Mountaineering. The Mountaineering Institute and Allied Sports Complex, Manali, offers comprehensive courses in mountaineering. For details, contact the director, of the complex at Manali 175131; tel. 42.

Skiing is in the developmental stage but is inexpensive and lots of fun. Usually good-to-excellent equipment is available at bargain rental rates. And, of course, the views are stunning. In Narkanda, near Shimla, the season usually runs January–mid-March. Beginner slopes, plus ski school (including minimal boarding and lodging and equipment) organized by HPTDC. Contact HPTDC in Shimla for details. At Solang Valley, 13 km from Manali, the season usually runs mid-December–early March. Himachal Pradesh's most promising ski resort. Contact the Manali Tourist Office for details. The Mountaineering Institute and Allied Sports Complex also offers comprehensive skiing courses at this same ski area.

 TREKKING. From a few days to a few weeks, trekking is the best way to discover the beauty of Himachal Pradesh. No matter where you are in the state, you are close to some spectacular walk. The *Himachal Pradesh Tourist Department* can supply you with brochures that suggest trekking routes if you want to go it alone. You can rent equipment in Manali or bring your own. You can spend your night in a tent or a rest house or bungalow. The four major trekking areas, which have treks of all lengths and degrees of difficulty, are Kullu–Manali; Lahaul; Chamba–Kangra; and Shimla–Kinnaur. The best months for trekking are generally early April–mid-June and mid-September–mid-October. In much of the summer, you have to contend with the monsoon. If Lahaul with its lunar landscapes entices you, the season usually begins in June and lasts through September, once the pass is cleared of snow.

If you want to trek under the auspices of a private company which would provide porters, guide, food, nearly all the works, contact one of the following:

Arohi Travels (Trek and Tour Operators), The Mall, Manali 175131, Kullu; tel. 139; Cable: AROHI.

Himalayan Adventurers Pvt. Ltd., Mayflower Guest House, Manali 175131; tel. 104; Cable: ADVENTURERS.

Both these outfits also conduct "jeep safaris"—go partially by jeep, then trek—covering more terrain in less time.

 WHITE-WATER RAFTING AND CANOEING. The white water is here in abundance, but the possibilities are still limited. The following private companies are paving the way, with excellent equipment and limited runs:

Himalayan Adventurers Pvt. Ltd., Mayflower Guest House, Manali 175131; tel. 104; Cable: ADVENTURERS.

Himalayan River Runners, 188–A Jor Bagh, New Delhi 110003; tel. 615736.

For canoeing courses, contact Regional Water Sports Center, Pong Dam, P.O. Sansarpur Terrace, Tehsil Nurpur, District Kangra 176501. The center is a branch of the Mountaineering Institute.

HOT SPRINGS. Manikaran. Hotel Parvati, Himachal Pradesh Tourism Development Corporation. Telephone 35 for details and reservation. 14 hot spring baths set up in individual clean cubicles. Open 24 hours.

Tattapani (51 km from Shimla). Popular sulphur springs that emerge from the Sutlej River. Regular bus service from Shimla. Baths are under construction. Contact Area Manager, Tourist Information Office, tel. 3311 or 3956.

Vashisht. Himachal Tourism Vashisht Baths, just outside Manali. Eight sulphur baths. Adjoining cafe serves tea, beverages. Open 7 A.M.–10 P.M. daily.

HISTORIC SITES. As in most of India, the state of Himachal Pradesh has many historic sites, including centuries-old temples and monasteries and later structures. Most of the temples and monasteries are open to visitors during daylight hours. When visiting, however, you must observe the religious rules and traditional customs. (See Behavior section under *Facts at Your Fingertips*.) There is generally no charge for entry, but when donations are requested, a few rupees may help your enjoyment. The following is a list of the major ones in Himachal Pradesh communities.

BHARMAUR

There are 84 temples nestled in a courtyard named after *churasi* (yogis) who came there to meditate centuries ago. *Laxshna Devi* is a wooden temple dedicated to Shiva that was built in the seventh century. *Nargingh Temple* is dedicated to Vishnu from the tenth or eleventh century. *Manimahesh Temple* is dedicated to Shiva and was built in the seventh century.

CHAIL

Chail Palace, former summer capital of the maharaja of Patiala, was built after World War I. Now a state-run hotel, it has great grounds with good walks and pleasant views.

CHAMBA

Lakshminarain is a stone temple complex, with three shrines dedicated to Shiva and three to Vishnu. The earliest was built in the tenth century, the last was constructed in 1828. Vishnu temples are of the Shikara type, with two overhead roofs; the others are in indigenous hill style.

DHARAMSALA

St. John's Church in the Wilderness, built in 1860, contains beautiful stained glass windows and a monument to Lord Elgin, the British viceroy who was originally from Scotland and asked to be buried in this church dedicated to the patron saint of Scotland.

Namgyal Monastery, a new Buddhist monastery with a towering golden image of Buddha, is the current seat of the Dalai Lama, the spiritual leader of Tibet, who fled Tibet after the Chinese invasion.

JWALAMUKHI

Jwalamukhi Temple, dedicated to the "Flaming Goddess," is an important northern pilgrimage center, with its flame kept perpetually burning by priests. The golden dome over the temple was a gift of Mogul Emperor Akbar.

KANGRA

Baijnath Temple (A.D. 800), a Shikara-style stone temple with a low pyramid shaped roof, is possibly the oldest Shiva shrine in India, conceivably constructed by Pandavas. Handsome carvings adorn interior pillars, including an unusual composite image of Vishnu and Laxmi.

KEYLONG

Kharding Gompa is the largest monastery in Lahaul, with colorful frescoes and murals and an enormous prayer drum containing strips of paper with the sacred mantra written a million times. It formerly was the capital of Lahaul.

KULLU

Bijli Mahavev Temple has a 60-foot-high spire that supposedly attracts lightning—divine blessings—which then shatters the Shiva lingam contained inside the temple. The priests reassemble the sacred symbol and wait for the miracle to occur all over again.

Basheshwar Mahadev Temple (in Bajaura, 15 km from Kullu) is a ninth-century pyramidical granite temple dedicated to Shiva and covered with exquisite stone carvings and sculptural detail, some of which was destroyed in the late 1700s.

Raghunathji Temple, built in the seventeenth century, houses the presiding deity of Kullu Valley.

MANALI

Hadimba Devi Temple, 600 years old, is a wooden shrine with a four-tiered pagoda-shaped roof. The temple is dedicated to the goddess Hadimba.

Vashisht Rishi and *Lord Rama* temples (in Vashisht, three km from Manali) are pyramidical stone temples, with sacred sulphur springs and temple baths.

MANDI

Panchvaktra Temple is of the Shikara style, with an unusual five-faced Shiva sitting in the meditation pose.

Bhutnath Temple, also of Shikara style, with a small lingam in the inner sanctum, is situated by the river in the old city.

MANIMAHESH

Manimahesh Temple (a 34-km trek from Bharmaur), constructed in the Shikara style, is one of the oldest and most beautiful temples in Himachal Pradesh.

MANIKARAN

Sri Ramchandra Temple was built in the sixteenth century and dedicated to Vishnu. *Sri Raghunath Temple* is also dedicated to Vishnu. All Manikaran, with its bubbling sulphur springs and legends connecting it to Shiva and Parvati who supposedly meditated in Manikaran for 1,000 years, is imprinted with a sense of spiritual history.

MASROOR

Here you will find 15 monolithic rock-cut temples in richly carved Indo-Aryan style. Partially ruined, these temples, with their rich ornamentation, still show clear resemblance to the famous Kailash Temple at Ellora in Maharashtra.

SHIMLA

Institute of Advanced Studies, former Viceregal Lodge, was constructed in 1884–88 during the time of Lord Dufferin. Sitting atop Summer Hill, the structure was built of Himalayan gray stone in English Renaissance (Elizabethan) style. No entrance is allowed without prior permission, but enjoy the beautiful grounds and views of Shimla.

Wildflower Hall (13 km from Shimla), former residence of Lord Kitchener built in 1903, is now a state-run hotel. Kitchener landscaped the present gardens, with their lovely grounds and walks.

ART GALLERIES AND MUSEUMS. *Bhuri Singh Museum,* Chambra, has an excellent collection of miniature paintings from the Kangra and Basoli schools, and the rescued murals from nearby Rang Mahal Palace, which suffered a fire years ago. Open 10 A.M.–5 P.M.; closed Mondays and official holidays.

Rierich Art Gallery, Naggar, houses a collection of paintings of the Russian artist Nicholas Roerich. Check with the tourist information office in Kullu (tel. 7) for the hours.

Himachal State Museum, near Chaura Maidan, Shimla, contains "hill" art and cultural art of Himachal Pradesh, including Pahari (mountain) and other miniature schools, of painting, sculpture, bronzes, costumes, textiles, and jewelry. Open 10 A.M.–1:30 P.M.; 2–5 P.M. Closed Mondays and official holidays.

THEATER AND DANCE. The *Tibetan Institute of Performing Arts,* located one km up the hill from Mcleod Ganj, in Dharamsala, occasionally offers Tibetan cultural performances. Contact the local tourist office for details.

SHOPPING. The *Tibetan Flea Market,* near Mcleod Ganj in Dharamsala, offers handwoven clothing and handicrafts every Sunday. In the Kullu Valley, famous for its shawls and woolen goods, the *Bhutti Weavers Colony* (six km from Kullu) is a cooperative venture of manufacturers of handicrafts. The *Akhara Baza,* a marketplace in the center of Kullu, is also good for regional goods.

COFFEEHOUSES AND SNACKS. In Shimla, the *Indian Coffee* House on The Mall, near Evening College, is a good place to meet and talk over coffee and snacks. Its run-down looks can be deceptive—just relax and let the charm seep through. Also try the *North Indian Coffee,* a few doors away, with the same ambience and same decor—or lack of it. Both are open 8:30 A.M.–9 P.M. A must stop eight km south of Mandi, heading toward Sundarnagar, is the *Roadside Indian Milk Bar,* a small building that you can identify by its brightly painted stones outside resembling enormous jelly beans. The place serves delicious chocolate milk shakes at about Rs. 3. All signs outside are in Hindi, which keeps this popular refreshment stand an Indian secret.

KASHMIR, JAMMU,
AND LADAKH

A Glimpse of Heaven

by
KATHLEEN COX

"Kashmir—only Kashmir!" These were the Emperor Jahangir's final words. To see his summer playground one last time; to die here, surrounded by the mighty Himalayas; to see again the stately Chenars that edged the emerald green lakes; to sit within his treasured gardens, lightheaded with the fragrance of spectacular flowers and mesmerized by the play of his exquisite marble fountains.

But the Mogul's final wish wasn't granted. On his last annual pilgrimage that took him from the heat and dust of the plains to his enchanted vale, Jahangir died. Satraps, nobles, and his imperial court hovered over him on his death bed and begged to know his last request. All he whispered was "Kashmir."

This Oriental super-Switzerland has lost little of the original charm that first attracted the Moguls. Just a breath of the invigorating air and you succumb to the spell of this conspiracy between mountain and nature—India's jewel of the East.

In the third century B.C., Kashmir formed part of Ashoka's far-flung Mauryan Empire. After Akbar grabbed it in 1587, the Mogul emperors never stopped paying lengthy visits, escaping from the unpleasant summer on the plains and taking refuge in this idyllic vale where they laid out, at lavish expense and with impressive technical ingenuity, their elegant "pleasure gardens." It's no surprise that the appeal of this valley survived the fall of the Moguls, also entrapping the British who flocked to Kashmir during the last decades of their rule in India.

In those days, since only the upper echelons could afford the time and expense involved in making the difficult journey, Kashmir never became an official "hill station." A semiautonomous state ruled by the maharajah of Kashmir and Jammu, it also remained a specifically restricted "Kashmiri" homeland, with the maharajah shrewdly passing an edict that prevented foreigners from owning land in his state. This edict gave rise to the houseboat—a Britisher's novel solution to the unfortunate restriction. This boat, aptly called "Victory," offered such an attractive alternative that, in no time, a flotilla of posh floating homes—each one outfitted in Victorian splendor—sat moored in Dal Lake.

Kashmir—slightly smaller than Great Britain, with under six million inhabitants—is in the heart of Asia. Few realize that it's farther north than Tibet. For thousands of years, caravans carrying precious merchandise passed from China and elsewhere through Kashmir on their way to the plains of India. This international flavor continues today. Here, you find a variety of races, national costumes, and traditions. The Kashmiri *pandit* (man of letters) forms the Hindu leading minority (Nehru was a Kashmiri pandit, as was his daughter, Indira Gandhi). The Kashmiri Moslems, representing about 90 percent of the population, are extremely devout, industrious, and hardworking. Their daily chanting bears witness to a strong brotherhood—a communal feeling—both joyful and profound.

Most Kashmiris wear an oversized loose cloak called *pheran,* which falls to the knees or ankles, worn over baggy trousers. In the cold winter months, they also wear a *kangri* under their cloaks, a portable heater that consists of a small wicker basket with a metal pan in which glowing coals are stored, kept in place by a leather strap hung around the neck.

EXPLORING KASHMIR AND JAMMU

As soon as you enter the Jammu region from Pathankot, you catch sight of the snow-capped peaks of Kashmir, the Per Panjal range. Jammu splits up naturally into three tracts—the mountainous, the submontane, and the plains. The inhabitants of these three divisions have their own dialects, customs, and dress. The Dogras inhabiting the plains speak Dogri, a mixture of Sanskrit, Punjabi, and Persian. The inhabitants of the "middle-mountains" are called Paharis and occupy themselves in agriculture and cattle breeding. Like the Kashmiris, they are hearty travelers and cover long distances without fatigue. The Gujars are seminomadic herdsmen. In summer, they drive their cattle or goats into the high mountains and make temporary flat-topped mud huts for themselves and their livestock; in the winter, they return to the lowlands.

Jammu, known as the "City of Temples," has long been a center of Indian culture in which the arts have flourished. For centuries, the Pahari painters have been well known for their lovely miniatures that show a dexterity of line and a matchless blend of color. In pre-Independence days, unlike Kashmir, Jammu was almost a closed part of the state. The maharajah liked to keep it strictly to himself—and the British raj, wisely enough, made no effort to prevent this. No European was allowed to enter without a government permit. Each winter, the

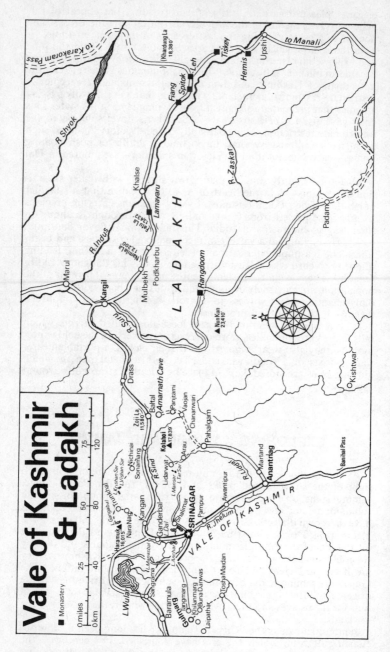

Vale of Kashmir & Ladakh

■ Monastery

0 miles 25   50   75
0 km 40   80   120

to Karakoram Pass

R. Shyok

Khardung La 18,380'

Leh

Tiskey

Upshi

to Manali

Fiang

Spitok

Hemis

R. Zaskar

Khalse

Lamayuru

Fatu La 13,432'

LADAKH

Padam

Marul

R. Indus

Namila La 12,200

Mulbekh

Podkharbu

Rangdoom

Kargil

R. Suru

▲ NurKun 23,410'

N

Drass

Kishtwar

Zoji La 11,580'

Amarnath Cave

Baltal

Panjtarni

Vaojan

Chananwari

Pahalgam

Nichinai

Sonamarg

R. Sind

Kolahoi ▲17,839'

Arau

Martand

Banihal Pass

Kangan

Lidarwat

L.Manisar

L.Tar Sar

Anantnag

L.Krishan Sar

L.Vishan Sar

Trunkhul

Gangabal L.

Ganderbal

Shalimar

Pampur

Awantipur

R. Lidder

R. Jhelum

Haramuk ▲16,015'

NaraNag

L.Dal

SRINAGAR

VALE OF KASHMIR

L.Manasbal

L.Anchar

L.Wular

Sangrama

Baramula

Gulmarg

Tangmarg

Khilanmarg

Buna Danwas

ToshaMaidan

Laipathar

maharajah moved down from the snowy heights of Kashmir and retired to his palace in Jammu, which enjoys the winter climate of the plains, standing 1,000 feet above sea level.

Although Jammu is primarily a transit stop to and from Kashmir, try to visit the multitowered Raghunath Temple, the largest temple complex in Northern India. Located in the heart of the city and surrounded by numerous other temples, Raghunath, constructed over a 25-year period beginning in 1835, is dedicated to Lord Rama (a Vishnu incarnation). A good portion of the interior is covered in dazzling gold leaf. Also see the Ranbireswar Temple, built in 1883 and dedicated to Lord Shiva with its 12 large crystal lingams, and the Dogra Art Gallery, which houses a lovely collection of miniatures in the Vasholi and Kangra styles. You can also check out the Vaishno Devi, and important Hindu shrine—three rock formations covered with gold canopies —set into a hilltop cave high above the Jammu plains. The "temple" is dedicated to the goddess Vaishno Devi, who supposedly took shelter here after killing a demon.

Srinagar, Capital of Kashmir

About 70 miles beyond the Banihal Pass, the gateway to the Vale of Kashmir, lies Srinagar, the capital of the state, nestled in the mountainous walls of the Himalayas at the center of the famous vale. This is the Venice of the East—a "Venice" ensconced miraculously in the midst of an eastern-style Switzerland (or is it Amsterdam?). Set against the winding Jhelum River with lovely Dal Lake sweeping off to the east, Srinagar brings to mind many water-based cities, while retaining a character completely its own.

Eyes linger on the tall riverside wooden houses, with their intricately carved verandahs and balconies jutting precariously over the Jhelum— majestic homes that frequently have their own private ghatlike front steps that lead down to the water. Many of these homes are old and weatherworn, but some still have brightly painted shutters and trim, and always you see that carefully worked Kashmiri gingerbread on the verandas.

Then there's the river, unfortunately muddy and polluted. *Dongas,* large flat-bottom vessels on which entire families live, compete for space on this waterway with lumber-laden barges, houseboats, ducks, swimming children, and *shikaras* (small boats used as water taxis with canopied roofs and fluttering curtains). You could spend days just watching the flow of life that moves back and forth throughout Srinagar.

Take a walk through the old city, giving yourself plenty of time to meander and follow on whim the narrow winding streets that often lead to a dead end or the river, the focus of life. Men in fur caps and women in dark *pherans*—their heads covered in a bright colored scarves or mysteriously veiled in black—walk along the crowded streets. Horse-drawn *tongas* (two-wheeled vehicles) prance by—the animals robust and jaunty, with the string of bells jangling around their neck adding to the festive air. Old men, frequently smoking their "hubbly-bubbly" (the Kashmiri hookah) sit inside small shops or open-air stalls that display all the artistry of Kashmir: furs and embroidered leather or fabrics, carved woodwork, paper-mâché objects, copper or silver urns and pots, shawls, and magnificent carpets.

Apart from the attractions of the old city and the river still spanned by its seven original wooden bridges, Srinagar has numerous landmarks. Early one morning, climb the stone steps that lead to the Shankaracharya Temple (built by a Hindu during the tolerant reign of Jahangir) at the top of a 1,000-foot hill on the southeastern edge of

Srinagar. You can still see parts of the original temple that existed here (the low enclosing wall and the plinth), believed to have been constructed by the son of Ashoka around 200 B.C. The existing temple provides a striking panorama, well beyond the city to the configurations of the Jhelum River and the adjoining Dal Lake.

There are also great views from the Hari Parbat Fort on top of a hill that is sacred to Hindus—Sharika Hill. Although the fortress dates from the eighteenth century, the wall around Hari Parbat was built by Akbar in the late 1500s. If you want to go inside, get permission from the director of tourism.

Srinagar, a predominantly Moslem city, also has its hefty share of historic mosques. See the Jamia Masjid, the largest in India. First built by Sultan Sikander in the thirteenth century and destroyed three times by fire, the last construction—maintaining the original design—was supervised by Aurangzeb in 1674. An attractive example of Indo-Saracenic architecture, its vast interior contains 400 cedar wood pillars, each made from a single tree trunk. Also, see the Pather Masjid, built entirely of limestone by Jahangir's wife, Nur Jahan, in 1620. And the pagodalike Shah Mamdan Mosque, one of the oldest mosques in the city (first constructed in the late fourteenth century) and also destroyed by fires and rebuilt, the last time in 1732—without a single nail or screw. The walls and ceilings are covered with delicate painted woodwork. Unfortunately, only Moslems are allowed inside. Finally, visit the Hazrat Bal on the western shore of Dal Lake, a new modern shrine that contains a sacred hair of the Prophet Mohammed, which is shown to the public on certain chosen days.

Dal and Nagin Lakes

For most, a visit to Srinagar means a vacation, however short, on a legendary houseboat. Although, it's possible to book your boat in advance (in high season this is advised), you can also wait and make a reservation at the Tourist Reception Center in Srinagar. But before you make your choice, it's wise to hire a shikara to see your boat first. The houseboats are moored on Dal and Nagin Lakes, and the Jhelum River. If you want peace and quiet, choose the Nagin or the remote end of Dal. If you're after the hustle and proximity of the city, stay on the southern end of Dal or right on the busy Jhelum—but be ready for noise!

Houseboats come in all sizes and price ranges, but the aura of most of them is genteel elegance. Even the new boats continue the original design—lovely fragrant carved walls and ceilings of cedar, a formal dining room, a handsome sitting room, and bedrooms, a sun deck on the roof, plus a cozy veranda from which you can watch the sun rise or set, depending on your location. A word of caution: staying on a houseboat sets you up as easy prey for the small tradesmen—touts—who paddle out in their shikaras transformed into floating stores—wide-eyed hawks casing the joint. Before you unpack, you're besieged with everything available in Kashmir, from a fresh cutting of local flowers (which is quite pleasant) to razor blades and mineral water. Prices can be exorbitant, so bargain for anything you want. And when you've had enough of the handicrafts, salespeople, and tailors, just say "no" with authority and send them away.

Mogul Garden

No trip to Srinagar is complete without a tour of the waterside Mogul gardens—a trip that should be made by shikara. Each small boat for private hire takes up to four passengers, but with two, it constitutes the height of pampered luxury. Once you've stretched out on the comfortable cushions under the shelter of the fringed canopy, you understand why this boat is dubbed the "gondola" of Kashmir. Your boatsman, with his heart-shaped paddle, glides you soundlessly over the calm water. You pass by ingenious floating vegetable gardens; stop, if you're in the right season, and snap off a gorgeous lotus bloom; follow the swooping course of an electric kingfish, and always remind yourself that this heaven is real.

At intervals all around the 12-square-mile surface stand the stately *chenars,* giant plane trees, which turn fire red in the autumn. The chenars, which were favorite trees of the Moguls who first planted them in Kashmir, form the backdrop to the first garden you visit: the Shalimar Bagh (Garden of Love), laid out in the early 1600s by Jahangir for his Queen Nur Jahan—four terraces of lawns and flower beds rising one above the other. A shallow water channel runs down the middle—typical Persian quadrant-style—and on the top terrace, reserved for the royal women, is a black marble pavilion, secluded and elegant. From May to October, you can watch an evening sound and lumiere show here.

A TOUR OF THE LAKES AND VALLEYS

Gulmarg

Gulmarg, the meadow of flowers, 32 miles northwest of Srinagar, was a favorite vacation spot of the Moguls and later of the British. At an elevation of 8,200 feet, this bowl-shaped valley, set high in the mountains and encircled by fir and pine-covered slopes, is not just a convenient base for numerous treks; it is an up-and-coming year-round resort. You can play golf in the warm months on one of the world's highest courses (originally developed by the British). You can sled (called "sledging") or ski in winter on assorted slopes with T-bar, puma, and chair lift, or trek with a *sherpa* up four km to Khilanmarg, with its breathtaking view and memorable run (a gondola will soon replace this novel, rigorous uphill climb). Although Gulmarg, with its snug circle of rustic hotels, is more like a frontier town than another Sun Valley or Chamonix, it is one of the best skiing bargains in the world. Lessons, lift tickets, and all equipment (fairly up to date, with outdoor clothes included) cost just a few dollars a day.

Gulmarg is also the place for invigorating walks and spirited pony rides. From its seven-mile-long Circular Path, which takes you through pine forests, you have a magnificent view of the entire valley of Kashmir, including Srinagar. You can also see the distant Nanga Parbat (over 26,000 feet). This giant, whose name means naked mountain, dominates the landscape for miles in every direction.

Wular and Manasbal Lakes

From Gulmarg, head northeast to Sangrama and then continue northeast until you reach Wular Lake, the largest freshwater lake in India. Set in magnificent high mountains, the Wular, which is the color of soft jade, is another popular vacation haunt. Here, too, the houseboat is an enticing accommodation. From the comfort of your private veranda, you can admire spectacular sunsets, and speculate over the legends connected to this ancient site. One legend claims that the Wular was formerly a city of such decadence that the mountains released a deluge that swallowed it up; when the water is low, you can see the remaining ruins, it is said. The Wular has evidently claimed enough lives that the deepest area is known as Mota Khon (Gulf of Corpses).

Just a few miles beyond the Wular is Lake Manasbal, a bird watcher's paradise (18 miles from Srinagar). The deepest lake in Kashmir, Manasbal is famous for its lotus blossoms that spread across the water in the summer.

Take the road that branches to the left at Ganderbal and head into the Sindh Valley, one of the most famous in Kashmir. As you travel along the sinuous terrain, the mountains come down precipitously on both sides, covered with that particular Kashmiri pine known as the budle tree. The average specimen stands over 100 feet tall.

Lidder Valley

Due south of Sonamarg is the Lidder Valley, with scenery that is less wild than in the Sindh but somehow more majestic. As you enter the valley via Baltal, you can take an arduous day-long trek to a height of 13,000 feet to the sacred cave of Amarnath, believed to be the former abode of Shiva. The pilgrim's rough-hewn treck, steps cut out of rock, leads straight to the object of worship—a stalactite, shaped like a lingam, hanging from the roof of the cave. At the year's most auspicious moment for worship—the night of the full moon between July and August when Shiva supposedly explained the secret of creation to Parvati—pilgrims pour in from every corner of India to offer their prayers to the god.

The Kolahoi Glacier

Lucky the traveler who takes the three-day trek from Pahalgam (equipment, porters, ponies, and guides are available here) up to the Kolahoi Glacier, the Matterhorn of Kashmir. This popular and relatively easy trek offers some of the most inspiring scenery in Kashmir. Besides seeing great panoramas, you also witness the agility of nomadic shepherds who move their flocks with sublime grace and speed. The actual journey that leads to the glacier takes you first to Aru, a tiny village situated at the foot of a meadow—a convenient stopping place. On the second day, you come to Lidderwatt, a camping site in a meadow forded by two small streams and surrounded by mountains. Here, the sun pours down from a subtropical sky while the encircling pines hold onto night well beyond daybreak. The third day takes you through a pine forest, then the view bursts wide open at Satlanjan. Here, you cross more narrow streams and finally see the milky green Kolahoi—craggy and daunting.

Snow Bridges

A word of warning for anyone who follows this enchanting village to the watershed: Beware of leaving too late in the year when melting snow can be dangerous. Up to the end of May or the beginning of June, you can rely on the snow bridges; after that, they can be deadly. And in its early phase, what is termed a snow bridge in Kashmir is just barely a bridge. During the winter, the ravines fill in and bridge over with snow, while the mountain torrent continues to force its way through a tunnel underneath. Until the thaw sets in, you can walk up and down these precipitous gorges on top of the snow, with the river crashing its way through beneath, unseen and frequently unheard. But once the snow starts to melt, these bridges become so slender at the middle of their arches they can snap at any moment, which can mean a drop of 15 to 20 feet. Or, the snow bridge may already may have broken up in the middle, leaving a gap of two or three feet, which you then have to jump across. The safest trip is across the giant snowbridge at Chananwari, a 10-mile pony trek from Pahalgam.

EXPLORING LADAKH

One of the prime adventure opportunities in India is remote and rugged Ladakh, lying between the two highest mountain ranges in the world: the Himalayan and the Karakoram. Ladakh can be approached by road, or you can fly straight to Leh, the capital. However, if you've got the time, the drive is the only way to go. The territory of Ladakh, about twice the size of Switzerland, represents 70 percent of the total area of Jammu and Kashmir and is one of the highest regions on earth—a good portion of it over 9,000 feet above sea level. With a total population of only 150,000, Ladakh has one of the lowest population densities in the world (two–three people per square mile). For the most part inhospitable and craggy, the otherworldly terrain is arid beyond belief, with mountain peaks soaring three to four miles high. The joint effects of elevation and isolation amid snowy mountains produce the most unusual climate in the world—a weird combination of desert and arctic. Burning heat by day is followed by piercing cold at night, with everything parched by the extreme dryness of the air. The annual rainfall rarely exceeds three to four inches; few rain clouds get over the prohibitive peaks. As you travel up and down the arid, windswept mountains for miles and miles, you see little sign of humanity, bird, or tree, just deserts of granite dust, bare crags, and mountains of different hues. Ladakh is rightly called the "moonland."

In spite of the harsh landscape, Ladakh offers a wealth of environmental intrigue. Pink granite contrasting with a deep blue sky, brisk sunshine, pure air, and green valleys dotted like cases in a vast desert. There are wild yak, the elusive snow leopard, the docile marmot, and blue sheep. But the greatest draw in Ladakh is the chance to witness a rich Buddhist culture firmly rooted in the majority of the people who live here, a culture that's fascinating to ponder. *Gompas* (monasteries) sit perched on high cliffs. *Ghortens* (stupas) and *manes* (sacred stone walls) keep evil spirits from entering a village; prayer flags flap in the cold, strong wind.

Ladakh is connected with Kashmir Valley by a black-topped road that usually remains open from the end of May to November, depending on the snowfall. The road passes through picturesque villages on the banks of the Sindh River, leaving the valley at Sonamarg. The first pass you cross to reach Ladakh is Zoji La (11,578 feet above sea level). On the other side starts the Drass Valley. Each side of the pass provides a startling contrast. You leave behind your last glimpse of forest-clad hills and suddenly stare into a vast mountainous landscape predominately stark, arid, and stony.

Kargil District

Kargil, with a population of about 5,000 predominately orthodox Shiite Moslems, is the second largest town in Ladakh and the headquarters of the Kargil district. Situated in the Suru Valley at the junction of the Drass and Suru rivers, Kargil's elevation of only 9,000 feet (low for Ladakh), reduced snowfall, and greater warmth have produced fertile fields that are rich in barley, wheat, and vegetables; rows of flourishing poplars and willows, and successful orchards. Kargil is famous for its mulberries and apricots.

Long ago, Kargil, the halfway point to Leh, used to be an important junction on the Asian trade route. Hundreds of caravans from China, Afghanistan, Turkey, and India laid over here, conducting intense bartering in the process—a heavy exchange of silk, jewels, ivory, and carpets. Now tourists who come overland to Leh often opt to stop here. Flanked by Shiite tombs (*Imambaras*) and mosques (over 400 years old), the ancient bazaar is crammed with local handicrafts (traveling hookahs, metalware, jewelry) and exquisite pashmina shawls and woven tweeds and blankets.

After crossing the Suru River, the road follows the Wakha Chu stream. Shergole, a tiny village 16 miles from Kargil, is your gateway to Buddhist Ladakh. There, built into a cliff and perched halfway up the mountainside, is a gompa containing some beautifully painted interior walls. Check to see if the lamas are present; it's worth a visit if they're around to let you in. Here, too, you begin to see the traditional prayer flags waving from the roofs of houses and handsome women decked out in their traditional Tibetan costumes.

Mulbekh

From Shergole, it's a few miles to Mulbekh and another gompa overlooking the Wakha Chu Valley and village. Inside are some beautiful frescoes, statues, and fascinating relics. Again, check to see if you can gain access before you start the climb. On the road below stands a huge statue of Maitreya, the future Buddha, carved out of rock, supposedly dating back to the first century when Buddhism first penetrated Ladakh.

Indus Valley

Once you leave Milbekh, the road cuts through a landscape of lunar dunes. You slowly chug up to the top of the 12,200-foot-high pass; the Namika-La. Wind your way back down to a valley and then proceed up and up again until you reach Fatu La, the highest point on the Srinagar-Leh road: 13,479 feet above sea level. The wind whips around stark, craggy peaks and across barren plateaus, rustling prayer flags mounted atop *chortens* (Tibetan stupas) constructed by Buddhists who have successfully negotiated the treacherous and lonely pass. As you head down to the Indus Valley, you execute one particularly sharp bend in the road. Suddenly, you see the distant whitewashed Lamayuru Gompa—Ladakh's oldest monastery, with caves dug into the rock—and there, nestled in valley below, the welcome green oasis of an old sleepy village.

Lamayuru Gompa

Formerly a large monastery with numerous buildings, all constructed in the tenth century, the Lamayuru has only one remaining intact structure. Inside in the head lama's chamber, monks who belong to the Griguna sect and follow the teaching of the Dalai Lama, pray before an enormous 11-headed image of Avolokiteeshvara. Also worth seeing are the mani walls built into the surrounding slopes—each stone carried and put into place by a Buddhist pilgrim. Note the mantra carved into the rocks: *Om Mani Padme Hum* (Oh Jewel in the Lotus Flower).

More than religiously significant, these walls protect the village from avalanches.

Alchi and Spituk Gompas

Near the village of Saspol, take the turn that leads to the eleventh-century Alchi Gompa, with six separate structures. You'll see an imposing collection of gigantic painted clay statues of the Buddha, ornately carved arches and doors, and hundreds of handsome small paintings, 1,000 years old, crammed onto many of the interior walls. Alchi is also unusual in that it is set in the lowlands, rather than on top of a hill.

About five miles from Leh is another important monastery, the Spituk Gompa, built 500 years ago on top of a hillock overlooking the Indus River. This monastery, the seat of the head lama of Ladakh, now contains a new gompa within its walls, plus exquisite *tankas* (Tibetan cloth paintings) and a separate chamber farther up the hill that pays odd tribute to Kali, the Hindu goddess of wrath. The numerous faces on the statue remain veiled except for one day of festive celebration in January. This chamber also contains an exceptional collection of old masks. Unfortunately, some rooms in the Spituk are now off limits to tourists.

Leh—From Buddhist to Military

Your next stop is Leh, seen first from a distance huddling in a narrow valley at the base of snow-covered peaks (part of the Karakoram Mountain Range). By the third century B.C., Leh (at 11,500 feet above sea level) was an important Buddhist center; later, it became a major commercial center on the "silk route" in Central Asia. Now the twentieth century has forced Leh to assume an infinitely less glamorous role as an important Indian military base. Even with the army, Leh has remained an isolated, compact town, with its 12,000 inhabitants trying hard to hold on to their original culture.

The most striking buildings in Leh are the sixteenth-century Leh Palace, still owned by the Ladaki royal family, and the Leh Gompa, perched on a mountain towering over the palace, as if asserting the supremacy of the spiritual realm. Large and rambling, this gompa contains a solid gold statue of the Buddha (weighing just over a ton), painted scrolls, ancient manuscripts, and handsome wall paintings. Higher up on the same ridge are the towers of an old fortification (now off limits).

The Leh bazaar may not offer great bargains (prices are better elsewhere), but it has much in the way of local color. Also, within the bazaar, see the Shiite Mosque, a good example of Turkish and Iranian architecture, built in 1594 by a son (Singe Namgyal) for his mother. Finally, just wander into the labyrinth of streets and alleys that take you through the old town on the lower slopes that lead up to the palace. On the plain below is the newer part of town.

Gompas Around Leh

Leh is an excellent base for excursions to several nearby monasteries and other worthwhile points of interest. Most of them are located on the road that heads southeast to the largest Buddhist gompa in Ladakh: the Hemis Gompa, 25 miles from Leh. The first stop on your route is the Tibetan Refugee Camp near Choglamsar, where refugees who fled Tibet after the Chinese invasion began the difficult process of establishing a new life in India.

At Shey, visit the fifteenth-century summer palace and monastery that belongs to the royal family of Leh. Make arrangements with the lama before you visit; the gompa is often closed. Inside is the largest Buddha statue in Ladakh—over 40 feet high. Made of copper and brass, gilded with gold and silver, and studded with jewels, the sitting Buddha with blue hair, beatific smile, and expressive almond eyes is a spiritual knockout. The Victory stupa, Ladakh's largest, is crowned in pure gold.

The next attraction is the 800-year-old Thikse Gompa, set atop a hill offering a panoramic view of the fertile Indus Valley. There are 10 temples containing more great relics and fine wall paintings. A large contingent of lamas and supposedly a few nuns live within the complex.

Last, but in no way least, is the Hemis Gompa. Built in the 1600s by King Singe Namgyal, this monastery is an imposing architectural tour de force—one that hits you suddenly. Prayer flags fluttering from tall pillars in the courtyard wave you forward. If possible, plan your visit during the Hemis Festival (usually in June or July), which marks the birthday of Guru Padmasambhava. This colorful event features masked dancers gyrating slowly to loud music (the forces of good) to fight off the demons. Hemis also has statues of gold, stupas studded with precious stones, and a great collection of tankas, including one claimed to be the largest in existence, exhibited once every 11 years (the next viewing is 1991).

Zanskar Valley, the New Frontier

Zanskar Valley, stretching out from a noble height of over 13,000 feet, is for adventurous, intrepid travelers who are willing to exchange comfort for a journey into a remote area where the ancient Buddhist culture is still largely undisturbed and intact. This district—a collection of isolated hamlets with magnificent gompas lying between the two branches of the Zanskar River—is well guarded by snowcapped peaks.

The climate is severe. A warm day can suddenly turn cold as ice. Winters are harsh, yet not totally unkind. With the cold, the normally endless trip into Leh for the people who live there is dramatically shortened. Once the Zanskar is frozen, they simply walk across, lopping off a good portion of a circuitous trek. "Fair Weather" roads in Zanskar are always difficult, even during fair weather. Still, if you want to see a place that is untouched and remote, go. Zaskar feels cut off from the world and from the rush of time.

To begin your journey through Zanskar, start from Kargil and head south through the Suru Valley, a fertile area with astonishing beauty. Pass the distant Nun (at 23,410 feet) and Kun (at 23,219), Zanskar's two highest peaks. Continue to follow the river until you reach Rangdum, an isolated hamlet with a seventeenth-century gompa set into the hills. Wind your way up to the Pensa La Pass—14,440 feet above sea level—where unexpected hot springs gurgle not far from the summit. A legend claims that these springs gave rise to the ancestor of the famous Zanskar stallion, now declared a protected animal.

Next is Sani, a tiny village. Be certain to visit the Karsha gompa, the largest and wealthiest monastery in Zanskar, with 500-year-old frescoes. Head to Padam, the former capital of the Kingdom of Zanskar and visit the numerous nearby monasteries. From Padam, head north to Stongdey to yet another gompa. Still farther north visit Zangla, even now ruled by a king who lives in his palace set in a hill.

After returning to Padum, head southeast to Phugtal, the site of one of two rare cave monasteries with temples that appear to spill out of the belly of the mountain. And finally, see Zongkhul—the second cave monastery—an unusual visual treat.

From Zanskar head back to Leh—or do a trek to Manali in Himachal Pradesh.

PRACTICAL INFORMATION FOR
JAMMU AND KASHMIR

WHEN TO GO. Winter is for skiing and snow-related adventures in Kashmir. Spring and early autumn represent a panorama of beautiful color, with ideal temperatures an extra dividend. In April/May, the snows in the upper reaches usually start to melt and the willows turn green. Almond trees bloom and flowers carpet the landscape. In September, autumn's dahlias and cosmos are in full bloom. The days are pleasant and the nights are cool. Summer is the time to trek, to ride horseback, to go rafting, to bike, to fish—the time to explore the remote magnificence of Ladakh. The passes here remain closed from sometime in October until May or June because of snow.

HOW TO GET THERE. By Air. *Indian Airlines* flies to Jammu, Srinagar, or Leh in Ladakh—even in winter, although flights are often delayed or canceled because of inclement weather. There are five flights from Chandigarh and daily flights from Delhi into Jammu. Daily planes from Delhi and Jammu fly into Srinagar. Five weekly flights fly into Srinagar from Chandigarh, two flights fly into Srinagar from Ahmedabad and Bombay, and three flights come from Leh. Two flights a week come from Delhi and Chandigarh into Leh.

By Bus. *Jammu and Kashmir State Road Transport Corporation* (J&KSRTC) shuttles deluxe buses from Delhi to Jammu. Buses leave Delhi from Ashok Yatri Nivas Hotel, 19 Ashok Rd. Buses also go from Delhi to Srinagar, leaving at 4:30 P.M. and arriving the next day at 5:30 P.M. In Delhi, the firm is at 218 Kanishka Shopping Plaza, 19 Ashok Rd.; tel. 343400, ext. 2243. In Srinagar, call 72698. The fare to Srinagar from Delhi is Rs. 200. A daily bus also runs between Srinagar and Leh, with an overnight halt in Kargil, when the pass is open (summer until early autumn).

By Train. From Delhi, the daily *Shalimar Express* to Jammu Tawi (no railway into Srinagar or Ladakh) takes 22 hours, and the faster *Himsagar Express* runs five times weekly. From Bombay, the *Jammu Tawi Express,* runs twice a week. From Calcutta, the daily Jammu Tawi Express. From Jammu to Srinagar, you can take the bus (numerous runs daily) or go by taxi. A fixed-rate taxi costs Rs. 650–Rs. 700, which can be shared by four people.

By Rented Car with Driver. From Jammu or Srinagar, the cost to rent a car with driver should be approximately Rs. 3 per km. In Leh, the cost of renting a jeep with a driver is approximately Rs. 300–Rs. 500 to do one day of local sightseeing. A jeep that carts you around all Ladakh can be costly. Delhi is 587 km to Jammu and 876 km to Srinagar; Srinagar is 434 km to Leh.

TOURIST INFORMATION. The *Jammu & Kashmir Tourist Department Corporation (J&KTDC)* is one of the best. They are out to please and have current information covering nearly every conceivable area of interest to the tourist. They also publish *Kashmir A–Z*, an excellent inexpensive directory that contains just about all the nitty-gritty information you need. If you're in Delhi before you head up to Kashmir, you'd be wise to check into the J & K tourist office. It's an example of efficiency and gracious service that you can expect in most of the big offices once you head north. The department has offices in major cities in India.

Tourist offices in Jammu, Kashmir, and Ladekh are open Mon.–Sat., 10 A.M.–5 P.M. Following is a list of the offices in the state.

Batote, 113 km from Jammu, tel. 42; *Gulmarg,* tel. 99; *Jammu,* Railway Station (no phone); *Kargil (Ladakh),* tel. 29, 35, and 67; *Katra,* 45 km from Jammu, tel. 3 and 5; *Kud,* 105 km from Jammu, tel. 7; *Leh,* tel. 95 and 97;

Pahalgam, tel. 24; *Ramban,* 148 km from Jammu (no phone); *Srinagar,* round-the-clock counter, tel. 77303 and 77305. Also an office at the airport.

FOREIGN CURRENCY EXCHANGE. Most of the Western-style hotels have money-exchange counters. Otherwise, head for a branch of the *State Bank of India* or *Jammu and Kashmir Bank,* open Monday–Friday, 10 A.M.–2 P.M.; Saturdays, 10 A.M.–noon.

ACCOMMODATIONS. You have a wide range of possibilities in the Jammu and Kashmir states—from fancy to rustic minimal. You also have the famous houseboats that run from grand to just barely seaworthy. But, as with the other Himalayan states, a visit should be for the adventure and the ethereal beauty of it all. Some of the most exquisite and remote areas offer few creature comforts (certainly no TV)–but what memories and what breathtaking views! Prices are based on double occupancy: *Expensive,* over Rs. 500; *Moderate,* Rs. 250–Rs. 500; and *Inexpensive,* under Rs. 250. Most of the Western-style hotels take major credit cards. Kashmir is popular, all of it, so book early. Government-run huts, especially in Gulmarg and Pahlagam, should be reserved two to three months in advance to play safe.

GULMARG

Expensive

Hotel Highlands Park. Gulmarg; tel. 30 and 91. 40 rooms. Many amenities: a bar, restaurant, room service, health club, five minutes from the golf course or ski runs, depending on the season. Nice rustic lodge-style hotel.

Moderate

Hotel Affarwat. Gulmarg; tel. 2. 18 rooms. New hotel with simple rooms, a restaurant, 24-hour room service, and a bar. Pleasant management.

Hotel New Zum Zum. Gulmarg; tel. 15. 20 rooms. Simple lodgelike hotel. Each room has a balcony. In winter, water is brought in buckets; otherwise, you have hot and cold water in your rooms. A restaurant and 24-hour room service. A good place to stay.

Hotel Ornate Woodlands. Gulmarg; tel. 68. 12 rooms, set up in three Indian-rustic huts. Restaurant. Off-season rates during March. On a hill.

Hotel Pine Palace. Gulmarg; tel. 66. 16 rooms plus a cottage. Simple rooms with "minimal-attractive" decor. Pleasant management. A bar, restaurant, and room service. Near the chair lift.

Inexpensive

J & K Tourist Huts. Gulmarg. Reservations: J&KTDC, Tourist Reception Center, Srinagar, 190001, India; tel. 76107. Charming one-bedroom huts with a sitting room, kitchen, a servant's room, and a bathroom. Perfect for Gulmarg. Numerous huts. You must book early (three months in advance from spring through early Autumn.

JAMMU

Moderate

Hotel Jammu Ashok. Opposite Amar Mahal, Post Box 60, Jammu Tawi, nine km from the airport, tel. 43127. 50 rooms, some air-conditioned; TV in rooms. A bar, restaurant, coffee shop, health club, and shops.

Asia Jammu Tawi. Nehru Market, Jammu, four km from the airport; 1½ km from downtown; tel. 43930. 44 rooms, some air-conditioned. A swimming pool, health club, room service, and restaurant. The best place in town.

Inexpensive

Hotel Premier. Veer Marg, Jammu, five km from the airport; in the heart of the city; tel. 43234. 21 rooms, some air-conditioned. A restaurant, bar, and 24-hour room service.

Tourist Reception Center. Jammu. Reservations: J&KTDC, Tourist Reception Center, Jammu; tel. 5421. Over 100 rooms, some air-conditioned. A good deal for the price.

KATRA

Moderate to Inexpensive

Asia Vaishno–Devi. Katra; 47 km from the Jammu Airport; tel. 61. 36 rooms, some air-conditioned. All rooms have balconies. Room service, a restaurant, and a health club. Vaishno-Devi is a famous place of pilgrimage (a 14-km trek from the hotel). Lovely setting. A well-run hotel.

Inexpensive

Tourist Bungalow. Katra. Reservations: also through J&KTC Tourist Reception Center, Jammu; tel. 5421. About 15 rooms. Good simple accommodations, considering the price.

PAHALGAM

Expensive

Pahalgam Hotel. Pahalgam, close to the downtown area; tel. 26 or 52. 41 rooms. Rates include all meals. TV, restaurant, disco, bar, swimming pool, health club, other amenities. Good views. Attractive hotel.
Woodstock Hotel. Pahalgam, near the downtown area; tel. 27. 60 rooms. Another nice hotel, with restaurant, bar, room service, disco, health club. Well run.

Moderate

Hotel Heaven. Pahalgam. 15 rooms. New modern hotel, with restaurant.
Hotel Mansion. Pahalgam. 20 rooms. A spiffy new hotel with a restaurant.

Inexpensive

Tourist Huts. Pahalgam. Reservations: J & K TDC, Tourist Reception Center, Srinagar 190001; tel. 76107. 10–15 one-bedroom huts each with a sitting room and kitchen. Reserve well in advance, very popular!
Tourist Bungalow. Pahalgam. Reservations: same address as above for the Tourist Huts. 10 rooms with attached baths. Again, very popular; book well in advance.

SRINAGAR

Expensive

Hotel Broadway. Maulana Azad Road, ½ km from downtown; tel. 71211. 97 rooms. Many amenities, including TVs, a restaurant, 24-hour room service, bars, a pool, and a shopping arcade. A modern new hotel, not great in character, but good service.
Oberoi Palace. Gupkar Road, four km from downtown; tel. 71241. 105 rooms with TVs. A grand old hotel. Not palatial; just the huge, former home of the maharajah, being spruced up. Vast lawns with views. A restaurant, bar, and shopping arcade. Ask for a room with a view.
Shahenshah Palace. Boulevard Rd. four km from downtown; tel. 71345. 74 air-conditioned rooms. Attractive hotel across from Dal Lake. A restaurant, coffee shop, and bar.

Moderate

Hotel Gulmarg. Boulevard, 1½ km from downtown; tel. 71331. 49 rooms. Nice older hotel with a restaurant. Dal Lake across the street.
Hotel Parimahal. Dal Lake, Boulevard, downtown; tel. 71235. 35 rooms. Another good hotel facing the lake. Restaurants, 24-hour room service, and a bar.
Shah Abbas Hotel. P.O. Box 273, Dal Lake Boulevard, downtown; tel. 77789. 84 rooms, some with a lake view. Restaurant, TVs, 24-hour room service, many amenities. Although the hotel is new and well run, it lacks a strong character.

Hotel Tramboo Continental. Boulevard, four km from downtown; tel. 73914. 54 rooms. Across from Dal Lake. Many amenities, 24-hour room service, and a restaurant. An excellent bargain—pleasant, comfortable, and clean.

Inexpensive

Cheshmashahi Hutments, Srinagar. Reservations: J&KTDC, Tourist Reception Center, Srinagar 190001; tel. 76107. Numerous single-bedroom huts, each with a sitting room, kitchen, servant's quarter, and bathroom. Book far in advance, they're very popular.

Tourist Reception Center Hotel Block (same reservations as above). Numerous rooms. Again, a very popular facility. Book early.

HOUSEBOATS Houseboats moored to the banks of Dal and Nagin Lakes are 80–125 feet long and 10–20 feet wide. An average-sized houseboat has a dining room, living room, one to three bedrooms with attached baths, and, in most cases, hot and cold running water. Most of the houseboats have terraces for sunbathing and lovely verandas. They are electrified and usually nicely furnished. Many kinds of houseboats are available. The approximate costs: *Deluxe Class* (Rs. 450 per double); *A Class* (Rs. 275 per double); *B Class* (Rs. 205 per double). There are lots of houseboats—lots of steal-you-blind houseboats as well as lots of houseboats surrounded by congestion and noise.

The following houseboat operators will give you the houseboat stay you imagine: gracious service and relative peace and quiet. You can rent the entire boat or just a bedroom and share, but given the intimacy of a boat, sharing is an important consideration. To play it safe, stick to the Deluxe, A, or B categories.

Reshu Boktoo & Sons, Sulaiman Shopping Complex, Dal Gate, Box 95, Srinagar (tel. 74547), has excellent boats on Nagin Lake. *Butt's Claremont Houseboats,* Nasim Bagh, Hazratbal, Srinagar 19006 (tel. 72325), also has *Butt & Sons,* Dalgate, Srinagar; (Claremont Houseboats) (tel. 72175), has very classy boats. *Abdul Rashid Major & Bros.* Nageem Bagh, Nagin Lake, Srinagar, 190006, Kashmir, has lovely smaller boats. *Siah Group of Houseboats,* Box No. 76, Srinagar, 190001 (tel. 74044); has nice, reliable boats closer to Srinagar, so expect more traffic and more noise.

TOURIST HUTS AND BUNGALOWS. The J & KTDC maintains other tourist huts and bungalows in hidden lovely places throughout this part of the state.

Jammu. *Mansar Lake,* 80 km from Jammu, tourist bungalow and huts; and *Surinsar Lake,* 42 km from Jammu, tourist bungalow.

For reservations: J&KTDC Tourist Reception Center, Jammu; tel. 5421. Bungalows, about Rs. 40; huts, Rs. 75–Rs. 100.

Kashmir. *Achabal,* former pleasure retreat of Empress Nur Jahan, now a camping ground, 58 km from Srinagar, tourist bungalow and huts; *Aharbal,* 51 km from Srinagar, near a beautiful waterfall, tourist bungalow; *Daksum,* 85 km from Srinagar, a forest retreat surrounded by mountains, tourist bungalow; *Kokarnag,* 70 km from Srinagar, botanical garden and hot springs high up in the mountains, tourist bungalow and huts; *Lake Manasbar,* 32 km from Srinagar, tourist bungalow; *Sonamarg,* 83 km from Srinagar, in a valley way up in the mountains, tourist bungalow and huts; *Verinag,* 80 km from Srinagar, Mogul ruins and hot springs, tourist bungalow; *Yusmarg,* 40 km from Srinagar, lovely valley in the hills of the Pir Panjal range, tourist huts.

For reservations in all of these huts and bungalows, contact: J&KTDC, Tourist Reception Center at Srinagar, 190001; tel. 76107. Bungalows, Rs. 40–Rs. 50; huts, Rs. 75–Rs. 140.

LADAKH

Accommodations have greatly improved in Ladakh in recent years, but this area still must be considered an "adventure" destination, with clean facilities, for the most part, not lavish amenities. For the sake of the environment and the culture, fancy hotels don't belong here. This is God's country, not taj or raj country. In most areas, moderately priced places operate under the European Plan with meals included.

Moderate

Welcomgroup Highlands Hotel. Kargil, Ladakh, tel. 41. 40 clean rooms. The best in town.
Kargil Sarai. Kargil, Ladakh. Limited rooms but clean.
Hotel D. Zojila, Kargil, Ladakh. Limited rooms but clean.

Inexpensive

Tourist bungalows operated by the state are located throughout the Kargil District of Ladakh. Sleeping bags are advised. Reservations: Tourist Officer, Kargil, Ladakh. These bungalows are at Drass, Kargil, Mulbek, Panikhar, and Padam-Zanaskar. All these facilities are simple, with sparse furnishings.

Rest houses are also available in this area. For reservations, contact Executive Engineer, Public Works Department, Kargil. Again, bring your own bedding. The cost is nominal. Rest houses can be found at Sankoo, Rangdum, and Bodh Kharbu.

LEH AREA

Expensive

Ladakh Sarai. Stok, Leh; tel. 181. 15 hand-made yurt circular tents. As fancy and expensive as you can get. $100 per person. Run by Tiger Tops Mountain Travel India Pvt. Ltd. (main office: 1/1 Rani Jhansi Rd., New Delhi, India; tel. 523057).

Moderate

Kang-Lha-Chhen. Leh, Ladakh; tel. 144. 24 basic rooms. Okay for the money.
Hotel K-Sar. Leh, Ladakh; tel. 148. 12 simple rooms.
Khangri Hotel and Restaurant. Nehru Park, Leh, Ladakh; tel. 51. 22 clean simple rooms.
Lharimo Hotel. Leh, Ladakh; tel. 101. 30 simple rooms.
Hotel Shambala, Skara, Leh; tel. 67. 24 rooms. The best of its price in the area.
Tsemo-la, Karzoo. Leh, Ladakh; tel. 94. 32 rooms.

LEH TOURIST BUNGALOWS. More tourist bungalows run by the state's tourist department. Again, sleeping bags are advised. Reservations: Assistant Director of Tourism, Leh, Ladakh. Cost: Rs. 25–Rs. 45. Bungalows are located at Khaltsi, Leh, Sakti, and Saspol. All these facilities are simple with sparse furnishings.

There is also a Public Works Department Rest House in Khaltsi. For reservation: Superintendent Engineer, Public Works Department, Leh, Ladakh.

 DINING OUT. In Kashmir, there is a strong hint of Middle Eastern cooking, and *kebabs* (small pieces of chicken, mutton, or balls of minced meat threaded on a skewer and cooked or fried) are great favorites. *Birianis,* typically Moslem dishes whose pedigree goes back to the Great Moguls, are prepared on all festive occasions. They are made from pigeons, chicken, or mutton with plenty of rice and butter and some spices. Other Kashmiri Muglai dishes to tickle your palate: *gushtaba,* a meatball curry cooked in a gravy of yoghurt and spices; *qabaragah,* meat made tender by marinating it in yoghurt and frying it on a fierce fire; *dum pukhta,* prepared in the same way but cooked very slowly in its own juice. You'll find the sweets rather syrupy. Kashmiri tea, drunk during or after meals, is of two kinds—the salty and the sweet. The former is of rosewood color and taken with cream. Sweet tea (*kahwa*) is milkless, often perfumed with saffron, and has almonds and cardamom floating in it. It is said to be very good for an upset stomach.

Prices, based on one person eating a three-course meal, excluding taxes, tip, or beverage, are *Expensive,* Rs. 50-plus; *Moderate,* Rs. 25–Rs. 50; *Inexpensive,* under Rs. 25. Most of the expensive hotels accept credit cards.

GULMARG

Expensive

Hotel Highlands Park. Gulmarg; tel. 30 or 91. Continental, Indian, Chinese, and Kashmiri cuisines. Lovely location; fairly good food. The best in town. Reservations advised.

Moderate

Khailan. Affarwat Hotel, Gulmarg; tel. 2. Indian and Continental dishes. Pleasant ambience.

JAMMU

Expensive

Bar-e-Kabab, Restaurant. Hotel Asia Jammu Tawi, Jammu; tel. 46373. Mughlai and tandoori specialties. Good ambience: outdoor eating with entertainment. Only open April–September, 7 P.M.–11 P.M. Reservations advised.
Peacock. Asia Jammu Tawi, Jammu; tel. 43930. Good Chinese, Continental, and Kashmiri food. Reservations advised.

Moderate

Cosmo Bar & Restaurant. Veer Marg, Jammu; tel. 47561. Good local restaurant serving Indian, Mughlai, Chinese, and Continental cuisines.

PAHALGAM

Moderate

Pine Grove Restaurant. Woodstock Hotel, Pahalgam; tel. 27. Indian, Continental, Chinese, and Gujarati food. Good, tasty cooking.

SRINAGAR

Expensive

Oberoi Palace. Gupkar Road, Srinagar; tel. 71241. Excellent Indian and Kashmiri food. Chinese and Continental dishes are also served. A large dining room in the former palace. Not grand, but pleasant. Hope they don't lose the chef. Reservations advised.

Inexpensive

Alka Salka. Sreerwami Road, Srinagar; no phone. Great food served all day long. The locals love the place.
Broadway Kolohoi Bar and Restaurant. Sonwar Bagh, Srinagar; tel. 77474. Reliable Indian, Chinese, Continental, and Mughlai foods.
Mughal Darbar. Shervani Road, Srinagar; no phone. Delightful, informal, popular restaurant serving tasty Kashmiri, Mughlai, and Continental foods. A great bargain.

LADAKH

Moderate

Dreamland Restaurant. Part of the Dreamland Hotel in Leh. Offers the best Chinese and Tibetan food in town.
Hotel Shambala also serves reliably good Ladakhi, Chinese, Continental dishes. Slightly more expensive.

 HOW TO GET AROUND. From the Airport. The airport is a short hop to downtown Jammu. A taxi ride should cost about Rs. 20.
    By Taxi. Metered taxis are available at negotiable rates.
By Auto Rickshaw. The most fun and cheaper than taxis, just make certain the driver uses the meter.

By Bus. *J & K State Road Transit Corporation (SRTC)* has mini-buses running regularly throughout the city. Speak to the tourist officer at the Railway Station in Jammu for fares and routes; tel. 43803.

By Rented Car with Driver. Contact the tourist department for a list of approved car rental agencies; tel. 43803. Figure the same rate per km at Rs.3, plus Rs. 50 for night-halt charges.

LEH

From the Airport. Taxis and jeeps are both available at the same rate of about Rs. 20. They are also available in Leh for short hops and longer sightseeing excursions. From Leh to Kargil, the fare is about Rs. 700 by taxi and about Rs. 800 by jeep (don't ask why). The taxi fare from Leh to Zanskar Valley (Padam) is about Rs. 3,500.

SRINAGAR

From the Airport. An airport bus takes you to the Tourist Reception Center in the heart of Srinagar for about Rs. 10. By taxi, figure about Rs. 60 to get into the thick of the city.

By Taxi. At Rs. 3 per km, this is the least-sensible way to travel if you plan to stay in the city, but it's okay for excursions around Dal Lake.

By Auto Rickshaw. Drivers here have the same reluctance to use the meter as elsewhere. Auto rickshaws should be much cheaper than taxis.

By Shikara (lovely Kashmiri gondola). This is the only way to travel here. Although rates are supposedly fixed, no *shikara* owner will agree to them. Negotiate in advance and figure on about Rs. 20 per hour. No more than five passengers are allowed in a shikara. Ideally, they are best for two stretched out in pampered style. They're slow, but who cares? For complete rates for various shikara trips, check with the tourist department.

By Tonga. This is another nice alternative. Robust horses with bells around the neck take you around town in two-wheel vehicles. Less expensive than the rickshaw. Haggle, but then enjoy yourself.

By Rented Car with Driver. Good and possibly necessary (if you can afford it) for long excursions. You can rent a car from *J&KSRTC* for approximately Rs. 3 per km (overnight halt charges, Rs. 50). Call 72698 for further details. Approved Tourist Taxi Operators of J&KTDC (tel. 76107) can also supply a list of reliable private agencies that rent cars with drivers.

By Helicopter. The J&KTDC operates *Westland Helicopter,* which offers a 15-minute round-the-city flight at Rs. 250 per person and a round-trip to Gulmarg at Rs. 500 per person. For details and reservations, contact the Tourist Reception Center, 77305.

TOURS. *J&KSRTC,* Tourist Reception Center, Srinagar, runs the following deluxe sightseeing tours; Call 72698 for further details and reservations.

City Forest and Shopping Tour, covering Shankaracharya Hill, Chesma Shahi Garden, and Zeathyar; central market; weaving factory; and museum, Rs. 12; Daksum via Achhabal and Kokernag, scenic spots including springs, day trip, Rs. 45; Gulmarg day trip, Rs. 45; Mogul Gardens-Shankaracharya Temple day trip, Rs. 28; Rahalgam day trip, Rs. 45; Sonamarg day trip, Rs. 43; Special Mogul Garden evening tour, Rs. 18.50; Verinag (Mogul ruins and springs) day trip, Rs. 46; Wular Lake day trip, Rs. 46; and Yusmarg (lovely valley) day trip, Rs. 38.

TOUR OPERATORS. Srinagar is the starting point for a lot of wonderful adventures. Like houseboat *wallahs,* there are good and bad private outfits ready to take you boating and trekking into the wilderness. Many are really just out to take you for a ride. Here is a list of really good adventurer packagers, who will give you a memorable *good* time:

Reshu Boktoo & Sons, Travel & Tour Operators, Box 95, Srinagar, India, tel. 74547. Good treks through Kashmir and Ladakh; jeep "treks" (week-long excursions from Srinagar via jeep to Leh and Ladakh); Shikara water treks. Personal attention.

Johenson Travels, Polo View, Srinagar; tel. 74000. Another reliable outfit.
Kai Travels Pvt. Ltd. Tara Bhavan, Srinagar; tel. 74180.
Sita Travel Service. Boulevard, Srinagar; tel. 77404. An excellent outfit that really knows the area and takes good care of tourists.
Sita World Travels. Maulana Azad Road, Srinagar; tel. 78891. Not so wildly adventurous, but reliable for standard excursions to the top spots.
Tiger Tops (Mountain Travel India Pvt. Ltd). The Bund, Srinagar; tel. 73015. Offers wildly expensive treks that are classy and cover all your needs and all the possible trekking routes.
In Leh, *J&KSRTC* runs a regular bus service from Leh to Kargil (a few hours' journey) and a bus from Kargil to Padum (a two-day trip).
Contact the tourist department at Leh (tel. 95 or 97) for a list of approved private agencies by hired jeep or car with driver. (Rs. 300–Rs. 500).
Artou Travels, P.O. Box 18, Leh, Ladakh (tel: 146) has an excellent reputation for treks from Ladakh.

 SEASONAL EVENTS. The three areas of Jammu, Kashmir, and Ladakh are each influenced by three specific religions: Jammu, Hindu; Kashmir, Islam; and Ladakh, Buddism. Each year, these areas observe the traditional cycle of festivals and religious observances that are celebrated throughout India. The following additional festivals are special to this state:
June. *Hemis Festival.* Ladakh's biggest monastery is the site of a two-day festival commemorating the birthday of Guru Padmasambhava, with masked dancers and eerie music. It's an intensely devout and culturally rich Buddhist festival, heavily attended. Contact the tourist department for details.
July/August. During the full moon, thousands of Hindu devotees trek to the Amarnath cave at Amar Yatra, approximately 48 km from Pahalgam, supposedly the abode of Shiva, to pray before the sacred lingam.

 **HISTORIC SITES.** Entrance to most places is generally free; where a donation is asked, a few rupees will do. Entrance to monasteries varies Rs. 5 to Rs. 10 per person.

JAMMU AREA

Bahu Fort. The oldest building in Jammu, constructed by Raja Bahu Lochan over 3,000 years ago; the interior temple is dedicated to Kali.
Raghunath Temple, dedicated to Lord Rama (Vishnu avatar). Largest temple complex in Northern India, it was started and completed 25 years later by his son. Much of interior is covered in gold leaf. The surrounding temples are dedicated to other gods and goddesses associated with the *Ramayana.*
Ranbireswar Temple, Jammu, constructed in 1883 by Maharajah Ranbir Singh, dedicated to Shiva. It has 12 crystal Shiva lingams.
Vaishno Devi. A 14-km trek from Katra leads to this important Hindu shrine, a cave dedicated to the goddess Vaishno Devi. The long narrow cave has three rock formations covered with gold canopies, representing the three divine aspects of the goddess; Maha Kali, Maha Lakshmi, and Maha Saraswati. An important pilgrimage site for Hindus.

LADAKH AREA

Alchi Gompa, 135 km from Leh, 5 km from Saspol. Six separate structures with a collection of gigantic painted clay statues of the Buddha, carved arches and doors, and hundreds of small paintings (1,000 years old).
Hemis Gompa, 49 km from Leh. Ladakh's biggest monastery built in the 1600s by King Singe Namgyal. Filled with gold statues, stupas studded with precious stones, and a great collection of *tankas,* including one claimed to be the largest in existence, exhibited once every 11 years.
Karsha Gompa, in Sani, Zanskar. The largest and wealthiest monastery in Zanskar, with 500-year-old frescoes.
Lamayuru. Ladakh's oldest monastery going back to the tenth century. Formerly numerous structures existed; now only one remains. Inside the head lama's chamber is an enormous 11-headed image of Avolokiteeshvara. Also see

the caves carved out of the mountains, with interesting interior furnishings of carpets and prized tankas.

Leh Palace and Gompa. Leh palace built in the mid-sixteenth century by Sovang Namgyal. Inside are old wall paintings depicting the life of the Buddha. Small corridors contain old tankas, statues. The gompa houses a solid gold statue of the Buddha, weighing over a ton.

Mulbekh Gompa and statue of Maitreya, the future Buddha, supposedly constructed in the first century, 25 miles from Kargil. Gompa contains beautiful frescoes and statues.

Sankar Gompa, 3 km from Leh, has an excellent collection of miniature gold statues and paintings.

Shergole Gompa, 16 km from Kargil, contains beautiful frescoes, statues, and relics.

Shey Palace and Gompa. Built by Senge Namgyal in the 1600s on the ruins of another fort, this palace is in decay, but there's a magnificent two-story statue of a sitting Buddha, made of copper and gold in the 1600s. The gompa contains beautiful frescoes. Make arrangements with the lama before visiting. The Victory Stupa is Ladakh's largest, crowned in pure gold.

Spituk Gompa, 5 km from Leh, was built 500 years ago. The current seat of the head lama of Ladakh, it has exquisite tankas and a separate chamber that pays tribute to Kali, the Hindu goddess of wrath. Her face is unveiled only one day in January.

Thikse Gompa, near Leh, is 800 years old. Ten temples with great relics and fine wall paintings.

Zongkhul and *Phugtal Gompus,* near Padum, are two rare cave monasteries that contain temples.

SRINAGAR AREA

Achabal, 58 km from Srinagar. All Mogul gardens are open from sunrise to sunset. A former Mogul garden, designed by a daughter of the Mogul Emperor Shah Jahan and the favorite retreat of Empress Nur Jahan. Now a grove with water cascades and fountains, a pleasant place to visit.

Amar Nath, 47 km from Pahalgam. A cave that was supposedly the abode of Lord Shiva, with a stalactite in the shape of a lingam created by water dripping through the limestone roof of the cave. Devotees make a special pilgrimage here during July/August.

Char Chenar. Shah Jahan's mogul garden is on an island in Dal Lake with a pavilion and three *chenars* (fire trees). There used to be a fourth.

Chasma Shahi (Royal Spring). The smallest Mogul garden, designed by Shah Jahan in the 1630s. Beautiful pavilions, illuminated at night. Fee, Rs. 1.

Hari Parbat Fort. Built in the eighteenth century by Atta Mohammad Khan, an Afghan governor; the surrounding wall was built by Mogul Emperor Akbar in the late 1500s. Among the numerous ancient structures are a temple dedicated to Parvati, a Moslem shrine and mosque, and a *gurdwara* built to commemorate the visit of Har Govind Singh to Kashmir. Permission to enter must be obtained from the State Archaelogical Department, Lalmandi Square, Srinagar. The fort, however, is poorly maintained; it's the exterior views that make a visit worthwhile.

Harwan, six km from Srinagar. Ruins of a Buddhist monastery dating back to the third century.

Hazratbal. White marble shrine built recently contains a sacred hair of Prophet Mohammed shown to the public on certain days.

Jamai Masjid is the largest mosque in Kashmir. First constructed by Sultan Sikander in the thirteenth century, it was destroyed three times by fire. The last construction was in 1674 by Aurangzeb in Indo-Saracenic architecture and laid out in the style of a Persian court mosque, with 400 cedar wood pillars, each from one tree.

Nasim Bagh (Garden of the Morning Breeze) is a Mogul garden of chenars originally laid out by Akbar in the early 1600s.

Nishat Bagh (Garden of Pleasure) is a Mogul garden designed by Asaf Khan, brother of Nur Jahan, in 1633. Ten beautiful terraces, formal gardens, a water channel with polished marble stepping stones, fountains, and pavilions. Persian in style and magnificence.

Shah Hamdan Mosque. First constructed in fourteenth century, suffered three fires. The last construction was in 1732 with no nails or screws used. Lovely carved windows and entrances. Only Moslems can go inside.

Shalimar Bagh (Garden of Love). Mogul garden constructed by Emperor Jahangir for his Nur Jahan in 1619. Four terraces with a water channel running from level to level. Typical Persian quadrant style. The black marble pavilion on top exclusively used by royal women. Sound and light show.

Shankaracharya Temple. The present temple was built during the reign of Jahangir by an unknown Hindu. It sits on the site of a temple originally constructed around 200 B.C. by a son of Ashoka. The low enclosing wall and plinth belong to the ancient temple.

 MUSEUMS AND ART GALLERIES. *Amar Palace,* Ram Nagar, Jammu, has an interesting collection of paintings in a former palace designed like a French chateau. Open 10 A.M.–2 P.M. and 3–5 P.M. in winter; 5–7 P.M. in summer. Closed state holidays. Free.

Dogra Art Gallery, Gandhi Bhavan, Jammu, houses nearly 600 paintings from Basholi and Kangra schools; plus sculptures, terra cotta pieces, murals. Summer, 7:30 A.M.–1 P.M.; winter, 10 A.M.–5 P.M. Closed Mondays and holidays. Free.

Leh Khar Palace Museum, Leh, is a former monastery with tankas, scrolls, statues, and armaments. Open summers only, 7–9:30 A.M. Rs. 5.

Shri Partap Singh Museum, Lal Mandi, Srinagar, was started by the maharajah of Jammu and Kashmir. Archaeology, natural history, and products of Kashmiri arts and crafts. Particularly interesting are the finds from Harwan, a Buddhist site of the third century. The collections of coins, carpets, embroideries, and textiles are all from the state. Open 10 A.M.–5 P.M.; closed Wednesdays and holidays. Free.

Stok Palace Museum, Stok, contains precious stones, tankas, twenty dresses, coins, and prayer instruments. Open 7 A.M.–6 P.M. Rs.20.

 WILDLIFE SANCTUARIES. *Dachigam National Park,* 21 km from Srinagar. Originally a royal game preserve belonging to the maharajah, this lovely park is now a protected sanctuary and home of the rare snow leopard, Himalayan black bear, brown bear, Kashmir stag *(hangul),* leopard cat, musk deer, and numerous birds. The best time to visit is June–October. Tourists are required to obtain special permits from the Chief Wildlife Warden, J & K Government, Tourist Reception Center, Srinagar tel. 75411.

Hemis High Altitude National Park (35 km from Leh) is the natural habitat of ibex, snow leopards, and numerous exotic flowers. Camping accommodations are available. Contact the Wildlife Warden, Leh.

 FISHING. Acclimatized varieties of trout attain greater size and are more plentiful than in their original European or North American habitat. Sturdy equipment is therefore required for fishing in Kashmir's fast waters. The trout fishing season is April 1–September 30, and the mahseer fishing season, August–September. Licenses are available from the *Directorate of Fisheries,* Tourist Reception Center, Srinagar (tel. 72862) and at Jammu, Nowabad Canal Road (tel. 47804). Both are open 10 A.M.–2 P.M. Monday–Saturday. License issued for a maximum of three days at Rs. 75 per rod per day.

This same office periodically publishes maps showing beats and the routes leading to them. It's not necessary to bring your equipment; rods, reels, lines, and lures may be hired locally. Fishing in the Sindh and Liddar rivers is usually poor from mid-May–mid-July owing to the cold water.

 GOLF. There are excellent golf courses in Srinagar, Gulmarg, and Pahalgam. *Srinagar Golf Club's* links: nine holes and double-flag 18 holes. *Gulmarg Golf Club's* course is good; it was redesigned to fill international standards and is probably the world's highest at 8,700 feet. Spring and autumn tournaments are held both in Srinagar and in Gulmarg (June and September). Contact *Kashmir Government Golf Club,* Maulana Azad Road,

Srinagar (tel. 76524) for reservations and temporary membership details; Rs. 20 per day.

Gulmarg Golf Club has temporary membership available; tel. 39 for details.
Pahalgam Golf Club, also has temporary membership available; tel. 51, for details.

SKIING is a popular sport in Gulmarg from December to March, when the meadow is covered by a thick blanket of snow 6–10 feet deep. The annual skiing competition is held in three stages during this period. There are now several ski lifts, and all equipment can be hired. Skiing courses are run by the Indian Institute of Skiing and Mountaineering. Information is available from any Government of India Tourist Office or from Commissioner of Tourism, J & K Government, Srinagar. An enjoyable winter holiday with lodge-style hotels, but don't expect European standards for skiing facilities—at least, not yet.

TREKKING. The soaring heights and scenic grandeur of the Inner Himalayas can best be viewed by hiking. Starting points of the seven treks indicated here (and there are many more) can be reached in comfort by bus or taxi. Guides, supplies, ponies, and *mazdurs* (porters) are available at all these points. Since good tents are for hire at several places in Kashmir, we suggest you carry tents even if there are tourist lodges and forest rest houses along the route. In this way, you will be completely independent. Light double-fly tents of medium size are recommended; they can be easily carried by pack ponies or porters and offer adequate resistance to hazardous weather.

For a list of reliable tour operators who'll give you a great personalized trek, even combined with a guide, see *How to Get There* section or contact the *Srinagar* or *Ladakh Tourist Department.* The tourist department will be able to help you arrange ponies and porters and will advise you about hiring charges, which should be fixed before you start. The best time to trek this region is generally mid-May–mid-October. Here are some of the more popular trek routes, rated by degree of difficulty.

KASHMIR

Trek 1. Pahalgam to Amarnath Cave via Chandanwari–Sheshnag–Panjtarni –(crossing Mahagunas Pass, 14,000 feet); 28 miles, four–six days. Elevation, 7,200–12,700 feet. *Moderate.*

Trek 2. Pahalgam to Kolahoi Glacier via Aru and Ladderwatt; 22 miles, four–six days. Elevation, 7,200–11,000 ft. *Easy.*

Trek 3. Pahalgam to Mansar Lake via Aru–Dandabari Glacier–Tar Sar Lake; 24 miles, five days. Elevation, 7,200–12,500 feet. *Easy* to *Moderate.*

Trek 4. Sonamarg to Gangabal Lake via Nichinai Pass, Vishensar Lake, 16 miles, seven days. Elevation, 8,500 to 12,500 feet. *Moderate* to *Difficult.*

Trek 5. Gulmarg to Alpathar via Khilanmarg, eight miles, two days. Elevation, 8,500–10,100 feet. *Easy.*

Trek 6. Gulmarg to Tosha Maidan via Buna Danwas and Gadala stream, 20 miles, 2½ days. At the end of the trek, visit the lakes near Chinmarg and Tosha Maidan Pass; there is hardly any difference in elevation. The return journey can be made via Riyar and Khag to Tangmarg, 2½ days. *Easy.*

Trek 7. Kangan to Gangabal via Wangat Valley–Nara Tag–Trunkhal, 21 miles, four days. Elevation, 6,800–11,700 feet. *Moderate* to *Difficult.*

LADAKH

Ladakh has extensive possibilities of high and difficult trekking and challenging climbing. There are innumerable towering peaks, most of them unnamed and unclimbed. The Suru and Zanskar valleys are excellent areas for trekking in the shadow of the high peaks of Nuń and Kun. The Zanskar valley can be approached from Kargil in about a week's trekking. The 14,000-foot-high pass of Penzi-La has to be crossed to reach the valley. There is a "jeepable" road following the River Suru up to Rangdoom Gumpa, about 130 km from Kargil. It is necessary to take all equipment, which can be hired in Srinagar.

You are well advised to contact the tourist offices in Srinagar, Kargil, Padum, or Leh to get a thorough briefing on the latest conditions of the routes, the streams en route, the location of bridges, and so forth before setting out. Also carry all the food you need. You'll find little to buy. There are numerous treks you can make, all of them incredible. Trekking in this area is best July–October. Here are three of the more popular possibilities:

Trek 1. Lamayuru to Padum. Via Chila–Hanupata–Photaksar–Shanpado Gongma–Linshat–Snertse–Pidmu–Pishu–Padam; eight days. *Difficult.*

Trek 2. Padam to Hemis via Tongde–Zangla–Foot of Sher Sher La–Chup-Cha–Shang Kong Ma–Kurna Sumdo–Nari Narsa–Lang Tang–Hankar Ning Ling–Skakdo–Hemis; two weeks. *Very difficult.*

Trek 3. Padum to Manail via Muney/Raru–Surley–Cha–Phugtal–Purney–Drangze–Karghyak–Gombo–Rangjon–Lartsa–Shingkun La–Gadi Shisa–Darcha–Manali, about 12 days. *Moderate to Difficult.*

 SHOPPING. Carpets, woodwork, and shawls take pride of place among the handicrafts of Kashmir. From Ladakh come soft, snug *pashmina* tweeds and shawls made of the belly-wool of the Himalayan goats, and Tibetan-style jewelry of jade and turquoise, set in beaten silver. The Kashmir Valley craftsmen produce decorative articles in papier-mâché in three grades. In the first, pure gold leaf is used; it is rarely exported owing to high customs rates. Here is your chance to buy on the spot at reasonable prices bowls, boxes, and trays of amazing richness of detail and beauty of Oriental design. Other products worthy of attention are *gaba* and *numda* rungs. Gaba are thin and light and can be hung up on the wall like tapestries. Numda are made of thick, light-colored felt with embroidered flower designs. Also good are embroidered wall hangings and fashion fabrics, leather and fur coats, bags, Kashmir silk, and carvings in walnut wood. Time and again you will be accosted by hawkers; first make sure they have a Tourist Department registration card, then start your bargaining session.

 SNACKS AND TEATIME. Asia Snacks. Bagh-E-Bahu, Jammu Tawi Fast food; good snacks. Local popular hangout. Open 10 A.M.–10 P.M.

Moma Mia's Hotel and Restaurant. On Nagin Lake, Srinagar. A houseboat moored to the western bank that serves espresso (not bad) from the sundeck. Nice ambience—and, of course, great views. Open all day.

 NIGHTLIFE AND BARS. Throughout the state, your best bet is always the better hotels where the bars are open during lunch and until late in the evening. If you're on a houseboat, bring your own—it's the most delightful bar in town.

WESTERN AND CENTRAL REGION

BOMBAY

City on the Move

by
KATHLEEN COX and RAVI KHANNA

Ravi Khanna is the New Delhi bureau chief for the Voice of America, which he has served for 15 years both in India and in the United States. As South Asia correspondent for the V-O-A, he was in India shortly after the assassination of Prime Minister Indira Gandhi in 1984 to cover the political scene and the country's mood under the leadership of Rajiv Gandhi.

Razzle-dazzle Indian-style: that's Bombay, the country's most "trendy" city. Its superb harbor provides the city with the country's busiest port. Its airport is also India's most active for international arrivals and departures. And Bombay is not only the financial hub of India, it is one of the largest manufacturing centers in the East.

The busy metropolis rests on the Arabian Sea, an island set off from the rest of India by a winding creek. Perhaps it's this separation that sets Bombay's culture apart from that of the rest of India. Bombay's culture is new, vibrant, and often aggressive, reflecting the affluence and energy of a busy city of nine million people. Here, Maharashtrians, Gujaratis, South Indians, Parsis, Goans, and peoples from north India are joined together in their new home. When people from different classes leave Bombay, they feel an instinctive bond with other Bombayites, irrespective of their community of origin—which in India means language or religious group, the first thing an Indian wants to know about a fellow Indian.

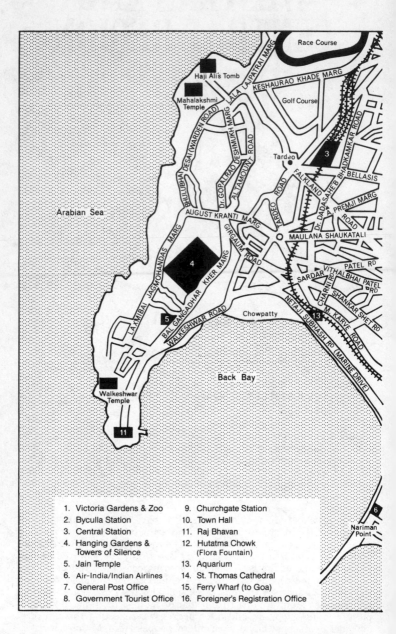

1. Victoria Gardens & Zoo
2. Byculla Station
3. Central Station
4. Hanging Gardens & Towers of Silence
5. Jain Temple
6. Air-India/Indian Airlines
7. General Post Office
8. Government Tourist Office
9. Churchgate Station
10. Town Hall
11. Raj Bhavan
12. Hutatma Chowk (Flora Fountain)
13. Aquarium
14. St. Thomas Cathedral
15. Ferry Wharf (to Goa)
16. Foreigner's Registration Office

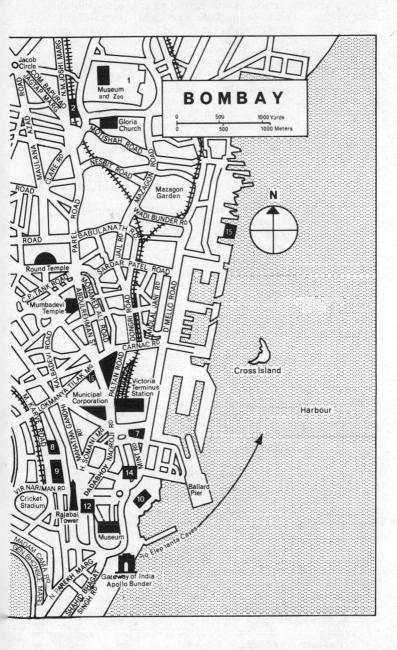

BOMBAY

| 0 | 500 | 1000 Yards |
| 0 | 500 | 1000 Meters |

Jacob Circle

Museum and Zoo

1

2

Gloria Church

MOTISHAH ROAD

NESBIT ROAD

MAZAGON ROAD

Mazagon Garden

WADI BUNDER RD

N

15

ROAD

ROAD

Round Temple

SARDAR PATEL ROAD

C.P. TANK ROAD

Mumbadevi Temple

CARNAC RD

16

Municipal Corporation

Victoria Terminus Station

Cross Island

Harbour

7

8

9

14

VIR NARIMAN RD

Cricket Stadium

Rajabai Tower

12

10

Museum

Ballard Pier

MADAM CAMA RD

GEN BHONSLE MARG

Gateway of India Apollo Bunder

to Elephanta Caves

While emperors, rajahs, and foreign invaders were warring along the river valleys and plains of India, the marshland islands (initially Bombay consisted of seven) remained untouched for many centuries by any but the fishing tribes. Yet the Arabian Sea connected these tribes—along with the inhabitants of the rest of India—to Africa. It was the sea that brought trade to the subcontinent even before the days of the Roman Empire and the sea that brought Europeans who first conquered, then modernized. The sea, in fact, created Bombay.

There were some Buddhist settlements near what is now Bombay, around the third century B.C., when the Mauryan Kings from the North ruled this area, but the seaports were more northerly and the big towns and elaborate courts were up on the plateau, above the Western Ghats, which rise sharply about 60 miles inland. The original inhabitants of the strip of land beneath the Ghats were joined by the Aryans, who were not fully absorbed until A.D. fourth century. It was then that the Maratha people emerged as a group and began to participate in the shaping of India's history.

But the strength and ruggedness of the Marathas came from the frugal hill areas, not from the soft lazy coast.

Maharashtra became the place of Hindu revival in the sixth and seventh centuries, exemplified in the creation of the Elephanta and some of the Ellora cave temples. Bombay's naval history may even have had a beginning at about the same time. The first people known to have taken an interest in Bombay's harbor were the Portuguese, 900 years later. (Vasco da Gama arrived at Calicut, farther south, in 1498.) Early in the sixteenth century, the sultan of Gujarat ceded the beautiful bay Bom Bahia—to Portugal. Had it not been necessary to add to the desirability of a royal princess, Bombay's destiny would have been different: Bombay or Mumbai or Mumbadevi—no one knows the exact derivation—was given as a dowry to Charles II of England when he married Catherine of Braganza. The British occupied the islands, began to join them, and established a fort and trading post. Shivaji, the greatest Maratha, made some raids on the British and used the booty to fight his wars with Emperor Aurangzeb. Although Bombay was within his territory, he was too occupied with the Great Mogul—chasing and being chased—to prevent the British from growing in strength. Eventually, Indians, who saw opportunities for trade and shipping, came to Bombay. The city grew in importance as other towns faded.

After many years of intrigue, betrayals, and mismanagement, the territory Shivaji had governed fell under the British. The *Peshwas,* the ministers who took over the rule of Maharashtra from the royal line, lost the Fourth Maratha War in 1818. The pride the British had in Bombay and their power over the western region are symbolized in Bombay's most celebrated landmark near Shivaji's statue, the Gateway of India, built to commemorate George V's visit in 1911.

An interplay of favorable circumstances made Bombay into India's industrial metropolis and one of Asia's busiest seaports. When the menace of Maratha sea raiders was finally broken, the East India Company's ships began to call at Bombay. Weavers from Surat settled there and, by 1850, the first cotton mills made their appearance. The outbreak of the American Civil War gave a further boost to this industry, as did a major land reclamation project in 1862 that joined the seven small islands into one. Soon coastal steamer services were started, followed in 1869 by the opening of the Suez Canal, which revolutionized Bombay's maritime trade with Europe. Since then, this go-ahead city never looked back and today Bombay claims 15 percent of all factories in the country and its textile industry accounts for 40 percent of the country's total.

In the past few decades, there has been a lot of reshuffling. In 1956, the Bombay State created at Independence was enlarged to include other Marathi- and Gujarati-speaking areas. Such a mammoth territory meant there were 48 million people talking in the main two languages, administered by one roster of government officials. A good deal of energy was wasted on linguistic controversy. Eventually the whole area was reorganized into Maharashtra and Gujarat states. The population of the state has grown rapidly since its reorganization, and the region is now among the most prosperous in India.

Exploring Bombay

Not far from the Gateway, beyond the Colaba market, is a village of the Kolis, one of the original fishing tribes. Although one word has a *c* and the other a *k,* you can see the connection. They speak Marathi, but they have their own ways. No one disputes a Koli woman's place in the bus line. The Koli women carry their fish all over town, walking with a fine stride, saris worn, Marathi fashion, skintight between their legs, and their hair slicked back, with flowers as if they are going for an outing or a movie. They do the marketing of the fish, and they keep the money. The men are sent out to master the waves and do their job of bringing home the fish; then they go to sea again. They are a very sociable group, spending lavishly on weddings and dancing and playing games all night on festive occasions.

The southern tip of the island is held by the Army and Navy. Within the military area is St. John's Church, called Afghan, because it was built to commemorate soldiers killed in the Afghan war. Its spire can be seen from all over Bombay. In the old churchyards near there, now dug up, you could read the gruesome story behind Britain's attempts to maintain its hold on India: cholera, plague, and malaria hit the families as soon as they entered the harbor. At low tide, you can walk to the lighthouse off the tip of the island, but be sure to come back before high tide. A club that civilians are allowed to use affords a refreshing open space to the pent-up South Bombayites.

In contrast to this part of the city is Churchgate, named for the gate in the old fort wall nearest St. Thomas's Cathedral. This area is all reclaimed land. The Mantralaya (State Secretariat), which by no means houses all the government offices, faces an inlet of the sea. Here also is the new, stunningly attractive, acoustically perfect Tata Theater, National Center for the Performing Arts, where regular performances of Indian classical music and dance are given. At Nariman Point is a rising modern complex of skyscrapers, housing offices, and hotels. Included are the Air India Building, with the country's only rooftop helipad, and a luxurious penthouse atop the Express Towers that Indian press baron Ramnath Goenka calls home.

Marine Drive

Between here and Flora Fountain (Hutatma Chowk)—hub of Bombay's pulsating life—are some of the city's most interesting institutions; the "Indo-Saracenic" Prince of Wales Museum and, in its grounds, the Jehangir Art Gallery; University Hall and the Rajabai Tower, which commands a panoramic view of Bombay's "Manhattan." Close to the harbor are the Mint, which you can visit, by special arrangement, and the Town Hall, with its wide sweep of steps.

Skirting along Back Bay is Marine Drive, famous as the Queen's Necklace, which can be seen at night from Malabar Hill's Hanging Gardens. The drive is a promenade in the evening; coconut hawkers from Kerala, wearing ankle-length white cloths wrapped around the waist, join the parade.

The wall in the sea has to be reinforced from time to time because the monsoon sea swings in with a ferocity that takes several people with it annually and would be capable of pushing the sea coast back to its original limits. Across the bay is Malabar Point where sits Government House, residence of the state governor, appointed by the Indian President. VIPs stay here, and a few special concerts and performances are held in this lovely spot.

Chowpatty Beach, with its statue of Tilak, a great political leader of this century, is one of the most important places in Bombay; it is the political nerve center. There are other places for big meetings in Bombay, but this site on the sea, accessible to thousands streaming in from all parts of the city and traditionally used for big festivals, gives a particular significance to any statement or decision made there.

This is where millions teem on big days like Ganesh Chaturthi. Rich and poor, frail and hearty move to the sea with clay or plaster or even silver or gold representations of Ganesh, the elephant-god. Families bring their statuettes from their dwellings to this location on the sea. On any evening of the year, Chowpatty is busy; yogis bury themselves in the sand, fishermen haul in their nets, children romp, and hungry working people flock to the stalls for *bhel-puri* (snacks) and colored drinks.

Not far from Chowpatty, at 19 Laburnum Rd. (off Pandita Ramabai), is Mani Bhawan, the home of Mahatma Ghandi when he visited Bombay. Today, the building is preserved as a national memorial and museum, containing a pictorial exhibit and a library, as well as a glassed-in preserved room where the Mahatma studied and slept.

Malabar Hill

The east side of Malabar Hill, which you see from Chowpatty, is covered with greenery topped by the Kamala Nehru (children's garden named for Nehru's wife). It's a long way round to get there. The hill road goes through Walkeshwar, a largely Gujarati neighborhood, where most saris are worn hanging down over the right shoulder. (The Gujaratis are a large group in the city and handle most of the trade.) Up on Malabar Hill and below it on the west side by the sea, are the mansions of wealthy industrialists who made their fortunes mainly in textiles. (Cotton grows in many places just north of Bombay and in what is now the state of Gujarat.)

B. G. Kher Road runs along the top of Malabar Hill. It leads past steep roads winding down to the Arabian Sea; all old novels of Bombay found a place for a car chase or two on these curving streets. On the hill is "Varsha," the residence of the chief minister of the state. Also on Malabar Hill is a temple with an interesting story behind it. A water tank in the temple is built around a fresh water spring which is said to have been created when the legendary Lord Rama's arrow struck the ground.

Bombay's Parsees

The greenery on the left as you go beyond the gardens is part of the Parsee Towers of Silence, the place where the Parsees dispose of their dead. (There is a model of the towers in the Prince of Wales Museum.) A park surrounded by a high wall conceals these bastions so that they are hardly visible. Even relatives of the deceased are not allowed to go beyond a certain point within the enclosure but may stay in the park where they can sit and meditate. Bearers carry the body to the top of one of these cylindrical towers where it is laid out to be immediately devoured by waiting vultures. The skeleton—after a few days' exposure to the elements—is then thrown down the tower's well where it is reduced to dust.

This strange method of disposal has a twofold explanation. The Zoroastrian religion—of which the Parsees are the last surviving community—respects the earth and the fire too much to pollute them with the bodies of the dead. Another of its tenets declares that rich and poor must unite in death.

The Parsees, who appear to be a numerous group in the city, are really a small minority, but their economic and cultural influence is considerable. They have done a great deal to build up Bombay's trade and industry; a large proportion of India's leading businessmen have been Parsee, and many of them philanthropists as well. Parsee means "from the City of Pars" in Persia, where this group came from to escape Moslem persecution 1,300 years ago.

An Open-Air Museum

Bombay, like most cities in India, is an open museum. Just listen to people speaking to each other and to their servants, how they ask a favor, how they quibble over prices, how they watch and take sides in a quarrel. In Crawford Market, at the junction of Dadabhoy Naoroji Road and L. Tilak Road, you will feel you are in an imaginary place. The bazaars, the hawkers with everything for sale, the goats bleating, the cotton-fluffing men twanging their beaters, the babble of languages —all but the horns of motor vehicles could be in ancient Babylon. An army of boys will carry your shopping or try to sell you shirt buttons and other odd items. They may be pests at times, but you can't say they are not practicing private enterprise. They have come to the golden city because it represents their best hope in life.

Keep up the fantasy and plunge into the opposite side of this Babel. For miles north of here are the homes of the multitude, but notice how many tiny shacks (with bedding rolled up on shelves) have bright shiny cooking pots and plants suspended outside in old tin cans. Traffic moves slowly enough in these sections to get good glimpses into the houses. They are enlivened outside with bright saris hung out to dry. One of the decrepit areas, Parel, was fashionable at one time. Look at the upper stories of houses in many old streets and you will see, above the shop signs, indications of better days. The crossing of the Quarter, let us say politely, of "courtesans," will not leave you indifferent.

The old Government House houses the Haffkine Institute, named after the Russian who came to India to work and discovered the cause of and cure for plague. Research is still done in the institute, and if you require snake-bite equipment, go there.

In Byculla, another older residential area, is the Jijamata Udyan. There is a zoo, but the profuse display of trees and plants is more than worth the trip. Outside the gates is a fine squat stone elephant taken from Elephanta, the island so named by the Portuguese. There is also a museum on the grounds. From here, you can cut across to the Race Course.

Environs of Bombay

If you arrive in Bombay by air, Juhu beach is the first strip of land you see as the plane comes down over the sea. A glimpse is all you get, but you must return to Juhu later, if only to have your fortune told. On the way, you cross the Mahim Creek. In this fishing village at low tide you can study the heavy ancient boats designed for the rough seas round about. On the far end of the causeway is a beautiful mosque, always white, always cool and noble. While you sun after a swim, you can have a snack of fried fish and see the performing monkeys. Juhu beach, once a secluded spot, is now crowded on weekends. When the tide turns, the undertow can become hazardous for the unwary. Pollution of sand and water is sometimes bad.

The local villages must be overlooked. They do not fit in with the idyll of palms, elegant leisure, and sun and sand as we would have them. Outside each hut is a string bed, and on that bed a man is often resting, with chores to be done lying all around him. When the villagers' city cousins come out for a day's picnic, it's fun.

Those who are interested in historical ruins should visit the fishing village of Bassein, farther north, ceded to the Portuguese in 1534 by Gujarat's Sultan Bahadur. This fortified town remained in their hands for 205 years, when it was conquered by the Marathas. British bombardment in 1780 damaged it heavily, but you still can see the civic and ecclestiastic vestiges of this once-prosperous Portuguese city. The *Porta do Mar* (Sea Gate) near the fort commands a splendid view of the sea.

Close to Bombay are spots of countryside totally different from the sea-blown open places in town. Aarey Milk Colony, the first Indian farm providing pasteurized milk on a bulk scale, is a popular Sunday family excursion.

The well-kept Krishnagiri Upavan garden, near Borilivi station, is a popular picnic spot, with a minitrain and a safari park with lions in their natural habitat.

The Elephanta Caves

An hour's launch ride from the Gateway of India is Elephanta Island, one of Bombay's major tourist attractions, as well as a reminder of India's past glories. Exactly who carved the cave temples on the island, originally called Gharapuri, or when, is not known. It is known, however, that the Portuguese renamed the island Elephanta after a large stone elephant found near the landing place. (The figure collapsed in 1814 and was subsequently moved to Victoria Gardens and put together again.)

Shortly before the time of Elephanta's excavation (between the sixth and eighth centuries) Bombay had experienced the Golden Age of the late Guptas, during which the talents of artists had a free scope. Sanskrit had been finely polished, and Kalidasa and other writers—under the Court's liberal patronage—had helped to bring about a revival of Hindu beliefs. It is the worship of Shiva, or Shaivism, that inspired these temples. That Shiva was well loved and the many ramifications of his personality well understood is shown by the polish and refinement of the artwork in the caves.

Crossing Bombay harbor on the way to Elephanta, you see centuries of India's life literally sailing before your eyes. The fishing sailboats in the harbor seem as much a part of the picture as do the modern liners. Tankers come full to Butcher Island, to the left of Elephanta. Their oil goes to Bombay's refineries. Behind them are the Tata electricity plant and the institute connected with atomic energy.

A flashlight and a knowledgeable guide on the island will help you to sort out the figures shown in the sculptures. You would have to be thoroughly familiar with Hindu mythology to understand fully each detail. But you cannot mistake the expressions on Shiva's faces, nor their intent. The powerful representations of strength, love, and spiritual peace at first seem buried in the dark halls. As you stay longer, they appear to grow and the walls to vanish, and you see them as a world in themselves. Part of the impression conveyed at Elephanta is the unity of dissimilar things, and likewise the differentiation one personage can undergo. Shiva gives good scope for such a portrayal.

The sculptures are great art, not only in the sense that they are beautifully executed, with a secure knowledge of the subject and a superb technique of the chisel. They show things we don't ordinarily think of as being there and combine apparently independent parts into new entities.

The outside of the main cave consists of a columned veranda 30 feet wide and six feet deep, approached by steps flanked by sculptured elephants. At each end of the façade is a pillar projecting from the wall, carved in the shape of a *dwarapala* (doorkeeper). The entire temple is 130 feet square. The main sculptures are on the southern wall at the back. Three square recesses contain giant figures of dwarapalas. The panel to the left shows a manifestation of Shiva combining the male and female forms, while on the right panel you see the figures of Shiva and his consort Parvati. The central recess in the hall contains the most outstanding sculpture, *Mahesamurti,* the Great Lord, an 18-foot triple image. The three faces represent the Hindu Trinity: Brahma, the creator, on the right; Siva, the destroyer, on the left, and in the center, Vishnu, the preserver. The multiheaded deity is a composite of the stern, just, loving, father-figure, an expression of the monotheistic tendency of Hinduism. On either side of the recess are pilasters carved with gigantic dwarapalas.

Other sculptures at the doorways and on side panels show Shiva's usefulness. Shiva brought the river Ganga (Ganges) down to earth—the story says—letting it trickle through his matted hair. The facts of the universe are played with in wild delight, represented through this god's acts. Shiva is depicted also as Yogisvara, lord of yogis, seated on a lotus, and as Nataraja, the multiarmed cosmic dancer. The beauty of this sculpture is in the grace, balance, and sense of relaxation conveyed in spite of the multiple action.

The fact that these sculptures were, in many cases, damaged by the Portuguese soldiery does not detract from their beauty. The serenity of facial expressions triumphs over the loss of arms and legs. In the magnificently fierce scene of Shiva destroying the demon Andhaka—he seems to be emerging from clouds in which his legs are hidden—one overlooks the broken rocks, so powerful is the remaining portion.

PRACTICAL INFORMATION FOR BOMBAY

WHEN TO GO. It is generally quite hot and humid in Bombay. The heat reaches a peak during what the Bombayites call the warm season—a mild understatement—between the end of March and the middle of June. From June to the end of September, it's monsoon time, but it's hot and muggy as soon as the rain is over. The most pleasant is between November to February.

HOW TO GET THERE. By Air. Planes of more than 50 international carriers land at Bombay Airport. *Indian Airlines* connects Bombay with major cities—Delhi (two hours), Madras (1½ hours), Calcutta (two hours), Hyderabad (1¼ hours), Bangalore (1½ hours). All flights are during daylight hours. From Delhi, there are five direct flights a day; from Madras, three flights; and from Calcutta, two flights. *Air-India* operates scheduled flights from Delhi, Madras, and Calcutta, day and night. Air-India offers a 25 percent concession to those who prefer to travel at night, that is, 11 P.M.–5 P.M. No off-season discounts are given by either airline. From Calcutta, Air-India operates twice a week. Among other international carriers that serve Bombay are *Alitalia, Pan*

Am, British Airways, Air France, Cathay Pacific, Gulf Airways, Kuwait Airways, Japan Airlines, KLM, and *Lufthansa.*

 TELEPHONES. The area code for Bombay is 022, which you need not dial within the city. If you are unable to get your number within the city, dial 199; for booking long distance calls, 183; directory assistance is 197. At public telephone booths, you dial the number and insert one 50-paisa coin, only after your party responds.

 TOURIST INFORMATION. The *Government of India Tourist Office* publishes a series of free booklets and maps on Bombay. These are available at any tourist information counter or at the main office in the city, located at 123 Carve Rd. (opposite the Churchgate Railway Station); tel. 293144. It is open Monday–Saturday, 8:30 A.M.–5:30 P.M. Every second Saturday of the month, it closes at 12:30 P.M., and it is closed Sundays and public holidays. Counters at both the international airport (tel. 6235331, ext. 253) and the domestic airport (tel. 6122053, ext. 278).

The *Maharashtra Tourism Development Corporation* (MTDC) is located on the ninth floor of the Express Tower, Nariman Point; tel. 2021713 or 2021762. It offers city and suburban tours daily, except Mondays, 9 A.M.–7:30 P.M. *India Tourist Development Corporation* (ITDC) is also located at Nariman Point; tel. 2023343. It offers tours and can provide accommodations. Certain travel agencies, such as *Sanghi International Travels, Travel Corporation of India,* and others offer ITDC-approved tours with guides. Contact the ITDC for details. No reservations are necessary, except for large groups.

 ACCOMMODATIONS. Hotels in Bombay are varied and well distributed throughout the city. They range from compact places with the barest essentials to grand and luxurious structures catering to the visitor's every need. Many new hotels have been built in the main city, but one should book well in advance for these, especially in the winter season, November and December. Hotel rates are based on double-occupancy, European Plan. Categories determined by price are: *Deluxe,* Rs. 900 and above; *First Class,* Rs. 700–Rs. 900; *Moderate,* Rs. 500–Rs. 700; *Inexpensive,* Rs. 500 under. Luxury taxes range from 5–10%.

AIRPORT AREA

Deluxe

Centaur. Adjacent to the domestic airport; tel. 6126660. 300 air-conditioned rooms. The hotel's wide range of facilities are excellent, with five restaurants featuring Indian, Chinese, and European cuisines. There is a swimming pool, shopping arcade, health club, tennis court, and putting green. A courtesy transport between the hotel and airport is also available.

Moderate

Hotel Airport Plaza. Conveniently located near the domestic Santa Cruz Airport. 80 clean, sparse rooms in a small motel with comfortable facilities and simple, modern decor. It has a reasonable restaurant, a swimming pool, and a disco. Free transfers from the airport.

Inexpensive

Hotel Imperial. 45 Telly Park Rd., Andheri East. The only passable hotel near the International Airport. 21 rooms with limited facilities; a restaurant and a bar.

Hotel Transit. Off Nehru Road, Ville Parle East; tel. 6129325. Located near the domestic airport. Restaurant and bar available.

BOMBAY
Deluxe

Oberoi Towers. Nariman Point; tel. 2024343. 931 rooms in one of India's tallest buildings, 35 floors, facing the sea, located in the new business hub of Bombay. Excellent guest services, eight restaurants, a bar, a fabulous seventh-floor garden swimming pool, and a coffee shop. Also available are a health club, beauty parlor, shopping arcade of 200 shops, and a convention facility.

Taj Mahal Intercontinental. Near Apollo Bunder at the Gateway of India; tel. 2023366. Actually two hotels with one check-in desk. The turn-of-the-century Taj, with 320 rooms, has been completely renovated but retains its Victorian grandeur, including ceiling fans and wicker furniture on the veranda. The adjoining 22-story Intercontinental, with 330 rooms, is among the best in India. Amenities include four restaurants and 24-hour coffee shop, health club, outdoor swimming pool, convention hall, and travel desk. The lobby is great for international people watching.

Welcomhotel Sea Rock. Lands End Bandra; tel. 6425454. 430 air-conditioned rooms. Well-appointed hotel with six restaurants, a travel desk, a club, a bar, and a full range of sports facilities. Transfers to and from the airport are also available. Member of the luxury Welcomgroup chain of hotels.

Expensive

Hotel Fariyas. 25 Arthur Rd., Colaba; Tel. 242680. 81 rooms. Centrally located, with a good range of restaurants, a roof garden, bar, and pool.

Hotel Natraj. 135 Netaji Subhash Marg; tel. 2044161. 83 rooms. Fine location and view. Restaurant and bar.

Hotel Poonam International. Shiv Sagar Estate, Annie Beasant Road Worli; tel. 4929954. 300 pleasant rooms with comfortable facilities.

Hotel President. 25 Cuffe Parade, Colaba; tel. 4951090. 300 rooms. Operated by Taj Group of hotels. Service and facilities are first class. Good Italian and Indian restaurants, a grill room, pleasant pool, terrace, and health club.

Moderate

Ambassador. Veer Nariman Road; tel. 291131. 173 rooms, some with air-conditioning.

Ascot Hotel. 38 Garden Rd.; tel. 240020. 70 air-conditioned rooms, not all with private bath.

Hotel Apollo. Landsdown Road at Apollo Bunder; tel. 202022. 55 rooms. Located just behind the Taj Majal International, this is a popular hotel for those who wish to be near the Gate of India. Hotel has a bar and a restaurant.

Bentley's Hotel. Oliver Road, near the harbor; tel. 241733. Air-conditioned and non-air-conditioned rooms. Breakfast included in the rates. Another Bentley's Hotel is located at Nataji Subhash Road; tel. 150693. Fan-cooled rooms; breakfast also included with the rates.

Ritz. 5 J. Tata Rd., Churchgate; tel. 220141. 73 rooms, some air-conditioned. Comfortable place near the main tourist office and the Churchgate Railway Station.

Sea Palace. 26 P. J. Ramachandra Marg (Strand Road); tel. 241828. Large building with some air-conditioned rooms and a restaurant.

Shelley's Hotel. 30 Ramachandra Marg; tel. 240229. Air-conditioned rooms for singles and doubles.

Inexpensive

The following offer basic amenities but are considered clean and comfortable.

Ascot Hotel. 38 Garden Rd.; tel. 240020. 26 air-conditioned rooms with attached baths.

Rex and Stiffles. 8 Ormiston Rd.; tel. 231518 and 230960, respectively. These two hotels share a building, with Stiffles occupying the first and second floors and Rex, the third and fourth. Basic comforts at each; some rooms are small and cramped.

There are no actual youth hostels for students in Bombay, but there is a **YMCA International Guest House** located at 18 YMCA Rd., near Central Railway Station; tel. 891191. The **YWCA International Guest House** is at 18 Madame Gama Rd.; tel. 2020445. Both offer bed and breakfast, and the YWCA takes in both men and women. Another YWCA is located at 34 Mostibai St.,

Byculla; tel. 372744. A **Salvation Army Red Shield Hostel** is located at 30 Meriweather Rd.; tel. 241824. It offers dormitory beds at a cheap price. Another Salvation Army hostel is also located in Byculla, at the Social Service Center, 122 Mauiana Azad Rd. It can be reached by the same telephone number.

JUHU BEACH

Deluxe

Holiday Inn. Bulraj Sahani Marg; tel. 571425. 210 air-conditioned rooms, with all amenities. Only two miles from the airport, this hotel faces the sea and has three restaurants, a coffee shop, and a range of sports facilities, including two swimming pools.

Moderate

Hotel Horizon. 37 Juhu Beach; tel. 571481. 140 air-conditioned rooms. Pleasant place but does not face the beach.

Sun-n-Sand. 39 Juhu Beach; tel. 571481. 132 air-conditioned rooms. Despite an uninviting foyer, this is an inviting place but with a cramped pool terrace.

Inexpensive

Kings Hotel. 5 Juhu Tara Rd., tel. 561803. 47 air-conditioned and comfortable rooms.

Sea Side Hotel. 39/2 Juhu Beach; tel. 561972. Doesn't face the beach, but the rooms are air-conditioned.

South End Hotel. 11 Juhu Tara Rd.; tel. 6125213. Fine budget value with both air-conditioned and fan-cooled rooms.

 DINING OUT. Bombay is a gastronomic high spot in which the traveler can sample all kinds of cuisines, from typical Indian dishes to Continental, Chinese, and Mughlai cooking. The most common Indian dish is *paubhaji,* a spicy mixed vegetable served with rice, available at most places, from street vendors to expensive restaurants. *Bhel-puri* is a popular snack available from almost every vendor at the beaches. The northern Mughlai cooking is so highly spiced at some restaurants that it seems to set off a volcano in your mouth, while the local Parsee cuisine is gentler in flavor. Bombay curry is, of course, a classic, and tourist-oriented hotel restaurants tone down the spiciness to your wishes. One of the features of Maharashtrian and Gujarati food is a sweet dish that is served as a first course and eaten with vegetable and *poori,* a mixture of whole meal and fine flour. Much less rice is eaten here than in other parts of India, and only a few places serve strictly vegetarian meals. Hotel dining rooms, as well as the independent restaurants listed in the expensive range, will accept major credit cards. For price ranges of classifications, see *Facts at Your Fingertips.*

Deluxe

Moghul Room. Oberoi Towers, Nariman Point; tel. 2024343. Classic Mughlai dishes, which can be softened in spiciness to your tastes. Extensive lunch buffet. Comfortable setting with Indian folk dances during dinner. Reservations suggested.

Outrigger. Also in the Oberoi Towers, same address and phone. Excellent Polynesian food in a ground-floor restaurant shaped like an outrigger canoe. Friendly service and pleasant ambience. Try their barbecue or seafood dishes. Buffet luncheon. Parties get special attention.

Roof Top Rendezvous. Top of the Taj Mahal International, Apollo Bunder at Gateway to India; tel. 2023366. Actually a supper club serving French and Continental cuisine that is well presented and tasty. Fine view of the harbor; entertainment and dancing to Western music in the evening. Reservations suggested.

Tanjore. Also in the Taj Mahal International. Fine regional dishes, as well as others (including Western), prepared at your request. Sup while seated on cozy sofas and enjoy top-rate Indian dancers and musicians. Very popular with the international crowd. Reservations suggested.

Expensive

Gaylord. Veer Nariman Road, Churchgate; tel. 220985 or 221259. Wide selection of Indian, Continental, and tandoori dishes; fully equipped bar; outdoor barbecue, either Indian (tandoori) or Western style.

Gulzar. Hotel President, 25 Cuffe Parade, Colaba; tel. 4951009. Largely Mughlai cuisine; recommended are dishes from Hyderbad and from the southern Mushal court. Fine traditional decor with entertainment during dinner.

Kabob Corner. Hotel Natraj, 135 Netaji Subhash Marg; tel. 2044161. A wide selection of tandoori dishes as well as other Indian and Continental foods.

Pasha. 55 Peddar Rd.; tel. 368332. Indian, Chinese, mughlai, and tandoori foods served. Bar serves only beer, but there's a posh permit room where you can sip your own spirits.

Talk of the Town. 1433 Marine Dr.; tel. 220883. Indian and Continental dishes served in pleasant surroundings, with live music and lit glass dance floor; outdoor garden.

Moderate

Chimney Restaurant & Bar. Filka Building, Daftary Road near the railway station in East Bombay; tel. 682973. Traditional Indian and Western foods served, with live music in the evenings. The restaurant also arranges for packed picnic lunches and snacks.

Chopsticks. 354 Linking Rd., West Bombay; tel. 5377789, 534729, or 539009. Good Chinese dishes (largely Cantonese) served either indoors or in an outdoor garden. Other Chopsticks restaurants, with similar offerings, are located at 90–A Veer Nariman Rd., Churchgate (tel. 2049284), and at the Jewel Mahal Shopping Complex, J.P. Road (tel. 625750).

Kwality Restaurant. India House, Kemps Corner; tel. 364991 or 369610. Indian, Continental, and tandoori specialties served from noon to midnight; soft recorded music, both Western and Indian. Other location: Band Box House, 252 C. Dr. Annie Besant Rd.; tel. 4936369 or 4938286.

Nanking Chinese Restaurant. Apollo Bunder, near Gateway of India; tel. 2022054. Wide selection of authentic Cantonese dishes.

Sher-E-Punjab Restaurant. 389–B Dr. D. B. Marg., Lamington Rd., tel. 361491, 380823, or 400004. Full range of Mughlai, tandoori, and Continental dishes served in pleasant surroundings with soft recorded music. Other location: 261–264 Sardar Bhagat Singh Rd.; tel. 265284 or 260431.

Inexpensive

Aroma Restaurant. 97 DaDa Saheb Phalke Rd., Dadar; tel. 449999 or 400014. Authentic Punjab dishes, with a family room for large gatherings.

Bristol Grill. Lakshmi Building, 22–A Sir P.M. Rd.; tel. 258462 or 291753. One of the few Bombay restaurants serving vegetarian dishes from southern India.

Gazebo "Open House." 537 Linking Rd., Bandra; tel. 546118. Feeling homesick? Relax; this place serves American fast food as well as confectioneries and ice creams, to the accompaniment of recorded Western music. Also caters to tourists with a take-out service.

New Yorker. 25 Chowpatty Sea Face; tel. 356108. Another place for homesick norteamericanos, serving pizza, sandwiches and Mexican fast food, as well as ice creams.

Oasis Chinese Restaurant & Bar. 211 S.V. Rd., West Bombay; tel. 400058. Traditional Cantonese dishes, with light recorded music.

Rasna Restaurant. Near K. C. College, Churchgate; tel. 220995 or 220790. Indian, Punjabi, Chinese, south Indian, Gujarati, and vegetarian snacks. Other amenities include a garden cafe, Indian fast food, and packed picnic lunches.

Samrat. Prem Court, J. Tata Road, Churchgate; tel. 220022 or 220942. Rather large place, serving strictly vegetarian Gujarati, Thali, and Punjabi dishes.

 HOW TO GET AROUND. From the Airports. Bombay is the foremost Indian city to provide separate airport terminals for domestic and international flights. Domestic airport (Santacruz) and International Sahar International airport are approximately three miles apart, but they share the same runways. A 24-hour **shuttle bus** links the two airports every 20–30 minutes. The airport departure tax is Rs. 100, and to the neighboring countries it is Rs. 50. No tax on domestic travel.

Regular **coaches,** run by an ex-servicemen's organization, go into the city center and cover all major hotels in between. The fare is Rs. 25 from both airports.

By Taxi. Taxis are available just outside the arrival hall, where one can pay in advance a fixed rate indicated at the counter itself for a particular place. From International Airport to downtown should not be more than Rs. 80, and from Santacruz, it should be around Rs. 65. Any complaint against taxi drivers can be reported to the traffic police or the tourist office by just giving the code number of the driver or the taxi number. During rush hour, the journey can take up to an hour.

By Train. Bombay city is interlinked with an extensive local electric train network. Rates are determined by the distance to the destination. At every station, the train stops for only 15 seconds. To avoid traffic jams and for economic traveling, use local trains, which are the best alternative, although they tend to get overcrowded during rush hours.

By Bus. *BEST* (Bombay Electric Supply & Transport) runs a bus service all over the city and into the suburbs, but buses tend to get crowded during peak hours. We suggest you keep change to buy tickets, which start at Rs. 0.50 and also are priced according to distance.

 FESTIVALS AND SEASONAL EVENTS. Bombay enjoys a rather full calendar of festivals, all celebrated with gaiety and great enthusiasm. The year starts with the festival of *Makar-Sankranti,* celebrated in **January** by kite flying and the exchange of sweets and vermillion. **March** brings the colorful spring and festival *Holi,* a day in which people throw colored water on each other and participate in folklore and music. *Shivratri* is also celebrated in this month. It is a day on which everyone worships Shiva. A night of vigil is observed with devotional songs and recitation from sacred books. *Guddi Pawa* is the day in **March/April** when the New Year is celebrated. In **May,** *Shivaji Jayanti* is a day when everybody participates in a procession through the streets. Shivaji was the great ruler of the state of Maharashtra, who protected it from British onslaught until he died. As a show of respect, a procession is arranged in the honor of the great leader.

August has a long series of festivals. It begins with *Naag Panch.* Live cobras or the painted images are worshiped on this day, which falls on the fifth day of the Hindu month Shravana. Also celebrated with religious observance by the public is Battis Shivala. *Janamashtami* is the nativity of Lord Krishna. A special feature of this day is that earthen pots holding curd are strung high across streets. Young men stand on top of each other forming a human pyramid and attempt to break the pots, while a merry and mixed audience watches. On *Coconut Day,* coconuts are offered to propitiate the sea, as fishermen set out in their boats. There is also the exchanging of sacred threads and a recitation from the scriptures rendered at a public place. The most famous festival is *Ganesh Chathurthi.* It's a colorful festival with a special feature in Bombay. The celebration includes worshiping Lord Ganesha in almost every house. A public procession is held in the streets, to the chanting of sacred songs and then Ganesha's image is immersed in the sea.

September marks the celebration of *Dusshera* and *Navratri,* a 10-day festival of fireworks, with colorful folk dances and music. It is celebrated at night for nine days to worship the mother goddess of the Hindu pantheon. Big fairs are held and temporary shrines are constructed for public worship. *Garba* and *Dandi Ras* (folk dances) are performed everywhere.

Diwali, in **October,** is a festival marking the beginning of the Hindu new year. On this night, every house is lit with candles and lamps to welcome the goddess of wealth, Laxmi. People exchange greetings and distribute candies. A social festival celebrated with fireworks and various cultural programs is organized. The Moslem festival *Ramadan* marks the end of the month of Ramzan during which every devout Moslem fasts each day until sundown.

All Moslem festivals are set according to the lunar calendar. But Christians make up a good percentage of Bombay's population. *Mount Mary's Feast* in **September** is celebrated with great solemnity at St. Mary's Church, Bandra. *Christmas* is also very special in the city. Office buildings and bazaars are lavishly decorated, colored lights festoon downtown, and parties and various cultural programs are held in hotels and public places.

TOURS. The MTDC offers five-hour **city tours** as well as all-day suburban tours daily, except Mondays. The city tour starts from the Taj Mahal Intercontinental Hotel (old section) at 9 A.M. and 2 P.M. This tour includes the nearby Gateway of India, Aquarium, Jain Temple, Hanging Gardens, Kamla Nehru Park, Mani Bhavan (where Gandhi stayed), Prince of Wales Museum, World Trace Center (closed Sundays), Worli Dairy, and Nehru Science Center. The cost is about Rs. 40 per person. MTDC is located at the Express Tower at Nariman Point.; tel. 2021713 or 2021762.

City tours are also conducted by *Sanghi International Travels,* 29 Patkar Marg (tel. 6425061); ITDC office, Nirmal Building, Nariman Point (tel. 2023343); and *Travel Corporation of India, Pvt., Ltd.,* first floor of Chandramukhi, Nariman Point (tel. 2021881).

MTDC daily **suburban tours** via luxury coaches also leave from the Taj Mahal Hotel, departing at 10 A.M. and returning about 7 P.M. The cost per person is Rs. 65, excluding food. It is suggested that you carry your lunch with you. This all-day tour includes Juhu Beach, Aarey Observation Point, Tulsi Lake, Kanhari Caves and National Park, Pawai and Vihar lakes, Worli Dair, and World Trade Center.

Tours are also available via **private air-conditioned car** or limousine with driver. A limousine for five people costs about Rs. 650 for four hours and about Rs. 850 for eight hours. Non-air-conditioned cars for four people cost about Rs. 300 and Rs. 500, respectively. Contact the MTDC for approved car operators.

MTDC also has three four-hour trips to Elephanta Caves, departing from Gateway of India at 9 A.M., 10 A.M., and 2:30 P.M. The cost is about Rs. 30 per person without food. Guides are available at the caves. During the monsoon (June–September) trips are suspended. Trips to other neighboring places such as Aurangabad, which include sightseeing, boarding, and lodging at Hotel Amarpreet, cost Rs. 765–Rs. 880. For those who prefer to stay in Ajanta Ambassador, the coach leaves daily at 8:30 P.M. from the tourist office. The cost to Mahabaleshwa, Panchgani, Shirdi, Pune, and Goa by luxury coach and launches ranges from Rs. 50 to Rs. 120. No advance booking is required unless it's a large group. Here are some excursions you may wish to consider:

Cheul. A morning launch from Ferry Wharf-Mazgaon Docks will take 1½ hours to Revas, on the mainland. A bus runs the remaining 20 miles to Cheul, the most ancient historic spot near Bombay, said to be over 3,000 years old. Gujaratis, Arabs, Portuguese, Konkan, kings, and Ahmednagar sultans have left vestiges of their various styles. The ruined Moslem Korlai Fort, on a cliff by the sea, faces across the Roha River. The Portuguese Palm Garden Fort, also in ruins, includes St. Barbara's, a fortified Franciscan church.

Kanheri Caves are situated near Thana, 28 miles away. They are reached by both train and motor vehicle. This is one of the largest groups of Buddhist caves in western India, numbering more than 100. A special feature of the caves is that they have been excavated from a huge circular rock. Climbing the flights of steps in the rocky mountain side, which connect the caves, is the most interesting part of the excursion. Caves 1, 2, and 3 are the most outstanding for their pillars, sculpture of Buddha idols, and stups. These caves are also included in various suburban tours.

The *Fort of Bassein,* 30 miles from Bombay, was constructed by the Portuguese in the fifteenth century. To reach the fort, travel by local electric train to Bassein Road and then by hired cars available at the station for seven miles. There are still a few battered structured standing, mostly churches and bunders (fortified walls) opening out on the fort. Manvi Bunder has a gorgeous view of the sea. Contact the MTDC office for arrangements.

Karla Caves are 100 miles by train to Lonavala and then 11 miles by road. Buses are available at the Lonavala railway station. The Buddhist rock-cut Chaitanya Hall of Karla dates back to the second century B.C. An inscription on the entrance attributes its excavation to Bhutapal of Vaijayanti. The caves are approached by a rough path of about two miles. Sedan chairs are available. Allow a full day for your visit.

Karla Bird Sanctuary, for lovers of wild life, is 61 miles away on the Bombay-Goa highway. State Transport buses go to Panvel and then to Karla. About 150 species of birds have been spotted at the sanctuary, 30 of which are migratory. The rare ashy minivet, a native of the Philippines, has been found here.

 **HISTORIC SITES.** *Gateway of India,* at Chhatrapati Shivaji Marg, is the landmark of Bombay, a 26-meter-high stone archway, designed by Wittett in the sixteenth century Gujarati style and built to commemorate the visit of King George and Queen Mary to India in 1911. An equestrian statue of Chhtrapati Shivaji and a statue of Swami Vivekanand have been installed here.

Haji Alis Tomb. Situated at the end of a causeway off Lala Laipaitra Marg, this tomb and mosque are devoted to a Muslim saint who drowned there while on a pilgrimage to Mecca. When a casket containing the immortal remains floated and came to rest on a rocky bed in the sea, devotees constructed the tomb and mosque at this spot. It can be visited only during the low tide.

Hantatma Chowk, formerly known as Flora Fountain, is the business center of Bombay, surrounded by offices, banks, shops, and colleges. On Sundays, there is a marked change; peace reigns in the area because most of the places are closed.

High Court, situated at K. B. Patil Marg, is an attractive building constructed in early Gothic style. The central structure rises 54.2 meters and is surrounded by a statue representing justice and mercy. It was completed in 1878.

Municipal Corporation Building, at Mahapatra Marg, is the V-shaped building standing opposite Victoria Terminal. It is designed in early Gothic style, blended with Indian motifs. The dome, its chief architectural feature, is 71.5 meters from the ground.

Rajabhai Tower, located at K. B. Patil Marg, is 79 meters high. Its university clock tower also houses the university library. Built in nineteenth-century Gothic style, it commands a fine view of the city.

Victoria Terminal, one of the largest buildings in Bombay, situated at Dadabhai Noroji Marg, was designed in the Gothic style. The imposing dome is surmounted by a figure symbolizing progress. A life-size statue of Queen Victoria is in front of the central facade. A clock on the top is 3.19 meters in diameter. The first train to steam out of Bombay went to Thane in 1853; since then, it has become one of the main railway stations.

 SPECIAL-INTEREST SIGHTSEEING. *Marine Drive,* at Nataji Subhash Road, is a promenade encircling the bay. The promenade is often referred to as the "Queen's Necklace" because of the sparkle of lights along it at night and their reflection on the water.

At *Nehru Planetarium,* situated at Lala Lajpat Rai Marg, one can get an entirely different perspective of the heavens. The planetarium projects images of the sky seen from anywhere on earth at the present or 2,000 years into the past or future. Open 3–6 P.M.; closed Mondays. Fee: Rs. 2.

Taraporewala Aquarium, located at Netaji Subhas Road, contains interesting specimens of marine life as well as freshwater fish. Shells, shellcraft articles, and fishery byproducts are also on display. Open 11 A.M.–8 P.M.; closed Mondays. Fee: Rs. 1.50.

 MUSEUMS. *Mani Bhavan,* a house where the great leader Mahatma Gandhi lived, has been converted into a museum. Located at Laburnum Road, it has an interesting collection of Gandhi memorabilia and contains a picture gallery and library of books by and about Gandhi. Open 9:30 A.M.–6 P.M. Entry fee: Rs. 1.

Nehru Science Museum, at Lala Lajpat Rai Marg, has a permanent gallery called light and sight gallery, consisting of exhibits related to the properties of light. It also has a Children's Science Park that contains antique exhibits, such as a railway engine, supersonic aeroplane, and steam lorry. Open noon–7 P.M.; closed Mondays. Entry fee: Rs. .05; free for students on educational tours.

Prince of Wales Museum. Bombay's principal museum, located at Mahatma Gandhi Road. It is divided into three sections: art, archaeology, and natural history. Miniature paintings of Rajasthan and the Deccan School of Art are exhibited in the circular gallery of the main building, designed in the Indo-

Saracenic style, with an imposing dome in the fifteenth-century western Indian style. The museum is named after Britain's King George, VI, who as prince of Wales laid the foundation stone of the museum in 1905. The Tata family collection forms part of the archaeology and art sections. The natural history section was started with part of an admirable collection of the Bombay Natural History Society. The picture gallery contains, in addition to ancient Indian paintings, some by European and contemporary Indian artists and copies of Ajanta murals. There is also a large collection of jade, crystal, china, lacquer, and metal objects, both ancient and modern. There are some excellent dioramas in the natural history section. The museum has an interesting collection of exhibits from the Maratha period. Open 10 A.M.–6:30 P.M. March–June and October–February; closes at 6 P.M. July–September. Closed on Mondays. Entry fee: Rs.1.50, free on Tuesdays.

Victoria and Albert Museum, situated in Byculla, is the oldest museum in Bombay. The three principal sections are those of natural history, archaeology, and agriculture. There is also a small collection of miscellaneous art objects. Most of the exhibits in the museum relate to Bombay and western India. There are displays of archaeological finds, maps, and photographs of Bombay's history. Open 10:30 A.M.–5 P.M. Mondays, Tuesdays, Fridays, and Saturdays; 10 A.M.–4:45 P.M. Thursdays; 8:30 A.M.–4:45 P.M. Sundays; closed Wednesdays. Entry fee: Rs. 1.50.

 ART GALLERIES. *Jahangir Art Gallery,* adjoining the Prince of Wales Museum at Mahatma Gandhi Road, is Bombay's main art gallery. In the same building are *Chemould* (upstairs), *The Connoisseur,* and *The Jehangir Nicholson Museum of Modern Art,* which features contemporary international shows. The *F.D. Apailwala Museum,* on Babulnath Road, Khareghat Colony, contains a small general collection in a former private residence. Most galleries are open 10 A.M.–7 P.M.

 PARKS AND GARDENS. Greenery and wild plants are a rare sight in Bombay, so its parks and gardens are cultivated with more care.

Ferozshah Mehta Garden (Hanging Gardens) at Bal Gangadhar Kher Marg, was laid out in 1881 on top of a reservoir that supplies water to many areas. A special feature of this garden is its topiary hedges that are pruned into animal shapes. A flower clock can also be seen here.

Veermata Jijabai Bhonsle Udyan at Dr. Babasaheb Ambedkar Road, known as Victoria Gardens, has a clock tower, ornamental gates, a varied collection of more than 300 wild plants and trees, and a sun dial, all adding to the beauty of the place, at a bandstand. From time to time, musical programs are performed. Elephant, camel, and pony rides are available for children. Closed Mondays. Open 8 A.M.–6 P.M.; rides, 3–5 P.M. Entry fee; Rs. 1.

Kamala Nehru Park at B. G. Kher Marg, was laid out in 1952. It is mainly an amusement park for children, named after the wife of the first prime minister of India. Civic receptions are also held here. On the slopes of Malabar hills, it offers a panoramic view of Marine Drive and Chowpatty Beach. It is illuminated on the Republic and Independence days.

Sanjay Gandhi National Parks is 35 miles from the city. Take the suburban local train to Borivli and a hired car for 11 miles to the park. The park is also known as Krishna Giri Upavan. The Lion Safari Park within gives visitors an opportunity to watch the Indian lion from special closed vehicles provided by the park. Open 9 A.M.–5 P.M. Closed Mondays and on Sundays if Monday is a public holiday. Entry fee: Rs. 5, adults; Rs. 2.50, children.

 BEACHES. Bombay beaches in the main city are no longer clean or maintained properly by the authorities. They are rather crowded and dirty. Suburban beaches are certainly a better alternative.

Chowpatty Beach, at the end of Marine Drive, is a popular beach in the center of the city, where the celebration of festivals such as Ganesh-Chathurthi immersion takes place. It is crowded most of the time, surrounded by kiosks and hawkers selling Bombay special snacks. The beach has become more of a venue for political meetings and gatherings than a place for swimming. The water is too polluted for that, anyway.

Erangal Beach is 35 miles from the city. Travel by suburban local train to Malad and then by road. Hotels and cottages are available.

Juhu Beach is 21 miles from the city. Travel by suburban local train to Santacruz and then by road. Best bus service also has special runs on Sundays and holidays. The five-mile beach is fringed with palm and coconut trees. A popular beach for all, it has a number of hotels, cottages, and restaurants. Horse, camel, and pony rides are also available. You can swim from October until May.

Gorai Beach is 59 miles via Borivli, Bhayander. The nearest railway station is at Borivli; then by road to Gorai creek and across by ferry. Then go by bus or horse carriage to the beach. Private shacks are available.

Madh, Marve, and Manori Beaches, the three famous "Ms", are 45 miles away. Take the suburban train to Malad and then go by road. All three beaches are a little distance from each other. There is a ferry service from Marve Beach to Manori Beach.

ZOO. Located at Dr. Babasaheb Ambedkar Road. Over 80 cages and enclosures are the homes for a prolific collection of animals and birds in Victoria Gardens. Animals range from elephants to the tiniest birds. Roaming around the zoo, thousands of visitors see fine specimens of tigers, lions, zebras, giraffes, bears, kangaroos, deer, antelopes, and chimpanzees, along with the rare and common bird collections. Open 8 A.M.–6 P.M. Closed Mondays. Entry fee: Rs. 1.

CHURCHES AND TEMPLES. *Afghan Church,* built in 1847, is known as St. John Church. It is dedicated to the British soldiers who fell in the Sind and Afghan campaigns of 1838 and 1843.

Ambernath Temple is located near Kalyan, 74 km by suburban electric train and then 1.6 km by road. It's an eleventh-century Chaulkyan temple with three entrances. Inside the temple is a broken figure of a Nandi, which is carved and adorned with ornaments. The floors also look richly ornamented. On the huge doorways are pillars carved with tracery and human figures.

Jain Temple, built in 1904, is located at the Ridge Road. This marble temple is dedicated to Adinath, the first *Tirthankara* (apostle). The walls of the temple are adorned with colorful paintings, depicting various incidents in the lives of 24 Tirthankaras of the Jain religion. On the first floor is a special shrine, dedicated to Parsavanath, carved out of black marble. The ceiling also shows the different planets as personified in Hindu mythology.

Mahalaxmi Temple, at Madav Bagh, is dedicated to the goddess of wealth, Laxmi. It is adorned with idols of various Hindu gods.

LAKES DISTRICT. The Bombay area has many artificial and natural lakes where one can go for a picnic and spend the day relaxing, hiking, or exploring. Here are four of the most popular and most scenic.

Powai Lake, about 15 miles from Bombay, is a wonderfully refreshing sight. Tall palm trees surround the lake. You can hire a boat or fishing craft owned by the Angling Association of India. This lake is totally dependent on the monsoon. On one side of the lake are rows of hills, each one higher than the other. To get to Powai, take a suburban Kurla train to Andherim and then by taxi. Best buses go to the lake on Sundays and holidays.

Tanso Lake is 65 miles by suburban train to Atgaon and then by road. Allow half-a-day to spend enjoying the scenery.

Tulsi Lake is about 12 miles from Bombay. Travel to Goregaon by train and then by road. Tulsi is the most beautiful of all the lakes in the Bombay area, surrounded by hills on all sides. On the eastern side, one can glimpse the Kaneheri Caves. Below the lake is Power-loom with a pretty garden laid out on a miniature terrace.

Vihar Lake is within a mile of Powai Lake. A stone clock at the site shows the time of the day by the shade it casts. The lake has plenty of crocodiles, lazying around only in remote parts. Nearby is also an amusement park and a one-story inspection bungalow is available.

SHOPPING. The best buys in Bombay are the handicrafts of western India, handwoven tie-dyed textiles from Gujarat, printed cottons from Nasik and Baroda, and handloom silks and saris from Aurangabad. Golden-bordered delicate muslins and silks of Khambat (Cambay) and Surat are also desirable, as are specialties of the Bombay region.

The two main shops are the *Government Emporium Handloom House* and *Khadi & Village Industries* at Dadabhai Narroji Road. Across the street and a short distance into Sir P. Mahta Road are *Uttar Pradesh Emporium* (for silks, brocades, and cottons), *Cottage Industries,* and *Bihar Emporia,* all good for textiles, as is *Central Cottage Emporium* near the Gateway of India.

Nearby, at Shivaji Maharaj Marg, behind the Taj Mahal Hotel, are many shops offering carpets and curios. Recommended is *Phillips Antiques,* opposite the Regal Cinema Hall, a treasure house for bric-a-brac and rare finds, much of them from the British raj period. *Crawford Market* is a colorful place for browsing and bargaining. The new *Craft Centre,* Nariman Point, has a number of state handicraft shops, as does the *World Trade Centre* at Cuffe Parade.

Most of the deluxe and expensive hotels have shopping arcades; the largest shopping arcade is at the *Oberoi Towers,* with 200 shops. Prices are, of course, much higher at these arcades than at the markets. At the famous *Thieves Market* (Chor Bazaar), you can bargain for items, from Victorian ceramic tiles to nautical instruments salvaged from sunken Portuguese ships to precious stones and jewelry.

Note: Genuine goods are available in all government-operated shops, where prices are fixed. These shops are open 10 A.M.–7 P.M. Bazaars are open until 9 P.M. Major credit cards are accepted at most shops. Although traveler's checks are almost universally accepted, it is best to keep some small change with you because some shops offer chips in lieu of change.

FILMS. As the center of the world's largest film-producing country, Bombay certainly has its share of movie houses as well as actors and actresses. India produces some 600 films a year, nearly half of them made in Bombay. Indian films generally are extravaganzas, containing a bit of everything from romance and music to drama and suspense. Such films are called *masala,* after the all-purpose word for spices that are added to practically every dish. Few of the Indian-made films are in English, but some have subtitles. There are also some cinemas, like the Foreign Film Theatres, that show films made in the United States or England. Since Bombayites are great moviegoers, it's best to get your tickets in advance. Check the local newspapers for listings. Admission to movie houses is Rs. 3–Rs. 6.

Perhaps more interesting is a visit to one of the film studios. Such a visit can be arranged with ease, for a small fee, by the ITDC (tel. 2023343).

NIGHTLIFE. Bombay has several discos, mostly in the international hotels, but they seem to lack the frenzy of such places elsewhere. The beat may be there, the music loud, and the lighting spectacular, but more often than not, the crowds needed to keep a disco lively are missing. These places are not crowded because the entrance or membership fees are high, making the places seem exclusive. The best of the lot is *Studio 29* in Bombay International Hotel, a hangout for some of Bombay's film stars and starlets. Also popular among visitors is *Xanadu* at the Horizon Hotel in Juhu, said to have the latest imported sound and light equipment. Other popular and safe places to visit are *Nineteen Hundred* at the Taj Hotel, with a very good design; *Cavern* at Sea Rock Hotel in Juhu; and *Take Off* at Hotel Santa Cruz, just opposite the domestic airport.

FORT COUNTRY OF
MAHABALESHWAR

Hills, Forts, and Cave Temples

by
KATHLEEN COX and RAVI KHANNA

After a tour of Bombay, with its rather fast pace, it's time for the visitor to head for the lush green hill stations around Bombay and relax. Tucked away here is a little hill station called Khandala. At the Karla Caves, you'll find rock carvings over 2,000 years old. And Khandala, Panchgani, Mahableshwar, and Matheran, are all picturesque places in the deep emerald green Western Chats.

Called the Fort Country of Maharashtra, the area was a stronghold of the legendary Shivaji, that great warrior. In the seventeenth century, Shivaji gave birth to Maratha power. Drawing inspiration from Hindu religious tales, he was fired by the idea of liberating his country from the grip of the Moslems. The tools were all there: a frugal, sturdy race of men and the hilltops of the Deccan Plateau, which could, with little effort, be made into impregnable small forts, excellent for highly mobile guerrilla warfare. The men under Shivaji were dedicated. They could scale the forts on these hills. They and their ponies could go where the elaborate Moguls could not.

There is the story of a Maharashtrian milkwoman, who, after the gates of one of Shivaji's forts were closed, climbed down a supposedly unscalable wall to return to her baby at home. Shivaji rewarded her and reinforced the defenses. In 1680 he died, leaving behind a new, powerful nation. The Maratha influence spread all over central India and became all-encompassing.

EXPLORING THE FORT COUNTRY

A few miles out of Bombay, you begin to move toward Kalyan and Ambernath. The eleventh-century Ambernath Temple, covered with beautiful designs, is one of best examples of Deccan temple architecture. A little difficult to find, the temple is in a valley between small hills and has a river running at the compound wall; a grove of trees completes this hidden, contemplative site. Constructed in 1060 to commemorate a king of the Silhara Dynasty and used for the worship of Shiva, this temple of exposed black rock has none of the commercial atmosphere of the paint and plaster city temples. Highly imaginative carvings, playful and spiritual, cover the temple, inside and out. Though the hall is not big, the sculptured dome makes it seem spacious. The *lingam* (phallus) shrine is in a crypt, which you climb down into. For worship, flowers are thrown onto the lingam and a temple priest throws water at intervals that flows out as holy water.

Once you are back on the main road, you head straight for the Western Ghats. On the left is the Matheran range, not yet accessible by road. At Panvel, a road branches off to Mahad, which is the old route to Mahabaleshwar. A small group of Jews have been living here for centuries, totally isolated from the outside world.

Matheran

Matheran is a resort, whose name means "woodlands overhead." The hill is an island of trees in an almost treeless plain. The approach to the town is in itself delightful. From Bombay, you can take a train to Neral, two hours out, where you see tiny toy trains that will take you to Matheran. The narrow-gauge railway of short, brightly painted wagons climbs leisurely through thickening woods. It's like a fairground joyride, with tunnels, sharp curves, and other thrills. Monkeys hop onto the train while little boys sell *jamun,* a small purple tree fruit.

Matheran is like going back in time. There are no cars, only rickshaws and horses. It feels good to shake off the city smells and sights and walk again. It's a picturebook town, complete with the resident ghost, but you can buy a crooked Pandhari stick to drive it away.

An Englishman, Hugh Mallet, collector of Thane, built this little town. Before he arrived in 1850, there were three tribes who lived on the hill. The tribes are still here, but, like everyone else, they have adapted themselves and now benefit from the tourists who come here.

Varieties of tall trees, some moss- and orchid-covered, shade you as you walk. From the tops of Louisa and Echo Points to the west, you can see Bombay, its oil refineries, the Elephanta caves, Karnala funnel —a 150-foot pillar rising from a much fought-over fort—and the sea. To the west of the hill is Parbal, which has a ruined fort. Between the hills roam panthers and wild boar. A path leading from One-Tree-Hill to the valley is named after Shivaji, who came to arrest an unworthy subordinate and stopped to worship at Matheran. Near the path is a Hindu shrine, from where three lingams are supposed to have emerged naturally, from the rock.

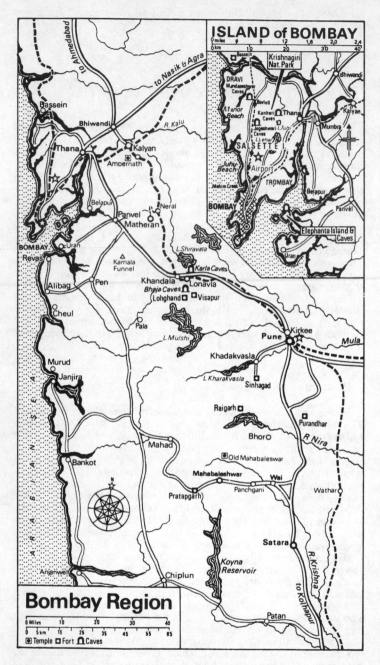

ISLAND of BOMBAY

DRAVI
Mandapeshwar Caves
Borivli
Manor Beach
Kanheri Caves
Bassein
Bhiwandi
Thana
Kalyan
Mumbra
Jogeshwari Caves
L. Tulsi
L. Vehar
SALSETTE I.
Juhu Beach
Airport
Mahim Creek
TROMBAY
Belapur
Panvel
BOMBAY
Elephanta Island & Caves
Uran

Krishnagiri Nat. Park

to Ahmedabad
to Nasik & Agra
Bassein
Bhiwandi
Thana
Kalyan
R. Kalu
Ambernath
Belapur
Panvel
Matheran
Neral
BOMBAY
Uran
Revas
Karnala Funnel
L. Shiravata
Pen
Karla Caves
Alibag
Khandala
Lonavla
Cheul
Bhaja Caves
Lohghand
Visapur
Pala
L. Mulshi
Pune
Kirkee
Mula
Murud
Khadakvasla
Janjira
L. Kharakvasla
Sinhagad
Raigarh
Purandhar
Bhor
R. Nira
Mahad
Old Mahabaleswar
Bankot
Mahabaleshwar
Wai
Panchgani
Wathar
Pratapgarh
Satara
Koyna Reservoir
R. Krishna
Anjanwel
Chiplun
to Kolhapur
Patan

ARABIAN SEA

Bombay Region

0 Miles   10   20   30   40
0 5 km 15   25   35   45   55   65
⊡ Temple ▢ Fort ⌂ Caves

The Karla and Bhaja Caves

The soft rolling hills quickly pass as the road levels out to the open planes between steep ranges. The solid black rock of the plateau, in some places 10,000 feet deep, is the home of many caves and forts. Four miles beyond Lonavla is a turning point to the left for Karla Caves, dedicated in 80 B.C. by Hinayan Buddhist monks, of the same sect that carved Kanheri. The main cave at Karla is the largest in the region. The sun window at the entrance was designed to slant the rays through its lattice work toward the *stupa,* a dome-shaped focus of worship at the end of the prayer hall. A drum built later at the entrance obscures some of the daylight.

Before the caves were rediscovered and protected by the British, wild animals had possession. The Peshwas had taken advantage of the holy site to put up a temple just outside the entrance, and there are small Hindu shrines tucked in along the ledge of the hill for good measure.

A fairly rough road leads to the Bhaja Caves. These 18 caves, in a lusher atmosphere than Karla, were probably meant for nuns. To the west of the caves is Longhand Fort. It was originally a Moslem fortification that Shivaji took twice, but lost again. Behind and above Bhaja Caves is Visapur Fort.

Toward Mahabaleshwar

Halfway to Mahabaleshwar from Pune is Sirwal, a watering place that was fashionable in the days when it took a week to travel from Bombay to Mahabaleshwar. Two miles beyond, there is an unmarked, but obviously Greek, templelike structure that resembles several temples of northern India of the fifth century. In ancient days, it was a tradition for charitable-minded people to chalk up good works for their future life. This small lonely hall contains two large water pots that have been neglected for years.

As you rise on the last ghat, the valley below becomes insignificant. On the right, shortly before the soil turns reddish announcing Panchgani, is a promontory called Harrison's Folly. Farther away is another outreach of land, Sidney Point. From here, you can look up to the top of the Krishna Valley, marked by a cone-shaped hill. A group of white spots to the left is Old Mahabaleshwar, a tiny village with three main temples.

For your first survey of Mahabaleshwar and its vantage points, follow the main road to the village and after buying a map, drive to the topmost point—Wilson Point—a flat open space. It was used during World War II by the army as part of its Jungle and Mountain Warfare Center. From here, you can view the mighty hills and dark-green valleys that would have been a rock garden for Mahabal.

Pune

Pune makes a wonderful base for a trekking holiday in the rugged low-lying hills that cover the surrounding areas. The former capital of the Peshwa administrations (1750–1817), it lies 119 miles from Bombay. Pune offers historical or pleasure explorations through monumental fortresses besides beautiful botanical gardens. A plateau 570 meters high in the Sahyadri hills near the west coast of India, Pune is a fascinating city with a bracing climate and healthy environment the year round. Known until recently as Poona, the city was the capital of the powerful Maratha empire and is closely associated with the great warrior King Shivaji (1630–80).

On the south edge of town is Parvati Temple, a white building prominent on a hilltop among smaller shrines. Easily climbed stairs lead up to it. From here, you can view the valley stretching to the first of the four ghats to be crossed on the way to Mahabaleshwar. It is said that after the defeat of the Marathas by Ahmed Shah Durrani at Panipat (1761), Balaji Bajirao was so heartbroken that he retired to Parvati Hill and died there.

Nonetheless, Pune recovered much of its former glory under Nana Peshwa in the latter part of the century. The saying *Jab tak Nana, tab tak Pune* (as long as Nana lives, Pune will live) expressed its faith in him. But the last year of the Empire was filled with strife, and in 1817, Pune finally fell to the British at the Battle of Kirkee. Under them, the city developed into the "monsoon capital" of Bombay Province and became a large military center.

Today, Pune is distinctly divided into the spacious cantonment and the crowded old city, where localities have been named after days of the week.

PRACTICAL INFORMATION FOR
THE FORT COUNTRY

WHEN TO GO. The best time to visit the hill stations and the cave temples around Bombay is from November to mid-June, when the weather is relatively mild and dry. During the rainy season, July–October, main highways may be open but those leading to the caves and other sights (particularly Matheran) may be inaccessible. We do not advise touring the region during that time.

HOW TO GET THERE. By Air. Daily *Indian Airlines* flights from Bombay to Pune take about 30 minutes. *Vayudoot*, the regional airline, also flies in three times a week.

By Car. Although the area is served by regular air flights and convenient trains, it is best seen by car in a day trip, or two, from Bombay. The distance from Bombay to the Kanheri Caves is 28 miles; to Ambernath, 46 miles; to Lonavala, 75 miles; and to Mahabaleshwar, 147 miles. From Lonavala to Pune, it is 39 miles, from Pune to Mahabaleshwar, 75 miles. (See *Bombay* chapter for car rentals with driver.)

By Train. The nearest points, such as Ambernath and Kanheri, are connected to Bombay suburban trains, schedules for which can be picked up at the Bombay station. Between Bombay and Pune (five hours), the *Mahalaxmi Express* and the *Deccan Queen* offer excellent service in first class; second class is also provided. These trains stop at Lonavala and Khandala stations. To go to places like Matheran, you change to a narrow-gauge, 14-passenger rail car at Neral, for which there is no regular schedule.

TOURIST INFORMATION. *Mahabaleshwar Tourist Development Corporation* (MTDC), Express Towers, Ninth Floor, Nariman Point, Bombay (tel. 2021713 or 2021962) offers all kinds of information as well as package tours to Pune and luxury coaches to Matheran, Panchgani, and Shirdi. A regional office of MTDC is located in the Central Building, Station Road, Pune. India Tourist Development Corporation (ITDC), will help also at Nariman Point, Bombay (2023343), provide guidance and help you hire a relatively inexpensive and comfortable private car with a driver.

ACCOMMODATIONS. If you don't take a day trip from Bombay, there is a wide selection of hotels, mostly in the *Moderate* range, at which to stay in the region. All have restaurants and some offer the American Plan (AP) with all meals included, so make sure you inquire before making reservations. Perhaps more important, ask if only vegetarian meals are served. See *Facts at Your Fingertips* for price ranges of classifications.

KHANDALA

Moderate

Hotel Dukes Retreat. Pune-Bombay Road; tel. in Bombay 269696, in Khandala 2187, 2189, or 2336. This comfortable retreat has 26 rooms, some with air-conditioning. Eight cottages and 18 suites. It also has a restaurant and garden cafe, recreation room, laundry, and games for children.

LONAVLA

Deluxe

Fariyas Holiday Resort. 8 Frichley Hill, Tungarli; tel. 2701–5. 90 air-conditioned rooms. Amenities include two restaurants, 24-hour coffee shop, indoor swimming pool, health club, children's amusement park, car rental, laundry, and valet service. The resort has well-kept grounds that include a lawn, garden, and nursery. AP available, as are package plans, according to the season.

Inexpensive

Adarsh Hotel. Shivaji Road; tel. 2353. 43 comfortable rooms, some air-conditioned, all with baths attached. Restaurant serves strictly vegetarian meals.

MAHABALESHWAR

Moderate to Inexpensive

Hotel Anarkali. Satara District; tel. in Bombay 4227306, in Mahabaleshwar 336, 429, or 430. Close to the center of town, this hotel has 37 non-air-conditioned rooms, a restaurant, laundry, and car rental services, as well as horse carriage rides. A 50 percent discount is offered off season.

Belmont Park Hill Resort. Willson Point; tel. 414. Only 14 double rooms at this resort, operated under AP, with Parsi and Continental meals provided. A get-together place that offers sing-alongs, bonfires, and table tennis.

Dina. Mahad-Goa Road; tel. 246. Bungalow-type hotel with 20 rooms, restaurant with a variety of cuisines, a playroom, laundry, and TVs.

Dreamland Hotel. Mahad-Goa Road, close to downtown area; tel. 228 or 239. 70 rooms (only four air-conditioned) and four duplex suites. Vegetarian restaurant, TVs, laundry, car rental, and children's playroom. Open October–mid June.

Fountain Hotel. Opposite Koyna Valley, Satra District; tel. 227, 425–7. AP only with the restaurant serving strictly vegetarian meals. Facilities include room service, indoor and outdoor games, a children's garden, laundry, hair dresser, and car rental. Open October–June.

Frederick Hotel. Bombay-Goa Road; tel. 240. Modest bungalow hotel with 32 rooms, restaurant, TVs, laundry, and car rental.

Mayfair. Mazda Bungalow, Myatt Road; tel. 366. Another small bungalow hotel with just 12 rooms. Operated under AP, with nonvegetarian as well as vegetarian meals. Facilities include TVs, laundry, children's play area, badminton court, garden, and car rental. Open October–June.

Regal Hotel. Bombay-Goa Road; tel. 317 or 444. Another AP-operated place with 31 rooms, vegetarian *thali* (all-you-can-eat) meals, laundry, children's playroom, and car rental. Open October–mid June.

PANCHGANI

Moderate

Amir Hotel. 188 Chesson Rd.; tel. 211 or 346. Close to downtown. 78 rooms, a restaurant, coffee shop, swimming pool, health club, and TVs.

PUNE

Expensive

Hotel Blue Diamond. 11 Koregaon Rd.; tel. 63775. A well-run, comfortable hotel with central air-conditioning for its 92 rooms and 12 suites. Amenities include two restaurants, coffee shop, bar, swimming pool, health club, laundry, travel agents, car rental, barber and beauty salons, bookshop, boutiques; folk and classical dances may be performed at the request of guests, who have the option of AP, MAP, or EP.

Expensive to Moderate

Amir. 15 Connaught Rd.; tel. 61840. 100 rooms, most air-conditioned. Indoor and outdoor restaurants, 24-hour coffee shop, bar, TVs in all rooms, health club, shopping arcade, barber shop, and car rental.

Moderate

Hotel Ashirwad. 16 Connaught Rd.; tel. 66142. Pleasant place one km from downtown. 42 rooms, some air-conditioned. Restaurant, car rental, room service, and laundry service.

Hotel Ranjeet. 870/7 Bhandarka Institute Rd.; tel. 59012 or 59142. Four km from Pune Railway Station. 25 rooms, half of them air-conditioned. Restaurant, room service, and bar permit room.

Inexpensive

Gulmohr. 15/A Connaught Rd.; tel. 61773–5. 32 rooms, only two air-conditioned. Restaurant, TVs in some rooms, bar permit room.

Shalimar. 12/A Connaught Rd., near the railway station; tel. 69191. 45 non-air-conditioned rooms, laundry, car rental.

Hotel Sutlej. Fergusson College Road; tel. 59065–9 or 59081–2. Centrally located between Pune and Shivajinagar. 35 non-air-conditioned rooms. The restaurant serves Indian and Chinese meals.

Hotel Suyash. 1547-B Sadashiv Peth, off Tilak Road; tel. 33414. 39 rooms, some air-conditioned. AP and EP. Facilities include restaurant, coffee shop, party room, and TVs with video films in rooms. Tourist cars available; city coach to airport.

 DINING OUT. Except for an independent restaurant in Mahabaleshwar, several in Pune, and a snacks place in Panchgani, it's best to take your meals at hotel dining rooms, where the food is often varied and well presented. It's advised to call ahead if you want to eat at a hotel at which you are not staying—not only to see if you can be accommodated but to determine the type of cuisine, particularly as to whether the food is strictly vegetarian. Independent restaurants here are all of the *Moderate* and *Inexpensive* classifications, based on price ranges listed in *Facts at Your Fingertips.*

MAHABALESHWAR

Moderate

Maikhana Restaurant. 92-B Masjid Rd.; tel. 223. Continental food served in a comfortable, air-cooled dining room seating 100 guests; beer bar. Open 10 A.M.–11 P.M.

PUNE

Moderate to Inexpensive

Amrapali. 1227 F.C. Rd., Lele Quarters; tel 59252 or 59021. Indian, Continental, and vegetarian meals served for lunch or dinner; air-conditioned and taped music. Open 11 A.M.–3 P.M. and 6:30–11 P.M.

Aspara. Udyog Bhavan, Tilak Road; tel. 440589. Centrally air-conditioned restaurant that also has a bar permit room, serving Chinese, Continental, and Indian dishes, 11 A.M.–3 P.M. and 6–11 P.M.

Chinese Room Oriental. Continental Chambers, Karve Road; tel. 34080 or 35179. Besides serving a wide assortment of Chinese dishes, this restaurant also has a bar permit room and is a station for delicious Indian-made ice cream. Try it. Open noon–3 P.M. and 7–11:30 P.M.

Chinese Room. 2434 East St., Pune Camp; tel. 63355. Cited by Famous Restaurants International for its fine food and service. Chinese food, of course, served in a 100-seat air-conditioned dining room. Open 11:30 A.M.–3:30 P.M. and 6:30–11:30 P.M.

Coffee House. 2 North Molodina Rd., Pune Camp; tel. 64974 or 67716. Despite its name, this 275-seat, air-conditioned dining hall serves Continental, Chinese, and vegetarian and nonvegetarian Indian and Mughlai dishes. Open 8 A.M.–11 P.M.

George Restaurant. 2436 General Thimmayya Rd.; tel. 61626. Western, Indian, and Chinese foods served either in an air-conditioned or non-air-conditioned room. There is also a juice and snack bar, ice cream parlor, and a pleasant garden. Open 9 A.M.–4 P.M. and 6–11 P.M.

Khyber. 1258/2 J.M. Rd.; tel. 51770 or 56149. Indian tandoori (barbecue) and Continental foods in air-conditioned room; beer bar and ice cream parlor. Restaurant also provides outdoor catering.

Kwality Restaurant. Bombay-Pune Road, Chinchwad; tel. 86090. Yes, there's one of India's famous chain restaurants located here, too, serving Indian and Continental meals. Open 11:30 A.M.–3:30 P.M. and 6:30–11:30 P.M.

Latif's Moghul Room. Rani Laxmi Bai Chowk, Maharaj Road; tel. 53247–9. Indian, Continental, tandoori, Chinese, and snack foods served in two rooms, one air-conditioned; beer bar. Open 7 A.M.–11:30 P.M. There is also a Latif's Cafeteria at 2434 East St.; tel. 60305. Similar foods and similar amenities. Open 11:30 A.M.–3:30 P.M. and 6:30–11:30 P.M.

Mayur Restaurant. S. No. 201 A/19 Chinewad (no phone). A small place with 40 seats serving only Indian foods. Open 11 A.M.–9:30 P.M.

Mazdana. 22 Dr. Amludhur Rd.; tel 28318, 23613, or 26712. A beautiful garden setting surrounds this restaurant that also displays antiques. The cuisine is Indian and Continental. Open for lunch and dinner.

Modern Cafe. 364/65 Shivajinagar, opposite Engineering College Hostel; tel. 59955, 59777, or 55888. All Indian meals prepared here, including vegetarian. Open 7 A.M.–10 P.M.

Oasis Restaurant. 595 Sachapir St.; tel. 26857. Indian, Mughlai, Chinese, and Continental foods served in a fully air-conditioned place that also has a bar permit room. Open 11 A.M.–midnight.

Poona Coffee House. 1256/2 Deccan Gymnkhana; tel. 59256 or 52970. More than a coffee house, this 320-seat restaurant also serves Indian, Chinese, and Continental foods, with live music provided. Open 9 A.M.–midnight.

Poona Restaurant. J.M. Road; tel 59051 or 59052. Perhaps the names of this restaurant and the Poona Coffee House should be exchanged, for this place serves only Indian food, including vegetarian. Open 11 A.M.–3 P.M. and 7–11 P.M.

Ruchira. J.M. Road, opposite Sambhaji Park; tel. 55440. A pleasant place with Indian, Punjabi, and tandoori dishes served to the accompaniment of live music. There is also a beer parlor and a bar permit room. Open 11 A.M.–midnight.

Shakun. 47/2 Poona Satara Rd.; tel. 440749. Punjabi and tandoori foods served. There is also a beer bar and bar permit room. Open 11 A.M. 11 P.M.

Sher-E-Punjab Restaurant. Alankar Theatre Building; tel. 65709. Specializes in Punjabi cuisine as well as other Indian dishes. Open 11 A.M.–11 P.M.

Restaurant Shreyas. 1242-B Apte Rd.; tel. 59023. Strictly Maharashtrian-style vegetarian foods served, either inside or on an open-air terrace. Open 5:30 A.M.–11 P.M.

 HOW TO GET AROUND. It is best to make arrangements in Bombay for travel in this region, whether by rented **car** with driver or in a package **tour.** If you want to visit only one section—the Kanheri Caves, for instance—you can do so in a day trip from Bombay. Both ITDC (tel. 2023343) and MTDC (tel. 2021713 or 2021762) can make the arrangements. In addition, several hotels have car rental services. Also, if you fly to one of the cities, there are also **motor rickshaws** to take you about at reasonable rates. Make sure, however, that the rate is established beforehand if the driver says the meter is not working.

TOURS. MDTC offers a variety of package tours of the region, either in luxury air-conditioned or non-air-conditioned coaches. Be prepared for blaring video tapes, however. Arrangements can be made either through MDTC (tel. 2021713 or 2021762 in Bombay) or through your hotel. Among the tours are

Mahabaleshwar—leaves daily at 7 A.M. and arrives at 2 P.M.; fare, Rs. 65 per person.

Matheran (Neral–Matheran–Nerali)—by taxi only; fare, Rs. 22.

Panchgani—luxury coach leaves daily at 6:30 A.M. and arrives at 2 P.M.; fare, Rs. 70.

Bombay–Shirdi–Bombay—luxury coach leaves daily at 10 A.M. and returns at 10:30 P.M.; fare, Rs. 150.

Pune—full-day sightseeing tour; fare, Rs. 16.

CAVE TEMPLES. *Mandapeshwar Caves* are about a mile from Borivli station, 15 miles away on the suburban line of the Western Railway (Churchgate or Bombay Central). They are the only Brahmanical caves in India that have been converted into a Christian shrine by the Portuguese. The three eighth-century caves are hewn out of rock. The third cave, on the west, a small *vihara* (monastery) was transformed in the sixteenth century into a Roman Catholic chapel.

Kanheri Caves are in a pleasant woodland five miles from Borivli station. They can also be approached by car. Although they belong to the early phase of Buddhist architecture, there are later additions, such as the fifth-century figure of the Buddha in the *Chaitya* hall of Cave No. 3. There are altogether more than 100 caves cut out of a huge circular rock. The main features of the caves are the flights of connecting steps cut into the rock and the stone seats where the monks used to meditate. The veranda of Cave No. 3 (second century) has in front two images of the Buddha, 23 feet high. Cave No. 10 was used for assemblies. The other caves are not worth intensive study. Available as an easy day's excursion by tour bus from Bombay.

Jogeshwari Caves (eighth century) are a mile from Jogeshwari station on the Western Railway's suburban line; on the island of Salsette, the original Bombay. Much defaced, they belong to the late period of Buddhist architecture. Brahmanical influence is evident; the shrines are isolated and stand in the center of a cruciform hall with several entrances. The long veranda has Elephanta-type columns, the square hall, 20 pillars.

The *Karla Caves* can be approached from Lonavla or Khandala on the Central Railway (Victoria Terminal). The outstanding feature of this group is the *Chaitya* cave, which is the largest and one of the best preserved of its kind in India (124 feet by 5 feet; height 46 feet). The Chaitya Hall's two giant pillars detached from the main structure have a group of lions supporting a large and badly damaged wheel. The fine railings and supporting elephants at each end (half life size and originally with ivory tusks) indicate an advanced stage of decorative art. The interior of the hall consists of 37 pillars, a vault, and a sun window. There are subtle variations in the carvings on the pillars. The sun window slants the rays and provides soft lighting on the stupa and pillars, creating a solemn atmosphere.

The 18 *Bhaja Caves,* about a mile from Malavli station (but just beyond Lonavla), were cut in the second century B.C. The face and entrance of the main cave (No. 12) are now open. The stilted vault is a fine piece of work. The last cave to the south has some good sculptures, including a prince on an elephant, a prince in a chariot, and the well-known dancing couple.

Bedsa Caves, (four miles beyond Malavli) are from a little later period than those at Bhaja. The chaitya here resembles the great hall at Karla, but is smaller. It has four pillars, about 25 feet high, with very lively carvings on them. Its ribbed roof is supported by 26 octagonal pillars 10 feet high.

Note. Bhaja and Bedsa Caves can also be approached by car, though there is a climb from the foot of Bhaja Hill. From Malavli station to Bedsa Caves, it's rough going; it's advisable to walk those four miles.

THE ELLORA AND AJANTA CAVES

Sacred and Secular Art Merge

by
KATHLEEN COX and RAVI KHANNA

Souvenirs of her glorious past still survive in India. The past lives on in India's continuity. There is no nostalgia for what was, no impatient anticipation for what will be. For the philosophy of the land dictates that to live for the moment is to share the spiritual joy of belonging. But the legends of India continue to inspire. One such legend surrounds the immortal rock-cut cave temples of Ajanta and Ellora.

Long forgotten and rediscovered by chance in 1819, the cave temples of Ajanta and Ellora must surely rank among the wonders of the ancient world. Here, over a period of 1,400 years—between the second century B.C. and A.C. twelfth century—great armies of monks and craftsmen carved cathedrals, monasteries, and whole cities of frescoed sculpted halls into the solid rock faces. Working with the simplest tools and an ingenious system of reflecting mirrors to provide them with light, they cut away hundreds of thousands of tons of rock to create the cave temples. The precision of their planning, their knowledge of rock formations, and the delicacy and profusion of their art have to be seen to be believed. It was an earth-shaking feat on the scale of the building of the pyramids coupled, if you can imagine it, with the creation of an art form "worthy of the Renaissance," and a religious fervor as intense as that of medieval Europe.

ELLORA CAVE-TEMPLES

(5TH C TO 8TH C AD)

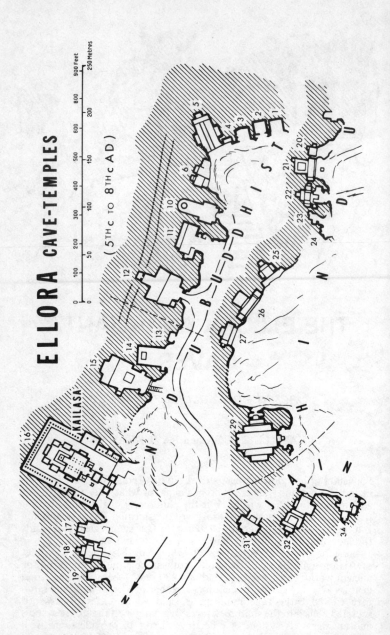

KAILASA

BUDDHIST

HINDU

HINDU

JAIN

N

The cave temples, between them, span three great religions—the Buddhist, the Hindu, and the Jain. They, by themselves, are reason enough to visit India.

First came Ajanta. It is believed that a band of wandering Buddhist monks first came here in the second century B.C. searching for a place to meditate during the monsoons. Ajanta seemed ideal because it was peaceful and remote from civilization. The setting was spectacular: a sharp, wide horseshoe-shaped gorge that fell steeply to a wild mountain stream flowing through the jungle below. The monks carved crude caves into this rock face for themselves, and a new temple form was born.

Over nine centuries, the cave temples of Ajanta evolved into a work of splendid art. Today, there are 29 caves in all; some of them were once monasteries, others were *chaityas,* or Buddhist cathedrals. All of them are intricately and profusely decorated with sculptures and murals depicting the many incarnations of Buddha.

Here, as a flickering light shines on the massive murals in the darkness, fables from the Buddhist texts come alive: Princes and princesses go about the splendid ritual of their lives; dancers perform to the sounds of a silent lute; richly caparisoned elephants and horses prance; celestial musicians play their instruments; great scenes of drama are enacted in courts, palaces, and bazaars; and a whole era comes to life again. But everywhere, at all times, spirituality flows deep and quiet below the surface. And the sensuous maidens depicted on the walls, your guide points out, were created to try the will power of the monks.

In the seventh century, for some inexplicable reason, the focus of activity shifted from Ajanta to a site 123 km to the southwest—to a place known today as Ellora. The cave temples of Ellora, unlike those at Ajanta, are not solely Buddhist. Instead, they trace the course of religious development in India—through the decline of Buddhism in the latter half of the eighth century, the Hindu renaissance that followed the return of the Gupta dynasty, and the Jain resurgence between the ninth and eleventh centuries. Of the 34 caves, 12 are Buddhist, 17 are Hindu, and five are Jain.

At Ellora, the cave paintings of Ajanta give way to sculpture, which often covers the walls in an exquisitely ornate mass. In the Buddhist caves, the carvings present a serene reflection of the Buddhist philosophy. But in the subsequent Hindu caves, they acquire a certain exuberance, a throbbing vitality. Gods and demons do fearful battle, Lord Shiva angrily flails his eight arms, elephants rampage, eagles swoop, and lovers intertwine.

The single most incredible edifice at Ellora is the Kailasa Temple—probably the world's largest monolith. Here, 85,000 cubic meters were scooped out of solid rock, laboriously by hand, to reveal a courtyard 45 by 30 meters—but leaving behind a lavishly carved main temple, and a three-story tower, cupola, and gateway—all linked together by an overhead vestibule. It is a tribute to the infinite genius of the ancient Indian craftsmen and their daring to have even conceived of such an idea. And they worked for hundreds of years. Today these cave temples are one of the wonders of ancient art. Though successive waves of invading Moslem armies badly damaged these artistic treasures, the cave temples that remain are enough to stagger the senses.

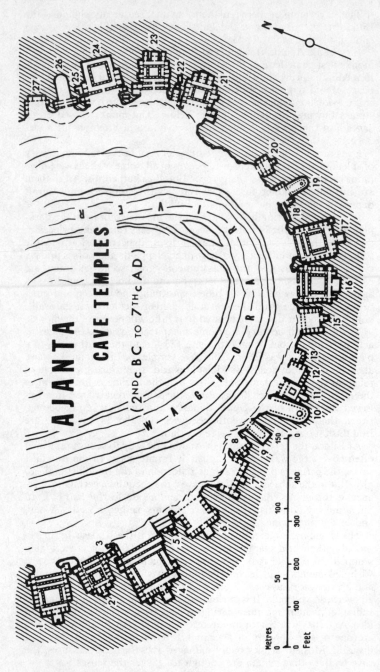

AJANTA

CAVE TEMPLES

(2ND c BC TO 7TH c AD)

EXPLORING THE CAVES REGION

If you wish to see the Ajanta and Ellora caves on your own, you have several ways of getting to them. But if you wish to play it safe, the best ways are the conducted tours from Bombay, Nagpur, Pune, and Goa by the Maharashtra Tourism Development Corporation. These tours are by air-conditioned and luxury buses that leave Friday and return Monday morning. The MTDC also conducts one-day tours from Aurangabad to Ajanta, Ellora, and around Aurangabad, respectively. A hired car or organized bus tour from Aurangabad is also a good alternative. To explore the caves at your leisure, you should use Aurangabad as a base for Ellora and Ajanta, 18 and 66 miles away, respectively. The quickest way of getting there is to fly (the train takes over nine hours). If you wish to enjoy the spectacular scenery on the way, a journey by train or car is well worth the effort. Both the rail line and the road run past Igatpuri, a hill station frequented by Bombayites seeking fresh air. From here, as you look southward, can be seen some of the highest mountains of western Indian and a few of Shivaji's hill forts.

By road, 90 miles out of Bombay is Nasik, which can serve as a good introduction to Buddhist cave art. The city, one of the holy cities of the Hindus, lies on the banks of the Godavari, a sacred river where every 12 years pilgrims by the thousands come for a purifying dip. The caves are on the east side of the town, near the river. Five miles southwest of the city are a group of 23 Buddhist caves known as Pandava Lena. These were executed in the A.D. first century and represent the Himayana style in which no statues of Buddha were permitted. A throne, a footstool, or footsteps were used to symbolize his presence. Each cave consists of three halls and a chapel laid out as one-story *viharas* or monasteries. Their setting is unusual and impressive, since they were chiseled out of a conical peak at the end of the Trimbuk Mountain. Caves 3, 8, and 15 are the real eye-catchers. In Cave 3, you find the stupa (a reliquary mound) and the *chakra* (wheel), symbols of Buddhism. There are images of Buddha in two other caves, but these were added later.

Ahmednagar, a historical Moslem city, lies on the route of visitors who are headed for the Ajanta and Ellora caves on the way back from Mahabaleshwar and Pune. Ahmednagar is named after Ahmed Nizam Shah, founder of the Nizam Shahi dynasty, who built it in 1490. Sixty years later, its main landmark, the fort, was erected by Hussain Nizam Shah. This battle-scarred citadel lies behind 1½ miles of walls. It gained notoriety when the British used it as a prison for Boer War captives in 1901 and in 1942, for Indian nationalist leaders, including Nehru. The Moslems left their mark with some monuments including Chand Bibi, the tomb of a royal minister six miles outside the city, and the Alamgir Dargah, the tomb of Emperor Aurangzeb, who died at Ahmednagar at age 97 in 1707 (his body was later removed to Aurangabad).

Aurangabad

Aurangabad takes its name from the Emperor Aurangzeb, the last of the great Moguls, who made it his capital. Here, since time immemorial, the sounds of history have thundered. And in the numerous fine monuments that lie in the region, you can see the influences of various empires, religions, and philosophies. Here lie the seventh-century Aurangabad cave temples—the historic medieval fortress of Daulatabad, with its miles of forbidding ramparts, once, oh so briefly, the capital of Hindustan.

Aurangabad today is a ghost town of legends, with its alleyways steeped in lore. It is the gateway to Ajanta and Ellora and is the most convenient headquarters for a trip there. And as a city in its own right, Aurangabad has many places if interest that will captivate the tourist. It is better to visit the caves here before visiting Ajanta and Ellora, for anything after them might well seem to be an anticlimax.

First there is the Panchakki. This pre-Mogul (seventeenth-century) monument is a mill where water was harnassed to turn large stones to grind flour. It serves as the tomb of a Moslem saint, Baba Shah Musafir, who was buried there in 1624. Baba Shah Musafir lies in a simple grave surrounded by gardens, fountains, basins, and an artificial waterfall.

Just two miles from the city center is a far more grandiose affair—the Bibi-ka-Maqbara, the mausoleum built in 1679 by Aurangzeb for his wife, Rabia-ud-Daurani. It is a rather pale imitation of the Taj Mahal, the masterpiece of his father, Shah Jahan, but it's impressive if you haven't seen the Taj. The exterior lacks symmetry and balance, and its interior decoration has nothing comparable with the wonder at Agra. Yet this royal resting place has its own splendor and grace.

Nearby also are Daulatabad and the Aurangabad caves. Daulatabad, a medieval fortress on a pyramid-shaped hill nine miles from the city, was originally known as Devagiri, the "Hill of the Gods." During the fourteenth century, it was renamed Daulatabad, the "City of Fortune," by the sultan of Delhi, Muhammad Tughlaq, who decided to move his capital there, 700 miles away. He moved the whole population of Delhi, too, a decision so mad that, after thousands died on this forced march, he ordered them to march back to Delhi. But Daulatabad remained, ruling the province from its mountain fort. The fort is surrounded by three miles of walls, and a visit here means a climb to the top of the rock, 600 feet high. When you get there, you are greeted by a huge cannon, 20 feet long, which somehow got there in the seventeenth century. One feature of the climb through the citadel is a spiraling tunnel 150 feet long near the top. Its upper entrance is crowned by an iron lid where defenders lighted a fire of hot coals to scorch besiegers in the tunnel. The Chand Minar pillar at the base of the fort was built as a victory column.

And then there are the Aurangabad caves, of which Caves 6 and 7 have the best sculptures. The other caves are separated by a mile of hills. At Aurangabad, the caves reproduce two forms of religious structures: the place of worship, or chaitya, and the monastery, or vihara. Carved out during the seventh century, the caves are later forms in Mahayana style. This style can be seen in such temples as Cave 1, with a Buddha on a lotus seat supported by snake-hooded demigods; or Cave 2, where a huge Buddha sits with his feet on a lotus; or Cave 3 with 12 carved pillars and another seated Buddha in front of his shrine. In the second group, which is a mile away, Cave 7 is interesting, with its huge figure of Bodhisattva Padmapani. (A Bodhisattva is a near-Buddha and one of the forms through which Buddha passed before he achieved enlightenment; *padmapani* means lotus-in-hand.) He is praying for deliverance from eight fears that are illustrated dramatically in stone: fire, the enemy's sword, the chains of slavery, shipwreck, attacks by a lion, snakes, a mad elephant, and death portrayed as a demon.

Ellora

Only 30 km from Aurangabad, Ellora represents what is perhaps the finest and most magnificent of Indian sculpture. Unlike Ajanta, where the temples were chopped out of a steep cliff, the caves at Ellora were dug into the slope of a hill in a north-south direction (they face the west and could receive the light of the setting sun). Many of the caves date back to the seventh century when Ajanta was abandoned and its creators moved to Ellora, 66 km away for some unknown reason. It was in this period that Buddhism started its gradual decline; that is why elements of Hinduism and Jainism can be found incorporated in the cave sculptures.

The style is post-Gupta. The 12 caves to the south are Buddhist, the 17 in the center are Hindu, and the five to the north are Jain. A description of the most eye-catching caves should serve as a good introduction to what you can expect when you visit Ellora.

The largest of the Buddhist caves is Cave 5, which is 117 feet by 56 feet. It was probably used as a classroom for young monks, and its roof is supported by 24 pillars. Since everything was carved out of the mountain, the word "supported" is more a way of expressing an optical illusion. Working their way down, sculptors first "built" the roof before they "erected" the pillars.

Cave 6 is unusual. It contains a statue of the Hindu goddess of learning, Saraswati, in the company of Buddhist figures. Cave 10 is the "Carpenter's Cave," where Hinduism and Buddhism meet again. Here, the stonecutters reproduced the timbered roofs of their day over a richly decorated façade that imitates masonry work. Light comes into the cave through an elaborate horseshoe window over a porch. Inside this chaitya, the only Buddhist chapel at Ellora, the main work of art is a huge image of Buddha. Despite this image and a number of Buddhist figures on a frieze over the pillars of the temple, this cave is dedicated to Viswakarma, the architect of the Hindu gods and the patron saint of Indian craftsmen.

Cave 11 (two stories) and Cave 12 (three stories) are remarkable for having more than one floor. The two caves comprise a monastery behind an open courtyard that leads to its façade, which looms nearly 50 feet high. Although this façade is simple, the interior is lavish. This block of rock was gouged into a ground-floor hall, a shrine on the story above it, and another hall on the top story with a gallery of Buddhas seated under trees and parasols.

The immediate successors to the Buddhist caves are the Hindu caves, and a step inside them is enough to pull the visitor up short. It's another world—another universe—in which the calm contemplation of the seated Buddhas gives way to the dynamic cosmology of Hinduism in which mythical gods seemingly come alive from stone. These sculptures are estimated to have been created around the seventh and eighth centuries.

Transfixed, the visitor watches the "action" as goddesses battle; Shiva flails the air with his eight arms; elephants big as life groan under their burdens; boars, eagles, peacocks, and monkeys prance around what has suddenly turned into a zoo; and lovers strike poses that leave the imagination somewhere far behind.

Kailasa Temple

The approach to Ellora is dominated by the awe-inspiring mammoth Kailasa temple, or Cave 16—one of the wonders of India. The Kailasa temple, a freestanding shrine, is carved out of solid rock with a small *gopuram* (altar) at the entrance and enormous pillars on either side—of Shiva, Parvati, and Gajalaxmi—with Ravana below shaking Mount Kailasa. The temple is dedicated to Mount Kailasa in the Himalayas, the abode of Lord Shiva, and in some oblique manner this monolith competes with the grandeur of nature's own creations.

The Kailasa is approximately twice the area of the Parthenon in Greece and 1½ times as tall. Exquisitely carved and sculpted with epic themes, no nobler monument exists of India's genius, daring, and skill. The world's biggest monolithic structure, its conception is simply breathtaking. Starting at the top of a cliff, an army of stonecutters removed three million cubic feet of rock to form a vast pit 107 feet deep, 267 feet long, and 154 feet wide, leaving a block in the center, which became a temple rising from the foot of what had once been a hill.

This replica of the home of Shiva stands in an open courtyard as three separate structures. The main temple rests on a base 25 feet high that appears to be supported by friezes of elephants. It measures 150 feet by 100 feet under a gabled front and a tower in three tiers beneath a cupola. An overhead bridge links the three buildings of Kailasa and its outer gateway. One gallery has a dozen panels that illustrate the legends of Shiva, while an adjoining panel tells the story of Vishnu as a man-lion, shredding the body of a demon with his claws. This demon was supposed to have been invulnerable to human or animal attackers, but Vishnu, by adopting a form that was neither man nor beast, destroyed the tyrant.

After this panel comes the masterpiece, the tale in stone of "Ravana shaking Kailasa," according to the epic *Ramayana*. Ravana was a demon who decided to show his strength by lifting Kailasa on his head. The mountain trembles in this sculpture, but Shiva remains unperturbed and catches Ravana merely by putting his foot down hard. Parvati is seen clinging to her husband's arm and looking slightly preoccupied.

Ajanta

Nestled on the slopes of a crescent hillside, hewn out of rock, are 30 caves where, two millenia ago, Buddhist monks found sanctuary and left a legend for posterity—Ajanta. The caves contain a series of wall paintings and sculpture, elegantly executed, with an aesthetic appeal that is timeless and craftsmanship that astounds scholars and art lovers even today. The antiquity of these caves ranges between 200 B.C. and A.D. 600, yet the remarkable unity of concept and sense of continuity remains unbroken. Despite their age, some of the paintings have retained their freshness and vivid detail wrought in rich earth colors, lamp black, and lapis lazuli.

The paintings depict the life and teachings of Buddha. A large segment is devoted to Buddha's earlier life as a prince surrounded by beautiful women, luxurious settings, and details of court life. Some of the exquisite paintings belong to this section.

The Ajanta caves are like chapters of a splendid epic in visual form. Natural light brightens the caves at different times of the day, and structural engineers are awestruck by the sheer brilliance of those ancient masters who, undaunted by the limitations of seemingly crude implements and tools, material, and labor, created this marvel of art and architectural splendor.

As at Ellora, monumental façades and statues were chipped out of hard rock. But Ajanta was given an added dimension by its unknown creators, a dimension expressed in India's most remarkable examples of cave paintings. The artists lovingly told the story of Buddha and, at the same time, portrayed the life and civilization they knew. Time has damaged some of these masterpieces, but the vivid colors and the flowing lines that remain continue to astound experts. True, this was religious art, but it was living art as well. When the electric spotlights flicker onto the paintings, the figures seem to awaken from their slumbers and come alive. Life was good then, and love was open. Modern art never succeeded in paying tribute to woman in the way it has been done at Ajanta.

There are 29 caves in all, but they are much smaller than those at Ellora, because the sculptors had to work on a much smaller site. The caves here have no courtyards; instead they were originally carved with steps leading to the river below. Only four caves are chaityas while the rest are viharas. The best paintings are to be found in Caves 1, 2, 16, 17, and 19, and the best sculptures are in Caves 1, 4, 17, 19, and 26.

The paintings at Ajanta are called "frescoes" although they were not executed in the true fresco technique developed in Italy. Here, a rough rock wall was covered with a plaster made from clay and cow dung mixed with chopped rice husks in a layer about a half-inch thick. On top of this layer, a smooth coat of lime was applied, and then the painter began his work. First, the composition was outlined in red and then an undercoating was applied. All the colors used at Ajanta were of local origin: red ocher, burnt brick, copper oxide, lamp black, or dust from green rocks that had been crushed. On this background, the painter then applied his colors. The outline was accentuated and highlights were added before the surface of the mural was polished to a shine.

The life of Buddha and the illustration of tales from Buddhist fables, or *jatakas,* are the two main themes of the caves at Ajanta. The total effect is that of a magic carpet transporting you back into a drama played by nobles, wise men, and commoners. The caves are numbered from west to east, not in chronological order.

The earliest cave, which dates back to 200 B.C., is Cave 13. However, it is only from A.D. 100 that the exquisite brush and line work begins. Caves 9 and 10 have a chaitya in a hall filled with Buddhas, dominated by an enormous stupa. In breathtaking detail, the *Shaddanta Jataka,* a legend about Buddha, is depicted in a continuous panel in Cave 10.

Opinions vary as to the most exquisite of the Ajanta paintings. The most popular are those in Cave 1, of the Bodhisattva Avalokiteshwara and Bodhisatvva Padmapani. Padmapani, or the "one with the lotus in his hand," is credited by the sculptures as being the alter ego of the Lord Buddha and who assumed the duties of the Buddha when he disappeared. The Avalokiteshwara is the most esteemed of the Bodhisattvas and is known as the Sangharatna, or "jewel of the order." Padmapani is depicted with his melon-breasted, sinuous-hipped wife, one of the most widely reproduced figures of Ajanta. The painting has been compared in technique to the work of Michelangelo and Correggio.

Cave 2 is remarkable for its ceiling decorations and its murals relating the final birth of Buddha. Buddha's mother, Queen Maya, dreams that an elephant with six tusks has entered her body. This dream is interpreted to mean that she is to bear a great son. In one panel, you see the birth of Buddha and the newborn child walking over lotus flowers with the king of gods, Indra, holding an umbrella over his head.

In Cave 4, sculpture is the main interest. It is the largest vihara in Ajanta, and depicts a man and a woman fleeing from a mad elephant, and a man giving up his resistance to a tempting woman. Cave 10 is believed to be the oldest cave at Ajanta, going back to second century B.C.

The mystical heights attained by the artist-monks reach their zenith in Caves 16 and 17, where the viewer is released from the bondage imposed by time and space. Transcending these barriers, one is faced by a continuous narrative that spreads horizontally and vertically, evolving into a panoramic whole—at once logical and stunning. There is an excellent view of the river from Cave 16, which may have been the entrance to the entire series of caves. One painting here is riveting. Known as "The Dying Princess," it is believed to represent Sundari, the wife of Buddha's half-brother, Nanda, who left her to become a monk. You can almost see the princess' eyes cloud over in death. One agrees with the art critic who said, "For pathos and sentiment and the unmistakable way of telling its story, this picture cannot be surpassed in the history of art."

Cave 17 possesses the greatest number of pictures undamaged by time. Luscious heavenly damsels fly effortlessly overhead, a prince makes love to a princess, and Buddha tames a raging elephant—all on the portico of the cave.

Another mural tells how Prince Simhala conquered Ceylon (now Sri Lanka), an island of beautiful ogresses who trapped the prince and his 500 companions. The captivity was a merry one, but Simbala sensed the trap and fled on a winged white horse with an ogress in pursuit of him. This beauteous witch enticed the king of Simhala's country into marriage and ate her husband for their wedding banquet. But Simbala drove out the ogress and conquered her island of Ceylon. Next to this painting is the scene of a woman applying lipstick, which never ceases to fascinate women visitors.

Another favorite is the painting in Cave 18 of a princess performing *sringar* (toilet). For its sheer exuberance and *joie de vivre,* the painting in Cave 2 of women on a swing is adjudged the best.

A number of unfinished caves were abandoned mysteriously, but even these are worth a visit. A steep climb of 100 steps takes you to the caves. You may also take the bridle path that is a gentler ascent with a crescent pathway running alongside the caves. From here, there is a magnificent view of the ravines of the Waghura River. For souvenirs of a memorable experience, you can pick up amethyst-veined rocks strewn generously on the hillside.

PRACTICAL INFORMATION FOR
THE AJANTA AND ELLORA CAVES

WHEN TO GO. The best season is autumn (September–November), when the region displays its colors after the rainy season. December–February is also a good season to visit. During monsoon (June–August), you should avoid going to these caves.

HOW TO GET THERE. There are three ways to reach these caves, with Aurangabad as the rest base.

By Air. Aurangabad is well connected from Delhi and Bombay. *Indian Airlines* connects Bombay to Delhi via Aurangabad and Udaipur. The fare is Rs. 858 from Delhi and Rs. 296 from

Bombay. *Vayudoot Airlines* also operates scheduled flights to Aurangabad three times a week (days vary) from Bombay at 6:45 A.M. The flight takes about 45 minutes, and the fare is the same.

By Train. Aurangabad is not directly connected to Bombay or Delhi. One first has to reach Manmad, which has regular services to Aurangabad. (The *Punjab Mail, Gorakhpur Express,* or *Panchwati Express* will bring you to Manmad.) From Manmad station, you change to the Ellora Express on a meter-gauge track, not a comfortable journey for 70 miles. The fare from Bombay to Aurangabad is Rs. 403 for first class and Rs. 97 for second class. After a tiring journey, if you don't plan to fly back to Bombay and are heading north instead, see Ellora first, then proceed to Ajanta and make Jalgaon your railbase. All Calcutta–Bombay trains stop at Jalgaon and Manmad. From Secundrabad (Hyderabad), a late-afternoon train pulls into Aurangabad early the next morning.

By Car. It is 250 miles from Bombay to Aurangabad via Pune. This is certainly a better alternative than the train. There is an excellent highway from Bombay to Aurangabad. You can hire a private car from offices of the India Tourism Development Corporation (ITDC), the Maharashtra Tourism Development Corporation (MTDC) or some travel agencies in Bombay. Allow four days for the trip, which includes two days for visiting the caves. Another alternative is a package tour by *luxury coach* offered by MTDC.

TOURIST INFORMATION. For visiting these caves, reservations can be made from Bombay at the MTDC office, Express Tower, 9th Floor, Nariman Point (tel. 2021733) or at its regional office in Aurangabad at Holiday Camp (tel. 4032). The Tourist Information Office can be contacted for hiring guides, for arranging private taxis, or obtaining guidance and information, at Krishan Vilas, Station Road (tel. 4817).

ACCOMMODATIONS. Since the Ajanta and Ellora Caves are such a popular tourist destination, there are some comfortable—even luxurious—hotels in the area, particularly at Aurangabad. True, the overall selection may be small, but what there is is more than adequate. Within a few miles of the caves, the accommodations are limited to a few small guest houses and lodges. Most are in the *Inexpensive* price range and offer basic amenities. Contact either MTDC or ITDC for details and arrangements. An exception is *Hotel Mokaro* at Jalgaon, two miles from the Ellora Caves (tel. 4278 or 3766), with 20 rooms, some air-conditioned, at *Moderate* rates, with meals included. For price ranges of classifications listed here, see *Facts at Your Fingertips.*

AHMEDNAGAR

Moderate

Ashoka Tourist Hotel. Pune-Aurangabad Road, Ahmednagar; tel. 3607, 4296, 4604, or 4796. One km from downtown. 32 rooms and five suites, most air-conditioned and with attached baths; restaurant and bar.

Hotel Natraj. 11 Nagar Aurangabad Rd.; tel. 6040 or 4701. One km from downtown and six km from the railway station. 24 double rooms with attached baths, some rooms air-conditioned. Restaurant and bar permit room.

Inexpensive

Hotel Archana. Borawake College Road, Shrirampur; tel. 2530 or 2531. Near the railway station and downtown. 25 rooms with attached baths. Restaurant and garden; taxi services.

Motel Suvidha. Nimgaon-Jali, Post Loni, on Nasik-Shirdi Road; tel. ASHWI 75. Six simple non-air-conditioned rooms with attached baths. Restaurant and permit room.

AURANGABAD

Deluxe

Ajanta Ambassador. Chikalthana; tel. 8211 or 8367; cable EMBASSY. Four km from downtown area on the way to the caves. 125 air-conditioned rooms and 20 suites in a rather new hotel. Amenities include two good restaurants (one in a garden). 24-hour room service, bar, barber shop, shopping arcade, swimming pool, tennis court, indoor games, and doctor.

Welcomgroup Rama International. Chikalthana; tel. 8241, 8244, 8340, or 8455; cable WELCOTEL. Centrally air-conditioned, with 75 rooms and three suites. Restaurant with banquet facilities, bar, poolside rose garden, swimming pool, beauty parlor, health club, croquet, golf, tennis, and secretarial services. Reduced rates April–September.

Expensive

Aurangabad Ashok. Dr. Rajendra Prasad Marg; tel. 4520–29; cable TOURISM. 10 km from the airport, three km from the railway station. 64 double rooms and one suite, some air-conditioned. Restaurant, bar, swimming pool, shopping arcade, room service, sports club, car rental, and laundry. AP and MAP available, as are apartments on a long lease.

Moderate

Hotel Amarpreet. Pt. Jawaharlal Marg; tel. 4615, 4306, 3986, or 3422. Centrally air-conditioned with 30 rooms, a restaurant, 24-hour coffee shop, bar, car rental, and children's play park. The hotel offers an off-season discount.

Hotel Nandanvan. Railway Station Road; tel. 3311–3. This hotel is the nearest to the Ajanta and Ellora Road leading to the caves, with 29 rooms (only two air-conditioned), two restaurants, bar permit room, car rental, and beauty parlor services.

Neelam Lodging & Boarding. Plot No. 2–1–6/7, Bhandkal Gate; tel. 4561–2. 28 rooms, some air-conditioned, restaurant, conference room, and two family rooms.

Hotel Raviraj. Dr. Rajendra Prasad Marg; tel. 3627, 3637, or 3939. 40 double rooms with attached baths, some rooms air-conditioned. Indoor and garden restaurants, bar, 24-hour coffee shop, arcade, and doctor on call.

 DINING OUT. Other than hotel dining rooms, the Ajanta and Ellora Caves area has little to offer in restaurants. If you wish to eat at a hotel other than the one in which you are staying, it is best to call to see if you can be accommodated. Many of the hotel restaurants also provide packed lunches for trips to the caves. At the cave sites, there are some snack food places you may want to try at your own risk. Other than that, we can list only two independent restaurants for this region, both in the *Moderate-Inexpensive* range, as set forth in *Facts at Your Fingertips.*

AHMEDNAGAR

Milan. 1072 Sarjepura; tel. 5621 or 5957. A small but clean place with 50 seats, serving Indian, Punjabi, and Continental foods. Restaurant includes an air-conditioned bar permit room and a terrace conference room. Open 7 A.M.–11 P.M.

AURANGABAD

Mingling Chinese Restaurant. Jalna Road; tel. 5991, 3895, or 4301. Despite its name, this fully air-conditioned restaurant serves tasty Indian and Continental dishes as well as Chinese food. There are periodic live music and dancing in the evenings. Open 10:30 A.M.–3:30 P.M. and 7–11:30 P.M.

 HOW TO GET AROUND. Chitkalthana Airport of Aurangabad is six miles from the city. Divisional Controller, *State Transport* (tel. 4032) runs buses from the airport and railway station to the city. Other modes of transport like **taxis** and **autorickshaws** run on meters. You can also have an amusing ride on horsedrawn *tongas. Tourist cars* can be rented from *Ajanta Travel and Tours* (tel. 4906 or 3968). *Tourist Taxi ITDC* (tel. 4143). Divisional State Transport Controller near the station can also be contacted regarding the bus service.

TOURS. Tour operators in Aurangabad are *Transport Syndicate,* c/o Rama International Hotel (tel. 4872) or *Print Travel & Transport,* Adalat Road (tel. 4707). Both arrange travel by private rented cars to Ellora, half-day trip to Ajanta Rs. 450–600. Renting a car and driver is better than taking the special full-day round-trip bus service to Ellora Caves–Daultabad Fort–Bibi ka Magbarad–Panchakki, which is run by MTDC. The bus picks you up from Aurangabad Railway Station at 9 A.M. and returns at 6 P.M. From Bombay to Aurangabad is a four-day trip, at a cost of Rs. 765 with accommodations at Hotel Amarpreet at Rs. 880 with accommodations at Ajanta Ambassador. The trip includes sightseeing by air-conditioned luxury coach to and from Bombay. Contact the MTDC office. It leaves daily at 8:30 P.M. and returns after four days at 7:30 A.M. An approved guide accompanies the tour. Other guides are also available near the caves or can be hired from the Government of India Tourist Office. Regular bus service to Ajanta in Aurangabad can be reserved at the railway station and bus stand. ITDC organizes daily tours with pick-up from main Aurangabad hotels; a three-hour trip to Ajanta costs Rs. 45 and a day tour to Ellora, including the caves and other sightseeing, costs Rs. 30. MTDC conducts daily Ajanta and Ellora visits and Aurangabad sightseeing from Holiday Camp.

CAVE EXCURSIONS. *Ajanta Caves* are situated on the Aurangabad-Jalgaon Road. These caves are famous for their exquisite murals and rock-cut carvings. To reach the caves, you either climb a staircase of about 100 steps or take a circuitous pathway. The paintings and sculpture inside the caves are of Buddhist origin. Five of the caves, Nos. 9, 10, 19, 26, and 29, are chaityas, or halls for group worship; the others are vharas, or caves for monks' quarters.

Ellora Caves, 66 miles from Aurangabad, are renowned rock-cut caves more than 10 centuries old. Of the 34 caves here, 12 are of Buddhist origin, 17 are Hindu, and five are Jain. Among the Buddhist caves, Nos. 5, 10, 11, and 12 are outstanding. Of the Hindu caves, Nos. 16, 21, and 29 are most worth visiting. No. 16, Kailash Temple, is the most famous, its intricately hewn monument is perhaps the world's largest monolith. Of the Jain group, Nos. 32 and 34 are most worth visiting.

Visiting Tips. All caves, except the painted ones, are open 9 A.M.–5 P.M., or until sunset, whichever comes earlier. Painted caves may be visited only 10 A.M.–1 P.M. Guide-lecturers are available at the sites at fees of Rs. 5 for each 1½-hour tour, or Rs. 15 for a full-day visit. If you have a flashlight, bring it along; if not, flashlights are available at minimal cost. It is also suggested that you visit the caves in the afternoon, when the sun falls on the grottoes. At both Ajanta and Ellora, chairs are available for aged or disabled visitors. A team of four *mazdurs* (porters) carry chairs to all the caves. Controlled fees depend on the number of caves visited and the distances between.

Photography. Except for professional movie cameras, no prior permission is required to take photographs inside the caves with the aid of flash bulbs. However, the use of camera stools or tables, or the erection of scaffolding is strictly prohibited, as is the use of burning or magnesium wire.

SHOPPING. Aurangabad is famous for its bidriwork (novelties of metal inlaid with intricate silver designs), nirmalware (painted articles on light wood) gold and silver lace, Himroo shawls, and silk saris. Organized and reliable buying opportunities: *Silk Mills Showroom, Shawl Factories* at Nawabpura, *Cottage Industries Sales Emporium* at Shahgunj, *Handloom Emporium* at Gulmandi, *Khadi Gram Udyog* at Sarafa, *Tourist Emporium,* opposite Holiday Camp, Station Road, and *Sajawat* at Eknath Mandir. Shops are open from 10 A.M.–8 P.M. Main shopping areas are closed on Sundays.

GUJARAT

Deserts, Lush Lands, and Lions

by
KATHLEEN COX and RAVI KHANNA

In Gujarat, India's westernmost state, desert tracts of the Indian sub-continent meet with the monsoon lands of peninsular India. Here you find India's largest marshland and Asia's only lion sanctuary.

Gujarat's lakes are a garden of water lilies. Its forests give shelter to thousands of birds. In spring, fragrant flowers bloom across the land-scape. In winter, mist rises from rivers that empty into the Arabian Sea. India's 5,000-kilometer coastline begins in Gujarat, wraps around the subcontinent, and ends in far-away Bengal. The hills, low and forested, rise gently to 1,000 meters. In upland hamlets are bred India's finest cattle, making Gujarat the home of India's dairy industry. From the Gulf of Khambhat, along the Kathiawad peninsula and the Gulf of Kutchhh, the western horizon is painted at sunset in a riot of color.

Women, in swirling skirts of black and red heavy fabric dotted with mirrors reflect Gujarat's passion for the bright and colorful: bounteous greens, earthy reds, and sapphire blues suffuse Gujarat's handicrafts and textiles, its folk dances, and its festivals. Even the Hindu temples, Jain shrines, Moslem mosques, and secular palaces are adorned with Gujarati ornamentation that sets them apart from monuments in the rest of India.

The northwestern border of Gujarat forms part of India's interna-tional frontier with Pakistan, while Rajasthan adjoins Gujarat on the northeast, Madhya Pradesh on the far east, and Maharashtra on the south. The 178,000-square-kilometer state has a population of 34 million. Of the original inhabitants, only the Bhil and the Gond tribes have survived. After the fall of the Gupta empire, various local dynasties ruled in different parts of Gujarat until the Moslem conquest of the entire area. When the British came in 1856, Gujarat and Maharashtra formed one huge bilingual state; in 1960, the two were divided into separate units.

With a large Jain population and a long period of Buddhist culture, from Ashoka's time to the end of the Vallabhi dynasty in A.D. 790, the people of this state are largely vegetarians. Masters of vegetarian cooking, Gujaratis make a variety of mouth-watering dishes out of the simplest lentils and vegetables. The Gujarati *thali* (vegetarian) dinner is an endless procession of savory vegetables cooked in aromatic spices, supported with a variety of crisply fried snacks and delicious confections made from sweetened burned milk or thick cold yogurt mixed with nuts. The farmhouse dinner is a Gujarati innovation. It consists of crisp hot *rotis* (flat unleavened bread) made from *jawar* or maize flour, huge dollops of butter, a pungent garlic chutney, and fresh vegetables steamed in an earthen oven. It is washed down with thick, sweetened milk flavored with sliced nuts and saffron.

The Gujaratis are, however, better known for their shrewd business sense exemplified by the citizens of Ahmedabad, the former state capital of Gujarat. The new capital, Gandhinagar, is 20 miles away on the banks of the Sabarmati river.

Some festivals of Gujarat are unique; others are slightly different from those in other states. (See "Fairs and Festivals" in *Practical Information,* below.)

Gujarat offers a scintillating range of fabrics. Textile weaving, vegetable-dye painting, tie-and-dye work, gold and silver thread work (*zari*), intricate silk embroidery, and patola- and tanchoi-type saris have been Gujarat's pride for centuries. The lacquered furniture of Sankheda, the mirror works of Kutchchh, bead-encrusted artifacts from Rajkot, and fine wood carvings from the vicinity of Ahmedabad have become popular with tourists, as have experimental paintings and murals at roadside art shows, the main markets, and the emporiums at Ahmedabad, Jamnagar, Surat, and Vadodara.

Just over the state line, going from Bombay to Ahmedabad is Sanjan, where a masonry flame-topped pillar marks the landing place of the Parsis in A.D. 745 after they had spent 19 years in Diu, and island south of Saurashtra. Why they left Diu is not known, but they set off in the same ships that had brought them from Persia. They had to keep moving the sacred fire for protection, and it was only after 700 years that they set it up permanently at Udvada, a little north of Sanjan. Now there are Parsi groups in almost every Gujarati town, and many of their last names are derived from the names of these towns.

Along the palm-fringed coast sliced by frequent banyan-lined rivers running into the Gulf of Cambay are many ancient ports. One major port is Surat. Known as the city of looms, it was India's busiest port in the seventeenth century. Surat lies at the mouth of the Tapti River. The Dutch, Portuguese, French, and English envied its prosperity. Surat today produces 70 percent of India's synthetic textiles. Most of its population is engaged in three professions—diamond cutting and polishing, gold and silver work called *zari,* and synthetic textiles. Surat is equally known for its distinctive cuisine.

In the nineteenth century, Surat's prosperity passed to Bombay.

The fort was built in the fourteenth century by Mohammed-bin-Tughlaq as a defense against the Bhils. After Akbar captured it from the Portuguese, it was a gateway for Mecca. Shivaji raided Surat four times; the size and elaborateness of the Dutch and English tombs indicate the amount of wealth the Europeans were anxious to defend.

On a hill overlooking the wide Narmada River and cotton fields on the other side, is Broach. The river was used for bleaching cloth, and the town's muslins went out in Broach's own ships. There has been a sudden spurt in the commercial life on this coast since oil was recently discovered at nearby Ankleshwar, as well as at Cambay, another old port at the apex of the gulf.

Baroda

About 118 km south of Ahmedabad lies the "garden city" of Baroda, which has boulevards lined with flaming gulmohurs. Once a princely capital, it acquired its original name, Vadodara, because of the profusion of banyan trees. "In the Heart of the Banyan Trees" was Baroda's original descriptive name. Modern Baroda is a lovely and progressive city of 460,000 inhabitants, containing many fine buildings, spacious gardens, and shady avenues.

The grand palace, set in a beautifully landscaped garden, is now a museum housing old furniture, weapons, artifacts and regal costumes, and original paintings and portraits by the nineteenth-century royal painter, Raja Ravi Varma. The Oriental Institute has a rich collection of ancient Sanskrit manuscripts, including one of India's great epics, *Ramayana.* The Baroda Gharana is an important school of Indian classical music. Baroda is also an industrial city with textile and petrochemical industries.

The reign of the family that governed Baroda until independence started in the early eighteenth century. Damaji Gaikwar was the son of a Maratha general in the Peshwa's army. He was allowed to levy one-fourth of the income of certain areas conquered by the army. Damaji II, along with the Peshwa, took Ahmedabad in 1753, ending Moslem rule in the region. The victors then divided the country. After Damaji II returned from the Battle of Panipat (against the Afghans), which destroyed much of the Peshwa's power, he chose Anhilwad Patan as his capital. His area dwindled in the course of controversies. By 1802, for receiving British help, he had to cede further land to the British, retaining small segments throughout Gujarat and Saurashtra.

The Kirti Mandir, or Royal Museum, contains remains of the family. The treasure—including the famous jewel "Star of the South"—is in the Nazar Bagh Palace, one of the spacious old dwellings of former times. In the collection is an embroidered cloth laid with stones, intended originally for the Prophet's Tomb. Two other palaces with well-kept gardens are the Pratap Vilas and Markarpura, which is south of the town. In the Lakshmi Vilas Palace, the *Durbar,* or audience hall, is beautified by mosaic decorations on the walls and by an Italian mosaic floor. There is a separate wooden gallery for women. The palace is a conglomeration of domes, towers, and spires—a wonderful example of architecture that strayed from the straight and narrow in trying to conform to the Indo-Saracenic style.

Dabhoi, 17 miles southeast, is a ruined town. Its walls, gates, and temples are the finest examples of the Gujarat style of Hindu architecture known for its city gates. The Malika Mata (Kali) Temple, built in the shape of a Greek cross, is covered inside with fine carvings. Within the town walls was a veritable botanical garden: peacocks and pelicans played at the reservoirs for which water was brought in by an aqueduct. Farms provided the population with food for long sieges.

Nearby, farmers, dressed all in white, and women in flared red skirts can be seen tending the fertile fields. Among these fields is the busy town of Anand. Much of Bombay's milk and butter comes from this cooperative dairy organization, which is helped by Danish experts and equipment under a UNICEF project.

Modhera

The sun temple of Modhera, 60 miles northwest of Ahmedabad, claims its place among India's most significant monuments. Built in A.D. 1026–27 on an exceptionally high plinth, it is designed to let the sun's rays penetrate the shrine. Full of grandeur and balance, its lines are enhanced by a wide bank of steps descending to a tank. A pillared porch leads to the Assembly Hall and shrine. Such is the design of the shrine that the Surya (Sun God) image—now missing—would be highlighted by the rising sun and the equinoxes.

On the road to Saurashtra is Sarkhej, deserted country retreat of sultans. Here are the tomb and mosque of Mahmud Begara, whose name arose from his enormous mustache shaped like the curved horns of a bullock. A great gourmet, he once exclaimed that if he hadn't been a sultan, he didn't know how he would have satisfied his hunger. Among this group of buildings is the tomb of Ganj Bakash, a saint and spiritual guide of Begara. Sarkhej's monuments, although Moslem, are almost purely Hindu inspired.

About 30 km northeast of Modhera is Patan, famous for its Patola silk saris, made from an intricately dyed yarn that, when woven, reveals exquisite geometric patterns.

Named after the Mahatma, Gandhinagar, on the west bank of Sabarmati, is the new capital of Gujarat. Government buildings, children's gardens, a thermal power house, legislative assembly, and Sarita Garden are some of the places worth a visit in this new capital.

Echoes of Ancient Egypt

Tourists are advised to travel 47 miles south of Ahmedabad to a place called Lothal, where archaeologists have recently brought to view the earliest known urban civilization of the subcontinent. This is, in fact, part of the bigger Harappan civilization that is found at Mohenjo-Daro and Harappa (now in Pakistan). What the archaeologists have actually excavated is part of the ancient port, complete with dockyard, streets, houses, underground drains, and a wall. Lothal was probably one of ancient India's important ports having maritime connections with Mesopotamia and Egypt.

Among the interesting discoveries at this site are two terra cottas— one representing an Assyrian with his typical square-cut beard, the other suggesting an Egyptian mummy. It is probable that when Mohenjo-Daro and Harappa fell into decadence, Gujarat continued to preserve the same civilization for several centuries until it merged in the all-assimilating culture of the Aryans.

Saputara, or the "abode of the serpents," is a picturesque hill resort overlooking a lush, green valley. It is situated at a height of 873 meters on the second highest plateau of the Sahyadri range. The wildlife sanctuary in the Mahal Bardipura forests, Gir waterfalls, Waghai, and Botanical Gardens are other attractions not far from Saputara.

Literally meaning a hundred kingdoms, Saurashtra is a region draped in romance and valor. In every city of Saurashtra, its rulers have left behind palaces, temples, mosques and museums, gardens, and sun-sparkling fountains. Parrots, which form the favorite motif of interior decoration and paintings of the region, flock by thousands and feed on the wild berries in the nearby bushes. Peacocks spread out their tails in the well-kept gardens.

From the centrally located university city of Rajkot, where Mahatma Gandhi spent his childhood, Saurashtra's many tourist destinations can be covered in day trips. The 50-year-old museum in Rajkot has invaluable antiques—furniture, crystalware, carpets, bronzes, hunters' trophies, and jewels. Junagadh, at the foot of the sacred Girnar Mountain, is a few hours' drive from here. Junagadh has many venerated Hindu and Jain temples. A Buddhist cave with spiral staircase and Ashoka edicts lie nearby. The alabaster-white palace here has a huge collection of Continental crystalware, chandeliers, and furniture upholstered with silver and gold-encrusted brocades. The Sakkar Bagh Museum also has a superb collection. Girnar Hills, the highest point in Gujarat at 1,117 meters, has venerated temples and a mosque. Junagadh is also a convenient base for visiting the beach resorts of Chorwad and Ahmedpur Mandvi, where you can have memorable views of the sunrise and sunset.

Southward from Junagadh lie the port town of Veraval and the sacred temple of Somnath at Prabbas Patan. Sacked and pillaged seven times and each time built anew to greater glory, the Shiva temple at Somnath, looking west to the Arabian Sea, is a magnificent edifice eulogized by the great historian-astronomer-mathematician Abu Raithan Al-Beruni. The museum reassembles the saga of the temple's destruction and rededication. Nearby is Bhalka Tirth, believed to be the place where Lord Krishna breathed his last. Coastal ships are built at Veraval.

Sasan Gir, the 1,400-square-kilometer forest preserve northeast of Somnath, is the home of the majestic Asian lion. In the clearings in the forest, you can see the royal beast in its natural habitat. In the middle of the forest is the vast Kamleshwar Lake. A primitive Negroid tribe lives by its shores.

Porbander—Gandhi's Birthplace

Westward along the coast is the small port town of Porbander, the birthplace of Mahatma Gandhi. Its narrow lanes are flanked by residential quarters with antique charm. Adjacent to the house in which Gandhi was born is Kirti Mandir, housing his personal effects, library, and a photo exhibition on his life and times.

Founded in 1713, nearby Bhavnagar was the capital of the former princely state. Today, Bhavnagar is a flourishing cotton exporting port. The Gandhi Smriti, a memorial, recalls Bhavnagar's association with the father of the nation. Other places of interest are the Central Salt and Marine Chemicals Research Institute, Lock Gate, Gaurishankar Lake, Vallabhbhai Patel Garden, and Takhteshwar Temple.

Jamnagar, founded in 1540 by Jam Raval, is an industrial town and an important naval base. Its fame rests on its tie-dye work in fabrics and pearl fisheries. Places of interest include the city lake, Lakhota Fort and Museum, Kotha Bastion, the Ayurvedic College, Digjam Aquarium, Khabhalia Gate, and Ranjit Institute of Poly Radiotherapy.

As the Saurashtra peninsula narrows northward into a small strip at Dwarka, you approach one of the most sacred Hindu shrines, the 50-meter-high Krishna Temple, the highest of its kind in India. Dwarka is believed to have been the kingdom of Lord Krishna. Over 2,000 generations have chanted hymns in this shrine. Among the other temples at Dwarka, the most beautiful is dedicated to Rukmani, Krishna's consort. Close to the port city of Okha on the Bet Dwarka islands are the Pat Rani temples.

Ahmedabad

Ahmedabad is a city that quietly blends the glorious past and a vibrant present, with an eye on a promising future. Ahmedabad means different things to different people. For architects, it is a remarkable repository of distinctive architectural styles—from the early Indo-Saracenic of the fifteenth century Moslem sultans to the experimental modern form of the legendary Le Corbusier. Rich detail, delicate tracery, and ornamental minarets impart a very Indian character to what had originally been foreign concepts. Continuity was the essence.

The city was founded in A.D. 1411 by Sultan Ahmed Shah. It was also the seat of the Mogul Viceroys of Gujarat-Jahangir, Shah Jahan, and Aurangzeb, all of whom later became emperors. In modern times, Ahmedabad was the home of Mahatma Gandhi, the apostle of peace and nonviolence.

Industrially, the city has seen many ups and downs over the centuries. It is said that Ahmedabad used to hang on three threads: gold, silk, and cotton. Later, when the British took over, the city was a desolate sight—empty buildings filled with rubbish and weeds and wild animals roaming within the broken-down city walls.

Today the city has nearly 75 mills that employ thousands and produce millions of meters of cloth. For some, it is the Manchester of the East. It has important claims to distinction in the history of India because of its survival for 500 years as a major center of trade and industry.

Although Ahmedabad is not as well known to Westerners as are India's larger cities— or even the smaller ones such as Agra, Varanasi, or Jaipur—it deserves to be much more widely appreciated.

Ahmedabad flourished under the Gujarat dynasty and after it had become a part of the Mogul Empire in 1572. As a Moslem capital, Ahmedabad was richly endowed with mosques and tombs, though some secular buildings survive, including the Citadel.

What is distinctive about Ahmedabad's architecture of that time is the strong Hindu and Jain influences on Moslem forms, probably more marked here than anywhere else in India. Communal tolerance was the rule in the city. Ahmedabad was a center of Moslem power and splendor and the home of a rich military official elite and of skilled Moslem weavers. But its wealth came from trade and industry, which were largely controlled by Hindu and Jain merchants and bankers. In early modern times, when Ahmedabad was on the important trade routes between the courts in northern and central India and the outside world, their commercial network extended as far as Constantinople and southeast Asia. They controlled Ahmedabad's export trade in textiles and the import trade in luxuries for the courts, collected revenue for the state, and financed princes and armies.

From the second quarter of the seventeenth century, the city fell into a century-long decline. From 1630 to 1632, a terrible famine depopulated Gujarat. Foreign traders—first, the Portuguese and later, the British—established new trading networks. Political turbulence created unfavorable conditions for Ahmedabad's trade and industry.

But today, the city of Ahmedabad is different. It is well connected by air, rail, and highway to the major Indian cities. It offers a wide variety of hotel accommodations from deluxe to simple lodges and tourist homes. The visitor who finds his way to Ahmedabad is rewarded with the discovery of one of the most colorful, exciting, and uncompromisingly Indian cities that is not on the beaten track of tourists.

Amidst all its color, its historical splendor, and its present-day business activity, there is a quiet corner in Ahmedabad that marks the city as the home of Mahatma Gandhi. On a peaceful stretch of the Sabarmati river, seven kilometers north of the city, Mahatma Gandhi set up a simple retreat in 1915. This was his Satyagraha Ashram, for many years the nerve center of India's freedom movement and the start of the famous Dandi March. Hridaya Kunj, his simple cottage, is now a national monument, preserved as it was during the mahatma's lifetime.

A Gandhi Memorial Center and Library and a sound-and-light spectacle offer an interesting display of his life and work.

Then there are the hills of Shatrunjaya that rise over the nearby town of Palitana. Covered with 863 shrines spanning a period of 900 years, the hills have rightly been called the "Abode of the Gods." The shrines, all Jain temples, are truly prayers in stone. Their finely carved spires and towers glisten in the sunlight. Their sanctuaries are dedicated to the *tirthankars,* or apostles of the Jains.

Pilgrims make the journey up the steep hill on foot; the aged and disabled use sedan chairs. At sunset, no one remains on the hill; even the priests withdraw, leaving the gods to themselves. It is possible to fly to Bhavnagar and drive 56 kilometers to Shatrunjaya. Those looking for fine ancient architecture must not miss the following: The Jumma Masjid (1423), which has been described as the most beautiful mosque in the East; the Sidi Saiyad Mosque (1430), celebrated the world over for its exquisite window of pierced stone tracery; the Rani Rupmati Mosque (1435), the Queen's mosque with its perforated stone screens; the Sarkhaj Rauza (1445–51), an elegant architectural complex of mosque, palace, tomb, and pavilions grouped around a great stepped tank; the Shining Minarets of Sidi Bashir's Mosque, an amazing phenomenon (when one minaret is shaken, the other vibrates too).

The Calico Museum of Textiles in Ahmedabad is one of the most famous textile museums in the world. It was privately founded in the 1940s by members of the textile family of the Sarabhai and today possesses an extremely rich and varied collection of Indian textiles from five centuries. In a building whose fascinating architecture combines Gujarat's traditional wood structures with modern functional forms that are well adapted to the presentation of textiles, the visitor can admire folk art embroidery, colorful applique hangings, rich brocades from the Mogul period, temple pictures painted on fabric, costumes, and carpets. Indian and international textile experts also engage in a wide range of research work here that has produced many valuable books on the history and techniques of textiles.

PRACTICAL INFORMATION FOR GUJARAT

WHEN TO GO. The best time to visit is November–March, when the temperature ranges between 55° and 85° F. Summers are very hot, so Gujarat is not recommended for visits then. Summer is also the time of the monsoons (June–August). Although rainfall then is moderate in much of Gujarat, it is quite heavy in the southern portion.

HOW TO GET THERE. By Air. Only domestic and regional airlines connect Gujarat with various parts of India. No international carriers fly here. You can be air linked either from Bombay or Delhi. *Indian Airlines* connects both Delhi and Bombay with Ahmedabad as well as with all the other cities of Gujarat. *Vayudoot,* the regional airline, flies from Bombay to Ahmedabad, Bhavnagar, Porbandar, Rajkot, and Surat and from Jaipur to Ahmedabad.

By Train. Ahmedabad is well connected with Bombay and Delhi by train. *Gujarat Mail* and *Saurashtra Mail,* offers first, second, and air-conditioned berths, and the *Chaircar* brings you in an overnight journey to Ahmedabad. For Baroda, you have to get off at midnight, so it's better to travel by the air-conditioned Delhi-bound Express or the Deluxe at Bombay Central. You can easily reach Gujarat in time to settle down and can manage a quick look-around before dinner. Saurashtra Mail will take you to Rajkot, Junagarh, Somnath, Dwarka, en route to Ahmedabad. First class offers large sleeping berths for four people and for two in a closed cabin. Meals and bedding are provided on demand at reasonable cost. Air-conditioned berths for sleeping are comfortable, especially during summer. Air-conditioned chair-cars have comfortable sliding big chairs. Second class is an open cabin for eight people with a common lavatory and cooler, and meals on demand.

By Car. The direct road from Bombay to Baroda (278 miles via Bhivandi and Shirshad) is the national highway, which is motorable, and it goes on to Ahmedabad. An alternative is to drive to Phalgat near Indore and then to cut across to Baroda. If you don't have your own vehicle, travel by train to Baroda or Ahmedabad and hire a chauffeur-driven taxi, but this is expensive. Rajkot is 162 miles from Ahmedabad, Anhilwad Patan sun temple, 78 miles from Ahmedabad via Modhera; Rajkot-Junagarh, 68 miles; Junagarh Gir Forest, 35 miles; Junagarh-Somnath (Veraval), 52 miles; Rajkot-Dwarka (via Jamnagar), 132 miles; and Ahmedabad-Palitana (via Dhanduka-Sihore), 135 miles.

TELEPHONES. The area code of Ahmedabad is 0272. You don't need to dial the area code if you're calling within the city. For directory assistance, dial 197.

TOURIST INFORMATION. Government of India Tourist Office counters are available for information at the airport itself (tel. 66277). For further information, contact Tourist Information Bureau, *Tourism Corporation of Gujarat Ltd.* (TCGL). H. K. House, Ground Floor, behind Jivabhai Chambers, opposite Gandhi Ashram Road (tel. 449683; telex 121–549 TCGL IN). Its regional offices are located at 1/847 Athugar St., Nanpura, Surat (tel. 26586), and Rang Mahal Diwan Chowk, Junagarh (tel. 834). You can also gather information at its Bombay-based office, Dhanraj Mahal, Apollo Bunder (tel. 243860); telex 011–2434 GUJI IN). The office provides free information and printed pamphlets on Gujarat and its various cities. Guides and accommodations at guest houses run by TCGL can also be arranged. TCGL provides city tours of Ahmedabad and nearby sightseeing, excursions, package tours, a special children's tour. A TCGL office is also located in Gandhinagar at Nigam Bhavan Sector 16. City tour information is also available from the *Municipal Corporation* at AMTS, Bus Stand, Lal Darwaza. In New Delhi, the TCGL office is located at Babakharag Singh Marg, Connaught Place, New Delhi.

ACCOMMODATIONS. Gujarat has a wide variety of hotels from which visitors can choose. Furthermore, the price ranges of hotels fit any budget. Some places offer the visitor the choice of staying under the American Plan (AP), with full meals included, or under the European Plan (EP), with no meals included in the rates. For price ranges of the classifications listed here, see *Facts at Your Fingertips.*

AHMEDABAD

Expensive

Cama. Khanpur, Ahmedabad; tel. 25281. One km from the downtown area. 55 air-conditioned rooms, including 13 deluxe and two suites, all with attached baths, and TVs. Facilities include a restaurant with live instrumental music as well as a poolside restaurant and a coffee shop, a car rental, beauty shop, sterilized water, doctor on call, and 24-hour room service.

Hotel Nataraj. Ashram Road, near the Income Tax Office; tel. 448747. Near the shopping area, this hotel has 25 air-conditioned rooms, two restaurants, and a coffee shop. A comfortable place to stay.

Moderate

Hotel Karnavati. Shree Cinema Premises, Ashram Road; tel. 402161 or 402170. Located one km from the downtown area, with 48 air-conditioned rooms; a bar permit room; restaurant; coffee shop; and postal, secretarial, laundry, and dry cleaning services.

Hotel Panshikura. Beside the Town Hall, near Underbridge, Ellisbridge; tel. 77611 or 77100. In the downtown area, with 21 air-conditioned rooms and a restaurant.

Rivera Hotel. Khanpur Road; tel. 24201. 65 air-conditioned rooms and seven suites. Facilities include a banquet hall, liquor shop, restaurant with live instrumental music, car rental, and laundry. AP and EP.

Inexpensive

Hotel Alankar. Opposite the Kalupuir Railway Station; tel. 383815. 26 simple rooms, in the center of the downtown area.

Ambassador Hotel. Khanpur Road; tel. 392244. Three km from the railway station. 30 air-conditioned rooms, with attached baths. Basic but clean.

BARODA

Expensive

Express Hotel. R. C. Dutt Road; tel. 67051. 1 ½ km from the downtown area. 64 rooms and two suites, all with attached baths and centrally air-conditioned. Two restaurants, coffee shop, pastry shop, 24-hour room service. AP available on application.

Hotel Surya. Sayahigunj, Baroda; tel. 66592, 63330, or 66514. Approximately five km from the airport and 2 ½ km from the downtown area. 34 air-conditioned rooms with closed-circuit TVs, a restaurant, and a courtesy coach to the airport and railway station.

BHAVNAGAR

Expensive

Welcomgroup Nilambag Palace. One km from downtown on road to airport; tel. 24340, 24422, or 29323. 14 air-conditioned, lovely rooms with attached bath. Restaurant with Indian and Western foods. Facilities include children's room, games room, library, and gardens for outdoor parties.

Moderate

Hotel Apollo. Opposite the Central Bus Station; tel. 25249, 29553, or 23136. 30 air-conditioned rooms with attached baths, channel music, and telephones. Has a restaurant, laundry, curio shop, and hair dresser.

JUNAGADH

Moderate

Lion Safari Lodge. Savangir, District Junagadh; tel. 21, 28. Operated by the GTDC, this lodge has 24 bath-attached rooms, some of which are air-conditioned. AP and EP available with an off-season discount of 10 percent from mid-June to mid-October. Only six comfortable rooms available, so reservations are a must. Restaurant features Continental and Indian cuisines, vegetarian and nonvegetarian. The lodge also arranges trips to the wildlife sanctuary and to local folk dances.

Inexpensive

Hotel Vaibhav. Near S.T. Stand; tel. 20330 or 20491. Near the railway station and the downtown area. 48 rooms, some air-conditioned. Has a vegetarian restaurant, 24-hour coffee shop, car rental, laundry, and catering services.

RAJKOT

Moderate

Galaxy Hotel. Jawahar Road; tel. 31781. Near the downtown area. 35 rooms, most air-conditioned. Has a restaurant for breakfast and snacks only, a laundry, and a car rental.

Hotel Tulsi. Kanta Stre Vikas Gruh Road; tel. 31791 or 31731. Four km from the airport. 36 rooms, some air-conditioned. Has a restaurant, money changing, car rental, laundry, TVs, and a doctor on call.

SURAT
Moderate

Hotel Oasis. Vaishali Cinema, Varachha Road; tel. 41124 or 41091. 1 ½ km from the downtown area. 27 rooms and three suites; some air-conditioned. Indoor and garden restaurants, coffee shop, swimming pool, health club, and wine shop.

Tax-Palazzo Hotel. Ring Road; tel. 43002 and 43018. 43 rooms, half of them air-conditioned. Two restaurants, a coffee shop, 24-hour room service, laundry, valet, and in-house TV movies.

 DINING OUT. Besides the hotel dining rooms, there are some independently owned restaurants in Gujarat, mostly in the *Moderate* and *Inexpensive* classifications. For price ranges of classifications, see *Fact at Your Fingertips.* If you wish to eat at a hotel at which you are not staying, it's best to call to see if you can be accommodated, particularly if it's at a dining room in a small hotel. Wherever you go, you can't order cocktails with your meal. Although there are liquor stores, Gujarat is a dry state as far as bars are concerned.

AHMEDABAD
Moderate

Kwality Restaurant. 9 Relief Rd.; tel. 20309. Indian, Continental, and Chinese foods served in this centrally air-conditioned restaurant, which can accommodate 25 people in its party room. Open 12–4 P.M. and 7–11 P.M.

"Patang." Chinubhai Center, Ashram Road; tel. 77899, 78866, or 77708. A wide array of Indian, Continental, Chinese, Punjabi, and Mughlai dishes accompanied by live Indian classical music. The restaurant also features cooking classes, cuisine demonstrations, and take-out services. Open 12:30–3 P.M. and 7–11 P.M.

Inexpensive

Havmor Restaurant. Opposite Krishna Cinema, Relief Road; tel. 380001. Indian dishes, vegetarian and nonvegetarian. Open 11 A.M.–11 P.M.

Neelam. Three Gates; tel. 348814. Chinese, Continental, and Punjabi foods served in a fully air-conditioned restaurant. Open 12–4 P.M. and 7–11 P.M.

P.D. Gati & Co. B.G. Railway Station; tel. 340456. A small place serving Indian foods 24 hours a day.

BARODA
Moderate

Kwality Restaurant. Sayaji Ganj; tel. 63508. Another in the Kwality chain, this one featuring Indian, Continental, Chinese, Italian, and Peshawari foods served indoors, in an outdoor garden, or catered in your quarters. Open 9 A.M.–11:30 P.M.

Volga Restaurant. Inside the Alankar Cinema Compound, Sayaji Ganj; tel. 63774 or 63993. A wide selection of tasty kebobs served Chinese or Mughlai style. Open 10 A.M.–11:30 P.M.

Inexpensive

Ishwar Bhuvan. Dania Bazar; tel. 541136 or 541184. Indian and Gujarati meals (*thali*) served 11 A.M.–10:30 P.M. An adjoining conference room accommodates 40 persons.

SURAT
Moderate to Inexpensive

Dwahalgiri Health Food Restaurant. Dwahalgiri Apartment, Athwalines; tel. 40040. Chinese, Continental, and Indian vegetarian and health foods served

10 A.M.–10 P.M. Proprietors of this restaurant also give advice on health foods to all diners.

Sahkar. Ajanta Apartments Corner, Ring Road; tel. 48917. Indian, Chinese, and Continental foods served 10 A.M.–midnight.

HOW TO GET AROUND. In Ahmedabad, *Municipal Corporation* runs **buses** from the airport to the city. Otherwise **taxis** are available; from airport to downtown, they should not cost you more than Rs. 50. **Auto-rickshaws** are also available, charges as per meter. For an amusing ride, take a horsedrawn **tonga.** Transport like private taxis can also be arranged by your travel agent or at a common taxi stand. Private taxis charge Rs. 2.50 per km. In Ahmedabad city, most of the important places are inside the city walls and within walking distance. The two farthest points, Chisti's Mosque near Shahpur Gate and Rani Sipra Mosque near Astodia Gate, are less than two miles from each other.

Local transport in Barado is the same as in Ahmedabad. Sightseeing can also be enjoyable on horsedrawn tongas.

At Junagadh, the rather irregular buses take you only four miles to the foot of Girnar hills, where you will find taxis, motor rickshaws, and tongas galore. To go to the Jain temples outside Palitana, you can hire a taxi or shuttle service, or go, after bargaining, by tongas. At Gir Forest, all arrangements are made by the Wildlife Sanctuary, Conservator of the Forest, Junagarh. To see Somnath Temple, hire a taxi at Veraval.

TOURS. In Ahmedabad, the Tourist Corporation of Gujarat Ltd. (TCGL), located on the ground floor at H.K. House, Ashram Road (tel. 449683), offers three separate city tours with the following itineraries:

Adalaj Stepwell–Gandhi Ashram–Hutseeing–Swaminarayan Temple–lunch –Badshah–No Hajiro–Jama Masjid–Teen Darwaza–Calico Museum–Sarkhej–Vishalla.

Adalaj–Mohera–lunch–Sharyas–Sarkhej Roja–Vishalla–Veechaar Museum.

Hutseeing–Swaminarayan Temple–Ratan Pole–Manek Chowk–Rani No Hajira–Jama Masjid–Badshah No Hajira–Teen Darwaza–Shopping on Ashram Road–lunch–N.C. Mehta Museum–Airport.

Most tours leave at 8 A.M. from TCGL and return at 2:30 P.M. daily, costing about Rs. 22. Full-day tours cost about Rs. 45. All are in air-conditioned coaches with a tour guide. TCGL also can arrange for tours via private cars or limousine with a driver and guide.

For children, there is a special *Bal Yatra* guide-accompanied sightseeing trip every Sunday at 8 A.M.; fare Rs.12.

Package Tours. The TCGL offers a selection of package tours throughout Gujarat that include accommodations at rest houses or hotels. All leave from Ahmedabad, but can be arranged through any regional tourist office.

The five-day *Saurashtra Darshan Tour* leaves Ahmedabad every Friday at 6:30 A.M. and returns at 8:30 P.M. the following Tuesday; fare, Rs. 435.

North Gujarat and Rajasthan Tour, also five days, leaves at 6 A.M. each Saturday and returns at 9 P.M. the following Wednesday; fare, Rs. 530–Rs. 645.

A five-day *South Gujarat, Ajanta, and Ellora Tour* leaves on the second and fourth Saturday of each month and returns the following Wednesday; fare, Rs. 660.

Mount Abu Tour, for two days, leaves on the first and second Saturdays and returns the following Sundays; fare, Rs. 195.

Nathwara Tour, also for two days, leaves every third and fourth Saturday, and returns the next evening; fare, Rs. 210.

FESTIVALS AND FAIRS. Gujarat is one state that offers fairs and festivals throughout the year, including many that are celebrated throughout the rest of India. Since most of the events are determined by the lunar calendar, contact the tourist offices for the exact dates. Fairs, which may be rooted in religion to commemorate events in honor of gods or goddesses, are truly secular social events in which all are invited to participate, providing a fine spectacle for tourists.

The year starts off with *Makar Sankrati* in **January–February** with kite flying and the exchange of greetings and vermilion.

Shavnath Fair, in **February** and **March,** is held during Mahashivatri at the foot of Mount Girnar. After a holy dip in the Mrigi Kund, pilgrims offer prayers at the temple. An awe-inspiring midnight ritual is a *Mahapuja,* in which holy men from all over the country ride about the fair on caparisoned elephants to the reverberating accompaniment of musical instruments.

During the colorful *Holi* festival in **March,** people sprinkle each other with dry colors and water. The festival is also marked by folk songs and dances.

Rathyatra, in **March–April,** is by far the biggest festival in Ahmedabad. It is highlighted by a day-long procession of thousands of devotees walking behind temple chariots accompanied by adorned elephants, camels, and trucks carrying mythological tableaux. The procession commemorates the visit of Krishna and Balram to Mathura.

Gokulashtami, the birthday of Krishna, is celebrated in **August** as a joyous festival, with feasting and merrymaking. Large fairs are held in Dwarka. A characteristic feature of this day in Gujarat is the performance of the folk dance, *Dandiya Ras.*

Tranetar Fair, in **August–September,** is a colorful three-day event held at the Trineshwara (three-eyed) Temple. The fair brings together tribal folk dancers in traditional costumes.

The most famous of all festivals is *Navratri,* in **September–October,** with its nine nights of music and dancing devoted to the nine forms of the mother goddess Ambaji. During the festival, there is a competition of *garba* dancing.

During *Diwali* in **November,** a myriad of lights adorn practically every house at night, culminating in firecracker bursts at dawn. The day preceding Diwali is celebrated as the new year, believed to be an auspicious day to enter any business transaction.

 TEMPLES. Gujarat is famous for its temple architecture. *Somnath,* one of the 12 Jyotirlingas or Shiva shrines, is a majestic monument by the seashore, ransacked and destroyed by Moslem invaders time and again but rebuilt on the same spot. It is believed that the temple was first built of gold, then silver, wood, and finally stone. The gates of the shrine were carried away by Mohammad Ghazni in A.D. 1026. The present temple is a recent reconstruction in the old style. Lord Krishna is said to have been cremated at the Triveni Ghat here.

The *Suraj Mandir* is a sun temple close by. A museum housed in the temple contains relics of the old somnath shrine.

Dwarka, is one of the four most sacred pilgrimage centers of Hindus. This is where Lord Krishna came, to leave Mathura and Brindaben and set up his kingdom. Archaeological excavations show that present-day Dwarka is the sixth city on this site having being submerged in the sea. Festival Janmashtami, the birthday of Lord Krishna, is celebrated here with great joy and abandon. It's a five-story temple supported on 60 columns and is crowned by a soaring, elaborately carved spire. Also famous here is an island near Okha port, where, according to legend, Lord Vishnu killed demon Shankhasur. *Nageshwar Mahadev* and *Gopu Talav Teerth* are two other important sacred shrines near Dwarka.

Bhalka Teerth, near Somnath, is the place where Lord Krishna, mistaken for a deer, was wounded by an arrow. The Dehotsarga at Triveni Ghat is where he was cremated.

Tulsishyam, in the heart of Gir Forest, 96 miles from Junagarth, is the scenic spot of Tulsishyam, with its hot springs and a temple dedicated to Bhim and his mother Kunti.

Madhavpur, also associated with Krishna, is believed to be the place where Krishna's marriage took place. The shrine is dedicated to the couple. The annual Madhavpur Fair celebrates the marriage with folk dances and music. The "elopement" of the couple is enacted in a colorful ceremony.

Modhera Sun Temple, 15 miles from Mehrana, is one of the finest examples of Indian architecture of its period. Built in 1026 during the reign of King Bhimdev I of the Solanki dynasty, the temple is dedicated to the sun god Surya and stands high on a plinth overlooking a deep stone-stepped tank. Every inch of the edifice, both inside and outside, is magnificently carved with gods and goddesses, birds, beasts, and flowers. The inner sanctum, which housed the presiding deity, was so designed that the first rays of the rising sun lit up the image of Surya.

Ambaji, situated on the Arasur Hill near Mount Abu, 120 miles from Ahmedabad, is dedicated to the worship of Shakti and is one of the most popular places of pilgrimage in Gujarat. Gujarat Bhavai, a folk drama, is frequently staged in the temple precincts.

Palitana is a breathtaking, picturesque temple city atop the holy mountain, Shatrunjaya, 36 miles from Bhavnagar. It is dedicated to Shri Adhishwara, the first trithanker of the Jains. Every Jain dreams of walking up the hill to build a temple, adding to the 900 odd temples already at the bejeweled crest of the mountain. As you walk up, or are carried up, you can see the marble temples glisten. The fantastic collection of temple jewels can be seen by special permission of the Hill Inspector or Manager of Anandji Kalyanji Trust or during deity-adorning ceremonies at Shri Adishwara Temple.

 CHILDREN'S ACTIVITIES. In Ahmedabad, the TCGL conducts a guide-accompanied tour for children, called *Bal Yatra,* every Sunday at 8 A.M.; fare Rs. 12. Contact the TCGL at H. K. House, Ashram Road (tel. 449683), for details on pick-up and return. Besides touring some of the parks, gardens, and museums, youngsters get to visit a Children's Traffic Training Park, in which they are educated on road safety and traffic rules, and the Vikram Sharabhai Community Center, a house where children can enjoy simple demonstrations in chemistry, physics, and other sciences.

In the city of Rajkot, *Bal Bhavan* is an institution for children's education through indoor and outdoor entertainment. Among the facilities are a library, theater, music and dancing rooms, swimming pool, aquarium, bird house, and playground. Contact the TCGL for details.

 HISTORIC SITES. Ahmedabad was founded in 1411 by Ahmed Shah, so it is natural that one of the city's earliest mosques was built by him. *Ahmed Shah's Mosque,* located in the southwest section of the Bhadra, was rebuilt after it was ransacked as a Hindu temple.

A *Siddi Sayyid Masjid* is a 500-year-old mosque on Relief Road, near the river. The mosque is famous for its latticed windows carved in single stone panels. The pattern of one whole window was formed from the entwined branch of a tree.

Rising above the Sarangpur Gate is the *Mosque of Siddi Bashir,* the architectural marvel of Gujarat. It has two minarets. Gently push one of them and both shake in unison. Each minaret is three stories high and delicately carved. Balanced stone balconies girdle the minarets of each story. Across the railway line, the *Raj Bibi Mosque,* too, had a pair of shaking minarets. The British demolished one of them to unravel the mystery.

Next to Jama Masjid of Delhi, Jama Masjid in Ahmedabad is considered the largest in India. Built in 1423, it has 300 pillars that divide the huge prayer hall into 15 large squares, each one surmounted with a dome.

 MUSEUMS. Gujarat has several museums worth visiting, notably in Ahmedabad and Baroda. Collections range from ancient artifacts and treasures to displays of present-day technology. The museums are generally well-maintained and most are free to the public. The following is a selection you may consider.

AHMEDABAD

The *Calico Museum of Textiles,* situated in Sarabhai House in the Shahi Bagh gardens, is considered one of the finest textile museums in the world—at least in the Far East. Its rare collection of fabrics dates to the seventeenth century. Included are Patola fabrics from Patan and south India, temple cloths, textiles from the Mogul period, handwoven cloths, brocades, and wooden blocks showing the Portuguese influence. Also on display are modern textiles illustrating the advance in the industry. A museum shop that sells reproductions of some of the pieces on display, as well as cards and books. Open daily except Wednesdays, 10 A.M.–12:30 P.M. and 2:30–5 P.M.; tel. 5100. Free.

N. C. Mehta Museum of Miniatures, at Sanskar Kandra, was designed by the noted architect Le Corbusier. It houses rare Indian miniature paintings, a collection amassed by a philanthropist who donated them to the museum. Also on display are regular-size paintings. Open daily except Mondays, 9–11 A.M. and 4–7 P.M.; tel. 78369.

Sabarmati Ashram, six km from Ahmedabad on the banks of the Sabarmati River, is a house where Mahatma Gandhi lived and worked for 15 years. Many of Gandhi's historical events, such as the Dandi March, commenced here. The ashram was founded in 1915 and today houses many of Gandhi's personal effects. It still makes handicrafts, handmade paper, and spinning wheels. Open 8:30 A.M.–6:30 P.M. daily. On Sundays, Tuesdays, Thursdays, and Fridays, at 8:30 P.M., there is a *son et lumiere* show in English with a small admission fee.

Shreyas Folk Museum is in the sloping green woodland that makes up the Shreyas Foundation. The museum has a fine collection of folk art and objects that illustrate the culture of Gujarat. On display are exquisite embroideries; unusual pots, pans, and other utensils; handicrafts; weapons; and bullock and camel carts. The museum also has a children's section that displays costumes, folk art, puppets, coins, and legends of various Indian states. Open afternoons only; call 78295 for details.

BARODA

Baroda Museum and Art Gallery is situated within Sayaji Bagh, a large park along the river. Founded in 1894, the museum has sections on art, archaeology, ethnology, geology, and natural history. The art gallery, in an adjoining building, contains Indian and European paintings. Open daily 9:30 A.M.–4:30 P.M.

Maharaja Fateh Singh Museum, located a little south of the town center along Nehru Road, has a unique collection of art treasures of the former rulers of Baroda. Also on display are the works by Murillo, Raphael, and Titian, as well as modern European and Indian paintings and sculptures and a fine collection of Chinese and Japanese art. Open daily except Mondays 9 A.M.–noon and 3–6 P.M. July–March, 4–7 P.M. April–June.

 PARKS AND GARDENS. *Deer Park,* on the outskirts of Ahmedabad, is adjacent to Sarita Udyan in Indrada village. It's a sprawling reserve for deer, those gentle-looking creatures that provide wonder and entertainment for children, as well as adults, of all ages.

Satira Udyan, in Gandhinagar, 23 km from Ahmedabad, is an ideal spot along the river for the picnickers. The area is under development for the provision of full recreational activities.

Sundervan Snake Garden, off M. Dayanand Road, Ahmedabad, may not be for everyone, for, as its name implies, this garden has a collection of snakes—from all over India. There is also a daily show that includes demonstrations with live snakes. For the less queasy, the garden is inhabited by freely roaming tame ducks and rabbits. And there's even a puppet show in the evenings!

 BEACHES. Gujarat's relatively unexploited coastline of about 1,000 miles is the country's longest, extending from Lakhpat to Umargaon. Along this coastline, beaches are gradually being developed into resorts, each with its own features, unique identity, and attraction.

Ahmedpur-Mandvi is an untouched beach located in Saurashtra, seven miles from Una railway station, providing entry to the Union Territory of Diu, which it borders. The beach has palm trees of a unique variety not found generally in India. The terrain and the landscape at Ahmedpur-Mandvi are as equally attractive as the beach. Tourist Bungalow is operated by Tourism Corporation. Attractive double and single rooms are also available at Samudra Beach resort. Sports include para-sailing and surfing.

Chorwad, an old summer palace resort of the erstwhile nabob of Junagarh is being converted into a luxurious sea resort, with a swimming pool, conference hall, and other facilities. The majestic palace rising on the seashore can make an exotic setting. At an interesting fishing community there, freshly caught fish and coconuts are on display. State Transport operates buses from Ahmedabad to Chorwad. Contact TCGL (tel. 449683) for details.

 WILDLIFE SANCTUARIES. Asiatic lions, those increasingly rare beauties, can be spotted at close range in the wildlife sanctuary at *Sasan Gir Forest,* the last major stronghold of the beasts. Also in the 500-square-mile forest are leopards, antelope, sambars, varieties of deer, and wild boar. Sasan Gir is reached daily by Indian and Vayudoot Airlines from Ahmedabad to Keshod, and then by road for 42 miles to the forest. There is also a narrow-gauge line of the Western Railway from Ahmedabad, as well as bus services from Junagarh and Veraval.

Visiting arrangements can be made by the TCGL offices, which offer two-day packages with pick-up at Keshod, transfers to the ITDC-operated Sasan Gir Forest Lodge, and escorted visits to the forest preserve. The ground package costs Rs. 950, including accommodations.

The best time for visiting the sanctuary is March–May, when you have a chance to see the animals lazing near water holes. The forest is closed during the monsoon season. Photographs are permitted, but there is a Rs. 25 charge for movie cameras. If you go by jeep, guides cost Rs. 7.50.

Valvadar Sanctuary, housing the exquisite black buck, consists of a grassland preserve through which visitors are driven by jeep. The black buck, one of the swiftest animals, can run at a speed of 60 mph. For arrangements and information on visiting the sanctuary, contact the TCGL offices.

 SHOPPING. Gujarat offers a scintillating range of fabrics, including woven textiles, vegetable-dye paintings, tie-dye work, gold and silver thread work (*zari*), silk embroidery, and various styles of saris. Also popular and lovely are mirror work on cloth, bead-encrusted artifacts from Rajkot, lacquered furniture from Sankheda, and wood carvings from Ahmedabad. In the *Manek Chowk* bazaar, Ahmedabad, you can find these items in shops next to jewelers, gold and silver shops, fruit markets, and vegetable stalls.

In Baroda, the best shopping area is *Leheripura Mandir Bazaar,* with its many shops dealing in fabrics, jewelry, and curios. In the *Fine Arts Faculty Building* of Baroda University can be found a wide selection of pottery, from antique to newly made pieces.

Bazaars generally are open 9 A.M.–7 P.M. daily, but main shopping complexes are closed Sundays. Bargaining is common at most shops (except government-operated stores), since prices are generally hiked when shopkeepers spot a tourist. Traveler's checks and credit cards are accepted only at the better places, hotel arcades, and government shops.

MADHYA PRADESH

India's Heartland

by
KATHLEEN COX and RAVI KHANNA

A journey into the heart of India carries you back to historic moments
of valor, glory, passion, and divinity. Madhya Pradesh's life is etched
in stone—arrested by the chisels of master craftsmen. This lovely state
is also studded with meandering rivers, extensive lush forests, hills and
ravines, and some of the rarest species of birds and beasts, including
the exquisite and elusive tiger. Conservationists have rated the Kanha
and Bandhavgrah National parks, with their undulating meadows and
abundant wildlife, as the finest in the country. Indeed, Madhya Pradesh
is the original Kipling country, the hunting grounds of Akela the wolf,
Kaa the python, and Sher Khan the tiger.

Long before the written word, the magic of this central state was
inscribed in colors that defied time, remaining as permanent reminders
inside nearly 500 labyrinthine caves of Bhimbetka. On the caves' walls,
a series of prehistoric paintings in vivid and panoramic detail sweep you
back to at least 8000 B.C. In fact, you can call this entire state a museum
without walls—one that contains over 1,800 man-made monuments,
including some of the world's finest. Here, you can visit the *stupa*
(shrine) at Sanchi, purportedly the best example of Buddhist architecture in India; the Bhimbetka rock shelter paintings that date back to
the Mesolithic Period (approximately 8000 B.C.); and the Gwalior Fort,
which Babur called "the pearl in the necklace of Indian forts." You can
also see the beautifully preserved medieval town of Orchra; Mandu, a
city built for joy by the Moslems in the fifteenth and sixteenth centuries

about which the Emperor Jahangir wrote, "Of all places in Hindustan none is more beautiful than Mandu after the rains"; and, of course, the unforgettable temples at Khajuraho, where the ecstasy of passion has been immortalized in stone.

The Historic Record

When the great Ashoka ruled over the Maurya Empire in the third century B.C., he laid the foundation of the great stupa at Sanchi. Shortly after his death, his empire collapsed and the Sungas took over, followed by the Guptas (A.D. 300–500), whose reign is referred to as the Golden Age. Repeated invasions of the Huns from Central Asia finally led to triumph over the splendor of the Guptas' Malwa Empire. The Huns, in turn, were defeated early in the seventh century by the famous Hindu emperor Harsha, who supposedly put 60,000 war elephants and 100,-000 horses on the battlefields to achieve his conquest. Despite the fear this man inspired on the battlefield, Harsha did have a benevolent streak. Every five years he distributed to the poor all his accumulated riches until finally he was reduced to begging.

The close of the tenth century witnessed a period of confusion from which emerged the Paramara dynasty with the great king Bhoja, a renowned Sanskrit scholar. The succeeding Chandellas created the magnificent temples at Khujaraho. The first Moslem invasions in the eleventh century ushered in a 400-year period of constant skirmishing between Moslems and Hindus—the latter reasserting themselves each time the Delhi sultanate showed any weakness; then, the stake in the battle was usually the fabled city of Mandu. The last of the great Mogul emperors, the fanatic Aurangzeb, managed to extend his rule through this part of India, but at such tremendous financial cost, his empire collapsed with his death. Next came the Marathas, who started life as peasants skilled in guerrilla warfare. They reigned over Malwa until the advent of the British at the close of the eighteenth century.

EXPLORING MADHYA PRADESH

The first stop on a tour of this state is Nasik (actually in the state of Maharastra and about two hours from Bombay). The road winds through forests, with the panorama of the hills and ravines of the Western Ghats spreading out over the horizon. On the right about five miles before Nasik, you come to the Pandu Lena Buddhist caves. From here you have a good view of the prosperous countryside dotted with stone houses and barns.

A holy city of the Hindus, Nasik lies on the banks of the sacred river Godavari. Lord Rama, hero of the epic *Ramayana,* spent the major part of his exile here. According to the Hindu legend, Nasik is also where Surpanakha, the sister of the demon king Ravana, lost her nose in an encounter with Lakshmana, Rama's brother. The Khumba Mela, the most important Indian fair, is held at Nasik every 12 years. At this time, millions of devotees from all over the country congregate to have a holy dip in the water, an act of purification that rids one of all sins.

Ages ago, recounts the legend, the gods and demons fought constantly for preeminence. Both discovered the existence of a *kumbh,* or pitcher, resting at the bottom of the sea. This kumbh contained nectar that would make any drinker immortal. To share the heavenly drink, the rivals pretended to make up their differences, but after the tremendous effort required to obtain the pitcher, Vishnu snatched it and ran off. During a 12-day tussle, four drops of nectar fell one each upon Nasik, Ujjain, Haridwar, and Allahabad. Since a day in heaven, the scene of the battle, equals a year on earth, each of these four cities, in rotation, now has the right to hold a Kumbh Mela, with a festival occurring every three years in each 12-year period.

The oldest shrine in Nasik is the Kapaleshwar Siva Temple. Before you cross the Godavari River, you see the blackened 200-year-old Sundar Narayan Temple. Although most of the shrines are on the opposite bank, some smaller temples plus a memorial to Gandhi are situated on an isle in the Godavari.

In Trimbak, 19 miles away and also in Maharashtra, you can walk to the source of the sacred Godavari River. Here, above a cascading waterfall tumbling down from the top of a long range of hills, Hindu devotees bathe in a cistern that collects the trickle of water. From this rivulet, the Godavari turns into an important water source that irrigates the plateau and extends all the way to the Bay of Bengal. Such obvious importance explains the river's prominence in Hindu legend and lore.

Sanchi

Sanchi sits on a hill crowned by a group of stupas and pillars that represent the peak of perfection in Buddhist art and architecture. This holy site occupies a unique position in the history of Buddhism. Originally consecrated by the Kushan rulers in A.D. first century, Emperor Ashoka sought to give permanence to this site by replacing the original wooden structures and railings with perfectly wrought stone embellished in forms and symbols that expressed Buddhist teachings. After he finished eight stupas at Sanchi, he built a nunnery for his queen, who came from Vidisha, espoused Buddhism, and entered the holy order of nuns. Meanwhile, his son, Mahendra, went to Sri Lanka spreading the faith to that island.

The glory that was Sanchi, seat of Buddhist learning and place of pilgrimage during the third century B.C., can still be experienced in the site's serene complex of structures. Every form of Buddhist architecture found expression here: stupas, temples, pillars, monasteries, and four magnificent *toranas,* or gateways. The master builders and carvers of these stupendous portals made of buff sandstone taken from the Udaigiri Hills drew inspiration from the *Jataka* tales (stories about the previous lives of the Buddha). The carvers, by trade silversmiths from Vidisha, brought to fruition on stone all the intricate, detailed skill of design and pattern consistent with their jeweler's art. The profuse carvings on the gateways depict the Buddha's incarnations and all the great moments in his life, which, in dramatic sequence, reveal the intense faith and supreme artistry of the creators of Sanchi.

After the decline of Buddhism in India, Sanchi went into oblivion. In 1818, Sir John Marshall, the director general of the Archaeological Survey of India, rediscovered the numerous remains. The architectural pieces and sculptures displayed here include the Ashoka pillar and images of the Buddha and Kushan.

At Sanchi, be certain to see the following:

Great Stupa No. 1. 36.5 meters in diameter and 16.4 meters high, this magnificent commemorative structure is a landmark in Buddhist architecture. Its construction was started during the reign of Emperor Ashoka but was completed by his successors in the second and first centuries B.C. The present stupa is a superstructure with a hemispherical dome that contains Buddhist relics built over the original earthen mound. It surmounts a high circular dome with a railing around its

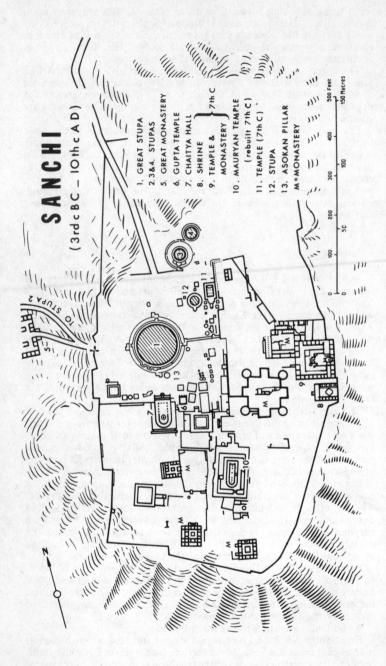

SANCHI
(3rd c BC – 10th c AD)

1. GREAT STUPA
2. 3&4. STUPAS
5. GREAT MONASTERY
6. GUPTA TEMPLE
7. CHAITYA HALL
8. SHRINE ⎫
9. TEMPLE & ⎬ 7th C
   MONASTERY ⎭
10. MAURYAN TEMPLE
    (rebuilt 7th C)
11. TEMPLE (7th C)
12. STUPA
13. ASOKAN PILLAR
M = MONASTERY

TO STUPA 2

0   100   200   300   400   500 Feet
0   50   100   150 Metres

base. The railing encompassing the dome has four elaborately carved toranas that are among the finest examples of Buddhist art.

Gateways. Bas-reliefs on the toranas depict tales of Buddha's previous incarnations and main events in his life in symbolic form—footprints, the Bodhi tree, the Wheel of Law, and the stupa motifs. The eastern gateway depicts the departure of Gautama (who eventually became Buddha) from his father's place, his mother's dreams before his birth, and the miracles of Gautama as Buddha. The western gateway shows the seven incarnations of Buddha. The middle architrave exhibits the preachings of Buddha's first sermon in the Deer Park at Sarnath. The northern gateway has on its top a broken Buddhist Wheel of Law. Its pillars depict the miracles of Buddha. Carvings on the southern gateway represent the birth of Gautama, with his mother, standing by the side of a lotus flower, flanked by two elephants pouring water over her head.

Stupa No. 2. Situated about .5 km from the Great Stupa, this shrine, standing on the edge of a hill, dates back to the second century B.C. It's surrounded by a well-preserved balustrade.

Stupa No. 3. Built 150–140 B.C., this stupa has a hemispherical dome surmounted by an umbrella. In the chambers of this stupa was found the relics of Sariputta and Mahamogallana, two of Buddha's first disciples.

Ashoka Pillar. Adjoining the southern gateway, the fragments on the Ashoka column depict an inscription in Brahmi characters instructing Buddhists to avoid schism. An outstanding feature of this pillar is its lustrous polish, dating back to the third century B.C. The Republic of India adopted the lion motif on the pillar as its state emblem.

Buddhist Vihara (monastery). The reenshrinement of the relics of the two disciples of Buddha—Sariputta and Mahamogallana—in the new vihara at Sanchi was one of the greatest Buddhist events of this century. The relics have been enshrined in glass caskets on a platform in the inner sanctum of the new temple.

Gupta Temple. Adjoining the Great Stupa, this is the earliest known structural temple in India. Dating back to A.D. fourth century, it's built of dressed stone slabs and has a flat roof.

Great Bowl. Carved out of one piece of stone, the Great Bowl was used to distribute food collected from the monks through begging.

Mandu

Mandu is a celebration in stone, of life and joy, of the love of the poet-prince Baz Bahadur for his beautiful consort, Rani Roopmati. Balladeers of Malwa still sing of the romance of these royal lovers. High up on the crest of a hill, Roopmati's pavilion continues to look down on Baz Bahadur's palace—a magnificent expression of Afghan architecture.

Perched along the Vindhyan ranges, at an altitude of 2,000 feet, Mandu, with its natural defenses, was originally the fort-capital of the Paramar rulers of Malwa. Later, toward the end of the thirteenth century, it came under the sway of the sultans of Malwa, the first of whom renamed it Shadibad, "the city of joy." And indeed, the pervading spirit of Mandu was gaiety, with its rulers building exquisite palaces like the Jahaz and Hindola Mahals, ornamental canals, and graceful baths and pavilions. Each of Mandu's structures is an architectural gem; some are outstanding, like the massive Jami Masjid and Houshang Shah's Tomb, which inspired the builders of the Taj Mahal centuries later. Under Mogul rule, Mandu was a pleasure resort, its lakes and palaces the scenes of splendid and extravagant festivities. The

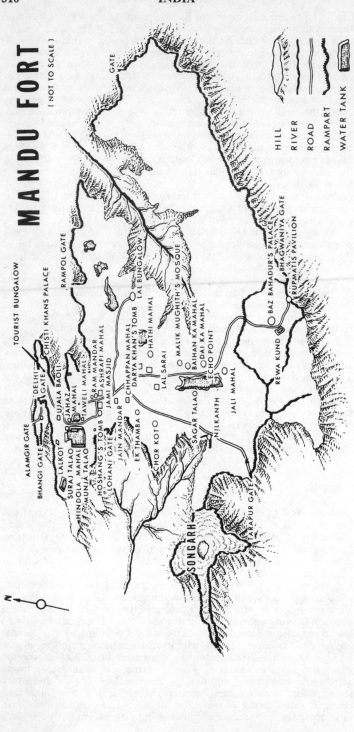

MANDU FORT
(NOT TO SCALE)

HILL

RIVER

ROAD

RAMPART

WATER TANK

GATE

TOURIST BUNGALOW

CHISTI KHANS PALACE

RAMPOL GATE

DELHI GATE

ALAMGIR GATE

BHANGI GATE

UJALA BAOLI

JAHAZ MAHAL

TAWELI MAHAL

RAM MANDAR

ASHRAFI MAHAL

JAMI MASJID

LAIKOT

SURAJ TALAO

HINDOLA MAHAL

MUNJA TALAO

HOSHANG'S TOMB

LOHANI MAHAL

JAIN MANDAR

EK THAMBA

CHOR KOTO

SAGAR TALAO

NILKANTH

CHHAPPAN MAHAL

DARYA KHAN'S TOMB

LAL BUNGALOW

HATHI MAHAL

LAL SARAI

MALIK MUGHITH'S MOSQUE

BAIHAN KA MAHAL

DAI KA MAHAL

ECHO POINT

JALI MAHAL

BAZ BAHADUR'S PALACE

BHAGWANIYA GATE

RUPMATIS PAVILION

REWA KUND

TARAPUR GATE

SONGARH

N

glory of Mandu lives on, in its palaces, mosques, legends, and songs chronicled for posterity.

Twelve gateways punctuate the 45-kilometer parapet of walls that encircle Mandu. Most notable of these is the Delhi Darwaza, the main entrance to the fortress city, approached through a series of well-fortified gateways with walled enclosures and strengthened by bastions, such as the Alamgir and Bhangi Barwaza, through which the present road passes. The Rampol Darwaza, Jahangir Gate, and Tarapur Gate are other main gateways.

Those with an appetite for royal architecture can feast on the following:

Jahaz Mahal. This 120-meter-long "ship palace," built between the two artificial lakes, Munj Talao and Kapur Talao, is an elegant two-story palace. It was probably built by Sultan Ghyas-ud-din Khalji for his large harem. With its open pavilions, balconies overhanging the water, and open terrace, the Jahaz Mahal is an imaginative re-creation in stone of a royal pleasure craft. Viewed on moonlit nights from the adjoining Taveli Mahal, the silhouette of the building, with the tiny domes and turrets of the pavilion gracefully perched on the terrace, is an unforgettable spectacle.

Hindola Mahal. An audience hall also from Ghiyas-ud-din's reign, this structure derives the name of "Swinging Palace" from its sloping sidewalls. Superb and innovative techniques are also evident in its ornamental façade: delicate trellis work in beautifully moulded sandstone columns. To the west of Hindola Mahal stand several unidentified buildings that still bear traces of past grandeur. Note the elaborately constructed wall called Champa Baoli that is connected to underground vaulted rooms in which cold and hot water were once available. Other places of interest in this enclave are Dilawar Khan's mosque, the Nahar Jharokha (tiger balcony), Taveli Mahal, and two large wells called the Ujali (bright) and Andheri (dark).

Ashrafi Mahal. This "palace of gold coins," which faces the Jama Masjid, was built by Hoshang Shah's successor, Mahmud Shah Khilji. Conceived as an academic institution (*madrassa*) for young boys, the study cells still remain in a fair state of preservation. In the same complex, Khilji built a seven-story tower to celebrate his victory over Rana Khumba of Mewar; only one story survives. The tomb, intended to be the largest structure in Mandu, is also in ruins.

Baz Bahadur's Palace. Built in the sixth century, the palace's unique features include a spacious courtyard surrounded by halls and high terraces that afford a superb view of the surrounding countryside.

Nilkanth Mahal. Located near the Nilkanth shrine, this palace, which belongs to the Mogul Era, was constructed by Mogul governor Shah Badgah Khan for Emperor Akbar's Hindu wife. On the walls are inscriptions, written during the time of Akbar, that refer to the futility of earthly pomp and glory.

Hoshang Shah's Tomb. India's first marble edifice is a refined example of Afghan architecture. Examine the magnificently proportioned dome, marble latticework of remarkable delicacy, and porticoed courts and towers that mark each corner of the rectangle. Shah Jahan sent four of his greatest architects to study the tomb's design. Among them was Ustad Hamid, who has been linked to the construction of Shah Jahan's Taj Mahal.

Jami Masjid. The great mosque of Damascus inspired the Jami Masjid, conceived on a grand scale with a high plinth and a huge domed porch projecting into the center. Similar imposing domes with seemingly innumerable domes filling the intervening space dominate the background. Most visitors are immediately struck by the vastness of the building and the simplicity of its construction. The great court of the mosque is enclosed by huge colonnades with a rich and pleasing variety of arches, pillars, number of bays, and domes above.

Roopmati's Pavilion. This graceful pavilion was originally built as an army observation post and later served as a retreat for the queen. From its hilltop perch, the queen could see Baz Bahadur's palace and the Narmada flowing through the Nimar plains far below.

Hathi Mahal, Darya Khan's Tomb, Dai ka Maha, Malik Mughith's Mosque, and Jali Mahal are some of Mandu's other fascinating monuments. Also visit Echo Point, the "Delphic Oracle" of Mandu, where a shout reverberates some distance and is clearly heard back.

The Lohani caves and temple ruins, not far from the royal enclave, also merit a visit. While you are there, pause at Sunset Point, in front of the caves. From here, you'll have a panoramic view of the surrounding countryside.

Gwalior Fort

Agra is only a crossroads stop on your trip south. Seventy-two miles away is Gwalior—and yet another chapter in Indian history, where the Moguls only played a minor part near the end of a long drama.

Gwalior is practically synonymous with its fort, one of the oldest in India (it is mentioned in an inscription dated A.D. 525). According to a legend, Suraj Sena, a local leader suffering from leprosy, met a Hindu saint, Gwalipa, on the rocky hill where the fort now stands. Gwalipa offered him a drink of water from Suraj Kund, a sacred pool. The drink cured the leper. Gwalipa then told Suraj Sena to build a fort on the hill (the derivation of the name Gwalior) and to use the name of Pal if he wanted his dynasty to survive. Suraj Pal's family flourished until one cynic refused to obey the tradition. Naturally, that was the end of the kingdom.

The grandeur of Gwalior dates back to another dynasty, the Tomars, who established their rule in the fourteenth century. A Tomar king, Man Singh (1486–1516) built the Man Mandir, a six-towered palace that forms the eastern wall of the fort and one of the sights of India. Three hundred feet long and 80 feet deep, it is decorated with perforated screens, mosaics, floral designs, and moldings in Hindu profusion. Beneath it, two underground floors were burrowed into the 300-foot-high hill of the fort, serving as air-conditioned summer quarters for Man Singh—and dungeons for the prisoners of the Moguls who, under the rule of Akbar, seized the fort.

Captured by the Marathas in 1784, Gwalior Fort became the scene of fierce fighting again in 1857, when it was the base for 18,000 Indians who rose up against the British in the Sepoy Revolt (Indian Mutiny), the beginning of India's struggle for independence. Under Tantia Topi and a woman hero, Rani Lakshmi Bai of Jhansi, the Indians made a valiant last stand. The rani's cenotaph is in Gwalior.

Man Singh also built the Gujari Mahal, a turreted palace of stone—now the home of an archaeological museum. This palace was also built for love. The king met a Gujar maiden, Mriganayana (the "Fawn Eyed"), famed for her skill as a slayer of wild animals. She agreed to marry him only if he brought the waters of the Rai River, the secret source of her strength, into the fort. For the sake of his bride, Man Singh built the Gujari Mahal and an aqueduct linking it to the Rai.

A visit to the Gwalior Fort requires an arduous climb up to the gates (elephants, bearing royalty, once used the road, which is too steep for cars). The fort contains a mosque on the site of the shrine of Saint Gwalipa; Chaturbhuj Mandir temple housing a four-armed idol of Vishnu; and five groups of gigantic Jain sculptures carved out of rock walls. The biggest, the image of the first Jain pontiff, Adinath, is 57 feet high with a foot measuring nine feet. It was constructed in 1440.

Vishnu also reigns in eleventh-century temples known as Sas Bahu (the mother-in-law and daughter-in-law temples). Another temple, the Telika-Mandir, with its 100-foot tower, is the highest building in the fort. This temple is an interesting blend of Dravidian architecture from south India, typified by the spire, with Indo-Aryan decoration on its walls. Finally, visit the Suraj Kund, the oldest Gwalior shrine, the pond that cured Suraj (Scna) Pal.

Outside the fort, Gwalior offers the tomb of Muhammad Ghaus, a Moslem saint worshiped by the Moguls, and the tomb of Tansen, one of Akbar's court musicians, which is still venerated by musicians. Lashkar, a mile from the fort, is a "modern" city built in 1809 on the site of an encampment. There you can visit two palaces, the Jai Vilas and the Moti Mahal, and a picturesque bazaar, the Inderganj Chowk. Gwalior is an ideal take-off point to many other destinations within the state.

Shivpuri

Steeped in royal legacies of the past, Shivpuri, former summer capital of the Scindia rulers of Gwalior, is 112 km from Gwalior on the Agra-Bombay Highway. A charming town, with palaces and artificial lakes, Shivpuri's fabled *chatris* (cenotaphs) are a reminder of former glory. These memorials to the Scindia dynasty are unique for their delicate filigree and inlaid marble work and their fusion of Hindu and Moslem architecture. Even before Shivpuri was a royal summer capital, its dense forests were the hunting grounds of the Mogul emperors, including Akbar, who captured great herds of elephants for his stables. Much later, tigers roamed the wooded hills, and royal *shikaris* (hunters) bagged many a magnificent beast. Shivpuri was also a natural choice for the summer resort capital. Shivpuri's royal ambience lives on in the exquisite palaces and hunting lodges and the graceful, intricately embellished marble chatris erected by the Scindia princes.

A sanctuary for rare wildlife and avifauna, Shivpuri is best known for its Madhav National Park. Driving through its 156 km of jungle is an enthralling experience, offering many glimpses of deer, blue bull, wild boar, and a variety of rare birds. The park, open throughout the year, is equally rich in waterfowl. An artificial lake, Chandpata, is the winter home of migratory geese, pochard, pintail, teal, mallard, and gadwall. The point where the forest track crosses the wide rocky stream that flows from the Waste Weir provides a good site for bird-watching. Species that frequent this spot are redwattled lapwing, large-pied wagtail, pond heron, white-breasted kingfisher, cormorant, painted stork, white ibis, lagger falcon, purple sunbird, paradise flycatcher, and golden oracle.

The cenotaphs of the Scindias are set in a Mogul garden, with quiet nooks under flowering trees intersected by pathways with ornamental balustrades, illuminated by Victorian lamps. The chatris of Madhu Rao Scindia and Maharani Sakhya Raje Scindia, the dowager queen, face each other across a water tank. With their shikhara-type spires and Rajput and Mogul pavilions, they synthesize the architectural idioms of the Hindu and Islamic styles. The white marble surface of Madho Rao Scindia's cenotaph follows the pietradura style, with lapis lazuli and onyx creating a spectacularly rich effect that is heightened by the delicacy of the trellis work on the sides. The dowager queen's cenotaph has a noble dignity of line and superb structural harmony. Both memorials contain life-size images of the Scindias, which ceremonially dressed retainers bless with flowers and incense each day. Each evening, classical ragas break the stillness that envelops the statues.

Rising from a natural eminence is Madhav Vilas Palace, the elongated rose-pink summer palace of the Scindias that was built on truly royal proportions. A fine example of colonial architecture, the "Mahal," as it is called, has remarkable marble floors, iron columns, graceful terraces, and a Ganapati *mandapa* (pavilion). From the turrets, the view of Shivpuri and the park beyond is spectacular.

At the highest point, deep within the forests of the park is the turreted George castle, built by Jiyaji Rao Scindia, that offers a lovely view of the lake. The best time to visit the castle is at sunset when the lake mirrors the changing hues of the day. Edging the forests of the Madhav National Park is the Sakhya Sagar lake, habitat of a variety of reptiles, including marsh crocodile or mugger, Indian python, and the monitor lizard. Bhadaiya Kund nearby is a scenic picnic spot at a natural spring, whose water is rich in minerals, with supposedly curative powers.

Other Sites Out of Gwalior

The medieval township of Orchha has hardly been touched by the hand of time. Lying 120 kilometers from Gwalior on the road to Khajuraho, Orchha is famous for its palaces and temples, built in the seventeenth and eighteenth centuries. Orchha was once the capital of the Bundela Rajputs, later under Mogul rule, and some of its palaces contain murals of the Bundela school. Particularly worth seeing is the Jahangir Mahal, a rectangular palace with eight minarets, which the Bundela raja, Bir Singh Ju Deo, built to commemorate the Emperor Jahangir's visit in the seventeenth century. See four important temples: the Chaturbhuj, Janaki, Laxmi, and Raja Ram mandirs. The Laxmi Mandir has exquisite paintings that adorn the ceilings and walls of three corridors. Vibrant in color and stylization, the paintings are in an excellent state of preservation and express religious themes and historical events, such as the 1857 uprising. The exterior of this temple is an interesting combination of temple and fort architecture.

The Madhya Pradesh State Tourism Development Corporation has converted the Sheesh Mahal into a hotel unit, giving visitors to Orchha the unique opportunity of experiencing the bygone splendor of this ancient city.

Datia is situated 69 kilometers from Gwalior on the Delhi-Madras main railroad line. Connected also by roads to Gwalior, Bhopal, and Jhansi, Datia is a town whose antiquity can be traced back to the *Mahabharata*. A town of great historic significance, highlighted by a seven-storied palace built entirely of stone and brick by Raja Bir Singh Ju Deo in 1614. The palace is considered one of the finest examples of Bundela architecture in the country. Within it are some fine wall paintings of the Bundela school. The Mogul frescoes in Datia's other attraction, the imposing Gopeshwar Temple, also reveal an interesting blend of cultures.

Surrounded by forested hills and lakes, Chanderi is a craft center famous for its saris and brocades. This city, 239 kilometers from Gwalior, has been influenced in its architecture by the Bundela Rajputs and the sultans of Malwa. The Koshak Mahal, built on the orders of Mohammed Khilji of Malwa in 1445, has an architectural style similar to the Jahaz Mahal in Mandu. The Jama Masjid and Shahzadi Ka Rouza were also built by the Malwa sultans, as was the Battisi Bandi built in 1485 by Sultan Ghyasuddin Shah. Northwest of Chanderi is the picturesque tank and temple complex of Parameshwar Tal, built by the

Bundelas. The old city of Chanderi, which has Jain temples of the ninth and tenth centuries, remains an important center of pilgrimage.

Narwar was once the capital of Raja Nal, whose love for Damyanti has been the theme of many legends and folksongs. Narwar lies 122 kilometers from Gwalior. Like Gwalior, it is dominated by a magnificent fort, standing on a hilltop, 500 feet above the town. The fort and Narwar's palaces are typically Rajput in style, with flat ceilings, fluted columns, and multifoil arches. Glass beads are an interesting interior embellishment.

Known as Padmavati in ancient times, Pawaya is a fascinating complex of ruins, 68 kilometers from Narwar on the Gwalior-Jhansi road. Pawaya's ruins still bear testimony to the days when it was the capital of the Nag Kings in A.D. 3. Particularly noteworthy is the life-size statue of Chaksha Manibhadra of A.D. 1. The ruins of the medieval fort built by the Paramars and the nearby Dhoomeshwar Mahadeo Temple are Pawaya's other attractions.

Bhopal and the Narmada River

Bhopal is the gateway to Indian antiquity at Sanchi. You can see caravans of camels ambling leisurely on the way to this lakeside capital of Madhya Pradesh, with a population of around half a million. Bhopal, nestling in rich foliage, is half hidden among mountains. A myriad of lights from houses along the lake are reflected in the lake's placid waters. Tall minarets and mosques stand majestically against the backdrop of shimmering city lights. It was in the eleventh century that the legendary Raja Bhoj (1010–53), fond of lakeside views, created a lake around which grew a sprawling city, Bhopal, named after him. Soon more lakes and gardens, parks and ponds were constructed, turning Bhopal into a beautiful city. Succeeding battalions of invaders seemed determined to erase it from the face of the earth, and Bhopal went into oblivion.

For a long while, Bhopal remained silent. But with the coming of the extravagant Moguls in the fourteenth century, the city was reborn.

The Afghan general of the Moguls, Dost Muhammed Khan, came here and was taken by its natural beauty. He set out a plan, and the new city of Bhopal began to take life on the ruins of the old city. Soon, the city, with its lakes, parks, gardens, and broad avenues, became a popular retreat. The Moguls made it a refuge for artists and musicians and a city of monuments and mausoleums. Their influence still lingers. Amuse yourself by watching a man, late in the night, with a *paan* in his mouth, an exquisitely carved silver purse in his hand, humming the lines of a poem. He has just come out of a *mushaira,* a symposium of poets.

Khan started the trend of creating picturesque lakes and raising beautiful monuments, with each ruler being more ambitious than his predecessor. Today, Bhopal is replete with fascinating monuments and lovely lakes. Centuries have passed, rulers have come and gone, but the monuments are still under construction. The sprawling Taj-ul-Masjid, started by Begum Shah Jahan in the 1600s, still incomplete, consists of an impressive main hall with an interarched roof, a broad facade, and a wide courtyard. Other monuments include the Jama Masjid, built by Qudsia Begum, which has tall dark minarets crowned with glittering golden spikes. The famous Moti Masjid is patterned on Delhi's Jama Masjid.

An outstanding feature of Bhopal, of course, is its two picturesque lakes. An overbridge divides one lake into two—Upper Lake and Lower Lake. The Upper Lake is over two square kilometers in size.

From the two high points of Idgah and Shamla you get a fabulous view of the sunset and the twinkling city lights on the lakes.

Bhojpur is also renowned for the remains of its magnificent Shiva temple and of two huge dams. The temple, known as the Bhojeshwar Temple, was constructed in a simple square plan, with each wall measuring 66 feet—an unusual design for such buildings. Its richly carved dome, though incomplete, has a magnificent soaring strength of line and is supported by four pillars. These pillars, like the dome, have been conceived on a massive scale, yet retain a remarkable elegance because of their tapered form.

Richly carved above, the plain doorway is a sharp relief from the two exquisitely sculpted figures that stand on either side. On the temple's other sides are balconies, each supported by massive brackets and four intricately carved pillars. The lingam in the sanctum rises to an awe-inspiring height of 7½ feet with a circumference of 18 feet. Set on a massive platform 21½ feet square and composed of three superimposed limestone blocks, the architectural harmony of the lingam and platform creates a superb synthesis of solidity and lightness. The temple was never completed, and an earthen ramp used to raise stones to dome-level still stands.

West of Bhojpur once lay a vast lake, but nothing remains today except the ruins of two huge dams that contain the lake's waters. The lake was destroyed by Hoshang Shah of Malwa (1405–34), who cut through the lesser dam, either intentionally or in a fit of destructive passion, and added an enormous fertile area to his possessions. According to a Gond legend, it took an army three months to cut through the dam and three years to empty it; then its bed was not habitable for 30 years. The climate of Malwa was considerably altered by the removal of this vast sheet of water.

Surrounded by the northern fringe of the Vindhyan ranges, Bhimbetka lies 40 kilometers south of Bhopal. In this rocky terrain of dense forest and craggy cliffs, over 500 rock shelters were recently discovered, extending back to the Mesolithic Period (about 8000 B.C.). Hundreds of paintings in the caves depict the life of the prehistoric cave dwellers, making the Bhimbetka group an archaeological treasure, an invaluable chronicle of the history of humanity.

Executed mainly in red and white with occasional greens and yellows and with themes taken from the everyday events of eons ago, most scenes depict hunting, dancing, music, horse and elephant riders, animal fights, honey collection, decoration of bodies, disguises, and household scenes. Animals, such as bisons, tigers, lions, wild boar, elephants, deer, antelopes, dogs, monkeys, lizards, and crocodiles, are also shown in abundance. In some caves, popular religious and ritual symbols occur frequently. The superimposition of paintings indicates that the same canvas was used by different people at different times.

The Narmada River has played a vital role in the history and development of Madhya Pradesh. Around it have sprung many places of historic and religious interest. Marble Rocks, soaring in glittering splendor, rise to 100 feet on either side of the Narmada, creating a scene of cool serenity. In his *Highlands of Central India,* Captain J. Forsyth speaks eloquently about the infinitely varied beauty of the rocks:

The eye never wearies of the effect produced by the broken and reflected sunlight, now glancing from a pinnacle of snow-white marble reared against the deep blue of the sky as from a point of silver; touching here and there with bright lights the prominences of the middle heights; and again losing itself in the soft bluish greys of their recesses.

Boating facilities are available from November to May, and although boating by moonlight is a thrilling experience, the Marble Rocks have been recently floodlit, adding a new dimension to their splendor. The Narmada, making its way through the rocks, narrows down and then plunges in a waterfall known as Dhuandhar, or the smoke cascade. The falls and the breaking of the water at the crest present an awesome spectacle.

Situated atop a hillock and approached by a long flight of steps, the Chausath Yogini Temple commands a singularly beautiful sight of the Narmada flowing through the Marble Rocks. Dedicated to goddess Durga, this tenth-century temple has exquisitely carved stone figures of deities belonging to the Kalchuri period. According to a local legend, this ancient temple is connected to the Gond Queen Durgavati's palace through an underground passage.

Jabalpur

A pleasure resort and the capital of the Gond Kings during the twelfth century, Jabalpur was later the seat of the Kalchuri dynasty. The Marathas held sway over it until 1817, when the British wrested it from them and left their impression on the spacious cantonment with its colonial residences and barracks. Today, Jabalpur is an important administrative center bustling with commercial activity. The places of interest in Jabalpur are Madan Mahal Fort, Sangram Sagar and Baj-namath, the Rani Durgavati Memorial and Museum, and the Tilwara Ghat from where Mahatma Gandhi ashes were immersed in the Narmada. Also of interest are the twelfth-century Mala Devi Mandir, Pisan Hari Jain Temples, and Roopnath. Jabalpur is the most convenient base for visits to the famous Kanha (173 kilometers) and Bandhavgarh (194 kilometers) national parks.

Omkareshwar, the sacred island, shaped like the holiest of all Hindu symbols, *Om,* has drawn a hundred generation of pilgrims. Here, at the confluence of the rivers Narmada and Kaveri, the devout have gathered to kneel at the temple of Shri Omkar Mandhata. And here, as in so many of Madhya Pradesh's sacred shrines, the works of nature complement those of man to provide an awe-inspiring setting.

Shri Omkar Mandhata Temple stands on a one-mile-long, half-mile-wide island that has been formed by the fork of the Narmada. The soft-stone construction has lent its pliable surface to a rare degree of detailed work, of which the frieze of figures on the upper portion is the most striking. Also intricately carved is the stone roof of the temple. Encircling the shrine are verandas with columns that are carved in circles, polygons, and squares.

The Siddhnath Temple is a fine example of early medieval Brahmanic architecture. Its unique feature is a frieze of elephants, carved on a stone slab, at its outer perimeter. Twenty-four avatars, a cluster of Hindu and Jain temples, are remarkable for their skillful use of varied architectural modes. The nearest airport is at Indore (77 kilometers), connected by regular flights with Delhi, Bombay, Bhopal, and Gwalior.

Maheshwar

Called Mahishmati when it was the capital of King Kartvirarjun, Maheshwar was a glorious city in the dawn of Indian civilization. This temple town on the banks of the Narmada was mentioned in the *Ramayana* and *Mahabharata.* Revived to its ancient position by the Holkar queen Rani Ahilyabai of Indore, Maheshwar's temples and mighty fort-complex stand in quiet beauty, mirrored in the river below.

A life-size statue of Rani Ahilyabai sits on a throne in the Rajgaddi within the fort complex. This is the right place to begin a tour of Maheshwar, for this pious and wise queen was the architect of its revived importance. Other fascinating relics and heirlooms of the Holkar dynasty can be seen in rooms that are open to the public. Within the complex is an exquisite small shrine that is the starting point of the ancient Dussehra ceremony still carried out today.

Peshwa Ghat, Fanase Ghat, and Ahilya Ghat line the river Narmada. Their steps lead down from the sandy banks to the river. Throughout the day, you can see a kaleidoscope of rural India in the pilgrims and holy men who sit at the ghats in silent meditation, in the rows of graceful women who carry gleaming brass pots down to the holy (life-giving) river, and in the ferry loads of villagers who cross and recross these surging waters. Lining the banks, too, are poignant stone memorials to the *setis* of Maheshwar, who perished on the funeral pyres of their husbands.

Crowned by soaring spires, the many-tiered temples of Maheshwar are distinguished by their carved overhanging balconies and their intricately worked doorways.

Maheshwari saris are renowned throughout India for their unique weave, introduced 250 years ago by Rani Ahilyabai. Woven mostly in cotton, the typical Maheshwari sari has a plain body and sometimes stripes or checks in several variations. The mat border designs have a wide range in leaf and floral patterns.

Indore

Indore, India's fourth-largest textile center, with a population of over one million, is a newcomer among cities in India. The area was given to Malhar Rao Holkar in 1733 by the Marathas Peshwas for whom he fought. While Holkar was away fighting, he left the affairs of state to his widowed daughter-in-law, Ahalyabai, whom he had saved from being a seti. Since her son was insane and died young, she became the ruler. At a time when all other states were floundering, her reign was a model of good administration.

Indore's outstanding temple is the Jain Kanch Mandir, or Glass Temple. Here every available surface is inlaid with mother-of-pearl, glass, and colored beads. Huge crystal chandeliers and carved silver tables add glitter, but paintings illustrating the dreadful punishments visited on sinners form a bizarre contrast with the scintillating interior. The ex-maharani's residence is the Manik Bagh. Guests were asked to stay in Lal Bagh, which was set in lovely grounds outside the city. The dignified old palace, with its graceful Audience Hall, is half hidden behind rows of bangle sellers on the main square of the city. The new palace is across the square. Around it the daily life of the small city carries on.

Ujjain

Ujjain, with a population of over 350,000, was described by Chandragupta II's court poet, Kalidasa, as "the town fallen from heaven to bring heaven to earth." Kalidasa also found "its palaces like mountains and its houses like palaces." Though the Gupta capital was Patiliputra, this was the city from where the emperor ruled for long periods. When Buddha was born, Ujjain was already a thriving city and the capital of a kingdom called Avanti. Legend goes that Shiva lived here after destroying a demon and thus Ujjain was born.

One of the four drops of heavenly nectar from the kumbh seized by Vishnu also supposedly dropped on Ujjain. Once every 12 years, millions of Hindu devotees congregate to celebrate the Kumbh Mela, the most sacred festival in the Hindu calendar.

Ujjain's literary, scientific, and religious life continued for centuries, and it was hundreds of years later that another poet was captivated enough to see it as "the very home of the golden age; paved with jewels, full of romance, with dancing girls in the temples and love in everyone's hearts." Politically, Ujjain went through swift transitions, from the hands of the Rajputs and the Moslems, to the Marath Scindias of Gwalior.

The Scindias rebuilt the Mahakala, the main temple, on the ruins of an earlier one destroyed by the Moslems. A fine old temple south of Mahakala is the Bridh Kaleshwar, small and compact, with a simple porch and shrine spire. Set in lovely seclusion is the Temple of Nine Planets, on the road to Indore at the confluence of the Sipra and two other rivers.

According to Hindu geography, the first meridian passes through Ujjain. A legend claims that the moon and Mars were born here. Ujjain's scientific work was done in an observatory built in the eighteenth century by Jai Singh II of Jaipur. It was called the Jantar Mantar. Jai Singh also built the Gopal Mandir, a Krishna temple almost buried in the bazaar. Not far away, yet hidden from the bustle in a cool garden of cypress trees and ponds, is the attractive Bohron-ka-Rauza, a mausoleum of the Bohra community of Moslems. Its walls are carved white marble and its large dome is well proportioned.

The Caves at Udaigiri

A group of two Jain and 18 Hindu caves are at Udaigiri seven miles from Sanchi. Hindu authorities regard the carvings of the boar incarnation of Vishnu in Cave No. 5 as the ultimate representation of the triumph of good over evil. Vishnu, with the head of a boar, is shown supporting Prithvi, the earth goddess he has rescued from the clutches of a snake demon. With self-assured poise, Vishnu stamps on the snake while rows of angels and demons look on.

Cave No. 7 was excavated on Chandragupta II's orders for his personal use. Cave No. 19 is the largest and the one with the most carvings. Cave No. 20 is unique because it is entered from below ground level and none of its compartments is high. The other caves are not as impressive and hardly merit a visit, unless you are a serious history buff.

The Satpura Mountain Range

From Bhopal, you recross the Narmada at a point halfway between Bombay and New Delhi, in the Satpuras Mountains. The town of Panchmarhi is on a plateau about 3,500 feet up, and it looks over red sandstone hills worn into strange shapes. Dhupgarh and Mahadeo peaks can be climbed on excursions from Panchmarhi. The first is a treat at sunrise, and the view from the second is even more spectacular, since you look across the Narmada in the opposite Vindhya Range.

The town's ancient history is limited to the legend of the Pandavas, the five brothers of the *Mahabharata* epic, whose supposed presence is given as an explanation for the hill's five caves—which may well have been Buddhist *viharas* (temples). The British used it as summer capital of the central provinces, but now it's simply a resort.

Mandla and Ramnagar

In the jungles, 60 miles south of Jabalpur, on the way to Nagpur, are two other Gond forts: Mandla, which the Narmada protects on three sides, and Ramnagar, 10 miles away, once a three-story palace. Both are in ruins. Mandla is near the source of the Narmada. It forms a deep lake near the town and is surrounded by a thick forest of primeval greenery.

We are back in Maharashtra again. Twenty-five miles northeast of Nagpur is Ramtek, or the Hill of Rama. The hill's chief temples, 600 years old, shine in the distance on top of the tapered hill and make a pleasant break in the long drive over the plains.

Nagpur, with its 866,000 population, means oranges to most Indians. The smell of oranges fills the air. Until the eighteenth century, the Gonds ruled here. But then Rao Bhonsle captured the throne. In a combined attack the peshwa of Pune and the nizam of Hyderabad sacked the city in 1765. Later, Nagpur was made the capital of the central provinces.

Gandhi's Ashram

About 50 miles from Nagpur is a tiny village, Little Sevagram, village of service, which has been the source and core of much of the country's thinking and action in the social revolution of the past 50 years. Here, Mahatma Gandhi settled in 1933, establishing his *ashram* (place of retreat) and putting his doctrines into practice. His simple hut became the nerve center of Indian politics for 15 years. Gandhi tackled practical problems, practically. To care for cows—India's sacred animal—he established a dairy and tannery where the tanning trade is respectable. He encouraged hand spinning of thread to make hand-woven cloth and worked out its system of distribution. But it was the eradication of untouchability that took up much of his time, and he scorned the idea of "unclean" occupations. His views started India on its road to equality.

The ashram he founded still exists. Sevagram is also the site of the Nai Talimi Sangh school, where 300 students live in the rural autarchy so eloquently preached by Gandhi. The students grow their own vegetables and weave the cloth for their clothing.

Two miles from Sevagram is another ashram in the village of Paunar. It was founded by Vinoba Bhave, Gandhi's land-reforming heir, and an important figure in the history of modern India.

PRACTICAL INFORMATION FOR

MADHYA PRADESH

WHEN TO GO. The best time to visit central India is from late October to late March. After that, it gets very hot, and the rainy season starts in June. Pachmarhi, in the hills, is best visited October–November.

HOW TO GET THERE. The three major cities of Madhya Pradesh—the capital city of Bhopal, Indore, and Khajuraho—are connected to Delhi or Bombay by air. Bhopal and Indore also have express and local train service. In addition, a bus runs to Indore via Bhopal from Bombay.

BHOPAL

By Air. Bhopal is connected by *Indian Airlines* and by *Vayudoot,* a regional airlines, from Delhi and Bombay. Flights originating in Delhi also operate to Gwalior.

By Train. Daily *Deluxe* and *Frontier Mail* trains connect Bhopal with Bombay and Delhi. Both trains are good and offer first- and second-class cabins, but only a few reserved seats. Otherwise, Bhopal is on the Delhi-Madras main line, with major trains going via Itarsi and Jhansi.

INDORE

By Air. Indore is connected by Indian Airlines and Vayudoot from Delhi. A Vayudoot "hopping flight" via Gwalior, Bhopal, Indore, and Bombay also leaves Delhi early each morning.

By Train. *Malway Express* leaves Delhi Railway Station at 7 P.M. daily and arrives the next afternoon in Indore.

By Bus. Indore is connected by bus from Bombay. On the 360-mile trip, the air-conditioned bus also goes through Bhopal and Mandu.

KHAJURAHO

By Air. A daily Vayudoot "hopping flight" links Khajuraho with Delhi, 1½ hours, on its way to Varanasi (Benares).

By Train. The nearest station on a train from Delhi (7 hours) and Bombay (20 hours) is at Jhansi, where Khajuraho is reached by regular bus service.

MANDU

Mandu is 62 miles from Indore, which has the nearest airport. Regular **buses** and air-conditioned **taxis** are available from Indore.

SANCHI

The nearest airport is at Bhopal (44 miles), from which regular **buses** and **taxis** are available. By **train,** Sanchi is on the Jhansi-Itarsi section of the Central Railway.

 TOURIST INFORMATION. Tourist information counters, whether operated by Madhya Pradesh Tourist Development Corporation (MPTDC) or by the India Tourist Development Corporation (ITDC), are located at each airport. In *Bhopal,* the MPTDC main office is at T. T. Nagar; tel. 62173, 62418, or 63552. An office is also located at 13 G.T.B. Complex, T. T. Nagar, New Market; tel. 64388. These offices provide tourist information for the state and can help you hire guides for city tours.

In *Khajuraho,* the ITDC office is located near the western group of temples; tel. 56.

A regional MPTDC office is located in the *Indore* Tourist Reception Center, behind Ravindra Natya Griha, Tagore Marg; tel. 38888. In *Ujjain,* it is situated in the Grand Hotel, Pachmarhi Prasthal Bungalow (tel. 100); in *Gwalior,* at Hotel Tansen, Gandhi Road (tel. 21568).

 **ACCOMMODATIONS.** With few exceptions, hotels in this central state of India are mainly in the *Inexpensive* and *Moderate* categories. But all offer at least the basic amenities. See *Facts at Your Fingertips* for price ranges of categories.

BHOPAL

Expensive

Hotel Panchanan. New Market Road; tel. 63047. Superior-class establishment with central air-conditioning, comfortable quarters, and a restaurant. Operated by MPTDC.

Ransom Hotel. Hamidia Road; tel. 72298 or 72299. 26 rooms, some air-conditioned. Facilities for banquets; a wide variety of cuisines in the popular restaurant.

Moderate

Jehan Numa Palace Hotel. Shamla Road; tel. 76080 or 76190; cable JEHANUMA. Located two km from downtown and 12 km from the airport, this hotel has 23 rooms, six of which are in an annex. All have attached baths.

Hotel President International. Berasia Road; tel. 75218. A good place to stay. Some air-conditioned rooms, a restaurant, and a bar.

Hotel Ramsons International. Hamidia Road; tel. 72298 or 72299; cable SETHIBROS. In the heart of the city, within 15 minutes walking distance of the railway station. 26 double rooms, some air-conditioned, all with attached bath. Restaurant, bar, banquet facilities, laundry.

Inexpensive

Pagoda Hotel & Restaurant. Hamidia Road; tel. 73949 or 74499; cable PAGODA. Situated in the downtown area, this hotel has 16 rooms, eight of which are double; some air-conditioned; all with attached baths. Pleasant restaurant and bar.

Nalanda Hotel, Restaurant & Bar. Ibrahimpura Street; tel. 73435. 2½ km from the railway station, seven km from the airport. 27 non-air-conditioned rooms; restaurant, bar, laundry.

Hotel Ranjit. Hamidia Road in the downtown area; tel. 751115 or 73066. 29 rooms, a restaurant, bar permit room, conference room, and car rental.

Hotel Shirez. Hamidia Road, near the Board of Higher Secondary Education; tel. 64513. 22 cheap but comfortable rooms, some air-conditioned.

GWALIOR

Moderate

Welcomgroup Usha Kiran Palace. Jayendraganj, Lashkar. 14 km from the airport, three km from the railroad station, tel. 23453. 23 rooms. A former guest house of the Maharaja of Gwalior. Some rooms are air-conditioned. Has a restaurant, bar, room service, nice grounds, billiards, archery, and badminton.

Inexpensive

Hotel Tansen, 6–A, Gandhi Rd.; tel. 21568. 24 rooms, a restaurant, bar, some air-conditioned rooms that also have telephones, and room service. Run by Madha Pradesh Tourism Development Corporation, Ltd.

INDORE

Expensive

Hotel Suhag. On Bombay-Agra National Highway; tel. 34111. The best available hotel in the area, with 83 centrally air-conditioned rooms, a restaurant, and a bar.

Moderate

Hotel Shreemaya. 12/1 R. N. T. Tagore Marg; tel. 34151–56; cable SHREEMAYA. A half-mile from the downtown area. 52 double rooms, 27 air-conditioned; all with attached baths and restaurant with south Indian cuisine.

Inexpensive to Moderate

Central Hotel. 70–71 Mahatma Gandhi Rd.; tel. 32131 or 32041; cable COMFORT. In the heart of the city, with 43 rooms, 12 air-conditioned.

DINING OUT. Hotel dining rooms are the best bet for meals in Madhya Pradesh, where decent independent restaurants are scarce. When you plan to dine at a hotel other than the one at which you are staying, it's best to phone ahead to see if you can be accommodated, particularly if it is a small hotel whose dining room is the most popular in the area. Prices for meals at hotels are commensurate with their classification. There are two independent restaurants in Indore that you may wish to try. Both are in the *Moderate* to *Inexpensive* category, as set forth in *Facts at Your Fingertips.*

Apsara. 1 R. N. T. Tagore Marg; tel. 21081 or 23026. Serves strictly vegetarian meals in its air-conditioned dining room; live music. Open 8 A.M.–10:30 P.M.

Mehfil Restaurant-N-Bar. 36 Sneh-Nagar Main Rd.; tel. 63097. Indian food is commendable in the restaurant, and the bar is a pleasant oasis.

GWALIOR

Moderate

Kwality. Motil Lal Nehru Marg; tel. 23243. Indian, Continental, and Chinese. Open morning until night.

Palace Dining Room. Usha Kiran Palace, Jayendraganj; tel. 23453. Continental, Chinese, tandoori, and Mughlai food. Breakfast, lunch, and dinner.

Hotel Tansen. 6 Gandhi Rd., tel. 21568. Indian, Continental, and Chinese food. Breakfast, lunch, dinner.

 HOW TO GET AROUND. From the airport at each city, you can take a Madhya Pradesh Transportation Corporation (MPTC) **bus,** or hire a **taxi** or **autorickshaw.** If the latter two are not metered, establish a price before getting in. For a pleasant experience, and only a bit slower, *tongas* **(horsedrawn carriages)** are also widely available in cities.

In Bhopal, to hire taxis or cars with drivers from private operators, contact the *Transport Office of MPTC,* 13 G.T.B. Complex, T. T. Nagar (tel. 64388); *Ashok Travels and Tours,* ITDC 22, Nishat Colony (tel. 64703); *Sanchi Travels,* T. T. Nagar (tel. 65868); or *Radiant Travels,* 7 Hamidia Rd. (tel. 74826).

In Gwalior, a car with driver can be hired from S.S. Travels, Welcomgroup Usha Kiran Palace, tel. 21136.

 TOURS. MPTDC offers a variety of tours throughout Madhya Pradesh and will help you plan your itineraries. Tours are conducted in luxury coaches, chauffeured cars (both air-conditioned and non-air-conditioned), and jeeps. Detailed information is available at each tourist information office. (See *Tourist Information* above.) Available are city tours and "theme tours" for specific interests, such as wildlife, monuments, pilgrimages, and scenic beauty. MPTDC's package tours for extensive touring include travel bookings, transport, accommodations, guide services, entry fees when necessary, and meals. Package tours of Bhopal and Sanchi cost Rs. 320–Rs. 550 per person; Bhopal–Khajuraho, Rs. 2,200–Rs. 4,000, round trip. Other round-trip tours from Bhopal include those to Bhimtek, Indore, Pachmarhi, Udaigir, and Ujjain.

 FESTIVALS. Unlike all other parts of India, Central India is no different when it comes to celebrating festivals, which go on throughout the year. *Basant Panchami,* in **February,** commences the welcome of spring, the best time for auspicious occasions like marriages to take place. On *Shivratri,* also in **February,** devotees worship Shiva with sacred songs sung in the temples. *Holi* is celebrated in **March,** when people throw dyes and water on each other in a day of merrymaking and enjoyment. In **August,** a 10-day festival, *Dussera,* is celebrated. For nine days, the mother goddess is worshiped, and on the tenth day, Ravana, the king of evil, is burnt, a symbol that good wins over evil. **November** brings *Diwali,* the festival of lights and firecrackers.

December. In Gwalior, the *Tansen Music Festival* honors Miya Thansen, Akbar's great musician in residence and one of India's most important musician/singers. This festival, which goes for days, celebrates the man and his music, which is performed by India's top talents. Check the Madhya Pradesh

State Tourism Development Corporation, Gwalior, (tel: 21568) for dates and details.

Folk dances are famous in central India. The Gonds, an ancient pre-Aryan tribe who inhabit the hilly forest regions of northeast Madhya Pradesh, still use stilts to cover long distances in their land of trackless jungles. From this tribal practice, a unique stilt dance has evolved. Other tribes, including the Bhils and the Banjaras, have a number of colorful dances, such as Dagle, Pali, Longi, Phag, (a sword dance), and the Loti, in which women balance pitchers filled with water on their heads. It's a spectacular sight. Such tribal dances can be seen during various fairs of festivals.

HISTORIC SITES. In Bhopal, view a panoramic sight of the city, with its minarets and mosques, from *Shamla and Idgah Hills.* It's best seen at sunset, but the view is also beautiful at dusk and in the evening, against the backdrop of glittering city lights and rippling water of the two lakes. *Upper Lake* and *Lower Lake* are four square miles in area and divided by an overbridge. MPTDC's Boat Club provides facilities for exciting trip by motor, sail, and paddleboats on the two lakes. The heart of the old city of Chowk is lined with old mosques and havelis that are reminders of a bygone, princely lifestyle. The shops in Chowk's narrow alleyways are treasure troves of traditional Bhoplai crafts.

In Gwalior, the *Gwalior Fort* is one of the oldest forts in India—one inscription dates back to A.D. 525. Temples were constructed in the eleventh and fourteenth centuries, and the lovely palaces were the work of a Tomar king, Man Singh (1485–1516), who built the Man Mandir (a palace topped with six towers) and the Gujari Malal (now housing an excellent museum). There are many other structures that make the fort worth a visit.

Udaigiri Caves, seven miles from Sanchi and two miles from Vidisha, are groups of rock caves carved into sandstone. An inscription says they were produced during the reign of Chandragupta II in A.D. 4–5. Characterized by richly carved facades on doorways, the shrines are progressively more spacious and ornate. (See *Exploring* section above for details.)

The city of *Ujjain* is one of the famous pilgrimages of India. The ancient Shikhar spires of the temples still dominate the city's skyline and the sacred River Shipra. A pilgrimage during Mahashivratri draws thousands of devotees to the *Mahakleshwar Temple.* At *Bade Ganeshjika* Mandir, a five-faced Hanuman idol is installed, along with an exquisitely sculpted image of the Ganesha (elephant-faced idol). *Chintaman Ganesh* is a temple of considerable antiquity, noteworthy in its carved pillars dating to the Paramaras period. Par Matsyendranath, dedicated to the memory of Matsyendranath, the historic Shivite leader of the Nath sect, has a scenic setting on the River Shipra. *Harsiddi Temple* contains an image of the goddess Annapurna. Constructed during the Maratha period, the temple has two pillars adorned with lamps in the Maratha style.

Along the *Narmada River,* there are many lovely natural sights to behold and enjoy. The *Handi Khoh* in Pachmarhi is an impressive ravine with a 300-foot precipice and dramatic steep sides. *Apsara Vihar* (Fairy Pool), formed by waterfalls, is an idyllic picnic spot also suitable for swimming. *Jalawataran* (Duchess Falls), two miles along the path from Belle View, tumbles down in three separate cascades. In Jabalpur, the river makes its way through marble rocks, narrows down, and then plunges in a spectacular waterfall called the *Dhiandhar Falls.*

MUSEUMS. With Madhya Pradesh steeped in history and religious customs, the museums in this state contain some eclectic collections. Museums are generally open daily, 10 A.M.–5 P.M., and, if not free, have an entrance fee of only a few rupees.

The *Central Museum,* in Nagpur, established in 1860, houses a wide variety of objects related to archaeology, art, ethnology, and geology, mostly collected in the state. The archaeology section shows, among other items, such antiquities as Copper Age implements and silver bulls, as well as Buddhist, Jain, and tribal sculptures and some interesting inscriptions, including one on a sacrificial wooden pillar.

Government Archaeological Museum, Bhopal, has a fine collection of sculptures from various parts of Madhya Pradesh. There is also a collection of paintings, from school buildings to paintings taken from the Bagh Caves.

Khandriya Sanghralya Museum, in Indore, contains some awe-inspiring Bhramanical and Jain images in stone and metal. Also on display are architectural fragments, pottery, coins, paintings, ancient manuscripts, arms, and historical documents.

Roopanker Museum of Fine Arts at Bharat Bhawan, Bhopal, houses works of art with special emphasis on folk and tribal art. Roopanker arranges special exhibitions, seminars, artist camps, lectures, and orientation courses in art.

Sanchi Museum, Sanchi, was built in 1919 to house antiquities recovered during the excavation of this site. The collection dates from Ashoka to the late Medieval period and includes a number of relic caskets, fragments of gateways, statues, and pottery.

Archaeological Museum in the Gujari Mahal, Gwalior, has good collections of sculptures, inscriptions, metal images, terra-cotta objects and archaeological pieces, including those recovered at the ancient sites of Besnagar, Pawaya, and Ujjain. It also contains an interesting collection of coins, paintings, among them copies of frescoes from the Bagh Caves (Buddhist caves from the sixth and seventh centuries). Open 10 A.M.–5 P.M. Closed Mondays. Nominal fee.

 WILDLIFE PRESERVES. *Bandhavargh National Park* lies in the Sal Forest in the heart of the Vindhyan Mountain Range. It presents an enchanting view of a wide variety of wildlife, including tigers, panthers, spotted deer, sambar, barking deer, wild boar, and bison. There are also the archaeological remains of the Kalchuri period; adjacent to the remains are a large number of prehistoric caves. Vehicles and elephants are available at the Forest Lodge for touring the park. Elephants accommodate four people, and rides cost Rs. 10 per hour each. Other entry fees: car, jeep, or station wagon, Rs. 10; minibus or van, Rs. 15. Personal guides, Rs. 3. A tax is also charged for photography, the rate depending on the use of the camera. The park is open daily except during the rainy season, July–October.

Kahna National Park can be reached by a regular bus service from Jabalpur, 100 miles away. Considered one of India's best parks, Kahna is the natural habitat of a large variety of wild animals, including tigers, panthers, sambar, cheetahs, black bucks, and barking deer. Entry fees: car, jeep, or station wagon, Rs. 10; minibus or van, Rs. 15. Photography charges depend on the size of the camera lens. Closed July–October.

 SHOPPING. A treasure of handicrafts may be found in Madhya Pradesh, where craftsmen have kept alive skills and traditions that go back hundreds of years. Small shops in bazaars and government-operated stores are located in practically each city and town, displaying handwoven brocades of Chanderi and Naheswar and *kosa* silks of Raigarh, along with leather toys and exquisitely wrought metal bells. Other specialties include silver jewelery, lacquer bangles, golden-thread embroidery, marble ashtrays, and boxes, and beaded tapestries of gods and goddesses. Bargain at the small shops in the bazaars. Shops are generally open daily, except Sundays, 9:30 A.M.–7:30 P.M. Bring rupees, including lots of small bills, for credit cards will be of use only in government-operated shops.

THE TEMPLES
OF KHAJURAHO

by
KATHLEEN COX and RAVI KHANNA

> Above, half seen, in the lofty gloom,
> Strange works of a long dead people loom,
> What did they mean to those who now are dust,
> These rioting figures of love and lust?
>
> *The Garden of Kama*

America wouldn't be discovered for 500 years; the groundwork for Chartres Cathedral wouldn't be laid for a hundred years, but in the year 1000, Central India was in its grand ascendancy, especially the region of Khajuraho, under the rule of the Chandella Rajputs. The Chandellas, like so many other Rajputs, traced their lineage back to the lunar god Chandra.

Chandra noticed Hemavati, the beautiful daughter of a Brahman priest, while she bathed in a moonlit pool. Hemavati's indiscretion led to her seduction, with the child of this unexpected alliance none other than Chandravarman, founder of the Chandella dynasty. Many years later, when Chandravarman came to power, his mother supposedly visited him in a dream. Build temples, she said—and build them he did, as did subsequent rulers.

During this time (A.D. 950–1050), India was the Asian Eldorado. People were rich, the land was fertile, life brimmed with pleasure. *Purdah* (the seclusion of women) hadn't yet cast its inhibiting pall on

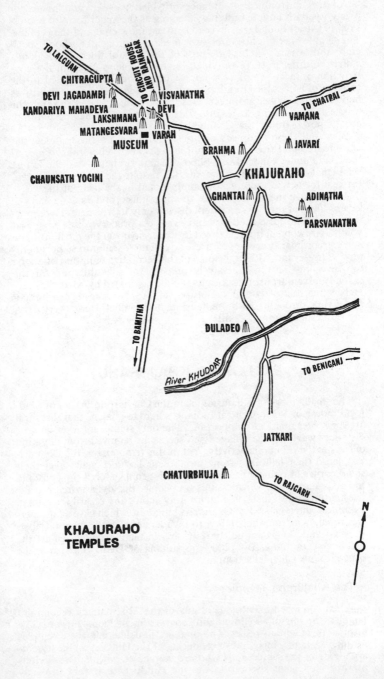

KHAJURAHO
TEMPLES

all the joy. Everyone lived the tenth-century-style good time: trooping off to fairs, feasts, hunts, dramas, music, and dancing.

All this untroubled abundance provided the perfect climate for creativity, with temple building emerging as the major form of expression. No strict boundaries existed between the sacred and the profane. The temple was the house of god, meeting hall, neighborhood social club, and gossip center. Offerings of the faithful filled the Rajput's coffers, and he, in turn, provided for his people, overseeing the construction of more temples—a happy, nonvicious cycle that led to the creation of 85 temples in a hundred years. And everyone of them was built at a time when architects and sculptors had passed through the classic and mannerist stages into the flamboyant baroque, the zenith of artistic power under the Chandellas.

What did these sculptors choose to represent on the temples that clustered around the now-tranquil village called Khajuraho? God, as the Hindu understands Him—Shiva, Vishnu, Brahma—and the Jainist saints that are all lavishly honored. But, despite the interest in heaven, the real focus was more earthbound, rooted in the facts of life.

And not just the hunt and war, feasting, music, and dancing, but the side of life that many Westerners discuss only in whispers. Here, portrayed with no false modesty and even less prudery, virile men and voluptuous women, immortalized in stone, cavort in the most intimate and extraordinarily erotic postures. To call these sculptures "pornography" is irrelevant. Although some of the decorative sculpture might be too revealing for the excessively innocent or too titillating for the sexually adventurous, most adults will be fascinated by what they see. Here is the best of Hindu sculpture: sinuous, twisting forms; human and divine, throbbing with life, tension, and conflict. Here, every carving exudes consummate skill.

EXPLORING KHAJURAHO

The small village of Khajuraho is in the Chattarpur district of Madhya Pradesh in North-Central India. It's hard to imagine that this rural area was ever politically important. The only significant river is some distance away, and the village itself seems far removed from any kind of substantial economic activity. Yet in this remote area, the Chandellas placed their temples—some monumental, some small. Over their small corner of rich civilization, in which people adored the gods and the gods showered their blessings on people, this dynasty reigned for five centuries until history, which rarely shows any regard for human happiness, intervened. The Chandella kingdom, which gave all its energies to enjoying life, succumbed to invaders of a stronger moral fiber. In the year 1100, Mahmud the Turk began the Holy War against the "idolaters" of India. By 1200, the sultans of Delhi ruled over the once-glorious Chandella domain.

The Khajuraho Temples

When you face the entrance of any of the 22 remaining Khajuraho temples, the row of ascending and separate finials looms upward, like a series of mountain peaks. The analogy is deliberate; these temples represent a highly imaginative rendering of the Himalayas, the legendary abode of the sacred gods who are worshiped within. The obvious upward movement also represents the Hindu path toward heavenly Nirvana: one first fulfills material obligations (the lowest peak), then social obligations, and then religious ones until one finally reaches the highest station and total peace, or nirvana. Also notice the placement of exterior carvings. That, too, is intentional. Human forms dominate the lower half, with abstract design—god's play—relegated to the celestial top.

The Khajuraho temples are of the Indo-Aryan type and are generally classified as *Nagara* or North Indian. But they have definite features that set them apart; indeed, no others like them exist in any part of India. Though dedicated to different deities (Shiva, Vishnu, or the Jain Tirthankaras—"perfect souls"), the general outline remains the same.

Each temple stands on a high platform and without the customary enclosure. The larger shrines (at least one in each group) have a central sanctuary for the honored god and one more at each corner for the lesser deities. The floor plan is divided into five distinct sections (three in the smaller temples). The appearance resembles a cross with two sets of arms. The visitor enters through the portico (*ardhamandapa*) into the assembly hall (*mandapa*), which leads to the sanctum where the idol is enshrined. There is a vestibule (*antarala*) to cross and then finally the *garbhagriha*, or cell-shaped sanctum. Around this shrine is the ambulatory or processional passage (*pradakshinapatha*). The smaller temples omit this last feature and the assembly hall. But the most noteworthy aspect of the Khajuraho temple is the *shikhara* (spire) surrounded and flanked by countless sister towers that push each other heavenward.

Although the floor plan and the silhouette of the temples are unique and noteworthy, the eye rightfully focuses on the soaring vertical lines that are beautifully balanced by two or three horizontal bands that are covered with hundred and hundreds of sculptured figures—gods and goddesses, celestial nymphs and handmaidens (*apsaras* and *surasundaris*), bold serpents and leonine beasts, and the array of human females (*nayikas*), usually made more sexy and alluring than their heavenly counterparts. And, of course, the major theme, which has given Khajuraho its reputation: the *mithuna* couples, "these rioting figures of love and lust," which, oddly enough, only account for 3–4 percent of the carvings.

How to interpret the preoccupation with the erotic? One explanation is rooted in religion, specifically the Tantric doctrine that was popular in the Chandella period. This cult, the antithesis of asceticism, emphasised the female as the dominant force of creation and taught that the senses are the equal of the spirit. The gratification of earthly desires is a step toward the attainment of nirvana. Another explanation is that the sculptors wanted to exhibit the full range of human life, which they certainly did. However, while many of the mithuna groups are explicitly carnal, others portray a wide spectrum of human emotion: jealousy, fear, modesty, and the tenderness and tranquility of love fulfilled.

Tour of the Temples

The temples are in three groups covering an area of about eight square miles. The Western Group is the largest and most important (the Khajuraho Archaeological Museum is located here, too). It includes the oldest (Chausath Yogini); the largest (Kandariya Mahadeo); plus the Devi Jagdambe, particularly "mithunaised." The Eastern Group, which is close to Khajuraho village, contains the Brahman and Jain shrines. The Southern Group is a mile south of the village and has only two temples, but they should be seen.

Western Group

Begin your tour with the Chausath Yogini Temple on the west side of the Shivsager Tank. The oldest temple at Khajuraho (some date it as early as A.D. 820 but 900 seems closer), it is dedicated to Kali, the goddess of wrath. Chausath means 64, which equals the number of female nymphs serving the fierce goddess. This temple is also built of granite (all the others are a pale, warm-toned sandstone), the only one oriented northeast–southwest instead of the usual north–south, and was once surrounded by 64 roofed cells for the figures of Kali's attendants, of which only 35 remain. Different in material and design, it is one of two temples at Khajuraho that does not follow the typical style.

Lalguan Mahadeva stands about a third of a mile from Chausath Yogini. This Shiva temple is in ruins and the original portico is missing, but it is of historical interest, since it is built of both granite and sandstone and represents the transition from Chausath Yogini to the later temples.

Kandariya Mahadeo is to the north of Chausath Yogini. This is the biggest and, by common consent, the best temple at Khajuraho and one of the best in India, representing the Indian "Golden Age" of temple art. Built in the typical Hindu five-shrine design, this temple is dedicated to Shiva; the inner sanctum houses a marble lingam with a four-foot circumference. The entrance archway is decorated with statues of musicians, lovers in fond embrace, crocodiles, and flying gods and goddesses. The ceilings, circles set in a square, are carved with scrolls and scallops; the pillars are ornamented with beasts and grotesque dwarfs; and flowers and pennants decorate the lintels and doorjambs of the sanctum. Outside, the three bands of sculpture around the sanctum and transept bring to life the whole galaxy of Hindu gods and goddesses, mithuna couples letting loose with every fantasy, celestial handmaidens, and lions. One art historian counted 872 statues—226 inside and 646 outside. This temple, with its imposing size, fine proportions, and inexhaustibly rich sculpture, is a high point of the Khajuraho tour.

Mahadeva Temple, also dedicated to Shiva, shares its masonry terrace with the Kandariya and the Devi Jagdambe. Although mostly in ruins, the temple still boasts a remarkable freestanding statue in the portico of a man caressing a lion.

Devi Jagdambe Temple was dedicated successively to Vishnu, Lakshmi, and then, because the sacred image of the goddess is black, Kali (the goddess of wrath). It is of the three-shrine design and, from the inside, seems shaped like a cross. The third band of sculpture has a series of mithuna themes of uncensored erotica. The ceilings are similar to those of the Kandariya, and the three-headed, eight-armed statue of Shiva is one of the best cult images at Khajuraho. Over the entrance to the sanctum is a carving of Vishnu.

Chitragupta Temple lies slightly north of the Devi Jagdambe and resembles it in construction. Facing east toward the rising sun, the presiding diety is Surya, the sun god, who finds his most grandiose tribute at Konarak. The temple cell contains his five-foot-high image with his chariot and seven horses that carry him away at dusk. He is also depicted above the doorway. In the central niche to the south of the sanctum is an image of Vishnu shown with 11 heads. The central head is his own, while the others represent his numerous incarnations. A profusion of sculpture—scenes of animal combats, royal processions, masons at work, and joyous dances—depict the lavish country life of the Chandellas.

The Vishwanath and Nandi temples face each other on a common terrace to the east of Chitragupta and Devi Jagdambe. There are two staircases; the northern flanked by a pair of lions and the southern, by a pair of elephants. Since it is an important Shiva temple, the Vishwanath has a simpler extra shrine to house the god's mount, the massive and richly harnessed statue of the sacred bull Nandi. It also supposedly had two original lingams (stylized phallic symbols)—one of pure emerald, the other of simpler stone. Only one, unfortunately the less valuable, remains. The Vishwanath is similar in dedication and floor plan to its larger sister, the Kandariya, but, unlike the latter, two of the original corner shrines remain. On the outer wall of the corridor surrounding the cells is an impressive image of Brahma, the three-headed Lord of Creation, and his consort. On all the walls, the form of the woman dominates, portrayed in all her daily tenth-century occupations: writing a letter, holding her baby, studying her reflection in a mirror, applying makeup, or playing music. The nymphs of paradise are voluptuous and provocative; the sexy scenes, robust. An inscription states that the temple was built by Chandella King Dhanga in 1002.

Parvati Temple, near Vishwanath, is a small and relatively unimportant shrine originally dedicated to Vishnu. But the original idol was supposedly replaced by the goddess Ganga standing on a crocodile. The name Parvati (wife of Shiva) is a misnomer.

The Lakshmana Temple, though dedicated to Vishnu, is almost in all respects similar to the Vishwanath. It is also a perfect example of the fully developed five-shrine Khajuraho style, since all four shelters for the minor gods are undamaged. The ceiling of the hall is charmingly carved in shell and floral motifs. The highly decorated lintel over the entrance to the main shrine shows Lakshmi, goddess of wealth and consort of Vishnu, with Brahma, Lord of Creation (on her left) and Shiva, Lord of Destruction (on her right). The planets are depicted on a frieze above the lintel. The relief on the doorway illustrates the scene of the gods and demons churning the ocean in order to obtain a pitcher of miraculous nectar from the bottom. The gods won the ensuing 12-day battle over the pitcher, drank the nectar, and gained immortality. Another doorway relief shows Vishnu in his 10 incarnations. The idol in the sanctum with two pairs of arms and three heads represents the same god in his lion and boar incarnations. Outside, two (not the usual three), sculptured bands display boar hunting, elephants, horses, soldiers, and—on the upper one—celestial maidens and some of those famous mithunas absorbed in their erotic pleasure.

Matangesvara Temple, south of Lakshmana, is the only "living temple," with worship taking place in the morning and afternoon. Its square construction and simpler floor plan is exceptional for Khajuraho. The temple has oriel windows, a projecting portico, and a ceiling of overlapping concentric circles. An enormous lingam, nearly 8½ feet tall, is enshrined in the sanctum.

Varah Temple, in front of the preceding shrine, is dedicated to Vishnu's Varaha-Avatar, or Boar Incarnation. The huge boar, snouty and stolid, is swathed and ringed with more than 600 carvings of gods and demons.

The Archaeological Museum is across the street from the Matangeswara Temple. Three separate galleries contain interesting sculptures and stone panels salvaged from ruined temples.

Eastern Group

This group lies close to the village and includes three Hindu temples (Brahma, Vamana, and Javari) and three Jain shrines (Ghantai, Adinath, and Parsvanath). This proximity of the cults attests to the religious tolerance of the times in general and of the Chandella rulers in particular. About halfway between the western group of temples and the village is a modern building housing a tenth-century idol of Hanuman, the monkey god.

Vamana Temple is northernmost and is dedicated to Vishnu's dwarf incarnation. The idol in the sanctum, however, looks more like a tall, sly child than a dwarf. The hall, a squat, heavily adorned pile of masonry and sculpture, contrasts strongly with the relatively plain-ribbed shikhara. The sanctum walls show total tolerance—almost all the major gods appear with their consorts in attendance. Vishnu in many of his forms, with even a Buddha thrown in. Outside, two tiers of sculpture are mainly concerned with the nymphs of paradise, who strike charming poses under their private awnings. The sculptors obviously enjoyed lavishing their energy on so many full-blown female bodies, so many ornaments, and so many handsome coiffures. Here, too, you see the unexpurgated mind at work.

Javari Temple is just to the south. It is small and of the simplified three-shrine design, but well proportioned and lovely. The two main exterior bands again boast hosts of heavenly maidens.

Brahma Temple is slightly to the south and opposite the Javari. Made of both granite and sandstone, it is considered one of the earliest temples. Its general outline, particularly that of the spire, suggests some other style of Indian temple. It was originally dedicated to Shiva, but the idol in the shrine was miscalled Brahma, and the name stuck.

The Jain Temples are to the south of this group, beginning with a little gem, the Ghantai. This open-colonnaded structure is only the shell of what was once a complete temple, but it is still one of the most attractive monuments at Khajuraho. Note the classicism and detail of the pillars. These slender columns seem decorated with French *passementerie*—bugles, braid, and bell-like tassels hang in graceful patterns. Adorning the entrance are an eight-armed Jain goddess riding the mythical bird, Garuda, and a relief illustrating the 16 dreams of the mother of Mahavira, the greatest religious figure in Jainism and a contemporary of Buddha.

Adinath Temple is east of Ghantai. A minor shrine, the porch is a modern addition, as is the statue of Tirthankara (perfect soul) Adinatha. The shikhara and its base are richly carved.

Parsvanath Temple, to the south, is the largest and finest of the Jain temples and probably the best construction, technically speaking, in all Khajuraho. Although Kandariya may have the best design, Parsvanath makes up for its lack of size and architectural perfection with marvelous sculpture. Its unrelievedly chiseled facades, turrets, and spires demand close inspection. The sanctum has a carved bull (Adinatha's emblem) standing on a pedestal. In 1860, another image was installed, that of Parsvanath. The outer walls have excellent statues of sloe-eyed beauties in naturalistic poses, occupied in feminine pursuits with children, cosmetics, and flowers. A statue of Shiva and Parvati is almost the epitome of love: her breast cupped in his hand, they regard each other with tenderness and desire. Almost all the exterior offers some of the best Hindu art in India. There is another temple in this group, the Shantinath, which is modern but does contain some ancient Jain sculpture.

Southern Group

There are only two temples in this group; the first, one of the major attractions of Khajuraho, the second, smaller and at a hiking distance or via car along a road.

Duladeo Temple, south of Ghantai Jain Temple, though built in the customary five-shrine style, looks flatter and more massive than do the typical Khajuraho shrines. It lacks the usual ambulatory passage and has no crowning lotus-shaped finials that are of a later period than the actual high point of Khajuraho statuary. The decoration is still graceful and well executed, particularly the multiple-figure bracket capitals inside and the flying wizards on the highest carved band outside. Here, too, in this temple dedicated to Shiva, eroticism works its way in.

Chaturbhuj Temple is nearly a mile farther south of Duladeo. Small, but with an attractive colonnaded entrance and a nice feeling of verticality, it enshrines an impressive large, four-handed image of Vishnu. The exterior sculpture, with a few exceptions, falls short of the Khajuraho mark.

Intermission

Although the temples are Khajuraho's major attraction and the compelling reason for any visit, lovely nearby respites from the intense concentration of sculpture do exist. See the Eastern Temples at sunset. Sit on the steps of the Vamana and watch the villagers come home from working the fields or fill their brass vessels at the nearby well. Walk into the adjacent Khajuraho village and meander around the streets crowded with boar, goats, buffalo.

One afternoon, take a three-mile ride by rickshaw to the tiny village of Rajnagar, with the maharajah's former fortress now a school set on the crest of a hill. Roam the narrow winding streets lined with charming whitewashed houses and shops. This easy excursion is a must if you are lucky to be in Khajuraho on a Tuesday, the day villagers from all around trek into Rajnagar for a daylong colorful bazaar.

PRACTICAL INFORMATION FOR KHAJURAHO

WHEN TO GO. Avoid June through August, when the thermometer climbs over 100°. Rainfall in July and August is also heavy. Best time to visit is from October to the end of March; the rainy season has ended then; and the temperature is delightful most of the time.

HOW TO GET THERE. By Air. The best way is the morning *Indian Airlines* flight, daily throughout the year, from Delhi (1½ hours) and Agra (40 minutes). The same flight continues to Varanasi and Kathmandu (Nepal). If you're in a rush, you could cover Khajuraho in a day, leaving Delhi or Agra in the morning and flying back early the same afternoon. But that's the speed demon's pace, which gives about five hours in Khajuraho, barely enough time to fly through the important temples. The best plan is to stay overnight. Take in the temples in the gentler light of late afternoon or early morning. Khajuraho can get hot by midday.

By Train. Trains from Delhi (seven hours), Bombay (20 hours) and Madras (30 hours) let you off at railroad stops at least 70 km away. The train involves a bus ride at regular intervals, which can take as much as five hours.

By Bus. Buses also make the run to Khajuraho. From Agra, 12 hours, once daily; Bhopal, 10 hours, two nighttime runs; Indore, 13 hours, one nighttime run; Jhansi, five hours, numerous daily runs.

By Car. It's a long ride, since Khajuraho is in the middle of village India. From Agra, 395 km; Varanasi, 415 km; Lucknow, 287 km.

TOURIST INFORMATION. Two separate tourist departments offer different information on Khajuraho. Both are helpful and worth a visit or telephone call. Get available brochures at the following offices:

Government of India Tourist Office, opposite the Western Temple Complex; tel. 47; winter hours: 10 A.M.–5 P.M.; summer: 8 A.M.–12 noon, 2:30–6 P.M. *Tourist Information Counter,* Khajuraho Airport; tel. 56; open only during arrivals and departures. *Government of Madhya Pradesh,* M.P. Information Center, Bus Stand; tel. 51; 10 A.M.–5 P.M. *Regional Tourist Office,* Tourist Bungalow, tel. 51, 10 A.M.–5 P.M.

ACCOMMODATIONS. Khajuraho has a limited number of hotels in all price ranges: *Expensive,* over Rs. 500; *Moderate,* Rs. 200–500; and *Inexpensive,* under Rs. 200. Rates are based on double occupancy. Most Western-style hotels take major credit cards. During peak season (October to the end of March) can be busy, so book in advance.

Expensive

Hotel Chandela. Khajuraho, M. P. tel. 54. Cable: CHANDELA. 102 rooms. Air-conditioned; cable TVs. Most Western amenities: room service, a swimming pool, a health club, a shopping arcade, restaurants, a 24-hour coffee shop, a bar, and modern decor.

Jass Oberoi. Bypass Road, Khajuraho, M.P.; tel. 66. Cable: OBHOTEL. 54 rooms. Air-conditioned; TVs. Most Western amenities: a health club, a swimming pool, tennis courts, 24-hour room service, restaurants, a bar, and modern decor.

Moderate

Hotel Khajuraho Ashok. Khajuraho, M.P.; tel. 24. Cable: TOURISM. 48 rooms. Air-conditioning; TVs. Some Western amenities: a swimming pool, shops, a bank, and a restaurant. ITDC-run.

Inexpensive

Hotel Payal. Khajuraho, M.P.; tel. 76. Feels less remote from the village and temples than do the Oberoi and Chandela. 25 rooms. Rate includes breakfast. Air-conditioning and fans; modern clean rooms. Restaurant. Well-run Madhya Pradesh Tourism hotel in a nice setting. Excellent value for the money.

Hotel Rahil. Near the Payal, Khajuraho, M.P.; tel. 62. 12 rooms. Fans. Clean and simple; hot and cold showers, restaurant. Good value for the money. Run by M.P. Tourism.

Tourist Village Complex. Khajuraho, M.P.; reservations: Regional Manager MPSTDC, Khajuraho, Madhya Pradesh. Eight cottages, two units per cottage. Cottages are a unique re-creation of a Bundelkhandi village with interiors trimmed in dark wood. Clean, sparce decor. Poor lighting, however, creates a dungeonlike atmosphere. Each cottage has a private porch with views. Outdoor restaurant. Check it out before you take a room. For some, it could be ideal.

DINING OUT. Khajuraho has limited restaurant facilities outside the Western-style hotels. A few outdoor cafes have limited menus. Most hotel restaurants serve Continental and Indian nonvegetarian meals and are open for breakfast, lunch, and dinner. Prices are generally in accord with the category of the hotel, with a three-course meal ranging from *Expensive* (Rs. 50 or more) to *Moderate* (Rs. 25–50). For an *Inexpensive* restaurant (under Rs. 25), try the **Raja Cafe,** an informal outdoor place opposite the Western Temples or the **Tourist Village Complex Restaurant,** also outdoors, and secluded, which has a limited Indian menu.

HOW TO GET AROUND. From the airport to Khajuraho center is about 6 km; to the pricy hotels, 4 km. A **taxi** should run about Rs. 20. Once you're in the small village, the best way to get around is by **cycle-rickshaw,** which comfortably carries two people. Drivers are supposed to follow fixed rates, but they like to keep this fact a secret. Negotiate hard or check with the Government of India Tourist Office (across from the Western Temple complex); an outside board lists the rates. Once you've seen the Western Temple complex, the other temples are spread around Khajuraho. Hire a rickshaw for a few hours (Rs. 25–40 per four hours) and have the driver take you from temple to temple, the old village and your hotel. **Taxis** are also available (Rs. 2 per km). You can engage a taxi at a flat rate for a number of hours or a number of kilometers. The tourist office can also give the scope of rates. In general, transportation costs in Khajuraho are reasonable by Indian standards. And, although rickshaw pedalers may try to get more than the government rate, it's hot and they work hard.

FOREIGN CURRENCY EXCHANGE. *State Bank of India* is open 10:45 A.M.–2:45 P.M. daily, closed Sundays; *Canara Bank,* Hotel Khajuraho Ashok 10 A.M.–2 P.M. Western-style hotels will also change well-known traveler's checks.

FESTIVALS. March. The *Khajuraho Dance Festival* gives you a week-long opportunity to see numerous forms of classical Indian dance performed by India's best dancers in culturally compatible outdoor surroundings. Contact tourist offices for specific details. Nominal fee. Buy tickets in advance.

TOURS. The Archaeological Survey of India conducts free lecture tours of the Western Group of Temples twice daily, except on Fridays and holidays. Tour starts at the gate of the Western Group of temples at 9 A.M. and 2:30 P.M.

You can also arrange for an excellent private guide (approved by the government). Make arrangements through the *Government Tourist Office* or at Raja Cafe (2–4 hours; about Rs. 50). Many of the guides are fluent in German, Japanese, Italian, English, and French. Don't get taken in by those who pose as guides inside the temple complex. They'll talk your head off, but the facts they tell are their own.

HISTORIC SITES. See all the 20 remaining tenth- and eleventh-century temples and their fabulous carvings. The best times of day to view the temples are early morning and late afternoon, when the light is softer and shadows highlight the delicate carvings. They are in three main groups, those of the west being generally acknowledged to be the best. Close to Khajuraho village is the eastern group, while three miles from there stand the southern groups. Out of these 20 temples, five are easily accessible—Kandariya Mahadeva Temple is by far the largest and the finest, the others being Lakshmana, Visvanatha, Chitragupta, and Devi Jagdambe. These temples are found in a group close to each other and make an imposing picture with their elegant spires against the sky. Temples are open from early morning to sunset. Western Complex, Rs. 2; others, free.

MUSEUM. The *Archaeological Museum* near the Western Group of Temples has three galleries: Jain, Buddhist, and miscellaneous, essentially sculptures collected on the temple sites. Tickets for the Western Group also include entry to the museum. Open 10 A.M.–5 P.M.; closed Fridays. Nominal entry charge.

SHOPPING. Opposite the Western Group of Temples is a square with numerous carts of so-called curios— most of which are new. Buy what you like and bargain hard. In general, Khajuraho is not a shopper's draw. Save your rupees for better quality items elsewhere.

SOUTHERN REGION

TAMIL NADU

Glories of Dravidian India

by
KATHLEEN COX

In almost any country, the south has a personality of its own, and India
is no exception. The pace of living in this sun-drenched state is more
leisurely and more traditional than the rest of the country.

The region covers the State of Tamil Nadu and some of its environs,
along the coast of the Bay of Bengal on the east and the Western Ghats
on the west. It was formerly a number of separate princely states that
were amalgamated, for linguistic reasons, after Independence.

The land of Tamil, founded by Dravidians over 5,000 years ago, is
primarily agrarian. It has frequent lush green vistas, charming narrow
waterways, vast groves of coconuts, bananas, and sugarcane, and innumerable tiny villages with huts of thatch, wood, mud, or brick—well-
tended homes that are pleasingly neat and tidy. Throughout the region,
you'll see colorful drawings on the ground or pavement in front of each
dwelling. Each morning the woman of the house, using her imagination, and white or colored powder, creates *kolams* (or *rangolis*) in
intricate geometric or flower designs. Traditionally, the powder was
made from rice and the design was then eaten by insects or birds. In
this way the woman pleased the gods by starting her day with an act
of charity. Even Madras, the capital, offers glimpses of the traditional
way of life that has all but vanished in many other cities of India. And
when Madras becomes too hot, the southern hill stations and the
beaches offer a great escape.

336

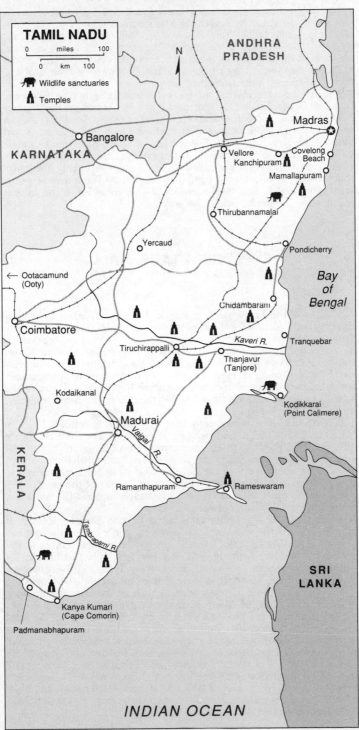

The difference between South India and the rest of the country is much greater than a few degrees on a thermometer. The south has been relatively unaffected by the waves of invasion that shaped India for centuries, even though it was the starting point of the last invasion of all—that of the Europeans. Alien empire builders either never reached the south during the long centuries of Indian history or their fury and zeal were spent by the time they got here.

The result is a fascinating survival of ancient India in its purest form. Nowhere else is classical dancing performed on the scale of the Bharata Natyam dances of Madras and other, smaller cities. Nowhere else can you experience the exuberance of medieval India as you can in old Madurai or Tiruchirappalli. The temples of South India can't be classified according to the dictates of Western architecture and esthetics. Their *gopura* (towers) are massive, and some—especially the more recent ones—have colors in combinations that no Westerner sees outside Miami Beach. But, as expressions of traditional India, the ancient temples are the heart and soul of any trip.

EXPLORING TAMIL NADU

MADRAS

Madras is the fourth largest city in India—outranked by Delhi, Bombay and Calcutta for the dubious distinction of cramming as many people as possible into one place. Fortunately, you don't feel the density in Madras. The city, which is divided in two by the Cooum River, sprawls over 68 square miles, with few tall buildings to mar the impression of an easygoing market town. The welcome sense of spaciousness is enhanced by Madras's waterfront on the Bay of Bengal, one of the world's largest and most attractive beaches set in the heart of a city, unspoiled and peaceful.

In spite of its large population, currently over four million, this city has a gentle pace and is made for people watching. The southerners are different from their northern counterparts, having the poise and self-assurance that comes from carrying the civilization of thousands of years. Saris aren't worn in the same manner as in northern India and though some men dress in the elegant white *dhotis* of the north, they often wear brightly colored *lungis* (cloth draped around the waist and worn long or pulled up between the knees).

That gracefulness is present in Madras in such liberal quantities is appropriate. In the Government Museum, you can see the famous bronze of the Chola period (tenth century) of Nataraja-Shiva in the cosmic dance pose. Although it's only two feet high, this beautifully executed statue seems to be constantly moving. It has rightfully become the symbol of Indian art that is recognized all around the world.

No visitor should dare leave Madras without seeing a performance of the Bharata Natyam. Many of these dance recitals are about Krishna, the most popular of Vishnu's nine incarnations, symbol of the ideal man. As they dance, the women appear to express their infatuation with the god, described in one prayer as "Lord Krishna, with eyes like lustrous pearls, head bedecked with peacocks' feathers and body of the hue of Heaven." The dancers exhibit perfect control over each muscle in their bodies, while executing intricate movements with clockwork precision. Once you've seen a Bharata Natyam dancer move her neck while keeping her head still, you'll respect the artistry and skill behind this classical Indian dance form.

Paradoxically, this least Westernized of India's Big Four cities is also its oldest European settlement. The written records trace the first European foothold in Madras back 500 years to the Portuguese, but the Portuguese were only latecomers. Legend claims that Thomas the Apostle ("Doubting Thomas") came here as a missionary to India and was martyred while praying in front of a cross engraved in stone on St. Thomas Mount (near the Madras Airport) in A.D. 72. This stone, called the "Bleeding Stone" because it supposedly sheds blood on December 18 (the day of St. Thomas's death), is now installed behind the high altar inside the lovely sixteenth-century Church of Our Lady of Expectation, erected on the foundation of an earlier church that St. Thomas is said to have built. His revered name has also survived in St. Thomé, a pleasant seaside residential section of southern Madras, while his body is believed to be entombed in the center of the San Thomé Cathedral Basilica, a handsome neo-Gothic structure with elegant arches and a 180-foot steeple, built in 1896. Inside, notice the image of Christ standing on a lotus flower (a typical Hindu pose).

From here, wander into the nearby inland district called Mylapore, the home of Tiruvalluvar, the Tamil poet who lived in the second century and wrote the *Kural,* the greatest of all works in the Tamil language. It's still recited reverently in South India. In Mylapore, you must visit the Kapaleeswarar Temple dedicated to Kapaleeswarar (Shiva). This structure offers an impressive contrast to the European architecture found in the cathedral. The sawed-off pyramid of its recently renovated *gopuram* (tower entrance) shatters the horizon far more violently than does the slim spire of San Thomé. This typical Dravidian temple, which was rebuilt about 300 years ago, is a riot of color. Although non-Hindus can't enter the sanctum sanctorum (inner shrine), they can enter the outer courtyard.

Fort St. George, the Original Madras

Strickly speaking, the history of Madras began with the history of the British in India. In 1639, 25 years before the British reached Bombay and 50 years before they arrived in Calcutta, the Rajah of Chandragiri gave Francis Day a lease to open a trading post for the British East India Company on the site of Madras, then known as Madraspatram. The following year, work began on Fort St. George that was finished in 1653. From this stronghold, Britain held Madras until India achieved independence, with the exception of a two-year period beginning in 1746, when Dupleix took it for France, only to lose it again in 1748. Fort St. George is tightly interwoven with the swashbuckling story of the struggle for India in the eighteenth century. Here, Robert Clive arrived in 1743 as a modest clerk for the East India Company. When Fort St. George surrendered to the French, Clive escaped and metamorphosed from a clerk into an officer in the army of the East India Company. By the time he was 30, he had become governor of Madras and was well launched on his meteoric career, which saw him preserve India for Britain only to die by his own hand in disgrace back in his native England.

Modern Madras has grown around Fort St. George, and the old fortress, which now houses the Tamil Nadu State Legislature and other political offices, is a good place to start a tour of this part of the city. Its 20-foot walls still guard the center of Madras and its busy commercial artery, Anna Salai (Mount Road). Inside the walls, you can stroll through the pages of history. Clive's house is still here, and Colonel Wellesley, who later became the Duke of Wellington, lived in another old home, which can also be seen within the fort.

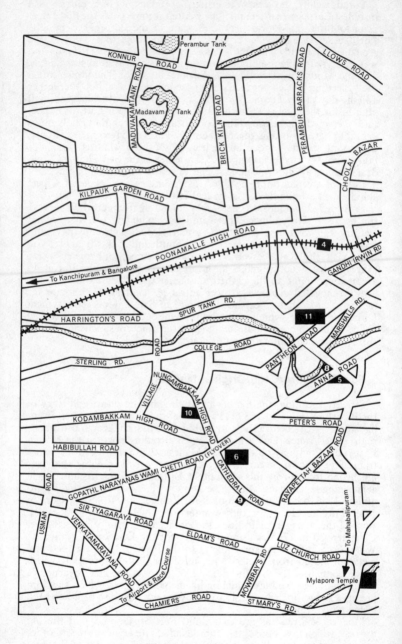

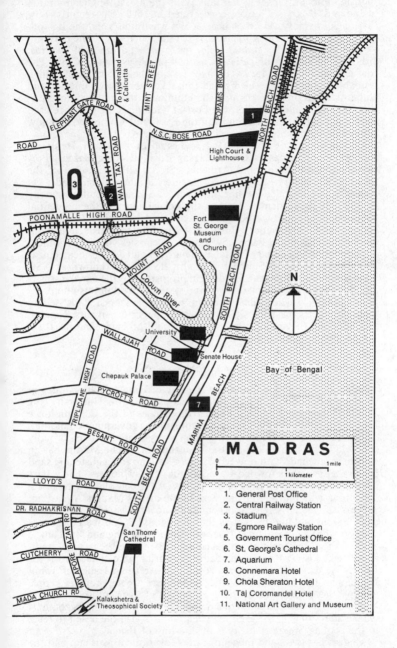

MADRAS

| 0 | | | 1 mile |
| 0 | | 1 kilometer | |

1. General Post Office
2. Central Railway Station
3. Stadium
4. Egmore Railway Station
5. Government Tourist Office
6. St. George's Cathedral
7. Aquarium
8. Connemara Hotel
9. Chola Sheraton Hotel
10. Taj Coromandel Hotel
11. National Art Gallery and Museum

Inside Fort St. George, you must visit the oldest Anglican church in India, St. Mary's Church, consecrated in 1680. The records show that one of its most generous benefactors was Elihu Yale, the Boston-born English merchant who also showed his generosity to the university that now bears his name. Yale, too, was a governor of Madras, although his term in office is not as memorable as that of Clive. The roof and walls of St. Mary's are five feet thick and bombproof, which probably explains why the French ransacked the sacred interior and committed the profane: turning the building into a military fortification. Finally, you can look at the Fort St. George Museum, once used as an exchange by the merchants of the East India Company, and now containing many interesting relics from that era.

George Town, the original Madras, lies north of the fort. Its streets still bear such names as China Bazaar Road, Evening Bazaar, Portuguese Church Street, and Armenian Street, all reminiscent of the four-century history of Madras as a center of international trade. On Armenia Street, notice the fine old Armenian Church, built originally in 1620. It subsequently became the cornerstone of the influential Armenian community. And don't miss the great Evening Bazaar (also called Parrys—pronounced Paris—after the former British confectionery factory that made Parrys Sweets, those candies you get on Indian Airlines). Evening Bazaar (which is in high gear all *day*) is located near Broadway and Nataji Subhash Chandra Bose Road (known as NSC Bose Road to taxi drivers). Produce in profusion fills the narrow streets and the senses. The odors change from street to street in this photographer's haven—a wholesale emporium of countless open stalls, selling fruit, vegetables, pastries, flowers, colorful paper ornaments, bangles, and whatever (if you look long enough you'll probably find it). It's a thoroughly fascinating bustle of bartering and noise.

Marina Beach and Other Sights

South of Fort St. George along the Bay of Bengal, Madras puts on its elegant face. South Beach Road runs past Madras University, the Senate House, the Chepauk Palace (the nabobs of the Carnatic once held court in this Moorish-style structure, now a government building). This is the Marina, the shore drive that every Madras citizen proudly tells you is the second-longest beach in the world. The Marina has an elegant promenade with flowerbeds along its lane and a glistening sand beach that is never crowded—at least not with swimmers. The waters off the Marina are infested with sharks. As a consolation, there's a swimming pool on the Marina, next to the dreary Madras Aquarium.

Near this aquarium is another memento of East India Company days, an old building known as the "Ice House." The Ice House was used to store ice brought all the way from New England by Yankee seafarers for the benefit of sunbaked businessmen in the pre-air-conditioned age. Also visit the Anna Samadhi, burial place of and shrine for Dr. C. N. Annadurai, the great orator and revered leader of Tamil Nadu, who died in 1969. The true "sight" here are the ordinary people who pay homage to one of the great heroes of their culture. It is said that when Dr. Annadurai died, a number of devoted followers committed suicide. Come in the evening when families visit the beach to relax in the cooling breeze that floats off the Bay of Bengal.

Madras has two good museums: the Government Museum and the National Art Gallery (both on Pantheon Road). The Government Museum has a vast collection of the best South Indian bronzes (see the famous Cosmic Dancer) all made by the lost-wax method, plus wonderful archaeological remains from excavations at the Amravati Buddhist stupa, part of which was constructed in the first and second centuries.

The National Art Gallery has a good collection of ancient and modern Indian art.

At the headquarters of the Theosophical Society, which was started at the turn of the century to encourage the comparative study of religion, philosophy, and science while promoting a universal brotherhood without regard to race, creed, or sex, you'll find an excellent library with old palm-leaf manuscripts and rare books. The grounds of the society, just over Elphinstone Bridge on the Adyar River, also have one of India's oldest banyan trees. This tree is mammoth—500 people can stand under its branches, which offer 40,000 square feet of shade.

Also in Adyar, visit the Kalakshetra School, where classical dance, as well as other important South Indian art forms, is taught. You can also see the ancient designs of Indian textiles reproduced anew.

The Madras Snake Park and Conservation Center, situated in beautiful Guindy Deer Park in Madras, was founded by Romulus Whitaker, an American who settled in India. The park gives the public a chance to see, photograph, and touch the common snakes of India (over 500 species), most of which are housed in an open "pit." Other reptiles— crocodiles, alligators, monitor lizards, and chameleons— also call the park home. Over a half million people visit the park each year. The entrance fees, apart from covering the cost of maintaining the park, are used for various wildlife projects and relevant surveys. The Snake Park has received numerous grants and the continued support of the World Wildlife Fund. While you're here, ask how the snake's skin is removed to make those articles that are hawked in abundance. You may decide to do without them.

The borders of Madras extend 37 miles south and 57 miles southwest to Mahabalipuram and Kanchipuram, respectively. No visit to the capital of South India should overlook these two monuments to the glory of the Pallava emperors.

MAHABALIPURAM

There's a good road between Madras and Mahabalipuram, on the Bay of Bengal. This city was once the main harbor and naval base of the great Pallava empire, the capital of which was in Kanchipuram. Although the reign of the Pallavas waned some 1,200 years ago, its gifts still stand on and near the shore of this "city of the seven pagodas," its European designation. Tiny Mahabalipuram, with its 4,000-plus population, offers a breathtaking display of masterful sculpture carved out of solid rock. In fact, the Pallavas developed four distinct kinds of sculpture: *rathas* (temple chariots), bas-relief sculptural panels, rock-cut caves, and freestanding temples. Here, humans worked nature into sublime art, although nature is now taking its revenge. The salt spray of the bay is carving the rock temples all over again.

The Five Rathas

The so-called pagodas of Mahabalipuram are actually seventh-century rathas, although, to a Western eye, they resemble small pyramid-shaped temples cut off by flat roofs. The walls of these freestanding, monolithic temples—each chiseled from a single rock—are a picture book of Hindu mythology. The five rathas, also known as the Pancha Pandava Rathas after the heroes of *Mahabaratham,* a Hindu epic, are dedicated to Durga, Shiva, Vishnu, and Indra. Near these delicate temples, life-size stone statues of an elephant, a lion, and a bull mount guard. These rathas, which are not overpowering in size, are well proportioned even though they are all unfinished. The finials are not in place.

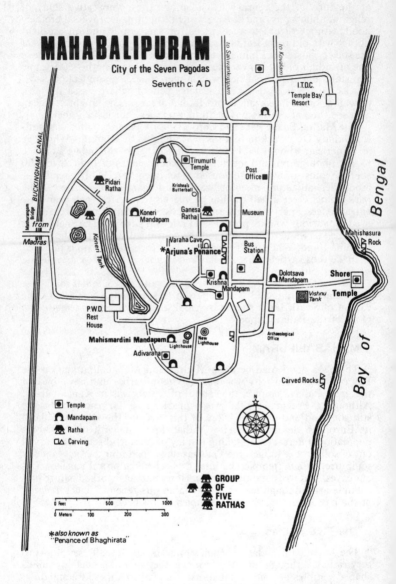

MAHABALIPURAM

City of the Seven Pagodas

Seventh c. A D

to Salavankuppam

to Kovalam

I.T.D.C. 'Temple Bay' Resort

BUCKINGHAM CANAL

Mathurapam Bridge

from Madras

Pidari Ratha

Tirumurti Temple

Krishna's Butterball

Post Office

Museum

Koneri Mandapam

Ganesa Ratha

Mahishasura Rock

Koneri Tank

Naraha Cave

Arjuna's Penance

Bus Station

Shore Temple

Dolotsava Mandapam

Krishna Mandapam

Vishnu Tank

PWD Rest House

Mahismardini Mandapam

Old Lighthouse

New Lighthouse

Archaeological Office

Adivaraha

Carved Rocks

N

Bay of Bengal

- ◉ Temple
- ⌂ Mandapam
- ⛩ Ratha
- ◁▷ Carving

GROUP OF FIVE RATHAS

| 0 Feet | 500 | 1000 |
| 0 Meters | 100 | 200 | 300 |

*also known as "Penance of Bhaghirata"

Rock-Cut Caves

In the nine rock-cut caves, you'll find some of India's most animated Hindu sculptures. Visit the seventh-century Mahishasuramardhini Mandapam and see the sculptural relief of the fight of the goddess Durga, riding a lion in her struggle against evil, which is represented by the image of Mahishasura, the buffalo-headed demon. Another bas-relief shows the god Vishnu is his cosmic sleep, lying on the coils of a serpent. Quieter pastoral scenes from the life of Krishna are carved into the Krishna Mandapam cave temple.

Bas-Relief

The pièce de résistance at Mahabalipuram is the "Penance of Arjuna," the world's largest bas-relief and a masterpiece of composition: two gigantic rocks (80 feet long with an average height of 20 feet); a crack runs in between. On either side of the crack are nearly 100 figures of gods, demigods, people, animals, and birds—nearly every real and mythological form of creation. This bas-relief has been called a fresco in stone, and its vitality makes its figures lifelike. The most prominent of its myriad characters is the group of elephants, one of them 17 feet long. Then there's Arjuna, the emaciated figure standing on one leg and doing penance—praying to Lord Shiva for a powerful weapon to destroy his enemies. All creation is witnessing his act.

Shore Temple

On the shore stands one of the oldest temples in South India, now protected against the erosion of the sea by a stone wall. Built by King Rajasimha in the seventh century, the temple comprises two shrines—one to Vishnu and the other to Shiva. It is a good example of the first phase of Dravidian temple architecture. Surrounded by a row of bulls carved out of solid rock, the Shore Temple stands with its back to the sea, rising up against blue waters with a white wreath of foam. There were once two or three more temples along the shore, but only one has withstood time and the sea for 12 centuries.

Mahabalipuram also has a fine beach and several good resorts; it's a relaxing slow-tempoed place to stay.

KANCHIPURAM

From the port of the Pallavas to their capital at Kanchipuram—one of India's holiest cities—is an easy 40-mile trip inland. On the way, stop at Thirukkalikundram, eight miles west of Mahabalipuram, where a small temple stands atop a 500-foot hill. There, every day just before noon, a priest feeds two white kites—birds that the faithful believe are the spirits of two saints. In the village at the foot of the hill, there is also a Pallaya rock temple dedicated to Shiva. And, along the route, notice more of those kolam (or rangoli) drawings on the ground in front of each Tamil Nadu dwelling.

The Golden City of Temples, Kanchipuram, is currently a charming, bustling village with numerous whitewashed homes featuring open porches stretched across the front with all the trim brightly painted. Kanchipuram contains no less than 124 shrines and is sacred both to Shiva and to Vishnu, which makes it an important stopping place for Hindus making their rounds of the seven holy cities of India (the other six are Hardwar, Ujjain, Varanasi, Mathura, Ayodhya, and Dwarka).

Kanchipuram is the "Varanasi of the South," and its religious architecture is a treat, even to the non-Hindu.

Kanchipuram's Pallava temples were built by its kings, who also founded Mahabalipuram. The kings patronized not only architecture and sculpture but all the arts, transforming their capital into one of India's greatest centers of learning. Hindu and Buddhist philosophies flourished side by side here. Since you would need a lifetime to visit and examine all the temples, here are a few of the best:

Kailasanatha Temple

The first temple built in Kanchipuram was the Kailasanatha Temple constructed in the early eighth century by King Rajasimha. A smaller temple built by his son, Mahendra, stands in the east end of the courtyard. Dedicated to Shiva, these sandstone temples are considered the finest examples of Pallava architecture. They are adorned with excellent sculptures—a big *nandi* (bull-headed god) on a raised platform, other nandis everywhere, and images of Shiva galore—as well as many lovely paintings on the walls. Note, too, the unusual tiny shrines built around the courtyard, each with its own shrine and pillared pavilion—58 exquisite monuments of fastidious labor.

Vaikunthaperumal Temple

Built a few years after the Kailasanatha Temple, the Vaikunthaperumal, with its three-story *vimana* (tower over the central temple), was built by King Nandivarman and is dedicated to Lord Vishnu, who is shown repeatedly: sitting, standing, and reclining—the figures often appearing one on top of another. Notice the sculptured panels of the *mandapa* (pavilion in front of the central temple); they recount the history of the Pallavas, including their battles with the Chalyukas. At that time, such nonreligious subject matter in a temple was unusual, possibly a first. In many ways, this temple, with its colonnade of lion pillars, marks the next stage in the development of Dravidian architecture. On its walls, you can also see more surviving Hindu murals.

Ekambareswara Temple

Although originally constructed by the Pallavas, this temple's most significant feature—its 196-foot *goporum* (tower entrance) with more than ten stories of intricate sculpture—was the result of a sixteenth-century addition by the Vijayanagar kings. This temple is also dedicated to Shiva; inside the courtyard is an important mango tree that is supposedly 3,500 years old. It is said that each leaf is different, the fruit of each branch offers a different taste, and when women wishing to become pregnant come here to pray, their wish is granted. Of the original 1,000 pillars that once stood in the mandapa only about 600 remain.

Sri Varadaraja Temple

Smaller, but probably more pleasing to the eye, is the 100-foot goporum of the Varadaraja Temple, originally built in the eleventh century but overhauled by the Vijayanagar kings 500 years later. Also known as the Devarajaswamy Temple, this edifice is dedicated to Vishnu, and its 1,000-pillared mandapa—all of it exquisitely carved—is one of the best. Be certain to see the massive chain carved from one stone, as well as the handsome pillars standing in the courtyard.

Sri Kamakshi Temple

In the heart of the old town, the Kamakshi, with its fancy gold-plated goporum, is dedicated to the goddess Kamakshi (Parvati). This temple is the site of an annual winter car festival, when numerous small deities from all the nearby temples are pulled by wooden temple cars in a procession, led by an elephant. The colorful event draws huge crowds.

Although Kanchipuram is most famous for its temples, it's also well known as a silk-weaving center. "Connjeevaram sari" (what the English formerly called Kanchipuram) is still synonymous with the best in Indian silk saris as well as silk by the meter.

Vellore

Thirty-five miles to the west of Kanchipuram is Vellore, on the banks of the Palar River. The heart of Vellore is its fort, built in the thirteenth century and still an excellent example of military architecture, despite a long and bloody history of battles. The last siege of Vellore occurred in 1806 during a sepoy mutiny caused by military grievances, antedating the great upheaval of the Indian Mutiny of 1857 by 51 years.

Across a moat, impressive gates lead into the fort. Inside, there's an exquisite temple of Shiva, probably built in the fourteenth century, which was not in use until a *lingam* (phallic symbol) was installed in 1981. Attractive sculpture adorns the temple's ceiling and pillars.

Thiruvannamalai

From Vellore, head south to Thiruvannamalai and one of South India's largest temples. Sprawling over 25 acres, the Arunachala Temple is dedicated to Tejo Lingam (Lord Shiva in his fire incarnation—one of the five elements he represents). Here, a goporum rises 200 feet with 11 sculpture stories. Behind it in the temple grounds is a magnificent pavilion of a 1,000 pillars.

The Arunachala Temple lies at the foot of a hill that bursts with celebration during the Karthikai Deepam festival during the full moon around the end of November. A huge bonfire, ignited on top of the hill and visible for miles, guides pilgrims to the shrine of a Hindu saint, Sri Ramana Maharisha, who spent much of his time here.

Pondicherry

Head east to Tindivanam, then south to Pondicherry. The atmosphere of a sleepy French provincial town is struggling to survive since this former tiny enclave was returned to Indian administration in 1954 after 250 years of French rule. Near its handsome Government House by the sea is a statue of Dupleix, the unsuccessful rival of Clive, who governed Pondicherry for 40 years in the eighteenth century. The French touch is completed with a statue of Joan of Arc.

Another influence that has begun to change Pondicherry was started by Sri Aurobindo, philosopher, poet, and patriot who withdrew to Pondicherry in 1910, after a political trial that lasted two years. With the help of a French woman, called "Mother," he founded the ashram that bears his name. His ideal, a superman who surpasses his fellowmen in the things of the spirit, is the antithesis of Nietzsche's; and his humanism is distinctly different from the philosophy of modern Western thinkers. The residents of the ashram, which can be visited, are supposed to be living according to the Master's (and Mother's) teachings—he died in 1950, she died in 1973—in a rarefied atmosphere of *sachidananda* (pure spirit). But the ashram and nearby Auroville, "the City of Dawn," an international commune of sorts, launched in 1968 by Mother, are embroiled in nonspiritual bickering. Much of Pondicherry's economy is Aurobindo-oriented. At Auroville, you see stabs at futuristic architecture in settlements called Aspiration and Revelation, in 17 different types of windmills, and in the Matri Mandir, a humongous sphere (an intended meditation hall) that has been under construction since 1971.

Chidambaram

Continuing south, you enter the South Arcot district—the southern India rice bowl—vibrant green with paddies where men lead water buffalo back and forth through lush, fertile fields. After about 40 miles, you reach Chidambaram. Chidambaram is the site of the oldest temple in South India, the Nataraja Temple, conceivably (no one knows for sure) built in the fifth century by a Chola king. Suffering from leprosy, according to legend, the king took the advice of a resident saint, bathed in a sacred tank, and recovered. Supposedly, he showed his gratitude by building the earliest stages of this temple (the sacred tank is inside) erected over a span of centuries. The Nataraja is dedicated to Shiva in various aspects, including the cosmic dancer prancing on the remains of evil and ignorance.

In the Chit Sabha (the inner sanctum) covered with gold plate, the presiding deity is identified by one of the five elements (all of which Shiva represents): air, known as the Akasa Lingam. What you see is a black curtain, standing for ignorance, that is raised three times daily. There are four other halls: the Nritta Sabha, Deva Sabha, Kanaka Sabha, and Raja Sabha. The Kanaka, also covered in gold plate, houses the famous Nataraja image of Shiva, the cosmic dancer cast in an alloy of five metals. The Nritta Sabha, the Hall of Dance, has over 50 pillars depicting dancing figures. Representing a heavenly chariot carved in stone, it contains an image of Shiva engaged in a dance contest with the goddess Kali. Shiva won. Deva Sabha is the Hall of Festivals, where all the processional deities are kept. Then, there's the Raja Sabha, some call it the most spectacular, 340 by 190 feet, with 1,000 pillars. Here the Pandyas and Cholas celebrated their victories. Two of the temple's four goporums of granite (no one knows how the granite reached Chidambaram; there's none within a 50-mile radius) are covered with sculptures illustrating the 108 dance positions of Bharata Natyam.

Vishnu is also worshiped at Chidambaram, although his Govindaraja temple is overshadowed by the shrine of Shiva. This temple is a more recent work, but it has an excellent statue of Lord Vishnu lying on a bed of snakes. The shrine closes at 11:30 A.M.

If you are lucky enough to be at Chidambaram in the early evening, visit the Siva-Sakthi Music and Dance School at 123 East Car Street. Inside this elegant old building with passive stone pillars, you might see a class of poised, talented girls learning the Bharata Natyam. Their instructress is a former dancer, regal, with perfect grace. As she provides the beat with a slap of her hands against a pillar, and the girls move with stunning grace, the effect is magic, memorable. A small donation would be an appropriate gift in return, although it's not required.

An interesting side trip from Chidambaram, is the old Danish trading port and town of Tranquebar, with its well-preserved fort and sleepy old colonial air. This town was Denmark's major Asian holding from 1620 until 1840, when the whole settlement was sold to the

British. Still well preserved are the fort, Dansborg Castle, two churches, and the houses of colonial administrators and merchants.

Thanjavur: Showplace of Chola Architecture

A few miles from Kumbakonam is Thanjavur (Tanjore), lying at the foot of what has been called India's greatest temple, the Brahadeeswarar Temple, dedicated to Shiva. Thanjavur was the capital of the Chola Empire from the tenth to the fourteenth centuries. A Chola king, Rajah Chola, who held the throne from 985 to 1016, built the greatest of the empire's 74 temples: the Bradadeeswarar, with its soaring tower (vimana) over the inner sanctum sanctorum—a tower that rises more than 200 feet. On its dome rests a single block of granite weighing 80 tons. The enormous hulk was inched up to the top along an inclined plane that began in a village four miles away, a technique used by the Egyptians to build the Pyramids. This is also the first of four Chola temples in Tamil Nadu to have a vimana soaring over the goporum.

The main shrine of the temple lies at the end of a paved courtyard and houses a huge lingam. This courtyard is guarded by another goporam tower. As you near the inner shrine of Brahadeeswarar, you will encounter India's second largest statue of Nandi the bull (the biggest is at Lepakshi near Anantapur). Sixteen feet long in black granite, Nandi is the mount of the god Shiva. Other sculptures inside the temple draw upon Vishnu and Buddhism as well as Shiva for thier subjects. The walls of the inner courtyard of the temple are covered with excellent frescoes of the Chola and the Nayak periods. These wall paintings are of special interest to lovers of Indian art because, for a long time, the earlier and more interesting Chola frescoes lay hidden under the upper layer of the Nayak paintings. Only when the modern archaeologist was able to expose the bottom layer did we come to know of the existence of an excellent school of painting in the Chola period, comparable to the famous frescoes in the Ajanta cave shrines.

Near the temple is a vast palace built by the Nayak and Maratha dynasties. Although much of the palace is in ruins, it does contain the celebrated Saraswathi Mahal Library with 30,000 volumes (8,000 of these are manuscripts written on palm leaves). In Tamil, Sanskrit, Marathi, Telugu, and a number of European languages, the manuscripts cover subjects from dancing to astronomy. The palace also has a superb collection of bronzes, poorly displayed in an old audience hall.

At Thanjavur also see the Schwartz Church built by a raja in 1779 to express his friendship for a Danish missionary, Rev. C. V. Schwartz, and the nearby Shiva Ganga Tank, known for its sweet water. Close to Thanjavur lies Thiruvaiyar, the nineteenth-century home of Sri Thyagaraja, saint and composer. He wrote more than a thousand songs in Carnatic (Southern Indian) music. In his honor, a major music festival is held here every January.

Tiruchirapalli

West of Thanjavur and 35 miles by road, you leave the "rice bowl" and enter the ancient Cauvery delta town of Tiruchirapalli (Tiruchi), built up by the Nayaks of Madurai. Tiruchi has always been a seat of power in South India and it bears the scars of wars fought to control it, particularly by the French and English.

The military and architectural heart of Tiruchi is its famous Rock Fort, rising 300 feet over the city on the banks of the Cauvery River. A staircase with 434 steps out into the rock, some of them tunneled, leads up to the summit and a temple dedicated to Lord Vinayaka (closed to non-Hindus). Along the way are various landings and shrines: an ancient temple dedicated to Ganesh (the elephant-headed god), a Shiva temple (called Thayumana Swamy Temple) with its hundred-pillared hall (also off-limits to non-Hindus), and cave temples cut into the rock—the two biggest were executed by Pallava sculptors who placed seven pillars across the facade and a square shrine at one end of a hollowed-out wall. Finally at the top, you are rewarded with a breathtaking view of the city and the countryside below.

Below the rock at the base of the fort, a "must" walk is through China Bazaar, the Big Bazaar, and down the interesting narrow side streets—all of which make up the heart of the Old City. You'll share the streets with crowds of people and the typical Indian array of animals, including donkeys. Have a "yard of coffee," so named for the way it is poured, at any of the *bhavans,* "French cafes"—Tamil-Nadu style.

Tiruchi has several other points of interest, including St. Joseph's Church, with its lovely Our Lady of Lourdes Parish, all done up in warm tropical colors and a gorgeous sandlewood altar. Also see the eighteenth-century Christ Church built by the Danish missionary, Rev. Schwartz; and the Teppakalum, a large tank, surrounded by a flower market and open-air stalls. Tiruchi is a busy place, industriously turning out hand-loomed cloth, cigars, mats, textiles, and several kinds of artificial diamonds.

Three miles to the north, though, the glory of religious India explodes again on Srirangam, an island in the Cauvery linked to the mainland by a bridge with 32 arches. Here, worshipers of Vishnu come to one of India's largest temples dedicated to their god—the Ranganatha Swamy Temple built between the fourteenth and seventeenth centuries. The people of Srirangam and the town itself exist primarily inside this 156-acre temple, which has seven sets of walls. It's a fascinating bustling complex. The temple itself really begins when you reach the mandapa behind the fourth wall. This is another of those 1,000-pillared halls (although only 940 remain). There are 22 towers around the temple, with the intended tallest nearing completion. This is very much a "living temple." Pilgrims from all over India come here every year in January for the Vaikunta Ekadasi festival. It is then that Heaven's Gate is opened and the idol of Ranganatha is brought into the mandapa from the inner shrine under a golden dome. This temple also houses a beautiful collection of jewelry.

Another temple, smaller but of more pleasing design, is about a mile to the east: a shrine of Shiva. Here, in the Mambukeswaram pagoda, is a lingam, the symbol of Shiva, submerged in water. This temple is also called Thiruvanaikkaval after the legendary elephant that once worshiped the lingam.

The water surrounding Srirangam island is not only holy but useful. In the eleventh century, a Chola ruler built a stone dam below the island to harness the Cauvery River. He built it so well that you can still see it today, a sturdy wall 1,000 feet long and 60 feet wide, serving the same purpose today as before.

Madurai

Madurai, 96 miles from Tiruchi, this is where you throw out all your points of reference and bases of comparison. In Madurai, architecture and sculpture are not passive monuments but living backdrops for scenes that must have been enacted in the cathedral cities of the Middle Ages. Although Madurai is not a pretty city, it's the beating heart of the land of the Tamils and the high point of a journey south from Madras to the top of India.

Madurai was thriving when Augustus took the throne of Rome (coins found here point to the existence of trade with Rome). Until the fourteenth century, it was the capital of the Pandya rulers of South India, who made it the mother city of Tamil literature with their generous patronage of poets and academics. Then the Nayaks ruled Madurai from the middle of the sixteenth century to 1743 and their majestic imprint is still fresh. The 10 tall goporams of the Meenakshi Temple raised during their dynasty are your first glimpse of Madurai, whether you arrive by car, train, bus, or airplane.

From the air, though, you can also see the two hills of rock marking boundaries between the "sweet place" (the meaning of "Madurai") and its surrounding green paddy fields. They are known as Yanai Malai and Naga Malai (the elephant hill and the snake hill). Two miles long, the Yanai Malai of gray and pink granite does seem to resemble a recumbent elephant. The sweetness of Madurai comes from the nectar that fell from the hair of the god Shiva on the city.

It is Shiva and his wife, Meenakshi, who are honored in Madurai's greatest landmark, the Meenakshi Temple. This, incidentally, is the first big Indian temple whose towers are being restored to their original polychrome colors. Concrete moldings and bright fresh paint have replaced the gentle pastels and crumbling stones of weathered Hindu sculpture. The result is fascinating. A few hundred incarnations of deities out of the Hindu pantheon leering at you from one of the Meenakshi goporams are not something you'll forget in a hurry. The goporams are lavishly covered with brilliant carvings of gods, goddesses, animals and mythical figures.

Rich Pandemonium

The temples are a city within a city that includes a fascinating bazaar, bustling from dawn to nightfall. As you set out to visit the Meenakshi Temple, you will find yourself in a human tide on which the Southern women float gracefully, flowers in their jet-black hair and bright saris draped around their straight bodies.

Although there are four entrances to the Meenakshi Temple, enter through the eastern entrance and stop, for a moment, to notice the mural on the upper-right in the entrance mandapa. In 1923, when paintings were added, the Indian artist included an image of Mahatma Gandhi. When the British insisted on its removal, the artist simply turned Gandhi into a holy man with long hair. He cleverly used watercolor that eventually disappeared, revealing Gandhi, as a young man—hands held together in the traditional *namaste* greeting.

The swirling life of the Meenakshi Temple never seems to stop. However, the temple is closed to devotees from 12:30 to 4 P.M.—a time when visitors are allowed to take photographs. Too bad, for then the temple seems dead. Madurai is known as the "city of festivals" and there seems to be one just about every day. Trumpets, drums, and religious chanting constantly fill the air but do not seem to disturb pilgrims taking a quick snooze under shady arcades.

Although nonbelievers are denied access to the two sanctuaries where Meenakshi and Shiva, in his incarnation as Sundereswarar, are enshrined, they can visit the rest of the temple quite freely. Hindus have no corporate worship and perform the *puja* (worship of the gods) either themselves or through the intermediary of a priest. It used to be possible to climb to the top of one of the goporums from where the panorama over the city of temples is extraordinary, but bomb threats have entered the arena and the goporums were temporarily closed at this writing.

A legend says that this temple was founded by Indra, the king of the gods, who found a lingam in the jungle and ordered his builders to house Shiva's symbol in a temple. When Indra set foot in the temple, he found that its tank was filled by some miracle with golden lilies. You can see this tank, surrounded by a colonnade (from which you get an excellent view of the goporums, as well). Worshipers bathe in the tank of the Golden Lily, where women perform some marvelous sleights-of-hand that enable them to change saris without ever appearing to be undressed. In the past, a bath in the lily tank served another purpose: tradition has it that a Tamil author's works were judged here by the simple expedient of placing his manuscript on the water. If it stank, it sank.

The high point of the Meenakshi Temple, however, is its Hall of a Thousand Pillars. Here, again, the figure is an approximate one; the exact number of pillars is 997. This hall was built around 1560 and is as great a work of structural engineering as it is of art. The pillars are a picture book in stone—and what pictures! They run the whole gamut of human expression from stateliness and grace to lusty humor and ribaldry. It has been said that visitors can wander through these pillars —which represent a grove of a thousand palm trees where a god was once found—and see something new no matter how often they return. Baroque is about the only European style approaching the exuberance of this Dravidian temple.

Outside the Hall of a Thousand Pillars are more pillars. But these are the famous "musical pillars" of the Meenakshi Temple, and they play musical notes when they are struck. The temple also contains a hall known as the Kambatti Mandapam, where Shiva in all of his various manifestations is represented on sculptured pillars.

At any time, this temple of Shiva and his wife is filled with worshipers pouring oil on minor gods, depositing flower offerings, and going through pujas in front of their deities. But its greatest day comes around the end of April during a festival celebrating the marriage of the sacred couple. The wedding is reenacted in the temple and then the images are paraded through the streets of Madurai. In all, the festive proceedings last three days. During the celebrations of the Tamil New Year (mid-April), the evening processions have a particular charm.

Once outside the majestic entrance goporums of the temple, you have still to see another example of the architectural mastery of the Nayaks. This is the palace or *mahal* of Tirumala Nayak, a blend of Hindu and Saracen architecture. Its curved dome, which soars without any visible support, is quite an accomplishment. In the evening, it is the location for an impressive *son et lumiere* presentation.

The modern city of Madurai lives side by side with its traditions. Spinning and weaving mills turn out some of the best cloth of all South India, and the city is an educational center as well. One of its two colleges was founded by an American Protestant mission (Madurai was the headquarters for missionaries as early as the seventeenth century when an Italian Jesuit came here and learned Tamil). Also, plan time to visit the Gandhi Museum, a display of many of his possessions that is touching in its simplicity and understatement.

Three miles outside Madurai is the famous Teppakulam (tank) with an island temple. It's a peaceful place, away from the hubbub and bustle. Eleven miles away is Azhagarkoil, with some excellent sculpture in the hall of a temple, dedicated to Lord Azhagar (Vishnu). Azhagar is the brother of Meenakshi in Hindu mythology.

Rameswaram

This side trip from Madurai can be the jumping point from South India to Sri Lanka. The sacred island of Rameswaram, said to be in the shape of Lord Vishnu's conch, is about 100 miles south from Madurai, with Sri Landa only 46 miles away on the other side of Palk Strait. This sliver of land, separating the Bay of Bengal in the north from the Indian Ocean, is one of the main goals of Hindu pilgrims who come here to pay tribute to Rama, the hero of the epic *Ramayana*. Rama came here in search of his wife, Sita, who had been kidnapped. Rama is one of the ten incarnations of Vishnu, and to many pilgrims, Rameswaram is as holy as Varanasi. It is built on the site where Rama worshiped Shiva to do penance for killing Ravana, the 10-headed demon king of Lanka. Rama wanted to set up a lingam to honor Shiva, so he told the monkey god, Hanuman, to find one by a certain hour, which he was unable to do. Sita, Rama's wife, made one of sand; that explains the lingam in the principal sanctum. When Hanuman returned with a second lingam, Rama saw the monkey god's disappointment and installed this lingam too. That in turn, explains the lingam in the northern sanctum. Rameswaram is so intimately linked with Rama that, to the Hindus, every grain of sand is considered sacred.

The temple of Rameswaram, rising above a lake as a vast rectangle about 1,000 feet long and 650 feet wide, is one of the most beautifully sculptured in India. It dates back to the twelfth century, although the process of building it took 3½ centuries, with the inspiration for its construction coming from one of the princes of Sri Lanka.

Here, you find a nine-story goporam, typical of Dravidian temples. But the corridors of the Rameswaram Temple are unique. They surround the rectangle, stretching out over a distance of 4,000 feet. Through occasional apertures, light filters into these corridors and flits over the carved pillars lining every foot on both sides. Each pillar is an individual composition carved out of solid granite—one of an army— and the total effect of the two ranks standing watch on the sides of the corridors is stunning. Leading authorities call this the most evolved of all Dravidian temples.

Also try to visit the Kothandaramasamy Temple near the southern-most tip of the island. This temple marks the location where Vibishana, the kidnapper of Sita and brother of Ravana, surrendered to Rama. It is the only structure on Dhanushkodi (the tip) that survived a devasta-ting cyclone in 1964.

Cape Comorin (Kanya Kumari)

At Dhanushkodi, two seas meet; at Cape Comorin (Kanya Kumari) at the southernmost part of India, the Bay of Bengal, the Arabian Sea, and the Indian Ocean all flow together. It was known to the ancients, too. Ptolemy called it *comaria akron* on his maps and Marco Polo knew it as Comori.

If time is a premium, this southern tip of India is overrated—crowd-ed with too many tourists and hustling hawkers selling junk. The distance from Madurai to the cape is a good 120 miles or more, depend-ing on the number of side trips. One possible stop is Courtallam, which lies in the Western Ghat mountain range. Its main claims to fame are the 300-foot waterfalls of the Chittar River and a small temple dedicat-ed to Shiva. The falls have a local reputation as a spa—bathing in them is supposed to invigorate a worn-out body. From here, it's a four-hour drive to Kanya Kumari.

To the southeast, also on the sea, is Tiruchendur, with a temple dedicated to Subrahmanya, built on the seashore. After driving through the Tirunelveli district, considered one of the oldest centers of civilizations in India (prehistoric burial urns have been discovered here), you reach Kanya Kumari. Here, the Western Ghats, which begin in Mysore, run into the sea, creating an obstacle course of jagged rocks that make the cape dangerous for ships. According to legend, this is where Shiva married the goddess Parvati, daughter of King Himalaya. The seven varieties of rice thrown at the wedding were transformed for eternity into the seven-colored sands of Kanya Kumari: red, brown, yellow, silver, orange, dark blue, and purple, as they have been preserved by Varuna, god of the sea.

The Kanya Kumari Temple, erected on a promontory of the cape, is revered by Hindus. Offshore lie the two rocks where Swami Vivekanda sat overnight in meditation before dedicating himself to improving the prestige of Hinduism by visiting America to expose Westerners to his faith. Also visit the Mahatma Ghandhi Memorial, constructed on the spot where the urn containing Gandhi's ashes was relinquished to the sea. The building was specifically designed so that on his birthday—October 2—at noon, the sun's rays fall through openings in the roof and shine directly on the center of his memorial. Then, for a quiet walk, meander through the fishing village near the Catholic church. The tiny community has an appealing quasi-Portuguese feel.

Just a few miles from Kanya Kumari is the Suchindram Temple, with its seven-story goporum and exquisite oversized water tank. This is one of the few temples that worships the trinity of Shiva, Vishnu, and Brahma. Non-Hindus can't enter the inner sanctum; the lingam inside is of three parts: the top represents Shiva, the middle represents Vishnu, and the bottom represents Brahma. The rest of the temple area (not off limits) is colorfully decorated and has musical pillars and an enormous statue of Hanuman.

Padmanabhapuram

Continue north to Padmanabhapuram, the ancient seat of the rulers of Travancore, who trace their ancestry back to A.C. 849. The Padmanabhapuram Palace, with its steep tiled roofs, white walls, woodcarvings, glossy black floors made from a crazy concoction including ash and eggwhite, and small courtyards, has an elegant pagodalike beauty that is reminiscent of Japanese domestic architecture. The palace also contains a museum with excellent old murals. In the adjoining Ramaswamy Temple, beautiful carved panels portray scenes from the *Ramayana*. From here, you can head back to Madurai or continue up the Malabar Coast into Kerala. (See *Kerala* chapter).

Kodaikanal and the Nilgiri Hill Stations

Tamil Nadu also has gentle, wooded hills framing a lake or two, which offer cool nights and a rest from temple-city intensity. Within the borders of this state are three of India's hill stations: Kodaikanal, only a short distance from Madurai; Ooctacamund (Ooty) and other delightful resorts in the Nilgiri Hills farther north; and Yercaud (east of Ooty) in the Salem district.

Kodaikanal is 75 miles from Madurai via a scenic road that runs through coffee plantations and forests as it climbs up through the Western Ghats to Kodai, at an altitude of over 7,000 feet. Europeans first discovered this spot in the Palni Hills in 1821. Fifteen years later, the collector of Madurai (the equivalent of a district governor) built a house that was soon followed by a rush of imitations. The descendants

of these nineteenth-century Europeans still flock to Kodaikanal for the
holiday seasons (April–June and September–October), when vacation-
ers can count on the cooperation of the climate and sun.

It's not just the weather that brings people to Kodai; the ride *is*
gorgeous. A wise man, Sir Vere Levenge, put a finishing touch on the
hill resort landscape by damming a stream to form a lake, with a
three-mile walkway and riding trail around it. Boating on the lake is
one of the popular pastimes in Kodaikanal. There are also tennis and
golf clubs and numerous walks you can take, but no elegant old-
fashioned hotels.

The Queen of Hill Stations-Ooty

The Queen of South India's hill stations is Ootacamund, "Snooty
Ooty," the capital of a chain of resorts in the Nilgiris or the Blue Hills
(*nila* means blue and *giri* means hill) on the northern edge of Tamil
Nadu.

With its green downs, gentle rains, and temperatures ranging between 50 and 60 degrees Fahrenheit most of the time, Ootacamund was
adopted as a summer home away from home at an early date by British
officials and planters in South India. After a few tentative attempts to
penetrate the Nilgiris, whose scenic beauties were previously enjoyed
only by the aboriginals, a collector of Coimbatore named John Sullivan
went up to Ootacamund in 1819. Sullivan liked it so much that he
became the first European to build a house there. By 1824, other
English people were settling in the hills, and they were followed by
Indian maharajahs. Then, the British governors of Madras made Ooty
their summer resort and built the Government House there. One of
them, the duke of Buckingham, brought his English penchant for
gardening with him, making life hell for the workers laying out the
gardens of Government House. One morning, informally unshaven and
dressed in old clothes, he started to give advice to one of the gardeners
who didn't recognize him. The gardener finally had enough. He turned
to him in disgust and said, "The way you go on, man, it would seem
you was the duke himself."

The Todas and other hill people encountered by Sullivan in 1819
would never recognize their Ootacamund today. Thousands of summer
houses are scattered over the hills, with the owners busy playing golf
and tennis or shopping on Charing Cross, the heart of Ooty. The town
boasts botanical gardens, an annual flower show, a number of hotels,
and a select circle of clubs where "snooty" of Ooty fulfills its name.

The downs of Ootacamund might well be in Devon or Yorkshire.
There are 50 miles of them, fortunately served by excellent roads, and
they offer golf, hunting, or just walking. Closer by are the 110-year-old
Government Botanical Gardens with more than 650 varieties of plants.
An artificial lake, conceived by Sullivan in 1823, gilds the lily of Ooty's
natural beauty. It measures only two square miles, but it offers pleasant
boating and good fishing. Near the shore of the lake is Hobart Park,
where weekly horse races are run in season.

Ooty is also a good jumping-off point for short and medium-length
side trips into the hills. The biggest of these is Doddabetta, 8,640 feet
high (most of it is done by car). Snowdon and Elk Hill (with its rock
temple) are the two runners-up in size, though heavily wooded Cairn
Hill is certainly the most beautiful.

Mukurthi Peak, a drive of 16 miles down the picturesque Mysore
Road, is the Todas' gateway to heaven. In days when female infanticide
still prevailed among them, the condemned babies used to be taken to
this hill to be done away with. Unlike the other Nilgiri tribes, these
handsome people did not turn to agriculture or handicrafts; they still

preserve their ancient way of life as herdsmen of the hills. Barely a thousand of them, they are recognizable by their flowing beards and long togalike robes.

About 40 miles from Ooty is the Mudumalai Game Sanctuary, with a full roll call of Indian wildlife.

Besides Ooty, there are two other hill stations in the Nilgiris. Kotagiri is 6,500 feet above sea level and 12 miles from Ooty, while Coonoor is 18 miles down the mountain railway line at an altitude of only 5,600 feet. The climate here is somewhat warmer than at Ooty. Coonoor is surrounded by tea plantations and has a shady park (Sim's Park) and some pleasant walks for hikers. Kotagiri is an island of green fields (including a golf course) surrounded by thick forests. It's one of the quietest spots in the Nilgiris and in all of South India.

Yercaud—the Jewel of the South

Northeast of Ooty is Yercaud, a quiet resort in the Servaroyan Hills (Sheraroy Range), about an hour's drive beyond Salem. At an elevation of 5,000 feet, the climate is inviting all year round. Yercaud has appealing vistas, gardens, waterfalls, and a lake. You can also arrange a trip to the Servaroyam Temple stop the third highest peak in the Sheraroy Range. During the annual festival in May, hundreds of tribal people from the Yercaud area arrive at the temple area, a festive and colorful event. Yercaud is also the least expensive hill station in Tamil Nadu, and the least "discovered."

PRACTICAL INFORMATION FOR TAMIL NADU

WHEN TO GO. This is a place to visit during winter. Here the thermometer never falls below 70° F but often rises to 90° F between November and February, and humidity can be high. When it's overcoat weather in Delhi (December–February), you can lie on the beach in Tamil Nadu. Summer (April–June) is forbidding, except in hill resorts like Ootacamund (7,500 ft.) or Yercaud (5,000 ft). The beach resorts of the South, like Mahabalipuram, are fun all year long, since you've got the water to cool off; but they are hot. Festivals, especially the spectacular "car" processions in major temple towns, are found year round, but most frequently in March–April. The best months for the hill stations are April–June and September–October.

HOW TO GET THERE. By Air. The following cities in India have direct daily *Indian Airlines* flights into Madras: Bangalore, Bombay, Calcutta, Cochin, Delhi, Hyderabad, and Trivandrum. Madras is also an international airport connecting the city to Colombo in Sri Lanka (*Air India* and *Air Lanka*), to Penang and Kuala Lumpur in Malaysia (*Malaysian Airline System*), and to Singapore (*Singapore Airlines* and Air India). In addition, daily Indian Airlines flights fly within the state to Coimbatore, Madurai, and Tiruchirapalli. Besides Madras, Coimbatore also has daily Indian Airlines flights to Bangalore, and Tiruchirapalli has daily Indian Airlines flights to Cochin and Trivandrum. *Vayudoot* also offers occasional flights from Coimbatore to Cochin, Mangalore, Madras, and Madurai and a flight (three times a week) from Thanjavur to Madras. Indian Airlines offers a special 30 percent discount on specified South India destinations (Coimbatore, Bangalore, Cochin, Madras, Madurai and Tiruchirapalli) when combined with travel from either Sri Lanka or Maldives provided you go there via Madras, Tiruchirapalli, or Trivandrum.

By Bus. *The Tiruvalluvar Transport Corporation* operates daily express deluxe coaches from Madras, to Bangalore, Ernakulam (Cochin), Mysore, Pondicherry, and Trivandrum and maintains an extensive network to every possible important destination within Tamil Nadu. As with most deluxe buses running throughout India, these buses are usually rolling television sets: Hindi movies blaring from the first kilometer to the last. So be prepared. Otherwise, the buses are more efficient, cleaner, cheaper, and faster than any train. For details, fares, and reservations, call *Express Bus Stand,* Esplanade, 561835/36.

By Train. There are some daily fast train services from India's principal cities to Madras (central). Some of the crack trains are the air-conditioned *Tamil Nadu Express* (reclining seats and so forth) four times weekly (journey time, 30 hours), and the *Grand Trunk Express,* with air-conditioned coaches, operating daily, both from Delhi. From Calcutta, the best train is the *Coromandal Express,* with air-conditioned coaches. From Madras (Egmore), you can reach Colombo by rail and ferry, which links Rameswaram with Talaimanar in Sri Lanka. The best train is the *Rameswaram Express,* which reaches Rameswaram in approximately 17 hours. Usually, you have to spend the night in Rameswaram to catch the ferry, which operates three times a week. The steamer from Rameswaram to Talaimanar Pier (Sri Lanka) takes 3½ hours. It does not run in December and January. Remember that with every train that involves an overnight ride, you must pay for a sleeper and *reserve* a berth. Otherwise, you might find yourself off the train. The seats are converted into berths, and you'll have no place to sit. Also travel at night via first class, first class air-conditioned, or second class air-conditioned. And always check to see if your class sleeper supplies bedding (it usually only comes with first class air-conditioned). Sometimes you can rent bedding for the night.

TOURIST INFORMATION. As soon as you get to Madras, go directly to the *Tamil Nadu Government Tourist Office* at 143 Anna Salai (Mount Road), Madras 600002 (tel. 840752, open 10:30 A.M.–5 P.M. Monday – Saturday. There's also a branch at the airport (8 A.M. – 8 P.M.) and another branch at the Central Railway Station Counter (7:15 A.M. – 7:15 P.M.). You can also contact the *Government of India Tourist Office* at 154 Anna Salai (Mount Road), Madras, 600002 (tel. 88685, open (9 A.M. – 5:30 P.M. Monday – Saturday), and at the airport, open around the clock.

These two bureaus have excellent information and maps on Madras and the rest of Tamil Nadu. They also offer excellent guides and can give you information about Tamil Nadu sightseeing tours. The staffs are extremely helpful. In the rest of the state, you'll find tourist offices in the following cities and areas. Most of them are open 10 A.M. – 5 P.M. Monday – Saturday.

Chidambaram. Railway Feeder Road, tel. 2739.

Coimbatore. Railway station, tel. 176.

Kanya Kumari (Cape Comorin). Beach Road, tel. 76.

Kodaikanal. Township Bus Stand.

Madurai. Hotel Tamil Nadu Complex, West Veli Street (near Central Bus Stand), tel. 22957; at the Railway Junction, tel. 24535; and at the Madurai Airport.

Mahabalipuram. Tel: 232.

Ootacamund. Super Market Building, Charing Cross, tel. 2416.

Pondicherry. Old Secretariate Building, Campagnie Street, tel: 4398 or 4406.

Rameswaram. Railway Station.

Salem. (near Yercaud) Tel: 66449.

Thanjavur. Hotel Tamil Nadu Complex, Gandhiji Road.

Tiruchirapalli. Hotel Tamil Nadu Complex, Cantonment, tel. 25336. Information also at airport and railroad station.

By Rented Car with Driver. Madras is 360 km from Bangalore, 1,355 km from Bombay, 1,616 km from Calcutta, 694 km from Cochin, 488 km from Coimbatore, 460 km from Madurai, 696 from Hyderabad, and 160 km from Pondicherry. Most roads in Tamil Nadu are good and wonderfully scenic. Once you arrive in Madras, if you have time to spare, we highly recommend you hire a car with a driver and really see the state. It's beautiful and culturally rich and deserves close inspection. The cost of hiring a car with a driver should run approximately Rs. 2 per km, plus night-halt charges (usually around Rs. 50 per night). Cars are available through the following agencies (book in advance): *India Tourism Development Corporation, Ltd (ITDC),* 29 Victoria Crescent, Commander-in-Chief Road; tel. 478884. *Tamil Nadu Tourism Development Corporation,* 143 Mount Rd., tel. 849803. *Holiday Tours* (Taj Coromandel Hotel), 17 Nungambakkam High Rd.; *Madras,* tel. 474849. *India Cabs,* 10

Nungambakkam High Rd.; tel. 471316. You can also contact the local *Tamil Nadu Tourist Office,* for a list of approved agencies.

 **ACCOMMODATIONS.** Hotel and guest house accommodations in Madras and the rest of Tamil Nadu run the gamut from expensive (by Indian standards) to cheap. Generally, with privately owned or managed hotels, a higher tariff translates into additional amenities (a telephone and a color television in your room and room service). But some of the most appealing hotels in Tamil Nadu are under 400 rupees a night. They may not have room service or a bar, but they have charm and offer fine hospitality. Indeed, guest houses and government-run hotels or lodges are comparatively inexpensive; the rooms can be clean and comfortable (albeit sparsely furnished), with the bonus of a lovely, sometimes remote, location. So keep this in mind when you travel: Expensive isn't always best; it usually means more West and less like India. Unless specified, all listings have Western toilets; the exceptions are those accommodations off the beaten path, where the room is more than satisfactory in other essential respects. The facilities are always clean. Room rates are based on double occupancy: *Super Deluxe,* over Rs. 900; *Deluxe,* Rs. 600–900; *Expensive,* Rs. 400–600; *Moderate,* Rs. 200–400; *Inexpensive,* under Rs. 200.

CHIDAMBARAM

Inexpensive

Apollo Lodge. 74 Sabanayagar St.; tel. 2907. 18 rooms, some air-conditioned. New modest hotel close to the south gate of the temple. All rooms have fans. No Western-style toilets, but clean, simple rooms. Management is eager to please.

Hotel Tamil Nadu. Railway Feeder Road; tel. 2323. 10 rooms and a restaurant.

Hotel Tamil Nadu. Arignar Anna Tourist Complex, Pichivaram (16 km east of Chidambaram; tel. 32. Clean, simple cottages with wicker furniture on the porch. Mosquito netting. Restaurant serving vegetarian and non-vegetarian Indian food. Peaceful setting on the edge of the backwaters; boats (running 6 A.M. – 10 P.M.) take you back and forth to the mainland. You can hire a boat for pleasure at Rs. 3 per hour per person.

COIMBATORE

Moderate

Hotel Surya International. 105 Race Course Rd.; (1.5 km from downtown); tel. 37751. 45 rooms, some air-conditioned; a shopping arcade, restaurant, 24-hour room service, and a lawn.

Inexpensive

Hotel Alankar. Sivaswamy Road, Rannagar; (two km from downtown); tel. 26293. 57 rooms, some air-conditioned, with TVs, and channel music. An ice cream parlor and restaurant on the premises. The best in town.

Hotel Tamil Nadu. Dr. Nanjappa Road; tel. 36311. 16 rooms, some air-conditioned. Restaurant.

COVELONG BEACH
(32 km from Madras)

Deluxe

Fisherman's Cove. Covelong Beach, Chingleput District; tel. Chingleput 268. A beach resort, with 42 air-conditioned rooms and 28 cottages with TVs. Off-season rates March 1 – December 14. Has a restaurant, bars, room service, shopping arcade, a beach, swimming pool, and tennis. Self-contained units. If you want nothing but a resort, this is it. The resort, however, doesn't necessarily catch the flavor of Tamil Nadu.

KANCHIPURAM

Inexpensive

Hotel Ashok Travellers Lodge. 78 Kamakshi Amman St. (near the Railway Station); tel. 2561. 12 rooms, not air-conditioned, and a restaurant and garden.

KODAIKANAL

Deluxe to Expensive

Carlton Hotel. Lake Road; tel. 252. 80 rooms, including cottages. Off-season rates July 1 – November 14; January 15 – April 14. Restaurants, health club, and lots of sports available, including boating on the lake. Lovely lawns. A Western-feel, if that's what you want. Hotel is set on the lake.

MADRAS

Super Deluxe

Welcomgroup Adayar Park. 132 T.T.K. Rd. (four km from downtown); tel. 452525. 160 rms. A modern structure with all Western amenities, including air-conditioning, cable TVs, room service, restaurants, a 24-hour coffee shop, bar, swimming pool, putting green, health club, and shopping arcade.

Welcomgroup Chola Sheraton. 10 Cathedral Rd. (four km from downtown); tel. 473347. 135 rooms. Modern hotel with all Western amenities; including air-conditioning, cable TVs, room service, restaurant, 24-hour coffee shop, bar, swimming pool, shopping arcade.

Deluxe

Taj Connemara Hotel. Binnay Road (one km from downtown); tel. 811051. 145 rms. Most Western amenities, including air-conditioning, room service, restaurants, a bar, and a swimming pool. Some older rooms furnished with antiques. Best of the fancy hotels, some ambience.

Taj Coromandel Hotel. 17 Nungambakkam High Rd. (two km from downtown); tel. 474849. 240 rooms. A modern structure; all Western amenities, including air-conditioning, cable TVs, room service, restaurants, a 24-hour coffee shop, bar, swimming pool, health club, and shopping arcade.

Expensive

Ambassador Pallava. 53 Montieth Rd., Egmore (½ km from downtown); tel. 812061. 125 rooms. A modern structure, with most Western amenities, including air-conditioning, TVs, restaurants, a 24-hour coffee shop, bar, swimming pool, health club, and shopping arcade.

Hotel Madras International. 693 Annasalai (Mount Road) (downtown); tel. 811811. 63 rooms. Recently renovated; has many Western amenities, including air-conditioning, TVs, 24-hour room service, restaurants, and a shopping arcade.

Savera Hotel. 69 Dr. Radhakrishnan Rd., (two km from downtown); tel. 474700. 125 rooms. Most Western amenities, including air-conditioning, TVs, room service, restaurants, a bar, swimming pool, and shopping arcade. Modern; good value.

Moderate

New Victoria Hotel. 3 Kennet La., Egmore (downtown); tel. 567738. 43 rooms, some air-conditioned; 24-hour room service, and restaurant. Pleasant management.

Hotel Palmgrove. 5 Kodambakkam High Rd., Nungambakkam (six km from downtown); tel. 471881. 89 rooms, some air-conditioned. Vegetarian restaurant and a bar. Good value.

Hotel Peacock. 1089 Poonamallee High Rd., (downtown); tel. 39081. 73 rooms, some air-conditioned; TVs in some rooms. A restaurant, bar, 24-hour room service.

Hotel Picnic. 1132 Poonamallee High Rd., (downtown); tel. 39021. 45 rooms, some air-conditioned; TVs in some rooms. Vegetarian restaurants and a bar.

Hotel Shrilekha. 49 Annasalai (Mount Road), (close to downtown); tel. 840082. 77 rooms, some air-conditioned. A restaurant and a bar.

Transit House. 26 Venkataraman St. T. Nagar; tel. 441346 (Rs. 275–300). Four rooms, air-conditioned, lovely garden, snack bar. Guest house ambience. (Off-season rates from April–September.)

New Woodlands Hotel. 72–75 Dr. Radhakrishnan Rd., Mylapore (seven km from downtown); tel. 473111. 160 rooms, some with TVs and air-conditioning. Restaurants and a swimming pool. Not bad for the price.

Inexpensive

Hotel Dasaprakash. 100 Poonamalee High Rd., (three km from downtown); tel. 661111. 100 rooms, some air-conditioned; vegetarian restaurant and ice cream parlor. Has old-world charm decor that is suffering from neglect. Beautiful lobby and grounds.

Hotel Kanchi. Commander-in-Chief Road, Egmore (close to downtown); tel. 471100. 60 rooms, some with air-conditioning and TVs. Two restaurants, a bar, 24-hour coffee shop. Good value.

Hotel Maris. 9 Cathedral Rd., (three km from downtown); tel. 470541. 70 rooms, some air-conditioned; vegetarian restaurant, bar.

Udipi Home. 1 Halls Rd., Egmore (near downtown); tel. 567191. 59 rooms; TVs in all rooms, vegetarian restaurant, pleasant ambience.

MADURAI

Expensive

Hotel Madurai Ashok. Alagarkoil Road; (four km from railroad station); tel. 42531. 43 air-conditioned rooms, a restaurant, and a bar. Reasonably good hotel run by ITDC.

Moderate

Pandyan Hotel. Race Course (four km from the center of town); tel. 42470. 60 air-conditioned rooms, a restaurant, bar, and shopping arcade. Best hotel in town.

Inexpensive

Hotel Tamil Nadu. Alagarkoil Road (four km from center of town); tel. 42461. Approximately 25 clean, spacious rooms. Restaurant, some shops. Very good value.

Hotel Prem Nivas. 102 West Perumal Maistry St., (in the center of town); tel. 31521. 60 clean, simple rooms; some with air-conditioning. Ask for a Western toilet. Nice vegetarian restaurant.

MAHABALIPURAM

Deluxe to Inexpensive

Silver Sands, Beach Village. On the beach; tel. 228. 60 rooms and cottages. Numerous descending off-season rates, depending on the time of year. Some air-conditioned rooms, and swings in most of the rooms. Has a restaurant, 24-hour cafe, free shuttle service to and from Madras at certain fixed times of the day, games, and cultural activities, including *Bharata Natyam,* Indian music. Nice shady drive into resort, numerous thatched huts, great Tamil Nadu decor. Terrific management. A room to fit every budget.

Expensive

Temple Bay Ashok Beach Resort. On the beach, ITDC Shore Cottages; tel. 251. 23 air-conditioned rooms, including cottages. A restaurant, barbecue, bar, swimming pool, and tennis courts. Modernish structure.

Moderate

Golden Sun Hotel and Beach Resort. On the beach; tel. 245. 35 clean, simple rooms, some air-conditioned. Nice grounds, with gardens; secluded and pleasant. A restaurant; cultural performances on request.

Ideal Beach Resort. On the beach; tel. 240. 15 clean, simple rooms, some air-conditioned. Beautiful gardens and a lovely swimming pool. A restaurant. Nice management. Good value. Off-season rate from May to August.

Inexpensive

Beach Resort Complex. On the beach. Tamil Nadu Tourism Development Corp.; tel. 35. 10 cottages, some air-conditioned. Stay in the new duplex cottage, with a living room downstairs and a bedroom upstairs. Great setup, but indifferent management. Still worth it. Avoid the restaurant.

OOTACAMUND

Expensive

Fernhill Palace. Fernhill Post; Nilgiris District (three km from downtown); tel. 2055. 71 rooms with TVs and fireplaces. Off-season rates from June 16 – March 14. Charming enormous building with grand style befitting the home of an ex-maharajah. 24-hour room service and a coffee shop, restaurant, bar; numerous recreational activities. Get into the old ambience and don't look too carefully at tarnished edges. Keep your eyes on the spectacular views instead.

Savoy Hotel. Nilgiris District (close to downtown); tel. 2572. 40 rooms, with TVs. Off-season rates from July 1 – March 30. Stay in a charming cottage. Lots of early Victorian style. Gorgeous grounds and gardens. A restaurant and bar; endless sports available.

Moderate

The Palace Hotel. Fernhill P.O., Nilgiris; tel. 2170. 22 rooms. Off-season rates June 15 – March 15. Some amenities. Lovely lawn, a restaurant, 24-hour coffee shop. Billiards.

Ritz Hotel. Orange Grove Road, Nilgiris; tel. 6242. 20 rooms in a nice older hotel with a restaurant and bar.

Inexpensive

Bamboo Banks Farm Guest House. Musinigudi P.O., Nilgiris (30 km from Ooty); tel. Musinigudi 22. Seven rooms and detached cottages. Situated in the Jungle Mudumallai Wildlife Sanctuary. Jungle Jeep rides, elephant rides, horseback riding, bird watching. Great place for the person who wants to be in a sanctuary and still have certain comfort.

PONDICHERRY

Inexpensive

Grand Hotel D'Europe. No. 12 Rue, Suffren (in the city on a quiet street); tel. 404. Six clean, bright rooms, but sparcely furnished; has mosquito netting. An old hotel that began in 1891, run by a fastidious Frenchman. Very nice ambience; excellent food. Rates include meals.

Hotel Mass. Maraimalai Adigal Salai (in town); tel. 7067. Fairly new hotel with 35 rooms but has neither the sense of the French nor the beach.

Park Guest House. Sri Auropindo Ashram; tel. 4412. 80 rooms, some air-conditioned. Ask for a room seaside, since this place is on the beach. If you don't mind pictures of "Mother" and other important members of the Sri Aurobindo Ashram staring down at you from the wall, the hotel is great. Clean and efficiently managed by a pleasant staff (all members of the ashram). A restaurant, gardens, beach, bike rentals. Each room has a fan and mosquito netting. Modern.

Government Tourist Home. Uppalam Road (on a quiet street); tel. 6376. 12 rooms, some air-conditioned. Neat and clean. A good bargain, considering the price.

RAMESWARAM

Inexpensive

Hotel Tamil Nadu. On the beach; tel. 77. 12 clean, decent rooms, some air-conditioned. The only place to stay. Balconies overlook the water. Restaurant.

THANJAVUR

Inexpensive

Hotel Parisutham Ltd. Adjacent to the Yagappa Theater; tel. 22318. 54 clean rooms, with fans and TVs. Good for the price. Room service, shops, and a restaurant.

Hotel Tamil Nadu. Gandhi Road; tel. 57. 15 large rooms, some air-conditioned, with fans. The balcony runs around an interior courtyard bordered by tall trees. Spartan government decor to the rooms.

TIRUCHIRAPALLI

Moderate

Hotel Sangam. Collector's Office Road (three km from downtown); tel. 25202. 40 air-conditioned rooms with TVs. A restaurant, garden restaurant, and bar; lovely lawns.

Moderate to Inexpensive

Hotel Aristo. 2 Dindigul Rd. (four km from downtown); tel. 26565. 31 rooms including cottages, some air-conditioned. Stay in a "theme" cottage. This place is Tamil Nadu/vintage California kitsch. Charming and a steal for the price. A restaurant and some other services; lovely lawns. The best in town.

Rajali Hotel. 2/14 Macconald's Rd.; tel. 31302. 78 rooms, most air-conditioned, 24-hour room service, TVs, restaurants, swimming pool, bar, and a health club. Very nice management. Another good hotel, but Western.

Inexpensive

Hotel Tamil Nadu. Cantonment; tel. 25383. 12 clean, simple rooms, some air-conditioned; others with fans. A restaurant and room service. Not bad, considering price.

YERCAUD (SALEM)

Inexpensive

Hotel Tamil Nadu. Tel. 273. 12 rooms. Off-season rates. Low-budget hill station. Simple accommodations; not overrun by tourists.

 DINING OUT. Rice is South India's staple food. Its curries, mixed with coconut milk, are hotter than in the north but not as rich; instead of fat, only a light oil is used in most dishes. Since many South Indians are vegetarians, you find a wide variety of tasty vegetable dishes. Some of the best—and least expensive—meals are found in simply decorated *bhavans* (Indian-style coffee shops) that serve delicious coffee and *thali* (named after the metal plate on which the meal is served). Thali is an epicurean's delight: generous servings of numerous tasty items (curried vegetables, rice, *dhal*, curd, *poori*). Sometimes the meal is served on a clean banana leaf. Bhawans also serve traditional *dogas, pakora, idli,* and vegetable cutlets. Just point to something intriguing and try it. In most cities, you can also get good nonvegetarian fare, including Chinese and Continental. But remember, part of exploring India should involve exploring the wonderful regional cuisine. Prices are based on a three-course meal for one person, excluding taxes, beverage, and tip: *Expensive,* Rs. 50 plus; *Moderate,* Rs. 30 – 50; *Inexpensive,* under Rs. 30. Most of the better hotel restaurants take major credit cards, even from nonguests. However, if you are not a guest, it might be wise to call at the smaller hotels to see if you can be accommodated. Listed here is a *selection* of hotel dining rooms, as well as independent restaurants.

CHIDAMBARAM

Inexpensive

Sri Mahalakshmi Vilas. On East Gate. Good vegetarian food; simple decor.

COIMBATORE

Moderate to Inexpensive

Hotel Alankar. Sivaswamy Road, Ramnagar; tel. 26293. Large choice of good Indian, Chinese, and Continental foods.

Hotel Surya International. 105 Race Course Rd.; tel. 37751. South Indian, tandoori, Mughlai, Continental, and Chinese cuisines. Another big-choice restaurant with reliable food.

KANCHIPURAM

Inexpensive

Hotel Ashok Travellers Lodge. 78 Kamakshi Amman St., near the railway station; tel. 2561. Adequate.

There are numberous *thali bhawans* (small cafes) around the center of town. Pick one that's crowded and have yourself an inexpensive good meal.

KODAIKANAL

Expensive to Moderate

The Silver Oak. At the Carlton Hotel; tel. 252. Indian and Continental, straightforward food, sometimes served indifferently. Reservations suggested for dinner.

Terrace. Same hotel. Dine outside on barbecue and tandoori specialties.

MADRAS

Expensive

Golden Dragon. Taj Coromandel, 17 Nungambakkam High Rd.; tel. 474849. Excellent Chinese dishes at lunch and dinner.

Kolam Restaurant & Grill. Hotel Connemara, Binny Road; Tel 810051. Good Indian and Continental food. Lunch buffet. Vintage British decor.

Kyber. Welcomgroup Adayar Park. 132 T.T.K. Rd.; tel. 452525. Poolside barbecue, specializing in tandoori cuisine and Continental grilled food. Reservations suggested.

Mysore. Taj Coromandel Hotel, 17 Nungambakkam High Rd.; tel. 474849. Excellent Indian food. Entertainment nightly. Reservations suggested.

The Residency. Welcomgroup Adayar Park, 132 T.T.K. Rd.; tel. 452525. Mughlai, Chinese, Continental. Candlelight and live band for dancing during dinner. Edwardian-style decor. Reservations suggested.

Sagari. Chola Sheraton, 10 Cathedral Rd.; tel. 473347. Chinese cuisine served in rooftop restaurant. Dancing at night. Reservations advised.

Moderate

Amaravathi. 1 Cathedral Rd.; tel. 476416. Good, spicy Indian food.

Buhari Hotel. 83 Mount Rd.; tel. 88391. Continental, Indian, and Chinese foods. Charming handpainted murals on walls. Private family dining booths. Vintage restaurant. A bit dingy, but reasonable food and nice atmosphere.

Chopsticks. Ambassador Pallava Hotel, 53 Montieth Rd.; tel. 812061. Chinese food, as the dinner name implies, and quite tasty.

Navaratna. Safire Basement, 614 Mount Rd.; tel. 477444. Excellent Gujarati and Rajasthani vegetarian food. 11 A.M. – 2:30 P.M.; 7:30 – 10:30 P.M.

Woodlines Drive-in-Restaurant. Cathedral Road; tel. 471981. Excellent South Indian vegetarian food.

Inexpensive

Chunking Chinese Restaurant. 67 Mount Rd.; tel. 86134. Chinese food here is excellent. No ambience, but a local favorite.

Ganga. 57 Armenian St. (no phone). Pure vegetarian and great snacks. Don't let the dark, too-low lighting deter you.

Mathura Restaurant. Tarapore Towers, 827 Mount Rd.; tel. 87777. Large, almost garish space saved by subdued lighting. Wide variety of excellent vegetarian food.

Matsya Restaurant. Udipi Home, 1 Halls Rd., Egmore; tel. 567191. Fine South Indian vegetarian food.

MADURAI

Moderate

Jasmine Restaurant. Pandyam Hotel, Race Course; tel. 42470. Good north Indian nonvegetarian food; also South Indian vegetarian, Chinese, and Continental.

Madurai Ashok, Alagarkoil Road; tel: 42531. More good North Indian nonvegetarian food, as well as South Indian and Continental cuisines. Breakfast, lunch, and dinner.

Inexpensive

New Arya Bhavan. 242 West Masi St.; tel. 22250. Excellent vegetarian food. Very popular places, morning until night.

MAHABALIPURAM

Expensive

Silversands Outdoor Cafe. Alagarkoil Road; tel. 228. Nice ambience with fine food. Indian, Continental, fish specialties. Lots of fun. Reservations suggested.

Moderate

Sunrise Restaurant. Beach Road (no phone). Charming thatched hut, with nice ambience and great food. Fresh seafood, including fish Masala and grilled crab. Not fancy.

Tina Blue View Restaurant. Beach Road (no phone). Upstairs restaurant offering view of water. Airy and simple restaurant. Good food; Indian and Continental.

PONDICHERRY

Expensive

Grand Hotel d'Europe. No. 12 Rue Suffren; tel. 404. Excellent French food; fixed menu. If you want to eat here, you must call or come by early in the day to see if the small dining room can accommodate you.

Moderate

Hotel Aristo. 30 E Nehru St.; tel. 4524. Good Indian and Western nonvegetarian food. Rooftop restaurant.

Inexpensive

Indian Coffee House. Nehru Street (no phone). Popular little restaurant serving vegetarian dishes throughout the day and evening.

THANJAVUR

Moderate

Hotel Parisutham Ltd. Near Tagappa Theatre, 55 G. A. Canal Rd., Thanjavur; tel. 22318 or 21466. Two good restaurants. One serves Continental, Chinese, and Indian foods; the other is a vegetarian restaurant.

Inexpensive

Hotel Karthik. 73 South Rampart St. (no phone). Fun restaurant where you get to eat your meal off a banana leaf.

Sathars Restaurant. Near the bus station (no phone). Simple restaurant serving excellent tandooris and spicy foods at low prices.

TIRUCHIRAPALLI

Moderate

Chogori Restaurant and Silent Spring. Rajali Hotel, 3/14 Macdonald's Rd.; tel. 31302. The best food in town. The chef works miracles with the excellent vegetarian, Chinese, nonvegetarian Indian, and Continental foods. But experience the exotic here, not food from home. Call to make certain you can get a table. Sample chicken Tangri kabab or Mughlai fish. Vegetarians, try Poriyal. Everything is delicious.

Chembian. Hotel Sangam, Collector's Office Road; tel. 25202. Good Indian and Continental foods. Reservations suggested.

Inexpensive

Sree Renga Bhavan. On China Bazaar (no phone). Excellent vegetarian food in a delightful restaurant open on the street. Popular place.

Vasantha Bhavan. On China Bazaar (no phone). Fine vegetarian food served in a friendly ambience.

SNACKS AND COFFEE. In Madras, **Ganga,** 57 Armenian St., has very good pure vegetarian snacks. Open all day. **Raj Ice Cream Parlour,** 36/1 Nungambakkam High Rd., tel: 472003. Ice cream, vegetarian snacks, juices. Open 10 A.M. – 1 A.M. In Madurai, **New Arya Bhavan,** 242 West Masi St. (tel. 22250), is a popular snack joint—good coffee, too. Open morning til night. In Tiruchirapalli, **Sree Renga Bhavan** and **Vasantha Bhavan** on China Bazaar, are the closest you'll come to a French cafes—Tamil Nadu-style. Excellent snacks and coffee in an open-air environment.

HOW TO GET AROUND. From the Airport. The Meenambakkam (Madras) Airport is about nine miles from the center of Madras. The PTC (public bus system) offers an airport minicoach service to most hotels and to the Egmore Railway Station. (Rs. 15; tickets issued on the coach). Service runs at frequent intervals, 5 A.M. – 10 P.M. You can also get into Madras by taxi, but insist that the driver turn on the meter (approximate cost: Rs. 30, plus a Rs. 5 flat charge for luggage). Or take an auto rickshaw, but again insist on the meter. The auto rickshaw should be cheaper; it won't be faster.

MADRAS

By Bus. PTC buses run 5 A.M. – 10 P.M. Fares are cheap. For fares and details, call 566980, ext. 36.

By Taxi. Taxis charge Rs. 3 for the first 1–8/9 km and Rs. 0.10 per each 1/9 of a km thereafter. Make sure the driver uses his meter.

By Auto Rickshaw. Cheaper and more fun. But again, these drivers really resist going by the meter. They're the best way to get around town.

THE REST OF TAMIL NADU

By Bus. The bigger cities (Coimbatore, Madurai, Thanjavur, Tiruchirapalli) have city bus services that are inexpensive, but not the fastest way to get around.

By Taxi. These same cities have taxis that usually don't have meters or drivers who refuse to use them. Haggle over the fare. Keep in mind the rates for Madras and let that be your guide.

By Auto Rickshaw and Bike Rickshaw. These are the preferred methods of transport, but with the same phantom or broken meters. So haggle and keep in mind that the auto rickshaw should cost less than the taxi, and the bike rickshaw should be cheaper than the auto rickshaw. In the temple cities (more like villages), your best bet is to hire a bike rickshaw for a few hours while you see the historic sights. (Rs. 40 for three – four hours should be tops.)

By Rented Car with Driver. If you fly into Madurai or Tiruchirapalli, you can arrange for a hired car and driver to meet you at the airport to take you around these interesting parts of Tamil Nadu. In Madurai, *South India Travel*

Agency (agents for SITA), West Veli Street; tel. 22345. In Tiruchirapalli, *Vaikai Travel & Tours Private Limited,* J. B. Shopping Complex, 35/B Promenade Rd.

TOURS. *The Tamil Nadu Tourism Development Corp. Ltd.,* (TTDC) at 143 Annasalai, VST Motors Building, Madras, 600002 (tel. 849803), sponsors a series of inexpensive Tamil Nadu deluxe bus tours with guides:

Madras City Sightseeing Tour. Daily, 2 – 6 P.M. Rs 25.

Temple Tour to Tiruverkadu-Mangadu. Tuesdays, Fridays, and Sundays. 6 A.M. – 9 A.M.; 10 A.M. – 1 P.M.; 2 P.M. – 5 P.M.; 6 P.M. – 9 P.M. Rs. 10.

Mamallapuram Tour (Kanchipuram–Thirukkalikundram–Mahabalipuram). Daily, 6:45 A.M. – 5:30 P.M. Rs. 70.

Tirupati Tour (Andhra Pradesh Temple). Tirupati–Tirumala–Tiruchanur. Daily 6 A.M. – 9 P.M. Rs. 145.

Tamil Nadu Three-Day Package Tour (Thanjavur, Velankanni, Nagore, Tirunallar, Poompuhar, Vaitheeswaran Koil, Chidambaram, Pitchavaram, Pondicherry). Rs. 175 per individual for single room accommodation; Rs. 150 per individual for sharing a double room. Friday – Sunday.

Tamil Nadu Seven-Day Package Tour (Tiruchirapalli, Srirangam, Kodaikanal, Madurai, Kanyakumari, Suchindram, Tiruchendur, Rameswaram, Thanjavur). Leaves Saturday and returns Friday. Rs. 950 per individual for a single room, Rs. 880 per individual sharing a double room, and Rs. 780 for each child as an additional member in a double room (no more than two children per double room).

South India Seven-Day Tour (Bangalore, Shravanabelagola, Belur, Halebid, Srirangapatna, Brindavan Gardens, Mysore, Mudumallai Wildlife Sanctuary, Ootacamund, Coonoor, Coimbatore, Hogenakkal, Thiruvannamalai). Leaves Saturday and returns Friday. Rs. 950 per individual for single room, Rs. 880 per individual sharing a double room, and Rs. 780 for each child sharing a double room (two children maximum).

The Madras sightseeing, Mahabalipuram tour, and Tirupati tour are also offered by the *India Tourism Development Corporation* (Ashok Travel and Tours) at 29 Victoria Crescent (near Ethiraj College), Commander-in-Chief Road, Madras (tel. 47888). Tickets are also available at the ITDC counter in the Government of India Tourist Office at 154 Anna Salai Rd.

If you wish to hire a guide, the best trained and most knowledgeable are available through the Tamil Nadu Tourist Office throughout the state. General rates: four hours for four people, about Rs. 35; eight hours for four people, about Rs. 50 plus a Rs. 15 lunch allowance.

SEASONAL EVENTS/FESTIVALS. Because the following festivals are set by the lunar calendar, contact the Tamil Nadu Tourist Bureau for exact dates.

January. *Pongal,* a colorful three-day festival that gives thanks to the sun, the earth, and the cow! Pongal is held at the close of the harvest season, which usually falls around the middle of January. A big deal throughout the state, the best Tamil Nadu festival. Bonfires and bulls and cows fancied up with beads and garlands. Lots of games and dancing.

January/February. In Madurai, the Vandiyur Mariamman Teppakulam (temple) holds its annual *Float Festival.* Decorated floats carry the sacred deities around the temple tank. This is a beautiful and interesting event.

February/March. The *Natyanjali Festival* is a five-day event in Chidambaram, dedicated to classical dance and Shiva, "The Cosmic Dancer." Also in March, the Kapaleeswarar Temple at Mylapore, Madras, holds an 11-day festival called *Arupathumoovar.* The eleventh day is the grand moment with over 60 sacred deities taken out in an elaborate procession.

March/April. Holding onto its French past, Pondicherry has a carnival—costumed good timers parading in the streets accompanied by bands playing festive music.

April/May. The temple city of Madurai holds its spectacular 10-day *Chitrai Festival* at the Meenakshi Temple to celebrate the marriage of goddess Meenakshi to Lord Shiva. Numerous deities are carried around in a chariot procession that also includes lots of traditional devotional music. A fascinating fair; heavily attended.

In May, Kanchipuram holds its annual 10-day festival with an even larger procession as deities from all the temples (and they're lots of them here) are

carried through the city. The procession occurs on the third day and is declared
an official city holiday, so every local resident gets to attend, along with all the
people who come to see the event. Also in May, Yercaud has an annual festival
at the Servaroyan Temple, a colorful event involving nearby tribal people.

August/September. *Ganesh Chaturthi* is celebrated throughout Tamil Nadu.
This festival involves Ganesh, the elephant-headed god. Processions and ritual
baths of the deity in rivers.

September/October. Navarathri is a nine-day festival, also observed
throughout Tamil Nadu involving the worship of Druga, Lakshmi, and Saraswathi.

October/November. *Deepavali.* A two-day festival throughout Tamil Nadu
and the rest of India, marks the start of the Hindu New Year. Fireworks and
lots of raucous celebrating.

December/January. A three-week festival of music and dance in Madras is
presented by the Indian Fine Arts Society, with great dance and music performed by India's best. At about the same time, in Tiruchirapalli, the *Vaikunta
Ekadesa* festival is another procession and deity celebration, held at the Srirangam Temple.

FOREIGN CURRENCY EXCHANGE. Most major hotels will cash traveler's checks; otherwise head to the
Bank of India or *State Bank of India,* which are located
in most cities. Hours are usually 10 A.M. – 2 P.M. Monday
– Friday and 10 A.M. – noon on Saturdays. Lines can be tedious, so bring a book.

RECOMMENDED READING. In Madras, pick up a
copy of *HALLO! Madras,* a monthly magazine for tourists, which is often waiting for you in a hotel room. You
can also purchase a copy at most leading book stalls for
Rs. 3. It tells you what's happening, how to get around, and what to see. An
informative pocket-size magazine.

If you plan to visit the temples in Tamil Nadu, get a copy of *House of God*
by N. S. Ramaswamy (Rs. 45, a paperback published by TravelAide). It's an
easy-to-read and informative book that gives you good details on the temples.
It's invaluable when there's no guide to explain all that carving in stone.

GARDENS AND PARKS. The Madras *Botanical Gardens,* adjacent to Saint George Cathedral on Annasalai
Road, Madras, is a restful place to visit. Started in 1835,
it is maintained by the Horticultural Society. *Children's
Park and Deer Sanctuary,* 8 km from the heart of Madras in Guindy, has a large
number of Indian antelope and numerous other animals, including monkeys and
reptiles. The best time to visit is early morning or early evening. Open sunrise
to sunset; closed Tuesdays.

Snake Park, Guindy (tel. 414821). Open 9 A.M. to 6 P.M., on Saturdays and
Sundays, 4 – 5 P.M. Rs. 0.50. Boasts an excellent collection of reptiles and good
demonstrations, including venom extraction on Saturdays and Sundays, 4–5 P.M.

In Coimbatore, V. O. Chidambaram Park contains a mini-zoo and children's
train; open sunrise to sunset.

The *Botanical Gardens* in Ootacamund, established in 1847 by the Marquis
of Tweedale, contains exotic and ornamental plants. *Children's Lake Garden*
has flowers and musical lights. Both open sunrise to sunset.

Pondicherry's *Botanical Garden,* planned in 1826, contains exotic plants
from all over the world, and an aquarium. Open sunrise to sunset.

Children's Park, in Thanjavur has a small diesel train to take the children
around. Open sunrise to sunset.

WILDLIFE SANCTUARIES. *Anamalai Wildlife Sanctuary* in Coimbatore District is open throughout the
year; the best time for viewing the elephants, bison,
tigers, wild boar, and crocodiles; 6 A.M. – 9 A.M.; 3 P.M.
– 6 P.M. You can make arrangements to go through the park on an elephant or
in a van. Forest lodging available.

Mudumalai Wildlife Sanctuary, in Nilgeris (60 km from Ooty) is open all
year, but the best season is February – May. The best viewing times are 6 – 9

A.M.; and 3 – 5 P.M. Herds of deer, bison, elephants, gaur, monkeys, and reptiles, including python, crocodiles. Tamed elephants are available for riding (6 A.M. – 8 A.M.; 4:30 – 6 P.M.). Forest accommodations are available.

Point Calimere Wildlife Sanctuary, Thanjavur district, is open all year. The peak season November – January. In April – June many birds have moved on. Deer, wild boar, flamingos, and lots of migratory birds.

Mundanthurai Tiger Sanctuary, Tirunelveli district, has its peak season January – September. The best viewing times: before 6 A.M. and after 3 P.M. Forest department provides tours to view the tigers. Forest rest house available.

Vedanthangal Water Birds Sanctuary (70 km from Madras) is the major bird sanctuary in India. Birds congregate here from October–November to March. Peak time December–January. The bird population depends on the monsoon, so check with the tourist office before you visit. Species include cormorants, egrets, storks, and herons. Rudimentary accommodations are available.

For more details and lodging reservations at any of the sanctuaries, contact the State Wildlife Warden, Forest Department, Administrative Office Buildings, Teynampet, Madras, 600006, Tamil Nadu.

 BEACHES. Tamil Nadu has great stretches of beautiful beaches. All the beaches are open to swimming, but at your own risk. Starting from Madras and heading south: *Elliots Beach* (11 km from Madras) is the best swimming beach near Madras. *Covelong* (38 km from Madras) is a lovely fishing village with a beach. In Pondicherry, there are good beaches all around the area. Mahabalipuram boasts beautiful stretches of sand with good local color—fishing boats and temples on the shore.

Rameswaram has many good beaches, but watch the currents. At Kanya Kurmari beaches, watch the current here too; it can be rugged!

 SPORTS. Chidambaram. Backwater **boating.** Inquire at the tourist office for details. You can also go boating with a boatsman: Rs. 3 per person per hour. Boats run 6 A.M. – 8 P.M.

Kodaikanal. Boating available on the lake. For **Golfing,** contact the club, tel. 323. **Fishing,** contact for license and details: Sub-Inspector of Fisheries, Kodaikanal. **Trekking,** contact the Trek Director, Department of Tourism, Government of Tamil Nadu, Madras, tel. 29111–216.

Ootacamund (Ooty). Boating available (8 A.M. – 6 P.M.) at the boat house on the lake. Fishing (trout): for license and a guide with a boat, contact. Assistant Director of Fisheries in Ooty, tel. 2232. Trekking: contact. Trek Director (see above). Golf, contact the Tourist Department for details.

Pondicherry. Boating on the Chunnambar River (8 km from Pondicherry). Boats available at the boat house for taking trips through local backwaters.

Yercaud. Boating and fishing on Yercaud Lake. For details, see the tourist department in Yercaud.

 HISTORIC SITES. In Madras, *Church of Our Lady of Expectations,* was built in the sixteenth century on the foundation of a church built by St. Thomas in the second century. The "Bleeding Stone" on which a cross is engraved is supposed to shed blood on the day that marks St. Thomas' death, December 18.

San Thomé Cathedral Basilica, Madras, is a neogothic structure with a 180-foot steeple erected in 1896. The interior has an interesting image of Christ standing on a lotus flower (Hindu pose).

Kapaleeswar Temple in Mylapore is typically Dravidian. Dedicated to Shiva, it was built in the 1600s. Painted in terrific bright colors. Non-Hindus can enter the courtyard, but only Hindus can enter the inner sanctum. Open 5 A.M. – noon; 4 – 8:30 P.M.

Parthasarathy Temple in Triplicane, eighth century, dedicated to Vishnu, was originally constructed by Pallavas and rebuilt by the Vijayanagar kings in the seventeenth century. Open 6:30 A.M. – noon; 4 P.M. – 8 P.M. Non-Hindus can enter the courtyard but not the inner sanctum.

Fort St. George, Madras, was built in 1640 by Francis Day for the East India Company. It now houses the Tamil Nadu State Legislature, offices of the ministry and secretaries to the government. See St. Mary's Church, consecrated in 1680, the oldest Anglican church in India.

In Chidambaram, *Nataraja Temple,* dedicated to Shiva, is the oldest temple in South India. It was built in the fifth century by a Chola king and covers 40 acres. The roof of the sanctum sanctorum is covered with gold plate.

In Kanchipuram, *Kailasanatha Temple* was built in the early eighth century by Pallava King Rajasimha. The smaller temple at the east end of the courtyard was built by his son. Dedicated to Shiva, sandstone temples are excellent examples of Pallava architecture.

Vaikunthaperumal Temple, Kanchipuram, was built in the eighth century by the Pallava King Nandivarman and dedicated to Vishnu. Unusual three-story vimina (tower over the central temple).

Ekambareswara Temple, Kanchipuram, was originally constructed by the Pallavas in the seventh and eighth centuries. The sixteenth-century Vijayanagar kings added the 10-story, intricately carved goporum (tower entrance). Dedicated to Shiva. The nearby mango tree is supposedly 3,500 years old.

Kanya Kumari Temple, Kanya Kumari, is dedicated to the virgin goddess Kanniyakumari, who protects the country. The eastern gate facing the Bay of Bengal is opened only five times a year, and a ritual bath at the Kumari ghat is considered sacred. Temple open 4:30 – 11 A.M.; 5:30 – 9 P.M.

Gandhi Memorial, Kanya Kumari, was constructed on the spot where the urn with Gandhi's ashes was kept on public view until relinquished to the sea. The building was designed so that on Gandhi's birthday, October 2, a ray of sun falls on the spot where the urn was kept.

Vivekananda Rock Memorial, Kanya Kumari, was built in 1970 to commemorate where Swami Vivekananda meditated before dedicating his life to spreading the ideals of Hinduism. A blend of all temple architectural styles in India. Ferry services to the memorial, 7 – 11 A.M.; 2 – 5 P.M. Nominal fee.

Suchindram Temple (13 km north of Kanya Kumari) has inscriptions dating to the ninth century. One of the few temples to worship the trinity of Shiva, Vishnu, and Brahma. Exquisitely carved seven-story goporum, lovely musical pillars, and a huge Hanuman (monkey god) statue, plus an enormous bathing tank. Very pretty. Non-Hindus can enter the courtyard but not the inner sanctum.

Padmanabhapuram Palace (45 km north of Kanya Kumari) was the ancient palace of the rulers of Travancore until A.D. 1333. Palace (open 9 A.M. – 5 P.M., closed Mondays and holidays; Rs. 0.50) contains excellent murals and stone sculptures.

In Madurai, *Meenakshi Temple* is dedicated to Shiva and is one of the biggest temple complexes in India. Most of the current structure was erected between the twelfth and the eighteenth century, but references to the temple date back to the seventh century. Open between 4:30 A.M. – 12:30 P.M.; 4 P.M. – 9:30 P.M. Photography, however, is permitted only after a Rs. 5 payment and during the hours the temple is closed: 12:30 – 4 P.M.

Tirumalai Nayak Palace, Madurai, was built in Indo-Saracenio style in the seventeenth century by Thirumalai Nayak. Beautiful courtyard surrounded by an arcade supported by vast pillars. All that's left of the once-enormous complex are two royal residences. Used to have quarters for the harem, relatives, a theater, a pond, and a garden. Open 8 A.M. – noon; 1 – 5 P.M. Rs. 0.40. Sound and light show every evening on the life of this Nayak king: 6:45 P.M., Rs. 1 to 3.

Rock-cut Caves, Mahabalipuram, are of seventh-century Pallava construction. The Mahashasuramardhini mandapam has a sculptural relief of the fight between the goddess Durga and Mahishasura, the buffalo-headed demon and the bas-relief of Vishnu in his cosmic sleep. In the Krishna mandapam are excellent scenes depicting the life of Krishna. The bas relief—the world's largest, (80 feet long with an average height of 20 feet—is also a Pallava construction.

Shore Temple, at Mahabalipuram has two shrines, one dedicated to Shiva and the other dedicated to Vishnu. Built by Pallava king Rajashima in the seventh century, it is an excellent example of Dravidian architecture.

In Pondicherry, *Auroville* is an international commune started by a French woman, now deceased, called "Mother," who was involved with Sri Aurobindo. Futuristic architecture can be seen here, especially the *Matri Mandir* meditation hall, a gigantic sphere under construction since 1971.

At Rameswaram. *Ramanathaswamy Temple* was built over a 300-year period starting in the twelfth century. An excellent example of Dravidian architecture, with the longest pillared temple corridor in all India.

In Thanjavur, Brahadeeswarar Temple, dedicated to Shiva, was constructed between 985 and 1016 by Rajah Chola. The first of four Chola temples in Tamil Nadu to have a vimana soaring over the gopora. The vimana is constructed from one single granite block.

At Thiruvannamalai. *Arunachala Temple* sprawls over 25 acres. It is one of South India's largest. Dedicated to Shiva in his fire incarnation, the goporum is 11 stories high. The exact date of its construction is unknown; parts existed as early as the seventh century.

In Srirangam, *Rangagantha Swamy Temple* was built between the fourteenth and the seventeenth centuries. A temple town with seven sets of walls leading to the most sacred areas. There are 21 towers. A fascinating complex teeming with life.

 MUSEUMS. Besides all the wonderful temples (museums in their own right), Tamil Nadu has some good art and sculpture collections worth seeing. Most are free, or have a nominal entrance fee; others accept a comparable donation. Listed here are some of the more important museums in the state.

MADRAS

Fort St. George Museum, South Beach Road. Featured here are costumes, prints, and paintings of the British in India. Open 10 A.M. – 7 P.M.; closed Fridays. Free.

Government Museum and National Art Gallery. Pantheon Rd., Egmore. The museum—over 1,100 years old—has sections devoted to geology, archaeology, anthropology, botany and zoology, besides numismatics, particularly related to South India. The collections are housed in three buildings. The front building contains the collection of arms and armor, prehistoric antiquities, specimens of anthropological interest, metal, wood, ivory work, and Hindu and Jain images. The sculpture gallery contains architectural pieces and Hindu, Buddhist, and Jain sculptures from Tamil Nadu, Andhra Pradesh, and Mysore. The most important is the collection of sculptures from the Buddhist site of Amaravati (first century B.C.), the earliest surviving sculptures from the south. In the galleries devoted to metal work are South Indian lamps, objects connected with household, and temple worship and images in bronze, among them the famous Nataraja and the beautiful set of Rama, Sita, Lakshman, and Hanuman. There is an interesting collection of woodcarvings from processional temple cars. The contents of the Arms Gallery are mostly from the palace at Tanjore and Fort St. George, and those of the prehistoric gallery include antiquities from the Iron Age sites of Adichannallar and Perumbiar. The Bronze Gallery contains some of the best of India's ancient icons and some excellent modern bronzes. Open 8 A.M.–5 P.M., closed Fridays, Rs. 0.50.

The National Art Gallery, set in a beautiful building (Indo-Saracenic style of architecture), houses an excellent collection of old and new art, including rare Rajput and Mogul miniatures.

MADURAI

Gandhi Museum has a picture gallery and some of Gandhi's personal possessions. Open 9 A.M. – 1 P.M.; 2 – 5:30 P.M.

Meenakshi Temple Art Museum in the 1,000-pillared hall contains temple art and architecture. Open 6 A.M. – 8 P.M., daily. Rs. 0.50 entrance.

PONDICHERRY

Government Museum is a celebration of Pondicherry history, starting with Chola bronzes and sculptures, moving to French cultural artifacts, and ending with current traditional Indian handicrafts. Open Monday through Saturday, 10 A.M. – 5 P.M.

POOMPUHAR

Art Gallery is housed in an exotic building designed to create the atmosphere of the second century. The ancient city of Poompuhar was once a major part of the Chola Empire, and this city gave rise to the Tamil epic *Silapathikaram.* This gallery, opened in 1973, depicts scenes from this epic. Check with the tourist department in Thanjavur for the exact hours.

THANJAVUR

Tanjore Art Gallery, Palace Buildings, contains ancient Chola statues in bronze and granite. Open 9 A.M. – 1 P.M.; 3–6 P.M. Closed Fridays.

 DANCE AND MUSIC. You should not leave Tamil Nadu without seeing a performance of the *Bharata Natyam*—the purest and in some ways the most beautiful classical dance form in India. In Madras, check the newspaper, *HALLO! Madras,* or call the Government of India Tourist Office (88685), which keeps a list of current cultural events. The following theaters and halls also have cultural events with some frequency:

Kalaivanar Arangam, Government Estate, tel. 565669; *Rajahannamalai Hall,* Esplanade, tel. 561425; *Rani Seethai Hall,* 603 Mount Rd., tel. 812522; *Museum Theatre,* Pantheon Road, tel. 812632; *Music Academy,* 115 East Mowbray's Rd., tel. 85619 or 812621.

In the last week of December, the Siva-Sakthi Music and Dance School, 123 East Car Street, Chidambaram, holds a formal Bharata Natyam program with its students. The students are young and talented. The building is old with pillars, perfect for this classic dance form.

 SHOPPING. Tamil Nadu has some wonderful markets in the big cities of Madras, Madurai, and Tiruchirapalli. The three best markets in Madras are *Jam Bazaar,* junction of Pycroft's and Triplicane roads (bustling fruit and vegetable market); *Evening Bazaar* (also called Parrys) near Broadway and N.S.C. Bose Road (wholesale markets); and *Burma Bazaar* at the eastern end of N.S.C. Bose Road along the harbor (best visited at night). You may not want to buy anything, but they're fun for browsing. If something strikes your fancy, haggle. In Madurai, just wander around the temple complex. The markets are fascinating; you'll find rows and rows of men sitting behind sewing machines sewing up ready-mades in minutes flat and stalls with all kinds of merchandise. It's fun just to wander and watch. In Tiruchirapalli, go to *China Bazaar* and *Big Bazaar* near the base of the fort.

Kanchipuram silk is the product to consider in Tamil Nadu. Check with the *Government of India Tourist Office* for a list of approved shops in Madras; when you're on the road, check in with the local tourist office. They're very good at steering you toward reliable, honest merchants. With silk, you don't want the lowest price; you want the best quality.

Curios—if you like interesting old pieces and you happen to be in Thanjavur, visit *V.R. Govindarajan,* 31 Kuthiraikatti St., tel. 20282. Great stuff cluttering up numerous rooms.

KERALA

Palm-Fringed Paradise

by
KATHLEEN COX

Just around the corner of Cape Comorin, the southernmost tip of India, begins a strange land of paradox. Kerala is one of India's most progressive regions, but it has all the ingredients of a tropical paradise, right to the palm trees waving over sandy beaches. A thin strip along the southwest coast, isolated by the wall of the Western Ghats, Kerala is unbelievably cosmopolitan, with a heritage of 3,000 years of relations involving the rest of the world. Phoenicians, Arabs, Jews, Chinese, and Europeans all landed on the shoreline to do heavy trading in this rich land that raised numerous valuable cash crops: tea, rubber, cashews, teak, and a wide assortment of spices, including "black gold" (pepper). Yet Kerala moves at a leisurely pace, like the slow moving boats that float through its network of canals and backwaters.

Kerala isn't for the hurried tourist, eager to chalk up a city a day. In the first place, it doesn't have that many cities. In the second place, the journey from one point to another is a good part of the fun. Forget the airline ticket to Cochin, with a quick hop to Trivandrum and the beach. Plan to travel into the Western Ghats—winding roads that take you by tea plantations and palm and rubber trees. Arrange for a languid cruise through the stunning backwaters. The state is small, but there's a lot to do.

Kerala didn't exist on the map until 1956, when it became one of India's smallest states, created out of Travancore-Cochin and the Malabar Coast district of Madras State. The result of this redrawing of the map of India is a slender but picturesque wedge along the Malabar Coast, which faces the Arabian Sea, with forest-clad mountains that rise as high as 5,000 feet at its back. Twenty-four million people live within its borders in an area of 15,000 square miles that is slightly smaller than Switzerland and about twice the size of Massachusetts. Though there isn't much room for newcomers, the population of Kerala has increased 20 percent over the past decade.

Despite Kerala's brief existence, it soon made a name for itself, becoming the first place in the world to adopt a communist regime in a free election: a political event that caused tremendous discussion and speculation, since Kerala also happens to be the most educated state in India. With a near-70 percent literacy rate (against a national rate of 36 percent), nine out of 10 children attend school, a startling figure anywhere in Asia. Although the communists lost control a few years back, the left is currently staging a comeback.

The scenery of Kerala is shaped by a partnership of geography and history. At least a quarter of its area is covered by forests that contain 600 varieties of trees, which makes timber an important industry—one in which woodsmen still use elephants as bulldozers. Up in the mountains are vast plantations of tea and cardamom (its name came from the Cardamom Hills of Kerala). Down below, pepper, coffee, rubber, cocoa, ginger, and turmeric—an essential spice in curry—grow in wild profusion. The mountains lord over a contrasting landscape of coconut trees and gray farmhouses built under palm-thatched roofs.

At times, when you travel through Kerala, it's hard to realize where you are. Towns and villages are heavily sprinkled with well-built churches, and one-quarter of the state's population is Christian. But nestling next to a church might be a house under a Chinese roof, gracefully bowed in the center with carved woodwork below the pointed ends. Or, at Cochin, you can even wander into a Jewish synagogue.

This human kaleidoscope developed over thousands of years. Behind the ramparts of the Western Ghats—there are only 16 passes through these mountains and none of them is easy—the Malabar Coast escaped domination by successive waves of empire builders who conquered ancient India by land. Long before Vasco da Gama, the Phoenicians came here to trade for spices, ivory, and sandalwood. Around 1000 B.C., King Solomon's ships visited Biblical Ophir, supposedly the village of Poovar, south of Trivandrum, the present capital of Kerala.

The spice treasure of Kerala, especially pepper, lured fortune seekers from a good many European countries. The Dutch preceded the Portuguese, although their stay was short. In 1516, the Portuguese signed a treaty with the rani of Quilon (wife of the rajah) and clung to it even though Arab traders, jealous of competition, talked the rani into harrassing the encroachers. The Portuguese did some harassing themselves. When they discovered that the Christians, who were sharing this part of India with them, had never heard of the Pope, these pious Catholics persecuted the "heretics."

In 1602, the Dutch, under the banner of the Dutch East Indian Company, reappeared and succeeded in forcing out the Portuguese in 1663 through skillful public relations with local chieftains. Still, the European procession was far from over. The British East India Company (on the Malabar Coast since 1684) opened its first settlement at Anjengo, south of Quilon. In the eighteenth century, the British won over the rajah of Travancore. By 1795, the Dutch were down and out. (Travancore was originally known as Thiruvazhum Kode, an alluring name that meant the abode of prosperity, but the British had difficulty with the pronunciation and solved the problem by substituting their corrupted phonetic version: Travancore.)

The People of Kerala

The people of Kerala who speak Malayalam seem unaffected by the Europeans' unending game of monopoly. One of the most important Hindu castes of Kerala, the Nairs (or Nayars), have traditionally been governed by the matriarchal system under which property is inherited through the female side of a family. This has given Nair women a proud position in Kerala society. The matriarchal system is now almost gone. In the past, though, the Nair male was quite a warrior—Nairs only gave up dueling under British pressure. The Nair family is a huge unit. Their ancestral home is known as the *tarawad,* and some Nair tarawads are handsome structures with rich carvings on their heavy wooden doors and door frames.

Kerala's Brahmans, the Namboodiris, have another unique family system. Until recently, only the eldest son was allowed to take a wife from his own caste (the others had to marry Nairs who are Kshatriyas, and their children had no right to the family's heritage).

Because there weren't enough Brahman eldest sons to go around, many Namboodiri women went through life unmarried. Now most Namboodiris marry within their own community, and the old system has died out. Another Hindu community, the Ezhavas, produced a great religious teacher, Narayan Guru Swami, who preached the revolutionary notion of one caste, one god.

Hindus, Christians, Jews, and Moslems, all form part of the human flow of Kerala. Most of the men dress in impeccable white *dhotis* (shirtlike garments) or colorful *longhis* (loin cloths), and the women wrap their alluring curves into multicolored saris. Soon, you even get used to the rather incongruous sight of the ever present black umbrella held over the head to ward off the equally ever present sun or the occasional shower that strikes unexpectedly.

The people of Kerala are worth watching when they relax, too. The Kathakali dance drama is one of India's most electric dance forms, and it originated here in this tropical state. Festivals crop up at regular intervals—with the most picturesque Onam, a four-day harvest celebration (August or September) that ends with races of exotic giant snake boats manned by 100 oarsmen.

EXPLORING KERALA

There's no fixed itinerary for visiting Kerala, but for convenience, we've arranged the main points of interest south to north.

Trivandrum and Environs

Trivandrum, built on seven hills, offers proud buildings that overlook quiet valleys. The main architectural landmark of Trivandrum is the Padmanabhaswami Temple, dedicated to Vishnu, a handsome example of South Indian temple architecture with a seven-story *goporum* (tower). No one knows the date of construction. One legend traces it back to 3000 B.C., but everyone knows how it was built. Four thousand masons, 6,000 laborers, and 100 elephants did the job in six months. In the main courtyard, the Kulasekhar Mandapam, there is some intricate granite sculpture; more sculpture can be appreciated on nearly 400 pillars supporting the temple corridor. Only Hindus may penetrate the sanctuary itself.

If you're an Indian art buff, visit Trivandrum's Museum and the Sri Chitra Gallery. The latter has a good collection of paintings as eclectic as Kerala itself. On its walls hang examples of the Rajput, Mogul, and Tanjore schools; copies of the Ajanta and Sigirya frescoes; and works from China, Japan, Tibet, and Bali, along with canvases by modern Indian painters. At a more earthy level, see the wonderful display of local arts and crafts in the museum, housed in a rambling palace with a Cubist pattern of gables. For travelers who wants their nature in easily digested form, there's a zoo and an excellent aquarium (also used by marine biologists and fishery experts). To see what life was like here before modern India, visit the Kaudiyar Palace, the residence of the maharajah of former Travancore-Cochin.

Trivandrum, the state capital and once a sedate city, now boasts an international airport that has brought an influx of tourists. Many of these recent arrivals spend languorous days on Kovalam beach, 10 miles south of Trivandrum. Here, you can take long walks on beautiful sandy beaches lined with palm-fringed lagoons and rocky coves. Or, just laze around and watch lungi-clad fishermen as they drag in nets filled with the day's catch, then push their slender wooden fishing boats out again with a Malayalam "heave-ho" chant.

Trivandrum to Quilon

Once you've experienced Kovalam, head north 32 miles to Varkala, a seaside town set against a backdrop of red cliffs with mineral water springs spurting down to the beach. Varkala is the goal of Hindu pilgrims bound for its Janardhana Temple, reputed to be 2,000 years old.

Varkala is also where Narayana Guru Swami, one of modern India's greatest Hindu religious reformers and saints, entered into *samadhi* (contemplative retirement) in 1928. Instead of the bewildering pantheon of Hindu gods, he preached a simple faith; "One Caste, One Religion, and One God." It's appropriate that this movement should have sprung up in tolerant and progressive Kerala. Now it's carried on by a brotherhood of his disciples. Their message is that of their leader: "Man must improve, whatever his religion."

Not far from Varkala lies a more mundane historical spot, Anjengo, where the British East India Company opened its first trading post on the Malabar Coast. You can visit the remains of an old fort built by these seventeenth-century merchants.

A dozen miles north, you reach Quilon, one of the oldest ports along the Malabar Coast. The ancients reached it long before, though: Phoenician, Persian, Greek, Roman, and Arab vessels all traded here. The most industrious were the Chinese. During the T'ang Dynasty (seventh to tenth centuries), China established trading posts in Quilon and, under the reign of Kubla Khan (thirteenth century), it exchanged envoys with this prosperous Indian city state (it became part of Travancore only in 1742).

To the visitor, Quilon offers its vista on Ashtamudi Lake, indented by red capes jutting from a shoreline of palms. Along the shore stand the Thevally Palace and Government House. Two miles from Quilon, you can wander through Thangassery, with its lighthouse, ruined forts, and slumbering Portuguese, English, and Dutch cemeteries.

Quilon is also the starting point of a beautiful stretch of inland waterways—53 miles of backwaters, called *kayals,* that snake through canals frequently shaded by the leaves of coconut palms. It's a lazy calm voyage that takes you all the way to Alleppey. You can go by public boat, very cheap, but it takes about a day. Or you can hire a launch for around $80 and make the journey in half the time. In either case, you'll travel by hidden villages and lush vegetation—a panorama of rural/waterside life Kerala style.

Alleppey

When you arrive in Allepey, a water-borne city (a miniature Cochin), you will find its canals teeming with numerous straw-roofed country boats introduced by the Chinese. Alleppey is a busy place. From coconut husks, it makes coir rope (the leading industry) and carpets (mats). It also thrives on the production of black pepper.

Also in Allepey, as in Cochin, you can see Chinese "fishing machines," immense contraptions consisting of a huge net lowered into the water on the end of a pole poised on a fulcrum. Once a catch has been lured into its meshes by a lantern on top of the "machine," it takes a half-dozen men on the other end of the pole to lift the haul out of the water. The boats, *wallams,* which serve as water trucks for the Kerala countryside, are Chinese in design. Flat-bottomed and built of planks stitched together with cords, they are about 40 feet long and carry nearly 20 tons. Like ferries, they are double ended, some with beautiful scrollwork on their bows. Cargo is carried under a roof of woven coconut fronds aboard these wallams. Although motor launches ply the backwaters of Kerala for tourists and travelers in a hurry, the wallam is still man powered. Its two-man crew drives it by punting, planting their long poles in the bottom at the bow and then walking a bit to propel their boat, just as bargemen (not gondoliers) still do on the canals of Venice. If you visit in August, you may just get to witness the Nehru Trophy Boat Race—a competition with those exotic snake boats.

Kottayam to Lake Periyar

From Alleppey, head for Kottayam. This small city has always been a busy base for Christian missionaries, and it boasts a number of old churches, including its Syrian Church: the Cheria Palli with colorful murals and numerous carved altars. From Kottayam, turn inland toward the east—the start of a beautiful side trip that takes you into swift change of scenery and ultimately to the Periyar Lake Wildlife Sanctuary (115 km). At first, you run through lush vegetation and palm-thatched villages dominated incongruously by churches built in an exuberant Portuguese colonial style.

After miles of low-lying palms and paddies, the road begins a winding climb up the Ghats, lined with prosperous tea plantations where plants are carefully pruned to a four-foot height (any higher, their leaves are no longer tender). These tea plantations, established early in the century by the British and now mainly under Indian management, are a flourishing industry. The picking of the tea by nimble-fingered women goes on for most of the year; then the baskets of young leaves go to factories for drying, rolling, fermenting, and sifting the leaves. About 50 miles from Kottayam, the road passes through Peermade, a hill station, and then it reaches Thekkady, close to Periyar Lake.

Periyar Game Sanctuary

The lake is a human-made touch added to the natural beauty of the Western Ghats: a reservoir created by a dam on the Periyar River. This lake, with its many fingers that wind around capes and hills, some rising 3,000 feet above its surface, is the heart of the 300-square-mile wildlife sanctuary.

Periyar offers one of the most sybaritic ways of seeing big game. Here, forget exhausting treks or long safaris. You lounge in a motor launch as it drifts around a bend and comes into sight of elephants or deer or bison stopping at the shores of the lake for a drink. During the dry season, when waterholes in the forest are empty, leopards and tigers also pad up to the water. One word of advice: either bribe all the Indian kids to be quiet—they love to scream and shout at a sighting—or hire a private launch.

Shooting, of course, is prohibited, but the hunter's loss is the photographer's gain. Elephant herds are so accustomed to *quiet* visitors drifting next door in launches that they hardly notice the intrusion. This is no place to be caught short of film, and specially built tree perches provide good observation posts. Elephants with their young graze beside deer, gaue (wild oxen) and sambar (large Asiatic deer); you may even glimpse tigers and bears. Of course, all the jungle's smaller creatures are photo material.

Cochin

Although Cochin is not a pretty city, it is one of those rare places where the twentieth century and ancient civilizations exist side by side. Cochin's past is so rich that it has a valid claim as a museum city. Cochin is also one of the three biggest ports on the west coast of India and the biggest in Kerala, handling over five million tons of cargo in a year, and a prosperous center of the coir industry. Stroll through the streets behind the docks lined with old merchant houses, *godowns* (warehouses), and open courtyards heaped with betel nuts, ginger, peppercorns, and hanks of coir. The air is filled with the smell of spices and the shouts of men pushing heavy carts. This Eastern scene has changed little over the centuries.

Cochin manages to pursue its various lucrative trades in its setting of wooden islands and canals winding past houses on stilts. Both in the past and in the present, Cochin has displayed a lively blend of people and architecture that is worth seeing. It's one of the few places in the world where you can visit a Jewish synagogue, Portuguese churches, Dutch buildings, and a couple of mosques and Hindu temples and see Chinese fishing nets all in the same day.

We use "Cochin" as a handy name for a cluster of islands and towns. Over on the mainland, three miles from the harbor but linked by bridges and ferries, lies Ernakulam, once the capital of the former state of Cochin. If you arrive by air, your terminal will be on Willingdon Island, a human-made island (it consists of material dredged in an ambitious harbor-deepening operation). On Vypeen Island, facing the sea, fishermen still use their Chinese cantilever contraptions. The coir makers work on Gundu Island in a cooperative where excellent samples of their products are on display, although businessmen dealing in coir make their homes in the residential quarter of Fort Cochin, where, in tropical India, you stumble onto an English village green, pseudo-Tudor houses, lawns, a club, and a perfect replica of a prosperous London suburb—except that palms betray where you are. Bolghatty Island is the most beautiful of the lot, and its colonial mansion, formerly used by the Dutch governor and later by the British Resident, is now a hotel (sadly rundown, it was just purchased by the Taj Hotel chain and is scheduled for renovation). Finally, there is Mattancheri, southwest of the harbor: the home of a dwindling Jewish community. History at Cochin is found in the most abundant quantities here and at Fort Cochin.

Fort Cochin is believed to be the oldest European settlement in India. It first saw the Portuguese flag in 1500; three years later, Alfonso de Albuquerque came with half a dozen ships bearing settlers and built Fort Cochin. He also brought five friars who built the first European church in India in 1510, still standing in Fort Cochin as St. Francis Church. Vasco da Gama first arrived in Cochin in 1502. He returned again in 1524 as Portuguese viceroy of the Indies. He died here and was buried in St. Francis Church. You can still visit his gravestone, but his remains were shipped back to Portugal in 1538 (he's buried in Lisbon). St. Francis Church, the oldest European church in India, reflects the colonial struggle for India. It was a Dutch Reformed church from 1664 to 1804, an Anglican church from 1804 to 1947, and now it's part of the Church of South India. The giant fans in the nave are operated from outside. The church contains Dutch gravestones and has the *Doop Book,* a register of baptisms and marriages from 1751 to 1894. You can look at a photographic reproduction of the vital statistics (the original is too fragile).

St. Francis is a sedate church in the Spanish style, but not nearly as flamboyant as the Santa Cruz Cathedral in Fort Cochin, which verges on the gaudy. The Santa Cruz was completed in 1904.

The White Jews of Cochin

Fort Cochin may be old but, compared to Mattancheri, it's an upstart. The first emigration of Jews to Kerala supposedly took place in the sixth century B.C., followed by a much bigger wave in the first century A.D., when Jews fleeing Roman persecution in Jerusalem came to Cranganore and settled there. One of the most impressive sights in the synagogue of Mattancheri are the copper plates presented to the Jewish community by King Bhaskara Ravi Varma in the fourth century A.D., who awarded them the village of Anjuvannam, a name meaning "five castes" (the Jews were considered the lords of five castes of artisans). Incidentally, both Jews and Christians have always been considered of high caste in Kerala. The plates state that Anjuvannam shall be the hereditary possession of Joseph Rabban and his descendants "so long as the world and moon exist."

The king's word was good, and the Jewish colony flourished, serving as a haven to Jews from the Middle East and, in later centuries, Europe. The Portuguese put an end to this state of affairs. When Albuquerque discovered the Jews near Cochin, he requested permission from his king to "exterminate them one by one" and destroyed their city at Cranganore. Moslem anti-Semitism flared up, too. It was with the arrival of the Dutch that the Jews of Cochin were able to live without fear once more—as they always had in India.

The synagogue in Mattancheri's Jew Town was built in 1568 after the expulsion of the Jews from Cranganore. It was considerably embellished in the mid-eighteenth century by Ezekiel Rahabi, who build a clock tower and paved the floor of the synagogue with hand-painted tiles of willow pattern (each one different), brought all the way from Canton in China. Indeed, the entire synagogue is beautiful, and the elder loves to show his visitors around.

Sadly though, the congregation has almost vanished; and, as an active synagogue, its days are probably numbered. Few of the pale, blond White Jews of Cochin are left (unlike the "Black Jews" from the mainland of India who are a mixture of Jewish and Hindu stock). Many of the White Jews emigrated to Holland and to England in the past two centuries, and others have gone to Israel.

Mattancheri also offers Cochin's other most interesting building—the "Dutch Palace"—built by the Portuguese (hence the quotation marks) in the middle of the sixteenth century. The Dutch Palace was taken over by the Dutch, who added some improvements before presenting it to the rajahs of Cochin, who used it as a palace. The rajahs, in turn, made more improvements, notably some excellent mythological murals. In one room, you can see the entire story of the *Ramayana* on the walls. The palace also contains a rare example of traditional Keralan flooring, which looks like polished black marble but is actually a subtle mix of burned coconut shells, charcoal, lime, plant juices, and egg whites. Both the synagogue and the palace are within easy walking distance of the boat jetty at Mattancheri.

While in Cochin, you must see a Kathakali dance-drama. There are many dance companies, and you can also attend a "short" two-hour performance at the Gurukalam Kathakali Yogam in Ernakulam, a tiny theater (bring mosquito repellent) that is weirdly magical. The dancers wear fantastic makeup and spectacular costumes. When the show begins, the stylized movements are larger than life—eerie, and wondrous —and an unequivocal delight. No surprise, since the performers begin rigorous training to master control of the eyeballs, neck, toes, fingers, and cheek muscles at age 5.

From Cochin to Trichur

After Cochin, the pace slows down again. Ten miles north is industrial Alwaye, the "Ruhr of Kerala." Here Travancore made a successful stand against Tipu Sultan, an invader from neighboring Mysore who came storming into Alwaye in 1790. Actually, Travancore was helped by a flood on the Periyar River, which forced Tipu to cancel his plans. Alwaye is also the home of the Union Christian College, one of the few started in India by Indians, not foreign missionaries. But the main reason to visit is that Alwaye is on the route to Kaladi, birthplace of Sankaracharya. Sankaracharya was an eighth-century saint and philosopher, the father of the *Advaita* doctrine of Hindu philosophy and one of the first of the monotheists who seem to flourish in Kerala— whether as Hindus, Christians, Jews, or Moslems.

Along the shore north of Alwaye, you reach old Cranganore, now known as Kodungalloor. The Cheraman Perumals, the early rulers of this part of the Malabar Coast, had their capital here, and an old building known as Cheraman Parambu is said to have been their palace. Kodungalloor was not always a drowsy seaside town. It was the first of Kerala's international harbors, and the heritage of its history includes a Portuguese fort, a number of Hindu temples (the best known are the Thiruvanchikulam and the Bhagavathi), and India's first mosque. Nearby Kottappuram adds a Christian touch: here St. Thomas the Apostle is said to have landed in India, and a church is dedicated to him.

Back inland once more, the main road and rail line run from Alwaye to Trichur, which has a zoo (quite a collection of snakes), an art exhibition in its town hall, an old palace, and a fort. Trichur is a must-see if you happen to be in Kerala during its Pooram festival, an annual affair occurring in April or May. This is one of South India's biggest shows, complete with processions, huge fireworks displays, and elephants decked out regally.

Kozhikode (Calicut)

The landscape reverts once more to coconut palms, tea, rubber plantations, and groves of tropical fruit trees as you head toward the sea from Trichur north to Kozhikode (Calicut). Kozhikode is rather remote from the rest of Kerala and, prior to 1956, it was not in the same state.

Long ago, it was a center of power of the Malabar Coast under its rulers, the Zamorins, a name meaning lords of the sea. The lovely city is noted for its block-printed cotton cloth and is the origin of the word *calico.*

The city, which has a large Moslem population, has always been a major port of the Malibar Coast, with its glory days as a trading center beginning when Vasco da Gama landed here on May 20, 1498, after rounding the Cape of Good Hope. The English first appeared in Kozhikode in 1615, and the British East India Company gained control of the city in 1792 following a treaty with Tipu Sultan.

For a last look at the Arabian Sea, take a train ride north to Cannanore, another harbor that has flown the flags of the ancient maritime powers. Vasco da Gama landed here, as well as at Kozhikode, starting the usual process of Kerala's colonial history from the Portuguese to the Dutch to the English, who made Cannanore their military headquarters until 1887. Cradled by the breakers of the Arabian Sea, Cannanore is a quiet spot that seems to be dreaming of the role it once played in Kerala's historical pageant.

PRACTICAL INFORMATION FOR KERALA

WHEN TO GO. Most of the year is pleasant in Kerala; even the monsoon season (May–June and October–November) is lush with gentle rain. During this time, it can be extremely hot and humid. In fact, the sun stays strong, most of the year, so be careful. The winter temperature is great—seldom rising above 85°F along the coast and a few degrees cooler in the hills, where light woolens are useful in the evenings.

HOW TO GET THERE. By Air. Cochin and Trivandrum have international flights to and from Maldive Islands. *Indian Airlines* has frequent flights to and from Bangalore, Bombay, Cochin, Dabolim (Goa), Delhi, Madras, Tiruchirapalli, Trivandrum. *Vayudoot* also connects Cochin with Coimbatore, Madras, and Mangalore.

From the Airport. The Kerala Tourist Development Corporation (KTDC) provides **bus** service to Cochin and Trivandrum at about Rs. 2. Inquire at the tourist information counter. A **taxi** to each city costs about Rs. 20.

By Bus. Various luxury coaches connect Kerala with important South Indian cities: Bangalore, Kanya Kumari (Cape Comorin), Madras, Madurai, Mangalore, Pondicherry, and so on. If you don't mind the near-constant blare and glare of video, buses are good; usually clean, and cheap, and much faster than the train. For details, contact: *Kerala State Road Transport Corporation* (KSRTC) in Ernakulam (Cochin), Bus Terminus, tel. 352033. In Trivandrum, call KSRTC, Central Bus Station, Thampanoor, tel. 63886. The *Karnataka State Roadways* and *Thiruvalliwar Transportation Corporation* (from Tamil Nadu) have luxury interstate buses. Inquire at the bus station in Ernakulam or Trivandrum.

By Train. Good rail connections link Cochin and Trivandrum with Bangalore, Bombay, Cannanore, Delhi, Madras, and Mangalore. For details, call Ernakulam (Cochin) Rail Station, 353100; from Trivandrum, call 62966 (days); 63066 (evenings).

By Car. To Cochin from Bangalore, 512 km; Ootocamund, 265 km; Madurai, 326 km; Madras, 694 km; Mysore, 470 km. To Trivandrum from Bangalore, 712 km; Bombay, 1613 km; Hyderabad, 1773 km; Delhi, 2900 km; Madras, 784 km; Madurai, 307 km; Mangalore, 633 km; and Mysore, 643 km. Kerala has some of the best and most scenic roads in India.

TOURIST INFORMATION. The Government of India and the state of Kerala have pretty good basic tourist information on Kerala, including some maps and some brochures. Before your visit, or when you arrive, contact the following offices:

Government of India Tourist Office, Willington Island, Cochin, Kerala; tel. 6045. Open 9 A.M.–5:30 P.M. Monday–Saturday.

Kerala Tourist Information Centre, Department of Tourism, Park View, Trivandrum, Kerala; tel. 6132. Open 10 A.M.–5 P.M. Monday–Saturday.

Kerala Tourist Information Counter, Central Bus Station, Thampanoor, Trivandrum; tel. 67224. Open 24 hours.

Kerala Tourist Information Counter, Railway Station, Thampanoor, Trivandrum (no phone). Open 24 hours.

Kerala Tourist Information Counter, Trivandrum Airport; tel. 3895. Open during flight times.

ACCOMMODATIONS. Kerala has a pretty good range of hotels in all price ranges in its two big cities, Cochin and Trivandrum. Throughout the rest of the state, there is not much choice. But what you find is adequate and reasonably priced. Rates are based on double occupancy: *Expensive,* over Rs. 400; *Moderate,* Rs. 150–400; *Inexpensive,* under Rs. 150. Most Western-style hotels take major credit cards (American Express or Diner's Club).

ALLEPPEY

Moderate

Alleppey Prince Hotel. A.S. Road, Alleppey 688007 (58 km from Cochin airport); tel. 3752. 30 air-conditioned rooms. Has a restaurant, bar, and swimming pool. Hotel can arrange backwater boat trips, Kathakali performances, and other cultural programs.

COCHIN

Expensive

Malabar Hotel. Willington Island, Cochin 682003 (five km from the airport, 12 km from downtown); tel. 6811. 37 air-conditioned rooms in this newly renovated hotel set on an island. Lovely and peaceful. Has a restaurant, bar, swimming pool, and other amenities.

Moderate

Hotel Abad. Chillikal, Cochin 682005 (three km from the airport, eight km from downtown); tel. 28211. 20 air-conditioned rooms. Has a restaurant, and coffee shop, but no bar. An adequate and well-run hotel in the Fort Cochin area.

Hotel Abad Plaza. Mahatma Gandhi Road, Ernakulam, Cochin 682035 (six km from airport, in downtown area); tel. 39729. 41 air-conditioned rooms with TVs. 24-hour room service, a restaurant, and many amenities. A new, modern hotel, without much character, but well run.

Bolghatty Palace Hotel. Bolghatty Island, Cochin; tel. 355003. Five rooms, some air-conditioned, four cottages. The main building, which is a former palace, is sadly neglected. Restaurant service and maintenance are indifferent. However, the building's exterior and the island are beautiful. The rumor is that this hotel may be handed over to a major hotel chain. As of this writing, the KTDC is running it into the ground.

Casino Hotel. Willington Island, Cochin 682003; (two km from the airport; five km from downtown); tel. 6821. 47 air-conditioned rooms, with TVs. Has a restaurant, bar, and other amenities. Another island hotel in a popular, pleasant setting. A good bargain.

Sea Lord Hotel. Shanmugham Road, Ernakulam, Cochin 682031, (seven km from the airport; near downtown); tel. 312682. 40 air-conditioned rooms with TVs. Has a restaurant and numerous amenities. A modern hotel, but the service can be sloppy.

Moderate to Inexpensive

Bharat Hotel. Durbar Hall Road, Cochin 682016 (five km from the airport; three km from downtown); tel. 353501. 95 rooms, some air-conditioned. Has a restaurant, 24-hour coffee shop, and some amenities. A popular, inexpensive hotel.

Grand Hotel. Mahatma Gandhi Road, Ernakulam, Cochin, (five km from the airport, three km from downtown); tel. 353211. 24 rooms, some air-conditioned. An inexpensive well-run hotel with a restaurant and bar.

International Hotel. Mahatma Gandhi Road, Ernakulam, Cochin 682035, (nine km from airport; near downtown); tel. 366010. 25 air-conditioned rooms with TVs. Has a restaurant, 24-hour coffee shop, bar, and lots of amenities. Simple decor, but a good bargain.

Inexpensive

Woodlands Hotel. Woodlands Junction, Mahatma Gandhi Road, Ernakulam, Cochin 682011, (six km from the airport, near downtown); tel. 351372. 65 rooms, some air-conditioned, TVs; vegetarian restaurant. A good hotel for the money.

KOTTAYAM

Moderate

Anjali Hotel. R.K. Road, Kottayam 686001 (two km from the railroad, close to downtown); tel: 3661. 22 air-conditioned rooms with TVs. Has restaurant, 24-hour coffee shop, bar, and many amenities. Will also arrange backwater cruise. A good bargain.

Inexpensive

Hotel Aida. M.C. Road, Kottayam 686039 (two km from the airport; five km downtown); tel. 3691. 40 rooms, some air-conditioned. Has a restaurant, bar, 24-hour room service, and a roof garden.

Hotel Ambassador. K. K. Road, Kottayam 686001 (two km from the railroad, close to downtown); tel. 3293. 20 air-conditioned rooms. Has a restaurant, bar, roof garden, 24-hour room service, and many amenities. A good bargain.

Hotel Triviny. T.B. Road, Kottayam 686001 (two km from the railroad, downtown); tel: 3393. 36 rooms, some air-conditioned. A simple hotel.

KOVALAM

Expensive

Kovalam Ashok Beach Resort. Kovalam 695522 (overlooking the beach); tel. 68010. 128 air-conditioned rooms, including cottages, with TVs. Has a restaurant, coffee shop, bar, shops, a great Ayurvedic massage and yoga center, swimming pool, and beach. Lots of amenities, but badly managed with indifferent service. Run by ITDC.

Moderate

Hotel Rockholm. Light House Road, Vizhinjam 695521; tel. 306. Seven simple, clean rooms, with balconies. On a cliff overlooking a beautiful cove. Good food; nice staff. The best bet in town.

Hotel Samudra. Kovalam (on the beach); tel: 62089. 50 rooms, 10 cottages. Has a bar and restaurant. Service often indifferent. Run by KTDC.

Inexpensive

Hotel Raja. Kovalam; tel. 584355. A small number of rooms and erratic service, but cheap!

There are numerous low-priced beach hut/hotels on the beach with only basic accommodations. If you're into local living, check them out when you arrive.

KOZHIKODE (CALICUT)
Inexpensive

Alakpuri Guest House. Maulana Mohammed Ali Road, (½ km from the railroad, near downtown); tel: 73361. 41 rooms, some air-conditioned. Has a restaurant, bar, and a nice lawn. Pleasant, but not on the water.

Beach Hotel. Beach Road, (one km from downtown, on the water); tel. 73851. 14 rooms, some air-conditioned. Has a restaurant, bar, and some amenities.

Sea Queen Hotel. Beach Road (one km from the railroad, one km downtown, on the water); tel. 60201. 28 rooms, some air-conditioned. Has a restaurant and bar.

LAKE PERIYAR
Moderate

Aranya Nivas. Thekkady, Idukki District; tel. Kumily 23. 26 rooms. Modernish hotel, near the lake and public boat launch. The restaurant is adequate.

Hotel Lake Palace. Thekkady, Idukki District; tel. Kumily 24. Wonderful former hunting lodge set on an island. Lovely rooms. Great service. Fixed-price meals are okay. The wild animals are a joy to watch. The place to stay.

Inexpensive

Periyar House. Thekkady, Idukki District; tel. Kumily 26. 40 rooms. Simple accommodations. Cheap and popular.

QUILON
Inexpensive

Hotel Shah International. Quilon 691001; tel. 75363. Large place with some air-conditioned rooms.

Hotel Sudarsan. Hospital Road, Parameswar Nagar, (one km from the railroad, downtown) 691001; tel. 73755. 35 rooms, some air-conditioned; a restaurant and a bar.

TRICHUR
Inexpensive

Hotel Elite International. Trichur 680001; tel. 21033. 93 rooms, some air-conditioned; room service, and a bar.

TRIVANDRUM
Moderate

Hotel Belair. Agricultural College Road, Vellayani Post Office, Trivandrum; (12 km from the airport, 10 km from downtown); tel. 3402. 25 rooms, most air-conditioned. Has a restaurant, coffee shop, swimming pool, lawn, and terrace.

Hotel Horizon. Aristo Road, Trivandrum 695014 (five km from the airport, close to downtown); tel. 6688. 47 rooms, some air-conditioned; TVs in rooms. Has a restaurant, bar, and amenities.

Hotel Luciya Continental. East Fort, Trivandrum 695023 (three km from the airport, close to downtown); tel: 73443. 104 rooms, some air-conditioned; TVs in air-conditioned rooms. 24-hour room service, a 24-hour coffee shop, restaurant, bar, and many amenities.

Inexpensive

Hotel Jas. P.B. No. 431, Trivandrum 695014 (seven km from the airport, downtown); tel. 64881. 44 air-conditioned rooms. Has a restaurant, bar, and room service.

Mascot Hotel. Palayam, Trivandrum (seven km from the airport; two km from downtown); tel: 68990. 41 rooms, some air-conditioned. Has a restaurant,

24-hour coffee shop, bar, health club, and some amenities. A good bargain for the price.

Hotel Pankaj. Opposite the Secretariat, Mahatma Gandhi Road, Trivandrum 695001 (five km from the airport, downtown); tel. 76667. 52 rooms, some air-conditioned. Has a bar, restaurant, room service, and some amenities. Popular.

Hotel Shanti Woodlands Thycaud, Trivandrum 695014 (five km from the airport, close to downtown); tel. 67129. 16 rooms, some air-conditioned, and a vegetarian restaurant. Nice hotel for the money.

GOVERNMENT GUEST HOUSES. Operated by the State of Kerala, government guest houses are simple but clean accommodations with nominal boarding charges (under Rs. 100) and nominal amenities. They can be found in Alwaye, Cannomore, Cheruthuruthy, Kozhikode (Calicut), Peermade, Quilon, Verkala, and Wynad. For details and reservations, contact the *Tourist Information Center,* Department of Tourism, Park View, Trivandrum, Kerala; tel. 61132.

DINING OUT. For all you beef lovers, Kerala has the real thing. It also has great seafood and Southern Indian vegetarian cuisine. In fact, this is a state—like Goa—that offers good good eating; both Indian and non-Indian. Most of the dining places are in the hotels, with major ones listed here. Prices are based on a three-course meal for one person, not including tip, taxes, beverages: *Expensive,* Rs. 50 plus; *Moderate,* Rs. 25–50; *Inexpensive,* Rs. 25 or under.

ALLEPPEY

Moderate to Expensive

Vemanad Restaurant. Alleppey Prince Hotel, A. S. Road, Alleppey; tel. 3752. Lunch and dinner. Kerala specialties, Continental, Chinese, and Indian cuisines. Excellent food. Call in advance. The hotel also has an *inexpensive* **Indian Coffee House,** with good basic nonvegetarian food and zesty Southern Indian coffee. A popular informal hangout.

COCHIN

Expensive

Hotel Abad Plaza. Mahatma Gandhi Road; tel. 361636. Indian, Continental, and Chinese cuisines; seafood; and beef. Great food, right down to the sundaes; Indian music and terrific service. Just hope the Abad hotels don't lose their chefs.

Rice Boats Restaurant. Malabar Hotel, Willington Island; tel. 6811. Variety of foods, served to you in a restaurant with "rice boat" decor. Reservations advised.

Moderate

Sea Lord Hotel Rooftop Restaurant. Shanmugham Road, Ernakulam; tel. 32682. Good fish and other selections in a variety of cuisines.

Moderate to Inexpensive

Grand Hotel. Mahatma Gandhi Road; tel. 353211. Japanese foods as well as international dishes.

Pandhal. Mahatma Gandhi Road, Ernakulam; tel. 355565. Fine nonvegetarian and vegetarian foods and local ambience.

Woodlands Hotel Restaurant. Woodlands Junction, Mahatma Gandhi Road, Ernakulam; tel. 351372. Very good vegetarian food in a pleasant setting.

Inexpensive

India Coffee House. Durbar Hall Road, Ernakulam; tel. 354724. Great coffee and good food, including snacks. Fast service.

KOTTAYAM

Moderate

The following three hotels have moderately priced good restaurants serving Indian, Chinese, and Continental cuisines:

Hotel Aida. M.C. Road, Kottayam; tel. 3691. Lunches and dinners.

Ambassador Hotel. K.K. Road; tel. 3293. Lunches and dinners.

Anjali Hotel. K.K. Road; tel. 3661. Lunches, dinners, and 24-hour coffee shop.

KOVALAM BEACH

Moderate

Rockholm Hotel. Light House Road; tel. 306. Best food in Kovalam. Eat indoors or in the delightful open-air restaurant set atop a cliff overlooking the beach.

Inexpensive

Try inexpensive beach huts for breakfast, lunch, or light dinner. Pleasant eating on the beach. Very informal.

LAKE PERIYAR

This is a place where the feast is with the viewing, not the eating. We recommend that you eat where you sleep. If you want to eat at the **Lake Palace** and you're not a guest, you must call (Kerala 24) to see if they can accommodate you. Fixed *moderate* to *expensive* menu of Indian and non-Indian foods.

TRIVANDRUM

Moderate

Annapoormai. Shanti Woodlands, Thycaud; tel. 67129. Excellent vegetarian foods.

Azad Hotel. Mahatma Gandhi Road, near Overbridge Junction. Indian and Moslem specialties. A popular local restaurant.

Hotel Horizon. Aristo Junction, Thampanoor; tel. 66888. There are two restaurants: Mira (indoors); and Galaxie (rooftop garden) serving international dishes.

Hotel Pankaj. Opposite the Secretariat, Mahatma Gandhi Road; tel. 66557. Rooftop restaurant serving Indian, Chinese, Continental, and South Indian lunches and dinners.

HOW TO GET AROUND. By Car. To get around Kerala, most visitors (unless they have time to spare) rent a car with a driver in either Cochin or Trivandrum. Rate for an Ambassador is Rs. 2 per km; with a Rs. 50 night-halt charge. Contact a tourist department center for a list of currently approved private transport companies. (See Tourist Information section for addresses.) You can also hire a car with a driver through KTDC in Trivandrum, tel. 76743; in Cochin, tel. 353234.

By Bus. Call the Kerala Road Transport Corp., Cochin 352033 (Trivandrum; 71029) for deluxe bus information. KRTC buses connect with most cities in Kerala and are cheap and clean. Unfortunately, video coaches are very noisy.

By Train. You can travel Cochin–Kottayam–Quilon–Trivandrum Kozhikode via train. In Cochin, for train information and reservations, call 353100; in Trivandrum, call 62966 (days) and 63066 (evenings).

By Boat. Kerala also has an interesting backwater canal network. (See under Tours, individual cities directly below.) You can get from some cities to the next via slow-moving delightful ferries.

ALLEPPEY

By Auto-Rickshaw. The best and cheapest way to travel around town.

By Boat. From Alleppey, you can take a public ferry backwater day-long trip to Quilon for less than Rs. 10. For details, inquire at the boat jetty or at the Tourist Department in Cochin or Trivandrum before you arrive. In addition, you can hire a lovely old wooden boat with a captain and do the trip in grand leisurely style, but for a far grander price (Rs. 600–700) for the day. Arrangements can be made through travel agents, tourist departments, and hotels.

COCHIN

By Taxi and **Auto Rickshaw.** Regular taxis are available, but the drivers hate to use the meters. Settle the fare in advance and bargain. It is better to use an auto rickshaw. They're much cheaper and more fun. Again, meters tend to be "broken." Fix the fare in advance. In either case, if you're trying to go from island to island, this is the least efficient and costliest method.

By Boat. The best way to island hop is via the ferries; it's faster, cheaper, and pleasant. Frequent service from early morning until about 10 P.M. There are ferries from Fort Cochin, Ernakulam, Mattancherry, Willington Island, plus numerous other runs. Ask at your hotel for specifics, or contact the local tourist office.

KOTTAYAM

By Auto Rickshaw. This is the best way to scoot around the streets of town. Cheap and fun.

By Ferry. This is another convenient starting and ending point for a backwater trip to Alleppey. Inquire at the boat jetty.

By Bus. From Kottayam, KTDC buses leave periodically for the Periyar Wildlife Sanctuary. Inquire at the bus stand.

QUILLON

By Auto Rickshaw. For those quick trips around town, this is the way to go.

By Boat. From here, you can take the day-long public ferry that weaves through the backwaters to Alleppey. Go to the boat jetty for information. You can also do shorter trips and you can rent a boat for the day.

TRIVANDRUM

By Taxi or Auto Rickshaw. By taxi to Kovalam Beach, figure Rs. 5 for the first km; Rs. 2 each additional km. For short trips, an auto rickshaw is easily half the price.

TOURS. Alleppey to Quillon. *All-day private boat trips* can be arranged through a travel agent or hotel. Or contact, well in advance, Manager, Kerala State Water Transport Corporation, Boat-Jetty, Alleppey. A wooden boat, spacious and comfortable with an interior cabin and a captain costs Rs. 600–700 for the day.

Cochin (Ernakulam). KTDC operates deluxe bus tours and some boat tours. Contact KTDC, Shopping Complex, Shanmugham Road, Ernakulam; tel. 35324. *Periyar Wildlife Sanctuary Tour,* two days by bus. Saturdays at 7 A.M. Rs. 100. Half-day boat trips, daily; 9 A.M.–12:30 P.M. and 2–5:30 P.M., in Cochin backwaters; visit St. Francis Church, Jewish Synagogue, Dutch Palace, Gondu, and Bolghatty islands. Fare: Rs. 15.

Trivandrum. KTDC conducts a series of bus tours that start at its reception center, Thampanoor (near the central railway station). Call 75031 for reservations and details. *Trivandrum Tour,* full-day tour departs at 8 A.M., except Mondays; Rs. 40. *Kanyakumari Tour* (Cape Comorin) is a full-day trip, starting at 7:30 A.M. daily; Rs. 60. *Ponmudi Tour* (Hill station) departs daily at 8:30 A.M.; Rs. 40. *Lake Periyar Wildlife Sanctuary* (two-day tour) departs Saturdays 6:30 A.M.; Rs. 100. *Kodaikanal Tour* (Tamil Nadu hill station) is a three-day trip starting 6:30 A.M. on the last Saturday of each month; Rs. 250.

FESTIVALS. *Pooram,* the most spectacular temple festival in Kerala, is held in April and May in Trichur. Elephants, sporting gorgeous gold-plated mail, carry Brahmans with ceremonial umbrellas and the temple deity, Vadakkunathan, in a procession accompanied by the beat of temple drums. Great festivities and fireworks. Contact the Tourist Department for exact dates for this and other festivals.

Onam, Kerala's biggest festival celebrating the harvest season, August–September. Lasting three days, it features dancing, singing, and exotic snake boat races at Alleppcy, Aranmula, and Kottayam. Boats of all descriptions—beak shaped, kite-tailed, curly-headed. A lot of hoopla!

On the second Saturday of August, snake boats compete at Alleppey for the Nehru Trophy in Nehru Trophy Boat Race. Big tourist draw.

Makaravilakka Festival, an important Hindu pilgrimage to the Ayyappa Temple at Sabarimala (180 km northeast of Trivandrum) is held November–January. The procession is made only by men and prepubescent and postmenopausal women. The arrival of the devotees who come from all over India is supposed to coincide with the conclusion of a 60-day fast. Many just make a five-km trek from the sacred Pampa River.

WILDLIFE SANCTUARIES. *Lake Periyar Wildlife Sanctuary* is set around an artificial lake. Inexpensive boat trips are available, but fellow passengers tend to squeal at the slightest sign of distant movement. Splurge and get a boat for yourself (Rs. 150). You can see elephants, leopards, tigers, langur, wild boar, deer, and numerous birds. You can also hire a guide and hike, there are lookouts to climb where you can just stand and gaze. Best time to visit is March–May. Contact Manager, Aranya Niwas, Thekkady, or the Field Director, Project Tiger, Kanjikuzhi, Kottayam (tel. 8409) for more details.

Neyyar Wild Life Sanctuary, 32 km from Trivandrum, is a large reservoir with boating available. There are elephants, sloth bears, wild boar, langur, tigers, leopards, birds. The sanctuary is also a crocodile breeding center and deer park. For more details, contact Wild Life Warden, Forest Headquarters, Trivandrum; tel. 60674 in Trivandrum.

Parambikulam Wildlife Sanctuary is situated around three dams, 48 km from Pollachi northeast of Trichur. Elephants, tigers, deer, gaur, otters, bears, tigers, and crocodiles abound. Facilities for boating and accommodations in a forest rest house are available. Details: Divisional Forest Officer, Teak Plantation Division, Thunacadavu Post; tel. Pollachi 33.

BEACHES. Kerala is aware of its prize beaches. They're beautiful—palm fringed, with towering cliffs and little coves. But watch out for the sun and current; they're stronger than you think.

Kovalam Beach, 18 km from Trivandrum, is lovely, with white sand, backed by cliffs. Watch out for the undertow while you're absorbed in the local color—fishermen bringing in the daily catch, sending out the boats. Beach huts sell food, and peddlars sell pineapples, bananas, coconut oil, beach mats, and handicrafts.

HISTORIC SITES. *Dutch Palace* in Mattancherry (eight km from Ernakulam) was built by the Portuguese and given to the maharajah in 1568. It's called Dutch because the Dutch later renovated it. The center of the building contains a large coronation hall, and seventeenth-century murals tell the entire story of the *Ramayana.* Three temples are dedicated to Vishnu, Shiva, and Pazhavayannoor Bhagavathi. Open 8:30 A.M.–12:30 P.M.; and 2–5 P.M. daily except holidays. Free.

Cochin Synagogue, Mattancherry, was originally constructed in 1568 and rebuilt in the late 1600s and 1700s after partial destruction. Beautiful Chinese floor tiles—no two alike—were added in 1762 by Ezekiel Rahabi, who also built the clock tower. The Cochin maharajah gave the synagogue the great scrolls of the Old Testament and copper plates. The entire building is a treasure vault. Open 10 A.M.–noon and 2–5 P.M. Closed Saturdays.

St. Francis Church, Fort Cochin, was the first European church built in India, constructed in 1510. Vasco da Gama was buried here. You can see his gravestone, but his remains were shipped back to Portugal. Sedate, stark architecture.

Vallia Palli, Kottayam, is a Syrian church that supposedly contains a cross brought from a church in Kodungalloor (Cranganore) that was established by St. Thomas.

Janardhana Temple, Varkala, 54 km north of Trivandrum, is claimed to be 2,000 years old. A famous pilgrimage center for Hindus, the temple is dedicated to Vishnu.

 MUSEUMS. *Chitra Art Gallery,* in Trivandrum, has an eclectic collection of paintings, including Rajput, Mogul, and Far Eastern art. Open 8 A.M.–5 P.M.; closed Mondays. Fee: Rs. 2.

Cochin Museum, Durbar Hall Road, Ernakulam. Emphasis here is on archaeology, models of temples, sculptures, and old photography and antiques from the nineteenth century. Open 9 A.M.–noon and 3–5 P.M.; closed Mondays and holidays.

Pazhassiraja Museum, East Hill, five km from Calicut. Copies of ancient mural paintings, antique bronzes, old coins, archaeological findings. Open 10 A.M.–5 P.M.; closed Mondays.

 DANCE AND THEATER. A trip to Kerala must include seeing a performance of the Kathakali dance form. *Katha* means story; *kali* means play, and that's what you see: a story/dance form over 400 years old—Indian pantomime performed in painted face and with great costumes. The performers start training at a very young age, learning how to control every muscle in their bodies and toes. Performances can run very long, but you can see an abridged version. Call for reservations and details.

Cochin. *Art Kerala,* Theosophical Society Hall, Pallimukka, Mahatma Gandhi Road, Ernakulam; tel. 32250. Dance performances at 7 P.M. Tuesdays, Thursdays, and Saturdays. Kathakali, Ottam Thullal, and Koodiyattom dance forms. *Cochin Cultural Center,* Durbar Hall Road, Ernakulam; tel. 31109. Daily Kathakali, 7–8:30 P.M. *Gurnkulam Kathakali Yogam,* Box 1740, Cochin, 682016; tel. 369471. Great tiny theater in Ernakulam; you get to see the performers apply their makeup. *Kathakali Club,* 22/212 Lavan Rd., Ernakulam; tel. 33357. Kathakali on the second Saturday of every month at TDM Hall, 6:30–10:15 P.M. *See India Foundation,* Kalathiparambil Lane, Ernakulam; tel. 31871. Daily Kathakali 7–8:30 P.M.

Trichur (In Cheruthuruthy, 36 km due north). *Kalamandalam Academy,* which is largely responsible for the revival of Kathakali dance, teaches other dance forms as well. Demonstrations on request.

Trivandrum. At *Trivandrum Kathakali Club, Drysyavedi,* and *Margi,* regular Kathakali programs are organized. Inquire at the Tourist Information Center for details.

 SHOPPING. Intricate and lovely ivory things—from cigarette cases to elephants—require the age-old method of hand carving. These and other items are available at shops and bazaars throughout Kerala. Bargain, but don't overdo it; if it's really cheap, beware—it's probably not ivory. Metal mirrors from the village of Aranmula are among the finest Indian curios, and the gold- and silver-brocaded fabrics of Kottarrare are special. Take a 30-minute drive to Balarama-Puram and see fabric as it was made centuries ago. In Cochin, great antiques, or let's say old curios, are sold on the street leading to the Jewish Synagogue. Some of the best treasures you'll find in India.

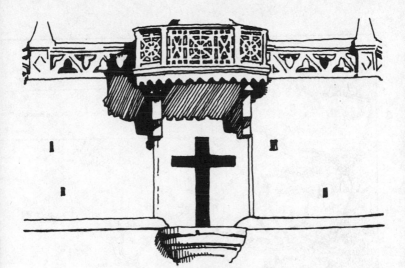

GOA

Tropical Gold Coast

by
KATHLEEN COX

If you think every paradise in the world is first discovered then ruined by the discoverers, go to Goa. No bigger than a thumbprint on the Malabar Coast map, this former Portuguese territory—the home of about one million easygoing, hospitable people, both Hindu and Christians—is in India, but not entirely of it.

The climate and scenery are resort perfect. Outside the monsoon season (June to September), which affects most of India, the temperature and weather stay high and dry. Most who visit Goa dream of becoming marooned in a charming village where the silvery sands of some of the world's most beautiful beaches are never more than a few steps away. The palm-bordered rivers move wide and lazily down to the Arabian Sea, while the towns are a pleasing blend of Portuguese and Indian. Houses gleam with a light wash of color set off by brightly painted pillared front porches and trim. Goa appears to be the epitome of well-cared-for tropical suburbia.

In the not-too-distant past, Goa was like an Asian Tangiers, with connections to Europe as well as the East. A constant flow of European products (legal and illegal) were uncrated in Goa's ports. Yet, after four centuries of heavy-handed Portuguese Catholicism, somehow only about 30 percent of the people became Christian. It also seems that the somewhat puritan atmosphere of India proper had trouble penetrating the borders. So most Goans remained much more liberated and better off materially than their neighbors in the rest of India.

389

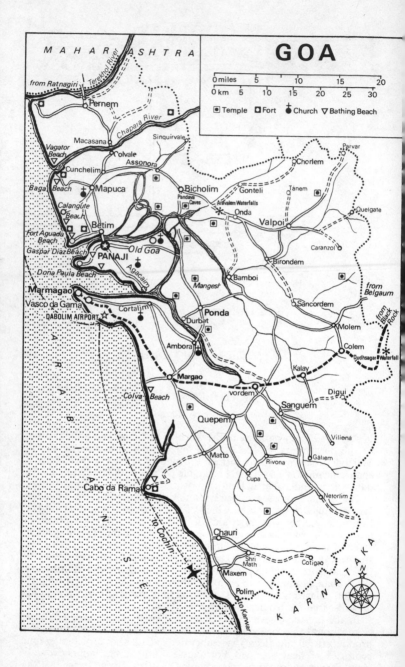

GOA

0 miles   5   10   15   20
0 km   5   10   15   20   25   30

▣ Temple ◻ Fort ✚ Church ⬤ Church ▽ Bathing Beach

The Portuguese were entrenched in Goa for 451 years, but they were ousted by India in a quick, nearly bloodless, operation in 1961—leaving behind a ghost town crammed with baroque churches and a plentiful, if artificial, economy. India has made changes. There are now many more schools, doctors, ever-present cows, the great novelty of a free press, free elections, and the pride of self-rule in a democracy.

Naturally, the Goans have suffered growing pains. Chief among them is the complicated and tedious unraveling of the colonial economy. Goa struggles to produce enough food to feed itself, and some whitewashed villages are almost deserted, with many able-bodied men seeking work in Bombay. But iron mines produce high-grade ore for export; delicious tinned prawns and shrimp sail off to the supermarkets; and conscientious agrarian and environmental planning is beginning to pay off with the occasional model farm and forward-thinking reforestation project. Although tourism also plays a growing role in reviving the economy, the state seriously attempts to keep an eye on Goa's beauty, holding back hoteliers who see rupee signs in architectural plans for mammoth resort monstrosities that would destroy the quaint peaceful charm.

A lively and unfortunately volatile topic among Goans is language: Should they speak Konkani, the traditional tongue, or Marathi, spoken next door, which would pave the way for absorption by the larger, more powerful Maharashtra? The issue is serious. Goans are fiercely loyal to their state (there are more than 300 Goan village clubs in Bombay), India takes second place in their heart.

A Historic Review

Early Goan history is a hazy maze of Hindu dynasties and subdynasties until the Middle Ages, when the Hindus stopped fighting each other and banded together to fight off the Moslems. Suddenly, everyone wanted a foothold on the Malabar Coast—the great source of spices and the important link in the Arabian trade routes. The Portuguese were the first Europeans to appear on the scene. Alfonso de Albuquerque arrived in 1510, fighting until he controlled the coast and had established a formidable and wealthy trading power. Silks and spices, porcelains and pearls, passed in and out of Goa's harbors until she rivaled Lisbon itself. "Golden Goa" was well known to the rest of the world.

Thirty years after Albuquerque came the most famous figure in Goan history, seeking not spices but souls: St. Francis Xavier. Born in a Spanish castle, doctor at the University of Paris, Francis left for Goa with a new title—apostolic nuncio to the East—when the king of Portugal requested missionaries for his overseas territories. With no possessions but a breviary and a crucifix, Francis transformed Goa by his preaching and his example before moving on to more distant lands. Ten years later, he died on the threshold of China, but his body was eventually returned to Goa, where it can be seen in a state of eerie quasi-preservation in the Bom Jesus Basilica.

At the end of the sixteenth century, life turned precarious for the Portuguese. They had to fight off newcomers of which there were many—Hindu, Moslem, Dutch, and British. By 1750, the proud baroque capital of Velha Goa (Old Goa) was battle scarred and plague ridden, so the population moved down river to Panaji. The Portuguese methods of rule degenerated as badly as did the buildings, with Goans suffering from the Inquisition, set up after Francis Xavier's death. This horrendous tool of injustice finally gave up the ghost in 1812. And the viceroyship, which was a political plus that enriched its possessor, did little for the Goans. Throughout the nineteenth and early twentieth centuries abortive revolts sprang up—fragile sparks of rebellion that were ruthlessly quelled by the Portuguese. In December 1951, India put a stop to what was, from her point of view, an intolerable situation. Operation Vijaya brought Goa back to India after a 451-year absence.

Daman and Diu, two other Portuguese vest-pocket enclaves, fell to India at the same time. Daman (22 square miles and 38,000 people), north of Bombay, and Diu (15 square miles and 23,000 people), across the Gulf of Cambay, share Goa's character, religions, and rural pursuits.

EXPLORING GOA

Let's face it—if you're in Goa, it's partially for the sun, sand, surf! Goa has 82 miles of coastline plus deep river estuaries, so you have quite a choice of public beaches. Closest to Panaji, the capital, are Miramar and Dona Paula beaches. At Miramar, closer of the two, the swimming is marred by a strong undertow and the view is marred by an unfortunate stretch of architectural eyesores erected before Goa wised up. The Dona Paula Beach is palm fringed and commands a fine view of the Mormugoa Harbor. Across the Mandovi River from Panaji is gorgeous Calangute Beach. This "queen of Goan beaches" is 16 km in length, with Baga, Anjuna, then Vagator cloistered in dramatic rocks and cliffs—a spectacular place to watch the sun disappear over the water. The Anjuna is also the scene of the weekly (Wednesday) "hippy" flea market, giving Goans a chance to buy brownies, apple pie, and all kinds of high-tech gear not normally available in the typical Indian bazaar. Another good public beach is the Colva, on the south coast near Margao. Here, the nomadic Lambanis, who travel the western states of India, set up shop on portable blankets cluttered with great handicrafts, jewelry, embroideries, and quilts.

Panaji, a pleasant whitewashed city, was only a sleepy village before the Portuguese transferred their capital closer to shore. The most important monument dating from the precapital days is the Secretariat Building—once a Moslem palace, then a Portuguese fort. Near the building stands the statue of the Abbé Faria, priest and hypnotist, portrayed in the act of mesmerizing a female patient. The best view of Panaji is from the Church of Our Lady of the Immaculate Conception or, if you're lucky, from the Portuguese-style villa of a Goan host who happens to live on the hillside. You can also get a good sense of Panaji from the banks of the wide Mandovi, where slow-sailing craft journey up and down the gray water.

The scenery around the capital is lush, with rice paddies, palms, groves of mango, and jackfruit. But plan for a leisurely pace, because of the number of linking ferries, usually crowded but still offering an easygoing, enjoyable ride. One easy excursion is to Velha Goa. The sixteenth-century Portuguese capital is a study in splendor and decay. Go by boat, if you can, so that, after you disembark, you can drive or walk through the Viceregal Arch, as each viceroy had to do before taking possession of his office. This arch, where Vasco da Gama gazes out from his niche in full regalia, was the symbolic entry to the city, as well as the gateway from the harbor.

The shell of the city covers about three square miles. Once it was the greatest commercial center east of Suez, rivaling Lisbon in grandeur. "Whoever has seen Goa, need not see Lisbon" was no careless boast. Now the great square, the site of the trials of the Inquisition, is little better than a neglected field.

The following is a convenient order for a tour of Velha Goa:

St. Cajetan, an Italian and contemporary of St. Francis Xavier, lent his name to this handsome church and convent of the Theatin Order. Constructed in the seventeenth century, the church was modeled after St. Peter's Basilica in Rome. The facade is neoclassic, with twin towers flanking the great dome, but the interior decoration is pure unrestrained baroque. The main altar soars nearly to the top of the edifice, the patron saint's altar is adorned with twisted columns, and the pulpit is an exercise in delicate carving. A large arched window, whose tiny panes are made of seashells, is interesting. In the crypt are the tombs of generations of Portuguese rulers.

Another curious feature, located beneath the raised platform that serves as a pulpit, is a tank, or a well, which has led many to believe that this was the site of a temple tank, meaning that this church replaced a former Hindu shrine. Many of the paintings that adorn the walls were brought from Europe in the fifteenth century; others were done locally.

The Se Cathedral, the largest church in Velha Goa, is an imposing white structure constructed between 1562 and 1652. Unfortunately, its facade is lopsided after the collapse of the north tower in 1776. The Cathedral's tiny congregation seems out of proportion to its 230-foot length and the magnificence of its decoration. The bell in the existing tower is referred to as the "Golden Bell" because of its rich tone, immortalized in a Portuguese poem. Notice also the Chapel of the Blessed Sacrament, the third chapel on your left as you face the altar. The closed blue doors combine three schools of art: the bottom panel is characteristically Hindu, the middle panel is Moslem, and the top panel below the arch is Greek. The main altar, dedicated to St. Catherine, is simple in shape with classical arches and Corinthian columns; richly gilded scenes in deep relief portray episodes in the saint's martyrdom. In the left nave are the chapels of St. Joseph, ornamented on every possible surface, of St. George, and of Our Lady of Necessity.

On the right is the chapel of the Holy Spirit, with its lovely altarpiece showing Mary surrounded by the black-bearded apostles on the day of Pentecost. Other chapels on this side are dedicated to St. Bernard, St. Anthony, and the Holy Cross. Almost hidden in this last chapel in the Mauresque style is a cross on which a vision of Christ is said to have appeared in 1919.

St. Francis of Assisi Church and Convent (built in 1661) is easily the best example of Portuguese religious art in Old Goa. The Franciscan Order was the first to arrive in Goa, even though nearly everyone thinks of Francis Xavier and the more spectacular results of the Jesuits in connection with Goa. True to the humility of their founder, the Franciscans went straight to the poor and downtrodden, whereas the Jesuits allied themselves with the resident Brahmans. The Franciscan church is simple and handsome, spacious and harmonious. The portal is pure Manueline style; inside, this theme is developed in rich stucco ceilings and a profusion of carvings. High above the main altar, Christ crucified is shown with his right arm detached from the cross in order to embrace St. Francis. In the convent next door, visit the museum and gallery with portraits of 16 Franciscan martyrs.

The Chapel of St. Catherine is an endearing little Renaissance church, one of the first erected by Albuquerque in 1510 to celebrate his arrival in Velha Goa on St. Catherine's Day.

The Bom Jesus Basilica took 10 years to build and is a striking example of Jesuit architecture. The interior is perhaps the richest of the churches in Old Goa, highly and heavily decorated, yet admirably proportioned. Built in the sixteenth century, the basilica is sacred to the Infant Jesus, but the Babe's statue is dwarfed by that of Ignatius of

Loyala, founder of the order of Jesuits, which stands above the gilded high altar.

Most will visit Bom Jesus not for its size or its style but for the relic on display. Here, in a splendor he constantly refused during his lifetime, lies the body of St. Francis Xavier. The body traveled after death almost as much as the saint had done in life, but in spite of each transfer (at least four) to this final resting place, the body resisted damage. Indeed, the deceased Francis suffered more from piety than anything else—both big toes were bitten off by female fanatics and an arm was severed at the request of a pope and carried off to Rome.

St. Francis owes his opulent casket to the generosity of the duke of Tuscany, who received the saint's pillow as a relic and sent the Florentine tomb in exchange. The entire chapel is covered with marble, inlaid with semiprecious stones, and decorated with paintings portraying the life of the saint. In recent years, the casket was cut open. Now, the curious or the worshiping can have a grisly glimpse of the head and shoulders of Francis.

Walk up the road from Bom Jesus to the Monte Santo or Holy Hill. Here you can see a number of other remnants of Portuguese glory. The most interesting is the Convent and Church of Santa Monica, which once housed more than 100 nuns, then slowly dwindled in importance until the last nun died in 1885. The church is refreshingly simple, in the Doric style, and contains a supposedly miraculous cross in one chapel. Its building is massive, more like a fortress than a nunnery.

Also on the Monte Santo are other churches, most of them ruined; and, on a less saintly level, a black stone whipping post where prisoners were given the Portuguese third degree. The best preserved of the group of churches is the little chapel of St. Anthony. Because St. Anthony is the patron saint of soldiers, the saint's image used to receive an annual salary from the commander of the army. One ill-advised general, who considered this a wasteful expense, cut off the payment. He died from a fall on the saint's feast day. The next general restored Anthony's stipend.

The amazing number of churches to the contrary, Goa is 68 percent Hindu and just 30 percent Christian. If there are few temples in proportion to the Hindu population, it's partially because the first wave of Portuguese destroyed them. The temples were rebuilt, but inland, at a safe distance from the foreign colonizers. In and around Ponda, there are seven temples within a three-mile radius. The most interesting is the small but lovely Shri Manguesh, set on a lush green hill. Dedicated to Shiva, the temple has an air of tropical elegance, with its blue pillars, tiles on the wall, old locally made crystal chandeliers, and large silver idols. The special Shri Mahadeva at Tambdi Surla (45 km from Panaji) in the foot of the ghats is the only example of Kadamba temple architecture (the Kadambas ruled from the eleventh to the thirteenth century) remaining in Goa. Built of basalt stone, the temple is in a tranquil setting on a river bank and site on a simple plinth with intricately carved pillars in the *mandapa* (pavilion). There is no use of mortar anywhere in the structure—stone is hammered into stone.

Once, dozens of mosques dotted the countryside, but the Portuguese, who showed no favoritism, pursued their policy of destruction and quickly demolished them. The only remaining mosque of any historic importance dates back to 1560 and is known as the Safa Shahouri Masjid, built by Ibrahim Adilshah of Bijapur. Unfortunately, an extensive garden with fountains that surrounded the mosque succumbed to the wrath of the marauding Portuguese.

Today, Old Goan homes are splendid sites, both inside and out. If you can plan your trip in advance, write the Tourist Department in Goa and ask to visit some of these well-preserved private showcases.

PRACTICAL INFORMATION FOR GOA

 WHEN TO GO. Goa can be lovely during the monsoon from June to September if you like rain plus warmth (and it does not rain perpetually). Otherwise, temperatures vary little, averaging 79°F. December, January, and February are great (a light wool sweater might be good to have in the evening). Because of various festivals, Goa is very crowded between late December and mid-January. Book well ahead.

HOW TO GET THERE. By Air. *Indian Airlines* has daily flights into Dabolim Airport, Goa, from the following major cities: from Bombay, 50 minutes; Delhi, 2½ hours; Cochin, one hour; Trivandrum, two hours; and Bangalore, one hour. *Vayudoot* also has occasional flights from Pune and Bombay to Goa. The airport is about a 30-minute trip from Panaji, the capital of Goa, passing through pleasant local landscape. Taxies and hotel transport are available at the airport.

By Bus. A bus can be a pleasant and comfortable way to travel; *unless* your only choice of bus is a video coach often called luxury, or super luxury. The Indians love these traveling movie marathons, but most of the films (maybe all) are in Hindi, and the sound is so loud it vibrates off the windows. So, if buses are your beat, bring earplugs (forewarned is forearmed). In every other respect, the bus is better than a train. It's reliable, clean, and fast. And best of all, it's easy to make reservations and get a ticket—easy by Indian standards.

The *Kadamba Transport Corporation Ltd.* (a government of Goa, Daman, and Diu undertaking), the *Karnataka State Road Transport Corporation, Maharashtra State Road Transport Corporation, Maharashtra Tourism Development Corporation,* and numerous private buses, can take you to and from the following major destinations: Bangalore, three luxury buses daily, 14 hours, Rs. 103; Bombay, 17 luxury buses daily, 17 hours, Rs. 150; Mangalore, five luxury buses daily, 12 hours, Rs. 66; and Mysore, one semiluxury bus daily, 17 hours, Rs. 92.

By Car. To drive to Goa is not impossible, obviously. But most drives from the major cities—Bangalore, Bombay, Mangalore, and Mysore—are long trips. Although the roads are good, by Indian standards, they are unlit and narrow. Don't travel at night or at dusk. Bullocks own the road; hit one and justice takes place on the ground, you see more. Besides, scenery throughout this part of India is so lovely, why miss it by traveling in darkness?

By Train. The train is more complicated to take than the bus and goes slower. The trains are often dirty and infrequently live up to their former romantic image. However, long-distance trains do provide an alternative to planes, and by traveling on the ground, you see more. From Bangalore, you can take the *Kittun Express* or *Mandovi Express,* Rs. 237 first class. From Delhi, you can take the *Jhelum Express, Koyna Express,* or *Mandovi Express,* Rs. 560 first class. From Bombay, take the *Miraj Express, Gomantak Express, Mahalaxmi Express,* or *Mandovi Express,* Rs. 260 first class. Second-class fares are about 25 percent of the first-class rate.

By Boat. An overnight ferry service operates between Bombay and Panaji. The trip takes about 22 hours and runs fairly regularly except during the monsoon (mid-May–mid-September). The boat is by no means glamorous, but it can be fun. We recommend the top accommodations: owner's cabin (Rs. 300), attached toilet and bath with two berths; or first-class deluxe A (Rs. 260), attached toilet and shower with two berths. The cheapest rate is the lower deck (lower class) at Rs. 48, with many other possibilities in between. Contact the *Shipping Corporation of India, Ltd.,* 16 Bank St., Fort, Bombay 400 023; tel. 256835. Telex; 011–4049.

TOURIST INFORMATION. Goa is a well-organized state when it comes to tourism. The *Tourist Department* is efficient, courteous, and responsive. If you want to see beautiful Goan homes, or if you want a list of hotels, contact the Tourism Department. Current information is available on almost every topic of interest to the traveler. *Goa Tourist Directory*, a free brochure published by the department, is especially helpful, supplying basic information about what to do and how to do it. It also contains minimal information on "sights" to see in Goa. Here's a list of department offices (hours usually 9:30 A.M.–4 P.M.):

Main office. Department of Tourism, Government of Goa, Daman, and Diu, Tourist Home, Patto, Panaji, Goa; tel. 5583.

Dabolim Airport. Tourist Information Office; tel. 2644.

Margao. Tourist Information Center, Municipal Bldg.; tel. 2513 or 3766.

Vasco da Gama. Tourist Information Center; tel. 2676 or 3119.

Panaji. Tourist Information Center, 5, Interstate Bus Terminus; tel. 5620.

Foreign Currency Exchange. Most banks and major Western-style hotels will exchange travelers checks. There's a *Bank of India* opposite Azad Maidan, Panaji, with branches in Margao, Papusa, and Vasco-da-Gama. Hours are usually 10 A.M.–2:30 P.M. Monday–Friday.

ACCOMMODATIONS. Goa has a great assortment of beach resorts to fit all budgets. And, when you've had enough sun and surf, you can head inland. Hotels, with rates based on double occupancy, are listed according to price category; *Super Deluxe,* Rs. 1500 and up; *Expensive,* Rs. 600–1500; *Moderate,* and *Inexpensive,* Rs. under 200. Book well in advance for December–February.

Super Deluxe

The Taj Aguada Hermitage. Sinquerim, Bardez; tel. 440–7; telex: 0194–206. 20 air-conditioned villas, each with its own lawn and verandah, set high on a hill. Jeeps take you to the nearby Taj Fort Aguada, with a beach, shopping arcade, restaurants, and all expected amenities. Each villa is set up to handle two separate parties, each with a double bedroom, but if you prefer seclusion, you can rent the entire villa: two bedrooms, a living room, dining room, and two bathrooms. Off-season rates, March 1–December 19.

Expensive

Majorda Beach Resort. Majorda, Salcette; tel. 20751–2; Telex: MBR 196–234. A modern well-designed resort with 64 rooms and four cottages; all air-conditioned. Two swimming pools, one in an interior courtyard, one outside; excellent beach, spacious lawns, numerous restaurants, a health club, and water sports. Full amenities. Off-season rates February 16–December 16.

Oberoi Bogmalo Beach. Bogmalo (five minutes from the airport); tel. 2192–2; telex: 0192–297 OBGA. Modern attractive resort, with 118 rooms, all air-conditioned, each with a private balcony. Has a swimming pool, health club, sailing, water skiing, restaurants, a shopping arcade, and all amenities. Off-season rates February 1–December 16.

Taj Fort Aguada Beach Resport. Sinquerim, Bardez; tel. 4401–7; Telex: 440194–206 TAJ IN. Modern resort hotel built into the ruins of the Portuguese fort. 120 air-conditioned rooms in the large, formal-style hotel or in cottages. An excellent beach and swimming pool, shopping arcade, health club, water sports, and restaurants. Off-season rates March 1–December 19.

Taj Holiday Village. Same address, and phone as Fort Aguada. Adjacent to the Aguada, but less formal. 86 red-tiled villas and cottages built along the lines of a Goan village. Some are air-conditioned, but all have fans and good ventilation. A swimming pool, excellent beach, restaurants, health club, and water sports. All amenities. Off-season rates March 1–December 19.

Welcomgroup Cidade de Goa. Vainguinim Beach, Dona Paula; tel. 3301–7; telex: 194–257 DONA In. Handsome hotel resort designed along the lines of a Portuguese hill town. 101 rooms, all air-conditioned, with varying Indian-style decor. Has restaurants, a swimming pool, beach, water sports, shopping arcade, health club. Also offers a unique 10-day health farm—a near-painless weight reduction program. Off-season rates from March 1–December 16.

Moderate

Hotel Baia do Sol. Baga Beach, Calangute; tel. 84; telex: 194–303 SOL IN. 22 rooms, including cottages (which are air-conditioned). Simple but adequate accommodations. Charming bar and restaurant. Has a beach, boating, and sailing. Off-season rates from June to August.

Estrela do Mar Beach Resort. Cobrowado, Calangute P.O., Baga (on the beach); tel. 14; telegram: Estrela. 10 rooms (with fans), a private balcony, and "beachy" decor. Has nice gardens and a restaurant and bar. Friendly service. Off-season rates from February 1 to November 30.

Hotel Fidalgo. 18th June Road, Panaji; tel. 3321–30; Telex: 0194–213 REST IN. New Hotel in Panaji. 122 air-conditioned rooms. Has a swimming pool, shopping arcade, restaurants, health club, and 24-hour room service. Off-season rates from April to September.

Hotel Mandovi. D. B. Bandodkar Road, Panaji; tel. 4481–5; telex: 0194–226. Old well-established hotel in Panaji. 63 air-conditioned rooms. Some amenities. Restaurant.

Hotel Nova Goa. Dr. Atmaram Barkar Road, Panaji; tel: 4575–9; telex: 0194–249 KAMS IN. In Panaji. 49 air-conditioned rooms with TVs. Has a swimming pool and a restaurant. Off-season rates from June 15 to September 15.

Prainha Cottages by the Sea. Dona Paula; tel. 4004; telegram: PRAINHA. 15 cottages (not air-conditioned). A quiet beach hideaway. An excellent bargain with excellent service. Restaurant. Off-season rates from June to September.

Varma Beach Resort. Calangute Beach, Calangute (near the beach); tel: 77; telegram: VARMA. 10 air-conditioned rooms with handsome decor. Good service.

White Sands Hotel and Cottages. Colva Beach, Colva (next to the beach); tel: 3253. 20 clean, simple rooms in duplex cottages. Has a restaurant and bar.

Inexpensive

Holiday Beach Resort. Candolim Beach, Bardez; tel: 88. 22 simple rooms (not air-conditioned). Has a restaurant, bar, and beach.

Sukh Sagar Beach Resort. Colva Beach, Colva (next to the beach); tel: 21888. 19 simple rooms (five air-conditioned). Has a restaurant and room service.

Tourist Cottages. Colva Beach (next to the beach); tel: 22287. (Run by Goa Tourist Development Corporation, contact Manager, Travel Division, Goa Tourism Development Corporation, Ltd., Tourist Hostel, Panaji, Goa.) Simple, clean, and cheap.

Tourist Resort. Calangute Beach, Goa; tel. 24. Also run by the Goa Tourism Development Corporation, Ltd.; contact manager at the same address. Simple, clean, and cheap.

Tourist Cottages. Farmagudi, Ponda (15 miles from the beach); tel. 177. Hilly serene location inland. New cottages, each with a fan and an Indian-style bathroom (Rs. 45).

Vagator Beach Resort. Fort Chapora, Vagator, Bardes; tel. 41. 30 clean, double-room cottages with attached baths. Friendly and helpful staff. Restaurant. Off-season rates from July to October.

 DINING OUT. Goan food is a taste feast. Portuguese dishes have been adapted with Indian Goan zest: a healthy pinch of red chili tempered with coconut milk. Excellent seafood—like pomfret *recheiado* in a red or green sauce or tiger prawns *baffad* (spicy-Goan style). Try squid, sardines, and stuffed fried oysters. The catch will be fresh if it's offered, and these dishes are not the same prepared anywhere else. Also, try *Feni,* the local brew, but watch out! It packs a punch. Prices depend on what you choose to eat. Shrimp is expensive; other fish dishes are not.

Most hotel dining rooms have mixed menus of Goan, Indian, and Continental foods, with price ranges according to their category—*Expensive,* Rs. 60 and up; *Moderate,* Rs. 25–60; and *Inexpensive,* less than Rs. 25. For out-of-hotel dining, you might try something from the following selection:

Expensive

Coconut Inn. Condolim (no phone). Great food and charming atmosphere in an old Goan-Portuguese interior filled with antiques.

Moderate

Beach House. Taj Village, Sinquerim, Bardez; tel. 4415. A Goan beach shack off the beach, with Goan and Indian cuisine; live music.

Goenchin. Dr. Dada Vaidya Road, Panaji, near Mahalaxmi Temple; tel. 5718. Typical Chinese food, with decor to match.

O Coqueiro Bar and Restaurant. Porverrim; tel. 5671. Excellent Goan restaurant with indoor-outdoor garden decor.

O Pescador. Dona Paula; tel. 4255. Fine Goan seafood.

HOW TO GET AROUND. Once you're in Goa, take advantage of the state's greatest natural resource: water. **Ferries** cross the Zuari River and the Mandovi River between Panaji and Betim while the new bridge is under repair. These ferries are usually crowded and slow paced, but picturesque and relaxing. Most of these ferries also carry cars. **Buses,** operated by *Kadamba Transport Corporation,* run between the main towns. Yellow-topped metered taxis are available in most central areas and from most hotels (Rs. 3.50 for the first km). Goa also has the standard **auto rickshaw** (Rs. 2 for the first km) plus the novel **motorcycle taxi** for the lone passenger. With all taxis and rickshaws, luggage fees and detention charges are extra. The standard waiting fee for a taxi is Rs. 6 per hour; for a rickshaw, Rs. 3.

Tourist taxis (luxury, air-conditioned and non-air-conditioned cars) can be hired from most hotels or from the Travel Division, *Goa, Daman, and Diu Tourism Development Corporation, Ltd.,* Tourist Hotel, Panaji; tel. 3396 or 3903.

Goa is a great state for leisurely **biking.** Bicycles are for hire at most public beaches in most towns, or ask at your hotel.

SEASONAL EVENTS. A religious feast is usually a great excuse to sing, dance, and hold a village fair. Goans love music; you ought to hear a *mando*—not quite a waltz and not quite a Portuguese *fado,* but with strains of both. What follows is a list of Goa's unusual festivals (most of them Christian):

January 6—*Feast of the Three Kings* at Reis Magos, Cuelim and Chandor.

February 2—Feast of Our Lady of Candelaria at Pomburpa.

Three days before Lent—*Carnival,* Goa's best party, with costumes, floats, music, and dancing. Unfortunately, in the last few years, this party has been subject to cancelation because of political disturbances.

Fifth Monday in Lent—*Procession of All Saints of the Franciscan Third Order,* another colorful procession of 40 statues of saints paraded through Old Goa—the only such procession held outside Rome.

August 24—*Festival of Novidades,* an offering of the first sheaves of the rice crop to the head of state.

August/September—Ganesh Chaturthi, a festive celebration of the birthday of Ganesh, the elephant-headed god.

October/November—*Deepawali,* the fireworks-and-all start of the Hindu New Year.

December 3—*Feast of St. Francis Xavier,* Patron saint of Goa at Old Goa.

December 8—*Feast of Our Lady of Immaculate Conception* at Panaji and Margao.

December 25—Christmas all over Goa.

HISTORIC SITES. The Director of Tourism has a list of old Goan houses with antique furniture and *objets d'art* that are privately owned but available for viewing on request. Contact the main office of the tourist department well in advance of your trip (see address under *Tourist Information*). If the cultural mood takes over suddenly, you can see the following churches and temples, at almost any time, sunrise to sunset.

Old Goan Churches. *Basilica of Nom Jesus* (sixteenth century), with the remains of St. Francis Xavier. *Se Cathedral* (1562–1652), dedicated to St. Catherine and the largest of the old churches. Richly embellished interior. *Church of St. Francis of Assisi* (1661), simple harmonious structure. Exquisite carvings and paintings. *Chapel of St. Catherine* (1510), constructed by Albuquerque to commemorate his arrival in Old Goa. *St. Cajetan Church* (seventeenth century), modeled on the design of St. Peter's Basilica in Rome.

Temples. *Shri Manguesh* (22 km from Panaji) in Ponda. Dedicated to Shiva; colorful interior. *Shri Mahalsa* (one km from Manguesh) The deity worshiped is Mohini, a reincarnation of Vishnu. *Shri Mahadeva* at Tambdi Surla (66 km from Panaji) in the foot of the Ghats. Only thirteenth-century temple remaining in Goa.

Mosque. *Safa Shahouri Masjid,* at Ponda, built in 1560.

MUSEUMS. Goa is not a museum-rich state, unless you define the term loosely and include the old churches and temples. But while seeing the churches, visit the *Archaeological Museum and Portrait Gallery* in Old Goa. The museum contains numerous sculptures of the early and late medieval periods collected around Goa, including friezes depicting self-immolation. The Portrait Gallery displays the portraits of the Portuguese rulers. There are also religious paintings on canvas and wood. Open 10 A.M.–noon; 1–5 P.M.; closed Fridays. Free.

WILDLIFE SANCTUARIES. There are three sanctuaries in Goa, all providing a day away from too much sand and surf. The *Bhagwan Mahaver Sanctuary* is the biggest (240 km) in Molem about 30–40 km due east of Margao. Thick forests with bison, cobra, python, deer, langurs (monkeys), and the elusive panther (don't expect to see one). It's also well populated by a rich variety of birds (crested serpent eagle, brown fish owl, green pigeon, shrike).

The *Bondla Sanctuary* is also a jungle resort (20 km northeast of Molem). A great sanctuary for kids or the "kid" in all of us, with minizoos, a deer park, wilderness trail, and elephant ride.

The *Cotigao Wildlife Sanctuary* is on the southeastern edge of Goa. Set in a hilly, forested terrain, it protects the same animals as does the Bhagwaver Sanctuary.

BEACHES. At *Miramar,* close to Panaji, watch the stiff undertow and avoid looking at the "modern" backdrop of concrete high rises. *Dona Paula,* also near Panaji, is palm-fringed with fine views of Mormugoa Harbor. *Calangute Beach,* across the Mandovi River in the Bardez district, is the "Queen of Goa (public) Beaches," with 16 km of sand. It includes the Basa, Anjuna, and Vagator beaches (each progressively farther north). The northern end of Goa is backed by dramatic cliffs for great sunset viewing. *Colva Beach,* south of Panaji and directly west of Margao, has long stretches of beautiful sand.

NIGHTLIFE AND BARS. Most hotels and resorts have their own bars. They usually close by midnight. Outside the hotels, try the *Haystack,* Arpora, near Anjuna Beach. Open every Friday evening from 8:30 until late; party atmosphere in a garden; Goan buffet dinner (that sometimes also features German goulash). Portuguese, Goan, and Spanish dancing and singing.

KARNATAKA

Oriental Splendor and Hindu Rococo

by
KATHLEEN COX

Within the borders of Karnataka (formerly Mysore), you can find the most colorful and most fascinating aspects of India, plus an occasional high level of comfort that can be Orientally sumptuous and Occidentally efficient. Although the lowlands can be hot in the summer, the plateau of Karnataka is situated at an angle where two mountain ranges converge into the beautiful Nilgiri Hills. One visit to this part of the state explains why Karnataka is called "the emerald land." It's green and gorgeous, with lush rice paddies and gentle sloping hills. The hill climate is pleasant and warm—in some places bracing—and even the rains that start in May are not the nonstop torrents experienced elsewhere, but quick showers are immediately followed by blue skies. There are rivers and waterfalls; forests filled with wild game and precious woods like teak, ebony, and sandalwood; and flowers everywhere. Much of the northern areas of Karnataka, at a superficial glance, seem right out of the American West—scrubby, near-barren land, studded with enormous boulders and dramatic craggy hills. However, your first sighting of a historic temple, tomb, or ancient fort reminds you that this is the exotic Indian subcontinent.

Karnataka, the size of New England, probably has been inhabited as long as anywhere else on earth. Thousand-year-old Hindu temples, decorated with carvings of amazing virtuosity; grandiose Moslem monuments; remains of lost civilizations; and some excellent modern city planning are just a few of the reasons to visit.

The scenes of village life are bound to linger. The 40 million people of Karnataka, called Kannadigas after their language known as Kannada, are sinewy and robust. Colorfully dressed women wait patiently to fill their jugs with water at the village fountain, which is also the social center.

The men, often scantily dressed in *longhis* (loin cloths) and *dhotis* (shirtlike garments), work in the fields walking slowly behind buffalo dragging plows that have not changed much in 3,000 years. In Karnataka, the climate makes it possible to live perpetually outdoors—the huts in the villages are often of rudimentary construction, and people think nothing of setting up their beds outside. Throughout much of the central and northern part of this exotic state, you encounter the delightful tribal nomads, the Lambanis—the women strutting their hips and wearing gay layered, mirror-covered, bejewelled skirts and blouses, and heavy silver jewelry on their ears, necks, fingers, arms, feet, and ankles.

The simplicity of the country is one extreme balanced by another: the grand palaces and formal gardens; the splendor of such festivals like Dussehra; and the relics of centuries of royal living—Hindu and Moslem. Scattered throughout the state in places like Belur, Halebid, Hampi, Aihole, Pattodkal, and Badami, you find some of the best religious monuments in India.

Parts of Karnataka are geologically among the oldest formations in the world. People have lived here at least 10,000 years, probably longer. And, because they have had little geographic possibility or incentive to move beyond their frontiers, they've remained faithful to the traditions of their forefathers. The state's history is intimately entwined in the great epic, the *Ramayana*. After India's first great emperor, Chandragupta Maurya, embraced Jainism, he retired to Shravarabelacola, renouncing all worldly possessions, including his empire. Many of the great names of India's early history, like the Cholas and the Gangas, ruled parts of Karnataka. Saints and philosophers followed each other on this auspicious soil. The Hoysala Dynasty (A.D. 1000–1300) was the first to control all of what is now modern Karnataka. They were great builders, creating the magnificent temples at Somnathpur, Belur, and Halebid. The Moslem hordes swept in here, too, with the Hoysala capital at Dwarasumudra (the modern Halebid) sacked by Malik Kapul in 1310 and again by Mohammed-bin-Tughlaq in 1327.

Power continued to swing back and forth between the Hindus and the Moslems. Vijayanagar, whose ruins are at Hampi, was Hindu; other places like Bijapur remained resolutely Moslem. Taking advantage of the general chaos, Hyder Ali, an adventurous commander-in-chief of the army, engineered a successful *coup d'etat* in 1761 and grabbed control. Then he and his son, Tipu Sultan, humbled the British who had their own expansionary plans. The two men added to the province (with the help of the French) and ruled it from Sriangapatna. In 1799, the British bounced back with a vengeance. Taking control, they eventually returned sovereignty to the old Hindu Dynasty in the person of Sri Krishnaraja Wadiyar III, ancestor of the last maharajah, who set up his capital in Mysore City. This family provided an unbroken line of enlightened rulers who made modern Karnataka a model state. The last maharajah was so popular that the new Republic of India retained him as the state's governor.

KARNATAKA

0   miles   100

0   km   100

N

MAHARASHTRA

Solapur

Bidar

Gulbarga

TO
HYDERABAD

ANDHRA PRADESH

Bijapur

Badami

Aihole

Pattadakal

Belgaum

GOA

Dharwar

Hampi

Hospet

Karwar

*Magod
Falls*

*Gokarna
Beach*

Kumta

Harihar

Chitradurga

*Jog
Falls*

Coondapur

Malpe

Sringeri

Belur

Helebid

*Nandi
Hills*

TO
MADRAS

Hassan

Bangalore

Mangalore

Mercara

Sravanabelagola

Srirangapatna

Somnathapura

Mysore

Sivasamudram

Talkad

Nagarhole

Arabian Sea

KERALA

Bandipur

Coimbatore

TAMIL NADU

EXPLORING KARNATAKA

Bangalore

Bangalore is a flourishing city of over three million inhabitants, capital of the state, an industrial center, and a garden spot. So little of Bangalore is old that at the end of the 1500s, nothing was there but a mud fort and a small bull temple, both built by a chieftain and founder of Mysore, Kempe Gowda, in the 1500s. The bull temple is reminiscent of the Dravidian style and contains a gigantic monolith of Nandi (15 feet high and 20 feet long). The mud fort was rebuilt in stone by Hyder Ali in the 1700s. It's in ruins today.

With the city and suburbs well planned in advance, Bangalore is not a sprawling, confused place. It feels orderly, serene, and regal, especially when you see the Vidhana Soudha, on the northern boundary of Cubbon Park. A sprawling white granite structure built in the neo-Dravidian style in 1956, it houses the State Legislature and the Secretariat. Permission is required to go inside. Bangalore is also the site of the prestigious Indian Institute of Science, established with the philanthropy of the Tata family (India's Rockefellers). In short, Bangalore is a snazzy city where Western-style luxuries such as a drive-in movie, 15 flavors of ice cream, and video game arcades exist, but with an Eastern flair.

Bangalore's charm peeks through tree-shaded gardens, manicured lawns, and ever-blooming fragrant flowers. The beautiful 240-acre botanical Lal Bagh Gardens, designed by Hyder Ali and Tipu Sultan, are landscaped with a variety of centuries-old trees, fountains, lotus pools, terraces, a Japanese garden, and an assortment of tropical and subtropical herbs and plants spread out over several acres. The huge Glass House at Lal Bagh is also the delightful arena for special exhibits.

Nandi Hills

The Nandi Hills, 37 miles from Bangalore, witnessed numerous savage battles for centuries. Now it's a much-appreciated health and pleasure resort. Two 1,000-year-old Shiva temples grace the charming landscape: one at the foot and the other at the top of the hill, and four rivers have their source here. Back in the 1700s, Tipu Sultan made these hills the site of his summer palace. Take a walk to Tipu's Drop, a 2,000-foot sheer cliff. Here, condemned criminals met a grisly fate—they were pushed over the edge.

Mysore

An excellent 85-mile-road leads from Bangalore to Mysore, the city of palaces. On the way, you pass through country strewn with strange-shaped boulders and pass near Ramnagar, the site of an experimental center for rural health, and Channapatna, which produces lacquered toys and spun silk. Finally, you reach the city of palaces, gardens, and Oriental splendor.

Mysore is 2,493 feet above sea level. No longer the official capital, it survives, nonetheless, as the principal residence of the former royal family, which makes it every inch a princely city. Mysore, beautifully planned and executed, gives little evidence of the crushing poverty so often associated with India. When you see what the maharajas accomplished in the way of public service, you will understand why his highness was appointed the first governor of Karnataka.

Maharajah's Palace

By far the most impressive Mysore building is the Maharajah's Palace, a massive edifice that took 15 years to build (started in 1857 on the site of the former wooden palace destroyed by fire). Here the Oriental decorative imagination runs wild. The palace, one of the biggest of its kind in India, is in the Indo-Sarcenic style—a gigantic synthesis of Hindu and Islamic architecture. Entrance gateways, domes, arches, turrets, colonnades, lovely Hoysola-like carvings, glittering chandeliers, and etched window panes—are all in magnificent profusion. On Sundays and holidays, the palace is illuminated with thousands of tiny lights that turn the palace into a glittering statement of wealth.

Inside the palace, you can see a few of the royal family's private rooms, plus the impressive Durbar Hall (*Durbar* is a feudal term for receiving the nobility). This hall is an elegant preservation of history, with its ornate ceilings and huge "grandstand" awning that overlooks the great court. The Marriage Hall (Kalyana Mandap), where the women sat behind screened balconies, has lifelike paintings of the Dussehra procession, and in the museum is the solid gold howdah (elephant throne) that the maharajah used during the festivals and other ceremonial occasions.

Public Buildings

Everything seems palatial in Mysore, even if the building in question turns out to be the Maternity Hospital, the Technical Institute, or even the Railway Office. The city's central square—Statue Square—just across from the palace, houses the marble effigy of the last maharajah's grandfather and predecessor, standing beneath a golden domed canopy.

Mysore also has an enjoyable wholesale bazaar (Devraja Market) near Krishnaraja Circle—a covered market of manageable size, with rows of hanging bananas, displays of other fruit, vegetables, and flowers galore, plus all the other foodstuffs India offers. It's bustling, noisy, and lots of fun.

Lalitha Mahal

As you head out of the center of Mysore toward Chamundi Hill, you see a dignified white edifice called the Lalitha Mahal, built in 1921 by the Wadiyars to house distinguished foreign guests. The palace has now joined the legion of those royal residences that have been converted into hotels, a second life that allows the mere ordinary, Indian, and foreign to taste some of that grandeur earlier reserved for royalty. These palaces are usually in superb locations, and the Lalitha Mahal is no exception. The interior is equally becoming a magnificent lofty dining hall with stained-glass dome, and an Italian marble staircase that is sublime.

Chamundi Hill

Continue to Chamundi Hill, named after the royal family's patron goddess, Chamundi. A good road leads to the top, but if you're spry and eager for exercise, climb the thousand steps (three centuries old).

About two-thirds of the way up is a 16-foot Nandi (Shiva's holy bull), constructed in the 1600s from a single piece of granite, including the garlands and bell around his neck.

The view from the top of the hill is superb: a beautiful panorama of all Mysore and the surrounding hills, lakes, and turrets of temples and churches. The Sri Chamundeswari Temple is dedicated to the royal Wadiyar family's titular deity. The base of the temple, dating back to the twelfth century, was supposedly built by the founders of Mysore; the ornately sculptured pyramidal tower was constructed in the 1800s. Next to the temple is the giant statue of Monster Mahishasura (Mysore is named after him), who was killed by goddess Chamundi, bringing peace to the country. Here he stands, built in mortar about 35 years ago, with sword and snake held aloof in each hand.

If possible, time your visit to Mysore to coincide with the 10-day Dussehra festival (September/October). The city is at its best, clothed in color, light, and joy. This is the same major Hindu celebration feted under different names all over India, but here it is a royal as well as a popular festival. The pomp, grandeur, and ceremony are not to be missed. Until a few years ago, the late maharajah sat on his jeweled throne every night of Duesehra; on the tenth day, he left the palace in a royal procession seated in his golden howdah atop a magnificently caparisoned elephant. The maharajah's son does not take part in the parade, but the infantry, cavalry, and camel corps still do. The torch-light and daylight parades are unique. *Theppotsava,* the worship of deities on decorated barges afloat in a flood-lit lake, is magical.

Brindavan Gardens

Only 12 miles northwest of Mysore are the Brindavan Gardens that extend in terraces beneath the Krishnarajasagar Dam, which anyone except possibly Louis XIV would compare favorably with Versailles. The place started life functionally—as an irrigation dam at the confluence of three rivers. The dam is 1¼ miles long and forms a 50-square-mile lake. It is constructed entirely in stone and crushed bricks and is ornamented with parapets and a niche for the river goddess. Even though the dam is one of the biggest in India, it commands only slight attention next to the gardens, exquisitely designed and alive with bright flowers and silvery fountains. An excellent time to go is at night, when the gardens are illuminated and hundreds of fountains and pools of all colors, sizes, and shapes bring out the best. (But beware of traffic jams.)

Srirangapatna

Srirangapatna is an island fortress between two branches of the Cauvery River and the former capital of the Mysore rajahs from 1610 to 1799. Hyder Ali and Tipu Sultan were its most famous residents. For 180 years, all this area of India was in a constant battle for control. The first to succeed were the British, on the fourth try in 1799, when Tipu Sultan lost his life in the skirmish.

Visit the fort and its imposing surroundings. The Moslems lived cheek to jowl with two Hindu temples, one of which, the Sri Ranganatha, is about 1,000 years old. Here, you can see the dungeons where captured British officers were imprisoned. The "Breach" marks the place where the British finally smashed through the fortifications and entered the town; the Water Gate was Tipu's last stand. See the ruins of Tipu's fortified palaces near the old parade grounds and the sultan's favorite mosque, the Juma Masjid, with its twin minarets. The top of the minarets offer a good view of the fort and another glimpse of Mysore.

Without doubt, the best monuments are outside the fort: Tipu's summer pleasure palaces (he indulged himself) and his mausoleum, the Gumbas.

Daria Daulat Bagh

The Daria Daulat Bagh Palace, set in a charming garden, doesn't look so impressive from the outside. Once inside, you'll think otherwise; there are carved ornate arches, liberally gilded wall panels, eighteenth-century colored frescoes. On the right of the entrance, you see Hyder Ali and Tipu riding at the head of their troops. On the left, there's a vain reminder of the victorious first battle against the British. All along the walls, in tiered bands, are scenes from the happy lives of the ruling Moslem nabobs obviously enjoying the comfort of their palaces, holding court, or simply looking important. These warmly colored frescoes are good sized, easier to admire than the Persian miniatures they closely resemble.

Gumbaz

About a mile from the palace is the Gumbaz, a beautiful monument to the preference of the Moslem rulers for taking their eternal rest in lavish style, too. In the center of a garden stands the cream-colored Gumbaz on its black marble pillars. The pillars support the lowest tier of the monument: a balconylike wall, delicately and minutely carved, surmounted at the four corners by miniature minerals. Above the veranda formed by the columns and this balcony is another tier, ornamented with arches and a carved plinth that, in turn, supports a third tier repeating the theme of the first on a larger scale—the whole crowned by a bulbous dome.

The interior is lacquered with Tipu's tiger-stripe emblem, and the doors are of ebony inlaid with ivory. Next to the elegant Gumbaz is a prayer hall in the same style.

Karapur Forest and Nagarhole National Park

An infamous event occurred in Karnataka in years past called *Khedda*, or "Operation Wild Elephant." The big pachyderms of Karnataka, considered the handsomest and strongest of the breed, were in great demand by maharajahs and princes who could afford them, circuses, zoos, and people wanting efficient working animals for construction projects. The arena for these roundups was in the Karapur forest, 49 miles south of Mysore, with the opponents—swarms of skilled tribesmen—against a herd of trumpeting mammoths.

Much of this area has now been flooded by a new dam, and kheddas are in decline. But in their time, they provided one of the most overwhelming spectacles of India. Hundreds of forest tribesmen would stalk the elephants. To the frenzied commotion of villagers beating bamboo poles against empty tins, drums, or gongs and with clouds of thick smoke billowing around them, the elephants would become dazed and frightened, moving unknowingly toward the trap set for them in the Kabini River. Once captured, they were trained.

Today, instead of the sight of animals in terror, you can watch wild elephants—untrapped and untamed—moving in peaceful security around the same forests. Kabini River Lodge, a joint venture between Tiger Tops India and the government of Karnataka, is a terrific resort at Karapur. Visitors stay in the renovated Victorian hunting bungalows of the maharajah of Mysore and the British viceroy. Excellent game-viewing tours by jeep take you through the Nagarhole National Park, with Colonel Wakefield and his staff skillful at stalking the wild beasts. Here, you're likely to spot the rare Indian gaur (bison), wild boar, sambar, barking deer, families of elephants (mothers, calves, "aunt" elephants, and tuskers), and maybe a leopard or tiger. You also have the unusual chance to paddle along the waterways in a *coracle,* a round, basket-shaped boat lined with buffalo hide. Coracles are so slow and quiet that you can approach very close to the families of wild animals and the abundance of birdlife (over 225 different species).

Sravanabelgola

Sixty-two miles north of Mysore is Sravanabelgola, presided over and dominated by the colossal statue of the Jain saint Gomateshwara. His monolithic image, 57 feet tall, watched over pilgrims for 1,000 years, ever since the time of the Ganga kings under whose patronage Jainism flourished. The religion has declined now in numeric importance, but the statue reminds us of its principles: Gomateshwara's nakedness suggests renunciation of all worldly things, and the still posture indicates perfect self-control. The gigantic image rises atop one of Shravanabelgola's two hills, Indragiri, where many smaller statues and a beautiful temple also stand. A rock-hewn stairway of 614 steps leads to the summit and the monolith, which is 26 feet across the shoulders and sports a 10-foot waistline, and 9-foot-long feet. As one critic said: "There is nothing grander or more imposing anywhere out of Egypt, and even there, no known statue surpasses it in height." Every 12 years, Jains from all over India gather here for the spectacular bathing festival where priests clamber up specially built scaffolding to pour hundreds of pots of 16 substances over Gomateshwara's head, including milk curds, honey, rice, fruit, and even gold and silver coins and precious jewels. The last festival was celebrated in February 1981.

Belur

Between Sravanabelgola and Hassan (35 miles), there is grassland and woodland that will make any New Englander or Englander feel right at home. From Hassan, it is only 22 miles through lush tropical landscapes to Belur, a flourishing city under the Hoysala kings during the twelfth century. The frontier-style town boasts only one reminder of that splendid time—but what a reminder! The Belur Temple of Lord Channakeshava, still a functioning temple dedicated to this Vishnu incarnate, stands almost as perfectly preserved as the day it was completed. (Started in 1116 by the Hoysala King Vishnuvardhana, it was completed 103 years later.) Legend claims that when Moslem conquerers came to Belur to destroy the temple, they left it alone, overawed by its magnificence.

Carved of soapstone, the Belur temple is like Somnathpur in design: star shaped, with the squat temple set on a platform. It is also flat on top, without Somnathpur's suggestion of a spire. Superbaroque Belur is a contemporary of Chartres, with more in common than meets the eye. In both cases, the patience of the anonymous medieval artisans seems infinite. Although each monument serves a different religion, they both share the desire to instruct the faithful through the only means open to them at the time: the image. At Belur we find gods and goddesses in all their varied aspects and incarnations and scenes from the great Indian religion epics. But, perhaps because the Indian's natural state is more religious, without the Westerner's tendency to separate religion from the realities of life, we also find hunters, dancers, musicians, and beautiful women dressing and adorning themselves.

Except at the bottom of the temple, the friezes are not as long and continuous as those of Somnathpur, and a series of semi-detached pillars and ornamented porches lend greater variety to the facade. The plan of the temple is the traditional porch-vestibule-shrine. The shrine has three doorways on the east, south, and north, with the eastern the loveliest of all. A railed parapet sculpted with eight exquisite friezes runs along the side of this doorway. On the rail to the right of the door are epic scenes and tiny musicians seated here and there. Above these ornamental rails are about 20 pierced stone windows showing a variety of scenes or geometric designs. The jambs of the northern doorways are carved with female bearers, and to the northeast is a chain of destruction: a double-headed eagle attacking a mythical beast that is going for a lion that is clawing an elephant that is seizing a snake that is swallowing a rat—followed by a sage pondering the entire spectacle. The southern doorway is crowded with gods, demons, and animals. Beyond the railed parapet are about 80 fine-chiseled separate images of goddesses. Each entrance is flanked by two pavilions with carved figures and at the sides, the crest of the Hoysalas: Sala, their ancestor, stabbing a stylized tiger.

Back in the center of the temple, notice the domed ceiling supported by four pillars—a majestic lotus bud with depictions of scenes from the *Ramayana*. Notice, too, the sculptures of the women at the top of the four pillars. Some of the jewelry they wear can be moved: the bracelets on an arm and a head ornament. The women are beautiful, voluptuous, full breasted, and full hipped, taking any number of graceful poses beneath the intricately pierced, scrolled, and scalloped stone canopies.

The nineteenth-century architect and critic, James Fergusson, summed up Belur this way: "These friezes . . . carved with a minute elaboration of detail . . . are one of the most marvelous exhibitions of human labor to be found even in the patient East. Here the artistic combination of horizontal with vertical and the play of outline and of light and shade far surpass anything in Gothic art." South of the main temple, a smaller shrine built over a period of 250 years, the Channigaraya Temple, is worth a good look. The other remaining Hoysala temple (Viranarayana) has rows of very fine images on its outer walls.

Halebid

A few miles from Belur is its sister temple at Halebid. The Hoysaleswara Temple was constructed a decade after Belur by the same king but left uncompleted after 180 years of labor. It, too, is a star-shaped plan but a double-shrine temple. At Halebid the sculptor's virtuosity reaches its peak—one can't "explain" this carving, but it is possible to say that these artists were able to treat stone like wood or ivory. One reason, apart from patience and talent, was that they worked in soft soapstone, which hardens with time. The friezes are breathtaking; first comes a row of elephants for stability, then one of lordly lions, then convoluting scrolls of swift horses. Above more scroll work are scenes from the religious epics that not only present philosophical ideas but mirror the living conditions of the time. Mythical beasts and swans follow. The largest frieze is also the most exuberant; based on a heavenly theme, it gives heavenly results. Here are the *apsarasis* or celestial maidens, clothed in jewels, with bracelets on each arm—sometimes they have as many as six arms. Sitting or standing in graceful postures under pierced canopies, the maidens are eight centuries old, yet eternally young. The walls are also graced by small turrets, beadwork cornices, columns and by what many consider Halebid's *pièce de résistance:* the entire Hindu pantheon brought to life in stone. Many of these carvings are on the west façade and include not only the gods and goddesses but many of their incarnations and such curious deities as Ganesh, the elephant god, with his papal-like tiara. There are 280 figures, mostly feminine, that rival the best in Gothic art.

Also take a look at the smaller Kedareswara Temple whose friezes are similar to the other's and executed with equal finesse. There is, in addition, a relatively unadorned early Jain temple, dedicated to Parsvanatha, whose finally polished pillars serve as fancy mirrors.

Sringeri

From Halebid, either head straight for the ancient temple city of Hampi, or, if time permits and your soul wants a break for reflection, meander there via Sringeri, Jog Falls (if they're running), and the district of Coorg. The road passes through majestic forest scenery. Then you arrive at Sringeri, situated on the bank of the Tunga River and scenically beautiful. Sringeri is also an important center of pilgrimage. Here St. Sankaracharya established a monastery to protect Hinduism (from the advance of Islam) and to help establish the Vijayanagar empire. In the lovely fourteenth-century Vidya Shankara temple, 12 zodiac pillars are so arranged that the sun's rays fall on the pillar that corresponds to that month. And the statuesque stone lions have stone balls inside the mouth. You can rotate them but cannot pull them out.

After passing through Sringeri, continue toward Jog Falls. You cross the river Sharavati, which leaps over an 800-foot precipice in four separate waterfalls—the "four R's." The "Rajah" is the grandest; halfway down, the violent "Roarer" meets it; close to them are the "Rocket," which is a multistaged one, and the "Rani," or Queen, which glides gracefully over the cliff. The columns of foam and spray created by all four of them make Jog Falls a myriad of prisms by day and hauntingly beautiful by moonlight.

One point: the falls are part of a hydroelectric scheme, so check that they will be "switched on" at the time of your visit.

Coorg

The mountainous area next to Kerala is Coorg, a former vest-pocket state of about 1,500 square miles and one of the greenest areas of Karnataka. Its 300,000 people are ethnically distinct. You wind your way through forests, coffee plantations, orange gardens and rice fields, frequently seeing no one for miles. Viewed from an elevation, the hills roll away in the blue haze of the distant horizon. Coorgis (called Kodavas), are handsome strong people who claim descent from legendary warriors. They're among the most adaptable and literate people in India.

Mercara is the capital, a quiet provincial town with a fortress and a temple looking over it from the hill. Hindu pilgrims consider the source of the Cauvery river at Talakaveri a place of great sanctity. Others will find it beautiful, too.

The West Coast railroad ends at Mangalore, the world's principal cashew-nut port. From here it's an hour's drive to Mudbidri and Karkal, housing remarkable Jain carvings and giant stone images. Farther up the coast is the modest seaside resort of Karwar, a good spot for salmon fishing (August–October).

Vijayanagar—Hampi

Across the center of Karnataka, northeast toward Hampi, is a different kind of tranquility—the tranquility of departed spirits. If you like ruins—not the battered fort or the tottering temple or even the Pompeii-like state of suspended animation—but real desolation that has you quoting Shelley:

> My name is Ozymandias, King of Kings
> Look on my works, ye Mighty, and despair!
> Nothing beside remains, round the decay
> Of that colossal wreck, boundless and bare
> The lone and level sands stretch far away . . . .

Then see Hampi (Vijayanagar).

In this once-proud city of Vijayanagar, the vista is extensive plains interrupted by red hills with craggy boulders, precariously balanced. But in all other respects the story is the same: Hampi is the shell of a colossal empire. The brilliance of Vijayanagar from the fourteenth to the mid-sixteenth century accentuates the debacle. Travelers then found it "as large as Rome" and "the best provided city in the world." And so well protected—surrounded by the turbulent Tungabhadra River and rocky ridges. Most notable of its rulers was Krishnadeva Raya (1509–29) whose military prowess, lavish hospitality, and love for the arts made him known beyond the confines of India.

Unfortunately, the reigning rajahs were continually at war with the Moslem sultanates of the Deccan, who eventually combined against the Hindu kingdom. Enormous armies clashed in 1565 north of the capital. A few hours of fighting was enough to destroy the place. Ramaraja, the last of a great dynasty, was decapitated. The city lost its life, too.

Plan at least a day to wander through Hampi. The ruins, spread over almost 15 square miles, include temples, palaces, baths, and pavilions. All of Hampi's architecture is in perfect harmony with its natural surroundings, blending into the hills, rocks, caves, and rivers. The most sacred buildings are on either side of the Tungabhadra River or on the peaks of the surrounding hills.

The Virupaksha Temple

The Virupaksha Temple, dedicated to Shiva and now considered the most sacred structure in Hampi, is still active—active with monkeys, too. When the bells are rung early morning and evening, the critters race into the interior courtyard for food. The temple, completed in the sixteenth century, has a nine-story goporam at one end of the formerly world-famous Hampi Bazaar that once sold heaps of precious jewels and diamonds. At the opposite end of the bazaar is a pavilion containing a destroyed Nandi.

On the surrounding hills are more temple complexes, including the Matanga Hill Temple, dedicated to a ferocious aspect of Shiva. This hill gives a good view of the original Hampi layout. Just below the hill and on the river bank is the Kodandarama Temple, which contains an image of Rama and is considered to be the most sacred bathing ghat on the Tungabhadra.

Vitthala Temple Complex

The most famous and imposing single complex, to be saved for a lingering visit at sunset, is the Vitthala Temple complex, the highest glory of Vijayanagara architecture. Constructed in the sixteenth century and dedicated to Vishnu, the walled rectangular courtyard contains the renowned chariot with lotus-shaped wheels: the entire vehicle intricately carved from a single granite stone.

Notice, too, the Vitthala Temple, with the elephant balustrades, and horses on the entrance columns, and its exquisite hall of imaginatively carved musical pillars, each hewn from a single stone. With the tap of the hand, each pillar duplicates the sound of a specific instrument. Music used to fill the temple—singing and dancing at sunrise and sunset. The sacred dancing was performed in the other detached hall in the southern part of the courtyard, its numerous columns all intricately carved.

Hazara Rama Complex

The other interesting temple complex takes you away from the sacred center of Hampi to the royal center, farther away from the river. This temple, in a rectangular compound, is called the Hazara Rama and is also dedicated to Vishnu. The Hazara Rama was for the private worship of the king. Surrounding this temple are the ruins of numerous civic buildings, royal residences, wells, aqueducts, and gigantic tanks. Of these, don't miss the Lotus Pavilion, the Queen's Bath, and the Elephant's Stables still in a reasonable state of repair.

As you leave Hampi and head for the bustling little city of Hospet, keep in mind as you enter the level plains that you have also entered the suburban area of the former empire. Little remains of this area—most of the dwellings for the common folk were built of wood, mud, or other perishable materials. Only a few temples have survived.

Belgaum, Badami, Aihole, and Pattadakal

On the way from Hampi to Bijapur is Belgaum, which dates back to the twelfth century, and to its east, a group of three enchanting villages: Badami, Aihole, and Pattadakal, glories of post-Gupta architecture (sixth to eighth centuries).

Belgaum's main attraction is its two Jain temples, heavy-looking, squat affairs. The first has a low wall at the entrance, carved with figures of musicians and a façade relieved with pillars and pilasters. The second has a low pyramidal roof that looks like an intricate layer cake and pillars with floral ornamentation. There is also an oval stone fort and a sixteenth-century mosque at Belgaum.

The three tiny temple hamlets of Badami, Aihole, and Pattadakal are off the beaten path, but what a peaceful trip they provide through simple yet exquisite villages that are the epitome of pastorale. The only intense or noisy gatherings crop up at the occasional "shandy" (market), usually held once a week on the outskirts of a tiny town. Villagers come from miles around to sell livestock, fruits, vegetables, clay pots, dried fish, colorful powders and spices, soaps, and incense. If you happen upon a shandy, stop and wander through; they're lots of fun.

Badami, a charming village and the former second capital of the Chalukyas, is nestled between red sandstone hills. The cave temples may not surprise anyone who has seen Ajanta-Ellora, but they should astound everyone else. All these temples were hewn out of solid rock, some as early as A.D. 550. And their setting is magical: carved into hills above a lovely reservoir with quaint, tiny temples dotting the edge. The four most important caves follow a set plan: a veranda with pillars, a hall with columns, and a small cell to enshrine the deity. Though the exteriors appear simple, with borders of grotesque dwarfs, the interiors are remarkable.

The first cave, possibly the earliest, is dedicated to Shiva and burrows deep into the rock. Dwarfs decorate the front of the veranda. Inside you see a Nandi bull (with a human body) on the left, and on the right, a unique carving of Nataraja (Shiva) as the Cosmic Dancer with 18 hands (the only one of its kind in India). The hands are so well placed that any right hand matches up with any left hand. In the panel near the Nataraja, look for Shanmukha riding a peacock. Below this image is a carving of two boys that, on close inspection, creates the illusion of four. The columns and the ceiling are so artfully turned and executed that it is hard to believe that the rock was removed from around them; this cave looks like all the others—looks constructed, not dug out.

The second cave is the smallest and is dedicated to Vishnu, with its sanctuary depicting the god's various incarnations. You see Varatha, (the boar), who rescued earth from a flood; Vishnu riding Garuda (an eagle); Vishnu as Trivikrama with one leg on the ground and the other kicked up in the air; plus Vishnu as Krishna depicted in scenes at the top of the wall.

Between the second and third caves is a path that leads to a rough excavation in which a Buddhist figure has been carved into the wall.

The third cave, also dedicated to Vishnu, is considered the finest excavation, with the same dwarfs waiting to greet you. Just inside the veranda on the left wall is an enormous image of Vishnu as Trivakrama, similar to the one in the second cave, yet the tallest of its kind in India. On the opposite wall is another huge image of Vishnu with eight hands. If you stand just inside the cave with your back to the shrine, you see, on the panel above the entrance, an image of Garuda with the beak and wings of a bird but a human face. Stand up close, it looks serious; step back, it grins. Examine all the columns covered with couples, (some of them are definitely sexy). Look for the traces of faded frescoes, the huge reliefs of Narasimha (the half-lion Vishnu incarnation) and Harihara (half-Shiva and half-Vishnu), and the image of Vishnu seated on a serpent. This is also the biggest cave, with a double row of pillars.

The final major cave is Jain and was probably built, or rather hewn, a hundred years after the others. Enshrined here are huge figures of Parasnatha (the Jain saint) and Mahavira (the founder of Jainism).

Aihole

The temples in Aihole are the oldest and most numerous: 150 shrines dating from A.D. 400 to 750, presenting the panorama of the genesis of Hindu medieval art. In an enclosure surrounding a tank, you'll find the U-shaped Durgan, the largest and most elaborately carved temple. Named for a fort, not the goddess, the Durgan is dedicated to Vishnu and was probably built in the seventh century.

The oldest temple is the Lad Khan where an eye accustomed to Hindu architecture will see much of the medieval temple form in an embryonic stage. The Suraya Naryana Temple, dedicated to the sun god, was built in the fifth or sixth centuries and contains an intriguing statue of the presiding deity surrounded by eight planets. Hit the stone in various places and it makes music. A short ride from these temples takes you to the Ravanaphadi (or Brahmanical) Cave. A carved Nandi guards the approach. Stone steps lead into the rock-cut cave with the dancing form of Shiva and other lovely statues.

Pattadakal

The temples of Pattadakal pick up where Aihole leaves off, with the evolution toward the high-towered, much-sculptured structure that is familiar in India. The sculpture, however, is not so much representative as decorative: pilasters, pillars, balconies, pierced work, and high relief of the faces of the towers. These temples are Chalyukan or Dravidian, and the best examples in each group are the Pampanath and the Virupaksha.

Bijapur

Bijapur, "The City of Victory," is a walled, medieval Moslem city boasting over 50 mosques, 20 tombs, and at least as many *mahals* (palaces). The architecture here is not the florid, overdecorated Oriental type often associated with Moslems, but Turkish—restrained and severe though grandiose in proportion.

The dominant building is the Gol Gumbaz, the vast mausoleum of Mohammed Adil Shah who ruled his kingdom from Bijapur in the seventeenth century. His mausoleum was built in the mid-1600s around the same time as the Taj Mahal. The dome of the tomb is the second largest in the world: 124 feet in diameter, with St. Peter's in Rome outdoing it by merely 15 feet. The square monument has arched entranceways on each facade and an octagonal tiered turret at each angle. The inside is severely bare except for four tall pointed arches supporting the dome. The acoustics of the enclosed space make it a remarkable whispering gallery, where any sonic message, from the flicking of a match to a shout, is repeated 12 times over.

Other monuments in Bijapur include the ornate tomb of Adil Shah's father; the Ibrahim Rauza, with its richly decorated walls and perforated stone windows; and the unfinished tomb of Ali Adil Shah. There are plenty of palaces: the Asar-I-Sharif, supposed to contain a hair of the Prophet Mohammad's beard; the Anand Mahal, where the harem lived; the Gagan Mahal, with its three magnificent arches; the Sat Manzil, a seven-story pleasure palace overlooking the city; and the Chini Mahal.

The Jama Masjid, built in 1565, is one of the finest mosques in India, remarkable for its harmonious proportions, its graceful minarets, the construction of the bulbous domes and the execution of the ornamental detail. Others are the Old Mosque, a converted Jain temple; the Andu Masjid, two-stories with a fluted dome; the miniature Makka; and the Mehtar Mahal, with its finely wrought gateway. Some of these buildings were sadly mutilated by Emperor Aurangzeb, but in spite of the ravages of time and men, Bijapur remains a splendid sight. The town is also notable for its many fine gardens.

If you're in Bijapur on Sunday, visit the Gandhi Market, where the nearby Lambanis set up shop in a center square selling colorful material and jewels. It's a photographer's paradise.

Bidar

Our last stop in Karnataka is Bidar. It is a deceptive city. The modern area is uninteresting, but head straight to the area containing the old inner fort and the inner city, the former capital of the fifteenth-century Bahmani kings. Its remarkable ruins are a monument to the time of its glory.

Spend a morning wandering through the remains of the inner fort; it should not be missed. See the beautiful Rangin Mahal (the Colorful Palace), with its small rooms and tile work; the Zanani Masjid, the oldest Moslem building in Bidar; the Gagan Mahal (Heavenly Palace), where you can meander down old stone steps into half-destroyed chambers and halls; the Royal Pavilion with more underground rooms; and the numerous other ancient constructions.

After seeing the fort, visit the nearby Bahamani Tombs of departed kings. Although not well maintained, they provide a sense of timeless grandeur. Two words of advice for Bihari: wear good walking shoes and bring a flashlight.

PRACTICAL INFORMATION FOR KARNATAKA

 WHEN TO GO. The climate here is near-tropical with warm days and balmy nights. The hot season begins late in March and ends in June, followed by the rainy season, which lasts until October. The other four months (November–March) are the cool season, when the daily temperature averages in the low 80s.

 HOW TO GET THERE. By Air. *Indian Airlines* connects most major cities with Bangalore or Hyderabad (in the northeast just inside Andhra Pradesh). Daily Indian Airlines flights also connect Mangalore with Bombay. *Vayudoot* has occasional flights: Bangalore to Hyderabad, Mysore, and Tirupati (also in Andhra Pradesh); Mangalore to Cochin (Kerala), Coimbatore and Madras (Tamil Nadu).

By Train. Trains can be fun; but they're not the fastest or most comfortable way to travel. A night on a train means making reservations early for the berth as well as for the sleeper. Make sure you have both reservations or you may be kicked off the train at bedtime. Travel second class air-conditioned or first class to get a reasonable night's rest. The telephone number of the railway station in Bangalore: 74173; for reservations: 79611. Daily trains from Bombay to Bangalore: *Udyan Express, Mahalakshmi Express, Sahyadhri Express* (24 hours). From Delhi (a couple of times a week) to Bangalore: *Karnataka Express* (40 hours). Daily trains from Madras: *Bangalore Mail, Bangalore Express, Brindavan Express* (six hours).

By Bus. *Karnataka State Road Transportation Corporation* runs regular buses (deluxe with video; be prepared for *noise*) to Bombay, Madras, Ernakulam (Cochin), and most important cities within Karnataka. For information and reservations, contact in Bangalore: Karnataka State Road Transport Corporation, "Transport House," Kengal Hanumanthaiah Road, Bangalore; tel: 73377.

By Hired Car with Driver. Ambassador car with driver (Rs. 3. per km plus night-halt charges, Rs. 50 per night) available through *Karnataka State Tourism Development Corporation Ltd.* Head office: 10/4 Kasturba Road, Bangalore, 560001, Karnataka; tel: 578901. Also available through *India Tourism Development Corporation Transport Unit,* Hotel Ashok, High Grounds Bangalore; tel: 79415. You can also contact the tourist department (see *Tourist Information*) for a list of reliable car-for-hire agencies. Obviously, you must make car arrangements in advance. Bangalore is approximately 566 km from Hyderabad, 540 km from Cochin, and 334 km from Madras. The roads are pretty good; however, don't expect the road signs to be in English.

 TOURIST INFORMATION. The Tourist Department throughout Karnataka tries to be helpful. Some departments have excellent brochures (most of which are available in Bangalore) on important monuments that you are likely to see if you intend to spend time in the state. The pamphlet on Bidar is especially good, as are the maps of the state and various cities. Most offices are open 10 A.M.–5 P.M., Monday–Saturday.

Bangalore. *Karnataka Tourism,* 9 St. Marks' Rd.; tel: 579139. *Tourist Information Center,* 52 Shrungar Shopping Centre, Mahatma Gandhi Road, tel. 52377. *Tourist Information Center,* Airport, HAL; tel. 51467. City Railway Station; tel. 51467.

Bijapur. *Hotel Adil Shahi,* Anand Mahal Road; tel. 934.

Hassan. *Tourist Officer,* Department of Tourism, B.M. Road; tel. 8862.

Hospet (Hampi). *Tourist Information Office,* Station Road, tel. 8537; or Manager, Hotely Mayura Vijayanagar, T. B. Dam, tel. 8270.

Mysore. *Mysore Tourist Center,* 2 Jhansi Laxmi Bai Rd.; tel. 23652. Deputy Director of Tourism, *Regional Tourist Office,* Old Exhibition Building; tel. 22096.

ACCOMMODATIONS. In many large cities of popular tourist areas in Karnataka, excellent facilities exist— some Western-style posh; some Eastern-style posh. Other undervisited areas have few options, but what's there is adequate. And remember that the benefit of the visit far outweighs the lack of carpeting in a room—or ought to. Karnataka is beautiful and culturally rich; forget deluxe amenities while visiting this overlooked state. Rates are based on double occupancy: *Expensive,* Rs. 600 plus; *Moderate,* Rs. 250–600; *Inexpensive,* under Rs. 250.

AIHOLE

Inexpensive

Tourist Home. Department of Tourism, Aihole; tel. 41. Eight simple, clean rooms. Its modesty is in keeping with its setting next to ancient temples. This is a village where time has stopped. Good food.

BADAMI

Inexpensive

Hotel Mayura Chalukya. Badami; tel. 46. 10 rooms. No air-conditioning. Restaurant.

BANGALORE

Expensive

Hotel Ashok. Kumara Krupa, High Grounds, (13 km from the airport, three km from the railroad station); tel. 79411. 187 air-conditioned rooms, TVs, 24-hour room service, a health club, swimming pool, tennis courts, numerous restaurants, and a coffee shop; golf nearby.

Holiday Inn Bangalore. 28 Sankey Rd., (11 km from the airport, three km from the railroad); tel. 73354. 204 air-conditioned rooms with TVs; swimming pool, restaurants, 24-hour coffee shop and many other amenities.

Taj Residency. 14 Mahatma Gandhi Rd., (five km from the airport, five km from the railroad); tel. 568888. 162 air-conditioned rooms, room service, health club, restaurants, bar, and numerous amenities.

Welcomgroup Windsor Manor. 25 Sankey Rd. (10 km from the airport, five km from the center of town); tel. 79431. 140 air-conditioned rooms with TVs, 24-hour room service, restaurants, bar, swimming pool, golf on request, and many other amenities. This is *the* hotel in Bangalore, done up to look like a Regency manor. Quite beautiful, but the most expensive one in town.

West End Hotel. Race Course Road (nine km from the airport; 1½ km from the railroad); tel. 29281. 135 air-conditioned rooms with TVs. Swimming pool, tennis courts, riding and golfing arranged, room service, restaurants, bar. Another lovely hotel; not grand but bungalow-style pretty, with great lawns and verandas. Has quiet class.

Moderate

Curzon Court. 10 Brigade Rd., (eight km from the airport; three km from the railroad); tel. 569997. 45 air-conditioned rooms with TVs; shopping arcade and a restaurant.

Hotel Bangalore International. High Grounds (14 km from the airport, two km from the railroad); tel. 258011. 57 rooms, some air-conditioned; TVs, 24-hour room service, a nice garden, and a restaurant.

Hotel East West. Residency Road, (nine km from the airport; six km from the railroad); tel. 53265. 96 rms, some air-conditioned; 24-hour coffee shop, restaurant, swimming pool, and health club.

Hotel Harsha. 11 Venkateswamy Naidu Rd., Shivajinagar (10 km from the airport; one km from the railroad); tel: 565566. 78 rooms, some air-conditioned; TVs, restaurants, a bar, and a swimming pool.

Shilton Hotel, St. Mark's Road (10 km from the airport; three km from the railroad); tel. 574471. 40 rooms, some air-conditioned; restaurant. Nice, friendly hotel. Popular and well run.

Woodlands Hotel Private Ltd. 5 Sampangi Tank Rd. (10 km from the airport; four km from the railroad); tel: 225590. 244 air-conditioned rooms. Has a restaurant, bar, and coffee shop. Indian hotel, but very nice.

Inexpensive

Barton Court Hotel. Mahatma Gandhi Road, (five km from the airport; three km from the railroad); tel: 575631. 22 air-conditioned rooms with TVs; restaurant.

Hotel Luciya International. No. 6 O.T.C. Road (12 km from the airport; three km from the railroad); tel: 224148. 66 rooms, some air-conditioned; a restaurant and bar. Sightseeing arranged.

Nilgiris Nest. 171 Brigade Rd. (seven km from the airport; four km from the railroad); tel: 577501. 24 rooms, some air-conditioned; room service and a restaurant.

BELGAUM

Inexpensive

Tourist Rest Home at Gokak Falls; tel. 132 (Reservations Assistant, Executive Engineer, No. 4 Subdivision, Gokak, Karnataka). Very few rooms; simple yet clean accommodations.

BELUR

Inexpensive

KSTDC Tourist Cottages. Temple Road, Belur. Very few rooms. Basic, but clean. Near beautiful temple. For reservations: Manager, Inspection Bungalow, Temple Road Belur, or Manager, Tourist Lodges, KSTDC, Kasturba Road, Bangalore.

BIDAR

Inexpensive

Hotel International, with 20 rooms, is scheduled to be ready in 1988.

Hotel Mayura Barid Shahi, Yadgir Road, Bidar; tel. 571. 14 rooms. Very good food. Adequate accommodations.

BIJAPUR

Inexpensive

Hotel Adil Shahi, Anand Mahal Road, Bijapur; tel. 934. 19 clean, simple rooms with overhead fans and mosquito netting. No great decor. Nice interior courtyard. Has a bar and a restaurant.

BRINDAVAN GARDENS

Moderate

Hotel Krishnarajasagar. K.R.S. Dam, P.O. Krishnarajasagar, District Mandya (in the Brindivan Gardens); tel. 22. Reservations can be made at Hotel Metropole in Mysore. 22 rooms, some air-conditioned, restaurant. Beautiful vantage point from which to see the illuminated fountains.

GOKARNA BEACH

Inexpensive

Inspection Bungalow. Gokarna. Minimal accommodations in a few rooms. But it's on the beach and the facilities are clean. Reservation: Assistant Engineer, Public Works Department, Kumpta, Karnataka.

GULBARGA

Inexpensive

Hotel Mayura Bahamani. Public Gardens, Gulbarga; tel. 644. 15 clean rooms, sparsely decorated; fan-cooled; Indian toilet.

Hotel Pariwar. Station Road, Gulbarga, tel. 21522. New, nice hotel. 45 adequate rooms, some with an Indian toilet, mosquito netting. Room service. Vegetarian restaurant. Excellent value.

HALEBID

Moderate

Tourist Cottages. Inspection Bungalow Compound. Four carpeted rooms; fan with mosquito netting available. Modern, but simple. Limited kitchen. Lovely garden, directly across from beautiful temple. Idyllic.

HASSAN

Moderate

Hassan Ashok. Bangalore-Mangalore Road (one km from the Hassan railroad); tel. 8731. Cable: TOURISM. 46 rooms, some air-conditioned; room service, a restaurant, and a bar.

HOSPET (HAMPI)

Inexpensive

Hotel Mayura Viyayanagar. Tungabhadra Dam; tel. 8270. A limited number of clean, simple rooms with mosquito nets and fans. Lovely arbored dining room.

JOG FALLS

Inexpensive

Hotel Woodlands. Tel. 22. 21 adequate simple rooms.

MANGALORE

Moderate

Welcomgroup Manjarun. Bunder Road (22 km from the airport; one km from downtown); tel. 31791. 100 rooms. Off-season discount from May to September. Restaurant, coffee shop, swimming pool. Fully air-conditioned. Bar, room service. Nice new hotel.

Moti Mahal. Falnir Road (16 km from the airport, one km from downtown); tel. 22211. 90 air-conditioned rooms. Numerous amenities including a restaurant, bar, swimming pool, 24-hour coffee shop, 24-hour room service, shops. Adequate, older hotel.

Inexpensive

Summer Sands Beach Resort. Chota Mangalore (on the beach); tel. 6253. 128 rooms. Swimming pool, mini-golf, health club, restaurant, bar. Charming local architectural design.

MERCARA

Inexpensive

Hotel Mayura Valley View. Tel. 387. Minimal accommodations in a few clean and adequate rooms. Lovely hill station.

MYSORE

Expensive

Lalitha Mahal Palace Hotel. (Eight km from the railway); tel. 23650. 54 rooms. Room service, billiards, swimming pool, tennis, restaurant, bar. Gorgeous old palace on the outskirts of the city. You won't want to leave. Ask for an old room with old furnishings for the full effect.

Moderate

Hotel Dasprakash Paradise. 105 Vivekananda Rd., Yadavagiri (two km from the railroad); tel. 26666. 90 rooms, some air-conditioned; a restaurant, bar, room service, and nice lawn. A good Indian hotel.

Hotel Metropole. 5 Jhansilakshmibai Rd. (one km from the railroad); tel. 20681; 18 air-conditioned rooms in an attractive older hotel. Restaurant.

Hotel Southern Star. 13–14 Vinobha Rd. (½ km from the railroad); tel. 27217. 108 air-conditioned rooms. 24-hour room service, swimming pool, restaurant, bar, 24-hour coffee shop, health club. New spiffy hotel.

Inexpensive

Hotel Highway Limited. New Bannimantap Extension (three km from the railroad); tel. 21117. 40 rooms, some air-conditioned; a restaurant and coffee shop. Nice hotel.

Kings Kourt Hotel. Jhansi Laksmi Bai Road (½ km from the railroad); tel. 25250. 20 rooms, some air-conditioned; a bar and a restaurant. New hotel, no soul but good service.

NAGARHOLE

Expensive

Kabini River Lodge. Nagarhole National Park. For reservations: Jungle Lodges & Resorts, Ltd. 348/349 Brooklands, 13th Main Road, Rajmahal Vilas Extension, Bangalore. Tel. 31020. 20 rooms. Food included in rates, plus numerous wildlife viewing-related activities. Excellent setup. The lodges used to be the former viceregal lodge and maharajah's lodge. This is one place where you have an excellent chance of seeing wild animals; you'll learn a lot, too. Col. Wakefield and his staff are gracious and intelligent. Jeep rides into the jungle. *Coracle* rides into the lake. Wonderful activities matched by wonderful ambience and attractive, rustic yet comfortable accommodations. Good food, too.

SRIRANGA PATTANA

Inexpensive

Hotel Mayura River View. River Side Cottage, Srirangapattana. Mandya District; tel. 114. Small number of rooms. No air-conditioning. But pleasant enough location to justify the simple, unadorned rooms.

UDIPI

Inexpensive

Travellers Bungalow. Udipi. Reservations: Executive Engineer, Udipi, Karnataka. Few rooms. Minimal facilities, but clean.

 DINING OUT. Except for Bangalore, Mangalore, and Mysore, don't expect a lot of dining options. Bangalore is about as Western as you can get, with almost too many American-style fast-food reminders. Throughout Karnataka, you *will* find reasonable food, but limited menus. In most cases, your best bet is to concentrate on enjoying the gorgeous surroundings and the intriguing culture and just eat in your hotel or experiment with wonderful *thalis* and *dosas*—South Indian vegetarian food. If you see a lot of people inside a small restaurant, you can expect healthy, cheap, good food. Prices are based on a three-course meal for one person, excluding beverage, tips, taxes; *Expensive,* Rs. 60 plus; *Moderate,* Rs. 30–60; *Inexpensive,* Rs. 30 and under. Dining rooms in better hotels, as well as expensive restaurants, accept major credit cards. Abbreviations: B, Breakfast; L, Lunch; D, Dinner.

AIHOLE/BADAMI

Inexpensive

Hotel Mayura Chalukya, Badami; tel. 46. Adequate restaurant with limited menu. Indian vegetarian and nonvegetarian omelets and simple Continental food. L, D.

Tourist Home in Aihole (tel. 41) might be able to feed you lunch or dinner if you're not a guest. Food will be simple and good.

BANGALORE

Expensive

Mandarin Room. Hotel Ashok, Kumara Krupa, High Grounds; tel. 79411. Great Chinese food. Reservations advised. L, D.

Prince's. 9 Brigade Rd., Curzon Complex; tel. 565678. Classy restaurant serving excellent Continental, Chinese, and Indian cuisine. Reservations required. L, D.

Wellington Room. Windsor Manor, 25 Sankey Rd.; tel. 79431. Mughlai, South Indian, and Continental cuisines. Dance band at night. Classy restaurant with former "regency" decor. Reservations required. L, D.

Moderate

Blue Fox Restaurant. 80 Mahatma Gandhi Rd ; tel. 570608. Good Indian, Continental, and Chinese food; popular. B, L. D.

Continental Restaurant. 4 Brigade Rd.; tel: 570263. Chinese food, very good. L, D.

Nanking Restaurant. 3 Grant Rd.; tel. 574301. Excellent pleasant, informal Chinese restaurant. Bar. Western music, which sounds okay in this Chinese restaurant in India. L, D.

Shipla Bar & Restaurant. 40/2 Lavelle Rd.; tel. 578273. Chinese, Continental, and Indian cuisines. Bar. Another good popular place. B, L, D.

Tandoor. 28 Mahatma Gandhi Rd.; tel. 578223. Specializes in Mughlai food. Bar. Very popular. L.

Topkapi Investment. 24th Floor, Public Utility Building, Mahatma Gandhi Road; tel. 578040. Good Chinese, Continental, and Indian food. L, D.

Inexpensive

Hotel R.R. Brigades. No 55/1, Brigade Road, Church Street; tel. 578229. Andhra style, South Indian food. Good, popular. A must, once. L, D.

Indian Fast Foods. 9 St. Patrick's Complex, Brigade Rd.; tel. 566176. You got it; American fast food (hamburgers, ice cream, hot dogs) Indian style. When you're too homesick, or just in the mood for an ethnic twist, this is the place. L, D.

Woody's. 177/178 Commercial St. Fast food—this time Indian-vegetarian style. L, D.

BIDAR

Moderate to Inexpensive

Hotel Barid Shahi. Anand Mahal Road; tel. 6571 Good Indian vegetarian and nonvegetarian food; some Chinese and Continental. L, D.

Kings Bar and Restaurant. An upstairs restaurant in the heart of town. Good Chinese, seafood, Indian (vegetarian and nonvegetarian). Feels very Indian. L, D.

Shilpa Bar and Restaurant. Also in the heart of town. Big menu: Chinese, Indian (vegetarian and nonvegetarian), some Continental. Somewhat Western restaurant, with private family rooms. Very good. L, D.

BIJAPUR

Inexpensive

Hotel Mayura Adil Shahi. tel. 934. Serves reasonable food. Chinese, Indian. Bar, too. L, D.

Hotel Samrat. Station Road. tel. 1620. Two restaurants: Shanti (vegetarian); President (nonvegetarian with a bar). Good enough and very inexpensive. L,D.

GULBARGA

Inexpensive

Kamakshi, in the Hotel Pariwar, Station Road; tel. 21522. Good Indian (vegetarian only) served in pleasant surroundings. L, D.
Kamat Cafe. In the heart of the town. Vegetarian food. Popular with the local folk. Good. B, L, D.

HOSPET

Inexpensive

Hotel Mayura Viyayanagar. Tungabhadra Dam; tel: 8270. Vegetarian and nonvegetarian food. B, L, D.
Shanbag Cafe. In the center of town near College Road and Taluk Office Center. Popular with locals; good Indian food. B, L, D.

MANGALORE

Expensive

Embers. Old Port Road; tel. 575001. Poolside dinnertime barbecue. Good. Reservations required.
The Galley. Manjarun, Bunder Road; tel. 25465. Continental, Chinese, and Indian food served in a British atmosphere. B, L, D. Reservations advised.

Moderate

Summer Sands Beach Resort. Chota Mangalore; tel. 6253. Varied menu of very good food. B, L, D. Reservations advised.

MYSORE

Expensive to Moderate

Gun House Imperial. Bangalore Nilgiri Road; tel. 20608. Very good Indian, Chinese, South Indian, and Continental food. Beautiful restaurant. L, D. Reservations advised.
Indra Cafe Paras. Sayyaji Rao Road; tel. 20236. Specialties: South Indian and Punjabi food. B, L, D.
Hotel Metropole. 5 Jhansilakshimibai Rd.; tel. 20681. Reservations advised. Good food: Italian, Indian, Chinese, and Continental. B, L, D.

HOW TO GET AROUND. Bangalore. Minimum charge for a **taxi** is Rs. 3.25; each km, Rs. 1.55. **Auto Rickshaw,** minimum charge is Rs. 1.45, less than a rupee per km. By city **bus** service, contact the tourist department for schedules and routes. **Mysore** and **Mangalore** offer a similar range of services and at similar rates. In all these cities, the auto rickshaw is the most fun and the most convenient form of travel. In most of the smaller cities and nearly all the villages, travel is by auto rickshaw, **bike rickshaw,** or **tonga** (horsedrawn cart). Bargain, but remember the bottom line: you're never really parting with a grand sum, especially considering the amount of pedaling required to carry you around in a bike rickshaw.

TOURS. The *Karnataka State Tourism Development Corporation* (KSTDC), 10/4 Kasturba Road, Bangalore (tel. 578901) conducts numerous tours from Bangalore, Hubli, and Mysore to various regions of the state. Buses are usually deluxe and very comfortable, providing an inexpensive way to see much of the state if you don't have a rented car and driver. In Mysore, KSTDC is located in Hotel Hoysala, Jhansi Lakshmi Bai Road (tel. 23652).

BANGALORE

Bangalore City Tour. Every day but Sunday (8:30 A.M.–6:30 P.M.). Tippu's palace, Bull Temple, Lalbagh, Kaveri Arts and Crafts Emporium, Vidhana Soudha, Museum, Venkatappa Art Gallery, Ulsoor Lake, Government Soap Factory, and Bannerghatta National Park. Rs. 25 per person.

Tirupati Tour (two days). Fridays and Saturdays, from June–March; Rs. 125, including lodging.

Ooty Tour (three days). Daily departures from April to July. Rs. 200, including accommodations.

Tour to Shravanabelogola–Belur–Halebid (one day). Every Friday and Sunday, July–February; daily, March–June. Rs. 55.

Nandi Hills Tour (one day). Every Sunday, July–February; daily, March–June. Rs. 30.

Tour to Hampi via Mantralaya and Tungabhadra Dam (two days). Every Wednesday and Friday. Rs. 120, including accommodations.

MYSORE

Hampi tour. Every Wednesday. Rs. 40.

Aihole, Badami, and Pattadakal (day tour). Every Thursday. Rs. 45.

Aihole, Badami, Pattadakal, and Bijapur (two days). Every Saturday and Sunday. Fare: Rs. 75, including accommodations.

Mysore local sightseeing (one day). Includes Somnathpura. Rs. 25.

Belur, Halebid, and Shravanabelagola (one day). Every Friday and Saturday. Rs. 50.

Ooty Tour (one day). Every day April–July. Rs. 50.

Government Sandalwood Oil Factory. 11 A.M.–1 P.M.; 3 P.M.–5 P.M. For other times, call 22856.

Government Silk Factory. 9 A.M.–11 A.M.; 12:30 P.M.–4:30 P.M. Closed Sundays. For other times, call 21803.

The following private organization runs excellent safari wildlife treks and tours in South India (many of their trips are in Karnataka): *Safaritan Travels Private Ltd.,* 26 and 27, 9th Main Road, Raja Mahal Vilas, Bangalore 560080; tel. 368624. Cable: WILDERNESS. Two-day tours to Ranganathittu and Nagarahole from Bangalore: Rs. 1205 per person; three-day tours: Rs. 1965 per person; numerous other trips. Safaris include jeep drives in forest, bird watching from floating *coracles,* naturalists who know their stuff, good food, and good lodging at, for example, Kabini River Lodge, a wonderful former maharajah's hunting lodge.

 SEASONAL EVENTS. March. In Nanjangud, the *Car Festival* is a procession of deities from the temple in small chariots. Festive Hindu occasion.

May/April. Melcote (52 km from Mysore) observes *Valramudi Festival.* Vishnu deity is adorned with a diamond-studded crown witnessed by thousands of devotees. Much festivity. *Karaga* is Bangalore's most popular festival, which symbolizes strength of mind represented by balancing contests (who can hold the most pots on the top of their heads). Very interesting.

In North Coorg, *Suggi,* is associated with the harvest, involving colorful local dances unique to this area.

August/September. *Ganesha Chaturthi,* throughout Karnataka, is a three-day festival celebrating Ganesha with songs and dances in the hopes that paying tribute to this god will return blessings and especially good fortune.

September/October. Mysore and the rest of Karnataka observe *Dussehra,* a 10-day festival that takes on tremendous pomp and pageantry. The festival celebrates the victory of goddess Chamundi over the demon Mahishasura. While the maharajah no looker takes part, the rest of the city does. The palace is lit up and glows. On the 10th day there is a fantastic procession including the camel corps, infantry, and cavalry.

November/December. *Kadalekaye Parishe* (Groundnut fair) held on the premises of the Bull Temple, Bangalore. Main event: who can consume the largest amount of groundnut. The temple bull is bedecked with a garland of groundnut to prevent him from ruining the local crops of this valuable product.

HISTORIC SITES. The state of Karnataka is rich in historical sites, predominantly temples, tombs, and ancient forts. Indeed, some places are temple villages in themselves. A few of these are in close proximity to each other and can be visited in a half day. Such is the case of Aihole, Badami, and Pattadakal, as well as Belur and Halebid. We've grouped these villages together so that you can better organize your visits.

AIHOLE-BADAMI-PATTADAKAL

Aihole alone has 150 temples dedicated to Hindu gods and goddesses. This temple village represents the cradle of Dravidian architecture. Aihole was founded by the first Chalukyan king around A.D. 450, and most of these temples are from 400 to 750. The simple towers of Aihole are precursors of the massive goporams in the south. See especially the temple of *Lad Khan,* possibly the oldest, the U-shaped *Durgan,* the *Suraya Naryana Temple,* the *Ravanaphadi* (Brahmanical cave).

Badami. This second capital of the Chalukyas was founded by Pulakesin I around A.D. 550. A beautiful, serene village with stunning cave temples dating back to the sixth century. A little-known must see, with caves so finely sculpted it's hard to believe they are chiseled rock.

Pattadakal (nine km from Badami). City founded by King Vikramaditya II in the beginning of the eighth century and the site of the Chalukyan coronation ceremonies. The next stage in temple evolution after Aihole, with 10 temples constructed from the 600s to the 700s. The *Papanath Temple* (A.D. 680) is the earliest example of pure Chalukyan style—a simple structure with plain pillars. The facades are decorated with themes from the *Ramayana.* The *Mallikarjuna Temple,* with Nandi standing out front, is decorated with scenes from the *Bhagavata.* The temple was constructed by a queen (Trilokya Mahadevi) of Vikramaditya II. The *Virupaksha Temple,* built in A.D. 740 by Lokamaha Devi, depicts scenes from the *Ramayana* and *Mahabharata.* See if you can find the carving that looks like an elephant from one side and a buffalo from the other.

Bangalore. *Bull Temple* (five km from Bangalore) is a monolithic bull built in the 1500s in the Dravidian style (15 feet high by 20 feet long) by Kempe Gowda, founder of Mysore. Supposedly the iron plate on its head keeps the bull from growing.

Nandi Hills (59 km) has 2,000-year-old Shiva temples, and is the former site of Tipu Sultan's summer palace. Walk up to Tipu's Drop, a 2,000-foot sheer cliff, where the condemned were pushed over the edge.

Tipu's Palace and Fort, just northwest of Lal Bagh, were originally built of mud in 1537 by Kempe Gowda; rebuilt in stone in the 1700s by Hyder Ali and embellished by his son Tipu Sultan. Good example of military architecture of the eighteenth century. Palace was the summer residence of Tipu Sultan. Open 8 A.M.–8 P.M.

Vidhana Soudha, on northern boundary of Cubbon Park, is an enormous white granite structure built in the neo-Dravidian style in 1956. Five-story building is crowned with a dome. On top sit three lions—India's national symbol. Permission is needed to go inside. Illuminated on weekends.

BELUR-HALEBID

Belur, (39 km from Hassan) is a former twelfth-century city under the Hoysala kings. *Belur Temple of Lord Channakeshava* (a Vishnu avatar and still a place of active worship) was begun in 1116 by Hoysala King Vishnuvardhana and completed 103 years later. Star-shaped and sitting on a platform, the squat temple is of soapstone. The guides are very informative, and Rs. 20 will make them very happy.

Halebid (16 km from Belur) was started by the same king 10 years after the construction of Belur began. It took 180 years of work. Has the same star-shaped pattern with a double shrine, again of soapstone, and a marvel of sculpture. Again, an informative guide (Rs. 20 maximum) will bring the gorgeous temple to life. The guides in both temple sites are witty and have a clearly developed "rap."

BIDAR

Bidar Fort, the site of the former capital of the fifteenth-century Bahmani kings, is a creation that mixes the Hindu and Moslem influences that are so much a part of this city. There's a small museum as you enter, with an archaeological department. The hours are "iffy"—sort of 8 A.M.–4 P.M. Try to get a guide to show you around. The Karnataka Tourism Department has a good pamphlet on all the monuments within the fort and around Bidar. The pamphlet contains excellent information and is intelligently written, but it has no map. Bring a flashlight and good walking shoes and plan for plenty of time (two–three hours). The place is usually empty of tourists, which is a shame, but it's nice to have the peace to soak up what glory remains.

Bahamani Tombs are not far from the fort. Visit early in the day to see the interior paintings (best in the morning light). A great sense of grandeur, but poorly maintained monuments. Again, a flashlight is a must. Buried here are eight former kings of Bidar. The tomb of Ahmed Shah-al-Wali Bahamani is 107 feet high and built on a square plane, with a dome that is three-quarters of an orb. No external decorations, but the interior was once quite colorful. You still see remnants of intricate floral designs and calligraphy. Also, set into the dome are supposedly nine diamonds—but you need a powerful flashlight to see them. Also visit the tomb of Sultan Allauddin Shah II. It originally glittered with the exterior covered with tilework, some of which still remains. Although just a shade of its former beauty exists, it's still quite lovely. Finally, visit the Chaukhandi of Hazrat Khalil-Ullah, on the way to the Ashtur tombs. Steps lead up to the entrance of an octagonal structure that encloses another tomb. This building was also formerly covered with tilework. Notice the beautifully carved granite pillars and the entrance decorated with floral motifs. The *Baridi Tombs* are situated to the west of Bidar on Nanded Road. Usually Moslem tombs are closed on the western side where a *mihrab* is built for saying prayers. Not so at the Tomb of Ali Barid (1542–1580). Legend claims that Ali Barid wanted his grave kept clean by the wind and sun, and kept it open.

BIJAPUR

Bijapur has 50 mosques and 20 tombs. This is a lovely Moslem-dominated city that is best appreciated with a government-approved guide. The *Gol Gumbaz,* built in the mid-1600s, encloses the second-largest domed space in the world, with a wonderful whispering gallery that can only be appreciated early in the morning when children have not arrived. The inscription on the entrance arch states that this tomb houses the mortal remains of Mohammad Adil Shah, who, on his death, became "an inhabitant of Paradise and also a Particle of the Firmament." There are great views of Bijapur from the top.

The *Jama Masjid,* built in 1565, has lovely proportions, graceful minarets, and lovely bulbous domes and is covered with ornamental detail. You can enter the courtyard, but only Moslems may enter the shrine itself. This is the largest mosque in the Deccan; 2,250 people can pray here, one to each painted block.

The *Ibrahim Rauza* has richly decorated walls and perforated stone windows. Built by Muhammad Adil Shah, it contains the tomb of his father, Ibrahim Adil Shah. Special acoustics enable the voice of the muezzin calling devotees to prayer to be heard from a mosque 200 feet away, while that same voice can't be heard outside the tomb. Try it.

HAMPI

Hampi, the ruins of the Vijayanagar empire, is also a place best appreciated with a government-approved guide, which can be arranged at the Hospet Tourist Bureau. A reasonable visit of the considerable ruins, spanning 15 miles, requires a day. The grand flourish of this empire lasted from the fourteenth to the mid-16th century. Do not miss seeing the *Virupaksha Temple* (visit early in the morning when the temple bells are rung and the monkeys come running to eat); the *Vitthala Temple Complex,* with its renowned stone chariot; and the *Hazara Rama Complex.*

MYSORE

Chamundi Hill is named after the royal family's patron goddess, Chamundi. See the 16-foot *Nandi,* constructed in the seventeenth century from a single granite boulder; the *Sri Chamundeswari Temple* dating back to the twelfth century, with a richly carved tower constructed in the eighteenth century; the *statue of Mahishasura,* built of mortar about 35 years ago (the goddess Chamundi killed this demon to bring peace to the country); and, finally, just see the view of Mysore.

Lalitha Mahal Palace, now a hotel, was built in 1921 by the maharajah for his foreign guests. Beautiful interior and exterior. Have tea, at least.

Maharajah's Mysore Palace, built in 1857 on the former site of a former wooden palace that burned down, is one of the biggest palaces in India. The architecture is Indo-Sarcenic, a synthesis of Hindu and Islamic design. On Sundays and holidays, the palace is illuminated with thousands of tiny lights. See the impressive Durbar Hall, with its ornate ceiling and huge "grandstand" awning. Also, the Kalyana Mandap (Marriage Hall), where women sat behind screened balconies; on the wall are lifelike paintings of the Dussehra procession. Plan at least an hour. Open 10:30 A.M.–5:30 P.M. Rs. 2.

SRAVANABELGOLA

Here, you'll find a colossal statue of the Jain saint, *Gomateswara.* The monolithic statue is 57 feet high and nearly 1,800 years old. The statue's nakedness is symbolic of the renunciation of worldly possessions.

SRINANGAPATNA

This is an island fortress and former capital of the Mysore rajah from 1610 to 1799. Its most famous residents were Hyder Ali and Tipu Sultan. Visit the fortress with the mosque inside; the summer palace called *Daria Daulat;* and Tipu Sultan's mausoleum, the *Gumbaz* (both are outside the fort).

SRINGERI

Sringeri is an important Hindu center of pilgrimage. See St. Sankaracharya's monastery, created just at the start of the Vijayanagar empire, and the fourteenth-century *Vidya Shankara Temple,* with its 12 zodiac pillars arranged so that the sun's rays fall on the pillar that corresponds to that month.

TALKAD

Talkad's 30 temples lie beneath a strange stretch of sand dunes on the banks of the Cauvery River. Two main temples are the *Vaidyesvara,* a Dravidian temple of granite perhaps built in the fourteenth century, with later additions; and the beautiful *Kirtinarayana,* possibly erected in 1117 (an example of the Chalukyan style temple). The sand is a result of deforestation, the construction of a reservoir in the fourteenth century, and the yearly monsoon.

 WILDLIFE SANCTUARIES. *Bandipur Wildlife Sanctuary,* 80 km south of Mysore, covers 689 sq km adjoining the Mudumalai forest. Once the private preserve of the maharajas of Mysore, it offers good opportunities to see herds of bison, elephants, spotted deer, elephants, and, if you're lucky, a tiger or a leopard. There are observation platforms for viewing, and jeep rides are available. For more details, contact the Mysore Tourist Office. The best time to visit is October–May. Entrance fees: Rs. 2 per adult; Rs. 1 per child.

Bannerghatta National Park, 22 km from Bangalore, is a new park covering 104 km, with a variety of wildlife, a crocodile farm, and a snake park. It also has a "Lion Safari," where lions roam freely as visitors are transported through in vehicles.

Nagarahole National Park, 96 km south of Mysore, comprises 572 sq km of forests and swamps that were once part of the exclusive preserve of the maharajahs. It has at least 250 species of birds and numerous animals, including antelopes, bears, jungle cats, barking deer, wild dogs, elephants, langur, mongooses, panthers, porcupines, sambar, tigers, and lots of reptiles. Vehicle and guides are available. Numerous tribesmen also live here (the Jenu Kurubas and Betta Kurubas). You can also trek, with permission from the Chief Wildlife Warden, Aranya Bhavan, 18th Cross, Malleswaram, Bangalore, tel. 31993. Van/jeep/mini-bus charge for viewing: Rs. 5 per km. Entrance fee: Rs. 2 per adult; Rs. 1 per child. Extra charge for a camera. Accommodations are available in the Cauvery Lodge.

Ranganathittu Bird Sanctuary, 18 km from Mysore, is made up of six islets in the Cauvery River. A large variety of birds (night herons, little cormorants, snake-birds, spoon bills), flying foxes, and reptiles. Entrance fee: per person Rs. 2. Additional charge for a camera. Boating is available at Rs. 1 per adult, Rs. 0.50 per child. Accommodations are available; contact: KSTDC Tourist Centre Badami House, opposite the City Corporation Offices, Bangalore 560002, tel. 578580. Riverside cottages with two rooms each, Rs. 45 per day.

BEACHES. There are good beaches in Karnataka that are just beginning to get ready for the influx of tourism: Near Mangalore, you'll find several fine beaches. In other parts of South Karnataka, Malpe has good sand and surf and Karwar has more excellent beaches, with *Lady Beach* nearby. There is also a good beach at Gokarna.

SPORTS. Bangalore has an 18-hole **golf** course, the Bangalore Golf Club, at High Ground. For more details and reservations, call 27121.

Horse racing is also held at Bangalore, from mid-May to the end of July, and again from November to March. Contact the Tourist Department for details.

GARDENS. *Cubbon Park,* Bangalore, covers over 300 acres of beautiful parkland laid out in 1864. Here you'll find many imposing Greco-Colonial style buildings, including the Public Library, the Attara Katcheri housing, the High Court, the Government Museum, the Technological and Industrial Museum; plus a delightful toy train to take children around the grounds and an aquarium.

Lal Bagh (so named because of the abundance of red roses) spreads over 240 acres in Bangalore. This botanical garden was originally designed by Hyder Ali in 1760 and added to by his son, Tipu Sultan. Has over 100 varieties of trees, hundreds and hundreds of flowers, and other plants. At the garden center is a stunning glass house reminiscent of the Crystal Palace in London. The foundation stone of this structure was laid by Prince Albert of Wales on November 28, 1889. Every year in January and August, flower shows are held here. You'll also find a 3,000-million-year-old rock called Peninsula Gneiss. Open 8 A.M.–8 P.M.

Brindavan Gardens, 19 km from Mysore, stretch out in terraces below the Krishnarajasagar Dam. At night, the gardens are illuminated with twinkling lights, fountains play, and, yes, channel music. The newest innovation has the lights responding rhythmically to the music—thanks to a computer. Gardens are illuminated for one hour weekday nights and two hours on Sundays and holidays. Entrance fee: Rs. 2 per person; car, Rs. 20.

Zoological Garden in Mysore has a large and varied collection of animals and birds in a five-km park. Open 7:30 A.M.–noon, 2:30–6 P.M.; on Sundays, 7:30 A.M.–6 P.M. Entry fee: Rs. 1.

MUSEUMS AND ART GALLERIES. Bangalore. *Government Museum,* established in 1887, is one of the oldest in India. Set in Cubbon Park, the museum has exhibits in archaeology, ethnology, geology, art, and sculpture and interesting exhibits from the Mohenjodaro ruins dating back to 5000 B.C. Open 10 A.M.–5 P.M. Closed Wednesdays and official holidays, Rs. .50.

Venkatappa Art Gallery, in Cubbon Park, exhibits the paintings of the court painter S. K. Venkatappa who painted in the late 1800s. Also exhibited are musical instruments that he crafted.

Mysore. *Sri Jayachamarajendra Art Gallery* is housed in the lovely Jaganmo-han Palace in Mysore. It has examples of various schools of Indian art, beautiful antique furniture, and decorated musical instruments. Open 8:30 A.M.–5:30 P.M.; tel. 23693.

SHOPPING. The skill of the old Karnataka craftsmen is still flourishing; inlaid furniture and ivory and sandalwood carvings are made in a variety of designs that delight the connoisseur. For hundreds of years, Karnataka has been the home of sandalwood. Statuettes and panels, beads, and pendants are executed in this delicately scented wood. Carved tables, screens, and dinner gongs are made in lovely designs.

In Bangalore the *Government Arts & Crafts Emporium* is at 23 Mahatma Gandhi Road. Commercial Street and Brigade Road in the Cantonment and Chickpet and City Market are good shopping areas. In Mysore City, the number one general shopping center is Deveraja Market. You might be able to pick up a length of material during your visit to the *Silk Weaving Factory* or a masterpiece in sandalwood at the *Chamarajendra Technical Institute;* both have showrooms. Bangalore silks are the world's finest; satin, organza, chiffon, and georgette are available by the meter.

FOREIGN CURRENCY EXCHANGE. Most of the better hotels will change traveler's checks. Otherwise, head for the nearest *State Bank of India, Reserve Bank of India, Bank of India,* or *Bank of Baroda.* Banking hours are usually Monday–Friday, 10 A.M.–2 P.M.; Saturdays, to noon. Lines are usually long; be prepared. Bring a book.

RECOMMENDED READING. *House of God, Select Temples of South India,* by N. S. Ramaswamy (a Travel Aide publication, Rs. 45). An informative paperback that can help you see your way through most of the important Karnataka temples, as well as temples in the rest of South India.

The Cave Temples of Badami, by A. M. Annigeri. Available in English, Hindu, French, and German, outside the caves sold by hawkers; 5 rupees' worth of delightful information, especially helpful if you're without a guide.

"Hampi–Splendours of Vijayanagar Empire," by George Michell and John Fritz. Helpful small pamphlet on the sites.

NIGHTLIFE AND BARS. There are classy bars at the West End Hotel on Race Course Road and Welcomgroup Windsor Manor, 25 Sankey Rd., Bangalore. They are usually open for lunch and then in the evening into the late night hours. Discos include the post *Prince's,* 9 Brigade Rd., Curzon Complex I Road, and the Knock-Out Disco, complete with psychedelic lighting, adjacent to the Blue Fox Restaurant, Mahatma Gandhi Road. You can also dance and drink, in African-hutlike decor, at the *Peacock,* Janardhan Towers, 2 Residency Rd. 7:30–midnight; also open for drinking, 11:30 A.M.–3:30 P.M.

In Mysore, three good choices for a drink in princely surroundings: *Gun Hill Imperial,* Bangalore Nilgiri Road; *Lalitha Mahal Palace;* and the *Lokaranjan Mahal Palace,* Lokaranjan Mahal Road.

ANDHRA PRADESH

India's "Melting Pot"

by
KATHLEEN COX

Andhra Pradesh is not on the itinerary of most Western visitors to India. It should be. The ancient Andhra culture reaches back into the great Indian epics: *Ramayana* and *Mahabharata*. Beautiful temples still stand from the earliest days of Hindu, Jain, and Buddhist worship, as do impressive Moslem forts, mosques, and palaces. A fine stretch of beach along the Bay of Bengal tempts you. Then there's Hyderabad, a fascinating city, with what many travelers regard as the liveliest market in all India.

If you're visiting Goa, Kerala, Madras, or any of southern India's many fascinating places, you'll find Andhra Pradesh on your route. Planes, trains, and buses from the north pass through Hyderabad on their way south. Spend four or five days in Hyderabad and its environs and enjoy the rich and varied culture, shopping, and delicious food.

Geographically, Andhra Pradesh includes fertile river systems in the north, the arid vastness of the Deccan plain, an extensive coastline along the Bay of Bengal, and the hilly Chittoor district of the south. Situated in central India, Andhra Pradesh has always been a "melting pot." Here many great forces in Indian history clashed, mixed, and created the unique character of this region. Hindu, Jain, and Buddhist sites are within a few kilometers of one another. Moslem buildings are fashioned from the stones of Hindu structures, and mosques and Moslem palaces are decorated with Hindu motifs.

427

Andhra's history reaches back to the time of Emperor Ashoka (c. 230 B.C.), when this state marked the southern boundary of his great empire. At Ashoka's death, Satavahana, a local chieftain, established a dynasty that would endure for four centuries. The Ikshavaku rulers who succeeded the Satavahanas lasted only 57 years, yet it was during their reign that Buddhist culture flowered. The Buddhist monastery in Nagarjunakonda Valley was built at this time—a major center of learning for all southeast Asia. The Pallavas of Tamil Nadu held sway over much of Andhra Pradesh for 3½ centuries until the Chalukyas supplanted them. Under successive Chalukyan kings, Andhra's Telegu culture came into its own. Each of India's major regions is fiercely proud of its language; yet all over India, Telegu is known for its gracefulness and intrinsic musical qualities.

In the thirteenth century, the Kakatiyas undertook bold projects to control the great river systems of northern Andhra. Then, in the fourteenth century, Moslem armies of the Delhi Sultanate swept through the Deccan plateau and captured two Hindu princes in Warangal. The princes were brought to Delhi, converted to Islam, and sent south to establish a Moslem stronghold in Andhra and Karnataka. But the new religion had less hold than the wish for power.

In 1336, one of the two "converts" established the Vijayanagar kingdom, and for close to two centuries Vijayanagar rulers struggled for power with their Moslem counterparts—the Bahmanis, whose kingdom across the Krishna River included the fabled diamond mines of Golconda. Tension between ambitious Hindu and Moslem forces placed much of Andhra in a state of constant strife. But, in years to come, these clashing elements would be reconciled and give rise to the region's vigorous mixed culture.

In 1518, Qutb Shahi broke away from the Bahmani kingdom and founded a dynasty responsible for the creation of Hyderabad and its memorable architecture. The dynasty ruled for 100 years until Aurangzeb's armies of the north conquered the area in 1687. Intrigue and treachery marked the next 40 years as the Mogul administration in Delhi tried in vain to maintain control over its new conquests in the Deccan. When Aurangzeb died in 1717, only seven years passed before Nizam-ul-Mulk took power and founded the Asafia Dynasty, known for its fabulously rich rulers (Nizams), who controlled the region—India's largest and most important princely state—until Independence in 1948.

EXPLORING ANDHRA PRADESH

When you visit Andhra Pradesh, expect variety in the scenery. The Eastern Ghats wind their hilly way along the eastern and northern borders; dense forests stretch along the east near the Bay of Bengal and farther west near Warangal. To the south is the Deccan plateau, which lies across all India at this longitude, and two important rivers that flow toward the sea: the northern Godavari and the southern Krishna. Sleepy canals serve as inland waterways. The weather remains humid year round, with relatively little variation in temperature. The environment is ideal for coconut palms, mango trees, and lush flowers. The world's third-largest artificial lake spills around the Nagarjunasagar Dam, a recently constructed gigantic hydroelectric project. Around Hyderabad City, huge granite boulders are strewn naturally on the bare plain as if by giants playing a game.

HYDERABAD

Today, Andhra Pradesh preserves vivid monuments from its complex past. There's no better place to begin than in Hyderabad. With upwards of 1½ million inhabitants, Hyderabad is India's fifth-largest city. Unlike so many of this nation's cultural attractions, Hyderabad doesn't have its origins in antiquity. The city derives its name from the romantic liaison of the Moslem ruler, Quli Qutb Shahi—the fourth king of the Qutb Shahi Dynasty that ruled from the forbidding fortress of Golconda. This king had a Hindu mistress named Bhagyamati (*bhagya* = lady luck; *mati* = harbinger). Early in his reign, he started building a new city because the Golconda stronghold had grown crowded and unhealthy. Six km to the south by the river Musi he found a site, which he named Bhagyanagar—city of good luck—after his mistress. Here he erected a palace for her and named it Hydermahal. Later, in 1589, Bhagyanagar was renamed after this palace—and Hyderabad was born.

The diamond mines of Golconda gave the Nizams unlimited resources. Hyderabad is filled with magnificent structures—palaces that have been converted to public buildings, hotels, hospitals, universities, and museums.

The Heart of Hyderabad

The center of Hyderabad is defined by four great arches facing the cardinal points. Charkaman (*char* = four; *karman* = gate) was constructed by Quli Qutb Shahi in 1592 when Hyderabad was still coming into being. Within the area defined by these arches, you'll find Charminar and Mecca Masjid, the city's two most striking structures, as well as a teeming market filled with Hyderabad's well-known pearl and bangle shops.

Charminar (four towers or minarets) is a rectangular granite edifice built in 1591. The building has elegant arches 50 feet high and four minarets 184 feet high and is designed in Indo-Saracenic style—which, like so much of Andhra culture, means it combines elements of both Moslem and Hindu art. The arches, domes, and minarets show Persian-Islamic influence, while various decorative motifs of leaves, petals, and flowers are done in Hindu style. At one time, an underground tunnel connected Charminar with Golconda Fort, some six km away.

Walk through the Charminar Market and you'll understand why Hyderabad is a shopper's paradise. Here you can buy all kinds of fabrics, especially cotton prints and lightweight shirts and drawstring pants made from *khadi* cloth. Hyderabad is also famous for *nirmal* toys: wooden figurines of people and animals painted in bright lacquer. There's also *bidriware:* trays, vases, boxes, and other objects made from an alloy of zinc and copper that turns gun-metal black—in vivid contrast to the silver patterns traced across its surface. For Rs. 250–600 you can buy a terrific example of this ancient craft. Ask someone to point you to *laad* (lacquer) bazaar, a bustling side street where bangles, pottery, nirmal toys, and bidriware are displayed in many stalls.

Best of all, Hyderabad is the unlikely world center for the pearl trade. Here in Charminar, in the heart of landlocked Andhra Pradesh, there are hundreds of shops dealing in pearl jewelry of all qualities and description. The pearls come from China and Japan: India's skilled jewelers and inexpensive labor make it a profitable enterprise. If you come looking for perfectly shaped natural pearls, you'll find them—but at no particular bargain. Instead, let the shopkeeper show you rice pearls, wheat pearls, flower pearls, seed pearls, Chinese bean pearls in various shapes and sizes. For less than Rs. 400, you can buy an attractive triple-strand necklace of rice pearls. You can try to bargain, but prices are set according to weight, so unless you're making a fairly substantial purchase, don't expect the shopkeeper to knock more than 10 percent off the asking price. The two most respected shops are Mangatrai and Omprakash & Sons, both in the Charminar area. Just ask—everyone knows where they are. Mangatrai has a new air-conditioned shop outside the Charminar Market on Bashir Bagh, opposite Hotel Naragjuna, where you can see the jewelry being made. Prices are the same; you'll be more comfortable, but you'll miss the fun of buying pearls in the picturesque Moslem market.

Mecca Masjid is the second-largest mosque in India (after Jama Masid in Old Delhi) and the seventh-largest mosque in the world. Its enormous colonnades are carved from single slabs of granite. Ten thousand people can gather under its double dome and in its vast courtyard for prayer. (Non-Moslems are welcome except during prayer services.)

Mecca Masjid is so named because soil was brought from the holy city of Mecca and mixed with Indian soil when construction was started in 1618. According to legend, completion of the mosque would herald the end of the Qutb Shahi Dynasty. Aurangzeb's forces defeated the Qutb Shahi armies, bringing central India under the sway of the Delhi moguls in 1687—the very year that construction of Mecca Masjid was finally completed.

Salar Jung Museum

The Salar Jung family served the Nizams of Hyderabad for five generations as prime ministers. In 1911, the last of the Nizams, Mir Osman Ali Khan, appointed the youthful Mir Yousuf Ali Khan to serve him as Salar Jung III. But this new prime minister was more devoted to art and literature than to his administrative duties. Within three years, he resigned his post and spent the rest of his life amassing an eclectic collection of some 45,000 objects, ranging from ivory furniture and jewel-crusted weapons to children's toys. When he died in 1949, he left his collection to the government of India. The museum is worth a visit.

The first room you enter is the Portrait Gallery. Here canvases depict the Nizam Dynasty. If you have a guide, he or she will tell you with the utmost conviction that Mahboob Ali Khan, the sixth Nizam, was so blessed that the mere mention of his name cured someone of the disastrous consequences of a poisonous snakebite.

At the far end of the room is a display case in which Safar Jung kept two dozen clay figurines, each modeled after one of his personal attendants. Possibly people of such great wealth and power too easily confused human lives with clay figures.

In other rooms, there are displays of magnificent silver and crystal pieces presented to Salar Jung by the British royal family, including a collection of stone sculptures from all over India: Chola, Pallava, Jain, and Buddhist art. In the gallery for wood carving you'll see elaborately carved furniture, plus a formidable representation of Garuda, the birdlike creature who is Lord Vishnu's mount (and the symbol of Indonesian Airlines.)

Two works of Western art draw the attention of curiosity seekers. *The Veiled Rebecca* by Benzoni, done in 1876, is a marble statue of a woman draped in a veil. It's more like a trick-or-treater done up as a ghost or a "wrapping" by the conceptual artist Cristo. The second bizarre piece is *Mephistopheles and Margaretta,* a German work of the nineteenth century. From the front, you'll stand face to face with

Goethe's satanic tempter. From the other side, all you see is the virtuous Margaretta. Good and evil back to back.

Don't miss the eighteenth century clock that presides over a covered courtyard. Children gather on benches to watch a mechanical blacksmith pound out the seconds on his anvil. On the hour, 10 soldiers file out of a sentry station to ring a brass bell the appropriate number of times. It's as much fun to watch the children as it is to watch the clock.

Golconda Fort

Five miles from the center of Hyderabad the ruins of Golconda Fort sprawled for many acres over the top of a granite hill. The fort's origins go back to the thirteenth century, but it was rebuilt by the Qutb Shahi Dynasty in 1525 where it remained their seat of power for 162 years until Aurangzeb seized the fort after a ten-year seige.

At one time Golconda was the center of one of the world's great diamond markets, making it the object of curiosity from Marco Polo and the first European visitors of the thirteenth and fourteenth centuries. Golconda's riches provided extra incentive to the northern moguls' dreams of expanding south. The Hope Diamond, the Orloff Diamond of Catherine the Great, and the British Crown's Kohinoor diamond all came from mines near the fort.

Climb the steep stone steps to a panoramic view of the city and surrounding countryside. Move on to Qutb Shahi Tombs where the seven rulers of the dynasty were laid to rest. Here, as at Charminar, you'll see Moslem architectural design joined with Hindu motifs in a style that's typical of Hyderabad. The dome and square base of the tombs are Moslem, as is the gallery of pointed arches. Hindu motifs include lotus leaves and buds, a chain and pendant design, projecting leaves, and cruciform capitals.

EXPLORING OUT OF HYDERABAD

Once you've seen Hyderabad, take in sights in the surrounding regions. Bidar Fort (see *Karnataka* chapter) is 82 miles northwest of the city and can be visited in a day's excursion. For those with two or three free days, an interesting tour can take in Warangal, Ramappa Temple, Nagarjunakonda, and Srisailam—a loop that will give you a vivid sampling of Hindu, Jain, Moslem, and Buddhist culture.

Yadagirigutta and Mahaveer Jain Temple

Warangal, your destination, is 140 km north of Hyderabad on the Hanamkonda Road. There are two worthwhile stops along the way. When you are 69 km out of Hyderabad, you'll pass through the town of Bhongir. A few kilometers more and you'll spot Yadagirigutta (in Telegu, *yada* means shepherd; *giri* and *Gutta* both mean hill), a small village perched at the foot of a rocky hill. Legend has it that Lord Vishnu revealed himself to the local saint, Yadava, by appearing in three forms of *narasimha* (*nara* = human; *simha* = lion). It is said that Lord Vishnu made this spot his abode, residing in a cave that, in time, became covered by thick forest. Many years later, Vishnu appeared to a local villager in a dream and guided him to the holy spot where the villager discovered a natural cave containing the three narasimha images. A temple was built to mark the sacred shrine for Hindu pilgrims.

It's worth a 30-minute detour to see *Lakshmi Narasimha Swami Temple,* an unprepossessing structure built around the legendary cave that serves as sanctus sanctorum. Even if there weren't a temple, the trip would be worthwhile if only to climb the hill at Yadagirigutta for a view of the Deccan Plateau spreading majestically in every direction. In some respects it's evocative of sections of the American plains; yet the view remains distinctly Indian, with palm trees, simple huts, oxen, and busy villages dotting the great expanse.

Enter the temple and pass on to the inner sanctum, flanked by silver portals. Inside the holy cave, you'll see Lord Vishnu in his half-lion, half-human incarnation slaying the demon Kiranyakasipa. Give yourself time to stand back and watch the pilgrims file in. They have come hundreds of miles to pray in this sacred cave.

Most temples sell *prassadum* (god's gift)—food that pilgrims buy to take home to relatives and friends as a way of sharing their blessings. Here, for only one rupee, you can buy a delicious *pulihara,* a tasty mixture of rice, tamarind, and spices served on a coconut leaf. It is clean, nourishing food—a fine snack for less than a dime.

From here on to Warangal, look for toddy tapsters clambering up the palm trees with pots and tools slung over their shoulders and tied around their waist. Just 15 km north of Yadagirigutta and 10 minutes off the main highway, you will come to Kolanapaka and the Mahaveer Jain Temple, a pleasant cluster of small buildings that houses magnificent sculptures of Jain deities. The temple is flanked by two elephant heads carved in bas-relief at the foot of the entrance. These are *dwarapalaka* (door guards) placed there to drive away visitors with evil intentions. Nevertheless, their spirit is far more one of *swagatham* (welcome) than of forbidding authority.

A few minutes inside this temple will reveal the power of Jain art. Sculptures of various Jain gods reside in closet-sized niches, seated in the Buddha-like lotus posture. Yet these Jain figures appear more muscular and energetic than the serene Buddha. Whereas Buddha usually seems content to keep his position through all eternity, those broad-shouldered, barrel-chested deities look ready to jump up at any moment and do something unexpected.

In the far left corner of the main hall is a charming sculpture of the subdeity Sri Bumiya Ji and his son Sri Manibadr Ji that looks like an amiable pumpkin and child. To the right is Mahaveer himself—the twenty-fourth and last Jain god—five feet high and solid jade! Mahaveer's lips curl in a wide, radiant smile. You will see few works of art of any religion that are so generously concerned with the joy of existence.

In Jain temples, there are often several sculptural representations of deities, all of them virtually identical. But here, the sculptures are sharply individual. To Mahaveer's right is Adeshwar, first of the Jain gods. The jewels in his forehead are valued at close to half a million dollars. And nearby is Shankeshwar, the second of the 24 gods—equally expressive, though less lavishly endowed.

All these gods have eerie, piercing eyes that, literally, bulge from their heads. Actually, each sculpture has a less startling set of eyes carved into the stone itself. What we see are called *chakshu* (spectacles) that have been added on to the deities to give them a startling, formidable presence. It makes us stop and take notice.

Warangal

Warangal, which includes the old town of Hanamkonda, was once the capital of the Kakatiya kingdom that controlled two-thirds of present Andhra Pradesh for most of the twelfth and thirteenth centuries. Warangal is best known for its mighty fort that now lies in ruins. Even so, enough remains to suggest the scope and ambition of the Kakatiya rulers.

Constructed between 1199 and 1261, Warangal Fort was surrounded by three walls. Driving through the Warangal area, you can still see traces of the outlying wall that once covered 127 km to encircle this stronghold. The middle wall is still visible in most parts; a sloped earthen mound facing out on a broad moat. These two walls served to impede large invading forces. The inner wall, an imposing stone fortification, turns a daunting vertical face to the outside; on the inside, the wall is built in steps so the Kakatiya defenders could rapidly mount the parapets to repel an attacking army. Marco Polo once passed through the triple-turning entrance and made his way to the dazzling royal court within.

When you arrive at the site of the Kakatiya court, you'll see a rugged hill nearby. Actually, it's one enormous boulder. This was an ancient religious site, named, appropriately, *orunallu* (one stone). Centuries later, Moslem rulers inadvertently transformed the ancient Telegu to Warangal.

Though the Kakatiya were ambitious builders, they were not completely practical. Their great buildings were erected on sand rather than stone foundations. In time, the great walls of Warangal Fort sank under their own weight; pillars tilted and fell, and the roof caved in. The awesome hall that Marco Polo visited is now a large field of broken columns and fractured statues. Goats graze among the solemn ruins. Still, it's a stirring sight.

Only the four grand entrance gates *(thorana)* remain standing. Each thorana is supported by four monolith pillars rising 30 feet. Perched on the crossbars atop these pillars are pairs of *hamsa,* the emblematic bird of India's ancient kings. Somewhere between a swan and a fat duck, the hamsa's blue blood is made clear in a legend not unlike *The Princess and the Pea.* It is said that if equal parts of milk and water were mixed together in a bowl, the hamsa would sup at it and remove only the water, skillfully leaving the milk untouched. Apparently, milk was too thick for the hamsa's delicate blood. Today, these remarkable birds are as extinct as dodos.

In 1323, the Kakatiyas submitted to the overwhelming might of Tuglaq Moslem invaders from Delhi. Sitab Khan was a military commander who was appointed district governor of the Warangal Fort area in the early fourteenth century. To celebrate his good fortune, he began to build Kush Mahal, which you can look at while you're exploring the fort.

The story of Kush Mahal is like a moral fable. Kush Mahal means happy home, and for Sitab Khan, happiness came from pillaging Hindu religious sites to gather construction materials for his Moslem dream house. If you look carefully, high up on arches that once supported the ceiling, you can see stones carved with the Hindu lotus, Sitab Khan's way of boasting of the temples he dismantled. On other stones, you can make out the Moslem crescent moon. Lotus and cresent moon—united by conquest. But Sitab Khan never had the chance to enjoy the happy home that looting built. He died before its completion.

The 1,000 Pillar Temple in Warangal will introduce you to Chalukyan temple design. Instead of the soaring grandeur of Tamil Nadu temple construction, here we have low star-shaped buildings—intimate and cloistered—built on a series of platforms. This is a Shiva temple (the Kakatiyas were great devotees of Shiva. Like virtually all Shiva temples of the south, there are three main architectural elements:

• The *mandipam* is a formal entrance hall used for festivals, marriages, and celebrations. The mandipam here is dilapidated because of an inadequate foundation. The ceiling has fallen, and pillars tilt at crazy angles.

• Passing through the mandipam, you come to a small central courtyard presided over by a monolith statue of *Nandi*. Nandi, the bull, is Shiva's vehicle—as much a part of the god's life and legend as Silver is to the Lone Ranger.

• Worshipers touch Nandi's flanks before entering the *temple* to pray at the Shiva *lingam* (phallic symbol). Hindu gods are each called by dozens of different names according to regional legends and language differences. Here Shiva is known as Rudresvara.

Many centuries ago, an underground passage connected this temple to Warangal Fort, some 11 km away. It's exhausting just imagining the effort that went into tunneling through all that stone and rocky earth.

The well beside the temple is still working after over 800 years. Both the well and the temple were completed in 1163.

Only a few minutes from the 1,000 Pillar Temple is Bhadrakali Temple. It overlooks a broad, shallow lake where fishermen stand waist-deep in the silty water to cast their nets. The temple and its stone image of Kali (or Durga, as she is called elsewhere)—with her eight hands all brandishing weapons—require only a brief visit. Most interesting, perhaps, is the opportunity you'll have to get a vivid glimpse of Indian life, for this is a popular pilgrimage spot.

Indian villagers in the Warangal area pay from their minuscule savings to go on packaged bus tours that bring them to several such temples and holy shrines in a few days. The buses bring their own cooks, utensils, and food. It's likely that you'll encounter one of these groups resting or eating on the covered stone terrace just outside the inner temple.

Palampet

In Palampet, 64 km from Warangal, Rudresvara Temple (popularly called Ramappa Temple) has some of the finest sculpture in India. The temple stands less than a kilometer away from Ramappa Dam, a mammoth wall of earth formed to link two chains of hills and thus create an artificial lake. Built by the Kakatiyas in 1213, the dam clearly indicates the Kakatiyas' strong belief that the gods meant for them to rule and control the land.

Like all Hindu temples, Rudresvara faces east, though now visitors approach it from its western porch where the goporam is currently under restoration. Before entering the temple, examine the basalt obelisk in the courtyard. The Telegu inscription proudly proclaims the creation of Ramappa Lake and of the Shiva temple. The top of the obelisk is adorned with different images on each of its four faces: (1) the shiva lingam, (2) Ganesha, Shiva's beloved son, (3) Nandi, and (4) a double image of the sun (representing the Hindu faith) and crescent moon (symbol of Moslem faith). The implication is that there's room on this planet for many religions, but the great god Shiva includes all faiths.

At one time, a canal diverted water from the nearby lake to form a shallow basin around the temple's outer wall—the architect's way of acknowledging that Hindu worshipers must bathe their feet before entering a temple.

Much of the pleasure this temple offers comes from the sculptural elements along the outer walls. The base of the temple has four layers of sculptured bands that wrap around the entire building. At the bottom is a procession of hundreds of elephants that represent the earthly power of the Kakatiya Dynasty. Only along the southwest wall is the procession interrupted to include a menagerie of snakes, birds, and other indigenous wildlife. Above the elephants is a row of open lotus blossoms, a sign of faith and, presumably, the divine favor shown to the Kakatiyas. The third strip of sculpture depicts various aspects of social life. Each of the hundreds of panels is unique. There are images of dance, music, wrestling, social customs, worship, and sexual intercourse. Above these lively images of twelfth-century life is a second strip of lotus flowers to remind believers that transient life is surrounded by the eternal kingdom of god.

Charming as these representations are, probably more striking are the black basalt human figures that peer down as brackets above the outer platform. Most other Hindu temples contain the repeated figures of Narasimha, the "human lion," perched triumphantly on an elephant's head. Here, an interesting feature has been added. Standing between the elephant's head and the squatting lion is a human form, further reminder that the Kakatiyas saw themselves as wielding the combined qualities of these creatures—the elephant's brute strength and the lion's warriorlike ferocity.

Flanking the three entrances to the temple are the most notable sculptures to be found at Palampet: pairs of lively female figures, almost life-size, carved from highly polished basalt. No matter what these women are doing, they seem to be dancing. Their simplicity, energy, and lithesome form reminds one of Matisse's dance panels, done near the end of his career. Beside the north porch, one of these women is caught in a crisis: a monkey has yanked her sari loose; with one hand she shoos away the mischievous creature, with the other, she tries to cover her private parts. Along the east porch, a woman hunter balances on one leg while an attendant removes a thorn from her foot. Also on the east porch is a dancing woman wearing the twelfth-century's version of platform shoes.

Inside the temple are more fine sculptures, though nothing is quite as impressive as the 12 figure brackets that stand outside. The four basalt pillars and the ceiling are crowded with scenes from the great religious epics. Particularly charming is a panel carved on the pillar to the right of the inner sanctum. Krishna, the playboy of the Hindu deities, has stolen all the clothing of a group of shepherd girls he saw bathing. The panel shows Krishna sitting merrily in a tree while the naked girls implore him to restore their clothes.

Even the most knowledgeable guide won't be able to account for all the legends and epics represented in this temple. Nevertheless, you'll be dazzled by the gaiety and sheer abundance of sculpture that makes Rudresvara Temple such an important site.

After you see the temple, you may want to stop at the Vanavihar Tourist Rest House for a snack or a cup of tea.

Less that one km away and overlooking the lake, it is a lovely spot to relax before your return to Warangal.

Nagarjunakonda

A day's drive from Warangal (240 km) or a shorter excursion from Hyderabad (144 km) will bring you to the town of Nagarjunasagar, where one of the world's largest dams blocks the Krishna River. In 1926, excavations in the Nagarjunakonda Valley uncovered relics from the early and middle stone age, as well as evidence of a great Buddhist civilization that flourished here during the third and fourth centuries. After Prime Minister Nehru set in motion the Nagarjunasaga Dam project in 1954, Indian archaeological teams devoted six hurried years to saving as many of the Buddhist treasures as they could. In 1960, the historic valley disappeared beneath the vast artificial lake created by the dam, but treasures from the Buddhist temples and learning center have been relocated and beautifully exhibited in the government museum set on Nagarjunakonda Island 10 km from the dam.

At Anupa, five km from the dam, a *vihara* (Buddhist monastery) has been partially reconstructed from stones and pillars unearthed during excavations of the valley. This vihara was created by the Buddhist scholar, Acharya (teacher) Nagarjuna, founder of the Madhyamika school of Mahayana Buddhism, as his instrument for teaching: a study center that attracted Buddhist scholars from as far away as Kashmir, Uttar Pradesh, Sri Lanka, and Southeast Asia. Here, Nagarjuna taught medicine, engineering, surgery, and astronomy, as well as pursued alchemical experiments in search of *amruth,* the heavenly herbal medicine said to produce immortality. (Legend has it that he succeeded and took a deep draught himself, a poetic way of saying that the spirit of the man lives on.) It's from Nagarjuna's teaching that Buddhism developed the doctrine of *Shunyata* (the void), the belief that we are surrounded by delusory forms and notions—that the truly enlightened reject illusion and experience all as a great, unchanging void.

The first thing you'll encounter as you approach the vihara site is a circular brick structure. This was once a *stupa,* an integral element in Buddhist worship that symbolizes the Buddha himself and his spiritual progress to nirvana, beyond all concepts and forms. The stupa's parasol-like crown was divided into eight sections representing eight great precepts of Buddha's teachings: 1) *Devatha:* devotion to God, to the Lord Buddha; 2) *Ghourva:* respect for one's guru or teacher; 3) *Ahimsa:* refusal to cause pain, injury, or physical punishment to one's fellow beings, which became an essential part of Gandhi's philosophy of nonviolence; 4) *Dharma:* obedience to sacred law; 5) *Moxa:* faith in salvation, striving for enlightenment; 6) *Araha:* renunciation of wealth and material needs; 7) *Kama:* renunciation of carnal desire; and 8) *Sanga:* commitment to the society of fellow Buddhists.

Turn from the remains of the eight-spoked stupa and you face a long brick wall that was once the main residential hall of the monastery. *Mahayana,* the form of Buddhism practiced by Nagarjuna, regards Buddha as both a teacher and a god, whereas *Hinayana,* the older and more orthodox sect, regards Buddha as supreme teacher but not as God. Both branches of Buddhist thought were given separate meditation chambers at Nagarjuna's monastery. To the left is a meditation room, or *chaitya griha* (*chaitya* = idol; *griha* = house), where Mahayanas could meditate before an idol in Buddha's image. To the right is an identical building, but it is a *stupa griha* (house with stupa), where Hinayanas could meditate on Buddha's teachings without having to worship before a carved representation of Buddha himself.

Just outside the door to the chaitya griha is a semicircular step ringed with a frieze of carved animal figures. This step, called "moonstone," symbolizes Buddha's concept that life is a fragile bubble (the curved stone suggests the bubble shape), a reminder that our task in life is to seek enlightenment before the bubble bursts. A second function of the moonstone was to divert one's attention before entering the sacred space. When one's eyes were drawn down to the curved step and the animal figures, one was supposed to empty one's mind of evil thoughts. Otherwise, the intense act of meditating might accidentally concentrate the "evil eye" with such force that the entire shrine might shatter.

Nagarjunakonda Museum

A pleasant 20-minute boat ride leads to Nagarjunakonda Island and a gem of a museum. In the entrance gallery of the museum, on the wall to the right, are photographs of the excavations that unearthed the collection that is housed here. One series of photos shows several jars—terra cotta, copper, silver, and gold—fashioned to fit inside each other in decreasing size. Inside the small gold jar, archaeologists found human bones, along with an inscription attesting that these were from the Buddha himself. The bones are not exhibited; they are kept in a secure vault on the island. But their very presence makes Nagarjunakonda a place of great importance to the Buddhist faithful.

At the entrance to the main exhibition hall, the visitor is greeted by a pair of chubby troll-like creatures. These are *Yaksha Padmanidhi* (*yaksha* = god of wealth; *padma* = lotus). Their heads are decorated with hanging lotus petals. A geyser of gold coins springs from the crown of each head, falling in a giant braid into each creature's left hand. It's an auspicious greeting: may you, too, be blessed with prosperity.

There are many appealing sculptures in this bright, spacious room. But if you want to learn a bit more about Buddha's life, you can begin by studying the fourth display on the left wall, which is divided into five sections, each depicting a crucial stage in the story of Buddha. Beginning on the far right of the panel you see Buddha's birth (in 566 B.C.); his Renunciation, when Buddha left behind his wife, family, and earthly riches to seek enlightenment; Mara's attack, the temptation of sexuality and various negative emotional forces; Buddha's first preaching at Sarnath; and Buddha's death.

As with so many artists, the sculptor who created this five-part narrative appears to have lavished particular attention on the forces of temptation. Mara's attack is depicted in the middle section: Buddha sits in the center of the scene while, to the right, sexual demons plot against him. To the left of Buddha, Kama (sex) tries to tempt him, and just below Kama, wicked cherubs representing pride and miserliness await their chance to besiege him. On the far left of this group, pride (in woman's form) glowers harshly; beneath her, a little demon, anger, joins the band of tempters. Buddha, of course, remains divinely unperturbed.

It's impossible to spend more than a few moments in the exhibition hall without being drawn to the 10-foot statue of Buddha that dominates the room. No need for description—it communicates without words.

The renunciation episode in Buddha's life is narrated with economy and understated emotion in display No. 48, which hangs in the exhibition room connected to the main hall from the right. The story is told in three sections proceeding from the bottom to the top. As a young prince, Siddhartha (Buddha) led a cloistered life that was calculated to shield him from the harshness of the external world. The bottom bas-relief depicts the day Siddhartha explored the marketplace. The scenes of human misery and mortality—an old man, a diseased man, a corpse, and an ascetic who had renounced the world—disturbed him, and he understands the shallowness of his youthful vision of life. The middle section shows Siddhartha spending the night reflecting on what he has seen and vowing to pursue the ascetic's path. In the top section, he leaves his father's palace in search of enlightenment.

Though the museum is small, it's easy to enjoy several hours here and outside in the pleasant gardens. But make sure you arrange in town for a government guide to accompany you before you go. The Andhra Pradesh Tourist Department provides guides at no charge, and they'll bring these storytelling friezes to life. (The booking counter for the boat shuttle is near the dam. It costs 10 rupees round trip. Try to book in advance at the government tourist department office.)

Amaravati

Another ancient Buddhist center, Amaravati, lies east of Nagarjunasagar on the right bank of the Krishna, a river inseparably linked with the history and culture of this region. Formerly an ancient Buddhist capital known as Dhyanakataka, Amaravati was a flourishing center of Buddhism in the first century B.C.—one of the four most important places of Buddhist worship in the country. Monasteries and a university brought devotees from as far away as China.

The ruins of the 2,000-year-old settlement are highly poetic, and much of the Buddhist culture is extremely elegant and remarkably well preserved. The stupa was originally the largest in the country. Although its size has been diminished (ravaged by the less spiritual), the richly carved panels and remaining friezes showing scenes of the life of Buddha are beautiful and worth your careful scrutiny.

Srisailam

Srisailam offers few of the conveniences that many Western travelers seek, but visitors who are willing to make a long day's excursion (from Hyderabad or Nagarjunasagar) or stay in a shabby government tourist house, will be rewarded by a firsthand look at the powerful emotion generated by Hindu worship.

Bhramaramba is the regional name for the goddess Durga (or Kali). Mallikarjunaswamy is the regional name for Shiva. Here Shiva and Durga exist in perpetual honeymoon—married anew every evening in a ceremony performed for thousands of pilgrims who flock here from all over India. This temple is particularly revered, for it holds one of the 12 *Jyothirlingams* in India. (Jyothi means light—in this case, spiritual light.) These 12 Jyothirlingams are said to have been formed by the divine force of nature itself.

In the central courtyard, a large map of India shows the location of the other 11 Jyothirlingams. These sacred places are scattered in every corner of the subcontinent.

This temple has no outstanding architectural or sculptural features, but its importance and popularity make it a memorable place to experience a Hindu prayer service. As you approach the temple, you'll see worshipers buying small baskets filled with coconut, fruits, and fragrant jasmine to offer the deity. Inside the low-ceilinged worship hall, devotees crowd along a metal railing, while a priest passes down the central aisle, chanting as he makes his way from the small Nandi statue toward the sanctus sanctorum, the small room that houses the sacred lingam. These quiet moments are merely a prelude to the actual ceremony. The priest enters the sanctus sanctorum and draws back a curtain to reveal the Jyothirlingam beneath a brass canopy covered with lotus blossoms. Instantly, an incredible clamor breaks forth—imagine a railroad train crashing through an orchestra that is playing *The Rites of Spring.* Drums, bells, curved horns, and brass gongs join in a deafening riot of sound. Numerous devotional candles are lit and passed over the lingam, as the Hindu faithful clasp their hands in prayer: wonder, reverence, and delight reflected in their faces.

This ceremony lasts for 10 minutes, after which the priest files past the worshipers once again, distributing jasmine flowers and collecting offerings. Worshipers are then invited into the sanctus sanctorum (non-Hindus can join them), where they kneel to kiss the lingam.

Note: It's best to attend the first prayer service at 5:45 A.M. to avoid the long lines that form by mid-morning.

There are several other temples here and numerous other shrines in the Srisailam area, but nothing else leaves the lasting impression of this joyful ceremony.

The Bay of Bengal

Unless you're journeying between Calcutta or Bhubaneswar and Madras, this area is off the beaten path. Nevertheless, it offers several interesting attractions. Visakhapatnam, or Vizag, as it is commonly known, is a thriving seaport flanked by long stretches of excellent beach. Rama Krishna Mission Beach is one of the cleanest beaches on India's east coast. Mount Kailas, six km away, overlooks another good beach.

From Vizag it's only a short trip (16 km) to Simhachalam (hill of the lion), famous for its eleventh-century Narasimha Temple. Devotees flock to this dramatic hillside setting to celebrate Lord Vishnu's heroic defense of Prahlada, his follower. They smear the Vishnu image with sandal paste until it's unrecognizable. Once a year, on the third day of Vaisakha (April–May), the idol is cleansed in a ritual called Chandana Visarjana, during which Lord Vishnu is revealed. The temple is known for its many elegant sculptures.

Bheemunipatnam is 35 km from Vizag by a road that runs along the beach. It is the site of a former Dutch trading settlement of the seventeenth century. A ruined fort remains, as well as Hollanders Green, the original Dutch cemetery. There's a good beach here. The spot hasn't been developed for super-tourism, but if you're willing to live in a modest guest house, consider Bheemunipatnam as the place to retreat and relax a few days.

Southeast Andhra Pradesh

The best approach to Tirupati in the hilly Chittoor district of southeast Andhra Pradesh is from Madras, in Tamil Nadu. Tirupati, with its temple of Lord Venkateswara in nearby Tirumala, is visited by millions of pilgrims every year. It's a popular temple, in large part because a visit here is said to bring good fortune.

Fortune is very much a part of the temple's history. In the days of the Pallava and Chola Dynasties, several rulers presented vast treasures at the hill temple. When Krishnadeva, the Raya king, visited the temple for the first time in 1513, he presented the deity with a jewel-studded crown, a necklace of pearls and precious stones, and 25 silver plates. Later that year, he returned to deliver a sword embedded with diamonds, rubies, and sapphires. The following year, glowing after a series of military victories, he buried the Lord's image in a pile of 30,000 gold coins.

This tradition of lavish offerings has made Tirumala the wealthiest temple in India. When you consider that India is a land of thousands of temples, this is no small distinction. Buses arrive from pre-dawn until evening, conveying thousands of pilgrims who wait patiently for their chance to pray in the temple and make offerings to the treasury. (Those who administer the temple treasury have distributed the money to fund a university, research institutions, health care, and social welfare organizations.)

On arriving in Tirupati, many pilgrims choose to walk to Tirumala by rock steps that have been traveled for centuries. There is also a winding road that cuts into the hills, providing magnificent views as you make your way by bus or taxi to Tirumala. Non-Hindus are barred from witnessing some parts of the worship, but if you want that blessing of wealth and want to experience India in all its spiritual intensity, the pilgrims' path from Tirupati to Tirumala offers a wealth of that sort, too.

PRACTICAL INFORMATION FOR
ANDHRA PRADESH

WHEN TO GO. From mid-October to late March is best. Temperature ranges from 60° F to 90° F with cooler evenings. Summer begins at the end of March, when temperatures climb above 100. Monsoon rains from June to August are welcome to farmers but not to tourists.

HOW TO GET THERE. By Air. Daily direct *Indian Airlines* flights into Hyderabad from Bangalore, Bombay, Calcutta, Delhi, and Madras. Occasional flights into Hyderabad from Ahmedabad, Aurangabad, Bhubaneswar, Pune, and Varanasi. Also daily Indian Airlines flights from Hyderabad or Madras to Tirupati, Vijayawada, and Visakhapatnam. From Tirupati, besides Madras and Hyderabad, flights to Vijayawada; occasional flights to Bangalore. From Visakhapatnam, daily flights to Calcutta.

By Bus. *Andhra Pradesh State Road Transport Corporation* (APSRTC) runs luxury coaches (many with loud unceasing video sets blaring) to most important southern Indian cities: Bangalore, Madras, and Bombay, plus numerous tourist spots in the state. For details and fares, contact in Hyderabad: APSRTC, RTC Cross Roads, Musheerabad; tel. 64571. *Indian Tourism Development Corporation* (ITDC) also runs deluxe interstate buses in and out of Andhra Pradesh. For details, contact ITDC 3–6–150/4 Lidcap Building Himayatanagar, Hyderabad; tel. 220730. *Tiruvalluvar Transport Corporation* from Tamil Nadu runs deluxe coaches to and from Tirupati, as does APSRTC. In Madras, contact either at the Express Bus Stand; tel. 561835.

By Train. To Hyderabad (the station is actually at Secundrabad), daily trains from Bombay are *Hyderabad–Bombay Express* and *Minar Express;* from Delhi, *Hyderabad Niz Express;* from Madras, *Navjivan Express;* from Bangalore, *Bangalore–Hyderabad Express.* To Waltair, there are numerous daily trains from Calcutta (Howrah Station). To Tirupati, two daily trains from Madras. Day trains are not hard to arrange. Sleepers with reserved berths (a must—don't just buy a sleeper ticket) involve early reservations. For details and fares, contact Railway Inquiry at Hyderabad; tel. 231352.

By Rental Car with Driver. Hyderabad is 566 km from Bangalore, 735 km from Bombay, and 680 km from Madras. A car with a driver costs about Rs. 3 per km, plus night-halt charges (usually under Rs. 50 a night). Cars are available through the following agencies: *Andhra Pradesh Tourism Development Corporation* (APTDC), Diamond House, Himayatnagar, Hyderabad (tel. 36282); *Indian Tourism Development Corporation*, Himayatnagar, Hyderabad (tel. 220730); *Sita World Travels* (tel. 223628); *Trade Wings* (tel. 30545); *Mercury Travel Ltd.* (tel. 34411); Indtravels (tel. 222034). *The State Tourist Information Bureau*, Himayatnagar, Hyderabad, 500029 (tel. 233384) can also recommend approved agencies.

TOURIST INFORMATION. If you're starting your visit to India in New Delhi, stop by the *Andhra Pradesh Tourist Information Centre* to make inquiries and pick up brochures at 1 Ashoka Rd., New Delhi; tel. 389182. Open 10 A.M.–5 P.M.; Monday–Saturday. The main office for the *Andhra Pradesh Travel and Tourism Department* is in Hyderabad at Gagan Vihar, First Floor, M.J. Road; tel. 556303. Open 10 A.M.–5 P.M., Monday–Saturday. The department can help arrange excursions and will give you brochures and suggest hotels. Other tourist offices:

Hyderabad Airport, tel. 556493; open 10 A.M.–5 P.M.; Monday–Saturday.

Nagarjunasagar. Tourist Information Officer, Hill Colony; tel. 3633. Open 10 A.M.–5 P.M., Monday–Saturday.

Tirupati/Tirumala. Tourist Information Officer, T.P. Area, Tirupati; tel. 2598. Open 10 A.M.–5 P.M., Monday–Saturday.

Visakhapatnam (Vizag). Tourist Information Officer, Hotel Apsara Arcade, Visakhapatnam; tel. 63026. Open 10 A.M.–5 P.M., Monday–Saturday.

Warangal. Tourist Information Officer, Tourist Rest House, Kazipet, Warangal; tel. 6201. Open 10 A.M.–5 P.M., Monday–Saturday. The Government of India also has a tourist office in Hyderabad at Sandozi Building Himayatnagar, Hyderabad 500029; tel. 66877. Open 9 A.M.–5 P.M., Monday–Saturday.

 **ACCOMMODATIONS.** Hyderabad has a good range of hotels in all price ranges. Throughout the rest of Andhra Pradesh, facilities exist, but not at the level or variety as in Hyderabad. Rates are based on double occupancy: *Expensive,* over Rs. 500; *Moderate,* Rs. 250–500; *Inexpensive,* under Rs. 250. Most Western-style hotels take major credit cards.

AMARAVATI

Inexpensive

Inspection Bungalow. Amaravati. Small number of rooms. For this price, clean is what you get. Very minimal. Reservations: District Collector, Guntar, Andhra Pradesh.

HYDERABAD

Expensive

Hotel Banjara. Road No 1, Banjara Hills, (seven km from the airport; five km from downtown); tel. 222222. 123 air-conditioned rooms, 24-hour room service, shopping arcade, restaurants, a coffee shop, and a bar. An attractive well-run hotel. The best place in Hyderabad, without question.

Baskar Palace. Banjara Hills. Scheduled for completion in 1988.

Krishna Oberoi Hotel. Banjara Hills. Scheduled for completion by 1988.

Moderate

Hotel Nagarjuna. Basheer Bagh (seven km from the airport); tel. 237201. 60 air-conditioned rooms with TVs, a restaurant, bar, coffee shop, and many amenities. Right on the street, however.

Hyd Inn. 5–9–24/82 Lake Hill Rd. (four km from the airport); tel. 237573. 30 rooms, all air-conditioned; room service, a restaurant, and some amenities.

Ritz Hotel. Hill Fort Palace Road (six km from the airport; ½ km from downtown); tel. 233571. 36 air-conditioned rooms with TVs, room service, crowded pool, restaurant, and bar. The Ritz is a converted palace, but it has seen better days. Could be charming; now it's merely acceptable.

Rock Castle Hotel. Banjara Hills (seven km from the airport; four km from downtown); tel. 33541. 22 rooms, some air-conditioned; some cottages. Has a bar, restaurant, room service, and lovely gardens. Ideal place for travelers who want a place with personality.

Hotel Sampurna. Mukramjahi Road (eight km from the airport, close to downtown); tel. 40165. 60 air-conditioned rooms with TVs, 24-hour room service, and many Western amenities. A good price for what you get, but the hotel has no particular character.

Secunderabad Club. Secunderabad; tel. 76351. In the old British cantonment area. A former officers' club, with a library of rare first editions from the high days of the raj. Spacious lounge rooms with cane furniture. Rooms are a bit shabby, but clean and adequate. A must for those who believe atmosphere takes precedence over a new coat of paint. Limited rooms, some air-conditioned. Bars and snacks, but no full meals.

Inexpensive

Hotel Ashoka. 6–1–70 Lakdikapul (five km from the airport, downtown); tel. 230077. 90 rooms, some air-conditioned; TVs, restaurant, room service, shopping arcade of sorts. Fine, for the price.

Hotel Deccan Continental. Minister Road (one km from the airport; one km from downtown); tel. 70981. 72 rooms, some air-conditioned; room service, restaurant, swimming pool, and other amenities. Not bad for the price.

NAGARJUNASAGAR

Until the Andhra Pradesh Tourism Department sets up its air shuttle service to and from Hyderabad, you must count on spending the night here if you want to see the Buddhist monastery and museum treasures. Unfortunately, accommodations are meager and indifferently administered.

Inexpensive

Right Bank Cottage. Nagarjunasagar; tel. 3633. 25 rooms, some air-conditioned.

Vijay Vihar Guest House. Nagarjunasagar; tel. 3625. Eight rooms, five cottages, all air-conditioned. The better of the slim pickings.

PALAMPET

Inexpensive

Vanavihar Tourist Rest House. Reservations through the Tourist Rest House in Warwangal. Four rooms. Indian toilets, no air-conditioning, but rooms are clean. Peaceful location overlooking the artificial lake. If you stay here, you must bring food from the market that the cook will prepare at no extra cost; this doesn't discount a tip. A five-minute walk to the temple.

SRISAILAM

Inadequate as Nagarjunasagar is, Srisailam has even less to offer. The thousands of pilgrims who visit daily either sleep outside or crowd into inexpensive *choultries.*

Inexpensive

Saila Vihar Tourist Rest House. Srisailam. Reservations through District Public Relations Officer, Kurnool; tel. 353. Five rooms. The only possibility in town, but you must be adventurous. Indian toilets. No air-conditioning. But sometimes, who cares?

TIRUPATI/TIRUMALA

Inexpensive

Bhimas Deluxe Hotel. 34–38, G Car Street, Tirupati; tel. 2501. 60 rooms, some air-conditioned; restaurant. Not bad.

Tourist Rest House. Alipari Road, Tirupati; tel. 2794. Adequate and inexpensive. Definitely no frills. Most visitors prefer to visit this area as a day excursion out of Madras, which offers a wide selection of accommodations in all price ranges.

VIJAYAWADA

Moderate

Hotel Kandhari International. Labbipet, Bunder Road (22 km from the airport, one km from downtown); tel. 61311. 80 air-conditioned rooms, room service, coffee shop, restaurant, and bar. The best in town.

Inexpensive

Hotel Manorama. 27–38–61 Bandar Road (22 km from the airport, downtown); tel. 77221. 69 rooms, some air-conditioned; restaurant, shopping arcade, TVs.

VISAKHAPATNAM (VIZAG)

Nearby Simhachalam and Bheemunipatnam are too small to offer more than simple guest house accommodations and a few very inexpensive Indian-style hotels without frills (certainly no air-conditioning). Most visitors will prefer to stay in Vizag, take in the beach, and make day excursions to these two towns.

Expensive

Park Hotel. Beach Road (15 km from the airport; four km from the railroad); tel. 63081. 64 rooms, air-conditioned, TVs, restaurant, swimming pool. Good hotel on the beach.

Moderate

Dolphin Hotel. Dabagardens (13 km from the airport; two km from the railroad); tel. 64811. 147 air-conditioned rooms with TVs, a restaurant, coffee shop, golf club, and swimming pool. Good.

Inexpensive

Hotel Aspara. 12–1–17, Waltair Main Road (12 km from the airport; two km from the railroad); tel. 64861. 69 rooms, some air-conditioned; three restaurants and a bar. Near town, but nice.

Ocean View Inn. Kirlampudi (16 km from the airport; three km from the railroad); tel. 64828. 30 rooms, some air-conditioned; TVs. Simple, but pleasant; beach nearby.

WARANGAL

Inexpensive

Hotel Ashoka. Main Road, Hanamkonda; tel. 85491. 40 rooms, air-conditioned; bar, restaurants. Clean, comfortable. The food is better than at many deluxe hotels.

Government Tourist Rest House. Kazipet Road; tel. 6201. Four rooms. Under renovation as of this writing: installation of Western toilets and air-conditioning. Should be ready by 1988.

 DINING OUT. Andhra Pradesh cooking, especially in Hyderabad, reflects the same historical and cultural influences mentioned earlier in the chapter. Moslem and Hindu, north and south all come together to produce a wide selection of tasty dishes. Generally speaking, you're likely to eat better in Hyderabad than anywhere else in India, with the exception of Goa. Prices are based on an average three-course dinner for one, not including beverage, taxes, or tip. *Expensive,* Rs. 50 or more; *Moderate,* Rs. 25–50; *Inexpensive,* under Rs. 25. Only Western-style hotels accept credit cards, unless noted.

HYDERABAD

Expensive

Kabab-E-Bahar. Hotel Banjara, Road No. 1, Banjara Hills; tel. 222222. Excellent barbecue specialties served beside an artificial lake. Very pleasant. Open 7:30 P.M.–midnight. Reservations advised.

Lambadi. Hotel Banjara, Road No. 1, Banjara Hills; tel. 222222. Hyderabadi specialties. A good place to order *haleem*—pounded wheat blended with spiced mutton and gravy. Open 1–3 P.M. and 8 P.M.–midnight. Reservations advised.

Shahnaz. Hotel Banjara, Road No. 1, Banjara Hills; tel. 222222. Continental and Chinese food. Open for breakfast, lunch, and dinner. Live music. Reservations advised.

Moderate

East & West Bar and Restaurant. Saifabad, opposite Telephone Bhavan. Good Chinese and Indian food. Major credit cards accepted. Lunch and dinner.

Golden Deer. Abid Road, near Palace Heights. Excellent Chinese meals and large portions. Lunch and dinner.

Golden Dragon. Near Park Lane Hotel, off Mahatma Gandhi Road. Another good Chinese restaurant. Lunch and dinner.

Manju Cafe and Bar. 4–1–873 Tilak Road; tel. 233180. Indian, Chinese, and Continental. 11 A.M.–11 P.M.

Palace Heights. Abid Road, eighth floor of a highly visible modern building. Fine view of Hyderabad. Offers choice of North Indian, tandoori, Chinese, and Continental dishes. Lunch and dinner.

Three Aces Bar and Restaurant. Abid Road; tel. 222480. North Indian, Chinese, and Continental dishes. Lunch and dinner.

Satkar. Hotel Sampurna, Makramjahi Road, Hyderabad; tel. 40165. A good Andhra nonvegetarian restaurant. Lunch and dinner.

Shahen Sha. Hotel Sampurna, Mukramjahi Road; tel. 40165. Continental and Mughlai; lunch and dinner.

Inexpensive

Samtrupthi. Hotel Sampurna, Mukramjahi Road; tel. 40165. Good vegetarian food. Open 11 A.M.–10 P.M.

Tirupati/Tirumala

Inexpensive

Bhimas Deluxe Hotel. 34–38, G Car Street, Tirupati; tel. 2501. Breakfast, lunch, dinner. Nonvegetarian and vegetarian food.

Simple vegetarian meals and snacks are available at any number of stalls or "hotels." In all likelihood, you'll be here on a day excursion and will eat a full meal before or after your visit.

VIJAYAWADA

Moderate

Hotel Greenlands Restaurant. 40–17–191/1 Bhavani Gardens; tel. 73081. Multicuisine, mainly Indian and Continental. Lunch and dinner. Outdoor dining.

Hotel Kandhari International. Labbipet, Bunder Road; tel. 61311. Good Indian, Chinese, Continental, and South Indian food. Lunch and dinner.

Hotel Mamata. Elura Road, opposite the Bus Stand; tel. 77221. Good Indian, Continental, vegetarian food. Breakfast, lunch, and dinner.

VISAKHAPATNAM

Moderate

Park Hotel Restaurant. Beach Road; tel. 63081. Good Indian, Chinese, and Continental food. Lunch, dinner.

WARANGAL AND PALAMPET

Inexpensive

Classic Bar and Restaurant. Hotel Ashoka; tel. 85491. The only place to go. Everything is well prepared. The vegetarian meal (Rs. 9) is as good as any you're likely to eat. Mutton do Piaza (Rs. 12) and Chicken Masala (Rs. 16) are memorable versions of these traditional dishes. Continental and Chinese dishes are also available. Just hope that the talented chef is not snapped up by one of the big hotel chains.

 HOW TO GET AROUND. From the Airport. Taxis into Hyderabad, Vizag, or Tirupati cost Rs. 50–Rs. 75. Regular bus service from the airport is much less, but it is also much less convenient.

By Taxi and Motor Rickshaw. Traveling about in Hyderabad, Vizag, or Tirupati, you can choose between motor rickshaw or taxi. For all but the most well-heeled traveler, taxis are an unnecessary expense. Rickshaws cost about 75 percent less (even when the driver claims that the meter doesn't work and insists on a set rate to squeeze you for a few more rupees). Rickshaws are also a lot more fun.

By Bus. There are local buses, too, throughout most of Andhra Pradesh, but they're a bit much to handle. Especially in Hyderabad, where you have to be a wild leaper to jump aboard.

By Boat. Another attractive option—at least for one leg of your journey—is the motor launch connecting Nagarjunasagar with Srisailam. It's simple, fast, cheap, and far more pleasant to travel the 100 km between these two towns by boat (three hours) than over rough country roads (4½ hours). Launch leaves

Nagarjunasagar for Srisailam at 6 A.M.; from Srisailam, the launch returns at 3 P.M., allowing you to do a loop of Hyderabad–Nagarjunasager–Srisailam–Hyderabad in either direction. The one-way fare is Rs. 100. From April–June, the worst months to be traveling in this area, the water level of the Kirshna River may make this excursion impossible. July–March boat service is usually in operation.

TOURS. *APTDC* is eager to help tourists visit the state. It has special government tours, in deluxe coaches, that will take you on the following excursions accompanied by a guide. Costs are approximate.

Hyderabad City Sight Seeing. Daily 8 A.M.–6 P.M., Rs. 35.

Nagarjunasagar. Twice daily. Numerous possibilities, one way, Rs. 25; overnight trip with air-conditioned accommodations, Rs. 100.

Yadagirigutta. Twice daily to the Laxminarasimha Swamy Temple. Rs. 25.

Tirupati. Every Friday at 4 P.M., returning at 6 A.M. on Monday. Again, numerous possibilities, including one-way, Rs. 100, and two-way transport and lodging, Rs. 275.

Manttalayam. Every Saturday at 10 A.M., returning on Sunday at 9 P.M. Tour to Raghavendra Swamy Temple, Alampur Temple, Pillalamarri. Rs. 125, including double-bed accommodations.

Srisailam. Every Saturday at 12 noon, returning on Saturday at 9 P.M. Rs. 100.

Warangal. Every Saturday and Sunday, departing at 7 A.M. and returning the same night at 9:30. Rs. 100.

With the tours to Nagarjunasagar and Tirupati, any tourist already at these places can pay Rs. 10 to join the local sightseeing with a guide. All tours originate in Hyderabad. For further details and reservations, contact APTDC, First Floor, Gagan Vihar, Mukhramjahi Road, Hyderabad (tel. 556493), at the airport counter (tel. 77192), or at the counters at either railway station.

SEASONAL EVENTS. As with the rest of India, Andhra Pradesh celebrates the major festivals: *Diwali* in **October/November,** a festival that marks the start of the Hindu New Year, and *Dussehra.* In Hyderabad, with its large Moslem population, the important Islamic holy days are also revered. But the following festivals are particularly special. Contact the tourist department for the exact dates.

January. Throughout Andhra Pradesh, *Pongal* is a three-day harvest festival. The sun is worshiped on the first day, then cows and bullocks (painted and decorated) are fed *pongal,* a rice concoction, as part of a ceremony of thanksgiving. Processions, lots of happy celebration.

April/May. Simhachalam observes the *Vaisakha Festival.* The sandpaste-covered image of Vishnu is cleansed in a ritual called *Chandana Visarjana,* revealing before crowds of devotees, the actual image of Lord Vishnu.

June/July. *Id-ul-Fitr* in Hyderabad is a festive celebration after the month-long fast of Ramadam. Feasting and lots of good fun.

$P£ **FOREIGN CURRENCY EXCHANGE.** You can change travelers checks at the better hotels, with minimum hassle. Or you can stand in a line, which is really more like joining a throng hanging around a teller's cage at a major bank, hoping sooner or later you'll get close to the window. Use the following banks throughout Andhra Pradesh: *State Bank of India* or *State Bank of Hyderabad.* Hours usually 10 A.M.–2 P.M. Monday–Friday; sometimes they're open Saturday mornings until noon.

RECOMMENDED READING. In Hyderabad, try to pick up a copy of *Glimpses of Hyderabad—A Guide:* It's not news, but it's still an informative paperback. Cost: Rs. 3.

HISTORIC SITES. Amaravati. Amaravati is a former Buddhist center that flourished in the first century B.C.— one of the four most important places of worship for Buddhists in India. Its stupa, which was originally the largest in India, is made of brick and covered with marble. Now mainly in ruins, it's still a peaceful site.

HYDERABAD

Charminar, a beautiful granite structure with a slender minaret rising from each corner, was built in 1592 by Quli Qutb Shahi, the founder of Hyderabad. The arches face the cardinal points: north, south, east, and west. The rooms above the arches may have been used as a college. The structure was possibly built as an offering to drive away an epidemic that was destroying the population of the then new city.

Golconda Fort, six km from Charminar, is a thirteenth-century fort rebuilt by the Qutb Shahi Kings in the sixteenth century and made their capital. It has great acoustics. A loud noise made under the dome of the front gate can be heard at the highest point in the fort. An ingenious water supply system—clay pipes and Persian wheels—carried water to roof gardens and palaces. Entry fee: Rs. 2.

Mecca Masjid is the biggest mosque in South India. Ten thousand devotees can pray inside. Construction was started in 1614 by the sixth Qutb Shah king, Abdullah Qutb Shah, and completed by the Mogul Emperor Aurangzeb. Colonades and door arches were made from single slabs of granite.

Qutb Shahi Tombs are memorials for seven of the Qutb Shahi kings. Structures have a strange infusion of Hindu influence. Note the lotus leaves and buds.

Venkateswara Temple is a marble structure, dedicated to Lord Venkateswara, completed in 1976 by the Birla Foundation. An excellent fusion of north and south temple architecture. Workmen from all over India were involved, including some craftsmen who were supposedly descended from the artists who worked on the Taj Mahal. The idols were made by south Indian sculptors. Open to all, regardless of faith, 8 A.M.–noon; 4–8 P.M.

KOLANAPAKA

Mahaveer Jain Temple is claimed to be 2,000 years old. Inside is a five-foot-high sculpture of Mahaveer, the last of the Jain gods, built of solid jade. Another deity, Adeshwar (the first of the Jain gods) has jewels in his forehead valued at half a million dollars.

NAGARJUNAKONDA

Arupa, five km from Nagarjunakonda, is a Buddhist monastery reconstructed from excavated ruins of a lost city and an important Buddhist settlement dating back to the third century. The original city was flooded by the Nagarjunasagar dam, which created the world's third-largest artificial lake.

PALAMPET

Rudresvara Temple (also called Ramappa Temple), dedicated to Shiva, was constructed by the Kakatiyas around A.D. 1234. This is a must-see if you're in the area. You'll find some of the best temple sculpture in India.

SRISAILAM

Bhramaramka Mallikarjunaswamy Temple contains a *Jyothirlingam,* which means natural lingam created by a god (one of 12 in India). The temple is enclosed in huge walls and gateways with bas-reliefs illustrating legends and avatars connected to Shiva. Parts of the temple complex extend back to the second century A.D. The daily *puja* is spectacular.

TIRUPATI/TIRUMALA

At Tirumala, *Sri Venkateswara Temple* is the abode of the "Lord of the Seven Hills" and home of one of the richest temples in southern India. The shrine is an essential pilgrimage, a great example of early Dravidian art. Non-Hindus are allowed inside. The temple sits on a peak, with its several *goporums* (towers) visible during the ascent. The main door, Vimana, over the sanctum sanctorum (inner shrine) and the temple flagpost are covered in gold plate.

Chandragiri Fort, 11 km from Tirupati, was important during the last days of the Vijayanagar empire. Built in A.D.1000. Inside are interesting remains of palaces and temples. Nearby, two palaces are used by members of the royal family.

Kalahahasti, east of Tirupati, is another important pilgrimage center and old temple with inscriptions that connect it to the Cholas in the 900s right through to the Vijayanagar Empire in the 1500s. The huge goporum was built in 1516. According to legend, the lingam inside the temple was worshiped by a spider *(sri),* a snake *(kala),* and an elephant *(hasti),* which obviously explains its name. The temple is dedicated to Vayu, the god of the winds.

At Simhachalam, 16 km from Vizag, the 11th century *Narashima Temple* is dedicated to Lord Vishnu in his incarnation as Narasimha in the form of a boar. The pillars in the mandapas have beautiful carvings.

WARANGAL

One Thousand Pillar Temple in Warangal, capital of Kakatiya Dynasty between the eleventh and twelfth centuries, was constructed in 1163 by Rudra Deva in the Chalukyan style, with each pillar richly carved. A six-foot Nandi stands out front. This temple is dedicated to Shiva.

Warangal Fort covers an enormous area; constructed between 1199 and 1261 by the Kakatiya rulers.

YADAGIRIGUTTA

Laxshmi Narasimha Swami Temple is situated on top of a lovely hill offering a good view of the Deccan Plateau. The temple is built around a cave where Lord Vishnu supposedly lived. In the inner sanctum, flanked by silver doors, Lord Vishnu lies in his half lion-half human incarnation slaying the demon Kiranyakasipa.

 MUSEUMS. Amaravati. *Archaeological Museum* holds Buddhist antiquities from third century B.C. to A.D. twelfth century. Open 9 A.M.–5 P.M.; closed Fridays.

Hyderabad. *Andhra Pradesh State Museum* in the Public Gardens was established in 1930. Collections of weapons, bidriware, bronzes, miniatures, manuscripts, and sculpture and a prehistoric section complete with a mummy. Open daily except Mondays and official holidays, 10:30 A.M.–5 P.M.

Birla Museum in the Asmangadh Palace at Malakpet, near the TV tower, houses bronzes, sculptures, paintings, armor. Excellent miniatures from the Deccani, Mogul, and Rajasthani art schools. In fact, you'll find art from all over the world here. Very eclectic displays. For hours, contact Director, Birla Archaeological and Cultural Institute, tel. 558347.

Salar Jung Museum has 38 galleries of priceless art treasures amassed in the early 1900s by Yousuf Ali Khan, aka Nawab Salar Jung. A lonely man, he surrounded himself with every conceivable notion of art: South Indian bronzes, miniatures from Shah Jahan's personal album, Nur Jahan's emerald and ruby dagger, and ivory furniture as well as Western Chippendale and Louis XIV, Persian carpets, even ordinary garden tools. A must-see, including the clock in the courtyard. Open daily except Fridays and official holidays, 10 A.M.–5 P.M. Rs. 2. Free guide service offered.

Nagarjunasagar. *Nagarjunakonda Island Museum* is designed in the model of a Buddhist *vihara* (monastery) and set on a hill. Here you can see the reconstructed relics of a third- and fourth-century Buddhist civilization: Buddhist stupas, actual relics of the Buddha, viharas, sacrificial altars, statues, even a peaceful garden. A boat takes you to the museum. Booking counter is near the dam. Rs. 10 per person. Departures 9 A.M. and 1:30 P.M.; return trips 1 and 5 P.M. Buy tickets *early!*—boats fill up fast. Museum is open 9 A.M.–4 P.M.; closed on Fridays. Admission free. For further details, call 3633 in Nagarjunasagar.

PARKS, GARDENS, ZOOS. *Lion Safari Park* and *Nehru Zoological Park* comprise 300 acres with almost 2,000 animals. Train ride and animal rides for kids. Also, see life-size fiberglass models of dinosaurs. Open 9 A.M.–5 P.M., closed Mondays. Rs. 1 per person for minibus ride through the lion safari. *Osmansagar* and *Himayatsagar* are two nearby lakes with gardens. Lovely for walks and picnics. Open sunrise to sunset. *Bagh-i-Am* is a beautiful public garden in the middle of Hyderabad containing plants from all over, a cypress garden, lotus pools, and a rose garden. Open sunrise to sunset.

BEACHES. You'll find lovely beaches around Vishakapatnam that are just opening up for tourism. Beaches extend north and south along the Bay of Bengal and include *Mount Kailasa, Rama Krishna Beach, Waltair,* and *Bheemunipatnam Beach.* Lovely coves and long stretches of sand grace each of these.

SHOPPING. Bidriware work, made from a special alloy with its vivid contrast of dull black and lustrous white, is a distinctive craft of Hyderabad. Attractive novelties inlaid with pure silver wire in intricate designs are manufactured from this alloy, which resembles gun metal in composition. Bangles, buttons, cigarette cases, trays, cuff links, fruit bowls, and so forth, are also made of this material. Nirmal toys are made of very light wood. Amusing specimens of animals painted with brilliant, metallike lacquer are manufactured for the delight of the children. Gold filigree work is another popular craft in this area. Ikat textiles (a process of tie-dye weaving) are also available.

Ivory and horn carving is also a cottage industry in Andhra Pradesh. Intricate designs in ivory combined with excellent workmanship go to produce exquisite articles like brooches, powder boxes, earrings, combs, and necklaces. Among other handicrafts are carpet and rugmaking. Carpets of Warangal are famous and have won prizes in various international exhibitions. These carpets are of three kinds: silk, cotton, and woolen. Their design conforms to Persian patterns.

The principal shopping centers are Abid Road and Pathergatty in Hyderabad, Rashtrapathi Road and Gandhi Road in Secunderabad, Chowrastra in Warangal and Hanamkonda. Best addresses: Government Cottage Industries Emporium, Gunfoundry, Hyderabad; Nirmal Industries, Khairatabad, Hyderabad; Weavers Cooperative Society in Warangal.

Hyderabad is the center of India's pearl trade. Near Hyderabad's famous Charminar area, there is a row of small shops whose display cases gleam with treasures from the sea. Pearls of every shape and hue are polished and sorted before being shipped throughout India.

Indeed, *Charminar Market* itself is one of the best in India. It's fun, interesting, and teeming with tempting items to buy—fabrics, bangles, bidriware—all the crafts and handiwork for which Hyderabad is famous. It's a place to bargain, a place to browse, and a place to get a good look at India.

TEATIME. Montgomery's Cafe, near Park Lane Hotel, Secunderabad, is a Hyderabad institution. This English tea room has survived from the days of the raj. Simple snacks and plenty of atmosphere. It's best to visit in the late afternoon or early evening.

NIGHTLIFE AND BARS. Most of the better hotels in Hyderabad have bars, generally open during lunch and from the early evening until 11 P.M. These two hotel bars are considered the tops: *Maikada,* Hotel Banjara, Road No. 1, Banjara Hills (tel. 222222), and *Rock Castle Hotel,* Banjara Hills (tel. 33541).

EASTERN REGION

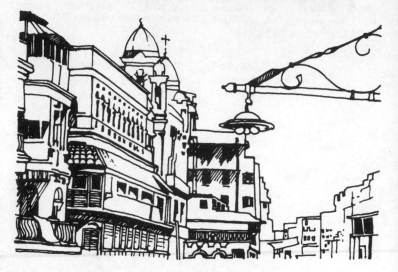

CALCUTTA

City of Astonishments

by
LISA SAMSON and AMIT SHAH

Lisa Samson is a free-lance writer and photographer whose photographs have been published in India and the United States. She has lived in Southeast Asia and has traveled extensively there and in India.

Amit Shah is a free-lance writer who has been associated with Fodor's for the past six years. His work has been published in more than a dozen publications in the United States and in India.

You are always unprepared for Calcutta. You have readied yourself for the grime, the filth, and the statistics of poverty that numb the most rational minds. You were right. They exist. A tourist brochure of a decade ago announced that "Calcutta assaults the senses like few other cities"; the burly, grimy, sweaty city is toiling, calculating, blind to suffering, and yet indispensable to the fabric of India.

You cannot remain objective about Calcutta. It is an intensely personal city, like New York, and you will not leave it without feeling a sense of bewilderment or coming under its bewitching spell. Revulsion is only for the ignorant. In Calcutta, you cannot hide from one of the largest cities in the world, a world of developing economies, of urban planning gone awry. For those who know its historic rise from obscurity in the 1700s to the beginning of its decline in the mid-1900s, Calcutta is a reminder of why and how the British Empire was created in India and what happened when the empire was dismantled.

Calcutta is a city of astonishments. Hundreds of refugees pour in across the Bangladesh border every day and make their way to the commercial nerve center, while migrants from across India come to the fabled city and revolutions threaten to disembowel the political structure altogether. Calcutta persists and surmounts.

You did not prepare yourself for Calcutta's inhabitants—the Bengalis—animated, laconic, intellectual, spirited, argumentative, anarchic, imaginative, and creative. They have dominated the city and have made it, for over 1½ centuries, the soul of India. They were among the first to react to the intellectual and political stimuli of the West and have produced, despite their sometimes desperate state, many of the most renowned filmmakers, writers, scientists, musicians, dancers, and philosophers in twentieth-century India. Blending the European humanism of the nineteenth century with the indigenous culture that was revived by Rabindranath Tagore, among others, Bengalis made the first organized efforts to oust the British in the early twentieth century, ultimately breaking away from Gandhian politics and choosing terrorism (a reason why the British moved their capital from Calcutta to Delhi in 1911).

Leisurely Visit Advised

The city is a dynamo—exhausting and exhaustive. It is not an "easy" travel destination but an essential one if you want to claim that you have visited India. Many Western travelers hurry through their visit to Calcutta and return home to spread misconceptions about India and this city on the flimsy basis of their short stay. A few years ago, a graffiti-splattered wall (in English) in Calcutta summed up the feelings of Indians about such tourists: "Calcutta Needs Development, Not Insults." Calcutta is the essence of India in many ways—its economic and developmental pitfalls coupled with its imagination and tenacity.

The Calcutta metropolitan district covers 883 square miles and has a population of nearly 11 million. It comprises two municipal corporation areas (Calcutta and Howrah), 32 municipalities, 62 nonmunicipal urban centers, and over 500 villages. By any count a huge cosmopolitan city, it sprang from three small fishing villages under the direction of the British East India Company.

A Bit of History

On November 9, 1698, Job Charnock, an agent for the East India Company, bought for a settlement three sleepy villages—Sutanati, Gobindpur, and Kali Kutta—for Rs. 1,200 from Sabarna Roy Choudhury, a local landowner. Charnock arrived in India in 1690 and started a "factory" at Sutanati. He negotiated the purchase of the first factory site with the Mogul Emperor Aurangzeb's emissary in 1690. An undistinguished man by all historical accounts, Charnock won the hearts of Bengalis by a personal deed: he rescued a young Bengali widow about to be burned at the funeral pyre of her dead husband, as was the custom of *sati*, married her, and lived and died in Calcutta. His grave is at St. John's Church, off Dalhousie Square. Through Charnock's real estate acquisition, the British gained a foothold in what had been the Sultanate of Delhi under the Moguls. Thus began the great drama known as the British raj in India.

The English built Fort William—near what is now Benoy-Badal-Dinesh Bagh (BBD Bagh)—and consolidated their position till 1756, when Siraj-ud-Daula, the nabob of Murshidabad, attacked the garrison. Many of the British residents fled. Robert Clive, fighting in Madras at the time, raced back to retake the city in 1757, but not before

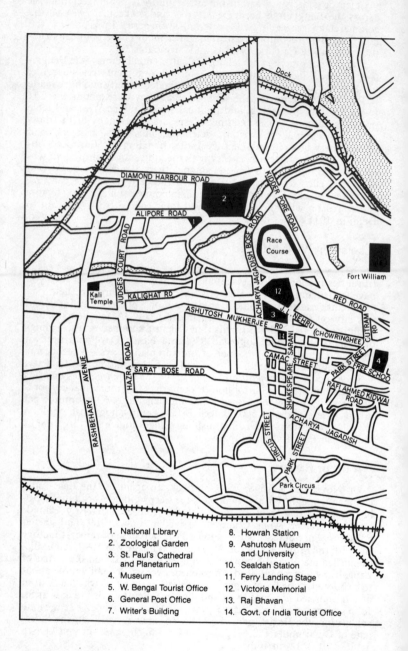

1. National Library
2. Zoological Garden
3. St. Paul's Cathedral and Planetarium
4. Museum
5. W. Bengal Tourist Office
6. General Post Office
7. Writer's Building
8. Howrah Station
9. Ashutosh Museum and University
10. Sealdah Station
11. Ferry Landing Stage
12. Victoria Memorial
13. Raj Bhavan
14. Govt. of India Tourist Office

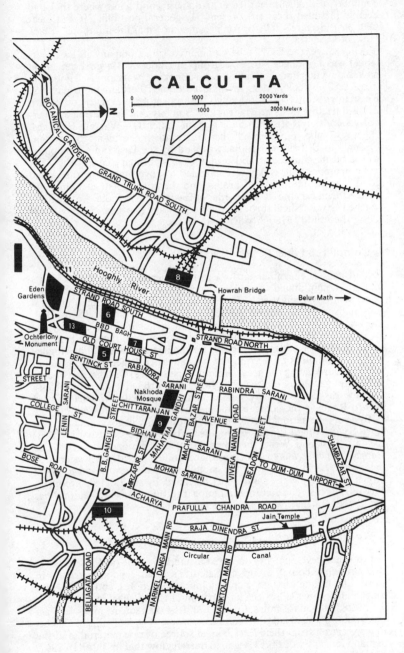

CALCUTTA

0   1000   2000 Yards
0   1000   2000 Meters

BOTANICAL GARDENS

N

GRAND TRUNK ROAD SOUTH

Hooghly River

Howrah Bridge

Belur Math →

Eden Gardens

STRAND ROAD SOUTH

Ochterlony Monument

BBD BAGH

Strand Road North

OLD COURT HOUSE ST

BENTINCK ST

RABINDRA SARANI

STREET

RABINDRA SARANI

COLLEGE STREET

LENIN SARANI

Nakhoda Mosque

CHITTARANJAN

MACHUA BAZAR STREET

BEADON STREET

SHAMBAZAR S

BOSE ROAD

B.B.GANGULI STREET

BIDHAN

MAHATMA GANDHI

AVENUE

VIVEKA NANDA ROAD

TO DUM-DUM AIRPORT →

MIRZAPUR ST

MOHAN SARANI

SARANI

ACHARYA

PRAFULLA CHANDRA ROAD

Jain Temple

NARIKEL DANGA MAIN RD

RAJA DINENDRA ST

MANIKTOLA MAIN RD

Circular   Canal

BELIAGATA ROAD

a number of Englishmen died in an underground cellar where they had been imprisoned (near the present-day general post office [GPO] near Dalhousie Square). This prison became known as the infamous "Black Hole of Calcutta."

After Clive, the East India Company (John Company in local parlance) was no longer simply a group of traders but a government in power, levying and collecting taxes, making wars, and negotiating treaties. The stockholders in London lobbied Parliament to pass the Regulatory Act of 1773, making Calcutta supreme over the other two English trading posts at Madras and Bombay and appointing a governor-general of British India based in Calcutta—Warren Hastings. Hastings, who represented the king and the crown government throughout British-held India, was paid by the East India Company, whose business interests and profits were of primary concern to him. Thus, mercantile interests were wedded to government for the public good. The accumulation of profits, and the government machinery to ensure them, became the first order of British rule in India. Colonialism reached a watershed through the acquisition of three small villages along the muddy Hooghly River in India.

Commercial and Political Hub

Throughout the nineteenth century, Bengal, with Calcutta as its capital, though difficult to govern, spread out from the eastern reaches of present-day Bangladesh. Because of the resurgent Bengali cultural nationalism, which fed the political nationalism of the late 1800s, Bengal became the commercial and political center of India and for the British east of the Suez Canal. The old pilgrim road that ran from the north (Chitpur Road) to the south (Kalighat) was named Chowringhee after the disciples of a hermit, Chowringheegiri. It became a fashionable boulevard facing the great *Maidan* (open space) with garden houses designed by Italian architects. In 1859, it was the first street in the city to have gas lamps. Today Chowringhee, renamed Jawaharlal (J.L.) Nehru Road, is the center of business and social life in Calcutta.

By 1905, the nationalist mood and the difficulty in governing the vast territory prompted Lord Curzon, the British viceroy, to partition Bengal into East and West, thereby splitting the nationalist forces. The Bengali response was so ferocious that a unified presidency was created again in 1912, but only after the capital of the raj was moved to Delhi and a new city, New Delhi, was designed by an English architect, Edwin Lutyens. The commercial impact of this change in capitals was far less severe than was the political impact.

World War II Ends Trade

But other developments occurred around the time of World War II that brought about the end of Calcutta's great economic trade—in cloth, silk, lacquer, indigo, rice, betelnut, tobacco, tea, and jutes. After independence in 1947, with the partition of East Bengal and the transfer of 28,000 square miles to India and 54,000 square miles to East Pakistan (now Bangladesh), trade grew worse. The jute mills of Calcutta were cut off from their East Bengal source of raw material, and the demand for synthetic fibers began to overshadow that for jute). In 1947, 17 million people were uprooted in eastern India; fewer than 30 years later, during the 1972 Bangladesh War, another large migration began that has continued in a steady stream. Decay had begun to set in. After a period of post-independence reconstruction under the Congress Party, the late 1960s brought Calcutta to a cathartic battle between the forces of change and the established, somewhat moribund, political forces.

One of the richest cities between Rome and Tokyo, in accumulated wealth and representations, Calcutta was once a leader of Indian exports, controlling 15 percent of the manufacturing industry, collecting over 30 percent of the national tax revenues, and surpassing the rest of India in the manufacture of light machinery. In the late 1960s–early 1970s, Calcutta went into a depression of monumental proportions. Manufacturing plants closed because of labor disputes, schools and colleges couldn't offer examinations because of student strikes, transportation creaked, basic services were overtaxed, and political violence wrenched the city in a frightening rage that peaked in 1970.

Left Front in Control

In May 1977, the Congress Party lost its grip on the political wheel of Bengal, and the Marxists (Communist Party of West Bengal), with a coalition group, the Left Front, were elected by an overwhelming majority. Much is heard about the Left Front in Calcutta—their work was probably invented by a Biblical Job. In power, they are pragmatists more than ideologues, and their balance sheet for the past decade has been mixed. The pressures from New Delhi (Congress), which controls the funds that could repair Calcutta's collapsing infrastructure and promote large-scale development, are enormous.

The Left Front's strategy of first consolidating its rural base in Bengal has worked, but in Calcutta, the politicization has practically crippled the legitimate functioning of public hospitals, government offices, and even the police. Some of the Left Front's gains are no mean achievements: doubling the rice production to the second state in India, increasing literacy in rural areas, providing health and legal benefits for sharecroppers, and decreasing the percentage of people below the poverty line. But even though the Left Front had its biggest electoral victory in the 1987 elections, urban Calcutta remains skeptical. Living in a city with over 11 million people, 150,000 "pavement dwellers," power shortages, and huge population increases, Calcuttans hope for long-term investment projects and less short-term lectures by politicians and urban development "experts." A recent poster, in English, summed up the feelings of many Calcuttans: Many say that Calcutta is a dead city. Yet, hundreds throng to Calcutta each day from neighboring states. Are they scavengers feeding on the mortal remains? No. They come in the hope for opportunities for a livelihood and survival. They do get them and settle down. They are not scavengers and Calcutta is very much alive.

EXPLORING CALCUTTA

Calcutta, unlike other metropolitan cities in India, is a relative newcomer, having sprouted from three sleepy fishing villages in the late seventeenth century. The course of British imperial history on the subcontinent is mirrored in Calcutta's own history and development.

If you come in by train, you're in for the experience of a lifetime. Howrah Station, situated on the west bank of the Hooghly River, is the major railway station in eastern India. A "permanent" population seems to reside on the platforms among the ferocious intensity of thousands on the move. This atmosphere extends to Howrah Bridge, a Calcutta landmark, built in 1941, a web of girders stretching 1,500 feet over the Hooghly. Passing over eight lanes of chaotic traffic, which includes all manner of transportation—rickshaws, cars, scooters, bicycles, pushcarts, and animal-drawn carts—two million people cross this single-span cantilevered bridge each day. Howrah, already a congested suburb of Calcutta, is becoming the fastest-growing population center in the metropolitan area.

A second Howrah Bridge at Hastings has been under construction for a number of years, and its completion is not expected for many more. Once over the bridge, you're near the Botanical Gardens. Spread over 270 acres and containing over 30,000 varieties of plants and trees, it is India's oldest (built in 1787). A 200-year-old banyan tree with over 600 branches taking root around the central tree creates a veritable forest—an awesome sight. Its circumference is 1,367 feet. Tour buses race through these gardens, which, with the view of the Hooghly, are an ideal spot for picnicking. If you can, hire a car and go there early in the day to avoid the crush of humanity that clogs the narrow street in Shibour that leads to the gardens. The road is lined with jute mills, once Bengal's main export industry.

About 6½ miles north of the gardens is Belur Math, the headquarters of the Ramakrishna Mission, a reform movement that has an impact far beyond Bengal. Ramakrishna Paramahansa, who died in 1886, forsook his Brahman status and preached the unity of religious faiths and an adherence to the altruistic values for all people. His disciple, Swami Vivekananda, established the mission in 1898. The Belur Math Temple resembles a church, a temple, or a mosque, depending on which angle you see it from. The temple is open 6:30 A.M.–noon and 3:30–7:30 P.M. daily.

A short distance north is Dakhineshwar Kali Temple (1847), a major pilgrimage site to which devotees continue to flock to see the temples of Shiva, Kali, Radha, and Krishna. It was here that Ramakrishna received his spiritual vision; his room is a museum. Open till 10 P.M.

Either on the way north of the city or returning south from Belur, a stop at Parasnath, one of Calcutta's most interesting Jain temples, is recommended. Built in 1867 on Budree Das Temple Street and dedicated to Sitalnathji, the tenth of the 24 *tirthankas* (prophets/reformers), it is a flamboyant structure filled with mirror-inlay pillars, stained-glass windows, marble floors in a floral design, a gilded dome, and chandeliers from nineteenth-century Paris and Brussels. In the garden, there are blocks of glass mosaics with European figures and statues that have been covered with silver paint. It is an unusual place of honor for the ascetic Jains. If you've been lucky and beaten the midday traffic back to the center of town, take a break to freshen up (without a doubt you will sweat in any season in Calcutta), have lunch (you might want to try one of the many brands of Indian beer—Bengal brews many of them), and when the midday heat abates a little, resume your sightseeing.

The Indian Museum (see *Museum* section), the Nehru Children's Museum, Victoria Memorial, and Birla Planetarium, are all within a few miles.

The British came to Calcutta to trade, and they needed political stability and an infrastructure to manage the indigenous population. Toward this end, they brought in soldiers, priests, and clerks. Their legacies remain in Fort William, on the east bank of the Hooghly near Strand Road; the fort is an irregular octagon enclosing three square miles, surrounded by a moat almost 50 feet wide. Built in 1773, and named after William III, it was said to be impregnable, a boast that has never been put to the test. Permission to visit is required from the commanding officer.

St. John's Church, built in 1784, is where Job Charnock, founder of Calcutta, is buried. In the garden, there is a monument to the victims of the "Black Hole" tragedy.

Nearby, St. Paul's Cathedral, with its soaring Gothic steeple, was built in 1847. Two earthquakes destroyed the previous steeples; the present one is a model of the one at Canterbury Cathedral. Florentine frescoes, the stained-glass western window, and a gold communion plate presented by Queen Victoria are of special interest. The hours of services are posted near the entrance gate.

Writers Building, on one side of Dalhousie Square (BBD Bagh), built in 1780, housed the "writers" or clerks of the East India Company. It was synonymous with mind-numbing bureaucracy from its inception and is, today, the dreaded bottomless pit of the present government's paper mill. The Gothic structure, with rows of Ionic pillars and groups of statues, is evocative of a Victorian architecture that is a photographer's delight.

Another sight of interest in this city that blends Victorian order and the anarchic bustle of a developing country is the Ochterlony Monument (Shahid Minar) at the northern tip of the Maidan near the Park Street Metro entrance on J. L. Nehru Road. This 158-foot pillar, erected to commemorate Sir David Ochterlony's victories in nineteenth-century Nepal, is designed with a curious blend of Middle Eastern architecture. Its base is Egyptian, its pillar is Syrian, and its cupola is Turkish! It was the focal point for political rallies (much like Nelson's at London's Trafalgar Square). You can climb a spiral staircase for a panoramic view of the city, but prior permission is required from the police commissioner. Inquire at the West Bengal Tourist Office. The Raj Bhawan (Government House), the residence of the governor and more or less a copy of Keddleston Hall in Derbyshire, is another such sight. Completed in 1802, it contains the throne of Tipu Sultan, the nemesis of the British, and a polished teak ballroom floor. Without an official invitation, however, tourists are not permitted. While in this area, stroll through the green expanse of Eden Gardens, which has lakes for boating and a wooden pagoda from Burma.

Leaving the center of the city, go south past the Calcutta Racecourse and the Maidan, where English officers once hunted wild game but which is now the "green lung" of the city, with almost two square miles of open parkland. The original forests were cut down to provide a clear field of fire for Fort William. Near the racecourse are the Zoological Gardens, opened in 1876, with some of the best collections of reptiles and white tigers in India. The zoo also has a children's zoo and an aquarium. Easy to walk around and attractive, it is open 8 A.M.–5 P.M. The entrance fee is Rs. 1. The air-conditioned snack bar, located near the entrance, is mobbed during the summer.

The Kali Temple at Kalighat, near a canal called Adiganga (the "real Ganga" because it is believed to be the original bed of the Hooghly) does not permit foreigners to enter. Built in 1809, the Kali is one of Hinduism's renowned pilgrimage sites, containing temples to Radha, Shiva, Krishna, and Kali. Human sacrifices were reputed to be common in the last century, but only goats are slaughtered now and offered to Kali with Ganges water and *bhang,* an uncultivated hemp.

Coming back north, there is a Nakhoda Mosque, built in 1926, the largest Moslem mosque in Calcutta, modeled after Akbar's tomb at Sikandra (Agra). The mosque can accommodate 10,000 people. It is open 6 A.M.–8 P.M. daily and is free.

The Agro-Horticultural Society's gardens are behind the National Library at Belvedere on Alipore Road. Founded in 1820, the gardens are in full bloom during December and January, and some flowers are out as late as early March. This is a soothing side trip.

At Muktaram Babu Street in Chorebagan (thieves' garden) is another site of historic interest, the famed Marble Palace, built in 1835 by Raja Mullick. A member of Bengal's landed gentry, with lands in what is now Bangladesh (then East Bengal), Raja Mullick chose to spend his money in the "second city of the Empire"—Calcutta. Lavishly built of Italian marble, the palace's dark walls are covered with paintings, clocks, statues, crystal, and china. The palace is said to contain paintings by Houdon, Gainsborough, Reynolds, and Reubens and a statue by Michelangelo. The grounds have aviaries and a family temple, as well as Roman fountains. Visitors are welcome. Inquire at the West Bengal Tourist Office for details. In mid-1987, the palace was open 10 A.M.–4 P.M., daily except Mondays and Thursdays. An appointment with the curator is needed (tel. 34–3310).

Calcutta's historical sights can keep you busy for days. Less well-known sights include Jorasanko Thakurbari at 5 Dwarkanath Tagore Lane, the house where Rabindranath Tagore lived and worked. Now a university, Rabindra Bharati, it actively fosters cultural activities. With its cupolas and balconies, Thakurbari (House of Tagores) was once known as a nerve center of intellectual life in Bengal. Today, part of it is a museum housing a splendid collection of Tagore memorabilia, open 10 A.M.–5 P.M. except Saturdays, when it closes at 1:30 P.M. Tagore —following Michael Madhusudan Dutt, Bankim Chandra Chatterjee, Ishwar Chandra Vidyasagar, Raja Ram Monun Roy, Sarat Chandra Chatterjee, Sri Ramkrishna, and Swami Vivekananda—brought about a renaissance in Bengali cultural, social, and political life in the nineteenth and early twentieth centuries. To walk the Thakubari's lanes, made for pedestrians and palanquin bearers rather than cars and buses, is to "feel" the old city.

South Park Street Cemetery is a treasure trove of British imperial history buried in Calcutta. Opened in 1767, the funereal obelisks are a testament to those participants in the British raj who made Calcutta their home. Among those whose graves are here are William Thackeray's father, Richmond; the linguist William Jones, founder of the Royal Asiatic Society; Colonel Charles Deare, who fought Tipu Sultan; and Anglo-Indian poet Louis Vivian Derozio. Bhowanipor Military Cemetery is the burial place of Charles Dickens's second son, Walter Landor Dickens, who died in Calcutta as a lieutenant.

PRACTICAL INFORMATION FOR CALCUTTA

WHEN TO GO. Calcutta, like most metropolitan cities in India, is best visited between October and March, when temperatures are between 98° F and 45° F. At an altitude of 20 feet and close to the sea, the capital of West Bengal can reach 100 percent humidity levels in the summer months (April–June) and during the rainy season (July–August), when the monsoon rains invariably flood city thoroughfares and Calcutta's antiquated, late nineteenth-century sewage and drainage system.

HOW TO GET THERE. By Air. Daily *Indian Airlines* flights connect Calcutta with all major cities in India. Calcutta is an international airport served by *Aeroflot, Air India, Bangladesh Biman, British Airways, Burma Airways, Druk Air, Royal Nepal Airlines, Singapore Airlines,* and *Thai International,* among others. India's feeder airline, *Vayudoot,* also has a number of flights to Calcutta. The state government is trying to upgrade and revitalize airport services to attract other international carriers to serve this city, which used to be a regular stopover for flights to and from Southeast Asia and the Pacific, including Australia.

After being lulled by the brisk efficiency of airports at Bombay, Delhi, and Madras, you should be prepared for long slow-moving lines in Calcutta's International Arrivals area. Airport personnel are less helpful here than at India's other international airports, and patience will be needed to surmount the aggravation caused by the airport authorities' lack of organization. If possible, use another international airport to enter India from abroad. The domestic section is reasonably well managed and should present no hazards.

How to Get to Town From the Airport. Coach service is available to main hotels and to the center of the city from the airport. The coach service and information desks are located in the baggage claim area, before you step out of the terminal, and are surrounded by insistent and aggravating touts and middlemen for private taxis. You should consult with the personnel at the service desks. Coach tickets are Rs. 14.

Taxis to the main hotels and to the center of town (Park Street vicinity) will cost Rs. 55–65. There is a taxi counter to the right of the exit gate of the terminal building. You may be tempted to get into a private taxi for a negotiated price, but you'll most likely end up paying up to twice what a metered ride would cost. Since taxi prices are fixed by the government and reflect the current cost of gasoline, they undergo frequent changes, and most meters are not adjusted to reflect the latest change. Taxis are required to carry a chart to reflect the current rates. As of mid-1987, the rate was 5 percent more than the metered amount. When you get in, make sure that the taxi driver or his assistant resets the meter.

There are hotel and tourist information counters at the airport. The Calcutta Airport also operates a tourist dormitory for budget travelers and those who arrive late at night, though reservations are difficult to acquire. Write to *Calcutta Airport Rest Rooms,* Calcutta Airport (tel. 57–2611). Rates are reasonable, with a single room going for Rs. 55 and a double room, for Rs. 75.

By Train. Calcutta is well connected by rail to all major cities. Howrah Station, the focal point of rail travel in the eastern region, is an extraordinary place, teeming with thousands of people, and the terminal for such folkloric trains as the Delhi-Howrah Mail (26 hours); Air-conditioned Express (same distance in 24 hours); the Rajdhani Express (fastest, in 22 hours); the Calcutta Mail (36 hours from Bombay); the Gitanjali Express (30 hours from Bombay); the Coromandel Express (25 hours from Madras).

Booking offices for *Eastern Railway:* For first-class air-conditioned cars, 14A Strand Rd., Calcutta 700 001 (near the GPO); for second class, 6 Fairlie Pl., Calcutta 700 001 (close to the Reserve Bank of India, a few blocks from the GPO). Tickets are also available at the railway stations (Howrah and Sealdah—the latter being the local commuter station in Southern Calcutta) although the lines and the waiting periods can be daunting. *Southeastern Railway* tickets are available for all classes from Esplanade Mansions, Esplanade East (near Raj Bhavan or Governor's House). Foreigners can avail themselves of *Indrail* passes for 7–21 days, payable only in foreign currency. (See *Facts at Your Fingertips* section for additional information.) Student discounts are also available for travelers under age 30.

By Car. India's oldest and most famous highway, the Grand Trunk Road, connects Delhi (1,328 miles), Bombay (over 1,332 miles), and Madras (1,063 miles). Consult the *Automobile Association of Eastern India,* 13 Promothesh Barua Sarani (tel. 47–5131). It can provide road maps and vital information on gas stations, lodging, detours, and the like enroute.

By Bus. *North Bengal State Transport Corporation* operates buses from Calcutta to North Bengal, various other parts of the state, Bihar, and Orissa. Booking offices are at Esplanade Bus Terminus, diagonally opposite the Central Cottage Industries Emporium at the hub of Calcutta's Chowringhee Road (J. L. Nehru Road).

 TOURIST INFORMATION. The *Government of India Tourist Office* at 41 Shakespeare Sarani (tel. 44–3521) and the *West Bengal Tourist Information Center,* 3/2 BBD Bagh (East) (tel. 23–8271) can provide you with all the information you require. The West Bengal Tourist Information Center has a free booklet, *Calcutta,* which lists the addresses and telephone numbers of airlines, trains, buses, ferries, travel agents, shipping companies, hotels, restaurants, medical services, banks, consulates, tourist information counters for all other Indian states, and so on. The other guide to pick up, *Calcutta Briefs*, is sold at local bookstores (try Cambridge or Oxford on Park Street) for Rs. 15 (a little over a dollar) and includes information on shopping, local performances and art exhibits, and notes on Bengali cuisine. It is simple, informative, and amusing.

TELEPHONES. The telephone system in Calcutta is highly erratic. Calls can take forever to connect, once connected are difficult to hear, and are frequently cut off in mid-conversation. Work is under way to improve the system, but the results are still a long way off. Persistence and patience are needed, since a call that is difficult to place in the morning may be easy to place in the afternoon.

ACCOMMODATIONS. The headlong decline of Calcutta's once-dominant position as the commercial and manufacturing center of India in the 1970s was strikingly reflected in the lack of new international-grade hotels in the city (despite the erection of numerous hotels elsewhere in the country). As India's business climate encouraged private-sector small companies and the public-sector companies diversified, the need of business travelers for accommodations increased dramatically. The state government is now addressing the lack of international-grade hotels. The Calcutta Metropolitan Development Authority (CMDA), the agency in charge of the city's development, is aggressively wooing major hoteliers to develop new properties in Calcutta. The good news for foreign travelers is that the *Welcomgroup*, whose headquarters is in Calcutta, is negotiating for a location for a 200-room hotel. The *Taj Group*, Welcomgroup's rival, has already started construction of the **Taj Bengal**, a 200-room hotel across the street from the Calcutta zoo in Alipore, a walk away from the National Library and overlooking the Calcutta Racecourse. Not to be outdone, the West Bengal Government, which owns **Great Eastern Hotel**, one of the aged hallmarks of British rule (150 years old) is planning to replace the structure with a 14-story hotel complex. The *Oberoi* group, which owns the best-to-date hotel, the **Grand**, completely refurbished its property in 1986–87, with an underground garage, additional restaurants, saunas, suites, and lawns. The four combined ventures will add an estimated 1,000 deluxe rooms to this city sometime in 1988 and 1989. Here, as in other parts of the country, you'll also find some hotels operated by the *India Tourist Development Corporation* (ITDC).

Note: All major hotels accept American Express, Visa, and Diners Club credit cards. Travelers carrying non-Indian passports are required to pay their bills in foreign currency. (See *Facts at Your Fingertips* for price ranges of category listings and other details.)

Deluxe

Airport Ashok. Calcutta Airport; tel. 57–4440, cable AIRPORTEL; telex AIROTEL 021–2271. Modern and luxurious, this 156-room hotel operated by the ITDC group has a full complement of services including a swimming pool and bar. Conveniently located near the airport, which is less than a mile away, it is far from the city center; therefore, it is recommended for short layovers and for travelers coming into Calcutta by air in the middle of the night.

Oberoi Grand. 15 J. L. Nehru Rd. (Chowringhee); tel. 23–0181; cable OBHOTEL; telex 7248, 7854. In the heart of the city. This hotel is the best in Calcutta with 300 rooms, newly renovated saunas, restaurants, and other luxurious appointments. Indian, Chinese, and Continental cuisines are served in the Moghul Room and Polynesia restaurants, and the coffee shop is open 24 hours a day. For entertainment, there is the Pink Elephant disco and the Chowringhee Bar. The hotel also has its own generator and is thus immune to the frequent power cuts in Calcutta.

Expensive

Great Eastern. 3 Old Court House St.; tel. 23–2311; cable GREASTERN; telex 021–3345. This is the old Imperial standby—Kipling stayed here in its high-ceilinged, spacious rooms. It is expensive for its quality, but has good restaurants, especially Chinese.

Hindusthan International. 235/1 Acharya Jagadish (A. J.) Bose Rd.; tel. 44–2394; cable MODERN; telex: CA 7464. Two miles from the downtown area.

Air-conditioned, with 212 rooms and the usual array of hotel services. Nevertheless, it is somewhat shabby and the prices are high for the services it provides.

New Kenilworth. 1 and 2 Little Russell St.; tel. 44–2647; cable NEW KEN; telex 021–3345. 100 rooms surrounded by spacious gardens, the old wing has been renovated and has 40 air-conditioned rooms. Good facilities and secluded (for Calcutta). During the winter, have your tea and meals in the gardens for a change of pace from the sanitized anonymity of the higher-priced hotels. Has refrigerator in each room.

Park. 17 Park St.; tel. 24–8301; cable PARKOTEL; telex PARK CA 7159. 170 air-conditioned rooms. It harbors the Jade Garden, a Chinese restaurant; Aquapark Pool with bar; the 007 Bar; and the Sujata Restaurant. Expensive for its plastic quality, but it is recommended for its prime location on Calcutta's "Broadway," Park Street, which has many restaurants, bars, and stores.

Moderate to Inexpensive

Fairlawn. 13/A Sudder St.; tel. 24–4460; cable FAIRHOTEL. In the heart of the city. 20 rooms, 18 of which are air-conditioned. This brightly colored, charming hotel is popular for its personalized service and ambience. New Market, Park Street, and Chowringhee are just minutes away.

Rutt Deen. 21/B Loudon St.; tel. 44–3884. 50 air-conditioned rooms and a garden.

INDIAN-STYLE HOTELS

Inexpensive

There are many Indian-style hotels with various levels of service and accommodations. We list some of them here without recommendation or disapproval.

Lindsay Guest House. 8B Lindsay St.; tel. 24–4640. 18 rooms, some air-conditioned.

Hotel Minerva. 11 Ganesh Chandra Ave.; 26–4505. 33 rooms, air-conditioning in most rooms; has a bar, restaurant, car rental counter, and currency exchange counter.

Hotel Shalimar. 3 S. N. Bannerjee Rd.; tel. 23–7193. Opposite the USIA Library. 20 rooms, all air-conditioned.

Shilton. 5A Sudder St.; tel. 24–3613. 28 rooms, some air-conditioned.

OTHER ACCOMMODATIONS

Inexpensive

International Guest House. Ramakrishna Mission Institute of Culture, Golpark, Ballygunge; tel. 46–3431. Far from the city center in southern Calcutta.

The **YMCA** has a "deluxe" section on Chowringhee (J. L. Nehru Road), between Metro Cinema and the Grand Hotel; tel. 23–3504. It has air-conditioned rooms but service is erratic.

The **YWCA International Guest House,** 1 Middleton Row (tel. 24–0260) accepts couples.

 DINING OUT. The passions of Calcuttans can be listed as politics, argument, *adda* (a spirited blend of gossip and intellectual discourse), cricket, and food. However, the best Bengali cuisine is available only in private homes, where the myriad ways to prepare fish, vegetables, and lentils will astound guests as well as tease their palates. Since it is difficult to be certain that you will meet a Bengali in Calcutta who will invite you home and lay out a sampling of the fabled Bengali delicacies—freshwater fish (*macher jhol*); sweets, especially *sandesh* and *rossogolla; chingri* (prawns) in coconut sauce; fish in rich yogurt sauce (*doi maach*); smoked *hilsa;* and so on—you may arrange for "home visits" through a travel agent such as Inder Zutshi of **Zutshi's Travel World Service,** 17 Kailash Enclave, New Delhi 110 048 (tel. 68–1448; telex 31–5176 ZWTS IN) in India, or Suraj Zutshi at 71 Keystone Ave., Reno, NV 89503 (tel. 702–323–0110) in the United States.

As in other metropolitan cities of India, restaurants usually have bars or a "permit room" (permits to serve liquor). There is no prohibition in Calcutta, but Thursdays are "dry" days and meatless days (no meat is served). Other cuisines that provide Calcutta with a pleasant flavor are Cantonese Chinese,

Burmese, all manner of North Indian and South Indian food, and Continental Western food, as well as the movable feasts of roadside stalls at the southern end of the Maidan. *Daab* water, fresh coconut juice, fresh fruit juices, and *lassis* (yogurt and fruit drinks) are available during the summer near the Lighthouse Cinema, off Chowringhee (J. L. Nehru Road) on Humayun Place. (See *Facts at Your Fingertips* for price ranges of categories.)

HOTEL RESTAURANTS

Expensive to Moderate

All the major hotels have restaurants. Among them the hotel restaurants are **Moghul Room** and **Polynesia,** the only Polynesian restaurants in Calcutta, both at the Oberoi Grand Hotel. Around the corner from the two is **Rang Mahal,** which has excellent Mughlai food. These restaurants have a bar and offer live music.

Maxim's and **Shah-en-Shah** are at the Great Eastern Hotel, the former being a sedate, somewhat scruffy dinner-dance affair, and the latter offering excellent tandoori dishes and live Indian music. Also at the Great Eastern is the **Chinese Room,** where the food is excellent but prices are high.

Golden Peacock at Hindusthan International and **Sujata** at the Park Hotel both have floor shows, but the food is not exceptional.

Jade Room at the Park offers good food in uninspiring surroundings.

Other hotel dining recommendations are **Fairlawn Hotel,** with a fixed-price dinner for about $2. The English breakfast for about $1.50 gets raves from English travelers. New Kenilworth's **Maikhana Restaurant** is excellent for lunch and has an open-air bar.

INDEPENDENT RESTAURANTS

Moderate to Inexpensive

Calcutta's recommended independent restaurants number about 25. Among them are

Amber, 11 Waterloo St.; tel. 23–3018. Open 10 A.M.–11 P.M. Excellent Mughlai and tandoori food, probably the best in the city, and a well-stocked bar. It is always crowded, so reservations are advised. Has convenient take-out facilities as well.

Bar-B-Que. 43 Park St.; tel. 24–9348. Open 10 A.M.–midnight. Uninspired Indian, Chinese, Continental, and tandoori fare. Bar attached. As of mid-1987, the restaurant was open only sporadically because of frequent management-labor disputes.

Blue Fox. 55 Park St.; tel. 29–7948. Open 10 A.M.–11 P.M. Popular with the city's smart set; full-service bar and good food and service, especially Continental.

Chungwah. 13/A Chittaranjan Ave.; tel. 27–7003. Open 11 A.M.–11 P.M. Recommended Chinese restaurant and bar.

Flury's. 18 Park St.; tel. 24–0300. Open 6:30 A.M.–8 P.M. The renowned tea room, with the city's best confectionery and selection of breads. It has a European ambience except that it can seat about 100. Stop by for a mid-afternoon break.

Kwality Ice Creams. 71 Strand Rd.; tel. 25–5680. The only restaurant on Calcutta's waterfront, it juts out over the river with splendid views at dusk of the Hooghly River with its slow-moving riverboats and the cantilevered Howrah Bridge. Good for snacks, this is strictly fast-food fare and is recommended for the view and as a place to stop as you stroll the harbor promenade.

Kwalitys. 17 Park St.; tel. 29–7849. Open 10 A.M.–midnight. Excellent for lunch. Tandoori and Mughlai dishes. Crowded surroundings.

Mocambo. 25–B Park St.; tel. 29–4152. Open 11 A.M.–11 P.M. Mainly a place for Calcutta's Westernized teenagers. Dinner dancing begins at 8 P.M. Tea is served at 4 P.M. and the dance floor is packed on weekends. Indian and Continental food; neither being memorable.

Peter Cat. 18 Park St.; tel. 29–8841. Open 10 A.M.–midnight. A favorite of Calcutta's business crowd, with a well-stocked bar, reasonable food, and courteous service.

Sky Room. 57 Park St.; tel. 29–4362. Open 10 A.M.–11:30 P.M. A long-standing favorite, it retains its excellent reputation for Indian and Continental food in a stylized decor—a ceiling of small winking lights designed to resemble the night sky.

Tandoor. 55 Park St.; tel. 29–8006. Until mid-1987, it was an excellent restaurant for tandoori dishes (especially the prawn tandoori) and a full bar. Labor disputes make its future uncertain.

Trinca's. 17B Park St.; tel. 24–8977. Open 10 A.M.–1 A.M. Well known as a place to hear the latest Western music played by Indian bands and singers, this remains a pleasant stop for snacks rather than full meals. Has a bar.

Vineet. 1 Shakespeare Sarani; tel. 44–0788. Open 11 A.M.–3 P.M. and 7–11 P.M. Excellent vegetarian food plus take-out service. Has live Indian music.

Other excellent eateries are **Anarkali,** 4B J. L. Nehru Road, for northern and eastern Indian food; **Abhinandan,** 24 Park Centre, for vegetarian food, and **Kathleen's,** a good bakery at 12 Free School St.

CHINESE FOOD

Chinese restaurants that are worth the effort in a city where Cantonese dishes, through years of amalgamation, have become "Calcuttonese" are **Waldorf,** on Park Street near the corner of Camac Street (tel. 27–1580); **Oasis,** 33 Park St. (tel. 29–9033), and **New Cathay,** 17–1 Chowringhee (J. L. Nehru Road) (tel. 23–3117).

BEST BETS

Every traveler knows the long-awaited thrill of finding restaurants, not listed in guidebooks, that serve memorable and delicious food for *moderate* prices. We recommend a few recent finds:

Aminia's. 1 Corporation Pl., opposite Elite Cinema. A greasy-spoon doing splendid business for over 30 years. Specialties are melt-in-the-mouth kebabs, huge *nans* (leavened bread), and a swirl of various meat curries. Has a separate section for women and families, if preferred, but not necessary.

Sabir's. 71 Biplabi Anukul Chunder St. A large, simple room with about 50 tables and chairs, lots of swiftly whirring fans, and some of the best north Indian fare for reasonable prices. Try the mutton *biriyani,* if nothing else.

Suruchi, on Elliot Road, a restaurant that lives up to its name "good taste"; the only Bengali restaurant of any standard in Calcutta, it serves a vast array of Bengali cuisine—from fresh fish, prawns, and rice to deep-fried breads and sweets.

Tulika's Ice Cream Parlour. 41 Chowringhee (on Russell Street, opposite the Assam House). A fast-food addition that carries over 15 imaginative sundae combinations and pizzas with extras. Essentially a carry-out place, but it has a few circular tables with stools. It's an enjoyable stop for dessert or for a midday break. Has take-out confectionery.

SWEETS AND TREATS

Bengali sweets—*rosogollah, sandesh, rosomallai, gulab jamun, sitabhog, shorbhaja,* and *barfi,* to name a few—are available at a variety of places, including **K.C. Das** at 11 Esplanade Rd. East and **Ganguram's** on Chowringhee (J. L. Nehru Road) near the Birla Planetarium. Bengal's unique *mishti lal dhoi* (sweetened red yogurt) is now available at the state-run **Mother Dairy** outlets throughout Calcutta and Bengal.

After savoring some of the city's gastronomic delights, one last taste treat awaits you, *paan*—a concoction of betel nut and other items wrapped in a paan leaf that has been spread with lime paste. This after-dinner digestive is an acquired taste, but one worth trying, especially after a huge Indian meal.

Paan is prepared in many different ways. Ask for *mitha paan* (sweet paan), which has sweet condiments (no *masala* or spices) and mint. It will be given to you folded into a trianglar shape that you pop whole into the back of your mouth. Next: chew! (Make your first bite a tentative one—sometimes the betel nut is so hard that you can do damage to fillings if you bite down too vigorously.)

Varieties of paan include one that contains *zarda,* a legal, mild narcotic. Restaurants will get it for you for a small tip. Paan shops are abundant in Calcutta, often selling cigarettes and soft drinks as well. We recommend the shop near Kwality's on Park Street, the one opposite the Waldorf restaurant on Park Street, and the one next door to the Amber restaurant.

HOW TO GET AROUND. One of the most amazing aspects of Calcutta is that the city, despite its catastrophic population boom, the resultant pressure on all city services, its crumbling infrastructure and its visibly deteriorating roads, keeps its inhabitants moving—by the millions. From one corner of this sprawling metropolis to another, Calcuttans move daily through a network of **buses, trams, cycle rickshaws, cars, motorcycles, trains, three-wheelers,** an underground **subway,** and **ferry boats.** Once, the port city of Calcutta was the commercial hub of the British empire east of the Suez. Transportation was always a crucial element in the imperial vision of draining the indigenous area's raw materials.

Calcutta still operates over 225 separate public bus routes, over 25 "special" tram routes with carriages for women only, and over 50 minibus routes (buses that travel an express route). Fares are based on the distance traveled. There are ferries on the Hooghly River (as the Ganges is called in this area). As of mid-1987, there were eight ferry landings around metropolitan Calcutta, shuttling workers between Calcutta and Howrah.

The average foreign traveler will be aghast at the overcrowded conditions of most forms of public transportation, especially city buses that tilt at gravity-defying angles owing to the weight of passengers clinging to the running boards. Yet, in all this seeming chaos, there is a commuter camaraderie, as in all parts of the world, and regular commuters have been known to start crossword puzzle clubs and informal vacation groups. A ride on one of these buses, preferably at midday (not at rush hour) atop a double-decker, can give you some sense of the Calcuttans' tenacity and spirit that you miss when you are enclosed in an air-conditioned car or coach.

Calcutta has a "first" in India in terms of mass transit. It is the **Metro,** the first subway on the subcontinent, built over a period of 15 years amid great controversy, long delays, and huge cost overruns. The butt of many a Bengali joke, it shuttles about 10,000 commuters each day over a six-mile route from the eastern Tollygunge section to the business district of Park Street. Unlike the crumbling vestiges of imperial rule that surround Calcutta, the subway is a symbol of what can be done if enough time and resources are made available to this spirited city. Trains arrive promptly every 15 minutes at spotless platforms, with announcements being made in three languages (Hindi, Bengali, and English). The doors open without a fuss, and air-conditioned cars disgorge their occupants, who cannot believe that such an efficient, clean system will remain so for long. The Metro officials plan a 10-mile system by 1990, from Tollygunge to Dum Dum (near the airport). Many Calcuttans use the Metro as a tourist attraction, much like the beginning years of Washington, D.C.'s system. Ride it for pleasure and for a fast ride down Chowringhee (J. L. Nehru Road). The fare depends on the distance traveled; the minimum is Rs. 1.50.

For a complete and authoritative guide to all bus and tram routes in the city, we recommend the *Calcutta and Howrah Guide,* sold for less than $1 at, among other places, the Oxford Booksellers on Park Street, next door to Kwality restaurant.

TOURS. The *West Bengal Government Tourist Office* at 3/2 BBD Bagh East, near Great Eastern Hotel, (tel. 23–8271) will provide you with an array of conducted and package tours. If you don't see printed information sheets at the office, ask; the tourist officers are helpful and informed. The ITDC at 4 Shakespeare Sarani (tel. 44–3521) also operates similar services. Tourist taxis are available from both locations. A full-day guided tour that takes in over 12 sights costs Rs. 26 (non-air-conditioned); Rs. 40 (air-conditioned). Tourist taxis cost approximately Rs. 250–Rs. 600, depending on the length of use, type of car, and distance traveled. Cars and drivers may be hired at deluxe hotels.

From October to March, the West Bengal Tourist Office has a number of package tours (including meals and accommodations) via train, bus, and boat to Rajasthan, North Bengal, and the Sunderbans (the swampy delta region of the Bay of Bengal that has the largest population of Indian tigers). The prices for these tours, which average a week, are reasonable. The tours are worth investigating if you are short of time and have a limited budget.

USEFUL ADDRESSES. Tourist Information. *Government of India Tourist Office,* 4 Shakespeare Sarani, tel. 44–3521; *West Bengal Tourist Information Center,* 3/2 BBD Bagh East, tel. 23–8271.

Foreigners' Registration Office. 237 A. J. Bose Rd., tel. 44–3301.

Rail. *Howrah* and *Sealdah* stations and booking offices at 6 Fairlie Pl. and 14A Strand Rd.

Travel Agents (recognized by the government). *American Express,* 21 Old Court House St. (tel. 23–6281); *Balmer Lawrie,* 21 Netaji Subhas Rd. (tel. 22–6871); *Marshall International,* 25 Camac St. (tel. 44–1034); *Mercury Travels (India),* 46C J. L. Nehru Rd. (tel. 44–3555); and *Travel Corporation of India,* 46C J. L. Nehru Rd. (tel. 44–5469). There are over 25 other government-recognized travel agents in Calcutta. A complete listing of these and other services listed in this section is available from the West Bengal Tourist Information Center.

Airlines. *Air India,* 50 J. L. Nehru Rd. (tel. 44–2356); *British Airways,* 41 J. L. Nehru Rd. (tel. 24–8181); *Indian Airlines* 39 Chittaranjan Ave. (tel. 26–0810); *Lufthansa,* 30 A/B J. L. Nehru Rd. (tel. 24–8611); *Pan American,* 42 J. L. Nehru Rd. (tel. 44–4643); *Thai International,* 18 G Park St. (tel. 24–9696); *Vayudoot,* 54 J. L. Nehru Rd. (tel. 44–7062).

An invaluable, quarterly updated listing of airline schedules is *The Complete Travel Handbook,* sold for Rs. 25 (about $2) at bookstores and by sidewalk vendors.

Consulates. *United States,* 5/1 Ho Chi Minh Sarani (tel. 44–3611); *United Kingdom,* 1 Ho Chi Minh Sarani (tel. 44–5171); *France,* 26 Park Mansion, Park Street (tel. 24–0958); *Federal Republic of Germany,* 1 Hastings Park Rd. (tel. 45–9141); *Nepal,* 19 Woodlands, Sterndale Rd. (tel. 45–2024); *Bangladesh,* 9 Circus Ave. (tel. 44–5208).

Emergency. Police or medical problems are tackled best through hotel desks and consular offices. The **police emergency** number is 100; **fire brigade,** 101; and **ambulance,** 102. These services are vastly overburdened, and the telephone system in Calcutta is one of the worst in India. Therefore, we recommend that you use your hotel's services.

FESTIVALS. Calcutta embodies Hindu India's "museum of festivals" and secular India's joy in celebrating its diverse cultures. There is a festival of some kind almost every week. The most spectacular and rambunctious is *Durga Puja,* celebrated for three weeks during **September** and **October.** Kali is one of Durga's incarnations. Each neighborhood has its own separate shrine with elaborate clay figures, some over a full story high, on bamboo and straw skeletons, that are uniquely constructed by a group of artisans in north Calcutta at Kumartulli, near Chitpur Road. At the close of the festivities, these statues are taken by open flatbed trucks, with surging crowds guiding them through the streets, to the Hooghly (*Ma Ganga*—Mother Ganges) and floated away. If you take a tour of neighborhoods at night to see the different forms that this colorful and imaginative folk art takes, along with the panoply of neon lights, jatras, and music, you won't be disappointed.

October and **November** bring *Diwali,* the festival of lights, which celebrates the return of Rama from his exile and his victory over Ravana, the demon, in the epic myth of the Ramayana. Almost all houses are lit with small terra-cotta oil lamps that ring the balconies and rooftop edges. Prayers are offered to Lakshmi, the goddess of wealth and prosperity, who is welcomed into households with crescendos of firecrackers. At least for another year, good has triumphed over evil.

In **December,** Christmas is celebrated not only by the Christians but by Calcuttans in general as *Boro deen* (the big day, as it is known in colloquial parlance). The weeks preceding Christmas provide an opportunity to hear some of the city's excellent amateur choirs at churches such as St. Paul's Cathedral, to shop in the well-stocked stores, and to visit the traveling exhibits at fairs that are set up in the Maidan during this season.

In **January** and **February,** Bengal is the venue for the *Gangasagar Mela* (the Festival of the River Ganges) when pilgrims come from all over India to celebrate the most important natural element in the mythology—the river, source of life, purifier, destroyer, and nurturer. Also in January-February,

Saraswati, the goddess of learning and the arts, is celebrated in a city that reveres intellectual life and thought.

March heralds the advent of spring and introduces the most boisterous of India's festivals, *Holi* or *Dol Jatra,* as it is called in Bengal. The festival of colors, when yellow hands, green hair, and purple faces are not uncommon as young and old, regardless of religious belief, spray and splatter each other with colored water and powder. It is advisable to enjoy the free-spirited fun with a companion or in a group to avoid being harassed if you don't wish to participate. While out in the city at this time, wear old clothes.

The Bengali's love of sweets takes an institutionalized form during some festivals that are peculiar to Bengal—*Bhai Phonta,* when sisters celebrate brothers; *Jamaishasti,* when sons-in-law are lovingly honored (and teased) by sisters-in-law; *Vijaya Dashami,* a variation of the Western Mother's Day, when the oldest women in a family are shown special reverence. These Bengali traditions bring Christmas-like festivities many times a year as celebrants offer gifts of sweets and clothes. Check dates locally, since they are based on the lunar calendar.

Other festivals of note are *Baisak,* the Bengali New Year in **April–May;** *Rath Jatra* (**June–July**), the chariot festival (see *Orissa* chapter for an extensive description). There are also Moslem, Sikh, and Parsi festivals. Check with the West Bengal Tourist Office for information. One of the most fascinating festivals in tribal India takes place in the neighborhood of Calcutta—the *Baul Festival* of song and prayer. The Bauls are wandering minstrels who worship Krishna and who, through their haunting songs, search for the divine in all of us. They carry on impromptu conversations with Krishna through their music as they travel from village to village through the winter and spring months. Baul music is being revived by individual groups in and around Calcutta in an effort to preserve it. Tagore's university at Santiniketan (110 miles from Calcutta) is one such place. Inquire at the tourist office for more information.

MUSEUMS AND GALLERIES. Calcutta's cultural energy is ever present in the diversity and range of its museums, galleries, and constantly changing exhibits. From November to March, book fairs, textile exhibitions, and different kinds of fairs dot the central Maidan and are akin to the great religious festivals in their frequency and number of attendees. Most of the museums and galleries listed here are free. When donations are accepted, Rs. 5 will do nicely.

Ashutosh Museum of Indian Art, College Street, is a small museum, located in the Senate House of Calcutta University. It is maintained by the university and includes an excellent and noteworthy collection of Bengal folk art, textiles, and terra-cotta clay models. The museum is open daily 10:30 A.M.–4:30 P.M. (Saturdays till 3 P.M.). It is closed Sundays and university holidays.

The Asiatic Society, 1 Park St., founded in 1784, is a research center for Indology. The library contains 20,000 volumes of rare Sanskrit, Arabic, Persian, and Hindi manuscripts. The society's collection formed the nucleus of the Indian Museum before that museum was created. However, it is possible to view only a limited part of the collection as of this writing because the society is trying to reorganize its collection after a long period of mismanagement during which much of the collection was pilfered. The society is planning to build an annex that will display part of its collection to the general public. If you are interested, write the director for official permission to peruse the stacks.

Birla Academy of Art and Culture, 109 Southern Ave., houses contemporary paintings, graphic arts, and photographs. Open daily except Mondays 3–8 P.M.

Birla Planetarium, J. L. Nehru Road, near Victoria Memorial, is a circular structure modeled after a Buddhist *stupa* (shrine) at Sanchi. Built in 1962, it was India's first planetarium and is one of the largest in the world. Daily programs are in English, Hindi, and Bengali. Open daily 12:30–8 P.M. The entrance fee is Rs. 5.

Bungiya Sahitya Parishad, 243/1 Upper Circular Rd., has collections of paintings of the Bengal School, sculptures, coins, and rare books in Sanskrit and Bengali.

Gurusaday Museum, Bratacharigram, Thakurpukur, off Diamond Harbor Road, about 12 miles from the city center, has exhibits including Bengali folk art, especially Kalighat *pat* (scrolls), similar to the murallike Orissan palm leaf paintings. Jamini Roy, one of India's foremost modernist painters, revived the form and incorporated the style into much of his work. Open 11:30 A.M.–4:30 P.M.; closed Thursdays.

The Indian Museum on Chowringhee (J. L. Nehru Road) is the oldest in India and one of the largest and most comprehensive collections in Asia. It opened in 1878, after being in construction for three years. Known locally as *Jadu Ghar,* the "House of Magic," the museum has 36 galleries in six sections: archaeology, art, ethnology, geology, industry, and zoology. It is considered to have one of the best natural history collections in the world. The archaeology section has a representative collection of antiquities from prehistoric times to the Mogul period, including relics from Mohenjodaro and Harappa, the oldest excavated Indus valley civilizations. The southern wing includes the Bharhut and Gandhara rooms (Indian art from second century B.C. to A.D. fifth century), the Gupta and Medieval galleries, and the Mogul gallery.

The coin collection, which you require special permission to see, contains the largest collection of Indian coins in the world. Gems and jewelry are also on display. The art section is on the first floor and has a good collection of Indian textiles, carpets, wood, papier-mâché, and terra-cotta pottery. A gallery on the third floor contains exquisitely drawn Persian miniatures, Indian paintings, and Tibetan monastery banners. The anthropology section on the first floor is devoted to cultural anthropology. The museum is planning a major change in the near future to establish India's first comprehensive physical anthropology exhibit in a major museum. The geological section is the largest in Asia. Some interesting specimens on display are an Egyptian mummy donated in 1880 by an English seaman, a fossilized 200-million-year-old tree trunk, the lower jaw of an 84-foot whale, and meteorites dating 50,000 years. The museum takes selected exhibits to rural areas for the benefit of villagers, most of whom will never be close to a museum. Open daily (March–November) 10 A.M.–5 P.M. and 10 A.M.–4:30 P.M. (December–February) except Mondays, when it is closed. Entrance is free on Fridays; there is a small fee other days.

Nehru Children's Museum, 94/1 J. L. Nehru Rd., adjoining St. Paul's Cathedral, has excellent exhibits for young and old that enliven mythology and history through the use of models and dolls. Open Tuesday–Sunday, noon–8 P.M. Closed Mondays.

Victoria Memorial, J. L. Nehru Road, was conceived in 1901 by Lord Curzon and constructed over a 20-year period. This "poor man's Taj Mahal" is designed in a mixture of Italian Renaissance and Saracenic architectural styles. Surrounded by spaciously laid-out gardens and Calcutta's great Maidan, Victoria Memorial is a haven from the bustle of this nerve-wracking city. The memorial houses an interesting collection of artifacts illustrating British roots in India. It includes Queen Victoria's writing desk and piano, pistols used by Warren Hastings, a governor-general, notebooks of Tipu Sultan, and prints, Indian miniature paintings, water colors, and Persian books. Open daily 10 A.M.–4:30 P.M. except Mondays. Cameras are not allowed; you must leave your cameras in the checkroom near the ticket booth. Small fee.

Other museums and galleries of interest are *Academy of Fine Arts,* Cathedral Road, next to St. Paul's Cathedral. Besides extensive galleries, plays are staged here daily. *Philatelic and Postal History Museum,* next to the GPO at BBD Bagh; closed Sundays. *Ramakrishna Mission Institute of Culture,* Golpark, Ballygunge. *Birla Industrial and Technological Museum* at 19A Gurusaday Rd. *Netaji Bhawan,* 38/2 Elgin Rd., originally the house where the nationalist, Subhas Bose, Bengal's favorite son, lived and worked. Historical exhibits are on display. *Art and Prints Gallery,* 31 Park Mansion. *Calcutta Painters,* 37C College Rd. *Society of Contemporary Artists,* 68/4 Purnadas Rd. *Rabindra Bharati Museum,* 6/4 Dwarkanath Tagore La. *Indian Society of Oriental Art,* 15 Park St.

For updated and current information on gallery offerings and museum exhibits, we recommend the Sunday edition of the *Telegraph* newspaper and *Calcutta: This Fortnight,* a free booklet available from the Government of India Tourist Office or the West Bengal Tourist Information Center.

 PUBLIC LIBRARIES AND READING ROOMS. Public libraries are always a boon to travelers. Without having to pay admission or buy a beverage, you can use a desk to write letters and journals or just rest awhile indoors, away from the sometimes too-exhausting city. Calcutta has over 150 such places (listed in *Calcutta and Howrah Guide,* Rs. 15, available at bookstores and newsstands). The *National Library* is at Belvedere, across from the Calcutta zoo, in the former viceregal residence. The biggest library in India, it contains over eight million manuscripts in various languages. The reading rooms are quiet and restful. Open 8 A.M.–8 P.M. Here are a few other libraries with the best locations and facilities: *American Library (USIA),* 7 J. L. Nehru Rd.; *Asiatic Society,* 1 Park St.; *British Council,* 5 Shakespeare Sarani; and *Ramakrishna Mission Institute of Culture,* Golpark.

Recommended Reading. Two books are informative supplements to your visit: *Calcutta,* published by the West Bengal Tourist Office in conjunction with IBH Publishing, is available at Oxford Booksellers on Park Street. Its quirky, often amusing, writing exhibits a loving feel for this chaotic yet mesmerizing city. Also available at Oxford is Geoffrey Moorhouse's *Calcutta* (New York: Holt, Rinehart, and Winston, 1985), which is essential reading for anyone who visits this astonishing city.

HOUSES OF WORSHIP. *Anglican:* St. Paul's Cathedral, Chowringhee (J. L. Nehru Road); *Roman Catholic:* Church of Christ the King, 5 Amir Ali Ave.; *Baptist:* Carey Church, 31 Bowbazar St.; *Congregational and Presbyterian:* Union Chapel, Dharamtalla Street; *American Methodist:* Methodist Church, Sudder Street; and *Jewish:* Shalome Jewish Synagogue, Synagogue Street. Additional listings of churches are available from any tourist information office.

There are also Hindu, Buddhist, Jain, and Parsi temples; Moslem mosques; and Sikh gurudwaras.

MEDICAL SERVICES. *Woodlands Nursing Home,* 8/5 Alipur Rd. (tel. 45–3951); *Bellevue Clinic,* 9 Loudon St. (tel. 44–6925); *S. S. K. M. Hospital,* 244 Lower Circular Rd. (tel. 44–9751). All leading hotels have English-speaking doctors on call.

SPORTS. If Calcuttans love politics, poetry, and processions as much as they love food, *adda* (gossip and intellectual conversation, a blend that is unmistakably Bengali) and argument—they love sports, especially **cricket,** even more. From November to February, the cricket season rules the day when work comes to a standstill and Eden Gardens overflows. With television the motto has become, "If you can't play, watch." Matches of people with various levels of skills—from international test matches to backyard alley games —are fielded every day. Bengal's obsession with sports also includes **soccer,** which was, until recently, the best-loved sport. You always know when a divisional soccer match is in progress near the Maidan; the roar of the crowd is like a "cathartic release of emotion," according to one local observer.

Clubs were formed during British times to set off the rulers from the ruled, and clubs continue to be an arena for much of Calcutta's passion for sports. A new hierarchy has been established through membership dues, and **sports clubs** continue to flourish. You have to be a guest of a member to attend, or you can apply for temporary membership. There are over 100 such clubs in Calcutta. The *Calcutta Cricket Club,* at 19/1 Gurusaday Rd., was founded in 1792 and is the oldest sports club outside England. The *Royal Calcutta Golf Club,* Golf Club Road and Tollygunge Road, is the oldest golf club in India.

Winter is also the time for **horse racing** and **polo.** The *Royal Calcutta Turf Club,* 11 Russell St., and the *Calcutta Polo Club,* 51 J. L. Nehru Rd., provide the organizational services for these two sports. The *Calcutta Racecourse,* built in 1819, is the scene of frenetic activity every Saturday, not just by the rich in box seats, but by ordinary racing enthusiasts perched atop the tallest tree branches on the outside of the track. Polo is played in sections of the Maidan.

Other sports include **rowing** at the *Lake* and *Bengal Rowing* clubs, both near Dhakuria Lake in Ballygunge; **horseback** riding at the *Tollygunge Club;* **swimming** at the *Saturday Club,* 7 Wood St., and the *Calcutta Swimming Club,* 1 Strand Rd.; **tennis** at the *Calcutta Cricket Club;* and **squash** at the *Calcutta Racket Club,* near St. Paul's Cathedral.

Calcutta offers much more in sports, from **rifle shooting,** to **fishing,** to **badminton,** to **table tennis,** to **rugby,** to **field hockey,** to **volleyball,** and more. Inquire at your hotel or call one of the clubs listed.

 SHOPPING. Calcutta's *Central Cottage Industries Emporium,* next to the USIA on J. L. Nehru Road, and the many state emporiums around the city offer the visitor an opportunity to browse through India's art, crafts, and fabrics. During the winter, craft and textile exhibitions are often held on the Maidan. Goods from all over India show up for sale there, making the exhibitions splendid shopping opportunities if you don't go when they first open (it sometimes takes a few days for all exhibitors to get set up) or too late, when goods have been picked over. Though the selection from other states is generally better in Bombay and Delhi, India's more heavily visited cities, Bengal's crafts and fabrics are best bought in Calcutta, the center of commerce in the eastern half of India.

Terra-cotta crafts from the Bankura, Birbhum, and Midnapore, districts of West Bengal, especially brightly painted figurines of animals and dancers and bas-relief plaques of deities such as Krishna and Radha, make unusual gifts, but one must pack these fragile items carefully. From Krishnanagar come clay figurines in both realistic and stylized shapes. Pottery bowls, mugs, plates, and serving bowls, glazed a rich aqua blue, are also nerve-wracking to travel home with, but their strong, simple lines have a certain appeal alongside the more ornately decorated crafts. More easily transportable (their diminutive size is said to allow them to be taken along in pockets on pilgrimages) and perhaps the most delightful of the crafts from Bengal are the frequently whimsical *dokra* figures made of a mixture of clay and metal, usually cast in the lost-wax method. The most popular forms of these Bengali folk bronzes are Hindu deities or animals. With their strangely proportioned shapes, dokra figurines exhibit a lively, carefree imagination at work, yet one that adheres to traditional notions of a particular deity's posture and gesture and the ornamentation that each would wear or hold. Shells are fashioned by shonkhari craftsmen into bangles, toe and finger rings, and exquisitely shaped demitasse spoons. Bell-metal work, bidri work, soapstone boxes and plates, and leather goods are some other indigenous crafts.

Textile buys are abundant in Calcutta. *Jamdani* weaving, a cotton fabric that is brocaded with cotton and *zari* (silver) threads is one of the more unusual weaves. Made on looms similar to the jamdani is the exquisite Baluchar brocaded silk from Murshidabad, with its deep purple or mauve background and ornately printed end pieces. For those who sew or have tailors back home, elegant Tussore silks are available by the meter.

Less luxurious but far more practical are the cottons of India that continue to be popular and provide a sensible antidote to the heat for those who have packed too many synthetics for travel in a tropical climate. In Calcutta's bazaars, more than in village bazaars, these items are plentiful. You can purchase men's *kurtas* (loose thigh-length shirts) that are popular with both men and women for the quality and coolness of their handwoven cotton fabric (*khadi*) and the freedom of their design. Women also find *salwar kameez* sets (loose dress-length tops worn with baggy pants that fit tightly at the ankle) to be especially comfortable, although they are not always as available ready-made as are kurtas. Thin cotton made into vests for infants and petticoats (which can be worn as dresses) for young girls are simply embroidered in colorful, juvenile designs. Once washed, these cottons become extremely soft. And for boys who are adventurous dressers, *kurta pajamas,* with a loose top worn over jodhpur-style pants, are a cool change from jeans and T-shirts. Tailoring is inexpensive in Calcutta, as it is all over India. If you have the time for fittings, take advantage of it. Lindsay Street, across from New Market, has a number of tailor shops. Inquire at your hotel desk for local recommendations.

Kantha embroidery is a Bengali needlework specialty in which a quilted surface is embroidered with all manner of shapes, from the more usual birds, animals, and trees to abstract designs. Some of Calcutta's destitute women have been organized to make embroidered bedspreads and pillow covers that have plain or multihued floral designs on heavy cotton. Though the embroidery work in them is not as fine as that in Kashmiri woolen shawls, it is vigorous, cheerful, and appealing.

Shopping in bazaars around Calcutta can be either an exhilarating—if exhausting—experience or a lengthy test of wills. Parts of the famous *Sir Stuart*

Hogg Market, better known as *New Market,* 19 Lindsay St., burned down a few years back, and many vendors have been relocated to J. L. Nehru Road, across from the Grand Hotel. The 110-year-old New Market houses about 2,500 stores under one roof, selling cotton *tangail* saris, Bankura clay horses, Malda brassware, leather from Santiniketan, silk from Murshidabad, Khadi cloth, poultry, cheeses, nuts, and other foods. It is one of Calcutta's most extensive bazaars. The new location lacks the bustling charm of the original New Market, and most visitors will find the undamaged part of the old area a more intriguing place to poke around. The bearers/touts at the old New Market are often difficult to discourage. (No matter how insistent they are, do not change foreign currency with them, and if they show you around the shops, you should be aware that they usually get a percentage of whatever you spend.) For those who are interested in leather goods, *Bata Shoes* has many outlets in Calcutta; the store at the Grand Hotel Arcade has the largest selection.

Other bazaar areas where Calcuttans go are *Gariahat,* 212, 214, and 216 Rash Behari Ave., *Barabazar,* in North Calcutta, and *Shyambazar,* 1A R. G. Kar Rd. On Sundays, traditionally the market day for Calcuttans, large wholesale markets spill from sidewalks into the streets in the North Calcutta area. At *Hathibagan,* 80, 81, and 82 Bidhan Sarani, even if one isn't interested in buying the goods being offered here—racing pigeons, parakeets, bright cotton children's clothes, inexpensive men's shirts and trousers, and plants—the energy and color are infectious. An unusual feature of the *Ultadanga Market,* 22 Ultadanga Rd., is that, because it caters primarily to small retail businesses, both vendors and buyers are men, and few women are seen on the streets. Taxis waiting to transport businessmen's large purchases line the side streets, except during the Puja festivals in the fall when the wholesale clothing market is so crowded with shoppers that the streets are closed to traffic.

Calcutta has over 90 markets, ranging from cattle, cut flowers, jewelry, and clothing markets to the daily necessities of produce, meat, and fish. A walk through some of these markets will enrich your perspective of the city, as well as allow you to snag some terrific buys. Bargaining is essential at all markets. Transactions are cash only; credit cards are not accepted.

Some specialty markets are on or near Chitpur Road, where there are shops that make musical instruments—sarods, sitars, harmoniums, *dholaks* (drums), and costumes for the traveling theatrical ensembles (*jatras*). At *Bowbazar,* the home of the jewelers' trade, one finds artisans who work in gold. Bentinck Street is known for its shoes and leather goods, and College Street, near the Ashutosh Museum, is the center for second-hand English and Bengali books. This street is packed tight with stalls overflowing with textbooks on every possible subject. Careful rummaging might turn up a first edition for a small price.

State-run emporiums lack the stimulating entrepreneurial energy of bazaar areas, but the quality of goods is usually better, and goods sell at fixed prices, with money going back to craftspeople without the usual percentage being deducted for middlemen. Credit cards, usually American Express and Visa, are accepted in emporiums. In some, such as the *Central Cottage Industries Emporium* and *Bengal Home Industries,* purchases are taken to a central location near the cashier, where they are wrapped and given to the shopper after they are paid for and just before the shopper leaves the store. This centralization eliminates the shopper's problem of carrying around a growing armload of goods while trying to see and buy more. Hang on to your receipts from each counter in the emporium; they are used as your claim ticket. Shopping bags with handles are not always available at Indian shops, and paper bags are often not sturdy, so some sort of large canvas or plastic bag is recommended when you are planning to do a lot of shopping.

Central Cottage Industries Emporium is at 7 J. L. Nehru Rd. (Chowringhee), next to the USIA Library, and, as the name implies, it has goods from all over India. Among other items, one can find colorful, intricate Mithila paintings from Bihar, beautiful handprinted writing paper and envelopes, and wooden toys. Bengal Home Industries is at No. 57, where you'll find a wide selection of Bengali handicrafts and items made in Bengal's cottage industries.

Also on this road are *Cauvery Karnataka Upahar,* at No. 17; *Kashmir Government Art Emporium,* at No. 12, which sells this lovely northwestern state's renowned crafts, such as papier-mâché objects covered with intricate brushwork designs in silver and gold, finely woven textiles, richly embroidered woolen shawls, and silk and woolen carpets in traditional patterns; *Rajasthan Handi-*

crafts, at No. 30E), offers silver jewelery and miniature paintings; and *Tripura Administration Sales Emporium,* at No. 58B, has leather and bamboo crafts.

Four shops on Lindsay Street make convenient stops: *Handloom House,* at No. 3, where textiles by the yard and by the piece are available; *Manjusha,* at No. 7/1D; *Uttar Pradesh Government Emporium* at No. 12B; and *Manipur,* at No. 15L.

The *Punjab Government Emporium* is at 26B Camac St. *Refugee Handicrafts* is now located at 2A and 3A Gariahat Rd. and sells, among other things, textiles by weavers who relocated from East Pakistan. Textiles are also available at *Khadi Gromodyog Bhavan,* 24 Chittaranjan Ave. At the *Assam Emporium,* 8 Russell St., one can get unusual baskets and honey from other northeast states. In south Calcutta, a new shopping center of emporiums has opened recently, the *CIT Market* on Dakshinapan near Dhakuria. Batik fabric, appliqued silk salwars and pillow covers, and woolen shawls highlight the Gujarat emporium located here, and the *West Bengal Emporium* has a good selection of dokra figurines on the second floor.

A unique purchase, a computer horoscope, is available at *Foresight Systems, Inc.,* 47–C Shakespeare Sarani (open Tuesday–Saturday, 10 A.M.–6:30 P.M.; Monday, 2 P.M.–6:30 P.M.). Rates vary from Rs. 75 to Rs. 500, depending on how much information is desired. A recent modernization of the ancient Indian horoscope methods, this office, with its computer setup in a temperature-controlled, dust-free glass enclosure, is a far cry from one's image of the spiritual Indian "fortune teller." Horoscopes are cast either in the Western astrological system or in the Indian configuration. To have a horoscope caste, you must know the location, date, and time of your birth.

Calcutta is the center of the tea trade in India. Tea auction houses flourish, as they have for almost 150 years. Packaged tea, loose or in teabags, is readily available at stores. The *Health Food Centre* near Kwality restaurant and opposite Magnolia restaurant, on Park Street, carries a reasonably priced selection of Darjeeling and other teas.

 ENTERTAINMENT. Calcutta takes its sustenance from the fervent creativity of its artists. Throughout the years of political strife and population and economic disasters, and browbeaten by the irritations and fatigue of daily life, Calcuttans have taken solace that their city has produced and keeps on producing some of India's most imaginative cultural representatives. It was here that Rabindranath Tagore wrote, becoming the first Asian to be selected for the Nobel Prize for literature. Tagore created a school of music, Rabindra Sangeet, whose two most famous expositions are the national anthems of India and Bangladesh. It is in Calcutta that filmmaker Satyajit Ray works and has brought a distinctively Bengali point of view of middle-class India to millions of viewers in the West. Here, too, Uday Shankar worked and brought Indian classical dance to the attention of the rest of the world, and Ravi Shankar, his younger brother, played, to the joy of thousands the world over. It is here also that Bengali journals and broadsheets are sold for pennies on the street, poets hawk their poems on street corners, and where theater, both traditional and modern, flourishes. Calcutta's entertainment possibilities are manifold.

To start out, look up *Calcutta: This Fortnight* (a free pamphlet from the West Bengal Tourist Office) and the Sunday edition of the *Telegraph* newspaper for daily listings of cultural and other entertainment news.

DANCE

Cities are often the best places to see performances of Indian classical dancing. Regional and national troupes gravitate toward the major cities, where the audiences are large. Calcutta is no exception. Besides the Bharat Natyam and Kathak, there are performances of the Manipuri and Odissi (Orissa) styles at the *Academy of Dance and Music,* 5 Dwarkanath Tagore La.; *Academy of Fine Arts,* near the Birla Planetarium; and at *Kala Mandir.* A smorgasbord of Indian dances at the *Oberoi Grand* is held nightly but is only for those who are not adventurous enough to experience the local culture in its authentic settings.

Two splendid versions of dance-dramas or performance arts that are unique to Bengal are the *jatras* and *Kavi gan.* Jatra (folk theater) is enacted outside the traditional dramatic set. The audience sits in the open air and the actors and actresses sing or act their roles, while a small orchestra sits to one side of the performance space and accompanies the action. Taken traditionally from mythology or from old Bengali novels, jatras also address historical and political issues these days. The action here is broad and the scope of emotions is great. Although once considered an unsophisticated form of entertainment by urban Bengalis, the jatra has been enjoying a revival that has brought some of Bengal's most popular film actors and actresses to the stage. *Rabindra Bharati University,* 6/4 Dwarkanath Tagore La., once part of Tagore's residence, offers courses in jatra, and the university's performances are worth seeing. Watch the newspaper listings during the winter months for the performance times.

Kavi gan is a stylized duet of poets who sing their responses in verse, *ex tempore,* on selected themes. Once immensely popular, it is a rare phenomenon now, though there are occasions that are advertised during the winter season.

FILMS

Movies are advertised each day in the English-language newspapers, the *Telegraph, Statesman,* and the *Amrita Bazar Patrika.* There are three to four shows a day, and it is advisable to plan ahead and purchase tickets in advance. The prices vary, depending on where you want to sit, the cheapest seats being up front. Calcuttans, as do other Indians, treat movies like Westerners treat television—they watch everything: the good, the mediocre, and the terrible.

Only a few major English-language movies are shown, while many B-grade films, never to be heard of in the West, are dumped into this accepting market. It is worth your time to find a Bengali who will accompany you and translate a movie by Satyajit Ray, Mrinal Sen, Ritwick Ghatak, Aparna Sen, or one of Bengal's more contemporary filmmakers.

MUSIC

Rabindra Sadan, A. J. Bose Road, near St. Paul's Cathedral; *Kala Mandir* and *Ramakrishna Mission Institute of Culture,* Golpark; and *Mahajati Sadan,* 166 Chittaranjan Ave. are some of the major venues for the world-renowned maestros of Indian music. These include Niser Hussain Khan, Latafat Hussain Khan, and Girija Devi, who follow in the tradition of Bade Gulam Ali, and Allaudin Khan, whose disciple was Ravi Shankar. There is also a developed folk music school in Bengal, known at Puratani (of old times). The subgroups are Panchali, Ramprasadi, Kirtan, and Toppa.

NIGHTLIFE AND BARS

The major Western-style hotels have **discos** for dancing as well as live music and dance performances in the main dining rooms during dinner. Some also feature floor shows. Calcutta's independent **bars** are not sprightly places. Most inhabitants buy their liquor at stores and entertain at home or go to restaurants with a bar service. Three bars that come closest to a comfortable, Western bar atmosphere are *Olympia,* 21 Park St. (tel. 24–9525); *Windsor Bar,* 207 A. J. Bose Rd. (tel. 44–3178); and *Saquis,* 177 Lenin Sarani (tel. 27–1580). These bars are open until about midnight; closed Thursdays.

THEATER

There is no permanent English-language theater in Calcutta. English plays are staged by amateur clubs, colleges, schools, and the British Council. The first Western-type drama was enacted in 1795, but public theater began in earnest in 1872 (before that date, private performances were staged by the wealthy and liberal, including the Tagores' Hindu Theatre). Bengali theater is the fulcrum of much of the city's cultural activities. Watch for performances at *Kala Mandir,* 48 Shakespeare Sarani; *Rabindra Sadan,* A. J. Bose Road, near St. Paul's Cathedral; *Star,* 79/3/4 Bidhan Sarani (tel. 55–1839); *Rungmahal,* 76/1B Bidhan Sarani (tel. 55–1619); Biswaroopa, 2A Raja Kissen St. (tel. 55–3220); and *Rangana,* 153/2 Archarya Prafulla Chandra Rd. (tel. 55–6846). The groups to watch for are Bahuroopi, People's Little Theatre, and Drama Libraries-Museums.

BENGAL AND BIHAR

Calcutta's "Suburbia" and a Troubled State

LISA SAMSON and AMIT SHAH

Calcutta's lack of "real" antiquities is sufficiently made up in the region surrounding it. After the British had merged Bengal with Bihar under the Bengal presidency in 1765, the modern-day states of Bengal, Bihar, and Orissa were one—the land of the bounty of the Ganges.

Like all great river deltas, Bengal was unquestionably a cradle of civilization. Ptolemy's geography mentions it as a seafaring nation. The Pala kings who ruled from the eighth to the twelfth centuries were patrons of the arts and learning; their artists traveled far south, even to Indonesia, and their religious scholars carried the Buddhist gospels to Tibet. During the Mogul period, Akbar conquered Bengal, but Bengal became virtually a separate kingdom under the independent nabob, Siraj-ud-Daula, who was routed in 1757 at Plassey, north of Calcutta, by Robert Clive through a series of treacherous conspiracies. The British thus won control over Bengal after the Dutch, the French, and the Portuguese had all made some efforts. The subsequent history of Bengal is synonymous with Calcutta and is outlined in that chapter of this guide.

Today, bounded by Sikkim and Bhutan in the north, east by Assam and Bangladesh, south by the Bay of Bengal and Orissa, and west and northwest by Bihar and Nepal, Bengal covers 54,469 square miles and has a population of over 54 million, an increase of nearly 24 percent since 1971.

473

Bihar, bounded in the north by Nepal, east by West Bengal, south by Orissa, and west and southwest by Uttar Pradesh and Madhya Pradesh, was part of the great Magadh empire from 500 B.C. to A.D. 500. Pataliputra (present-day Patna) was designated by Chandragupta Maurya as the empire's capital city. Maurya's grandson, Ashoka, later became the evangelist of Buddhism. During A.D. fourth and fifth centuries, Pataliputra formed part of the great Gupta Empire, which saw the revival of Hinduism. Factional and fractious battles denied Bihar a stable rule until the eighth century, when the Palas of Bengal won paramountcy. In 1193, Bihar was overrun by Moslem invaders and remained part of the sultanate in Delhi till the second half of the fourteenth century. In 1529, Babur, the first of the Moguls, wrested it from the Lodhi rulers and was eventually ousted by the English in 1765, more because of weak-kneed, indolent nabobs than any British supremacy. In 1912, the British separated Bihar and Orissa from Bengal and divided the three into separate provinces in 1936. Today, Bihar has a total population of over 70 million within 107,803 square miles and has had an average population increase of 24 percent since 1971.

Bihar—Mineral Rich and Land Poor

Rich in minerals, producing about 40 percent of the nation's mica, coal, copper, and iron ore, Bihar is still one of India's poorest states. Only 26 percent of its cultivable lands are irrigated. It also has a sizable tribal population, one of the largest concentrations in India. Bihar, one of the major pilgrimage sites of Buddhism as well as Hinduism, is an extremely troubled state. It is also one of the most corrupt. Feudal armies belonging to wealthy landlords clash with peasant militias and sharecroppers of lower castes. Escaping the cycle of poverty, some 400,000 leave the state each year to labor in Calcutta's jute mills and shipyards, pulling handcarts, working as construction crews in the Himalayan foothills and as farm laborers in the prosperous Punjab. Caste bigotry, illiteracy, crime, and corruption are endemic. Forty percent of the population is below the official poverty line of $500 a year (about Rs. 6,250) for a family of four. The current five-year plan outlays $4 billion in investments in Bihar to shore up the crumbling infrastructure. That amount is less than $15 per person (about Rs. 188).

No one is sure what approach would be most meaningful—implementation of land reform laws, attacking political corruption and feudal bigotries, or expanding investments and development areas in north and central Bihar. All these problems are reflected in the weak focus on tourism. The tourist information centers are ill equipped, ill informed, and frequently closed. From the following sections, it is clear that the range and scope of the sightseeing attractions in Bihar are wide: from festivals and fairs, to abundant wildlife and the many sanctuaries, to the rich cultural heritage, to folk craft, to historical architecture, and to picturesque landscapes. Travelers should not be deterred, but should be aware of the difficulties of traveling here.

Bengal does not have Bihar's problems. All its problems seem concentrated around metropolitan Calcutta. In early 1987, however, the Darjeeling district did show signs of political unrest among the Gorkhas, who wanted an independent state, Gorkhaland, supported by the Gorkha National Liberation Front (GNLF). For a while, it seemed that the violence would curb the traffic of tourists to these pine-clad hills with their staggeringly beautiful vistas of glacier-fed rivers, serrated hillsides full of flowers and tea, majestic Himalayan peaks, and clean, crisp air. The disturbances now seem to have abated, and in mid-1987, travelers were visiting the area for the traditional summer-in-the-hills vacations as they did in years past.

PRACTICAL INFORMATION FOR
WEST BENGAL AND BIHAR

 WHEN TO GO. Darjeeling and the surrounding region can be visited almost all year round (although December to February might bring scattered snowfall and freezing temperatures), but the rest of West Bengal and Bihar are ideal between October and March, when the weather is dry and sunny and the mornings are crisp and pleasant. The average temperature ranges from 50°F to 85°F. The Chotanagpur Plateau and the Hazaribagh region are slightly cooler because of their altitude and forestation. Darjeeling and its environs are delightful in the summer, from April to June, but remember that the tourist traffic from the humid plains reaches its peak during this period.

 DARJEELING PERMITS. Those who fly into Darjeeling's Bagdogra Airport can get a permit at the airport to visit for up to 15 days. Those who come overland by road or by train must get a Restricted Area Permit (apply for it when you get your visa). Permits can be obtained by contacting the *Foreigners' Registration Office,* 237 Acharya Jagadish (A. J.) Bose Rd., Calcutta (tel. 44–0549). It is advisable to get all permits for visiting and trekking here. (See *Facts at Your Fingertips* for additional permit information.)

 HOW TO GET THERE. By Air. There are direct *Indian Airlines* flights daily from Calcutta, Patna, and Delhi to Bagdogra, the nearest airport for the Darjeeling region. Patna is linked to Delhi and Calcutta through daily flights, as well as with Kathmandu (Nepal), Lucknow, Guwahati, and Ranchi. *Vayudoot*'s air services connect Calcutta to Jamshedpur daily except Sundays, and to Ranchi, Cooch Behar, and Patna three times a week. Darjeeling can also be reached from Calcutta by train—to New Jalpaiguri, which is about 50 miles from Darjeeling and about three hours by taxi, climbing a steep and winding gradient of hills. Taxis cost about Rs. 375–400 (approximately $30). Express buses from Bagdogra or New Jalpaiguri are around Rs. 30.

By Train. Bihar's capital, Patna, 10 hours from Calcutta, and Gaya are on the main lines of the railways between Delhi and Calcutta. The *Rajdhani* stops at Gaya four days a week. The Howrah-Ranchi overnight mail train takes eight hours. Trains also connect Jamshedpur (Tata Steel Express), and north Bihar (Mithila Express), home of the now-famous Mithila painting done by the women of the area. Complete train information is available in Calcutta through *Eastern Railway* offices at 14A Strand Rd., near the general post office (GPO); 6 Fairlie Pl., near Benoy-Badal-Dinesh Bagh (BBD Bagh); and *Southeastern Railways* at Esplanade Mansion, near the Great Eastern Hotel. The expansive network of rail connections between Calcutta, the port, and the industrial and agricultural hinterland is a colonial legacy. Take advantage of them to savor the experience of reasonably comfortable travel in trains through rural Bengal and Bihar.

By Car. Calcutta is 453 miles from Darjeeling by road (National Highway 34) via Berhampur, Malda, and Siliguri. Ferry crossings near Malda over the Padma River (which separates Bangladesh and India) provide a memorable sight of riverboats winding down the great river—the lifeblood and nemesis of agricultural Bengal. Ranchi is 278 miles from Calcutta, through the "rice bowl" regions of Burdwan to the low hills of the Chotanagpur Plateau (on National Highway 33). Patna is 370 miles from Calcutta and 620 from Delhi on the oldest highway in India, the Grand Trunk Road. Mostly a truckers' route, it is congested and hazardous. Bodhgaya is 312 miles from Calcutta via Asansol.

By Bus. Buses galore connect Calcutta to destinations on all sides of the axis—to Siliguri (north), to Santiniketan via Rampurhat (west), and to Digha (south). Buses leave from *Esplanade Terminus* on Jawaharlal (J. L.) Nehru Road (Chowringhee) in Calcutta, diagonally opposite the Metro cinema hall (tel. 23–1916). It is advisable to go there in person to get information, since telephones are unreliable in Calcutta. An excellent schedule book for airline flights and train timetables is the *Complete Travel Handbook*. It is available at all major booksellers and at *Oxford Booksellers* in Calcutta on Park Street, next to Kwality restaurant.

The *West Bengal Tourist Bureau* runs a number of long-distance tours in air-conditioned coaches between September and March. Fares are reasonable. Inquire at 3/2 BBD Bagh East (tel. 23–8271) for complete information.

 **ACCOMMODATIONS.** The various tourist lodges and bungalows run by the West Bengal Tourist Development Corporation (WBTDC) can be booked as far ahead as three months (we advise that you book at least a month in advance) through the West Bengal Tourist Office at 3/2 BBD Bagh East, Calcutta 700 001 (tel. 23–5917 or 5168) and through tourist bureaus at Siliguri, Hill Cart Road (tel. 21632), or Darjeeling, 1 J. L. Nehru Rd., (tel. 2050). Calcutta, being the administrative headquarters, would be the most logical and secure place to make and confirm reservations. Reservations cannot be made on your arrival at most individual lodges. For your peace of mind, confirm bookings through Calcutta. Inquire about off-season discounts, up to 25 percent between May and August and November to March (depending on the geographic and climatic location) at selected lodges throughout the state. The WBTDC in Calcutta has a free booklet with detailed listings of over 40 lodges. It is updated regularly and can be useful if you intend to shop around for inexpensive accommodations in picturesque locales.

Bihar, with its unpredictable state government bureaucracy—in early 1987, the state government employees went on strike and closed offices, including tourist offices, for over a month—does not have a centralized reservations office for accommodations. If you are going to Bihar from Calcutta, the Bihar government's shabby offices at 26B Camac St., Calcutta 700 017 (tel. 44–0821), can provide you with a meager stock of information. In Patna, the state capital, the Government of India's Tourist Office at "Tourist Bhawan," Beerchand Patel Path (tel. 26721), can be of help.

Note: Addresses and telephone numbers are listed in as many places as possible. However, we recommend that you contact the state-level tourist office for information on reservations for tourist bungalows and lodges. Hotel chains have centralized booking systems. See *Facts at Your Fingertips* for these addresses and telephone numbers.

WEST BENGAL

All reservations for tourist lodges and bungalows in West Bengal are made through WBTDC in Calcutta.

Bakkhali

Inexpensive

The Tourist Lodge. Tel. KAKDWIP 76. A beach house with decks running right to the beach and shaded by casuarina groves. 48 beds. Breakfast and lunch charges (very low) added to the rates regardless of whether you eat these meals. The restaurant is attached.

Cooch Behar

Moderate

Hollong Forest Lodge. P.O. Box Madarihat, Jalpaiguri. Near the Jaldapara Wildlife Sanctuary, with seven double-bedded rooms. Meals are not included, but can be provided. Since Phuntsholing, in Bhutan, is approachable by road through this area, Indian nationals on vacation consider this a favored spot. Make your reservations in Calcutta a few months in advance.

Nilpara Forest Bungalow. P.O. Hasimara, Dist. Jalpaiguri. Two rooms are available with minimal furniture. Good for backpackers; bedrolls and kitchen utensils are provided. You have to carry your own provisions or pay the caretaker to arrange simple meals.

Madarihat Lodge. P.O. Madarihat, Dist. Jalpaiguri; tel. 30. Eight rooms and a restaurant.

Darjeeling

This "queen of the hill resorts of the east" has a number of hotels at various prices. A room with a view will give you a spectacular glimpse of the Himalayan peaks, especially Kanchenjunga, the third-highest peak in the world, when the clouds slip off for a few minutes, even on a cloudy day.

Deluxe

Oberoi Mount Everest. 29 Gandhi Rd.; tel. 2626; cable: OBHOTEL. Castle-like with 70 rooms, good food, a health club, babysitting services, and splendid views. Considered the best in the "high-living" strata.

Hotel Sinclairs. 18/1 Gandhi Rd.; tel. 2930; cable: SINCLAIRS. A modern hotel, with teak-planked floors and teak furniture—the twin of Sinclairs at Siliguri. It is a full-service hotel with 54 rooms and excellent service.

There are also a number of moderately priced bungalow-type hotels on the hillsides overlooking the panoramic ranges.

Windamere Hotel. Bhanu Sarani (the Mall); tel. 2841; cable: WINDAMERE. 27 rooms. Has a magnificent view not only of the surrounding ranges and valley but of the Mall (the promenade of this town). Fireplaces are lit in every room each night and hot-water bottles are slipped under covers to warm the bed. There is a bar, garden, excellent food, and arrangements for local tours. This is a favorite hotel for travelers, representing the bygone pace and luxury of the raj-types on holiday during the blistering summers in the plains.

Moderate to Inexpensive

Alice Villa. H. D. Lama Road; tel. 2381. A no-frills hotel that has been doing business for over 25 years. Rooms with fireplaces.

Bellevue Hotel. Overlooking the Mall; tel. 2129; cable: BELLEVUE HOTEL. Full-services hotel with 43 rooms.

Swiss Hotel. On Gandhi Road, below the Oberoi Mount Everest; tel. 265. A cozy, small hotel with lots of charm.

Hotel Tiffany's. Franklyn Prestage Road; tel. 2840. Only seven rooms, so try for those on the second floor with the views. Rates include breakfast and dinner.

WBTDC Tourist Lodges in Darjeeling

Moderate

WBTDC pragmatically maintains a number of lodges in Darjeeling, since the tourist traffic does not abate except during the hard winter months. The following is a sample that tourists may wish to consider:

Darjeeling Tourist Lodge. On Bhanu Sarani, Darjeeling; tel. 2611; cable: DARTOUR. 61 beds. Rooms in this lodge have great views and are well heated with electric heaters.

Lowis Jubilee Sanitorium. Dr. S. K. Pal Road; tel. 2127. 215 beds. Rates include bed tea, breakfast, and dinner.

Maple Tourist Lodge. Old Kutchery Road, Darjeeling, tel. 2090. 36 beds.

Shailabas Tourist Lodge. Off S. K. Pal Road; tel. 2684. Under renovation in mid-1987, this 53-bed lodge was originally a maharaja's palace with lovely gardens and a panoramic view of Darjeeling.

Inexpensive

Darjeeling Youth Hostel. Dr. Zakiy Hussain Road; tel. 2290. 46 beds at rock-bottom prices; no restaurant. Separate dormitories for men and women, with balconies girdling the building; large fireplaces.

Tiger Hill Tourist Lodge. P.O. Ghoom, Senchal; Tel. 2831. About seven miles from Darjeeling and 2½ miles from Ghoom railway station, home of the famous "Toy Train." 20 beds and an attached restaurant. There are fabulous views of Kanchenjunga at sunrise and, on clear mornings, with the aid of binoculars, you might see Mount Everest.

Digha

On the coast, near the Orissa border, overlooking the Bay of Bengal, this resort has a number of *inexpensive* accommodations. The **Tourist Lodge**, P.O. Digha, District Midnapore, (tel. 55 or 56), has 46 beds, with one compulsory meal at an extra charge. The restaurant is attached. Inquire in Calcutta at the *West Bengal Tourist Office* about cottages that have kitchens attached and rent for about $2. You could carry canned foodstuffs from Calcutta, buy some meals at the lodge's restaurant, and eat fruits from the local vendors. The price for all this will add up to one of the cheapest beach vacations of your life!

Durgapur

Inexpensive

Durgapur Tourist Lodge. P.O. Durgapur, District Durdwan; tel. 5476 or 5760. 24 beds (double) in both air-conditioned and non-air-conditioned rooms. The restaurant is attached.

Kalimpong

Moderate

Kalimpong Park Hotel. On Ringkingpong Road; tel. 304; cable: KALIM-PONG PARK HOTEL. With 20 rooms, a restaurant serving Nepalese and Tibetan, as well as Chinese, Indian, and Continental food; a bar, garden, and travel counter.

Inexpensive

Four tourist lodges are located here: **Kalimpong Tourist Lodge** (tel. 384), with 15 beds; **Tashi Ding Tourist Lodge,** with 10 beds (an annex of the Kalimpong Lodge); **Shangri-La Lodge** (tel. 230), with 23 beds; and **Hill Top** (tel. 654), with 20 beds. All four are recommended for their splendid views and good services for the basic budget traveler.

Kurseong

Tourist Lodge. 20 miles from Darjeeling; tel. 409. Eight beds at *Inexpensive* rates. This is the only recommended accommodation here.

Maithan

Maithan Tourist Hostel. 16 miles from Asansol. Basic *Inexpensive* rooms. Food is available on request.

Malda

Tourist Lodge. Off National Hwy. 34 north from Calcutta; tel. 2213. Has 26 beds for *Moderate* prices, in air-conditioned and non-air-conditioned rooms.

Mirik

The **Tourist Hostel and Cottages.** 30 miles from Darjeeling; tel. 37. *Moderate* to *inexpensive* double rooms and suites in cottages and rock-bottom dormitory-style beds. Cottages have attached kitchens, but eating at the restaurant is more convenient.

Murshidabad

The **Tourist Lodge.** At Berhampore, near Murshidabad; tel. 439. Has 26 *Moderate*-priced beds in air-conditioned and non-air-conditioned rooms. The restaurant is attached.

Santiniketan

Tourist Lodge (tel. 399). With 97 beds in air-conditioned rooms, this comfortable lodge is *Inexpensive* and ideal for this small but frequently visited area. Food is authentic Bengali and available at the adjoining restaurant. Lunch and dinner, which cost about a dollar (Rs. 13) are added to the price of the room. Also inexpensive is **University Guest House**, in a crunch, with 28 beds. For reservations for the guest house, write Registrar, Viswa Bharati, Santiniketan, P.O. Bolpur District, Birbhun, West Bengal.

Siliguri

Moderate to Expensive

Hotel Sinclairs. P.O. Pradhannagar, Siliguri 734 403; tel. 22674; cable: SINCLAIRS. Seven miles from the Bagdogra Airport, less than a mile from the railway station; 48 rooms. Facilities include a bar, restaurant, swimming pool, car rental, and airlines booking counter.

Inexpensive

Tourist Lodge. On Hill Cart Road; tel. 21028. With 21 beds and the usual restaurant attached to the lodge, as is the standard for all WBTDC lodges.

There are also about eight Indian-style non-air-conditioned hotels, all on Hill Cart Road. Among them are **Ranjit Hotel** (tel. 22056), **Saluja Hotel** (tel. 22029), **Delhi Hotel** (tel. 22918), **Air View Hotel** (tel. 21160).

Vishnupur

In one of the oldest towns in Bengal, the only accommodation is the **Tourist Lodge,** Vishnupur, District Bankura (tel. 13), with 28 beds at *Inexpensive* rates. Breakfast is charged regardless of whether you eat it. Other meals are available at the adjoining restaurant. There is also an **Inspection Bungalow** of the Public Works Department; inquire in Calcutta about its availability.

BIHAR

Reservations for tourist bungalows or lodges in Bihar should be made through Bihar Tourist offices at Patna, if possible.

Bodh Gaya

The best in town is ITDC's *Inexpensive* **Ashok Traveller's Lodge,** Bodh Gaya 824 231 (tel. 25), near the museum, with 12 rooms and attached baths. There's also the tourist bungalow; the **Japanese Monastery,** with dormitory-style accommodations, which is usually filled with Japanese tourists; and the **Burmese Monastery,** with very basic rooms, if you're truly hard pressed for accommodations.

Gaya

A comfortable and *Inexpensive* **Circuit House** is available through permission of the district magistrate. There's also a **Rest House** with 16 beds. Near the bus depot.

Hazaribagh

Surrounded by low-lying hills and forests, this small town has gained recognition as a tourist stop because of its natural beauty and its rustic way of life. Basic accommodations are available at the **Public Works Department (PWD) Bungalow,** Collector, Hazaribagh PWD Inspection Bungalow.

Other *Inexpensive* Indian-style hotels with attached restaurants are **Standard, Magadh, Ashok,** all in the central bazaar area. There is a **Tourist Lodge** (tel. 236), reserved through the Assistant Tourist Information Officer, Tourist Information Center, Government of Bihar, Hazaribagh.

Jamshedpur

Moderate to Expensive

One of the industrial-belt cities, called the "steel city," it has a company hotel, **TISCO** (Tata Iron & Steel Company) at 7B Road with 26 rooms, open to travelers not on company business only if there's a vacancy. A restaurant is attached.

Inexpensive

Boulevard. Sakehi Boulevard; tel. 25321. A Western-style hotel with 19 rooms, about a quarter of which are air-conditioned; bar facilities; and a restaurant.

Nalanda

Inexpensive, no-frills accommodations are available at **Inspection Bungalow.** Apply to the Superintendent, Archaeological Survey of India, Eastern Survey, at Patna. For **Nalanda Rest House,** apply to the Divisional Officer, P.W.D. Cooks are available at both these provincial government lodgings. Other rock-bottom accommodations are **Youth Hostel,** Pali Institute, with six rooms, and **Rash Behari Vidalaya Hostel.**

Parasnath

Dak Bungalow (without food) is atop a mountain. Contact the Tourist Information Center, Government of Bihar, Hazaribagh (tel. 236), for reservations. Another **DAK Bungalow** is near the Grand Trunk Road, three miles from Parasnath. Both are *Inexpensive*

Patna

The capital city of Bihar has a few international-grade hotels. All accept credit cards.

Deluxe

Maurya Patna. South Gandhi Maidan, P.O. Box 137, Patna 800 001; tel. 22061; cable MAURYA; telex 022–214. This Welcomgroup hotel has 80 rooms with full amenities. Reservations can be made through Welcomgroup's central reservations system in major cities. See *Facts at Your Fingertips.*

Moderate

Hotel Chanakya. At Birchand Patel Marg; tel. 23141. 42 air-conditioned rooms with full services, including car rentals.
Hotel Pataliputra. At Birchand Patel Path; tel. 26270; telex 022–311. 56 rooms.
Hotel Republic. Lawlys Building, Exhibition Road; tel. 22021; telex 022–261. 35 rooms.
Hotel Satkar, Fraser Road; tel. 25771. 50 air-conditioned rooms.
In the process of being approved by the Government of India Tourist Office are **Avantee Hotel,** opposite Dak Bungalow on Fraser Road (tel. 31851; cable: AVANTEE), 40 rooms, a shopping arcade, and a car rental desk. **Manita Hotel-Motel,** Ghoswari, Chanipapur, Bakhtiarpur (tel. 61 or 62, cable MOTEL). 20 rooms, two restaurants (one open-air), and a car rental desk; **Hotel President,** Fraser Road (tel. 25722), 36 rooms; **Hotel Samrat,** Fraser Road, with 71 rooms and full services including a rooftop restaurant.

Rajgir

Two **Tourist Bungalows** (tel. 39), with double rooms and attached baths; also, **P.W.D. Rest House and Youth Hostel.** Both are *Inexpensive*

Ranchi

Moderate

Hotel Arya. Four miles from airport and two miles from railway station. 28 rooms, an attached restaurant, and a car rental desk.

South-Eastern Railway Hotel. At the railway station. 22 rooms, attached baths, tennis courts.

Inexpensive

Hotel Yuvraj. One mile from the airport and less than a mile from the railway station. Has 45 government-approved rooms, a car rental desk, a restaurant, and a liquor permit.

DINING OUT. With meals provided at most of the hotels—either as part of the rates or for a few rupees extra—dining out is mainly dining in, in this part of India. There are a few places to stop for tea or snacks in Darjeeling, Bengal, all in the *Moderate* to *Inexpensive* price range. Several Tibetan restaurants offer the local fare of *moo-moos* (dumplings), *tomba* beer, and a grain dish called *thukpa.* Most of these places are one-room affairs with curtained cubicles. Other places to consider are

Chowrasta. At Chowrasta (the square). A very good south Indian vegetarian open-air restaurant. Fine views and wide selections of *dosas* (pancakes) and lentil and vegetable dishes.

Glenary's. On Nehru Road; tel. 2055. The best confectionery and tearoom in Darjeeling; also serves Chinese, Indian, and Continental foods and has a bar. Go for the breads and pastries and, of course, Darjeeling tea.

Keventers. On Nehru Road, opposite the Planter's Club, on a different hillside level from Glenary's; tel. 2026. Great for milkshakes, snacks, and tea. A favorite of the local school and college crowd from the exclusive public (read "private") schools of the area. Has a terrific view from its tables on the open-air terrace.

In Jamshedpur, **Kwality** (tel. 23930). The only restaurant in town. It serves Indian, Chinese, and Continental foods throughout the day and evening. It also has a confectionery counter and a well-stocked bar.

In Bihar, there are no recommended independent restaurants outside the major hotels, which all have full-service dining rooms.

USEFUL ADDRESSES. West Bengal. *West Bengal Tourist Office,* 3/2 BBD Bagh East, Calcutta 700 001 (tel. 23–8271); and 1 Nehru Road, Chowrasta, Darjeeling (tel. 2050). Information counters are located in Calcutta at the Calcutta Airport and Howrah Railway Station; in Bagdogra at the airport; and at the railway stations in Siliguri and New Jalpaiguri. *Government of India Tourist Office,* 4 Shakespeare Sarani, Calcutta 700 071 (tel. 44–3521); *Automobile Association of Eastern India,* 13 Promothesh Barua Sarani (tel. 47–5131); *Indian Airlines,* 39 Chittaranjan Ave., Calcutta (tel. 26–0810); *Vayudoot,* 54 J. L. Nehru Rd., Calcutta (tel. 44–7062).

Bihar. *Bihar Tourist Information Centre,* 26B Camac St., Calcutta 700 017 and Fraser Road, Patna (tel. 44–0821 in Calcutta, tel. 25295 in Patna); *Government of India Tourist Office,* "Tourist Bhawan," Birchand Patel Path (tel. 26721); information counters at Patna Airport, Patna Junction Railway Station; *ITDC Transport Unit,* Hotel Pataliputra, Birchand Patel Path, Patna 800 001 (tel. 23238); *Indian Airlines,* Patna (tel. 22554); *Vayudoot,* South Gandhi Maidan, Patna 800 001 (tel. 22554).

WHAT TO SEE AND DO. Bengal. The *Himalayas* cast their giant shadows over the travelers' itineraries in this region. Darjeeling, or Dorje Ling, the "place of thunderbolts," at an altitude of 7,012 feet, is the most picturesque and Oz-like town in north Bengal. It is a three-hour drive up a winding road from Bagdogra airport or Siliguri train station. The road climbs 4,921 feet over a 52-mile stretch, bordered by tea estates, hydrangeas, primroses, carnations, roses, ferns, and thickets of bamboo. The wisps of clouds over the valley and the dark green of the plains are all visible in the crisp, cool air at this altitude.

There is a "toy train," a narrow-gauge mountain railway with a few small compartments and a powerful steam engine. It is said to be one of the slowest train journeys in the world, from New Jalpaiguri to Darjeeling, sometimes taking 12 hours, at 5–6 miles per hour. The best way to experience this unusual and memorable train ride is to take it from Darjeeling to Ghoom and back. Ghoom, at 7,407 feet, is one of the highest railway stops in Asia. On clear days, you can glimpse the ragged ridges of Kanchenjunga. "The Ghoom Loop" is a whirling knot of tracks alongside the mountain, as the train loops around and around on its descent to Darjeeling.

One of the charming features of a hill station such as Darjeeling is that you can walk and take your time seeing the sights. The *Natural History Museum,* within walking distance of Chowrasta, houses a remarkably comprehensive collection of fauna of the region (4,300 exhibits). Open 10 A.M.–4 P.M. (Wednesdays, till 1 P.M.); closed Thursdays. There is a small entrance fee.

Lloyd's Botanic Gardens, opened in 1865, has one of the world's most impressive collections of different species of orchids (2,000) in its Orchid House. The terraced gardens have Sikkim spruce, geraniums, arum-lilies, alpine plants, azaleas, rhododendrons, magnolias, and a variety of Himalayan conifers. Admission is free. The gardens are open 6 A.M.–5 P.M. daily. *Victoria Falls* is one of the most pleasant half-hour walking trips here. Though the falls are only in full glory after the monsoons (October–November), the surrounding trail will enchant nature lovers with its mosses, lichens, orchids, cherry, maple, birch, alder, and juniper.

Another garden is *The Shrubbery,* planted by a governor of West Bengal in 1976 at Jawahar Parbhat (formerly Birch Hill) behind Raj Bhawan (Governor's House), northwest of the town square. From here, you get a magnificent view of the Kanchenjunga range and the Singla Valley.

About two miles from here is the five-mile-long ropeway at North Point, connecting Darjeeling to Singla Bazaar, an attractive picnic and fishing spot. Round-trip fares are Rs. 15 per person. You can reserve a seat by calling the officer-in-charge (tel. 2731), *Darjeeling-Rangeet Valley Ropeway Station,* North Point.

The Himalayan Mountaineering Institute, on Jawahar Road West, is a unique contribution to mountaineering that India established after 1953, when Mount Everest was first climbed. Tenzing Norkay, the first Sherpa to climb Mount Everest with Edmund Hillary, was the first principal of the institute. The institute trains hundreds of mountaineers of all ages and nationalities. An excellent museum. Displays of equipment, photographs, and notebooks, not only from successful climbs but from legendary and tragic efforts, such as Mallory's, add to the lore and lure of the mountains that overlook it. Open 8:30 A.M.–1 P.M. and 2–4:30 P.M. daily, except Mondays. Entrance fee is Rs. 1.

Near this area is the *Happy Valley Tea Estate,* about two miles from the center of town. Open 8 A.M.–noon, and 1–4:30 P.M. daily except Sundays (till noon); closed Mondays. Here you can see the production of the famous Darjeeling tea—from the green leaf stage, through the withering, drying, pressing, fermenting, rolling, and grading of the orange pekoe, flowery orange pekoe, and other blended teas.

Next to the Himalayan Mountaineering Institute is the *Himalayan Zoological Park,* with Tibetan yaks, Siberian tigers, Himalayan black bears, deer, red pandas, and an aviary. This "high-altitude park" is tiny and the cages seem all too small. However, since you have little chance of seeing these animals in their natural surroundings, take a look.

Near the Mall (the central promenade, ringed with benches) is *Observatory Hill,* with Tibetan Buddhist shrines, prayer flags, and a magnificent view of the mountain ranges and the surrounding valleys. Also nearby is *Step Aside,* the house where Indian nationalist leader Chittaranjan Das died in 1925. Excursions around Darjeeling include the Batasia Loop at Ghoom (three miles). *Dhirdham Temple,* near the railway station, whose architecture is inspired by the Pashupatinath temple in Kathmandu. The *Ghoom Buddhist Monastery* (five miles), with the 15-foot-high Maitreya Buddha (the "Buddha to come"). The oldest monastery in this region, it has palm-leaf and paper manuscripts. Also in Darjeeling is the *Bhutia Basti Monastery,* north of Observatory Hill.

Tiger Hill (seven miles), at 8,432 feet, is the place for a sunrise view. The golden glow of the early morning sun changes the color of snowcapped peaks to crimson, pink, and shining gold, as you stand at an observation deck shivering, wrapped in blankets over your coat, and sip coffee laced with brandy. Tour buses and jeeps go there each morning, but you have to get out by 4:30 A.M. Check with the tourist office and any travel agency. It is best to spend a night at the Tourist Lodge at Tiger Hill to make the simple hike to the observation deck. Twenty-four miles away is Bijanbara at 2,500 feet, on the Rangeet River, a wonderful site for picnics. Kalimpong, 32 miles away, at 4,100 feet, is a serene hill town. The road from Darjeeling descends near the Teesta River and winds through tea estates. At *View Point,* you can see the confluence of the Rangeet and Teesta rivers, two Himalayan glacier-fed rivers, charging to the plains. There are flower nurseries; the Tharpa Choaling Monastery, where photography is prohibited; and Guripur House, where Rabindranath Tagore wrote many of his world-famous poems. Kurseong, 20 miles away, at 4,860 feet, provides a sweeping view of the plains, especially from Eagles' Crag. *Senchal Lake,* six miles, is a popular picnic spot. The entrance fee is Rs. 0.50. Also near Kalimpong is *Tadakh Orchid Centre* (16 miles). Over 110 varieties of hybrid, as well as local, orchids are cultivated here. Mirik, at 5,800 feet and 30 miles away, is India's newest hill resort (opened to tourists in 1979), with a 77-mile-long lake that is open for boating and fishing. Both jeeps and bus tours go to Mirik every day for about Rs. 25 per person (round trip).

Going south, *Murshidabad,* the capital of Bengal during Mogul times, is 137 miles north of Calcutta. The local Moslem architects built vaulted arches and sloping parapets embellished with terra-cotta decorations because stone was scarce and erosion was high from the heavy rainfall. The ancient towns of Gaur, Pandua, and Malda have the remains of the *Adina Mosque,* one of the greatest displays of medieval Moslem architecture outside Damascus. Also of interest are *Katra Mosque* in Murshidabad and *Hazarduari,* the palace of the nabob of Murshidabad, built in 1837, which contains firearms, china, and plates that are reputed to crack if poison is placed on them. Nearby is Malda, the "English Bazaar," as it was once known, a foreign settlement for the Dutch, English, and French since 1680.

Santiniketan, 110 miles northwest of Calcutta, is the "abode of peace" that Tagore envisioned as a place to merge the traditional rural values of hard physical work with intellectual and imaginative creative work. Besides the university, which is a center of fine arts and performing arts in Bengal, there are the hot springs of Bakreswar.

Vishnupur, the "terra-cotta capital" of Bengal, is only 91 miles from Calcutta. Thirty miles south of Calcutta is *Diamond Harbour,* a former Portuguese pirate stronghold that has a natural harbor and is an ideal picnic area. Farther south are the beach towns of Bakkhali (82 miles) and Digha (116 miles) and the Sunderbans (see *Wildlife Sanctuaries*). On your way toward Bihar, stop at Maithan on National Hwy. 2, where the red soil of Bihar merges with the green paddy of Bengal, and a giant reservoir (one of the five built as part of the Damodar Valley Corporation in the 1950s) marks the division of an industrial hinterland and a predominantly rural state—Bihar.

BIHAR

The first stop in Bihar, just across the Bengal border, is the sacred *Parasnath Hill.* This is the eastern center of Jain worship, and Parasnath, a *tirthankara* (perfect soul) is said to have gained nirvana on this hill. Fifty miles east and southwest are Hazaribagh and Ranchi, two of Bihar's small but pleasant towns surrounded by dense forests (see *Wildlife Sanctuaries*), making them good vantage points for establishing itineraries.

Hundru Falls, one of the highest falls in Asia, is 27 miles from Ranchi; when the Subarnarekha River is in its postmonsoon highmark, the falls are spectacular. South of Ranchi is the steel town of Jamshedpur; 95 miles west is Netarhat in the middle of the Chotanagpur Plateau, a scenic and relaxing spot, at 3,622 feet.

Aside from its wild virgin forests, Bihar is noted for being the ancient seat of Buddhist learning and culture. At *Bodhgaya,* nine miles from Gaya, stands the peepal tree (the Bodhi tree) underneath which, 2,500 years ago, Gautama, prince of Kapilavasta, attained enlightenment and became the Buddha. The original Bodhi tree died, and saplings from it form the present tree. The Emperor Ashoka erected a shrine near the Bodhi tree that was replaced in the second century by the Mahabodhi Temple. The temple has been renovated many times, adding contours through the centuries. It shows the influence of various Buddhist countries, especially the curvilinear Burmese style. The surrounding railings are richly carved, and ornamented votive *stupas* (shrines) surround the main temple. The carvings are from the *Jataka* tales ("birth stories") and depict the Buddha's previous incarnations. The north side is flanked by the "jewel walk" or Chankramana—a raised platform with carved lotus flowers, where the Buddha is said to have paced back and forth, meditating and deliberating about whether he should reveal his wisdom and knowledge to the world. Bodhgaya is a pilgrimage spot for both Hindus and Buddhists. The Hindus consider Buddha to be an incarnation of Vishnu. On the banks of the Niranjana River, where Siddhartha, a worldly young prince came to seek the ultimate truth, modern-day visitors stand in awe, looking at and touching the relics and objects of veneration of one of the world's oldest religions. Near the Chankramana is the *Tibetan Monastery,* built in 1938. A six-foot-high metal drum painted in golds and reds, the Dharma Chakra, or wheel of law, is the main object on view. For forgiveness of all past sins, turn the wheel three times, from left to right. There are also Chinese, Japanese, and Thai Buddhist temples here.

Nine miles north of Bodhgaya is Gaya, a dusty little town at a major rail junction. Second only to Varanasi in sanctity for Hindus, Gaya attracts pilgrims from all over India, who come here after the deaths of their parents to offer *pindas* (funeral cakes) to the souls of the departed. This offering symbolically releases the dead from earthly bondage and is essential in Hindu ritual.

The center of the pilgrimage is the *Vishnupada Temple,* said to have been built over the footprints of Vishnu. Renovated in 1787, the structure is 97 feet high and has eight rows of sculpted pillars supporting the *mandapa* (hall). Non-Hindus are not allowed in the inner sanctum, but the exterior is well worth the visit. There's a banyan tree nearby under which the Buddha is said to have meditated for six years. Half a mile away is *Bramanjuni Hill,* with 1,000 stone steps. Climb to the top and you'll see Gaya's rooftops and Bodhgaya's spires. Twelve miles away is the *Surya Temple* to the Sun God, at Deo, on the Sone River, where pilgrims come to celebrate the Chhatha Vrata festival (see *Festivals* section).

About 31 miles from Gaya are the *Barabar Caves,* on which E. M. Forster based his Marabar Caves in *Passage to India.* These are the earliest specimens of Buddhist rock-cut shrines, dating back to 200 B.C.; two of them bear inscriptions of Emperor Ashoka. A little over 62 miles from Gaya is *Sasaram* and one of the finest Moslem mausoleums. Sher Shah, the builder of the Grand Trunk Road, the oldest highway in India, is entombed here under a five-tiered hexagon with arches, latticework cupolas, and a 150-foot dome. It stands in the middle of a lake with fountains. Two other excursions from Gaya, to Rajgir (40 miles) and Nalanda (41 miles) complete this tour.

Rajgir is one of the ancient towns associated with Buddhism. It was here that the first Buddhist Council met after Buddha attained enlightenment and where his teachings were written down. Buddha spent 12 years here, as did Mahavira, the founder of the Jain religion. Today, it is a health spot known mainly for its hot springs. Besides the hot springs, you can see ruins from an aerial chairlift (four miles). The Japanese have built a new monastery, *Vishwa Shanti Stupa* (World Peace Stupa), whose four Buddha statues depict birth, death, enlightenment, and teaching. There are Burmese and Thai monasteries; *Venuvena,* the bamboo park where Buddha and his disciples lived; and Jain and Hindu temples, among others. The *Cyclopean Wall,* originally 30 miles of perfectly joined stones that girdled the city, is now in ruins. Also, there is the *Ajatshatru Fort,* built in the fifth century B.C. by a king whom Buddha had cured of a plague of boils.

The most famous center of ancient Buddhist scholarship is Nalanda, the "place that confers the lotus" (*nalam*)—a symbol of spiritual learning. Between the fourth and twelfth centuries, Nalanda was one of the most celebrated university towns. The Chinese traveler-scholar Hiuen T'sang spent 12 years here in the early seventh century and recorded that there were 10,000 monks and students and 2,000 teachers. He also left detailed descriptions of the vigorous university life, where nine million volumes of manuscripts were available for students from as far as Japan, Sumatra, Java, and Korea. In 1199, an Afghan marauder, Bhaktiar Khilji, torched the university and massacred its residents. Buddhism in India suffered a severe blow, and monks fled to caves or out of the country. Painstaking excavations have uncovered large areas of the university complex, including six temples and 11 monasteries. The most imposing is the *Sasiputa Stupa* (the Great Stupa), built by Ashoka to honor Ananda, Buddha's first disciple. Also excavated is *Sarai Mound*, with frescoes of horses and elephants. Thai Buddhists have recently constructed a temple, *Wat Thai Nalanda*, here.

From the tranquility of the Buddhist excavated sites to the ancient capital, Pataliputra (present-day Patna), is not an altogether pleasant experience. Patna, an overcrowded city of over two million on the banks of the Ganges, stretches for over eight miles. It is the logical jumping-off point for your travels in Bihar, since it is linked to all major Indian cities. While you are here, you should take a quick tour of the city. *Golghar,* a beehive-shaped building, previously a granary built in 1787 to store grain following a famine in 1770, is a squat, impressive structure, 88 feet high and 410 feet wide, with 13-foot walls. Two staircases lead to the top, from where you can see the Ganges and Patna over the rooftops. *Harmandirji* is a shrine consecrating the birthplace of Guru Gobind Singh, the tenth and last Sikh guru. One of the holiest of Sikh shrines, it contains some personal belongings of the guru and Sikh scriptures.

Gulzaribagh is the site of a former opium factory used by the British East India Company, which made hefty profits with this lucrative trade from China. It is now a printing office for the government. You can visit the opium storage areas if you are a history buff. Three miles from the Patna Railway Station is Kumhrar, where excavations have unearthed relics of four continuous periods 600 B.C.–A.D. 600.

Moslem mosques in Patna are *Patherki Masjid* and *Shershahi Masjid,* the oldest is the Patna, built in 1545. Other places of interest are the Bihar Institute of Handicrafts and Designs and Birla Mandir. Daily tours are operated by the Bihar State Tourism and ITDC. From Patna, trips can also be arranged for Nalanda, Rajgir, Gaya, Bodhgaya, and Vaishali (see *Useful Addresses*).

 WILDLIFE SANCTUARIES. Bengal and Bihar both stretch north to south, from the Nepalese foothills to Orissa. Bihar has more national wildlife sanctuaries than does any other state in India. With the burgeoning need for land to support the population, the federal government's efforts to strike a balance between the need to reforest tracts of land and the need to maintain and increase the dwindling wildlife and provide meaningful programs to ensure these goals have received marginal publicity. The richness of India's wildlife can be seen in Bihar's 12 and Bengal's eight sanctuaries. Only the most easily accessible ones are listed here. (See *Facts at Your Fingertips* for a general overview of India's sanctuary program.)

Note: Unless otherwise stated, inquire about reservations at the Bihar and Bengal tourist offices in Patna and Calcutta.

BENGAL

Jaldapara. Ninety miles from Siliguri across the new New Teesta Bridge at Jalpaiguri is a sanctuary for bison, deer, elephants, tigers, leopards, barking deer, and Indian one-horned rhinoceroses. Lying below Bhutan and covering 62 square miles of *terai* (sub-Himalayan forests), its rich bird life includes the lesser florican, great stone plover, and jungle fowl.

Sunderbans. These dense mangrove swamps in the delta region are only a few hours by bus from Calcutta (steamer and overnight information are provided by the tourist office at Calcutta). Sunderbans, the "beautiful forest," has the largest population of tigers (200) in India. Over 1,500 square miles, this estuarine land has tigers swimming placidly but stealthily in its channels, along with crocodiles, deer, and wild boar.

BIHAR

According to the latest census, Bihar has 138 tigers. The largest tiger reserve is in the 600 square miles of dry deciduous forests of the Palamau Tiger Reserve (Betla Sanctuary), where the world's first tiger census was taken in 1932. It is accessible from Ranchi or Hazaribagh. Chital, tigers, elephants, panthers, wild boar, sambar (antlered Indian deer), and pythons find a natural habitat here. The Tourist Department runs tours from Ranchi. If you go by private car, van, or jeep and require accommodations, write to the Field Director, Palamau Tiger Reserve, P.O. Daltonganj, or the state tourist offices at Patna and Calcutta.

Hazaribagh Sanctuary. In the undulating forests of the Damodar Valley, once the private lands of a local maharajah, is this 98-square-mile reserve for nilgai, tigers, sambar, leopards, boar, panthers, hyenas, and spotted deer. It is accessible from Hazaribagh, about 10 miles away on National Hwy. 22. Contact the Divisional Forest Officer, Hazaribagh, or the Tourist Information Center, Hazaribagh (tel. 236), for tour information.

Other sanctuaries in Bihar are **Lawalong,** 128 square miles (accessible from Gaya although best reached from Hazaribagh), which has tigers, panthers, sambar, deer, and nilgai; accommodations are at a Rest House at Lawalong. **Mahuadan,** 40 square miles, with wolves, wild boar, and spotted deer, is 50 miles from Daltonganj. **Bhimbandh,** 422 square miles, is 37 miles from Monghyr in North Bihar; it has sambar, tigers, panthers, boar, bears, nilgai, and langur monkeys, as well as hot springs. **Dalma,** 120 square miles (16 miles from Jamshedpur and 68 miles from Ranchi), has elephants, boar, and mouse and barking deer. **Rajgir,** 22 square miles (63 miles from Patna), has leopards, nilgai, barking deer, and langurs. It also has a number of hot springs in the nearby pilgrimage town, the first recorded capital of Magadha in the sixth century B.C., a place of worship associated with Buddha and the Jain teacher, Mahavira. **Topchanchi,** five square miles, has a beautiful lake and a nearby Forest Rest House, near National Hwy. 2. This tiny reserve has langur, panthers, wild boar, and barking deer. Less accessible from larger towns are **Udaipur,** in North Bihar, 11 square miles, with varieties of water birds; **Valmiki Nagar,** 286 square miles, with panthers, boar, tigers, and hog deer; **Kaimur,** 830 square miles, 115 miles from Patna; and **Gautam Buddha,** 160 square miles, 25 miles from Gaya.

MUSEUMS. Ava Art Gallery. Hill Cart Road, on the way to Ghoom, Bengal, has a fine collection of embroidery and art belonging to Mrs. Ava Devi. Open 8 A.M.–noon and 12:30–6:30 P.M. daily. Small fee.

Himalayan Mountaineering Institute, on Jawahar Road West, Bengal. Excellent retrospective through displays of equipment, photographs, and other memorabilia of Mount Everest and other twentieth-century Himalayan expeditions. Open daily 9 A.M.–5 P.M. in summer; 9 A.M.–4 P.M. in winter; closed 1–2 P.M. and all day Tuesdays. Fee.

Natural History Museum. Meadowbank Road, Darjeeling, Bengal, has 4,300 exhibits of the fauna of Darjeeling, Sikkim, Tibet, Bhutan, Nepal, and the Eastern Himalayan region. Very well presented. Open 10 A.M.–4 P.M. (Wednesdays from 1 P.M.); closed Thursdays. Small fee.

Tenzing's House, on D. B. Giri, Bengal, was the home of the Sherpa who scaled Mount Everest with Edmund Hillary in 1953 and became the first to do so. Now a museum.

Bodhgaya Site Museum, in Bihar, has a collection of archaeological exhibits excavated from the local area. Entrance is free to the museum, which has a fine collection of gold, bronze, and stone statues of Buddha.

Jalan's Quila, in Bihar, has a rich collection of jade, Chinese paintings, and silver filigree work of the Mogul period. Prior permission is needed, since this is a private collection.

Arabic and Persian manuscripts are part of the collection at the **Khuda Baksh Oriental Library,** Bihar. The library also has Rajput and Mogul paintings; a tiny Koran, only one inch wide; and books rescued from the plunder of the university at Cordoba, Spain.

Most exhibits at **Nalanda Museum,** Bihar, date from the seventh to fifteenth centuries. An excellent collection of Buddhist and Hindu relics excavated from the destruction of the university in the twelfth century. The great seal of the university, panels depicting the avatars of Vishnu, stone and copper plate inscriptions, and pottery are also on display.

Patna Museum, Bihar, has a good collection of metal and stone sculptures from the Maurya and Gupta periods, terra-cotta figurines and a 52½-foot fossilized tree that dates back 2,000 years. Also has a Tibetan section.

FESTIVALS AND SEASONAL EVENTS. The festivals of a predominantly agricultural society celebrate myth and nature. The Vedic gods were of three kinds— celestial, atmospheric, and terrestrial. Bengal and Bihar have a full calendar of events celebrating the different categories. As in other parts of India, exact dates for most festivals are difficult to pinpoint, since they are set by the lunar calendar.

BENGAL

The Leocha and Bhutia peoples in the Darjeeling region celebrate *Makur Sankranti,* the New Year, in **January,** with fairs and folk dancing all along the Teesta River.

In January and **February,** *Vasant Panchami* is celebrated to honor Saraswati, the goddess of learning. Saraswati is believed to have invented the Indian stringed musical instrument—the *veena.* She is always depicted sitting on a graceful swan with a veena, looking serene and sophisticated. In a particularly whimsical and delightful variation in Bengal, books, pens, paint brushes, and musical instruments—all symbolizing aspects of human knowledge—are kept at her shrines. This is a major festival in and around Calcutta, especially at Santiniketan, Tagore's university, where cultural tradition is given prominence.

March is the harbinger of spring and is marked by a literal splash of colors during *Holi,* or *Dol,* as it is called in Bengal.

In **April,** Bengalis celebrate their New Year, *Poyla Baisakh.* Also in April is *Charak Mela,* a rural spring fair.

For Moslems in the north Bengal Murshidabad region, *Id-ul-Fitr,* the end of Ramadan, after the end of a month of fasting during daylight hours, is an occasion for feasting during **June/July.** The *Rath Yatra,* or chariot festival, honoring Jagannath, lord of the universe, with his brother, Balabhadra, and sister, Subhadra, is one of India's most eye-catching celebrations (see the *Orissa* chapter for details). Bengal celebrates this festival with chariots and processions in Calcutta and at Serampur.

In mid-**August,** Vishnupur is the site of *Jhapan,* celebrating the serpent goddess Manasa. Groups of snake charmers and handlers demonstrate tricks and feats on platforms, in bullock carts, and by the roadside.

In August/**September,** Vishnupur also celebrates *Inrapuja,* the festival of the warrior god Indra, god of thunder.

September/**October** brings *Durga Puja,* or Dussehra, as it is known elsewhere in India. The 10-day celebration of Rama's victory is visually breathtaking and deafening, with music and fireworks. (See the *Calcutta* chapter for details on the making of images for this major event.) During this period, Vishnupur also celebrates *Ravana Badh.*

October/**November** bring *Diwali,* the festival of lights, and the celebration of Lakshmi, goddess of prosperity, and Kali, signifying strength and depicting the horrors that mortals have brought on themselves. Images of bamboo and clay, profusely and intricately adorned, are created in every locality in Calcutta and in the state of Bengal.

In **December,** at Santiniketan and rural Bengal, *Paus Mela* (fair of the Bengali month of Paus) is energetically celebrated.

BIHAR

In **November,** about a week after Diwali, Bihar celebrates its most important event of the year—*Chhatha Vrata,* the sun festival. The harvest season begins and the first crop is offered to the sun—the lord of the crops. The banks of the Ganges, at Patna, are the festival's most accessible vantage point. The sun played a most significant role in the epic *Mahabharata,* when Draubadi, exiled with the Pandavas, fed 88,000 by worshiping the sun. The 88,000, as legend has it, helped the Pandavas regain their lost kingdom, and good and justice triumphed over evil. Other Bihari festivals are *Holi* and *Buddha Purnima,* which marks the life of Buddha from birth to enlightenment to death, celebrated at Bodhgaya and Rajgir, the Buddhist pilgrimage towns.

In **March/April,** there is a Jain festival, *Mahavira Jayanti,* dedicated to Mahavira, the twenty-fourth tirthankara of the Jains. It is celebrated with great fanfare on Parasnath Hill.

July's *Rath Yatra,* the chariot festival, is best seen in Bihar at Jagannathour near Ranchi.

In **August** is *Ganesh Chaturthi,* a harvest festival with the god of plenty, the plump and docile elephant-headed Ganesh. Images are brought into houses and stored for good luck.

One of the world's largest cattle fairs takes place in **November** at Sonepur near Patna, on the banks of the fertile Ganges. The fair lasts for a month, and cattle are brought, by road, walking, from all across India. Decorated with crimson, orange, purple, and gold ribbons, their horns festooned with garlands and silver leaf, and their ankles circled with bells, cattle wade the river onto the shore, accompanied by the blowing of conch shells. This kind of fair is at the heart of a rural tradition and it is here that you will see an India that is vigorous, imaginative, and alive.

 SPORTS. Trekking in the low Himalayas (unlike the arduous treks in the high Himalayas of northern India and Nepal) is accessible to most travelers to Bengal. Darjeeling is the vantage point, the best trekking months being April and May, October and November. The spring months get a few showers, but the fall months are dry, with excellent visibility. For the novice, one-day treks around Darjeeling to Tiger Hill, seven miles away, at 8,482 feet, through villages and past the brilliance of orchids and rhododendrons, is recommended. There are a number of other short trails.

For the hardy and the more experienced, the 100-mile Darjeeling–Manaybhanjan–Tonglu–Sandakphu–Phalut trek offers breathtaking views of Kanchenjunga and the Everest peaks. There is a road to Manaybhanjang (16 miles) from Darjeeling. Tonglu, at 10,100 feet, overlooks four of the five highest peaks in the world—Everest, Kanchenjunga, Makalu, and Lhotse. This trek ends in Phalut (11,200 feet) on the West Bengal–Nepal–Sikkim border.

Treks like these usually take eight to 10 days, and you need a trekking permit. Previously obtainable from the Foreigners' Registration Office in Darjeeling, it is now advisable, because of the coordination of all permits, to get the permit from Calcutta at the *Foreigners' Registration Office,* 237 A. J. Bose Rd. (tel. 44–0549). Trekking agencies will arrange for porters, food, guides, tents, sleeping bags, and so on. The recommended ones are *Summit Tours* and *Himal Ventures,* both at Indreni Lodge, 7 Chowrasta (tel. 2710); and *Kanchenjunga Tours,* 1 D. B. Giri Rd. (tel. 3058). Contact these agencies four to six weeks in advance, since trekking in these regions is very popular. Bring as much of your own gear as possible to avoid disappointments owing to faulty equipment. Hiking boots, insulated socks, and sleeping bags are easily transported and are essential, even for day treks.

There is excellent **fishing** in the Teesta and Rangeet rivers. The best times are October–December and March. Permits are required. Inquire in Calcutta, Bagdogra Airport, or at the *Travel Corporation of India* (TCI), Gandhi Road, Darjeeling (tel. 2694). Kalijhora, 18 miles from Siliguri on National Hwy. 31A, is a picturesque fishing spot on the Teesta River. Permits for fishing here are obtained from the Divisional Forest Officer at the *Siliguri Tourist Office.*

Lepong Racecourse, 5 miles from Darjeeling, is one of the highest racecourses in the world and possibly the smallest. **Horse** and **pony riding** are popular in Darjeeling, particularly for young children, but hard bargaining is necessary to establish a base rate and the number of hours.

Binar has limited avenues for unorganized sporting events. Clubs at Patna offer temporary memberships for their facilities, but these are limited to **swimming** and **indoor games.** ITDC is developing **river running** (rafting) and plans to have dinghies with outboard motors to circumvent the waters from Hardawar (in the north) to Patna in the plains. Seasonal wild game **hunting** permits are also offered, but the scarcity of firearms and the restrictions to protect wildlife make this an uncertain sport. If you are interested, inquire at approved travel agents in Patna and Calcutta and at the *Government of India Tourist Office.*

 SHOPPING. Bengal and Bihar, as do all sections of this colorful subcontinent, offer a mosaic of local crafts whose distinctive items can be purchased in their places of origin, as well as through government emporiums in larger towns, where the prices are fixed by state regulation.

Baluchar, "figured muslin," as it is known in Bengal, is woven in the Murshidabad region of north Bengal and is one of the finest materials to emerge from Indian looms. Cotton fabrics are brocaded with *zari* (silver threads), and colors of deep purples and maroons highlight the weaving. Borders are ornamented with floral motifs and figurative works. Baluchar is a Moslem weaver's craft. In Murshidabad, the renowned Moslem center of pre-British Bengal, weavers under royal patronage made the town of Murshidabad synonymous with silk and cotton weaving. Murshidabad is also known for its gold and silver inlay work on wood, primarily as bases for hookahs (water pipes). Carved, painted, and stained ivory has long been an art form in Murshidabad, but it is illegal to import ivory into the United States.

Bengal's potters at Bankura, Birphum, and Midnapore make painted dolls, animal figures, and smooth, blue-glazed earthenware. Metalwork, *dokra* figures of metal and clay, soapstone carvings, bamboo crafts, and quilts are all found in Bengal's bazaars. Unique to Bengal and little known to most tourists are *sholapith* toys. Sholapith is the core of a plant that grows wild in marshy areas of Bengal, and delicate images of deities and flowers are fashioned from it. It is also commonly made into traditional headgear for weddings in Bengal. Another Bengali craft is *shonkari* (shell craft), most often seen as bangles and toe rings.

If you visit Santiniketan or Vishnupur, you may come across the rural tradition of narrating stories with the aid of painted scrolls. As in Orissa, these *pats* are common in rural Bengal, with separate pieces depicting scenes of the story. In Calcutta, you can see them in a museum.

Vishnupur and Santiniketan also produce leather goods, bell metal wares, fine Tussar silks and terra-cotta figurines that are common in most Bengali households.

Darjeeling's crafts are different from those in the rest of Bengal. Nepalese and Tibetan brasswork and jewelry, gems, woodwork, carpets, and wool weavings are the mainstays. And, of course, you can buy the renowned Darjeeling tea directly from some of the tea estates after having taken a tour to see their production methods.

Shopping areas in Darjeeling are *Manjusha Emporium,* on Cart Road, open seven days a week; *Tibetan Refugee Self-Help Centre,* also off Cart Road, toward Ghoom; and shops along Nehru Road and Chowrasta.

BIHAR

Patna is well known for its wooden inlay work on metal, ivory, and stag horn. Artisans also use wood chips of unusual grain and color to decorate table tops, wall hangings, and trays.

Bihar has recently "discovered" a cottage industry that has become a lucrative and widely known art form—Mithila paintings. The women painters of Mithila (for it is primarily the women who paint) in north Bihar create highly original paintings, previously done on mud walls but now done on paper and canvas. Growing out of myth and ritual, the forms are striking in their simplicity of execution and in the complexity of their images. Some paintings are available throughout India in government emporiums, but it is becoming increasingly difficult to find good examples of this art.

ORISSA

Natural and Spiritual Beauty

by
LISA SAMSON and AMIT SHAH

"Every standing tree is an ovation to life" is not an inscription on an ancient temple wall but a painted roadside sign put up by the Department of Forestry in the state of Orissa. The sign's ambiguous language testifies to one of Orissa's claims to fame: its abundant natural beauty. It also suggests the spiritual underpinnings, Buddhist and Hindu, that were the motivational factors for much of the man-made wonders to be seen here. Once a center of Buddhist learning and propagation, Orissa is one of Hinduism's most active pilgrimage sites. Some say that to see Orissa is to see India, and certainly, visitors to Orissa have much to choose from. In the temple cities of Bhubaneswar, Puri, and Konarak, you can see the unusual Orissan temple architecture, with its strange shapes and fabulous and frequently erotic sculptures. On the coast and in the north, west, and south, you can indulge yourself, as ancient Orissans must have, in the pleasures of nature.

For many years, Orissa has attracted tourists primarily to its three temple cities—the "golden triangle" of Puri, Konarak, and Bhubaneswar, so named because they are located on the coast within 50 miles of one another, forming a triangle. It is here that Hinduism's distinctive Orissan temple architecture reached its peak in tenth century A.D. The state also has a large number of important Buddhist and Jain sites, such as the beautifully preserved rock edicts of Emperor Ashoka at Dhauli, which date from about 260 B.C.; the first-century B.C. caves at Khandagiri, cut out and used by monks as meditation cells; and the ruins of the seventh-century Buddhist university at Ratnagiri-Lalitagiri. In these architectural monuments, you can trace the history of Orissa from its early Buddhist and Jain roots through the flourishing Orissan civilization between the fourth and thirteenth centuries, when the great Hindu temples were built. But there is much more to explore in Orissa.

In the past few years, Orissa has begun to develop other rich offerings for travelers: its fertile countryside, idyllic coastal towns, forested mountains, deep-cut gorges, varied waterways, and wildlife preserves. Orissa's unpopulated beaches, which stretch from Chandipur near the West Bengal border to Gopalpur-on-Sea; its hot springs at Atri and Taptapani; its wildlife preserves of Chilka Lake, Simlipal, and Ushakothi; and its Biological Park and Botanical Garden at Nandankanan, are just a few of the natural sights that are becoming more popular with tourists.

Bounded by Bihar on the north, by West Bengal on the northeast, and by Andhra Pradesh and Madhya Pradesh on the south, Orissa consists of an extensive plateau in the interior that drops to a rich alluvial coastal plain crisscrossed by large rivers, including the great Mahanadi. The plateaus and hills in the north and south of the state have peaks that rise from the plateau elevation of 3,000 feet to as high as 5,500 feet, at times creating spectacular waterfalls. In the west, a rich mineral belt yields chromite, manganese, and graphite. Through the central part of the state, five rivers descend from higher reaches, cutting rocky gorges and creating fertile green valleys as they flow to the Bay of Bengal. Along the coast, which has beautiful isolated beaches, one also finds fertile land as one leaves the hills to the west and approaches the sandy stretches that adjoin the Bay. Rice paddies; cashew and mango groves; sugarcane fields; and jute, casuarina, and sal forests dot this primarily agricultural state in which its 26 million people live in relative prosperity. Though over 80 percent of the population cultivates rice, forests of sal, teak, sandal, and bamboo occupy 43 percent of the state's area. Historically slow to industrialize, Orissa now boasts a growing number of medium-sized industries based on minerals, sugar, glass, textiles, and handloom weaving that have begun to provide a secure economic base for this predominantly agricultural state. Steel plants at Rourkela, the Hirakud Dam Project on the Mahanadi River (one of the largest earth dams in the world), and the profusion of high-tech electrical small firms around Bhubaneswar assure this state of steady growth into the twenty-first century.

Looking Backward

Orissa, known in earlier times as the land of Kalinga, is noted in some of the most ancient Indian epics. Legend has it that Kalinga, one of the five sons of a sage, traveled as far as the hills of the Eastern Ghat and, looking down on the lovely countryside below him, decided to settle his people here, "where Nature abounds in wanton profusion." An early Kalinga king is believed to have sided with the Kauravas in the Mahabharata war, recorded in the great Indian epic of the same name. Part of the state is still called Kalinga by local people.

The recorded history of Orissa began in 260 B.C., with the edicts of the Mauryan Emperor Ashoka carved in rock at Dhauli, near Bhubaneswar. Ashoka, once known as Ashoka the Terrible, is said to have looked down from the hill at Dhauli to survey the plains of Kalinga strewn with the carnage of the Kalinga Wars that he had begun as conflicts of conquest. Horrified at what he saw, Ashoka repented for his deeds and converted to Buddhism, then the religion of Orissa. He actively propagated the Buddhist philosophy of nonviolence far beyond the borders of India. Soon after Ashoka's death, Orissa reasserted its independence. In the first century B.C., Kharavela, the third Chedi king and perhaps the greatest king to rule Kalinga, extended his empire from near Agra in the north to Kanya Kumari in the south, bringing Jainism to Orissa.

It was during his reign that the Khandagiri and Udayagiri caves (near Bhubaneswar) were carved by Jain monks out of the rock faces of these hills, to be used as meditation cells. Many of these tiny cells are covered with friezes; the Hathi Gumpha (the Elephant Cave) at Khandagiri bears a Pali inscription carved in the rock that records Kharavela's reign. Some say that relics of Ashoka and Kharavela were preserved in Dhauli and Udayagiri and, therefore, that the hills that flank Bhubaneswar became sacred spots. After Kharavela, the Chedi dynasty of Kalinga declined, and Jainism was again replaced by Buddhism in about A.D. 100.

The zenith of Orissan civilization and architecture was reached between the fourth and thirteenth centuries, when the Kesari and Ganga kings brought Hinduism to this Buddhist land. The Lingaraj temple at Bhubaneswar and the Jagganath Temple at Puri were constructed during the brilliant Kesari period. The Ganga kings ruled from the twelfth to the fifteenth century, during which time the magnificently engineered Sun Temple at Konarak was built on what were then coastal dunes. Moslem incursions into the state, prompted partly by a need to keep the Moslem armies equipped with war elephants that could be found in the Orissan wilds, culminated in the occupation of Orissa in 1568. The Afghans controlled Orissa until Akbar's Hindu general, Man Singh, annexed it for the Moguls in 1592. During their control, the Moslems destroyed many temples of the "idol worshipers." Of Bhubaneswar's 7,000 temples that once lined the banks of the sacred Bindusagar Lake, only about 500 are in some sort of preservation today.

The Dutch came to Pipli, now a village of craftsmen near the coast, and the British East India Company came to Balasore near the West Bengal border in the seventeenth century. In 1751, the Moguls ceded Orissa to the Marathas, who held it until the British took it over in 1803. They did little to improve the economic condition of the country or of the people. After Indian independence, the modern state of Orissa was shaped by encompassing some 26 small kingdoms. Its move toward industrialization has involved some impressive strides in irrigation and energy production, and the capital, Bhubaneswar, is developing steadily in light industry and high-tech companies.

Tribes

Descendants of the people who lived in Orissa before the Aryan invasions over 3,000 years ago, the Adivasi tribals of Orissa are numerous. Over 60 tribes, each marked with its own culture, are concentrated in the forest and hill regions of the state, and many still live in much the same way that they have for thousands of years. Once forced back from their hereditary land into less fertile places, they are now protected by the Indian government under the Protection of Aboriginal Tribes regulations.

Many of the tribes, especially those in the northwestern industrialized area, are beginning to leave their traditional hunting and agricultural lifestyles to seek jobs in places like the iron fields. It is difficult to say how much longer these people, who have held onto their traditions through thousands of years of dynastic changes, will be able to continue passing them on to future generations.

EXPLORING ORISSA

The Temples

Located in a triangle along the coast, which is referred to as the "golden triangle," are the cities of Bhubaneswar, Puri, and Konarak, famous for their stunning examples of Orissan temple architecture and for their spectacular religious celebrations. Many of the temples were constructed during the golden age of Orissan temple building, the eighth to the thirteenth centuries. Taken together, the Orissan shrines, especially those at Bhubaneswar, represent a coherent development of the Nagara style of Indo-Aryan architecture.

The Orissan temple consists almost entirely of a vaulting spire that thrusts upward in a pinnacle among much lower replica turrets that seem like mere surface wall decorations. The temple contains the *jagamohan,* or porch, which is usually square with a pyramidal roof. Immediately following the jagamohan is the *deul,* the cubicle inner apartment that enshrines the deity and that is surmounted by the soaring tower. Sometimes one or two more halls—*natmandir* (the festival hall) and *bhogmandir* (the hall of offerings)—are set in front of the porch.

The architecture of Orissan temples may seem strange and heavy, but the sculpture on these temples is graceful, often unashamedly erotic, and steeped in mythology. There is musical, dancelike, animated quality to many of these sculptures. Beautifully detailed, the statues range from voluptuous, amorous couples to musicians; to fierce beasts; to historical scenes; to birds, flowers, and foliage, all of which alternately tease and soothe the viewer.

Bhubaneswar and Its Environs

The capital of Orissa since 1956, Bhubaneswar is known as the "Cathedral City of India" and has over 500 temples in various stages of preservation. In Bhubaneswar and its immediate environs are presented a nearly 2,000-year panorama of Orissan art and history. From the third century B.C. to A.D. 1500 one can witness in the rock edicts of Dhauli, the caves at Khandagiri, the ruins at Sisulpalgarh, and the temples of Bhubaneswar a rarely preserved architectural record of the many dynasties that flourished and died out.

In Bhubaneswar, the greatest of the temples, the Lingaraj, is off-limits to non-Hindus. Its huge tower is visible from miles away, but the closest foreigners will get to it is a viewing stand erected during the period of the raj when Lord Curzon, the British viceroy, visited the temple. Other temples to visit are the ornate Parsurameswara, said to be the oldest surviving temple in the city; the Mukteswar, with the unmatched intricacy of its carved detail; the Rajrani, with its embracing couples; and the Brahmeswar.

Using Bhubaneswar as a base, you can travel easily into the surrounding countryside to explore the important Buddhist sites of Dhauli and Khandagiri or go farther afield to Konarak and Puri. The roads between the three major cities pass through Orissan villages with monochrome mud huts decorated, by women, in complex rice-paste designs dedicated to Laxmi—the goddess of beauty—along paddy fields green in the hot sun, past irrigation canals and ponds thick with water hyacinth, and—between Puri and Konarak on Marine Drive—

past groves of casuarina, cashew, and mango, alongside the sea. Within minutes of leaving the fast-growing metropolitan area, you see images of the rural Indian landscape that appear timeless. As wooden bullock carts creak under their loads of hay, and as farmers stand in watery ditches separating young rice shoots for replanting, and as children play among themselves with handmade toys, you catch the continuation of the cycles of life, which thousands of years ago inspired the artisans who sculpted the temples of Orissa.

Six miles west of Bhubaneswar, the twin hills of Khandagiri and Udayagiri are worth a visit, especially for a short drive at dusk. You can see the mount at Dhauli and Bhubaneswar's rooftops from here. The caves and inscriptions are worth visiting more for their historical significance than for their artistic merit.

Dhauli, about four miles southeast of Bhubaneswar, overlooks the Kalinga Plains. The irrigation canals, neatly lined palm trees, and the sculpted paddy fields offer a serene view of what was once the scene of tremendous bloodshed that finally persuaded Emperor Ashoka to convert to Buddhism in the third century B.C. This view, with its historical associations, is moving, and the rock edicts, in which Ashoka calls all men his children, are well preserved.

Konarak

The sleepy town of Konarak is home to one of India's most fabulous temples—the Sun Temple or "Black Pagoda," so named because of the dark patina that covered it over the centuries. Legend shrouds the Sun Temple. Constructed in the thirteenth century by King Narasimha, probably as much as a monument to himself as to honor Surya, the sun god, it is an architectural and engineering wonder. Built in the shape of Surya's chariot, with 24 huge chariot wheels and pulled by seven straining horses, this is a breathtaking temple. Those who are willing to rough it a little to see the temple lit at night and almost deserted in the early morning should plan to stay overnight in one of the two simple government tourist lodges.

Puri

Puri, on the coast, is a seaside town that contains one of the holiest sites of Hinduism. In the ninth century, the seer Sankaracharya designated it as one of the four pilgrimage sites (*dhams*) for Hindus. Pious Hindus believe that a pilgrimage to Puri is an obligation and that if one stays here for three days and nights, one will gain freedom from the cycle of births and rebirths. The central attraction of Puri is the enormous Jagannath Temple.

It is here also that one of the most spectacular of India's temple fairs, Ratha Yatra, the Car Festival, is celebrated. Held in mid-summer and attracting crushing hordes throughout the weeks of the celebration, the festival swells the already huge number of pilgrims to the Jagannath Temple to unbelievable proportions. Non-Hindus are not allowed to enter the Jagannath Temple. One can see into the compound from nearby rooftops, however. An outstanding feature of the temple is that, since its early beginnings, all castes were equal here but with the presiding Brahman priests more equal than others.

Buddhist Excavations

In addition to the rock edicts at Dhauli, there are other Buddhist sights of interest in Orissa. About 62 miles north of Bhubaneswar is the

finest, the Ratnagiri-Lalitagiri complex, where Buddhists built Puspagiri, a university, in the seventh century. In A.D. 639, the Chinese
pilgrim, Hiuen-T'sang, described Puspagiri in detail, stating that it was
one of two Buddhist universities in Orissa. The ruins of sculptured
portals and pagodas have been excavated and are in good condition.

Natural Beauties

Orissa's natural beauties are many, although few have the kind of
Western accommodations that are available in Bhubaneswar and Puri.
However, some of them are near areas with such accommodations and
so can be visited in one day.

Near the West Bengal border is Chandipur, which has one of the best
beaches in India. Here, the sea recedes three miles each day at low tide.
See it before it is unavailable for such casual visits. It's located in
Balasore district and is in the middle of a raging controversy with the
central government in New Delhi, which would like to set up a National Test Range for missiles, rockets, and pilotless target aircraft. The
residents of Balasore have resisted the government's promises of reloca-
tion and compensation. This might not be an attractive locale for very
long.

Simlipal Tiger Reserve in the center of Mayurbhanj, the northernmost district of Orissa, is breathtakingly beautiful. Aside from the wild
animals (tigers, leopards, elephants, bison, and sambars) there are vast
tracts of sal forest, cascading waterfalls, and lush grasslands. Popular
with Bengalis and Biharis because it is near their borders, one needs
to book a stay here long in advance.

Ushakothi is another of Orissa's many wildlife sanctuaries. Located
in the northwest corner of the state, it can be reached on National
Highway 6 not too far from the huge Hirakud Dam.

Hirakud Dam, in the northwest corner of the state, is one of the
largest earth dams in the world, and its reservoir forms the largest
artificial lake in Asia. Harnessing the mighty Mahanadi River, this
hydroelectric project provides flood control and irrigation for rural
Orissa and inexpensive power to the state's burgeoning industrial sector.

Toshali Sands, between Puri and Konarak on Marine Drive, bills
itself as Orissa's ethnic village resort. Its guests can enjoy the tranquil
beauty of an almost deserted beach without having to be at the far
reaches of civilization.

Chilka Lake, a huge lake on the coast south of Puri, is favored by
many migratory birds and is a renowned sanctuary. However, check
with local tourist officers about visiting the sanctuary. The practice
shelling at the nearby military gunnery range drives birds away for
weeks.

South of Chilka Lake is Gopalpur-on-Sea, a quiet seaside resort with
good surf and sailing and a prewar quaintness. Like Toshali Sands, it
offers a lovely beach without requiring that you forgo the creature
comforts.

If your time is limited, Nandankanan Biological Park, near Bhubaneswar, is a lovely spot in which to see some of what the wilds of
India have to offer. Wild animals found throughout India are kept here
in their natural habitat. The park also boasts a botanical garden and
a lake for boating.

Hot springs are located in various places throughout the state, but
two can be visited in day trips. Taptapani, 40 miles from Gopalpur-on-
Sea, is in a forest, and water from the spring is channeled into a nearby
pond. Atri, a little over 25 miles from Bhubaneswar, has the additional
attraction of the Temple of Lord Hatakeswar.

PRACTICAL INFORMATION FOR ORISSA

WHEN TO GO. From October to mid-March is the best season for visiting Orissa, when the monsoons are over and temperatures are at their most temperate. Near the sea and in the western hills, this period can be extended until mid-April. In the higher reaches of the Simlipal Range, where the Simlipal Tiger Reserve is located, the temperatures are cool and enjoyable even in May and June. These cooler times are also drier periods, and unpaved roads—or roads under repair—and unplanted fields create extremely dusty conditions. In the higher elevations, cooler evening mists can be quite penetrating, so be prepared to be damp after evening outings.

Note: When you prepare for your journey to Orissa, we recommend that you read Alistair Shearer's *The Traveler's Key to Northern India* (New York: Alfred A. Knopf, 1983), which contains two well-researched and illuminating chapters that will benefit those who are interested in architectural history.

HOW TO GET THERE. By Air. *Indian Airlines* has flights to Bhubaneswar from Bombay, Calcutta, Delhi, Hyderabad, Nagpur, Raipur, and Varanasi. *Vayudoot* has flights from Calcutta, Hyderabad, Rajahmundry, and Vishakapatnam to Bhubaneswar and Jeypore (no service between Calcutta and Jeypore), and from Bhubaneswar, Calcutta, and Ranchi to Rourkela. From Bhubaneswar, you can reach Konarak (40 miles) by car or bus, and Puri (39 miles) by train or road.

How to Get to Town From the Airport. Taxis are available for getting to Bhubaneswar, at a fare of approximately Rs. 40. The transfer from Bhubaneswar to Puri by taxi is approximately Rs. 400. Some of the larger hotels in Puri provide transportation from Bhubaneswar.

By Train. The *Howrah–Puri Express* and *Howrah–Puri Passenger* are first-class express trains that connect Bhubaneswar and Puri with Calcutta. The *Kalinga–Utkal Express,* also a first-class train, connects Bhubaneswar and Puri to Mathura in Uttar Pradesh via Jhansi (Khajuraho is 110 miles from Jhansi). Rourkela, in the northern industrial belt, can be reached on the *Bombay–Calcutta (Howrah) Gitanjali Express,* a second-class train. Other towns along the coast that are of interest to tourists are served by the *Calcutta (Howrah)–Madras Central* line trains. The *Vizianagram–Raipur* line passes through the western section of the state. There are air-conditioned coaches on some of these trains.

By Bus. Buses of the *State Transport and Orissa Road Transport Company* travel between all parts of the state. The Orissa Tourism Development Corporation (OTDC) operates daily buses between Bhubaneswar and Rourkela for Rs. 65. Privately run "video coaches" are fast becoming a popular means of transport with Indians, particularly for long-distance overnight bus rides. Unless you have a particular penchant for seeing Indian films, the noise level in these buses makes them less desirable than is the normal bus service.

USEFUL ADDRESSES. Orissa is one of the few states that has designated tourism as an industry. One of the boons of this designation is that OTDC is well represented throughout the state, even in smaller towns, and has a number of excellent publications that are regularly updated. *Tourism Directory Orissa* is an invaluable and inexpensive book, and the *Tourist Map of Orissa* is also helpful.

OTDC Addresses. *Bhubaneswar,* Jayadev Marg, near the Panthanivas, Bhubaneswar 751014; tel. Bhubaneswar-50099. *Puri,* Station Road, At P.O. Puri, District Puri; tel. Puri-2131. *Konarak,* Tourist Bungalow, At P.O. Konarak, District Puri; tel. Konarak 21. *Cuttack,* Arunodaya Market Building, Link Road, Cuttack; tel. Cuttack 23525. *Berhampur,* Old Christian Street, Berhampur, District Ganjam; tel. Berhampur 3226. *Rourkela,* U.G.I.E. Square, Rourkela, District Sundargarh; tel. Rourkela 3923.

ACCOMMODATIONS. There are Western-style hotels in Puri, Gopalpur-on-Sea, and Bhubaneswar. Some of the state guest houses (*panthanivas*) and circuit houses are also very good. A minimum of seven days' notice should be given to the executive officers running these places. But, except at the height of the tourist season and during festival times, one can find accommodations on arrival. For price ranges of categories, see *Facts at Your Fingertips.*

BHUBANESWAR

Expensive

Hotel Kalinga Ashok. Gautam Nagar, Bhubaneswar 751014; tel. 53318. 35 rooms, 29 of them air-conditioned. This hotel is operated by the ITDC and has a bar, restaurant, and conference facilities.

Hotel Konark. 86/A–1, Gautam Nagar, Bhubaneswar 741014; tel. 53330. Has 72 rooms, restaurants that feature live music, a 24-hour coffee shop, and banquet, conference, and secretarial facilities.

Hotel Oberoi Bhubaneswar. Plot CB–1, Nayapalli, Bhubaneswar 751013; tel. 56116. Newly opened, this hotel has 66 air-conditioned rooms, a swimming pool, tennis courts, and a jogging track.

Moderate

Panthanivas Bhubaneswar. Jayadev Marg, Bhubaneswar 751014; tel. 54515. Recently expanded and now with upgraded facilities, this 72-room OTDC-run hotel is conveniently located near the OTDC office.

Hotel Prachi. 6, Janpath, Bhubaneswar 751001; tel. 52521. With its pleasant surroundings, Prachi has 48 rooms, a swimming pool, tennis court, restaurant, and Indian Airlines and Air India counters.

Hotel Swosti. 103, Janpath, Unit 3, Bhubaneswar 751001; tel. 54178. 48 rooms, a restaurant, central air-conditioning, and banquet and secretarial services.

CHILKA LAKE

Moderate

Ashoka Hotel. Tel. 8 and 9, located at Balugaon.

The OTDC runs a **Panthanivas** (tourist bungalow) at Rambha, tel. 46 and one at Barkul, tel. Balugaon–60.

Inexpensive

Hotel Chilika. Tel. 68, at Balugaon.

CUTTACK

Moderate

Hotel Ashoka. Ice Factory Road, College Square, Cuttack 753003; tel. 25708. Convenient to the railway station and downtown. 50 rooms, some of which are air-conditioned.

Hotel Trimurti International. Link Road, Cuttack 753021; tel. 22918. Offers 38 centrally air-conditioned rooms. Both these hotels have bars, restaurants, small conference halls, laundry facilities, and travel desks.

Inexpensive

Hotel Anand and **Hotel Orienta,** both in the downtown area (no phones).

GOPALPUR-ON-SEA

Expensive

Oberoi Palm Beach Hotel. Gopalpur-on-Sea, District Ganjam. Eight miles from the Berhampur railway station. A 19-room bungalow-style beach hotel, with tennis, surfing, good restaurants, and a bar.

KONARAK

Facilities at Konarak are simple. The only reason for staying here overnight is to see the Sun Temple at night, when it is lit dramatically (May–September, 6–10 P.M.; October–April, 5:30–9:30 P.M.), and early in the morning, before it gets crowded. Prices are *Moderate to Inexpensive.*

OTDC's Travellers Lodge has four simple but comfortable rooms with connecting baths and can provide Indian and Western-style catering from the nearby Panthanivas. The service is hospitable and charming. **Panthanivas Tourist Bungalow,** also run by OTDC, has 10 rooms and limited facilities. Both the Travellers Lodge and the Tourist Bungalow are conveniently located near the Sun Temple. Konarak has only an open-air restaurant that serves appetizing meals for a few rupees. For the experience, try the **Sun Temple Hotel** (a restaurant), which serves authentic Bengali food on banana leaves and has bottled soft drinks.

PURI

Expensive

South Eastern Railway Hotel. Chakratirtha Road, Puri; tel. 2063. 200 yards from the beach, 32 rooms with baths. With its beautifully maintained lawns and gardens, its lovely view of the sea and its air of belonging to an earlier, less-complicated era, it is easy to understand why this hotel has long been the favorite seaside hotel in Puri.

Toshali Sands. Puri-Konark-Marine Drive, P.O. Baligwali, Puri 752002; tel. 2888. Between Konarak and Puri. Reservations can be made in Calcutta, Manjusa, 43, Sarat Bose Road, Calcutta 700020; tel. 483605 and 440118. 40 rooms spread out in separate bungalows. A delightful new hotel billing itself as "Orissa's Ethnic Village Resort." An exceptionally beautiful place with a well-trained staff. Its architecture, gardens, and interior design combine to make it a showplace of Orissan art and architecture. Facilities include a swimming pool, cultural shows, angling, billiards, access to an uninhabited beach, bicycles, a health club, and conference hall.

Hotel Vijaya International. Chakratirtha Road, Sea Beach, Puri 752002; tel. 2701 or 2702. Near the downtown area. 44 rooms, half with air-conditioning, and a restaurant.

Moderate

Hotel Holiday Resort. Sandy Village, Chakratirtha Road, Puri; tel. 2440. Reservations can also be made from Calcutta through Honey Holidays, 12/1 Lindsay Street, Flat 17, Calcutta 700007; tel. 242437. All rooms are located in cozy cottages, surrounded by beautiful gardens. A dining hall and bar are currently available, extensive facilities are under construction.

Hotel Prachi Puri. Swargadwar, Gourbarsahi, Puri 752002; tel. 2638. 37 rooms, some with air-conditioning, and a restaurant.

Mahodadhinivas. Puri; tel. 2507. A tourist bungalow, one of OTDC's more expensive hotels but still in the moderate range.

ROURKELA

Inexpensive

Your best bet is to stay at **Rourkela House** (contact the manager, Steel Authority of India, Rourkela Steel Plant, tel. 5076), or **Annex to Rourkela House,** Sector 20, Rourkela 15; tel. 5129. **Apsara Hotel** on New Road is also a possibility. New Station Road, Rourkela 1; tel. 2111.

SIMLIPAL TIGER RESERVE

Inexpensive

To stay in the reserve is to rough it; no catering services are available. However, the caretaker helps visitors cook their food, provided that they carry provisions. Contact the Field Director, Simlipal Tiger Reserve Project, Baripada 757 002; tel. 173, for permission to visit the park and to reserve at seven of the 10 **Rest Houses** in the reserve. Be sure to make reservations at least four weeks in advance, since this area is frequented by travelers from West Bengal and Bihar. For reservations at the other three Rest Houses, contact the Deputy General Manager, Simlipal Forest Development Corporation, Ltd., Baripada; tel. 272.

TAPTAPANI

Inexpensive

OTDC runs a **panthanivas** that features hot water provided by the nearby hot sulphur spring. Contact Tourist Officer, Brahmapur, District Ganjam.

USHAKOTHI

Inexpensive

Forest Rest House at Badrama may be used by those who wish to visit this wildlife sanctuary. Contact the Deputy Forest Officer, Bamra, District Sambalpur.

 DINING OUT. Throughout Orissa, meals are generally taken at one's hotel. Most of the hotels just listed have restaurants that serve three meals a day of either Indian, Bengali, or Continental foods. If you wish to dine at a hotel other than the one at which you are staying—particularly if it's a small one—call ahead to see if you can be accommodated. Prices for meals are listed in the price categories for hotel accommodations in *Facts at Your Fingertips.*

 HOW TO GET AROUND. By Car. Orissa has some beautiful scenery, and its roads have improved considerably in recent years. As is the case in most of India, however, the monsoon rains do great damage to roads, so a road trip is recommended only toward the end of the cool season (February–March) when work crews have repaired the worst problems and before the summer heat dries out the landscape. At this time, the vibrant Flame-of-the-Forest trees are covered with velvety orange blossoms, and the scent of the blossoming cashew and mango trees fills the roadways with their heady scents. The Marine Drive connecting Puri with Konarak is an especially beautiful stretch of road, bordered on one side with casuarina groves and mango and cashew trees and on the other by the sea.

National Hwy. 5 runs through the state near the coast and National Hwy. 6 cuts through the northern hills from Bangriposi to Keonjhargarh and Sambalpur, crosses the Mahanadi River near the Hirakud Dam, continues into Madhya Pradesh. Along Hwy. 6 from Bangriposi to Keonjhargarh, where the road skirts the edge of the Simlipal Forest, the combination of farmlands under cultivation, small villages, and densely wooded hills with mountains in the distance conveys a strong sense of the hardships and beauty of rural Orissa. Motoring here, as in the rest of India, is a hair-raising adventure because of the long-distance bus and truck drivers. Some distances for motorists: Bhubaneswar to Gopalpur-on-Sea (via Kurda–Rambha–Chatarpur), 125 miles; Bhubaneswar to Puri (via Pipli), 41 miles; Bhubaneswar to Konarak (via Pipli), 39 miles.

 TOURS. Private **taxis** are available, and the OTDC Office in Bhubaneswar can arrange **cars** for touring whose rates vary from Rs. 300 to Rs. 500 for a full day, depending on whether the car is air-conditioned and the distance one goes. Conducted sight-seeing tours by **bus** are operated in all the major tourist destinations. OTDC runs a number of conducted all-day tours to major destinations in the state, such as Bhubaneswar–Khandagiri and Udayagiri Caves–Nandankanan–Dhauligiri, for Rs. 30.

 FESTIVALS AND DANCING. Festival times are always opportunities to experience, in a unique way, the culture of India through the rituals of religion. In addition to their sacred aspects, these festivals are often occasions for colorful village fairs (*melas*) that draw rural people from miles around to the temple towns. Throughout Orissa, most spectacularly in Bhubaneswar at the Lingaraj Temple, Shiva is celebrated in the cooler months of **February–March** during the festival of *Shivratri*. Pilgrims flock to this festival and offer prayers at nearby Bindusagar Lake, which is said to be filled with water from every sacred river and tank in India. Also celebrated during this cooler period is the boisterous, colorful festival of *Holi*.

In Puri, one of India's major pilgrimage towns, there are frequent temple festivals, the most spectacular of which is *Ratha Yatra,* celebrated in June–July, depending on when the full moon falls. Continuing through much of the summer, Ratha Yatra attracts thousands of pilgrims to this charming seaside town. The most impressive aspect of the festival to Lord Jagannath, lord of the universe, is the procession of three huge chariots carrying the images of Lord Jagannath, his brother Balabhadra, and sister Subhadra through the streets of Puri. Shaped like temples, these fantastically decorated chariots are so large that thousands of devotees are needed to pull them through the streets. In former years, some followers, having worked themselves into a religious frenzy, threw themselves to their deaths in front of the huge wheels. Having been taken to Gundicha Mandar, the God's Garden House, where the images rest for seven days, the three are returned to the Jagannath Temple in a similarly spectacular procession. At the end of these festivities the huge chariots are dismantled and their parts are sold to pilgrims. Because it is such a magnet for Hindu pilgrims, this festival is recommended if you want to experience the intensity of a particularly exhilarating, exhausting religious celebration.

Odissi, the classical dance form of Orissa, is perhaps the most lyrical style of Indian dance. Watching the dancers performing their graceful, codified gestures and postures, you are reminded of the dancelike sculptures that cover Orissan temples. It is as if one of the lovely dancing maidens on the Sun Temple at Konarak had suddenly come to life. Through the calculated movements, the dancers' bodies seem to represent a variety of statues.

In addition to classical Odissi dance, *folk dances* and *tribal dances* are still performed during festival times throughout Orissa. Despite the modernization of Orissa that is changing other aspects of their lives, the tribal people hold on to their music and dance.

 HISTORIC SITES. *The "Golden Triangle": Orissa's Temple Cities.* Although some of the Orissan temples, such as the Lingaraj Temple in Bhubaneswar and the Jagannath Temple in Puri, are closed to non-Hindus, others are accessible except for their inner sanctums. Signs are posted indicating the restrictions.

BHUBANESWAR

Of the city's many temples, the most spectacular is the eleventh-century *Lingaraj Temple,* considered to be the ultimate in Orissan temple architecture. Closed to non-Hindus, its exterior carvings can be viewed from a raised platform on its periphery (bring binoculars and a few rupees as an "offering"). It is set in a huge walled-in compound that measures 520 by 465 feet and holds at least 70 smaller votive shrines. Like the great Jagannath Temple in Puri, the Lingaraj compound is a world in itself. Dating from about A.D. 1000, the Lingaraj Temple originally consisted only of the porch and shrine; the dancing hall and the hall of offering were added about a hundred years later. The curvilinear tower (*vimana*), built without mortar, rises to a height of 147 feet. The tower is divided into vertical sections; at the top, just below the lineal spire, are figures of a lion crushing an elephant. The tower is hollow, and the top is reached by an interior staircase hewn out of walls that are seven feet thick. The inner walls of the shrine, which have no adornment, house the *lingam* (phallic symbol) of Shiva. Outside, the sculpture is profuse, representing a high point of Hindu decorative art.

Near the Lingaraj Temple is one of Bhubaneswar's many sacred tanks (man-made ponds). The biggest of these tanks, *Bindusagar,* 1,300 feet long and 700 feet wide, is surrounded by a stone embankment. It is a magnet for pilgrims who believe that it is filled with water from every sacred stream and tank in India and can therefore wash away sins. It is said that 7,000 temples once stood on the shores of Bindusagar.

The *Vaital Deul Temple* (mid-700s–early 800s), near Bindusagar, is one of the earlier temples. Unlike other temples in Bhubaneswar, its double-storied and barrel-shaped roof shows the influence of Buddhist rock architecture.

Half a mile to the east of the northeast corner of the Lingaraj is "The Grove of the Perfect Being." In this mango grove are more than 20 temples including the oldest surviving temple in the city, the *Parasurameswar;* the diminutive *Mukteswar,* considered the gem of Orissan architecture; the *Siddheswar;* and the *Kedareswar.* The Parasurameswar was built in A.D. mid-600s and is decorated with sculpture that is executed with great vigor.

The *Mukteswar* (A.D. 10th century), called a "dream realized in sandstone" and the smallest temple in Bhubaneswar, bears very fine sculpture. An emaciated hermit teaching, a lady riding a rearing elephant, cobras darting their heads, and lions fighting are some of the themes represented. The most distinctive feature of the temple, its *torana* (arch gateway), shows the influence of Buddhist architecture and is intricately carved with peacocks and feminine figures in languorous positions.

Adjoining the Mukteswar is another of Bhubaneswar's many sacred tanks. Beyond it stands the *Kedareswar Temple,* with its eight-foot statue of Hanuman, the monkey god, and another of the goddess Durga standing on a lion. Northwest of the Mukteswar is the Siddheswar.

About half a mile from the Lingaraj is the *Brahmeswar Temple* (A.D. 11th century), built around the same time and sumptuously carved.

Standing by itself in green rice fields is the *Rajrani* (A.D. 11th century), perhaps the most harmoniously proportioned temple in the city. So enchanting are its erotic sculptures that it has been suggested that it was built by some early Orissan king as a pleasure dome rather than as a temple.

In addition to its temples, Bhubaneswar is the site of new and sprawling development being fueled by a burgeoning electronic and high-tech industrial complex. This growth has given rise to central bazaars and shops full of Orissa's handicrafts, especially textiles, wood and stone carvings, and intricate paintings (*patta chitras*) traditionally executed on leaf, now on canvas, that, until recently, were available only rarely in urban areas. Shopping in the evening is an added adventure after a day's sightseeing. The OTDC office and your hotel desk can provide directions and information. The *State Museum,* the *Tribal Museum,* and *Handicrafts Emporium* are also places of interest.

AROUND BHUBANESWAR

Three miles to the west of Bhubaneswar are the hills of Udayagiri and Khandagiri, with caves dating back to the second century B.C. These caves are of great interest because of their antiquity. Believed to have been cut by Jain monks who built them to meditate in, many of the caves feature rough sculpture. In front of the *Hatigumpha Cave* is a Palli inscription of Kharvela, one of Orissa's early princes, which describes the events of his 13-year rule. The *Ranigumpha Cave* (Queen's Cave) and the *Ganesh Gumpha* are the most interesting. These three caves are located on Udayagiri, the hill to the right of the road. To the left is Khandagiri hill and the *Ananta Cave,* with its veranda and decorated pilasters. From the top of this hill, you can look across the plains to Bhubaneswar and Dhauli.

DHAULI

Four miles southeast of Bhubaneswar, Dhauli is where Emperor Ashoka is said to have looked down on the carnage of the Kalinga Wars and resolved to put an end to such killing. His conversion to Buddhism, begun here, had profound effects on the propagation of Buddhism outside India. A huge elephant carved out of a large rock, representing the Buddha, Emperor Ashoka's "Rock Edicts" stating that all men are his children, a Hindu temple to Shiva, and the Buddhist Peace Pagoda, built in the early 1970s by Japanese Buddhists, are located here.

PURI

The beach and the *Jagannath Temple* are the town's central attractions. The Jagannath Temple, abode of Jagannath, lord of the universe, is a majestic structure, 210 feet high, that is tiered and layered with carvings. Like the

Lingaraj in Bhubaneswar, entry to the temple is prohibited to non-Hindus (so strictly is this rule enforced that former Prime Minister Indira Gandhi was refused admittance because she had married a Parsi and was thus outside the faith). You can view this imposing structure from the roof of the Raghunandan Library opposite the eastern gate of the temple. A few rupees donation is expected. If the library is closed, the Jaya Balia Lodge up the street from it will sometimes let visitors climb to its roof. Binoculars are recommended. The temple stands in a compound 652 by 630 feet surrounded by a 20-foot-high wall. It is composed of the traditional porch and shrine, surmounted by a conical tower 192 feet high. The hall of offerings and the pillared hall of dance were added several centuries after the original temple was built in about 1030. Just as in Bhubaneswar, the compound is covered with smaller votive shrines.

The famous chariot festival of *Ratha Yatra* that occurs here has earned Lord Jagannath a place in the English lexicon as *juggernaut.* As giant chariots (40 feet high with seven-foot wheels) roll relentlessly down the narrow streets of Puri, carrying images of Jagannath, Bahabhadra, and Subnadra and pulled by thousands. In the past, devotees worked into a frenzied state of ecstacy were trampled to death or trampled others.

Lord Jagannath's abode is a land of superlatives. Devotees lavish this holy city of Hinduism with their offerings:—the temple kitchen, reportedly the largest kitchen in the world, feeds Mahaprasad, its unique steamed cuisine, to over 10,000 people daily and, during festival times, to 25,000.

The other attractions at Puri are its bustling *bazaar area* and its sea beach where *nullias,* wearing conical straw hats, help nonswimmers into the surf and back to safety. The beach is mainly used by pilgrims and as a promenade; sunbathing and swimming in swimsuits and bathing trunks by Westerners will draw unwelcome stares. Nearby Balighai Beach is more isolated. Those who stay at the nearby Toshali Sands Resort can enjoy its lovely, remote beach unencumbered by curious and prying crowds.

KONARAK

The Archaeological Survey of India is doing restoration work on the *Sun Temple,* the most spectacularly engineered of all the temples of Orissa, which is located on the coast, not far from Puri. The irritation one feels initially because scaffolding surrounds part of the temple, built in the shape of the sun god's chariot, soon gives way to an interest in watching the stonecarvers at their work. As impressive as the temple is now, it was once even more splendid. Of the original temple compound, only half the main temple, the audience hall, remains in anything approaching its original shape. The original compound consisted of a dancing hall, an audience hall, and a tremendous tower that must have been 227 feet high if it conformed to traditional proportions of Indian temples. Part of the tower still existed as late as 1837, when the English archaeologist Fergusson visited it, but it had fallen by 1869. The Audience Hall had to be filled with stone slabs and sealed off to prevent its collapse. Its construction in this location so near the sea (which has since receded two miles from the site) on sandy soil is the main reason why it has crumbled; the salty air and the softness of the sand dunes are the major culprits.

The original architect, Sibai Santra, directed 1,200 workmen to lay the foundation of this temple, but the sand dunes on which it was being built did not provide him with much hope of success. Legend has it that having failed in his attempts to raise the structure, he fell asleep on the nearby beach, crestfallen and dejected. When he awoke, he found an old woman offering him a plate of hot food. Seizing the plate, he dipped his fingers into the center of the steaming porridge and burned them. The woman chided him, saying, "My son, your manner of eating is like Sibai Santra's manner of building the temple. You must start from the edges and not in the center, as he throws stones into the middle." A wiser man, Sibai Santra started the construction afresh, and we have the privilege of seeing his vision in stone.

The Sun Temple is constructed in the form of a huge chariot with 24 huge wheels pulled by seven straining horses. Every area of the temple is intricately carved with some of the most fantastic sculpture to be seen in India. Platforms, horses, colossal-sized elephants, pillars, and boundary walls of the main plinth are covered with mythical animals, whimsical depictions of daily life, war, trade, erotic sculptures of amorous dalliances—the panoply of a culture's finest instincts: its imagination, mythology, history, and knowledge of the life cycle.

Each structural feature of the temple has a hidden meaning. The seven horses of the chariot represent the seven days of the week, the 24 wheels are the 24 fortnights of the Indian year, and the eight spokes of each wheel are the eight *pahars* into which the ancients divided day and night.

As was usual with temples of this period, both the spire, which was supported by the half-ruined structure (near the pagoda), and the audience hall, which remains, stood on a high plinth. Now that the hall has been blocked off, the entrance to the shrine is inaccessible. Three flights of steps lead up to it from the east, north, and south, and the main door on the west leads to the principal temple. The three-tiered roof, with space between each tier for closer inspection, is covered with elaborate carvings. The walls rise to about 45 feet before they begin to contract inward toward the flat ceiling.

A spectacular sight at night, the temple is lit with floodlights 8–10 P.M. during the summer (May–September), and 5:30–9:30 P.M. in the winter (October–April). At these times, you can't enter the temple compound, but you may view from the outside the unforgettably majestic image of this architectural and artistic wonder rising dramatically out of the silent, deserted, shadowy grounds. To get a leisurely close-up look at the Sun Temple and its fabulous, intricate carvings, arrive between 7 and 8 A.M., before busloads of pilgrims and other tourists.

The Archaeological Survey of India provides a guide service, but be sure to ask the guide for an identification badge, since many less-informed free-lance guides are eager to take you around. At the entrance to the compound, vendors sell well-researched guidebooks to the Sun Temple and other Orissan monuments for a few rupees. These publications are also available at the Archaeological Museum, located near the OTDC Travellers Lodge. This small museum, run by the Archaeological Survey, has a rare collection of ruins from the temple; it shouldn't be missed.

RATNAGIRI-LALITAGIRI

At Ratnagiri-Lalitagiri, the seat of Puspagiri, the A.D. seventh-century Buddhist University, excavations are gradually revealing a magnificent sight. Stupas, monasteries, and stone sculptures are in excellent condition.

 BEACHES. *Gopalpur-on-Sea,* an enchanting seaside resort nestled at the foot of cliffs, is located eight miles from Berhampur, which is a railhead on the South Eastern Railway route, connecting it conveniently to Bombay, Calcutta, Hyderabad, Madras, and Puri. Berhampur is also on bus lines from Bhubaneswar, Puri, and Rourkela. Gopalpur-on-Sea can be reached by regular bus service from town. Travelers who need assistance should contact the OTDC Tourist Counter at the Railway Station (tel. 3870) or the Tourist Office, Old Christian Street (tel. 3226). This is a delightful spot to spend a beach vacation, with water sports equipment provided and first-class treatment given. It is recommended for those who don't mind its isolation from other tourist centers.

Toshali Sands, located on Marine Drive between Konarak and Puri, is a beautifully designed "ethnic village resort" surrounded by a thick coconut grove and well-maintained gardens. Although not on the beach, its guests have access to a nearly deserted beach a short distance away through groves of casuarina that seem to sigh with the slightest breeze. Hotel shuttles provide transportation between the hotel and the beach. The hotel also picks up guests who arrive in Puri on the train. Tour buses pick up guests for trips into Puri or Konarak, which makes Toshali Sands a convenient, though slightly isolated, location from which to see the sights of both places. Those who are in good physical shape and have a little time on their hands should consider borrowing one of the bicycles available free to guests and cycling to Puri. Although the trip is long, the route along Marine Drive is wonderfully scenic, bordered by casuarina groves and cashew and mango trees on one side and the sea on the other. Cycling is a terrific way to enjoy its sights and smells.

HOT SPRINGS. Atri. A holy place 25 miles from Bhubaneswar, this lovely hot spring is also the sight of the
Temple of Hatakeswar.

Taptapani. 30 miles from Berhampur, and thus a
convenient outing from Gopalpur-on-Sea, this hot sulphur spring is located in
a forest setting. The nearby panthanivas (travelers' lodge) has its hot water
supplied by the hot spring.

WILDLIFE SANCTUARIES. The hills, forests, and waterways of Orissa are rich with breathtaking scenery and
unusual wildlife. Though the infrastructure for visiting
these locations is being developed at present, one can't
go expecting much more than the basics. But in a state that is predominantly
agricultural, a trip outside the temple cities of Bhubaneswar, Puri, and Konarak
provides a means of placing these centers of spectacular monuments in the
context of a countryside that seems to have changed little since the Kalinga
Wars. And what better excuse to get into the countryside than to explore one
of Orissa's wildlife sanctuaries?

Nandankanan. This lovely zoological park, situated in the Chandaka Forest
12 miles from Bhubaneswar, is highly recommended for those who are interested in seeing some of India's wildlife but are on a tight schedule. Here tigers,
including the rare white tiger; lions; panthers; leopards; pelicans; peafowl; pythons; and gharial crocodiles are on exhibit in their natural habitat. Across the
lake from the zoological park is a botanical garden. One of the OTDC-run tours
out of Bhubaneswar includes a visit to Nandankanan, which is also connected
to Bhubaneswar by regular bus service.

Simlipal. In the hilly Mayurbhanj district in northern Orissa is the less
accessible Simlipal Forest. This lush sanctuary, which covers 1,700 square miles,
has a core area of approximately 550 square miles that has been established as
the Simlipal National Park. All of this core is a tiger reserve, one of India's
earliest and largest. Scenery in this park, with its valleys, gorges, waterfalls, vast
grasslands, rivers and streams edged with ferns and mosses, and thickly wooded
slopes, with their abundance of sal trees and orchids, is ample reason for at least
a short visit. Tigers, elephants, Indian wolves, leopards, sambar and deer, hill
mynas, peafowl, parakeets, and a variety of snakes all make their home here.
Jeeps are necessary for traveling within the park and should be arranged for
through the field director. Not to be missed are the waterfalls of Barehipani (in
the park), which plummet from a height of 1,400 feet and Jaranda (500 feet);
the vast grasslands of Bachhurichara; and the Meghasani Peak, which reaches
almost 4,000 feet. During the festival of Makara (January 13–14), the Santal
tribes located in this area join together to feast and dance in large number.

Chilka Lake. On the coast between Bhubaneswar and Gopalpur-on-Sea,
Chilka Lake spreads its aquatic beauties over 680 square miles, making it the
largest inland lake in India. Its brackish water, dotted with islands bearing such
whimsical names as Honeymoon and Breakfast islands, is rich with marine life
and enticing to fishing and boating enthusiasts. Migrating to Chilka in the
winter months (November – March) are flocks of ducks, pelicans, golden plov-
ers, cormorants, flamingoes, ospreys, and other migratory birds from as far
away as Siberia. Water transport facilities are available through the OTDC at
Barkul and Rambha and through the Revenue Department at Balugaon.

Ushakothi. The best time to visit this sanctuary is at night when, from the
vantage point of special watch towers erected near watering holes and saline
tanks, you can see its elephant, tiger, black panther, deer, and wild boar populations. You may get permission to visit from the Forest Range Officer, at P.O.
Badrama. Guides are also available from this office.

MUSEUMS. In Bhubaneswar, the *Orissa State Museum*
has palm leaf manuscripts and a few sculptures from
temple ruins. *Tribal Research Museum* has ornaments,
weapons, and dresses of Orissa's many tribes. Konarak
has an *Archaeological Museum* near the Sun Temple that features sculptures
from the temple. All are open 10 A.M. – 5 P.M. except Mondays.

SPORTS. As was just mentioned, **beaches** and **wildlife sanctuaries** are a special attraction of Orissa. **Bicycling** for travelers who are in good physical condition is an ideal way to take in the rural scenery and lush paddy fields along the road that skirts the sea between Konarak and Puri. Check with your hotel or the local tourist office for bike rentals.

SHOPPING. Shopping for the various crafts of Orissa could be a way of exploring some of the smaller villages in the state, although Bhubaneswar will provide the best selection of crafts for most tourists. The *Orissa State Emporium,* Utkalika, in the Eastern Tower Market Building and, for Orissan textiles, the *Handloom Weavers Cooperative,* in the West Market Building, are recommended in Bhubaneswar. After the capital, *Cuttack,* a center for delicate silver filigree work, is one of the best places for crafts in Orissa. You can bargain for inexpensive souvenirs in local bazaars, outside temples, in the village outside the entrance to the Sun Temple in Konarak, and along Bada Danda Road in Puri. Also in Puri is the *Arts and Crafts Emporium,* which sells at fixed prices. Stone carvings of the statuary at Konarak; Khiching soapstone carvings of Hindu deities; brightly colored papier-mâché masks of Japannath, Balabhadra, and Subadhra from Puri; *pattachitra* paintings; terra-cotta work, including toys; and the meticulous and gaily colored applique work used to make sun umbrellas and wall hangings from Pipli are just some of the arts and crafts from which to choose. Of all the beautiful Orissan textiles, the unusual double *ikat* design, in which warp and woof threads are tie-dyed in complementary patterns and then woven together, is most treasured.

ASSAM, MEGHALAYA, AND THE NORTHEAST STATES

Foothills of the Himalayas

by
LISA SAMSON and AMIT SHAH

The northeast states of Arunachal Pradesh, Assam, Manipur, Megh-alaya, Mizoram, Nagaland, and Tripura are some of the most visually beautiful and culturally fascinating areas of this tremendously diverse country. However, they have been troubled areas of India for many years, an Achilles heel of sorts to the central government. Connected to the rest of the subcontinent by a narrow corridor of land, encompassing foothills of the Himalayas, marshy grasslands, and wild mountainous areas, these seven states are home to the largest and most varied concentration of India's tribal peoples and site of one of its ancient Hindu states.

Almost engulfed by Burma, Bangladesh, and China, the seven states have been all but inaccessible to foreign travelers for years. In fact, travel restrictions to Assam and Meghalaya—the two states that had been open to tourists—have been tightened increasingly over the past few years. Political strife in the northeast, fueled by long-simmering internal disagreements or resulting from pressures brought about by conflicts in Bangladesh that overflow into India, erupt periodically into open conflict between disputing internal factions or against the central government.

As a result, regulations for access to these areas change frequently, making travel in this area somewhat of a gamble. Some travelers' long-planned trips, notably to Assam's wildlife sanctuaries of Kaziranga and Manas, have been canceled at the last moment because of adverse local conditions.

Events of 1986–87 offer equal doses of both optimism and pessimism for the future access of tourists to this area. The Union Territories of Arunachal Pradesh, which borders China in the extreme northeast, and Mizoram, a pointed finger-shaped area wedged in between Bangladesh's Chittagong Hill Tracts and Burma's Chin Hills, recently became two of India's newest states. Carved out of Assam and the North East Frontier Agency (NEFA), these are the last of the area's Union Territories to gain statehood.

Becoming India's twenty-third state has brought an end to Mizoram's seemingly intractable 20-year-old conflict with India's central government and repatriation of thousands of guerrilla fighters who lived in exile in the Chittagong Hill Tracts of Bangladesh. In elections held in early 1987, the Mizos voted in the leader of the Mizo National Front, the guerrilla organization, as their chief minister, thus completing their break with Assam (from which Mizoram was separated in 1972, becoming a Union Territory). With this severance, the Mizos began to exercise their long-fought-for right to choose their own leaders and direct their internal policy. With statehood, it is hoped that Mizoram will have the opportunity to rechannel its energies to internal development, the first step toward making it a more accessible location for outsiders.

Arunachal Pradesh's statehood, perceived by neighboring China as provocation, has given rise to troop buildups on both sides of the Sino-Indian border. For many years, India and China have disagreed about their physical boundaries in this northeast area (there are also Sino-Indian border disputes in the northwest area of Jammu and Kashmir). The newest confrontation suggests a less optimistic beginning for India's twenty-fourth state. With an international disagreement of this nature, it will continue to be difficult to get the government's permission to visit this area.

In terms of nature, wildlife, and tribal culture, the northeast is an area of great riches—a fascinating area of exploration for the naturalist, wildlife enthusiast, anthropologist, political scientist, musicologist, or dance or religious scholar. An abundance of rare and endangered animals are sheltered in sanctuaries here, and there are unusual sites, some of them to be found in the more accessible areas of Assam and Meghalaya.

EXPLORING ASSAM

Through Assam winds the magnificent Brahmaputra River, its name meaning "son of Brahma," lord of the universe. And an apt name it is, providing life-nourishing water to irrigate the rich alluvial plain through which it runs or meting out devastation during the monsoons, when rains have risen its crest to over 40 feet above its natural level. The river traverses east to west and makes Assam one of the most fertile areas of India. Rice grows in abundance here, but it is for tea that Assam is better known. Tea plantations abound in Assam, their low-lying green foliage dwarfed by the tall shade trees above them. At harvest time, women with woven baskets strapped to their heads move slowly through the tea plants, picking the tender leaves, all the while

seeming to swim through a waist-high sea of green. Tea grew wild in
this area for centuries; the first organized tea estates were established
by the British in the 1800s. Almost 800 such estates now blanket the
hillsides of Assam, producing about 50 percent of India's tea.

Assam is not just a picture postcard state continuing traditions of the
raj, however. Rich oil fields were discovered in the area surrounding
Digboi, where the first oil refinery in Asia was built and where 50
percent of India's crude oil is now produced.

A Bit of History

Assam's ancient history, which is not well documented, is largely
discussed in terms of the plains people, not the numerous tribes who
populated the surrounding hills. In the thirteenth century, the Ahoms
of Burma gained power in Upper Assam, gradually conquering the
lands once ruled by the Kacharis. Moslem invaders in the 1500s were
defeated by the Ahoms, but, in the 1600s, Lower Assam was ceded to
Aurangzeb, the great Mogul emperor. A constant location of conflict,
Assam came under the control of the East India Company in 1826 and
remained under British control in one administrative guise or another
until 1947. Since Independence, conflict has continued. What was once
Assam and the North East Frontier Agency (NEFA of Assam) has
been restructured, creating the states of Nagaland (in 1963), Meghalaya (in 1972), and Mizoram (in 1987) from parts of Assam and
Arunachal Pradesh (in 1987) from the NEFA.

Guwahati, the traditional capital of Assam (Dispur, part of Guwahati, is now the temporary capital), is said to have been the ancient city
of Pragjyotishpur, meaning "Light of the East." It sits on the southern
bank of the Brahmaputra and is one of the few locations that is accessible to foreign travelers. Various religious and scholarly centers are
found nearby. Hajo, 15 miles away, attracts Buddhists and Hindus,
who come to worship the remains of Buddha at the Hayagriba Madhab
Temple, and Moslems who come to worship at the Pir Giyasuddin
Aulia, believed to be one-quarter as holy as the great mosque in Mecca.
Navagraha, in the eastern part of Guwahati, was once a center of
astrology and astronomy.

Huge Wildlife Sanctuaries

What most attracts people to Assam, however, are the two great
wildlife sanctuaries near Guwahati—Kaziranga and Manas. Swaying
on top of an elephant, you traverse the grasslands of these two splendid
parks in the hopes of seeing some of its rare wildlife. Kaziranga, bounded by the Brahmaputra River and the Mikir Hills, is best known as the
home of the largest population of Indian one-horned rhinoceroses.
These massive beasts were mistaken for the legendary unicorns by
Marco Polo, who proclaimed them "hideous." On the verge of extinc-
tion in the early 1900s, the rhinoceros population has increased steadily
since 1908 when this sanctuary was set aside for them as a forest
reserve. Not known for being sweet tempered, the powerful rhinoceros
creates vibrations in its wanderings that are an ample warning that it
is not to be taken lightly. The elephants you ride through the parks,
well acquainted with the moody rhinoceros, keep a respectful distance.
Kaziranga also has wild elephants and water buffaloes—another impressive animal—sambar, swamp deer, bears, and a great variety of
birds.

Manas Wildlife Sanctuary, a beautiful spot, watered by many rivers
and streams, is an excellent place for those who are interested in fishing.
Considered to be among the loveliest of India's wildlife sanctuaries, it

was set up in 1928 as an original tiger reserve and is part of "Project Tiger." Sharing the riverine sanctuary with the tiger are one-horned rhinoceroses, wild buffaloes, sambar, and the unusual pygmy hogs and hispid hares. Manas has a great variety of birds; spectacular daily flights of great pied hornbill wing across the Manas River into neighboring Bhutan.

EXPLORING MEGHALAYA

When one learns that Meghalaya has the world's wettest spot—Cherrapunji—with an average annual rainfall of almost 450 inches (37 feet), one can understand why the state is known as the "abode of clouds." Meghalaya, once a part of Assam, encompasses the Khasi, Jaintia, and Garo Hills, which are also the names of their principle tribes. The tribes are of different ancestry: the Khasis are Austro-Asiatic, the Jaintias are Mongolian, and the Garos are Tibetan. Although they are from different backgrounds and embrace different customs, they share a common link in that their social organization is matrilineal; power and land are passed down through the women in all three tribes.

Shillong, the capital, is one of India's finest hill stations, its environs having been compared by foreigners to the Scottish Highlands. Lying at 5,000 feet, it has an invigorating, healthy climate. During the hot, dry season on the plains, it is a popular vacation spot for Indian families. Its natural beauties include waterfalls cascading from fantastic heights, mysterious underground caves, and small streams that persistently carve out dramatic gorges. Meghalaya's forests of pines and firs, which are filled with rare orchids and butterflies, shelter the rare golden cat. And there are blue lakes whose banks invite you to picnic.

Against the background of the almost fairy-tale beauty, Meghalaya's tribes continue to pass on their culture. Music is an important part of tribal life, making festival months joyous and entertaining. Particularly impressive is the Wangala or "100 Drums" Festival, which is celebrated after harvest time in the Garo Hills. This celebration is now organized by the state as a means of encouraging the continuation of tribal culture.

EXPLORING ARUNACHAL PRADESH, MANIPUR, MIZORAM, NAGALAND, AND TRIPURA

The remaining five states that make up the northeast are a mosaic of cultures. The many tribes found here (40 distinct tribes or subtribes make up one-third of the population of the tiny state of Manipur) are kept in relative isolation from the outside world. However, the British missionary work in the area has had a profound effect. The majority of the tribes of Manipur, Mizoram, and Nagaland are converts to Christianity; the Mizo language was even given a Roman script by Christian missionaries.

In other respects, each state is different. The hilliest area of northeast India is Mizoram, which is bounded by Burma on the east and south, Bangladesh and Tripura on the west, and Assam and Manipur on the north. On its steep hills grow over a thousand varieties of medicinal plants, and many rivers and streams cut gorges through the hills. The Mizos are of Mongolian origin and are believed to have arrived in Mizoram in the eighteenth century from the Chin hills of Burma. Despite its protracted conflict, the literacy rate of Mizoram is surpassed only by Chandigarh, Kerala, and Delhi, and its society has no distinctions based on class or sex. Dances and music are very important, and younger Mizos have enthusiastically taken to Western music.

The "land of jewels," as Manipur is known, which shares its borders with Burma, Nagaland, Mizoram, and Assam, was once a princely state. Like many of the northeast states, Manipur's climate is inviting year round and the scenery is gorgeous. Although a majority of the hill people are Christians, those who live on the plain are primarily Hindus. Manipuri dance, one of the great classical dance dramas of India, reenacting the story of Radha and Krishna, evolved here. Light steps and hand poses that are decorative rather than descriptive make it a lyrical, enchanting dance. Men, women, and children participate in the dancing, which is performed for all major events to the sound of cymbals and drums. Polo and field hockey are favorite sports in Manipur.

Bounded by Burma in the east and Arunachal Pradesh, Assam, and Manipur, Nagaland is one of the smallest Indian states. Its hilly land is populated primarily by about 16 tribes and subtribes, each with a distinctive language and culture. Dimapur was the one-time capital of the Kachari rulers, and relics of their kingdom can be seen. During World War II, Naga tribesmen played an important role in halting the invasion of India by the Japanese at Kohima. The tennis court of the deputy commissioner's bungalow was the scene of this struggle. It is now lined with scores of white crosses in memory of those "who gave our today for your tomorrow," according to an inscription.

An intriguing story about Manipur, Mizoram, and Nagaland was recently reported in *India Today,* the most widely read newsweekly in India, similar in format to *Time* and *Newsweek.* According to the report, in the 1950s, members of the Kuki tribe began to convert to Judaism, believing themselves to be descendants of one of the lost tribes of Israel. Now over 4,000 in all three states, their number is steadily increasing. They have a synagogue in Imphal, Manipur, and follow Jewish teachings. A prime aim of this group is to emigrate to Israel. In 1983, the Israeli government allowed four Kuki tribe members to visit Israel to attempt to authenticate their claims and to receive formal religious instruction.

Tripura has a vastly different makeup from the other small states. An ancient Hindu princely state dating back 13 centuries, Tripura traces its origins to the days of the Mahabharata. It was ruled by maharajahs until 1949. Its low hills and plains adjoin, and are almost surrounded by, Bangladesh. Recently, this proximity placed it in an international refugee situation, when thousands of Buddhist tribesmen, the Chakmas, entered Tripura to escape from the Bangladesh army. A decade-long conflict between the Chakmas and the government of Bangladesh stems from problems with the original partition of India and Pakistan in 1947. Believed to support a guerrilla force of some 7,000, called the Shanti Bahinis, the Chakmas who have entered Tripura fill refugee camps along the border with Bangladesh.

The last of these states, Arunachal Pradesh, borders Tibet on the north, Assam on the south, Bhutan on the west, and Burma on the east. A wild and mountainous area, it is the most isolated spot in the northeast, and most of it is covered with forests.

It is sensible, but unfortunate that tourism is not being encouraged in these northeast states. Their temperate climate, rare wildlife, natural beauty, and intriguingly disparate indigenous populations would make them prime areas to visit. One hopes that the progress made in the past few years toward calming the political turmoil here might eventually allow the area to develop its potential as an accessible spot for those who are interested in wildlife, nature, and tribal culture.

PRACTICAL INFORMATION FOR
ASSAM AND MEGAHALAYA

NOTE: Permission is so rarely given to foreign tourists who want to visit Arunachal Pradesh, Manipur, Mizoram, Nagaland, and Tripura that the areas are considered off-limits. Continuing tensions along the Sino-Indian border and various internal conflicts within these volatile states have made them inaccessible for many years. Visits to the two exceptions, Assam and Meghalaya, are increasingly being restricted. According to tourist authorities in Calcutta, fewer than 150 permits were issued to foreigners to travel to Meghalaya in 1986. Permission to travel to Meghalaya and to see Assam's two wildlife sanctuaries is considered only for those traveling in a group of six or more. An authorized tour agent must be used for visits to the sanctuaries, and a government liaison officer is assigned to the group.

With the recent buildup of troops along the Arunachal Pradesh border with China, one can expect that travel in this scenically beautiful and culturally fascinating area of India will continue to be all but inaccessible for some time to come. For this reason, we are including only Assam and Meghalaya in this *Practical Information* section of this edition. See the preceding essay for information on the history of the five inaccessible states, two of which were recently granted statehood.

It is critical that those who wish to travel to the northeast apply early for permits, three months at a minimum and six months to be safe. In addition, because political events in this area are volatile, sudden changes in access are common, sometimes causing long-planned trips to be canceled at the last moment. Trip-cancellation insurance is strongly recommended for those who plan to travel in this area (see *Facts at Your Fingertips*).

 WHEN TO GO. Assam is best visited between October and May. The wildlife sanctuaries of Kaziranga and Manas are usually closed during the monsoon season (July–September). Kaziringa's best season is February – May, while Manas is best from January to March. For those who are interested in fishing in Manas, February and March are the prime months. Temperatures range from 70° to 90° F in the summer and 48° to 78° F in the winter. Cool nights in the summer make a light wrap necessary, and lightweight woolens are recommended for winter visits.

In Meghalaya, which boasts the world's wettest spot, Cherrapunji, is extremely rainy between late May and mid-August. September – March is recommended for those who prefer to visit a drier climate. As in Assam, a light wrap is needed for summer evenings and lightweight woolens are recommended for the winter.

 TRAVEL PERMITS. For Assam. Travel to either Kaziranga or Manas Wildlife Sanctuary in Assam is restricted to groups of six or more people, and permission is given only to those who participate in a tour offered by an approved tourist agent. Go to one of the government-approved tour agencies listed in the *Calcutta* chapter or in the international listings in *Facts At Your Fingertips*. You can apply in advance through your consulate (six months in advance, to be safe) or to the *Assam Tourist Information Centre,* Government of Assam, in Calcutta or Delhi (see *Useful Addresses* below for locations). Applications are processed in seven days.

On their arrival at Guwahati's Borjhar Airport, travelers to Manas and Kaziranga are met by a liaison officer who accompanies them while they are in Assam.

For Meghalaya. Tourist permits to visit Meghalaya for one to two weeks are processed only for groups of six or more. Apply to the *Under Secretary to the Government of India, Ministry of Home Affairs,* Lok Nayak Bhawan, New Delhi 110 003. With this permission from New Delhi in hand, one must visit the *Meghalaya Tourist Information Centre,* 9 Russell St., Calcutta 700 071 (tel. 29–0797), to get the permit to enter the state. This permit, which allows visits of up to two weeks, is issued the same day. It is recommended that you arrange your trip through a tour agency.

HOW TO GET THERE. By Air. *Indian Airlines* has flights connecting New Delhi, Calcutta, and Patna with Guwahati, and Assam. Jorhat, the town nearest to the Kaziranga Wildlife Sanctuary, is connected by Indian Airlines to Calcutta and Guwahati. Guwahati is also connected to various cities in the northeast that are currently off-limits to foreign travelers: Agartala, Dibrugarh, Dimapur, Imphal, Lilabari, and Tezour. *Vayudoot* has a flight from Calcutta to Shillong, Meghalaya, and Guwahati.

Although it's possible to get to Assam by **car** or **train,** the distances are so long (630 miles by train from Calcutta and 1,200 miles from Delhi; 700 miles by car from Calcutta), and permission to do so is so infrequently given, that only air travel is recommended.

How to Get From the Airport. Groups of foreign tourists entering Assam to go to Manas and Kaziranga are met by a liaison officer of the state government who is appointed to them for their stay. Transportation is arranged in **minibuses** or other appropriate vehicles to take you to these wildlife sanctuaries. In Shillong, **taxis** and a state-run **bus** service go from Umroi Airport into town, a distance of 10 miles.

USEFUL ADDRESSES. Assam. *Directorate of Tourism,* Government of Assam, Ulubari, Guwahati, Assam 781 007; tel. 27102 or 31022.

Assam Tourist Information Offices, Calcutta: 8 Russell St., Calcutta 700 071; tel. 24–8341; or, at the same address, Assam House, tel. 29–8341. Guwahati: Tourist Lodge, Station Road, Guwahati 781 001; tel. 24475. Kaziranga: P.O. Kaziranga Sanctuary, District Sibsagar, Assam 785 109; tel. 23/29. New Delhi: Assam Information Center, B–1 Baba Kharag Singh Marg, New Delhi 110 001; tel. 32–5897.

Tourist Information Counters. Arrival area, Borjhar Airport, Guwahati.

Government of India Tourist Office, B. K. Kakati Road, Ulubari, Guwahati 781 007; tel. 31381, Cable: INDTOUR. *Government of Meghalaya Tourism Information Office,* G. S. Road, Ulubari (near Chariali), Guwahati; tel. 27276. *Indian Airlines.* Guwahati, Paltan Bazar; tel. 23128. *Vayudoot,* Guwahati; tel. 25757.

Meghalaya. *Directorate of Tourism,* Government of Meghalaya, Police Bazar, Shillong 793 001; tel. 26054. *Tourist Information Center,* Government of Meghalaya, Meghalaya State Transport Corporation Building, Police Bazar, Shillong 793 001; tel. 26220. *Government of India Tourist Office,* G. S. Road, Police Bazar, Shillong 793 001. *Meghalaya Tourism Development Corporation* (MTDC), Shillong Tourist Hotel, Polo Road, Shillong; tel. 26220; Cable: MEGTOURCOR, Telex: 237–222. Meghalaya House, 9 Russell St., Calcutta 700 071; tel. 29–0797. Meghalaya House, 9 Auranozeb Rd., New Delhi 110 011; tel. 37–5394 or 301–5605.

ACCOMMODATIONS. Under current restrictions, accommodations in Kaziranga or Manas, in Assam, are arranged by tour agents through whom one must travel. Information for these areas will prove useful should these restrictions be lifted in the future. (For price ranges of hotel categories listed here, see *Facts at Your Fingertips.*)

GUWAHATI

Expensive

Hotel Kuber International. Hem Barua Road, Guwahati 781 001; tel. 32601 – 5; cable: HOTELKUBER; Telex: 0235–251. Western-style amenities with nicely appointed rooms and revolving rooftop restaurant. Accepts major credit cards.

Hotel Nandan. G.S. Road, Guwahati 781 008; tel. 31281 – 6; cable: NANDAN. Diners Club.

Urvasi Airport Hotel. Borjhar, Guwahati 781 015; tel. 82293; cable: PORTLAND.

Moderate

Hotel Bellevue. Mahatma Gandhi Road, P.O. Box 75, Guwahati 781 001; tel. 28291; cable: BELLEVIEW. Overlooks the Brahmaputra River. American Express, Diners Club.

Stadium Guest House. Dr. B. Baruah Road, Guwahati 781 007; tel. 23312.

Inexpensive

Tourist Lodge. Station Road; tel. 24475. Operated by the Government of Assam.

JORHAT

Jorhat, which has the airport nearest to Kaziranga Wildlife Sanctuary, has the *moderately* priced **Paradise Hotel,** Solicitors Road, Jorhat 785 001; tel. 821 (PBX), 610, 1366; cable: PARADISO. Diner's Club and Visa. Also *moderate* is the **Eastern Hotel,** Galari, Jorhat 785 001; tel. 490, 327.

KAZIRANGA WILDLIFE SANCTUARY

Kaziranga Forest Lodge, run by the ITDC, **Tourist Lodge Number 1,** (Western-style), and **Tourist Lodge Number 2** (Indian-style) are all booked through the Deputy Director of Tourism, Kaziranga Sanctuary, Sibsagar District, Assam 785 109; tel. 23; Cable: TOURISM. The Forest Lodge is the better and more expensive facility.

MANAS

Reservations for rustic accommodations at the **Forest Lodge** and **Tourist Lodge** are made through the Field Director, Tiger Project, Barpeta Road, Assam; tel. 153; Cable: WILDLIFE.

Tourist Bungalow, Barpeta Road. Reservations are made through Tourist Information Office, Barbet Road; tel. 49.

SHILLONG, MEGHALAYA

Expensive

Pinewood Ashok. Shillong, Meghalaya 793 001; tel. 23116. Cable: PINEWOOD. Run by ITDC, it has single and double rooms and family cottages, a bar, restaurant, and shopping arcade. Accepts major credit cards.

Moderate to Inexpensive

Shillong Club, G.S. Road, Shillong 793 001; tel. 26938.

Shillong Tourist Hotel. Polo Hill, Shillong 793 001; tel. 24933.

The state tourism department maintains two **Tourist Bungalows** that are *moderate* and situated on a cliff. For reservations, contact Director of Tourism, Meghalaya, Police Bazar, Shillong 793 001.

DINING OUT. Since tourists to Assam and Meghalaya are experiencing increasing restrictions, your dining here will be most likely confined to the dining rooms of hotels. Most of the dining rooms in the better hotels serve Continental (Western-style) foods as well as Indian fare. And in many of them, the price of the meals is included in the rates. If you would like to try eating at a hotel other than the one in which you are staying, it is advisable to call first to see if you can be accommodated. Phone numbers for most of the hotels are listed in the "Accommodations" section.

 HOW TO GET AROUND. As was just stated, all groups that are headed for Assam's two main wildlife sanctuaries must work through a tour agent and are accompanied by a liaison officer. The following information will be of use should these restrictions be lifted. In Guwahati, the Directorate of Tourism conducts **tours** on the weekends to Kaziranga and Manas from the Tourist Lodge near the railway station, where reservations are accepted (tel. 24475). Fees (Rs. 168 to Kaziranga, Rs. 145 to Manas) include transportation, food, accommodations, and an elephant ride to and from the sanctuary. Modest fees are charged for still photography equipment used in the sanctuaries; the fees vary, depending on the type of equipment used, with telephoto lenses being charged a higher rate. The best way to see the wildlife is on elephant back. The directorate also conducts local tours and, in good weather, river cruises on the Brahmaputra. **Cars** can be hired through one of the following: *BSS Travels,* Fancy Bazar (tel. 23544); *Rhino Travels,* Pan Bazar (tel. 27838); or *Sheba Travels,* G.N.B. Road (tel. 22135). Approved guides are available through the Directorate of Tourism (tel. 27102).

However you travel, the roads to Manas and Kaziranga pass through green forests and alongside lush tea plantations, skirting the Brahmaputra and other rivers that run through this state, occasionally crossing them on bridges that date from the Ahom Period (thirteenth–eighteenth century), making the journey itself memorable.

The *Government of Meghalaya's Directorate of Tourism* (MTDC) offers conducted tours in and around Shillong, as well as some day excursions to Meghalaya's popular tourist spots, such as Cherrapunji and Jakrem. Also see the "Festival" section for information on the directorate's excursion to Tura during the celebrations of the Garo Hills' harvest festival as well as other excursions originating in Calcutta (contact them at 9 Russell St.). **Taxis** can be hired at the *Tourist Taxi Association,* Police Bazar, and trained guides are available through the Directorate of Tourism, Police Bazar, or the *Government of India Tourist Office. Meghalaya Transportation Corporation* operates **buses** in the city and has daily service to Cherrapunji.

 FESTIVALS AND FOLK DANCING. In Assam, three main festivals, or *bihus,* are energetically celebrated: *Bohag Bihu,* which occurs in April and is the Assamese New Year, *Magh Bihu,* and *Kati Bihu.* Music, dancing, and communal feasting are integral parts of these celebrations. During Bohag Bihu, festivities full of ritual and song continue for a week.

Elsewhere in the northeast the many tribal groups celebrate various festivals to the accompaniment of music and dance. The *Wangala,* or Hundred Drum Festival, is celebrated in the Garo Hills of Meghalaya after the harvest in late fall. Beginning with a ceremony led by the village priest, it builds to a climax during which tribal members dance to the pulsing rhythms of 100 drums, gongs, flutes, and trumpets. The festival continues for many days. The MTDC sponsors a four-day excursion from Shillong to Tura to see this festival. Contact Manager, MTDC, Shillong Tourist Hotel, Polo Road, Shillong 793 001 (tel. 26220, cable: MEGTOURCOR, Telex: 237–222) or the government tourism representatives in Calcutta (see address in *Useful Addresses*). The colorful *Nongkrem Dance,* another religious dance, is held in Smit, nine miles from Shillong, and the *Laho Dance* is celebrated in Jowai, after the fall harvest.

HISTORIC SITES. Travel in Assam and Meghalaya outside the towns of Guwahati and Shillong is increasingly restricted. At present, foreign visitors to Assam's *Kaziranga Wildlife Sanctuary,* which lies 135 miles northeast of Guwahati along the Brahmaputra River, and *Manas Wildlife Sanctuary,* 110 miles southwest of Guwahati, must come in groups of six or more. These are two of India's finest wildlife sanctuaries, in whose evergreen forests and wet grasslands one rides on the back of elephants to see the rare one-horned Indian rhinoceroses, wild buffaloes, sambar, and wild elephants. Golden langur monkeys, pygmy hogs, and hispid hares inhabit Manas, and both sanctuaries have a wide variety of birds. Manas is also a tiger reserve and is part of India's Project Tiger.

Guwahati, the gateway to India's northeast, is picturesquely situated on the banks of the Brahmaputra River, surrounded by green hills. A number of interesting pilgrimage sites are nearby. *Kamakhya Temple,* its swelling, beehive-like shape dominating Nilachal Hill, is dedicated to Kali and is a center of Tantrism. On Peacock Island, in the middle of the Brahmaputra River, is the *Umanada Shiva Temple,* where thousands come during Shivratri celebrations in February–March. A few miles outside Guwahati is Hajo, where temples of various faiths coexist, including the Hayagrib *Madhab Temple,* sacred to Hindus and Buddhists and believed by them to contain relics of the Buddha (some believe it was here that he attained nirvana). *Navagraha,* meaning nine planets, on Chitrashala Hill to the east of Guwahati, was once the center of astronomical and astrological study. Twenty miles away, on the far side of the river (reached by ferry), is Sualkuchi, the center of Assam's handloomed silk industry. The *Assam State Zoo* has examples of Assamese wildlife, including the one-horned rhinoceros.

Kaziranga Wildlife Sanctuary. This sanctuary, one of the best known in eastern India, is home to the largest number of India's rare one-horned rhinoceroses. In 1908, when there were hardly a dozen of these powerful, armored animals alive in the area, Kaziranga was declared a forest reserve. Today, the rhinoceroses, numbering close to 1,000, coexist with wild elephants, tigers, wild buffaloes, leopards, and barking deer in Kaziranga's 200 square miles of forests and grasslands. Gliding and darting over its *jheels* (swampy flats with ready areas surrounding shallow pools of water), are a rich variety of water birds, including floricans, purple herons, black-necked storks, egrets, adjutants, ring-tailed fishing eagles, river terns, and pelicans (near Kaziranga village there is a pelicanry).

At **Mihimukh,** a few miles from the forest lodges, you can see rhinoceroses, buffaloes, and swamp and hog deer. If you take the time to travel deeper into the sanctuary, you can see these animals in wilder surroundings. Currently, anyone traveling to Kaziranga must go through an approved tour agency that makes all arrangements for transportation and accommodations. Should these restrictions be lifted in the future, arrangements can be made by contacting the *Tourist Reception Officer,* Kaziranga, Wildlife Sanctuary, Assam; tel. 3.

Manas Wildlife Sanctuary. Covering 170 square miles in the foothills of the Himalayas, bordering the isolated, mountainous country of Bhutan, Manas is laced with many streams and rivers. The Manas, Beki, and Hakua rivers flow through it, contributing to Manas's reputation of being one of India's most beautiful sanctuaries. The best season here is from January to March, but those who want to do some fishing will find February and March the best months (fishing is permitted at a small daily charge). The birds in the sanctuary are exceptional. The early morning sight of large flocks of great pied hornbills crossing the river to feed on the Bhutan side is memorable. Manas has an abundance of waterbirds, such as the white-capped redstart, which can be seen on the pebble-covered river banks, and, on the river, the merganser, egret, ruddy shelduck, cormorant, and a variety of ducks. Wildlife in the sanctuary includes tigers, Indian rhinoceroses, wild buffaloes, elephants, swamp deer, and the rare pygmy hogs and hispid hares. There are also some golden langur monkeys living in small groups (usually nine or less) in the evergreen forests. At present, all foreign visitors to Manas must go through approved tour agents. Should this restriction lift, reservations for accommodations and vehicles can be made through the Tourist Information Officer, Barpeta Road, Assam, Tel. Barpeta Road 49.

At both wildlife sanctuaries, photographers shoot either from the top of elephants (the best means of transportation through the sanctuaries' grasslands) or from specially constructed observation towers. Daily fees for photography are levied (Rs. 5 for a still camera and Rs. 500 for a 35mm motion-picture film camera), based on the type of equipment to be used (telephoto lenses are charged a higher rate).

Visits to **Meghalaya,** "the abode of the clouds," are also restricted to groups of six or more. Shillong, its capital, is one of the finest of the Indian hill stations, to which people flock to avoid the heat of summers on the plains. Compared often to Scotland's Highlands, it is a slow-paced, relaxing setting in which to unwind from the hustle and bustle of Calcutta and Delhi, and its surrounding areas are home to some of India's oldest and most fascinating peoples, the Khasi, Jaintia, and Garo tribes.

Cherrapunji, 35 miles from Shillong, is considered the world's wettest spot, with a torrential 450 inches (37 ½ feet) annual rainfall, though another location in Meghalaya, Mawsynram, has recently broken that record. At Cherrapunji you see the *Mawsmai Caves* and *Kynrem Falls.* At Mawsynram, there is an interesting rock formation resembling a Shiva lingam that appears to be anointed continually with water from a breast-shaped rock overhead. Meghalaya will delight the nature lover, with hot springs at Jakrem and Garampani; caves at Mawsynram and Tura; Crinoline, Elephant, Bishop and Beadon, Spread Eagle, and Sweet Falls; and numerous lakes, including the lovely Umiam Lake, fed by fast-running streams and rivers. Rare orchids and butterflies are splashes of color against the panoramic scenery of this moist, green, jewel of a state.

MUSEUMS. The *Assam State Museum's* collection includes costumes of Ahom kings, sculpture, pottery, coins, art, and archaeological artifacts. It is open 9:30 A.M.–3:30 P.M. Tuesday–Saturday, 9:30 A.M.–12:30 P.M. Sundays; closed Mondays. Guwahati also has many small museums. The following are open 10 A.M. – 4 P.M. Monday – Friday, 10 A.M. – 1 P.M. Saturdays, and are closed Sundays: *Assam Forest Museum, Assam Government Cottage Industries Museum,* which displays traditional crafts, and the *Anthropological Museum* (Department of Anthropology, Guwahati University, tel. 88248). The *Department of Historical and Antiquarian Research,* which has a collection of old manuscripts, and the *Museum of Animal Husbandry* at the Assam Veterinary College are open 10 A.M. – 4 P.M. Monday – Saturday; closed Sundays.

Meghalaya's State Museum in Shillong includes anthropological, cultural, botanical, and wildlife exhibits. Open 10 A.M. – 4:30 P.M. in summer and till 4 P.M. in winter. Closed Sundays and holidays.

SHOPPING. Assam is known for its exquisite wild silks that include the rough *endi,* a gray or off-white silk frequently made into shawls, and *muga,* the finest of the wild silks, which is naturally gold in color. *Pat* is another of Assam's beautiful silks. Baskets and other bamboo crafts, traditional tribal musical instruments, and traditional weapons are also treasures to be considered. And it goes without saying that one should pick up a number of packets of Assamese tea! In Guwahati, shopping areas are *Fancy Bazar, Pan Bazar,* and *Ambari,* with the *Government Emporium* (tel. 23439) located in Ambari. Shops are closed on Sundays.

A *hatt* or bazaar is held three times a week in Shillong. Tribal women bring in their produce from neighboring villages, often in intricately woven baskets that they wear on their backs. Beautiful bamboo work, unusual baskets, Chinese shoes, and traditional dresses called *Jainsem* are available here. Rare butterflies are used in many souvenir items, though the beauty of the butterflies is sometimes overshadowed by unattractive methods of display. *Police Bazar* and *Bara Bazar* are Shillong's shopping areas, where you'll find a number of northeast state emporiums. Wild honey is also available here in the northeast (It can also be bought in the Meghalaya Emporium, 9 Russell St., Calcutta).

SIKKIM

Tiny State with Giant Vistas

by
LISA SAMSON and AMIT SHAH

There is a Sikkimese legend that goes something like this: Stars are the laughter of the Sikkimese that, having risen far into the sky, have frozen into the myriad stars.

Something in this tiny state, one of India's newest, snuggled into the eastern Himalayas, makes you believe—or want to believe—in this legend. Perhaps it is the high altitude or the disconcerting lay of the land, which seems continually to rise or fall, never leveling out for any distance. Or perhaps it is the strange effect of witnessing ancient religious rituals that are so bound up in the Sikkimese's daily life. For in Sikkim is a people who, despite the constant incursions into their country by aggressive neighbors, continue to exhibit a gaiety that gives credence to the legend.

Sikkim has always been vulnerable because it contains the best natural passes through the Himalayas and therefore the routes of choice for trade between India to the south and Lhasa, Tibet, to the north. For centuries, this tiny kingdom has been caught in a series of disputes over who should rule it. Since 1975, however, Sikkim has been the twenty-second state of India. Inside its 2,745-square-mile area is an odd combination of forces; masses of Indian military troops remain perpetually on alert on the Tibetan border and a basically peaceful people go about their daily lives following the nonaggressive tenets of Mahayana Buddhism. It is your impressions of the people and of the spectacular natural beauty of their land that will remain with you long after you return home.

Before the eighth century, the Lepchas, Sikkim's original people, lived here. According to some anthropologists, they were a rare society in that war had no place in their culture. Through the centuries, invasions from Tibet brought the Bhutias to Sikkim, who now make up over 60 percent of the population, and by the British, who, in turn, brought the Nepalis. These three groups—the Lepchas, Bhutias, and Nepalis—now form the people that call themselves Sikkimese.

Theirs is a magnificent country dominated by Kanchenjunga, the third-highest mountain in the world, which is revered by them as the presiding deity, the home of gods. And, indeed, from many a monastery vantage point, one can feel the greatness of this majestic mountain. In its shadow are other great beauties—forests thick with over 500 species of orchids, beautiful birds and butterflies, red pandas, blue sheep, rhododendrons, and blue poppies. In this visually lovely land, the people have been nurtured by Buddhism, which finds its expression in simple yet beautifully ornamented monasteries and shrines and festivals that are filled with colorful dances. Between the natural scenery and the traditional culture, there is much to enchant you.

PRACTICAL INFORMATION FOR SIKKIM

 WHEN TO GO. The best times to visit Sikkim are March – late May, and October – mid-December. Summer temperatures range from 68° to 76° F and winter temperatures fluctuate between 26° and 50° F. As in other mountainous areas, it is recommended that you wear layered clothing that can ensure your comfort at a variety of altitudes, with their accompanying variation in temperatures.

 PERMITS. An *Inner Line Permit* from the Under Secretary, Ministry of Home Affairs (Foreigner's Section, Lok Nayak Bhavan, Khan Market, New Delhi 110 003) is needed by all foreigners wanting to visit Sikkim. Application should be made, in duplicate, at least six weeks before one's intended date of arrival in Sikkim. An additional copy of the application should be sent to the Liaison Officer, Sikkim Tourism Office, Hotel Janpath, Room No. 10, New Delhi, to expedite it. In your application include information regarding the purpose of your visit; when and where you wish to travel; and your name, home address, and passport and visa numbers. Those who wish to sightsee are given a seven-day permit that is easily extended for an additional three days by applying to the Inspector General of Police in Gangtok and stating why you need the additional time. Those who wish to go trekking are given a 15-day permit. East Sikkim beyond Rongali and North Sikkim beyond Phodan are restricted areas because of their sensitive military location vis-à-vis the Chinese presence in Tibet.

 HOW TO GET THERE. By Air. The nearest airport to Sikkim is Bagdogra in West Bengal, 77 miles from Gangtok, Sikkim's capital. Bagdogra is reached via *Indian Airlines* from Calcutta, a flight of under one hour, and from Delhi, Guwahati, Imphal, and Patna. India's feeder airline, *Vayudoot*, operates a twice-weekly helicopter service from Bagdogra to Gangtok (in Gangtok, contact Jossi and Jossi, Lall Market Road, for information), but, normally, one travels from Bagdogra overland to Gangtok, a trip of approximately five hours. Taxis are available from the airport to Gangtok, and the Sikkim Nationalised Transport (SNT) runs a bus service that costs a few dollars. Check with the Sikkim Tourist Information Counter at the airport.

By Train. The nearest stations to Gangtok are Siliguri Junction, 71 miles away, and New Jalpaiguri, 77 miles away. From Siliguri, the SNT operates regular **bus** service. Private buses that also go from Siliguri to Gangtok are *North Bengal Services, Apsara, Sikkim Beauty,* and *Sikkim Glory.* If you arrive at Siliguri, check with the *Sikkim Tourism Office* at SNT Colony, Siliguri; tel. 21496.

ACCOMMODATIONS. All hotels listed here are in Gangtok, which is the center for visitors to Sikkim. For rate categories and classifications, see *Facts at Your Fingertips.*

Expensive

Hotel Mayur. Gangtok, Sikkim 737 101; tel. 2752, 2558; cable HOTEL MAYUR. Full facilities.

Hotel Nor-Khill. Gangtok, Sikkim 737 101; tel. 2386, 2720; cable NORK-HILL. Rated as a four-star hotel by the Indian Government, with all the amenities.

Hotel Tashi Delek. Mahatma Gandhi Marg, Gangtok, Sikkim 727 101; tel. 2991, 2038; cable TASHIDELEK. Also rated as a four-star hotel, this one boasts a roof garden and an airlines counter.

Moderate

Hotel Tibet. Paljor Stadium Road, Gangtok, Sikkim 737 101; tel. 2523, 2568; cable HOTEL TIBET.

Siniolchu Lodge. Located above the bazaar, it has a good view of Gangtok and the surrounding mountains; tel. 2074.

Inexpensive

Karma. Has attached baths and communal baths; the difference in price is about $1; no phone.

Orchid. Most rooms have attached baths; tel. 2381.

In West Sikkim: **Hotel Mt. Pandim** (P.O. Pelling, West Sikkim, at Pemayangste, tel. 73) has a terrific view of the Himalayas.

DINING OUT. Hotel restaurants are recommended for the duration of your stay in Sikkim. The hotel dining rooms offer Continental as well as Indian foods and, in some places, Chinese cuisine. If you wish to eat at a hotel other than the one at which you are staying, you should telephone to see if you can be accommodated. Those who go on long treks will, of course, have their provisions arranged for them by the trekking services.

HOW TO GET AROUND. For travel in and around Gangtok, **cars, coaches, Land Rovers,** and **jeeps** are available for hire through the SNT. Contact the SNT booking office near the Tourist Information Center in Gangtok. The SNT also operates **buses** in Sikkim. Sightseeing **tours,** which include a tour of Gangtok and a 2½-hour tour to the Rumtek Monastery are offered by the *Department of Tourism.* Contact the Department of Tourism, Gangtok Bazaar, tel. 2097 and 2064.

USEFUL ADDRESSES. Gangtok Department of Tourism (see "How to Get Around" section). *Sikkim Tourist Office,* Hotel Janpath, Room 10, Janpath, New Delhi 110 001. *Tourist Information Center,* 4C, Poonam, 5/2 Russell St., Calcutta 700 017; tel. 24-0223, 24-7512. *Sikkim Center,* Fourth Floor, Air India Building, Nariman Point, Bombay 420 021. *Sikkim Tourist Office,* SNT Colony, Siliguri; tel. 21496.

FESTIVALS AND FOLK DANCING. The Hindu Nepalese celebrate *Durga Puja* in **October/November** as do Indians in other states, by worshiping images of the goddess Durga for four days and then taking these images, with great pageantry, to the river for immersion. During Buddhist festivals, fabulous masked dances are performed by monks. The two most significant of the Buddhist festivals are the celebration of the magnificent mountain, Kanchenjunga, revered by the Sikkimese as the mountain god and the protective deity of Sikkim, and **New Year's** festivities, when good is shown to triumph over evil. The Sikkimese celebrate in dance and song throughout the year. The Department of Tourism in Sikkim arranges folk dance performances for tourists.

WHAT TO SEE. Like Leh, Ladakh, Bhutan, and Nepal, Sikkim is a Himalayan "Shangri-la" that offers you the spectacular scenery of the Himalayan peaks and valleys, and a culture that is rich in intriguing religious ritual and art. Individual tourists are allowed to enter Sikkim for sightseeing purposes, and you may plan your own itinerary. Anyone who wishes to go trekking must be in a group accompanied by a Government of Sikkim guide and must trek over certain routes. Areas of north and east Sikkim are restricted owing to their proximity to Tibet.

The Buddhist monasteries, called *gompas* (solitary places) by the Sikkimese, are a main attraction, with their simple lines elaborately decorated with carvings, their vividly colored frescoes, and their arresting images of the Tibetan Buddhist pantheon. The power of Buddhism is felt in the darkened interiors of these shrines, lit by devotional lamps and reverberating with the sounds of monks at prayer. Outside many of these monasteries, built in isolated locations, one is treated to breathtaking views of the mountain ranges that surround Sikkim.

GANGTOK

At 5,000 feet, Gangtok, the capital city of Sikkim, is called the "lofty hill" by Sikkimese. Some sights to see here are

Deer Park. Near the Secretariat to the south of the town center, Deer Park has Himalayan spotted and musk deer and a breathtaking view of the mountains and Gangtok.

Doddul Chorten. Near the Orchid Sanctuary, contains religious relics and is a place of worship. Surrounded by 108 prayer wheels, devotees go round in clockwise fashion to cleanse themselves of sin.

Enchey Monastery. Built in 1840, this monastery has splendid frescoes and religious sculptures. At this high spot north of the city, you get one of the best views of Kanchenjunga.

Orchid Sanctuary. Near the Sikkim Research Institute of Tibetology, this botanical area displays over 500 varieties of orchids. The best time to see it is April–May or December–January, when the orchids are in full bloom.

Sikkim Research Institute of Tibetology. A traditional-style building of great beauty, this institute houses the world's third-largest collection of Tibetan books on Mahayana Buddhism. It also has precious religious icons and tankas (Tibetan cloth paintings). Buddhist scholars from all over the world come here to study.

Tashi View Point. A little over five miles north of Gangtok, this point has a fine view of the mountains.

AROUND GANGTOK

Phodang Monastery. Several miles north of Gangtok is one of the five principal monasteries of Sikkim and one of the most beautiful. Recently restored, it contains magnificent old murals. **Rumtek Monastery,** southwest of Gangtok, is the state's largest monastery. Built on land that was given by the then-chogyal (king) of Sikkim to the ninth incarnation of the original Gyalwa Karmapa of Tibet when this head of the Karmagupa sect of Buddhism sought refuge in Sikkim after the Chinese occupied Tibet. Phodang Monastery is an exact replica of Chhoful monastery in Tibet.

WESTERN SIKKIM

In an area popular with trekkers is some of Sikkim's most awe-inspiring scenery and two of Sikkim's most revered monasteries, as well as a historic site and a spectacular mountain.

Pemayangtse Monastery. Located at Gyalshung, this shrine was built in the seventeenth century. All other monasteries belonging to the Nyingma sect are subordinate to Pemayangtse, which means "the Sublime Lotus." Covering the ceilings and walls of the monastery are thousands of vivid images of gods and demons. As with many other monasteries in Sikkim, the view of the surrounding mountain ranges is spectacular from here.

Tashiding Monastery, an hour by car from Pemayangste, is on the top of a small hill between the Rangit and Ratong rivers. So holy is it that the Sikkimese believe that just by gazing on the *chorten* (shrine), Thongwa-Rangdot, one can be cleansed of sin. The spring festival draws thousands of believers to view the chorten and another greatly revered object, *Bumchu,* which is a sacred container of holy water, said to be blessed by a holy man after having said 5 billion Mane mantras. The water contained in it is believed to be self-replenishing, having stayed "sweet" for 300 years.

Yaksum. En route to Dzongri, this is an important historical site, where the first ruler of Sikkim was crowned in A.D. 1641.

Dzongri, at 13,000 feet, is where one gets perhaps the penultimate view of Kanchenjunga. With Mount Padim, opposite it, rising to 21,958 feet, and the Khangla ridge, the sunsets here are to be treasured the rest of one's life.

SPORTS. Trekking is obviously a main reason for coming to this isolated state. Those who want to trek should contact one of the travel agencies listed in *Facts at Your Fingertips.* You must take one of the routes set out by the Government of Sikkim, such as the Pemayangtse–Dzongri, Pemayangste–Gangtok, Naya Bazar–Gangtok, or Nay Bazar–Pemayangste treks, and travel with a guide.

SHOPPING. *Government Cottage Industries Institute,* high up on the main road above Gangtok, is set up as a training facility to encourage young artisans in the traditional arts and crafts. It specializes in Lepcha weaving, wood carving, paintings of typical Sikkimese designs, and handwoven carpets, blankets, and shawls. Open Monday–Saturday 9:30 A.M.–12:30 P.M. and 1–3:30 P.M. Don't miss the good Sikkimese rum and liqueur made in Rangpo.

BHUTAN

A Real "Shangri-la" Nation

by
LISA SAMSON and AMIT SHAH

This tiny nation of 1.2 million, considered by many to be one of the world's "Shangri-las," is nestled in the dizzying elevations of the magnificent eastern Himalayas, occupying 18,000 square miles of spectacular natural scenery dominated by towering Himalayan peaks, thick forests, fertile valleys, and well-stocked glacier-fed rivers and streams. Since Bhutan opened its doors to tourism in 1974, this exquisite scenic beauty, combined with the intriguing expressions of its age-old religious and cultural traditions, have exerted a strong fascination over visitors.

With centuries-old fortress-monasteries rising above rivers and valleys, tranquil Buddhist monasteries filled with elaborate artwork and clinging to rock faces, and a landscape filled with the soothing incantations of monks at prayer and the tinkling sound of animals' bells, Bhutan offers the traveler the opportunity to visit, if only briefly, a country that continues to be steeped in legend and dreams, not yet fully wakened to the realities of the twentieth century. In a world that debates the pros and cons of nuclear weaponry, the sheltered Bhutanese continue their passionate enjoyment of archery, once used to defend their nation against outside aggressors, and now practiced as a competitive sport.

What is immediately apparent in Bhutan is that it has been, and remains in many ways, an isolated kingdom. In the 300 years between 1626 and 1921, only a handful of European expeditions penetrated the daunting Himalayan passes that surround Bhutan. Today only a small airport at Paro, which accommodates daily flights from Dhaka, Bangladesh, and Calcutta, India, and a road from India's eastern state of West Bengal connect Bhutan to the rest of the world. Bounded on the north by Chinese-occupied Tibet, the east by India's Arunachal Pradesh, the south by Bengal, and the west by Sikkim, Bhutan, by the grace of its geographic location, continues to be able to maintain a strict control over its interactions with outsiders.

Travel here is restricted to those participating in prepaid tours, usually of at least six people, that are closely monitored by government-assigned guides. Like neighboring Sikkim, the eastern section of the country remains off-limits to visitors; but in late 1987 plans were under way to open this area to trekkers and rafters. All tourism is controlled by one governmental organization, the Bhutan Tourism Corporation. By this calculated lack of freedom of access, the Bhutanese ensure that the traditions that have set them apart from the rest of the world will continue to be preserved for many more generations and that its evolution into a modern state will be carefully planned and controlled.

Early History Uncertain

Druk Yul (the Land of the Thunderbolt Dragon), as Bhutan is called by its inhabitants, has a vague history. Its original natives are today represented by the Sharchops, who live in the eastern areas and are said to have come from Assam. Ngalops, descendents of Tibetans who came as conquerors many centuries ago, make up a large portion of the population. The Bhutanese religion and culture are strongly related to that of Tibet. The Buddhism practiced here is related to lamaism, having been greatly shaped by Guru Rimpoche, who is reported to have flown from Tibet to Paro's Takstang Monastery on the back of a tigress sometime in the eighth century. Within the past century, Nepalese have settled in southern Bhutan.

Written history in Bhutan began with the introduction of Buddhism in the seventh century, and there are still temples in Bumthang, an area of central Bhutan, from this time. But it was not until the early 1600s that Bhutan's many Buddhist sects were joined under a leader, Shabdrung Nawang Namgyel, who united the country in 1630 and established the Drupka sect of Kagyupa Mahayana Buddhism. Through conflicts with Tibet, China, Bengal, and Britain, Shabdrungs headed the Bhutanese until 1900, when these lineages ended. At that time, two districts of the country, Paro and Tongsa, were preeminent. In 1907, the head of Tongsa, Ugyen Wangchuk, became the hereditary ruler. Today's ruler, Jigme Singye Wangchuk, is the fourth in this line that has been credited with the founding of modern Bhutan.

Through various treaties negotiated between 1774 and 1910, first the East India Company and then the British government exercised the right to guide Bhutan's external relations while refraining from interfering with its internal administration. From the British, the Bhutanese also received a yearly subsidy. On gaining independence from Britain in 1949, the Government of India signed a similar treaty with Bhutan. In 1969, at the recommendation of King Jigme Dorji Wangchuk, the absolute monarchy of Bhutan was changed to a form of "democratic monarchy" that continues today. The National Assembly, with 151 members, meets twice a year. The majority of its representatives are elected from the population at large; the remaining members are either elected by Bhutan's regional religious bodies or are high government officials. In 1971, Bhutan became a member of the United Nations.

From Tropical Plants to Alpine Flowers

Bhutan's 18 districts stretch from the lowland terrain to northern mountain peaks reaching 24,000 feet. Its vegetation, growing in fertile valleys fed by streams and rivers of melted snow or on hillsides, reflects this dramatic rise in altitude and the resultant variations in climate. At different altitudes are mango, banana, and orange groves; rice paddies and fields of maize and wheat; oak, blue spruce, hemlock, and cypress forests filled with orchids and rhododendrons; and, high above all, tiny alpine flowers. Yaks, goatlike blue sheep, Himalayan bears, snow leopards, elephants, bison, rhinoceroses, deer, and golden langur monkeys populate the various terrains.

It is an enchanting and enchanted land, this land of the Drupkas, the thunder people. Men wear *khos,* knee-length robes; women wear *kiras,* ankle-length dresses; and the many Buddhist monks wear dark red robes. During festivals, costumed men in ancient masks reenact old battles between good and evil, imparting the lessons of old legends to all those who attend.

Throughout the country are strange, fairy-tale-like castles, the massive Bhutanese *dzongs,* which were built as centers of defense. Large enough to hold hundreds or even thousands of people, these square structures, constructed without nails, were built in conformity with their surroundings. Whether erected in strategic sites at the confluence of rivers or rising from mountainsides, these dzongs helped fend off repeated attacks by Tibetans and other aggressors. Inside, they contained monasteries and administrative offices, and many continue to be used in this fashion. Scattered throughout Bhutan are also *lhakhangs,* Buddhist temples, whose peaceful, darkened interiors are filled with dramatic religious artwork and sculpture. Many of these temples, as well as some monasteries, have been built at the sites of caves where holy men are reported to have performed a variety of pious acts, thus making the ground blessed.

The Himalayan mountain range provided Bhutan with a natural barrier to keep outside influences at bay for centuries. Modernization is now coming to Bhutan. New roads are making increasing portions of the country accessible, small private-sector industries are growing, as is tourism, with the infrastructure that supports it (although only 2,000 foreigners were allowed entry in 1986). But with a government whose five-year-plan for 1987–1992 lists the "preservation and promotion of the national identity and cultural heritage" as a top goal, one can expect that Bhutan will continue to preserve the rich culture that is its heritage.

PRACTICAL INFORMATION FOR BHUTAN

WHEN TO GO. The best times to visit Bhutan are March–June or September – November. No matter what the season, the evenings are generally cool. Because the weather is always subject to dramatic changes in temperature from day to night and at different altitudes, layered clothing is recommended to accommodate the variance in temperatures.

PERMITS. Applications for visas must be made at least six weeks in advance. The main office for processing applications is the *Bhutan Travel Corporation,* Royal Government of Bhutan, Box 159, Thimphu, Bhutan. In India, applications may be sent to *Bhutan Travel Service,* c/o The Royal Bhutanese Embassy, Chandragupta Marg, Chanakyapuri, New Delhi 110 021, or *Druk Air Corporation,* 51 Tivoli Court, 1A Ballygunj Court, Circular Road, Calcutta. Visa applications are sent to those who have made reservations for a tour of Bhutan.

One photograph is required, and a $20 fee is charged for the visa at the point of entry into the country.

HOW TO GET THERE. Visitors to Bhutan must enter **by air** on the national airline, *Druk Air,* which operates Dornier propeller planes that fly into Paro, Bhutan, from Calcutta, India, every Friday, and Dhaka, Bangladesh, Thursdays and Sundays. It is anticipated that by 1989 there will be flights to Paro from Delhi, India.

USEFUL ADDRESSES. *Bhutan Tourism Corporation,* Box 159, Thimphu, Bhutan; tel. 2647; cable BTC THIMPHU. telex 31–62377 SARC IN.

Bhutan Travel Inc., 120 East 56th St., Suite 1430, New York, NY 10022; tel. 212–838–6382; telex 220–896 BTS UR.

Bhutan Travel Service, Calcutta, India; tel. 57–3776.

Bhutan Travel Service, c/o The Royal Bhutanese Embassy, Chandragupta Marg, Chanakyapuri, New Delhi 110 021, India; tel. 609112; telex 31–62263 Druk-in.

Druk Air Corporation, 51 Tivoli Court, 1A, Ballygunj Circular Road, Calcutta 700 019, India; tel. 434419 or 574876.

The Royal Bhutanese Embassy, House No. 58, Road No. 3A, Dhanmondi R.A., Dhaka, Bangladesh; tel. 505418.

ACCOMMODATIONS AND DINING. Although there are a growing number of privately owned hotels in Bhutan, such as the Welcomgroup of India's **Hotel Druk** in Phuntsholing, tours coming here generally use one of the following: the **Olathang Hotel** in Paro, the **Kharbandi Hotel** in Phuntsholing, and either the **Motithang Hotel** or the **Bhutan Hotel** in Thimphu. These hotels are built in the traditional Bhutanese style and are decorated with art of the country. Meals are included in the price of a tour and are eaten in whichever hotel one happens to stay, although some good restaurants are opening up in the private hotels. Buffets are frequently served and include vegetables, rice and noodle dishes, and chicken, mutton, and pork dishes. Fresh and canned fruits from Bhutan's orchards are available.

Hotel bars are stocked with Western liquors, as well as Bhutanese and Indian beers, rums, and whiskeys. There are no "dry" days here.

TOURS. Open to tourists in 1974 under carefully regulated conditions, visitors to Bhutan must be included in a **tour** to enter the country. Travel arrangements within Bhutan are organized through tour operators and therefore are part of the tour package. You can arrange to stay on after a tour, to see more of the area covered by the tour, or, with special permission, to visit Central Bhutan. The cost of such an extended stay in mid-1987 was $170 per day inclusive of hotel, food, car, driver, and guide. You cannot travel unescorted.

Although tours are usually taken by minibus or car, you might find yourself using an unusual variety of transport such as horse, yak, or shanksmare, depending on the tour. If you prefer to set your own pace, you can hire a car and driver for $40 per day during your participation in a tour, but you are expected to follow the tour group's itinerary for the day. For information on tour operators who offer trips to Bhutan, including those who arrange treks, contact the *Bhutan Travel Service* (see the "Useful Addresses" section). Many tour operators listed in *Facts at Your Fingertips* also offer tours and treks to Bhutan.

The Bhutan Travel Service organizes a seven-day tour, the "Journey to Druk Yul," which originates in Dhaka, Bangladesh, twice a week (cost, $1,150 in mid-1987). Visitors generally fly into Paro from Dhaka or Calcutta on Bhutan's national airline, Druk Air, aboard a twin-engine propeller Dornier plane, although some tours come in overland from Bagdogra, arriving first in Phuntsholing. It is expected that by 1988 there will also be flights from Delhi, India, to Paro.

FESTIVALS AND FOLK DANCING. Buddhism is at the heart of festivals in Bhutan, which generally occur in the spring and fall, with **April** and **October** offering the largest number and the most spectacular of the festivals. Some tours are regularly organized around these festival times, especially those to Paro during its spring festival and to Thimphu and Central Bhutan during the fall.

Bhutanese festivals often go on for days, with celebrations including dance, song, and sporting events. Masked dancers, richly attired, act out parts of ancient Buddhist religious myths and legends. Hero dancers symbolically slash through the ignorance of the world with their swords, jesters work the crowds to teach onlookers the role of humor in everyday life, and somber cemetery dancers reminder all of the temporal nature of this life. During intervals between these energetic dances, which are performed by men, women sing old songs while dancing quieter round dances. No matter how large or small, every festival includes an archery competition, reminding you that at one time Bhutanese warriors were acclaimed as the best archers in the Himalayas.

Folk dancing performances are included in many of the tours to Bhutan.

WHAT TO SEE. Unless you arrange a custom tour for six or more people, what you see in Bhutan will be determined by the itinerary of the tour you join. No matter what tour you go on, however, the spectacular beauty of this mountain kingdom will surround you, whether you choose to see city sights or join a trek (most treks also offer some amount of sightseeing). Everywhere are massive *dzongs,* Bhutan's strategically placed fortress-monasteries, which also serve as administrative centers for the government, rising from towering mountainsides or from between rushing rivers; ancient Buddhist temples, known as *lhakhangs,* with vivid religious art and traditional rites preserved by generations of red-robed monks. In late 1987, Bhutan declared the interiors of these temples off-limits to all but proven Buddhists. Other sites worthwhile are forests abounding with rhododendron, the national flower; and glacier-fed streams teeming with trout. You shouldn't leave Bhutan without seeing the mask dances in which dancers in fabulous costumes swirl to the haunting sounds of drums, cymbals, gongs, and long horns.

CENTRAL BHUTAN

The windy valley of Wandiphondrang, with its rich, lovely pasturelands, is the gateway to central and eastern Bhutan. It has a dzong perched on top of a ridge between two rivers.

Tongsa, in the Mangde River Valley, is the ancestral home of Bhutan's royal family. The *Tongsa Dzong,* considered by some to be the most impressive dzong in Bhutan, is massively built in tiers and strategically located to guard the only east-west route through Bhutan. Building began in 1543, but it wasn't completed till the seventeenth century. Its many levels encompass over 20 temples, many of which are opened to visitors, and the roofs of these temples have golden symbols over their altars. It is now a state monastery.

Bumthang is where Buddhism originated in Bhutan; therefore, Bumthang is the center of the culture and history of the country. Its monasteries, some of the earliest in Bhutan, contain Buddhist art dating back to the seventh century. *Jakar Dzong,* built in the seventeenth century and rebuilt after an earthquake and fire in the 1800s, is also here.

PARO

Paro Valley is dominated by Mount Chomolhari to the north whose glacier water feeds the Paro Chu River that flows through the fertile valley. *Rimpong Dzong,* located on a mountainside here, played a critical part in repulsing Tibetan incursions. It now houses the Paro monastic body and administrative offices. *Ta Dzong,* once a watchtower used in the defense of Rimpong Dzong, is now the location of the National Museum.

At *Paro Dzong, Paro Tsechu,* one of the two largest festivals in Bhutan, is celebrated in the spring. This festival is now open only to group travelers. Those who are fortunate enough to attend this celebration will be astounded by the size and beauty of the Thongdel, a huge *tanka* (cloth painting) depicting Guru Rimpoche and two celestial attendants, which is exhibited beginning at dawn on the last day of the festival. Made by monks, it is appliqued in silk with gold threads and is truly a national treasure. Many times the height of a person, it fills a huge wall of the dzong when displayed, and it takes the monks hours to unfurl it and then carefully roll it up at the end of the celebration.

Taktsang Monastery (or Tiger's Nest), a cluster of gravity-defying structures that cling to a cliff 3,000 feet above the Paro Valley, and, therefore, is at an elevation of 9,840 feet, is one of the most dramatic monasteries in Bhutan. The monastery was built around a cave where Padmasambhava, better known as Guru Rimpoche, the "Precious Teacher," is believed to have landed, having come from Tibet on the back of a tigress. It was founded in the eighth century, originally as a convent. Kyichu Lhakhang, built sometime during seventh century, is a sacred monastery and one of most revered in Bhutan.

PUNAKHA

Temperate, with mango and banana groves and orange orchards, Punakha is home to the head lama and 500 red-robed monks in winter. *Punakha Dzong,* built in 1637, houses several temples and sits majestically overlooking the confluence of the Pho Chu and Mo Chu rivers. Also in Punakha is *Machhin Lhakhang,* where the embalmed body of Shabdrung Nawang Namgyel is enshrined, with rites conducted today in the same manner as they were in his time.

THIMPHU

Now the capital and center of government, religion, and commerce, Thimphu lies at an elevation of 7,500 feet in the Wangchu River valley. The *Memorial Chorten,* located centrally, is dedicated to the previous king, Jigme Dorji Wangchuck. Shaped in the style of a traditional *chorten* (shrine), it contains paintings and sculptures. Over 300 years after its erection in 1641 by Bhutan's first leader, Shabdrung Nawang Namgyel, *Tashichhodzong,* the seat of Bhutan's government, was rebuilt in 1961 by Jigme Dorji Wangchuk, the father of modern Bhutan. The largest structure in all Bhutan, Tashichhodzong houses the country's various government ministries, the National Assembly, and the office of the reigning monarch. Its walls bear intricate religious paintings and sculpture that illustrate the tenets of the Buddhist faith. It is also home to the central body of monks during summer months. The yearly *Thimphu Tsechu* (festival) is celebrated in the courtyard in front of the Assembly Hall. *Simthokha Dzong,* the model for all Bhutanese dzongs, was the earliest fortress-monastery, built in 1627 by Shabdrung Nawang Namgyel. Today it serves as a center for the Dzongha language and religious study.

BEHAVIOR. The farthest east that visitors can travel in Bhutan is to Mongar and Lhuntsi. There are a few other restrictions to keep in mind. Throughout Bhutan, you must not wear shoes in temples. Some temples are off-limits to visitors, and in others women are prohibited from entering certain rooms. Still photography is permitted in most areas, but you are not allowed to photograph religious images. Unless you have permission, motion picture photography is not permitted. Consult the Bhutan Travel Service before going or with your guide while in Bhutan. Tipping is prohibited in Bhutan.

MUSEUMS. Located high on a cliff above the Paro Valley is *Ta Dzong,* Bhutan's national museum. Once a lookout post for the defense of Rimpung Dzong against Tibetan aggressors, Ta Dzong was turned into a museum in 1967. Ornately embroidered tankas are a highlight of the collection, which also includes religious masks, ornaments, and other examples of the rich artistic heritage of Bhutan.

 SPORTS. Archery is the national sport, and almost every village has an archery range. Archery competitions, a vital part of every village festival, feature archers who attempt to hit a small target from 450 feet.

Trekking. The jutting peaks of the Himalayas may be inaccessible to most, but for the hardy and physically fit, Bhutan offers a range of treks that explore some of them. Treks can be arranged for groups of six or more; each group is provided with an experienced guide, a cook, assistants, pack animals, and all the necessary equipment except for sleeping bags, water bottles, and whatever is needed in one's day pack. The treks vary in length and difficulty, from the four-day Samtengan trek that includes a gradual climb through pine forests and villages, to the more strenuous 16-day Lingshi, Laya, and Gasa trek. Trekking from the wilderness areas of Soi and Lingshi, you hike to the home of the yak-herding Layas, a people whose reclusive nature and distinctive dress and customs set them apart from other Bhutanese. Laya women are especially distinctive, wearing petite conical-shaped bamboo hats over their long hair (other Bhutanese women keep their hair short). After a respite at the Gasa hot springs, this challenging trek terminates in Gasa's beautiful, thick forests. Many of these treks include some sightseeing.

Mountaineering. Access to the daunting mountain peaks, rising to 24,000 feet, is strictly controlled. Interested parties should apply one year in advance to Manager—Mountaineering, *Bhutan Travel Corporation,* Box 159, Thimphu, Bhutan. Peaks that are open to mountaineers are Mounts Jitchu Drake, Masagang, Namsela, and Kanglum.

River running. With its abundance of beautiful snow-fed rivers and streams, Bhutan could well evolve into a prime spot for river rafting in the next few years, although at present, there are no facilities for it. Check with the Bhutan Travel Corporation for developments in this area.

 SHOPPING. Traditional crafts of Bhutan are sold in Thimphu at the *Handicraft Emporium.* Exquisite textiles, baskets, carvings, and metalwork—many fashioned in the same manner as they have been for centuries—are to be found here. In Thimphu, visit the *Sunday Market* to enjoy the energy and color of a market day in Bhutan. Paro also has a bazaar area. You are not allowed to take antiquities out of the country, and items appearing to be old must have a certificate from the Department of Antiquities Preservation indicating that they are not antiques. If you shop in the Handicrafts Emporium, such items will come with the necessary certificates. Shops are open 8 A.M.–8 P.M., including Sundays.

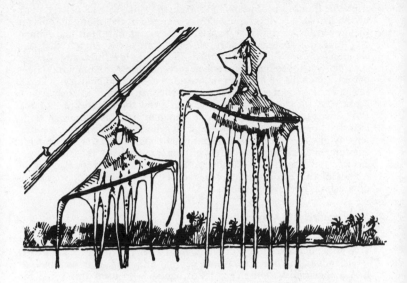

ANDAMAN AND NICOBAR ISLANDS

Vacation Retreats in the Making

by
LISA SAMSON and AMIT SHAH

One descends from the heavens to Port Blair, Andaman Islands, like the monkey god, Hanuman, is believed to have done in his valiant quest to rescue Sita, the lovely wife of Rama. The *Ramayana's* most mischievous character, Hanuman is said to have used these exquisitely beautiful tropical islands as his bridge to Lanka, and his name has been lent to the Andaman Islands (from *Handuman*), the larger island group of this Union Territory. Only his pressing task of rescuing Sita can explain why this fun-loving, self-indulgent god didn't linger here, enjoying the invigorating sea breezes, the vast tracts of dense forests, and the stunning marine life found in coral beds that surround many of these islands. The modern-day traveler to India, having no such epic responsibilities, would do well to stay here for a time to explore the natural beauty and historical sights of these islands.

The Andaman and Nicobar Islands form the peaks of a submarine mountain range that stretches for hundreds of miles into the Bay of Bengal, separating it from the Andaman Sea. Rising out of shimmering turquoise waters speckled a darker blue, where coral beds spread out from white sandy beaches, these islands hold the promise of evolving into one of India's most beautiful, relaxing vacation spots in the next decade. The islands, inaccessible to all but the indigenous aboriginal tribes for thousands of years and then used primarily as a penal colony by the British, are developing slowly. At present the changing policies that govern accessibility to the islands by foreign nationals place much of the islands' natural beauty off-limits, but not so much that one shouldn't go now, before aspects of the fragile loveliness are altered.

Ptolemy, the Roman geographer, recorded the Andaman and Nicobar Islands in his first map of the world in the second century. I'Tsing, the Buddhist scholar, referred to the Nicobar Islands in the seventh century as the "land of naked people." And the adventurer, Marco Polo, inaccurately stated that the Andaman Islands were one large island. Though their existence has long been recorded, the reputed ferocity of some of the various aboriginal populations, the inhospitable environment, and the lack of "sweet" water on many of the islands long ensured their isolation from the rest of the world. Even today, only 38 islands of the 293 are inhabited and of these, many support only a diminishing number of tribes.

Inhabited by Aborigines

Until the 1600s, the various aboriginal tribes, which date back to the Paleolithic age, lived alone on the islands. Then the Mahrattas annexed the islands in the late seventeenth century and used them as a base to harass the British, Dutch, and Portuguese who used this route for trade. The British attempted to establish a settlement in the Andamans in the late 1700s, but were successful only after the Indian Mutiny in 1857, when they built a permanent penal colony at Port Blair. In the Nicobar Islands, France, Denmark, Austria, and Great Britain all had some vague rights at various periods from the seventeenth century onward.

The Danes in particular were tenacious in their attempts to occupy the islands until they relinquished them to the British in 1869. The Japanese were in control of the Andaman and Nicobar Islands from 1942 till 1945. They allowed Subhas Chandra Bose, the Indian nationalist who formed the Indian National Army (INA), to fly the Indian tricolor for the first time. Bose had aligned with the Japanese to fight for Indian independence, but his group fell afoul of Japanese territorial ambitions, and the INA had a short-lived tenure at Port Blair. From the time the islands were liberated by the Allies until Indian independence in 1947, they were again controlled by the British.

Once a Penal Colony

Arriving today in Port Blair, the capital, one finds it difficult to comprehend the sense of dread felt by the political activists and criminals who were deported here when the British used it as a penal colony. Known by them as Kala Pani or "Black Waters," there is little now to indicate the brutalizing punishment that was meted out to these prisoners except what can be seen at the Cellular Jail, now a national museum, whose stark simplicity testifies to those bleak times.

Today Port Blair, a relatively modern town for India, is the only metropolitan locale on this island chain that is accessible to foreign tourists. Its population consists primarily of Tamils, Assamese, Bengalis, Burmese, and Malays, many of whom count as their ancestors those prisoners who were once deported here.

India's history since independence is also uniquely etched into the demographics of the Andamans because displaced persons from East Bengal, evacuees from Burma, Indian emigrants from the former British Guiana, and, more recently, refugees from Bangladesh (formerly East Pakistan) have been relocated here. What growth has occurred in population over the past decades has done so largely through emigration, not from an increase in the aboriginal population.

Tribal Reserve Areas

The inaccessibility of the tribal population, preserved for thousands of years by their unwillingness to have contact with others, is now preserved by the Indian government under the Protection of Aboriginal Tribes regulations. Of the islands' six tribes, five are confined to their traditional habitation areas, which have been set aside by the government as "Special Primitive Tribal Reserve Areas." Contact with any of the tribes is completely restricted by the government, even to ethnologists.

In February 1987, a more remote tribal group with whom a government-sponsored party of local officials, sociologists, and anthropologists were trying to make contact, rebuffed the attempt by firing arrows with poison tips at the boat bearing the party. The existence of these ancient peoples, some of whom exist exactly as they did in the Stone Age, is an intriguing and provocative fact, but, in general, the closest you can come to their culture is a visit to the small but informative Anthropology Museum in Port Blair. Here you can learn of the Andamanese, Onges, Jarawas, and Sentinelese, who are the five Negrito tribes of the Andamans, and the Mongoloid tribes of the Nicobars, the Nicobarese and the Shompens.

As is true of much of what is accessible to tourists in these islands, you can get only a glimpse of the treasures that are here, but that glimpse alone is fascinating and haunting.

Few Islands Accessible

If you come to the Andaman and Nicobar Islands expecting to see the spectacular natural beauty particular to such isolated, undeveloped tropical islands, you will not be disappointed as long as you get out of Port Blair. In Port Blair, you don't expect to find the unusual, curious collection of museums and tourist sights that are there. Although few of the hundreds of islands are accessible to foreign tourists, those that are offer some of the world's most spectacular coral reefs, guaranteed to dazzle and enchant even experienced divers. Here are the colors you dream of spread out in warm, clear waters. The rich variety of marine life, from the vibrantly colored parrot fish to the shy seahorse, is mesmerizing. As schools of fish dart and glide through a background of intensely colored coral, you will understand the stories of divers who, becoming enraptured with such beauties, fail to remember their limited oxygen supply.

To experience the marine beauties of the islands, you must put up with some frustration at the limits placed on travel here. However, measured against the possibility of upsetting the fragile ecology of these islands in a rush to develop them too quickly, these are frustrations that you must take in your stride. Currently, only day trips are permitted to the islands; because of the time it takes to get to them, you have only a few hours to explore the reefs. But with the vivid colors and intriguing shapes and the sometimes amusing, sometimes compelling, activity of the myriad marine animals you see, the few hours spent here will yield a surplus of memorable images on which you will reflect long after you return to the mainland.

Other water sports, such as windsurfing and sailing, can be enjoyed in the Andamans. They are all arranged through the larger hotels, since there is little evidence of a tourist industry here other than these hotels.

Cellular Jail

Sightseeing in the Andamans, though limited, offers some interesting finds. The primary attraction is the Cellular Jail, where thousands of men and women who fought for independence were interred, some of them for years, in tiny, spartan, isolated cells. Built by the British, it was completed in 1906 and part of it is still in use until the new local jail is completed.

Looking down from the central guard tower into the current prisoners' garden or walking through the grounds alongside some of the elderly Freedom Fighters who occasionally come back to visit, one senses how contemporary is this part of India's history, compared to what one sees on the mainland. Of the original seven wings of the jail, only three remain, the others having been destroyed in 1943 by an earthquake. A number of small museums are worth visiting for the information on the islands that they provide. In addition to the Anthropological Museum, there are the Marine and Forest Museums.

Rare Beauties Protected

The Andaman Islands are not the bustling, glamorous "resort" vacation spot that Thailand's Phuket is fast becoming. Rather, they are a peaceful vacation spot that offers outdoor activities associated with beach resorts but with restrictions to protect their rare beauty. At times, one wonders if the tourist is really here to stay or if, like the early Danes and British who came to colonize the islands, tourists will ultimately give up and leave the local population to enjoy this bit of paradise without further outside influence.

The fact that these islands aren't yet a developed tourist haven adds a great deal to their charm but is also the source of some irritation. The government has plans to expand the tourist facilities and is considering a variety of recommendations to take greater advantage of the islands' richness of botanical and marine life. Right now, however, tourists are set down in an environment that is uncluttered with the amenities of other island resorts. Although the hotel staffs are solicitous of your needs, you have a refreshing if frustrating feeling that to the rest of the islanders you just don't matter much. The sleepy, soothing atmosphere makes it a reviving spot to come to after the more boisterous encounters you have had on the mainland.

PRACTICAL INFORMATION FOR

ANDAMAN AND NICOBAR ISLANDS

 FACTS AND FIGURES. Different sources provide different information on the Andaman and Nicobar Islands. In fact, one government official, when asked to explain why a government tourist publication stated that there were 293 islands in the group while a bulletin board in the same office gave the number as 306, responded that it all depended on what one defined as an island. Whichever figure you accept, these idyllic islands are scattered over about 500 miles in the Bay of Bengal in two groups that run north-south. The Andaman Islands lie to the north and the Nicobar Islands are to the south; in between is the 90-mile-wide Ten Degree Channel. Port Blair, the capital city, on South Andaman Island, is 778 miles from Calcutta, 738 miles from Madras, and 744 miles from Vizag. The southernmost tip of the chain, the Great Nicobar Island, is only about 90 miles from Sumatra in Indonesia.

Covering almost seven-eighths of the approximately 5,100-square-mile area of the Andaman and Nicobar Islands are lush rain forests, thick with unusual and sometimes rare evergreen deciduous and tropical trees and plants. These dense forests are divided into "protected" areas (60 percent), which are worked for lumber (one of the islands' primary exports) and "reserved" areas (40 percent), which were set aside as tribal land by the government's Protection of Aboriginal Tribes regulations.

Only 26 islands in the Andamans and 12 islands in the Nicobars are inhabited. The population of 223,000 (the government's approximate 1986 figure) is concentrated on the Andamans, primarily around Port Blair. The population of the Nicobars, according to the most recent official census taken in 1981, numbered 30,500, including about 22,200 Nicobarese and Shompen tribesmen. The islands' total tribal population makes up 10–20 percent of the population. Because many of these primitive tribes still shun contact with outsiders, exact numbers are difficult to determine.

 WHEN TO GO. The climate in the Andaman and Nicobar Islands is tropical and temperate with temperatures varying between 62° and 86°F throughout the year. Constant sea breezes bring relief even during hot spells. The relative humidity is 75 percent, and the annual rainfall, which is about 120 inches, is spread evenly over eight months, from mid-May to mid-September during the South Western monsoons, and from early November to mid-December during the North-Eastern monsoons. The ideal time for vacationing here is mid-December–mid-May, when conditions are optimum for enjoying water sports and the islands' natural beauty. Because of the lack of large seagoing boats, mid-February–mid-May is best if you want to include a trip to Cinque Island. During these months, the seas are usually calmer, which makes it possible for smaller boats to ply the waters. The local authorities are considering plans to import some larger boats, which would make Cinque accessible for a longer period. They hope to implement these plans in 1988.

 PERMITS. Foreign tourists who wish to visit the Port Blair Municipal area and the islands of Jolly Boy and Cinque are not required to get permission from the Government of India before they arrive in Port Blair, provided they stay no more than 15 days. However, you will need to get a 15-day permit when you arrive. Because there is no counter for the government official who is responsible for filling out these permits, you should ask for the airport duty officer. If you can't locate this official while you wait for your luggage to be unloaded at the edge of the runway, walk up the hill to your left to the *Departure Building* and go through the breezeway and around front to your left. A guard at the entrance to the Departure Building may stop you, but persist in your inquiries until someone comes forward who can help. Don't be tempted to forgo this formality, despite the time it takes to locate the proper authority, because your entry into Port Blair will be stamped into your passport and will be checked on your departure. This permit is also obtainable in Delhi at the Ministry of Home Affairs and in Calcutta at the Writers' Building. However, we recommend that you get it in Port Blair to avoid the frequently long lines at offices in these two major cities.

Regulations governing access to other areas in the Andaman and Nicobar Islands are revised with some regularity. As of this writing (mid-1987), the 15-day permit from the Port Blair officials allows you to stay in the Port Blair municipal area and to go on day trips to Jolly Boy and Cinque Islands. Foreign nationals are not allowed to visit the Nicobar Islands or the "Special Primitive Tribal Reserve Areas." Groups of six–20 tourists may obtain permission, through the Immigration Department in Port Blair, for day trips to the Grub, Snob, Redskin, and Boat islands.

You may apply for permission to stay in the Andaman and Nicobar Islands for longer than 15 days or to visit other areas (excluding the restricted tribal areas) in Great and Little Andamans by writing to the Director, *Ministry of Home Affairs* (ANL Division), Government of India, North Block, Second Floor, New Delhi 110 001.

HOW TO GET THERE. By Air. *Indian Airlines* operates 737 jet service to Port Blair from Calcutta on Tuesdays, Thursdays, and Saturdays. This early-morning flight (6:20 A.M.) returns to Calcutta (9 A.M.). There is also a Monday flight from Calcutta to Car Nicobar via Port Blair. Madras flights to Port Blair are on Wednesdays, Fridays, and Sundays (6:20 A.M.), with return flights the same day (9:25 A.M.).

How to Get From the Airport. When you arrive in Port Blair, airline **vans** transport you from the plane to the edge of the runway, where there is a shed, a parking lot, and not much more. After claiming your luggage and getting your permit to visit the islands (if you haven't already done so), either take the **taxi** sent by individual hotels or hire one of the private taxis in the parking lot next to the arrival shed. Depending on where you are staying, the fare to hotels should be Rs. 25–35. You'll have to do some bargaining, since taxis often do not run their meters.

By Ship. Regular sailings by passenger ships from Vizag, Madras, and Calcutta take approximately three days. The Deluxe Cabin Class costs about Rs. 600 (U.S. $46). Food is not included in the fare. Information can be obtained from the *Shipping Corporation of India,* 13 Strand Rd., Calcutta 700–001, tel. 232354, telex 021–7311; 245 Madame Cama Rd., Bombay 400–021; tel. 202–666, telex 011–237; M/s K.P.V. Shanik Mohammed Rowther and Company (agent of the Shipping Corporation of India), 202 Linghi Chetty St., Madras 600–001, tel. 510–346, telex 041–200; and M/s A.V. Bhanejiraw & Burud Pattabiramayva and Company, Box 17. Vishakapatnam 530–035, tel. 62661, 65584, 65597, telex VMO495 210.

Officials in Port Blair state that Indian Airlines is considering a proposal that would make Port Blair more accessible from other ports in India. Specifically, it is possible that there will be Delhi–Bhubaneswar–Port Blair and Madras–Port Blair–Nicobar car service in 1988.

ACCOMMODATIONS. Since traveling to the Nicobar Islands is still restricted, your stay must be prearranged when you apply for a permit. The Andaman Islands, however, have some lovely places to stay—most with modern Western amenities and accoutrements. Even Indian-style hotels have a charming, relaxed atmosphere. For price ranges of categories listed here, see *Facts at Your Fingertips.*

Deluxe

Andaman Beach Resort. Corbyn's Cove, Port Blair, Andaman Islands 744 101; tel. 2599 or 2781. Run by the Travel Corporation of India (TCI), it is the pioneer of the resort hotels in the Andamans. (TCI also offers inclusive tours to the Andamans.) This resort's charming, relaxed facilities include 32 double rooms, banquet and conference facilities for 100, and a lounge/game room. Equipment for snorkeling, scuba diving, windsurfing, fishing, and other water sports is available. The beautifully maintained gardens are just one indication of the care that the management takes of this hotel.

Asiana Hotel. South Point, Port Blair, Andaman Islands 744 101; tel. 2937. The newest resort hotel on the Andamans. Open for business in 1986 though not yet completed. It sits high over the sea, halfway between Corbyn's Cove and Marine Hill.

Bay Island Hotel. Marine Hill, Port Blair, Andaman Islands 744 101; tel. 2881. WelcomGroup's lovely resort hotel has 40 comfortable rooms. Designed by Charles Correa, one of India's foremost architects, the hotel is built on a steep hill directly overlooking Ross Island and looks like a cluster of tribal huts. Open breezeways connect buildings containing rooms with the central building that houses the lobby, a bar, and a restaurant. Most rooms have balconies with a view of the sea. The bar and restaurant are open-air and offer spectacular wide-angled views of the sea. A dip in the seawater swimming pool, nestled at the bottom of the hill on which the hotel is built, is a refreshing way to end a day of sightseeing. Though the hotel doesn't have its own water sports equipment, the travel desk can arrange for snorkeling equipment.

Moderate

Megapode Nest and **Nicobarese Cottages.** Located in Haddo, Port Blair, both are medium-priced accommodations that have some air-conditioned rooms.

Inexpensive

One of the inexpensive, government-run accommodations, the **Corbyn's Cove Guest House** has the loveliest location on a hill overlooking the cove. Two of the others are located in Haddo, **Guest House Number 1,** and **Tourist Home,** and one is on Marine Hill, **Tourist Home.**

For reservations for the Corbyn's Cove Guest House, Megapode Nest, Nicobarese Cottages, and the Tourist Homes, write to Deputy Director (Tourism), Secretariat, Andaman and Nicobar Administration, Port Blair, Andaman Islands 744 101. Reservations for Guest House Number 1 are made through the Executive Engineer, North Division, Port Blair, Andaman Islands 744 101.

There is also a **youth hostel** for students. For reservations, contact Warden, Youth Hostel, Port Blair 744 101.

DINING OUT. All restaurants in Port Blair are part of the hotels, and they combine Indian, Chinese, Continental, and Burmese cuisines. Buffets are common for lunch and dinner. Because most food and drink is flown in from Calcutta and Madras, the prices are higher and fresh fruits are not always available.

USEFUL ADDRESSES. *Government of India Tourist Office,* Middle Point, Port Blair, Andaman Islands 744 101; tel. 3006.

Tourist Information Center, Tourist Home; tel. 2380.

Indian Airlines Office, G–55, Middle Point, Port Blair, Andaman Islands 744 101; telephone booking: 2205.

Island Travels, Aberdeen Bazaar; tel. 3034.

HOW TO GET AROUND. The easiest and fastest way to travel is to hire a **car** and driver through a travel agency (inquire at your hotel desk) for Rs. 25/hour (about U.S. $2). A full day runs Rs. 250. Also, your hotel desk can contact the **taxi** stand in Port Blair, which operates daily until 8 P.M. **Bicycles** may be rented as well. Bicycling is a leisurely way of exploring, but it is recommended only to those who are in good physical shape, since Port Blair and its immediate surroundings are hilly. Inexpensive conducted **bus tours** that take in the sights of Port Blair and include a trip to Corbyn's Cove are offered through the *Department of Information, Publicity and Tourism.* Contact the Public Relations Officer (tel. 2596) at the Commissioner's Secretariat, or the *Tourist Information Center* (tel. 2380) for reservations.

WHAT TO SEE AND DO. Because foreign travelers are not permitted to visit the Nicobar Island group, the following information concerns the Andaman Islands only.

The primary interest of travelers to these islands is to see the fabulous natural beauty that abounds and to enjoy a beach holiday in a largely undeveloped, relaxing environment. The **coral beds** throughout the islands support some of the most spectacular underwater marine life to be seen anywhere in the world, and the multihued waters in which they are found are astonishingly clear and bath-water warm. From close to shore you can snorkel out to where the sea floor is covered with coral. Water temperatures range from 78° F on the surface to about 60° at a depth of 130 feet. There is good visibility to 50 feet below the surface; at a depth of 80 feet, there is a visibility to about 15 feet. Whether you snorkel from the surface or skin dive, the anemones, angelfish, sweetlips, parrot and squirrel fish, brain coral, and sea fan are vividly displayed in languid waters.

Coral beds are easily accessible at *Jolly Boy* and *Cinque* islands, both of which are uninhabited islands of great beauty. Convenient day trips can be arranged through the travel desks at the larger hotels or by contacting either the *Tourist*

Information Center, Tourist Home, Haddo (tel. 2380), or *Island Travels,* Aberdeen Bazar (tel. 3034). Boats to Jolly Boy leave from Wandoor Beach for the approximately one-hour ride to the island. The fare is Rs. 50 per person, and a small fee is charged at the entrance to Wandoor Beach. The departure time can vary, although it is scheduled at 9:30 A.M. and returns 2–3 P.M. Cinque Island can be reached either from Port Blair, a trip that takes 3½ hours by boat, or from Chiriya Tapu, a two-hour trip by boat. Since these islands are so isolated, have the hotel prepare a picnic lunch or take along food from shops in Port Blair. Drinking water and other beverages should also be taken.

At the time of writing, the management of the *Andaman Beach Resort* was especially knowledgeable about the Islands' underwater attractions and was active in organizing **scuba-diving** and **snorkeling** expeditions. If this is your reason for coming to the Andamans, contact them. The information and arrangements they provide will prove invaluable.

Although some snorkeling equipment is available through hotels and Island Travels, we recommend you bring at least a well-fitting mask and snorkel. The much-advertised "glass-bottom" boat is no more than a motorized dinghy with a small plexiglass section through which passengers sitting in the middle of the boat can peer.

If **sunbathing** and **swimming** are of interest, the best spot near Port Blair is *Corbyn's Cove,* a peaceful spot at the southern end of Port Blair. The beach, like that of the other islands to which day trips are permitted, has clean white sand, gentle surf, and clear, warm waters. Ringing the crescent-shaped beach are tall palms that cast long shadows across the sands in the late afternoon. Across the road from the beach, you can enjoy a snack at the Andaman Beach Resort Hotel.

The natural beauty of the Andaman Islands has, in the past, made it a good spot for a camping beach vacation, but, as of this writing, overnight camping anywhere in the islands has been curtailed.

The Department of Information, Publicity and Tourism organizes daily **harbor cruises** that leave the Marine Jetty in Port Blair at 3 P.M. This 1½-hour sundown cruise takes you around the Port Blair harbor and out to Viper Island, where the penal settlement was located before the *Cellular Jail* was constructed. Contact the Marine Department, Port Blair (tel. 2528), or the Tourist Information Center, Tourist Home (tel. 2380), for reservations.

To enjoy their flora and fauna or to bask lazily in the sun are the main attractions of the Andaman Islands. Aside from these seaside attractions, there are some historic sights, small museums, and a few other tourist sights to explore. Dominating the island's recent history, located just north of the Aberdeen Jetty, is the *Cellular Jail,* now a national memorial to the Indian Freedom Fighters who were interred here by the British before independence (open 9 A.M.–12; 2–5 P.M., Mondays–Saturdays). Built by the British between 1886 and 1906, the original design was a seven-winged building radiating out from a central guard tower. It contained 698 small cells in which prisoners were kept in solitary confinement. Today, to the right and left of the entrance to the compound, there are galleries of photographs of many of these Freedom Fighters, grouped according to the incident for which they were imprisoned. Various prison artifacts, such as a device for holding prisoners while they were being flogged, and information regarding food rations and work responsibilities, testify to the harsh treatment meted out to these "criminals." Within the compound, you can visit the gallows and the narrow whitewashed cells on the upper floors of the unoccupied wing on your right as you enter. If you climb to the top of the central guard tower, you can see the lists of names of the Freedom Fighters inscribed in stone. You can also look out over the three remaining wings of the prison (the others were ruined in an earthquake in 1943), one of which is temporarily being used as the local jail, and out to a distant treelined shore with the sea beyond.

The *Anthropological Museum,* housed in a nondescript and somewhat run-down building in Port Blair, is a small treasure house of information on the islands' tribal peoples. Here you will find models of tribal villages, everyday tribal artifacts, and photographs of the various expeditions that have made contact or, in some cases, have not been successful in making contact, with the islands' six tribal groups. A powerful remainder of the fragility with which such groups cling to their traditional cultures are two photographs of a tribal couple, the first taken in their tribal dress, the second taken in Western dress. Publications for sale provide anthropological information on the tribes, including an impressive bibliography published by the Anthropological Survey of India, which lists all the available literature on the islands. A small research library on the second floor, rumored to be the one place in Port Blair that stays open past 8 P.M., has an extensive collection of books on the islands, as well as general books on anthropology, sociology, economics, and politics and a wide variety of current periodicals. The museum is open 9 A.M.–noon, 1–4 P.M., and is closed Saturdays and holidays.

Another museum that, though small, offers an impressive amount of information is the *Forest Museum.* Located near Chatham Saw Mill, it displays the rich variety of local woods and illustrates how each is put to use by the lumber industry. Dioramas display how old methods combine with new as elephants and bulldozers work together to transform raw logs into finished goods. Dominating the two-room museum is a large tree fashioned out of pieces of all varieties of trees, from the velvety red *padauk* to the unusual marblewood. Hours at the Forest Museum are 8:30 A.M.–4 P.M. daily.

Having seen the Forest Museum, you should next visit *Chatham Saw Mill,* the oldest and one of the largest saw mills in Asia. Informal tours are given to tourists who show up on their own. You walk through most of the buildings at the saw mill, following the process of turning huge logs into finished planks of wood. Timber is unloaded from boats coming from various places in the islands, sawed into planks on large pre-World War II band saws, trimmed and planed, and then cured in huge temperature-controlled kilns. Once seasoned, the planks are sorted by grade, arranged in towering stacks, and stored in huge warehouses while awaiting shipment to the mainland's auction markets. You are also allowed to watch artisans in cavernous workshops turning premium-grade wood into furniture. Photographs are not permitted.

Finally, a museum that provides information on life under the sea is the *Marine Museum,* near Marine Park (open 8:30 A.M.–4 P.M., closed Saturdays). Any novice diver will appreciate the museum's display of the coral that is found in the waters offshore. The muted colors of the preserved fish specimens don't prepare you for the vivid color you see when snorkeling or diving, but the variety of species of marine life on display attests to the richness of the underwater life here and can help you identify some of what you will encounter in the coral reefs. A short distance from the museum is *Marine Park,* a pleasant strip of land that runs along the sea and has modest, well-maintained topiary gardens, a pastel-colored assortment of playground equipment, and a vigorous statue of the Indian nationalist, Subhas Chandra Bose.

There are few other attractions in or around Port Blair. Some of the islands' unusual animal life, including the saltwater crocodile-rearing farm, can be seen at the *Mini Zoo* (open 7 A.M.–noon; 1–5 P.M., closed Mondays). *Sippighat Farm* (open 6 A.M.–11 A.M.; noon–4 P.M.; closed Mondays), is a government-run 80-acre demonstration farm on which spices and other cash crops are grown for propagation all over the islands. Enroute to Cinque Island, you can visit *Chiriya Tapu,* also known as Bird Island, a picturesque spot with panoramic views of the sea and the surrounding islands. It cannot be visited by foreign nationals except as part of a journey to Cinque Island. Another scenic spot is *Wandoor Beach,* where you board the boat that takes you to Jolly Boy.

Because tourism in the Andaman and Nicobar Islands is under development, policies governing access to sights outside Port Blair are constantly being reevaluated. On your arrival in Port Blair, contact the *Government of India Tourist Office,* which is helpful, or your hotel's travel desk to get the most up-to-date information. At present, the Directorate of Tourism office is able to provide only a map of Port Blair. A reputable travel service, if you don't have a travel desk at your hotel, is *Island Travels,* Aberdeen Bazaar; tel. 3034. Many tours are offered by the Tourist Information Center, Tourist Home (tel. 2380).

 SHOPPING. In Port Blair, the *Cottage Industries Emporium* (open 9 A.M.–1 P.M.; 1:30–5 P.M., closed Mondays and Fridays) has a sparse display of wood and shell items for sale in its sleepy showroom. It is advisable, therefore, to check shops near the *Aberdeen Bazaar* for these items. Although some of these places seem to carry only cheap "shell art" at first glance, you can find some beautiful shells in their natural state, such as mango shell, chambered nautilus, nancowry, spiney murex, and king shell if you poke around. Since tourism is only now becoming important to the islands' economy, local raw materials, such as the unusual varieties of woods, are rarely used in native crafts. When available, items of marblewood and padauk are beautiful and, in the case of the latter, a pleasure to touch. Hard bargaining and comparison shopping are suggested at these shops.

NEPAL

NEPAL

Reaching the Ultimate Heights

by
KARL SAMSON

Karl Samson is a free-lance travel writer and photographer whose work has been published in newspapers and magazines in the United States and in Asia. For much of the past two years, he has been traveling in Southeast Asia, Nepal, India, Ladakh, and in Europe.

Nepal, a country where myths endure and mysteries persist, is a land of striking contrasts. Bananas and papayas ripen in the warm subtropical sun not 25 miles from the glistening snowcapped peaks of the world's highest mountains. Cows, unperturbed by blaring car horns, steal vegetables from produce vendors who line the crowded, narrow streets of Kathmandu. Buddhist monks circle a *stupa* (shrine) under the all-seeing eyes of Lord Buddha, while pious Hindus line up beside an ornate temple to the goddess of smallpox, which stands only a few feet away. Throughout the country, the Middle Ages coexist with the twentieth century. It is just these contrasts that have attracted tourists since the country first opened its doors to the West in 1951.

Nepal stretches for 500 miles along the northeast border of India and is only 100 to 150 miles wide. It is bounded in the east by Sikkim and West Bengal, in the south and west by Bihar and Uttar Pradesh, and in the north by the Chinese Autonomous Region of Tibet.

Divided into three geographic regions, Nepal offers a diversity of environments from the hot, humid subtropical lowlands of the Terai to the frigid, snowbound peaks of the high Himalayas. In between these

539

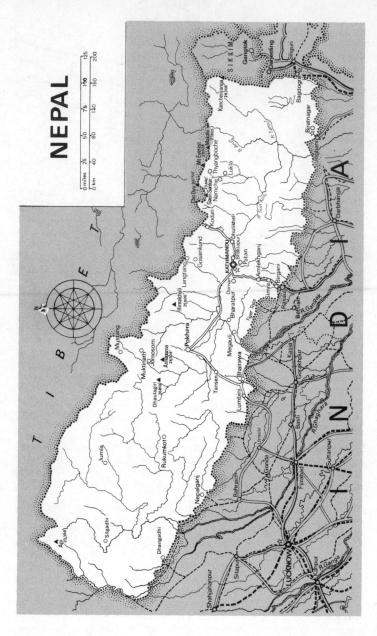

NEPAL

0 miles 25 50 75 100 125
0 km   40   80 120 160 200

two extremes lie the rolling hills and green valleys that give Nepal its image of being a true Shangri-la.

Running the entire length of Nepal like a backbone are the Himalayas, the tallest mountains in the world and some of the youngest. Mount Everest, known as Sagermatha in Nepal, towers to 29,028 feet and straddles the border with Tibet. In addition to Everest, there are more than 100 other peaks over 20,000 feet tall. Although in Nepal's capital city of Kathmandu, the Himalayas are mostly obscured by the high hills surrounding the city, many nearby locations offer spectacular views of the mountains.

The most striking aspect of the midland hills of Nepal is the endless terracing. For centuries, the farmers of this country have been building terraced fields into the steep hillsides. The country has more agricultural terraces than does any other nation in the world. It is in this temperate climate that is ideal for agriculture that most of the country's approximately 17 million people live. Nepal is primarily an agricultural country, with 93 percent of the population working the land. However, because so much of the country is mountainous, only 26 percent of the land is under cultivation. Much of that land would never be considered for agriculture in any other country, but with the extensive system of terraces, Nepal's farmers have made the most of their land and climate.

Along the southern border with India extends the Terai, Nepal's fertile rice-growing region. This low-lying region, which averages only about 250 feet above sea level, is an extension of the Indo-Gangetic plains of northeastern India. With relatively easy access to India and the best roads in Nepal, the Terai supports most of Nepal's limited industries. This region is also home to some of Asia's rarest wild animals. In Royal Chitwan National Park, live royal Bengal tigers and Indian one-horned rhinoceroses.

Just as the geography and climate of Nepal are diverse, so, too, is the ethnic makeup of the country. Each of the numerous castes and ethnic groups has its own language and style of dress and often is predominant in a specific region of the country. The Sherpas, well known for their help on mountain expeditions and found primarily in the Everest region, are primarily Buddhists and speak a Tibeto-Burman language. Other important groups include the Newars, who live mainly in the Kathmandu Valley, and the Tharus, who live in the Terai. Rais, Gurungs, Magars, Limbus, and Tamangs also make up a large part of Nepal's population.

Gurkhas, known and admired throughout the world for their valor in battle, are not of one specific ethnic group but are primarily Gurungs, Magars, Rais, and Limbus. The Gurkhas have served valiantly in the British, Indian, and Nepalese armies, distinguishing themselves in both world wars.

Since the late 1950s when the Chinese invaded Tibet, thousands of Tibetans have taken refuge in Nepal. The addition of their culture to the Nepalese lifestyle has added a new and unusual dimension to an already exotic cultural melting pot.

Many myths and legends persist in Nepal; by far the most widely known is that of the Abominable Snowman, known as the *yeti* in Nepal. The yeti has been known for centuries from records kept in Sherpa monasteries high in the mountains. However, despite numerous expeditions to search for the yeti, no one has been able to provide hard evidence of its existence. Still, the legend persists.

Nepal is also the home of living gods. The king of Nepal is considered an incarnation of the Hindu god Vishnu. It was this sacred position that prevented the king from being dethroned when the Rana prime ministers took control of the country in the mid-nineteenth century. Nepal's other living god is a young girl known as the Kumari, the virgin goddess who lives a life of isolation in a beautiful old home on Kathmandu's Durbar Square. Whenever the Kumari first bleeds, a sign that she is human after all, she is replaced by another specially chosen young girl.

With its medieval cities, colorful religions, high mountains, and sweltering lowland jungles, Nepal is a compact country of amazing diversity. Over the centuries, its mountainous geography has played an integral role in its economic, cultural, religious, and military development. Today, these many unusual contrasts are making Nepal one of the world's most interesting destinations.

A Bit of History

Although Nepal is an ancient country, its early history is inextricably bound up in the region's myth and folklore. Few historical records are available to document the legends that often refer to historical figures as well as gods and goddesses. It is known that more than 2,000 years ago, advanced cultures were living throughout the region now occupied by modern Nepal.

According to legend, the Kathmandu Valley was formed when a powerful god from China emptied the waters of the lake that once filled the valley. Modern geological exploration has determined that the Kathmandu Valley was indeed a vast lake at one time. However, the lake had drained long before humans appeared in the area. The rich soil of this ancient lake bed has accounted for the development of the valley as the cultural center of Nepal.

The earliest known inhabitants of the valley were the Ahirs, or shepherd kings, who occupied the area as long ago as the eighth century B.C. The primitive people are believed to have migrated into Nepal from northern India. The Indian epics *Ramayana* and *Mahabharata* both refer to the Kirantis, who occupied the eastern foothills of the Himalayas. Records show that the Kirantis probably moved into the valley about 700 B.C., but little is known about them.

In the Terai region west of the Kathmandu Valley, the Shakyas, a Rajput clan from northern India, had founded the city of Kapilvastu by the sixth century B.C. The beauty of this city was renowned and its culture flourished. It was here, in the city's Lumbini Gardens, that Prince Siddhartha Gautama was born in 567 B.C. The prince would later become enlightened while sitting beneath a bo tree and become known as the Buddha.

Ashoka, the emperor of India who embraced Buddhism and helped spread this religion throughout the subcontinent, visited Lumbini in 250 B.C. and erected a stone pillar. Legends contend that Ashoka continued on to the Kathmandu Valley to erect the four stupas surrounding Patan. However, there are no records to support this belief.

About A.D. 200, another powerful north Indian tribal group, the Lichhavis, began moving into Nepal. With their center of power in the Kathmandu Valley, the Lichhavis ruled until about the ninth century. Under the Lichhavis, Nepal saw its first flowering of art and architecture and became a powerful and prosperous country. The pagoda style of temple architecture developed at this time, and many temples and palaces were constructed. Unfortunately, few of these buildings have survived. However, some excellent stone carvings from this period can still be seen at Changu Narayan and other places.

Nepal's medieval period then began with the rise of the Malla dynasty, which lasted until the eighteenth century. The Malla kings were great patrons of the arts and culture. Trade, industry, architecture, and religion all flourished during this period. Most of the beautiful temples and palaces of the Kathmandu Valley were built by the Mallas.

By the middle of the fifteenth century, the powerful king Yaksha Malla had extended his domain to include parts of Tibet and India, as well as the Kathmandu Valley and much land to the east and west. However, with the death of Yaksha Malla, the power of the Mallas slowly began to wane. Having divided the valley's cities among his sons, Yaksha Malla had unknowingly set in motion the decline of the Malla dynasty. The sons and their descendants fought among themselves and slowly weakened the city-states that they had created. By the middle of the eighteenth century, these individual kingdoms were unable to unite against the advancing army of Ghorka ruler Prithvi Narayan Shah, who stormed across Nepal from the west.

Prithvi Narayan Shah, fearing an invasion by the British who had taken control of India, set out to unify the many tiny kingdoms of Nepal so that country could better defend itself against the British threat. Between 1744 and 1768, he succeeded in conquering all of Nepal's many kingdoms and, for the first time in history, Nepal was a unified country.

British India was not the only threat to Nepal. Because of trading disputes, relations with Tibet had deteriorated. When Nepal annexed part of Sikkim (then a part of Tibet) and looted several Tibetan monasteries, Tibet turned to China for help. In 1792, war broke out between Nepal and China. Nepal's small army was no match for the 70,000 Chinese troops sent to Tibet, and a treaty requiring a ransom to be paid to China every five years was eventually signed.

In 1814, border disputes along its southern border brought about a war with British India. The treaty that ended the war in 1816 gave much of the disputed land to the British, but, in 1860, most of it was returned to Nepal. Today's borders are those established in 1860.

In 1846, a bloody massacre in Kathmandu allowed the prime minister, Jung Bahadur Rana, to usurp power from the king. The king and queen fled to India, and Jung Bahadur installed the crown prince as king. Because the Nepalese believed their king to be an incarnation of the god Vishnu, Jung Bahadur maintained the monarchy but removed all its power.

The title of prime minister was made hereditary, and the Ranas ruled Nepal for the next 104 years. The period of Rana autocracy was a time of almost uninterrupted peace for Nepal. For many years, the Ranas enjoyed popularity both at home and abroad. Although Nepal was officially isolated from the rest of the world during this period, the Ranas made several trips to Europe. Jung Bahadur Rana, after visiting England, instituted many civil and military reforms. However, to maintain power, the Ranas withheld education from the people. By ignoring the public welfare of Nepal, these despostic rulers amassed substantial fortunes and reduced the country to an impoverished condition.

Eventually, infighting among Rana family members and pressure from a newly independent India began to take its toll on the prime ministers. Public support in Nepal waned as unemployment and food prices rose. The inefficient government of the Ranas had brought itself to the brink of revolution.

In November 1950, King Tribhuvan took refuge in the Indian Embassy and was later flown to Delhi. Mohan Shumsher, ruling prime minister at the time, installed the king's grandson as the new king. Despite the support that Ranas had received from other nations, no country was willing to fight against the wishes of India in this situation, and India refused to recognize the new king.

Nepalese in India and at home began an open revolt against the Rana government. Protests in Kathmandu and attacks along the border by insurgents based in India quickly undermined the government. In February 1951, King Tribhuvan returned to Nepal, and more than a century of Rana rule officially came to an end.

Nepal Today

During the more than a century when the Ranas exploited Nepal and its people for their personal gains, little thought was given to developing the country. Political isolationism had left Nepal with few international relations. When King Tribhuvan regained power, he was faced with the immense task of creating a new system of government, solving the country's many economic problems, and opening relations with the rest of the world. Even now, nearly 40 years later, the country is still struggling with many of the same dilemmas.

King Tribhuvan died in 1955, the year Nepal joined the United Nations, and his son, Mahendra, ascended to the throne. In 1975, King Mahendra's son, who had been educated in England, the United States, and Japan, became King Birendra Bir Bikram Shah Dev. As the current ruling monarch of this independent kingdom, he wields nearly absolute power in matters of state. He is supported by a partyless political system based on the Panchayat, or village council, that is ostensibly a democratic form of government. However, dissatisfaction and frustration with the ineffective Panchayat system has led the people to demand a more representative and democratic form of government.

A landlocked country, Nepal has for years acted as a buffer between its two large and powerful neighbors, India and China, both of which have sought to influence Nepal's government for their own benefit. However, Nepal has managed to maintain good relations with both countries for some time. With the hope of preserving peace in the region and continuing good relations with both neighbors, King Birendra, on his coronation, proposed that Nepal be declared a zone of peace. In his address calling for the zone of peace, King Birendra stated, "We need peace for security, we need peace for independence and we need peace for development. . . . We believe that only under a condition of peace will we be able to create a politically stable Nepal with a sound economy." This proposal, which adheres to a policy of nonalignment, has been supported by more than 73 countries.

It was not until 1951 that Nepal began to take serious notice of the outside world. Before then, it had diplomatic relations with only four countries. After Nepal opened its doors to the Western world, it was still quite a few years before many people other than mountain climbers visited the country. It took the construction of Kathmandu's international airport and the beginning of flights from Bangkok in 1968 to open the eyes of tourists to this unique Himalayan kingdom. Since 1968, tourism has become the country's single largest source of foreign exchange. This relatively rapid escalation of tourism in a country that had been shut off from the rest of the world has had a huge impact on the culture of Nepal. However, the effects are still confined mainly to Kathmandu and the country's few other tourist destinations. Outside these areas, life goes on much as it has for hundreds of years.

It is this unchanging lifestyle that presents Nepal with many of its economic problems. The same rugged mountains that allowed many small independent kingdoms to develop over the years have inhibited economic development. The lack of communication within the country is one of the greatest problems facing Nepal today.

There are only 3,500 miles of roads in Nepal, and these are not always passable. Nepal's population of 16 million people is evenly distributed over much of the land, and many of these people still live far from the nearest road. About 40 small airstrips have now been opened throughout the country to provide many isolated regions with a direct link to Kathmandu. Still, much of the country remains remote and inaccessible.

Because so much of the population is inaccessible, the government has a difficult time providing the people with even the most basic services, such as medical facilities. In Nepal, there is only one doctor for every 32,000 people. Consequently, infant mortality is high and life expectancy is short, about 50 years. Poor hygiene and unsanitary housing conditions are responsible for the spread of many infectious diseases. Only a small percentage of the population has access to piped drinking water, and gastrointestinal illnesses are rampant. Inadequate food supplies and illiteracy compound the health problems. Ignorant of medical treatment, people often do not seek help for health problems. Malnutrition is chronic, especially among children, who make up nearly half of the country's population.

Despite the country's many health problems, the population continues to grow at an annual rate of 2.6 percent. In parts of the Terai region, the annual growth rate is nearly six percent. With 94 percent of the population working in agriculture, the land is approaching the limits of its abilities to provide food and employment. In the higher regions of the Himalayas, there are already annual food shortages, and many of the region's people are forced to migrate to the lowlands for the winter. Grain produced in the Terai is being exported to India, despite the food shortages in Nepal. The lack of roads makes it difficult to ship the needed foodstuffs to remote mountain villages.

With the increasing demand for food, farmers have moved onto more marginal land, continuing the terracing they have done for centuries. However, as more and steeper land is cleared for crop production, the erosion problem escalates. Nepal has more terraces than any other country in the world. It also has the worst erosion problem. Entire mountainsides are being washed away by the country's annual monsoon rains, and severe flooding in the lowlands is one result of the overfarming in the hills and mountains.

Erosion is further aggravated by deforestation, caused by the country's dependence on wood as its primary source of fuel. It is predicted that by the year 2000, when Nepal's population reaches 30 million, there will be no more forests left in the country. In the past 30 years alone, the land area under forests has decreased by 40 percent.

Although exploration for fossil fuel deposits has recently begun in Nepal, the lack of adequate roads makes exploitation of any resources difficult. Perhaps Nepal's only real hope lies in its huge hydroelectric potential. On a per-capita basis, Nepal has the highest hydroelectric potential in the world. Several large generating plants have gone into operation in recent years, and more are under construction with the help of foreign aid. Although there is little hope of providing all the widespread population with electricity, Nepal could substantially lessen its dependence on wood from the rapidly disappearing forests. The country is also looking toward India as a major purchaser of electricity, which would provide Nepal with another source of foreign exchange. With adequate amounts of energy, Nepal would also be able to initiate some large-scale industries.

Because Nepal's industrialization is limited, unemployment is high. Small cottage industries produce such items as clothing, carpets, and souvenirs for the tourist industry. Medium-scale industries exist mostly in the Terai, with jute products being the Number One export item. One hindrance to Nepal's plans for future industrialization is the lack of skilled labor.

During the century when the Ranas controlled Nepal, the education of the people was ignored, and only a few members of the aristocracy were allowed an education. Since the overthrow of the Ranas, Nepal has been struggling with its staggering illiteracy rate, which has hampered the country's development. Even now, only about 25 percent of the population is literate. The government hopes that by focusing on vocational education, it can train the people in areas that are necessary for the further progress of the country's economy.

Many other nations have taken a keen interest in assisting Nepal with the numerous problems facing the developing nation. Agricultural, medical, educational, and industrial programs have been implemented throughout Nepal by numerous foreign aid agencies. Farmers are being assisted in land management and crop production. Reforestation programs are being implemented with foreign aid. Nepalese doctors are being trained abroad, and foreign doctors and nurses are volunteering their services to help bring adequate health facilities to remote regions of the country. Laborers are being trained in new skills to help them set up alternative industries to produce in Nepal some of the products that are currently being imported.

In addition to the foreign aid, the Nepalese government continues to implement programs of its own aimed at bolstering the nation's economy by improving communication, developing employment opportunities, educating the people, raising agricultural production, providing medical facilities, controlling population and conserving natural resources.

EXPLORING NEPAL

The visitor to Nepal must keep in mind that this is a very poor Third World country. The living conditions of the people are far below what we in the West would consider the acceptable minimum standards. Sanitation is almost nonexistent. For many of the people here, children included, begging is a way of life. However, in the midst of this extreme poverty, there is also great beauty and charm. The culture, history, and natural beauties of Nepal offer the visitor many memorable experiences. It is this very contrast that makes Nepal such an enchanting country.

If you have never visited a Third World country, it will be a shock. But, on closer inspection, you are likely to become enthralled with the colorful friendly people, the intricate mosaic of the green fields and terraces, the unique architecture of the country's many ancient temples and palaces, and the ever present peaks of the Himalayas.

Most explorations of this country begin with the Kathmandu Valley, the country's cultural, commercial, and administrative capital. At an elevation of 4,500 feet, Kathmandu has a pleasant climate year round. Even in the middle of winter, it rarely freezes in the valley. However, because Kathmandu is in a low valley, the beautiful Himalayas are only partially visible. For an unobstructed view, it is necessary to venture into the surrounding hills. Several small towns perched on the high ridges offer spectacular views of the mountains, with sunrise and sunset excursions particularly popular.

For one of the most extraordinary and closest views of the Himalayas, a trip to Pokhara, a 30-minute flight west of Kathmandu, is a necessity. This quiet rural valley on the edge of a picturesque lake is Nepal's answer to Kashmir. Bananas, papayas, banyans, and poinsettias grow throughout the valley, giving it a lush tropical feel the year round.

Down in the tropical lowlands of the Terai region, Chitwan National Park offers a chance to view some of Asia's rarest animals in the wild—Bengal tigers, one-horned rhinoceroses, crocodiles, sloth bears, and other rare creatures make their home in this nature preserve. Also in the Terai region is Lumbini, the birthplace of Buddha, which is a popular pilgrimage site for Buddhists and an interesting excursion for anyone interested in Buddhism or the ancient culture of Nepal.

For the adventurous, Nepal has some of the most exciting attractions in the world. The Himalayas, which are the highest mountains in the world, offer almost unlimited opportunities for trekking, white-water rafting, and mountain biking. However, because of the inaccessibility of the snows in Nepal, there is little in the way of winter sports.

Kathmandu

Originally known as Kantipur, Kathmandu is believed to have been founded in A.D. 723 by King Gunakama Deva. With few historical records from so long ago, however, there is some dissent over the founding date of the city. Some scholars say the city was founded as late as the twelfth century. Nevertheless, there is a great deal of evidence to show that there were developed communities in the valley 2,000 years ago.

Kathmandu probably derived its name from the Kasthamandap, a wooden temple erected in the early seventeenth century by King Laxmi Narsingha Malla. The Kasthamandap stands at the southwest corner of Kathmandu's Durbar Square. According to legend, the large open structure was constructed from a single tree. The name means wooden pavilion.

In the early morning, produce vendors surround the ancient Kasthamandap, and devout Hindus stop to leave offerings at the small Maru Ganesh shrine beside the building. Ganesh is the elephant-headed god of good luck. Ganesh shrines are found on nearly every street in Kathmandu, but this beautiful little temple, with its shining gilded roof, is one of the finest. Whenever a new king is crowned in Nepal, one of his first acts is to visit this temple with offerings.

Behind and to the right of this pagoda-style temple is an old building with intricately carved windows and doorways. Through the low doorway is a small courtyard filled with more beautifully carved windows.

This is the Kumari Bahal, the home of the living goddess, Kumari. This virgin goddess is a small girl believed to be the incarnation of the goddess Kumari. The goddess is sometimes seen waving to visitors from an upstairs window. It is forbidden to photograph her within her home.

The child is chosen from among the goldsmith caste of Buddhists and lives an isolated life in this building. She leaves her home only on a few special occasions, the most important being the festival of Indra Jatra, when the king, considered an incarnation of the god Vishnu, receives her blessings. When the Kumari first shows signs of blood, indicating that she is actually human, she is replaced by a new Kumari.

Palace Not in Harmony

Across the busy square from the Kumari Bahal is a large white building that looks out of place with its Grecian pillars and painted facade. This is the Gaddi Baithak, which was built in 1908 by one of the Rana prime ministers who ran the country for more than 100 years after usurping power from the royal family. This is just one of the many European-style palaces built by the Ranas during their years of rule. Many of their other extravagant palaces have now been converted into government office buildings and hotels.

Directly in front of the Gaddi Baithak is a three-tiered Shiva temple perched atop a nine-stage platform. Steps lead up to the temple, which offers a splendid panorama of Durbar Square and the surrounding neighborhoods. This temple is an excellent vantage point for observing the bustle of activity in the square. Rickshaws, motorcycles, taxis, and cars haphazardly negotiate their way through the square, managing to avoid hitting the pedestrians and vendors who thread their way back and forth across the flagstone pavement. Vendors selling a wide assortment of curios arrange their wares on the platforms of the square's many temples, while children amuse themselves with imaginative games.

From an upper window of what appears to be an old house on the north side of the square, colorfully painted statues of the god Shiva and his consort Parvati peer down on the chaos in the square. This building is a temple built in the domestic style, meaning that it resembles a house. There are only a few of these domestic-style temples scattered around Kathmandu. Most of the important temples in Nepal are pagodas, and it is believed that the pagoda style of architecture made its way to China and Japan after developing in Nepal.

At the foot of the tall Shiva Temple can be seen a small, white, plastered shikhara-style temple. This type of temple architecture originated in north India. Shikharas are most often constructed of plastered bricks or stones.

Heart of Old Kathmandu

Behind the Shiva and Parvati temple is Hanuman Dhoka square, the heart of old Kathmandu. Bordering Hanuman Dhoka, which means the gate of Hanuman, is the old Royal Palace. Near the palace's Golden Door, which is guarded by two large painted stone lions, is a curious red figure atop a short pedestal. This is the image of the monkey god Hanuman from which the square derives its name. The statue of the monkey god Hanuman has been the object of the people's devotion ever since it was installed in 1672 by King Jaya Pratap Malla and, over the years, it has become covered with oils and red powder. It is no longer possible to distinguish any of the features of this statue, which is protected by an umbrella and usually wrapped in a scarlet cloak.

Just inside the beautiful golden door is another striking statue. This one is of the black-skinned half-man, half-lion god Narsingha, who is depicted slaying the demon Haranyakashipu.

The royal palace is built around 14 large courtyards. Nasal Chowk, the largest and the one into which the golden door leads, is able to hold as many as 10,000 people. It is here that the coronation of the king is held. Although parts of the royal palace date back to the 1500s, most of it was built about 300 years ago. Much of the palace now houses the Tribhuvan Memorial Museum, which is dedicated to the king who led the revolt against the Ranas in 1951.

At the south end of the courtyard is the nine-story Basantapur Tower. With beautifully carved windows on each floor, this building commands a spectacular view across the roof of the palace and of all Kathmandu beyond. From here, you can easily see the unusual round-roofed pagoda temple to Hanuman at the opposite end of the courtyard.

Erotic Art "Protects" Temples

Just outside the golden door is the large Jagannath Temple, with its carved wooden roof struts depicting erotic scenes. One explanation for the erotic carvings, which can be seen on many of Nepal's temples, is that because the goddess of lightning is easily embarrassed by such scenes, she turns away without striking, and the temples are thus protected.

Along the palace wall opposite Jagannath Temple is a stone inscription in 15 languages, placed here in 1664 by King Pratap Malla. Among the languages used in the inscription are English and French.

If you walk straight out from the golden door, you will find on your left at the end of the wall a huge golden mask hidden behind a lattice work of intricately carved wood. This is the White Bhairav. Each year on the festival of Indra Jatra, the screen is opened and a big pot of local rice beer is place behind it. During the day's celebrations, people drink the beer through a long straw that passes through the mouth of the mask.

On the far side of the square from the White Bhairav is a small building that houses a terrifying bas-relief of the Black Bhairav. With its ferocious fangs and necklace of human skulls, this is the most frightening incarnation of the god Shiva—an appropriate visage for the god of destruction and terror. In the past, the Black Bhairav was used as a lie detector. It was believed that anyone telling a lie in front of this statue would immediately bleed to death.

Atop a pillar between the images of the Black Bhairav and the White Bhairav is a bronze statue of King Pratap Malla surrounded by his four sons. The statue was placed atop its square stone pillar in 1670.

Temple Entrance Forbidden

Just to the north of the palace complex is another large, ornate temple. This is the Taleju Temple, which only the royal family and certain priests can enter, except one day each year when it is open to the Hindu public. Housed within its walls is an image of the goddess Taleju Bhawani that was brought here from India in the 1500s. Taleju Bhawani was the family deity of the Malla kings, and it is believed that human sacrifices once took place here.

The three gilded roofs of the temple are topped by a gilded pinnacle and a gold umbrella. Large bronze faces of the goddess gaze from the windows of the building's upper floors. From each of the temple's three roofs hang small bells. Within the walled compound surrounding the temple are many small pagodas.

Just outside the colorfully painted gateway to the Taleju Temple is the small, unusual Kakeshwar Mahadeva Temple. Originally constructed in 1681 and renovated after the 1934 earthquake, this temple has a typical Nepalese-style first floor with a plastered shikhara-style second floor.

A flagstone road, Makhan Tole, leading past the Taleju Temple will take you into the bazaar section of old Kathmandu. Here vendors, shoppers, and an occasional stray cow crowd the dark streets. Shops selling Tibetan carpets, *tankas* (paintings with a Buddhist theme), masks, and other unusual items open directly onto the street. Flute sellers carrying what appear to be upside-down Christmas trees made of bamboo and wooden flutes stand in the sun playing beautiful melodies on their instruments. Devout Hindus on their way to a temple stop to buy garlands of marigolds and poinsettias as offerings to the gods. Small brass images of Nepal's many gods stare out of shop windows on a street scene little changed by the passage of time.

Makhan Tole, which leads diagonally away from Hanuman Dhoka Square, also contains a few more temples of interest—an excellent place to combine some shopping with sightseeing.

Three Small Squares

Indra Chowk is the first of three small squares along the length of this street. A domestic-style temple with a facade of red, green, and white tiles faces the busy square. Inside the temple is a silver image of Akash Bhairav. Four statues of ferocious-looking beasts gaze down from their second-floor perches. Unfortunately, non-Hindus are not allowed to enter this temple.

In the second square, Kel Tole is one of Nepal's holiest and most ornate temples—the temple of the White Machendranath, which is worshiped by Buddhists and Hindus alike. Buddhists revere the White Machendranath as a form of the *bodhisattva* Avalokiteshwara. Bodhisattvas are enlightened beings who choose not to enter Nirvana but remain on earth to help others achieve enlightenment. Hindus worship the White Machendranath as an incarnation of Shiva.

The temple is well hidden within a small courtyard. A small Buddha on a stone pillar and two metal lions mark the entrance. In front of the small pagoda-style temple stand two bronze statues of the goddess Tara and an incongruous Greek statue of a woman. An ornately embossed and gilded facade surrounds the doorway of the temple, where people congregate with offerings for the small image of Machendranath. Several metal banners hang from the pinnacle of the gilded roof to just below the lowest tier. Known as *dhvajas,* these banners provide a pathway for the gods to come down to earth. Many of Nepal's temples are equipped with these gilded banners.

In Asan Tole, the third and busiest of the three squares, there are four small temples. The three-story Annapurna Temple enshrines a holy silver pitcher. Other temples in Asan Tole are dedicated to Ganesh, Narayan (Vishnu), and Uma Maheshwara.

A short distance beyond Asan Tole, the road ends at a small lake. This is the Rani Pokhari, the queen's pond. In the middle, connected to the bank by a causeway, stands a Mogul-style Shiva temple constructed by Rana Prime Minister Jung Bahadur. Many frightening ghost stories are told about this quiet pond, and on winter mornings, when a thick fog hangs over Kathmandu, it is easy to imagine spirits rising from the mists over the water.

Temples "On Parade"

Stretching south from the Rani Pokhari is the Tundikhel, one of the largest parade grounds in the world. Along its length there are temples, the Martyr's Memorial, statues of Rana rulers, a marketplace, a park, a grandstand, and a pasture for the city's many goats and cows.

A block west of the Tundikhel's southern end is what appears to be a minaret. This tower, known as Bhimsen's Tower, or *Dharahara,* was built by Prime Minister Bhimsen Thapa in 1832 as a memorial to a dead queen. During the earthquake of 1934, the tower collapsed but was later rebuilt.

Kalmochan Temple, near the Patan bridge, is another Mogul-style building erected by Jung Bahadur Rana, who built the temple in Rani Pokhari. With its four ferocious gilded beasts standing on the roof, Kalmochan is an imposing structure. Two statues, one of Jung Bahadur Rana and another of Garuda, stand in the courtyard, which is usually empty. The Nepalese believe that the temple is built above a mass grave containing the remains of people killed in a massacre ordered by Jung Bahadur Rana. Consequently, they avoid the site, and it is in need of repair.

Nearby is a large, though plain, temple that also sees few worshipers. This is the Tripureshwar Mahadev Temple, constructed in the nineteenth century by the wife of Jung Bahadur Rana to honor her husband.

The Rana prime ministers were admirers of both Mogul architecture, as can be seen at the Rani Pokhari and Kalmochan Temple, and European architecture. Another of their extravagant Victorian palaces can be seen just east of the Tundikhel. Singha Durbar, an immense white structure fronted by a reflecting pool, had more than 1,000 rooms when it was built in 1901. Unfortunately, much of the palace was destroyed by fire in 1973. Now used as a government office building, Singha Durbar has been greatly restored, and work continues to return it to some of its former grandeur.

The current residence of the king of Nepal is the Narayanhiti Royal Palace at the north end of Durbar Marg, a popular shopping street. Little can be seen of the king's residence but the unremarkable annex that was built in 1970.

PATAN

Just across the Bagmati River to the south of Kathmandu is the ancient city of Patan (also known as Lalitpur). From its position above the valley floor, Patan offers some of the valley's best views of the Himalayas. Patan is more widely known, however, as a city of exquisite temples and talented artists and craftsmen.

According to legend, Patan was founded by the Indian emperor Ashoka, a Buddhist, who is said to have visited the Kathmandu Valley in 250 B.C. Standing at the four corners of old Patan are four Buddhist stupas, simple hemispherical mounds of brick and earth, said to have been erected by Ashoka.

There is still a strong Buddhist influence in Patan, and many of Nepal's most outstanding Buddhist temples can be found here, along with outstanding Hindu temples and old palaces. The old buildings date mostly from the fourteenth to the eighteenth century. At that time, Patan was an independent kingdom ruled by the Mallas. Quite a few of the city's buildings have been restored, some more than once. The earthquake that struck the Kathmandu Valley in 1934 razed many of Patan's temples, almost all of which have been reconstructed.

As in Kathmandu, Durbar Square is the heart of the city, and it is here that a tour should begin. The most striking building on Durbar Square is the Krishna Mandir, a four-story stone temple that is considered one of the finest examples of Nepalese art and architecture. Graceful finials top the numerous peaked roofs of the temple, and excellent carvings depicting scenes from India's ancient epics, *Ramayana* and *Mahabharata,* are depicted on the temple's friezes. Atop a pillar in front of the Krishna Mandir is a large bronze statue of Garuda, the vehicle of Vishnu, which was placed here by one of the Mallas when the temple was completed.

Palace Complex

Across the street from the Krishna Mandir is an extensive palace complex built in the seventeenth century. Divided into three main courtyards known as *chowks,* the palace, which is the oldest one in the Kathmandu Valley, is a stunning example of Nepalese craftsmanship.

The entrance to the northern chowk is notable for its beautiful "golden" gate, an excellent example of the fine metalwork characteristic of this period. Mulchowk, the central courtyard, houses the entrance to the Taleju Bhawani temple. The main doorway to this temple is flanked by life-sized bronze figures of the Hindu deities Ganga (standing on a crocodile) and Yamuna (standing on a tortoise). In the Sundarichowk is the royal bath, a large sunken pool surrounded by intricate stone carvings and a miniature version of the Krishna Mandir, which stands across the street. The water spout of the bath is another fine example of Newari metalwork.

Directly across the street from the entrance to the royal bath is an unusual octagonal stone Krishna temple built in 1723 in the shikara style. Beside this temple is a huge bronze bell erected in 1736. In the past, the bell was used to signal alarms during worship at the main Krishna Mandir.

Several typical Nepalese pagoda-style Hindu temples are also to be seen on Durbar Square. The three-story Hari Shankar Temple, to the north of the bell, is dedicated to Vishnu and Shankar. Two prostrate stone elephants guard the entrance to this temple. To the right stands the Char Narayan Temple, believed to have been built in 1566, the oldest temple on the square. Two stone lions and two guardians of Narayan, Ajaya, and Vijaya, flank the steps leading to the entrance of this two-tiered pagoda.

Cobra-Coiffed King

Between the Hari Shankar Temple and the Char Narayan Temple is a bronze statue of King Yoganarendra Malla perched atop a tall stone pillar. The king sits beneath a cobra with a flared hood, and on the cobra's head rests a small bird. Although this king lived during the early eighteenth century, popular belief holds that the king will not die until the bird flies away and that some day he will return to the royal palace, which always has a window and door left open for his return.

Several other interesting temples are to be found within a few minutes' walk of Durbar Square. Two large maps have been erected on the square to help visitors orient themselves and locate these other temples. Not far from the square is the five-tiered temple of Kumbheshwar. Hindus believe that the god Shiva resides in this temple during the six months of winter before returning to his summer home on Mount Kailash in Tibet. The only other five-tiered pagoda in the Kathmandu Valley is Nyatapola Temple in Bhaktapur.

The temple of the Rato (red) Machhendranath was first built in 1408. Once a year, the dark red wooden image of Machhendranath is taken out of the temple and paraded through the city on a huge chariot. Both Hindus and Buddhists worship Machhendranath. Nearby is the Minanath Temple, which holds a Buddhist image of Bodhisattva Lokeshwara.

Another noteworthy Buddhist temple is the Mahabuddha, the "temple of 1,000 Buddhas," named for the images of the Buddha featured on the golden-colored bricks of which the temple is constructed. The structure is in the shikhara style. Another such smaller shikhara can be seen in the same compound. The small building was constructed from bricks left over after the main temple, destroyed in the 1934 earthquake, was rebuilt.

Golden Temple

Hiranya Varna Mahavihara, known as the Golden Temple, is a Buddhist monastery near Durbar Square. It contains one of the most beautiful and ornate examples of Buddhist art in the Kathmandu Valley. Two large painted lions guard the temple's nondescript entrance, which gives no hint of the treasures that are hidden within. In a tiny courtyard stands a small shrine with ornate silver doors and a gilded roof. Behind this temple is the main building, protected behind an iron gate. The intricately embossed, gilded walls, from which the temple derives its popular name, shine in the sun. A three-tiered roof, also gilded, crowns this spectacular building.

Although Patan is full of beautiful and unusual temples, it is not known only for its historical offerings. It is also a city of artists and craftspeople. A large percentage of the city's population is employed in the home manufacture of handicrafts. Brass and bronze statues, copper pots, wood carvings, and wool carpets are all manufactured in Patan.

BHAKTAPUR

With few vehicles crowding its narrow ancient streets, Bhaktapur retains more of a medieval feel than does either Kathmandu or Patan. Also known as Bhadgaon and the city of devotees, Bhaktapur has been extensively renovated with aid from West Germany. The city's temples, royal palace, and ancient homes look now much as they did in the seventeenth and eighteenth centuries. Bhaktapur is a quiet city in which people go about life much as they have for hundreds of years. Located nine miles east of Kathmandu, the city was founded in A.D. 889 with streets laid out in the design of a conch shell.

At the heart of the city is Durbar Square, (yes, that's the square's name here, too), entered through a large gate on its western side. Statues of Bhairav and Hanuman flank the gate, and many other images decorate the colorful archway. There are several other gateways of special interest within Durbar Square. Immediately to your left, behind two ornate stone lions, are seventeenth-century statues of the god Bhairav and goddess Ugrachandi Durga.

To your right as you face these statues is another pair of stone lions guarding the entrance to the National Art Gallery. Behind these lions are statues of Hanuman Bhairav and Narsingha Narayan. Within the art gallery are excellent examples of Nepalese paintings and stone carvings from the thirteenth to the nineteenth centuries. Most of the pieces displayed here depict Hindu and Buddhist Tantric deities. The gallery is housed in the old royal palace, which extends for much of the length of Durbar Square.

Nepalese Art at Its Best

The main entrance to the royal palace is the stunning Golden Gate. This magnificent gilded gateway is considered the finest example of Nepalese art in the country. Constructed in the mid-1700s by King Ranjit Malla, the Golden Gate features intricately wrought gods, demons, and mythical animals. Facing the gate is a bronze statue of King Bhupatindra Malla seated with his hands together in a gesture of devotion to the goddess Taleju Bhawani, whose temple is behind the Golden Gate.

The shining gateway also leads to the oldest section of the royal palace—the palace of 55 windows. Constructed in 1427 and renovated in the seventeenth century, the palace is known for its third-floor balcony, which consists of 55 ornately carved windows positioned side by side.

In front of the palace is the shikhara-style stone temple of Batsala, which is covered with detailed carvings. On either side of the temple are two large bells. The smaller of the two bells is known as the bell of the barking dogs. Whenever the bell is rung, the dogs in the neighborhood begin barking.

Behind the Batsala Temple is the oldest temple in Bhaktapur, the Pashupatinath Temple, which is a replica of the famous Pashupatinath Temple in Kathmandu. Erotic carvings decorate the roof struts of this temple.

Pagoda-Style Temple

Down a short street behind the Pashupatinath Temple is Taumadhi Square, which is dominated by the tallest temple in Nepal. The Nyatapola Temple is one of the finest examples of Nepal's pagoda-style temples. With its five-tiered roof and five-stage platform, it is beautifully symmetrical. On each of the five platforms of the temple stand a pair of stone statues, each of which is said to be 10 times stronger than the pair below. At the bottom are the wrestlers, Jaya and Patta, who were said to be 10 times stronger than ordinary men. Above them are two elephants, then two lions, two griffins, and finally, at the top, two demigoddesses, Baghini and Singhini. Because the temple was never officially inaugurated, its doors have remained closed since its construction in the early eighteenth century.

Also in Taumadhi Square is a large temple dedicated to the god Bhairav. A third pagoda-style structure on the square has been converted into a cafe, which offers excellent opportunities for unobstrusively observing the life of this square.

Ten minutes' walk from Taumadhi Square is Dattatreya Square, where some of the most intricately carved windows in Bhaktapur can be found. The peacock windows that grace the Pujari Math Hindu monastery are renowned as the finest examples of the Nepalese woodcarvers' art. Pujari Math stands beside the unusual three-story Dattatreya Temple, which is said to have been built from the trunk of a single tree. What makes this building unique is a small room, on the second story of the temple, that abuts the main section of the temple.

On the opposite side from Pujari Math is the Brass and Bronze Museum, which houses a collection of examples of Nepal's fine brass and bronze work dating from the eighteenth century. Oil lamps, water pots, cooking pots, ritual vessels, and other metal objects are on display in this restored building. In the vicinity of Dattatreya Square are many old houses that have been restored as part of the West German project.

Potters, Weavers at Work

Bhaktapur has traditionally been known for its pottery and hand-woven fabrics, and it is still possible to observe the city's potters and weavers at work. The center of pottery manufacturing is only a short distance from Taumadhi Square. Potters spin their heavy wooden wheels by hand and quickly shape their pots, bowls, and vases, which are then lined up to dry in the sunny streets.

Within the dark houses of Bhaktapur can often be heard the rhythmic clacking of hand looms. Here the women stay busy weaving the black and red saris that are characteristic of this area.

On Dattatreya Square, you can also watch woodcarvers carry on the ancient art that has produced the intricate windows of Nepal's many old buildings. At Taumadhi Square, tanka painters can be seen creating highly detailed Buddhist images on canvas.

KATHMANDU VALLEY

According to legend, the Kathmandu Valley was formed when the Chinese god Manjushree used his sword to cut through one of the hills surrounding the lake that filled the Kathmandu Valley at that time. In the southern part of the valley beyond Patan is Chobar Gorge, through which the waters of the valley drain. This narrow gorge is believed to be the gash made by Manjushree in ancient times. At the lower opening of the gorge is a small temple. People can often be seen bathing at this sacred spot. In recent years, the natural beauty of this setting has been ruined by a large cement factory that constantly spews smoke into the air and has covered the vicinity with a fine layer of cement dust.

Manjushree drained the ancient lake, the legend goes, so that he could better worship a flaming lotus flower that floated on it. This burning flower was the Adi Buddha, or primordial Buddha. When the waters had receded, the lotus rested on a high hill in the middle of the valley. On that hill was later built the huge Buddhist stupa of Swayambunath.

The hill on which this beautiful stupa sits is now a pleasant forested park. Swarms of small monkeys live here and scavenge the food offerings left by devoted Buddhist and Hindu pilgrims who daily visit the hill's many shrines. The top can be reached either by walking up the steep steps on the east side of the hill or by taking a roundabout road that leads up from the southwest. Those who choose to climb the steps will be rewarded with the site of the stupa's large eyes peering down at them as they make the steep ascent. Along the way are several brightly painted stone Buddhas, many small *chaityas* (miniature stupas) and stone statues of various animals that are vehicles of deities. At the entrance to the hill is a large colorful gate, behind which is a small building containing a large prayer wheel. To the right of the gate is a long wall of smaller prayer wheels. Tibetan people can often by seen here spinning the prayer wheels before making the climb to the top. Along the steps, other Tibetans, refugees, and pilgrims, may be seen carving prayer stones or weaving colorful belts, which they sell to passing tourists.

With its all-seeing eyes of the Buddha gazing out in four directions, Swayambunath is an extraordinary sight. Multicolored Tibetan prayer flags flutter in the breezes as pilgrims circle the stupa. Originally built more than 2,000 years ago, Swayambunath is a large white hemisphere of brick and earth crowned by a gilded copper spire consisting of 13 concentric circles and an intricate metal umbrella. Remember to circle the stupa only in a clockwise direction. To walk counterclockwise is considered sacrilegious.

Prayer Wheels and Shrines

All around the base of the stupa are prayer wheels and small shrines containing images of different Buddhas and their consorts. Over the years, many other shrines have been built around Swayambunath. One of these is an ornate temple to Hariti, the Hindu goddess responsible for averting smallpox and ensuring fertility. On Saturdays, the shrine is packed with worshipers who have come with offerings to ask special favors of the goddess.

Also on this hill are several Buddhist monasteries that contain beautiful wall murals and large statues of Buddha and various Bodhisattvas. Another Hindu temple on the hill is dedicated to Saraswati, the goddess of learning.

You have an excellent view of the entire Kathmandu Valley from Swayambunath. In the distant eastern side of the city, it is possible to discern the valley's other large stupa, Boudhanath, which is the holiest site in the country for Tibetan Buddhists. Boudhanath, though not as old as Swayambunath, is much larger—one of the largest stupas in the world. Once again, the all-seeing eyes of the Buddha peer out from their tower atop the white hemisphere of brick and earth. Within the stupa is an unknown relic placed there when the shrine was constructed. Some people believe that it actually contains a piece of bone from the body of the Buddha.

Nepal's Most Sacred Temple

Not far from Boudhanath is Pashupatinath, the most sacred Hindu temple in Nepal. Dedicated to the god Shiva, the temple complex stands on the banks of the sacred Bagmati River, which is a tributary of the Ganges. Hindus regularly come to Pashupatinath to bathe in the waters of the river. It is here that many cremations are performed. The ashes are then sprinkled on the river so they can eventually join the holy Ganges. Each year in late February or early March, thousands of pilgrims visit Pashupatinath on the holy day of Shivaratri. From all over India and Nepal, thousands of Hindus, including many *saddhus* (wandering holy men), come to worship Shiva and bathe in the waters of the Bagmati.

Although the main temple is open only to Hindus, it is possible to catch glimpses of this ornate structure from across the river. Intricate silver doors and walls surround the lower level of the two-tiered temple, which is crowned with gilded roofs. Within the building is a huge Shiva lingam, and outside stands an equally large gilded bull, Shiva's mount, Nandi.

Numerous small white shrines on the bank opposite the temple contain small stone lingams. A paved path leads up a wooded hillside behind these stupas to several other shrines dedicated to various gods and goddesses.

When you arrive at Pashupatinath, you are likely to be approached by a young Nepali man speaking excellent English. He will want to give you a guided tour of the grounds. If you do not want his assistance, you must be insistent. Otherwise he will follow you, diligently explaining the temples and expect payment for his services at the end of the tour. If you accept his tour, NRs. 30–40 is sufficient payment.

Just over the wooded hill from Pashupatinath is Guheshwari Temple, dedicated to Shiva's consort, Parvati. However, this temple is also open only to Hindus, and little of the building is visible from beyond the high walls of the courtyard.

North of Kathmandu is another sacred and unusual pilgrimage site dedicated to the god Vishnu. In the middle of a small pond is a 15-foot-long stone statue of Vishnu sleeping on a bed of huge snakes. Carved in the seventh century, it is believed that the statue was later rediscovered by a farmer plowing his fields. A Nepalese legend holds that the reigning king will soon die if he visits Budhanilkantha.

Animals Offered for Sacrifice

Farther along the picturesque road that leads past Shesh Narayan is the temple of Dakshinkali, which is dedicated to Kali, the goddess of terror. Every Tuesday and Saturday, Hindus visit this small temple to offer animal sacrifices to Kali. After being sacrificed, the animals are taken home and prepared for dinner, thus serving a dual purpose. Hindus believe that animals sacrificed in this manner will have a much better life in their next incarnation. A trip to Dakshinkali is definitely not for the squeamish. The gruesome nature of the shrine is in striking contrast to the tranquil atmosphere of the surrounding forested hills.

Kirtipur, a small medieval town of historical significance, makes a pleasant stop on the way back to Kathmandu from Dakshinkali. Perched atop a high hill, this fifteenth-century town was once a fortress guarding the valley below. In his campaign to unify Nepal during the eighteenth century, King Prithvi Narayan Shah was forced to make three attempts before he was able to capture Kirtipur. Among the town's ancient temples and houses, old lifestyles persist.

Dating back to the fourth century, the Changu Narayan temple complex, eight miles east of Kathmandu, is a shining example of the art and architecture of the Lichhavi period. Several of the stone statues here were carved in the fifth and sixth centuries, making this one of Nepal's most extensive repositories of art from this early period in Nepalese history. Although it is difficult to reach this hilltop shrine, which requires a 45-minute walk through beautiful countryside, it is well worth a visit.

Elephant Rides and Picnics

Close to Changu Narayan is Gokarna Safari Park, which has pleasant natural surroundings for hiking and picnicking and offers elephant rides and horseback riding. Here in the park's forested hills can be seen several species of deer, as well as monkeys. For anyone who does not have enough time to visit Chitwan National Park in the Terai region of the country, this small park offers visitors the experience of exploring the forest from high atop an elephant. Gokarna is also home to one of the two golf courses in the Kathmandu Valley.

Two other parks offer pleasant hikes and quiet surroundings for picnicking and escaping the hectic activities of Kathmandu. Nagarjun Royal Forest encompasses the forested mountain just to the northwest of Kathmandu. At the top of the park's Jammacho Peak stands a small white Buddhist stupa, which can be seen from the valley floor. It is a two-hour walk from the park entrance to the stupa at the top. A lookout tower beside the stupa provides excellent views across the valley and over the snowy Himalayas to the north. Along the trail may be seen many species of birds and an occasional deer.

Six miles south of Patan is the Royal Botanical Garden in Godawari. Although the gardens are not impressive, it is a quiet place for a picnic. Several paths wind through the shady grounds and past a small stream.

The National Museum, which is located near Swayambunath stupa, houses exhibits of the culture and arts of Nepal. Nearly 1,500 years of the country's art are on display here, including wood, stone, brass, and bronze sculptures. Many fine paintings and old books are also shown. In a separate building, there are natural history exhibits as well as displays of the arms and armor of past kings and their armies. Another wing of the museum is dedicated to the late King Mahendra.

HIMALAYAN HORIZONS

It comes as a disappointment to many people, but there are only limited views of the Himalayas from Kathmandu. To view the full grandeur of these spectacular peaks, it is necessary to make an excursion from the Kathmandu Valley. However, it is possible to expand your Himalayan horizons by simply getting off the valley floor. In Kathmandu, the Soaltee Oberoi and Everest Sheraton offer good views from their upper floors. In Patan, which is situated on a hill just south of Kathmandu, the new Hotel Himalaya Kathmandu affords splendid views of the mountains.

Tour companies in Kathmandu offer several alternatives for sunrise and sunset excursions into the hills that surround the Kathmandu Valley. From these heights, it is possible to see for hundreds of miles in every direction. Nagarkot, which is known especially for its colorful sunrise vistas, is at an altitude of 7,500 feet and is 22 miles east of

Kathmandu. From Mount Everest in the east to Dhaulagiri in the west, nearly 20 mountain peaks over 20,000 feet tall are visible from this beautiful natural setting of pine forests and pastures. The Tara Gaon Resort Hotel, run by the government of Nepal, provides simple overnight accommodations here. There are also numerous small lodges offering the most basic accommodations (no showers and shared toilets).

Although not as high as Nagarkot, the old town of Dhulikhel, 18 miles east of Kathmandu on the road to the Chinese border, offers spectacular sunsets as well as sunrises. However, because Dhulikhel is only at 6,000 feet, it is not possible to see Mount Everest or the Annapurnas and Dhaulagiri. Thus, only about 15 peaks over 20,000 feet are visible here. Dhulikhel has two small resorts offering comfortable accommodations and food—the Dhulikel Mountain Resort and the Himalayan Sun-and-Snow.

View of 25 High Peaks

About 18 miles northwest of Kathmandu is Kakani. At 6,700 feet, this town is surrounded by green terraces, forests, and alpine scenery. The peaks that are visible extend from Dhaulagiri in the west to Gauri Shankar in the east. Tara Gaon Resort Hotels have another facility here.

On the old mountain highway to the Indian border lies the town of Daman, at nearly 8,500 feet above sea level. Many people consider this to be the finest spot for viewing the Himalayas. At least 25 peaks over 20,000 feet tall are visible here. An unobstructed view from west of Dhaulagiri to east of Mount Everest is the reward for making this long trip. High-powered telescopes mounted on a viewing tower in Daman allow close-up views of the mountains.

If the view from your plane as you flew into Kathmandu seemed more exciting than any of the vantage points on the ground, you can take Royal Nepal Airlines' "Mountain Flight" for an hour of extraordinary vistas. This flight leaves several times each morning, weather permitting, from October to March, at times extending to April or even May. During the flight, which covers the eastern Himalayas, 18 peaks over 20,000 feet tall can be seen, including Mount Everest.

For leisurely close-up views of the mountains, nowhere in Nepal is better than Pokhara. Many people consider Pokhara's vista of Machhapuchhare and the Annapurnas to be one of the finest in the world. Tour agencies in Kathmandu offer overnight trips to Pokhara by plane or car, although it is a long and grueling trip by road.

Jungle Safaris

Contrary to what many people believe, Nepal is not an entirely mountainous country. Running the length of its border with India is the Terai—an extension of the low-lying Indo-Gangetic plains. In the center of this region, which averages over 250 feet above sea level, is the Royal Chitwan National Park. The park covers nearly 400 square miles of grassy river valleys, dense forests, and low hills. Created in 1973 from what had been a royal hunting reserve, Chitwan provides protection for some of Nepal's rarest wildlife. The park is now closely guarded to prevent poaching or the destruction of the habitat. Local villagers are allowed into the park only once a year to harvest the tall elephant grass that grows there. These people depend on the grasses for roof thatching and walls for their primitive huts.

Many animals also depend on the elephant grass for food and shelter. Four species of deer, the Indian one-horned rhinoceroses, royal Bengal tigers, and leopards all make their homes in the park, as do wild boars, monkeys, sloth bears, and mongooses. More than 350 species of birds, including giant hornbills, peacocks, eagles, and parakeets, live in this diverse habitat.

Several private lodges operating within the boundaries of the park offer elephant-back safaris, dugout canoe rides, and nature walks. An elephant ride here can be a thrilling experience. The giant one-horned rhinoceroses, of which there are nearly 200 in the park, may weigh two tons. The elephant drivers, called *mahouts,* are skilled at finding rhinoceroses for visitors to photograph. Although not usually frightened by elephants, the rhinoceroses may occasionally become excited and charge, but actual attacks are rare.

"Tiger, Tiger . . . "

Unlike the animals of Africa's plains, those in Chitwan are not found in large herds. Deer and rhinoceroses are usually found alone or in pairs. The elusive tiger is one of the park's most solitary creatures. Because it is a nocturnal hunter, it is usually seen only in the early morning or late afternoon and then only by the lucky.

The best time of year to visit the park is between October and March. In March, the Indian bison, or gaurs, come down from the Churia Hills in the southern part of the park. These large beasts, which resemble American bisons, bring their newborn calves with them.

Mid-January is not a good time to visit because hundreds of villagers enter the park to harvest the elephant grass and burn the cut fields. With so much human activity in the area, the wild animals move into the forests and are much more difficult to locate.

Chitwan National Park can be reached by air, road, or river. Tiger Tops, the oldest lodge in the park, has an airstrip nearby. The flight from Kathmandu takes only about 30 minutes. Other lodges are best reached by car. The trip from Kathmandu by car takes about 4½ hours. For the more adventurous, most lodges offer raft trips down the Trisuli River. River trips can be for one or two days, including a night's camping along the river. There are easy floats with only a few exciting rapids to be negotiated—a great addition to a Nepalese jungle safari.

POKHARA

In Pokhara, the Himalayas seem close enough to reach out and touch. With spectacular mountain views, a picturesque lake, green fields, and giant pipal trees everywhere, Pokhara offers a refreshing, relaxing atmosphere that is perfect for recuperating after a hectic schedule. People often just sit here for days, gazing up at the dozen or so magnificent snowcapped peaks at the north end of the valley. Its natural setting is definitely Pokhara's main attraction. Nowhere else in Nepal is it so easy to get so close to the majestic Himalayas that attract people from all over the world.

Dominating the valley is the pyramid-shaped peak of Machhapuchhare, the Fishtail Peak, which rises up directly from the valley floor. Machhapuchhare derives its name from the fish-tail shape of its summit. Unfortunately, that shape cannot be seen from Pokhara. It is necessary to trek two days into the hills outside the valley before the "fish tail" can be properly viewed.

Machhapuchhare is a sacred peak and consequently has never been climbed, although one expedition ascended to within a few yards of the peak. Arrayed behind Machhapuchhare are the glittering peak of Dhaulagiri, the world's fifth-highest mountain, and the Annapurnas. Annapurna I is the sixth-highest peak in the world. Other peaks that are visible from Pokhara include Hiunchuli, Gangapurna, and Lamjung Himal.

Pokhara is a small city located on the edge of picturesque Phewa Lake, which stretches for nearly two miles through the valley. On one side of the lake are forested hills, and on the other side, green terraces cling to the foothills that rise up toward the peaks of the Himalayas. Boats can be rented here with or without an oarsman. Few experiences can match the serenity of floating on this beautiful lake with the reflection of the snowy Himalayas reflected in the calm waters. On a small island in Phewa Lake stands a pagoda-style temple surrounded by trees that make a pleasant excursion by boat. Two other smaller lakes, Begnas and Rupa, are also nearby.

One of the best ways to explore Pokhara is on a bicycle. The quiet, uncrowded streets are well paved and never too steep. For a much more leisurely trip around town, a horse and carriage can be rented by the hour.

Unusual natural phenomena abound in the Pokhara area. Just to the south of Phewa Lake are David's Falls. These mysterious waterfalls cut their way through a steep, narrow ravine before suddenly disappearing into a large dark hole in the ground. The Seti Gorge, a similar ravine, cuts through the river valley just to the east of town. From the middle of the Mahendra Bridge, it is possible to look down into the gorge, which is barely six feet wide. Far below, the river courses through its narrow chute. North of town is one of Nepal's only known limestone caves, the Mahendra Cave, which is full of stalactites and stalagmites.

LUMBINI: THE BIRTHPLACE OF BUDDHA

At this isolated spot near the Indian border, the Lord Buddha was born more than 2,500 years ago. Since that time, it has been one of the most sacred pilgrimage spots for Buddhists, although it was only in recent decades that archaeologists began extensive excavation of the area. A stone pillar, erected in 250 B.C. by the Indian emperor Ashoka, marks this formal royal garden as the birthplace of Siddhartha Gautama, the prince who would later become "the Enlightened One."

In addition to the Ashoka pillar, there is a brick temple that contains ancient stone carvings depicting the birth of the Buddha. A small pond nearby is said to be the pool where Buddha's mother, Maya Devi, bathed before giving birth. Several shrines have recently been built here in Lumbini by different countries. Funding is coming from many sources to develop Lumbini as a major pilgrimage center, and archaeological excavations continue in the area.

Bhairawa, a short drive from Lumbini, can be reached by a 45-minute flight from Kathmandu. It is also possible to drive by way of Pokhara, but the trip is arduous. Currently, there are only a few basic accommodations in Lumbini.

PRACTICAL INFORMATION FOR NEPAL

WHEN TO GO. The climate of Nepal varies widely according to season and elevation. The best time to visit is October–April, when the visibility is likely to be good for mountain viewing and the daytime climate in the valleys is mild. This is also the time of most of the major festivals and the best season for trekking in all but the highest elevations. Kathmandu and Pokhara are pleasant even in the middle of winter. Neither area receives snow, and the temperature rarely, if ever, goes down to freezing. In the high elevations frequented by trekkers, it can get extremely cold at night, but, during the day, it is usually comfortable in the sun.

From March onward, visibility gradually deteriorates until the onset of the monsoon, which lasts from early June to early October. Cloud cover is usually constant during the monsoon, and rains can be torrential. Landslides and blocked roads are likely to occur from June to September. In Kathmandu, which is at 4,500 feet, winter temperatures can reach 68° F and summer temperatures, 86° F. The Terai region, which is an extension of the Indo-Gangetic plains along the Indian border, is warmer and more humid throughout the year. By March, temperatures in the Terai can reach 100° F. Nepal's best weather comes in late October and November, but this is also the busiest tourist season, so be sure to make your hotel reservations in advance. Midwinter—December and January—can bring cold nights, but the days are generally pleasant and sunny. More and more tourists are coming to Nepal at this time of year.

WHAT IT WILL COST. With new luxury hotels going up each year, Kathmandu is fast losing its reputation as an inexpensive city to visit. The cost of a first-class hotel room is approaching $100 per day, putting Nepal on a par with popular tourist destinations around the world. However, it is still possible to visit Nepal if you are on a budget.

Two people can expect to spend roughly $125–$150 per day for deluxe hotel accommodations, three à la carte meals a day, and a hired car and guide for city sightseeing. For moderately priced accommodations, three à la carte meals a day, and city sightseeing by tour bus, a couple can expect to spend $90–$110 per day. The cost of jungle safaris in Chitwan National Park varies from $150–$300 a day for two people. In Pokhara, Nagarkot, or Dhulikel, prices are lower than in Kathmandu. However, there are no deluxe or first-class accommodations in any of these places, so daily expenses will be less than $100 for two people.

It is possible for a couple staying in one of Kathmandu's many inexpensive hotels to get by on $55 or less per day if they avoid the high-priced hotel restaurants and do their sightseeing with regularly scheduled tour buses. Young travelers on a tight budget can get by on $25 or less for two people.

Hotels. *Deluxe* hotels cost $75–$95 per day. *Expensive* accommodations will run $45–$60. *Moderate* hotels are $35–$45, and *Inexpensive* hotels cost less than $30. These prices are all for double rooms.

Restaurants. In Kathmandu's best restaurants, most of which are located in the major hotels, in à la carte dinner without drinks will cost $8–$12. However, several fine restaurants in Kathmandu offer a variety of cuisines at prices that are much lower than those in the major hotels. Dinner without drinks at one of these first-class restaurants will cost $5–$8. In addition, in the many small restaurants in the Thamel neighborhood that are frequented by budget-minded travelers, a dinner will cost $2–$5.

Taxis. Taxis in Kathmandu are equipped with meters, and 10 percent is added to the price on the meter. A trip almost anywhere in the city will cost NRs. 15 or less. The trip from the airport into town will cost NRs. 20–25. However, taxi drivers prefer not to use their meters, especially at night, when they demand much higher rates than normal. Bargaining is necessary in this case. Tipping is not necessary. The motorized rickshaws charge a few rupees less than the taxis and are metered. Tricycle rickshaws must be bargained for, and the price for a short trip should not exceed NRs. 10.

Drinks. Nepal produces a wide variety of alcoholic beverages. The local liquors are inexpensive, and a mixed drink in a restaurant or bar costs only NRs. 30–40. Imported liquors are about double that price and are readily available in hotel bars and first-class restaurants. Beer in Nepal is not expensive. A liter bottle of local beer costs NRs. 40–50 at hotels. Coffee in Nepal is usually instant.

Cigarettes. Imported cigarettes, both American and British, are readily available in and near major hotels in Kathmandu. A pack of imported cigarettes costs NRs. 35–40, whereas a pack of local cigarettes is less than NRs. 10.

Magazines and newspapers. *Time* and *Newsweek* (Asian editions) are widely sold in Kathmandu. They cost NRs. 27 and 24, respectively. The daily *International Herald Tribune* provides excellent coverage of world news for NRs. 16. *USA Today* is also available for the same price. Other foreign magazines are not readily available, but the American Library in Kathmandu has a wide assortment, although these are usually a few weeks old.

Haircut and shampoo. A woman's shampoo and set costs about NRs. 75, and a haircut is about the same price. A man's haircut costs about NRs. 30.

TRAVEL DOCUMENTS. All travelers to Nepal must be in possession of a valid passport. A seven-day visa, which can be renewed for up to three months, is obtainable at any border upon your arrival. However, it is better to obtain a full 30-day visa in advance from an overseas Nepalese embassy or consulate. These embassies and consulates are located in Washington, D.C.; New York; London; Paris; Bonn; Bangkok; Delhi; Calcutta; Rangoon; Tokyo; Cairo; Riyadh; Islamabad; Beijing; Lhasa; Moscow; Dhaka; and Hong Kong. Visas can be extended locally for up to three months for NRs. 75 per week. Special permits are required for trekking and mountaineering expeditions, and some areas of the country are off-limits to foreigners. The Central Immigration offices in Kathmandu and Pokhara issue permits and visa extensions. A trekking permit costs NRs. 60 per week. Passport-size photos are necessary, both for extending visas and for acquiring trekking permits.

HEALTH. Typhoid and cholera inoculations are not required but are strongly recommended. Make sure your tetanus inoculation is current. It is also advisable to have an injection for paratyphoid and a gamma globulin shot for hepatitis. Precautions against malaria should be taken if you visit the Terai region (Chitwan National Park) in the warmer months. Because malaria-carrying mosquitoes come out only at night, it is best to stay inside after dark and sleep under a mosquito net.

HOW TO GET THERE. By Air. Because Nepal is a landlocked country with its capital located behind a high mountain barrier, it is best reached by air. Kathmandu is served by *Royal Nepal Airlines, Thai International, Indian Airlines, Burma Airways, Pakistan International Airlines,* and *Biman Bangladesh Airlines.* There are daily flights from India (New Delhi, Varanasi, Patna, or Calcutta) and several flights weekly from Bangkok. Flights are also available, less frequently, from Hong Kong, Dhaka, Rangoon, Colombo, and Karachi.

By Overland. It is still possible to make the long overland trip from Europe to Nepal. However, because of the political situation in Iran, U.S. citizens cannot make this trip. This grueling journey is only for the most adventurous and usually takes 60–90 days. Two companies offering this trip are *Sundowners International,* 267 Old Brompton Rd., London SW5, England, and *Hann Overland,* 185 Streatham High Rd., London SW16 6EG, England.

The **train** service from Calcutta to the border post of Raxaul requires several changes and a degree of stamina. **Bus** service is also available through India to the Nepalese border, including direct express links between Kathmandu and Patna or Delhi. The Indian-built mountain highway, from the Nepalese border town of Birganj (a Rs. 20 rickshaw ride from the Indian border at Raxaul) to Kathmandu is called the Tribhuvan Rajpath. Opened in 1956 and not carefully maintained since then, the Rajpath offers 160 miles of mountain driving hardly equaled anywhere else in the world. Taking eight hours by bus or taxi, the serpentine route hairpins up to a pass of 8,000 feet before descending into the Kathmandu Valley at 4,500 feet. Most buses now take a longer, but much less hair-raising, route.

CUSTOMS. All baggage must be declared and is subject to inspection. Entry formalities are rather easy going, but exit procedures can be strict; a special watch is kept for the illegal export of antiques or drugs. If you bring in more than the minimal amount of photographic or video equipment, it may be necessary to list the items on a special form, which will be checked by customs when you depart.

At the Airport. Visitors will find Nepalese officials courteous and helpful, and it is possible to get through all the formalities in a relatively short time. On landing, you will need a passport and a disembarkation card. Here you can apply for a seven-day visa costing $10 if you have not already gotten a visa before entering the country. Two passport-size photos are necessary for the visa, and additional photos are required if you extend the visa. Also at the airport is a tourist information center.

Major hotels offer free airport transfer services; otherwise the taxi fare into town is NRs. 25–50, depending on whether the taxi driver uses the meter or a set fare is negotiated. It is cheaper to use the meter.

On your departure, there is a NRs. 150 departure tax for international flights and NRs. 30 for domestic flights. The airport also has a small duty-free shop, where purchases may be made in U.S. dollars.

ACCOMMODATIONS. In recent years, Nepal has become popular as a tourist destination, and deluxe hotels have begun to flourish in Kathmandu. These hotels offer all the amenities one would expect from top-class hotels in the Indian subcontinent: excellent restaurants, bars, and coffee shops. Convention facilities, health clubs, tennis courts, and swimming pools are provided by most hotels.

The local hotel association uses a grading system of one to five stars, which assures that a five-star hotel will have a well-trained staff and excellent services. However, below the four-star level, there is a great deal of variation in quality. Outside Kathmandu, accommodations can be basic.

In recent years, Kathmandu has just about caught up with the rest of the world in hotel prices. The *Deluxe* hotels range in price from $70 to $90 a day for a double. In Pokhara, the best hotels cost only $40 a day for a double, but these hotels do not offer the amenities of Kathmandu's top hotels. In Chitwan National Park, prices range from $150 to $330 a day for a double, which includes all meals and activities in the park. Hotels add a 10–15 percent government tax, depending on the quality of the hotel, and some hotels also add a 10 percent service charge.

KATHMANDU

Deluxe

Hotel de l'Annapurna. Durbar Marg; tel. 21711. 150 rooms, centrally located near the old city and shopping areas. Good facilities, with four restaurants, the largest hotel swimming pool in Kathmandu, tennis courts, and a shopping arcade.

Everest Sheraton. Baneswor; tel. 220567. 158 comfortable rooms near the airport. Good views from the upper floors. A wide range of facilities, including nine restaurants and bars, conference facilities, a swimming pool, health club, tennis courts, cultural shows, and a disco. Rooftop barbecues, as well as restaurants offering spectacular views. Complimentary shuttle bus service to the city center.

Hotel Himalaya Kathmandu. Sahid Sukra Marg, Patan; tel. 521887. 120 rooms, all with spectacular views of the Himalayas—the best views in the valley. Two restaurants also offer good views. Conference facilities, Japanese garden, swimming pool, tennis courts, shopping arcade. Free shuttle bus service to Kathmandu.

Hotel Kathmandu. Maharaj Gung; tel. 412103. 120 comfortable rooms, one of the newest hotels in Kathmandu—on Embassy Row. Two restaurants, a bar, tea lounge, swimming pool, health club, and shopping arcade. Free shuttle bus service to the city center. Affiliated with Gokarna Safari Park, which has a golf course.

Hotel Soaltee Oberoi. Tahachal; tel. 211211. The largest hotel in Nepal, with 281 rooms. Extensive facilities, four restaurants, two bars, a gambling casino, cultural shows, live music, shopping arcade, swimming pool, health club, tennis courts, playground for children, and babysitting. The hotel is away from the city center, but a free shuttle bus service is provided. Good views of the mountains from upper floors.

Hotel Yak & Yeti. Durbar Marg; tel. 413999. 111 elegant rooms, located in the city center near the shopping areas. Good conference facilities, swimming pool, tennis courts, health club, and a small lake for boating and fishing. Part of the hotel is converted from a nineteenth-century Rana palace. Good restaurants.

Expensive

Hotel Blue Star. Tripureswar; tel. 214135. 90 air-conditioned rooms. Extensive conference facilities, restaurants, and bars; an indoor swimming pool; health club, shopping arcade; and supermarket. Conveniently located midway between old Kathmandu and Patan.

Dwarika's Kathmandu Village Hotel. Battisputali; tel. 414770. This delightful compound has 19 individually decorated rooms featuring intricately carved antique windows like those seen in old palaces. The buildings are typical Newari-style houses. This is the only hotel in Nepal to have received the coveted Pacific Area Travel Association Heritage Award for cultural conservation efforts. Quiet shady gardens with brick terraces. Located near Pashupatinath Temple. This is the closest Nepal has to a bed and breakfast inn.

Hotel Malla. Lekhnath Marg; tel. 410320. Near the present Royal Palace and shopping area of Tramel. 75 good rooms and facilities. Attractive decor evokes the architecture of old Kathmandu, delightful gardens, but no swimming pool. Several good restaurants.

Hotel Shangrila. Lazimpat; tel. 412999. 50 comfortable rooms. Small and quiet hotel or "Embassy Row." Has several restaurants and a conference hall. Barbecues are held in the award-winning gardens.

Hotel Shanker. Lazimpat; tel. 410151. 158 ornately decorated rooms in a restored Rana palace behind the present Royal Palace. Hotel has beautiful exterior, but interior is in need of upkeep. Large pleasant lawn for afternoon tea. Many windows are blocked to prevent photographs of the Royal Palace. Poorly managed, but atmospheric.

Moderate

Hotel Narayani. Pulchowk; tel. 521711. 88 plain but air-conditioned rooms. Reasonable facilities, swimming pool, and good views of the mountains.

Summit Hotel. Kupondole Height; tel. 521894. 34 rooms with traditional Nepalese decor in a quiet residential neighborhood. Restaurant, bar, terrace barbecues, good views, pleasant gardens, swimming pool. Excellent value.

Tara Gaon Resort Hotel. Boudha; tel. 410409. Near Boudhanath Stupa, east of Kathmandu. 19 large rooms with huge round windows looking out to the mountains. Restaurant, snack bar, lounge with fireplace. Operated by the government.

Hotel Vajra. Bijeswari; tel. 224545. Near Swayambunath Stupa. 39 rooms. Traditional Nepalese architecture and artwork. Rooftop and terrace gardens, restaurant, library, art gallery, cultural shows, and avant-garde plays. Good value.

Inexpensive

The hotels in this category are simpler and have fewer modern facilities. They are, nevertheless, comfortable for the more experienced traveler. Services are usually limited. Some have restaurants attached to the hotel. Hotels in this category have been proliferating in Kathmandu even faster than those in the deluxe category. These hotels cater mostly to young travelers on tight budgets. The newer hotels tend to be much smaller than those built 15 or 20 years ago, and the older hotels tend to be in need of repairs. The **Kathmandu Guest House,** Thamel (tel. 413632), 80 rooms, once voted as "the most popular cheap budget hotel" by *The Traveler* magazine, is no longer the good value it used to be. Complaints are common.

The best values include **Hotel Manaslu,** Lazimpat (tel. 413470), 45 rooms in a restored Rana palace. **Hotel Ambassador,** Lazimpat (tel. 414432), 30 rooms, on "Embassy Row." **Hotel Makalu,** Dharmapath (tel. 223955), 30 rooms, centrally located. **Hotel Nook,** Kantipath (tel. 213627), 28 rooms, near old Kathmandu. **Hotel Gautam,** Jyatha (tel. 215014), good Indian restaurant. **Hotel Greenwich Village,** Kupondole Height (tel. 521780), small in a quiet section of Patan. **Hotel Oasis,** Patan Dhoka, Patan, (tel. 521711), operated by the management of the Hotel Narayani.

POKHARA

Moderate to Expensive

Hotel Dragon. Pardi Lake Side; tel. 52. 20 basic rooms. Clean but slightly run-down; service in restaurant is poor. Away from the lake and the airport.

Nothing really to recommend it, but the Hotel Association of Nepal gives it two stars.

Fish Tail Lodge. Tel. 71. 35 comfortable rooms in a resort setting on the banks of Phewa Lake. Spectacular view of Machhapuchhare, the Fish Tail Peak, from which the hotel derives its name. Reflections of the Annapurnas and Machhapuchhare shimmer on the waters of the lake. This is the most peaceful setting of any hotel in Nepal. The hotel is reached by a small barge, and rowboats are available. The ski-lodge-type restaurant with a large fireplace features a variety of cuisines. Has regularly scheduled cultural programs. Operated by the management of the Hotel de l'Annapurna in Kathmandu.

Hotel Mount Annapurna. Tel. 27. Near the airport. 32 basic rooms. Simple restaurant serving a variety of cuisines, bar, rooftop terrace with stunning views, garden. Basically not much better than much less expensive accommodations on the lake.

New Hotel Crystal. Nagdhunga; tel. 35. Near the airport, 70 rooms with good views, air-conditioning, and carpeting, but basically plain. A spacious lawn surrounded by poinsettia bushes is ideal for relaxing and gazing at the Himalayas, which rise from the valley floor only 25 miles away. Reasonable restaurant; cultural programs.

ROYAL CHITWAN NATIONAL PARK

Moderate to Expensive

Chitwan Jungle Lodge. Durbar Marg; tel. 410918. Located far to the east of Tiger Tops is this 22-room compound of Tharu-style thatched roof huts. All are comfortably furnished and have attached baths. Programs at this isolated jungle lodge include elephant rides to observe wildlife, dugout canoe rides on the nearby river, bird-watching walks, and hikes in remote sections of the park. Nepalese and European food is served, and there is a full bar. Knowledgeable naturalists are ready to answer questions about the park and its wildlife. Overnight rafting trips can also be arranged. Much less expensive than Tiger Tops.

Gaida Wildlife Camp. Durbar Marg; tel. 215840. Located between Tiger Tops and Chitwan Jungle Lodge, Gaida's 20 thatch-roofed huts with porches are on the banks of the Dungla River. This area is known for the large numbers of rhinoceroses that live here. Gaida also operates a tented camp farther inside the park. Accommodations and costs are similar to those at Chitwan Jungle Lodge. Rafting trips are available.

Tiger Tops Jungle Camp. Durbar Marg; tel. 212706. This unique tree-top hotel, 20 rooms, which pioneered jungle safaris in Chitwan, is located in the western section of the park and has an airstrip nearby that allows visitors to fly directly from Kathmandu. Although there is no electricity, accommodations in the rustic lodge are comfortable. There is also a tented camp, 10 tents, on a river island some distance from the lodge. Many people enjoy the tented camp more than the lodge because it offers more of a safari atmosphere. Unusual accommodations are also available in a local Tharu village, where visitors stay in a typical village longhouse, 12 rooms. Local tribal life, as well as the park's jungle wildlife, can be observed here.

The management of Tiger Tops is now operating the Karnali Tented Camp in far-western Nepal. Recently 16 rhinoceroses from Chitwan were relocated to the Royal Bardia Wildlife Preserve, where Karnali is located. Many of the same wild animals found at Chitwan are also found here.

Just outside the park's boundaries, in the village of Sauraha, there are numerous lodges offering basic accommodations. You can stay at these inexpensive lodges and make day trips into the park, but, because of the number of people in the vicinity of the village, wildlife can be scarce. Some of the better lodges here are **Hotel Elephant Camp,** Durbar Marg (tel. 223976); **Hotel Wildlife Camp,** Thamel (tel. 411045); and **Park Cottage,** Jyatha (tel. 213214).

OTHER DESTINATIONS

Moderate

Dhulikhel Mountain Resort. Dhulikhel; tel. 411031. 16 comfortable rooms in nine cottages perched on a ridge high above the Kathmandu Valley. All rooms have picture windows looking out on the wide expanse of the Himalayas, particularly breathtaking at sunrise and sunset. Restaurant offers a wide variety of cuisines.

Himalayan Horizon Sun-n-Snow Hotel. Dhulikhel; tel. 180114. 12 comfortable rooms in typical Newari-style buildings that look out on the Himalayas. Large terrace and restaurant with a wall of glass. Excellent for viewing sunrises and sunsets over the mountains.

Inexpensive

Tara Gaon Resort Hotel. Nagarkot; tel. 410409. Small resort with simple accommodations. The most extensive views of the Himalayas in the Kathmandu area. Spectacular sunrises. Reasonable restaurant.
Tara Gaon Resort Hotel. Kakani; tel. 41409. Similar facilities to Tara Gaon at Nagarkot. More good views of the Himalayas from a beautiful natural setting amid forests, pastures, and terraces. Restaurant serves a variety of cuisines.

 DINING OUT. Unlike India, Nepal has not developed a wide variety of cuisines. Many of the popular foods in Nepal are actually of Tibetan origin. Most Nepalese food is simple and rather bland. The staple meal of the nation is *dal bhat tarkari,* which is white rice, lentils, and mildly spiced sautéed vegetables. Because meat is expensive, it is not eaten often, and beef is not eaten at all. However, buffalo, lamb, goat, and chicken are readily available. Nepal's mild climate ensures that a wide variety of vegetables are available year round. Most foods are cooked in mustard oil or clarified butter.

Momos, steamed dumplings filled with vegetables or meat and dipped in a hot sauce, are popular. Some shops in the markets specialize in different types of momos. *Kothays* are similar to momos but are fried like an Indian *samosa.* *Thukpa* is a simple, popular noodle soup. *Gyakok* is an elaborate meat and vegetable soup served in a large metal pot with coals underneath to keep it hot. *Sikarni* is a delicious dessert of spiced and sweetened yogurt.

Sweet milk tea is the most popular drink, and tea vendors can often be seen going from shop to shop with their teapot and glasses. *Chang* is the local beer and is made from rice, barley, or millet. A distilled liquor, *rakshi* is also made from the local grains.

Most of the better restaurants in Kathmandu are located in the major hotels and accept credit cards. Prices are based on the cost of a meal for one person, without drinks or tips. Categories are *Expensive,* $8–12; *Moderate,* $5–$8; and *Inexpensive,* less than $5.

Telephone numbers, when available, are included in this list. However, except for the deluxe hotel restaurants, reservations are not necessary. Since meals are included with the lodgings in places outside Kathmandu, those dining rooms are not included.

Expensive

Amber Restaurant. Durbar Marg; tel. 216282. Fine Indian cuisine with live music to accompany the evening meal.
The Apsara. In the Hotel Malla; tel. 410320. Features Continental cuisine with a Nepalese touch.
Downtown. Everest Sheraton Hotel; tel. 220567. For those feeling a bit homesick, this dining room features American food.
Al Fresco. Hotel Soaltee Oberoi; tel. 211211. The best place for Italian food, including fresh pasta and pizzas.
The Chimney Room. Hotel Yak & Yeti; tel. 413999. Perhaps out of the borscht circuit, but good Russian cuisine is featured here.
Ghar-E-Kabob. Durbar Marg; tel. 216282. Tops for the tandoori style of Indian cuisine. Also live music in the evenings.
Gurkha Grill. Another Hotel Soaltee Oberoi dining room, decorated like a Gurkha officers' mess hall. Continental cuisine, with nightly dancing.
Himalchuli. Also in Hotel Soaltee Oberoi, decorated with Tibetan wall hangings. Features Nepalese music and dance performances. The food is a blend of the two countries.
La Marmite. Durbar Marg; tel. 213458. Kathmandu's only restaurant serving exclusively French food.
Sunkosi. Durbar Marg; tel. 215299. Wonderful Nepalese *sikarni* served at this restaurant, with a brick interior reminiscent of old Kathmandu.

Moderate

Anan. Khichapokhari. Modest restaurant serving primarily Nepalese and Tibetan fare.

Arirang Korean Restaurant. Durbar Marg. As the name says, the food is Korean.

La Dolce Vita. Thamel. Italian food, and not bad.

Fuji Restaurant. Kantipath. Also, as the name says, Japanese food is served here.

Kasthamandap Restaurant. Hotel Mandap. Nepalese and Tibetan dishes are featured.

Koto Restaurant. Durbar Marg. Exclusively Japanese fare.

Nanglo. Durbar Marg; The fare here is Chinese, and rather good.

New Kabab Corner. Hotel Gautam. This dining room features Indian food, particularly the tandoori style.

Old Vienna Inn. Thamel. Continental cuisine with a limited menu.

RaRa Restaurant. Durbar Marg; tel. 216006. Japanese food, including a sushi bar.

Ras Rand. Lazimpat. Principally Chinese food, but a few Nepalese dishes are available.

Tibet's Kitchen. Thamel. Tibetan food prepared over an open barbecue-type pit.

HOW TO GET AROUND. By Air. *Royal Nepal Airlines* (RNAC) services some 40 domestic airports throughout the country. Daily services are operated to the major tourist destinations, such as Meghauli (for Tiger Tops), a 30-minute flight south of Kathmandu, and Pokhara, a 35-minute flight west of the capital. Flights into the numerous small mountain airstrips, primarily used by locals and trekkers, are often disrupted because of poor weather conditions. These flight cancellations can cause a backup of passengers that can take days to clear, so be sure to leave plenty of time in your travel plans for unexpected delays if you are planning to use one of these remote airstrips. It is often a better idea to fly in and walk out to avoid the possibility of getting stuck a long way from your connecting flight out of the country.

For the popular destinations, RNAC has a dual pricing system, which has tourists paying much more than local residents. Some sample round-trip domestic airfares: Kathmandu to Pokhara, $80; to Meghauli (for Tiger Tops), $90; to Bhairawa (for Lumbini), $37; to Lukla (for Sagarmatha National Park and trekking), $110.

By Car. There are only about 3,500 miles of roads in Nepal. About half are considered all-weather roads, and even these are often closed by monsoon rains. Major road routes include the Tribhuvan Rajpath, 160 miles from Kathmandu to Birganj on the Indian border; the Prithvi Rajpath, 160 miles from Kathmandu to Pokhara; the Arniko Highway, 65 miles from Kathmandu north to Kodari on the Chinese border; the Mugling Narayanghat Highway, 100 miles from Kathmandu to Chitwan National Park. Distance along these roads can be deceptive; the 160-mile journey from Kathmandu to Pokhara can take six hours. A road from east to west along the whole length of the southern border has been under construction for many years with the help of several nations, but there are still a number of gaps in the road.

Self-drive **cars** are not readily available nor are they advisable in Nepal, unless you have extensive experience driving on narrow mountain roads that are busy with large trucks and buses. However, you can hire a car and driver for about $45 per day through local travel agents.

In the Kathmandu Valley, there are many different options for getting around. Organized **tours** are by far the best way to see a lot in a short time. However, if you prefer to do your exploring on your own, a **bicycle** is probably the best means of transport, although cycling can be a real challenge on the crowded, bumpy roads of Kathmandu. Bicycles can be hired by the day for NRs. 10. **Taxis** can also be hired for the day at a rate of NRs. 400–500. Metered taxis and motorized **rickshaws** are available throughout the city, as are tricycle rickshaws. **Buses** are available to virtually any spot accessible by road, but they tend to be slow, crowded, and uncomfortable. Definitely for the hardened traveler only.

TOURS. Nepal is included by many of the tour operators who have programs for India. There are also a number of operators specializing in adventure and trekking tours.

Tours from the U.S.: *Shiba Travel,* 1776 Broadway, Suite 1603, New York, NY 10019; tel. 800–223–1622 or 212–586–8847.

Lindblad Travel, Inc., 1 Sylvan Rd. North, Westport, CT 06881; tel. 800–243–5657 or 203–226–8531.

Tours of Distinction, 141 East 44th St., New York, NY 10017; tel. 212–661–4680.

Abercrombie & Kent, 1000 Oakbrook Rd., Oakbrook, IL 60521; tel. 800–323–7308 or 312–887–7766.

Zutshi's Travel Service, 130 Vine St., Reno, NV 89503; tel. 702–323–0110. Contact: Suraj Zutshi.

Tours from Canada: *Canadian Himalayan Expeditions,* Crossways Travel, 2340 Dundas St. West, Toronto, Ontario M6 P4 A9; tel. 416–535–2993. Contact Joe Pillar for specialized tours and trekking.

Tours from the U.K.: *Trailfinders,* 46 Earls Court Rd., London W8 6EJ (tel. 837–9631), is a clearinghouse for information on adventure travel and is well worth contacting.

Other operators are *Kuoni Travel,* Kuoni House, Dorking, Surrey RH5 (tel. 0306–885044); *Explorasia,* 13 Chapter St., London SW1 (tel. 630–7102); *Royal Orchid Holidays,* Thai International, 41 Albemarle St., London W1 (tel. 491–7953); and *Alta Holidays Ltd.,* Alta House, 152 King St., London W6 0GU (tel. 741–8041).

In the more comfortable field are *Swan Hellenic,* Beaufort House, St. Botolph St., London EC3A (tel. 247–0401), and *Serenissima Travel,* 2 Lower Sloane St., London SW1 W8BJ (tel. 730–9841).

TOURING ITINERARIES. Because it is a small country, Nepal can easily be seen in one to two weeks. During the busy tourist season of October and November, it is wise to have confirmed hotel reservations. At other times, it is easy to make arrangements once you have arrived in the country.

One-Week Tour

Day 1. Sightseeing in Kathmandu; evening cultural program.

Day 2. Mountain flight or sunrise excursion to see the Himalayas; see Patan's Durbar Square, Tibetan Refugee Center, handicrafts center, and Swayambunath Stupa in the afternoon.

Day 3. Visit Dakshinkali, Shesh Narayan, Chobar Gorge and Kirtipur in the morning; the restored city of Bhaktapur, Boudhanath Stupa, and Pashupatinath in the afternoon.

Day 4. Travel to Chitwan National Park for a jungle safari.

Day 5. Elephant rides, dugout canoe trip, nature walks, bird-watching in the park.

Day 6. Travel to Pokhara; take an afternoon boat ride on Phewa Lake.

Day 7. Get up early to see the sunrise over the Himalayas, tour Pokhara, and return to Kathmandu in the afternoon.

Two-Week Tour

Day 1. Sightseeing in Kathmandu; evening cultural program.

Day 2. Morning mountain flight to view the Himalayas; see Patan's Durbar Square, Tibetan Refugee Camp, handicrafts center, and Swayambunath Stupa in the afternoon.

Day 3. Trip by car to the Chinese road on the spectacular Kodari Highway.

Day 4. Visit the restored city of Bhaktapur in the morning; travel to Dhulikel or Nagarkot for sunset over the Himalayas and spend the night.

Day 5. Sunrise over the Himalayas; visit Changu Narayan Temple on the way back to Kathmandu; see Boudhanath Stupa and Pashupatinath in the afternoon.

Day 6. Visit Dakshinkali, Shesh Narayan, Chobar Gorge and Kirtipur in the morning; in the afternoon, visit Budhanilkantha Temple.

Day 7. Raft trip down the Trisuli River; spend the night camping beside the river.

Day 8. Go to the Royal Chitwan National Park for a jungle safari and take an elephant ride through the jungle.

Day 9. Elephant rides, canoes rides, nature walks, bird-watching.

Day 10. Travel to Pokhara, take an afternoon boat ride on Phewa Lake, and see the sunset over the Himalayas.

Day 11. See the sunrise over the mountains and the sights in Pokhara in the morning; relax by the lake in the afternoon.

Day 12. Take a day hike or pony trip through the foothills outside Pokhara; visit old villages.

Day 13. Travel to Lumbini, birthplace of Buddha.

Day 14. Return to Kathmandu.

Three-Week Tour

Same as the two-week tour but spend one week trekking.

Now that it is possible to travel to Tibet from Nepal, many Kathmandu-based agents are offering trips to Lhasa and other cities in this remote country. Trips can be arranged for anywhere from four days to several weeks.

Among the best-known travel agencies in Kathmandu are *Adventure Travel Nepal,* Durbar Marg (tel. 221379); *Yeti Travels,* Durbar Marg (tel. 221234); *Annapurna Travel & Tours,* Durbar Marg (tel. 222339); *Natraj Tours and Travel,* Durbar Marg (tel. 222014); *Malla Travel & Tours,* Lekhnath Marg (tel. 410635); *Nepal Travel Agency,* Ram Shah Path (tel. 413188).

For trekking agencies, see *Trekking* section.

 CURRENCY. The Nepal rupee is divided into 100 paisa. The currency exchange rate is approximately NRs. 21.70 to U.S. $1, or NRs. 32.08 to £1. Currency notes are in denominations of 1, 2, 5, 10, 20, 50, 100, 500 and 1,000 rupees and coins are of 5, 10, 25 and 50 paisa and 1 rupee.

Banks are open Sunday through Friday, 10 A.M.–4 P.M. It is advisable to buy only the internationally well-known types of travelers' checks, such as *American Express, Bank of America,* or *Cooks,* since banks may refuse to accept others. Credit cards can be used in the major hotels, a few of the better restaurants, and some of the antique, curio, and rug shops. Leading hotels usually add a 10 percent service charge and a 10–15 percent government tax, depending on how many stars the hotel has. Most hotels insist on being paid in foreign currency; if they accept rupees, they insist on seeing a currency-exchange receipt. Be sure to request one of these receipts whenever you change currency. Only 10 percent of the money you have changed into Nepalese rupees can be changed back to foreign currency and then only if you can produce sufficient receipts. Only Indian and Nepalese citizens can exchange Indian rupees.

 TIPPING. Major hotels usually add a 10 percent service charge to the bill, so tipping the many employees who have been seeing to your needs is not necessary. However, if you wish to tip bellhops, NRs. 5 to 10 is usually sufficient. In first-class restaurants, if the service and food were particularly good, a 5–10 percent tip is acceptable. It is not necessary to tip taxi drivers.

TIME. Nepalese time is 5 hours 45 minutes ahead of Greenwich Mean Time, noon in London being 5:45 P.M. in Nepal. Nepal is 15 minutes ahead of Indian Standard Time.

MAIL AND TELECOMMUNICATIONS. The General Post Office on Kantipath in Kathmandu is open 10 A.M.– 5 P.M. daily. It is closed on Saturdays and public holidays. Nearby is a telecommunications office with international cable and telex facilities. Leading hotels and travel agents also have telex facilities. Satellite telephones provide fast and inexpensive overseas services.

An airmail postcard costs NRs. 4 to America or Europe. A 20-gram airmail letter to America costs NRs. 8 and to Europe, NRs. 7. It is easiest to buy stamps at your hotel desk and place your cards and letters in the post box provided. Cards and letters, although they take a while to reach their destination, usually do go through. However, it is a better idea to carry souvenirs home rather than have them mailed. Mailing packages yourself from the special foreign post office can be a tedious, time-consuming, and aggravating experience and is best avoided. There are shipping companies that can package and forward any large items for you. *Sharmasons* is one of the most reliable shipping agencies.

BUSINESS HOURS. Government offices, museums, and banks are open 10 A.M.–5 P.M., February–November, and 10 A.M.–4 P.M. the rest of the year. Shop hours are generally 9 A.M.–8 P.M. On Saturdays, government offices and banks are closed. As in India, the numerous public holidays can be an unexpected nuisance.

All major hotels have money exchange counters that are open every day. In addition, two exchange bank counters in Kathmandu are open every day of the year: *Rastriya Banijya Supermarket Branch,* New Road, 10 A.M.–5 P.M. and *Rastriya Banijya Thamel Branch,* Thamel, 7:30 A.M.–7 P.M.

ELECTRICITY. The supply of electricity in Kathmandu is now fairly reliable since a nearby hydroelectric generating plant was opened. Outside the Kathmandu Valley, it can be erratic. Current is 220 volts/50 cycles, so a transformer is necessary for using American appliances such as hair dryers and electric razors.

USEFUL ADDRESSES AND PHONE NUMBERS. The police telephone number (emergencies) is 211999 in Kathmandu. But when you need help, it is best to contact the management of your hotel first because few of Nepal's police officers speak English.

Tourist Information Center, Gangapath, tel. 220818.
Central Immigration, Maiti Devi, tel. 412337.
American Embassy, Pani Pokhari, tel. 411179, 411601, 413836.
British Embassy, Lainchaur, tel. 414588, 410583.
Indian Embassy, Lainchaur, tel. 410900, ext 230.
Air India, Kantipath, tel. 212335.
Biman Bangladesh Airlines, Durbar Marg, tel. 222544.
British Airways, Durbar Marg, tel. 222266.
Burma Airways, Durbar Marg, tel. 224839.
Royal Nepal Airlines, New Road, tel. 214511.
Thai International Airways, Durbar Marg, tel. 224917.

WHAT TO SEE AND DO. For many people, Nepal means one thing—the majestic *Himalayas.* With Mount Everest towering over them all, these are the highest peaks in the world and form a backbone running the entire length of the country. There are many options for viewing this spectacular mountain range. Several small towns in the hills outside Kathmandu offer pleasant accommodations for leisurely viewing of the mountains. The most popular are sunrise and sunset trips to Nagarkot, Dhulikhel, and Kahani. For a more exciting view of the Himalayas, Royal Nepal Airlines offers a morning "Mountain Flight" that provides a close-up view of Mount Everest and many other peaks. However, Pokhara is the best spot for just sitting and absorbing the breathtaking splendor of these mountains. Situated on a picturesque lake, Pokhara is a quiet rural town less than 25 miles from Machhapuchhare Peak, sometimes called the *Matterhorn of Nepal.* Surrounding this picture-perfect sacred mountain are the impressive peaks of the Annapurnas and Dhauligiri.

The *Kathmandu Valley* has often been described as a living museum. Not only are there dozens of old temples and palaces featuring the unique art and architecture of Nepal, but there are also the colorful people, many of whom still follow a lifestyle that has changed little in hundreds of years. Durbar Square and Hanuman Dhoka Square are the center of old Kathmandu. On these two adjacent squares are some of the finest examples of Nepal's characteristic pagoda-style temple architecture. Intricately carved wooden window lattices decorate many of the old buildings, both here and in the old streets that radiate out from this point. In the bazaars of Asan Tole, Indrachowk, and Kel Tole, there are many Hindu and Buddhist temples, as well as open-fronted shops selling a wide variety of unusual items.

Jungle safaris are also a popular attraction in Nepal. At Royal Chitwan National Park, several lodges provide visitors with the opportunity to see some of the rarest animals of the Indian subcontinent, including the one-horned rhinoceros and the royal Bengal tiger. Rafting down the Trisuli River is a popular way of getting to the park. Several other rivers in Nepal provide exciting white-water adventures.

Lumbini, the birthplace of Buddha, is another location of interest. Archaeological excavations continue to uncover ancient ruins in this area.

 FESTIVALS. Nepal is a land of festivals. Hardly a day goes by without a festival being celebrated somewhere in the kingdom. The Nepalese are a devoutly religious people, and their numerous Hindu and Buddhist deities are the focus of most of the country's largest festivities. Other festivals are dedicated to ancestors and deceased relatives or other family celebrations. The planting and harvesting of the crops and the change of seasons are also cause for much celebration. Festivities usually include ritual bathing in sacred rivers and lakes, visiting temples with special offerings, and feasting or fasting. The period from August to October, after the harvest is in, is a particularly busy festival time. Most Nepalese festivals are based on the lunar calendar, so the exact date changes from year to year. Following are some of the more important festivals and the dates on which they will be celebrated in 1988.

February 16. *Shivaratri* is one of Nepal's most important festivals and, as the name implies, it is dedicated to the god Shiva. Hundreds of thousands of Hindus from Nepal and India make the pilgrimage to worship at Pashupatinath Temple in Kathmandu. There is much feasting and ritual bathing in the holy Bagmati River.

Sri Panchami, on **February 23,** serves a dual purpose. It is the first day of spring, according to the Nepalese calendar, and it is also a day for honoring Saraswati, the Hindu goddess of learning. Students all over the Kathmandu Valley visit shrines dedicated to Saraswati. In the morning, the Saraswati Temple at Swayambunath is a particularly good place to observe students worshiping.

Tibetan New Year also occurs in **February.** At Boudhanath Stupa east of Kathmandu, Tibetans who have spent the winter here hold festivities before making the long trip back to Tibet. Tibetans and Sherpas perform folk songs and dances.

February 25– March 3 is *Holi Purnima.* During this festival, which has little religious significance, people throw colored water on each other. There is much laughter and fun, but it can get messy. Watch your camera and clothes.

April. *Chaitra Dasain,* for the goddess Durga, is celebrated with animal sacrifices. Dasain is held again in October with many more festivities.

Bisket Jatra on **April** 13, is the biggest festival in Bhaktapur and falls on the Nepalese New Year. A week of celebration includes chariot processions, feasting, and the ceremonial raising of a huge wooden pole.

Nava Barsha (Nepalese New Year), **April** 13, a national holiday, is celebrated with much music and dancing.

White Machhendranath Jatra, also begins on **April** 13. A tall spire of green foliage is mounted on a huge chariot bearing the image of the White Machhendranath and pulled through the old sections of Kathmandu for four days. This festival is celebrated by Hindus and Buddhists alike.

Red Machhendranath Jatra, beginning **April** 20, is Patan's biggest festival and is similar to the celebration of the White Machhendranath in Kathmandu. A large chariot is pulled through the city for several days.

May 1 celebrates *Buddha Jayanti (Baishakh Purnima).* On this full-moon day, Buddha's birth, enlightenment, and death are celebrated at Buddhist shrines throughout Nepal. In Lumbini, the birthplace of Buddha, there is a special fair. In the Kathmandu Valley, Swayambunath Stupa is the best place to observe the festivities.

August 28 kicks off *Gaijatra.* This carnival-type festival lasts for eight days, during which time cows and teenagers dressed as cows parade through the streets. Gaijatra is meant to help family members who have died during the year complete a smooth trip to heaven. Cows are believed to be helpful in this journey. Dancing, singing, and humorous performances satirizing current sociopolitical situations are all part of this festival.

September 2 is *Krishnastami,* the birthday of Krishna, an incarnation of the god Vishnu. Celebrations are held at the Krishna Mandir in Patan and at Changu Narayan Temple east of Kathmandu. There is a procession through the streets of Patan, as well as singing and dancing. It is also a day of fasting.

Teej, **September** 14, is a women's festival during which Hindu women in Kathmandu visit Pashupatinath Temple to worship Shiva and Parvati. Ritual bathing in the sacred Bagmati River is meant to wash away all the sins of the past year.

Indrajatra begins **September** 24. Lasting for eight days, this festival is dedicated to Indra, the Hindu god of rain. Masked dancers perform nightly in Kathmandu's Hanuman Dhoka Square, and the huge mask of the White Bhairav is displayed for the only time during the year. The king visits the Kumari, Nepal's living goddess, before she is paraded through the old city in an ornate chariot. Several other chariots are also pulled through the streets of old Kathmandu.

October 18 starts *Bada Dasain (Durga Puja).* Lasting 10–15 days, this is Nepal's biggest and most important festival. Celebrated at the end of the monsoon season, Bada Dasain is dedicated to the goddess Durga and the triumph of good over evil. In Hanuman Dhoka Square, there are many bloody animal sacrifices to Durga. In rural villages, giant swings are set up for the children.

November 8 begins *Tihar (Lakshmi Puja).* This five-day festival is marked by the worship of different animals, including crows, dogs, and cows. Lakshmi, the goddess of wealth, is also worshiped, and, on one day of the festival, thousands of tiny butter lamps line the streets as each household welcomes the goddess.

Mani Rimdu is also held during **November.** Celebrated most enthusiastically in Namche Bazaar, this Sherpa festival features masked lamas performing traditional dances in the courtyards of monasteries throughout the region near Mount Everest.

December 29 notes the *Birthday of H. M. King Birendra,* with a huge parade, fireworks, and many other festivities. At the main rally on the Tundikhel parade grounds in Kathmandu, groups of people from all over the country dress in their traditional costumes and perform songs and dances.

TOURS. Guided bus tours cover most of Nepal's main attractions. Dozens of local travel agents based in Kathmandu offer daily sightseeing excursions to Kathmandu, Patan, and Bhaktapur, as well as other sights of interest to tourists who wish to visit in and around the valley.

Popular guided bus tours, costing NRs 75–100, include the following half-day trips:

Kathmandu, Swayambunath, and Patan. Kathmandu's Durbar Square area, the ancient Buddhist stupa of Swayambunath atop a hill outside the city, Patan's Durbar Square area, and the Tibetan Refugee Center where wool rugs are made.

Bhaktapur, Boudhanath, and Pashupatinath. Excellent West German restorations of temples and palaces in Bhaktapur, the huge stupa sacred to Tibetan Buddhists at Boudhanath, and the most sacred Hindu temple in Nepal, Pashupatinath.

Dakshinkali, Chobar Gorge, and Shesh Narayan Temple. Animal sacrifices at Dakshinkali every Saturday and Tuesday, ancient stone carvings and sacred ponds at Shesh Narayan, and the narrow gorge where the waters of the Kathmandu Valley cut through a large hill.

Other popular tours include sunrise and sunset mountain-viewing trips to Dhulikhel, Nagarkot, and Kakani. These trips cost NRs. 100–125. The trip to the Chinese border at Kodari takes an entire day and costs NRs. 300. This exciting mountain drive affords great views of both the Himalayas and the life of Nepal's village people.

Overnight tours to Pokhara can also be arranged for NRs. 800–1,000.

Two- and three-day jungle safaris in Royal Chitwan National Park are popular. There are several lodges within the park or just outside the park's boundaries. The cost of these trips ranges from $75 to $300 for a two-night stay, which includes all meals, elephant rides, dugout canoe rides, jungle hikes, bird-watching, and cultural programs.

Royal Nepal Airlines offers a morning mountain-viewing flight daily between October and March (sometimes as late as May). The flight provides a close-up glimpse of Mount Everest, as well as dozens of other Himalayan peaks. The cost is $65 when booked through the airline and $75–$80 when booked through a travel agent.

MUSEUMS, GALLERIES, AND LIBRARIES. The *National Museum* (tel. 211504), just west of Kathmandu near Swayambunath Stupa, has an interesting collection of artworks dating back to the fifth century. Stone statues of gods and goddesses display the skill of the early Lichhavis. Bronzes, wood carvings, religious paintings, and beautifully illustrated old books are among the displays in the art gallery. Another wing of the museum contains natural science displays and an arms and armor display. There is also a memorial museum dedicated to the late King Mahendra. The museum is open every day except Tuesday, 10 A.M.–4 P.M. in winter and 10 A.M.–5 P.M. the rest of the year. The entrance fee is NRs. 3 and NRs. 8 if you carry a camera.

The *Tribhuvan Museum* (tel. 212294), devoted to the life of former King Tribhuvan, and a numismatic collection are housed in part of the old Royal Palace in Hanuman Dhoka Square, Kathmandu. Although the museum is of little interest to tourists, it is necessary to buy a ticket to see the inside of the old palace. In addition to the beautiful window carvings that line the palace's courtyards, there is Basantapur Tower, which rises nine stories above the ground and affords spectacular views of the city. The museum is open 10:15 A.M.–4:15 P.M. daily except Tuesdays. The entrance fee is NRs. 5 and NRs. 8 if you carry a camera.

The *National Art Gallery* (no phone), Durbar Square, Bhaktapur, has an excellent collection of traditional and religious art, which is partially housed in the old Palace of 55 Windows. Open 10 A.M.–5 P.M. daily except Tuesdays. The entrance fee is NRs. 5 and NRs. 8 with camera.

The *Brass and Bronze Museum* (no phone), Dattatreya Square, Bhaktapur, houses many fine examples of Nepalese metal crafting of the past two centuries. Open 10 A.M.–5 P.M. daily except Tuesdays. The entrance fee is NRs. 5 and NRs. 8 with a camera.

Swayambunath Museum (no phone), beside Swayambunath Stupa, is a small collection of old stone statues. Open daily. Free.

The *Natural History Museum* (tel. 212889), located near the foot of Swayambunath Hill, has an extensive collection of stuffed and preserved birds, mammals, reptiles, insects, and plants from all over Nepal. Open 10 A.M.–5 P.M. daily except Saturdays. Free.

Several art galleries in Kathmandu specialize in the contemporary art of Nepal. *Shrijana Art Gallery, October Gallery* and *NAFA Art Gallery* are some that regularly have exhibits and sales.

There are two English language libraries in Kathmandu. The *American Library* (tel. 221250) on Juddha Sadak (corner of New Road) has an excellent selection of current periodicals and newspapers from the United States; there is also a small collection of books. The *British Council Library* (tel. 213796) on Kantipath requires a local sponsor for membership. The *Kaiser Library* (tel. 213562), housed in an old Rana palace just off Kantipath, includes old books in many languages. This was once a private collection.

In Pokhara, there is a cultural museum that features life-size dioramas and photographs of several of that region's different ethnic groups. Open daily except Tuesday. *Craft of Pokhara,* a small craft shop and gallery near the airport, has displays with information about many of the local handicrafts.

SPORTS. By far the most popular sport among visitors to Nepal is **trekking**, and a trip to this mountainous country is not complete without at least some sort of trekking experience, even if it is just a short hike through the hills outside Kathmandu. It is advisable to make arrangements before your arrival with one of the tour operators listed in the *Tours* section above.

Rafting has also become popular in recent years. A number of companies in Kathmandu offer rafting expeditions of lengths varying from one day to 10 days or more. There are trips for every level of experience on Nepal's many beautiful rivers that wind their way down from the high Himalayas to the plains of India. Rafting companies provide everything necessary for a gentle float or a wild white-water adventure. November–March are the best months for rafting. The average cost of a rafting trip is $50.

Some of the better rafting companies include *Great Himalayan Rivers,* Hotel Woodlands (tel. 222683); *Himalayan River Exploration,* Durbar Marg (tel. 222706); and *Lama Excursions,* Durbar Marg (tel. 410786).

Mountain biking is rapidly gaining popularity as more of these rugged bicycles become available for rent in Nepal. Many of the country's trails and unpaved roads are ideal for exploring on a **bicycle.** Mountain bikes can be rented from *Mountain Bikes Nepal* (no phone), Thamel, Kathmandu, for NRs. 50 per day. This company also offers organized trips.

Golfing in Nepal is limited to two nine-hole courses in the Kathmandu area. The Golf Club (tel. 212836) is located near the airport, and the second course is located at Gokarna Safari Park (tel. 412103). The greens fee for nonmembers at each course is NRs. 75.

Horseback riding and **elephant rides** are also available at Gokarna Safari park. Horses are rented at NRs. 80 per hour and elephants at NRs. 100 per hour.

It is also possible to ride elephants at Chitwan National Park, and horses can be rented in Pokhara from *Pokhara Pony Treks* (tel. 253).

Pokhara also has **rowboats** for rent on Phewa Lake. Boats are available with or without an oarsman. At Chitwan National Park **dugout canoes** provide rides on the park's meandering rivers.

TREKKING. Nepal's most popular outdoor sport, and the main reason many people visit this country, is trekking. It was not until recently that any roads were built in this rugged, mountainous country. Even now, most of Nepal's tiny rural villages are connected only by well-worn trails that wind through green valleys and over steep mountains. Thousands of miles of trails lace the Himalayas and their foothills, and many of these paths are open to adventurous foreign travelers who come in search of mountain vistas and the Nepal of past centuries. More than half of Nepal's population lives in the hills and mountains on small farms carved out of the steep hillsides. These people, far from roads and electricity, live a lifestyle that has not changed in centuries. Different ethnic groups inhabit different parts of the country. It is this cultural diversity, along with the spectacular Himalayas, that is attracting more and more trekkers each year.

Trekking in Nepal can be as easy or as difficult as you want it to be, and trips can last from a few days to three months. There are dozens of agencies headquartered in Kathmandu that will arrange treks of various lengths and budgets. Some of the better known ones include *Above the Clouds Trekking,* Thamel (tel. 41291); *Amadablam Trekking,* Lazimpat (tel. 410219); *Mountain Travel,* Durbar Marg (tel. 212808); and *Sherpa Cooperative Trekking,* Durbar Marg (tel. 223348). These and other agencies specialize in group treks that include guides, porters, and cooks. They will make all the preparations for you, including obtaining trekking permits, and can provide all the necessary equipment for the trek. Although it is possible to contact these companies before you arrive in Nepal, it is not necessary. People often arrive in Nepal without any intention of trekking, but when they discover how easy and how much fun it can be, they are anxious to go themselves.

On group treks arranged through an agency, porters will carry everything except what you want to carry yourself such as a camera, canteen, and snacks. Each night, tents will be set up for you and dinner prepared. In the morning, after breakfast, you will start out on the trail while the porters break camp. Even with their heavy loads, the porters will easily catch up with you. A long lunch break provides ample opportunity for slow walkers to catch up and even get in a bit of rest before continuing to that day's destination. Usually no more than six hours a day are spent walking, and this is at a leisurely pace. A trek of this type, when arranged in Nepal will cost about $50 per day.

More adventurous and more experienced hikers with plenty of time can strike out on well-marked trails with just a guide or a porter. On the more popular trekking routes, it is not necessary to carry any food. In the villages that are scattered along the trails, small inns provide inexpensive rooms and meals. Several good books that describe these popular hiking routes are complete with information on walking times and the availability of lodging and food. A guide will be able to provide most of the same information for a specific area. This type of trek costs about $5–$10 per day, which includes the cost of a guide or porter. All equipment necessary for trekking, including backpacks, boots, sleeping bags, tents, down jackets, rain gear, stoves, and cookware, can be easily rented in Kathmandu or Pokhara for a few rupees a day.

The best months for trekking are October and November. After the monsoon ends, the forests and fields are green, the skies are clear, and temperatures, even at high elevations, are moderate. During March and April, also popular months for trekking, the wildflowers are in bloom in the middle elevations. Particularly beautiful are the white, pink, and red flowers of the huge rhododendron trees that grow in thick forests throughout Nepal. During the winter months, the skies are clear and the snowy peaks sparkle in the bright sun. By day, the temperature is ideal for walking, but at night, it can drop below freezing. Above 9,000 feet, snow can be a problem. May and June are a good time to visit the higher altitudes of the Himalayas. The snows have melted and the monsoon has not yet started. During the monsoon months from June to September, many trails are washed away by the heavy rains. Landslides and swollen rivers also make travel nearly impossible. Land leeches are quite common at this time.

Before beginning a trek, you must obtain a trekking permit. These permits are easily obtained from the *Central Immigration Office* in Kathmandu or the *Immigration Office* in Pokhara. The permits cost NRs. 60 per week, and you must submit two passport-size photographs and your passport with the application. Special permits, obtainable from the *Nepal Mountaineering Association,* are necessary for mountaineering expeditions. The more well-known peaks are often booked for years in advance, but many lesser peaks are readily available.

TREKKING ROUTES. There are three main trekking areas in Nepal. Within each region, many different treks are possible, depending on your abilities, interests, and available time. Where you begin your trek is up to you. You can begin trekking just outside Kathmandu, but new roads now make it possible to start much farther into the mountains. This is also true in the Pokhara region. Several small airstrips are scattered throughout these main trekking areas and can be used if your time is limited. However, because of weather conditions, these airstrips are often shut down for several days at a time. Be sure to leave plenty of room in your schedule if you plan to use one of them.

The most popular trek in Nepal is the **Pokhara-to-Jomosom Trek.** This route climbs up from the valley floor past terraced hillsides and small villages. As the trail climbs higher into the foothills of the Himalayas, it passes through dense rain forests, rhododendron forests inhabited by large langur monkeys, evergreen forests, and small terraced valleys and eventually reaches the barren, high desertlike regions along the Kali Gandaki River. This is the edge of the Tibetan Plateau; beyond this, there are no forests for 1,000 miles.

Because different ethnic groups inhabit the numerous small villages along this trek, each settlement has a different character. Building styles change from town to town, crops vary, and people look and dress differently, depending on their cultural heritage. For centuries, this trail has been a major trading route between the highlands of Tibet and the lowlands of Nepal and northern India. Many of the towns, especially those beyond Jomosom, look as if they have been around for thousands of years. For more than 2,000 years, the tiny village of Muktinath, 16 miles beyond Jomosom, has been a pilgrimage site for Buddhists and Hindus. Several small temples have been built here, and one of them houses the mysterious water and stone that burn. These eerie blue flames, caused by natural gas seepage, are considered holy, and thousands of pilgrims make the journey to see them every August. Nearby are the ancient towns of Jarakot and Kagbeni, both occupied by Tibetan people. This trek can be made in 16–20 days.

Another possible trek in this region is the classic **Around Annapurna Trek,** which takes about 25 days and includes much spectacular scenery before crossing the 17,700-foot Thorong Pass. Below this pass is Muktinath, where the trail joins the Jomosom-to-Pokhara trek.

For many people, nothing will do but to make the trek to Everest Base Camp. This high-altitude camp sits at the base of Mount Everest, with several other peaks rising up around it. This is the land of the Sherpas, the sturdy mountain people who have assisted so many mountaineering expeditions and treks. The Sherpas, being of Tibetan origin, are Buddhists; consequently, this region is full of Buddhist monasteries, which are one of the main attractions for trekkers. To reach the high elevations of Khumbu near Everest Base Camp, it is necessary to cross nearly 150 miles of rugged foothills known as the Solu region. Although there are many picturesque villages, forests, and terraced valleys throughout the Solu, there are few glimpses of the mountains. To save themselves the long, grueling hike into the Khumbu region, with its spectacular scenery, many people choose to fly into the airstrip at Lukla. This places you within two days' walk of Namche Bazaar, the gateway to the Khumbu region and Sagarmatha National Park. However, because Lukla is at 9,275 feet, a day's rest is necessary for acclimatization. At this elevation, altitude sickness is a real problem, and precautions must be taken to prevent becoming ill.

The third popular trekking area is the **Helambu–Gosainkund–Langtang** region just north of Kathmandu. These three distinctive regions offer a variety of trekking experiences. Each area is ideal for a one-week trek, or the areas can be combined for two- or three-week treks.

Helambu, which follows the northeast rim of the Kathmandu Valley, is a hilly region of moderate elevation, with many forests and terraced hillsides. Because it is south of the main Himalayas, with high mountains in between, there aren't many views of the snow-clad peaks from here. In the spring, when the rhododendrons are in bloom, Helambu is particularly stunning.

PHOTOGRAPHY. A wide variety of film is now available in Kathmandu, although prices are quite a bit higher than in the United States. It is better to bring an adequate supply of film to this highly photogenic country. Although Nepal is a small country, most visitors find much more to photograph than they had expected. From the spectacular panoramas of the Himalayas to the ancient buildings to the smiling children playing in the streets, Nepal offers a wealth of photographic opportunities. Kathmandu now has quite a few computerized one-hour film processing centers for color print film. These centers usually provide acceptable service, but it is best to carry your undeveloped film home with you. Most airports will hand check film and cameras, so it is not necessary to expose them to the possible damaging effects of X rays. Lead-foil film-storage bags to protect film from X rays are also available at camera shops.

Overexposure of photographs can be a problem in Nepal because of the intense light at high altitudes. A UV or skylight filter is a necessary accessory if your camera is equipped to accept filters. A polarizing filter, which will cut high altitude glare even more than a UV filter, can come in handy.

In museums you will be required to pay a separate fee, usually NRs. 5 – 7, to take your camera inside. Otherwise, you must lock it up in one of the lockers that is provided. In some Hindu temples, photography is prohibited. There are notices posted in English in these places.

MEDICAL NOTES AND FACILITIES. Medical facilities in Nepal are extremely limited, and those that are available often are far below Western standards. There is only one doctor for approximately every 30,000 people in Nepal. Because of the general lack of hygiene and sanitation throughout the country, it is advisable to take several precautions to ensure that you don't get sick.

Gastrointestinal illnesses are the most common problem for tourists and Nepalese alike. Frequently encountered disorders vary from upset stomachs and abdominal cramps to diarrhea and vomiting accompanied by fever. These symptoms may be brief (24 hours) or more long-term and are attributable to a variety of organisms. Most common, however, is the sort of illness that comes on quickly and disappears with equal speed. Rest and plenty of fluids are the best treatments for such an illness, which is commonly caused by a change in diet and different bacteria in the environment. To minimize your risk of getting ill, avoid street stalls, eat only fruits that have been peeled, and avoid uncooked vegetables unless you know that they have been treated to kill bacteria (this is a common practice at better restaurants, which usually post a notice in the menu that their salads have been treated).

However, much more serious illnesses, such as hepatitis, cholera, typhoid, dysentery, and giardiasis can also be spread by contaminated food and water. It is advisable to have inoculations against hepatitis, cholera, and typhoid before arriving in Nepal. However, your risk of contracting any of these illnesses is slight.

Rabies is also common in Nepal. Dogs and monkeys are the two most commonly encountered carriers of this serious disease. It is advisable to give both of these animals a wide berth, if possible. Most important, do not harass or otherwise disturb baby monkeys or puppies; the mothers are much more likely to attack you to protect their young. If you are bitten by an animal, immediately wash the wound for 20 minutes with running water to remove all saliva. The postexposure rabies vaccine should be taken as soon as possible. In

Kathmandu, the vaccine is available at the *Kalimati Clinic* (tel. 214743) and the *CIWEC Clinic* (tel. 410983).

Trekkers who hike to elevations above 9,000 feet may develop altitude sickness. Symptoms of altitude sickness include shortness of breath, headache, nausea, vomiting, weakness, and insomnia. More serious cases can develop into pulmonary and cerebral edema, which can cause death. The only cure for altitude sickness is to descend to lower elevations. A slow ascent is the best way to avoid the illness. The *Himalayan Rescue Association* (tel. 215855) by Kathmandu Guest House has an informative pamphlet on this subject.

If you need a doctor while in Nepal, first ask at your hotel. English-speaking doctors are on call with all the major hotels. For more serious illnesses or hospitalization, the *Patan Missionary Hospital,* Lagankhel, Patan (tel. 521034, 521048, 522266), is staffed by English-speaking doctors.

The Kalimati Clinic, Kalimati, Kathmandu, offers postexposure rabies vaccine and gamma globulin injections for the prevention of hepatitis. It is supervised and staffed by American volunteers.

The CIWEC Clinic, Baluwatar, Kathmandu, is staffed by American doctors and Western nurses.

For a more extensive list of English-speaking doctors in Nepal, contact the U.S. Embassy.

DRINKING WATER. Do not drink tap or stream water in Nepal unless you are certain that it has been boiled, filtered, or treated. Hotels usually provide each room with a bottle of water that is safe for drinking and brushing teeth. In restaurants, it is best to stick to hot tea, coffee, or bottled drinks. Soda water and mineral water are also widely available. When trekking, take extra precautions, such as boiling *and* treating water, if possible. Iodine is the best water treatment and is available in Kathmandu.

POLLUTION REPORT. Even this Himalayan kingdom, once thought of as Shangri-La, is no longer free of environmental pollution, although the air pollution problem is mostly confined to the Kathmandu Valley. Often a thick haze hangs over the Kathmandu Valley, obscuring the nearby mountains from view. An ever increasing number of diesel trucks and buses fill the city's air with their black smoke, and brick and cement factories on the outskirts of the valley further aggravate the problem. Add to this the smoke of domestic cooking fires (nearly everyone in Nepal still relies on wood for cooking), and the air in Kathmandu can become unpleasant.

A more irritating aspect of Kathmandu's pollution problem is the dust that constantly irritates the eyes during the drier months. Noise pollution is another serious problem. Constantly blaring car horns can quickly frazzle the nerves of any traveler who came here for a quiet mountain vacation.

LANGUAGE. The national language, Nepali, is rooted in Sanskrit and is of the Indo-Aryan family of languages. Distinct dialects are spoken in many districts. Among the most important of these are Newari, Sherpa, Gurung, Magar, Limbu, and Tamang. Since the influx of Tibetan refugees, Tibetan is being spoken more widely. English is widely understood in cities and towns where great importance is placed on an English education for children. Along popular trekking routes, innkeepers usually speak English, but other people you encounter along the trail likely will not.

RELIGION. Nepal is the only officially Hindu country in the world. The country's constitution recognizes Hinduism as the official religion, and 90 percent of the people are adherents. However, Buddhism also has an old history in Nepal (the Buddha was born in Lumbini, Nepal, in 623 B.C.) and is tolerated by the Hindu majority. In fact, the two religions are intricately entwined in Nepal, which can be confusing for visitors to this highly religious country.

Often a temple site may be sacred to both Hindus and Buddhists. Certain deities are worshiped by members of both religions. The White Machendra enshrined in a small temple in Kathmandu is considered by Buddhists to be Avalokiteshwara, a Bodhisattva, and by Hindus, an incarnation of Shiva. Even the Buddha is considered by Hindus to be an incarnation of Vishnu. Other deities worshiped by both Hindus and Buddhists include Saraswati, Banesh, Taleju, and Guheshwara. Many other Hindu gods also have Buddhist counterparts.

BEGGING. Beggars are becoming much more common in tourist-visited areas of Nepal. Traditionally, beggars have taken up positions near large temples. People who come to worship at these temples will often give a few paisa or a rupee to these destitute people. *Saddhus,* wandering holy men, are also seen at Hindu temples, and visitors often give alms to these ascetics. Away from temples, beggars fall into two categories—those who sit quietly on the street with their bowl in front of them and those who follow and harass tourists. The former are likely to be the more legitimately in need of handouts. Children will often approach with outstretched hands chanting, "One rupee, one rupee," or, "One pen, one pen." Do not give in to the demands of these children; they are usually not truly in need. They have learned that this is an easy way to get money from rich tourists. There are, however, many homeless children on the streets of Kathmandu who are genuinely in need of help. It is better to buy them a little food than to give them money. There are dozens of relief and development agencies working in Nepal, any one of which would be grateful for whatever contribution you can make. At the airport, in the departure lounge, several boxes are set up for donations of any remaining Nepalese currency you might have, since it is illegal to take money out of the country.

BEHAVIOR. Nepal is a relaxed and informal country. There are few customs that the visitor need be aware of. Perhaps it is most important to remember that Hindu temples are often off-limits to non-Hindus. These temples are usually marked with a sign in English. Other temples forbid any leather goods, such as shoes, belts, or camera cases, within their walls. In others, it is necessary to take off your shoes before entering—a custom that is often followed in Nepalese homes as well. If people are sitting or sleeping on the ground, do not step over them; this also applies to food that is on the ground or floor. When giving or receiving something, do not use your left hand. Instead, try to use both hands. Do not offer food to a Nepalese person if you have already taken a bit of it. Foreigners are considered "contaminated" and, therefore, food they have tasted is also contaminated.

 SHOPPING. It is easy to be overwhelmed by the myriad shopping opportunities in Nepal. Street after street is lined with shops full of unusual arts and handicrafts. Street vendors display their assortments of curios and souvenirs in any available space, whether it is a crowded shopping square or a temple compound.

Nearly everyone is willing to bargain, and discounts of 50 percent or more are possible. Street vendors are willing to drop their prices much more than are shopkeepers, and among shopkeepers, Tibetans drive a much harder bargain. Remember, don't ask a street vendor how much something costs unless you are ready for the hard sell.

Nepalese and Tibetan antiques used to be a great attraction, with lots of genuine bargains possible. However, it is now illegal to export Nepalese antiques. If you purchase something that even looks antique, it might be a good idea to ask the shopkeeper about getting an export license from the Department of Archaeology. Without the export seal from the government, your purchase could be confiscated when you try to leave the country. Tibetan antiques, however, can be exported if an export license is acquired.

Many of the most unusual and attractive items for sale in Nepal are actually of Tibetan origin. Tibetan carpets, handmade at several refugee camps in Nepal, are one of the best shopping values and can be purchased for a fraction of what they cost abroad. These beautiful carpets come in various sizes and qualities. Those having 100 knots per square inch and, colored by vegetable dyes, are the finest quality and most expensive. Much more common are the 85-knot rugs using vegetable or chemical dyes. There are also 65-knot rugs available. At the *Tibetan Refugee Center* in Patan, it is possible to observe these carpets being made.

Tankas, colorful paintings depicting Tibetan Buddhist themes, can be as finely detailed as any Indian miniature painting. These wall hangings are painted on canvas and are often bordered with silk. In the past, tankas were carried by wandering monks. At *Local Handicrafts & Workshop* on Taumadhi Square in Bhaktapur and *Mannie's* on Durbar Marg in Kathmandu, you can watch tankas painters at work.

Prayer wheels, small cymbals, handbells, and other ritual items of Tibetan Buddhism are available in a wide assortment of qualities. Generally, the best deals on such items are at Boudhanath and Swayambunath stupas.

Colorful Tibetan felt boots; wool coats and vests; and hand-knitted sweaters, socks, hats, and gloves are inexpensive and warm. Outlandishly colorful cotton clothing is reminiscent of Kathmandu's days as a hippie hangout. Shoulder bags in all shapes and sizes are also good buys.

Brass and bronze statues of Buddha, Hindu gods, and other figures, widely available, are cast at the *Patan Industrial Estate,* where prices are fixed and usually lower than in shops. There are many small woodcarving factories here, and most have showrooms offering good prices.

It is highly advisable to carry all your purchases home with you. If you must have something shipped, do not rely on the shop to forward your purchase, but use a reliable shipping agency. Some of the companies that provide packing and shipping are *Sharmasons Packers and Movers,* Kantipath; *Van Pack Movers,* Durbar Marg; *Atlas Packers and Movers,* Durbar Marg; *Universal Packers and Movers,* Durbar Marg; and *Shrestha International Cargo,* Thamel.

HINDI-ENGLISH VOCABULARY

Although English is the *lingua franca* of India, and is spoken by almost everyone who has received a high-school education, you may find yourself in a position where no one understands your English (although this is highly unlikely unless you stray by car far from the usual tourist paths). There being more than a dozen major languages and hundreds of dialects, we are quoting below only a few expressions of courtesy in Hindi, understood in most parts of India, together with the more current terms in art and architecture, religion, etc., you will come across in this volume. They are mostly of Sanskrit origin, the sacred language of the Indo-Aryans. Some are from Arabic and Persian.

You know more words of Indian origin than you think: they entered the English vocabulary during the presence of the East India Company and during subsequent British rule, spread everywhere English is spoken and were eventually absorbed into other languages.

Various

atcha	(ach-*cha*)	O.K.
bagh	(b*a*g)	a garden
baksheesh	(baksh*eesh*)	a tip, a reward
dhoti	(dhoetee)	skirtlike garment worn by Indians
ha (nasal)	(h*a*)	yes
howdah	(how-d*a*h)	the seat fixed on an elephant's back. It usually accommodates two in front and two behind.
ji	(*jee*)	a respectful suffix (Gandhi*ji*); also used as an address (ha-ji=yes sir).
mahout	(*ma*hoot)	elephant driver
maidan	(*ma*-eh-*dan*)	plain
mehrbani se	(may-her-banee-say)	please
nahin	(na*heen*)	no
namastey	(na-ma-stay)	word for all greetings
nawab	(*na*wab)	title given to important Moslem land-owners
ram-ram	(*ram-ram*)	equivalent of "hello"
sahib	(sa*heeb*)	master
Shri (or Sri); Shrimatee	(Shree/Shree-m*a*-tee)	Mr; Mrs
shukriya	(shookr*ee*ya)	thank you
wallah	(wal-*lah*)	a fellow (rickshaw wallah)

Art-Architecture

chaitya	(*cha*-eet-ya)	a Buddhist prayer hall
dravida	(dra-*vee-da*)	Southern or Dravidian style of architecture
dvarapala	(Varapala)	door guardian statue
ghazal	(*gha*-zal)	poetry set to music, originating from Persia and now usually sung in Urdu
geet	(geet)	light popular song
ghats	(*gha*ts)	terraces on a sacred river bank (also mountains)
gopuram	(go-poo-ram)	monumental gates of South Indian temple enclosures
gurudwara	(goo-rood-wara)	Sikh temple
jagamohan	(jag-mohan)	in Orissan architecture an enclosed porch preceding the sanctuary

Kathakali	(katha-kalee)	classic dance form of Kerala
mandir	(mandeer)	Hindu temple
mandapa	(mandapa)	porch
Manipuri	(maneepooree)	classical dance form of Manipur (Assam)
mithuna	(meethoonaa)	statues of amorous couples
Nagara style	(Nagaara)	the Northern or Indo-Aryan type of temple characterized by the tower
stupa	(stewpaa)	Buddhist sacred mound
sitar	(seetaar)	stringed instrument with movable frets, played by plucking the strings
torana	(towrana)	gate of a temple enclosure
vihara	(*vee*har)	a Buddhist monastery

Religion

ahimsa	(a-heem-saa)	non-violence, harmlessness
apsara	(aapsaaraa)	a damsel of Indra's heaven
ashram	(*aash*raam)	a hermitage
avatar	(ahvatar)	one of the various incarnations of Vishnu
Bodhisattva	(Bodheesatt*va*)	potential Buddha who before final enlightenment ministers to humanity
Brahma	(Bramma)	the creator of all things in Hindu Trinity
Brahmin	(Br*am-man*; nasal "n" pronounced)	the first, or priestly class in Hinduism
Buddha	(B*oodha*)	Prince Siddhartha, born on the Nepalese border about 563 B.C. Buddha means "the Enlightened One"
Devi	(Dayv*ee*)	Parvati, consort to Siva in her benevolent form
dharma	(Dh*arm*aa)	path of conduct
dharmachakra	(dhar*ma*chakra)	the Buddhist Wheel of the Law, an ancient solar symbol
Durga	(Doorg*a*)	Parvati, consort of Siva in her form as a destroyer of evil
guru	(gooroo)	spiritual teacher
hatha yoga	(haatha yog)	the mystic path of physical exercise
hinayana	(heenayana)	"small vehicle": early Buddhism with emphasis on the doctrine, rather than on worship
Jainism	(Ja-ay-nee-sum)	a religion founded by Mahavira in the 6th century B.C. preaching solicitude for all life
jatakas	(Ja-ta-kas)	tales about the Buddha in his previous incarnations
Kali	(Kalee)	the goddess Parvati in her terrible form
kirtan	(*keer*tan)	religious songs
Krishna	(Kreesh-n*a*)	hero of the epic Mahabharata. One of Vishnu's incarnations
Kshatriya	(sh*a*t-ree-y*a*)	the second, or warrior, caste in Hinduism
Lakshmi	(laksh-mee)	Goddess of wealth and beauty, the consort of Vishnu
lingam	(leengum)	sacred symbol of Siva
mahayana	(maha-yeah-na)	"great vehicle". Later from Buddhism, with emphasis on Buddha's divinity
mantra	(*man*tra)	a word or sentence used as an invocation
maya	(ma-yeah)	escape from material reality, an illusion
moksha	(mawksh*a*)	release from all material desires

mudra	(moodra)	ritual gestures denoting mystic powers
Nandi	(Nandee)	the sacred bull, Siva's mount
Nirvana	(Neervana)	eternal bliss
Pariahs	(paree-ahs)	the untouchables or outcasts of Hinduism (this practice is now banned in India)
Parvati	(Parvatee)	wife of Siva
prana	(pran; nasal "n" pronounced)	Breath of Life, sustaining the body
puja	(pooja)	wishful prayer performed before a god's image
Puranas	(pooranas)	Hindu mythology. There are eighteen Puranas and a number of epics which include the *Ramayana* and the *Mahabharata*
Rama	(Raam)	hero of the Ramayana
rishi	(reeshee)	Hindu sage
sadhu	(sadhoo)	a celibate holy man
samadhi	(samadhee)	the deepest form of yoga meditation
samsara	(saamsaaraa)	the cycle of life and rebirth
Saraswati	(Sa-ras-wa-tee)	Goddess of wisdom
Siva or Shiva	(Seeva or Sheeva)	God of the Hindu Trinity. The destructive and creative aspect
Sudra	(soodra)	the fourth main caste in Hinduism (farmers and artisans mostly)
sutra	(sootra)	a sacred text
swami	(swam-ee)	a teacher of certain branches of Hinduism
tandava	(tan-da-va)	Siva's cosmic dance, symbolic of his function of creation and destruction
Tirthankara	(Teerthankara)	one of the twenty-four Jain patriarchs who attained perfection
Trimurti		physical shape of the Hindu Trinity (Brahma, Vishnu, Siva)
twice-born		a term used to denote high-caste Hindus who are said to have a second birth when invested with the sacred thread of their caste
Vedanta	(Vay-dan-ta)	an inquiry into the aim of all knowledge; a metaphysic of intuition
Vedas	(Vay-das)	the four most ancient Hindu scriptures
Vishnu	(Veesh-noo)	the Preserver of Mankind in the Hindu Trinity
yoga	(yoga)	a discipline of meditation by which the powers of man over himself are developed
yogi	(yogee)	a follower of yoga

Index

INDIA

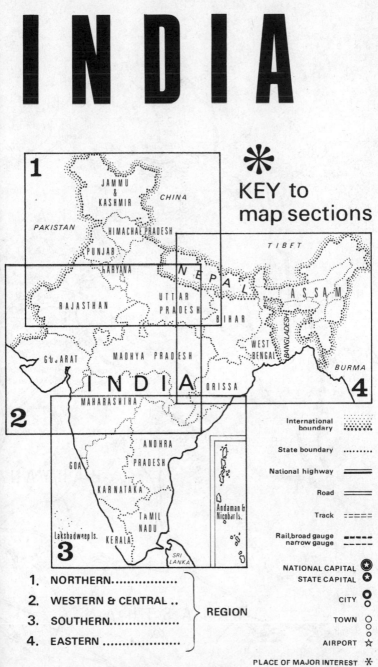

1

JAMMU & KASHMIR

CHINA

PAKISTAN

HIMACHAL PRADESH

PUNJAB

HARYANA

RAJASTHAN

UTTAR PRADESH

NEPAL

TIBET

ASSAM

BIHAR

BANGLADESH

GUJARAT

MADHYA PRADESH

WEST BENGAL

BURMA

I N D I A

ORISSA

4

MAHARASHTRA

2

ANDHRA PRADESH

GOA

KARNATAKA

TAMIL NADU

Andaman & Nicobar Is.

Lakshadweep Is.

KERALA

3

SRI LANKA

✳ KEY to map sections

International boundary	∵∵∵∵
State boundary	....
National highway	━━━
Road	══
Track	═════
Rail, broad gauge	▬▬▬
narrow gauge	▬ ▬ ▬

NATIONAL CAPITAL ◉
STATE CAPITAL ◉

CITY oo

TOWN ○○○○

AIRPORT ☆

PLACE OF MAJOR INTEREST ✳

1. **NORTHERN**.................
2. **WESTERN & CENTRAL** ..
3. **SOUTHERN**.................
4. **EASTERN** ....

REGION

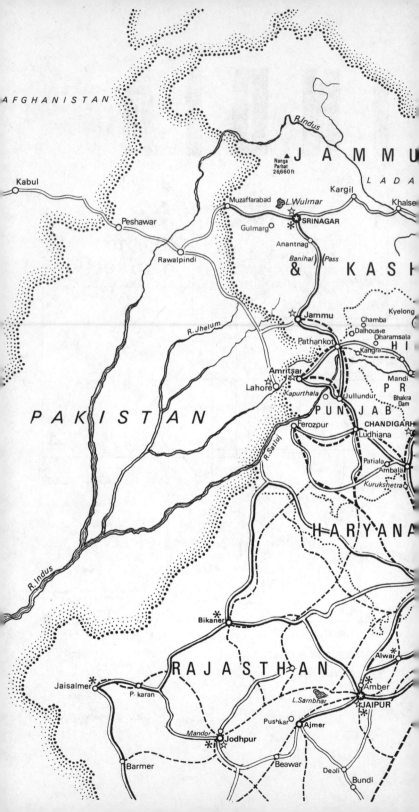

Karakoram
Pass

H

Leh

C H I N A

M I R

Manali

CHAL

Kulu

E S H

Narkanda

SIMLA

Gangotri

Jamnotri

Chakrata

Kedarnath

Mussoorie   Badrinath

Tehri   Joshimath

Dehra Dun

Rishikesh

Hardwar   Nanda Devi

Lansdowne   Pindari Glacier

aharanpur   Ranikhet   Almora

Ramnagar   *   Naini Tal

CORBETT
NAT.PARK

Meerut

Rampur

Moradabad

DELHI *

Bareilly

Aligarh

Shahjahanpur

Brindaban

hura   U T T A R   P R A D E S H

aratpur   *Agra

Fatehpur Sikri   Kanauj   Fyzabad

Dholpur   LUCKNOW   Gorakhpur

Kanpur

Gwalior

Datia   R.Ganga

ivpuri   R.Yamuna   Sarnath

Jhansi   Allahabad   Varanasi

Ramnagar

T I B E T

N E P A L

Lumbini

PAKISTAN

Bikaner

Didwana

L. Sambhar

Jaisalmer   Pokaran

Pushkar   Ajme

Mandor

R A J A S T

Jodhpur

Beawar

Barmer

Bhilwara

Sadri

Chittorgarh

Mt Abu

Udaipur

Abu Rd.

G U J A R A T

Modhera

GANDHINAGAR

Bhuj

Viramgam

Ahmedabad

Bagh Caves

Mandvi

Dholka

Godhra

Okha   Jamnagar

Wankaner

Dwarka

Rajkot

Cambay

Baroda

Dabhoi

Gondal

Bhavnagar

Broach

Porbandar   Junagadh   Jetpur

Palitana

Ankleshwar

Mangrol

GIR FOREST
NAT PARK

Surat

Veraval   Somnath

Dhulia

Chandor

Manm

A r a b i a n   S e a

Nasik

Sinnar

Igatpuri

Ahmednagar

BOMBAY

Ambarnath
Matheran

Lonavla

Karla Caves

Poona

**2   WESTERN &
CENTRAL REGION**

Mahabaleshwar

Wai

0 miles   100   200

0 km   100   200   300

BOMBAY

Nasik
Manmad
Ellora Caves
Sinnar
Aurangabad
Ambarnath
Matheran
Lonavla
Karla Caves
Poona

R. Purna
R. Dudna
R. Godavari
Nander

Ahmednagar
Bir

Nizamaba

MAHARASHTRA

Mahabaleshwar
Wai

Osmanabad
Bidar

A N

Ratnagiri

Sholapur

Secunderabad
HYDERABAD
Golconda

Kolhapur

Bijapur

R. Krishna
Raichur

P R A

Bagalkot
Aihole
Badami
Pattadkal

Belgaum

Kurnool

GOA
PANAJI
Hubli

Hampi
Tungabhadra Dam

Guntakal

Karwar

Anantapur

Jog Falls
Shimoga

K A R N A T A K A

Mudabidri
Karkal

Halebid
Belur Hassan
Sravanbelgola

BANGALORE
KOLAR GOLD FIELDS

Mangalore

Channapatna
Krishnarajasagar
Mercara
Nanjangud
Srirangapatna
Mysore
Somnathpur

Cannanore
Tellicherry
Mahe

Wildlife *BANDIPUR*
Sanctuaries
MUDUMALAI
Ootacamund
NILGIRI HILLS
Coonoor
Erode

T A
Salem

Calicut

K E R A L A

N A D U

Coimbatore

LAKSHADWEEP ISLANDS

Trichur

Kodaikanal

Cochin
Ernakulam
Thekkady
Madurai
Alleppey
Kottayam
PERIYAR WILDLIFE SANCTUARY

Tuticorin

Courtalam
Quilon
Varkala
Tinnevelly

TRIVANDRUM
Nagercoil
Kovalam Beach
Cape Comorin

3 SOUTHERN REGION

0 miles   100   200
0 km   100   200   300

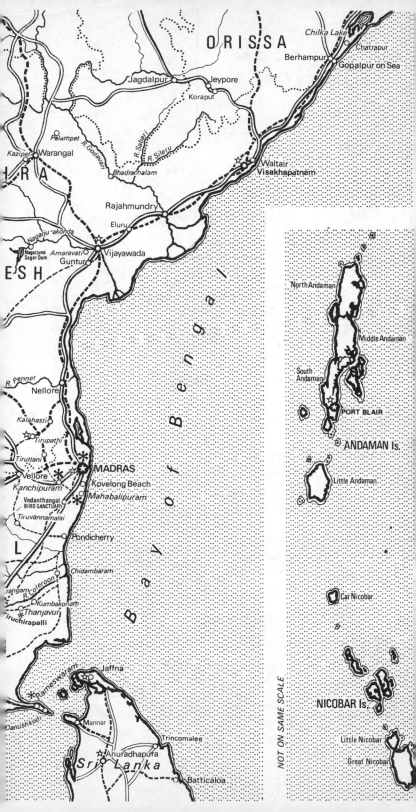

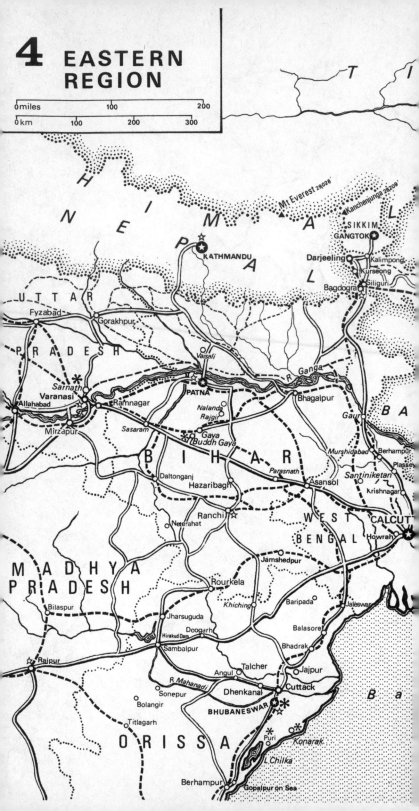

4 EASTERN REGION

0 miles 100 200
0 km 100 200 300

HIMALAYA

T I

N E P A L

Mt Everest 29028

Kanchenjunga 28208

SIKKIM
GANGTOK

KATHMANDU

Darjeeling
Kalimpong
Kurseong
Bagdogra
Siliguri

UTTAR

Fyzabad
Gorakhpur

Vaisali

PRADESH

Sarnath
Varanasi
Allahabad
Ramnagar
PATNA
R. Ganga
Bhagalpur

Gaur

Mirzapur
Sasaram
Nalanda
Rajgir
Gaya
Buddh Gaya
B I H A R
Murshidabad
Berhampur
Plassey
Santiniketan
Daltonganj
Parasnath
Krishnagar
Hazaribagh
Asansol
Ranchi
Neterahat
W E S T
CALCUT
B E N G A L
Howrah

M A D H Y A
Jamshedpur
Rourkela

P R A D E S H
Bilaspur
Khiching
Baripada
Jaleswar
Jharsuguda
Balasore
Doogarh
Hirakud Dam
Sambalpur
Bhadrak
Raipur
Angul
Talcher
Jajpur
R. Mahanadi
Cuttack
Sonepur
Dhenkanal
B a
Bolangir
BHUBANESWAR
Titlagarh
O R I S S A
Puri
Konarak
Berhampur
L. Chilka
Gopalpur on Sea

BA

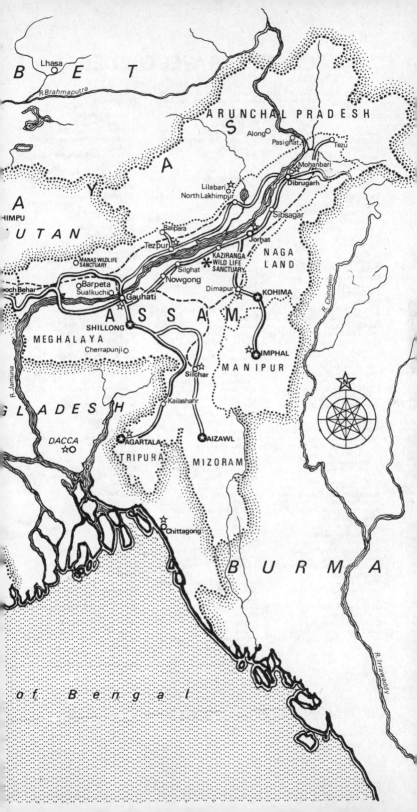

FODOR'S TRAVEL GUIDES

Here is a complete list of Fodor's Travel Guides, available in current editions; most are also available in a British edition published by Hodder & Stoughton.

U.S. GUIDES

Alaska
American Cities (Great Travel Values)
Arizona including the Grand Canyon
Atlantic City & the New Jersey Shore
Boston
California
Cape Cod & the Islands of Martha's Vineyard & Nantucket
Carolinas & the Georgia Coast
Chesapeake
Chicago
Colorado
Dallas/Fort Worth
Disney World & the Orlando Area (Fun in)
Far West
Florida
Fort Worth (see Dallas)
Galveston (see Houston)
Georgia (see Carolinas)
Grand Canyon (see Arizona)
Greater Miami & the Gold Coast
Hawaii
Hawaii (Great Travel Values)
Houston & Galveston
I-10: California to Florida
I-55: Chicago to New Orleans
I-75: Michigan to Florida
I-80: San Francisco to New York
I-95: Maine to Miami
Jamestown (see Williamsburg)
Las Vegas including Reno & Lake Tahoe (Fun in)
Los Angeles & Nearby Attractions
Martha's Vineyard (see Cape Cod)
Maui (Fun in)
Nantucket (see Cape Cod)
New England
New Jersey (see Atlantic City)
New Mexico
New Orleans
New Orleans (Fun in)
New York City
New York City (Fun in)
New York State
Orlando (see Disney World)
Pacific North Coast
Philadelphia
Reno (see Las Vegas)
Rockies
San Diego & Nearby Attractions
San Francisco (Fun in)
San Francisco plus Marin County & the Wine Country
The South
Texas
U.S.A.
Virgin Islands (U.S. & British)

Virginia
Waikiki (Fun in)
Washington, D.C.
Williamsburg, Jamestown & Yorktown

FOREIGN GUIDES

Acapulco (see Mexico City)
Acapulco (Fun in)
Amsterdam
Australia, New Zealand & the South Pacific
Austria
The Bahamas
The Bahamas (Fun in)
Barbados (Fun in)
Beijing, Guangzhou & Shanghai
Belgium & Luxembourg
Bermuda
Brazil
Britain (Great Travel Values)
Canada
Canada (Great Travel Values)
Canada's Maritime Provinces plus Newfoundland & Labrador
Cancún, Cozumel, Mérida & the Yucatán
Caribbean
Caribbean (Great Travel Values)
Central America
Copenhagen (see Stockholm)
Cozumel (see Cancún)
Eastern Europe
Egypt
Europe
Europe (Budget)
France
France (Great Travel Values)
Germany: East & West
Germany (Great Travel Values)
Great Britain
Greece
Guangzhou (see Beijing)
Helsinki (see Stockholm)
Holland
Hong Kong & Macau
Hungary
India, Nepal & Sri Lanka
Ireland
Israel
Italy
Italy (Great Travel Values)
Jamaica (Fun in)
Japan
Japan (Great Travel Values)
Jordan & the Holy Land
Kenya
Korea
Labrador (see Canada's Maritime Provinces)
Lisbon
Loire Valley
London

London (Fun in)
London (Great Travel Values)
Luxembourg (see Belgium)
Macau (see Hong Kong)
Madrid
Mazatlan (see Mexico's Baja)
Mexico
Mexico (Great Travel Values)
Mexico City & Acapulco
Mexico's Baja & Puerto Vallarta, Mazatlan, Manzanillo, Copper Canyon
Montreal (Fun in)
Munich
Nepal (see India)
New Zealand
Newfoundland (see Canada's Maritime Provinces)
1936 . . . on the Continent
North Africa
Oslo (see Stockholm)
Paris
Paris (Fun in)
People's Republic of China
Portugal
Province of Quebec
Puerto Vallarta (see Mexico's Baja)
Reykjavik (see Stockholm)
Rio (Fun in)
The Riviera (Fun on)
Rome
St. Martin/St. Maarten (Fun in)
Scandinavia
Scotland
Shanghai (see Beijing)
Singapore
South America
South Pacific
Southeast Asia
Soviet Union
Spain
Spain (Great Travel Values)
Sri Lanka (see India)
Stockholm, Copenhagen, Oslo, Helsinki & Reykjavik
Sweden
Switzerland
Sydney
Tokyo
Toronto
Turkey
Vienna
Yucatán (see Cancún)
Yugoslavia

SPECIAL-INTEREST GUIDES

Bed & Breakfast Guide: North America
Royalty Watching
Selected Hotels of Europe
Selected Resorts and Hotels of the U.S.
Ski Resorts of North America
Views to Dine by around the World

AVAILABLE AT YOUR LOCAL BOOKSTORE OR WRITE TO FODOR'S TRAVEL PUBLICATIONS, INC., 201 EAST 50th STREET, NEW YORK, NY 10022.